Trashing the Economy

Other books by Ron Arnold
At the Eye of the Storm: James Watt and the Environmentalists
Ecology Wars
The Grand Prairie Years (historical novel)
Edited:
Stealing the National Parks
People of the Tongass
Storm Over Rangelands
The Asbestos Racket
It Takes A Hero

Other books by Alan Gottlieb
The Gun Grabbers
Alan Gottlieb's Celebrity Address Book
Gun Rights Fact Book
The Rights of Gun Owners
With George Flynn:
Guns for Women
Edited:
The Wise Use Agenda
Fear of Food

Trashing the Economy

HOW RUNAWAY ENVIRONMENTALISM IS WRECKING AMERICA

Ron Arnold
Alan Gottlieb

FREE ENTERPRISE PRESS
BELLEVUE, WASHINGTON

Distributed by Merril Press

Trashing the Economy

Second Edition
Published by the Free Enterprise Press

Typeset in Times Roman on AMSi computers by the Free Enterprise Press,
Bellevue, Washington. Cover design by Northwoods Studio.

The Free Enterprise Press is a division of the Center for the Defense of Free
Enterprise, 12500 N.E. 10th Place, Bellevue, Washington 98005. Telephone
206-455-5038. Fax 206-451-3959. E-mail address: CompuServe 74123,3036.

This book distributed by Merril Press, P.O. Box 1682, Bellevue, Washington
98009. Additional copies of this book may be ordered from Merril Press at
$19.95 each. Phone 206-454-7009.

LIBRARY OF CONGRESS CATALOGING-IN-PUBLICATION DATA

Arnold, Ron.
    Trashing the economy : how runaway environmentalism is wrecking
America / Ron Arnold, Alan Gottlieb. — 2nd ed.
        p.   cm.
    Includes bibliographical references and index.
    ISBN 0-939571-17-X : $19.95
    1. Green movement—United States. 2. Environmental protection—
Societies, etc. 3. Conservation of natural resources—United
States. 4. Environmental protection—Economic aspects—United
States. I. Gottlieb, Alan M.   II. Title.
GE197.A76   1994
330.973'092-dc20   94-38261
                                                           CIP

Contents

Ron Arnold • Alan Gottlieb

Foreword to the Second Edition

We are pleased to release the second edition of *Trashing the Economy* so soon after publishing the original. It has already become the standard reference for those interested in tracking the environmental movement. We have added substantial materials to many of the profiles, such as Defenders of Wildlife. We virtually rewrote the profile on Greenpeace. We have made corrections, improved the index and cleaned up a number of typographical errors. The second edition, changed as it is, sends our original message more powerfully:

Runaway environmentalism is wrecking America. The first edition of this book made that startling case in a hard-hitting narrative based on years of research and investigation. The second edition is even harder-hitting. It is the skeleton key to secrets that the environmental movement does not want the public to know. It contains heavily documented profiles of more than sixty environmental organizations, including many histories, sources of funding, interlocking boards of directors, personal biographies of leaders—and exactly how they kill jobs and trash the economy, detail by detail, fact by fact.

Nothing like this book has ever before been dared. It is the road map to a concentration of money and power unlike anything America has ever seen. It has but one message: The environmental movement is not what it seems. It is not Saving the Earth, it is Trashing the Economy. This is the story of a runaway movement grown so arrogant and aggressive it is killing the goose that lays our nation's golden eggs.

Trashing the Economy has taken us three years to complete. It was made possible only by the volunteer help of hundreds of informants, some of whom spent months of their time and substantial amounts of their own money digging out hidden facts about the most powerful superlobby on Capital Hill, some at serious risk to themselves.

Much of our material came from whistle-blowers and defectors from the environmental movement itself—government memos and organization letters dropped over our transom, personal interviews, financial statements, computer network printouts, closed conference proceedings.

Most of our information came from activists in the wise use movement that has grown up to challenge the legitimacy of environmentalism. These are the people who have suffered most at the hands of unfeeling environmentalists. They do not live in glass towers in New York or Washington, D.C. They are the true guardians of the environment, the farmers and ranchers who have been stewards of the land for generations, the miners and loggers and oil drillers who have built our civilization by working in the environment every day, the property owners, workers and technicians and professionals who provide all the material basis of our existence. This is their story. The devotion of these people to the jobs, private property, communities and lives of others has kept us going through a deluge of vicious attacks by environmental organizations intent on keeping the public in the dark about their inner workings. This book belongs to our activist friends who have helped in more ways than we could ever acknowledge.

Because what we found was so shocking, we have included footnotes citing the sources for every major fact we describe— more than 1,250 footnotes. We know that footnotes break up the flow for the average reader, but there was no other way to enable the skeptical to verify what we discovered. We placed the footnotes at the end of each chapter rather than at the bottom of the page or in the back of the book. This book is too important to leave its assertions untested. We urge every reader to check everything we say *at the source*—to challenge every one of the more than sixty environmental groups we profile and evaluate the responses yourself.

In some ways this book resembles a directory of the environmental movement. You can certainly use it that way, one profile at a time. However, it is also a coherent narrative which, read from front to back, unfolds a story of stunning magnitude. It is a long book, but the public deserves to know the truth. However, we received more than twenty times the material you will find included in this book. Do not think that this is the whole story of the dark side of the environmental movement. What we did include has been told as completely as possible. Because we expect readers to skip around as well as read straight through, you will find minor repetitions in a few profiles.

Of the hundreds who have helped assemble our materials, four stand out for their selfless contribution of time, resources and effort: Teresa Platt of the nonprofit Fishermen's Coalition based in San Diego; Erich Veyhl of the Washington County Alliance, a citizen group in Maine; Ann Corcoran, publisher of the *Land Rights Letter* in Maryland; and Kathleen Marquardt of Putting People First in Washington, D.C.

Teresa Platt spent more than a year researching Earth Island Institute with the assistance of colleagues Steve Medina, Hector Eribez and Arturo "Tury" Acevedo. The network these devoted activists put together was able to locate the crew members of the *Maria Luisa*, the tunaboat on which environmentalist Samuel LaBudde filmed his phony 1988 "dolphin-slaughter" videotapes that devastated the U.S. tuna fishing fleet, and uncovered the intriguing truth behind his false claims.

Erich Veyhl has long been a crusader for private property rights and has gathered an incredible wealth of documents revealing the chicanery of government and environmental groups to destroy America's property rights. Erich provided us with invaluable evidence and astute advice for the profiles of National Parks and Conservation Association, the National Audubon Society and the Nature Conservancy.

Ann Corcoran, a former Washington lobbyist for the National Audubon Society, generously gave her time for interviews, provided crucial documents and reviewed the manuscript of the profiles of the National Audubon Society, the Nature Conservancy, and the subprofile on the Conservation Fund.

Kathleen Marquardt and husband Bill Wewer of Putting People First in Washington, D.C. provided much of the research for our profile of People for the Ethical Treatment of Animals. We are indebted to Bobby and Joan Berosini of Las Vegas for court documents in their legal battle against PETA.

Ron Arnold ● Alan Gottlieb

Other outstanding contributors include Joe Wrabek of Cascade Locks, Oregon, who provided key documents and his eyewitness experience for the subprofile of the Trust for Public Land and the story of the Columbia River Gorge.

Margaret Reigle, founder of Fairness to Land Owners Committee in Maryland, gave us valuable information on her experience with wetlands regulation and unique insights as one of the leaders of the property rights movement.

Some people's contributions are beyond our ability to express thanks. If it had not been for Charles S. Cushman, founder of the National Inholders Association, we doubt that today's broad uprising against the environmental movement would be so successful. He was among the first to challenge the damage to private property rights by environmentalists. He remains a paramount wise use leader in helping grassroots resistance groups that have arisen in response to environmentalist abuses all over the nation. Without Chuck's pioneering activism, advice and friendship over the years, we could never have written this book.

William Perry Pendley has long been a leading defender of property rights and wise use in the courts as President and Chief Legal Officer of Mountain States Legal Foundation. His inspiration and advice helped make this book possible.

Mark Meyer, a student who is part of the Center for the Defense of Free Enterprise intern program at the University of Washington, helped with newspaper research and Infotrak file retrieval, and he also proof-read the manuscript.

So many groups in the Wise Use Movement helped that we cannot give them all the credit they are due. We are particularly indebted to Leon Favreau's Multiple Use Association in New England, Bob Voight's Maine Conservation Rights Institute, and Ron Schiller's High Desert Coalition in California for organizing conferences which resulted in substantial materials for this book. Kraig Saunders provided vital documents and critique. Numerous wise use leaders are mentioned in the text, and to each of these people we extend our hearty thanks and admiration. To those many others who helped, but remain uncredited in the text, you know who you are and you have our gratitude.

A few of our sources must remain unnamed, particularly informants in government and the environmental movement, because they fear for their safety.

What merits this book may have belong to the fine people who helped. All errors of fact or judgment rest solely with the authors.

> Ron Arnold
> Alan Gottlieb
> *Liberty Park*
> *Bellevue, Washington*

Dedicated
to all those who lose their jobs or their property
because of the culprits exposed in this book.

Getting Trashed

The American Dream is in trouble.

Not since the Great Depression of the 1930s has the average citizen felt such alienation from "The System."

We have seen jobs that were the foundation of America's wealth dying off. We have seen Los Angeles in flames. We have seen secession measures on ballots in California and Kansas—rural communities trying to break away from hated urban governments—with similar moves under consideration in Alaska and Michigan's Upper Peninsula. We worry about the vigor and even the viability of our country.[1]

We have seen a Presidential campaign in which Bill Clinton and Al Gore won with only 43 percent of the popular vote—and the victorious Southerners ushered in the Bubba Era without carrying either Texas or Florida. George Bush, who proved he knows how to wow them on the hustings four years earlier, ran a campaign so dull it was memorable mainly for a debate during which he looked at his watch to see if it was time to leave yet. The television infomercial came out of retirement to convince nearly twenty percent of the electorate it should vote for a protest candidate with big ears and a bigger pocketbook. His potent message was that people are fed up with greedy businessmen, lazy workers, and careerist politicians beholden to special interests. During that whole alienated election, more than 30 percent of those contacted refused to even talk to a *poll taker*. A Knight Ridder newspaper reporter characterized the Clinton election as "a mandate to give the American people hope—or else."

Or else.

Americans are realizing with outrage that their home is no longer the nation that their fathers and grandfathers once built in steel mills and automobile factories and household appliance plants—the land of hope and optimism, the one nation in the world where anything might be possible.

Political leadership, too, has lost its power to inspire us. The Congressional election of 1992 turned out the old rascals for a batch of new rascals—and saw the largest turnover in members of Congress in several generations. Gridlock is gone—and the power of Congress is growing rapidly into we know not what.

Even when jobs are not vanishing by the hundreds of thousands, clouds of mistrust hang low over the Potomac; even as politicians give themselves more control over our lives, confidence in government fades like a ghost in pale fog.

But lingering economic woes agonize us most. Many speak indignantly of the eroding work ethic, the incredible vanishing middle class, wage cutbacks, bureaucratic quagmires, trade deficits, interest rates, make-work jobs, taxation and the problems of the service economy. A 1991 series of articles by the *Philadelphia Inquirer* which examined the worsening lot of the middle class prompted 20,000 anxious letters to the editor and orders for 400,000 reprints. Who would believe that just two years later we would see such giants as IBM, Sears, Boeing and Eastman Kodak hemorrhaging high-quality jobs by the thousands?

Recessions come and go, but a sticky mood of deterioration pervades even the best of recent times. When unemployment worsens, frightened, frustrated workers drive their old clunkers past the crumbling ruins of shut-down factories where they used to make a living, counting new empty storefronts and vacant office spaces on their way to the unemployment line. They wonder who the people are who have time to go out and protest over the spotted owl, wetlands, protest against this and that; they wonder why there is anyone who cares more for obscure plants and animals than for people and jobs.

When jobs perk up a little, shoppers who would prefer Ralph Lauren fashions still buy at K-Mart where they can at least find Jaclyn Smith's line of clothing; those who don't eat meat are still not necessarily vegetarians. Even when we can manage to crack a smile at the situation, it comes out gallows humor. He: "What's the latest on the economy?" She: "There's light at the end of the cliff."

We get the usual political promises and the usual cynical retorts. Vice President Al Gore told CNN, "The biggest new market in the history of world business is the market for the new products and new processes that will make possible economic progress without environmental destruction. Millions of jobs are at stake unless we can lead the environmental revolution and create the new jobs that will come out of this revolution." Commentator Rick Henderson mused in *Reason* magazine that abandoning existing technology, retooling factories and diverting expertise to suit environmental bureaucrats was likely to have a few costs, too. "Using Gore's logic," Henderson wrote, "the Los Angeles riots were an economic godsend—think of all the jobs rebuilding the city will create!"[2]

The *New York Times* recently commented, "The nation's plant workers, homemakers, miners, students, farmers and business people are searching for ways to turn the economy around and bend government to their will, some with what comes across as now-or-never determination."[3]

That's an interesting way for the *New York Times* to state peoples' problem: "to turn the economy around and bend government to their will." What has happened to America that ordinary people have to fight their government for control and for economic survival with now-or-never determination? What has happened to America that the electorate would welcome a President into office with *Or Else* hanging over him?

Something is wrong, dreadfully wrong. Something is sapping the strength of our once powerful nation. Somebody has slipped a monkey wrench into America's industrial gears and all the teeth are breaking off.

But who? Who would do such a thing? And how did we let it happen?

The answer is stunning: The Monkey Wrench Gang is the much-admired environmental movement. And we let it happen by trusting our own government too much.

If that sounds preposterous, reserve your judgment a while. This book is not another conspiracy theory. It is built around detailed profiles of the top environmental groups in America, telling who runs them, where they get their money, what they do with it, and exposing the economic damage they cause, campaign by economy-trashing campaign and program by job-killing program. Never has such a factual analysis of the environmental movement been published—taking names and kicking butt, as the vernacular goes.

We all realize that the environmental movement has become a major fact of American life. Even the FBI, which monitored some Earth Day 1970 organizers as potential subversives, ran an environmental exhibit in its lobby for Earth Day 1990. Vice President Al Gore wrote a best-seller titled *Earth In The Balance* reflecting his impeccable environmentalist credentials. Some 20,000 lawyers in the U.S. call themselves "environmental" attorneys. Environmentalists have become very Establishment. And very willing to trash the economy: A 1980s Sierra Club poll found 40 percent of respondents said they favor environmental goals "regardless of cost to the economy."[4]

Regardless of cost to the economy.

Think about that.

We have all felt Green Guilt poking at us, poking at us. We have all seen the skyrocket popularity of John Javna's *50 Simple Things You Can Do To Save The Earth*. We know it's not nice to fool with Mother Nature. We even find journalists opening stories with the lead, "Child abuse, wife battering, alcoholism, divorce, single-parenting, toxic waste"—a commentary on just how embedded the environment has become in our social anxieties.[5]

But when we see overkill at work we don't take it very seriously. Who could believe *Earth Island Journal* meant it when the editors began their *50 Difficult Things* list:

1. Dismantle your car.
2. Become a vegetarian.
3. Grow your own vegetables.
4. Have your power lines disconnected.
5. Don't have children.

And who could believe that a respected environmental scholar would recommend abandoning all our rights and freedoms for the sake of the environment? William Ophuls, a former United States Foreign Service Officer, decided that "the golden age of individualism, liberty, and democracy is all but over," and thus concluded in his 1992 book *Ecology and the Politics of Scarcity Revisited*, "The need for a world government with enough coercive power over fractious nation states to achieve what reasonable people would regard as the planetary common interest has become overwhelming." Mr. Ophuls subtitled his book, "The Unraveling of the American Dream"—in his view an unraveling that is necessary to save the earth.[6]

That's just a few shrill extremists. The rest of the environmental movement is more sensible.

Is it?

Many of us won't even ask that question. We think the environmental movement certainly can't be trashing the economy. Environmentalists are out to protect nature, to prevent pollution, to protect wildlife, to preserve beautiful surroundings. We need those things in order to survive. Nature is the basis of our economy. Clearly, environmental organizations get no money for saving old growth forests, for saving the whales, for fighting for clean air, pure water, pristine land—they have no economic interest at stake, thus they are irreproachable.

That sounds right. But it's not. Economics is not about money. Economics is about the allocation of scarce resources to individual wants. Ponder that. *Economics is about the allocation of scarce resources to individual wants.* Saving beautiful surroundings is as much an allocation of scarce resources to individual wants as your purchase of a home or payment of a doctor bill or rental of a movie on videocassette. Those are all economic decisions.

Every act of environmental protection is an economic decision. Putting old growth trees in a nature preserve rather than allowing foresters to convert them into homes is an economic decision. Banning exploration for oil and gas on the Outer Continental Shelf rather than using it to heat homes and run automobiles is an economic decision. Expanding a national park by demolishing the homes and businesses of next-door neighbors is an economic decision. Protecting wetlands by regulating private property out of all commercial or residential development is an economic decision. And every one of those items is on the agenda of the Clinton Administration.

Making such human choices—the allocation of scarce resources to individual wants—is what environmental organizations do every day. And in making their choices they are inevitably and unavoidably economic competitors trying to allocate scarce resources to their individual wants against the individual wants of all the industries that feed, clothe, shelter and employ us.

Environmental organizations have an economic stake in every issue they raise. Their individual wants are just that: individual wants. They are no more innocent than their opponents. They are just as open to skepticism and critique.

And, as we shall see, there is also a great deal of money for environmental groups at stake.

In the name of protecting nature—a goal Americans embrace wholeheartedly—over the last two decades Congress passed more than 300 major environmental laws and regulations with thousands more at the state and local levels, and we're adding more every year.

Those laws didn't just protect the environment. There were unwanted side effects.

Some laws tried to protect nature by creating harsh restrictions on business. Some infringed on private property rights with confiscatory land-use regulations. Some made it impossible to use the resource-rich federal lands that comprise one-third of our nation's area—700 million acres. Other laws expanded this surprisingly socialistic government-owned land-base by condemning private property to create federal nature preserves, thus removing it from the tax rolls. Every one of these laws killed jobs and trashed the economy in some specific way.

As Franklin G. Reick, president of Fluoramics, Inc., said, "If this country is destroyed, it will be destroyed by mindless bureaucrats and Kafkaesque regulation much sooner than by the pollution we all want cleaned up."

The Institute for Policy Innovation wrote, "The rapid growth of government regulations may very well be the single most important obstacle to U.S. competitiveness here and abroad."[7]

The artificial resource scarcity and high cost of doing business created by this New Environmental Regime has sapped the American economy of its profit margin, leaving nothing for growth—trashing the economy. These varied laws have slowly, gradually, invisibly come home to roost, unexpectedly squeezing the life out of America's free enterprise system, all in the name of environmental protection.[8]

Storing mounds of dirt can be illegal. To move a rock in a stream or cut down a tree in your own yard can bring heavy fines. A farmer using water to grow blueberries or cranberries can be fined and imprisoned for despoiling "wetlands." Bill Ellen was convicted and sentenced to six months in federal prison for creating ten duck ponds on Maryland's Eastern Shore where he managed a private wildlife sanctuary because in the process, he "knowingly filled wetlands without any federal authorization," according to Assistant U.S. Attorney Jane E. Barrett, who helped prosecute Ellen. When supporters sought a Presidential pardon for Bill Ellen, environmental groups furiously insisted he go to jail.[9]

Cities find themselves unable to foreclose on companies that fail to pay real estate taxes because, upon foreclosing, they legally become the owner of record and hence are responsible for the clean-up costs of previous polluters. Service stations close down by the thousands because owners cannot afford to comply with new rules forcing them to replace underground gasoline storage tanks that are in perfectly good condition. Every day a new piece of the American economy crumbles under some absurdly harsh environmental regulation.

Regardless of cost to the economy.

That wasn't the way most of us wanted it. Everyone was concerned about the way we were depleting our natural resources and abusing our environment. But we didn't want to trash the economy while saving the planet. Economists in particular worried about solving the problem. As a team of analysts wrote:

Economists have a double concern in the matter: that the viability and healthfulness of the environment be preserved, and that the measures taken to protect the environment be effective and not reduce the flow of ordinary goods and services any more than is necessary. This second concern is the economist's special province, and for that reason his adrenalin begins to flow when he hears some of the more alarmist proposals for meeting the "environmental crisis." Is there really an environmental crisis, or only a problem that we can deal with soberly? Is the environmental problem so severe that the growth in the output of goods and services must be brought to a halt while millions in this country and hundreds of millions throughout the world still live in poverty?[10]

But all of us aren't sober economists. We see the flow of goods and services being brought to a halt all around us, and we have a hard time understanding why. The reason is complex, but a good part of it came from the perception of *environmental crisis*, loudly purveyed for two decades by the organized environmental movement—familiar names such as the Sierra Club, the Audubon Society, and the National Wildlife Federation. Those exemplary groups and others like them hawked crisis as if it were a commodity during two decades of artfully overheated debate. Congress followed them calorie for calorie: Virtually every immoderate law that the environmental movement conceived, drafted, and lobbied, Congress dutifully passed.[11]

Environmentalist-produced television programs taught a whole generation to respond to every environmental problem as if it portended the end of the world—fill a wetland, kill the earth; endanger a species, kill the earth; farm with agrichemicals, kill the earth; build a single family residence, kill the earth; get out of bed in the morning, kill the earth. Environmental crisis became an everyday feeling. It gave us the present anti-business, anti-growth climate in America. The environmental movement, instead of solving the problem, in a very real way *became* the problem.[12]

Jeremy Burgess, a science writer and supporter of environmentalism, asks: "Is it just me, or does everyone else feel guilty for being alive, too?" Eco-prophet Theodore Roszak, author of *Person/Planet: The Creative Disintegration of Industrial Society,* warned: "Shrill environmentalists risk losing their audience—and their cause." He asks "Have we pushed scare tactics and guilt trips as far as they can take us?"[13]

But neither Burgess nor Roszak nor any other environmentalist asks: "Are we trashing the economy for a false image of harmed nature and failing to see the consequences?"

America, although still sleepy-eyed, is waking up to that possibility. A CNN/*Time* magazine poll in 1992 found that 51 percent of respondents felt that the environmental movement "had gone too far" in their demands on government and industry, yet 50 percent felt that it was important to protect the environment.[14]

We are beginning to notice the organized environmental movement in a new way. We are beginning to notice that it has grown immensely rich and powerful, funded by big industry, big foundations and big law firms, contrary to our fond memories of two decades ago. We are beginning to notice that You Can Never Be Green Enough—that the endless thrust to make things "better" inevitably radicalizes the "betterers," so they can never be satisfied.

There is no way the air can ever be clean enough, the water ever pure enough, the land ever perfect enough. We always need a new law to make it cleaner, purer, better. We are beginning to notice that our old friends the Sierra Club and the Audubon Society and the Natural Resources Defense Council are shifting steadily to the left. President Clinton is finding out the hard way that you can never outrun an environmentalist to the left. We see environmental groups treat every problem as The Crisis of the Century or The Doomsday Scenario. We see that every place where people want to make a living is suddenly recognized as the habitat of The Last Big Old Tree or The Last Cute Little Animal or even The Last Ugly Bug. We are beginning to notice that anything alive is more important to the organized environmental movement than people.

You Can Never Be Green Enough.

We are beginning to notice that the big mainstream environmental organizations have lost their way, no longer just *identifying* crises, but *fabricating* them, so there will be something to do with all their huge fund-raising infrastructure. Just as the environmental Vice President Al Gore got lost in the woods hiking at Coolfont Resort in West Virginia,[15] so his environmental movement got lost in the woods hiking to political power. And we are beginning to wonder if that isn't a little crazy.

Trashing Business

Hardly anyone would deny the need to protect the natural world. The ideal of man and nature living together in productive harmony is shared by virtually everyone. Even the village idiot realizes that nearly all human activities affect the environment. Most of us feel that we have a right to be here and the brains and the good will to treat nature with human decency—albeit somewhat short of treating it with perfection. The organized environmental movement, on the other hand, has become increasingly aggressive in manipulating large political, social and economic issues—and the target is human activities, because they *are* short of perfection.

When your only goal is to slow or stop human activity, there is a certain inevitability to your results. You end up doing nothing but hurting people. That is the net effect of all environmental laws, regardless of the good intentions of those who wrote them.

Consider the mindless way businessman Jeffrey Fowler was treated by officials of the Anaheim, California, environmental bureaucracy: Someone spilled nearly a gallon of gasoline in the parking lot of the small industrial building he leases to a cluster of small businesses ranging from gardening services to computer companies. A neighbor smelled the strong odor and called the Orange County-City Hazardous Materials Emergency Response Authority, which came out and mopped up the gasoline without notifying Fowler. A few days later he received a bill for $1,531.65 from the Authority. Alarmed, Fowler sought and found the actual culprit and notified the Authority, which refused to pursue the guilty party, saying the landowner was responsible. Spilling hazardous materials is a crime under California law, but it is the only crime not subject to due process. Fowler was prosecuted for the offense. In a frustrated letter seeking help he wrote to us, "This legal logic would be equivalent to charging a property owner with murder if a dead body was dumped on his front lawn." We receive dozens of such letters every month at the Center for the Defense of Free Enterprise.

On the other hand, many Americans have noticed that *big* business does very little to defend itself from environmentalist attack, trying to buy them off instead. Employees of large timber, mining, and other basic resource firms are most incensed at the timidity of their corporate leaders. These employees and others who have to struggle to maintain their economic footing forget that most successful business leaders enjoy getting away from it all *in nature.* Corporate nabobs like to build their second homes in the better parts of nature. In fact, the in-joke definition of an environmentalist is "someone who just bought a vacation home and doesn't want anybody building on the vacant lot next door."

Corporate executives not only build second homes, they also go to extravagant expense to visit wild scenic places and they often have deep sympathy for any rare or endangered species that might live there. And is it perhaps too outlandish to suspect that certain large well-capitalized corporations are giving huge amounts of money to environmental groups for the exact purpose of devising and lobbying restrictive laws with which only large well-capitalized corporations can afford to comply? You don't have to be a rocket scientist to realize that if you're big enough you can use environmental regulations to bankrupt your competition—the small and medium-sized firms that are the most technologically innovative in our economy.

The real tragedy is that many so-called "environmental" laws do not protect nature at all, but only harm industry. Rod H. Bolton, president of Electronics Solutions, a unit of Zero Corporation in San Diego, told us how his firm purchased a required $20,000 degreaser to clean up computer chips in an environmentally protective manner. In order to get approval to operate that environmental protection machine, his company had to go through five layers of bureaucracy and pay $22,000 for permits for a device that only cost $20,000 in the first place—and had to wait 16 months for his final permit. Then, state government tightened the operating cleanliness rules to impossible standards so bureaucrats could walk into the plant and levy exorbitant fines because a worker left a paint can lid open too long ("toxic" fumes) or some other minor infraction.

"Business has simply become a source of money to fund government's environmental projects and perpetuate their empires," said Bolton. "Environmental regulation has become a revenue source, not a way to protect nature."

Regardless of cost to the economy.

Another San Diego executive at the same meeting, William Stewart, vice president and senior counsel with Cubic Corporation, agreed with Bolton. "Business is being treated merely as a 'deep pocket.' We see firms leaving the state because of what they perceive as the government abusing the regulatory process."

A 1991 poll conducted by the California Business Roundtable revealed that 23 percent of California businesses said they were planning to move all or some operations outside the state within the next five years. Among the top reasons for leaving was predatory regulatory policies, along with crime, taxes, and traffic.[16]

Government programs are notorious for failing in their original purpose because bureaucrats build great bureaucracies, not great societies. Environmental programs are not exempt from this inherent fault. When companies faced with "greenmail" tactics cannot find other states with less greedy bureaucrats, they leave the United States altogether. This "capital flight" is a serious consequence of overzealous environmental regulation. Another serious consequence is the bite it takes out of the average American pocketbook each year—while failing to help the environment.

The Cost of Environmentalism

Environmental regulations on business cost each family more than $1,000 a year, or about $110 billion annually, according to former chairman of the Council of Economic Advisors Murray Weidenbaum. Other analysts say it is many times that amount. Robert Crandall, a senior fellow at the Brookings Institution, attempted to put a cost on environmental protection by reviewing all the major economic studies since the early 1970s. He found the excess to be *several hundred billion* dollars a year. Economists Michael Hazilla of American University and Raymond J. Krupp of Resources for the Future, a Washington-based environmental think tank, put the total cost of federal air and water legislation in 1990 at $320 billion—$79 billion in direct costs, the remainder from curtailed job growth, lowered savings rates, and reduced capital formation. This stupendous reallocation of resources, asserted Hazilla and Krupp, reduced our Gross Domestic Product by 5.8%.[17] Rochester Institute of Technology says all expenses associated with regulation exceeded $400 billion in 1991, or a cost-per-family of $4,200.

The Environmental Protection Agency itself estimated that complying with its regulations was costing Americans $115 billion a year, or a remarkable 2.1 percent of Gross National Product, versus 0.9 percent in 1972. Every American is paying on average about $450 more in taxes and higher prices, or $1,800 for a typical family of four—about half their annual expenditure for clothes and shoes. EPA's regulation has cost the nation $1.4 trillion in the past twenty years and compliance costs will total another $1.6 trillion in the 1990s alone, not counting the 1990 Clean Air Act Amendments that could add another $40 billion. Superfund cleanup is estimated to cost as much as $1.25 trillion, with about 85 percent of that stupendous amount earmarked for "transaction costs" which for the most part means lawyers' fees.[18]

That does not count the loss of property values due to environmental regulation for wetlands and endangered species or outright condemnation for nature preserves.

Nor does it factor in the economic losses from environmentalist pressure to reduce allowable timber harvest, mining operations, petroleum exploration, or livestock grazing on federal lands—and all of these are economic activities the Clinton Administration has said it will stop.

But taking Weidenbaum's calculations as a conservative figure, it is fair to say that Congress would never pass the $110-billion annual hidden budget for environmental compliance if it showed up on government expense sheets—but those compliance costs have been pushed off into private budgets.[19]

Today the Environmental Protection Agency is charged with administering the Clean Air Act; the Clean Water Act; the Resource Conservation and Recovery Act; the Toxic Substances Control Act; the Noise Control Act; the Quiet Communities Act; the Safe Drinking Water Act; the Asbestos Hazard Emergency Response Act; the Medical Waste Tracking Act; the Comprehensive Environmental Response, Compensation, and Liability Act; the Emergency Planning and Community Right-to-Know Act; the Marine Protection, Research, and Sanctuaries Act; and the Insecticide, Fungicide, and Rodenticide Act. The EPA says it costs $131 billion a year to comply with those regulations.

Behind each one of these laws stands an environmental group that lobbied it into existence and made sure the costs were pushed onto private budgets. Congress never acts, it only *reacts*.

Congress reacts these days mainly to the wishes of the powerful environmental lobby (and we will see just how incredibly powerful it is in the profiles to come): Congress passed the 1992 budget that financed the payroll for 122,400 federal regulators—the largest number ever. And that is considered *understaffed* considering the huge excess of laws they have to enforce against businesses.

The question is not "Shall we pay to protect the environment so that man and nature can live together in productive harmony?"—everybody would answer "Yes" to that. The question is "What portion of the costs now being imposed are excessive?" Everybody would like to know the answer to that. Although the actual number is clouded in confusion, there are studies that provide clues.

The 1990 legislation to cure the alleged damage from acid rain was lobbied into law by environmental groups that totally ignored a $500 million study by the National Acid Precipitation Assessment Program (NAPAP), a study that Congress itself ordered and paid for. The study found minimal damage from acid rain in actual examinations on the ground by respected and qualified scientists. Fewer than 300 lakes of the 7,000 studied were found to be acidic to any serious degree. Less than 1 percent of the forest decline on the Eastern Seaboard was due to acid rain. There was a *problem* of unacceptable proportions, but certainly not the *crisis* that was so loudly touted in environmental group fundraising mailers. NAPAP research director J. Laurence Kulp said the cost of the 1990 clean air law that was supposed to cure acid rain is $4 billion a year—but the benefits are barely $100 million. And the good effects on nature are so small as to be unmeasurable. Only a lunatic would willingly enter into a contract with such unfavorable terms—unless the real intent was to trash the economy.

The new Clean Air Act Congress passed in 1990 is nearly 800 pages long—compared to fewer than 50 pages for the previous Clean Air Act. It came out of the Bush administration which was trying to prove that George really was the environmental president. The Office of Technology Assessment estimates that new fuel and auto emission standards cost $2 billion to $6 billion dollars a year, yet only 12 million people—not quite five percent of the total population—actually suffer from elevated smog levels for more than 100 hours a year—and all of them are in California. All other problem areas could meet EPA levels by cutting emissions on one or two days a year. The law was unreasonably harsh, as everyone in Congress realized, but they didn't dare ease up on George Bush's proposal for fear that the powerful environmental lobby would eat them alive. So now the private sector has to pay over $100 billion each year to meet the new law's excessive demands.

Former Deputy Administrator of EPA John Quarles said of the permit process for the new Clean Air Act, "It may become an administrative nightmare." The Act affects some 150,000 small businesses. Just doing the paperwork to get one set of the permits will cost the average small business between $10,000 and $15,000, and buying the monitoring devices to track emissions will cost anywhere from $10,000 to $50,000. Every little auto-body repair shop will have to buy $100,000 worth of equipment to catch spray paint fumes. The result of this single law will be the death knell for tens of thousands of local mom-and-pop businesses that cannot afford to comply with the Act.

Solid-waste disposal regulations and toxic waste cleanup cost $5 billion to $9 billion a year. Part of the rationale for the tough regulations was that such wastes were predicted to cause an additional 1,100 cancers each year. If the money spent actually prevented half of those cases—an optimistic estimate—it would add up to a cost per avoided case of $10 million to $18 million.

Regardless of cost to the economy.

The Clinton Administration has sworn it will toughen the Clean Air Act to limit emissions to 1990 levels by the year 2000.

Michael J. Bennett, veteran journalist and author of *The Asbestos Racket*, says we will spend $150 to $200 billion needlessly removing asbestos from buildings—$60 billion for schools alone, and the overall economy will sustain between $1 trillion and $2 trillion in lost property values. And the asbestos issue has also warped our legal system into a nightmarish travesty of justice. In truth, 95 percent of the asbestos used in this country is essentially harmless. The 5 percent that is seriously harmful is the blue asbestos imported from South Africa during World War II and used primarily in shipyards to wrap pipes. So asbestos removals in most instances were a complete waste of time and money, and actually exposed people to more hazard by stirring up the dust of old asbestos than they would have by simply containing it in place.

But because of environmentalist legal activism, asbestos claims can be made in the courts because of mere exposure to the substance *before any harm appears*—the theory being that it takes years for certain asbestos-related cancers to show up. That may seem like a compassionate accommodation to a real problem, but the entire juridical tradition of American law has required that an *actual harm* be done before a court may accept a case. Now, however, anyone can simply say they have been exposed to asbestos and file a lawsuit on the *mere expectation* that a future harm might occur and the courts need not turn it away for lack of merit. Productive companies such as Johns Manville and Fibreboard have been subjected to thousands of these "maybe-I'll-get-sick-someday-but-pay-me-now" lawsuits. Nobody objects to lawsuits being filed for harms actually suffered, but the potential is now there to turn our entire justice system into a jungle, with even knowingly predatory claimants being able to bring costly litigation against anyone else for the mere expectation that they may suffer some harm some day. That unexpected outfall of environmental activism alone could bring our entire economy to a slow, grinding, agonizing halt.[20]

Regardless of cost to the economy.

The Clinton Administration has sworn it will tighten asbestos laws.

The late Dr. Dixy Lee Ray, the marine biology professor who went on to become chairman of the Atomic Energy Commission and Governor of the State of Washington, told the Wise Use Leadership Conference in mid-1992 that we had developed a new zeal to clean up the environmental messes and excesses of the past—the good news—but it was costing far more than anyone expected for unimpressive results—the bad news. "We have already spent $11 billion to clean up fewer than three dozen of the 1,200 hazardous waste sites designated for cleanup."

One of these sites, she said, is the Missouri town of Times Beach, which was evacuated because the dirt of the streets was found to contain dioxin in concentrations comparable to "one drop of vermouth in five carloads of gin." Dioxin was treated by the media as a manmade horror chemical at the time, but is now widely recognized as a naturally occurring substance created whenever combustion of natural substances occurs. A $400 million government study has concluded that dioxin is everywhere and has been doing no detectable harm. Thus, after being stampeded into needlessly evacuating a whole town at a cost estimated to exceed $230 million—and lifelong mental and emotional anguish to former residents—with no benefit, we found that the dioxin "crisis" so loudly merchandised by environmental groups a decade ago was a mild problem that could have been handled with little expense and no disruption to peoples' lives. It was a nasty slap in the face to hear Dr. Vernon Houk, the government scientist who originally recommended the evacuation, later tell an environmental conference in Missouri that the Times Beach scare and evacuation was unnecessary. "It was the result of an unfortunate scientific misunderstanding," Houk said. *An unfortunate scientific misunderstanding!* A whole town of families lost their homes and way of life because of a stupid government mistake. The families of Times Beach felt utterly betrayed by their government, alienated, thrown away, despised. And there was nothing they could do about it, no restitution, not even so much as an apology.

A dioxin story that broke September 28, 1992 shows us the mind games the media can play to manipulate public perception. The single actual event being reported was a conference in which scientists evaluated a report to be used by the Environmental Protection Agency to rewrite dioxin control regulations. The *Los Angeles Times* slanted their version of the story, "Scientists Urge Study of Dioxin Danger Beyond Cancer." The *New York Times* headlined theirs, "Panel Finds No Wide Threat of Cancer Caused by Dioxin." It's amazing what a difference a few time zones can make.

However, environmental groups still try to peddle fear of dioxin as a fund raising gimmick and press for more government studies, hoping that one will someday come up with the politically correct result.

Regardless of cost to the economy.

The Clinton Administration has sworn it will tighten dioxin laws.

Then there are the predatory environmental groups that consciously use the regulatory system as a fund raising device for their own organizations. One of their favorite ploys is to identify a chemical that the government is methodically phasing out for low but unacceptable levels of toxicity and then to raise an alarm that the government is not acting fast enough on the chemical, thereby endangering millions of people. In exactly such a stunt, the Natural Resources Defense Council severely damaged the apple orchard business—one of America's few remaining mom-and-pop industries—by claiming on CBS News *60 Minutes* that Alar, a growth regulator chemical, was "the most potent carcinogen in our food supply," when in fact Alar has never caused a single case of cancer and no test has ever shown it to cause cancer in any laboratory animal—one of its by-products, UDMH (unsymmetrical dimethylhydrazine), had been shown to be a weak carcinogen in one strain of laboratory mice, but does not cause cancer in rats. Even though such a low level of toxicity does not constitute an imminent hazard, the Environmental Protection Agency was diligently following its normal decertification procedure to gradually remove Alar from the market, and the NRDC discovered that fact. NRDC hired Washington, D.C.-based Fenton Communications to treat a low level problem as if it were The Crisis of the Century.

The sensational skull-and-crossbones story hit the small screen and 40 million of its viewers: "Alar is the most potent carcinogen in our food supply" said CBS News *60 Minutes'* Ed Bradley, and the public jumped to the conclusion "my child will die of cancer if he or she eats apples." Mothers everywhere immediately dumped the apple juice sitting in the refrigerator down the sink—whether Alar had ever touched the apples or not. School lunch rooms removed apples from the menu. The Alar panic caused the apple market to disappear for months and drove thousands of small orchardists into bankruptcy. Devastated apple orchardists sued the Natural Resources Defense Council, CBS News *60 Minutes* and Fenton Communications for damages in the hundreds of millions of dollars, but were ultimately thrown out of court. Florida recently passed a product disparagement law to stop such abuses.[21]

Why do we go to such lengths to destroy the industries that feed, clothe and shelter us? Robert Crandall of Brookings told *Fortune* magazine that it's "a desire to purge ourselves of guilt for succeeding too well in taming nature." In short, some people who feel guilty just want to stop growth for the sake of stopping growth.[22]

That's bad enough, but it's not even the *tip* of the iceberg.

Trashing Our Cities

The City of Columbus, Ohio, found itself faced with unmanageable environmental costs. Unlike other cities that continue to work in the dark, the mayor and city council of Columbus commissioned a unique study that revealed environmental regulation was trashing its municipal economy at an unbelievable rate. By the year 2000, households will be paying over $850 a year for new environmental regulations atop the City charges they pay now, plus the $1,000 a year they pay now on the federal regulations that Murray Weidenbaum pointed out.

The report, prepared by a blue ribbon Environmental Law Review Committee, began, "The City of Columbus has been affected during the last several years by changes in both federal and state environmental mandates. For example, between 1988 and 1990, there were 67 environmental mandates from the Federal and State government."

The City of Columbus had to obey five categories of unfunded mandates:

Lands: Resource Conservation and Recovery Act (RCRA); Underground Storage Tank (UST); Solid Waste Disposal (Ohio HB 592); Explosive Gas Monitoring; Infectious Waste. **Water**: Clean Water Act (CWA); Safe Drinking Water Act (SDWA). **Air**: Clean Air Act (CAA). **Chemical**: Toxic Substances Control Act (TOSCA); Federal Insecticide, Fungicide and Rodenticide Act (FIFRA); Asbestos Hazard Emergency Response Act of 1986 (AHERA). **Multi-purpose**: Superfund Amendments and Reauthorization Act of 1986 (SARA Title III).

The report went on, "More importantly, the federal government is actively pursuing compliance with these legislative mandates. U.S. EPA Administrator, William Reilly, has set the enforcement tone for the federal government by the '...aggressive enforcement...' stance that he adopted even in his confirmation hearing. In addition, the State of Ohio has begun to adopt similar legislative mandates with which the City must comply or face legal action.

"Unfortunately, very little or no funding has been provided at either the state or federal level to assist the City in complying with these laws and regulations, And, costs of compliance are escalating. Environmental costs may be 85% higher in the year 2000 than in 1987 if full compliance with environmental mandates is achieved."

You can bet that President Clinton's EPA Administrator will make it tougher than that.

Most of the new mandates purport to improve the nation's health and safety risks, but in fact they do little at stupendous cost. The mandate that EPA promulgated on radon in drinking water is a case in point. It was said to avoid some 83 lung cancer cases a year at a total capital cost of $2.4 billion and an annual cost of $310 million. But EPA's figures are absurd. The Association of California Water Agencies, representing some 400 public water providers, say the actual cost to California alone would be $3 billion in capital and $540 million a year. And the estimate of saving 83 cancer deaths bears no resemblance to reality. Canadian scientists have found no correlation between raised radon levels and raised lung cancer deaths. In fact, it seems that increased radon levels *prevent* lung cancer—states such as Pennsylvania, Iowa, Minnesota, Florida and Utah found an *inverse* relation between radon levels and lung cancer death rates. The higher the average levels of residential radon, the lower the lung cancer death rate. So, if we actually obey the EPA's mandate in all our cities, we will spend many billions of dollars to *promote* lung cancer! The late columnist Warren Brookes acidly noted, "The only beneficiaries of such madness are regulators and politicians who will reap special interest contributions from those selling the equipment needed to carry out this mindless Washington mandate."[23]

The Environmental Law Review Committee concluded, "Because of these changes, the costs to the City of Columbus over the next ten years is expected to be $1,088,484,880 in 1991 dollars just to comply with the environmental mandates that have already been enacted into law. An additional 20 federal laws are either proposed or are in the development phase." With normal inflation, the real cost was estimated at over $1.6 billion. The entire city budget for 1991, by contrast, was $591 million.[24]

City officials called for rules that tackle real rather than "perceived" risks to human health in order to keep costs down in the rising tide of federal mandates combined with dwindling federal assistance.

The *Columbus Dispatch* asked, "Are the regulations worth it?" The cost of complying with new water regulations alone, the newspaper reported, was estimated to send water and sewer bills to triple their current levels. However, Richard C. Sahli, executive director of an environmental group calling itself the Ohio Environmental Council said, "Clean, safe water is more important than money. The bottom line has got to be: Is the water safe?" Despite the fact that no massive outbreaks of disease related to drinking water have occurred in this country for generations, environmentalists want tough new standards. Critics say this is mere treatment for the sake of treatment. The water is safe now, and this is just a way of expanding environmentalist empires and bureaucracies. The data used by lawmakers to come up with the new laws was faulty. "It's bad science," said Kenneth Button, who runs Columbus' water quality assurance lab. Some of the new laws, said Button, were designed to eliminate one case of cancer in a million, even where the cancer research is not conclusive.

City of Columbus officials are taking their case to the other major cities of the United States, encouraging them to do similar studies so the nation will have some idea what these Washington-imposed mandates will cost us all. The Municipality of Anchorage, Alaska performed its analysis and released a report in late 1992 showing the economic devastation it is suffering from federal environmental mandates.[25]

Regardless of cost to the economy.

The Clinton Administration has sworn it will set tougher standards for cities, including a horrendous water runoff standard.

Trashing Development

Increasing the out-of-pocket cost of regulation to the average American is not the only way environmentalists trash our economy. *Preventing* economic growth—lost opportunity costs—is another way to bring about industrial collapse. Ominous trends are developing that have the potential for stopping all development everywhere—total gridlock. The obstacles to development include not only headline-grabbing federal laws such as the Endangered Species Act and Wetlands Regulations but also a bevy of new State Growth Management Acts that destroy traditional local control over land use decisions. In most states, the power to control land-use has been vested in the local government, under the assumption that local government is most responsive to and cognizant of the development needs and desires of residents. This vesting has formed the core of local governmental powers, which, experts have noted, "through land-use, extend to many areas of public policy, including: housing, economic development, public finance, transportation, environmental protection, energy conservation, and even banking practices."[26]

However, nine states have adopted state land-use planning and growth management legislation, responding to environmentalist constituencies demanding state coordination and direction of local planning decisions, under the "web-of-life" rationale that land-use decisions can have larger-than-local ramifications that are rarely considered by local governments.

These nine states have each taken a distinctive approach to state control of land-use:

Florida: Adopted an intergovernmental approach with three major parts. 1) State and regional control was established in the 1972 Environmental Land and Water Management Act. 2) The 1975 Local Government Comprehensive Planning Act required local plans but did not provide for consistency between state and local plans. 3) The 1985 State Comprehensive Plan mandated a top-down plan with 300 policy statements local governments must follow.

Georgia: Required comprehensive planning by state, regional and local authorities. This was a bottom-up approach to seek consistency among state and local plans. It provided for a regional role in compiling plans, but the regions have no enforcement authority.

Hawaii: Passed a two-part law. 1) The Land Use Law created four land classifications and regulations for each classification. 2) The State Plan gives county control over urban districts, state control over agricultural districts, and joint control over conservation and rural districts.

Maine: Set state standards for local planning and appropriated money for local government planning. State is empowered only to review local plans and recommend changes. The law is procedural, not substantive.

New Jersey: Passed a complex law built around a state-prepared map of land use areas, with seven classifications and consistency achieved between local and county plans through an innovative "cross-acceptance" process. Cross-acceptance is a negotiated review of the state map, which is adjusted by county and municipal planning agencies. Participation in cross-acceptance is not mandatory, but eligibility for state infrastructure funds is related.

Oregon: This law created state planning goals and required local plans to conform. The state originally had authority to recommend critical areas, but it was repealed in the mid-1980s. Counties conduct local planning.

Rhode Island: Law requires local planning to conform to state goals. No state map is mentioned in the law, but the state planning agency keeps one updated.

Vermont: Another two-part law. 1) Act 250 is a state planning act containing 10 criteria for larger-scale development—about one-third of all developments require state permit approval. 2) Act 200 requires regional plans to be consistent with state plans and offers incentives to local governments to conform to 32 state planning goals.

Washington: A complicated law imposes state goals on local (county) plans. Conformity is required of 12 urban counties (out of the total of 39 counties), although three more may voluntarily comply. Urban growth areas must be specified in the plans. No new regional layer of review was enacted.

Washington and Florida have the most oppressive Growth Management laws because they combine with other Open Space ordinances to wreck average people. A typical Washington State horror story appeared in a local newspaper:

> After spending more than 30 years cultivating her little farm along the Sammamish Slough, Betty West may be forced to leave.
>
> The people of King County have decided they want West's property for a park, and the County Council is expected to approve a plan to begin condemnation proceedings to force the 68-year-old widow off her land.
>
> A trial will be held, and a jury will decide how much the county must pay West for her property. Her cottage will then be torn down, and her 2-acre blueberry farm will be allowed to revert back to wilderness.[27]

Pacific Legal Foundation, the Sacramento, California-based public interest law firm championing private rights, has set up a permanent office in Bellevue, Washington in the expectation that the state will be the site of *the* major showdown over land rights in America. Furthermore, the four largest Washington counties are experiencing secession movements as rural separatists strive to remove themselves from the hated urban requirements of the Growth Management Act.

In addition, six states have gubernatorial growth control commissions: New York, Pennsylvania, Maryland, Virginia, West Virginia, and California have either a Growth Strategies Commission or are considering growth management legislation.

In all cases, environmental advocacy groups have generated the popular constituency for these new centralizing laws. As one expert stated, "environmental advocacy groups have been active in these states, and enjoy wide support. Environmental land-use concerns can be a particularly strong impetus to state growth management when development is perceived to have damaging effects on the environment." Environmentalist groups have made it a priority to identify LULUs—Locally Unwanted Land Uses—and give them maximum bad publicity to generate opposition to development and support for laws that stop development. That's a LULU!

The thrust to bring Growth Management Acts to all states has intensified in recent years. In 1989, the Jessie B. Cox Charitable Trust gave $40,000 to One Thousands Friends of Oregon, an anti-growth environmental organization, "for participation of three New England statewide groups in the National Growth Management Leadership Project." The project was designed to train state cadres in lobbying tactics and to network them with the large national environmental groups.[28]

The Associated General Contractors of America became so concerned about the economic damage and delays being caused by environmental lockdown that they began a nationwide survey of delays and related costs in early 1992. Here is a compendium of just a few problem areas they found:

Alabama: A $43 million project was delayed because of a regulatory dispute.

Arizona: Three projects totaling $212 million were delayed for Clean Air Act and Endangered Species red tape. Eight more projects totaling $170 million were held up for archaeological approval by the Bureau of Indian Affairs and lack of landfill cleanup.

North and South Carolina: Five projects worth $83 million were halted for a mishmash of wetlands permits, Coastal Areas Management Act permitting, U.S. Coast Guard permitting, Clean Water Act certification, and Fish & Wildlife permitting.

Florida: Two projects worth $23 million were stopped for soil contamination studies and environmental investigation.

Illinois: Thirty-four projects amounting to $51 million were stopped for a variety of environmental regulatory reasons.

Mississippi: Three projects worth $33 million were halted in this depressed economy for Department of Environmental Quality reviews, among other hang-ups; a $19 million project was stopped for wetlands reasons.

Nebraska: A $30 million project was stopped for wetlands mitigation.

New Mexico: Three projects totaling $40 million were bogged down in environmentalist lawsuits.

North Dakota: Three projects worth $45 million were held up for wetlands permits, archaeological site studies, and wildlife mitigation measures.

Oklahoma: Seven projects totaling $259 million were trashed by endangered species regulations, an environmentalist lawsuit, environmental impact statement requirements and hazardous materials permitting.

Pennsylvania: Four projects totaling $48 million were locked down because of EPA's Superfund Cleanup regulations, wetlands re-analysis, and environmental impact statement requirements.[29]

Some of these projects will never be finished. Environmentalism will kill them. Some will die because the developer was run out of money by the bureaucracy—which prints the money and never dies. Others will eventually be allowed to continue, but at costs that escalate alarmingly with every passing day, adding needless burdens to our economy that do nothing to protect the natural world.

None of these projects is in a natural area such as a national park or a national forest. All are in urban zones where similar developments were common until the flood of environmental laws after 1970 began to put the brakes on all development. To a reasonable person, none of these projects would do any harm to the environment whatsoever. But the laws are no longer administered by reasonable standards: they rely upon technical factors. The developer has to prove he won't violate those technicalities. The technical parameters are as elastic as Silly-Putty when supporting the regulator's demands but unbending as glass when the developer tries to use them to make his own case. Development is being choked to death by people who have their own but don't want anybody else to have development. Our children will have no new places to work except vacant lots that nobody can build on.

Regardless of cost to the economy.

The Clinton Administration has sworn it will limit real estate development as part of a national growth management package.

Trashing Property Rights

The most provocative environmental laws are those that result in the loss of private property rights. The Nobel Prize for Economics in 1991 went to the University of Chicago's Ronald Coase, whose seminal 1960 essay, *The Problem of Social Costs*, argued that property rights could protect the environment better than a regulatory bureaucracy.[30]

The environmental movement, on the other hand, is actively destroying private property rights on a massive scale. For example, rules for protecting wetlands are so strict that millions of land owners—that's right, *millions*—are discovering to their horror that they cannot do anything with their own land, and can't sell it to anyone else—the rules scare away all potential buyers.

Wetlands were once protected according to the biological functions they performed. And wetlands used to be wet. That was before the environmental movement got hold of them. Now officials focus on definitions dreamed up by environmental groups in language so broad and vague that nobody can comply with them.

The new policy says that a North Dakota corn field where pools of water collect for a week each year during normal spring run-off is a wetland. The new policy says a muddy patch between railroad tracks in the center of the main street in an Idaho town is a wetland. The new policy says that irrigation ditches dug by farmers in Nevada and California, some of which have been in use for a century, are wetlands. Most horrifying, the new rules say that ordinary building lots for new homes in densely populated urban centers are wetlands. Land owners watch as their life savings disappear in environmental red tape, and in extreme cases, they *cannot even enter their own property on foot!*

Peggy Reigle left her job as vice president of finance at *The New York Daily News* and bought an abandoned 138-acre farm for $400,000 near rural Cambridge, Maryland, looking forward to the day she could sell 14 lots on part of it and build her dream home on the remainder. When she went to offer the lots for sale, she discovered that wetland laws barred her from developing on or near a little swale that ran through the farm and nobody would buy her lots for fear their home-building projects would be stopped. Her $400,000 investment is useless. Peggy Reigle's dream home has turned into a nightmare.

In frustration and outrage, Reigle formed a little protest group, the Fairness to Land Owners Committee, which has quickly grown to a nationwide membership of 8,800 property owners in 30 states. Her aim is to limit protection to only the most valuable wetlands and allow development on the rest, providing compensation for property rendered useless by wetland laws. "It's a national crisis," Reigle told the *New York Times*. "Landowners, and I mean moms and pops, not oil companies and miners, are being abused by restrictions that no longer make sense. Their lives have been devastated and their land is being held hostage by these laws."[31]

The highly technical definitions of "wetland" used to classify private property are so bizarre that the average person would never guess that building lots which look like perfectly dry ground had been designated "wetland." Yet orthodox environmentalists insist that puddles where rainwater remains for more than seven consecutive days in a year must be "protected" as if they were precious relics. Whenever environmentalists say "protect" they mean "control."

In effect, government is making private property owners provide a public good—the protection of wetlands—at private expense without compensation. Environmental groups such as the Sierra Club and the Natural Resources Defense Council argue that people like Peggy Reigle are not entitled to just compensation for their loss because they still hold title to the land—and that any development of nature would harm the property of others, which is not a constitutionally protected activity. The question is whether regulating private property for a public good constitutes a taking for which just compensation is due under the U.S. Constitution's Fifth Amendment. This is known as the "regulatory taking" issue.[32]

It entered the environmental movement in a study by the Task Force on Land and Urban Growth published in 1972 by the Citizens' Advisory Committee on Urban Growth, a body established by presidential order in 1969. The study, *The Use of Land: A Citizen's Policy Guide to Urban Growth*, was sponsored by the Rockefeller Brothers Fund and the task force chairman was Laurance Rockefeller. Get used to seeing the Rockefeller name in close association with environmentalism: It will appear again and again in our profiles.

The study began with a quotation from Aldo Leopold:

> It is time to change the view that land is little more than a commodity to be exploited and traded. We need a land ethic that regards land as a resource which, improperly used, can have the same ill effects as the pollution of air and water, and which therefore warrants similar protection.[33]

The main recommendation of the report was that the federal government would become the recipient of "open space" land through mandatory exactions on developers, donations, and grants in lieu of federal estate taxes. And a national lands trust would be established and noncompensatory greenbelt plans would extend government regulation to all private property. Environmental protection areas would be protected not by purchase but through the police power of the federal government.

The police power is defined by legal scholars as "the right of the sovereign to legislate on behalf of its citizens to protect their health, safety, welfare and morals."[34]

The Rockefeller report envisioned that ownership of land should be separated from development rights. Development rights should be created and allocated to the land by society through government, i.e. a thoroughgoing eco-socialism for land. For many years various Rockefeller foundations have funded environmental groups willing to adopt this agenda (See the chapter on Money). *The Use of Land* was edited by Rockefeller protégé William K. Reilly, who went on to become the Bush administration's Environmental Protection Agency administrator.[35]

Around 1987 a number of environmental organizations realized that an old common-law doctrine called "the public trust" was a way to invoke the police power to destroy private property rights without incurring payment of just compensation, and began using it in the courts. Essentially, the public trust doctrine says that there are interests so profoundly important that they cannot be entrusted either to private owners or to the elected members of the legislature but only protected by the courts, which have the power to strike down any law that protects private property.

The theory behind the public trust doctrine is that the government can only alienate into private ownership those lands and resources that are not essential for the public. Properties such as navigable waters are essential for public use and therefore cannot be owned by a private individual or corporation. Thus, if the courts find that a private property owner has harmed or plans to harm some aspect of the public trust, they can issue an order stopping all use of that private property without paying just compensation, because there is no right to harm the public trust and therefore nothing has been taken from the private property owner.

Clearly, the public trust doctrine can be stretched into any shape a clever lawyer is able to conceive—the definition of what is "essential for the public" can be pushed indefinitely. Necessity is always the tyrant's plea.[36]

Environmentalists claim that landowners are too narrowly focused on the pursuit of profits to recognize a wider societal duty to protect environmentally sensitive land. John Echeverria, chief counsel for the National Audubon Society, said, "The nub of the issue is whether the government can regulate property to prevent a public harm without giving rise to a compensation claim. I do not know that we can pay for every economic knock that people suffer."[37]

Consider Mr. Echeverria's last thought.

"I do not know that we can pay for every economic knock that people suffer."

He is perfectly aware his movement is making people suffer economic knocks.

He does not know if they can pay for it.

But he wants it done anyway.

Regardless of cost to the economy.

The public trust doctrine is the perfect tool to avoid paying. With no economic penalty to be borne for their actions, the environmental movement's incentive is strong to eliminate every last scrap of private property in America. Environmental lawyers have pressed literally hundreds of cases in recent years invoking the public trust doctrine for environmental protection, expanding the concept of "essential for public use" to encompass virtually all private property.[38]

Even where condemnation procedures allow for payment of just compensation, government says your property is valued higher when it wants to collect taxes, and it says your property is valued lower when it wants to buy it. Land owners are becoming the new persecuted class.

This reversion to feudal property arrangements, in which the sovereign holds all power over property, represents the cutting edge of a sword that could very realistically bring about an absolute eco-socialism in this country within a few years. The basic theory of property embraced by the American Founding Fathers—John Locke's "labor theory of property" by which an individual preempted absolute ownership of land good against the world and all its governments by mixing his labor with it to create human improvements—is utterly ignored in the public trust doctrine.

The public trust doctrine acts as a cloud on the title of all property now held privately in the United States, just waiting for some environmental lawyer to invoke it. It is a legal way to nationalize any land a court sees fit and to avoid paying just compensation for any taking of any size.

The courts have yet to give a definitive answer, ruling on different occasions for both the public trust doctrine and private property rights.[39]

A federal appeals court ruled in April 1992 that the Environmental Protection Agency exceeded its authority to regulate wetlands when it fined a Midwestern developer $50,000 for filling in a depression in an "isolated" wetland. In *Hoffman v. EPA*, Judge Daniel Manion of the U. S. 7th Circuit Court of Appeals rejected the argument that the commerce clause of the U. S. Constitution, which gives the federal government the right to regulate interstate trade, extends to protection of migratory birds on wetlands not associated with a river or lake. Virginia Albrecht, the attorney for Hoffman Homes Inc., the developer, said the decision shows that EPA needs to have a solid legal foundation when it interferes with private property.[40]

In New Jersey, state tax Judge David E. Crabtree lowered the assessed valuation of a 240-acre urban tract from $20 million to $1 million because it couldn't be developed due to state and federal wetland regulations. The "wetland" was smack in the middle of the Giants Stadium complex, surrounded with office buildings, luxury high-rise apartment buildings and an outlet shopping mecca—not exactly the "precious heart of biological diversity" environmentalists whine about. But the Federal law said it was a wetland and that was that. The state of New Jersey had almost condemned the parcel once to widen the New Jersey Turnpike, which runs right beside it, but dropped that plan in 1987 after it learned that new Federal restrictions under the Clean Water Act made the state's project impossible to complete. The owners, the estate of Jerome Sisselman, a tombstone maker who died in 1980, asked the city of East Rutherford to reduce their taxes to a level that reflected the economic trashing their property had suffered from the wetland regulations. The city rejected their plea in 1990, so the Sisselman family sued. The court rejected the city's rejection. Judge Crabtree's decision said that because of wetlands regulations, the property must be taxed as undevelopable land, and reduced the annual taxes from $300,000 to $17,000—a permanent loss of $283,000 each year in tax revenue. A lawyer in the case said the tract was the most valuable undeveloped real estate in New Jersey before the decision. Municipalities throughout New Jersey were horrified at the precedent which will cost them untold millions in lost revenue when all other victims of wetlands press for similar treatment. East Rutherford city attorney Kenneth Porro said the decision may be appealed: "This is a valuable, valuable property." The private owner and the cities are both screwed, plain and simple. Urban governments that have heretofore so smugly supported environmentalists now have something new to think about: where are their property taxes coming from in the no-property Age of the Environment?[41]

The nub of this debate centers around two contradictory views on private property rights. Traditional American values treat private property rights as sacred, rights of the individual good against the world. The Founding Fathers were adamant on the point. John Adams saw private property as the most important single foundation of human liberty:

> ...[P]roperty is surely a right of mankind as really as liberty....The moment that idea is admitted into society that property is not as sacred as the Laws of God, and that there is not a force of law and public justice to protect it, anarchy and tyranny commence. Property must be sacred or liberty cannot exist.[42]

Most of the thirteen original states adopted constitutions prefaced by Bills of Rights which included the natural right of property. The most famous, the Virginia Bill, declared that "all men are by nature equally free and independent, and have certain inherent rights, of which, when they enter into a state of society, they cannot by any compact deprive or divest their posterity; namely, the enjoyment of life and liberty, with the means of acquiring and possessing property, and pursuing and obtaining happiness and safety." Massachusetts declared that "all men are born free and equal and have certain natural, essential, and unalienable rights; among which may be reckoned the right of enjoying and defending their lives and liberties; that of acquiring, possessing, and protecting property; in fine, that of seeking and obtaining their safety and happiness." Even after American political theorists abandoned the theory of natural right, drafters of constitutions continued to paraphrase the Virginia and Massachusetts Bills. Most states adopted some declaration of the natural right of property.[43]

Every state constitution, along with the federal Constitution's Bill of Rights, protects property rights by requiring due process and just compensation for the taking of private property for public use. There is little doubt that this fundamental regard for private property is one of the cornerstones on which America's historic prosperity and vitality has been based.[44]

Environmentalists deny that any such natural right or juridical right exists. Property, as "deep ecologists" write, is at best a leasehold from the state based on the social contract and upon the "biospheric contract." "No one may hold property in any way that harms another, and no one may use property in any way that harms the biosphere," is the most cogent summary of this position. "No one should use property in any way without the input of others," is an oft-expressed corollary.

The socialist mentality has found a fitting home in environmentalism. The libertarian notion of holding property rights as good against the world, or to exclude others from trespass, or to do with as one pleases, is unacceptable, intolerable, and unarguable to hard-line environmentalists. This monumental slide back into feudal notions of the state as ultimate authority over the use and disposition of land, of course, means in practice that there are no property rights of any description, for it is all too easy to assert that there is no way to use a given property without harming others or harming the biosphere in some way. This core belief of environmentalism is openly discussed primarily among academics, and rarely in the political arena—yet. If you can't own property, you *become* property.[45]

The practical worry of environmental group lawyers is that if property owners' demands for just compensation are met, the cost of environmental protection could cripple their pet regulatory programs and end the cushy jobs of their former leaders—about whom more later—who now feed at the public trough in positions of government authority. They are particularly sensitive over the backlash against environmental laws from people such as Peggy Reigle because she is not a big corporation and her organization's pathetically microscopic $20,000 annual budget receives nothing from any big corporation. The credibility of little grass roots advocates rising up in wrath against the mighty environmental movement is hard to combat. Ordinary citizens are beginning to perceive the vast power now entrenched in the hands of the environmental bureaucracy, and are openly worrying that democratic society, private property and free markets may not survive environmentalism.

Clinton sub-cabinet officer George T. Frampton, former president of the Wilderness Society, frankly admitted to the *New York Times* that many Americans "believe environmentalism has replaced Communism as the No. 1 enemy. They have fixed on environmentalism as the green phase of international socialism." Such candid acknowledgments are causing the environmental movement to lose its edge even as it assumes imperial power in the Clinton Administration.[46]

And the crass disregard of highly-placed environmentalist icons for the plight of abused property owners is adding to the sense of frustration and outrage against environmentalism. When Peggy Reigle told her story on ABC News *Nightline*, Ted Koppel's guest, then-Sen. Albert Gore brushed it off as a small problem of no real consequence. What's a dream home, anyway? America's Peggy Reigles are just *people*. We're talking *the environment* here.

Regardless of cost to the economy.

The Clinton Administration has sworn to give the environment higher priority than property rights.

But *is* Peggy Reigle's personal disaster just a flyspeck? All the way across the country from Cambridge, Maryland, Marty Sevier tried to save a big real estate deal near Seattle, Washington from bogging down in wetlands that are wet only because of technical definitions that have lost touch with reality. Sevier is senior director of development for Glacier Park Company, a Burlington Resources subsidiary set up to liquidate land long held by Burlington Northern Railroad. IntraWest Development Corporation, a Canadian company, took an option to buy 600 acres of Glacier Park's land in the Kent Valley near busy population centers, freeways and Seattle-Tacoma airport. It was ideal for industry and warehouses, and zoned for the purpose. But after a study showed that 450 out of the 600 acres would be nearly impossible to develop because of the "wetlands" on them, IntraWest nixed the deal. Marty Sevier told a *Seattle Times* reporter, "The wetlands have killed virtually every deal we've tried to do in the valley in the last year."

Glacier's 600 acres were reappraised downward in 1991, from $68 million to $34 million, reducing tax payments to local communities by $400,000. Glacier is having the appraised value further reduced by another $20 million, leaving its land worth $14 million or less. That will mean further reductions in taxes, shifting the tax burden to homeowners and local businesses. Gary Volchok, a land broker, said that 3,300 acres of the 4,000 industrially zoned acres still left undeveloped in the valley cannot be built on because of wetlands that aren't wet. The lost tax revenue to the adjoining cities of Renton, Kent and Auburn caused by these "wetlands" amounts to $2.5 million.[47]

Trashing Finance

Compounding this trashing of the local economy is the reluctance of banks to lend money to developers unless they already have permits in hand and have preleased more than 50 percent of a building. That's a Catch 22. The bureaucratic process has become so mired in wetland and other environmental controls that it takes at least two years and sometimes twice as long to get a building permit. Marty Sevier's problem property lies in King County, Washington, which also suffers the delayed building permit syndrome. A county official there noted that if all the stalled permits were moved through his agency, it would generate $872.2 million—nearly a billion dollars—worth of construction work and purchases. Carroll Asbell of King County's Building and Land Development Division, said, "That's more than the U.S. lends to some countries. This is what would be spent on everything from kitchen cabinets, salaries, studs, drywall, or brick and mortar." He was fired for his honesty.[48]

As a result of endless environmental delays, the nearby city of Bellevue has seen real estate development dry up to the point that eleven city employees in the building permit department had to be laid off for lack of anything to do. The destructive cumulative impact of wetlands on the economy of just this small valley area in Washington State is estimated at over $100 million and more than $1 billion in King County where the valley is situated. Estimates for the state of Washington exceed $5 billion lost. And Glacier Park Company's national portfolio of 17,657 acres from Washington to Florida faces the same wetlands prohibitions, as the New Jersey case portends. EPA guidelines effectively define more than 70 percent of U.S. land as "wetlands." Three-quarters of all undeveloped private real estate in America are now "off limits" and their assessed valuations are going nowhere but down, dragging the nation's tax revenues with them.

Every time a city or a specific industry is hurt by environmental restrictions, the overall economy's financial structure is also weakened. Karr McCurdy, assistant vice president and geologist with Pittsburgh's Mellon Bank Basic Industries Group, points out that environmental legislation has a negative impact on an industry's financial standing. When financial ratings go down, capital does not flow to affected companies, but becomes dammed up behind environmental restrictions. That hampers the circulation of money through the entire economy.

Take coal, a basic energy mineral: "The financial industry is finding it increasingly important to monitor changes and developments in environmentally related legislation which may have a negative economic impact on coal producing concerns," McCurdy said. The cost of environmental compliance can rarely be fully passed on to the customer. What actually happens is that higher cost producing coal mines simply shut down, cheaper alternative fuels take over coal's market share, and surviving coal companies have to pay higher interest rates to borrow money. "This increasing cost scenario will result in lower sales revenues and operating profit margins, both of which will combine to have an even larger negative impact on profitability," McCurdy said. "Lower profits translate into increased financial risk and a higher cost of capital."[49]

Every basic industry in America is finding its financial condition affected by environmental legislation: Agriculture, fisheries, forest products, mining, petroleum, livestock and all other natural resource producers. You can only push the nonproductive cost of doing business up so high before the whole economy collapses.

Trashing Our Farms

Our farms are particularly vulnerable to assault by wetlands controllers. Even though farms are theoretically exempt from wetlands regulation, in practice they are attacked through numerous loopholes such as "pothole lakes" and "riparian zone" exceptions, and farms are all in areas where there is water from some source. With the definition of wetlands so elastic that it can even include "moist soils," Uncle Sam's environmentalists can effectively nullify property rights on 70 percent of U.S. private land, which works out to at least half of all farmland. That's *most* of the eastern United States and more than 40 percent of California. Federal wetland policy has also shut down or reduced commercial development, reduced the availability of land for housing—causing prices to either skyrocket or collapse, depending on the situation. Existing homes go up in price, undeveloped land goes down, and in places like California where environmental regulations are completely insane, the market just gives up and goes totally to hell. And with the amount of farming land reduced, the per capita price of food goes up.[50]

Consider what happened to farmer Rick McGown of Missouri: He faced prosecution because he repaired a sunken levee on his property, thereby restoring 150 acres of brushland to corn production, yielding an incredible 150 bushels an acre. The Army Corps of Engineers that took him to court had declared his farm to be "wetlands" because it contained "catttails," according to a biological report. When those cattails were examined more closely, they turned out to be wheat sorghum, a common crop plant in Missouri, but something totally unknown to the incredibly intelligent Army Corps of Engineers "biologists." It's this kind of imbecile-with-a-machine-gun mentality that so threatens America's economy today. McGown's neighboring farmer friend Allen Moseley has the same problem, as do thousands of other farmers all over America. Environmentalism is destroying our food base.

The bureaucrats and environmentalists have power—if they only had a brain and they only had a heart. It's beginning to sound like that song from *The Wizard of Oz*. McGown told the *New York Times* that the government was in actuality only "using the Clean Water Act to capture farmers' property."[51]

Consider what happened to a Louisiana farmer who mortgaged his home and converted an unauthorized trash dump into commercial crawfish ponds that provide habitat for river otters. Robert Szabo, an attorney for the National Wetlands Coalition, an industry lobbying group, said the Army Corps of Engineers denied the farmer an "after-the-fact" permit. Szabo said, "I guess if a crawfish pond is found to be destruction of a wetland, you just begin to see how pervasive this can be, and to some people fairly nonsensical."[52]

The Wetlands Regulations, which were derived from the Clean Water Act, said the *New York Times*, have created "a web that has now entangled farmers, environmentalists and Federal agencies in legal disputes across the country. What a runaway bureaucracy wants them to do, farmers say, is convert good cropland into bogs and marshland...with total disregard of property rights guaranteed under the Constitution."

Regardless of cost to the economy.

The Clinton Administration has sworn it will enforce stricter wetlands regulations and refuse to recognize any property rights or pay any just compensation in wetlands cases.

Trashing People

What doesn't get taken out of production by wetlands could be trashed by the Endangered Species Act. If you own land which is home to any species, plant or animal or bug that has been classified by the U.S. Fish and Wildlife Service as "endangered" or "threatened," the law restricts that land from residential, commercial, or even agricultural development. When the Endangered Species Act of 1973 was passed, probably not a single member of Congress had any inkling of the time bombs they had set ticking. Most of them were thinking about saving the whooping cranes and bald eagles and other such beloved creatures. They weren't thinking about insects, salamanders and weeds, although numerous obscure species now crowd the Endangered Species list.

Most people would willingly try to save even these creatures if it were not for the punitive way the law was drafted. Under terms of the Endangered Species Act it is unlawful to kill, harm, harass or annoy any creature listed as endangered or threatened. "Harm," has been defined to include any acts that destroy, damage or modify habitat used by an endangered or threatened species. The problem is, once a general habitat for an endangered species is identified, you can't "harm" a particular part of it even if the endangered species doesn't use that part. That can have disastrous results for *people*. The federal government spent $177 million in 1991 shuffling paper to enforce the Endangered Species Act, but that doesn't begin to reveal the true human cost of this law. Consider the following story:

The Hill Country of Central Texas is about to be nationalized. No, not by some new dictator roaring up in an army of tanks and guns. By nine rare creatures protected by the Endangered Species Act that environmentalists put on a list brought into Austin in the briefcase of a federal bureaucrat. Two of the nine protected creatures, the black-capped vireo and the golden-cheeked warbler, are small songbirds that winter in Mexico and points south and return to the Austin area in March to nest. Even though the biggest threat to these declining bird populations is the brown-headed cowbird that lays its eggs in the smaller birds' nests and crowds out the young, people are being punished for the decline. Incidentally, the other seven species were cave-dwelling invertebrates—the kind of creatures most people call bugs and worms.

The golden-cheeked warbler was entered as an emergency listing to the Endangered Species list on a handwritten petition by a member of Earth First!, the eco-terrorist band that has burned livestock auction barns, shot livestock on the range, and nearly killed sawmill worker George Alexander with a hidden spike in a tree that caused a bandsaw to break into deadly shrapnel. The petition wasn't challenged by anyone, so it went on the list. There are an estimated 1,100 to 2,300 breeding pairs of warblers.

Ben Love, a Texas rancher from the Trans-Pecos region, said "I think there is little disagreement that this listing was done for the sole purpose of stopping development in western Travis County, Texas." He's right. The consequences of this Earth First! listing have been devastating. Part of the habitat for the warbler is mature juniper, which covers the Texas Hill Country west of Austin by the hundreds of thousands of acres. "Harming" that habitat could mean anything the bureaucrats want it to mean.

Margaret Rodgers, an elderly lady who owns a ranch west of Austin, was clearing a fencerow of invading young junipers so she could rebuild the fence. The vigorous juniper had crowded the fenceposts and rearranged the barbed wire so badly that her livestock could get out—a problem familiar to every Hill Country rancher. Some busybody saw her at work and called the U.S. Fish and Wildlife Service, which is the federal agency responsible for enforcing the Endangered Species Act. Robert M. Short, a Fish and Wildlife bureaucrat, responded to the report of the secret informer by writing this letter to Mrs. Rodgers:

> It has come to our attention that clearing of a strip of woodland has recently occurred on a tract of land located south of FM 1431 in the vicinity of Lago Vista, Texas. We understand that you are one of the joint owners of the property. Information available to us indicates that this property supports prime habitat for the federally-listed endangered golden-cheeked warbler. Destruction of habitat of an endangered species may constitute a "take" of that species as defined by the Endangered Species Act, which prohibits "take" of a federally-listed species.[53]

Despite the fact that Mrs. Rodgers was cutting immature juniper growing up under her fences, which is not "prime habitat" for the little warbler, Short warned Mrs. Rodgers that she was in violation of the Endangered Species Act and threatened her with criminal and civil penalties. "Section 11(b)(1) provides for a fine of not more than $50,000 or imprisonment up to one year, or both," Short wrote. "Section 11(a)(1) permits assessment of up to $25,000 as a civil penalty for each violation."

Texans did not take kindly to the Fish and Wildlife Service for this highhanded action. "If you can't clear your fencerows," said Ben Love, "you can't keep your cattle, horses, sheep and goats in." Enforcement to protect just that one species of songbird would clearly destroy the entire livestock economy of Central Texas.

Yet that is exactly what the law demands.

We called Mrs. Rodgers when the incident was made known to us. She told us that the Nature Conservancy had already bought out adjoining parcels of the ranch owned by relatives, but she had refused their offers to buy her land. Perhaps that casts light on who the informer was and why bureaucrat Short was so helpful to Mrs. Rodgers in explaining the penalties: Did the U.S. Fish and Wildlife Service have an agreement with the Nature Conservancy to apply enough pressure to Mrs. Rodgers to convert her into a "willing seller?" We will examine collusion between government and private environmental groups in detail in our profile of the Nature Conservancy.

One facet of the federal takeover of Central Texas is called the Balcones Canyonlands Conservation Plan, which would spend $125 million confiscating 65,000 acres of private land west of Austin. It was cooked up by a self-appointed executive committee comprised of Sierra Club and Audubon Society members and local government officials. This committee used the authority of the Endangered Species Act section 10A to set up a huge preserve which would protect the habitat from development forever by taking it out of private ownership, or putting it in the ownership of environmental groups such as the land-buying Nature Conservancy. The head of the committee was David Braun, head of the Texas Nature Conservancy. Where were the land owners on this committee? Guess.

Perhaps the idea of the Balcones Canyonlands Conservation Plan was not really to protect those precious endangered species at all. The front page of the August 1991 *Austin Sierra*, newsletter of the Austin Regional Group of the Sierra Club, stated: "The biggest benefit of the plan will be the creation of permanent open spaces for public recreation, water quality enhancement, and wildlife protection, regardless of whether or not the species survive."

What was that last part? *Regardless of whether or not the species survive?* Do we detect a little shuck and jive here? Could the warbler and the vireo just be a cover for a big land grab?

The federal government has threatened all use of a vast area of Central Texas for human purposes, in effect stealing the land without paying for it. And the same thing is brewing in Southern California because of another small bird, the gnatcatcher; in the Gulf Coastal States because of the Red Cockaded Woodpecker; and virtually everywhere else by some critter or another. The Sierra Club and the National Wildlife Federation say that plants and animals are more important than people.

Regardless of cost to the economy.

The impact of their beliefs extends far beyond the Texas Hill Country. In the tiny village of Manacaparu, Brazil, seventeen-year-old Gilson Ramos walked late one evening in August from his palm-thatched cottage down to the banks of the Amazon to tie up his canoe. It was high water season, when the world's mightiest river floods. Fish dispersed by the swelling waters attracted an 18-foot-long jacare, a South American cousin to the familiar alligator. In the dark, Gilson thought he grabbed his canoe, but it was the jacare's tail. As a barefoot, 12-year-old neighbor later told a *New York Times* reporter, "The jacare took Gilson away and ate him up."

Gilberto Mestrinbo, governor of Amazonas state, summed up the feeling of his people about meddling environmentalists from the United States and other developed countries of the world: "Environmentalists care more about plants and animals than about people." Mestrinbo is leading a campaign to sue Brazil's environmental protection agency for compensation for the loss of Gilson. And he is fighting to end the 25-year-old ban on hunting wildlife species in Brazil, a law forced upon the nation by pressure from American environmentalists. "We need a jacare hunting season," said Governor Mestrinbo. "It would be great for tourism and would give locals more income. Environmentalists are only interested in restrictions that block development of Amazonas"—Brazil's largest and least developed state.

Governor Mestrinbo said, "Our region contains minerals worth $1.6 trillion, tropical hardwoods valued at $1.7 trillion, huge deposits of natural gas, and fertile areas that would allow Brazil to increase its farmland by 70 percent. Yet we have been condemned to eternal misery solely because some environmentalists insist that the Amazon remain untouchable."

American environmentalists aggressively press to turn all of Amazonas into a vast nature museum. Already, 37,000 square miles of Amazonas and Roraima states has been turned into a park—situated in the middle of the world's last great untapped mineral province, a park the size of Portugal, with proven deposits of gold, tin, and diamonds. Advocates of the wise use of resources failed in a recent attempt to reverse the government decision to put the land off limits to settlement and development. Only the Yanomami tribe may live there, a Stone Age band of about 10,000 individuals, and even they are not allowed to use the vast wealth under their bare feet.

And back in the little village of Manacaparu, for Eloi Soares de Oliveira, a neighbor of the bereaved Ramos family, the most incomprehensible environmental law is the ban on hunting jacares. "We are surrounded on all sides by jacares," Soares said. "Surrounded on all sides."[54]

This is definitely getting crazy. A brain. A heart. Where are you now that we need you, Tin Man and Scarecrow?

Trashing Industry

Industry provides all the things we need to live. America seems to have forgotten that basic fact. Let us explain it in simple terms anyone can understand, as we heard it once told by a mining engineer:

People need *things*. *Things* are made of *stuff*. *Stuff* comes out of the *ground*. *Industry* gets the *stuff* out of the *ground* and turns it into *things*. Then people can *use* the *things*. Whatever it is, animal, vegetable, or mineral, the *things* we need to live are made of *stuff* that *industry* gets out of the *ground,* one way or another. If that sounds patronizing, it is—we Americans have grown so remote from our natural and industrial roots, so soft and stupid, we *need* a patron.

It's as if every adult American had been afflicted with the blind sight of the sixth grader in Oakland, California, whose entry into a 1980s Farm Poster Contest announced "We Don't Need Farmers Where I Live Because There's A Safeway Right Across The Street." That's forgivable in a twelve-year-old, but not an adult with a college degree working in a professional job. Yet that's what many supposedly grownup Americans think today. They are people who use things made by industry every day and never even realize it, much less say "Thank you, industry." Environmentalism is a kind of impervious Mindwrap that protects them from economic reality. Minds stuffed with fluffy. Emotions that regard industry as evil men running evil factories whose only product is pollution. Souls that believe all the material goods of industry just come out of some little black box like magic. With a society as disconnected from the real world as that, we have no chance of survival. We will act to mock, and devalue and destroy the very sources of our food, clothing, and shelter, just as we see the environmental movement doing all around us.

At a conference once, we asked a highly intelligent reporter who was interviewing us, Eric Brazil of the *San Francisco Examiner,* what the mining industry had done for him today—just picking an industry at random to make a point. He stunned us with an uncomprehending abstraction: "Well, I suppose that some mining industry stock transaction may have increased the portfolio of some of the readers of Hearst newspapers." We stared in disbelief and said, "Didn't the mining industry provide the metal for the presses that will print the story tonight that you're writing today?" With a shock of recognition he said, "I see your point." Unfortunately, not everyone is as bright as Eric Brazil.

How many of us realize that land is the fundamental source of what keeps us alive? And that industry is the fundamental instrument that gets modern society's stuff out of the ground and makes it into things we can use? There is no more basic way to trash the economy than to do what the environmental movement is doing: to stop industry from getting stuff out of the ground, whether animal, vegetable or mineral—bread, hamburger, lumber, chardonnay, videocassettes, hospitals, cars, airplanes, buildings, condoms, gasoline, clothes—you use it, it comes out of the ground one way or another.

Phil Davidson's family runs a sawmill in the timber town of Mapleton, Oregon, about 60 miles south of Portland. Like many small and middle sized sawmills, he has traditionally purchased substantial amounts of timber from the National Forests, which were established for the purpose of providing a timber supply from part of the federal lands. Davidson watched his company and his town decimated by environmentalists entering the political process to stop the sale of federal timber. His story has been repeated in hundreds of towns throughout the Pacific Northwest. It isn't by accident. The National Audubon Society pressed lawsuit after lawsuit to kill off Phil Davidson and everyone like him, blocking access to raw materials under the guise of protecting salmon runs, rare plants, and finally, the spotted owl that everyone has heard of. Randall O'Toole, a Portland, Oregon-based environmental activist, candidly admitted to *Newsweek* that "cumulatively, the environmental movement is interested in shutting down the timber industry." O'Toole was distancing himself from that viewpoint, but his credible assertion was based upon inside knowledge.[55]

To have such an ambition is an outrage. To have such an ambition and use false pretenses to achieve it is despicable. But, according to Sierra Club Legal Defense Fund analyst Andy Stahl, the spotted owl is merely a surrogate for preventing the harvest of old-growth timber. He told an environmental law conference, "When it comes to protecting old growth, I've often thought that thank goodness the spotted owl evolved, for if it hadn't, we'd have to genetically engineer it. It's a perfect species to use as a surrogate."[56] Stahl was evidently unaware that his presentation was being videotaped and transcribed. What kind of twisted organization is the Sierra Club that it can use such deliberate cunning to destroy the livelihood and lives of so many fellow humans?

The gall that environmentalists exhibit in denying any blame for the economic catastrophe they caused is equally outrageous. A 1991 Wilderness Society report on the devastated Northwest timber economy said in essence that the spotted owl was not to blame, the industry was dying anyway because of automation, so what's the big deal? In fact, much of that "automation" is the result of political fears—forest firms are changing from making ordinary lumber from ordinary trees to making flakeboard and other forest products that can be manufactured from small-diameter non-controversial trees such as aspen. These products are made on huge high-technology presses requiring a few computer-trained operators rather than the larger blue-collar crew of the ordinary sawmill. There are plenty of trees to support ordinary sawmills, but the Sierra Club and its cohort won't let loggers use them. So the only viable alternatives are innovative products such as flakeboard.

The Wilderness Society report only referred to big timber firms with the capital to automate their way out of the political problem of choked-off timber supply. It didn't even mention the major fact of the spotted owl problem: What happens to the medium and small firms—*most* of the people affected? They are the thousands of small logging contractors, and the thousands of family log-trucking firms, and the hundreds of little independent sawmills. They didn't automate, because they couldn't. Most Northwest terrain is unsuitable for the automated tree snippers used in Southern forests, and the diameter of Northwest trees is generally too big for anything other than a chainsaw, which cannot be automated. Log trucks likewise resist automation. Independent sawmills can rarely raise the capital to buy high-tech computerized equipment, especially when the prospects for adequate timber supply to recoup the investment are dimmed by political uncertainty. The Wilderness Society conveniently forgot these victims of their overweening power. And when the log supply was curtailed, even the automated sawmills shut down. These productive people simply vanished from the economy because they could not buy any timber—it's "protecting" the spotted owl. That timber could support both people and owls with intelligent management, but environmental dogma won't let it.

Regardless of cost to the economy.

The Clinton Administration has sworn to prevent any consideration of economic impact in the designation of endangered species.

The popular perception that development is encroaching on nature and destroying it is the exact opposite of what has really happened during the past twenty-five years. In fact, nature protection designations have proliferated so wildly they are destroying economic development everywhere, not just in the Pacific Northwest. Every time an environmental group draws a line around a new place on a map and convinces Congress to "protect" it, thousands of people are pushed out of productive employment. Little by little, one area after another has been pushed off-limits to economic resource use.

Perhaps the most stupefying example of using the spotted owl as a surrogate for shutting down the timber industry came from Lake Washington Technical College near Seattle. A middle-aged man who had lost his job in the timber industry to the spotted owl enrolled in the college's recreational vehicle repair program. When the Sierra Club eliminated his job, they told him to go get retrained, so he did, but not without anguish. This out-of-work logger struggled for months before moving to Seattle, fighting to maintain his self-esteem, worrying about feeding his family, and wondering what new career he should pursue. He picked recreational vehicle repair because he was mechanically inclined and it seemed like a more secure future than another forest job, given the political realities of eco-power.

But there was a joker in the deck. The educational system of the state of Washington is funded in large part by revenues from state-owned forests. When the Sierra Club used the spotted owl as a surrogate to shut down the timber industry, it also severely hurt the educational system. The former logger found that his retraining program at the state-supported college would fold for lack of funds before he could complete it—the Sierra Club had shut down his retraining program with the same blow that killed his logging job. The logger told a reporter, "It took me six months to get over my fears. I came here. I moved my family. I started to get over my fears and now you come in here and tell us this course isn't going to exist anymore?"[57]

Now environmentalists like Stahl are using the Red Cockaded Woodpecker as a surrogate in the South, "biodiversity" in Wisconsin and other Lakes States, and the "Northern Forest" project in New England to put the timber industry out of business.

Government As Enemy

Jim Little runs cattle on the 30,000 acre Bear Valley allotment in Idaho. The land is bisected by Bear Valley Creek near the headwaters of the Salmon River, where the spring chinook salmon spawn. The chinook run is newly listed as an endangered species. Protection measures will increase Little's operating costs more than 20 percent.[58] That will squeeze the surplus out of his ranch. He'll slowly drift down the road to economic ruin. Environmentalists are doing everything they can to speed his departure. The Nature Conservancy, Earth First! and the Audubon Society have pushed ranchers to the brink of extermination with demands to take private and government lands out of livestock production.

The Audubon Society's slick television special, *The New Range Wars*, falsely depicted cattle ranchers as depredating the land and maligned cattle as ecology-wreckers. It was part of the environmental movement's efforts to make federal rangelands "Livestock Free by '93!" Getting the public to support that campaign required the depiction of ranchers as a "rape, scrape and run mob," and as receiving private subsidies for grazing on public lands. In fact, ranchers have one of the best records of land stewardship and conservation of any human endeavor. And in fact, there is no subsidy whatsoever in grazing on federal lands—the grazing fee the rancher pays the government is twice the value of what he receives in the form of grass, because the rancher already owns the water that gives the federal lands the value they have. The fact is that eliminating U.S. grazing leases would simply destroy a whole way of life for no real benefit. But truth doesn't matter to environmental groups.

As a respected veterinarian noted:

> Everybody in the livestock industry is aware of the slogan "Cattle Free by '93." The environmental movement seeks to ban the leasing of public lands by the U.S. government to livestock producers for grazing. If this goal is realized, it will have devastating effects on the livestock industry in the western states, where many ranching operations are dependent on such leases. Thousands of ranching families will be deprived of their way of life and their ability to earn a living. Many larger agricultural enterprises will be severely set back, impacting both owners and employees.[59]

Telling the truth about the environment can be hazardous. Prominent Nevada rancher Wayne Hage wrote a book in 1989 titled *Storm Over Rangelands*. In it he argued that the major federal range management agencies—the U.S. Forest Service and the Bureau of Land Management—were submitting to pressure from environmental groups and systematically seizing the range rights of ranchers. Federal bureaucrats are denying access to water owned by the ranchers and severely cutting back grazing allotments that have been contractually assured for more than 100 years, Hage asserted. Hage documented government abuses of private rights by federal bureaucrats who used false claims of "damaging the environment" as an excuse to encroach little by little on the rancher's grazing rights, slowly weakening the rancher's position until he went bankrupt and could be thrown off the range completely. Hage also asserted that powerful environmentalist interests were behind the assault on private rights.

More to the point, Hage detailed the long chain of private rights in federal rangeland which established conclusively that the federal government was in the wrong. He showed that it was not the rancher who was being subsidized by low grazing fees, but the wasteful bureaucracy that was being subsidized by the private rancher with a federal land grazing permit priced twice as high as the grass was worth. Hage pointed out that environmentalist efforts to raise federal grazing fees to the same level as private grazing leases was comparing apples with oranges. The private grazing lease is priced so high because the lessor owns all the values. But the federal grazing allotment is filled with values the private permittee already owns—the water, the roads, the fences, the stockwatering ponds, and so forth. Why, Hage asked bluntly, should a federal permittee pay again for what he already owns?

Hage's book also examined the history of wildlife populations in federal grazing lands, revealing that ranchers had been such good stewards of the environment that game animals such as grouse, bighorn sheep and antelope have increased dramatically. The phony claims of "damaging the environment" were especially galling to ranchers who had for generations protected wildlife through predator control and building water catchments so animals could survive the dry season, only to have some new federal bureaucrat fresh from employment with an environmental group come onto a rancher's allotment, photograph a naturally bare rocky spot and put it in the rancher's Range Condition File as "proof of overgrazing."

Hage's book caught on like a firestorm in a summer prairie. Thousands of ranchers who thought they were the only ones suffering at the hands of federal bureaucrats suddenly realized that they were all in the same predicament. Hage went on the lecture circuit with his book telling other ranchers how to defend themselves. He was an instant hit. His arguments were so powerful that environmentalists could not rebut them.

Hage told his audiences that the private rancher with a grazing permit on federal lands in many cases owns more of the values in the "federal" land than the government does—water rights, roads, fences, wells, pipelines, stockwatering ponds, mineral rights, cattle chutes, ranch houses, bunk houses and cook houses are commonly owned by the private permittee and not by the federal government. In such cases, why should a federal agency dictate to the private rancher? Why don't the managing agencies, the Bureau of Land Management and the U.S. Forest Service that charge stiff grazing fees, recognize these private rights instead of trying to steal them? The Internal Revenue Service always recognizes private rights in federal lands—to tax them. One hand of the government doesn't know what the other hand is up to—except that they're both groping in private pockets. Hage urged ranchers to stand up for private rights in federal lands— anathema to the Bureau of Land Management and the U.S. Forest Service. This challenge to centralized power did not go unnoticed by the government and several key environmental groups.

Hage found himself being harassed by the U.S. Forest Service, one of the federal agencies on his Pine Creek Ranch in Central Nevada. Ranchers throughout the West tell of federal agents coming on their allotments, opening gates and running the permitee's cattle out into forbidden areas, then calling the ranch house and telling the permittee to come reclaim his "trespassing" cattle— and pay an exorbitant fine for the privilege. The income to the federal bureaucracy from these myriad phony trespass cases is tremendous. This is the grazing version of bureaucrats using environmental regulations as a revenue source rather than as a way to protect nature.

One day in the summer of 1991, Wayne Hage got a call from a Toiyabe National Forest bureaucrat telling him that a large fraction of his herd had mysteriously trespassed into a forbidden area and that he should come get them. Hage went to see what had happened and found his herd being guarded by an army of federal agents armed with automatic weapons. Perhaps they thought these were battle bovines or combat cows. Or perhaps they thought Mr. Hage would arrive in a temper and they could end the theory of private rights in federal lands then and there.

At any rate, the Forest Service confiscated Wayne Hage's cattle and sold them at auction—ignoring brand-inspection laws that require the seller to be the owner of the cattle. The government, violating its own laws, thus destroyed the value of Hage's ranch and shattered his finances. Hage filed a lawsuit in the United States Court of Claims asking for just compensation for the property of which he had been deprived, including his extensive private rights in the federal lands, water rights foremost.

Immediately, the Sierra Club, the National Wildlife Federation and the Natural Resources Defense Council filed for status as intervenors in the case, arguing that all ranchers should be removed from their federal grazing allotments without compensation of any kind and that rancher-owned water rights should be taken by the federal government without compensation. If anyone mistrusts Wayne Hage's allegations that the federal government was acting on pressure from environmental groups, the brief these groups filed in this case should remove all doubt. They certainly made Wayne Hage's ranch livestock free by '93. And they're trying to destroy the entire livestock industry with similar tricks on all federal grazing allotments.

Regardless of cost to the economy.

Then came one of the most astonishing conflicts of interest in American legal annals: The Attorney General of the State of Nevada, Frankie Sue Del Papa, contracted with the staff attorney of the National Wildlife Federation, Thomas Lustig, to represent the state as an intervenor in the Hage lawsuit. It is astonishing because the Attorney General takes an oath of office to defend the laws of the state, and water rights in Nevada are owned by the state. Nevada state water rights are transferred into private ownership through state courts as adjudicated water rights. If private water rights in Nevada are abandoned or forfeited, they return to the state, not to the federal government. Wayne Hage owns adjudicated water rights with a chain of title going back in the state of Nevada for a century.

And yet the Nevada Attorney General hired an environmental group staff lawyer to argue that Nevada state water rights ought to be given to the federal government. Why? A little probing into the background of Frankie Sue Del Papa revealed that she is a long-time environmentalist, actively sitting on the advisory board of the Trust for Public Land, a frequent partner of the Sierra Club in lawsuits that end up with court awards of land or cash to the Trust. It seemed clear to many Nevada ranchers that Attorney General Del Papa was intervening on the side of the three environmental groups solely to give the Hage ranch and its water rights to her pet environmental group. The web of power spun by the environmental movement is impressive—and, to some, frightening. Numerous property rights organizations called for the resignation or impeachment of Del Papa.[60]

Nevada State Senator Dean Rhoads, chairman of the Public Lands Committee, approached Del Papa and urged her to withdraw her motion as an intervenor in the Hage case. She replied, "Over my dead body." Senator Rhoads allowed as how that might be arranged. The Legislature of the State of Nevada subsequently launched an investigation into allegations of conflict of interest against Del Papa. The U.S. Claims

Court judge later threw Del Papa and her environmentalist cohort out of court, denying their motion to intervene.

The federal government then obtained a felony indictment and conviction of Mr. Hage on charges that he damaged and removed government property—for cutting brush choking his own ditches on his own privately-owned right of way. The Ninth Circuit Court of Appeals overturned the conviction as "not proved." But it shows the length our government will go to silence a critic.

Unsympathetic observers have said that Wayne Hage brought his martyrdom on himself. If standing up for one's rights is equivalent to martyring oneself, then we can begin to see why the *New York Times* thought that citizens must protect themselves from their own government with desperation.

Trashing our Minds

Perhaps the most insidious and devastating effect of environmentalism is its systematic corruption of our minds. By flashing warnings against all human activity across our every waking minute, environmental organizations thwart and mock and act to destroy all human activity. Green Guilt has become a way of life.

We are told that global warming is going to destroy all life on earth. But we are not told that there is a very serious debate among experts as to whether global warming is even happening—and if it is, whether it holds any harm in store. Although exhaustive records of temperatures in the United States for the past century reveal no change whatsoever, advocates of the doomsday scenario insist that *worldwide* the mean temperature has risen about one degree in the past century. That is debated, but let's say it has. Do we hear that the world is rebounding from "The Little Ice Age," a drop in global temperature estimated at 2 degrees Fahrenheit, that brought harsh winters from 1400 to 1850? No. Because that would show any increase to be a return to normal, not a catastrophe. Do we ask what the Earth's normal temperature is? No. Because the answer is that it is always changing up or down, a dynamic system, not some ideal condition frozen in time forever. We are today in an interglacial era that has lasted nearly 10,000 years, and human history lies mostly in a severe Ice Age that prevailed during the past 2 million years. We're far more likely to see the return of the glaciers than a tropical Earth. Do we ask what would really happen if the worst possible increase in temperature came, let's say an average rise of 25 degrees Fahrenheit? No. Because that's less than the global cooling since the age of the dinosaurs, when the whole world was such a tropical paradise that reptiles unable to generate their own body heat could spread from the north pole to the south. A future in which the whole planet looked like Hawaii is less fearsome. Increased deserts? No. Deserts are caused by global cold, not global warming. Deserts came only with the Ice Ages because atmospheric water was locked up in the polar ice caps, and would green up again if the polar ice caps melted and the warmer climate evaporated the oceans at a higher rate leading to greater global rainfall—just look at the fossil evidence and you will find that deserts come with global cooling, not global warming. Global warming is a manufactured crisis to justify any measures to stop human activity. Yet the Clinton Administration has sworn to limit carbon dioxide emissions to 1990 levels to reverse global warming.[61]

We are told that man-made chemicals are depleting the ozone in the upper atmosphere, creating an ozone hole which will let in more ultraviolet radiation and kill all life on earth except for a few resistant creatures such as cockroaches and spiders. Do scientists who disagree get quoted in the daily newspapers or network television news programs? No. Because they would point out that the ozone hole over Antarctica has always been there, and that we only became able to detect it in the recent past. It is a natural feature formed around the South Polar Vortex, a vast air current generated at the South Pole by the rotation of the earth, and influenced by the magnetic field of the earth which bends into the South Pole and the absence of sunlight over Antarctica during the winter months when there is not enough solar energy to cause the formation of ozone from natural atmospheric components. And did anyone point out that the supposed ozone hole over North America—actually precursor conditions, the ozone is perfectly intact, but the newspapers couldn't deal with anything that wasn't all black or white—was primarily the result of volcanic dust from the recent eruption of Mt. Pinatubo in the Philippine Islands? No, because that would make the doomsday scenario less frightening. The ozone hole is a manufactured doom. Yet the Clinton Administration has sworn to ban all ozone-depleting chemicals regardless of the cost to the economy.

We are told that acid rain is devastating our lakes and forests on the Eastern Seaboard in the downwind track of fossil fuel-burning power generating plants. As we noted above, the $500 million study of the National Acid Precipitation Assessment Program (NAPAP), that Congress itself ordered and paid for, found minimal damage from acid rain in actual examinations on the ground by respected and qualified scientists. Do we hear environmental groups saying, "Well, we were wrong. What we thought was a crisis is really only a problem that can be cured without penalizing the power industry and increasing costs of energy." No. Because that would hurt their fund raising and soften the image of industry that they are trying so hard to make people hate. Do we hear anything about all the millions of beneficial uses that our power plants yield, of the homes they warm, or the light they shed, of the cultural wealth they generate? No. Because environmental groups must cultivate the belief that the only product of industry is pollution. And that *blame* is the only proper response to any industry at all. Acid rain is a manufactured doom to make us hate industry. Yet the Clinton Administration has sworn to halt all acid emission regardless of cost to the economy.

We are told that our Native American forebears had a better philosophy than Western civilization and a more benevolent lifestyle—in short, were great prophets of environmentalism. One famous statement by Chief Seattle, a head of the Suquamish tribe near Puget Sound in Washington state, in an 1855 letter to President Franklin Pierce has become an icon of environmentalism. In early 1992, *Brother Eagle, Sister Sky: A Message from Chief Seattle* stood at No. 5 on *The New York Times Book Review* best-seller list; it sold more than 250,000 copies since its publication by Dial Books for Young Readers in 1991. The 1992 Earth Day U.S.A. Committee, based in New Hampshire, asked 6,000 religious leaders from around the world to read Chief Seattle's letter:

The Great Chief in Washington sends word that he wishes to buy our lands. How can he buy or sell the sky? The wealth of the land? The idea is strange to us.

We don't own the freshness of the air, or the sparkle of the water, so how can he buy them from us? Every part of the earth is sacred to my people; every shining pine needle, every sandy shore, every mist in the dark woods, every clearing and humming insect is holy in the memory and experience of my people.

We know the white man does not understand our ways. One portion of the land is the same to him as the next, for he is a stranger who comes in the night and takes the land, whatever he needs.

The earth is not his brother, but his enemy. When he has conquered it, he moves on. He leaves his father's grave and his children's birthright is forgotten. There is no quiet place in the white man's cities; no place to hear the leaves of spring or the rustle of insect wings. I have seen a thousand rotting buffaloes on the prairies left by the white man who shot them from a passing train. The dogs of appetite will devour the rich earth and leave only a desert.

Whites, too, shall pass. Perhaps sooner than other tribes. Continue to contaminate your bed and you will one night suffocate in your waste.

The sacred corners of the forest are heavy with the sons of many men, and the views of the ripe hill are blotted by talking wires. Where is the thicket? Gone. Where is the eagle? Gone.

And what is it so say goodbye to the swift and the hunt, the end of the living and the beginning of survival?

It is a masterpiece of environmental thought. It is revered by many as the perfect rebuke to industrial civilization. It makes today's children ashamed of themselves and their parents. It makes them hate their life. It makes them want to tear down all that industry has built and restore the beautiful life of Chief Seattle.

The letter is so perfect to our modern ears that it sounds like the work of a modern movie writer. Because it is. A scriptwriter named Ted Perry wrote it in 1971 for an environmental film called *Home*. Chief Seattle never said most of it.

Perry, now a professor at Middlebury College, was hired by the Southern Baptist Radio and Television Commission to take the speech of Chief Seattle and strengthen its environmental theme for their film. "I never tried to pretend that Chief Seattle said the things I wrote," Perry told the Associated Press. "I was inspired by Chief Seattle and I told the producers to identify me as the author of the words. But they said it would be more authentic if people thought Chief Seattle had said it."

The phony letter is based upon an actual 1854 speech of Chief Seattle, but the real speech contains virtually none of those words, as attested by the only known translation, written by Dr. Henry Smith, who published his recollections in 1887— 33 years after Chief Seattle gave the speech.

Northwest historian David Buerge said, "Chief Seattle is probably our greatest manufactured prophet." Buerge is one of a group of reputable historians frustrated that their work has failed to stop the myth from spreading around the world. He points out that there were no bison within 600 miles of Chief Seattle's home on Puget Sound; what's more, the letter is dated about 15 years before the first railroad crossed the

Plains from Omaha to Sacramento. The great buffalo slaughter that our script writer deplored so eloquently took place *more than a decade after Chief Seattle died.*

Murray Morgan, who has written half a dozen books about the Pacific Northwest, said "It's deplorable how people have felt free to shove words in his mouth. Very little of it is accurate."

Earth Day U.S.A. Committee spokeswoman Denise Gauther said, "It was really the right message for us. The important thing is the words were said." By whom does not appear to matter. The Committee ignored the historians and decided to send the phony version out anyway, noting that the letter was "attributed" to Chief Seattle.

Dial Books was only slightly more honest. They printed an explanation at the end of *Brother Eagle, Sister Sky*, saying that "the origins of Chief Seattle's words are partly obscured by the mists of time." The creator and illustrator of the book, Susan Jeffers, frankly admitted, "Basically, I don't know what he said—but I do know that the Native American people lived this philosophy, and that's what is important."[62]

Native American people also practiced unspeakably barbaric tortures, systematically burned enemy villages, crops and people and some tore the beating hearts out of living sacrificial victims. There is always a dark side to nature worship.

Isn't it important to tell the whole truth? Should we believe that lies intended to make Western culture reject its own beautiful arts and bounteous industry don't matter? Is publishing a known fraud without so much as asking where it really came from acceptable educational practice for our children?

Thus the environmental movement trashes our minds.

Manufactured prophets.

Manufactured crises.

Manufactured dooms.

Trashing the Economy with lies, deceit, fraud.

The growing mythology of eco-apocalypse has provoked an organized backlash to orthodox environmentalism: More than 1,500 varied groups with a total membership of perhaps 3 million all over America have sprung up to defend property rights, jobs and economic survival, and access to federal lands for commodity use and motorized recreation. These three segments form a movement for the wise use of resources as opposed to no-use of resources—the Wise Use Movement.

They are facing an uphill battle trying to tell the public that environmentalism is not the sweetness and light we thought it was. Development is not encroaching on nature and destroying it as much as nature protection is encroaching on human development and destroying it. People are losing out.

We could go on and fill this book with environmentalist-caused horror stories. Some have urged us to do just that. We have received enough correspondence from devastated people to fill several books with poignant tales of human suffering caused by environmentalist Economy Trashers. We regret that we could not tell every one of these tragic stories. Every person matters. But it is just as important that readers understand who is to blame, and that is why we have filled the bulk of this book with profiles of the guilty—the Economy Trashers themselves and all their allies—and there are plenty of horror stories to verify our assertions.

Trashing Our Jobs

One of the key Economy Trashers is the Environmental Grantmakers Association (EGA), a quiet consortium of over a hundred large Establishment foundations allied with a large number of top environmental groups. It has become something of a Command Central for much of the environmental movement within the past few years. Through the power of the purse, which contains many billions of dollars, these powerful foundations guide their environmental movement colleagues according to their own agendas. *Money* magazine said that in 1991, environmental groups "took in $2.5 billion."[63]

With the rise of the Wise Use Movement to challenge the legitimacy of the environmental movement, the Environmental Grantmakers Association became concerned. In October 1992, EGA met at the plush Rosario Resort in the San Juan Islands in Washington State's inland sea to address those concerns along with its regular agenda items. They were surprised by a demonstration of seventeen placard-carrying protesters desperately trying to tell the foundation executives that their money was being used to kill jobs and communities. The demonstration had been organized by Charles S. Cushman of the National Inholders Association, who was alerted to the meeting by friends in the wise use network and chartered a boat to take the protesters into the resort's private harbor.

The protesters were asked to leave the resort, but EGA official Jon Jensen allowed them to give a short talk to any conference attendees who wished to listen. About forty gathered around a grassy spot outside the conference center for twenty minutes to hear the anguished stories of people losing their property, their jobs and their communities. But the EGA sessions were closed to the public.

One of the final closed sessions of the three-day annual retreat was titled "The Wise Use Movement: Threats and Opportunities." Individual audio tapes of this session, we later discovered, can be purchased for $11.00 each from Conference Recording Service, 1308 Gilman Street, Berkeley, California 94706, Phone; (510)527-3600, Fax: (510)527-8404. The presenter was Debra Callahan, Director of the Environmental Grass Roots Program at the W. Alton Jones Foundation in Virginia, seventh largest source of environmentalist funding nationally, dispensing over $7.4 million through 97 separate grants in 1990 alone.

Callahan first checked her audience—"Are any of you associated with wise use groups?"—then, assured there were no infiltrators, told the room full of environmental group leaders "about some of the information-gathering that's been going on about the wise use movement, the property rights movement, from all across the country." She was clearly worried about what she had discovered.

"Our foundation put together a report about eight months ago. I'd like to update you on what we have learned in about the last four months in continued research."

The additional research, had been performed by media strategy firm MacWilliams Cosgrove Snider of Boston, under sponsorship of the Wilderness Society, and distributed as "The Wise Use Movement: Strategic Analysis and Fifty State Review." Callahan, referring to the report, said her foundation had previously thought of the resistance to environmentalism as coming from "command and control, top heavy corporate-funded front groups," but that "what we're finding is that wise use is really a local movement driven by primarily local concerns and not national issues...And in fact the more we dig into it, having put together over a number of months a fifty-state fairly comprehensive survey of what's going on, we have come to the conclusion that this is pretty much generally a grass roots movement, which is a problem, because it means there's no silver bullet.

"The movement is growing quickly at the grass roots as it finds its base around the country, in some states more quickly than others, but again"—and here her voice became very emphatic and she tapped the rostrum—"*this is happening in every single state. We think of this as being a Western phenomenon. It's not true.*

"In New England it's about the Adirondack Mountains, it's about private property rights movements, it's about the Northeastern forests. In the Southeast it's about coastal zone management and coastal development. It's about shrimpers in Louisiana not liking turtle exclusion devices. In the Midwest it's about farm lands. In coastal Louisiana and Texas it's about minerals development, coal mining...All over the country it's like a gas—it's filling the available space.

"Generally speaking, you see as many women as men"..."As far as age range, same thing is true.

"What people fundamentally want, what people fundamentally believe about environmental protection" Callahan said polls reveal, "is that no, it's not just jobs. And no, it's not just environment. Why can't we have both?

"The high ground is capturing that message, okay? The Wise Use Movement is trying to capture that message. What they're saying out there is that 'We are the real environmentalists. We are the stewards of the land. We're the farmers who have tilled that land and we know how to manage this land because we've done it here for generations. We're the miners and we're the ones who depend for our livelihood on this land. These environmentalists, they're elitists. They live in glass towers in New York City. They're not environmentalists. They're part of the problem. And they're aligned with big government. And they're out of touch. So we're the real environmentalists.'

"And if that's the message that the Wise Use Movement is able to capture, we are suddenly really unpopular. The minute the wise use people capture that high ground, we almost have not got a winning message left in our quiver."

Judy Donald of the Washington, D.C.-based Beldon Fund said, "There are, as Deb has made clear, ordinary people, grass roots organizations who obviously feel their needs are being addressed by this movement. We have to have a strategy that also is addressing those concerns. And that cannot come from environmentalists. It can't come from us. That's the dilemma here. It's not that people don't get it, it's that they do get it. They're losing their jobs."

Barbara Dudley, then executive of a church-related fund, now head of Greenpeace, said, "This is a class issue. There is no question about it. It is true that the environmental movement is, has been, traditionally—this has been in the past an upper class conservation white movement. We have to face that fact. It's true. They're not wrong that we are rich and they are up against us. We are the enemy as long as we behave in that fashion."

"Wise use," Callahan continued, "is a term that was coined by a figurehead named Ron Arnold who actually showed up here yesterday or the day before with these people who had yellow placards and they were walking around in a circle, and they were saying, you know, 'your grants are taking away our jobs' and that sort of thing. He had ten folks [there were seventeen] who are real people out there with placards, who've lost their jobs, who live in communities where there's real economic stress because of transition—economic transition—based on resource extracting issues.

"And they were saying, and they were looking us straight in the eye, 'Hey, because of the work that you've been engaged in, we're hurting. We're losing our jobs. And it's not right.' And how do you say to somebody, 'No, I don't want you to have your job.'"[64]

Listen to the tape yourself. Hear their words yourself.

No, I don't want you to have your job.

It's not that they don't get it, it's that they do get it. They're losing their jobs.

They're not wrong that we are rich and they are up against us. We are the enemy as long as we behave like that.

No, I don't want you to have your job.
What has happened to the environmental movement?
No, I don't want you to have your job.
What has happened to our philanthropic foundations?
No, I don't want you to have your job.
Burn those words into your memory, America.
No, I don't want you to have your job.

Explaining Eco-Class Warfare

It is worthwhile to think about *why*. What is it that allowed the Economy Trashers into power—aside from their immense foundation grant wealth, that is? Our nation spent two decades—the 1960s and the 1970s—building up mythic images of human destructiveness, wailing that this was the last decade before doomsday, and in self-righteous revenge passing laws against loggers, farmers, miners, fishermen, oil drillers, ranchers, real estate developers, car makers, manufacturers of all kinds, small business—against everybody that feeds, clothes and shelters us. Everybody that provides material goods for us. And we never thought about the consequences. Why?

Why would we let such a disaster creep up on us unawares? For one thing, America has changed.

First we've grown affluent, gratified, and forgetful of our basic needs. Psychologist Abraham Maslow taught us about the Needs Hierarchy, the observable fact that as people grow able to satisfy their basic needs for food, clothing, shelter and physical security, those basic needs no longer motivate as powerfully and a new set of needs arise.

These new higher level needs are non-material and arise in a more or less regular order: The need for love, for a sense of belonging, for self-esteem, and for "self-actualization"—to be all that one can be. When these higher level needs are themselves gratified, they too no longer motivate as strongly and a new and final highest-level set of needs arise: The knowledge needs and the aesthetic needs— the need to know, to understand the universe we live in, and the need to live in beautiful surroundings, to create beautiful things, to live a beautiful life.

In the 1960s the science of ecology entered our culture to fill an overarching knowledge need, because it seemed to explain everything in nature, and later the science was elevated to an aesthetic—a key to beauty, to a promise of ultimate gratification, to a life of perfect harmony.

But Maslow discovered in his long career as a clinical psychologist that there are unexpected consequences of growing all the way to the top of the needs hierarchy. People at the highest levels, he found, tend to feel an "independence of and a certain disdain for the old satisfiers and goal objects, with a new dependence on satisfiers and goal objects that hitherto had been overlooked, not wanted, or only causally wanted." Old gratifiers "become boring, or even repulsive." New ungratified needs are overestimated. Lower basic needs already gratified are underestimated or even devalued. In a strikingly prophetic passage, Maslow warned:

> In a word, we tend to take for granted the blessings we already have, especially if we don't have to work or struggle for them. The food, the security, the love, the admiration, the freedom that have always been there, that have never been lacking or yearned for tends not only to be unnoticed but also even to be devalued or mocked or destroyed. This phenomenon of failing to count one's blessings is, of course, not realistic and can therefore be considered to be a form of pathology....This relatively neglected phenomenon of post-gratification forgetting and devaluation is, in my opinion, of very great potential importance and power.[65]

Environmentalism is today's essential expression of post-gratification forgetting and devaluation. Enough of us have gone all the way up the Needs Hierarchy that we as a culture are now acting to devalue, to mock and to destroy our food, clothing, shelter and freedom.

Even our best thinkers fall into the trap. Witness Peter Drucker, the reigning guru of business management wisdom, in his new book *Post-Capitalist Society*: He maintains that the central means of production in our economy is no longer capital, natural resources, or labor. "It is and will be knowledge," he says. "Instead of capitalists and proletarians, the classes of the post-capitalist society are knowledge workers and service workers."[66]

No doubt. But what will they eat or wear or live in when they have devalued and mocked and destroyed the production of capital, natural resources and labor? Even knowledge and service workers get grumpy when they miss dinner.

Peter's next book may be titled *Post-Society Society*.

The pathology hits everyone. It seems that everything we do acts to devalue and mock and destroy our food, clothing, shelter—and freedom.

An Ethic of Genocide

There is a more ominous dimension to post-gratification forgetting and devaluation. As Dr. Kent Adair of Stephen F. Austin State University observed, "People have lost faith in the ability of reason, lost faith in science, lost faith in technology, lost confidence in their institutions and lost confidence in themselves.

"People have been overwhelmed rather than satisfied by the world they have created and are looking for seemingly new answers to give them a sense of confidence in the future. History has repeated itself. Belief in Man and belief in religion has again died, or is at least sick. We have lost confidence in our society and in ourselves."

Other observers see the same thing from different angles. At a conference in Virginia in 1992, a clinical social worker drew a psychological portrait of modern America. It was a variation on the theme of "the lonely crowd" which emerged in sociology 40 years ago, and in American theater before that. It depicts the "atomization" of Americans, which creates millions of lonely people living cheek by jowl. Loneliness, in turn, generates odd compensating behavior, a hunger for contact, closeness, intimacy. So we watch TV talk shows such as Oprah Winfrey and Phil Donahue, we join the conspicuous fellowship of Christian evangelical churches rather than mainstream denominations, we cherish family values that are vanishing—and we seek a sense of belonging in the environmental movement, deep ties to a nature we feel like we've lost, some personal connection to the beauty of the primitive.[67]

From this deep sense of unmet emotional need and deep-seated uneasiness about ourselves, about our world, we feel there must be some Utopia out there somewhere, a place where the perfect life can be led at the top of the Needs Hierarchy. There must be something bigger than ourselves that we can believe in. We desperately crave it, our hearts and souls need it. When faith in all things human and divine is stripped away, as has happened many times in history, the only Utopia we can turn to is Nature—untouched, pristine, primitive, glorious Nature. If Man cannot assure perfection, we feel, Nature can. Today, the urge to liberate nature from human exploitation is a natural consequence of dissatisfaction with the modern world. As we go up that last step of the Needs Hierarchy, from the knowledge needs to the aesthetic needs, we devalue even knowledge and want to strip away all sophisticated knowledge in favor of the alluring beauty of primitive forms.[68]

The goal of liberating nature from human exploitation is as revolutionary as anything the world has ever seen. Social analyst Robert Nisbet wrote in 1982:

> It is entirely possible that when the history of the twentieth century is finally written, the single most important social movement of the period will be judged to be environmentalism. Beginning early in the century as an effort by a few far-seeing individuals in America to bring about the prudent use of natural resources in the interest of extending economic growth as far into the future as possible, the environmentalist cause has become today almost a mass movement, its present objective little less than the transformation of government, economy, and society in the interest of what can only be properly called the liberation of nature from human exploitation. Environmentalism is now well on its way to becoming the third great wave of the redemptive struggle in Western history, the first being Christianity, the second modern socialism. In its way, the dream of a perfect physical environment has all the revolutionary potential that lay both in the Christian vision of mankind redeemed by Christ and in the socialist, chiefly Marxian, prophecy of mankind free from social injustice.[69]

The goal to transform government, economy, and society in order to liberate nature from human exploitation has potential far more revolutionary than anything the world has ever seen. The reason is that "to liberate nature from human exploitation" is a goal with an implicit ultimate consequence. It is not limited to banning chlorofluorocarbons so we can save the ozone layer, or to forbidding use of the internal combustion engine to prevent the greenhouse effect, or to shutting down Third World development to save tropical rainforests. It is not limited to the mere reform of government, economy, and society in order to make them less exploitive of nature. It implies the destruction of human civilization.

While this logical consequence of environmentalism remains invisible to the pop culture bandwagon environmentalist, leaders of the movement recognize it clearly. Environmentalist philosopher Christopher Manes even subtitled his book *Green Rage: Radical Environmentalism and the Unmaking of Civilization*. Unmaking civilization is revolutionary indeed.

To go back to the primitive is one of humanity's most powerful urges. But it is not the final consequence of environmentalism. Building a powerful mythology of the primitive fosters one final problem. As mythologer and classicist Edith Hamilton wrote in 1940:

> Nothing is clearer than the fact that primitive man, whether in New Guinea today or eons ago in the prehistoric wilderness, is not and never has been a creature who peoples his world with bright fancies and lovely visions. Horrors lurked in the primeval forest, not nymphs and naiads. Terror lived

there, with its close attendant, Magic, and its most common defense, Human Sacrifice. Mankind's chief hope of escaping the wrath of whatever divinities were then abroad lay in some magical rite, senseless but powerful, or in some offering made at the cost of pain and grief.[70]

Environmentalism has taken on many of the aspects of "some magical rite," and its solutions resemble "some offering made at the cost of pain and grief." *No, I don't want you to have your job.* To liberate nature from human exploitation implies that most common regression, Human Sacrifice. *No, I don't want you to have your life.* Unthinkable? David M. Graber, a research biologist employed by the National Park Service, wrote in his book review of Bill McKibben's *The End of Nature* for the *Los Angeles Times*:

> Human happiness, and certainly human fecundity, are not as important as a wild and healthy planet. I know social scientists who remind me that people are part of nature, but it isn't true. Somewhere along the line—at about a billion years ago—we quit the contract and became a cancer. We have become a plague upon ourselves and upon the Earth. It is cosmically unlikely that the developed world will choose to end its orgy of fossil energy consumption, and the Third World its suicidal consumption of landscape. Until such time as homo sapiens should decide to rejoin nature, some of us can only hope for the right virus to come along.[71]

Mr. Graber's hope, offensive as it is, nevertheless has become a common-place among environmentalists. Even so august a personage as Prince Philip of the United Kingdom, President of the World Wildlife Fund International, a few years back told the British journal *First*, "In the event I am reborn, I would like to return as a deadly virus, in order to contribute something to solve overpopulation."[72]

It sneaks up on you. The novice environmentalist sees only the lofty and noble dream of a perfect physical environment. Then, headline after headline—acid rain, global warming, the ozone hole, oil spills—the environmentalist begins to harden. Negativity sets in. Perceptions change. There is a distinct shift toward seeing man as the systematic destroyer of the good, the systematic doer of evil. The image of humanity changes. A profound misanthropy develops—and the environmentalist is unaware of it. Finally, like Mr. Graber, the radicalized environmentalist feels—consciously or otherwise—that in order to liberate nature from human exploitation one must eliminate all humans.

While environmentalism may sound appealing in its early purifying let's-clean-things-up stage, it inevitably becomes self-annihilating. We have jumped on its bandwagon with a vengeance. Nearly every American today claims to be an environmentalist. Virtually no American understands the anti-human implications of becoming an environmentalist—of saving nature *from* people instead of *for* people—until it's *their* life and livelihood on the chopping block. Willy-nilly, we have become a nation of Economy Trashers. Only now are average Americans beginning to realize that liberating nature has consequences—the gradual elimination of jobs, economic activity, human use of the earth, and, ultimately, the disappearance of all food, clothing, shelter, and freedom. And, conceivably, the planned extinction of the last human.

Now does it seem so preposterous that runaway environmentalism is wrecking America?
No wonder the average citizen feels so alienated from "The System."
The system has become self-defeating, frustrating and hopeless.
It must be changed.

We can only hope that we are not too late.

Getting Trashed—Footnotes

1 "Secession," *Time*, May 11, 1992, p. 9.

2 "Bewarin' O' The Greens," by Rick Henderson, *Reason*, August/September 1992, p. 5.

3 "Shadows blot mood of voters," by B. Drummond Ayres Jr., *New York Times*, February 9, 1992.

4 "With Friends Like These..." by Paul Rauber, *Mother Jones*, November 1986, p. 47.

5 "Art that exposes family crises," by Charlene D. Daniels, *USA Today*, October 6, 1991, p. 5D.

6 *Ecology and the Politics of Scarcity Revisited: The Unraveling of the American Dream*, William Ophuls, W. H. Freeman and Company, New York, 1992, p. 278.

7 "The Growing Regulatory Burden: At What Cost to America?" by Ronald Utt, IPI Policy Report No. 114, November 1991, Institute for Policy Innovation, Lewisville, Texas.

8 *The Doomsday Syndrome*, John Maddox, McGraw-Hill, New York, 1972.

9 "'Wetlands' Send Man Up The River," by Richard Miniter, *Insight*, December 14, 1992, p. 7.

10 *Economics of the Environment: Selected Readings*, Edited by Robert Dorfman and Nancy S. Dorfman, W. W. Norton & Company, New York, 1977, p. *ix*.

11 See such titles as *Soil Erosion: Crisis in America's Croplands?*, Sandra S. Batie, The Conservation Foundation, Washington, D.C., 1983; "The Toxic Tornado," by Peter A. A. Berle, *Audubon* 87, no. 6 (1985), p. 4; *Omega: Murder of the Ecosystem and Suicide of Man*, Paul K. Andersen, comp., W. C. Brown, Dubuque, Iowa, 1971; "Our Vanishing World: 17,500 Species Are Becoming Extinct Each Year," by Boyce Rensberger, *Washington Post National Weekly Edition*, October 27, 1986, p. 38.

12 See the critique of the environmental movement in *Doomsday Has Been Cancelled*, J. Peter Vajk, Peace Press, Culver City, California, 1978.

13 "Green Guilt and Ecological Overload," by Theodore Roszak, *New York Times*, June 14, 1992, p. D1.

14 "Gunning for the Greens," by Andrea Dorfman, J. Madeleine Nash, and Dick Thompson, *Time*, February 3, 1992, p. 50-52.

15 "Gore gets lost in woods," Associated Press A-Wire, November 10, 1992.

16 "Why California Firms Flee to Nevada," Michael McCabe, *San Francisco Chronicle*, March 11, 1992.

17 "How Zealous Greens Hurt Growth," Louis S. Richman, *Fortune*, March 23, 1992, p. 26.

18 "You can't get there from here," by Peter Brimelow and Leslie Spencer, *Forbes*, July 6, 1992, p. 59.

19 "Return of the 'R' Word," Murray Weidenbaum, *Policy Review*, Winter 1992, pp. 40-43.

20 *The Asbestos Racket: An Environmental Parable*, Michael J. Bennett, The Free Enterprise Press, Bellevue, Washington, 1991.

21 "Florida bill to protect growers," Seattle Times, Friday, May 6, 1994, p. F6. See also *Fear of Food: Environmentalist Scams, Media Mendacity, and the Law of Disparagement*, Andrea Arnold, The Free Enterprise Press, Bellevue, Washington, 1990.

22 "How Zealous Greens Hurt Growth," by Louis S. Richman.

23 "Putting a price tag on green mandates," Warren Brookes, *Washington Times*, August 19, 1991.

24 *Environmental Legislation: The Increasing Costs of Regulatory Compliance to the City of Columbus*, The Environmental Law Review Committee, May 13, 1991, Columbus, Ohio.

25 *Paying for Federal Environmental Mandates: A Looming Crisis for Cities and Counties*, compiled for the United States Congress by Municipality of Anchorage, Alaska, Tom Fink, Mayor, September, 1992.

26 *State Growth Management Legislation: A Comparative Analysis of Legislative Approaches and Administrative Provisions*, by Jim Neumann, Woodrow Wilson School of Public and International Affairs, Princeton, New Jersey, June, 1991, p. 1.

27 "County going after widow's small blueberry farm," by Edwarde Hegstrom, *Bellevue Journal-American*, January 10, 1993, p. 1.

28 *National Guide to Funding for the Environment and Animal Welfare*, Edited by Stan Olson, Ruth Kovacs & Suzanne Haile, The Foundation Center, New York, 1992, p. 99.

29 *Survey of Environmental Lockdown—Preliminary Finding*, Associated General Contractors, Washington, D.C., May, 1992.

30 "You can't get there from here," by Peter Brimelow and Leslie Spencer.

31 "When the Bad Guy is Seen as the One in the Green Hat," Keith Schneider, *New York Times*, February 16, 1992, p. E3.

32 *Grand Theft and Petit Larceny: Property Rights in America*, Mark K. Pollot, Pacific Research Institute, San Francisco, 1993.

33 *The Use of Land: A Citizen's Policy Guide to Urban Growth*, William K. Reilly, editor, A Task Force Report Sponsored by the Rockefeller Brothers Fund, New York, Thomas Y. Crowell, 1973, p. 7.

34 See the classics in the field, *A Treatise on the Limitations of Police Power in the United States*, Christopher G. Tiedeman, 1886, and *The Police Power, Public Policy and Constitutional Rights*, Ernst Freund, 1904.

35 *Property Rights and Eminent Domain*, Ellen Frankel Paul, Transaction Books, New Brunswick, 1987, p. 27.

36 Milton wrote, "So spake the Fiend, and with necessity / The tyrant's plea, excus'd his devilish deeds." *Paradise Lost,* Book IV, line 393.

37 "This Land is My Land," by H. Jane Lehman, *Los Angeles Times*, October 4, 1992, p. K1.

38 "The Public Trust Doctrine and Coastal Zone Management in Washington State," by Ralph W. Johnson, Craighton Goeppele, David Jansen, and Rachael Paschal, *Washington Law Review*, Volume 67, Number 3, July 1992.

39 *Takings: Private Property and the Power of Eminent Domain,* Richard A. Epstein, Harvard University Press, 1985. See also *The Taking*, Joseph Gughemetti and Eugene D. Wheeler, Hidden House Publications, Palo Alto, California, 1981.

40 "Courts Weigh in On Wetlands," *Land Letter*, published by The Conservation Fund, Arlington, Virginia, May 20, 1992, p. 4.

41 "Tax Judge Lowers Assessment Of Undeveloped Wetlands Tract," by Jerry Gray, *New York Times*, May 1, 1992, p. B5.

42 John Adams, *Defense of the Constitutions of Government*, in , *Works*, edited by C. Francis Adams, vol IX (1854), Little, Brown, Boston, 1850-56, p. 560.

43 *Private Property: The History of an Idea,* Richard Schlatter, Rutgers University Press, New Brunswick, New Jersey, 1951, pp. 188-9.

44 *Private Property: The History of an Idea*, Richard Schlatter.

45 The environmental faction known as "deep ecology" is, however, outspoken on the issue. See Bill Devall and George Sessions, *Deep Ecology: Living as if Nature Mattered,* Peregrine Smith Books, Salt Lake City, 1985.

46 "When the Bad Guy is Seen as the One in the Green Hat," Keith Schneider.

47 "Already squeezed by financing, builders stuck in wetlands bog," John H. Stevens, *Seattle Times*, Wednesday, February 12, 1992, p. B5.

48 "BALD's backlog builds to a billion," by Barbara Clements, *Bellevue Journal-American*, April 17, 1992, p. 1.

49 "Enviro Regs Influence Lending," *Coal Voice*, National Coal Association, January-February 1992, p. 7.

50 "Bogged Down in Wetlands," by William G. Laffer, *Free Market*, November 1991, p. 6.

51 "For Farmers, Wetlands Mean a Legal Quagmire," by William Robbins, *New York Times*, April 24, 1990, p. B6.

52 Personal communication by Ron Arnold with National Wetlands Coalition.

53 Robert M. Short to Margaret Rodgers on Department of the Interior letterhead provided to the authors by attorney.

54 "Animosity in the Amazon," *New York Times*, June 13, 1992.

55 "Who's Who: 20 for the future," *Newsweek*, September 30, 1991, p. 62.

56 *Sixth Annual Western Public Interest Law Conference*, "Old-Growth's Last Stand," Saturday, March 5, 1988, University of Oregon School of Law, Eugene, Oregon, transcript, p. 13-14. Complete transcript available from For The Record, Eugene, Oregon, (503)345-6168.

57 "Hard times hit technical school," Bellevue *Journal-American*, January 10, 1992, p. 1.

58 "Face to Face with the Sockeye," Patricia Peak Klintberg, *Beef Today*, February 1992, p. 10-11.

59 "The Way I See It," by Robert M. Miller, D.V.M., *Western Horseman*, May, 1992, p. 74.

60 "Group Calls for Resignation of AG Del Papa," *Carson City Appeal*, June 10, 1992, p. 1.

61 For an excellent discussion of the scientific issues in this section, see *Trashing the Planet*, Dixy Lee Ray, Regnery Gateway, Chicago, 1990.

62 "Earth Day Letter Disputed," *The New York Times*, April 21, 1992.

63 "Best Charities," *Money*, December, 1992, p. 122-123.

64 "Preservationists acknowledge growing grass roots opposition, plan strategy," by Erich Veyhl, *Land Rights Letter*, January/February 1993, special supplement. Transcribed from tapes of the EGA conference.

65 *Motivation and Personality*, Abraham H. Maslow, Second Edition, New York, Harper & Row, 1970, p. 61.

66 "Finding New Heroes for a New Era," by John Huey, *Fortune*, January 25, 1993, p. 65.

67 "In the typical U.S. family, even those who live together live alone," William Thorsell, *The Globe and Mail*, Toronto, Canada, September 26, 1992, p. D6.

68 "The New Utopians," by Jigs Gardner, *Chronicles*, January 1992.

69 *Prejudices: A Philosophical Dictionary*, Robert A. Nisbet, Harvard University Press, Cambridge, 1982, p. 101. Nisbet is Albert Schweitzer Professor of the Humanities, Emeritus, Columbia University.

70 *Mythology*, Edith Hamilton, Little, Brown & Company, Boston, 1940, p. 14.

71 David A. Graber, "Mother Nature as a Hothouse Flower," *Los Angeles Times* Book Reviews, Sunday, October 22, 1989, p. 1-9. Quote is on p. 9.

72 *First*, a quarterly of strategy and politics, Summer 1988, London, p. 29.

Meet the Economy Trashers

"If you'll give the idea a chance, you might agree that the extinction of *Homo sapiens* would mean survival for millions if not billions of other Earth-dwelling species," said an article in the fringy environmentalist magazine *Wild Earth*.[1] An interesting approach to population control. That's what the media love about the environmental movement: its rationality, its temperance—its sheer asininity.

It might come as a surprise to the average American, but the very same idea can be found in the respected pages of the huge and time-encrusted *Audubon* magazine. Avowed misanthrope Richard Conniff wrote in a 1990 *Audubon* article, "Among environmentalists sharing two or three beers, the notion is quite common that if only some calamity could wipe out the entire human race, other species might once again have a chance." Unlike *Wild Earth's* Voluntary Human Extinction Movement (VHEMT, pronounced "Vehement"), *Audubon*'s Conniff paused to reflect that, "The trouble with this noble and self-sacrificing stance is that it almost always winds up being compromised so that some select group of *other* people gets wiped out."[2]

The milk of Conniff's human kindness curdles easily, however. He concluded his *Audubon* article, "China recently turned down court appeals by two Sichuan farmers found guilty of selling four giant panda skins. With only one thousand pandas left in the wild, I have little spirit for opposing the death penalty, which is what the farmers got by way of a bullet to the back of the head."

An interesting approach to population control.

Mr. Conniff once dedicated a book, "To hell with you all."

To hell with you all.
No, I don't want you to have your job.
Regardless of cost to the economy.
One way or another, those themes run through all environmentalism.

The goals of the environmental movement are stated less colorfully but perhaps more usefully by Edith C. Stein in *The Environmental Sourcebook*:

> The environmental movement challenges the dominant Western worldview and its three assumptions:
> ● Unlimited economic growth is possible and beneficial.
> ● Most serious problems can be solved by technology.
> ● Environmental and social problems can be mitigated by a market economy with some state intervention.
> Since the 1970s we've heard increasingly about the competing paradigm, wherein:
> ● Growth must be limited.
> ● Science and technology must be restrained.
> ● Nature has finite resources and a delicate balance that humans must observe.[3]

We feel that fairly represents the debate.

The competing paradigm's three themes dominate the entire environmental movement. That includes more than twelve thousand nonprofit groups centered on the environment or related areas, according to the Internal Revenue Service. They command billions of dollars in resources and incredible political clout. This book profiles twenty-five membership groups, each of which has an annual income in excess of a million dollars, five influential non-membership and five specialized organizations, equally well-endowed—35 powerhouses of the movement.

Each environmental group has its own special story. Each has its own origins, strategies and preferred operating style. And yet they coalesce into a single movement, not monolithic and solid like a potato, but instead, well-textured with friendly rivalries and spiteful enmities, cozy clusters and antagonistic factions—a wide variety that forms distinctive axes of influence, discrete currents in the movement's overall flow.[4]

The money that flows into these groups is phenomenal. The Foundation Center, which keeps track of major non-profit grants in America, listed 2,937 grants of $10,000 or more with a total value of $237.7 million made by 429 foundations to environmental groups in 1989 and 1990. *The Chronicle of Philanthropy* published figures for 1990 that showed the top 12 environmental groups alone to have combined incomes of $519 million, over half a billion dollars.[5] *Money* magazine said that in 1991, environmental groups "took in $2.5 billion."[6]

As a movement, these groups are like no other in number of laws they have written, number of court cases they have won, number of regulations they have imposed—and number of jobs they have killed. They are private, and yet their activities shape broad public policy that trashes the economy. Paradoxically, many are closely connected to the most powerful corporations in the world and America's most elite family foundations—and most are subsidized by exemption from income tax obligations. They are the only important power center in American life not controlled by an internal canon of ethics or by government regulation.

For all their media coverage they are barely known and even less understood. This book is an unprecedented look into America's largest superlobby, revealing a world of deceit, treachery, violence, and ruthless drive to dominate.

The environmental movement is not what it seems.

What we will find in fact is a self-enriching power-hungry leadership using nature slogans to betray a naive public into a new brand of economic slavery. What the environmental movement is really doing, despite its carefully groomed image of Saving the Earth, is Trashing the Economy.

So, while this book is built around profiles of the twenty-five top membership groups, five top non-membership groups, and five important specialized groups, it also contains sub-profiles of more than twenty-five related or otherwise influential organizations—more than sixty groups in all.

Although these rankings change annually as incomes fluctuate, the list of top national environmental groups as of the beginning of the year 1994 was:

1) **The Nature Conservancy**, $278.49 million, 708,000 members;

2) **National Wildlife Federation**, $82.8 million, 4 million members;

3) **World Wildlife Fund**, $60.7 million, 1 million members;

4) **Greenpeace**; $48.7 million, 1.7 million members and supporters;

5) **Sierra Club**, $41.7 million, 550,000 individuals;

6) **National Audubon Society**, $40.0 million, 542,000 individuals;

7) **Natural Resources Defense Council**, $20.4 million, 170,240 members;

8) **Humane Society of the United States**, $19.2 million, 975,000 members;

9) **Cousteau Society**, $17.7 million, 350,000 members;

10) **Environmental Defense Fund**, $17.3 million, 250,000 individuals;

11) **The Wilderness Society**, $16.0 million, 300,000 individuals;

12) **Clean Water Action**, $11.6 million, 600,000 members;

13) **National Parks and Conservation Association**, $11.2 million, 260,000 members;

14) **Conservation International**, $10.9 million, 55,000 members;

15) **People for the Ethical Treatment of Animals**, $8.8 million, 325,000 members;

16) **Defenders of Wildlife**, $6.5 million, 75,000 members plus 13,000 contributors;

17) **Center for Marine Conservation**, $5.6 million, 110,000 members;

18) **Environmental Law Institute**, $4.3 million, 1,900 associates;

19) **Union of Concerned Scientists**, $3.7 million, 100,000 members;

20) **Friends of the Earth**, $2.4 million, 50,000 members.

21) **Izaak Walton League of America**, $2.0 million, 52,700 members;

22) **Fund for Animals**, $1.8 million, 200,000;

23) **Earth Island Institute**, $1.5 million, 32,000 members:

24) **National Toxics Campaign**, $1.5 million, 1,400 groups;

25) **Environmental Action, Inc. /Environmental Action Foundation**, $1.3 million (combined), 16,000 members.[7]

Five important non-membership environmental groups also do their best to trash the economy with conferences, studies, books, and other intellectual assaults:

1) **World Resources Institute**, $10 million;
2) **Resources for the Future**, $7.8 million;
3) **The Keystone Center**, $4.1 million;
4) **Rocky Mountain Institute**, $1.2 million; and
5) **The Foundation on Economic Trends**, $606,921.

One important non-organization that doesn't show up in the money and membership tabulations is **Earth First!** This eco-terrorist faction trashes the economy by sabotage and violence, has no official members, calling itself a "movement" rather than an organization to shield its supporters from prosecution, although an **Earth First! Foundation** has been granted a 501(c)(3) tax status by the Internal Revenue Service.

In addition, a number of specialized groups with million-dollar budgets must be included:

Worldwatch Institute, $3 million, a non-membership global anti-development organization.

INFORM, Inc., $1.5 million, 1,000 members, a "social responsibility" organization centered on waste issues.

League of Conservation Voters, $1.3 million, a political action committee.

Zero Population Growth, $1.3 million, 30,000 members, a population control organization.

Rainforest Action Network, $1.2 million, 35,000 members, a direct action network.

We have organized our profiles of rich and powerful groups so they contain subprofiles of offshoots or closely cooperating groups. For example, The Conservation Fund ($13.8 million) and the American Farmland Trust ($3.4 million) you will find profiled under The Nature Conservancy, the common thread being Patrick F. Noonan, who has served as a leader in all three. The Sea Shepherd Conservation Society ($980,000) is treated under our profile of Greenpeace because its leader Paul Watson got his start in Greenpeace and founded his new group because he was kicked out of the old. The Trust for Public Land ($22.7 million) appears in the Sierra Club and Sierra Club Legal Defense Fund profile because the three work together so systematically they are virtually partners.

We subprofile the Population Crisis Committee, Planned Parenthood and the Smithsonian Institution under World Wildlife Fund; LightHawk, the Northern Forest Lands Council, American Rivers, Inc., the Natural Resources Council of Maine and the Conservation Law Foundation under National Audubon Society; the American Humane Association and International Fund for Animal Welfare under the Humane Society of the United States; Citizen Action, United States Public Interest Research Group, Public Citizen, Inc. and National Environmental Law Center under Clean Water Action; the Citizens' Clearinghouse for Hazardous Wastes under National Toxics Campaign; the

Animal Liberation Front under People for the Ethical Treatment of Animals; the Rails to Trails Conservancy under National Parks and Conservation Association; the Marine Mammal Fund under Earth Island Institute; the Environmental Grantmakers Association in the chapter on Money; the Earth Communications Office and the Environmental Media Association in the chapter on Media.

Just remember that there are similar outfits all over the country, such as:

Ocean Alliance, $1 million, 3,000 members;

Renew America, $850,000, 6,000 members;

Wildlife Habitat Enhancement Council, $416,000, 80 corporate and conservation organizations, 15 individuals;

National Coalition Against the Misuse of Pesticides, $300,000, 1,200 members;

Farm Animal Reform Movement (FARM), $150,000, 12,000 members;

and literally thousands more, such as the Society for Ecological Restoration, the Greenbelt Alliance, the Consultative Group on Biological Diversity, and Land-of-Sky Regional Council—and on and on.

Categorizing environmental groups by field of interest tends to be an academic exercise because so many organizations cover more than one subject. However, the Environmental Data Research Institute (EDRI), a nonprofit organization that provides information on funding to the environmental community, tracks ten issues which it uses as the framework of its database: Agriculture, Energy, Climate and Atmosphere, Biodiversity, Water, Oceans and Coasts, Solid Waste, Toxic Substances and Waste, Endangered Lands, and Development. Each environmental organization is assigned to one of those fields in the database.

The Environmental Sourcebook compiled by Edith C. Stein in cooperation with the EDRI adds Population, making eleven database fields. The animal rights factions are not granted a field in Stein's sourcebook, but they include themselves in the environmental movement.[8]

Analysts such as Rik Scarce consider that "Animal Liberation is a vital part of a bigger environmental picture." Scarce includes the Humane Society of the United States, People for the Ethical Treatment of Animals, the Animal Liberation Front, the Band of Mercy and In Defense of Animals as legitimate members of the environmental movement's radical wing.[9]

There is little agreement among environmentalists about how their movement should be analyzed, largely because they are so involved in the *content* of their actions that they cannot see the *context* of their actions, which is how it affects the human econosystem.

About Movements

You can't understand the environmental movement without understanding the fundamentals of movements themselves. We've all heard of the civil rights movement, the consumer movement, this movement and that movement. But what is a movement? What is the thing in itself, regardless of what *kind* of movement it may be? What do all movements have in common, what constitutes movement-like behavior, *what makes a movement a movement*?

Common sense tells us that a movement is a groundswell of public opinion that organizes itself into constituent groups that seek to influence public policy. That's true, but it's not very helpful in understanding how they work. How do movements work?

Probably the best answer you will find came from the work of two academics, anthropologists who have studied movements since the 1960s, Luther Gerlach and the late Virginia Hine. As professional colleagues they wrote two important books together, *People, Power, Change: Movements of Social Transformation* and *Lifeway Leap: The Dynamics of Change in America*. As these titles tell us, when we say "movements," we're really saying "movements of social change." All movements are attempts to redistribute power.

Gerlach and Hine discovered that movements, regardless of their subject matter—political, social, self-help, religious, or whatever—all behave remarkably alike, and according to definite patterns. Movements can be characterized by the acronym SPIN (Segmentary Polycephalous Ideological Networks). The environmental movement is a SPIN.

Segmentary. A movement contains many segments, that is, many different groups or organizations. If it has only one organization, it is not a movement. True movements have many organizations. The environmental movement has more than 12,000 groups in the United States, according to the Internal Revenue Service's *Cumulative Index of Nonprofit Organizations*. A little more than 3,000 groups are listed in various directories such as *The Nature Directory* by Susan D. Lanier-Graham, *The Environmental Sourcebook* by Edith Carol Stein, the *World Directory of Environmental Organizations* edited by Thaddeus C. Trzyna, *The Conservation Directory* published annually by the National Wildlife Federation, *Directory of National Environmental Organizations* published by U.S. Environmental Directories, and the Environmental Protection Agency's in-house *Directory of U. S. Environmental Organizations*.

The ten major issues the Environmental Data Research Institute tracks— Agriculture, Energy, Climate and Atmosphere, Biodiversity, Water, Oceans, Solid Waste, Hazardous Substances and Waste, Endangered Lands, and Development (and don't forget Population and Animal Rights)—reveal something about the segmentation of the movement, but little about its real structure or function.

Each of the groups profiled in this book, of course, is a segment of the environmental movement in its own right, but we have also attempted to identify larger clusters of groups which form natural power axes and give the movement its characteristic shape—not categorized by the issues they're active in, but by their actual impact on the economy—and also to identify the most significant connecting links between the environmental groups themselves and the outside world, in particular, money sources and allies.

Each segment of a SPIN is self-sufficient. You can't destroy the network by destroying a single group or leader. The center of a network is everywhere. Movements tend to be dynamic, with groups forming and dissolving, here today and gone tomorrow, with a few becoming large and permanent—we have profiled only the biggest and most permanent groups in this book. However, reading through even a few of the profiles will reveal how fluid the overall movement has been over time. Leaders move from one group to another, groups form, dissolve, merge, split. Movements thrive by splintering, like a dandelion going to seed. A SPIN gains its energy from temporary coalitions, from the constant combining and recombining of talents, tools, strategies, numbers, contacts.[10]

Polycephalous Leadership. Polycephalous means "many headed" in Greek. A movement has many heads, many leaders, and no one can speak for the whole movement. If it has only one leader, it is not a movement. True movements have many leaders.

Nobody is "the official leader" of a movement, which makes some think there are no leaders, or think they are conspiracies. Neither is true. Those who think the environmental movement is a monolithic conspiracy simply don't know the facts. This book will enlighten them. As we shall demonstrate, movement structures are linked by exact individuals and exact events, and unless you know *who, what, when* and *where*, you can only guess about *why*. The environmental movement's leaders have been reasonably clear in writing about their *why*, and, if you know where to look, they've left a revealing paper trail—and an even more revealing trail of defectors and other informants—about their *who, what, when* and *where*.

Denis Hayes, organizer of the first Earth Day, once described the rotating lobbying leadership of the environmental movement during the 1970s: "We put together the Clean Water Act and there was no ambiguity: NRDC was the lead organization, people took their assignments from them, and we all reported in. For the coalition against the SST, Friends of the Earth was the leader, we all took our assignments from them, and we reported in. For the Clean Air Act, Environmental Action was the leader. We all took our assignments and we reported in. It all ran like fairly smooth clockwork." Movement leadership is polycephalous.

This fluidity of leadership can even be found within a single organization: Earth Island Institute has two co-executive directors who share the duties.

Just as there are clusters of groups that work closely together and share leadership, as Hayes noted, there are movement leaders who disagree with each other on goals, methods and ideology to the point they refuse to work together. Turf fights are legion within the environmental movement, as in all movements. There are more forces that tear a movement apart than hold it together, which is why so few movements succeed in turning their political clout into real political power.

Likewise, there is no such thing as a "card carrying" member of a *movement*. One may have a membership card in a movement *group*, but not the movement. Groups have members. Movements have *participants*. This is a fundamental distinction, because anyone who claims to be in a movement *is in a movement*. Just saying so makes you a participant.

Conversely, if one denies that one is part of a movement, that does not necessarily make it so. Some animal rights activists, for example, claim they are not part of the environmental movement, but their behavior belies their words—their groups frequently come to the aid of the Sierra Club or the World Wildlife Fund when the issue is animal rights.

Similarly, for a critic to say that somebody else is not a movement participant doesn't *ever* make it so. Nobody can kick anybody out of a movement. Each group thrives or withers according to the ability of its leaders and the accidents of daily life which gain or lose supporters. One group cannot force another group out of a movement. Groups can distance themselves from undesirables or isolate them or attack them publicly—the pariah group is still a node in the network and all the rest are powerless to eject it—one of the reasons why movements are such powerful instruments of social change. The cutting edge group and the trailing edge group both may displease the mainstream, but there's nothing the mainstream can do about it short of assassination, which often backfires and makes the dead immortal, as the murders of Malcolm X and Dr. Martin Luther King amply demonstrated in the Civil Rights Movement. Earth First! upsets some mainstream environmentalists, but nobody can kick the radicals out of the movement.

Anyone, on the other hand, can be kicked out of a movement *group*, as the career of David Brower clearly illustrates: he was kicked out of the leadership of the Sierra Club in 1969 and of the Friends of the Earth in 1980—and he *founded* the Friends of the Earth.

Ideology. A core of shared beliefs lies at the heart of every movement. Even though environmentalists disagree about many things, they all share a few central beliefs. Because the movement is so diverse, it is hazardous to propose a list of Environmentalism's Articles of Faith, but a noted environmentalist rashly did the job for us and a prominent environmental journal published it.

Environmentalist Victor B. Scheffer worked for the United States Fish and Wildlife Service for more than thirty years. His 1969 book *The Year of the Whale* received the Burroughs Medal for outstanding environmental writing. He wrote two noted nature books, *Natural History of Marine Mammals* (1981) and *Spires of Form: Glimpses of Evolution* (1985) and an accomplished analytical work, *The Shaping of Environmentalism in America* (1991).[11]

Scheffer is a credible spokesman. In a *Northwest Environmental Journal* article titled "Environmentalism's Articles of Faith" Scheffer wrote what may be the clearest statement of the environmental movement's ideology. We reprint its core statements here without comment.[12]

1) *All things are connected.* "Now we technological beings have spun a web of change around the whole earth and nearby space. Our artifacts range in scale from radiations and molecules to mountains and lakes. Yet never will we understand completely the spin-off effects of the environmental changes that we create, nor will we measure our own, independent influence in their creation."

Scheffer adds: "I use the word *nature* for the world without humans, a concept which—like the square root of minus one—is unreal, but useful."

2) *Earthly goods are limited.* "This truth finds expression in the term 'carrying capacity,'" writes Scheffer. "As applied to people, carrying capacity is the number of individuals that the earth can support before a limit is reached beyond which the quality of life must worsen and *Homo*, the human animal, becomes less human. One reason we humans—unlike animals in the wild—are prone to

exceed carrying capacity is that our wants exceed our needs."

3) *Nature's way is best.* "Woven into the fabric of environmentalism is the belief that natural methods and materials should be favored over artificial and synthetic ones, when there's a clear choice. Witness the vast areas of the globe poisoned or degraded by the technological economy of our century."

4) *The survival of humankind depends on natural diversity.* "Although species by the billions have vanished through natural extinction or transformation, the present rate of extinction is thought to be at least 400 times faster than at the beginning of the Industrial Age. Humankind's destruction of habitats is overwhelmingly to blame."

Scheffer adds that "No one has the moral right, and should not have the legal right, to overtax carrying capacity either by reducing the productivity of the land or by bringing into the world more than his or her 'share' of new lives. Who is to decide that share will perhaps be the most difficult social question for future generations."

5) *Environmentalism is radical* "in the sense of demanding fundamental change. It calls for changes in present political systems, in the reach of the law, in the methods of agriculture and industry, in the structure of capitalism (the profit system), in international dealings, and in education."

In our critique, we assume that Scheffer's statement, or something essentially like it, expresses accurately or mostly accurately the ideology actually shared by all environmentalists, giving proper recognition to differences of emphasis or belief between movement segments. Where we have found significant disagreements, we describe them in the individual group profiles below.

The ideology, in order to generate dedication and deep commitment, must revolve around superindividual claims, so that movement participants feel they are fighting not for themselves but only for a cause. As sociologist Lewis A. Coser has noted, "The consciousness of speaking for a superindividual 'right' or system of values reinforces participants' dedication, mobilizing energies that would not be available for mere personal interests and goals. Individuals entering into a superindividual conflict act as representatives of groups or ideas. They are imbued with a sense of respectability and self-righteousness since they are not acting for 'selfish' reasons."[13]

As many commentators have noted, the self-righteousness of environmentalism fosters a religious zeal. Religion-like references are a dime a dozen in environmental writings.[14] Alston Chase, for example, in his book *Playing God in Yellowstone*, went so far as to assert that John Muir, "along with his older friend Emerson and their contemporary, Henry David Thoreau, were the first apostles of a loose collection of ideas that formed a new religion of nature." Chase was careful to note that they never became a formal church, never broke openly with Christianity, and did not share exactly the same views. But he emphasized that Emerson and Thoreau both felt that "nature was nearly synonymous with God. Modern urban industrial society, therefore, in cutting people off from nature, was denying God." Chase felt it was important for critics of environmentalism to recognize that "From the time of Emerson, Thoreau, and Muir this distinctive environmental religious perspective continued to grow.

Slowly it was distilled into beliefs characterized by antipathy to progress, science, and the Judeo-Christian religious tradition."[15]

Whether or not one regards environmentalist fervor as having a religious dimension, the zealous ferocity of its most devoted adherents cannot be imagined by anyone who has never borne its brunt. To question Environmentalism's Articles of Faith is to bring down upon oneself a wrath of intense psychic violence—"green rage," as author Christopher Manes aptly dubbed it. Particularly among the unstructured grassroots environmentalists typically found on university campuses, the ideology has grown into a passionate hatred of anything and anyone thought to harm nature or that questions environmentalist beliefs.

As in all movements, environmentalism's ideology makes compromise appear as a moral stain. Environmental groups usually demand complete surrender from their opponents rather than striking a compromise in which both sides trade value for value. For example, the National Parks and Conservation Association once sent the leaders of a town in Maine its position statement on a proposed addition to Acadia National Park which perfectly exemplifies this attitude: "It is not acceptable to trade-off one point against another, such as deleting the Northern Lot in order to acquire the Merchant's Cove Lot, and say that a 'compromise' has been struck." *No, I don't want you to have your property.* The comprehensive solution is the only acceptable solution.[16]

Networks. Movements, said New Age guru Marilyn Ferguson, can be visualized as "a badly knotted fishnet with a multitude of nodes of varying sizes, each linked to all the others, directly or indirectly." The nodes are groups. Each group is connected to every other group in the movement by an imaginary line, the line representing potential or actual communication. The resulting pattern is a network. There are no command lines in a network, only communication lines—that is, nobody in a network can give orders to or make demands upon anybody else in a network and expect to get results.

Movements are organized so that the nodes—groups or individual participants—are tied together not through any central point, but rather through intersecting sets of personal relationships and intergroup linkages. Movement groups constantly split, combine, and proliferate. Because it is much more difficult to visualize a complex and fluid network than a linear hierarchy, it is tempting to revert to thinking of movements as conspiracies, but it simply isn't so. We have to make the mental effort to see things as they are. These are the major features of networks:

A) Personal ties between members. Movements profit from pre-existing ties of kinship, friendship, or other close association. People in movements often cross back and forth in the activities of two or more movement groups. Many have commented on the phenomenon of "The same dozen neighbors form the membership of the same dozen local environmental groups."

B) Personal ties between leaders. Movement group leaders may tie the movement together through hundreds of loose and indirect friendship paths. Speeches or visits by one leader to another's group, taking a job in another group for a time, joining in a coalition with another group on a specific issue, all serve to tie a movement together. For example, Brock Evans went from being a leading Washington lobbyist for the Sierra Club to a similar job with the Audubon Society, and his many friendships in both organizations cemented the movement in so many ways they could not be counted.

C) Johnny Appleseeds. A successful movement will produce a few charismatic leaders who travel widely to talk to various groups. They spread the ideology, planting seeds everywhere they go. Not all segments of the movement in any city may gather to hear any one of these "traveling evangelists," but each draws an audience from more than one wing of the movement. You can trace the growth of a movement in the ripples left behind by these traveling evangelists like a stone skipped over water.

D) Organizers. Fortunate movements will be blessed with a number of savvy activists who know how to organize new or existing groups for specific fights and, occasionally, for permanent growth. These people go out from a home base and visit another location long enough to work with local talent, get things going, and then return home, where they continue giving long distance advice by telephone, facsimile machine, or computer modem network.

E) Rituals. Every movement develops rituals that bind it together. The environmental movement uses outings, group meetings and conferences, rallies, marches, boycotts, demonstrations, news conferences. Such rituals develop a sense of common purpose that feeds the movement.

F) Webs of Interests. There are always interests that will try to take advantage of a successful movement, usually trading money donations for influence. The environmental movement is webbed to nine major interests: 1) foundations; 2) corporations; 3) law firms; 4) university departments of environmental studies; 5) the media; 6) government, 7) sympathetic constituencies such as consumer groups, population control organizations, and others whose main purpose is distinct from but congruent with environmentalism; 8) eco-entrepreneurs whose businesses rely upon or profit by environmental regulations, a new breed of corporate socialists who look to regulations as a legal anti-competitive edge; 9) public relations firms with social change orientations that devise and execute environmentalist campaigns for specific issues.

About the Web of Interests

Foundations. More than 1,000 foundations give money to environmental groups. With the money comes policy making power. As in most other human enterprises, in the environmental movement the Golden Rule applies: who has the gold rules. Golden Donors control the environmental movement's agenda to a large extent—but not completely. Greenpeace, for example, picketed the elitist Environmental Grantmakers Association, and the Nader Bunch remains aloof by cultivating its own money machine. Remember, it's a complex network with exact connections, not a monolithic conspiracy.

Even within the organizations which cozy up to the big money, internal managers call the shots to a substantial degree, sometimes getting contrary and drawing down the wrath of foundation funders who send their cash elsewhere. In the chapter on money we provide thumbnail sketches of more than two dozen major foundations that fund the environmental movement.

There are a good number of left-wing foundations which push the environmental agenda ever further toward left-wing looneyism, opposing President Clinton's capital gains tax cut, demanding minute regulation of every aspect of every business and generally opposing free enterprise of any kind. However, foundations frequently find their meetings dissolving into shouting matches about some environmental wacko such as Jeremy Rifkin and his book *Beyond Beef* alienating the public and giving opponents in the Wise Use Movement an issue. Jeremy won't be getting any money from these folks for a long time. But there's always a foundation wackier than the corresponding environmental group, so the problem will not go away.

In some cases, it is difficult to tell where the foundation leaves off and the environmental group begins because of shared memberships on boards of directors. In the larger Establishment family foundations including those of the Rockefellers and Mellons, everybody sits on everybody else's boards, as we will detail below. Even some of the most far-out left-wing eco-groups enjoy such incestuous relationships: Adele Simmons, the president of the immensely wealthy MacArthur Foundation, sits on the board of directors of the ultra-leftist Union of Concerned Scientists. The old interlocking board phenomenon of the Standard Oil Trust days is still very much in vogue among environmental groups and their most golden donors.

The Environmental Grantmakers Association, a cartel of 160 golden donors (1993), has evolved into a sort of Command Central for the environmental movement in the past five years. Its meetings are the planning, strategy and monitoring center for more than fifty mainstream environmental groups as well as more fringy networks such as Earth First!—but not including some of the more grassroots-oriented groups such as Greenpeace USA, which does not belong to EGA, doesn't like it, and actively opposes it.

Corporations. More than 100 companies from Citibank to Nike allow Earth Share, a federation of 40 environmental groups, to canvass employees at work—a privilege formerly extended only to the United Way.

Many hundreds of corporations give large direct grants or corporate foundation grants to environmental groups. The motive is not always simply to do well by doing good. For some of the larger companies, regulation is a competitive edge against smaller rivals, and nobody can ram regulations through Congress better than the environmental movement.[17]

Several corporations are members of the Environmental Grantmakers Association, including the Chevron Companies, Patagonia, and L. L. Bean.

Law Firms. The contribution money that goes from the 20,000 environmental law firms in America to the environmental movement cannot be traced. Lawyers are clever folks and have been known to hide contributions to environmental groups by having their spouses sign the checks and other cute tricks. The likelihood that there is merely a little trickle of money in this pipeline is vanishingly small.

However, fee awards and other court-ordered payments are matters of public record and amount to many millions won by private law firms for the pockets of environmental groups every year. See the profiles of the Sierra Club and Clean Water Action for details.

University Environmental Departments. One doesn't think of the huge amount of money in the form of grants to university environmental departments as part of the wealth of the environmental movement, but it is indeed. Studies performed by dozens of environmentalist-wracked universities end up as evidence in courtroom battles or in the pages of eco-group propaganda. Scientists on the payrolls of environmental organizations may also pick up a pile of cash by doing some of the work on such studies.[18]

There is also the recruitment function, a valuable business consideration, which university environmental departments perform for the movement. University departments crank out trained, indoctrinated and ideologically reliable troops for government environmental jobs, staff positions in environmental groups, and leadership positions for the future—or merely as voters to create a Green Majority.[19]

In some cases, university environmental department faculty members actually sit on the boards of directors of environmental groups. For example, Professor V. "Vim" Crane Wright of the University of Washington's Institute of Environmental Studies sits on the board of directors of a political action committee, the League of Conservation Voters.

The Media. Some of the media just plain give money to environmental groups, such as the *New York Times*, the *Washington Post* and the *Los Angeles Times*. Of course, they say it doesn't affect their objectivity. You believe that, don't you?

Most of the media give millions of dollars worth of free publicity to environmental groups out of ideological agreement. Some do it just because there are occasionally real news stories about the environmental movement.

In general, there is precious little skepticism about environmental groups in any medium—newspapers, magazines, books, movies, television, radio. Reporters and editors just swallow eco-ideology whole and feed it to us with a spoon. Some are out-and-out eco-partisans with no pretense of objectivity.

We have yet to see a major newspaper do an investigative journalism hit piece against a major environmental group, and there's plenty to write about. They just won't do anything that might hurt their darlings. Environmental groups have easy access to editors to assure damage control when Wise Use Movement opponents dig up real dirt about eco-nasties.

Government. The Environmental Protection Agency estimates that about $3 billion a year goes from the federal government to pay for activities related directly to an environmental group or cluster of groups—conferences, national park brochures that promote the National Parks and Conservation Association, grants for nature studies, endless "educational" programs that indoctrinate our children. Any bets that's all the federal money going into the environmental movement? Even the Freedom of Information Act can't find it all. We know, we've tried.

Sympathetic Constituencies. Consumerists, population-control advocates, labor unions, urban liberals, and a host of others have been known to come together to form coalitions with environmental groups. Coalitions are by nature temporary and centered around a single issue, but the contacts and solidarity generated by fighting together lingers after the issue is settled and the coalition disbanded.

Eco-entrepreneurs. The web of service and supply industries that have grown up as a direct result of environmental laws and regulations—wetlands consultants, endangered species detection technicians (who have been known to dig up a rare plant and put it on private property they wanted to take), environmental cleanup firms, hazardous waste removal and treatment companies, smokestack scrubber manufacturers, recyclable package designers and so forth. The motives of these companies to give money to environmental groups are too transparent to require comment.

Depending on which economist you believe, these may be productive enterprises or costly parasites actually imposing a hidden tax on productive enterprises. Our concern is reporting their financial donations to their allies in the environmental movement.

Public Relations Firms. A substantial network of leftish social change public relations firms routinely devises and executes environmentalist campaigns. For example, Fenton Communications of Washington, D.C., created the Alar scare campaign for the Natural Resources Defense Council, as well as the Ancient Forests media campaign. Millions of environmental movement dollars go to these public relations firms and never appear in total estimates of the wealth of the overall environmental movement because they do not flow through environmental organization balance sheets, but come directly from foundations.

This web of interests is a vital part of the environmental movement's network—remember the acronym SPIN that describes all movements: Segmentary, Polycephalous, Ideological Networks. The *whole* network has to be understood before you can form any realistic appraisal of the force of a movement to promote social change and the redistribution of power.

Movements can only thrive when there is a cause that calls for social change and when there are people ready to make those changes: Leaders, followers, group members, supporters, webs of interests, non-participant approvers in the general public.

The cause that calls for social change is always some *perceived crisis.* As a kite flies only against the wind, movements rise only against a perceived wrong that must be set right. While movement leaders emphasize the innovations and improvements on their agendas, the truth is more basic. There is always an identifiable wrong to fight against at the root of every movement.

Movements are fundamentally reactionary—in the sense of reacting against some wrong with the intent of setting it right. Regardless of what the agenda says, movements are always *against*. The environmental movement arose against violations of nature by industrial civilization.

One last note on movements: The "Lifestyle" version of environmentalism that became popular in the 1960s and '70s—living simply, wasting no resources, going back-to-the-land, living in hippy communes, raising ecological consciousness, becoming a professional university student staying indefinitely in the ivory tower, that sort of thing—is sometimes looked upon as the real grassroots power of the environmental movement. We don't think so. Despite the fact that many of the environmental movement's most extreme zealots dwell in this unstructured segment, their psychic energy is dissipated in philosophical discussions, internal squabbling and loud arguments with opponents rather than in forcing social change on others. Movements are movements only if they transfer power. Living in voluntary simplicity or personal poverty as an unstructured individual or an ecological community may make a political statement, but it transfers no political power. Only when the grassroots organize and transfer political power do they have any social meaning. Even millions of lifestyle environmentalists making political statements but doing nothing to transfer political power are as meaningless as Michael Jackson's moonwalk: entertaining, and it *does* look like forward progress—if you're easily fooled by illusions.

At Issue

Is the environmental movement wrecking the economy? The only fair way we can answer that question is to examine a representative cross section and see if the results are consistent with our premise. Before we can do that we have to define the premise with reasonable exactitude. What do we mean by trashing the economy?

It is not the same as asking the dollar cost of all damage done by the environmental movement. The total dollar damage cannot even be estimated, much less ascertained, and even if it could, dollars could not replace lost livelihoods, destroyed customs and shattered ways of life. Where we can determine the number of jobs killed and economic activity trashed, we report them.

Some of the impacts of environmentalism are huge but diffuse so they can only be surmised, for example, the decline in nationwide property values and tax revenues caused by wetlands regulation or some other preservation scheme. Not only do economists of equal qualification disagree on such dollar costs, but there is also no way to determine the lost value of economic opportunities foregone because of environmental restrictions, for example, how much economic benefit would have been generated if the private businesses and hundreds of homes in Ohio's Cuyahoga Valley National Recreation Area had not been nationalized and torn down after it was established in 1975.

We are asking a more fundamental question. Is the environmental movement wrecking the economy? Economics is not about money or dollar cost, economics is about the allocation of scarce resources to individual wants. The economy is the system by which we allocate scarce resources to individual wants. To trash the economy is to trash the system by which we allocate scarce resources to individual wants. Is the environmental movement trashing the system by which we allocate scarce resources to individual wants?

First, are environmental groups intervening in private property and free markets sufficiently to eliminate the profit margin of the American society? Second, are environmental groups working to do more than hamper markets—to overthrow the market system entirely and create an eco-socialist society? Or, third and even more horrendous, do environmental groups work to disassemble the motors of civilization itself, for example, by violently crippling scientific, engineering and production capability so that industrial society slowly crumbles from lack of nourishment?

The question of an incipient eco-socialism is most troubling, and much more than mere name-calling. The clearest—and most profound—analysis of socialism was written by the economist Ludwig von Mises, whose *Human Action* had a lot to say about it. There are two patterns for the realization of socialism, he begins.

The first pattern (we may call it the Lenin or the Russian pattern) is purely bureaucratic. All plants, shops, and farms are formally nationalized; they are departments of the government operated by civil servants. Every unit of the apparatus of production stands in the same relation to the superior central organization as does a local post office to the office of the postmaster general.

The second pattern (we may call it the Hindenberg or German pattern) nominally and seemingly preserves private ownership of the means of production and keeps the appearance of ordinary markets, prices, wages, and interest rates. There are, however, no longer entrepreneurs, but only shop managers (*Betriebsführer* in the terminology of the Nazi legislation). These shop managers are seemingly instrumental in the conduct of the enterprises entrusted to them; they buy and sell, hire and discharge workers and remunerate their services, contract debts and pay interest and amortization. But in all their activities they are bound to obey unconditionally the orders issued by the government's supreme office of production management. This office tells the shop managers what and how to produce, at what prices and from whom to buy, at what prices and to whom to sell. It assigns every worker to his job and fixes his wages. It decrees to whom and on what terms the capitalists must entrust their funds. Market exchange is merely a sham. All the wages, prices, and interest rates are fixed in appearance only; in fact they are merely quantitative terms in the government's order determining each citizen's job, income, consumption, and standard of living. The government directs all production activities. The shop managers are subject to the government, not to the consumer's demand and the market's price structure. This is socialism under the outward guise of the terminology of capitalism. Some labels of the capitalistic market economy are retained, but they signify something entirely different from what they mean in the market economy.

It is necessary to point out this fact in order to prevent a confusion of socialism and interventionism. The system of interventionism or of the hampered market economy differs from the German pattern of socialism by the very fact that it is still a market economy. The authority interferes with the operation of the market economy, but does not want to eliminate the market altogether. It wants production and consumption to develop along lines different from those prescribed by an unhampered market, and it wants to achieve its aim by injecting into the working of the market orders, commands, and prohibitions for whose enforcement the police power and its apparatus of violent compulsion and coercion stand ready. But these are *isolated* acts of intervention. It is not the aim of the government to combine them into an integrated system which determines all prices, wages and interest rates and thus places full control of production and consumption into the hands of the authorities.[20]

It is clear that we must take pains to distinguish between Interventionists and Eco-socialists in our analysis of the environmental movement.

By and large, the Interventionist environmental organizations seek to Trash the Economy by promoting social change. They seek to make people think differently about the issues, to persuade through education and public relations campaigns, to compel change by lobbying governments for new laws, and by going to court to insure that their legislation is enforced. They tend to frame every issue as the crisis of the century, to scream in front of the television cameras and twist arms behind closed legislative doors until they get their way. Their way is to convince Congress to cripple business and industry with stringent regulations and then go to court and enforce their will with punitive lawsuits, but to retain a hampered market system.

To hell with you all, mainstream version.

It is thus a misrepresentation to lump all the anti-technology factions as socialists or communists, "watermelons"—green on the outside, red on the inside. While a recognizable coterie still suffering from the collapse of world communism may be looking to environmentalism as a new vehicle for old ideology, the environmental movement itself appears to us to be complex and opportunistic, and perfectly capable of using interventionist, eco-socialist or eco-terrorist methods to achieve its ends—whatever works, as Greenpeace recommended.

Early activist Keith Lampe wrote in 1969, "Capitalism, phased out, cannot be replaced with socialism or communism because these forms, too, are growth-and-progress oriented. We have very little recent politico-economic inheritance to work from."[21]

The environmental movement, to such activists, was a counter-revolution against the Industrial Revolution requiring an anti-growth-and-progress political expression such as feudalism or the God-King states of early Mesopotamia and Egypt or even earlier tribal forms.

However, to correctly present the mainstream of eco-socialist thinking as it stands today, we quote a thoughtful essay by respected environmentalist Amy MacDonald published in *Habitat: Journal of the Maine Audubon Society*:

> In abandoning anti-communism as the organizing principle of this country, it has been suggested that we will need to find a new enemy against which we can rally—such as environmental destruction. Certainly environmental degradation poses a more serious threat to Americans now than the phantom of communism that obsessed us for two generations....
>
> If environmental protection is incompatible with economic freedom, with what does that leave us? The Green Party in the U.S. suggests a voluntary code of behavior for business, but by definition that would be unenforceable. The most convincing argument for public ownership of resources—socialism—is that without it, there can be no ironclad safeguards for our environment....
>
> Almost all environmental battles boil down to the tension between private property rights and the public good. It is the chief failing of our democratic system that so few citizens see the state as the embodiment of the public good; most, in fact, view it with suspicion. Any form of socialism, therefore, strikes most Americans as anathema. But it may be something we are forced to examine if, as political theorist William Ophuls predicted some 13 years ago in *Ecology and the Politics of Scarcity*, "The golden age of individualism, liberty, and democracy is all but over."[22]

We take that as a fair representation of the current eco-socialist viewpoint.

Our third category, unmaking civilization by sabotaging industry in the name of nature, is the domain of the radical environmentalist. In an April 1990 report titled "Eco-Terrorism: The Dangerous Fringe of the Environmental Movement," the Heritage Foundation worried that the radical environmentalists' "extremist philosophy is leading to a guerilla movement that is destroying property and injuring the innocent and one day will kill innocent workers or park employees."[23]

Major arson attacks against laboratories across the nation, livestock auction buildings in the West, destruction of logging and mining equipment, and other violent attacks have become routine events every year. Most sabotage against industries never makes headlines because firms do not want to give the ecoteurs any media glory and encouragement. Serious sabotage against society in general, on the other hand, makes big headlines, such as Earth First!'s destruction of electricity transmission towers that left more than 90,000 Santa Cruz, California customers of Pacific Gas and Electric in the dark.[24]

In his book *Eco-Warriors*, Rik Scarce wrote, "One veteran eco-warrior who requested anonymity stated that the day might come when shooting timber company executives would replace monkeywrenching as the most drastic means for saving old-growth trees; another activist saw the possibility of shooting timber workers in the field rather than executives. Yet other trends in precisely the opposite direction are at work as well; the renunciation of tree spiking by Earth First! in southern Oregon and northern California was greeted with enthusiasm by many in the movement (and condemnation by others)."[25]

The perception that drives the radical environmentalists was clearly stated at the end of *Eco-Warriors*:

> Most radical environmentalists assume an uncharacteristic air of pessimism when asked about the world fifteen or twenty years from now. Judi Bari [of Earth First!] puts the consensus position succinctly: "I believe the Earth is going to rise up and throw us off....The Earth's failure to be able to sustain this kind of life will cause it to collapse. I'm sure life will survive that, but I don't think that humans will. I don't know if we deserve to."[26] The immanency of the end of much of the non-human world as it has evolved over millions of years is the fundamental threat against which eco-warriors struggle. Tropical rainforests fall at an incredible pace so that we might have teak dining tables. Whales are going extinct, and dolphins die for our tuna sandwiches. Once sprawling populations of plains buffalo and tule elk, now reduced to a few thousand in number, become hunters' prizes. Acid rain from power plants and car exhausts is found at the highest, most inaccessible lakes and granite peaks. Children die early and painful deaths from pesticides, toxins, and radioactive wastes that find their way into their drinking water and even into their mothers' milk.[27]

In short, we're talking about three kinds of environmental organizations Trashing the Economy: 1) Interventionists; 2) Eco-socialists; and 3) Eco-terrorists.

The Problems of Critique

In any such investigation there is the danger of mischaracterizing a complex field by oversimplification. We have seen many critiques of the environmental movement, and, although we sympathize with the intent of all, most of them, we must admit, fail miserably, either by projecting the motives of a few radicals onto the whole movement or by neglecting the huge variety of groups that comprise its adherents and thus failing to correctly identify all the multifarious axes of power flowing in the overall movement.

As Stephen Jay Gould once wrote, "Professions are big, and everyone makes a stupid statement now and again. As an honorable opponent, you cannot use a single dumb argument to characterize an entire field."[28] We have tried to gather under one cover not only a representative cross-section of stupid statements and dumb arguments by environmentalists, but also a representative cross-section of stupid conduct and dumb deeds by environmentalists trashing the economy.

But we propose that it is not unfair to present arguments exclusively *against* the environmental movement such as you will find in this book. We make no effort to balance the environmental movement's good deeds against its bad. The environmental movement has had nearly thirty years in which to make its case. We have no obligation to make it for them again. This book has a point of view, and we make no claim to be detached observers. Yet, our arguments are all based on facts and heavily annotated with published materials, unpublished documents and personal interviews with informants. Environmentalists are free to rebut them if they can. You've heard the argument *pro* in the environmental debate for years. This book is the argument *con*. Make up your own mind.

Why Certain Groups Were Included

As you can see from the list above, we have counted the major animal rights organizations as well as more traditional environmental groups. The Environmental Data Research Institute has no category for animal rights in its database and does not track such influential groups as the Fund for Animals or the Humane Society of the United States or People for the Ethical Treatment of Animals, but it does include Defenders of Wildlife in the Biodiversity database field. It's not a matter of excluding wild-eyed radicals, because EDRI also lists the violence-prone groups Sea Shepherd Conservation Society and Earth First!

Some people object that lumping animal rights groups with the environmental movement is unfair. The facts disagree. As *Animals' Agenda* noted, "Though there's still a contingent within the animal rights movement that doesn't want environmental problems mixed in with 'its' issues, most humane activists consider themselves part of the environmental movement. Grassroots groups across the country jumped with ease into local Earth Day celebrations..."[29]

In addition, Elliot Katz, a Long Island veterinarian who moved to California's Big Sur and became a guerilla veterinarian, treating animals without a licence and receiving vegetables or other goods as payment, founded the group In Defense of Animals in 1983. Katz's group now has 50,000 members. It files lawsuits and appeals of environmental impact statements, common tactics of the environmental mainstream. Katz says that today, "a major thorn in [the research establishment's] side is how animal advocates work with environmental laws and EIRs to slow down their projects and to cost them."[30]

Aside from the observable fact that animal rights activists participate in more general environmental activities and numerous mainstream groups come to the aid of animal rights groups in specific issues, their Economy Trasher philosophies coincide: protecting the environment is so important that it doesn't matter if you harm people's livelihoods or trash the economy in the process. Wildlife protection groups have long espoused the fundamental notion that animals have legal rights of some sort, however limited. Establishment environmental philosophers consider all of nature to have "rights."[31] It would be foolish to omit the animal rights groups from our Economy Trasher list. They have power, they are well networked with mainstream groups, they have already done tremendous damage to the economy and bode ominously to do much worse.

However, we did *not* include certain rich and powerful organizations such as Ducks Unlimited ($68 million in 1990), the North Shore Animal League ($26.1 million) or Chesapeake Bay Foundation ($5.1 million) for several reasons. Ducks Unlimited does not inject itself into the political arena in the role of hard-line green group on a full-time basis, although they are evolving in that direction. The Economy Trasher behavior they do exhibit is nearly identical in nature to other more consistently hard-core groups that we *do* profile: Ducks Unlimited, which *The Environmental Sourcebook* also does not list, somewhat resembles the National Wildlife Federation. Chesapeake Bay Foundation is large but regional, like numerous others in our subprofiles, such as the Northern Forest Land Council.

Who Are The Environmentalists?

There are leaders, there are zealous adherents and there are followers.

They don't have the same agendas.

Today more than 80 percent of all Americans say they are "environmentalists." These are overwhelmingly good-hearted people who do not want to trash the economy. But organization leaders act as if this rather vague statistical expression of friendliness toward the natural world were a mandate for all they do. It is not. Only about 5 percent of all Americans actually belong to an environmental group of any kind, and even fewer are aware of the radical anti-jobs, anti-technology, anti-people agendas of their revered organization leaders and their zealous adherents. Most environmental group members have no idea that the groups they support are doing the things we will detail in the profiles that follow.

Who is an environmentalist? The 80 percent of Americans who tell pollsters they are environmentalists are a mere statistic without any substantive meaning—their names are not on environmental group mailing lists so there is no way to recruit their financial support or political activism. Anyone can say they are anything, and such polls have no criteria for determining what constitutes being "an environmentalist."

The Americans who are environmentalist enough to put their money where their mouth is, i.e., join an environmental group and pay dues, can be counted with a modicum of accuracy: Assuming the environmental groups are being honest in their reporting, there are about 15 million memberships total in our top 25 groups, not allowing for an unknown amount of overlap. An unknown number of people belong to two or more environmental groups. How many individuals are counted more than once in this 15 million total we have no way of knowing.

On the basis of 15 million members and a total U.S. population of about 250 million, that's approximately 5 percent of the population. A little over 5 percent of the whole country is a respectable fraction for a movement of social change—if the numbers are realistic, which there is no way to know.

One of the imponderables is the number of "lifestyle" environmentalists who are zealous adherents to the cause but are not members of any organization. They may vote, go to local council meetings and apply pressure as individuals, thus furthering the movement in small ways, but there is no way to count them or assess their results. In examining the observable results of environmentalism's Trashing the Economy such as laws passed, court cases won, administrative practices adopted, businesses sabotaged, we find only organized groups behind the results—even if the organization is nominally informal, such as Earth First! "Lifestyle" environmentalists may have helped push somewhere along the way, but we can't even detect, much less analyze, their impact. They simply don't seem to matter.

Detailed demographic data on the environmental movement's dues-paying members are scarce, said a 1990 *Washington Times* news story. "One of the few attempts at characterizing environmentalists was done in 1982. Research and Forecast Inc., a New York market research firm, found that environmentalists were most likely to be white, urban dwellers with more than one college degree and a service industry job." Members of the Nature Conservancy, the Wilderness Society, the Natural Resources Defense Council and Environmental Action comprised the group surveyed, which is reasonably representative of the top twenty-five membership Economy Trasher groups profiled in this book.[32]

The demographics of the Sierra Club mailing list are impressive, with median household incomes above $40,000 (34.3 percent earn above $50,000), educational achievement levels above four years of university work, and 87.8 percent holding professional managerial jobs. So we are looking at the higher if not elite ranks of American society when we look at the organized environmental movement's members: better educated people of ample money and liberal privilege who benefit from—and are totally oblivious to—all the productive resource enterprises they try to destroy.

To hell with you all.

The demographic data on the *leadership* of the environmental movement, on the other hand, are complete. We know all their names and addresses—and incomes and personal histories. We can characterize these leaders without fear of error. The mainstream environmental movement leadership is lily-white, highly educated, overwhelmingly professional, and well versed in the ways of power. The environmentalist leadership is not only found heading up well known organizations such as the Sierra Club, Audubon Society, or National Wildlife Federation, those very same people are also found in government, on the boards of directors of top corporations, in high society, and wherever else they damn well please to be.

These people are accustomed to wielding political power, many coming from Eastern families long listed in the Social Register. Many of them are lawyers educated in the best schools, many from Ivy League backgrounds. Yale, for example, gave the world Gus Speth, head of the World Resources Institute; Richard Ayres, co-founder of the Natural Resources Defense Council; Charles Elkins, director of the EPA's Office of Toxic Substances; the late Senator John Heinz, a noted environmental advocate who was also a scion of the famous ketchup family; John Bonnie, former EPA counsel; William Butler and James Tripp, both counsels for the Environmental Defense Fund; and Peter Seligmann of Conservation International. And don't forget that President Clinton went to Yale Law School. Perhaps most importantly, many of them live in Washington and saunter back and forth between leadership positions in environmental public interest groups and government agencies that control environmental issues.

This revolving door between government and the environmental movement has serious implications for the future of America. Pressure to eliminate private property, restrict free markets, and take the limits off government can be brought to bear from inside and outside of government—by the same people.

The Environmentalism Industry

The *New York Times Magazine* said, "the major environmental groups have become industries unto themselves, with well-paid professional staffs wielding extraordinary influence on Capitol Hill and in federal agencies."[33]

Environmental organizations are businesses. Money is their fuel. Non-profit organizations must make a profit, contrary to popular belief—they just don't pay income tax on it or distribute it to shareholders. If environmental groups don't make a profit they will go out of business, just like their tax-paying victims. In addition, a number of environmental groups are not completely tax-exempt: Political Action Committees and lobbying groups must pay taxes on certain parts of their income, which makes it doubly important for them to watch the bottom line.

Like any business, environmental organizations have professional managers operating the business and skilled employees doing the work: management and labor. Like any manager, the leader of an environmental group must be expert at planning, strategy, operating, staffing, budgeting, controlling and supervising. Like any employee, the staff members of an environmental group must be trained, qualified, and motivated to do the work. In our profiles of the top environmental groups we have examined the top management in detail where information was available, and listed the number of staff, distinguishing between professional and clerical where information was available.

Direct mail is the lifeblood of most environmental organizations. They hire professional public relations firms just like Exxon does, and they have to find the sales pitch that works just like du Pont does, and they have to get a successful return or go bankrupt just like every business. They are just as prone to exaggeration in advertising as for-profit businesses, and for the same reason: to get your money.

Direct mail fund raising has a standard formula that must be followed if money is to come back in those expensive little Business Reply Envelopes they send you. The message of the direct mail letter must appeal to three base emotions: Fear, Hate and Revenge. We are *not* telling you what we think is the proper way things should run, we are reporting a well-known fact of the direct mail business. You'll find that formula taught in any direct mail textbook.

Thus, every environmentalist fund raising mailer must present you with a *crisis*—a problem won't do, because only crisis carries *a sense of urgency*, and without urgency, recipients will not respond. That crisis must *frighten* you as well as having time-sensitive urgency. If you are not frightened, you won't send money.

Then the direct mail letter must present you with a bogeyman against whom to focus your anger, somebody who is at fault for the crisis that now has you frightened. Environmentalist direct mail pitches all use industry or private property as the bogeyman that you must hate.

Once you've been frightened and made to hate the bogeyman, the successful direct mail appeal must offer you a way to get revenge against the bogeyman—the payoff for your contribution. The more soul-satisfying the revenge, the better the letter pulls.

All this must be dressed up in an appeal that appears to have a high moral tone, but which—without you realizing it—works on your lower emotions. If you do direct mail environmentalism any other way, you're wasting your time and postage.

If you analyze every environmentalist direct mail package that brought back money, you'll find its appeal letter was a disguised moral message based on fear, hate and revenge. Environmental groups that use direct mail successfully thrive by evoking the basest emotions in your heart without you ever realizing it.

Another fact of business life: Environmental groups must maintain well established financial ratios just like any business—they are different only in subject matter. Because memberships constitute fundamental income sources to all but a handful of environmental groups, the members-to-staff ratio is critical. Most environmental advocacy groups figure they must maintain at least 1,500 members per staff position. When memberships fall off, staffs are cut just like in an automobile factory when car sales fall off—if the management is worth its salt.

Environmental groups have management-labor problems just like any other business firm. Friends of the Earth staffers even formed a labor union in 1983 because management was planning cutbacks.

Environmental group memberships typically fall off at a rate of about 30 percent per year; very few groups suffer less turnover, some suffer more. That means a group with 100,000 members must recruit an average of 30,000 new members every year just to stay in the same place. Growth is a matter of direct mail gurus finding the right combination of good pitches and good lists, which is a blend of astute management and dumb luck.

Environmental groups, like many non-profit organizations, also rely not only on rank-and-file members, but also on philanthropy, which means they require leaders and staff skilled in writing grants and sucking up to golden donors. The cocktail party circuit is where most contacts are made between environmental leaders and high-dollar contributors; eco-managers need a wardrobe with L. L. Bean attire at one end and black tie togs at the other.

Clearly, running an environmental organization requires business skill as well as zeal. There is nothing magic about the Nature Conservancy or the Sierra Club. The people who run environmental groups are not saints any more than the people who run General Motors or the local shopping mall. Environmentalists want your business. They'll do what's necessary to get it.

Environmentalism is a business. Like all businesses, part of the *modus operandi* of every environmental group is to put competitors out of business— but its competitors are more often the businesses that feed, clothe and shelter us all than they are other environmental groups. Environmentalists want your business. They'll do what's necessary to get it.

Regardless of cost to the economy.

What you are about to read will be news to members of the environmental movement as much as it is to anyone. The supporters of environmentalism are ignorant of the facts about their movement—about its real operating methods, its faults and malefactions, about its cumulative impact on our economy, about where all the movement's money comes from and what the leaders do with it. Where demographic studies on environmentalism exist at all, they are designed to help woo more money and members in their direction. There is only the most rudimentary data base of research on where environmental groups get their money and what they do with it because they are not willing to reveal such possibly embarrassing facts.

As a result, the environmental movement has grown intellectually moribund. There is little communication among environmental organizations on their economic impact. There is not a single forum or publication for the candid discussion of economic problems caused by environmentalism. They will admit of no harm to the economy. The greatest of faults, as Carlyle said, is to be conscious of none.

To hell with you all.

Every citizen in the country needs to know something about the environmental movement, if for no other reason than to heed the old maxim "Know the enemy." That the environmental movement is the enemy of the people will become abundantly clear in the profiles that follow. Environmental organizations are not what they seem.

You're likely to find your blood boiling as we unfold the secrets behind this popular movement. You'll see the way environmentalists *really* think and operate. You'll discover how they create issues out of thin air, and then manipulate the facts, the media and the public. You'll see how the movement's positions on everything from animal welfare to global warming have radicalized over the past two decades, and what dirty tricks and lies—and illegal acts—they resort to in order to consolidate their political power.

Meet the Economy Trashers—Footnotes

1 Quoted by Daniel Seligman, "Down With People," *Fortune*, September 23, 1991, p. 215. *Wild Earth* is a publication of the Cenozoic Society, a group co-founded by Dave Foreman after he left Earth First!

2 "Fuzzy-Wuzzy Thinking About Animal Rights," by Richard Conniff, *Audubon*, November 1990, p. 127-28.

3 *The Environmental Sourcebook*, Edith Carol Stein, Lyons & Burford, New York, 1992, p. 6.

4 Numerous directories list environmental groups. See *World Directory of Environmental Organizations*, Third Edition, edited by Thaddeus C. Trzyna with the assistance of Ilze M. Gotelli, California Institute of Public Affairs in cooperation with the Sierra Club and IUCN—The World Conservation Union, 1990.

5 "The Philanthropy 400," Special Report, *The Chronicle of Philanthropy*, November 19, 1991, p. 1.

6 "Best Charities," *Money*, December, 1992, p. 122-123.

7 All money and membership figures were derived from the Annual Reports of the respective groups, or from their IRS Form 990 Annual Reports, or from standard reference works such as *Public Interest Profiles* or *The Encyclopedia of*

Associations or *The Environmental Sourcebook* or from telephone interviews by the authors with organization officials. They are as up to date as our sources.

8 *The Environmental Sourcebook*, Stein.

9 *Eco-Warriors: Understanding the Radical Environmental Movement*, Rik Scarce, The Noble Press, Inc., Chicago, 1990.

10 *The Aquarian Conspiracy*, Marilyn Ferguson, J. P. Tarcher, Los Angeles, 1980, p. 216.

11 Although basically uncritical and merely laudatory, Scheffer's historical account is useful. See *The Shaping of Environmentalism in America*, Victor B. Scheffer, University of Washington Press, Seattle, 1991.

12 "Environmentalism's Articles of Faith," by Victor Scheffer, *Northwest Environmental Journal*, Vol. 5:1, Spring/Summer 1989, pp. 99-108.

13 *The Functions of Social Conflict*, Lewis Coser, The Free Press, New York, 1956, p. 112.

14 See for example *A Theology of the Earth* (lecture at the Smithsonian Institution, October 2, 1969) René Dubos, Washington, D.C., Government Printing Office.

15 *Playing God in Yellowstone: The Destruction of America's First National Park*, Alston Chase, Harcourt Brace Jovanovich, New York, 1987, pp. 301-02.

16 Memorandum, Destry Jarvis to Maine Delegation, Town Officials, Committee Staff, Re: Isle au Haut Legislation, February 9, 1981.

17 "Oiling the works: How Chevron bought its way into environmentalism's power circle," by Eve Pell, *Mother Jones*, March-April 1991, p. 39. *Mother Jones* is a non-profit magazine funded largely by foundation grants.

18 "The Role of Foundations and Universities in Conservation," Russell E. Train, *Horace M. Albright Lectureship in Conservation*, no. 7, 1967.

19 "Education for Environmental Concerns," by Robert S. Morrison, *Daedalus* 96, no. 4 (1967), p. 1210.

20 *Human Action*, Ludwig von Mises, Yale University Press, Hartford, 1949, revised edition 1963, third revised edition published by Henry Regnery Company in 1966, pp. 717-718.

21 "Earth Read-out," by Keith Lampe, November 27, 1969, quoted in *The Environmental Handbook*, Ballantine Books, New York, 1970, p. 7.

22 "Are Democracy and Environmental Protection Incompatible?" by Amy MacDonald, *Habitat: Journal of the Maine Audubon Society*, January 1990, p. 19.

23 *Ecoterrorism: The Dangerous Fringe of the Environmental Movement*, Doug Bandow, The Heritage Foundation Backgrounder, 764, p. 10.

24 "Environmental Demonstrations Take Violent Turn," by Elliott Diringer, *San Francisco Chronicle*, April 14, 1990, p. A3.

25 *Eco-Warriors*, p. 266.

26 Rik Scarce interview with Judi Bari, Ukiah, California, August 31, 1989.

27 *Eco-Warriors*, p. 267.

28 "Impeaching a Self-Appointed Judge," by Stephen Jay Gould, *Scientific American*, July, 1992, p. 118-121.

29 *Animals' Agenda*, July/August 1990.

30 Rik Scarce interview with Katz, Corte Madera, California, March 1, 1980.

31 *The Rights of Nature*, Roderick Frazier Nash, University of Wisconsin Press, Madison, 1989.

32 "Who is an environmentalist?" *Washington Times*, April 19, 1990.

33 *New York Times Magazine*.

The Profiles

The Nature Conservancy ▆▆▆▆▆▆▆▆▆▆▆

The Nature Conservancy (Founded 1951)
    Annual budget: $278,497,634   Net Assets $855,115,125 (1993) [1]
        Staff: 1,150 total
      Members: 708,000 individuals; 405 corporations
     Tax Status: (501)(c)(3)
   Headquarters: 1815 North Lynn Street
              Arlington, Virginia 22209
              Phone: (703)841-5300 Fax: (703)841-1283

The Top of the List, the Number One Economy Trasher. This richest of all environmental groups—with total assets of $855 million—is one of the least known. A 1990 marketing study showed that the public didn't know the group's name or understand what it does. [2]

Yet the Nature Conservancy's 708,000 members belong to an outfit that operates 8 regional offices: in San Francisco, California; Boulder, Colorado; Winter Park, Florida; Honolulu, Hawaii; Boston, Massachusetts; Minneapolis, Minnesota; Albany, New York; and Chapel Hill, North Carolina, along with 50 state chapter offices. [3]

Wealth this big keeps a low profile for a good reason. If the public knew what it was really up to, they'd be up in arms against it. As *Rolling Stone* commented, the Nature Conservancy is a "relatively obscure but smart and effective environmental group. Unlike some organizations, it expends no energies on publicity-seeking stunts or shrill fund-raising mailings." [4]

The Nature Conservancy is so secretive because it is a big money nonprofit upperclass real estate firm. TNC buys private land in the United States, sometimes at the request of the federal government, and then sells the bulk of it—about two-thirds—to that federal government at substantial markups. *Outside* magazine called TNC "Century 21 with a built-in buyer." TNC also builds commercial housing developments on its "saved" properties. TNC has also operated commercial farms, including cotton plantations, on its "saved" properties. TNC also runs a "save the rainforest" project with no accountability to prove it did anything beyond selling its donors a promise of pie-in-the-sky. [5]

This group has been known to hide behind phony front companies to get land from owners who would not have knowingly sold to an environmental group. It has also been known to join with higher-profile groups to politically intimidate owners into selling.

The Nature Conservancy has so many disgruntled former employees that a veritable army chanted in our ears, "Conservation has been taken over by Big Money." If this profile has any theme, that's it.

Conservation has been taken over by Big Money.

Since its founding in 1951, the Nature Conservancy has bought more than 5 million acres of private land in the United States, largely through outright purchases and gifts from donors, and 20 million acres in Canada and throughout Latin America in "debt-for-nature" swaps in Costa Rica, Ecuador and the Dominican Republic.

The Nature Conservancy keeps about a third of the land it buys, and manages what it does keep with professional staff members. In Texas, the Nature Conservancy keeps only 10 percent; some 90 percent of the land it acquired there is now in government hands.[6] Nevertheless, its holdings of 1,631 nature preserves in the United States form the largest private sanctuary system in the world, according to the *New York Times Magazine*.[7]

Rich? TNC pays its 17 officers an annual total of $1,786,432 (average $105,084). Its other 1,130 or so employees are paid salaries totaling $45,824,545; pension plan benefits, $1,913,453; other employee benefits, $3,832,110 (1992). That's more than $53 million for the hired help. What's more, TNC owns $138,228,753 worth of endowment investments, has $49 million parked in U.S. obligations, $27 million in bonds, $138 million in its common stock portfolio, $36 million in life income trusts, $29 million in mutual funds, $26 million in planned giving investments, and $102 million in land investments. Keep that in mind the next time you get a direct mail fund raising appeal from The Nature Conservancy. They really need the money, poor babies.[8]

The Nature Conservancy descended from The Ecological Society of America, a small group founded in 1917 by academics at the University of Illinois, mostly botanists and zoologists. They were interested in preserving places in which to collect scientific specimens. In 1946 a faction spun off a new unincorporated organization called the Ecologists Union, which was incorporated on September 11, 1950 in Columbus, Ohio, and renamed The Nature Conservancy. The group named itself after the British government's Nature Conservancy preserve system, but decided to "stay private and buy preserves with private funds." TNC was incorporated on October 22, 1951 as a non-profit corporation in the District of Columbia. It was granted exemption from income taxes under §501(c)(3) of the Internal Revenue Code on March 23, 1982.[9]

In 1953 TNC accepted the gift of a 60-acre tract in the Mianus River Gorge in the suburbs of New York City, and still manages it as its oldest private reserve—now expanded to 440 acres. The gift confirmed the original intent of the Conservancy, to privately acquire and protect its own natural sites.[10]

Back in those old days, from TNC's inception in 1951 to the early 1970s, it was as American as motherhood and apple pie, using small donor funds to preserve small selective nature tracts and manage them privately under local chapter control. The donations did not stay small for long. An early grant of $100,000 from Mrs. DeWitt Wallace, co-owner of the *Reader's Digest*, was soon complemented by additional grants from foundations, corporations, and individuals.[11]

In 1970, the group took the first step that eventually led it astray: TNC bought three islands off Virginia—the Smith, Myrtle, and Ship Shoal Islands, which front for 12 miles along the coast above the point where the Chesapeake Bay meets the Atlantic Ocean. The coast of Virginia is rimmed with marshes, lagoons, and bays behind the barrier islands. The beaches are on the islands, and that is where the people want to be. The only way to get to the beaches in 1970 was by private boat.

The Smith Island Development Corporation petitioned the Virginia Assembly to build a bridge across Cape Charles, the southernmost tip of the Delmarva [Delaware-Maryland-Virginia] Peninsula, to Smith Island, then run a road connecting Myrtle and Ship Shoal. "From there," said the developer, "the commonwealth could keep pushing the road north until it eventually connected all eighteen islands."[12]

A new bridge to the islands would not only please beach lovers, it would also generate more revenue for the Chesapeake Bay Bridge Tunnel, built in 1964, which would help the entire state's economy.

But a bright young man named Patrick F. Noonan had become the Nature Conservancy's director of operations, and he had other plans. He realized that the purchase of these three islands could be the start of something big. So he got the Conservancy to pay $1.25 million for the 8,800 acres, much of the money provided by the Mary Flagler Cary Charitable Trust, an East Coast philanthropic foundation that originally got its money from the Rockefeller Standard Oil Trust and Henry Morrison Flagler's railroad, steamship and luxury hotel empire in Florida. The Conservancy told the *New York Times* that the Smith Island Development Corporation "had plans for 15,000 single family, apartment and motel units on the islands."[13]

With its purchase the Nature Conservancy destroyed hundreds of millions of dollars worth of economic growth and thousands of jobs—not just with those three islands, but with what followed. Pat Noonan began an acquisition campaign that lasted into the 1980s and spent almost the entire permanent capital of the Conservancy—$25 million—to buy 14 of the 18 barrier islands, containing 40,000 acres along sixty miles of the Eastern Shore of Virginia and stopping all development—except for the Conservancy's own development of upscale vacation homes and condos available only to the very rich. They called it the Virginia Coast Reserve (VCR).

The people of the Virginia Shore generally hated the Nature Conservancy. They felt the organization was tying up lands which could have otherwise been developed for the Shore's economic benefit. They were also irritated by the intrusion of outsiders—"come-heres" in local parlance—and the Nature Conservancy were consistently outsiders of the worst sort, arrogant, we-know-better-than-you-how-to-care-for-this-land, secretive, rich and openly hostile. The county commissioners deeply resented the tax-exempt status of TNC's lands, something the poor counties could ill afford. Everyone was annoyed when the Conservancy curbed the locals from hunting, fishing, camping and joy riding on the islands.[14]

When David E. Morine started with the Nature Conservancy in January of 1972, it had only 48 full-time employees. After eighteen years as a professional environmentalist, he wrote his 1990 memoir, *Good Dirt*. Morine was hired by Patrick Noonan and still exhibits a good dose of hero-worship. He said of Noonan, "All during the seventies Pat attacked the Virginia Barrier Islands with more force than any hurricane. He was then [beginning in 1973] president of the Conservancy, and as director of land acquisition, I followed behind and picked up the pieces. The Conservancy's whirlwind acquisition efforts blew away the developer's plans for a new Ocean City. Once the Conservancy gained control of the islands, the assembly scrapped all proposals for roads and bridges."[15]

No brag, just fact. During the first six months of Noonan's presidency, he bought Parramore Island, the largest of the Virginia barriers islands from several owners including James Wheat of Wheat First Securities in Richmond for $1.6 million. He also bought up a large stretch of the Chattahoochee River in Georgia. His local chapters were buying up prime developable land from Maine to California in a planned pattern to block economic growth. "Haphazard preservation is as bad as haphazard development," Noonan used to say.

How did the Nature Conservancy get the political power to thwart the Virginia legislature? How did the Nature Conservancy manage to buy up all this land from local people who wanted reasonable development and who had become frightened by the Conservancy's 1970 lockup of Smith, Myrtle, and Ship Shoal Islands? Simple. The Conservancy used a bogus front group.

In 1975, a decoy company called Offshore Islands Inc. donated Metompkin Island to the Conservancy. Norfolk, Virginia, banker M. Lee Payne, admitted, "We created Offshore Islands Inc. just as a front so the Nature Conservancy could proceed with buying the islands." The Conservancy said that Payne is man who conceived the idea for a fake front company.[16] Payne also personally owned fifteen parcels comprising approximately 1,600 acres in Accomack County.[17]

Beginning in 1979, something called the Allegheny Duck Club, which was actually a partnership of Seward Prosser Mellon of Ligonier, Pennsylvania, Richard P. Mellon of Pittsburgh, Pennsylvania, and their late sister Constance Brown of New York City, began secretly buying up Virginia coastal land through surrogates. The surrogates included William M. Robinson, an attorney with the Pittsburgh firm of Reed Smith Shaw & McClay; attorney Mason R. Walsh, Jr. of Ligonier; M. Lee Payne; Tom Wilcox, an Oyster, Virginia, attorney; and John Norling, a real estate broker also from Oyster. The Conservancy's surrogates bought the entire town of Oyster. The communities didn't know. Even some of the Conservancy's staff didn't know.

Conservation Editor George Reiger of *Field & Stream* magazine wrote, "So much secrecy surrounds the inner workings of TNC [that] TNC Virginia biologist Rod Hennessy quit TNC when he discovered those bird-watching trips he had been conducting were nothing more than real estate safaris for Allegheny Duck Club members." Reiger is a long-time TNC member and a resident of Accomack.[18]

Just buying up the islands through ersatz fronts was not enough. Development was encroaching along the mainland marshes behind the barrier islands. That had to be stopped. But how? The Conservancy had already sunk $10 million into buying up the islands. Buying up the mainland frontage could cost another $100 million. There had to be a cheaper way.

David Morine tells us, "The more Pat pondered the problem, the clearer the solution became. There were only six deepwater frontages along the entire Eastern Shore. Pat reasoned that whoever controlled these six deepwater frontages controlled development. 'No developer's going to invest a lot of money for frontage on the Eastern Shore if he can't get access to the beaches.'"[19]

Noonan resigned as Conservancy president in the summer of 1980— succeeded by William Blair, Jr.—to assume the presidency of the Conservation Fund, but still served as a consultant. By the end of 1984 he had secretly orchestrated the Conservancy's acquisition of over 12,000 acres surrounding the six deepwater frontages, using the spurious front group again. As Morine gloated, "We now controlled the most developable land on the Eastern Shore."[20]

In December 1985 the Nature Conservancy announced it had signed a contract to obtain the property of the Allegheny Duck Club along a 100-mile stretch between the Atlantic Ocean and the Chesapeake Bay. E. Gregory Low, executive vice president of the Nature Conservancy (1992 salary $101,450, benefits $17,782), said his organization would trade lands of equal value to the Mellon group in unspecified locations. The Conservancy had plans to develop its coastal land into high-priced, low-density vacation homes and make a bundle of money, but the board of supervisors of Accomack County, Virginia, didn't like the deception.

Chairman of the board of county supervisors Dr. William Turner said, "We now are suspicious of the Conservancy. We thought they had done a good job of conservation on the Barrier Islands. But Low admitted to me that they do a lot of private duck hunting with their Yankee friends. We don't need them."

Turner demanded that the Conservancy reveal to the board of supervisors the details of its connection with the Mellon family and the Conservancy's political connections in the area. He noted that the Mellons had been known to close down steel mills and foreclose loans—and wasn't too sure how such people would treat the folks who had lived on this coast for generations.

Dr. Turner's doubts were well founded. TNC refuses to sell any of its real estate to locals. One top TNC official told a colleague, "We're going to get all of those people out of there and put our kind of people in." His kind of people is multibillionaire John Kluge of Metromedia Company, to whom TNC *has* sold property. The Conservancy denies it.[21]

One Eastern Shore resident feared, "All of us will end up being the servants to these goddam rich people." A Shore rent farmer named Ronnie Kellam sent his rent checks to Box RKM, Ligonier, Pennsylvania, which is the address of the Richard King Mellon interests. Patrick Noonan personally owned four properties in Accomack County: 143 acres at White's Neck; the Finney land of 15 acres; the Fox parcel of 24.15 acres; and the Burton property of 66.15 acres. Noonan's mentor Mason Walsh, Jr. personally owned two parcels of Virginia Shore property in Northampton County, 150.04 acres and 1.99 acres, both near Townsend.

Dr. Turner added that residents of the islands were considering a class action lawsuit against the Nature Conservancy because it is a tax-exempt organization intending to engage in commercial development while effectively blocking others.[22]

Here the pattern that was to shape a number of future environmentalist land trusts emerged: Create an exclusive private nature preserve as a magnet for profitable upscale adjacent residential and commercial development, then use the profits to finance still more nature acquisition. But do it quietly.

In one Virginia barrier island case, wrote *Field & Stream* editor George Reiger, the Conservancy struck a deal with the island's principal owner and developer: it accepted a charitable contribution of *undevelopable* tidal wetlands in exchange for the builder's meaningless promise of 'compatible development' in the dunes and maritime scrub. In addition to his multi-million dollar tax deduction, the developer got to advertise the rest of his holdings as 'being adjacent to a federal wildlife refuge,' since TNC got the **Fish and Wildlife Foundation** to accept title to the tidal wetlands which were then turned over to the U.S. Fish and Wildlife Service."[23]

The Nature Conservancy raised a flurry of newspaper headlines over the deception, but escaped prosecution for fraud. Some talk even surfaced that the Smith Island Development Corporation, which supposedly posed the original "threat" of building a road to connect the barrier islands, had itself been a totally fictitious entity dreamed up by the Nature Conservancy as a straw man to scare members into donating money for "saving" the Virginia shore—no documentation can be found in state corporation and tax records that such a business ever existed.[24]

Environmentalists seem to think they are above the law, and when they have enough money behind them, they are.[25]

Conservation has been taken over by Big Money.

How did a young man named Patrick F. Noonan, the president of an obscure environmental group called the Nature Conservancy, achieve this monumental land grab? Where did he get that kind of expertise? And where did he get that kind of money?

A sizeable fraction of the money behind the Nature Conservancy is that of the Mellon fortune. The Mellon family is one of the top three philanthropic dynasties in America. Their giving ranks far behind the first-place Rockefellers, but far ahead of the third place du Ponts, whose fortune has been split between so many heirs that any one family member falls far down the list of the nation's golden donors. The Mellon money was amassed first by old Judge Thomas Mellon, son of a destitute farmer from Poverty Point, Pennsylvania.[26]

One of Judge Mellon's eight children, son Andrew William Mellon (1855-1937), became one of the richest men in America in his day, an officer and director of many industrial firms. He created the Aluminum Company of America (ALCOA) by taking over a small Pittsburgh firm that owned the rights to a new electrical process for refining aluminum ore. He formed the Gulf Oil Company with his brothers Richard and William. He owned coal interests, steel interests, banking interests, and a lot more.[27]

Andrew Mellon had the reputation of being ruthless and rapacious even among such tough-minded competitors as Andrew Carnegie and John D. Rockefeller. He treated labor abominably, meeting a 1915 strike at Alcoa in Massena, New York, with a private army of Pinkerton men and hired spies. If immigrant labor rebelled at their wretched working conditions, he brought in blacks from the sharecropper South. He provided no benefits at all for former employees. He was not a nice man. Even his wife hated him, separating from him after nine years of tending their two children, Paul and Ailsa, in the nursery while Andrew tended his millions in the den.

Through Andrew's rough business genius, the family today owns holdings in more than a hundred large American corporations, including Alcoa, Koppers, Carborundum, General Reinsurance, First Boston, and the Mellon National Bank. Andrew Mellon also served as a high-ranking government official. He financed the construction and donated paintings to found the National Gallery of Art in Washington, D.C., possibly as a gambit to derail a court action then being pressed by the federal government against him for income tax evasion. He was also secretary of the treasury (1921-1932) and ambassador to England (1932-1933).

Richard King Mellon, son of Andrew's brother Richard B. Mellon, became head of the family financial empire as president of the Mellon National Bank in 1934. He had been groomed for the position all his life, sent to Princeton and thence to the business world where ten years after graduation he held directorships in 34 major corporations. He also carried on the family tradition of philanthropy. But he held a totally different view of corporate responsibility than his father.

When he saw Pittsburgh's steel mills choking his neighbors to death in the killer smogs of the post-World War II 1940s, he decided to put an end to the air pollution once and for all. He formed the Richard King Mellon Foundation in 1947, focusing its assets and benefactions primarily on the needs of Pittsburgh and western Pennsylvania, what he called the "Renaissance" redevelopment program. Because of his great wealth and power, he was able to virtually force the corporate elite of the region to clean up the city and successfully demanded government help in doing it. By 1962 he could look out his window and see a sparkling redeveloped city where before there had only been grime and gloom. He said, "We cannot get away from the fact that the very basis of our industrial society rests upon the environment in which we live." He was an early advocate of the Wise Use philosophy, that man and nature can live together in productive harmony—without feeling the necessity of damning industry while helping nature.

He died in 1970 at the age of seventy, and his widow Constance took over control of his foundation. In 1977 she changed the direction of the foundation's grants radically: She announced that concern for the city of Pittsburgh would continue, but as a secondary objective. For reasons that will become apparent, the Trustees changed the major emphasis of the foundation to land conservation and wildlife preservation on a national scope. "The prime concern of the foundation's efforts in conservation focuses on funding acquisitions of significant natural wilderness areas, both to protect lands from development and to assist in wildlife preservation," an annual report stated. "It is a consequence and reflection of the genuine concern on the part of the foundation's Trustees for preserving this country's natural heritage." In 1977 the foundation allocated 42 percent of its total outlays to land acquisition, most of it going to the Nature Conservancy.

Richard P. Mellon, an adopted son of Richard King Mellon, became chairman of the board of the foundation when Constance Mellon died in 1980. Seward Prosser Mellon, the other adopted son, became president of the foundation. It was Prosser, as he is known to friends, who helped set up the Allegheny Duck Club as a phony front for the Nature Conservancy. He took Patrick Noonan under his wing as protégé, grooming him for big things, assigning Mason Walsh, Jr., the foundation's chief counsel, as Noonan's personal adviser—and Walsh, as you will recall, was one of those surrogates secretly buying up land for the VCR. In 1980 the Richard King Mellon Foundation's board gave the Nature Conservancy a $15 million grant for initial funding for the Conservancy's "Rivers of the Deep South" program, and a $25 million grant in 1983 to launch its National Wetlands Conservation Project to "identify critical areas from the Atlantic coastal wetlands to the forests of Hawaii."

It was becoming abundantly clear that nature preserves had a magnetic attraction for adjacent upscale development that could be very, very profitable.

In short, the Nature Conservancy for many years was driven by the agenda of the Mellon Money.

Masters of Illusion

The Nature Conservancy is perhaps the most dangerous of all environmental groups, not only because it is the richest, but also because it appears to be harmless and idealistic.[28] As we have seen on the Virginia coastal barrier islands, it is more interested in deals than ideals.

We have investigated dozens of complaints about the Nature Conservancy from private landowners all over America who feel abused. We found a particularly nasty case in a federal court in Indiana. Professor Frederic A. Gibbs, M.D., now deceased, was once a prestigious neurologist and pioneer of the electroencephalogram (EEG) test. Apparently he had grown mentally confused and disabled in his waning years and at a time when he was not competent, parties assisted him in changing documents that attempt to leave his entire estate including a large farm to the Nature Conservancy. The Gibbs family sued the Nature Conservancy for undue influence and fraud and is struggling to retrieve ownership of the land and estate for the family heirs. The Gibbs family's detailed allegations of the Nature Conservancy exercising undue dominion and control over the elderly Dr. Gibbs as presented in the court documents are horrifying. The Gibbs family won the lawsuit.[29]

We have also had a number of complaints from rural parties who felt cheated and tried to sue the Nature Conservancy. They tell us they received threats of massive retaliation from the Nature Conservancy in the form of libel lawsuits and in some cases, we are told that TNC lawyers have even threatened to sue small-town lawyers for malpractice if they accepted cases from critics. The Nature Conservancy with its vast wealth and top-notch lawyers can be quite intimidating.[30]

Many others tell us they sold their property to the Conservancy at bargain basement prices for the tax write-off only to see it quickly sold at huge profits to the government, or, more astonishingly, to developers who stripped it and built it up.

In addition, TNC developed 80 acres of low-cost housing in one of their "Last

Great Places" on Block Island in Long Island Sound for teachers and blue collar workers to encourage them to live in this isolated spot.

In fact, TNC gave a session to the National Association of Home Builders Show in Atlanta in 1990 titled "Doing Deals with Land Conservancies" in which TNC past president Frank D. Boren told how they could help developers get around President Bush's recent pledge of no let loss of wetlands. Mr. Boren suggested they use TNC to vet a prospective property: "You're out of your mind if you don't check our data bank first—which is free, doesn't cost you anything—before you hit an endangered species on your land."[31]

At the same session, TNC's director of Trade Lands program, Richard S. Friedman, urged developers to buy TNC sites next to its bird preserve on Elkhorn Slough in California's Monterey Valley, where commercial agriculture, mostly strawberries, was using pesticides they wanted to get rid of. "I've got one 350 acre parcel under option," said Freidman, "and we'll probably put ten to twenty houses about 350 feet above sea level with good views of Monterey Bay, take the strawberries out, reforest that with native vegetation and put some trails in down to the preserve. I'd like to convince people not to put their homes next to a golf course. This time have your homes next to a flyway to watch those ducks come in and those geese, which are dwindling populations."

Many critics have seen the pattern, including George Reiger of *Field & Stream*. "The Conservancy," he said, "will be able to make so much money from selling these...farms, woodlands, and wetlands, it will be able to buy and develop even more farms, woodlands, and wetlands in other states!"[32]

Reiger also revealed that the Nature Conservancy inspects on average 400 properties and acquires 1,000 acres of them *each day*.

TNC's ledgers showed that as of June 30, 1990, it was holding $53.5 million in land "for resale to the government."[33]

TNC's ledgers showed that they received $90,693,000 from sales of land to government agencies in 1992. That's nearly the *total* budget of the second largest environmental group in America, the National Wildlife Federation at $94.4 million.[34]

The Nature Conservancy is not what it seems.

For one thing, it is not the sweetness-and-light outfit of its membership brochures: the Nature Conservancy never lets unflattering comments go unpunished. George Reiger of *Field & Stream* found out the hard way. TNC Chief Operating Officer Bill Weeks (1992 salary $122,000, benefits $20,372) and Leigh H. Perkins, chairman of Orvis Company, the Manchester, Vermont outdoor mail order firm, a big *Field & Stream* advertiser and member of the Nature Conservancy board of directors, pressured the magazine, which caved in and told Reiger no more critiques of the Nature Conservancy.

TNC loyalists are evidently more willing to believe the group's brochures than its ledgers.

The worse for the truth. Most magazines do not have the guts to print the truth about the Nature Conservancy's phony deals: A *National Geographic* feature waltzed around the issue with euphemisms and oblique references, although it was clear that Noel Grove, the writer, knew exactly what was going on—and he even admits it in private. The power of the Mellon money Old Boy Network, which is very tight with the highfalutin Grosvenors of the National Geographic Society—Patrick F. Noonan sits on their board of trustees—can defeat the bald truth any day.[35]

Playing Rough

The Nature Conservancy also uses its financial and political clout to intimidate private property owners into selling. Their favorite harassment ploy is to covertly play "good cop-bad cop" in joint actions with openly aggressive environmental groups. TNC rigs deals with activist accomplices to raise huge stinks about specific land developments that then become politically impossible so that selling to TNC is the only alternative.

A case in point is the attack on Donnell Pond, east of Ellsworth, Maine. Prentiss and Carlisle, a timber company based in Bangor, owned a substantial portion of the land around the pond. In the summer of 1987 they had contracted with Patten Corporation, a Vermont-based developer, to put in 150 camp lots on their land, although Patten had less than a sterling track record for abuses. This project had been designed for minimum impact-maximum conservation, scattering the sites over 1,500 acres so that for each camp lot there was an average of nearly ten untouched acres in the project. Most people regarded it as a model development.

But not the Maine Chapter of the Nature Conservancy, which, with its 12,000 members, is the state's largest eco-group. It wanted absolutely no development on that pond. Period. So TNC set about to wreck the Patten Corporation's plans. Conservancy Maine Director Mason Morfit and Associate Director Kent Wommack worked with the belligerent Natural Resources Council of Maine (NRCM) and with Edwin Meadows, then director of Maine's Bureau of Public Lands—but formerly a trustee of the Nature Conservancy—to stop Patten's project dead in its tracks. Here's how it worked:

Attack Phase I. The NRCM mounted a screaming publicity campaign with the usual eco-sales pitch: "The last magnificent wilderness pond in Maine is about to be overwhelmed by a tidal wave of destruction by heartless out-of-state developers." Reading NRCM's propaganda, you could just visualize a dozen pulp mills, thousands of thirty-story apartment houses and hundreds of honky tonks built on concrete stilts in the middle of the pond, each dumping millions of tons of raw sewage, solid waste and sulfuric acid in the water each day. Whoosh! There goes the neighborhood.

Attack Phase II: The state offered $2 million for the property, but the owners refused the lowball price. In order to put a big hammer in the state's hands, NRCM supporters lobbied the state legislature to consider new controls over private property. Private lands that had been open to public use through the generosity of the owners might be denied all development rights. Owners might be able to do nothing with their land. Nothing. Nada. Nichts. Zero. Zip.

Except keep the title and pay taxes. That way, the state would not owe just compensation and the public could have play without pay. With this threat of virtual destruction of all property rights hanging over the whole state, the plan went into:

Attack Phase III: Edwin Meadows, playing the kindly bureaucrat, who, far from being stung by the developer's rejection of his ridiculously low price, amiably suggested to Patten executives that they meet with the low-key environmental group, the Nature Conservancy. "I know the private sector is not always comfortable dealing with state agencies," he told a magazine reporter. With TNC's economic know-how, especially knowledge of tax advantages, and their business-like approach, they could work something out, Meadows said.[36]

Patten executives did not know that Meadows was once a trustee and paid officer of the Nature Conservancy and was leading them to his old group's butchering block. The Nature Conservancy met the Patten executives with cold-eyed disdain. There will be no development of any kind on Donnell Pond, the developers were told. Patten was in shock.

The Natural Resources Council of Maine kept up its publicity. Lobbyists kept on the legislative pressure. Patten caved in.

On April 1, 1988—All Fools' Day—the Nature Conservancy completed contracts on behalf of the state of Maine to give Patten $1.4 million and 12,000 acres of forest land elsewhere in exchange for control over 7,000 acres in the Donnell Pond area. Patten retained 343 acres, plastered with a conservation easement that restricts development to eight camp lots.

Wommack told *Down East* magazine, "We didn't plan it that way, but it worked out as the old good-cop, bad-cop routine. The Natural Resources Council played the bad cop, then we could come in as a friendly cop, providing a forum that allowed Patten to do the right thing and feel good about it."

Wink, wink, nudge, nudge.

Funny how the Nature Conservancy can develop its own "Last Great Places" but doesn't want anybody else to develop their own great place.

We guess not all Great Places are created equal.

Selling our Birthright

There is another illusion, one infinitely more threatening. TNC appears to be buying land in legitimate deals and preserving it as a selfless protector of nature, putting its money where its mouth is, even if it does make a few million bucks in commercial real estate development now and then, which, after all, is just good old American competitive capitalism at work, even if a little odd for a nonprofit. None of the publicity in the standard profiles of environmental groups, such as that published in *Public Interest Profiles*, even mentions the most important fact about the Nature Conservancy: that it serves as a major conduit for nationalizing private land by selling the bulk of its purchases to the federal government at high "management fees" (profits).[37]

Patrick Noonan—hiding behind TNC's early reputation—not only shifted the Conservancy from small-is-beautiful to huge lands deals, from local control to rule from the top, but most significantly, he also shifted the Conservancy from its original keep-it-and-manage-it policy to getting the federal government to buy TNC land and pay them a tidy profit—never asking whether public ownership of land was in the best interest of either the public or the environment. It was ecologist Garrett Hardin, recall, who said, "The tragedy of the commons is averted by private property."

Noonan, with the guidance of Harvard Ph.D. Robert Jenkins as his science director, decided to adopt a "protect whole ecosystems" approach for the Conservancy. Jenkins has been called "the soul of the Conservancy" for his role in creating its present philosophy. David Morine sketched that new philosophy in this passage from *Good Dirt*. After exulting over Noonan's victory in secretly acquiring all the islands and the most developable mainland parcels for the Virginia Coast Reserve, he wrote:

> The rest of the conservancy was nervous. We had invested close to $25 million, the bulk of our permanent capital, into this one preserve.
>
> "Don't worry," Pat told us. "The VCR will make an excellent U. S. Fish and Wildlife refuge. You can sell it to the Feds and get all of your money back."[38]

Noonan, as a matter of fact, had taken Secretary of the Interior Cecil Andrus on a duck hunt on the VCR in 1979, trying to get him interested in making it into a new National Wildlife Refuge, with no luck. The Reagan Administration put a halt to that racket.[39]

But the Conservancy had been buying land, holding it, and then peddling it to the Feds since the year Noonan became president. The Nature Conservancy made its first really big deal with the federal government in 1973. TNC knew that Union Camp Corporation, a New Jersey-based forest products firm, was preparing to dispose of a 49,000 acre pulpwood tract it owned in the Great Dismal Swamp in North Carolina and Virginia valued at $12.6 million. TNC suggested that it might make more sense tax-wise and public relations-wise for Union Camp to donate the cutover land—which still contained thick forest growth of non-commercial species—for conservation than to sell it to developers. Union Camp agreed. TNC then approached the Weyerhaeuser Company, another big timber company, to see if they could work the same deal there. They could, 11,000 acres worth. Three years later, the Nature Conservancy deeded the combined land to the Feds. The U.S. Fish and Wildlife Service used it to create the Great Dismal Swamp National Wildlife Refuge. The splashy deal brought the Nature Conservancy to the attention of the federal government as an avenue for acquiring land that might otherwise be unavailable to them.

Mike Ford, chief of the Bureau of Land Management's Lands Branch explained, "We have found people prefer to deal with land trusts rather than with the government. We use their expertise to take advantage of many once-in-a-lifetime opportunities to acquire priceless properties we would have missed without the Nature Conservancy's help."

William Weeks, who came on staff in 1982 and is now the Conservancy's Chief Operating Officer, was quoted by the late columnist Warren Brookes as saying, "We buy these properties when they need to be bought, so that at some point we can become the 'willing seller' (to the government). This helps the government get around the problem of local opposition." Weeks strongly denies he ever said it. The documents say enough.

The principle, as TNC insider David Morine wrote in his book, is "leverage and rollover, leverage and rollover." The leverage is land bought low and sold high, the rollover is using the profit to buy more land low and sell it high, *ad infinitum.*

But what, exactly, is the federal government trying to do nationalizing more private land? The Feds already own more than a third of the entire nation, the largest share of any Western democracy and a strangely socialistic feature in what is widely perceived to be a capitalistic free enterprise society.

The Nature Conservancy poor-mouths about its sell-it-to-the Feds project, saying it loses money all down the line, but in fact it makes out like a bandit with federal deals. The only loss that showed up in TNC's 1992 financial report was $2.2 million on "trade lands." What are trade lands? The report says, "TNC sells certain real property, which has little ecological value, and uses the proceeds to support the acquisition of sites which contribute to the protection of biodiversity." That's all they're losing money on. The rest of their $278 million annual revenue came from somewhere. TNC's Form 990 IRS report says $76,318,014 of it came from government sales. And even if they didn't make a dime, what the hell are they doing as shills nationalizing private land anyway? If they're so public-spirited, why don't they *give* it to the government? Their profit merely adds insult to injury. But it's very real.

The 2,851-acre Cox Ranch near Las Cruces, New Mexico, is a case in point. In a very complicated and questionably illegal transaction, the Bureau of Land Management exchanged $4.237 million worth of federal land to the Nature Conservancy for the Cox Ranch, which the BLM's own appraiser had valued at only $2.65 million. The difference is clear profit for the Nature Conservancy.

How could the Nature Conservancy make such a sweetheart deal? Because it had a sweetheart in the Bureau of Land Management: BLM New Mexico State Director Larry Woodward, who sat on the Nature Conservancy's New Mexico board of directors. Insider trading, environmentalist style. On August 31, 1987, Mr. Woodward signed an agreement between the BLM and TNC explicitly stating that the Nature Conservancy would make a profit on the Cox Ranch deal:

> The Nature Conservancy will purchase the Cox Ranch for a price below appraised Fair Market Value, but will exchange the property to BLM for lands equal to the full Fair Market Value of the Cox Ranch. Any difference between the cost of purchase and total proceeds from the sale of exchange lands will be applied to reimbursement of the Nature Conservancy of its overhead and direct expenses.[40]

Woodward tentatively agreed to a price of $4.5 to $4.9 million. This arrangement was such a blatant violation of BLM regulations and federal law that BLM's Chief of Land Appraisal Dave Cavanaugh insisted that Woodward get an objective outside appraiser. Jack Donnell was hired and on June 10, 1988, turned in his valuation of the Cox Ranch at only $2.65 million. The Nature Conservancy's appraiser, Gene Price, came up with a valuation at the same time of $4.5 million. TNC knew it could play hardball, and indicated that the BLM would lose the deal at $2.65 million.

Woodward pressured Cavanaugh into increasing the Donnell appraisal to $3.525 million, with the excuse that Mr. Donnell had not assumed any market value increase since 1986. The Nature Conservancy wouldn't go for the $3.53, so in October 1988 Woodward gave TNC 14 separate parcels of land valued by BLM at $4.23 million for $3.81 million, a 10 percent "pooling" discount. This was the final sale price for the Cox Ranch, with $288,000 held on account by BLM as "owing"—the difference between the $3.81 million "pooling" discount price and Cavanaugh's revised appraisal of $3.52—an amount the Nature Conservancy could work off over time.[41]

Then the Nature Conservancy gave the owners of the Cox Ranch BLM lands worth $2.82 million, or about 80 percent of Cavanaugh's inflated final appraisal. Thus, when the deal was done, the Nature Conservancy came out with a net gain of $1.417 million worth of lands from the BLM—minus the $288,000 held on account.

The taxpayers didn't do so well. They paid the Nature Conservancy a cash-flow profit of $1.13 million, plus $700,000 to cover the tax credit earned by the Cox family for selling 20 percent below Fair Market Value. And, as things turned out, cash sales of those 14 parcels BLM sold to TNC for $3.813 million have produced prices 72 percent above the BLM valuation. The Nature Conservancy, long after Patrick Noonan set the pattern, and even after President William Blair was succeeded by Frank Boren in 1987, did very well for itself peddling private property to the federal government.[42]

The Nature Conservancy challenges this account, denying vehemently that it makes a profit on any of its megadeals. However, the Inspector General of the Interior Department called the Cox Ranch deal "legally questionable" in a June 28, 1991 report on his investigation into environmentalist land trust profiteering.

The Cox Ranch fiasco was not an isolated incident. The Conservancy took the 321,703-acre Gray Ranch in New Mexico's southwestern boot heel out of production in a January 1990 purchase that demoralized ranchers throughout the state. The U.S. Fish and Wildlife Service had been working in cahoots with the Nature Conservancy to get them to buy the ranch at an inflated price and sell it to the federal government to establish the Animas National Wildlife Refuge, at a healthy profit for the Nature Conservancy, as in the case of the nearby Cox Ranch. Livestock grazing on the Gray Ranch has been more than cut in half, reducing historic grazing levels by 3,000 yearlings, with a loss of $50,000 a year in tax revenues to the county.

Media mogul Ted Turner was reportedly buying into the Gray Ranch with the Conservancy, and his credentials in helping environmentalists stop all economic activity are impeccable.[43] The range condition on the Gray Ranch when purchased by the Nature Conservancy was rated "good to excellent" over its entire area, showing outstanding stewardship of the range by all its previous private owners and no need to reduce livestock production—other than to satisfy Economy Trasher dogma.[44]

In a fascinating sidelight to the uproar generated by TNC's Gray Ranch purchase, Bureau of Land Management bureaucrat John D. Tabb said, "The BLM does not advocate the purchase of the Gray Ranch in New Mexico." A careless reader might not notice that the U.S. Fish and Wildlife Service, another agency within the Department of the Interior, *did* advocate the purchase. An ingenious whipsaw between two government agencies to misdirect attention away from the Nature Conservancy's endless complicity in the nationalization of private land.[45]

"The Nature Conservancy is a serious threat to the livestock industry," said Al Schneberger, executive director of the New Mexico Cattle Growers' Association. The net loss of grazing land caused by the Nature Conservancy is giving great concern to the livestock economy all across America. The New Mexico Cattle Growers Association passed a resolution in June 1992 opposing the activities of the Nature Conservancy in New Mexico, seeking to end its non-profit status, requesting the state Attorney General to investigate the organiza-tion, and urging all landowners "to cautiously approach any transaction with The Nature Conservancy with an eye to the future of our Nation and its freedoms."[46]

The Conservancy made a bid for a large chunk of eastern Oregon in 1991, seeking to buy out the MC Ranch in Lake County, and portions of the Roaring Springs Ranch on the west slope of Steens Mountain in Harney County, and the Kueny Ranch at Fields in Harney County's Pueblo Valley. Local tax bases were threatened until county commissioners voted to impose normal taxes on the Nature Conservancy and to disallow its pleas that it deserved special treatment because it was a nonprofit organization.[47]

The Nature Conservancy's relationship with the government has even been formalized. A splashy Memorandum of Understanding affirmed "a policy of cooperation and coordination" between TNC and the Bureau of Land Manage-ment.[48] The pact was signed amid much ado in Tucson, Arizona, March 23, 1990. The Bureau's "cooperation with others" is important in the "acquisition and exchange of lands deemed important for public ownership," and "TNC has the experience and capability to assist the BLM in the acquisition of privately owned lands," said the Memorandum. The Nature Conservancy has become a surrogate for government because it is an appealing front for the many people who mistrust the government and refuse to sell to the bureaucrats. The Nature Conservancy will buy your land, and at the right price, the Nature Conservancy is always a willing seller to the government.[49]

When ranchers expressed dismay and formally asked BLM to reassure them that the Memorandum did not herald an attempt to remove all livestock from traditional grazing allotments, they received a non-answer from an acting deputy assistant director of support services: "While the BLM would completely agree that livestock grazing continues to be a legitimate use of the public lands, we also realize that the public considers some western lands to contain such critical resource values that their careful conservation and stewardship is warranted. The BLM has not abdicated any of its decision authorities in this agreement. We do recognize and acknowledge that the meaning of multiple use and stewardship continues to be refined through our open management processes." A disgusted rancher said he felt "some junior official has just told us to go mind our own business and that interests of those who want to kick us off are more important."[50]

The line between the Nature Conservancy and the government is a thin one, and getting thinner. In New Mexico, Mike Spear, the U.S. Fish and Wildlife regional director in New Mexico, was on the state board of trustees of the Nature Conservancy. Bureau of Land Management state director for New Mexico Larry Woodward, who sat on the Nature Conservancy's board, was forced to resign in October 1990 for the appearance of a conflict of interest. Texas Public Works Department Commissioner Tim Hixon was on the Nature Conservancy's national Board of Governors. The Memorandum of Understanding carries a lot of weight—the power and majesty of the United States government sits on the shoulders of the Nature Conservancy.

In addition, Robert Miller, the Chief, Realty Division of the U.S. Fish & Wildlife Service for the New England Region, had fed appraisals and other inside information to The Nature Conservancy's Philip Tabas, Eastern Region Legal Counsel (1991 salary $79,882, benefits $10,432) since at least 1986. In 1994, Miller became an employee of The Nature Conservancy as real estate officer— bringing a stupendous fund of insider information into the private environmental group. Tabas had carried on a long correspondence with Miller, reminding him on one occasion (letter of November 7, 1986) that he had "pretty broad authority to pay what we both agree to for the property, even '...in excess of the approved appraisal value,'" and asking on another occasion (letter of January 24, 1990) that Miller use his influence to promote a TNC property to a higher federal purchase priority, writing, "if there is anything you can do with the powers that be in your national office to revise the James River project to a higher ranking, it would make the job of securing Congressional funds for this project that much easier." Such incestuous relationships with government appear to pervade The Nature Conservancy.

William Perry Pendley, president and chief legal officer of Mountain States Legal Foundation, alleges this pact "between the governmental agency responsible for managing 342 million acres of federal land and a nongovernmental entity engaged in massive land purchases" violates the Federal Advisory Committee Act, which was adopted "to remedy perceived abuses of insider relationships between private parties and public officials." Pendley has called on the Bureau of Land Management for "an immediate review" of the memorandum's legality and to open BLM meetings with the Nature Conservancy to the public.

Natural Reaction

At times, the Nature Conservancy buys land with no idea how to manage it and creates an ecological disaster. The Carrizo Plains Natural Area, a 180,000 acre preserve that used to be a lush stretch of vigorous shortgrass country between San Luis Obispo and Bakersfield, California, is an object lesson in preservationist folly. We say *used to be*. Today it is reverting to a wind-scoured desert of tumbleweeds, killed by the Nature Conservancy's failure to understand the very nature it appointed itself to conserve.[51]

In 1988 the Nature Conservancy bought its first 82,000 acre tract in the Carrizo Plains area from a ranching firm, Oppenheimer Industries, for $14.2 million, the start of a Bureau of Land Management plan to buy up 180,000 acres with $50 million. The area was planned by sixteen different groups and paid for with money from assorted sources: The Conservancy put up $4.6 million of the purchase price, $4 million came from BLM, $4.6 more was essentially borrowed from the American taxpayer, and Texaco was legally blackmailed into putting up a million dollars if they wanted to develop an energy cogeneration plant in the general vicinity.

When the Conservancy bought out the ranchers who previously owned the land, they had a sea of beautiful shortgrass. They took the cattle off the land. Cattle, according to Economy Trasher dogma, degrade and destroy the natural prairie. The lush shortgrass would be thicker, stronger, more natural in a few years, they assured everyone. They were wrong. Without livestock grazing, there was nothing to retard the growth of tumbleweeds and loco weed and other noxious plants.

The very next season, visitors noticed that the good grasses were thinner, crowded by burgeoning tumbleweeds. Leaf hoppers, pernicious insects, began to proliferate. The next season there were fewer patches of shortgrass to be seen, and bare areas began to appear between huge clumps of tumbleweed. Within three years, the shortgrass was all but gone, its seeds laying dormant in the desert sand. Nothing remained but bare ground and a vast crop of tumbleweeds and leaf hoppers, all blowing across the plain to adjoining private ranches where they stack up against fences until they break them down, spreading the ravenous insects to nearby farm ground.

In the mordant pun of one New Age wag, "My Karma ran over my Dogma."

The private ranches where cattle still safely graze provide a stark contrast to the nature preserve. Much of the Carrizo Plains Natural Area is now a sere brown desert with widely scattered clumps of tumbleweed and blowing dust. The private ranch on the other side of the fence is knee deep in thick lusty shortgrass, fertilized by cow manure, weeded by cows, managed for profit by a greedy capitalist out for nothing but money, as the recycled rhetoric goes. Who has done a better job?

The Carrizo Plains Natural Area teaches us a valuable lesson, if we are still able to learn: Before the ranchers got here, the Carrizo Plains were bare ground and tumbleweed. When ranchers brought in their cattle and began to suppress the weeds through grazing, the shortgrass that had struggled for millennia for bare survival exploded into a green miracle. A local rancher asked wryly, "Why is it that city folks can understand that their lawns need to be mowed and fertilized with steer manure, but not our grasslands?"

The beautiful grassy plains that inspired the Nature Conservancy were an artifact of man and cattle. Yes, those "two greatest enemies of the earth, man and cattle" had created the sea of grass that environmentalists coveted. But the Nature Conservancy didn't know. So they took it away from the ranchers with relentless pressure to sell out. And in their ignorance they destroyed it, ranch by ranch—the Washburn, the KCL, the American Ranch, the Goodwin, the Van Meter, the MU. Nature knows best. Now it is indeed a natural area, reverted to its original desert condition, no different from millions of acres in the Southwest. The values that made it unique and worth preserving were destroyed by preservationists who didn't understand man's role in shaping a beautiful ecology.

The Carrizo Plains Natural area provides us with another object lesson in preservationist folly. Back in 1988, when TNC began to buy up ranch land for the natural area, Steve McCormick, a director of the Conservancy (1992 salary$108,976, benefits $$18,648), said, "I don't think we'll squeeze the ranchers out. The Conservancy won't put pressure on people to sell their property. If they don't want to sell, we won't buy. Where ranchers do want to hang on to their property, the Conservancy works with them."

It was a flat lie. It sucks in dozens of good-hearted people bouyed up by loans from the Nature Conservancy—to run a potato farm in Idaho or a sheep operation in Wyoming and then, after a few years of prosperous operation, they find themselves greeted with a notice from the Conservancy that they can't grow as many potatoes this year or run as many sheep because some endangered flea has been discovered fifty miles away—and within a short time they find the Conservancy can no longer work with them at all.

Ask Marcus Rudnick. He owned one of the ranches that the Conservancy "worked with." The Nature Conservancy secretly connived with the Bureau of Land Management to drastically reduce the number of cattle he could graze on his allotment, driving him to economic ruin. Rudnick bitterly accuses the Conservancy and the BLM of working in cahoots to force him off the Plains. He and his partner decided they had to sell out: after all, the feds were offering $5 million—$4.4 million put up by BLM and $600,000 by the Conservancy.

Now Marcus is renting the ranch back from the Conservancy. He can remember one good year when he ran 6,000 steers and had grass left over. Now BLM is quibbling about turning out 300 head on the same ground. The Nature Conservancy got everything Marcus Rudman held sacred: his 23,000 acres of deeded land, his grazing rights on 35,000 BLM acres, and his human dignity. TNC got the county, too: all those values are gone from the tax rolls now.

In a similar nature-stupidity situation at the other end of the nation, the Nature Conservancy opposed the reforesting or cleanup of the Cathedral Pines in Connecticut after they were ravaged by storms. Claiming that the site would be a natural classroom for studying regeneration after devastation, the Conservancy kicked up its own storm of protest from local citizens who wanted the area managed for recreation rather than turning it into a museum that would inevitably attract insects and other pests as it decayed—aside from the fact that forest regeneration patterns in New England are among the most studied and best understood natural cycles on earth.[52]

To hell with you all.

Nature Conservancy abuses are nationwide. In late 1992, the Missouri Department of Natural Resources admitted that it had manipulated land purchases at six state parks to allow the Nature Conservancy to realize nearly $500,000 in profits.

Missouri State Auditor Margaret Kelly released an audit saying the department's Division of Parks, Recreation and Historic Preservation "conspired" with TNC between 1983 and 1987, apparently violating provisions of the Missouri Constitution and misleading the landowners who sold to the Conservancy.

In her audit, Kelly cited a deal in which the parks division negotiated to buy land with a $91,000 appraised value for a $67,985 sale price. The Conservancy bought the land for the sale price, and the parks division bought the land eight days later for the appraised value, allowing the Conservancy to realize a profit of $23,015. Other deals were included in the audit.

"The only reason to involve the Conservancy was to move money back to them," a state official said.[53]

The Boss

Anyone who still doubts that the environmental movement wields immense economic and political power should poke into the background of John C. Sawhill (1992 salary $185,000, benefits $17,118), the current president and chief executive officer of the Nature Conservancy who took over from Frank Boren. Sawhill is no blue-jeaned hippy carrying a protest sign in a street rally, although he might sit on the board of directors of the companies that paved the street, that made the card stock for the protest sign, and his organization might receive grants from the company that manufactured the blue jeans. His wife Isabel is an appointee in the Clinton Administration. Before coming on board as Conservancy president in 1990, Sawhill owned a partnership in McKinsey & Company, a big-money international management consulting outfit.

In fact, the Nature Conservancy had hired McKinsey & Company to propose management improvements so the organization could expand. The McKinsey report that came back recommended that the old-line conservation advocates on staff be dismissed and replaced with new marketing-conscious personnel. TNC took the recommendations to heart: they hired Sawhill as President, gave McKinsey selections a substantial presence on the board of directors and have methodically pushed aside conservation champions such as Dr. Robert Jenkins— although his scientific reputation provides too much credibility for TNC to fire him outright, he's been shoved off into a corner where he is reportedly not happy. Another member of the McKinsey firm, Robert W. Fri, had taken over the presidency of Resources for the Future in 1986. Carter Bales, an officer with McKinsey, is also a member of TNC's Board of Governors. TNC has a $50,000 contract with McKinsey and reimbursed them $104,291 in 1992 for travel expenses. The McKinsey Connection is powerful indeed.

Sawhill is Big Money personified. He sits on the board of directors of RCA, Pacific Gas and Electric, Consolidated Edison, Philip Morris (*there's* an ironic twist for an "environmentalist"), Crane Corporation and General American Investors. John Sawhill is also a trustee of Princeton University, chairman of the board of the Whitehead Institute for Biomedical Research at Massachusetts Institute of Technology and the Manville Personal Injury Settlement Trust, and a member of the board of advisors of the Center for Energy and Environmental Policy. He was cochairman of the Aspen Institute's Committee on Energy. This guy may be low profile, but he's no local yokel. Where ever he goes, he leaves a tremor of power in his wake.

Part of the reason is that Sawhill has spent a good deal of time in the federal government and has grown accustomed to quietly bossing people around and expecting unquestioning obedience. He was associate director of energy and natural resources in the Nixon administration's Office of Management and Budget from 1972 to 1974, head administrator of the first Federal Energy Administration in the Ford administration from 1973 to 1975, and deputy secretary of energy in the Carter administration from 1979 to 1980. He was a member of the Council on Foreign Relations. He has been a member of the Trilateral Commission from August 1979. From 1975 to 1979 he was president of New York University. When it comes to political power, Sawhill needs no guide map to congressional and administrative offices and no introduction when he walks in the door. As we shall see, such incestuous relationships between environmental organization leaders and government are the rule rather than the exception. There is a virtual revolving door between the two.

The Nature Conservancy has muscle in many invisible places because of Mr. Sawhill and the McKinsey Connection. It also has officers and a board of governors that extends its reach into nearly every high place in the land: Officers (salaries): Anita Attridge ($104,000); Carol Baudler ($80,000); Michael Coda ($108,000); Niels Crone ($109,000); Michael Dennis ($99,000); George Fenwick ($91,268); Robert Jenkins ($100,000); John Sawhill ($185,000); W. William Weeks ($122,000); Geoffrey Barnard ($108,000); Charles Bassett ($90,654); J. Martin Carovano ($88,879); Dennis Donald ($88,410); John Flicker ($99,600); Steven McCormick ($108,976); Bruce Runnels ($96,869); Kelvin Taketa ($106,776). Total officer compensation, $1,786,432; average officer salary $105,084. Other salaries: $45,824,545; pension plan benefits, $1,913,453; other employee benefits, $3,832,110.

Conservation has been taken over by Big Money.

Governors (all serve without compensation except Sawhill): Peter S. Ashton; Carter F. Bales, Christopher T. Bayley; David C. Cole; Ian M. Cumming; Daniel P. Davison; Daniel R. Efroymson; Mary Fleming Finlay; Wilbur E. Garrett; I. Lamond Godwin; Artuo Gómez-Pompa; Ralph J. Gutiérrez; John W. Hanes, Jr.; James R. Harvey; Richard E. Heckert; Sherry F. Huber; Kate Ireland; Samuel C. Johnson; James C. Kennedy; Barbara A. Lipscomb; Orie L. Loucks; Robert L. Mitchell; Alfredo Novoa Peña; Wendy J. Paulson; Leigh H. Perkins; John C. Pritzlaff, Jr.; Winthrop P. Rockefeller; John C. Sawhill; H. Norman Schwarzkopf; John M. Seidl; John B. Sias; Daniel Simberloff; John G. Smale; Richard S. Weinstein; John C. Whitehead; Joseph H. Williams; Ward W. Woods; Gail Walling Yanney.

Conservation has been taken over by Big Money.

The combined stock portfolios of these governors and officers encompass virtually every Fortune 500 corporation.

The staff members are no slouches, either. According to the *New York Times Magazine*, the Nature Conservancy's Arlington, Virginia, headquarters "has an abundance of Ivy League M.B.A.'s, lawyers, biologists and real-estate experts."[54]

They recruit through the classified ads in your big-city daily newspaper.

Here's an actual sample:

> **Real Estate Specialist**
> Implement all phases of land acquisition for private conserva-
> tion org. Requires grad degree & 3+ yrs exp in rel field; xclnt
> real est & negotiating skills; success w/lrg, complex real est.
> transactions; frequent overnite travel; strong commitment to
> conservation. NS office, $29K-39K. DOQ plus ben. Send
> resume & cover letter to
> The Nature Conservancy
> Field rep position, 217 Pine St. #1100, Seattle 98101. EOE.
> Minorities encouraged to apply.

The Conservancy lobbies at the state and federal levels—at the federal level only the appropriations committees to keep the money flowing to buy land—participates in initiative and referendum campaigns, gives congressional testimony, conducts a media outreach program, and engages in direct action. It also offers a speakers program and training and technical assistance.

The bimonthly *Nature Conservancy Magazine* goes to members and supporters, while *On the Land* is a bimonthly internal newsletter. State newsletters originate in all 50 states.

The Nature Conservancy is also expanding into partnerships with for-profit firms to bolster revenues in bad economic times, one with the Nature Company, which sells art, maps and gadgets with ecological themes in 60 stores and a catalog with a circulation of 4 million.[55]

TNC also has a deal with the telephone industry: MCI will donate 5 percent of any customer's monthly phone bill to the Nature Conservancy at the customer's request. TNC expects the deal to bring in about $400,000 a year. TNC also has a deal with MasterCard to receive a percentage of each credit card purchase made by a Conservancy member who uses a special "affinity" charge card.

The bottom line is that the Nature Conservancy is a Green Destroyer. This tweedy, benign-sounding group is an insidious menace that has hounded troubled home owners and businesses and applied behind-the-scenes pressure to turn stubborn ranchers and farmers into "willing sellers" through the National Heritage Program, the brainchild of TNC vice president Robert Jenkins.

Database Tentacles

For years there was a terrific turf battle within the environmental movement to see whose computerized database system would become standard. The Nature Conservancy won because of its Natural Heritage Program, a joint venture with more than 40 state governments to inventory, list and save natural wonders, rarities, and the habitats of endangered plants and animals. The money to do this comes from state, federal, foundation and private funds. The way it works is this: TNC sends in a four-person team to each state—a botanist, zoologist, ecologist and data-processing specialist. They ransack all available records, texts, theses, museums and herbarium collections to establish just what the state has to protect. They examine real estate records and potential preservation sites for government acquisition. Then they enter it into their database. The Conservancy is very proud of its equipment, powered by Hewlett-Packard 3000 minicomputers running Revelation Technologies' Advanced Revelation DBMS to prioritize its land purchases.

The Conservancy's Biological and Conservation Data System is distributed across 76 locations in the U. S., Canada, the Caribbean, and Latin America. It consists of 45 integrated files subdivided into 2,000 data fields. The database holds information pertaining to 65,000 plant and animal species in 400,000 locations. The Conservancy is planning to expand into a local-area network system based on Banyan and AST Research servers.[56]

This database is "so fine-grained," says the *Wall Street Journal*, "that, in some states, it records the precise locations of individual eagle nests and clumps of globally endangered plants."[57] Is your land on their computerized data base? Call them and ask. It could save you money—and your property rights.

The Conservation Data Center Network is an elaborate Conservancy-owned system operated to train government agents to identify and track private property to enforce land use controls. A Conservancy document stated:

> The Conservancy hires and trains at its national office a program coordinator and other professionals who then become the staff of the program in the capital of the state or nation where the program will be housed. The Conservancy supervises this staff under contract. The goal is for this staff to transfer to government employment (or otherwise permanently establish themselves) after the initial phase, which is generally two years. This transfer ensures that expertise is not lost and is a pivotal part of the way in which the network functions.[58]

In essence, the Nature Conservancy constructs a land use control database in a state or nation, then gives the data system to the government. An example is the Maine Natural Heritage Program, begun by the Maine Chapter in 1983 and transferred to state government in 1989. A Conservancy newsletter announced, "Under a Memorandum of Agreement signed with the Department of Economic and Community Development (DECD), the State Planning Office (SPO) and the Department of Environmental Protection (DEP), and Department of Inland Fisheries and Wildlife (IF&W), the Conservancy-state partnership establishes the Maine Natural Heritage Data System as an integral part of state government.... From the state's perspective, the availability of the comprehensive information contained in the Heritage data base facilitates a variety of planning and regulatory functions."[59]

Who elected the Nature Conservancy land use controller?

Getting a private tract listed by the National Heritage Program focuses government attention on the property and creates the expectation that it will some day be declared an undevelopable preserve, thus destroying its marketability as productive land and severely distorting its price, inflating it if federal purchase is certain, depressing it if not.

Money

Substantial funding for the Nature Conservancy comes from corporations, corporate foundations and the family foundations of wealthy industrialists.

Corporate contributions make up 10 percent of the Nature Conservancy's funding sources, foundation grants 20 percent, and individual donations 70 percent (percentages rounded). TNC spends 52 percent of its revenues buying and managing lands and 2 percent on direct mail fund-raising. Program spending was 88 percent of income; fund raising was 8.5 percent of income; administration was 7.0 percent of income.

In 1990, it seemed that the *Fortune 500* were falling all over themselves to give huge amounts of money to the Nature Conservancy. As we shall see in the detailed accounting below, Dow Chemical and Exxon gave in the $250,000 to $499,999 range; Allied-Signal, Inc., W. Atlee Burpee Company, BP Oil, Enron, Newmont Gold Company, and Times-Mirror Corporation gave in the $100,000-$249,999 range; Boeing $50,000-$99,999.

TNC's "Corporate Associates" (donors of $1,000 or more) included Aldus Corporation, America West Airlines, Amoco, ARCO, The Arizona Republic/The Phoenix Gazette, Burlington Northern, Inc., Burpee, Champion International Corporation, C & P Telephone, Cluett, Peabody & Company, Conoco, Fleet/Norster, Huber, Liz Claiborne, Marshall & Marshall Lumber, Inc., Orvis, Pacific Gas Transmission Company, Patagonia, Phillips Petroleum Company, Roseburg Forest Products Company, Sears, Security Pacific Corporation, Standard Alaska Production Company, Standard Insurance Company, Tabasco, U.S. Trust, Waste Management, Weldon Materials, Inc., Wells Fargo Bank, and Willamette Industries, Inc.; ($10,000 or more), L. L. Bean, Chevron, Coca-Cola, Du Pont, Eastman Kodak, J. P. Morgan, and Philip Morris ($5,000-$9,999).

The Mildred Andrews Fund of Cleveland, Ohio, gave $10 million, the largest single environmental grant in America in 1989. The Champlin Foundations gave $2 million to the Rhode Island Nature Conservancy. The Amoco, John D. and Catherine T. MacArthur, and William Penn foundations gave $1 million to $1,999,999; and the Pew Charitable Trusts gave $500,000-$999,999.

Here is a detailed description of as many of the major grants for 1989 and 1990 to the Nature Conservancy as we were able to uncover. Most of the grant descriptions for all the groups that follow are taken verbatim either directly from copies of the grants themselves when environmental groups made them available, or from various compilations by the Foundation Center, the *Taft Corporate Directory*, or *The Journal of Philanthropy*.

Do not blame us for the bizarre wording of the various grant purposes. They are written in *foundationese*, an esoteric language spoken in Nonprofitland and described by Dwight Macdonald in a marvelous set of articles in *The New Yorker* some years back. As he pointed out, sentences in foundationese are often reversible, like a trench coat. "Democracy is essential if a healthy economy is to function effectively," for example, which actually came out of a foundation annual report. As Macdonald noted, it "gives just as good wear either way."[60]

The Abell Foundation, Inc. gave $200,000 in 1989 to the Baltimore office in a

2-year grant "to increase the permanent revolving capital fund for preservation projects through 1) a survey of special interest groups and public attitudes, 2) management workshops and 3) planning of a regional conference for the implementation of a common environmental agenda. This grant was shared with the Maryland Environmental Leadership Forum." Translation from foundationese: Here's some money to help your fundraising and membership recruitment by 1) a direct mail survey containing a donation coupon and business reply envelope; 2) some fancy meetings that will attract a few high-dollar donors and train your cadre at the same time; and 3) a really big prestigious meeting that will roust high-dollar donors by the dozen.

The **Achelis Foundation** gave $20,000 in 1989 for the Long Pond Greenbelt Project.

The **Amoco Foundation, Inc.**—the big oil company's corporate giving philanthropy—gave headquarters $100,000 in 1989 for general purposes.

The **Mildred Andrews Fund** gave $10,000,000 (yes, that's 10 million dollars) in 1989 for general support.

ARCO Foundation—Atlantic Richfield's corporate oil industry philanthropy—gave TNC's San Antonio, Texas, office $25,000 in 1989 for the Clymer Meadow Preservation Project; $25,000 in 1989 to the Baton Rouge, Louisiana office for the White Kitchen Wetlands Preservation Project; $10,000 to headquarters in Arlington, Virginia, "for acquisition of ecologically endangered land;" $15,000 to the Arizona Chapter for the "Streams of Life Preservation Program;" $15,000 to the California Chapter for the Carrizo Plain "Let's Make a Desert" preservation project; and $10,000 to the Washington Chapter for the Skagit Bald Eagle educational/preservation program.

The **Ashland Oil Foundation, Inc.** gave $10,000 in 1989—unspecified purpose.

The **Baton Rouge Area Foundation** gave $25,000 in 1989 for a challenge grant for acquisition of Bluebonnet Swamp.

The **Bodman Foundation** gave $35,000 in 1989 for the Biological and Conservation Data System and acquisition of land within dwarf pine barrens on Long Island.

The **Borden Foundation**—the dairy company's corporate philanthropy—gave $11,500 in 1989—unspecified purpose.

The **James G. Boswell Foundation**—the family philanthropy of a respected California Central Valley farm magnate—gave TNC's California Field Office $30,000 in 1989 for the Santa Cruz Island Reserve, and $25,000 to the Idaho Field Office for the Garden Creek acquisition.

The **Lynde and Harry Bradley Foundation, Inc.** gave $50,000 in 1989 for purchase of designated Wisconsin lands.

The **Buchanan Family Foundation** gave $20,000 in 1989—unspecified purpose.

In 1989 **Burlington Northern** railroad's corporate foundation gave TNC $25,000 for its Montana chapter; $25,000 for its Arizona chapter; $20,000 for its Washington chapter; and $10,000 for its Minnesota chapter.

Cargill Foundation—the giant agribusiness corporate philanthropy—gave $10,000 in 1989.

The **Champlin Foundations** gave $2,000,000 in 1989 for Rhode Island purchases.

Close Foundation, Inc. gave $25,000 in 1989 for the South Carolina Chapter.

Collins Foundation gave $40,000 in 1989 for Columbia Gorge land preservation.

Columbus Foundation gave $140,000 in 1989 to preserve Big Darby Creek Watershed.

The **Community Foundation of New Jersey** gave $25,000 in 1989—unspecified purpose.

The **Compton Foundation**—funded by an heir of the Ralston Purina fortune—gave $50,000 in 1989 for TNC's Latin American Division; $38,000 to the Honolulu office for general operating support; $10,000 to the San Francisco office for general support, and $30,000 to the Colorado Field Office for the Rivers of the Rockies program.

Cooke Foundation gave $200,000 for the Islands of Life Campaign in Hawaii.

The **Arthur Vining Davis Foundation** gave $100,000 in 1989, a 3-year grant for Leadership Development and the Florida Wetlands Protection Initiative.

The **Eleanor Naylor Dana Charitable Trust** gave $10,000 in 1989.

Charles Englehard Foundation gave $25,000 in 1989.

The **Ford Motor Company Fund**—the automotive corporate foundation, not the family foundation—gave $10,000 in 1990.

The **Mary D. and Walter F. Frear Eleemosynary Trust** gave $10,000 in 1989 for the Islands of Life Campaign in Hawaii.

The **Wallace Alexander Gerbode Foundation**—the fortune of missionaries to Hawaii who grew rich in sugar cane and pineapple plantations—gave $100,000 for development of a Pacific Program.

The **Ann and Gordon Getty Foundation** gave $65,000 in 1989.

The **GTE Foundation**—the telephone corporate philanthropy—gave $10,000 each to the Honolulu and Indianapolis office in 1989.

The **Halliburton Foundation, Inc.**, gave $25,000 for the Tallgrass Prairie Preserve Campaign, intended to turn portions of the Great Plains into a federal park.

The **James Irvine Foundation**—which came from a ranching fortune—gave $225,000 in 1989 "toward research, education and outreach programs at the Carrizo Plain preserve." How ironic, ranch money destroying ranches.

The **W. Alton Jones Foundation, Inc.**, a charity based on an oil fortune, gave $25,000 in 1989 to the Virginia Chapter and $50,000 to the Nature Conservancy International in 1989 for the Self-Sufficiency Project.

The **Joyce Mertz-Gilmore Foundation** gave $20,000 in 1989 for the Venezuela Self-Sufficiency Project.

The **J. M. Kaplan Fund, Inc.** gave $125,000 in 1989 primarily for New York State Field Office work.

The **Peter Kiewit Foundation**—the corporate giving program of the giant construction firm—gave $24,500 to establish a Natural Heritage System inventory program in Nebraska.

The **F. M. Kirby Foundation, Inc.** gave $13,000 in 1989.

The **John D. and Catherine T. MacArthur Foundation**—a Chicago insurance company fortune—gave $375,000 for the Parks in Peril programs in seven high priority national parks in Bolivia, Colombia, Ecuador, and Peru.

The Marbrook Foundation gave $10,000 in 1990.

The Robert R. McCormick Charitable Trust gave $500,000 in 1989 for conservation activities in metropolitan Chicago area.

The McInerny Foundation gave $25,000 in 1989 to expand an education program in the Conservancy's Hawaii preserves.

The Merck Company Foundation—the pharmaceutical giant's corporate giving program—gave $10,000 in 1989.

The Minneapolis Foundation gave $38,600 in 1990.

The Charles Stewart Mott Foundation—Mott was a co-founder of General Motors and this foundation was built on GM money—gave $67,000 in 1990 to maintain and enhance properties acquired in the vicinity of the College and Cultural Center in the Flint, Michigan area; and $63,000 in 1990 to protect biological resources in Latin America by assisting local conservation groups in building self-sustaining financial capacity to support conservation efforts within their own countries. Translation of that last piece of foundationese: Here's some seed money for a fundraising campaign to build a captive environmental movement in Latin America that responds to American environmental group direction.

The Spencer T. and Ann W. Olin Foundation gave $20,000 in 1989.

The Oregon Community Foundation gave $11,890 in 1990.

The David and Lucille Packard Foundation—computer money—gave $200,000 in 1990 to the Western Region office in San Francisco for acquisition of the Parrott Ranch.

The William Penn Foundation—originally founded by Otto Haas of the industrial chemicals firm Rohm and Haas—gave $900,000 in 1990, a 3-year grant for the Campaign for the Delaware River.

The Howard Phipps Foundation gave $20,000 in 1989.

The Prince Charitable Trusts—a meatpacking fortune—gave $35,000 in 1989 to the Chicago office for a capital campaign and $10,000 to the Boston office for start-up funds.

The Procter & Gamble Fund—the multi-product giant's corporate philan-thropy program—gave $15,000 in 1990.

The Prospect Hill Foundation, Inc. gave $25,000 in 1990 "to implement tax-free forest land exchanges across state borders," and $12,500 for the Rhode Island land preservation fund. Translation out of foundationese: "Here's some money for a clever land-laundering gimmick to take more private land out of production and maybe sell it to the feds."

The Scherman Foundation, Inc. gave $35,000 in 1989 for a 2-year grant for general support.

The Shell Oil Company Foundation gave $10,000 in 1989.

The Jules and Doris Stein Foundation gave $15,000 to the St. Louis, Missouri office, and $10,000 to the Nature Conservancy of Rhode Island, both for general support.

The Stratford Foundation gave $46,688 in 1989.

The Surdna Foundation, Inc.,—which got its money from John Andrus (Surdna is Andrus spelled backwards), who built a vast fortune in pharmaceuticals, real estate, gold mining, and lumber—gave $50,000 in 1989.

The Times Mirror Foundation—the corporate philanthropy of the Los Angeles Times newspaper empire—gave $50,000 for acquisition and preservation of the Carrizo Plains project. The *Los Angeles Times* gives excellent coverage to the Nature Conservancy.

The Timken Foundation of Canton—the industrial bearing firm's corporate philanthropy—gave $25,000 to purchase land in Big Darby Creek.

The Town Creek Foundation, Inc.—the donor of which is Edmund A. Stanley—gave $10,000 in 1990.

The Union Pacific Foundation—the railroad's corporate philanthropy—gave $10,000 in 1989.

US WEST Foundation—the telephone corporate philanthropy—gave $15,000 in 1989 for the Waldron Island conservation project.

The Victoria Foundation, Inc. gave $35,000 in 1989 for purchase and protection of wildlife habitat surrounding Manumuskin River through the New Jersey Critical Areas Campaign.

The Wells Fargo Foundation—the bank's corporate philanthropy—gave $10,000 in 1989.

The Weyerhaeuser Company Foundation—the timber giant's corporate philanthropy—gave $10,000 in 1989.

Tell us they don't call the shots.

Conservation has been taken over by Big Money.

Direct corporate giving, in a look-back to 1985, found Aetna Life & Casualty Foundation, Inc. giving $3,000; AT&T direct corporate contribution of $10,000; Amoco, $10,000; ARCO Foundation, $18,890; BankAmerica Foundation $1,500; Burlington Northern Foundation, 93,000; Chevron, $32,500; Citicorp, $2,500; Exxon, $85,000; Ford Motor Company Fund, $4,000; General Electric Foundations, $3,000; General Motors Foundation, $5,000; Georgia-Pacific Foundation, $2,500; GTE Foundation, $41,000; Johnson and Johnson Family of Companies Contribution Fund, $1,500; Mobil Foundation, $6,000; Monsanto Fund, $5,123; Morgan Guaranty Trust Company of New York Charitable Trust, $3,000; PepsiCo, $125; Philip Morris Companies Inc. In The Public Interest, $7,000; Procter & Gamble Fund, $10,000; Standard Oil Company Contributions, $10,000; Texaco Philanthropic Foundation, Inc., $5,000; Union Pacific Foundation, $27,500; United States Steel Foundation, Inc., $5,000; Unocal Foundation, $12,000.

Free enterprise giving to destroy private property and hamper free markets. But, not, we must note, to destroy industrial civilization and not to impose a thoroughgoing eco-socialism. It is clear that the Nature Conservancy is interested in maintaining civilization and its material wealth—albeit it only in the interests of those who are most civilized and most wealthy. It is obvious that the Nature Conservancy wants primarily the interventionist model imposed on America but might tolerate an eco-socialism if favorable terms could be worked out. It is plain that if the Nature Conservancy is no longer completely an artifact of the Mellon money, it is definitely an operational arm of what we characterize as the Mellon Interventionist Axis, which is an unmistakable power stream in the complex currents of the overall environmental movement.

Charitable Delusion

When the Interior Department's Inspector General released his 1992 report revealing the Nature Conservancy's great wealth and underhanded dealings, the organization frantically scurried around to dream up something that would make themselves look a little human. They decided "to help transform a typical low-income housing project into a compatible development showcase for some of the neediest residents" near their Virginia Coast Reserve. These are the locals the Mellon elite wouldn't even talk to the previous year.

In fact, Executive Director John Sawhill wrote in the 1992 Annual Report of this first contact with ordinary people who have real needs, "We have entered uncharted territory and must proceed with caution." Actually, the Environmental Protection Agency, Old Dominion University, and an upscale design firm did all the work on the "compatible development showcase." But the Nature Conservancy takes all the credit because it's their land.[61]

So now the Nature Conservancy has its own Potemkin Village, just like Catherine the Great of Russia when she visited the Crimea in 1787 and Count Grigori Potemkin built strings of phony front towns to create a festive Arabian Nights atmosphere for her entourage, which included the Emperor of Austria, the King of Poland and innumerable European diplomats. The serfs got dressed up in costumes provided by the Count and waved as Catherine's "Cleopatra fleet" went by their Potemkin Village, then put their rags back on in the shacks behind the facade and returned to the potato fields.

Perhaps some of us will visit the Nature Conservancy's Potemkin Village in Virginia. Talk to the serfs. Then drive back to plantation headquarters in Arlington and see if Executive Director Sawhill will spare us a few minutes. Compliment ol' Massa how good he treatin' de folks.

Conservation has been taken over by Big Money.

The Nature Conservancy sprouted an offshoot in 1980 that has become the National Park Service's private acquisition surrogate:

The Conservation Fund
Annual Budget: $13,886,902 (1993)[62]
Staff: 19 professionals on contractual basis
Non-membership
Tax Status: 501(c)(3)
1800 N. Kent Street, Suite 1120
Arlington, Virginia 22209
Phone: (703)522-8008 Fax: (703)525-4610

The Conservation Fund is small—no membership—well-funded, and *very* quiet. It's not listed in the standard reference *Public Interest Profiles*. Its huge income would place it as Economy Trasher Number Eleven if it was a membership group. It pays Officers and Directors compensation of $400,000, other salaries $1,084,714, pension plan $64,160, other benefits $86,318. It is headquartered near the Nature Conservancy, and headed by Patrick Noonan, who left his position as president of the Nature Conservancy in 1980. Noonan created the Conservation Fund with Mellon money and the help of his closest colleague, Mason Walsh, Jr., chief counsel for the Richard K. Mellon Foundation.

The professional staff of 19 are not employees in the strict sense, but work on a "contractual services" basis. They include a general counsel; 2 attorneys; real estate director; ecological assessor; Director of Civil War Battlefield Campaign; Western Greenways representative; New England representative; Georgia representative; editor, *Common Ground* and *Land Letter*; Coordinator-President's Commission on Environmental Quality; public relations; land use planning/graphics; scientific director; scientist; microbiologist; fish pathologist; auditor; CPA service. The Conservation Fund paid these 19 folks a total of $1,691,000 in 1991, which amounts to $89,000 each if you divide it up evenly, which they didn't.

Ed McMahon, American Greenway Director, receives $66,500 salary, $7,989 benefits; Ken Olson, Director of Special Programs $80,000 salary, $10,851 benefits; Joe Hankins, Director of Aquaculture $56,700 salary, $6,977 benefits; Larry Seltzer, Director of Freshwater Institute $77,500 salary, $9,304 benefits; Henry Little, Director of Gift Lands, $56,364. Chief Operating Officer John Turner gets $68,000 salary, $3,743 benefits.

Conservation has been taken over by Big Money.

TCF was established to network with government and private organizations and agencies to regulate activities on land, including parks, wildlife habitats and historic sites. Its projects include:*American Greenways*, promoting open space corridors to link natural, historic and recreation areas. In practice such areas fall along highways, rivers, and trails transversing and connecting urban, suburban, and rural areas. Usually they begin as combined public and private lands, but soon the private lands are targeted for government condemnation or for strict land use controls so they meet the aesthetic standards desired by environmentalists. Greenways have the potential of nationalizing nearly a third of the private land in America.[63]

TCF also operates a project called the *Civil War Battlefield Campaign*, tightly regulating private lands near government-owned historic battlefield lands.

TCF's *Conservation Leadership* project increases the effectiveness of nonprofit conservation organizations. The *Land Advisory Service* provides specialized skills in environmental land planning. The *Freshwater Institute* uses new techniques to regulate groundwater reserves.

Hush-Hush Deals

The Conservation Fund and the Mellon Foundation bought or helped arrange the sale of at least four select parcels of land around Shenandoah National Park in Virginia in 1990 and 1991. It was no accident that the Conservation Fund and the Mellon Foundation bought the Shenandoah land: A letter dated June 29, 1990 from

National Park Service Director James M. Ridenour to Richard King Mellon Foundation Trustee Mason Walsh, Jr., said, "We are requesting that the Richard King Mellon Foundation and the Conservation Fund purchase the Coleman Gore Estate property."

A year later the Richard King Mellon Foundation purchased an adjacent private tract through the Conservation Fund after Noonan and Shenandoah National Park Superintendent Bill Wade visited the site to arrange the deal.

In a clever "land laundering" deal in October 1991, the Conservation Fund sold a tract of land for $65,000—that it had originally bought for $60,000—to the Virginia Department of Transportation, which swapped it with Shenandoah National Park. The public was none the wiser for the Conservation Fund being behind the transaction along with the Mellon fortune. There goes the Park Service nationalizing more private land—by the dark of night.

The idea that the National Park Service could be a bad guy is astonishing to most Americans. The agency's public reputation is clean as a hound's tooth. Behind closed doors, however, it is a ravenous bureaucracy building an empire of vast acreages taken not from the unsettled public lands out West, but from the private homes and farms and businesses of people all over America. Every one of the National Park Service's many divisions—those handling 1) nature parks, 2) historic parks, 3) urban parks, and 4) recreation areas—has become a sophisticated land grab institution systematically and continually searching out private property and taking it by power of condemnation or regulation into the federal domain.

The horror stories told by inholders—owners of private property within government boundaries—are summarized in a Public Broadcasting System *Frontline* program titled *For the Good of All*, showing how the Cuyahoga Valley National Recreation Area in Ohio grew like a cancer from promises that "no private property would be taken" to the needless seizure and destruction of nearly every one of the more than 500 homes and businesses within the boundary lines—to create "open space" for urban recreationists from nearby Akron.

The same horrors have been perpetrated in so many places that an organization was founded in 1978 to resist the government's threats against private property owners: the National Inholders Association, founded by Yosemite National Park inholder Charles S. Cushman. Cushman's success has been so stunning in organizing one threatened community after another against the Park Service's threats that he has been tagged by bitter environmentalists as "Mr. Rent-A-Riot."

Those living outside the boundaries of National Park Service lands but nearby find themselves victimized by "greenlining," putting environmental sanctions on private property that forbids new structures or changes to existing ones so that the "character of the area" is not "damaged." The late syndicated newspaper columnist Warren Brookes wrote a 1991 7-part series, "Big park coming to you?" in which he warned against National Park Service efforts to turn the entire nation into "one big park." The National Park Service, far from being the friendly caretaker of our magnificent natural heritage, is in fact the voracious and ferocious destroyer of private property rights in every corner of America.

Backfire

Somebody who knows is Ann Corcoran, a one-time Washington lobbyist for the National Audubon Society. She earned a master's degree from Yale's School of Forestry and was a dedicated environmentalist.

But today, because of the National Park Service's excesses and connivance with the Conservation Fund, Ann Corcoran has become a one-woman commando force working with angry property owners all over America against property-grabbers in the environmental movement which serve as surrogates for a number of federal agencies. Ann is one of a growing number of defectors from the environmental movement who sees land trusts for what they are: a blatant attempt by the wealthy elite, using tax breaks, to steal American land from its private owners and lock it up in government ownership. Ann Corcoran felt betrayed by a movement she gave her honest efforts to. She now publishes the *Land Rights Letter*, a rich source of information on all property issues, fearless in exposing environmentalist chicanery.

Ann's conversion came after she and her husband Howard bought a 158-acre farm on a hilltop that borders on the Antietam Civil War Battlefield near Sharpsburg, Maryland and spent their savings restoring it to operating condition. "I was just going to raise the kids and the cows, and that sort of stuff," she told a farm magazine writer.[64]

Then one fine day early in the Bush administration, Ann went to a landowners meeting at the Battlefield headquarters with the National Park Service and state officials who were trying to explain their wonderful new plan for protecting Antietam. The meeting took place on January 19, 1989, organized by the Washington County Farm Bureau and the County Extension Agent to find agreeable solutions.

"This was in my naive days when I still thought there was hope for working out something agreeable to the landowners," Ann said.

At the meeting, T. Destry Jarvis sat down behind her—he'd been a lobbyist for the National Parks and Conservation Association when she was with Audubon. Ann turned around to the familiar face and said, "Destry Jarvis, what are you doing out here?" She thought this was a local meeting.

Destry—seeing a friendly face—started talking. "Ann, I'm not with NPCA anymore. I work for Patrick Noonan now. The Conservation Fund has big plans for your county."

"Oh, really?" Ann asked. "Like what?"

"We're going to Greenline your county."

"Greenline? I'm not familiar with that."

The meeting was called to order and the conversation broke off.

Later, during a break, Jarvis stood in the hall with Ann and explained that greenlining was a land protection approach which uses a little direct acquisition and a lot of land use regulation. He told Ann how Noonan had already starting buying farms in the area. The strategy was simple. The Conservation Fund buys land around the Battlefield, then donates it to the Park Service.

At that time Ann was not aware of the pattern of purchase and donation. She did not pick up on Jarvis's remark. She was riveted by the alarming fact that the Conservation Fund had been buying up land in her neighborhood with no public fanfare.

The next day she began looking into county land records and found that the Conservation Fund had very quietly bought up two farms around the Antietam

National Battlefield—one inside the boundaries, one outside—and planned a future purchase to surround her property. She was about to become an "inholder" subject to an array of regulations that would essentially eliminate her property rights and her ability to run a working farm—without paying her just compensation.

She used the Freedom of Information Act and discovered that the Park Service had asked the Conservation Fund to act as its surrogate.

Jack Lynn, Conservation Fund spokesman, admitted, "The Park Service asked us to acquire the Antietam property so we did."

There was more to it, much more. One of the properties near the Corcorans' land had been bought at a bargain basement price of $195,000 by two employees of the Department of Housing and Urban Development, *one of whom, Tom Low, was then on loan to the Conservation Fund.* (Exactly what is a federal employee doing "on loan" to a private environmental group?) They subdivided the property, sold the bulk of it to the Conservation Fund for $302,000—at a profit of $105,000. The late columnist Warren Brookes called this caper the "green Robin HUDscam."

Ann had by this time ravelled out the background of Patrick Noonan with the Nature Conservancy and its elaborate land control schemes—when Destry Jarvis called and wanted to meet with her again.

She went to a luncheon with Jarvis and Ralph E. Grossi, president of the **American Farmland Trust** along with Ed Thompson, the AFT's attorney (see subprofile below). Ann was astounded at the discussion. Destry had badly misread his earlier meeting with Ann and now obliquely suggested that she "act as the local Judas Goat to lead the other landowners in her community to the slaughter," as she describes it.

Environmentalist land grabs work much easier when a local landowner greases the skids by praising the land grab group, offering to put some of their personal land into "protected" status and throwing the populace off guard.

Ann smiled through the whole luncheon, remaining pleasantly noncommittal. She was not about to let her investment and her life be ruined. She and her husband immediately bought an option on the crucial piece of the puzzle—a long narrow farm that would have made a sandwich of their property—before the Conservation Fund could get to it.

Patrick Noonan was not amused.

Destry Jarvis suddenly found his services no longer required by the Conservation Fund (now he's a top aide to the Director of the National Park Service).

Tom Low, one of Noonan's lieutenants—the one on loan from HUD—called Ann and said, "I understand you have an option on this property."

"That's right."

"Pat Noonan wants to talk to you."

He asked for an immediate meeting with Ann and Howard Corcoran at their home. On Palm Sunday. The Corcorans didn't know what to expect.

Noonan showed up on Palm Sunday accompanied by Low. Noonan was charming and Low scowled in a corner. Noonan talked for two hours about conservation and how wonderful land preservation was. He scarcely mentioned the crucial farm property, made a little political chit-chat, got up and left. The Corcorans could hardly believe it.

Ann concluded, "He's sizing us up."

A little more digging revealed a two-inch-thick state study for construction of an 800-acre convention center with upscale hotel accommodations, fine restaurants, swimming pool, golf course—a destination resort. Antietam Battlefield was historic, Harpers Ferry wasn't far away, the C&O Canal wasn't far and the whole Antietam area is only an hour from Washington. The proposed resort would make a wonderful magnetic attraction for upscale spenders. But along with the convention center plans came the restrictions on everybody who lived there. You have to control the "local yokels," make sure they don't smell up the place with their working farms or build a housing development anywhere on their property, Ann said.

Ann exposed the whole thing to the community. Everybody was up in arms. The Conservation Fund withdrew.

"You can't work these things in daylight," said Ann Corcoran. "They scurried like little rats out of here."

She subsequently found the Antietam pattern repeated so many times in so many places around the country, and raised such a stink about it that the Interior Department was forced to issue a July 26, 1990 memo forbidding this "insider trading" project. The systematic abuses were what convinced her to start publishing her *Land Rights Letter*.[65]

Such tricky deals, as noted above about the Cox Ranch, came under scrutiny from the Interior Department's top cop, Inspector General James R. Richards. In March 1991 Richards began an audit "to assess the propriety of...land transactions conducted with the aid of third-party nonprofit organizations" by the National Park Service, Bureau of Land Management, and U.S. Fish and Wildlife Service, all of which are administered by the Interior Department. Richards intended to determine "whether the Government is buying land at inflated prices, thereby allowing excessive profits to be made, and whether the acquired lands are actually needed by the Federal agencies."

Richards released his final audit on June 5, 1992. The Inspector General found that the Interior Department paid $7.1 million more than was warranted to land conservation groups for 71 acquisitions since 1985. The IG also concluded that "the government's interests were not always adequately protected and that non-profit organizations benefited unduly from some of the land acquisition transactions."[66]

The audit identified 317 land acquisitions with a value of $222 million that nonprofits were involved in between October 1, 1985 and September 30, 1991. Auditors sampled 130 of the transactions worth $134 million involving the Bureau of Land Management, Fish and Wildlife Service, and National Park Service. Payments to nonprofits above the fair market value were also discovered in another $48 million worth of purchases, which led to the review of 89 Fish and Wildlife Service transactions. The Inspector General concluded that the Fish and Wildlife Service paid $5.2 million more than the approved fair market value of $44 million on 64 transactions. Nonprofits received another $1.9 million to facilitate seven other transactions, essentially as unauthorized "finders' fees."

The Fish and Wildlife Service admitted that it had failed to follow its own appraisal procedures in four cases.

Interior Secretary Manuel Lujan, Jr. said on the day the audit was released that he would ask the Office of the Solicitor "to determine our legal authority to pay added charges, such as interest and overhead." Third parties, he said, would not be paid more than fair market value for land acquisitions.

The Nature Conservancy and the Trust for Public Land criticized the report and denied any wrongdoing, claiming the audit was "an effort to make land conservation more difficult by recommending additional administrative restrictions on those agencies entrusted with conserving our national parks and other public lands." Environmentalists seem to like federal restrictions on everybody but themselves.

So far, nobody in the government has lost their job over this scandal, and no environmentalist is in jail.

Horror stories happen at the local level, too. A typical example came from King County in Washington State: A 1989 Open Space Bond Issue won funds to create numerous greenways connecting existing reserves. One, a 630 acre $5.3 million project, was a wildlife and hiking corridor linking Cougar, Squak and Tiger mountains. The land acquisition proceeded until it got down to the last 38 acres, but that contained the homes of H. B. and Jennie Trimble, Garry McLenaghan, Katie Liston, and Blaine and Peg Petty. When negotiations with the Trimbles broke down, the King County Council voted May 11, 1992 to condemn the property. The government offered less than $9,000 per acre for land in a location where comparable sales have exceeded $30,000 an acre. The couple had no opportunity to testify; they weren't even notified of the impending action until phoned by a local newspaper reporter. The other three couples face similar action—now their property is an island in a sea of government eco-property.

The Pettys have lived in their home more than thirty years. The County wants 20 of their 24 acres—but not their house—leaving their once-isolated home next to a privacy-smashing trailhead parking lot, convenient to vandals. Katie Liston can't find a comparable home for what the County is offering them—one of her children was paralyzed in an automobile accident two years earlier and volunteers spent thousands of hours and dollars making the home completely wheel-chair accessible. The McLenaghans might be able to stay, but they'd have to give up land they had counted on as their retirement nest egg.

This is not prevention of development, it is The De-Development of America, a war on private property. We are sacrificing people to animals—to the bears and coyotes and county council members.

The Conservation Fund's Board of Directors consists of: Patrick F. Noonan, president, $148,500 salary, $16,542 benefits; Kiku Hoagland Hanes, secretary (she married into the Hanes underwear fortune) $55,000 salary, $9,800 benefits; Joann Porter, assistant treasurer, $64,500 salary, $10,006 benefits; Hadlai Hull, treasurer; David Sutherland, vice president, $64,000 salary, $6,426 benefits; and directors Wallace B. Dayton; Gilbert Grosvenor (National Geographic Society); Charles Jordan, $14,400 compensation; Ann McLaughlin;William Spencer; Alfred Taylor, Jr.; Hubert Vogelman.

The Conservation Fund publishes the *Land Letter*, which "provides comprehensive coverage of national land policy for natural resource professionals in government, nonprofit conservation organizations, and the private sector." Noonan bought the *Land Letter* from Bill Chandler, a former lobbyist for the Nature Conservancy. It sells for $165 a year for 34 issues, and is one of the best sources of information on current environmental legislation, administrative actions, and litigation.

The Fund also publishes a bimonthly newsletter, *Common Ground*, "including current events, trends and ideas on conservation," with a circulation of 10,000.

Contributions for the year ended December 31, 1991 were $5,732,000, which was 81 percent of total revenue of $7,120,000. Administrative costs were $761,000 or 11 percent of revenue, fund raising costs were $192,000 or 3 percent of contributions, and $5,290,000 went to program services.

The ARCO Foundation gave the Conservation Fund $10,000 in 1989 for the Greenways for America program in Texas and California.

The Bodman Foundation gave $25,000 in 1989, the second payment of a two-year pledge toward an "ornithological program, specifically for preservation projects focusing on species in Northeast and on Long Island."

The Compton Foundation, Inc. gave $10,000 in 1989.

The Charles Engelhard Foundation gave $25,000 in 1989 "for a Civil War Battlefield project"—to take Ann Corcoran's Antietam land, perhaps?

Richard King Mellon Foundation gave $700,000 in 1990 in support of the Richard King Mellon Land Conservation Revolving Fund.

The Howard Phipps Foundation gave $10,000 in 1989.

The Prince Charitable Trusts gave $50,000 in 1989 for publication support.

The San Francisco Foundation gave $20,000 in 1990, a 2-year grant to recognize and assist creative greenway demonstration projects in Northern California.

Virginia Environmental Endowment gave $30,000 in 1987 to help launch the Commonwealth Revolving Fund and implement the Waterfall Project in Page County, Virginia.

That only accounts for $880,000. Where the Conservation Fund got the rest of its $5,732,000 contributions, public relations person Jack Lynn refused to say. He was particularly emphatic about it. The Fund is among the most secretive of all environmental groups—one disgruntled former employee told us they even keep things in the office locked away from their own staff members and that Patrick Noonan is fanatical about maintaining secrecy inside and out. "It's damn paranoid in there," said the source. Particularly about money. Others may have better luck requesting this public information; Mr. Lynn's direct office number is (703)683-2996. The public has a right to know. Perhaps Congress can look into it for us all.

The Richard King Mellon Foundation's 1990 contribution of $700,000 comprises more than ten percent of TCF's total 1991 budget, so we can add the Conservation Fund to the Mellon Interventionist Axis without fear of mischaracterization.

Tell us they don't call the shots.

Conservation has been taken over by Big Money.

That's not all of Noonan's mischief. He also finds time to be chairman of the board of another land-control outfit called the

American Farmland Trust (1980)
Budget: $3,500,000
Members: 16,000
Tax status: 501(c)(3)
1920 N Street, NW, Suite 400
Washington, D.C. 20036
Telephone: (202)659-5170
FAX: (202)659-8339

It's another private organization that buys up land and sells it to the government—and places severe restrictions on commercial farming operations—while pretending to be preserving the rural farm way of life. Noonan's Mellon Foundation colleague Mason Walsh, Jr. serves as AFT executive committee chairman. But Mellon money, although plentiful in the American Farmland Trust, is not the base.

The American Farmland Trust is largely a Rockefeller Axis artifact, founded by Douglas P. Wheeler, who has held a long string of environmental organization positions, most recently in the World Wildlife Fund (see profile). Ralph E. Grossi, a Washington denizen who owns a ranch in Marin County, California, is President. AFT is part of the vast environmentalist network supported by Laurance Spelman Rockefeller (b. 1910, third of the five sons of John Davison Rockefeller, Jr.), whose **Rockefeller Brothers Fund** or his**American Conservation Association** (see profile in Money chapter) could be credited as the Twin Mother Ships of the environmental movement. Oh, yes, Patrick Noonan also sits on ACA's board of directors. Interlocking directorates.

The Rockefellers, as everyone knows, are the richest and most powerful family in the United States. Their power lies in the many interlocking corporations, financial institutions, foundations, and leading individuals they have controlled over the years. They include Exxon (originally Standard Oil of New Jersey), Mobil (Standard Oil Company of New York), Chevron (Standard Oil of California), Standard Oil of Indiana, Creole Petroleum in Venezuela, Chase Manhattan Bank, Metropolitan Life Insurance and Equitable Life Insurance. Eastern Airlines was a Rockefeller company for many years before it went bankrupt. John D. Rockefeller, Jr. donated the land for the United Nations headquarters in New York—which multiplied the value of the slums he owned nearby manyfold. Rockefeller Center in New York City and Rockefeller University were eponymous family projects.[67]

Laurance is the venture capitalist and environmentalist of the Rockefeller brothers. After taking a degree in philosophy at Princeton, he became the most business-minded of the five Rockefeller brothers, becoming a co-founder of Eastern Airlines in 1938 and an associate with McDonnell Aircraft Corporation. During World War II he served in the Navy, and afterward engaged in a wide range of businesses from resort hotels to nuclear equipment and computers. He was appointed to the federal Outdoor Recreation Resource and Review Commission in 1958, and brought in aides from his two environmental groups, Jackson Hole Preserve, Inc., and the American Conservation Association. He served as chairman of the New Citizens' Advisory Committee on Recreation and Natural Beauty in the Johnson Administration, which was renamed the Citizens Advisory Committee on Environmental Quality during the Nixon years—Rockefeller's total committee service lasted from 1969 to 1973.[68]

The Rockefeller Brothers Fund is also a key money resource for the Conservation Foundation (where Laurance Rockefeller was a trustee)—now merged into the World Wildlife Fund—the American Conservation Association (where he is chairman and director), the National Parks and Conservation Association, the Natural Resources Defense Council, Worldwatch Institute and the World Resources Institute. From these pivotal groups, Rockefeller has bankrolled, groomed, tutored and linked a legion of environmentalist leaders including William Kane Reilly (former Environmental Protection Agency Administrator), Patrick Noonan, James Gustave Speth (former chairman of the President's Council on Environmental Quality), Russell Train (former Administrator of the Environmental Protection Agency and current chairman of the World Wildlife Fund), and many other protégés who make up his "Permanent Green Government," as the late columnist Warren Brookes dubbed it. But why would the Rockefellers, the Mellons and other wealthy people want a Permanent Green Government?

The purpose statement of the Rockefeller Brothers Fund itself gives us the best answer: "To support efforts in the U.S. and abroad that contribute ideas, develop leaders, and encourage institutions in the transition to global interdependence and that counter world trends of resource depletion, militarization, protectionism, and isolation which now threaten to move humankind everywhere further away from cooperation, trade and economic growth, arms restraint, and conservation." That's foundationese for "To make the world safe for our big money."

The Foundation Center further describes the Rockefeller Brothers Fund: "There are five major giving categories: 1) One World, with two major components: sustainable resource use and world security, including issues related to arms control, international relations, development, trade, and finance; 2) New York City; 3) Nonprofit Sector; 4) Education; and 5) Special Concerns."[69]

In Laurance's father, John D. Rockefeller, Jr., we see the archetype of elitist environmentalism. The story of how he donated Grand Teton National Park to America is instructive: In 1926, John D. Jr., his wife Abby and three youngest sons Laurance, Winthrop and David visited Yellowstone National Park under assumed names "so they could mix with the people"—but with Yellowstone superintendent and future National Park Service Director Horace Marden Albright as guide.[70]

Albright had coveted the Grand Tetons for the Park Service for some time. Back in 1882, only a decade after Yellowstone National Park was established, General Philip Sheridan suggested extending the park's boundaries to including the adjacent Jackson Hole region. In 1898, Charles Wolcott, director of the U.S. Geological Survey became the first to suggest a separate Grand Teton National

Park. In 1918, Congressman Frank Mondell of Wyoming introduced a bill to include the Tetons and the northern portion of Jackson Hole in Yellowstone National Park, but Idaho Senator John Nugent killed it.

The U.S. Forest Service administered the land. The Forest Service opposed the park. The locals opposed the park. Albright tried wooing the locals during the 1920s, but without success. He persuaded prominent author Struthers Burt to write glowingly of the Tetons in national publications. The argument was framed in terms of the Park Service's aesthetic vision and the Forest Service's utilitarian ethic. Stalemate.

Now, with John D. Rockefeller, Jr. in tow, Albright had his main chance.

Driving to Jackson Lake and the Grand Teton mountains, Rockefeller asked him, "Why are those telephone lines on the west side of the road, where they mar the view of the mountains?" Albright explained that the Forest Service, which owned that stretch of road, needed telephone service for the communities ahead. And "Why is that ramshackle old building allowed to stand over there where it blocks the view?" Albright explained that it was on private land and its owner considered it colorful. Mrs. Rockefeller became depressed as they drove into Jackson Hole, passing a dance hall, gasoline station, dilapidated cabins, billboards, and signs advertising cattle range for sale. "It's so ugly in such a beautiful place," she said of the community.

At the end of the tour, John D. Jr. asked Albright, "What would it take to clear up all of this?" Albright ordered a key underling to perform a secret study of the private properties, then went to New York and told Rockefeller a buyout of the offending buildings would cost $397,000. "No, no, that's not what I had in mind at all" said Rockefeller, "I'm only interested in the ideal proposition. I wanted to know about the land on both sides of the river, and to the north." That, calculated Albright, would cost over $2 million. Rockefeller didn't bat an eyelash. He pledged to buy the whole thing and give it to the government, working in cahoots with Albright to grease the appropriate political skids with Congress to accept the donation and designate it a national park.

The land acquisition process was a model of things to come. Rockefeller's talented people set up a phony front corporation, the Snake River Land Company of Salt Lake City, and through their network of contacts with Rockefeller's Colorado Fuel and Iron Company had quietly gotten the word spread around the Jackson area that it was a cattle company. Albright enlisted an old lawyer friend named Harold Fabian to supervise the land purchasing, but since he was based in Salt Lake City, they needed someone to do the actual purchasing who was respected in the Jackson Hole area, who knew what land might be available, and its fair price. Fabian and his associates settled on the leading banker in Jackson, Robert E. Miller, president of the Jackson State Bank. His bank also held mortgages on many of the properties Rockefeller sought.

The Snake River Land Company told Miller to pay fair prices, but also had an arrangement that would allow him to make a larger profit if he got all of the needed lands under a certain price. Miller was never told that Rockefeller money was behind the Snake River Land Company, nor did he know the true purpose of the land purchases he was making. In fact, he personally opposed creation of a Teton National Park and favored the Forest Service proposal to lease parcels of the Teton National Forest to individuals.

The phony front company thus succeeded in hornswoggling a banker into buying up land for a purpose he opposed from people who would never have sold had they known what Rockefeller intended to do to their community. Rockefeller won. The locals lost. Grand Teton National Park was dedicated in 1929.

However, the Rockefellers had not donated *all* the land they secretly bought up. And they kept buying it up. Soon they owned a substantial portion of Jackson Hole. The story is well known, but seldom told plainly: a respected conservation encyclopedia pussyfoots around the shady deal like this:

> The formation of Grand Teton National Park in 1929 brought most of the mountain range under federal protection; to Rockefeller fell the challenge of gaining control of the private farms and ranches within Jackson Hole before further encroachments could threaten its value as the Tetons' "frame."[71]

But the locals didn't want to be "framed" and they caught onto the project. Residents, farmers and ranchers rose up in arms against the big lockup that would take Jackson Hole off the tax rolls and endanger the property rights of those who had been surrounded by Rockefeller's secret purchases. Now the issue was cast in terms of struggling Western ranchers, farmers and residents against the power of eastern wealth. Congress refused to act.

In 1940 John D. Rockefeller, Jr. incorporated in New York **Jackson Hole Preserve, Inc.**, a nonprofit organization, to handle their interests in the national parks. Laurance became trustee and president. They offered their land to the government to enlarge Grand Teton National Park. Congress refused to accept it.

Then, after a little back-room politicking, the situation suddenly changed. Over a storm of protest, President Franklin D. Roosevelt established Jackson Hole National Monument by proclamation in 1943 and accepted the Rockefeller donations in principle. There's more than one way to skin a cat. If you've got the money and power. Now the debate was switched to a question of the relative power of the executive and legislative branches of government and the rights of the states against the national government.

In 1949 Rockefeller was finally allowed to sign over his land; the next year Congress agreed to add Jackson Hole to Grand Teton National Park.

Jackson Hole Preserve, Inc., built the Jackson Lake Lodge next to the park in 1955 at an expense of $6.5 million and the Rockefeller interests operated it thereafter as a national park concessioner. Yes, Virginia, there is such a thing as a non-profit luxury resort developer.

Conservation has been taken over by Big Money.

A long time ago.

Although Jackson Hole Preserve, Inc. has since grown into a general environmental movement philanthropy, Grand Teton National Park remains to this day virtually a Rockefeller fiefdom—the Rockefellers own the National Park concession—with Jackson Lake Lodge, Jenny Lake Lodge and Colter Bay Village operated by the profit-making New York-based management company, Rockresorts, Inc.

This is no big secret. *Forbes* magazine wrote as recently as 1988, "In Wyoming the Rockefellers gave 34,000 acres for use as a national park. But make no mistake, there was an eye toward the bottom line. The land donations enhanced the value of the resorts."[72]

The same thing has happened near other Rockefeller gifts to the nation for national parks; the Rockefellers developed luxury resorts near the donated lands that became Virgin Islands National Park in 1956 (Caneel Bay Resort and Cinnamon Bay Campground on St. John and Little Dix Bay resort in the British Virgin Islands).

Laurance Rockefeller donated 52 acres of personal lands in 1969 in Hawaii for Haleakala National Park, then pressured Hawaii Governor John A. Burns to donate a key state tract and, as a board member of the Nature Conservancy—yes, Laurance was a long-time board member of TNC—convinced them to raise $500,000 to acquire private lands in the Kipahulu strip that brought the park from the volcanic crater to the ocean (Rockresorts, Inc. managed the Kapalua Hotel on Maui for three years while 250 condominiums were built around it).[73]

Rockefeller bought and contributed half the property that became Great Smokey Mountains National Park in North Carolina. Rockefeller also donated some of the land that became Shenandoah National Park in Virginia—then restored reachable Colonial Williamsburg to its original glory (there are five official hotels—the Williamsburg Inn, Williamsburg Lodge, The Motor House, the Governor's Inn and The Cascades—of the The Colonial Williamsburg Foundation, which is, of course, a Rockefeller nonprofit foundation with offices in Rockefeller Center, New York).

The Rockefeller interests purchased Dodenburg Mountain on the Hudson River and presented it to Palisades Interstate Park in October 1951. Laurance Rockefeller personally owns the Woodstock Inn and Resort in Woodstock, Vermont.

By the time John D., Jr. died on May 11, 1960, his lifetime philanthropy for the environment amounted to nearly $70 million.[74] Laurance followed in amounts many times greater.

We saw the Big Eastern Money land grab happening at Antietam, but with Mellon money. It was the Rockefellers who originated the strategy which we first met in the Nature Conservancy's Virginia Coast Reserve.

If preservation and resort development seem contradictory, think through the strategy. In fact, they are the perfect complement to each other. The principle, copied by the Nature Conservancy from the Rockefeller pioneers before them, is simple: Create exclusive preserves as a magnet for profitable upscale adjacent development, so you can make piles of money to finance still more acquisitions and end up with a vast land-control empire. Lock up land to prevent any competitor from developing it (and government ownership is the best guarantee of *that*), and exploit the high-dollar visitors who come to see what you've locked up. Then buy up more land around the magnet to keep competitors from developing it and to enlarge the attracting power of the magnet—and sell that to the government at a profit.

In effect, you reap profits from natural areas as if you owned them, but you pay no taxes on the land—and if your adjacent development is run by a nonprofit corporation, you could end up rich beyond the dreams of avarice and paying no taxes at all. Even if you run it with a for-profit firm, you won't do badly. The rack rates at Caneel Bay run about $500 a day for an ordinary room—it costs so much because it's the perfect hideout for celebrities: there are no phones in the rooms and nobody can find out if you're even registered.

Even if your corporate socialist empire is operated by a for-profit firm, you could sell the company for a fortune, as Laurance Rockefeller sold Rockresorts, Inc. to railroad giant CSX in 1988—and CSX knows hotels, having owned West Virginia's historic Greenbrier Hotel, site of many a cozy environmentalist strategy session, for more than 80 years. CSX outfoxed Rockefeller by quickly trying to dump his chain of the world's most exclusive resorts, hiring the investment banking firm of Wasserstein, Perella & Company to find a buyer. CSX evidently didn't want to get into the shady land-donation business.[75]

But if this model of creating a world safe for the environmental elite is to work, it must control Two Nasty Things: single-family housing expansion (urban sprawl) and commercial agriculture. Both of these Two Nasty Things demagnetize a luxury resort. Any rationale that will control these Two Nasty Things must be made into accepted public dogma. So we are taught to worry about endangered species, because the Desert Tortoise and the Golden-cheeked Warbler can be used to stop single-family housing and commercial agriculture. We are taught to revere wetlands because they can be used to stop single-family housing and commercial agriculture. We are taught to worship biodiversity because it can be used to stop single-family housing and commercial agriculture. And we wonder why those big wealthy family foundations pay out all that money to sponsor nature programs on the Public Broadcasting System. And we wonder why those big wealthy family foundations promote a Permanent Green Government.

Once you grasp the nature of the elite's land control empire, many apparent contradictions within the environmental movement become understandable, particularly the odd blend of big money families and anti-industry activists. We will meet many protégés of the Rockefellers and Mellons and other big money families—including the Alexander Graham Bell telephone fortune in the form of Bell's son-in-law Gilbert Grosvenor and his successors in the **National Geographic Society**—in the profiles that follow. We'll even meet the **Smithsonian Institution**, which, we will discover, is a very large government environmental organization.

We will also see a substantial internationalism in the environmental movement, not only because Planet Earth is essentially one ecosystem, but also because much of the big money backing the environmental movement is concerned with making the world safe for big money. Among the Rockefellers, this concern is most clearly expressed in the prestigious liberal establishment organization, the Trilateral Commission, formed in 1973 by David Rockefeller and some 200 other "eminent private citizens" to develop good relations among North America, Western Europe and Japan—thus the term "trilateral." In its own words, the Trilateral Commission was "formed by private citizens of

Western Europe, Japan and North America to foster closer cooperation among these three regions on common problems." Those problems include political relations, international economic issues, and Third World development.

University of Texas political analyst Marvin Olasky wrote that the Commission's "major concerns are international economic management, science and technology issues, and security challenges to Western Europe, North America, and Japan. Annual plenary sessions are 'always addressed by the head of state or the chief of government of the nation where the session is held;' and, according to the *Economist,* the 'vision of the commission as a proto-world government or tool of multinational capital is still cherished on the right and the left.'"[76]

The Trilateral Commission received a great deal of publicity when Jimmy Carter picked twenty-five trilateralists to serve in the highest posts of his administration. Among present or former trilateral members are John Anderson, George Bush, Zbigniew Brzezinski, Henry Kissinger, Cyrus Vance, Walter Mondale, and Andrew Young. Corporate executives include those from Exxon, General Motors, Ford, Coca Cola, Bank of America, Cargill, Bechtel, General Electric, CBS, *Time*, Barclay's Bank, Rio Tinto Zinc, and Mitsubishi.[77]

This powerful elite concentrates on promoting their business relationships in the trilateral countries and controlling Third World development, some for transparent reasons; for example, the Rockefellers have a lot of investments in Latin America. It should thus come as no great surprise to find that Rockefeller foundations give large grants to American environmental groups working in Latin America to buy up or tie up land as well as promote stringent environmental controls over business. Every little bit to limit the competition helps, you know.

As *The Economist* noted, left- and right-wing conspiracy theories surround the Trilateral Commission as if it were the Devil Incarnate—about the only thing the Communist Party USA and the John Birch Society have in common is a seething, irrational hatred of trilateralism. Don't get caught up in that. Conspiracy theories are almost always wrong. When you know where *all* the environmental movement's money comes from and goes to, the Trilateral Commission is just one of hundreds of special interests protecting its hind end and using environmentalism as a catspaw. Read our chapter on Money for details.

Which is to say that we should not become hypnotized by the glitterati, as dazzling as they may be. There is far more to the environmental movement than the big money elite, as we shall see. It is an exceedingly complex network, and can best be understood by detailed knowledge of all its major parts, which is what this book is about. To characterize the environmental movement as just a cabal of rich capitalist Trilateralist One Worlders who control all environmental groups from a hidden central point is perhaps a favorite war cry of commie pinkos and redneck crackers who are not noted for their research skills (or even their reading achievement scores), but it is no more true than that they are all a bunch of unwashed weird-lifestyle radicals.

The elite is certainly present and influential—and the exact groups they influence are easily identifiable, so we have listed them in the chapter on

Money—but like all movements, the environmental movement is *segmentary*, and contains many factions that are unrelated except through a common vision. The movement is not controlled from one central point, or even from several pivotal points. It would be much less effective if it were. There are many segments and many leaders and no one can even *speak* for them all, much less control them all.

The closest thing to a Command Central in the environmental movement is the Environmental Grantmakers Association, a cartel of eco-money foundations and corporations (and even one church) that exercises considerable influence over environmental group programs through the power of the purse, and we tell all about it in the chapter on Money. But fourth-largest group Greenpeace, for example, will have nothing to do with the Environmental Grantmakers Association and has even picketed one of its meetings. We should strive to see all the connections that really exist, but we should resist making connections that do not.

So let's look into the details of the American Farmland Trust. The main thing AFT does is get property rights—particularly development rights—out of the hands of private farmers and into the hands of governments, mostly state governments. Total support and revenue for 1990 was $3,482,308. When added to the Trust's revolving fund used to buy out private property rights, the total balance sheet for the year added up to $5,868,013.[78]

Like the Nature Conservancy and its 405 corporate members, the American Farmland Trust has lots of corporate donors. Giving gifts to the AFT of $10,000 or more were the Archer-Daniels-Midland Foundation; H.J. Heinz Co. Foundation; and the Prudential Foundation. Gifts of $5,000 to $9,999 came from Nabisco Brands and Pioneer Hi-Bred International, Inc. Gifts of $2,500 to $4,999 came from Conoco, Inc.; Du Pont; Freeport-McMoRan, Inc.; IMC Fertilizers, Inc.; Patagonia, Inc. (which also gave $10,000 to the eco-terrorist organization Earth First!). Gifts of $1,000 to $2,499 came from Agway Foundation; Cenex Foundation; Crestar Bank, DeKalb Genetics Corporation; Henry & Henry; RMI Direct Marketing; Salad King, Inc; Select Sires, Inc; and USX Foundation. Matching gifts came from BP America Inc.; Champion International Corporation; Chemical Bank; Digital Equipment Corporation; The Equitable Foundation; General Cinema Corporation; John Hancock Mutual Life Insurance Company; Lotus Development Corporation; Morgan Guaranty Trust Company of New York; Pfizer Inc.; Rockefeller Family & Associates; Transamerica Foundation; and The William and Flora Hewlett Foundation.

Laurance Rockefeller's **American Conservation Association, Inc.** of New York City (Annual grants in excess of $2 million)—the donors of which are Laurance S. Rockefeller, Laurance Rockefeller, the Rockefeller Brothers Fund, and Jackson Hole Preserve, Inc.—gave AFT $50,000 in 1989. You need to control those Two Nasty Things, remember.

Archer-Daniels-Midland Foundation gave $35,000 in 1989. Archer-Daniels-Midland is the largest food ingredient processor in the nation. It is an interesting observation that when Nelson Rockefeller went through Senate confirmation hearings after President Gerald Ford appointed him Vice President of the United States, the only major holding outside of Rockefeller investments that Nelson listed was a substantial amount of Archer-Daniels-Midland Company stock. It may be a mere coincidence that after Nelson Rockefeller was confirmed as Vice President, agricultural policies favored the products of Archer-Daniels-Midland Company and from time to time their stock price has appreciated notably. Mrs. Nelson A. Rockefeller remains on the foundation's board of directors to this day.

The **ARCO Foundation** of Los Angeles (Assets $221,858—the low number reflects only a residual: Arco pays in more than $16 million annually that gets paid out during the same fiscal year) gave the AFT $10,000 in 1989.

The **Compton Foundation** (Assets $62,534,943), which got its money from the Ralston Purina fortune, gave AFT $31,000 in 1989.

The **Geraldine R. Dodge Foundation** of New York City (Assets $137,953,811) gave AFT $25,000 in 1989.

The **William and Flora Hewlett Foundation** (Assets $559,792,927) from their computer fortune, gave AFT $150,000 in 1990, a 3-year grant for support of environmental policy work.

The **J. M. Kaplan Fund, Inc. of New York City** (Assets $85,564,577) gave AFT $75,000 in 1989.

Kraft General Foods Foundation gave $10,000 in 1989.

The **Charles Stewart Mott Foundation** of Flint, Michigan (Assets $929,505,650), which is General Motors money, gave AFT $67,800 in 1990.

The **Ruth Mott Fund** of Flint, Michigan (Assets $2,249,107), also GM money, gave AFT $20,000 in 1989.

The **William Penn Foundation** gave $350,000 in 1990, a 3-year grant for a farmland preservation program in southeastern Pennsylvania and southern New Jersey.

The **Prudential Foundation** of Newark (Assets $96,224,000) gave AFT $10,000 in 1989 for farming survey on sustainable agriculture.

The **Winthrop Rockefeller Trust** of Little Rock, Arkansas (Assets $86,438,344) gave the AFT $50,000 in 1989.

The **San Francisco Foundation** (Assets $226,099,459) gave AFT $15,000 in 1990 to preserve prime farmland in eastern Contra Costa County.

Surdna Foundation gave $25,000 in 1989.

Among many others.

The Board of Directors of the American Farmland Trust consists of chairman Patrick F. Noonan; vice chairs Edward H. Harte and Richard E. Rominger; secretary/treasurer Alfred H. Taylor, Jr.; executive committee chairman Mason Walsh, Jr.; Stephen S. Adams; Robert B. Anderson; Dwayne O. Andreas; Louis R. Benzak; Dennis Collins; Doyle Conner; Joan K. Davidson; William M. Dietel; Jean Wallace Douglas; Gilbert M. Grosvenor; Thomas L. Lyon; Ralph Morris; Betty Peacock; Mrs. David Rockefeller; Obie Snider; and John Winthrop.

The American Farmland Trust is one of the organizations in the Rockefeller Interventionist Axis, perhaps the most powerful stream in the great turbulence of the overall environmental movement. Like the Mellon Axis, the Rockefellers only become eco-socialists when it's *your* property. Likewise, they are not civilization destroyers, but carry out their Economy Trasher agenda as establishment interventionists.

Oh, yes, we almost forgot: There are *more than 900 land trusts* like the Nature Conservancy in the United States. And they all take from the property owner and submit the bill to the taxpayer: For example, the Sonoma Land Trust, less than two months after reaching a $700,000 agreement to limit development on a remote Alexander Valley ranch in California, asked county taxpayers to take over the deal for $900,000. County Supervisor Ernie Carpenter said, "I feel it's a bad policy for the land trust to be getting a 30 percent premium on the very first deal they bring to the county's open space district."[79]

The Nature Conservancy. The Conservation Fund. The American Farmland Trust. And 900 other land trusts.

Job killers.

Economy trashers.

The Nature Conservancy—Footnotes

1 1993 New York State filings, Annual Financial Report, dated February 7, 1994.

2 "The secrets of Gray Ranch," by Bruce Selcraig, *New York Times Magazine*, June 3, 1990, p. 28.

3 *Public Interest Profiles 1992-1993*, Congressional Quarterly Inc., Washington, D.C., p. 550.

4 *Rolling Stone*, May 3, 1990.

5 "The secrets of Gray Ranch," *New York Times Magazine*.

6 "Why we cannot buy our way out of environmental dilemmas," by Tom Wolf, *Los Angeles Times*, July 21, 1991, p. M2.

7 "The secrets of Gray Ranch," *New York Times Magazine*.

8 TNC 1992 Form 990, Part IV, Investments, Securities and Investments, Other.

9 "Quietly Conserving Nature," by Noel Grove, *National Geographic*, December 1988, p. 837.

10 "The Nature Conservancy Game," by Bil Gilbert, *Sports Illustrated*, October 20, 1986, p. 86.

11 *Protecting the Environment: Old Rhetoric, New Imperatives*, Jo Kwong Echard, Capital Research Foundation, Studies in Organization Trends #5, 1990, Washington, D.C., p. 173.

12 *Good Dirt*, David E. Morine, Globe Pequot Press, Chester, Connecticut, 1991, p. 160 ff.

13 "Conservation group buys three islands off Virginia," Associated Press, *The New York Times*, December 8, 1970.

14 Personal correspondence between a local reporter and a citizen investigating the Conservancy, dated October 22, 1985, confidential source.

15 *Good Dirt*, p. 164.

16 "Conservancy asked to reveal land plans," by Linda Cicoira, *The Norfolk Virginian-Pilot*, January 18, 1985, p. D1.

17 List provided by Accomack County Assessor Kendall Bradley in 1985.

18 "Unnatural Developments," by George Reiger, *Field & Stream*, August 1990.

19 *Good Dirt*, p. 164.

20 *Good Dirt*, p. 164.

21 "Development for a favored few?" by Warren Brookes, *Washington Times*, January 25, 1991, p. F1.

22 "Officials Oppose Eastern Shore Development," by Doris O'Donnell, *Tribune-Review*, Greensburg, Pennsylvania, January 13, 1985, p. B1.

23 "Unnatural Developments," *Field & Stream*.

24 Conversation with the Virginia Department of Consumer Affairs and Interview with Ann Corcoran of the *Land Rights Letter.*

25 "Hosanna for the unsung heroes," editorial by Robert E. Burns, *U. S. Catholic*, June 1988, p. 2.

26 Almost any encyclopedia will provide a similar sketch of the Mellons. See *Encyclopedia Britannica*, Micropedia, Volume 7.

27 *The Golden Donors: A New Anatomy of the Great Foundations*, Waldemar Nielsen, E. P. Dutton, New York, 1985, p. 183-187.

28 See such uncritical pieces as "Last bit of Eden teeters on brink of development," *New York Times*, April 2, 1992, p. B7.

29 Erich L. Gibbs and Frederic A. Gibbs, Jr. v. The Nature Conservancy and the First National Bank of Valparaiso, Case Number H92-0371, filed November 13, 1992, United States District Court for the Northern District of Indiana. Case set for trial October 12, 1993.

30 A hint of the Nature Conservancy's dark side was presented in "The best and worst of public interest groups: from lifting up the poor to shaking down the elderly," by Rita McWilliams, *Washington Monthly*, March 1988, p. 19.

31 Tape #100, "Doing Deals With Land Conservancies," by Boren and Friedman, January 19, 1990, live recordings of NAHB 46th Annual Convention & Exposition, Atlanta, Georgia. Available from NAHB, Washington, D.C.

32 "Lost in Locustville II," by George Reiger, *Field & Stream*, October 1986, p. 21.

33 "Shared Concerns: An NCIB Special Report on Selected National Environmental and Conservation Organizations," (report) National Charities Information Bureau, New York, 1992.

34 1992 Annual Report, the Nature Conservancy.

35 "Quietly Conserving Nature," *National Geographic*, p. 818.

36 This entire story can be found in "Protecting the Future," by James P. Brown, *Down East*, 1989 Annual, p. 84.

37 *Public Interest Profiles* is published annually by the Foundation for Public Affairs, affiliated with Congressional Quarterly, Inc. in Washington, D.C.

38 *Good Dirt*, p. 164.

39 Ron Arnold interview with U.S. Fish & Wildlife personnel, 1981, while writing the book *James Watt and the Environmentalists.*

40 Woodward to Nature Conservancy, August 31, 1987.

41 Memorandum of Understanding dated September 19, 1988 between the Bureau of Land Management and the Nature Conservancy. Obtained through the Freedom of Information Act from the U.S. Department of the Interior by the New Mexico Land Use Alliance.

42 "Why IG is probing land trusts," by Warren Brookes, *Washington Times*, May 30, 1991, p. G1.

43 "Ted's fonda buffalo, too," by Thomas Jaffee, *Forbes Informer*, April 27, 1992, p. 18.

44 "The Gray Ranch, A Review of Selected Aspects Associated With Possible Federal Acquisition of the Gray Ranch in New Mexico to Establish The Animas National Wildlife Refuge," by Al Schneberger, Jed Elrod, and Ronald J. White, New Mexico Department of Agriculture, August 1990.

45 "Rancher concerns downplayed," by Fred Wortham, Jr. *Western Livestock Journal*, May 7, 1990.

46 *Resolution*, New Mexico Cattle Growers' Association, Albuquerque, New Mexico, June 1992.

47 "Battle lines form over Oregon ranches," by Debora Thomas Hood, *Western Livestock Journal*, July 15, 1991, p. 1.

48 "Historic wildlife agreement signed," *Los Angeles Times*, March 24, 1990, p. A27.

49 "Stockmen wary of 'Conservancy' pact," by Fred Wortham, Jr., *Western Livestock Journal*, April 16, 1990, p. 1.

50 "Rancher concerns downplayed," by Fred Wortham, Jr., *Western Livestock Journal*, May 7, 1990, p. 1.

51 "This dying ground," by Lee Pitts, *Livestock Market Digest*, November 18, 1991, p. 1.

52 "Conservancy conserves desolation, kicking up another kind of storm," by Nick Ravo, *New York Times*, August 18, 1989, p. A18.

53 "Land Purchases Are Manipulated," by Tom Uhlenbrock, *St. Louis Post-Dispatch*, October 8, 1992, p. 6A.

54 "The secrets of Gray Ranch," *New York Times Magazine*.

55 "The selling of the green," by Jerome Cramer, *Time*, September 16, 1991, p. 48.

56 "Database keeps earth's inventory," by Gary H. Anthes, *Computerworld*, July 23, 1990, p. 28.

57 *Wall Street Journal*, May 24, 1989. Quoted in *Public Interest Profiles 1992-1993*, Congressional Quarterly Inc., Washington, D.C., p. 550.

58 Natural Heritage Program / Conservation Data Center Network: Brief Technical Description, Nature Conservancy, Arlington, Virginia, 1989.

59 "Maine Natural Heritage Program expands to state," *Maine Legacy*, February 1989, p. 1.

60 As quoted in *The Golden Donors: A New Anatomy of the Great Foundations*, Waldemar A. Nielsen, E. P. Dutton, New York, 1985, p. 304.

61 1992 Financial Report, Nature Conservancy.

62 Source: Virginia Division of Consumer Affairs.

63 "Property Rights: The Debate Is Joined," *Organization Trends*, Capital Research Foundation, Washington, D.C., March 1992.

64 Personal interview by Ron Arnold at a conference in Bangor, Maine, 1992.

65 Subscriptions to *Land Rights Letter* are available from P. O. Box 568, Sharpsburg, Maryland 21782, phone 301-797-7455.

66 "Department of Interior Land Acquisitions Conducted with the Assistance of Nonprofit Organizations," Document Number 91-I-833, Office of the Inspector General, Washington, D. C., June 5, 1992.

67 *The Rockefellers: An American Dynasty*, Peter Collier and David Horowitz, Holt, Rinehart and Winston, New York, 1976.

68 *The Story of the Rockefeller Foundation, 1913 to 1950*, Raymond B. Fosdick, Harper & Bros., New York, 1952.

69 *National Guide to Funding for the Environment and Animal Welfare*, edited by Stan Olson, Ruth Kovacs & Suzanne Haile, The Foundation Center, New York, 1992, p. 193.

70 This section is derived from *The Birth of the National Park Service: The Founding Years, 1913-33* by Horace M. Albright as told to Robert Cahn, Howe Brothers, Salt Lake City, 1985, p. 215-16.

71 "Rockefeller, John Davison, Jr. (1874-1960), and Laurance Spelman Rockefeller (1910-)," by Alfred Runte, *Encyclopedia of American Forest and Conservation History*, edited by Richard C. Davis, Macmillan Publishing Company, New York, 1983, p. 582.

72 "On the right track?" by Edwin A. Finn, Jr., *Forbes*, May 16, 1988.

73 *A History of Early Land Acquisition for Kipahulu Valley as an Extension of Haleakala National Park*, Mark Tanaka-Sanders, District Ranger, Kipahulu Valley, Maui, Hawaii, 1991.

74 *A Contribution to the Heritage of Every American: The Conservation Activities of John D. Rockefeller, Jr.*, edited by Nancy Newhall, Knopf, New York, 1957.

75 "Rocky times for Rockresorts," by Edward F. Cone, *Forbes*, October 31, 1988, p. 8.

76 *Patterns of Corporate Philanthropy: Public Affairs Giving and the Forbes 100*, Marvin Olasky, Capital Research Foundation, Washington, D.C., 1987, p. 244.

77 *Trilateralism: The Trilateral Commission and Elite Planning for World Management*, Edited by Holly Sklar, Black Rose Books, Montreal, 1980.

78 American Farmland Trust Annual Report, 1991.

79 "Land trust's ranch deal could cost county $900,000," by Tom Chorneau, *Santa Rosa Press Democrat*, November 12, 1992, p. A1.

National Wildlife Federation ▐▬▬▬▬▬▬

National Wildlife Federation (Founded 1936)
     Annual budget: $82,816,324 (1993)
          Staff: 608 total
      Members: 4 million members
    Tax Status: (501)(c)(3)
  Headquarters: 1400 16th Street, NW
               Washington, D.C. 20036
               Phone: (202)797-6800 Fax: (202)797-6646

The Number Two Economy Trasher. While the Nature Conservancy is the biggest environmental group in terms of sheer wealth, the National Wildlife Federation is far and away the biggest in terms of members. While the Nature Conservancy toils quietly in the basement of the environmental movement, the National Wildlife Federation reveals the movement's intent on the rooftops through high-profile action and a vast publication program.

The NWF is not an organ of the Mellon Money Axis or the Rockefeller Money Axis like the Nature Conservancy and American Farmland Trust, respectively, but has its own distinctive web of big money connections. The National Wildlife Federation occupies a position in the Establishment Interventionist Axis: It does not eschew owning and managing its own private wildlife areas although it acts to interfere with property rights generally and specifically acts to nationalize private land into government nature preserves.[1]

And although it acts to regulate business and stop market activities on federal lands, it does so in the interest and with the cash of a substantial spectrum of large corporations, including Arco, Du Pont and Ciba Geigy. It avoided becoming the instrumentality of a single monied enclave like the Nature Conservancy / Mellon Money symbiosis because its structure is a consortium of originally independent state hunting and conservation groups and outdoor recreation organizations dating back more than 50 years.

In 1936, at the conclusion of the first North American Wildlife Conference, the 1,500 delegates ended three days of work by creating the General Wildlife Federation. Its first president was Jay "Ding" Darling, who originated the idea of the federation and organized a 1934 meeting of leading industrialists and munitions makers, asking for subscriptions to a national consortium of organized sportsmen. The federation, with local, county, and state groups as members, was to act as a clearing house of information and also as a lobbyist on wildlife and conservation issues. The federation created the wildlife stamp as a fund raising device rather than ask for membership fees. Darling drew the first stamps himself in 1938, the year his group incorporated as the National Wildlife Federation.[2]

Renaming the organization and giving it the lofty mission "to educate the public about conservation as well as the symptoms and the solutions to environmental abuse and neglect" was not enough to assure success.[3] After Darling resigned the presidency in 1939, the National Wildlife Federation lost its sense of mission.[4] It drifted, and in 1946, when the American Wildlife Institute dissolved its debts, the federation was reactivated and went on smoothly to become the largest membership conservation group in America, and the most clearly grass roots organization of the time.[5]

The Federation grew during the 1970s because it developed a new category of individual membership to supplement its state and local chapter structure. By 1980, the NWF had attracted over three-quarters of a million individual members. These were more interested in wildlife appreciation than in hunting and fishing, which created serious internal frictions. Some state affiliates, such as the Pennsylvania Federation of Sportsmen, remained interested in hunting and fishing exclusively; affiliate Michigan United Conservation Clubs reflected the newer appreciative interest.[6] This split set the stage for the National Wildlife Federation to make the transition from early conservation group to modern environmental organization.[7]

The *Washington Post* in a 1990 story said the Federation's early support from local hunting and fishing groups "has resulted in the largest membership of any conservation group and a generally conservative agenda. But under [president Jay] Hair's leadership, the group has widened its focus beyond protecting wildlife habitats and become more aggressive in lobbying on a wide range of environmental issues."[8] Just how objective and completely revealing this story was is questionable, however, because the Washington Post Company is a contributor to the National Wildlife Federation.

The National Wildlife Federation, although it began with grass roots members and a program of public education about wildlife that was the envy of the world, has become one of the most dangerous Economy Trashers in the country. It has evolved from a conservation group relying on private benefactors and private solutions into just another environmental group pushing for stronger government regulation and greater limitation on individual stewardship. It runs five departments: Development (fund raising); International; Public Affairs; Research and Education; and Resource Conservation.

NWF trashes the economy not only with its anti-industry lobbying, but also with a bevy of lawsuits against resource producers,[9] constant pressure campaigns to sway administrative agencies,[10] and a gigantic publication program that effectively teaches young people to hate everything industrial. Ranger Rick's Nature Club and Ranger Rick's Wildlife Camp indoctrinate youngsters along with the CLASS program (Conservation Learning Activities for Science and Social Studies); Earth TREK carries on the work with teens. The Institute for Wildlife Research finishes the job.

NWF's joint campaign with other environmental groups to convince the Bush administration to adopt its "no net loss" policy for protecting wetlands is the reason Peggy Reigle can't build her dream home in Maryland and that Marty Sevier is watching Glacier Park Company's land values shrink toward zero. As nationally syndicated columnist Alston Chase commented, "Established megaguilds such as the Sierra Club and National Wildlife Federation have become bureaucracies that pursue agendas almost exclusively devoted to extending the power of the federal government over land and industry."[11]

Except *their* land and industry, that is. An interesting tale reveals the shameless hypocrisy of this enormous eco-group: Years ago, in 1975, Dr. Claude Moore, an honorary president of the National Wildlife Federation, donated a 357-acre conservation sanctuary in Virginia that was home to 185 species of birds. So far, so good. However, in 1986, NWF decided it needed a prestigious seven-story $40 million heat-efficient ecologically sensitive building in downtown Washington, D.C. to showcase its new green look. The Federation was preparing to desert its traditional conservation field work for Washington lobbying. It needed money for the building fund. What did NWF do?

Of course. It sold the donated tract of Dr. Moore for $8.5 million to a developer who wanted to put 1,350 housing units on the site. The money was used to help build their new tower of power. Dr. Moore was appalled. He sued to stop the loss of what a guidebook published by the Smithsonian Institution had called "a gem of a wildlife area." He alleged that the Federation broke a contract explicitly restricting the preserve's use in perpetuity. He lost. In 1988, a Virginia court issued an opinion that found no evidence of fraud on the part of the Federation. The National Wildlife Federation at the time had 17 staff lawyers.

Former National Wildlife Federation President Ray Arnett was shocked by the crass power trip. "NWF was known as the largest conservation education association in the world," said Arnett. "Now they have moved more into advocacy, lobbying."

The animosity created by the Federation's treachery has given potential donors pause about making gifts like Dr. Moore's. The betrayal itself, however, is a classic example of an old line conservation group metamorphosing into an environmental group, with all the usual anti-technology, anti-civilization, and anti-human rhetoric hiding a self-serving elitist agenda.[12]

Executive Power

Jay Hair has been executive director of this shameless group for more than 10 years and, with his annual salary of $232,640 (benefits $42,689, expenses $15,507), is the highest paid environmentalist executive in America. During the recession in 1991, he told reporters that he chose to forego an increase in his salary and chopped $35,000 from his office budget (but not his salary), and—sob!—cancelled a planned trip to Thailand and Vietnam. Poor baby. He also chopped his staff from 780 employees to 608, but kept his own job. While his group was suffering from an economic slump he himself helped create with unrelenting anti-industry activism, Hair blamed the recession on Operation Desert Storm against Saddam Hussein. "The whole point is that wars are really bad for the environment, the people and the economy," he told the *Washington Post*.[13] You would think that someone who made such a sophomoric statement would be a dolt, but Jay Hair is supremely intelligent.

It's *Dr.* Jay Hair, thank you. He holds a Ph.D. in zoology from the University of Alberta in Canada. He took his undergraduate degree in biology and his M.S.

in zoology from Clemson University. He was administrator of the Fisheries and Wildlife Sciences Program at North Carolina State University before coming to the National Wildlife Federation. Oh, yes, and Dr. Hair also worked for the federal government for a while, as a special assistant with the U.S. Department of the Interior working on a national fish and wildlife policy. There's that incestuous revolving door between government and environmental groups again. But that's not enough. Jay Hair is a member of the Environmental Protection Agency's Biotechnology Science Coordinating Committee. He's an adjunct of the government.[14]

During Dr. Hair's tenure the NWF has tripled its income and at least tripled its political power. With the help of a three-year grant from the Pew Charitable Trusts, the Federation built on state affiliate influence through its Institute for Conservation Leadership, which "trains individual leaders, develops more effective local conservation organizations and helps to link a state's conservation organizations into an effective network capable of statewide action." In practice, that meant installing new ideologically sound greenie leaders in the place of the old line state affiliate directors, many of whom have been unceremoniously booted out.

For a tax-exempt organization, the National Wildlife Federation gets heavily involved in politics. The Federation, for example, viciously attacked several agency-head nominees of the Bush Administration, including James F. Cason, nominated to be Assistant Secretary of Agriculture in charge of the Forest Service and Soil Conservation Service,[15] and Cy Jamison, nominated as Director of the Bureau of Land Management.[16]

NWF also sells an "Activist Kit" with information on how "to contact members of Congress and officials in federal agencies on urgent conservation programs" and "how to keep track of important legislative and regulatory actions." The political action package includes booklets describing how best to contact politicians and the media, it contains lists of all members of Congress and all members of key Congressional committees, and organizing cards to assemble information. The Federation also operates a Legislative Hotline, with a message updated twice weekly to provide a summary of the latest news from Capitol Hill and federal agencies. Through its Resource Conservation Alliance, Federation activists carry on grass roots lobbying. The Federation is skirting the legal restrictions of its tax-exempt 501(c)(3) classification by this thinly disguised promotion of grassroots lobbying, which is properly the province of a 501(c)(4) lobbying organization whose contributions are not tax-deductible to donors.

But politics is practically the National Wildlife Federation's middle name. NWF was one of the lead organizations that assembled the *Blueprint for the Environment,* a staggering set of political policy recommendations for increased taxpayer funding of environmental causes, increased government management of our daily lives, increased regulation, fewer private rights, and diminished roles for the non-member individual in environmental decision making. NWF President Jay Hair was one of the elite six environmental group leaders who met with President-Elect Bush on November 30, 1988, to give him their two-volume, 1,500-page *Blueprint for the Environment,* a distinctly political visit.

The political document was billed as "a cooperative effort by America's environmental community." Its preparation had been directed by a twenty-member steering committee of the most exalted environmental organizations' representatives. Steering Committee chairman was Thomas B. Stoel, Jr. of the Natural Resources Defense Council, while William Howard of the National Wildlife Federation and Jan Hartke of Global Tomorrow Coalition served as Vice Chairs, Tina Hobson of Renew America was Personnel Chair, and Elizabeth Raisbeck of the National Audubon Society was Development Chair.

The environmental movement got the idea from the conservative Heritage Foundation, which had given the Reagan Administration's transition team "a check list of what they wanted to do office by office," said Tina Hobson, who directed consumer affairs for the Carter Administration's Department of Energy and now heads Renew America, a left-wing environmental group. "That's where we got the list of agencies they wanted to defund, the programs they wanted to jettison. And basically, except in the environmental area, they got everything they wanted."[17]

Voting members of the steering committee consisted of Richard Ayres (Natural Resources Defense Council), Ruth Caplan (Environmental Action), Mike Clark (Environmental Policy Institute), Peter Coppelman (The Wilderness Society), Clifton E. Curtis (The Oceanic Society), M. Rupert Cutler (Defenders of Wildlife), Christopher Flavin (Worldwatch Institute), Robert L. Herbst (Trout Unlimited), Jack Lorenz (Izaak Walton League), Michael McCloskey (Sierra Club), Bob Pollard (Union of Concerned Scientists), Paul Pritchard (National Parks and Conservation Association), Susan Weber (Zero Population Growth), Cynthia Wilson (Friends of the Earth), and Andrea Yank (Natural Resources Council of America). It was as close to a monolithic union as the environmental movement has ever come. It was also a rare inside glimpse into who in the environmental movement thought who else was important—membership on the steering committee was by invitation only, and consisted solely of organization heads or their hand-picked executives.

The *Blueprint* was the environmental movement's political manifesto, and is highly instructive.[18]

It called for actions that would force private parties to bear the expense of environmental programs to achieve "public" benefits. It was a plan to gradually eliminate private property, free enterprise, and individual liberty, and to impose a thoroughgoing ecoligarchy to rule over every aspect of American life. According to the editor:

> While twenty major groups served on the Blueprint Steering Committee, more than one hundred actually participated in the process of developing recommendations. Thirty-two different task forces organized the work on their respective topics and coordinated the volunteer efforts of hundreds of individuals. *Blueprint for the Environment* became the umbrella under which groups with different approaches to specific problems could come together and work for the national welfare. It was that umbrella—and the seven million voters represented by the groups under that umbrella—that

united the Blueprint Executive Committee in its meeting at the White House with the President-elect. It is that same umbrella, now in book form, that will continue to unite the Blueprint groups and all Americans in their ongoing efforts to encourage responsible federal environmental action at home and abroad.[19]

The original *Blueprint* contained 511 recommendations, all reflecting a strong reliance on government power. By the time the *Blueprint* came out in book form, "More than 750 detailed recommendations, assembled by cabinet department or agency," had "already been delivered to representatives of the new administration." It was a political dissemination campaign unparalleled in American history.

Each of the original *Blueprint* recommendations, contained on a single sheet of paper, is directed to a specific assistant secretary or administrator within a specific cabinet office. The front side contains the particular office to which the recommendation is directed, a brief recommendation statement and several paragraphs of explanatory text. The back side contains the budget saving or expenditure that results from this specific recommendation, both the House and Senate committees and subcommittees involved with the particular issue and relevant studies on the topic. It also lists other related federal programs, some of the best sources of expertise from among the Blueprint participants, and, on occasion, specific implementation steps and a budget history of the office or program involved.[20]

The first set of recommendations dealt with population control. The President of the United States was to "establish an official population policy for the United States, and encourage all other nations to do the same" with the "overall objective [of] stopping population growth worldwide." These days Vice President Al Gore would just have to get rid of two of his four children, no doubt. The President was to restore "financial support for multilateral organizations" like the United Nations Population Fund and International Planned Parenthood Federation, to force a population control component upon economic assistance programs administered by the Agency for International Development, and by forcing the World Bank, the Inter-American Development Bank, the Asian Development Bank and other funding institutions to make population control a condition for receiving funds.

A large number of the *Blueprint's* recommendations pressed for immense increases in federal funding. It urged an annual slush fund of at least $150 million for the National Park Service to condemn private property near existing national park units and bring it into federal ownership. It asked to triple the budget of the Federal Energy Regulatory Commission for environmental purposes. It pushed a "re-funding" budget of $6 million for the Council on Environmental Quality and a supplemental appropriation of $3.8 million to hire more environmentalists. It recommended that the Forest Service be given unspecified millions to force private nonindustrial forestland owners to have conservation plans by 1993, and to take more land out of commercially productive classifications "by greatly expanding the Research Natural Area program and the National Wilderness Preservation

System," (Wilderness already locks up more than 90 million acres, and they want to triple that). It asked for $30 million for the Water Bank Program to convert—"restore"— working farms into natural wetlands. It wanted vastly increased funds to reclassify commercial grazing lands as non-commercial natural preserves. It asked for more money to stop commercial marine fishing, to stop the use of pesticides and fertilizers, to create an EPA National Ecological Research Center, an EPA Aquafund to supplement Superfund, and dozens of additional Economy Trasher budget-busters.

Another section of the *Blueprint* sought to tighten federal regulation. It wanted the Secretary of Commerce to set national water efficiency standards for plumbing fixtures, the Secretary of Energy to lower the amount of electric energy consumed by fluorescent and incandescent lamps, a ten-percent per gallon increase in the gasoline and diesel fuel tax with 10 percent of this revenue "designated for low-income needs," and a multitude of regulatory Economy Trasher restrictions on everything from pesticides, mining activities, and wildlife refuges to acid rain, clean air, sediment in rain runoff, groundwater, solid waste reduction, and private land near historic sites.

Yet another portion of the *Blueprint* called for broadly expanded federal bureaucratic planning. The President should order a new mission plan for the National Forests to halt all timber operations and convert all historic commodity production programs to nature preserves—no stick of commercial timber to be cut or grown on federal lands. Range management was to be expanded "beyond its traditional emphasis on livestock and forage production to a broader perspective that emphasizes a full range of values and uses, including watersheds, wildlife and fish, riparian areas, soils and recreation"—decoded, that means to phase out all cattle grazing on federal lands. River conservation is to be planned and all agencies required to file their plans with the Federal Energy Regulatory Commission, an end-run to actually remove major hydroelectric dams and "restore" rivers to their original condition. The Secretaries of Interior, Agriculture, and Commerce should coordinate fisheries planning between all their staffs—which would create an incredible tangle of red tape. The Administrator of the National Oceanic and Atmospheric Administration should require planning by the coastal states to comply with federal demands. The Bureau of Land Management should be restructured to phase out all commercial uses of federal land including mining, livestock grazing, petroleum development, and even motorized recreation. The National Park Service should close down many of its visitor units to the public for the sake of a new scientific research program.

A final segment of the *Blueprint* called for private provision of "public" benefits. "The Director of the Bureau of Land Management should work actively to provide public access to those lands that will support recreational usage"— meaning the Director should open adjacent private lands to public trespass without owner consent or compensation. The National Park Service should request an annual appropriation of at least $150 million "to complete land acquisitions and land protection actions for the established units of the system," i.e., to condemn private land near national parks in an empire building orgy of stupendous proportions. The National Park Service should also support a "Park Protection Act" to shut down all businesses within five miles of any national park, national monument, historic area, without the owners' consent or compensation.

That is about as blatant an Economy Trasher agenda as one could ask for. It certainly gives us some idea whether the environmental movement is proposing actions that would hamper the market economy to the point of collapse and whether it is proposing actions that would integrate government interventions into full control of production and consumption.[21] With President Bill Clinton at the helm, we can expect to see this wish list become law.

As practical examples of the National Wildlife Federation promoting the *Blueprint*, which it drafted with other groups, NWF worked to prevent "most oil and gas leasing in National Wildlife Refuges;" It led the effort to carve Atchafalaya National Wildlife Refuge from private land in Louisiana; it lobbied with state affiliate organizations to have Congress designate millions of acres of non-developable wilderness across the country; it won a lawsuit stopping coal leasing in the Fort Union region of North Dakota until restrictive rules could be imposed; it forced numerous industries and local governments to reduce direct and indirect discharges into the Great Lakes; in 1988, NWF advocated substantial cuts in sulfur dioxide and nitrogen oxide emission and tougher limits for motor vehicle emissions to strengthen the Clean Air Act as part of the National Clean Air Coalition, and also recommended that the Bush administration's clean air proposals eliminate provisions that sulfur dioxide/nitrogen oxide emission trading be "scrapped."

Job Killer Supreme

NWF has global ambitions: It influenced Congress to deal with environmental impacts in foreign countries on projects funded by the World Bank; it successfully lobbied Congress to restore funding for the United Nations Environment Programme; it forced the Agency for International Development to publish "Our Threatened Heritage," a series of international environmental propaganda programs.[22]

Clearly, those three items show that the National Wildlife Federation is so powerful it carries substantial foreign policy clout of its own. Another example: NWF pressure led to a precedent-setting decision by the Inter-American Development Bank not to release funds for a road project in Brazil until local citizens were consulted. This effort to interpose "the rights of local people into play whenever a development project is planned," does not extend to his homeland—Dr. Hair's army of lawyers does its best to centralize decision-making in Washington, D.C. and to hell with the American citizen who's going to lose his job or see his community destroyed by anti-industry laws drafted and lobbied by Dr. Hair's cohort of Economy Trashers.

The Federation stopped all economic development on 170 million acres in 17 western states in 1989 by winning a lawsuit in the U.S. Court of Appeals. The decision reversed a 1988 ruling that the NWF had no standing to sue the Bureau of Land Management over commercial development of public land, including mining and oil and gas leasing, because the environmental group could not prove the development would cause direct harm to its members. The Appeals Court said the Federation does have standing, based on affidavits submitted by individuals in the group stating that they use the land for recreation. Although the original decision lifted a ban on developing the land, the Appeals Court refused to reinstate it, "because the case should proceed with dispatch" through lower courts which would try the merits of the case. The Federation had brought the lawsuit in 1985 alleging that the Bureau of Land Management violated federal law by granting development rights without holding public hearings. Despite the Appeals Court's refusal to reinstate the development ban, Department of the Interior spokesman Bob Walker said that private developers and agency officials did not know how to proceed. "This leaves a lot of people in limbo," he said. The National Wildlife Federation destroyed thousands of jobs with this victory over the economy.[23]

Memberships make up only 19 percent of the National Wildlife Federation's funding sources. Sale of goods, mostly nature education materials, comprises the bulk of the $77.2 million NWF raked in during 1991. Donations and bequests accounted for 14 percent or $12.4 million in Fiscal Year 1990. Ranger Rick memberships brought in 14 percent; *Your Big Backyard* earned 6 percent, and other income, including $2.2 million worth of investment income, amounted to 8 percent.

The National Wildlife Federation has been one of the leaders of the new eco-commercialism, participating in a bevy of "affinity group" deals that bring piles of money in from unrelated services. For example, NWF is part of the telephone donation scheme offered by MCI to its customers: Anyone using MCI can donate 5 percent of their monthly telephone bills to NWF. Three other groups also participate in the MCI program: Ducks Unlimited, the Nature Conservancy, and the National Audubon Society. Debra Shriver, consumer-markets spokesman for MCI told *Time* magazine, "The program lets us support the environmental movement and try to capture the younger demographic audience we are looking for."[24]

NWF has also licensed its logo for use on toys, T shirts and stuffed animals at K-Mart, Sears and other stores. The Federation also has a deal with American Greetings Company to sell a series of birthday cards made from recycled paper and bearing pictures of endangered species.[25]

NWF derives its national strength from 51 state and territorial affiliate groups. Each affiliate is supposedly an independent, self-governing organization, but an internal shakeup that began in 1989 sought to oust the old-line sportsman faction from state leaderships and impose its own Washington D.C.-picked green-ideology leaders into affiliate power positions. Thirteen regional executives controlled by national headquarters work with the affiliates to keep them in line with central policy. These regional executives are assisted by the staff of attorneys, scientists, and resources specialists in the federation's Washington D.C. headquarters. NWF operates natural resource centers in Anchorage, Alaska; Boulder, Colorado; Atlanta, Georgia; Ann Arbor, Michigan; Missoula, Montana; Bismark, North Dakota; and Portland, Oregon. NWF is also affiliated with the National Wildlife Federation Endowment.

NWF is the most potent environmental group when it comes to media and publications. Its issue-oriented radio advertisements have swayed public policy for years, as have its annual television public service announcement campaigns featuring The Muppets, and "You Can Make a Difference," a special report that airs periodically on the Discovery Channel. Its classroom curriculum materials make industry-haters out of our children with great skill: NATURESCOPE is a series of teaching manuals on the environment, and the CLASS Project is an environmentalist curriculum for middle schools.

Just as Dr. Jay Hair is a wizard of propaganda, so he is a consummate master of the microphone, ready with those Velcro soundbites that stick in your ears. He combined those talents at a special briefing breakfast for the Environmental Media Association in 1990, addressing the heads of the Big Three networks and Fox Broadcasting. Dr. Hair urged the TV community to integrate environmental messages into its programming permanently.

"I think that you in the entertainment community may be the most important audience I have ever addressed," Hair said. "You and the work you do touches the lives of million of people every day. Your contribution to the cause of environmental protection may be more important than what I do in advocacy."

He said the challenge the industry faces is to "inspire and educate" the young people to become more responsible and environmentally aware citizens.

He said that in spite of the big media bash of Earth Day 1990, the destruction of the environment continues at an alarming rate.

"The last TV special is not going to be 'The Simpsons,' 'The Cosby Show,' or 'The Best of Johnny Carson,' or reruns of 'Dick Tracy,' 'Batman,' or 'Total Recall.'

"The last issue that ought to be addressed before society will read: 'The Environment: The Day The Earth Died.' I hope you never produce that TV documentary," Hair said, suggesting that the way to prevent that occurrence is to educate the public on the need to keep the global support system alive.

The response? Paul Witt, one of the executive producers of ABC's "Time Warner Presents The Earth Day Special," said "We have the ability to empower the public to effect change through example and illustration. Showing fictional characters living in an environmentally responsible way gives other people the tools to do likewise."[26]

No one commented on what showing fictional characters hating industry might give people.

The real result? The Environmental Media Association pressured Marshall Herskovitz, co-executive producer of the ABC series *Thirtysomething*, to develop a plot line about halting construction of an incinerator. You can argue all you want about the merits of incineration as the best of all waste disposal methods, but nobody who watches *Thirtysomething* will ever even wonder about it. Stop construction. That's the only message allowable. Stop construction. Any construction.[27]

There's a lot more of this anti-technology fallout profiled in the Media chapter. NWF publishes a bevy of periodicals including *International Wildlife* and *National Wildlife*, both bimonthly magazines; *Ranger Rick*, a monthly magazine for ages 6-12; *The Leaders*, a monthly newsletter, *Your Big Backyard*, a monthly publication for preschoolers; *Conservation Exchange*, a quarterly newsletter, *Conservation 92* (or the last two digits of each year), a biweekly newsletter for public policy activists.

NWF also publishes an annual *Conservation Directory*; and a series of books and booklets including *America's Wildlife Hideaways, Backyard Naturalist, Colors in the Wild, Endangered Animal Species* (a children's book), *The Joys of Songbirds; Naturescope Library, Phantom Reductions: Tracking Toxic Trends, Treasures of the Tide, The Unhuggables, What Do Animals See, Hear, Smell and Feel?* (another children's book), and *Your Choices Count: NWF Citizen Action Guide*. NWF also publishes a number of newsletters, including *EnviroAction* 3 times a week when Congress is in session; *EYAS* 3 times a year; and the quarterly *Gene Exchange*.

Economy Trashing Experts

A report by the National Wildlife Federation can kill thousands of jobs with just a few sheets of paper. Charter fishermen on Lake Michigan understand. A report by NWF of toxins in Lake Michigan created panic and destroyed their business for months. It claimed that pollution was so bad that eating just one meal a week of 20- to 30-inch lake trout increases one's cancer risk to one in 10. The report recommended that sport fishermen sharply reduce consumption of Lake Michigan fish and that pregnant women and children not eat any fish from the lake. Of course, the report was part of a fund-raising campaign for NWF.[28]

The "report" was a mere gimmick to make money for the Federation. The report had been culled from results of studies done on animals and the Federation extrapolated the risk to humans, a simple juggling of statistics using a completely unreliable method. The Illinois Department of Public Health and Michigan's departments of Natural Resources and of Public Health and Agriculture strongly disagreed with the report and said fish advisories issued by the four states bordering Lake Michigan were satisfactory.

But the damage had been done. Consumers did not wait to hear the public health department's reaction to the NWF report. Panic hit the sport-fishing industry, wholesalers and food brokers. Summer bookings of charter fishing companies went to hell. Supermarkets went frantic trying to find out where their fish was coming from. The fish business hit rock bottom and stayed there—nobody would buy *any* fish, even from unimplicated areas, because the National Wildlife Federation had frightened them into worrying that it might be from Lake Michigan.[29]

The National Wildlife Federation's report had no merit. No extra cases of cancer were reported. No danger existed. There was simply nothing wrong with the fish. As former EPA director William Reilly once told a reporter in a fit of candor that environmental activists often "exaggerate and hyperbolize to get an issue on the agenda."[30] Yet the power of the National Wildlife Federation had destroyed jobs and income in the billions of dollars. The National Wildlife Federation Trashes the Economy again.

NWF's board of directors includes a number of prominent and well-connected members of the elite: Chairman Robert H. Gardiner, vice-chairmen Carl Reidel, Gene G. Stout, and Phillip W. Schneider, treasurer Francis A. DiCicco, and secretary Joel T. Thomas. Other members of the board include Richard J. Baldes, Virginia B. Ball, Gerald R. Barber, Mary Frances Berry, Magalen O. Bryant, Dean L. Buntrock, John M. Campanelli, Dan E. Cunningham, Maurice K. Goddard, Lena Guerrero, Don F. Hamilton, Emily M. Kress, John F. Lentz, Raymond L. Linder, Tom Martine, Elizabeth W. Meadowcroft, Gordon G. Meyer, William S. Naito, Jean Richardson, Rudolph J.H. Schafer, and Thomas L. Warren.

The National Wildlife Federation joins some peculiar but effective partnerships, a recent one with John Denver's Windstar Foundation, a deep ecology lock-it-up-and-kick-'em-out cutting edge industry-bashing establishment. A joint conference in Washington, D.C. in 1990 "featured ancient forest guru Lou Gold and the Reverend Jesse Jackson."[31]

Another vehicle of unusual power is their Corporate Conservation Council, a group limited to 20 giant industry members who are invited to join by the NWF.[32] They hold an annual closed-door forum, where top corporate and environmental leaders speak off-the-record. Most of the industry members are also heavy contributors to NWF. What are they buying? Critics wonder whether the industry leaders who go to these cozy sessions are making deals in violation of the Sherman Antitrust Act, a question that Congress should certainly look into. It is a well documented aim of Economy Trasher National Wildlife Federation to limit industrial growth, not to promote it. Making sure that some firms get limited first would be a natural concern of corporate leaders who deal with powerful environmental lobbying pressure groups such as the National Wildlife Federation. The Federation lobbies stringent rules on industries that only big well-capitalized firms can comply with, thus pushing medium and small business competitors of their donors out of the market. How these sessions could do anything other than result in restraint of trade is hard to see. Perhaps these firms will one day be invited to explain to a judge why their complicity with the environmental movement is not a violation of the Sherman Antitrust Act of 1890.

One interesting crack in this wall of corporate eco-solidarity appeared right after the catastrophic Exxon Valdez oil spill in Alaska's Prince William Sound. The spill was exactly the doomsday disaster that the National Wildlife Federation had been waiting for. It was perfect for fund-raising—a natural for a direct mail bonanza. Only some reasonable connection between the spill and NWF had to be made in the public's mind in order to convince them that NWF was the natural place to send money. The presence of Exxon on their Corporate Conservation Council now became an embarrassment. NWF had to do something, so they sued Exxon for punitive damages and to establish a multi-billion dollar fund to oversee the cleanup of Prince William Sound. Some of the rhetoric got pretty harsh. National Wildlife Federation Vice President for Resources Sharon Newsome told a press conference that Exxon was negligent in failing to prevent a spill and that they fraudulently misrepresented their ability to clean up the damage.[33]

Exxon (originally a Rockefeller company, remember), seeing their former colleague going for their jugular—a multi-billion dollar slush fund is costly even for Exxon—resigned from the Corporate Conservation Council, saying the environmental group was unfairly critical of the Exxon Valdez oil spill. The Federation, knowing where the direct mail money was, slapped back with a stinging response, calling Exxon a "corporate pariah" that should keep an open dialogue with environmentalists. Even after this clear demonstration of the environmental movement's lack of loyalty or any sense of fairness, Exxon still gives piles of money to environmental groups that do nothing but trash Exxon jobs and hurt their shareholders.[34]

Crisis Creators

This presents us with an object lesson: Those who are in the business of making us perceive that there is an environmental crisis stand to gain from that perception. In this case the National Wildlife Federation found a real crisis about spilled oil. The same principle applies to the Federation's Fish Story about toxic fish that weren't toxic—and to global warming, the ozone hole, and anything else that might frighten people about the environment. Power-and-pressure groups such as the National Wildlife Federation quite obviously gain money and members—wealth and clout— from creating a crisis mentality. Scientists seeking grants to study the crisis profit too, but less obviously. Ideologues who want to transform society gain credibility, attention, and political entré.

This creates what we call The Going Concern Effect. If you are an environmental organization leader such as Dr. Jay Hair with millions of members and millions of dollars in annual income, at some point you realize that winning political conflicts is relatively easy. You have an agenda, you have skilled lobbyists, you have a huge pressure group to back up your lobbyists, you have clever lawyers to take test cases to court, and you have targets that cannot run away. You hold the moral high ground, fighting for a superindividual cause, and the public is riding your bandwagon *en masse*. You are a Going Concern. Then you realize that it's too easy to win. As German sociologist Georg Simmel wrote in 1908:

> A group's complete victory over its enemies is thus not always fortunate in the sociological sense. Victory lowers the energy which guarantees the unity of the group; and the dissolving forces, which are always at work, gain hold....Within certain groups, it may even be a piece of political wisdom to see to it that there be some enemies in order for the unity of the members to remain effective and for the group to remain conscious of this unity as its vital interest.[35]

Thus, a major task of the successful environmental group becomes The Search For Enemies. Commenting on Simmel's idea, American sociologist Lewis Coser said:

Following up the idea that outside conflict increases group cohesion, Simmel now claims that struggle groups may actually "attract" enemies in order to help maintain and increase group cohesion. Continued conflict being a condition of survival for struggle groups, they must perpetually provoke it.

Moreover, he implies, outside conflict need not even be objectively present in order to foster in-group cohesion; all that is necessary is for the members to perceive or be made to perceive an outside threat in order to "pull themselves together."[36]

Thus, environmental groups inevitably become struggle groups. If you are fighting for a cause, fighting becomes your occupation. The facts don't matter. You can't have an oil spill every day. Perceived threats are good enough. Sometimes you have to cook up a Fish Story. It becomes a sociological necessity. When there is no conflict, environmental groups must generate it in order to keep their Going Concern going. They must perpetually provoke conflict. Environmental groups leaders were very intelligent about selecting industrial civilization as their scapegoat: It provides a rich and seemingly endless list of individual targets for conflict. Cultivating a crisis mentality in the society at large does wonders for environmental groups: it fosters group cohesion, income, and a healthy mailing list that keeps the cash register jingling merrily.

A secondary result of The Going Concern Effect is that struggle groups tend to attract struggle junkies. As sociologist Herta Herzog once noted, "The opportunity for expressing aggressiveness is also a source of satisfaction."[37]

Thus we find a vociferous minority attracted to environmental struggle groups for personality maintenance purposes and satisfaction of aggressive urges. The headlines are full of the names and faces of vociferous struggle junkies who regard environmentalism simply as a license to kill industrial civilization. They press for public policy that destroys industry and they escape all harm themselves. It is the perfect setup.

The National Wildlife Federation does not have to follow the laws it imposes upon industry with its lobbying—it operates no productive enterprises. The NWF has no responsibility to supply the needs of humanity in an environmentally sound manner, yet sets itself up as judge, jury, and executioner for all who do. Dr. Jay Hair and his crew do not feed, clothe, shelter, or provide for anybody. They stand aloof and command that others do their bidding, carrying no burden themselves. They and their cadre of struggle junkies are vultures waiting for an industrial accident to happen so they can mobilize their recruitment campaigns and fatten on the disasters of others. If they can't find one, they make one. Fish Stories.

Freedom of Information Act records indicate at least $915,377 in grants to the Federation from the Environmental Protection Agency and Department of Energy during 1976-1982 in amounts as high as $451,600. Later data is not available.

Program spending was 90.2 percent of income; fund raising was 5.4 percent of income; administration was 4.7 percent of income (all in 1991).[38]

The NWF operates computerized services including databases, online and mailing list services. It maintains an 8,000 volume library, a Conservation Hall of Fame and a Wildlife Gallery of Art.

Foundations and corporations which got their wealth from entrepreneurs working the free enterprise system but which now seem to want nobody else to have that opportunity lavish their wealth on the National Wildlife Federation. Institutions named below but without dollar amounts specified were obtained from corporate or foundation annual reports that did not state the amount or purpose of their contributions.

American Conservation Association.

Amoco's corporate foundation gave $46,000 in 1989 "for environmental conservation."

ARCO Foundation.

Baltimore Gas & Electric Company.

Beldon Fund.

Broyhill Family Foundation.

Capital Fund Foundation.

Ciba-Geigy Corporation.

Coca-Cola Company.

Combustion Engineering, Inc.

Dow Chemical.

Duke Power Company.

E. I. du Pont de Nemours and Company.

Exxon Corporation.

Fanwood Foundation.

General Electric Company.

General Motors Corporation corporate foundation gave $10,000 in 1990.

Hechinger Foundation.

IBM Corporation.

W. Alton Jones Foundation.

The Joyce Foundation (which was based on the fortune of timber baron William T. Joyce and his two firms, the Tremont Lumber Company and the William T. Joyce Company) gave $375,000 in 1990 for "research, policy, and education activities of the National Biodiversity Policy Center" to shut down timber harvest, and another $56,000 in 1990 for "work on state level implementation of model water quality standards," the grant shared with the Great Lakes Natural Resource Center in Ann Arbor, Michigan.

Mars Foundation.

Miller Brewing Company.

Mobil Oil Foundation.

Monsanto Company.

The Kenneth T. and Eileen L Morris Foundation gave $10,000 in 1989.

The Charles Stewart Mott Foundation (Mott was one of the founders of General Motors) gave a $60,000 in 1990 for a "Model Great Lakes Water Quality Standards Project to coordinate basin-wide policy reform through adoption of uniform water quality standards" which will generate false alarms and work to enforce treatment for the sake of treatment as in Columbus, Ohio, rather than for any real public safety reason, and gave $40,000 in 1990 for "Multilateral Development Bank Action Project to strengthen effectiveness of Third World conservation organizations," (General Motors also funds the Trilateral Commission at about $5,000 annually).

Mutual of Omaha, Inc.

Pennzoil Company.

The Pew Charitable Trusts, (based on the fortune of John Howard and Joseph Newton Pew, founders of Sun Oil Company, now The Sun Company, Inc.) gave $100,000 in 1990 for "technical assistance to develop analytical capacity to understand environmental implications of international agreements."

Riggs National Corporation.

Stone Foundation.

3M Company.

The Town Creek Foundation gave $10,000 in 1990.

The USX corporate foundation gave $25,000 in 1989 for a capital grant.

The Washington Post.

Waste Management, Inc.

The Weyerhaeuser Company's corporate foundation gave $12,500 in 1989 for general support.[39]

You may have been shocked to find the *Washington Post* on this list. One of the reasons that environmentalists have been able to get away with unscientific claims, exaggerations and outright fraud is that a biased press is "among those egging the environmentalists on," in the words of Hugh Ellsaesser, atmospheric scientist with the Lawrence Livermore National Laboratory.[40] Brent Bozell III and Tim Graham of the Media Research Center agree. They reported that newspapers whose foundations donate money to a group also give that group more coverage than newspapers whose foundations did not contribute. And more favorable coverage. Fairness doesn't matter to the media.

The *Washington Post* is particularly obnoxious about its unfairness, as noted by ombudsman Richard Harwood: "You are not 'entitled' to a letter to the editor, to an op-ed piece or even to a paid advertisement; if we don't like it, we don't print it. To ask for 'equal time' on the evening news or in the morning newspaper is, very often, to bay at the moon. You have no 'right' to fair treatment, no 'right' to be quoted accurately or in context or even quoted at all in news reports, broadcasts or commentaries. If you are offended by a Herblock cartoon, your remedy may lie with the United Nations but not here. If your reputation is soiled in a front-page story under a four-column headline, it is most unlikely to be cleansed in the same spot (if it is cleansed at all). The First Amendment to the Constitution, as the Post's executive editor [the now-retired Ben Bradlee] once put it with accuracy and candor, protects our irresponsibilities as it protects innocuous speech." Environmentalists get royally treated. Critics of environmentalism get royally screwed. Freedom of the press belongs only to those who own the press.

The unholy alliance between the *Washington Post* and the National Wildlife Federation is not unique. You'll find the *New York Times* giving money to the Sierra Club in their profile. The Media Research Center reported funding linkages between the Environmental Defense Fund and the New York Times Company Foundation, between the National Audubon Society and the New York Times Company Foundation and Times Mirror Foundation (The *Los Angeles Times*), and between the World Wildlife Fund and the Times Mirror Foundation and New York Times Company Foundation.[41] The Times Mirror Company and *National Geographic* give large amounts of money to the Nature Conservancy. The media power of the environmental movement is overwhelming, and for a good reason: The media have a lot of money invested in the environmental movement.

The corporate world rushes to give money to the NWF, which uses it for lobbying to put the corporate world out of business: Exxon, Mobil, Dow Chemical, Du Pont, Monsanto, Weyerhaeuser and General Motors.

It's been a pattern for years. Take a 5-year look-back to 1985: Atlantic Richfield's corporate foundation gave NWF $16,422. Exxon gave $7,500. Mobil's corporate foundation gave $33,000. Standard Oil gave $1,000. Big oil was solidly behind the National Wildlife Federation and still is.[42]

Maybe they're suicidal. Or maybe they don't give a damn about their stockholders and employees. The NWF often denigrates opposing studies as "industry-funded." But they get so much of their money from corporations that their studies are no less "industry-funded."

All across America the National Wildlife Federation has trashed hundreds of thousands of jobs with lawsuits, wetlands regulations, mining fights, endangered species battles and dozens of other campaigns.

Dr. Jay Hair gets paid $240,000 a year to kill the jobs of the less fortunate.

That's the National Wildlife Federation.
Job Killers.
Economy Trashers.

National Wildlife Federation—Footnotes

1 "The next half-century: a golden opportunity for conservation leadership," *National Wildlife*, June - July, 1986, p. 25.

2 *Ding: The Life of Jay Norwood Darling*, David L. Lindt, Iowa State University Press, Ames, Iowa, 1979.

3 *Protecting the Environment: Old Rhetoric, New Imperatives*, Jo Kwong Echerd, Capital Research Center, Washington, D.C. 1990, p. 159.

4 *The Stories Behind the Organization of the National Wildlife Federation and Its Early Struggles for Survival*, Carl D. Shoemaker, National Wildlife Federation, Washington, D.C., 1960.

5 *A Conservation Saga*, Ernest F. Swift, National Wildlife Federation, Washington, D.C., 1967.

6 "Affiliate action: lots of muscle at the grass roots," *National Wildlife*, April - May, 1986, p. 34.

7 "Federation's growth gives muscle to conservation programs," *National Wildlife*, June - July, 1985, p. 25.

8 "From Fringe To Political Mainstream," by Michael Weiskopf, *Washington Post*, April 19, 1990, p. A1.

9 "We sue, but only as a last resort," *National Wildlife*, April - May, 1985, p. 33.

10 "A wilderness of lawsuits," by James Kelly, *Time*, September 14, 1981, p. 18.

11 *Washington Times*, November 16, 1990.

12 "From Conservation to Environmental Movement: The Development of the Modern Environmental Lobbies," Robert Cameron Mitchell, Resources for the Future, Quality of the Environment Division, Discussion Paper QE85-12, June 1985.

13 "War and Recession Taking Toll on National Environmental Organizations," by John Lancaster, *Washington Post*, February 15, 1991, p. A3.

14 *Public Interest Profiles, 1992-93*, Congressional Quarterly, Washington, D.C., 1992, p. 539.

15 "Environment Activists Hit Bush Choice for U. S. Post, by Mark Stein and Louis Sahagun, *Los Angeles Times*, May 21, 1989.

16 "Environmentalists Hit 'Shocking' Appointment," by John Lancaster, *Washington Post*, July 11, 1989, p. A23.

17 *Environmental Action*, November/December 1988.

18 "Bush supporters reassured after Jackson meeting," Frank Murray, *Washington Times*, December 1, 1988, p. A3.

19 Introduction, by T. Allan Comp, editor, *Blueprint for the Environment: A Plan for Federal Action*, Howe Brothers, Salt Lake City, 1989, pp. xi-xii.

20 *Blueprint for the Environment*, p. xii.

21 "Revived 'Standing' Can Make Political Plaintiffs Stand Down," by L. Gordon Crovitz, *Wall Street Journal*, April 18, 1990, p. A23.

22 "NWF supports environmental safeguards in foreign aid," *International Wildlife*, April - May, 1986, p. 34.

23 "Federal Wilderness Ruling Puts Industry in 'Limbo,'" by Paula Yost, *Washington Post*, June 21, 1989, p. A3.

24 "The Selling of the Green," by Jerome Cramer, *Time*, September 16, 1991.

25 "Wildlife Promoted In American Greetings New Line," by Joan E. Rigdon, *Wall Street Journal*, October 9, 1990.

26 "Hair Rallies Showbusiness Exex To Support Environmental Issues," by Jane Lieberman, *Variety*, June 21, 1990.

27 "And Now a Message From an Advocacy Group," by Richard Stevenson, *New York Times*, May 27, 1990.

28 National Wildlife Federation news release, June 29, 1989.

29 "For Charter Fishermen, Report Poisons Business," by Lauren Ina, *Washington Post*, August 22, 1989.

30 "Boss of EPA sees risks as unavoidable," by Jennifer Spevacek, *Washington Times*, March 17, 1989.

31 *E, The Environmental Magazine*, January/February 1991.

32 *Non Profit Times*, April 1990.

33 "Exxon, Alyeska Sued by Wildlife Group," by Rose Gutfeld and Allanna Sullivan, *Wall Street Journal*, August 18, 1989.

34 "Exxon Resigns From Panel Of Environmental Group," Associated Press, *Wall Street Journal*, October 30, 1989.

35 *Conflict*, Georg Simmel, an essay originally Chapter Four of *Soziologie* (1908), translated by Kurt H. Wolff, the third edition (1923), published in *Conflict* and *The Web of Group-Affiliations*, The Free Press, New York, 1955, p. 98.

36 *The Functions of Social Conflict*, Lewis A. Coser, The Free Press, New York, 1956, p. 104.

37 In P. F. Lazarsfeld and F. N. Stanton (eds.), *Radio Research 1942-43*, Duell, Sloan and Pearce, New York, 1944.

38 *Money* magazine, December 1992, p. 122.

39 *Grants for Environmental Protection and Animal Welfare*, 1991-1992, The Foundation Center, New York, 1991.

40 "Global 2000 Revisited," Hugh Ellsaesser, p. 22.

41 "Bottom Line to headline?" by Brent Bozell III and Tim Graham, *Washington Times*, August 15, 1989, p. F3.

42 *Patterns of Corporate Philanthropy: Public Affairs Giving and the Forbes 100*, Marvin Olasky, Capital Research Foundation, Washington, D.C. 1987.

World Wildlife Fund

World Wildlife Fund (Founded 1961; predecessor in 1948)
Annual budget: $60,791,945 (1993)
Staff: 244 total—172 professional; 72 support
Members: 1 million members
Tax Status: (501)(c)(3)
Headquarters: 1250 24th Street, NW
Washington, D.C. 20037
Phone: (202)293-4800 Fax: (202)293-9211

The Number Three Economy Trasher. *Animals' Agenda* said, "The powerful World Wildlife Fund (WWF), is one of the wealthiest groups in the international arena."[1] That shouldn't be too surprising for an organization that gets 20 percent of its income from your federal tax money, another 10 percent from industry, and half from foundations.[2] *Philanthropy* said, "Their effect on environmental policy has been enormous. And many of these environmental organizations have received significant support from foundations and even corporations."[3] Major donors Chevron and Exxon donated more than $50,000 in 1988, and Philip Morris, Mobil and Morgan Guaranty trust gave large contributions to the World Wildlife Fund.[4]

This American nonprofit group is only one of 29 international corresponding World Wildlife Fund organizations and a home office in Gland, Switzerland. The United Kingdom's Prince Philip, Duke of Edinburgh, is President of the World Wildlife Fund internationally, lending a prestige that can hardly be critiqued without a bit of *lèse majesté*. No offense, Prince, but you know how fond we scoundrels from the Colonies are of raising a little hell now and then.

The American unit of the World Wildlife Fund concentrates on "international field activities, including protection of endangered wildlife and wildlands, especially in the tropical forests of Latin America, Asia and Africa; international trade in wildlife, ecologically sound development; conservation of natural resources; and environmental public policy and opinion," according to its literature. It operates affiliate Fairfield Osborn Center for Economic Development.

It is another one of those marvellous revolving door organizations: In July 1990 it absorbed the Conservation Foundation, which had given the Bush Administration William K. Reilly, its Administrator of the Environmental Protection Agency. In addition, WWF's president, Kathryn S. Fuller (salary, $185,000, benefits, $16,650), worked at the office of the Legal Counsel at the Department of Justice and helped start Justice's wildlife section, becoming head of the section in 1979.

WWF's chairman of the board, Russell E. Train, a former Environmental Protection Agency Administrator, is also a ranking member of the Rockefeller bloc— he sits on the board of directors of Laurance Rockefeller's American Conservation Association and of the Rockefeller Brothers Fund. The World Wildlife Fund is solidly in the Rockefeller Interventionist Axis.

Because the Conservation Foundation merged with the World Wildlife Fund, formalizing an affiliation dating back to 1985, it's necessary to devote a little attention to the Conservation Foundation. Don't confuse it with the Conservation Fund, which is the Mellon Interventionist Axis-Patrick Noonan offshoot of the Nature Conservancy that we examined above. The Conservation Foundation was something else—*really* something else. It was also solidly in the Rockefeller Interventionist Axis. Former EPA Administrator William Reilly was president of the Conservation Foundation for 16 years until his appointment to the Bush Administration in 1989.

Who is William Kane Reilly? He grew up in the affluent community of Fall River, Massachusetts, he was graduated from Yale in 1962, got a law degree from Harvard and an urban planning degree from Columbia. David Brooks, editorial writer for the *Wall Street Journal,* said of Reilly, "He is a polished, well-mannered, and genial man, who seems conciliatory even when he is not. A member of the Cosmos and University Clubs, he has an aristocratic languor about him. For 16 years he was president of the Conservation Foundation, one of the more genteel environmental groups, supported by the Rockefeller and Mellon Foundations. His nickname around the [Bush] White House is Clean Air Head, for he is not known for a sharp intellect."[5]

But that sells Bill Reilly short. He is one of Laurance Rockefeller's key protégés, long groomed for power in the Permanent Green Government. The fact that he is out of government does not mean we have seen the last of him. His bureaucratic assignments began during the Nixon Administration when he sat on the President's Council on Environmental Quality. In 1972, Laurance Rockefeller named Reilly executive director of the Task Force on Land Use and Urban Growth, where he was editor of its report, *The Use of Land: A Citizens Policy Guide.* This report urged policy makers to use environmentalism as a stalking-horse for federal land use controls.

As *Insight* magazine reported, "The trick was to assert federal control without compensating owners for the uses they would lose. The constitutional requirement to pay owners for such government 'takings' had traditionally been a powerful constraint."[6]

Reilly's 1973 report said, "It is time that the U. S. Supreme Court re-examine its precedents that seem to require a balancing of public benefit against land value loss...and declare that, when the protection of natural, cultural, or aesthetic resources or the assurance of orderly development are involved, a mere loss in land value is no justification for invalidating the regulation on land use."[7]

Reilly's report laid out the basics of using "biological diversity" as a rationale for growth management, i.e., limiting The Two Nasty Things, single-family housing and commercial agriculture, or virtually any economic use.

Reilly did well in this job and was rewarded with the presidency of the Conservation Foundation, the most exclusive and prestigious environmental think tank of all—and Laurance Rockefeller was a board member of the Conservation Foundation for many years.

Reilly may be no Einstein, but he's not a bad Napoleon. Reilly turned the Conservation Foundation/World Wildlife Fund into the fastest growing conservation organization in America during his tenure, tripling its budget and doubling its membership, according to the left-wing newspaper *In These Times*. "Corporations like Chevron have been well served by an identification with WWF. Mutual of Omaha, Ralph Lauren, Rolex and Jaguar have all teamed up with the WWF to tap into conservation's 'popular appeal' and 'enormous audience.'"[8]

Using the influence of the Rockefeller family, Reilly tapped the industry coffers of such corporate sponsors as Du Pont, Dow, Exxon, Monsanto and Times Mirror, which earned him the suspicion of many environmentalists who called the Conservation Foundation an industry front. The truth of that suspicion will become evident as we unfold the many ways in which large firms can use large environmental groups to bankrupt smaller competitors. CF under Reilly's direction sponsored mediation on environmental policy issues and encouraged dialogue between environmentalists and industry, according to *Industry.Week* magazine.[9]

The result was that industry leaders learned the paradigm of preserving nature to act as a magnet for upscale adjacent development—and to support expensive environmental restrictions that would harm their less-well-capitalized competitors instead of themselves. Reilly is not as dumb as his critics think. Nor are his industrial contributors as innocent.

In These Times wrote of the Conservation Foundation, "While the organization prides itself on its 'moderate' and 'responsible' positions, many environmentalists consider it an industry front. One reason is that the Conservation Foundation is heavily indebted to industry coffers. Its list of corporate sponsors is a shocking catalog of environmental wasters—DuPont, Dow, Exxon, Monsanto and General Electric.

"Samuel P. Hayes writes in his book *Conservation and the Gospel of Efficiency* that the Conservation Foundation forms a fifth column within U.S. society, claiming neutrality and objectivity while advancing industry efforts to delay or oppose regulations. The foundation has supported deregulation, the use of cost-benefit and risk analysis and regulations that gain industry compliance through incentives rather than penalties.

"'Industry knows these laws aren't going away,' Reilly told the *Los Angeles Times*. 'And environmentalists have come to realize that it's going to take cooperation from industry to get the laws working.' According to this view, less adversarial approaches, like soliciting cooperation rather than demanding compliance, are more successful. Environmentalists, Reilly believes, should spend less time protesting, boycotting and screaming and more time exploring the 'costs' and 'benefits' of various 'options.'"[10]

The notion that big industry would use the Conservation Foundation to *oppose* regulation is charmingly naive. Government regulations, as most economists constantly point out, behave in practice as if they were valuable private property rights belonging to the regulated, creating restrictions so harsh on a well-developed industry that they prevent less-well-capitalized newcomers from entering the market and therefore discourage innovation and competition—the perfect, if expensive, mechanism to keep the status quo. It's like a protection racket in which the payoffs are legal and the government is your hit man.[11]

Once William Kane Reilly stepped out of the Conservation Foundation into the magic phone booth of the EPA, he shed the garb of mild-mannered conservationist and turned into a veritable caped crusader—if one were to bestow a comic-book title upon him it would have to be "Captain Eco-Nazi." *Organization Trends* quoted a typical anti-free enterprise adage from The New Reilly: "The land market...is the principal obstacle to effective protection of private open space. Open spaces should be insulated as completely as possible from the market forces that now press them into development. One way to accomplish this...is for owners of open spaces to give up or sell part of their property rights."[12]

One should not be too perplexed by such a statement from a Rockefeller protégé. After all, it was the original Rockefeller, John D., who perfected monopoly capitalism in his Standard Oil Trust, saying that competition was wasteful and should be eliminated through government-sanctioned monopolies. He sincerely believed that even though the public should pay aplenty for the benefits of monopoly's orderly markets, those benefits should be real.[13] He wanted to deliver genuine benefits to the public, but he didn't want anybody else to, that's all. His behavior was not too different from the motto Greenpeace adopted a hundred years later, "whatever works." He knew how to buy judges, public officials of all sorts, and legislatures. He knew how to get extra-curricular help from the federal government. He proved, perhaps more than any other American businessman, that there is a difference between corporate capitalism and free enterprise. William Kane Reilly learned from experts. It's no surprise that he wants some of us to surrender our private property rights.

Reilly may be genial on the outside, but behind his desk he was a real command-and-control SOB during his EPA incarnation. He ordered assistant EPA administrator James M. Strock to refuse a petition by Washington Legal Foundation—a legal think tank and public interest law firm active in pro-free enterprise issues—that would revise the U.S. Sentencing Commission's guidelines involving environmental offenses. The legal foundation asserted that the commission's guidelines were "being exploited by overzealous EPA officials and federal prosecutors in order to impose overly harsh prison sentences on small businessmen for minor regulatory offenses." For example, John Pozsgai, a self-employed truck mechanic—a hardworking immigrant from communist Hungary—was sentenced to 27 months in federal prison for placing topsoil on his wooded property where he planned to build a repair garage.[14]

That was the longest sentence in U.S. history for an environmental offense because EPA bureaucrats under Reilly's direct orders decided that portions of Pozsgai's lot were a marginal wetland. In fact, the only water on the whole property came from a storm drainage ditch and a broken sewer pipe that had been neglected by the city of Morristown, Pennsylvania. The lot opened onto no federal navigable water, there was no nature preserve, there was nothing but a seep of foul, stinking sewer water just below the surface of the ground, infected with coliform bacteria. Pozsgai cleared the area of tons of old truck tires and other junk illegally dumped there before he bought the property.

Reilly's case against Pozsgai stunk as much as the leaky sewer. But it is certainly an example for all the small competitors of big business. Big business can afford to obey the stringent pollution standards they support, knowing full well their small competitors cannot. The paradigm works: What you can't profit from, prevent anyone else from profiting from. Use nature protection as a hammer to destroy the competition. Criminalize free enterprise.

Crush the little guy. Caress the big guy. So what else is new?

Reilly's Eco-Police buddies in the Justice Department imposed a sentence on John Pozsgai greater than the average sentence imposed under the guidelines for burglary, larceny, embezzlement, fraud, drug offenses, auto theft, counterfeiting, bribery and prison escape, according to the U.S. Sentencing Commission's own data—for cleaning up a stinking mess and trying to turn it into a profitable business site. He was caught committing—gasp!—free enterprise. Now he's a political prisoner. What country is this?

Welcome to Eco-America, Hungarian immigrant John Pozsgai. We hope you can tell the difference between our authoritarians and the ones you escaped, John—ours have degrees from Harvard, Yale, and Columbia and are protégés of the Rockefellers and Mellons.

The World Wildlife Fund since Reilly's departure, under Kathryn Fuller's presidency, has prospered. Today WWF lobbies Congress, participates in regulatory rulemaking, sells merchandise, does research, writes grants to get money from foundations, runs a debt-for-nature program, operates its own foreign policy, offers a speakers program, and wows them in the media. WWF directly influenced President Bush's acid rain and wetlands policies, says the *Washington Post*.[15]

But its major programs fall in the international arena. Between 1987 and 1989 WWF negotiated the first debt-for-nature swap, in cooperation with the Nature Conservancy, and has been instrumental in spreading both the interventionist model and the eco-socialist model of environmentalism throughout the world.

Kathryn S. Fuller has been with WWF since 1982, originally as a consultant, later as director of its TRAFFIC (U.S.A.) office, which monitored wildlife trade.[16] Her American outfit is affiliated with other World Wildlife Fund organizations in 29 countries around the world. Although WWF retained its Rockefeller Interventionist Axis ties after Reilly's departure and the merger with the Conservation Foundation, the organization properly falls within a deeper power stream in the overall environmental movement: the Global Interventionist Axis.

World Environmentalism Models

The world environmental movement became a recognizable feature of global society during the late 1960s and early 1970s, primarily in the form of international commissions convened to address environmental issues. The Pearson Commission (chaired by Canadian prime minister Lester B. Pearson) came in the heyday of a broad optimistic multilateralism—the "One World" vision of the Trilateral Commission—reflected in the title of the Pearson Commission's 1969 report: *Partners in Development*.[17] The future looked endlessly rosy. Big money felt it could make the world safe for big money using environmental restrictions.

By 1972 the United Nations Conference on the Human Environment held in Stockholm gave up on economic progress. Its report cited adverse impacts of development, urging an end to economic growth. It was the era of The Computer That Cried Wolf, the nickname tagged onto the 1972 Club of Rome study, *The Limits to Growth*.[18] The study's computerized world models assumed relationships between population, resources, pollution, agriculture, technology, and capital that inevitably led to a crash of one sort or another, no matter how the global population and economy expanded. The assumptions they fed the computer were completely Malthusian.

For those who have never read the musings of Thomas Robert Malthus, English economist and demographer, here is the core of his basic premise, from his seminal work *An Essay on the Principle of Population*, fifth edition, 1817, published by John Murray, London, volume 3, book iv, chapter v, pages 126-28:

> It is an evident truth that, whatever may be the rate of increase in the means of subsistence, the increase of population must be limited by it, at least after the food has once been divided into the smallest shares that will support life. All the children born, beyond what would be required to keep up the population to this level, must necessarily perish, unless room be made for them by the death of grown persons. It has appeared indeed clearly in the course of this work that in all old states the marriages and births depend principally upon the deaths, and that there is no encouragement to early unions so powerful as a great mortality. To act consistently, therefore, we should facilitate, instead of foolishly and vainly endeavoring to impede, the operations of nature in producing this mortality; and if we dread the too frequent visitation of the horrid form of famine, we should sedulously encourage the other forms of destruction, which we compel nature to use. Instead of recommending cleanliness to the poor, we should encourage contrary habits. In our towns we should make the streets narrower, crowd more people into the houses, and court the return of the plague. In the country, we should build our villages near stagnant pools, and particularly encourage settlements in all marshy and unwholesome situations. But above all we should reprobate specific remedies for ravaging diseases; and those benevolent, but much mistaken men, who have thought they were doing a service to mankind by projecting schemes for the total extirpation of particular disorders.... The necessary mortality must come, in some form or other; and the extirpation of one disease will only be the signal for the birth of another perhaps more fatal. We cannot lower the waters of misery by pressing them down in different places, which must necessarily make them rise somewhere else: the only way in which we can hope to effect our purpose, is by drawing them off.

Malthus was dead serious, a fact his apologists have tried to mask. Even Karl Marx and Frederick Engels, founders of communism, detested Malthus. As Engels wrote in *Outlines of a Critique of Political Economy* (1843), "The implications of this line of thought are that since it is precisely the poor who are the surplus, nothing should be done for them except to make their dying of starvation as easy as possible, and to convince them that it cannot be helped and that there is no other salvation for their whole class than keeping propagation down to the absolute minimum. Or if this proves impossible, then it is after all better to establish a state institution for the painless killing of the children of the poor....Charity is to be considered a crime, since it supports the augmentation of the population."

So, when we say "Malthusian," we are not just talking about someone who believes that food and resource production cannot keep pace with uncontrolled population growth, we are also talking about people who actively recommend cutting off the production of information, resources, technology and medicine so that undesirables will die off. Malthus personally campaigned for repeal of England's Poor Laws. He himself was not poor, of course. He was educated at Cambridge, took holy orders, later married well, and took a professorship of history and political economy at the East India Company's private college in Haileybury, Hertfordshire, where he lived comfortably for the rest of his life.

To the Malthusian Club of Rome, an elite group of wealthy and influential leaders from around the world, growth was the problem, and the solution lay only in a "no-growth" or "steady-state" global society. If you program the computer for *The Limits to Growth* to say you can't win, it will always tell you that you can't win, no matter what happens in the real world. This model was adopted by many mainstream American environmental groups as an intellectual basis for meat-axe ban-all-growth policy, particularly the litigating groups such as the Natural Resources Defense Council, the Environmental Defense Fund, and the Sierra Club.

The Club of Rome's meat-axe model of world growth prevailed into a period of major setbacks that demoralized the international community. During the mid-1980s, a debt crisis threatened global economic security, economic growth was absent or feeble in large regions of the world, economic growth failed to resurge following the decline in world oil prices contrary to economists' confident predictions, and the world's greatest creditor nation, the United States, almost overnight became the world's largest debtor. Developing countries became net exporters of capital. Military expenditures grew apace, along with protectionism. The happy multilateralism of the 1960s was in retreat.

The Brundtland Report

The next major shift in world environmental models came on April 27, 1987, when the United Nations World Commission on Environment and Development released its report, *Our Common Future*, signed by eminent commissioners from 21 countries.[19] The commission, headed by Gro Harlem Brundtland, prime minister of Norway, tacitly acknowledged that the previous world model had been a version of the old hacker chestnut, "Garbage In, Garbage Out," and politely rejected the Club of Rome's no growth scenario for the garbage it was. The Brundtland Report, as it became known, advocated growth. Indeed, said the commission, growth is an urgent necessity if poverty is to be reduced and environmental impacts curtailed:

It is impossible to separate economic development issues from environmental issues; many forms of development erode the environmental resources upon with they must be based, and environmental degradation can undermine economic development. Poverty is a major cause and effect of global environmental problems. It is therefore futile to attempt to deal with environmental problems without a broader perspective that encompasses the factors underlying world poverty, and international inequality.[20]

If that reads like an eco-socialist political tract, there may be a reason: The commission's chair, Gro Harlem Brundtland, was not only the first woman to serve as prime minister of Norway, she, in the flashy argot of *Time* magazine, "is a postmodern green neosocialist philogynic philosopher-queen."[21]

Brundtland also figured prominently in the 1991 International Conference on the Future of Socialism, which tried to read the dried tea leaves clinging to the shards of the shattered Soviet empire. Their tentative conclusion was that environmentalism might be a convenient vessel in which to paddle past the debris of Karl Marx and Vladimir Lenin to the less discredited "social democracy" of revisionist Eduard Bernstein with its combination of private initiative and social reform, the sort of socialism practised in the Scandinavian countries.

Not everyone in the Brundtland commission was an eco-socialist, however. The United States delegate, William Ruckelshaus, is a well-known interventionist—and is a member of the board of directors of the World Wildlife Fund (as well as chairman of Browning-Ferris Industries, second in size only to Waste Management, Inc. in the waste disposal field).

To the Brundtland commission we owe the current buzzword, *sustainable development*. Generically, it means to develop only in a manner that does not damage future ability to develop, but that, as we shall see, is a splendidly elastic idea. As a technical concept, sustainable development can mean using resources only at the rate they can be replaced in nature, like cutting forests no faster than they grow or rotating crops so that the soil can rest and recharge without losing its fertility. As a political concept, sustainable development can mean forbidding any further use of oil because it can never be replaced in nature, or stopping the cutting of forests until every tree is mature rather than balancing the cubic volume of annual harvest with the cubic volume of annual regrowth. One way you get industrial civilization thriving forever. The other way you get Ecotopia where we preserve resources so future generations can't use them either.

The Brundtland report was so totally immersed in the interventionist and eco-socialist milieu it was unconscious of the fact that it left no room for markets and free choice as anything but a problem. The commission's report offered six types of substantive proposals, each of which is worth examining:

First was a set of diagnostics concerning the basic *sources* of environmental problems. The commission proposed that national governments and international agencies ensure that all policies, programs, and budgets support development that is economically and ecologically sustainable. The secretary-general of the United Nations was requested to provide a high-level center of leadership for the system to assess, advise, assist, and report on progress toward this goal.

Second was a recommendation to police the *effects* of environmental problems. Existing bureaucracies in environmental protection and resource management agencies should be given greater enforcement powers. The United Nations Environment Programme (UNEP) should be strengthened.

Third was *global risks*. A "Global Risks Assessment Programme" was to expand and rigorously reinforce the capacity to identify, assess, and report on risks of irreversible change to natural systems, and threats to the survival, security, and well-being of the world community. The commission recommended a new international program for cooperation among nongovernmental organizations (NGOs), scientific bodies and industry groups. NGOs include private environmental groups, which were particularly pleased with this recommendation.

Fourth, *informed choices*. The commission posed a large role for NGOs, the scientific community, and industry to actively inform the public on environmental matters. Such groups would be given "expanded rights," not specified.

Fifth, enlarging the *legal means* for change. The report devoted 22 articles to proposed new legal principles, and made suggestions for a universal declaration on environmental protection and sustainable development, and for the subsequent drafting of a new international convention "setting out the sovereign rights and reciprocal responsibilities of all states on environmental protection and sustainable development." This declaration and charter would impose new restrictions on the signatories, including an obligation to alert and inform neighboring states in the event of an accident likely to have a harmful impact on the environment.

Sixth, and last, *future investments*. The report approved World Bank efforts at reorientation of its programs toward greater environmental concern, and recommended that others follow the example.[22]

In short, the Brundtland report blamed capitalism and free markets for generating "the global problématique;" it linked the deteriorating environmental situation to global macroeconomic conditions and to the policies of the World Bank, the International Monetary Fund (IMF), and other bilateral and multilateral financial and external aid agencies.

The Brundtland report emphasized the interlocking nature of resources, environment, economy, and military expenditures, giving a nod in passing to the traditional issues of population growth, food supply and agriculture, species extinction, deforestation, soil erosion, desertification, nuclear safety, wood fuels, the greenhouse gases and climate warming, urbanization, the use of the global commons (oceans, space, Antarctica), and all the other hand-wringers—a real grab bag of gloom and doom.

The final analysis of the report stated:

> The next few decades are crucial. The time has come to break out of past patterns. Attempts to maintain social and ecological stability through old approaches to development and environmental protection will increase instability. Security must be sought through change. The Commission has noted a number of actions that must be taken to reduce risks to survival and to put future development on paths that are sustainable. Yet we are aware that such a reorientation on a continuing basis is simply beyond the reach of present decision-making structures and institutional arrangements, both national and international.[23]

Although we will hear "The next x years are crucial" as the most tiresome eco-battle cry in the pages that follow—we have heard it endlessly for the past century—this version was a call for a new world government with the power to enforce environmental law with armed officers and troops if necessary. The slogan of "sustainable development" was sufficiently vague that each segment of the environmental movement could reasonably claim that it meant whatever they wanted it to mean—it could be a justification for interventionism, eco-socialism, or outright dismantling of civilization. A respected analyst, Ian Burton, director of the International Federation of Institutes for Advanced Study in Toronto, said of the Brundtland report, "This amounts to what I would describe as a call for the reradicalization and revitalization of the environmental movement."[24]

That is exactly what happened.

Carnival in Rio

The latest model of world environmentalism arrived in June of 1992 when more than 100 heads of state and 50,000 others streamed into Rio de Janiero, Brazil for the Earth Summit, the reradicalized, revitalized environmental movement's circus of the mind. The big eco-bash was formally known as the United Nations Conference on Environment and Development, or UNCED.

After years of feverish preparations and the expenditure of vast piles of cash, the Malthusians won big at UNCED. Two formal treaties came out of the Earth Summit, one governing climate change and the other on biological diversity.

The Group of 77, which represents the Third World, tried to shift the Rio agenda toward economic development, but were outflanked by environmental groups—those pesky NGOs. However, with the help of the Vatican, the Group of 77 thwarted the U.S.-led campaign to put population control, which they saw as genocide, at the top of the agenda.

Aside from the two formal treaties, the Earth Summit participants also endorsed several nonbinding documents, including a Declaration of Principles and Agenda 21, a long laundry list of policy recommendations ranging from population control and sustainable development to the creation of new global organizational frameworks for environmentalism. Vice President Al Gore, who headed the U.S. congressional delegation to Rio, declared UNCED a "tremendous success." Gore said, "I believe deeply that substantive policy and program changes necessary to protect the Earth's environment will come more easily after the Earth Summit."

UNCED's agreement to create a "sustainable development commission within the United Nations" will function as a subsidiary of the Economic and Social Council (Esosoc) and, Gore explained, be "empowered to have hearings, to have public proceedings, and receive evidence about the behavior and policies of countries around the world in order to assess whether and to what extent they are consistent with the agreements reached at Rio."

Despite the attacks of Greenpeace denouncing the Earth Summit as a failure, Gareth Porter of the Environmental and Energy Study Institute said, "the majority of environmental groups believe that the Rio meeting was by and large a success.

"Even if the agreements adopted by the Earth Summit fall short of what is needed, they do provide institutional mechanisms and benchmarks for holding governments accountable for progress in integrating environment and development and in forging more effective North-South cooperation. Moreover, the Earth Summit itself represents a fundamental transformation of world politics. The conference raised the issue of sustainable development and environmental protection to the top of the global political-diplomatic agenda, both for governments and for people of the world."

Gus Speth of the World Resources Institute said, "This is a watershed event. The right issues are being raised. And new people are being forced to deal with these issues."

Robert Engelman, director of the Population and Environment Program of the Population Crisis Committee, said, "On the first occasion the nations of the world sat down in one place following the end of the Cold War, the topic was the preservation of the planet's natural riches, not only for all people living today but for all future generations.

"UNCED also marked the first time an international dialogue among nongovernmental organizations, and between NGOs and government delegations, was an integral aspect of a major UN conference. The U.S. government deserves credit for involving, and being willing to listen to, NGOs throughout."

If you wonder what the hell Engleman's NGO is, and you should, it's

The Population Crisis Committee (1965)
Annual budget: $4 million (1990); $3.2 million (1991)
Staff: 39 professional and clerical
Tax status: 501(c)(3)
1120 19th Street, N.W., Suite 550
Washington, D.C. 20036
Phone: (202)659-1833 FAX: (202)293-1795

This is one of those "Web of Interests" groups in the Sympathetic Constituency category that poked its nose into the environmental movement in an obviously big way during the Earth Summit. President J. Joseph Speidel says it was established "to encourage and expand those activities that promise the greatest impact on reducing world population growth."

The PCC supports projects that cannot be funded by government resources but which promise maximum impact in reducing fertility through its Special Projects Fund. It encourages governments and private organizations to adopt or increase population control programs.

This group publishes *The Population Briefing Paper* periodically to about 60,000 recipients, which covers family planning, public health, public policy, and other population issues, focusing on one topic per issue.

The Population Crisis Committee is distinctly Malthusian, supporting measures that would deny resources to the Third World that might support population growth.

The Population Constituency

Population control groups generally favor one of three major approaches to solving overpopulation: the *population rate approach*, the *development approach* or the *resource approach*.

The population rate approach is centered on lowering birth rates. The technique of choice is family planning and success is measured by contraceptive use. This approach largely ignores the influence of other factors such as natural resource availability, technical innovation or capital growth. It also tends to conflict with the traditional values of many cultures and creates serious clashes over religious beliefs, social systems and political controls.

The development approach says that development itself slows population growth by offering alternatives to childbearing for satisfaction and security. Demographers cannot explain the effect completely, but point out that industrialized nations need fewer children in the urban work environment and that education, improved health care, and womens' rights probably influence declining birth rates in North America and Western Europe. However, observations in nations which have strict anti-contraception laws such as the Muslim countries have shown there is no drop in population growth rates with development.

The resource approach says that if a population cannot be sustained without depleting the resource base and degrading the environment, an area is overpopulated. The model employed in this approach was developed by Paul and Anne Ehrlich and is stated: Environmental impact = Population x Affluence x Technology. The solution to overpopulation is to cut off the production of information, resources, technology and medicine by restricting them politically. The standard is protecting the environment, not improving human life. People, well-being and technology are bad by implicit definition in the Ehrlich model. The only way to reach the ideal of zero environmental impact is zero population, zero affluence and zero technology.

Of the three approaches, the resource approach is most Malthusian and a prime candidate for human rights abuses.

Many single-issue population control groups enter the environmental movement's venues. All of us have heard of **Zero Population Growth** ($1.6 million annual budget) which espouses Malthusian solutions (see profile on pages 584-587). Believe it or not, there is actually a group called **Negative Population Growth** in Teaneck, New Jersey, with an annual budget of $250,000. Major Washington, D.C.-based outfits include the **Center on Population Options** with $2,046,505 in 1990; the **Centre for Development and Population Activities** with $3,315,263; the **Population Institute** with $1,325,597; the **Population Reference Bureau** with $2,998,771; the **Population Resource Center** with $1,114,000; **National Abortion Rights Action League** with $2,662,403; **Population-Environment Balance** with $650,000 a year to lobby against "the adverse effect of population;" the **Pathfinder Fund** in Watertown, Massachusetts with $14,682,750. Major New York City groups include the **International Women's Health Coalition** with $1,600,000; the **Global Committee of Parliamentarians on Population Growth and Development** with $1,200,000; the **Alan Guttmacher Institute** with $4 million; and the biggie of the Malthusians, the **Population Council**, with an annual budget of $40 million.

Then, of course, there's **Planned Parenthood** with $383 million a year and 8,855 staffers. You may not think Planned Parenthood is an environmental group, but its leaders do: As long ago as 1970, Planned Parenthood in conjunction with the Ecology Center of Berkeley, California, published *Grass Roots— Directory of Environmental Conservation Organizations* and has actively participated in Earth Day events since.

Friends of the Earth's *Environmental Handbook* contains a section titled "Suggestions Toward an Ecological Platform" that reads like a Planned Parenthood brochure: "Stabilizing the U.S. population should be declared a national policy. Immediate steps should be taken to:

1) Legalize voluntary abortion and sterilization and provide these services free.

2) Remove all restrictions on the provision of birth control information and devices; provide these services free to all, including minors.

3) Make sex education available at all appropriate levels, stressing birth control practices and the need to stabilize the population.

4) Launch a government-sponsored campaign for population control in the media comparable to the present antismoking campaign.

5) Offer annual bonuses for couples remaining childless and eliminate tax deductions for more than two children."[25]

Garrett De Bell, who edited *The Environmental Handbook* for Friends of the Earth, is now an environmental consultant hired in June 1990 by movie giant MCA/Universal to inject ecological themes into the movies and television.[26]

The population control constituency is a substantial part of the environmental movement's web of interests.

The leaders of the World Wildlife Fund have taken part in all of the above global conferences, either as representatives or behind-the-scenes funding and policy sources. The Malthusian leaning of WWF has been made clear on numerous occasions, among the most memorable of which was the following quotation by international WWF President Prince Philip of the United Kingdom in *People* magazine:

> Human population growth is probably the single most serious long-term threat to survival. We're in for a major disaster if it isn't curbed....I was in Sri Lanka recently, where a United Nations project set out in the late 1940s to eradicate malaria. It's an island and it was therefore possible to destroy the mosquito carrying the disease. What people didn't realize was that malaria

was actually controlling the growth of the population. The consequence was that within about 20 years the population doubled.[27]

Debt For More Debt Swaps

The World Wildlife Fund-United States makes its own foreign policy, the key instrument of which is the debt-for-nature swap. The concept of "debt-for-nature" swaps was coined by Thomas E. Lovejoy III in an October 1984 *New York Times* opinion piece to "solve global environmental ills," particularly in the Third World.[28]

Lovejoy at the time was vice president for science of the World Wildlife Fund-U.S. (1973-1987), but then became assistant secretary for external affairs of the Smithsonian Institution. He received his B.S. and Ph.D. in biology from Yale (where else?). Lovejoy is president of the Society for Conservation Biology and chairman of the U.S. Man and Biosphere Program. He founded the public television series, *Nature* and served a year as Clinton administration Interior Department science advisor.

Debt-for-nature swaps, in Lovejoy's own words, "capitalize on the discount at which debt of many nations sells on the secondary market. One of the first such swaps involved purchase at 35 cents on the dollar of sovereign debt of Ecuador by two U.S. conservation organizations, the World Wildlife Fund and the Nature Conservancy. In a process prearranged by Fundacion Natura, an environmental group founded in Ecuador [in 1978], the debt was then donated to that foundation. Fundacion Natura in turn took it to the Central Bank for conversion to bonds at face value in local currency. The income was and is used for protection of national parks and reserves, environmental education and related activities."[29]

Read Lovejoy's words again if it sounds like a scam. It is. It is a direct imitation of a practice invented by sophisticated entrepreneurs to buy foreign debt on the secondary market at a deep discount—but not so deep that it would lose the leverage required to convince the debtor nation to swap the debt instrument, convert it to cash in local currency at face value, *and use it for economically beneficial developments such as factory construction*. These secondary-market swaps were originally meant for things the country wanted in the first place, but couldn't afford. Billions upon billions of dollars of debt have been converted in this fashion for commercial purposes. It is a cheap way for developing countries to reduce their foreign debt by internalizing the note (but not eliminating it). It reduces a nation's daily outflow of hard currency in interest payments, which helps stabilize internal inflation. It makes the country more creditworthy on world debt markets while recycling funds to use for development a second time.

Lovejoy knew a good thing when he saw it. He realized that a sufficiently rich and influential environmental organization could enter the secondary market and compete for the sovereign debt of developing nations—and take the secondary debt market away from economic development. He also realized that a link-up between such a rich and influential American organization and a private environmental organization in the debtor nation could exert sufficient leverage to persuade local politicians and central bank officials to put vast areas of their country off limits to development in national parks and other nature reserves, with the payoff being a rise in the prices of the remaining land and resources.

By creating artificial scarcity in land and the resources it contains, you drive up the price of the residual land and the resources it contains. And if some rich Norteamericano sees fit to develop a luxury resort near your remote national park and pay for the roads to get to it, why, then, you might even develop a little Rockefeller-style economic activity, too. Such malice may be of low stature, but it has very long arms.

Lovejoy also saw that the secondary debt market offered a sophisticated way for American environmental groups to fund—and control—their counterparts around the world. Once in place, the debt-for-nature swap gave the American environmental organization a legally beholden counterpart in another nation, a counterpart which could not refuse to help impose some favorite interventionist or eco-socialist economic model on the developing nation and hamper the growth of a market economy. To date, at least nine nations have been leveraged into executing debt-for-nature swaps: Bolivia, Brazil, Costa Rica, Ecuador, Philippines, Dominican Republic, Madagascar, Poland, and Zambia.

What really happens in one of Dr. Lovejoy's debt-for-nature swaps? Here are the actual steps of a specific swap, with the concrete people and events in place.

Step One: An environmental group, i.e., the World Wildlife Fund, identifies or helps to create a private environmental group, i.e., the already-existing Fundacion Natura, in some foreign country where it seeks to impose the American model of interventionism or eco-socialism, i.e., Ecuador. (In this case, The Nature Conservancy acted in concert with WWF to perform a single swap with Fundacion Natura.) In early 1987 the World Wildlife Fund, with its extensive Rockefeller connections, makes contact with old friend Roque Sevilla Larrea, director of Fundacion Natura, and explains to him Dr. Lovejoy's idea of debt-for-nature swaps. Señor Sevilla is enthralled, and, using his own extensive political connections along with the Rockefeller influence, goes to the Monetary Board of the Republic of Ecuador and gets the agreement of the Ecuadoran government to cooperate "in the exchange of indebtedness up to U.S. $10 million, into monetary stabilization bonds denominated in *sucres*, the interest on which will be devoted exclusively to financing Fundacion Natura's activities."[30]

Step Two: William K. Reilly of the merging Conservation Foundation/World Wildlife Fund sends one of his officers to the commercial bank which holds the Ecuadoran note on a loan in the amount of $9 million. They negotiate an agreeable discount rate at which the bank is willing to sell the note for cash, which Dr. Lovejoy says was 35 cents on the dollar. A Spanish-language article by Fundacion Natura's Señor Sevilla tagged the discount rate at 15 cents on the dollar, not 35 cents on the dollar as quoted by the *New York Times*.[31]

Step Three: Then Reilly sends an officer to an American philanthropic foundation with compatible international goals, i.e., the John D. and Catherine T. MacArthur Foundation in Illinois, and asks Murray Gell-Mann, their board member in charge of environmental grants, to provide all or part of the cash for a debt-for-nature swap set to close in 1989. Dr. Gell-Mann, a Nobel Prize-winning physicist, agrees and arranges a series of grants that will help fund the project. The merged Conservation Foundation / World Wildlife Fund receives a MacArthur Foundation grant in the amount of $735,000 "for a program linking conservation and sustainable development in seven priority areas in Colombia, Peru and Ecuador," scheduled for 1989.

Simultaneously, Frank Boren, head of the Nature Conservancy, has his staff request a MacArthur Foundation grant, and receives one also scheduled for 1989 in the amount of $375,000, publicly announced as assistance for "the Parks in Peril program in seven high priority national parks in Bolivia, Colombia, Ecuador and Peru."

Other philanthropies were approached by TNC and WWF to help with this debt-for-nature swap. The Compton Foundation—funded by an heir of the Ralston Purina fortune—gave $50,000 in 1989 for TNC's Latin American Division. The German Marshall Fund of the United States gave WWF $37,500 in 1989 "for a conference in Europe on approaches linking Third World debt relief to conservation." W. Alton Jones Foundation, Inc. (based on oil money) gave WWF $990,000 in 1989 "for Indonesia, Madagascar and Latin America environmental program." Charles Stewart Mott Foundation (General Motors money) gave WWF $50,000 in 1990 "for program of small seed grants to grassroots nongovernmental conservation organizations in Latin America and Caribbean." The Mildred Andrews Fund gave TNC $10,000,000 in 1989 for general support—ten million bucks would sop up any little pools of uncovered debt left lying around.

Step Four: The Nature Conservancy, the World Wildlife Fund and Fundacion Natura formalize their agreement on December 14, 1987 that the two American organizations will absorb $9 million of Ecuador's foreign debt to the commercial bank and give it to the Ecuadorian environmental group. Fundacion Natura has obtained the agreement of the Junta Monetaria (Monetary Board) through Resolution No. JM-259-FN on October 8, 1987 to exchange Ecuador's indebtedness. The Nature Conservancy and World Wildlife Fund buy the $9 million of Ecuador's debt from the commercial bank for 15 cents on the dollar, an amount more consistent with the agreement document than Dr. Lovejoy's statement of 35 cents on the dollar. That's almost $1.5 million for $9 million worth of debt. The World Wildlife Fund's share of the principal amount was $1 million, according to the agreement document, with the Nature Conservancy paying the rest—both groups having raised the funds from foundation grants, mostly from the MacArthur Foundation. When the World Wildlife Fund draws diagrams of this process, they insert pictures of happy grassroots U.S. families to indicate where the money came from, a cheerful illusion.

Step Five: The two American environmental groups then donate the debt instrument to Fundacion Natura.

Step Six: Señor Sevilla takes the note, which is now legally the property of his foundation, to the Central Bank of Ecuador, which redeems it, as prearranged, in local currency at 100 cents on the dollar, i.e. $9 million worth of *sucres*.

Step Seven: But Fundacion Natura does not get the $9 million worth of *sucres*. Instead, the Central Bank converts the redeemed note to interest-bearing government monetary stabilization bonds in that same amount, $9 million worth of *sucres*. The bonds are amortized over eight years, the same as external debt, with the interest rate adjusted semiannually. The agreement document states, "The Bonds will be delivered to Fundacion Natura, which shall be entitled to receive all payments of principal and interest thereon in accordance with the terms of the Bonds."

Step Eight: Sevilla's group, now endowed with the income and principal from $9 million worth of local currency, uses the money to:

1) Design boundaries, develop management plans, and perform nature interpretation and environmental education—in short, tell other people what to do;

2) Buy nature reserves; and

3) Train "a cadre of Ecuadorian conservationists through the organization of in-country workshops, field courses and related activities," according to the agreement document.

The interest payable on the bonds for the first year was dedicated to seven directing-buying-training projects specified by the World Wildlife Fund: Cayambe-Coca Ecological Reserve, Cotacachi-Cayapas Ecological Reserve, Sangay National Park, Podocarpus National Park, Cuyabeno Wildlife Reserve, Yasuni National Park, and Galapagos National Park.

Interest in later years was committed to projects determined by Fundacion Natura—but only if approved by the World Wildlife Fund-U.S., based on progress reports. Principal paid on the bonds was committed to "establish an endowment fund in support of Fundacion Natura's general activities," according to the agreement document. The swap was completed in August of 1989.

In other words, Ecuador paid Fundacion Natura to buy up or politically tie up about 5 million acres of land in the Andean and Amazonian regions of Ecuador so it can never be developed—just like the Nature Conservancy does in the United States—and to generate environmentalist propaganda for Ecuadoran consumption.[32]

That's what a debt-for-nature swap *really* looks like.

What did everybody get out of it?

The U.S. commercial bank got hard currency for a problematic or uncollectible loan through a normal transaction on the secondary market and took the appropriate write-off.

The debtor nation liquidated some of its foreign debt, which increased its creditworthiness on the international debt market, but had to internalize the face value of the foreign debt through Central Bank bonds in local currency, which conserves the nation's hard currency funds which must be used to pay foreign debt.

The philanthropies asserted their control and got a client with popular projects that fit their international ideological goals.

The two American environmental groups got multiple benefits: They wrote successful grants to big philanthropies, they fulfilled their members' expectations of "protecting nature" with innovative programs, they placed a foreign environmental group under contractual legal obligation to do things their way, they set up a power network in a foreign country upon which to base future activities.

The foreign environmental group got an endowment plus a network upon which to base future activities plus a political commitment from its government to allocate various public resources to the group's political will plus the public relations perception that their activities were generating economic productivity, e.g., national parks and tourism.

The U.S. Internal Revenue Service allows a charitable deduction equal to the value of local currency received in such an exchange. The debt-for-nature swap is an extremely sophisticated way to build the environmental movement into a worldwide force for interventionism or eco-socialism. Environmental imperialism at work.

In October of 1989, the government of Ecuador authorized a new exchange of up to $50 million in sovereign debt for social, cultural and environmental purposes.

What debt-for-nature swaps do to national sovereignty is soft-pedaled. The non-profit sector—the so-called "Third Sector," third after the private sector and the government sector—of most developing countries is very small. In the United States it comprises more than ten percent of all economic activity and can drive national policy in substantial ways. By increasing the political clout of "Third Sector" groups in various foreign countries through debt-for-nature swaps that enrich and empower cooperating private non-profit foundations—NGOs (Non-Government Organizations)—the American environmental movement can effectively work to impose its interventionist and eco-socialist policies over a significant part of the world.

The U. S. World Wildlife Fund was instrumental in getting debt-for-nature swaps in Costa Rica,[33] Ecuador,[34] Mexico,[35] Brazil,[36] and many other nations. They have tried to push eco-tourism by pointing out that nature tourists to poor countries where WWF wants to stop development are richer, stay longer, and spend more money—scant consolation for trashing the commodity economy.[37] Tourist industry jobs typically pay less than half the wages of a commodity-related job and you can't eat, wear or build houses out of tourists—at least not legally.

The trashing of the world economy by the WWF is coming under closer scrutiny now, with even world commentators issuing words of caution.[38] However, WWF operates according to a sophisticated and highly self-conscious strategic plan that calls for a systematic trashing of the world economy, quietly, incrementally, lethally—and World Wildlife Fund-U.S. has something called a Country Plan for all its target nations. Even planning experts have commented on the organization's skill in the field.[39]

The Bush administration went so far as to include debt for nature as an integral part of its Latin American Initiative on debt and trade. Once certain economic conditions are met, the United States will engage in major debt-for-nature swaps with bilateral debt. Dollar obligations will be converted into local-currency environmental trusts. However, the Bush administration did not follow the World Wildlife Fund model of giving the debt instrument to an existing private environmental group in the foreign nation.

Instead, it set tough conditions before environmental trusts can be created. These conditions are: an IMF agreement; a World Bank structural adjustment loan; if necessary, reform toward an open investment regime; and a satisfactory agreement with commercial bank creditors. However, there is no specific legislation to prevent the environmental trust from being or becoming a private environmental organization such as the World Wildlife Fund. And, the trusts are rigged to *exclude* sustainable development such as ecologically sound mining with landscape restoration, petroleum production using slant drilling to reach beneath a sensitive area without entering it, low-input farming and ranching, visitor accommodation construction and road-building so tourists can get to natural sites.

Before we go on to the operational details of the World Wildlife Fund-U.S., it behooves us to consider the originator of the debt-for-nature swap concept and what he's doing now.

The Smithsonian Institution

Most people think of the Smithsonian as a museum in Washington, D.C. Indeed, from its 135-year-old "castle" on the Mall, the Smithsonian Institution operates the world's largest complex of museums and research institutes, including 15 museums and galleries, the National Zoological Park and research facilities in 8 states and the Republic of Panama.

But the Smithsonian is much more than a keeper of artifacts and specimens. Funded by the U.S. government and by private sources, it has also become an immensely powerful environmental organization, but one we never think of as such. A good part of the reason is Dr. Thomas E. Lovejoy III.

Dr. Lovejoy is a Yale-trained tropical biologist who serves as the Smithsonian's Assistant Secretary. He has not only involved the Smithsonian in his brainchild, the debt-for-nature swap, but has also turned the venerable institution into a center of rabid anti-industry propaganda. His victories include a huge media bash sponsored by the Smithsonian Institution in September 1989 titled, "Global Environment: Are We Overreacting?" (see the Media chapter).

Consider Dr. Lovejoy's masterwork, the Smithsonian Rainforest Project. The fundraising blurbs for this Economy Trasher project treat all human activity as destruction. They begin with the usual headlines: "In the next ten minutes 800 acres of the world's tropical rainforest with perish. Every second one and a third acres of tropical rainforest falls to man's blade or fire."

Then the body copy tells a horrifying tale: "Economic and social pressures have often moved developing nations in Asia, Africa and Latin America, and their international business partners, to treat rainforests as jungle barriers to progress. They clear for crop farming, cattle ranching, logging and resettlement."

People respond by sending money to the Smithsonian in carloads.

Stop and think about that a minute. Dr. Lovejoy has said the greatest horror we can commit in a tropical rainforest is crop farming, cattle ranching, logging and human settlement. The respected Smithsonian Institution has told us *it is a ruination that needs the redemption of our contributions* for our fellow humans to raise food to feed themselves, to grow fiber to clothe themselves, to make lumber to shelter themselves and to own land they can call home, their own.

What has happened here? A fundraising blurb has just pried money out of our pockets with a sales pitch that says providing food, clothing, shelter and a place to live is "destruction." We just gave fifty bucks to an outfit for complaining against farmers, ranchers, loggers, and home-dwellers. We just donated cash to an American environmental group that will use our money to go into every developing nation and gain control of its local environmental groups to stop all farming, stop all ranching, stop all logging, and stop all dwelling. When the Smithsonian is done, those nations won't be developing any more. What the hell is going on here? Have we lost our marbles?

That ought to be a no-brainer, but our fellow citizens cannot see the logical equivalency in the Smithsonian's impassioned plea. Go to the library and examine a few recent issues of *Smithsonian* magazine. Look for other evidences of this low-life anti-human bias. See if you aren't burned at the environmentalist propaganda being paid for by the U.S. government.

Back to the World Wildlife Fund-U.S.

Public Interest Profiles, contrary to *Philanthropy*, as quoted at the beginning of this profile, says of WWF-U.S. funding: dues provide 62 percent of all funding sources; the federal government, 10 percent; big industry , 2 percent; foundations, 10 percent; WWF's investment portfolio, sales of products, and individual contributions yield them the balance of their total budget. WWF puts out two newsletters, *Focus*, a bimonthly, and *TRAFFIC (U.S.A.)*, a quarterly.

WWF also puts out fund-raising mailings by the ton. A recent one warned that "The powerful oil and development lobbies have targeted America's wetlands as their next environmental victim." Environmentalist fund-raiser mailings are not known for their strict adherence to fact. What really happened in this case was that they were responding to a move by President George Bush, who announced revisions in the regulations aimed at establishing general building permits for wetlands of low ecological value while preserving areas typically regarded as true wetlands—marshes, swamps, and bogs. But the World Wildlife Fund is no friend of private property rights, so they set out on a campaign of lies and distortions to hide the real impact of the Wetlands Regulations.

It was the Conservation Foundation/World Wildlife Fund under William Kane Reilly that had pressured George Bush into his 1988 campaign pledge of "no net loss" of the nation's wetlands. It was the Conservation Foundation/World Wildlife Fund under William Kane Reilly that in 1988 convened representatives of environmental groups, government, and industry to implement the President's campaign pledge. This unofficial panel's recommendations for controlling floods, preserving water quality, and supporting a range of wildlife were incorporated—without public hearings or comments—into the 1989 *Federal Manual for Identifying and Delineating Jurisdictional Wetlands*, used by the U.S. Army Corps of Engineers and other agencies in deciding whether permits should be issued to private land owners who wish to build on or otherwise alter their land. Yes, that procedure was illegal—a violation of several Government In The Sunshine laws requiring public notice in the Federal Register and allowing for public participation—but what the heck, laws are just laws, and this is *the environment* were talking about. The Conservation Foundation's recommendations became the law. And what a law.

When the revised manual took effect, it became painfully evident that "wetlands" had been defined so broadly that it gave the Army Corps, the EPA (which became Reilly's personal fiefdom), and other federal agencies vastly expanded jurisdiction. Wetlands no longer had to be wet. Now they only had to support vegetation that needed water! Or had to be covered by standing water for more than 7 consecutive days in a year. Or just have "moist soils." By the new improved elastic definition, your home surroundings are likely a wetland because of standing water, so is the Arizona desert because flash floods cause "moist soils" that linger under rocks for a week, and so is the top of the Empire State Building because mosses of a type found in wetlands grow up there in the Art-Deco crevices.

I don't think we're in Kansas anymore, Toto. We just entered Eco-Oz—but this Oz is backed up by federal marshals with big guns who will put you in jail, take your property rights away from you and not pay you a penny's worth of "just compensation."

Under the new manual, the number of privately owned wetlands in Maryland instantly rose from an estimated 275,000 to 1 million acres—40 percent of the state's Eastern Shore—half of Vermont became "wetlands;" half of all farmland and 70 percent of all land in the United States fell under the Army Corps' jurisdiction. The Conservation Foundation, with an unofficial and illegally inserted set of recommendations, managed to threaten three-quarters of all private property in the nation.

Thousands of developers and private property owners experienced long delays in getting building permits, disastrously increased housing costs, and severe devaluations of their properties.

That was why President Bush announced his revisions in the regulations. President Bush's revisions were the reason the World Wildlife Fund cut all those trees to make the paper to put out its huge fund-raising mailing warning its members about the oil and development lobbies targeting wetlands—but, of course, it did not warn its own members that the WWF had targeted *their* private property rights. The WWF tried everything to misdirect the public's attention from the stupidity of their regulations, even wringing their hands that horrible floods would result from a definition saying that wetlands had to be wet.[40]

After President Bush sounded his note of caution, the World Wildlife Fund quickly released a lengthy study defending the 1989 manual. WWF did its level best to prevent property owners from having any effect on the manual. "Only certain kinds of evidence [for identifying wetlands] would be considered adequate, and no other evidence could be used," said the WWF study. "The proposed revisions [by President Bush] would further impose on the government agencies the burden of finding or producing this evidence." How worried the WWF is about burdens that might fall on government. How careful the WWF is about putting all burdens on the private property owner.

Of the 40 scientists who prepared the World Wildlife Fund's study, 13 are past or present employees of the Environmental Defense Fund, the National Audubon Society, the Nature Conservancy, the Wilderness Society, and the Coalition to Restore Louisiana Wetlands. Another 19 work or have worked for the Army Corps, the EPA, the Fish & Wildlife Service, and other federal and state agencies. The study was as biased as a flat tire, done by scientists bought and paid for by environmentalist organizations protecting their own incomes on the back of private property owners. The study was funded by the Mary Flagler Cary Charitable Trust (remember the Nature Conservancy's first funding for the Virginia Coastal Reserve), Gaylord Donnelley, and the Elizabeth Ordway Dunn, John D. and Catherine T. MacArthur, Richard King Mellon, and Curtis and Edith Munson Foundations.

The World Wildlife Fund's program to stop development using the endangered species act caused such a public backlash that the organization had to hastily assemble a "report" claiming that only 19 out of 75,000 projects were actually killed—which totally ignored the thousands of projects that were delayed at such expense they died of attrition and were not listed.[41]

Fundraising Tactics

Interesting aspects of the WWF's fundraising include licensing the use of its panda logo to manufacturers of cookie jars,[42] socks,[43] children's fashions,[44] a line of jewelry and neckties under the WWF label,[45] and the use of charity auctions—one jewelry manufacturer raised $411,000 in 1991.[46] Exploiting the name of the World Wildlife Fund has become big business.[47] *Animals' Agenda* even accused WWF of selling out by forging links with corporations guilty of environmental offenses.[48] To balance things, The Direct Marketing Association gave its prestigious Echo Award to the World Wildlife Fund in 1990 for one of the year's most imaginative and effective junk telegram campaigns,[49] and the year earlier gave WWF its Echo Award for a "save-the-rain-forest" junk telephone call campaign,[50] and a year earlier a Bronze Echo Award for junk mail fund raising (on the horrors of the animal skin trade).[51] The World Wildlife Fund is expert in junk mail, junk calls, and junk cables.

The World Wildlife Fund's Board of Directors is made up of chairman Russell E. Train; cochairmen Lawrence S. Huntington and Melvin B. Lane; executive committee members include president Kathryn S. Fuller; treasurer Hunter Lewis; secretary Anne P. Sidamon-Eristoff; and executive committee members William T. Lake, George H. Taber, William H. Whyte, and Edward O. Wilson. Train's vice president Doug Wheeler was named California's director of natural resources in 1991.

Douglas P. Wheeler is an excellent case in point of the fluidity of movement leadership. His current official title is Secretary for Resources, State of California. Before that he was vice president of the World Wildlife Fund, executive vice president and vice president of the Conservation Foundation, executive director of the Sierra Club, founder and president of the American Farmland Trust, executive vice president of the **National Trust for Historic Preservation**, Deputy Assistant Secretary of the Interior, and the legislative counsel and legislative attorney for the Department of the Interior. Out of government, into the environmental movement, back into government.

Rockefeller protégés and Reilly colleagues are *everywhere* in the land control business.

Other board members include: Anne T. Bass, Edward P. Bass, Joseph F. Cullman III, Raymond F. Dassmann, Marshall Field IV, Caroline M. Getty, Lena Guerrero, Frances C. James, Thomas H. Kean, Richard D. Lamm, H. Eugene McBrayer, Scott McVay, Adrienne B. Mars, Cruz A. Matos, Gilman Ordway, Arthur Ortenberg, Julie Packard, William D. Ruckelshaus, Gerald E. Rupp, Oscar Arias Sanchez, Lloyd G. Schermer, Helen B. Spaulding, Rodney B. Wagner, Susan M. Williams, and Rosemary M. Young. Laurance S. Rockefeller served on this board for many years. Recognize any of those names? You could play American Elite Trivial Pursuit for hours connecting that list to money and positions of power.

Program spending was 88.4 percent of income; fund raising was 8 percent of income; administration was 3.4 percent of income (all in 1991). The Fund maintains a library of 10,000 volumes and 400 journal subscriptions on the environment run by Barbara K. Rodes, research librarian.

The Conservation Foundation / World Wildlife Fund in their merger year 1989/90 received funding from Cummins Engine ($15,000), General Electric ($25,000), Heinz ($15,000), Procter & Gamble ($12,000), and Waste Management ($50,000 or more, the record is unclear). After the merger, the World Wildlife Fund received funding from Chevron ($50,000) and Exxon ($85,000).

The following accounting tabulates grants made to both the Conservation Foundation and the World Wildlife Fund since they merged in 1989/90, the years for which the most recent non-profit tax returns are available.

The ARCO Foundation gave CF $35,000 in 1989 for "conflict resolution programs," and another $10,000 in 1989 for "Greenways for America program in Texas and California."

The AT&T Foundation gave CF $10,000 in 1989.

The Champlin Foundations gave CF $200,000 in 1989 "toward purchase of lots to be used for affordable housing for essential persons on Clock Island as part of Successful Communities Program. Grant shared with Block Island Community Development Corporation."

Geraldine R. Dodge Foundation, Inc. gave CF $50,000 in 1989 "for second-year funding of Successful Communities growth management program in New Jersey, with major focus on Clinton Township; technical assistance includes development of model ordinances, land trusts and master planning to retain open space, historic buildings, scenic views, agricultural land and other valued features."

Ford Foundation gave WWF $56,200 in 1990 "to assist community managed nature reserve in Irian Jaya."

Ford Motor Company Fund gave WWF $10,000 in 1990 "for Eastern European environment."

General Electric Foundation gave CF $25,000 in 1989.

The Wallace Alexander Gerbode Foundation gave WWF $65,000 in 1989.

German Marshall Fund of the United States gave WWF $37,500 in 1989 "for conference in Europe on approaches linking Third World debt relief to conservation. Grant shared with Conservation Foundation."

The Ann and Gordon Getty Foundation gave WWF $65,000 in 1989.

H. J. Heinz Company Foundation gave CF $15,000 in 1989.

W. Alton Jones Foundation, Inc. gave WWF $990,000 in 1989 "for Indonesia, Madagascar and Latin America environmental program."

The John T. and Catherine D. MacArthur Foundation gave WWF $735,000 in 1989 "for program linking conservation and sustainable development in seven priority areas in Colombia, Peru and Ecuador;" and another $530,000 in 1989 "for planning of new biosphere reserves, training of local leaders, environmental education, development of new Institute of Natural History and support of state and federal natural resource use planning in Oaxaca."

The Richard King Mellon Foundation gave CF $50,000 in 1989 "toward National Celebration of the Outdoors."

Joyce Mertz-Gilmore Foundation gave CF $20,000 in 1989 for general support; another $20,000 for "Global Change and Biological Diversity Project that will produce educational materials about effects of warming on wild plants and animals for conservationists."

Mobil Foundation, Inc., gave WWF-U.S. $10,000 in 1989.

Charles Stewart Mott Foundation gave WWF $50,000 in 1990 "for program of small seed grants to grassroots nongovernmental conservation organizations in Latin America and Caribbean."

New York Times Company Foundation.

The David and Lucille Packard Foundation gave CF $30,000 in 1990 "for advancing wetlands policy implementation."

Howard Phipps Foundation gave CF $50,000 in 1989; $50,000 to WWF in 1989.

Prince Charitable Trusts gave CF $25,000 in 1989 for project support; another $20,000 in 1989 for Aquidneck 2000 Plan.

The Procter & Gamble Fund gave CF $12,000 in 1990.

Rockefeller Brothers Fund gave WWF $35,000 in 1990 for Eastern European Environmental Program, to help strengthen management of environmental institutions in region, to promote technology transfer and environmentally sound foreign investment, and to build support in U.S. for such endeavors.

The Florence and John Schumann Foundation gave CF $200,000 in 1989, a 3-year grant for efforts to advance national wetlands policy.

The Schumann Fund for New Jersey, Inc. gave CF $75,000 in 1989, a 3-year grant for Clinton Township Project of Successful Communities Program.

Shell Oil Company Foundation gave CF $15,000 in 1989.

The Times Mirror Foundation gave WWF $15,000 in 1989 for annual support.

The Weyerhaeuser Foundation gave CF $10,000 in 1989.

World Wildlife Fund. The Smithsonian Institution.

Job killers.

Economy trashers.

World Wildlife Fund—Footnotes

1 *Animals' Agenda*, May 1989.

2 *Research Centers Directory*, 17th Edition-1993, entry number 2215.

3 *Philanthropy*, the Philanthropic Roundtable, March/April 1990.

4 "Buying In," by Eve Pell, *Mother Jones*, April / May 1990, p. 23.

5 "Saving the Earth From Its Friends," David Brooks, *National Review*, April 1, 1990.

6 "'Wetlands' Sends Man Up the River," by Richard Miniter, *Insight*, November 29, 1992, p. 7.

7 *The Use of Land: A Citizen's Policy Guide to Urban Growth*, William K. Reilly, editor, A Task Force Report Sponsored by the Rockefeller Brothers Fund, New York, Thomas Y. Crowell, 1973, p. 7.

8 *In These Times*, January 18-24, 1989.

9 *Industry Week*, March 19, 1990.

10 *In These Times*, January 18-24, 1989.

11 See, for example, "Why the Privatization Movement Failed," by Robert H. Nelson, *Regulation*, July/August 1984.

12 "Property Rights: The Debate is Joined," *Organization Trends*, Washington, D.C., March 1992.

13 *The Age of the Moguls*, Stewart H. Holbrook, Doubleday & Company, Garden City, N.Y., 1956, p. 8ff.

14 "Throwing Away the Key," by Dan Gifford, *Voice*, December 11, 1990, p. 25.

15 "From Fringe To Political Mainstream," by Michael Weiskopf, *Washington Post*, April 19, 1990, p. A1.

16 "Fuller to head conservation organizations," by Stephen H. Wyman, *Washington Post*, February 20, 1989, p. B9.

17 *Partners in Development*, Lester B. Pearson, Praeger, New York, 1969.

18 *The Limits to Growth*, Donella H. Meadows, Dennis L. Meadows, Jørgen Randers, and William W. Behrens III, Universe Books, New York, 1972.

19 Nations signing: Algeria, Brazil, Canada, Colombia, Côte d'Ivoire, Federal Republic of Germany, Guyana, Hungary, India, Indonesia, Italy, Japan, Nigeria, Norway, People's Republic of China, Saudi Arabia, Sudan, United States, USSR, Yugoslavia, and Zimbabwe. William D. Ruckelshaus was the commissioner for the United States.

20 *Our Common Future*, World Commission on Environmental and Development, Oxford University Press, Oxford and New York, 1987.

21 "Norway's radical daughter," by Nancy Gibbs, *Time*, September 25, 1989, p. 42.

22 "Report on Reports: Our Common Future," reviewed by Ian Burton, *Environment*, June 1987, pp. 25-29.

23 *Our Common Future*, p. 22-23.

24 "Report on Reports: Our Common Future," p. 28.

25 *The Environmental Handbook*, edited by Garrett De Bell, Ballantine Books, New York, 1970, p. 318.

26 "Saving the Earth—With the Help of Film and TV Characters," by Daniel B. Wood, *Christian Science Monitor*, July 25, 1990.

27 "Environment," *People*, December 1981, p. 56.

28 "Aid Debtor Nations' Ecology," Thomas E. Lovejoy 3d, *New York Times*, October 4, 1984.

29 "Applying Third-World Debt to the Environment," by Thomas E. Lovejoy, *New York Times,* December 26, 1990, p. A25.

30 Debt-for-Nature Agreement dated December 14, 1987 between World Wildlife Fund-U.S. and Fundacion Natura. Document provided by the Smithsonian Institution, Washington, D.C.

31 "Por Que Canjear Dueda Por Naturaleza," por Ec. Roque Sevilla Larrea, Fundacion Natura, Ecuador y Dr. Alvaro Umana Quesada, Ministro de Recursos Naturales, Energia y Minas, Costa Rica.

32 "Ecuador Gets Aid for Debt, Environment," by Michael Weisskopf, *Washington Post*, April 6, 1989.

33 "More money for Costa Rica's parks," by Marjorie Sun, *Science,* March 25, 1988, p. 1482.

34 "Ecuador debt bought in swap," *New York Times,* April 6, 1989, p. C18.

35 "BankAmerica to forgive loans in deal to aid rain forests," by Martha M. Hamilton, *Washington Post,* June 12, 1991, p. C1.

36 "Bank of America to donate loans," *American Banker*, March 13, 1992, p. 6.

37 "Nature tourists in WWF survey spend more, take longer trips," by Nadine Godwin, *Travel Weekly,* February 18, 1991, p. 16.

38 "Ecology vs. economics: time to reconsider," by Ricardo Bayon, *World Press Review,* August, 1990, p. 14.

39 "Strategic planning for the World Wildlife Fund," by G. J. Medley, *Long Range Planning,* February, 1988, p. 45.

40 "Pollution, floods foreseen in wake of wetlands plan," by Rudy Abramson, *Los Angeles Times,* January 17, 1992, p. A4.

41 "Wildlife protection stops few projects, study asserts," by Tom Kenworthy, *Washington Post,* February 11, 1992, p. A19.

42 "Panda, snowy owl, penguin to grace cookie jars, magnets," by Lisa Casey Weiss, *The Weekly Home Furnishings Newspaper*, February 3, 1992, p. B2.

43 "High Point gets sock license for World Wildlife Fund," *Women's Wear Daily*, April 12, 1990, p. 8.

44 "Animal attractions: children's fashions designed by Cynthia McKinney for Harlequin support the World Wildlife Fund," *Women's Wear Daily,* February 25, 1991, p. 14.

45 "World Wildlife jewelry line is launched by Manhattan," *Daily News Record,* October 4, 1991, p. 5.

46 "Bulgari raises $411,000 for WWF," *Woman's Wear Daily,* November 22, 1991, p. 9.

47 "Wildlife charity exploits its name," by Liz Warner, *Marketing,* November 12, 1987, p. 4.

48 "Money questions for conservationists," by Merritt Clifton, *The Animals' Agenda,* November 1991, p. 36.

49 "Cabling for help," *Fund Raising Management*, December 1990, p. 20.

50 "Saving the rain forest," *Fund Raising Management,* December 1989, p. 20.

51 "Horror stories in the skin trade," *Fund Raising Management,* December 1988, p. 52.

Greenpeace

Greenpeace (Founded 1971, lobbying arm in 1987)
  Annual budget: $11,411.050 (Greenpeace Fund, Inc., (1992)
           $37,805,230 (Greenpeace, Inc., (1993);
      Staff: 250 staff members plus 20 interns (reorganized in 1992)
           Offices in 30 countries
    Members: 1.7 million members and supporters U.S. (1993),
           4.5 million worldwide
  Tax Status: Fund is (501)(c)(3) Greenpeace, Inc. is (501)(c)(4)
  Headquarters: 1436 U Street, NW
           Washington, D.C. 20009
           Phone: (202)462-1177 Fax: (202)462-4507

The Number Four Economy Trasher is very open about destroying free enterprise. "I don't believe in the market approach.... It results in treating toxics or pollution as a commodity...When companies have a bottom line of profit you won't have them thinking about the environment." So said former Greenpeace USA Executive Director Peter Bahouth (salary $53,900) in the left-wing newspaper *In These Times* in April 1990.

Anti-capitalist rhetoric shouldn't come as much of a surprise from a group reconstituted from the 1969 Don't Make a Wave Committee, a bunch of American Vietnam War draft dodgers who fled to Vancouver, British Columbia, and, with some Canadian supporters backed by American Quaker money, tried to stop U. S. nuclear tests on the Aleutian island of Amchitka with a halibut seiner renamed *Greenpeace*. Various West Coast Quaker groups gave money, including the Palo Alto Meeting of Friends and the Eugene Meeting of Friends.

Canadians were worried about possible tidal waves and earthquakes from the underground atomic blast and American Quakers had tried to stop nuclear tests twice before by sending the boats *Phoenix* and *Golden Rule* into test zones but were quickly arrested and their boats seized. However, if a Canadian boat were to sail into a test zone and stayed outside the actual territorial limit, American authorities could do nothing about it.

The Don't Make a Wave Committee had talented planners and fundraisers, for all their radicalism—but the radicalism stuck in the public's mind. As Robert Hunter wrote in his official history of the organization, one of the original patriarchs of Greenpeace was former Philadelphia lawyer Irving Stowe, "a Jew who had joined the Quaker religion" and rabid America-hater.

Stowe's reasons for leaving America were, of course, Vietnam, refusal to pay taxes that went into the war effort, anger over corruption of the political system, and "creeping fascism." He tended to let all his personal views spill out in his interviews. His public denunciations of American imperialism and atrocities were beginning to embarrass other members of the committee. There were fears that he was stirring up anti-Americanism for its own sake, not because of the specific issue of Amchitka. In fact, Irving Stowe's attacks on America were to leave such a lasting impression in Vancouver that for years afterward, Greenpeace would be viewed as a tool of Peking or the Kremlin, a reputation that was not helped much a few years later when Stowe traveled to China and came back singing its praises.[1]

When early Greenpeace radical Rod Marining said, "I'm not a Red, I'm a Green," he was not expressing tender love toward free enterprise.

The Quaker principle to "bear witness" was not enough for Greenpeace, which tries to make *everybody* bear witness—with the Greenpeace point of view, of course. Confrontation, civil disobedience, staged films of animal abuse, inflammatory lies and physical harassment are Greenpeace's methods despite its avowed adherence to Quaker principles of non-violence. It is inextricably entwined with the ecoterrorist organization, Earth First!, quietly sharing staff, activists and offices. It is definitely outside the Rockefeller Axis and the Mellon Axis. It does not overlap the big-industry-funded sportsman/greenie melange of the National Wildlife Federation in the Establishment Interventionist Axis. Regardless of its international nature, Greenpeace is too radical to be a Global Interventionist. It is not interested in promoting one business against the interests of another or using nature preserves as a magnet for profits and political clout. It simply wants all economic activity nationalized—or stopped outright—while it gets rich.

Although Greenpeace is currently losing members and making a strong bid to mainstream itself, it falls decisively in a Radical Eco-Socialist Axis along with a few other groups in the overall environmental movement. They have virtually cornered the youth market in the environmental arena. What's their secret of success?

"The secret to [Greenpeace co-founder] David McTaggart's success is the secret to Greenpeace's success: It doesn't matter what is true, it only matters what people believe is true. You are what the media define you to be. Greenpeace became a myth, and a myth-generating machine."[2]

So said Paul Watson, one of the co-founders of Greenpeace. That squib from a long 1991 article in *Forbes* magazine gives us the aromatic top-note of what Greenpeace is all about—perception is reality and the facts don't matter. As we'll see, they don't think much of the law, either.

Greenpeace was formed in 1971 in British Columbia when the original Don't Make a Wave Committee dissolved itself and its core members incorporated as the Greenpeace Foundation. The group of transferred Committee originals consisted of America-hater Irving Stowe; Jim Bohlen, an American composite-materials researcher who fled to Canada when his son reached draft age; Paul Cote, a Canadian lawyer; Terry Simmons, a cultural geographer from California; and Bill Darnell, who gave the group its name.

As Robert Hunter wrote, the story goes that at the end of a 1969 organizing meeting to find a boat for the Amchitka protest, Irving Stowe got up to go home and gave his usual V sign, saying "Peace."

The youngest member of the committee, a twenty-three-year-old Canadian named Bill Darnell, said, "Make it a *green* peace."

Everyone paused. That had a certain ring to it. Not just peace, but an ecological peace.

"That sounds good," said Jim Bohlen. "If we ever find a boat, that's what we'll call it, *Greenpeace*."[3]

The *Greenpeace*, incidentally, didn't have much luck at first. The United States cancelled the test at Amchitka during their first voyage, and the detonation occurred during their second trip while the boat was still a thousand miles away—the blast came off without a hitch, caused no tidal wave, no earthquakes, and resulted in headlines making the Greenpeace crew out as fools. But the fledgling group's skilled use of the media to stir up anti-American sentiment in Canada convinced the U.S. to stop testing in Amchitka for political reasons. They won by losing.

Bohlen and Stowe also organized the first British Columbia Chapter of the Sierra Club, investing the Canadian wing of the organization with a radicalism it had not yet learned at home.

The 1971 Greenpeace Foundation elected impulsive, individualistic, heavy-handed E. Bennett Metcalfe as chairman, a veteran Canadian Broadcasting Company freelance writer and CBC West Coast theatre critic who had once run his own public-relations firm. Other members included Robert Hunter, the *Vancouver Sun's* token hippy opinion columnist and later official historian of Greenpeace; Patrick Moore, a radical University of British Columbia student working on his Ph.D. in ecology; Paul Watson, whom Hunter described as "a muscular seaman who had knocked about the world on freighters, and who would have been a perfect candidate for the [Amchitka] voyage, except that he had North Vietnamese flags stitched to his army jacket, wore Red Power buttons, Black Power buttons, and just about any kind of antiestablishment button that could be imagined." Watson also "wrote for the underground press, and had been busted in at least a dozen demonstrations, some of them staged by the Vancouver Liberation Front." Watson in fact did none of that except write, but he was to later become a big thorn in the side of Greenpeace.[4]

The early group's biggest asset was America-bashing Irving Stowe, not for his rhetoric, but for his talent as a fundraiser and money manager. He pinched pennies, turned pennies into dollars and was incorruptible in their administration.

The last of the founders was mythically wealthy Canadian businessman and former tennis champion David McTaggart. Of the Greenpeace originals, David McTaggart and Paul Watson have in the years since been graced with something close to sainthood by avid radicals. But the myth-generating media cannot hide that Greenpeace is pushing the art of Trashing the Economy to new lengths.

To Greenpeace, pollution is a sin, not a cost of civilization, and should be outlawed, not taxed—even if that means shutting down all industry everywhere and eradicating industrial civilization totally. Eco-socialism can only arrive on foot. Greenpeace refuses to give any of its many research grants to cleaning up pollution, saying that its role is to eliminate the industrial processes that create pollution rather than clean it up. That means eliminating industries.

The base-note of the Greenpeace perfume is provided by co-founder David McTaggart and sniffs of his checkered past. McTaggart, unlike his storybook image in the Greenpeace fund-raising mailers, is not quite the successful tennis idol and real estate executive who saw the light at age 39 and decided to save the planet. In fact, *Forbes* magazine described him as "a failed real estate promoter who left investors and relatives in the lurch and departed before his projects failed." In a long article, the business magazine told how one of his customers, Bruce Orvis, a cattle rancher near Stockton, California, lost almost $3 million in a bloated scheme cooked up by McTaggart.

After beating a hasty retreat to Colorado where he rigged an even more grandiose land development project and accumulated big debts from his lavish lifestyle McTaggart ran out on his third wife, Betty Huberty (he's had four wives now) after selling her Mercedes 280SL sports car and keeping most of the proceeds—and the skunk even snitched the wedding ring he'd given her. He absconded to the South Seas in his 38-foot ketch, narrowly escaping a lawsuit for securities fraud brought by Wells Lange, charging that McTaggart bankrupted him and his brother in a $1.5 million investment by understating the project's liabilities and leading them to believe that other investors existed when they did not.

Greenpeace co-founder E. Bennett Metcalfe recruited McTaggart, who had answered a Greenpeace news release in an Auckland, New Zealand, newspaper, over the phone from Vancouver. McTaggart took $9,000 from Metcalfe to outfit his boat so it could take part in the second Greenpeace "direct action," a protest against French nuclear testing on Mururoa atoll. When Metcalfe later flew to Auckland, McTaggart not only resisted accounting for the nine grand, but had also been thrown in the slammer on a charge of smuggling Swiss watches into New Zealand on his boat. Greenpeace paid $1,000 to spring him. So much for Saint David.

McTaggart vehemently denies all of the above—from his posh Italian villa.

Metcalfe says, "I invented McTaggart, really. I often see myself as a kind of Dr. Frankenstein, who created a monster."

Greenpeace next went to confronting whaling vessels with its little high speed Jacques-Cousteau-brainchild "Zodiac" boats in daredevil exploits to destroy the whaling industry in Japan, the Soviet Union and Iceland. Soon Greenpeace and whales became synonymous. Greenpeace sought a ban against whaling with the International Whaling Commission, but couldn't muster the two-thirds majority vote. So they recruited new anti-whaling members for the IWC. How?

Bag-man Francisco Palacio says he used funds from a Greenpeace and World Wildlife Fund steering committee to provide several million dollars worth of luxury travel and accommodations to civil servants and politicians from such small Caribbean states as Belize, St. Lucia, St. Vincent, Antigua, Costa Rica and the Seychelles, nations that had not previously shown any interest in whaling. They joined the IWC, giving their proxies to Greenpeace agents whose votes succeeded in imposing a ban on whaling. When asked by Michael Klint of Danish TV-2 whether the Greenpeace money amounted to bribery, Palacio replied, "Well, you know the results. Did the new countries support the cessation of commercial whaling? Yes. It's very simple. Yes." Uta Bellion, Chairman of Greenpeace International, countered, "Greenpeace never bribed any country to join the IWC."

Greenpeace International was formed in 1979 after an acrimonious lawsuit between Greenpeace Canada and Greenpeace USA. The settlement established David McTaggart in control of the International. It now has branches in 30 countries in Asia, Australia, Europe, New Zealand, North America, South America, and Russia, with a total membership of approximately 4.5 million and income of about 150 million U.S. dollars. There are twelve voting members of the Stichting Greenpeace Council, composed of global Greenpeace affiliates, which sets all policy regarding campaign issues. It is one of the biggest multinational green industries in the world, with corporate headquarters in Amsterdam and 400 full-time employees.[5]

Greenpeace Fund, Inc. (formerly Greenpeace USA), the American tax-exempt organization, has 7 regional offices in the United States and a lobbying affiliate, Greenpeace, Inc., (formerly Greenpeace Action) with a combined income of $48,777,308.

In June 1992, Greenpeace, Inc. bought substantially all of the assets of Greenpeace Fund, Inc. and absorbed most of its staff, which had been terminated by Greenpeace Fund, with the intention "of pursuing its goals through the consideration and funding of grants to other organizations and individuals," leaving what appears to be an empty shell filled with money, $25,047,761 total assets. A recent IRS report revealed that Greenpeace Fund had $770,000 invested in certificates of deposit, $2,414,154 in U.S. Government securities, and $99,000 in municipal bonds. Total investments at the beginning of 1992 were $3,523,023.

Greenpeace Fund paid $10,300,000 to Greenpeace International in 1991, which gave back grants of $3,917,192.

In September 1991 David McTaggart resigned his $60,000 a year position as chairman of Amsterdam-based Greenpeace International, replaced first by Helsinki civil rights lawyer Matti Wouri and subsequently by staffer Uta Bellion, who had joined Greenpeace in 1986. McTaggart remains in control behind the scenes.

Fund-raising Tactics

According to Robert Bidinotto, staff writer for *Reader's Digest*, "Greenpeace has become the darling of the liberal media, and the entertainment industry's charity of choice. The cable music network VH-1 financed and is airing dozens of free commercials for the group, many narrated by Hollywood celebrities."[6]

Greenpeace Germany, second-largest branch operation after Greenpeace USA, brought in revenues for 1990 of $36 million and 700,000 members, of whom 320,000 permit Greenpeace to automatically debit their bank accounts annually for the dues of 50 Deutsche marks, about $30.[7]

While the environmental movement was still growing in the late 1980s, the eco-thug faction was growing fastest. *E, the Environmental Magazine* commented, "While total membership in U.S. environmental organizations has grown steadily from about 4 million in 1980 to about 20 million today—counting overlapping memberships—Greenpeace, the Sea Shepherds and Earth First! have grown at about five times the mainstream rate, and their support continues to skyrocket.

"Greenpeace, the fastest grower, had 240,000 U.S. donors in 1980. At last count, it had 1.5 million donors in the United States and 2.5 million worldwide."[8]

Nowadays Greenpeace and Earth First!, but not Sea Shepherds, are shrinking. To keep the money flowing, Greenpeace uses the services of high-tech professional direct mail fund-raising consultants. Craver, Mathews, Smith & Co. is the firm of choice for many environmental groups including the Sierra Club, the Natural Resources Defense Council and Greenpeace Fund. Craver, Mathews, Smith & Co. (CMS), which started in Washington, D.C., is a prominent liberal direct mail firm that has handled left-of-center candidates and organizations such as the National Organization of Women, the National Abortion Rights Action League and the American Civil Liberties Union. CMS was fired as consultant for the Democratic National Committee when they aided the Draft Kennedy committee in 1980, but was rehired in 1981. They handled John Anderson's presidential campaign in 1980, Morris Udall's presidential campaign in 1976, and have also acted as consultants for Sen. George McGovern, Sen. John Culver, and Sen. Birch Bayh.

Roger Craver—the "C" in CMS—sits on the editorial board of *Campaigns and Elections* magazine. Robert Smith—the "S" in CMS—like the other principals in his firm, worked in the Common Cause organization. Smith was also a former community organizer for New York City and other private youth groups. He has a B.A. in political science and sociology from the University of California at Berkeley.[9]

Ken Smith (no relation to Robert) came on board in 1981 and in 1982 opened a second CMS office, in Marin County, California. That office split away in late 1993 to become Dodd Smith Dann, now handling Greenpeace, Defenders of Wildlife, and the Wildlife Conservation Society, leaving CMS with the Sierra Club, the Cousteau Society and many others. William Dodd was once circulation director for *Mother Jones*, and Chris Dann came from a long career in public television.

These national consulting firms have been the real secret of success behind much of the environmental movement. They have been one of two major factors in the success of Greenpeace Fund—not the headlines and sexy mythology and David McTaggart's exploits.

The other of the two factors in Greenpeace's financial success is Ralph Nader's Citizen Action and Public Citizen, Inc., which together coordinate door-to-door canvassing for Nader groups *and for Greenpeace*—see the profile of Clean Water Action for details.

If people don't know where to send the money, headlines go into the recycling bin and sexy mythology evaporates when it's time for dinner and in most places McTaggart is just David Who? Craver, Mathews, Smith & Co. and Dodd Smith Dann tell people where to send the money.

Forty-three million times in 1990. Greenpeace USA raised $64 million that year, 60 percent of it from the 43 million direct mail packages designed by Craver, Mathews, Smith. These slick forest-gobbling mailers hew to the established verities of direct mail science: You need a bogey-man and you need a sense of urgency. Direct mail fund-raising only works when you can get people's negative emotions aroused. Direct mail gurus have known for many years that you have to play on your audience's fear, hate and desire for revenge if you want them to send money. It's the oldest rule in the direct mail fund-raising game, and Craver, Mathews, Smith is expert at exploiting negative emotions for Greenpeace.[10]

They mail their targets messages that work. Bogeymen? "Whalers have already slaughtered 94 percent of our whales." Of course, it's not true. Urgency? "Half the world's shorelines have been destroyed." Of course, it's not true. Like Paul Watson said, "It doesn't matter what is true, it only matters what people believe is true." And former Craver, Mathews, Smith director Bill Dodd told *Forbes* magazine, "You need a sense of urgency and you need an enemy." Lies and exaggerations create the sense of urgency, and business is the perfect bogeyman. Whatever works.

Direct mail is not a get rich quick scheme, it's a get rich in a reasonable length of time scheme: If the first mailing gets back enough to pay for the postage and printing, it's doing well. The not-so-great package will get back about 1 percent, a good package will get back 2 percent, a rare great package will get 3 percent or more. A good return for environmental group direct mail solicitations is 1.5 percent, about the same as any other. If Greenpeace sends out a million solicitations, that means it gets back 15,000 responses—with money. The average donation amount is $25, meaning the package brought back $375,000.

Then you have to subtract the costs of the mailing to see what the net income is. Postage for a typical Greenpeace package is 11 cents per piece, the subsidized postal rate for tax-exempt groups. For a million pieces, that's $110,000 for postage. Package design, layout, printing, stuffing, bundling and mailing costs about $200,000 from a firm like Craver, Mathews, Smith. The cost of renting a prospecting list for a million piece mailing is about $65,000. That's a total cost of $375,000 for a total income of $375,000. Input equals output. It's a wash.

Did Greenpeace just lay out more than a third of a million bucks to get its money back dollar for dollar with no net gain? Not at all. Direct mail rarely makes money on the first mailing. But those 15,000 people who responded are believers. When the next mailing goes out to them they will respond at a typical rate of 50 percent, not 1.5 percent. The money that comes back then is also much cheaper. You don't have to lay out the $65,000 to rent a list, because names that respond to you become your property, and on the second go-round, you only mail to your own list. Then, too, you may be able to recycle some of the design features from earlier mailings. And sell the names on your list to other direct mail outfits, which generates royalty income.

In addition, direct mail is the perfect educational medium. It gets your message across to a million readers absolutely straight, unfiltered by the media and unscathed by negative comment. You may only get money responses from 15,000 people, but you reached many times more with your ideology.

Direct mail may be inefficient as a cost-effective method of fund-raising, but it is powerful at getting recruits and keeping their money coming in. Greenpeace Fund and its lobbying arm Greenpeace, Inc. combined spent $12.9 million on fund-raising campaigns in 1991. Most tax-exempt organizations follow accounting standards and reveal how much of their costs go to fund-raising and how much to programs. Greenpeace refuses to reveal their cost of fund-raising to the public, but they are readily available on the annual IRS Form 990 financial report that all non-profits must submit. Its advisory fee to Craver, Mathews, Smith in 1991 was $1.3 million. And that is exclusive of mail house costs for distribution ($565,030), list maintenance ($91,178), graphics ($83,128) and fulfillment ($83,655).

However, Greenpeace didn't plan its biggest fund-raising event at all. In 1985 agents of the French government blew up Greenpeace's ship *Rainbow Warrior* in Auckland, New Zealand, in an effort to stop them from obstructing nuclear testing. Fernando Pereira, a photographer, was on board the ship when French frogmen blew it up. He was killed. Greenpeace had a martyr. Within two years, Greenpeace was rich, with American revenues tripling to $25 million. France paid Greenpeace over $20 million in compensation, but the money was not used to buy a new *Rainbow Warrior*, as members were led to believe. According to Frans Kotte, former chief accountant of Greenpeace in Amsterdam—who was fired January 1, 1993 in a dispute—it was transferred to an account of another foundation called Ecological Challenge. The new ship was actually paid for out of membership contributions. Chairman Uta Bellion says the compensation money was kept as a "safety net."

Pereira was later reported to have been a contact for the terrorist Second of June Movement gang, and for the Soviet KGB in planning the "Hot Autumn" anti-cruise missile protests in Western Europe. Even though that didn't get much press, it took some of the glow off his sainted martyrdom. But not before Greenpeace raked in tons of money on his death.

Greenpeace is the archetypal "Eco-Thug" organization that behaves as if it were above the law of all nations. It is intimately entwined with the ecoterrorist group Earth First!, according to that group's leader, Michael Roselle. Its illegal direct action campaigns against industry have won it fame, money, power and hero worship, much to the consternation of the corporations that support most environmental groups. As the *Washington Post* noted, Greenpeace "was particularly effective in inspiring fear in corporate boardrooms with its credo of 'whatever works' and such stunts as plugging up the discharge pipes at a Dow Chemical Co. plant."[11]

In its heyday of eco-commando fervor, Greenpeace activists pulled off spectacular industrial sabotage stunts such as steering rubber dinghies ("Zodiacs") between whale harpooners and whales, parachuting off smokestacks, spraypainting fur seals, blockading roadbuilders, blowing up billboards, unfurling painted cracks on dams and generally raising hell. Where industry has never been anything but a giant wimp in justifying itself to the public, Greenpeace gave a world desperately short of heroes somebody who would stand up for what they believed, and the world media cheered, even though the ultimate success of the Greenpeace agenda would enslave those very media in a zealous eco-censorship that would make Stalin's manipulations look like freedom of the press.

Greenpeace has grown rich since its early quixotic assaults on industry got headlines, and it's trying to get respectable. The *Washington Times* said, "The National Wildlife Federation still has more money and members. But Greenpeace is gaining a virtual monopoly over one of this country's most valuable natural resources: its young people. Greenpeace is a cultural phenomenon—a 1990s Pied Piper trying to lure a whole generation toward a promised land of total political transformation."[12]

The lure nowadays is mostly lies. The best example is a visit by the Greenpeace vessel *Rainbow Warrior* to San Diego, California, in early 1992. On February 6 the old tub wheezed into San Diego harbor proclaiming "War with the tunamen." At issue was the assertion that the American tuna fleet was mercilessly killing dolphins to the point of extinction and a tough new law before Congress had to be passed—a law that would make it illegal to capture dolphins in any way. This "Encircle Bill" would be used against all foreign countries and eradicate the tuna fishing industry worldwide. Greenpeacies docked the *Rainbow Warrior* at a downtown pier and held an "Open House" to spread their propaganda. Crowds showed up.

Greenpeace miscalculated this one, but good. The 100-boat American tuna fleet was nowhere to be found. It had been destroyed, forced to sell out, reflag, and scatter all over the world. The bulk of the fleet had gone to the Western Pacific as a result of the "dolphin-safe" movement pushed by Greenpeace and other groups several years earlier. San Diego's last sixteen huge tuna fishing vessels had departed in the summer of 1991. All that was left was the families and former crews of tuna boats.

And they were angry. Very, very angry.

For they knew that the whole "dolphin-safe" campaign had been a fraud. Tuna fishermen had long used dolphins as "scouts" to find schools of mature yellowfin tuna, and learned quickly that some of the friendly sea mammals inevitably became entangled in their purse seine nets along with the tuna catch. The industry itself had lowered dolphin mortality with huge investments of time, money and new net technology.

The truth was that the number of dolphins killed in tuna nets had never presented the slightest danger to their survival—most modern catches killed no dolphins at all. But by the time marine biologists could document those facts, Greenpeace and Earth Island Institute, among other groups, had pressured tuna cannery firms to shut down their San Diego plants and had convinced Congress to pass strict "dolphin-safe" laws. The most convincing testimony presented to Congress had been a video clip surreptitiously taken by Samuel LaBudde, an environmentalist with Earth Island Institute (see profile) who had signed aboard a tunaboat as a mechanic and cook, a video clip showing a whole net full of dolphins being slaughtered without mercy to get the few yellowfin tuna that had also been caught.[13]

Before Greenpeace knew what hit them, their San Diego war with the tunamen had turned into a community war against Greenpeace. Hundreds of demonstrators suddenly appeared on the street in front of the *Rainbow Warrior's* dock carrying signs reading "Greenpeace—Nazis of the 90s," and "Greenpeace already killed our jobs—yours is next!" and "Greenpeace is lying to you! We don't kill dolphins!"[14]

The demonstrators were the wives and children of tunamen, retired fishermen, dispossessed vessel owners and their friends and neighbors from miles around. They gave out anti-Greenpeace literature, including the critical *Forbes* magazine article quoted above. The demonstration had been called by Roland Virrissimo, ex-captain and present vessel owner—whose ship was forced to move to the Western Pacific. The tunaboat *Odette Therese*, owned by Roland's brother Bobby, mysteriously exploded at dockside in Panama in 1990, killing four men.

Some of the demonstrators went on board the *Rainbow Warrior*. There, the wife of Angelo Souza confronted the Greenpeacies about the film they were showing the San Diego public, the Sam LaBudde film that had convinced Congress to decimate the U.S. tuna fishing fleet. Mrs. Souza told the viewers, "I have been involved with the tuna industry for over thirty years. I have gone to sea with my captain husband. The vessel and crew in this video are not Americans. This is not how Americans work. This whole film is a fraud. It is an old boat with a new owner and an inexperienced crew. Even the film was rigged, it was spliced from two different trips. It's common knowledge among fishermen that Sam LaBudde lied about that dolphin slaughter. It's not typical of anything. You're all a bunch of liars! And you've destroyed the jobs of thousands of innocent people with your lies!"

A Greenpeace spokesperson admitted it was the largest demonstration ever mounted against his organization.

Then the *Rainbow Warrior* visited San Pedro, California and left hazardous waste in port. Richard Gillaspy, enforcement supervisor for the Los Angeles Fire Department's Hazardous Waste Control Program said the Greenpeace ship left 50 gallons of photographic chemicals, cleaning solvents, oil and paint at Berth 93 on February 10, 1992. The *Rainbow Polluter*. Do as I say, not as I do, eh?[15]

There's more to phony film-making. Greenpeace, according to independent Iceland-based journalist and filmmaker Magnus Gudmundsson, likes freedom of the press for itself, but not for anybody else. In 1990 Greenpeace filed lawsuits against three German publications that said things about Greenpeace it didn't like. Gudmundsson himself has been the target of Greenpeace legal actions—trying to stop him from showing a film he made that says Greenpeace staged brutal animal-killing scenes in its fund-raising propaganda movies. Gudmundsson filed a countersuit. Both parties won their respective claims and were awarded modest damages.

Gudmundsson filmed his 1989 anti-environmentalist documentary *Survival in the High North,* which he paid for with his own funds, to dramatize the battle between hunting peoples of the North Atlantic and environmental groups such as Greenpeace. His interviews with Inuit whale hunters and Faeroe Islanders reveal the stark reality that seal hunting and whale hunting for them is not sport, but a matter of survival—Greenpeace was in effect advocating genocide by cutting off their main supply of meat with its anti-whaling campaign. The film also depicts the bleak aftermath of welfare dependency and suicide faced by the dwellers of Iceland, Greenland and the Faeroe Islands after campaigns that devastated their seal hunting business through bans on sealskin imports to Europe.

In his film, Gudmundsson also explores the evidence brought forward in 1986 by Leif Blaedel, a prize-winning Danish journalist, that revealed Greenpeace faked footage in its film *Goodbye Joey* by using paid torturers in gruesome scenes intended to inflame passions against kangaroo hunters. Blaedel produced court records from Dirranbandi, Australia, to confirm that the ghastly scenes were faked by Greenpeace producers. The court records existed because the paid kangaroo torturers were caught, prosecuted, and fined for tormenting the animals for the Greenpeace film. Even though the public record showed the film was fraudulent in 1983, Greenpeace Denmark sent it out as late as 1986. *Forbes* magazine reported that Greenpeace media director Peter Dykstra claimed that "Greenpeace stopped distributing the film in 1983, when it discovered the film's 'integrity problems.'"

The most important part of Gudmundsson's film, however, was a segment using footage taken—with the written permission of Greenpeace—from Greenpeace's 1970s fund-raising film *Bitter Harvest*. It is a harsh scene in which a person Gudmundsson testified is a Greenpeace stooge dressed as a harp seal hunter, face blackened to prevent positive identification, drags a baby seal away from its protesting mother and leaves it skinned alive to die an agonizing death. Gudmundsson shows evidence that the scene was staged, playing separate clips together indicating that the same event was filmed several times from different angles, just like a Hollywood production.

Even back in the 1970s when the footage still had its initial shock value, critics wondered how Greenpeace could possibly have convinced a real harp seal hunter to cooperate in making a film that would certainly put him out of business—aside from the fact that what they wanted to film was contrary to the humane killing techniques actually used by real harp seal hunters. The one witness to the actual filming of the Greenpeace footage, Dr. Harry C. Rowsell—whom Greenpeace quotes as saying the film is from a real seal hunt—actually says the scene was staged, according to Gudmundsson.

Greenpeace vehemently denies everything Gudmundsson says about them, and has dragged him into courts in Iceland, the United Kingdom, and Norway demanding damages for libel. It cost Gudmundsson about $40,000 in legal fees to defend himself for speaking out. The case heard in Oslo, Norway resulted in a May, 1992 ruling that Gudmundsson's claim that Greenpeace knowingly made false statements that hunters skinned live seals was proven beyond a doubt. Gudmundsson was acquitted of all seven counts of libel.[16]

Greenpeace announced it was fully satisfied with the verdict even though the court confirmed that the organization deliberately falsified information in its documentary. Small consolation for what happened then: Its 15,000-person membership in Norway collapsed overnight to 35 activists. Greenpeace income also plummeted. The chairman of Norwegian Greenpeace, Bjørn Økern, resigned and stated that Gudmundsson was right about Greenpeace's fund raising tactics and that none of Greenpeace's money was used for "environmental protection." Økern also termed Greenpeace "an ecofascist group." Økern also resigned his seat on the board of directors of Greenpeace International.

Barbara Dudley, executive director since 1992, was previously executive director of the North Shore Unitarian Universalist Society Veatch Program, a member of the Environmental Grantmakers Association. Greenpeace does not have a political action committee (PAC). Greenpeace publishes a bimonthly newsletter, *Greenpeace*.

Greenpeace Fund received the following grants:

The Max and Victoria Dreyfus Foundation, Inc. gave $10,000 in 1989.
Town Creek Foundation, Inc. gave $10,000 in 1990.
Greenpeace.
Job killers.
Economy trashers.

The Sea Shepherd Conservation Society (1977)
Budget: $980,000[17]
Members: 32,000
Staff: 1 paid, administrator/accountant
3107A Washington Boulevard
Marina Del Rey, California 90292
Phone: (310)301-7325. FAX (310)574-3161

It is Paul Franklin Watson's overglorious inclination to think of Sea Shepherd in terms of Isaac Asimov's futuristic science fiction *Foundation* series: Greenpeace is the giant and dominating Foundation, jealously trying to eradicate the rebellious and self-righteous Second Foundation (offshoot Sea Shepherd), which takes the role of keeping the First Foundation true to its original goals.

There is a certain bizarre truth to this literary allusion. Watson was ousted from Greenpeace for violating the organization's principle of nonviolence by wrestling a club from a harp seal hunter, and has since annoyed Greenpeace by actually doing what the bigger organization only wishes it was doing.[18]

Watson tells his version in a self-congratulatory autobiography, *Sea Shepherd: My Fight for Whales and Seals.* Essentially, Greenpeace co-founder Patrick Moore felt that Watson was too much of an activist and threatened to kick him out if he were elected president. Moore was elected and set out to make good on his promise. The usual fuss about paying off debts and other internal politics added to the fracas. The club incident Watson described thus: "I had picked up a sealer's club and had thrown it into the water." Greenpeacers told him he had no right to appoint himself a one-man vigilante squad and booted him out.[19]

However, Watson told us privately that his ouster was actually triggered by a quarrel with Moore over actress Brigitte Bardot when she was visiting a Canadian ice floe with them to film an anti-seal hunting commercial. Watson refused to allow Moore to travel in the helicopter with La Bardot because there was only room for her and the film crew. Moore had to fly with Watson, much less glamorous—somehow appropriate that Sea Shepherd was spawned from a bit of internal petty ego rivalry contesting who had the biggest reproductive apparatus. There is a certain sassy twinkle to this story that is characteristic of Watson, which sets him apart from pretentious Greenpeace and, despite his many wretched excesses, makes him the eco-terrorist we love to hate.

Paul Watson to many is Dr. Derring-Do, anarchist Captain of the Ocean Sea, kamikaze headband and romantically unruly hair waving in his slipstream—a legend in his own mind, the Messiah of Marine Mammals ramming driftnetters, sinking whalers, symbolically firing an antique Civil War cannon grafted onto his ship's deck. Greenpeace on helium. A filmmaker named Ron Precious immortalized Paul in several award-winning documentaries. Watson has repeatedly sold the film rights to his autobiography *Sea Shepherd,* now owned by Wes Craven Productions, hoping it will be used as the basis of a sequel to Carolco's long-shelved *Warriors of the Rainbow,* a dramatization of the Greenpeace story to be—someday—directed by Renny Harlan. Watson is skeptical of the outcome, but says the money helps.[20]

Robert Hunter, a co-founder and one-time president of Greenpeace, characterized Watson in his official history of the group, *Warriors of the Rainbow*, as a member of the violence-prone Vancouver Liberation Front. Watson says he wrote about the VLF but never actually joined—he was a communications major not long out of school when he helped found Greenpeace.

Hunter also remembered that Paul had been irresistibly attracted to the 1973 armed FBI confrontation with American Indian Movement leaders at Wounded Knee, South Dakota. Watson got a Bureau of Indian Affairs press pass into the scene of the seventy-one-day siege and then slipped into the village at night where he volunteered as a medic for the Indians.

Paul loved melodramatic touches such as getting initiated into the Oglalla Sioux tribe in a sacred sweat lodge ceremony where he had a vision telling him to fight whalers and other users of sea mammals. He got his license to Trash the Economy straight from the Great Spirit.

The Wounded Knee siege was important combat experience, Watson says, and prepared him for what was to come. During the standoff, he also filed reports to *Vancouver Sun* columnist Bob Hunter, who wrote pieces based on Watson's material that appeared in the paper every other day.

Watson's role as a writer has never been emphasized, but we believe it is a powerful part of his success. He wrote for the alternative Vancouver newspaper *Georgia Strait* from 1970 into the 1980s and served as correspondent for Defenders of Wildlife from 1975 to 1979. His books *Sea Shepherd* and *Earthforce* have substantially influenced the green movement.

The question of Paul Watson's predilection for violent actions to protect nature has attracted much attention. We asked him about it, and he said, "I don't particularly like violence per se, but where it is necessary I will take measures to destroy equipment without hurting people. Sea Shepherd is not a pacifist organization. We have always carried guns on board our ships, but take pride in the fact we have never used them— except for our Civil War cannon, which makes a lot of noise, but fires no shot."

Watson puts out a good line of nonviolent talk in his newsletter, but he once told a reporter that when he was young and saw his playmates shooting birds, "I got the impression that instead of going out to shoot birds, I should go out and shoot the kids who shoot birds."[21]

When we asked him about that, he said it was not his exact quote, but that he had actually shot a kid in the jean-clad butt with his b-b gun when he was 12 years old to save a bird. Most of us who grew up in rural areas—Watson grew up in New Brunswick—bear reminders of old b-b gun fights, so this episode may or may not be significant. With Paul Watson, you're never quite sure whether you've got Gandhi or Godzilla.

Watson floundered around for a while after being drummed out of Greenpeace, starting an outfit he called Earthforce Environmental Society in June of 1977 in Vancouver and fiddled about for four months trying to save elephants in Africa. His friends Elmer "Jet" Johnson (flamboyant founder of Greenpeace USA) and Bruce Bunting, a veterinarian from Michigan, also disillusioned with Greenpeace, co-founded the new group, the three experimenting with post-Greenpeace directions.

A year later Watson changed the name to Sea Shepherd Conservation Society and refocused it on marine issues where his skills lay. The name came from an article Watson had written for the Greenpeace newsletter titled, "Shepherds of the Labrador Front," another decisive result of Watson's role as a writer.

He went to Cleveland Amory of the Fund for Animals, whom he had known for some time, and asked for help with a campaign to protect seals. Amory asked how he could do it. Watson said he could put a crew on the ice with parachutes or buy a ship to get through the ice to Newfoundland and the Labrador seal hunt. Amory liked the ship idea better, and came up with $120,000 with which Watson bought the 206-foot British fishing boat *Westella* in Kingston-on-Hull on December 5, 1978 and rechristened it the *Sea Shepherd* on December 15.

Britain's Royal Society for the Prevention of Cruelty to Animals donated a grant of $48,000 on December 20, and Watson used it to fit out the boat for hunting seal hunters. Thwarting seal hunters by spraying red batik dye on a thousand pups and parking in the mouth of an inlet to block ships' passage got eight protesters arrested and raised media coverage across the world. It proved to be merely the prelude to more risky exploits.

The idea of going after the well-known whaling ship *Sierra* and ramming it would make more great media theatre. Watson methodically hunted down the vessel, found it by sheer luck 200 miles off the coast of Portugal and chased it to the port of Leixoes for a controlled situation for the ramming. When they reached shore on Tuesday, July 17, 1979, he told his 19 crew members, "Look, I can't guarantee you're not going to get hurt, but I can guarantee you're going to jail after we ram the *Sierra*. You have ten minutes to either stay or get off the boat." Ten minutes later 16 of the crew stood on the Leixoes dock.

Those who stayed were chief engineer Peter Woof, third engineer Jerry Doran, and Alex Pacheco, co-founder of People for the Ethical Treatment of Animals (see profile). Pacheco was only 18 at the time and uncertain of his goals. Watson told him, "Alex, I want you to get off the boat and do the photography to document what we do here and be a spokesperson." He then rammed the *Sierra*. Portuguese Coast Guard authorities ordered the three pirates to sail the *Sea Shepherd* into the harbor at Leixoes, where it was seized as security to pay for damages to the *Sierra*. The port captain charged Watson with negligence. Watson replied that it was not negligence, he had struck the vessel exactly where he intended. The port captain said, "I see. Well, we have received no complaint from the owners of the *Sierra*, so you are free to go."

The next day Watson received a call to visit with Greenpeace boss David McTaggart at a posh hotel. At the poolside McTaggart angrily told Watson, "You just caused us a lot of trouble. We were going to protest the *Sierra* and now you've sabotaged those plans." Watson claims that McTaggart requested the *Sea Shepherd* crew to atone for their sin by breaking into the hotel room of the *Sierra*'s agent and stealing his briefcase, which contained evidence Greenpeace could use to steal Watson's thunder. According to Watson, McTaggart said, "If you don't do this, you're through in this movement, because we have the means to make this a world issue and you don't. Do this, or we'll stick it to you." McTaggart could not be reached at his Italian villa for comment.

Watson returned to Vancouver and toured the United States to work the media. Then, when the *Sea Shepherd* was turned over to *Sierra* owner Andrew Behr, damages and fines for his offense against the *Sierra* turned out to be $750,000. Watson decided he would never let his ship be sold to pay reparations to a whaler. He went to Portugal on Christmas to steal it back. However, he found that under Portuguese law all the fuel had been pumped out of it and all the navigational equipment removed. So on December 31, 1979, with Peter Woof, he opened the seacocks, let the ocean in, and scuttled the *Sea Shepherd* at the Leixoes dock.

On February 5, 1980, two men and a woman went to Lisbon, rowed a skiff across the Tagus River to where the *Sierra* had been towed and was tied up. They blew up the whaling vessel. At 10 a.m. that morning a woman called the United Press International in Lisbon from a phone just across the border in Spain and said,

"The *Sea Shepherd* is avenged! Make no mistake about it—this was no accident, this was a deliberate act of sabotage! The *Sierra* will kill no more whales! We did it for the *Sea Shepherd!*"

Watson says the two men involved were U.S. military personnel using naval mines. On April 27, 1980, the same trio blew up the *Isba I* and *Isba II*, two of Spain's five whalers, and sank them in the harbor of Marin near Vigo, Spain. Mines on two other whalers failed to detonate, according to Paul Watson.[22]

It has been all downhill from there.

Watson did manage to get another British flag vessel, *Sea Shepherd II* (registration number 5305912, 194 feet, beam 32.10 feet, gross registered tonnage 658), a converted side trawler, originally the *St. Giles.*

Until 1981 Watson operated essentially under the aegis of Fund for Animals, then turned to building Sea Shepherd Conservation Society into a functional entity on its own. He was helped by close friends and board members Peter Brown and Benjamin L. White, Jr., owner of a Virginia arborist company.

An unusual aide-de-camp was a young man named Scott Trimingham, who came on board in 1982 and served as President for nearly a decade, although, as a devoted pacifist, he never went out on any campaign. As Irving Stowe was the financial godsend for Greenpeace, Trimingham was an excellent administrator, fundraiser and development officer for the Sea Shepherds and helped increase the group's membership from 2,000 to 15,000. The Sea Shepherds operated out of Trimingham's Redondo Beach home for many years.

As time went on, the Sea Shepherd Society grabbed clubs and rifles from the hands of sealers, cut drift nets, and staged confrontations with Soviet and Taiwanese drift net ships.[23] After Watson issued a warning in Reykjavik, two unidentified supporters operated an undercover sabotage of harbor-bound Icelandic whaling ships on November 9, 1986—half of the nation's fleet.[24]

Later Paul Watson bragged about sinking the two Icelandic whaling ships.[25]

Then Watson said that Sea Shepherd member Rodney Coronado of Morgan Hill, California, was directly involved in the multi-million-dollar sabotage, along with a British citizen. Watson refused to identify the British participant other than to say his first name was David.[26] The *Sea Shepherd Log* later identified David as David Howitt.[27]

When Greenpeace called Watson a terrorist for his action, Watson responded, "What do you expect from the Avon ladies of the environmental movement?"—a jab at their door-to-door fundraising methods. He flew into Iceland on January 21, 1988 and brazenly dared authorities to arrest him, which they did, which apparently surprised him. The Public Prosecutor of Iceland questioned Watson closely, and the results were remarkable.

The Ministry of Justice of Iceland issued a press release the next day stating, "At the questioning Paul Watson admitted that he has given some remarks that connect him with the sabotage, but in spite of this he now claims that he neither took part in the planning nor the execution of the sabotage."[28]

Watson says he never changed his story at all, insisted in a news conference that he was involved, and believes Iceland did not prosecute because they didn't want the publicity. Believe which story you will, but we still suspect that when bigtime prison doors loomed, Captain Derring-Do became The Chicken of the Sea. He says no. In any event, the Ministry of Justice of Iceland deported him and declared him *persona non grata*, refusing him entry permanently.

David Howitt and Rod Coronado were conspicuously absent on this visit to Iceland, but Watson claims he told Icelandic authorities that if they wanted them there, he would get them there. Watson is insistent on accepting responsibility for the sinkings. Coronado remarked of the incident, "A reporter called Paul to see if Sea Shepherd wanted to accept responsibility. Of course, if lightning struck a whaling ship, Paul would accept responsibility for it."[29]

Watson takes credit for inventing tree spiking. In an *Earth First! Journal* article he said, "I was the person who first thought up the tactic of tree spiking and as such I feel obligated to defend this child of my imagination."[30]

The idea, Watson said, came from an incident in 1977 when a sawmill had to shut down for a day because its bandsaw ran into a cannonball fired by Captain Cook into a tree two centuries earlier. It reminded him of an accident his father had: "As a child I witnessed my father break a chainsaw on a horseshoe that had been nailed to a tree a century before and became over time internal armor protecting the heart of the elderly and noble being. I was delighted."

He claims to have spiked some trees in the mid-1960s to protect them from developers but was not successful. He had better luck in 1982 spiking 2,000 trees at Grouse Mountain Resort in Vancouver, British Columbia, to prevent timber harvest to expand a ski area. A publicity campaign led local sawmills to state they would not buy any of the logs, and the deal was off. Watson says he told Earth First! leaders Dave Foreman and Mike Roselle about tree spiking at a 1982 meeting and they went off with it.

The objective of tree spiking isn't to break the blade or hurt anyone, Watson told us, but to cause expensive downtime. "Trashing the economy," he chuckled.

Watson takes his economy trashing seriously, as a cause, not a money-making scheme. Listening to him hold forth on Greenpeace, however, is to hear profound disgust gnawing at him. "They're a bunch of frauds and they constantly copy us," he told a *Los Angeles Times* reporter. "I can determine what Greenpeace's agenda is going to be tomorrow by announcing today what we plan to do next." He was upset not so much for being copied as for having to prod wealthy Greenpeace into action—another subtext reference to his Asimov-inspired Foundation/Second Foundation imagery. "They're into megabucks, they're big business, so we're a serious threat because we're in business to put ourselves out of business."

Greenpeace co-founder Jim Bohlen replied, "I've known the guy for fifteen years and he's absolutely insane, out of his mind."[31]

Probably not. Just dubious about greenies who use the environment to get rich.

In 1990, during a North Pacific drift net campaign, Watson's crew sank a short piece of a long drift net and rammed two Japanese ships. Fishermen aboard one vessel reacted by throwing knives.[32]

In 1991, off Trinidad, Watson came alongside a Taiwanese drift net vessel to investigate and express disapproval, but its captain out-brashed Watson and rammed him, seriously damaging both ships. It had evidently never occurred to Watson that his victims might fight back.

In February 1991, the *Sea Shepherd II* rammed a Mexican tuna boat, the *Tungui* in Guatemalan waters because it was killing dolphins.[33] Watson claimed the captain of the *Tungui* had killed 1,000 dolphins in the previous month, but the captain said he had only encircled 1,000 dolphins with his purse seine net while tuna fishing, and successfully released more than 99 percent while making rich tuna catches. The Mexican navy was called out to defend the *Tungui*.[34]

Alston Chase once wrote in his syndicated column about the Sea Shepherds, "They have not lost their sense of humor. A few years ago, the Sea Shepherds' crew was under siege by irate Faeroe Islanders, angry that these ecoteurs were interfering with whaling. The Faroese attacked with guns and tear gas. Capt. Watson responded by loading his ship's water cannon with lemon meringue pie filling and attempting to fire at his foe. It is hard to get mad at a guy who can conceive such sweet revenge."[35]

Watson's "humor" is infuriating to many. But his derring-do plays well in America, even in Peoria—because we are not hungry. To the Faroese, the whaling operation that Watson made light of with his lemon meringue water cannon was a matter of survival, a diligent search for protein because there is little else to provide it. The 17 inhabited Faeroe Islands are volcanic rock covered by a thin layer of moraine or peat soil. These islands support a population of 44,000 whose economy is based on fishing, mostly for cod. There are no indigenous land mammals—sea mammals provide a crucial part of the Faroese diet, and the whale species they hunt enjoy thriving populations that are neither endangered nor threatened. The Faroese rely upon puffins and other small seabirds to supplement their food supply. Only 6 percent of the land is cultivable, producing mainly potatoes and grass for sheep—wool is used in a small home-spinning and knitting industry.[36]

Watson claims the Faroese kill pilot whales for sport, which they deny, and ridiculed the plight of this struggling culture by wasting food to make a joke of them. Very funny, Paul.

Alston Chase wrote again of the Sea Shepherd in July 1991, "according to reliable sources, activists aboard the Sea Shepherd are carrying firearms for the first time."[37]

Watson had told Chase they had always carried weapons, and that the charge was not news. Up to 1990, the Sea Shepherd Society ostensibly followed a "prime directive" to destroy only "implements of death" (such as whaling ships), explicitly proscribing firearms and explosives and forbidding any action that "could result in a possible physical injury to human life."

However, a supposed revision of the Society's "prime directive" announced in 1991 enjoins Sea Shepherds only to "avoid at all costs, short of immediate self-defense, the causation of bodily physical injury or death of any who opposes us."[38]

Paul Watson told us the prime directive—humorously modeled after the Prime Directive of the *Star Trek* television series—had not been changed. In fact, he clearly stated in the Fall 1991 issue of *Earth Island Journal* that "We do indeed carry weapons;" "We...carry one shotgun and a rifle;" "We recently had two automatic rifles donated to us...(later allegedly given away);" and "These weapons are also legal, registered and declared upon entry and departure from each port."[39] Watson faxed us government documents to prove it.

Watson told *Outside* magazine that he keeps two Chinese assault rifles locked on board. "We're going up against the Taiwanese, who have openly threatened violence against us. We may have to defend ourselves. My responsibility is to protect my crew."[40] The two rifles were donated to a law enforcement agency.

Watson told us he is a member of the National Rifle Association.

In February 1992, a United States-flag Sea Shepherd Society ship, the *Edward Abbey* (official hull number 985122, home port Long Beach) attacked the Costa Rican fishing boats *Albatros, Mariela* and *Aztec* near Coco Island.[41] The three captains filed a complaint stating:

> On February 23 as we approached Coco Island we were intercepted by a ship flying the United States flag under the name *Edward Abbey* at about 11:30 a.m.
>
> This ship furiously tried to sail against us several times, forcing us to change our course. We tried to establish radio contact with it but were repeatedly ignored.
>
> As part of their hostile actions, they shot bullets with a red substance at us. Some hit our boat, others hit two of our crew members, Martin Dijeres Dijeres and Juan Mayorga Montes, causing them great pain. The American ship also fired live ammunition in the air a few times.
>
> Finally, the American ship also shot a mortar round at us that landed some 10 meters away from our boat.[42]

Watson says the "bullets with a red substance" were paint ball bullets from the popular game. No live ammunition was fired, he says, and the "mortar" was the Civil War cannon that makes a lot of noise but contains no cannonball. The Tuna Commissioner of Costa Rica issued a news release stating:

A new concept of imperialism, not much different from that of the last century, exists today. In the name of ecology, environmentalism and other principles, some people intend to sacrifice the countries of the Third World.

Environmentalists will defend their principles even if it means trampling the sovereignty of any nation that dares stand in their way. They are not concerned with the hunger affecting the poor neighborhoods of Puntarenas, Caracas or Mexico City. What's more, they will not stop at cold-blooded murder. For them it is only a modus vivendi that allows them to raise millions of dollars to defend principles for which they will sacrifice us.

It is time to defend our sovereignty and that our authorities act and capture this armed ship.[43]

Mick Kronman, a freelance reporter for *National Fisherman* magazine and *Underwater USA* magazine, interviewed Peter Brown of the Sea Shepherd Conservation Society about this incident. The Sea Shepherds believed that the Costa Rican boats were fishing illegally in a national park near Coco Island. During the interview, Mr. Brown made the following statements: "The fishermen are full of shit. In fact, we should have used real bullets on the damn bastards, not paint bullets. These fishermen are pigs. They're raping the environment for the sake of a buck." When Kronman wrote that in his magazine articles, the editors deleted it. Kronman verified in writing the quotes to Teresa Platt, president of the nonprofit Fishermen's Coalition.[44]

Scott Trimingham, the Sea Shepherd Society's president and chief fundraiser, resigned in June 1990. He told us that because of his pacifist beliefs, he could no longer support the organization. A laudatory tribute to Trimingham appeared in the Spring 1991 *Sea Shepherd Log*, saying publicly that he was leaving because he needed time with his family.[45]

Trimingham told *Outside* magazine, "We had rules about not hurting anyone, about not using weapons. I left because those rules and that philosophy seem to be changing."[46]

Watson says the real reason Trimingham left was disagreement over administration. Trimingham wanted to use direct mail solicitation, and Watson didn't. Trimingham tried a mail campaign and gained over a thousand new members, but Watson told him they were costly and not as loyal as those who sought out Sea Shepherd on their own, and nixed further direct mail campaigns. Other business disputes precipitated the final rupture.

More recently, the Sea Shepherds suffered a serious internal split when Ben White and other leaders tried to change directions toward releasing captive marine mammals. The conflict centered on the dolphin act at Steve Wynn's Mirage casino operation in Las Vegas. Sea Shepherd President Ben White screamed they'd never condone captive dolphins under any circumstances.

In the Summer 1991 issue of *Sea Shepherd Log*, Watson's staffer Lisa Lange fumed over the horrible conditions she and President Ben White found in the Mirage's dolphin act: "Steve Wynn is guilty of jailing wild animals in unnatural surroundings and this is unforgivable. Nearing the end of our visit, Wynn was waxing generous, getting ready to write us a substantial check [$50,000] for our 'good intentioned' work, when [Wynn's aide] Ms. Onie informed him that in our last issue we referred to his facility as 'Steve Wynn's killing tanks.' Never have we witnessed a donation slip through our fingers so quickly. (In case any of you wonder, we'll take his money and use it to shut him down. No donations are ever accepted with strings attached.)"[47]

Those in big business who give money to environmental groups should replay that statement, see if it rings any bells: "we'll take his money and use it to shut him down." Get it? Knock, knock. Anybody there in the executive suite?

Watson didn't want to get into the animal release business, and White did. The fact that White had soured a $50,000 donation may have had something to do with it as well. The group's newsletter tells the story: "Early in 1992, Ben White resigned from the board of directors of the Sea Shepherds. He accused the board of not supporting his plan to aggressively liberate dolphins from marine aquariums." We originally thought Watson had fired White, but during a subsequent debate with Ron Arnold at Northwestern Law School, White verified that he had resigned as reported.

Paul Watson aroused our suspicions because shortly after White left, he wrote: "I apologize to Steve Wynn for the overzealous actions of our former director....My own investigations of the Mirage have shown that Steve Wynn is an ally and not an enemy to the dolphin....[The dolphins were captive-bred, so releasing them would be a death sentence.] Our case against the Mirage is closed. We welcome Steve Wynn as an ally."[48] Wynn gave the $50,000.

How do you spell ally? G-o-l-d-e-n D-o-n-o-r.

When Norway's Prime Minister Gro Haarlem Brundtland announced in 1993 that her nation would resume limited whaling on non-threatened species, Watson went ballistic. He sailed to Norway and attempted to scuttle the *Nybraena*, a fishing/whaling vessel. On June 3, 1994, Watson and Lisa Distefano were convicted and sentenced to 120 days in jail, which they appealed from a safe distance in the United States, not showing up in Norway for the hearing.[49]

In July 1994, Watson encounterd the Norwegian Navy, which was blockading the Sea Shepherd vessel *Whales Forever* to prevent them interfering with whaling operations. Watson's ship and a large naval vessel collided—each accuses the other of ramming. *Whales Forever* fled after two shots were fired over its bow. Norway claims Watson sent a false Mayday message stating "several persons reportedly hit by gunfire," but no Coast Guard records show it. [50]

Of more than passing interest, the Sea Shepherds recently acquired the *Mirage*, an 11-meter, 2-person diesel-electric military submarine, diving depth 300 meters, formerly with the Norwegian Navy (what irony), now fitted with various underwater cutting tools.

Windup

The group puts out a quarterly newsletter, *Sea Shepherd Log*. It lists affiliates as Earth Island Institute and Fund for Animals, in recognition of informal cooperation. A previous informal relationship with Earth First! was terminated after Dave Foreman left its leadership.[51]

The leaders of the Sea Shepherd Conservation Society are Paul F. Watson, Founder and President; Carroll Vogel; Rosemary Waldron; and Lisa Distefano (Director of Orcaforce).

The Sea Shepherd Conservation Society lies in the Deep Ecology Eco-Terrorist Axis of the environmental movement.

The Grainger Foundation, Inc. gave the Sea Shepherd Conservation Society $25,000 in 1989 "for special program fund."

Gordon Lightfoot, the Canadian singer, claims he donated $20,000 in 1989.

Steve Wynn of the Mirage Hotel and the Golden Nugget in Las Vegas in mid-1992 gave $50,000.

The Sea Shepherd Conservation Society.

Job killers.

Economy trashers.

Greenpeace USA—Footnotes

1 *Warriors of the Rainbow: A Chronicle of the Greenpeace Movement*, Robert Hunter, Holt, Rinehart and Winston, New York, 1979, p. 17.

2 "The not so peaceful world of Greenpeace," by Leslie Spencer with Jan Bollwerk and Richard C. Morais, *Forbes*, November 11, 1991, p. 174.

3 *Warriors of the Rainbow*, p. 7.

4 *Warriors of the Rainbow*, p. 11.

5 *Eco-Warriors: Understanding the Radical Environmental Movement*, Rik Scarce, The Noble Press, Inc., Chicago, 1990, p. 51.

6 "Environmentalism: Freedom's Foe for the '90s," Robert Bidinotto, *The Freeman*, November 1990.

7 "The not so peaceful world of Greenpeace," by Leslie Spencer with Jan Bollwerk and Richard C. Morais, *Forbes*, November 11, 1991, p. 174.

8 *E Magazine*, January / February, 1990.

9 *The Gun Grabbers*, Alan Gottlieb, Merril Press, Bellevue, Washington, 1986, p. 127.

10 "In the mail: solicitation techniques of environmental mailers," by James R. Rosenfield, *Direct Marketing*, September 1991, p. 19.

11 "From Fringe To Political Mainstream," by Michael Weiskopf, *Washington Post*, April 19, 1990, p. A1.

12 *Washington Times*, March 12, 1990.

13 "Drive to stop killing by tuna fleets is given new impetus," by Scott Armstrong, *Christian Science Monitor*, April 14, 1988, p. 3.

14 "Tunamen fight back," by Dennis Potter, *Fishing Boat World*, June 1992, p. 14-15.

15 "Greenpeace ship leaves hazardous waste in port," by Caroline Brady, *San Pedro News-Pilot*, a Copley Los Angeles Newspaper, February 25, 1992, p. 1.

16 "Greenpeace Found Guilty of Falsifying Information," *The New Gun Week*, Friday, July 31, 1992, p. 9.

17 Personal interview with Paul Watson, September 25, 1994, telephone interview September 26, 1994. Much of this subprofile is based upon these long discussions.

18 "A militant turn for conservationists," by Charles Fenyvesi, *U. S. News & World Report*, November 24, 1986, p. 72.

19 *Sea Shepherd: My Fight for Whales and Seals*, Paul Watson as told to Warren Rogers, W. W. Norton & Company, New York, 1982, p. 151.

20 *Sea Shepherd Log*, Spring, 1991, p. 4.

21 *Omni* magazine, February 1981.

22 *Sea Shepherd*, p. 250.

23 "Sea Shepherd mission: Sink those drift nets," by Nancy Klingener, *Miami Herald*, May 29, 1991, p. 4B.

24 "A militant turn for conservationists," by Charles Fenyvesi, *U.S. News & World Report*, November 24, 1986, p. 72.

25 "Modern-Day Pirates Fight the Whalers," by Bella Stumbo, *Los Angeles Times*, June 13, 1987, p. 1.

26 "Anti-Whaling Group Names Iceland Saboteur," by Douglas Martin, *New York Times*, November 13, 1986.

27 "Sea Shepherd Returns to Iceland," by Paul Watson, *Sea Shepherd Log*, March 1988, p. 1.

28 "Press Release," Doms og Kirkjumalardaduneytid, Reykjavik, January 22, 1988.

29 *Eco-Warriors: Understanding the Radical Environmental Movement*, Rik Scarce, The Noble Press, Inc., Chicago, 1990, p. 198.

30 "In Defense of Tree Spiking," *Earth First!*, September 22, 1990, p. 8.

31 "Modern-Day Pirates Fight the Whalers," by Bella Stumbo, *Los Angeles Times*, June 13, 1987, p. 1.

32 "Conservation vessel rams 2 ships in Pacific," *New York Times*, August 16, 1990, p. A11.

33 "Conservation group says its ship rammed a Mexican tuna boat for taking dolphins," UPI, *Los Angeles Times*, February 18, 1991.

34 "Tuna boat attacked," Reuters, *San Diego Union*, February 19, 1991.

35 "Sea Shepherds may give piracy a good name," by Alston Chase, *Washington Times*, August 30, 1990.

36 "That sinking feeling," *Time*, November 24, 1986, p. 45.

37 "A disturbing shift from pacifist tactics," by Alston Chase, Universal Press Syndicate, as published in the *Seattle Times*, July 1, 1991, p. A13.

38 "Prime Directive," *Sea Shepherd Log*, Spring 1991, p. 2.

39 *Earth Island Journal*, Fall 1991.

40 "Slow boat to trouble," by Trip Gabriel, *Outside*, September 1991, p. 54.

41 "Barco de Sea Shepherd fue el que ataco a pesqueros," by Miguel Munoz, *La Prensa Libre*, Puntarenas, Costa Rica, March 6, 1992. En espanol.

42 *Denuncia*, Central Pacific Regional Fishing Center, Puntarenas, Costa Rica, March 3, 1992. En espanol.

43 "Ambientalistas Atentan Contra la Soberania Nacional," Armando Rodriguez Gutierrez, Comisionado del Atun. En espanol.

44 Mick Kronman to Teresa Platt, May 20, 1992.

45 "A Tribute to Scott Trimingham," *Sea Shepherd Log*, Spring 1991, p. 3.

46 "Slow boat to trouble," by Trip Gabriel, *Outside*, September 1991, p. 54.

47 "Steve Wynn's-Dolphins Lose," by Lisa Lange, *Sea Shepherd Log*, Summer 1991, p. 5.

48 "Mirage Hotel file closed," by Captain Paul Watson, *Sea Shepherd Log*, Fall 1992, p. 8.

49 *Conviction* dated June 3 1994, Lofoten Herredsrett. In Norwegian.

50 *"Sendte ut Mayday—i 11 knop,"* VG, July 7, 1994, p. 7. In Norwegian.

51 *The Environmental Sourcebook*, Edith C. Stein, Lyons & Burford, New York, 1992, p. 184.

Sierra Club

Sierra Club (Founded 1892)
  Annual budget: $41,716,044 (1992)
        Staff: 325 total—180 professional, 145 support, plus volunteers
    Members: 550,000 individuals
  Tax Status: (501)(c)(4)
  Headquarters: 730 Polk Street   408 C Street, NE
                 San Francisco, California 94109   Washington, D.C. 20002
                 Phone: (415)776-2211   Phone: (202)797-6800
                 Fax: (415)776-0350   Fax: (202)797-6646

Economy Trasher Number Five. As "the only member of the 'Group of 10' without tax deductible status, the Sierra Club is the most free-wheeling lobbying and political apparatus of any of the environmental groups," said the *Washington Post*. "The Group of Ten" is the somewhat pretentious name that ten environmental groups in Washington, D.C. gave their informal coalition which banded together in 1981 to coordinate strategy during the Reagan administration. By rank, they are 1) National Wildlife Federation; 2) National Audubon Society; 3) Sierra Club; 4) Wilderness Society; 5) Natural Resources Defense Council; 6) Environmental Defense Fund; 7) Izaak Walton League of America; 8) National Parks and Conservation Association; 9) Friends of the Earth; and 10) Environmental Policy Institute.[1]

The Sierra Club arrived at its "most freewheeling" status after a hundred years of drifting relentlessly to the left of the conservation spectrum. Founded by a number of California notables including naturalist John Muir and University of California paleontologist Joseph LeConte, it remained a local hiking group of the San Francisco elite for many years and it had no axe to grind with industry.[2]

Muir had advocated wilderness protection for the Sierra Nevada through government ownership since the 1870s and was influential in establishing Yosemite National Park in 1890.[3] After the Yosemite success, Muir's supporters in the East immediately began thinking about an organization to protect the remainder of the Sierra. Simultaneously, students and faculty at the University of California in Berkeley were planning an alpine club. The two factions got together and on June 4, 1892, twenty-seven men signed the articles of incorporation in San Francisco. Muir served as its first president.[4]

Its outings became its hallmark. The first "High Trip," in which 96 hikers explored the high country of Yosemite in 1901, grew into a Club tradition, with some 200 Clubbers hauled to the mountains each year. It evolved in the mid-1950s into a diverse outings program following the philosophy that those who know the places will defend them.

The Club originally acknowledged no polarization between the preservationist and the entrepreneur. John Muir's expeditions in his later years, including the famous trek to Glacier Bay in Alaska, were funded by railroad magnate Edward H.

Harriman and Muir even lobbied the California legislature to grant Harriman's Southern Pacific Railroad a monopoly on rail access to Yosemite.[5]

Early Club directors and presidents included the subdivider Duncan McDuffie, the mining lawyer William Colby, and the petroleum engineer Alexander Hildebrand. Historian Susan Schrepfer noted, "These defenders of the Sierra negotiated and at times compromised with developers. They were not always opposed to the demise of wilderness, not even in their 'Range of Light' [the Sierra Nevada for which the Club was named]."[6]

The legendary battle waged by the Sierra Club in 1908 to prevent the construction of a water-supply dam in Hetch-Hetchy Valley near Yosemite was not typical of the early Club. Preservationist John Muir had a difficult time convincing fellow Club members to go along with him, which they finally did only half-heartedly. Muir had a penchant for alienating supporters with remarks such as the peroration he once delivered to some alligators, "Honorable representatives of the great saurians of older creation, may you long enjoy your lilies and rushes, and be blessed now and then with a mouthful of terror-stricken man by way of a dainty!"[7]

To hell with you all.

Gifford Pinchot, humanitarian, utilitarian and first Chief of the U. S. Forest Service, joined the Hetch-Hetchy battle as a titanic opponent of Muir.[8] Because the proposed reservoir was to provide a reliable water supply for San Francisco, which had been devastated by fire after the 1906 earthquake largely because of an inadequate water system, Pinchot was able to gain the support of powerful figures of the day. The moral issue went to people's hearts, and Congress authorized the dam to be built in 1913. Muir died the year after. The Hetch Hetchy Reservoir was filled.[9] It supplies domestic and irrigation water to this day, although environmentalists have recently renewed their efforts to have it torn down—Muir's revenge.[10]

The Hetch Hetchy battle precisely captured the essence of the preservationist philosophy of John Muir as opposed to the conservation philosophy of Gifford Pinchot. Pinchot coined the phrase, "Conservation is the wise use of resources." Muir called for an end to commodity use of natural resources, a ban to be enforced through government ownership and regulation.[11]

The ignominious defeat of the preservationist philosophy left the Club a political moderate for many years. William E. Colby, a Muir protégé, served as Club director from 1900 to 1949 and got along cordially with federal land agencies. Colby and the Club campaigned for the expansion of Sequoia National Park to include the watersheds of the Kern and Kings rivers, and got a bill passed in 1926, but they had been forced to exclude Kings Canyon. In 1940 Colby and the Club convinced Interior Secretary Harold L. Ickes that Kings Canyon National Park should be established. In 1941 the Club blocked logging in Olympic National Park.

In 1946 the Club had 3,500 members and was restricted to California. The Club in 1947 began to stir politically again, and reversed its earlier policy favoring roads into the Sierra, removing from its bylaws the clause "to render accessible the mountain regions" that John Muir himself had put there. It was drifting leftward, but as late as 1949, Club president Bestor Robinson could be heard saying, "Never let your love of nature overshadow your concern for human needs. I want wilderness to contribute to the American way of life."[12]

Outdoor recreation became popular in the 1950s and the pressures changed the Club more. Despite the qualms of a few, in 1950 Club chapters were formed outside the state, an Atlantic Chapter and a Pacific Northwest Chapter, the first steps toward becoming a national organization. New voices in the 1950s pushed the Sierra Club closer to its present position. Leaders criticized recreational developments in the national parks and began to sound the theme of exclusion—*my* uses, not *yours*. They clashed with the Forest Service over logging in the national forests and over wilderness protection in the North Cascades. In 1956, the Club joined with the Wilderness Society to seek wilderness legislation rather than administrative protections, resulting in the Wilderness Act of 1964.

Also in 1956, the Club began a serious political campaign for a Scenic Resources Review to force government agencies to catalog all natural areas so they could systematically and continually be removed from commodity production and their recreational use limited to hiking. The Club's pressure helped produce the Outdoor Recreation Resources Review Act in 1958 (see the profiles of the Izaak Walton League of America, pp. 467-475, and the National Parks and Conservation Association, pp. 362-402, for the details of this act).

Loren Eisley, archaeologist, paleontologist and philosopher, helped create the Club's expensive "Exhibit Format" books (1960-1968) on the redwoods and the Galapagos Islands, among other places, as part of an abortive "Earth National Park" campaign, a logical extension of the web-of-life theory just emerging with the popularization of the science of ecology.

The inspiration for that series had been photographer Ansel Adams' *This Is the American Earth*, a Sierra Club extravaganza which showed its leaders that art book lovers would fork over fifty bucks to adorn their coffee tables with nature photography packaged in poetry, visionary prose and fine printing—and it would reinforce their political campaigns. The twenty-volume Exhibit Format book series, more than anything, made the Sierra Club a household word.

The man whose vision made it happen and whose book-designing skills made it successful was David Ross Brower, mountain climber in his youth, activist in his maturity, who had met Adams in the Sierra Nevada in 1933—and who became the Sierra Club's first executive director in 1952.

Brower was a dynamic leader and the epitome of the amateur naturalist as head of a conservation group. He had been born in Berkeley in 1912, grew up there and attended the University of California at Berkeley from 1929 to 1931, but dropped out to work. He learned about the Sierra Club on a trip to the Sierra and joined in 1933.[13]

Brower was an expert climber, recording a number of first ascents in the Sierra Nevada and one of Shiprock in New Mexico. During World War II he served as a first lieutenant in the Tenth Mountain Division in Italy.

After joining the Club, Brower began doing editorial work for the *Sierra Club Bulletin* in 1935. It didn't pay much, so he worked as an editor for the University of California Press from 1941 to 1952.

He led the Club to victory in a four year battle (1952-1956) over dams proposed for Dinosaur National Monument. The Club had become a militant national organization.[14]

Brower's watershed year was 1960 when he published his article, "A New Decade and a Last Chance: How Bold Shall We Be?" in the Sierra Club Bulletin, presenting a new apocalyptic vision that "What we save in the next few years is all that will ever be saved." Those "next few years" stretched on for more than thirty years of increasingly hysterical extremism.

Brower led many historic battles of the Sierra Club—in the 1960s he was instrumental in establishing the Club's Washington lobbying office, fought against the redwood industry to carve a new Redwood National Park out of their private property, and most fatefully, damned proposals to dam the Grand Canyon, recommending the safe, clean alternative of nuclear power. Brower changed his views late in the '60s, and fought the Sierra Club's approval of California's Diablo Canyon as the site for a nuclear power plant.

Brower was the first but not the last environmental leader to relish being called an extremist. Extremism to Brower meant distrust of authority, public attacks on misguided expertise, and avoidance of compromise. The sword had been drawn. It has slaughtered countless jobs.

But that sword cut both ways. In 1966 the Sierra Club lost its tax-deductible status because of its lobbying, which violated the law. To some extent the impact was ameliorated by the Sierra Club Foundation, which had been formed in 1960, and could accept tax-deductible donations for educational use only. But the Club's balance sheet deteriorated severely. David Brower was a genius at campaigning but an abysmal businessman. His insistence upon more lobbying and continuing the production of the hugely expensive Exhibit Format book series nearly bankrupted the Club.

An anti-Brower faction grew on the board of directors. It was more than his disastrous money mismanagement. The directors feared his opposition to the Diablo Canyon nuclear power plant.

Brower, after working for the Sierra Club in various capacities for 53 years, was caught with his hand in the cookie jar one time too many: As *Mother Jones* noted, "In asking Brower to resign in May 1969, the board cited his 'general intransigence, willful failure to follow board directions, unauthorized expenditures...and contemptuous disregard for club offices.'"[15]

Success and power had gone to his head. A tall, patrician man, Brower increasingly cloaked himself in imperial arrogance. Sitting in his fine redwood home high in the Berkeley Hills he grumped that the Golden Gate Bridge framed in a stunning view out his living room window should be torn down. He took out Club ads in large newspapers at great expense without authorization, took increasingly strident positions, quarrelled with his superiors, alienated all but the most left-wing of the Sierra Club leaders. Even his old friend, Ansel Adams, admitted it: "He intensely believed in what he did, but he acted with complete disregard for financial realities—the bottom line had become unimportant." Adams was one of the board members who voted for his ouster.

Michael McCloskey, a lawyer, took his place, ending the era of Club leadership by amateur naturalists and beginning the professionalization of the environmental movement. Brower went on to found Friends of the Earth (see profile) and after being thrown out of it, founded Earth Island Institute (see profile).

Michael McCloskey took the reins of the Sierra Club and proved himself a consummate demagogue. He revived the bitter images of John Muir's defeat at the hands of Gifford Pinchot in the Hetch Hetchy dispute. It became the Club's "Remember the Alamo!" battle cry. The point was to convince environmentalists to shut down all commodity use of the National Forests, which had been established for the benefit of homesteaders, to protect watersheds, to supply grazing and timber for actual settlers, and to prevent large monopolistic interests from establishing landed estates.[16] By creating a new universe of discourse in which the public forgot this original mission of the National Forests, McCloskey convinced Club members that they were fighting the Hetch Hetchy battle all over again, this time with a chance of winning:

> Pinchot had fought John Muir on establishing new parks in the national forest land because this is what he had in mind all along. Rather than places for people, for wildlife, for beauty, where the lessons of ecology were respected, where timbering is subordinate, Pinchot waited until a way could be found to get the loggers in. The seeds of his thinking have produced our present disaster—where forestry in our national forests means a relentless effort to sell off nearly all marketable commodities on terms not too unacceptable to industry, and let the public use the residue. [We need] a call to arms—for the public to recapture control of its forests, to assert a new future for some of the earth's finest forest land, and to find stewards of a public trust who can be trusted. We must begin all over again.[17]

The clever rewriting of history and the intelligent reframing of issues was McCloskey's forte. He had a gift of debate unmatched in the movement's annals. In a single decade, McCloskey's legal genius reshaped American law into the image of the new environmentalism. His almost-fantastic accomplishments included:

Forest-related issues: Roadless Area Review and Evaluation (RARE) I EIS requirement (1972); RARE I: 56 million acres of wilderness inventory, 12 million acres of study areas in logging moratorium (1973); 1.5 million acres added to National Wilderness Preservation System (1973); 3.7 million acres in New York State's Adirondacks with greater protection (1973); California Wilderness Act, 105,000 acres (1974); Eastern Wilderness Act, 250,000 acres in 16 instant areas, 17 study areas (1974); Tongass Timber Sale cancelled (1976); Alpine Lakes Wilderness (1976); Boundary Waters Canoe Area: suit banned logging in outer zone (1976);

National Parks issues: Gateway East National Recreation Area created (1972); Golden Gate National Recreation Area (1972); 83.5 million acres recommended for d(2) wilderness status in Alaska (1972); Grand Canyon National Park expansion (1974); Big Thicket Preserve in Texas (1974); Cuyahoga Valley National Recreation Area in Ohio (1974); Big South Fork Cumberland National Recreation Area (1974); Yosemite National Park Master Plan rejection (1974); Hells Canyon National Recreation Area (1975); Congaree National Monument (1976); Land and Water Conservation Fund increased to $900 million (1977); administration support and action on Mineral King area transfer to National Park status (1978); Redwood National Park expansion (1978).

Public Land Law issues: Killed the National Timber Supply Act (1970); killed Rep. Wayne Aspinall's Public Land Law Review Commission bill (1972); Model Forest Practices Act in California (1974); Monongahela lawsuit: curbed cutting "immature" timber (1975); National Forest Management Act (1976); provisions for even-flow restriction of clearcutting, new classification of marginal lands, provisions to preserve natural diversity (1976); Bureau of Land Management Organic Act with strong wilderness provisions (1976).[18]

Many of these projects were carried out by coalitions that McCloskey helped form.

McCloskey's pioneering use of the lawsuit as an environmentalist weapon paralleled the successes of the Environmental Defense Fund and the Natural Resources Defense Council. In 1970 the Sierra Club Legal Defense Fund was established as a separate but affiliated organization to institutionalize the advocacy function. Following the United Nations Conference on the Human Environment in 1972, the Club established an office of international affairs in New York, which became the Sierra Club Earthcare Center.

This list of Executive Director McCloskey's leadership achievements does not include Sierra Club victories in pollution control, wildlife, or energy, which are also extensive. Mike McCloskey is arguably the best star pilot in the galaxy of environmental leaders and one of the most cunning warriors the movement has ever had. He started the Club using computers in the late Seventies during the fight for the Alaska Lands Act to quickly target members and supporters most likely to help out with a phone call or letter to a key Congressman on the eve of an important vote. He also used this campaign to cut through the turf fighting between the heads of the different environmental groups that couldn't work together, and helped build the Alaska Coalition headed by Chuck Clusen that attracted more than 50 groups and built a network of thousands of volunteers around the country.[19]

In 1988, after he had been kicked upstairs into the position of Chairman, McCloskey participated on the steering committee of the *Blueprint for the Environment* report and chaired its Council on Environmental Quality Task Force. Shira Flax, a ranking staffer, participated as chairman of the Disarmament Task Force. McCloskey also served as a member of the National Clean Air Coalition that pushed for strengthening the Clean Air Act of 1970 and pressured the Bush administration through reviews and criticisms into presenting its strangling Clean Air Bill that passed Congress in 1989.

Mike McCloskey's Sierra Club was one of the forefront advocates of the Endangered Species Act of 1972, probably the single most destructive economy trasher law on the books. Under the Act, it is a federal crime to destroy the habitat of plant and animal species listed as "endangered" or "threatened." The Secretaries of the Interior and Commerce are responsible for determining which species should be listed. Generally, an "endangered" species is one determined to be currently in danger of extinction; a "threatened" species is one not currently in such danger but likely to become so within the foreseeable future.[20]

This law enables environmentalists to delay, prevent, or impose outrageously costly "mitigation" penalties on development by petitioning to have a species listed. Since anyone can petition the government to add species to the list, finding potential candidates to stop specific developments has become a big business for environmentalists. Actual businesses have been established to "discover" newly endangered species on proposed development properties. Environmentalists systematically use the Act as a kind of legal blackmail to trash the economy.[21]

It is not unusual to find that, long after a development project has been killed at a horrendous cost in jobs and money, the allegedly "endangered" species suddenly turns out to be alive and well in huge numbers in a nearby valley or stream or forest. The classic example is the Tellico Dam farce. In 1978, the U.S. Supreme Court ruled that the Tennessee Valley Authority must halt construction of the Tellico Dam because construction would destroy the home of the endangered snail darter, which was later found thriving in large numbers in other parts of the South.

But such discoveries do not embarrass environmentalists, who appear to be beyond shame. The case of the Dusky Seaside Sparrow ended in snail darter fashion, even though environmentalists tried to put blinders on the public by saying of the bird that it was

living on borrowed time. Man-caused habitat changes pressed in—cattle grazing, canal and road building, burning and drainage for agriculture, flooding and pesticide spraying for mosquito control. The advent of the close-by Cape Canaveral space-flight center and the development it spawned were a major blow. Site-tenacious, the dusky race existed nowhere else and would not move. Its numbers fell. By 1976, no more evidence of nesting could be found.[22]

That was written quite a while after renowned ornithologist Roger Tory Peterson, in the 1980 edition of his authoritative *Field Guide to the Birds,* noted that the Dusky was actually rather common: "Any Seaside Sparrow on St. Johns River near Titusville, Florida, is the species." The doomsayers got a further slap in the face when scientists John C. Avise and William S. Nelson found that mitochondrial DNA from the supposedly "extinct" dusky seaside sparrow was an exact match with existing populations of seaside sparrows up and down the Atlantic coast.[23]

The fact that no such studies were required when environmentalists demanded the Dusky be listed demonstrates the extent to which environmental organizations have gained credibility as legitimate spokesmen on such issues, despite their history of emotionalism, exaggeration, baseless allegations, and outright fraud. Their total power over the development economy is awesome. The Sierra Club Legal Defense Fund was to use hype and minimal regard for scientific proof again in the Pacific Northwest old-growth battle that centered around the Northern Spotted Owl (see profile of the National Audubon Society).

Perhaps the most important lesson we can learn from McCloskey's list of accomplishments is that the growth of environmental legislation has systematically prevented new economic development and burdened existing economic enterprises for more than two decades and that no one has calculated—or even thought about—the cumulative economic impact. When we hear appeals to save the last forest we are listening to a twenty-five-year-long campaign that hops from one place to the next, putting one forest after another off limits to commercial timber harvest and regrowth, and never counting all the "saved" forests—or the costs of having saved them. When we hear appeals to clean up the air or the water we are listening to a twenty-five-year-long campaign to make the air and water cleaner and cleaner and cleaner so that now we are measuring single molecules of impurity that have no health effect whatever and are merely demanding treatment for the sake of treatment.

Lobbying Tactics

In the 1980s, David Gardiner became the Sierra Club's top Washington lobbyist. He was one of the leaders who shaped the Club's lobbying strategy: the Club chooses a set of eight legislative priorities every two years to coincide with the term of Congress, then brings to bear all the pressure of its impressive and high-demographics membership. These eight priorities are pragmatically selected on the leadership's estimation of their winnability, an approach the Club learned from McCloskey. That way the Club builds a reputation for success and that helps pry money out of high-dollar contributors.

McCloskey's pragmatism was behind the Club's shift away from support for nuclear power as a safe, clean alternative to dams in the Grand Canyon. David Brower's opposition to nuclear power was the last straw that got him fired in 1969—because the board feared that opposing nuclear power would alienate its members. But when the climate of public opinion shifted, so did the Sierra Club. In 1979 the Club voted against the Diablo Canyon nuclear power plant site and endorsed the Nuclear Weapons Freeze, opposing any further government funding for the production or testing of destabilizing weapons.

Even here the canny McCloskey's pragmatic hand can be seen: By endorsing the Freeze, the Club prevented its San Francisco Bay Chapter from supporting local nuclear free zones, which would offend the larger national membership. The board argued that the unilateral nature of nuclear free zones without Soviet nuclear free zones would conflict with the club's support for a bilateral nuclear freeze. McCloskey also engineered the shunting of a proposal to oppose Star Wars to committee—his membership was not yet willing to go that far against defense.

Fund-raising Tactics

The peddling of illusion seems to have become one of the Sierra Club's prime operations. The Club's Peter McAllister told a gathering of environmentalists in 1988, "We're all in marketing and advertising and we have to play it for all it's worth."[24]

The Sierra Club itself gets rich from many pockets. In 1992 the Club took in $15,506,00 in memberships, $12,912,308 in contributions and grants, $5,123,285 from program service revenue including book sales and more than 275 outings, $156,332 in interest on temporary investments and $654,624 in dividends and interest from securities. The Club had $7,979,267 in investments (it is not uncommon for contributors to donate shares of stock in profit-making corporations to non-profit groups instead of cash, and these donations of stock yield the usual dividend income). Estate bequests amounted to $348,938 in 1992.

The Sierra Club uses most of the high-tech fund-raising gimmicks you'd expect from a soap manufacturer or Sears Roebuck. Like the Cousteau Society, it is a client of Craver, Mathews, Smith & Company, which helps it raise money with direct mail campaigns. In addition, the Sierra Club uses huge bull pens of motor-mouth telemarketers who endlessly call targets and read a fund-raising script that asks donors to give to the Sierra Club till it hurts, usually hyping some current issue.

The Sierra Club also issues its own VISA credit card. With each use, banks donate a fraction of the consumer's purchase to the environmental group, ranging from one-half of 1 percent to 5 percent of the amount charged. Edward Shelton, president of American Bankcard Services, which markets the Sierra Club's card, said, "The club expects to get $20 to $40 a year per cardholder." The use of such "affinity cards," as they are known in the trade, is growing, says Mr. Shelton, because by tapping loyalties, banks can encourage card-switching and increase their market share. Affinity cardholders usually beat the industry average of 37 uses a year. So your bank, which won't loan to a home builder because the Sierra Club is suing him over endangered species or to a business that employs hundreds of people because environmentalists have damaged their industry's risk exposure through lawsuit after lawsuit, is *giving* money to the environmental movement.[25]

The greenmail lawsuit against industry, like the bounty-hunter lawsuit against the federal government, is another big source of Sierra Club money. It works like this: First, you draft a law that will make a certain economic activity a crime, you lobby it through Congress with provisions for citizen lawsuits against industries that break the new law, and then, having created the universe of discourse on the subject, you sit on a dead branch and wait for a company to break your law. Then you sue them, and when they lose or they're ready to fold, you stick them up for big donations to the Sierra Club.

This usually works—Coors Brewing signed a 1991 agreement to avert a Sierra Club lawsuit by contributing $160,000 to the Trust for Public Lands, a private land-buying environmental group something like the Nature Conservancy that works in tandem with a number of bigger muscle groups like the Sierra Club. But the U.S. Justice Department went to court in 1990 to stop the Sierra Club from collecting a $4.2 million penalty from Unocal Corporation. Unocal's refinery in Rodeo, California, north of Oakland, was the victim of a six-year Clean Water Act lawsuit filed by the Sierra Club Legal Defense Fund over discharges into San Francisco Bay. There was a serious question about whether the discharges were harmful in any way, but, like most companies, Unocal thought it would be cheaper to cut a deal than pay an army of lawyers for six *more* years as the case made its way through appeals courts. Under terms of the negotiated settlement, the Sierra Club would have recovered $1.3 million in legal fees and Unocal would give $4.2 million to the Trust for Public Land, the California Water Pollution Cleanup and Abatement Account, and other organizations. The Feds said that water pollution penalties must be paid directly to the Treasury for general purposes.

The Sierra Club objected, not only because it would not get its greenmail loot, but also "because the Justice Department's approach would allow the oil company to take a substantial tax write-off for a pollution fine." Let's not leave the economy holding any penny we can steal from it, boys! Or perhaps the message should be the reverse, like the popular bumper-sticker: Don't steal—The government doesn't like competition.[26]

It is appalling that such power over the economy lies in the clutches of a tiny clique of people in a private environmental organization. Even the most basic resources are totally at the mercy of environmental litigators. The Viceroy Gold Corporation, a Canadian company, gave in to environmentalist greenmail tactics in a California battle out of what appears to be moral cowardice. Viceroy Gold began the process of obtaining permits to mine in a tiny area known as the Castle Mountain Project within the borders of the East Mojave National Scenic Area, a designation lobbied into existence by a number of environmental groups to prevent economic activity. The Bureau of Land Management, the federal agency that administers the area, had approved the mining permits in 1987, in accordance with strict environmental regulations. But the environmental movement saw an easier target than robbing a gold mine: robbing a gold mining company.

The Sierra Club Legal Defense Fund, representing the Wilderness Society, the California Wilderness Coalition, the Desert Protective Council, the Sierra Club, Desert Survivors, and Citizens for a Mojave National Park, filed an appeal and threatened to sue if Viceroy refused to meet their demands. Viceroy asked for a meeting in June 1988 and soon folded, giving the groups a $2 million greenmail payoff in 1990 and agreeing to extremely costly mining techniques far beyond reasonable protections for the environment. But when you expect to mine 750,000 ounces of gold worth nearly $290 million, it may be worth a few million bucks of shareholders' money to get the monkeys off your back. Viceroy executive Chris Mitchell, said, "We would rather see the money go into environmental enhancement than into the pockets of lawyers." Chris, what do you think those guys in the Sierra Club Legal Defense Fund are?

Ed Hastey, state director of the Bureau of Land Management, said that Viceroy "paid off" the environmentalists, "not a good way of doing business." Norbert J. Riedy of the Wilderness Society said, "We didn't want the mine there at all, but we also saw it would get permits." So these Economy Trashers did what any good thugs would do, they ganged up with a few partners and staged a stickup. Viceroy executives emerged from the rape with a smile on their face, pretending all was well, saying they hoped environmentalists "can use this as an educational tool for a better understanding of the mining industry." You bet, Viceroy, they now understand they can get you to lie down and play dead. The Wilderness Society's Riedy learned this: "Gold companies have enough profit to make considerable environmental compromises and we intend to use this example to press for similar measures elsewhere."

Very educational, Viceroy. You did our mineral economy a big favor.

One wonders exactly what is meant by "an environmental compromise" as practised by the Wilderness Society or the Sierra Club. A firm comes into an economic arena with millions of dollars of investment capital, a technological infrastructure, a payroll of people expert in doing a good job, and the legal obligation to work under strict regulations and publicly reveal all the money they handle. Environmental groups come into that economic arena with nothing other than the political clout to stop all economic activity. They insist that a firm obey their wishes. They offer nothing in return for concessions other than the right to continue to do business until the next environmental group comes in for its pound of flesh. In another context, this behavior would be called blackmail and its practitioners called gangsters.

The Sierra Club also uses the simple vexatious lawsuit as a means to impose its ideology on every aspect of life—and death. One of the Sierra Club's most appalling achievements to date has been to file suit to prevent construction of a hospice for terminally ill patients in Monterey, California. The infamous case has become known among disgusted lawyers—and it takes a lot to disgust a lawyer—as *Sierra Club v. The Terminally Ill.*[27]

Hospice of the Central Coast is a nonprofit organization which provides a total support system and health care program for terminally ill patients and their families. It spent four years publicly planning for a new center, securing a donation of land from the Pebble Beach Company and raising $4,100,000 from the community to help construct the proposed new $6 million, 28-bed facility. The land—fewer than five acres of a 140-acre tract—is not visible from any surrounding area.

In addition, a forestry management plan developed by experts hired by the company was reviewed by other experts from the city and the State Department of Fish and Game, who found that it satisfied the California Environmental Quality Act (CEQA).

The company even invited the Sierra Club to help design the project. The Club refused.

In November, 1990, the city planning commission found that the project created no unresolved environmental impacts and approved a permit. The Sierra Club, which did not attend the public hearings, at the last minute appealed this decision and then, when its appeal was rejected by the city council, filed suit, alleging that the city had violated the CEQA by issuing a land use permit without requiring an environmental impact report.

The Monterey *Herald* editorialized that "this is a classic case of an environmental impact report being demanded in the hope that it will either delay a project to death or kill it outright."

The Sierra Club denied any attempt "to delay or stop the hospice from being built in Monterey," but emphasized the "threatened habitat" near the hospice being "one of only three small native pine forests left in the Continental United States."

To hell with you all.

In 1983, pesky old David Brower came back to haunt the Sierra Club. He lobbied the membership to put him on the board of directors and enough people voted for him to give him a seat. Brower was still chairman of the board of Friends of the Earth at the time and brought his antinuclear agenda to the Sierra Club. It was not welcome.

In 1984 Brower recruited other antinuclear activists in the Club to apply pressure to make ending the arms race one of the Club's lobbying priorities. At the next board meeting, in February of 1985, eight other priorities were confirmed, and the board didn't even discuss the nuclear issue. Brower helped get up a subgroup calling itself the Nuclear Concerns Coalition which circulated a petition that was eventually signed by more than 2,000 Club members, and that pressured the board to reconsider at its November meeting.

Sierra Club leaders are cunning, however. Michelle Perault was then president and accepted a motion from her husband, director Phillip Berry, to accept the nuclear issue as a priority—but an "unfunded priority." Of course, nothing happens with an "unfunded priority." Brower pressed for putting the funding question—$50,000 for an antinuclear lobbyist on Capitol Hill—to the membership. The board agreed, although it voted 14 to 1 against recommending funding. Guess who the lone dissenter was.

Perrault took no chances with Brower and sent out thousands of flyers to Sierra Club leaders all over the country, warning against requests for donations from the Coalition, and positioning the Club as a reasonable body trying to fend off extremists who were damaging the Club's credibility and effectiveness. The Nuclear Concerns Coalition pulled back under the withering fire, but came back later, again to no avail—by then the Soviet Union was collapsing and the Cold War ended with a whimper, not a bang, taking the guts of the antinuclear movement with it.

Oh, yes, if you'll skip below to the list of the Sierra Club's current board of directors, you won't find David R. Brower's name on it.

Carl Pope, former staffer and current executive director ($77,142 annual salary), took over from Michael Fisher, who assumed office in 1987 after two years as senior associate of Sedway Cooke Associates, a San Francisco-based urban and environmental planning firm. He was executive director of the California Coastal Commission from 1978 to 1985—there's that revolving door again, out of government into the environmental movement. Under Pope's new leadership, the Sierra Club has given a large number of grants to other environmental groups, including $38,000 to the Wilderness Society, $1,500 to NRDC, $2,000 to the Natural Resources Council of Maine and more than two dozen others.

Although the Sierra Club lies outside the Rockefeller clique's inner circle, it has received millions of dollars from the Rockefeller foundations in past years. And its leaders share some characteristics with the Rockefeller protégés. With leaders such as Michael Fischer and William Kane Reilly and their urban planning degrees, it's not hard to see why the environmental movement is so in love with centralized planning as a model for reshaping society—even with the collapse of the Soviet Union, they are not about to give up the dream, which led the late newspaper columnist Warren T. Brookes to call members of the Green Movement "Watermelons:" Green on the outside, Red on the inside. There's only one difference: Even old line Communists think the enviros are crazy. Lev Timofeyev, author of *The*

Anti-Communist Manifesto, told us during a conversation from his apartment in Moscow that environmentalists startle even hard-line right-wing Communist Party stalwarts with their blind faith in planning and government control.

Trying to keep their ideological purity has become an obsession. After considerable agonizing, the Sierra Club turned down $700,000 from McDonald's, which wanted to sponsor an environmental educational project. McDonald's sought another environmental organization to fund.[28]

Keeping their ideological purity is also tearing the Club apart. According to a December 1993 *New York Times* story by Keith Schneider, when the Club's chief lobbyist in the Pacific Northwest, William Arthur, cut down fir and pine on 10 acres he owned in Pend Oreille County, Washington, and sold it to a log exporter for $10,000, purists in the 40,000 Atlantic Chapter called for a virtual end to logging in the Northern Rockies. Others, including Atlantic Chapter leader Margaret Hays Young called for a ban on all logging in all national forests, period. Other Club leaders were alarmed at the radicals' efforts to get elected to the board of directors, saying the Club had won in the past by incrementalism, trashing the economy little by little so few people noticed. This new hardline stance would draw strong opposition from the public, worried Dr. John Osborn, conservation chairman of the Northern Rockies Chapter. No kidding, John.

The Sierra Club Legal Defense Fund (1971)
Budget: $8.7 million (1991)
Non-membership
Tax status: 501(c)(3)
180 Montgomery Street, Suite 1400
San Francisco, California 94104
Phone: (415)627-6700

SCLDF is a public interest law firm that many call "the Great Litigating Arm of the Environmental Movement." "Sue early and sue often" could be its motto. Its annual budget of $9.3 million (1990) and staff of 80 make it a formidable force in the courts. The Legal Defense Fund's chairman Michael Traynor ($132,916 annual salary) replaced Rick Sutherland who was killed in an automobile accident in the summer of 1991. Traynor previously served on the Fund's board for 17 years, including 2 years as chairman.

The Sierra Club Legal Defense Fund was established to make public policy through the courts. The idea was not to follow the law, but to make the law by forcing issues in case law. From its inception, the SCLDF was supported largely by the Ford Foundation, including grants of $98,000 in 1971, $143,000 in 1972, and $192,000 in 1974. Even though the Ford Foundation announced it intended to discontinue support of public interest law firms in 1974, it nonetheless provided an additional grant of $85,000 in 1976 and kept giving money through 1979.[29]

The Sierra Club Legal Defense Fund pioneered the bounty-hunter subsidy from federal taxpayers that has netted them millions of dollars. Thanks to the diligence of SCLDF, environmentalists are being paid handsomely by you and me for Trashing the Economy—by means of the environmental lawsuit.

More than 130 federal statutes and the Equal Access to Justice Act provide for payment of fees in suits against the federal government. None of the statutes require an annual public report on legal fees and recipients. Accountings are difficult to obtain.

Records obtained through the Freedom of Information Act indicate that since 1985 at least 105 payments have been authorized for three top environmental groups: the Sierra Club Legal Defense Fund with 53 payments; the Natural Resources Defense Council, 34 payments; and the Environmental Defense Fund, 18 payments—figures which may reflect multiple payments for single cases.

The Sierra Club Legal Defense Fund reported legal fee collections of $2.3 million total in fiscal 1990 and 1991.

The Natural Resources Defense Council listed legal fees totaling $1.65 million for fiscal years 1989 and 1990.

And the Environmental Defense Fund reported $186,000 in fiscal 1989 and 1990.

The Seattle Audubon Society and other groups have asked the courts to award them legal fees for initiating the spotted owl lawsuit that is decimating the timber industry in the Pacific Northwest. They want to be paid to put people out of business, recompensed for destroying an industry, rewarded for ruining whole communities.

Our federal government has already paid legal fees in other environmental-group cases running into the hundreds of thousands of dollars. The total bounties paid to environmentalist lawyers aggregate in the millions. During the period 1981-1983 alone, fee awards totaling $3.8 million were disbursed to environmental group lawyers in 154 cases. A single award of $1.2 million in fees went for one surface-mining case alone.

Former Deputy Attorney General D. Lowell Jensen points out that the taxpayer subsidy is often billed at the "silk-stocking" rates charged by top corporate law firms. Environmental groups may then use these fees in other litigation that qualifies for additional subsidies.

Most shocking, the bounty-hunter laws have attracted a school of sharks who created a new legal specialty: Federal Attorney Fee Inflating. There are actually attorneys who specialize in winning higher fees for environmental lawyers. They go to court demanding not only high hourly rates for environmental lawyers—much higher than the $75 an hour cap established by the Equal Access to Justice Act— but also to obtain special bonuses and windfalls by taking advantage of little-known clauses in federal laws. Such attorneys have even generated a new jargon all their own. You may see lawyer magazines talking about "How to Enhance Your Lodestar." What's a lodestar? The lodestar is the base from which bonuses are calculated. The higher the lodestar, the higher the bonus. Your taxes at work.

The result has been situations in which the primary lawsuit took 186 hours, but the fees dispute took 350 hours. In another case, a Sierra Club chapter's lawyer demanded and won a $10 an hour cost of living adjustment over and above the $75 an hour cap set by the Equal Access to Justice Act in addition to a $57,667 fee for blocking a military project in Maine where the economy badly needed the jobs. Environmentalists are above the law, and even judges put them on a special pedestal.

Incredible as it seems, there is even a journal for such predators, the *Federal*

Attorney Fees Awards Reporter. It puts one in the frame of mind that must have affected Shakespeare when he wrote that wonderful line in *Henry VI, Part II*, "The first thing we do, let's kill all the lawyers."

Supreme Court Justice White noted in the benchmark case on such environmentalist lawyer fees that Congress apparently established "counsel fees so as to encourage private litigation." It certainly did.

The Natural Resources Defense Council, the Environmental Defense Fund, the National Wildlife Federation and the Sierra Club Legal Defense Fund were part of a 28-member "public-interest" alliance that opposed Senate efforts to cap fees at $75 an hour in the mid 1980s.

The alliance's statements to the Senate Subcommittee on the Constitution said the members use the money for "continuing and...if possible, increasing the legal representation the organization offers." Increasing representation is possible because a staff attorney paid a salary that works out to $25 or $30 an hour can bring in a one-case award at two to six times that much. One winner can sustain other old and new initiatives.

Michael Greve, executive director of the Center for Individual Rights, a Washington-based public interest law firm, said, "Fee awards above actual costs have greatly enhanced the environmental movement's litigation capacity and, hence, the frequency of lawsuits."

Jensen testified that "It is not uncommon for attorneys to be awarded fees that exceed their hourly rates for private clients."

Many environmental lawsuits are brought to change or initiate federal regulatory policy. Such suits also pull into court, at their own expense, those directly affected.

In 1989, the Environmental Protection Agency was ordered to pay $110,000 for the Sierra Club in litigation that forced the adoption in 1984 of regulations governing radionuclides. Radionuclides primarily concern uranium miners and nuclear power firms, yet other industries had to enter the lawsuit at customer and stockholder expense to protect their interests, including the coal-fired portion of the electric-power industry.

In 1992 the Environmental Defense Fund was the plaintiff in a suit against the Environmental Protection Agency over periods of haze in the Grand Canyon. The settlement will require a power-plant operator to invest $530 million to install scrubbers on a plant that already meets standards of the Clean Air Act. Twenty-year operating expenses are estimated at $1.8 billion. The settlement will affect electric rates in wide areas of the West, including Los Angeles. The plant operator spent at least $1.5 million in court defending its interests.

One of the bounty-hunters' most-used statutes is the Surface Mining Control and Reclamation Act (SMCRA). A $1.2 million award on appeal came in a long-running case over the establishment and operation of an applicant-violator tracking system for new mining permits. In addition, the General Accounting Office found that from its passage in 1977 through early 1989, bounty-hunter attorney fees from the act totalled more than $1.2 million to "public interest" lawyers and groups in 12 suits.

Who are the law firms and environmental groups that raked in this taxpayer largesse? The GAO report listed the following payments: Galloway & Greenberg, $619,310; Yablonski, Booth & Feldman, $258,615; Tom FitzGerald, $64,875; Dow, Lohnes & Albertson, $39,409; National Wildlife Federation, $33,409; Environmental Defense Fund, $30,952; Center for Law and Social Policy, $30,952; Morgan & Foley, $30,084; Advocates for the Public Interest, $26,815; Sierra Club Legal Defense Fund, $20,981; Environmental Policy Institute, $19,048; Council of Southern Mountains, Inc, $13,128; Harmon & Weiss, $10,485; Onek, Klein & Farr, $9,802; L. Gilbert Kendrick, $6,640; and the National Trust for Historic Preservation, $3,679. Total $1,217,506.

Bruce Fein, former general counsel of the Federal Communications Commission, wrote in the journal *Law and Contemporary Issues,* "The inescapable result is a costly and unrestrained growth in litigation against federal agencies." Fein called generous fees a "reward for litigious meddlesomeness by those who simply do not like the results of our political and administrative processes." He contended that net result is "to shift policymaking from the legislative and executive branches to the judicial branch in a clear circumvention of the political decision-making process."

The Sierra Club Legal Defense Fund publishes a quarterly newsletter called *In Brief.*

The Sierra Club's empire falls into a distinct channel of the environmental movement that could be characterized as the Establishment Eco-Socialist Axis. It is neither an artifact nor an instrumentality of either the Rockefeller Money Axis or the Mellon Money Axis. The Sierra Club clearly falls within the Establishment in terms of its leaders' backgrounds and relationships and its working within the framework of politics and law. However, the Sierra Club pursues policies that have both Interventionist and Eco-Socialist features, making the classification a judgment call—and we see more Eco-Socialist features than Interventionist. The Sierra Club refuses to support or countenance any profit-making commodity uses of public or private lands, which could be an extreme form of Interventionism. Every piece of legislation created by the Sierra Club consolidates power in the State and harms free markets and capitalism, which could be more than Interventionism. Both of these positions move the Sierra Club away from the Interventionist Axis and place it mostly in an Establishment Eco-Socialist Axis, but to a somewhat lesser degree than the Wilderness Society. However, the Sierra Club does not envision the destruction of industrial civilization like the eco-terrorist axis, even though that may be the actual incremental result of everything it does.

The Trust for Public Land (1972)
Annual budget: $23,516,506
Staff: 170 professional and clerical
Tax status: 501(c)(3)
116 New Montgomery Street, Fourth Floor
San Francisco, California 94105
Phone (415)495-4014 FAX (415)495-4103

This San Francisco-based Economy Trasher grew up a few blocks down the street from the Sierra Club and works hand in glove with the old-line environmental group. Huey Johnson, a former Secretary for Resources for the State of California, was the founding president of the Trust. He went on to become president of the Resources Renewal Institute of San Francisco and an environmental columnist for the *San Francisco Examiner*. TPL today operates out of an office in the same block as the Sierra Club Legal Defense Fund.

It is a nonmembership group run by President Martin J. Rosen with a staff that for many years included the son of Senator Bennett Johnston (D-Louisiana). TPL's balance sheet on March 31, 1991 showed total assets of $66,085,000 and total revenues of $23.5 million. Six regional groups participate with TPL in acquiring and preserving private land in urban and rural areas and converting it to public use. Its magazine *Land and People* goes out three times a year to a circulation of 25,000. TPL also publishes *The Conservation Easement Handbook*. It is also cozy with the Rockefeller and Mellon folk.

The Trust for Public Land is another eco-profiteer that buys land at distress prices and then sells it to the government at Fair Market Value, reaping a tidy gain. TPL works a great deal with the U.S. Forest Service. The Forest Service can be a ferocious predator when it's out to absorb some more private land into its already vast domain.

Ask Janet and Bill Rogers, who bought 160 acres of remote land near Zenia, California on a high ridgetop. They loved the place and began to work it, planting a garden and an orchard of fruit trees, digging wells and beginning their dream home. Then they discovered an unpleasant fact: They had bought one of the last remaining parcels of private land in a county where the federal government owns 90 percent of the land. Their farm was surrounded by federal property, and ranchers had grazing permits on that land, meaning that the cattle from their allotment could easily drift through their gateless fence and make short work of their garden. The obvious solution was to put up a gate in the fence so the neighbors' cattle couldn't trespass. So the Rogerses put a gate on their road.

Unfortunately, the fact that their home was surrounded by federal property made their private land an "inholding," private land within a government area. They did not know that long-time Forest Service policy has been to eliminate all inholders and take their property, by condemnation in the courts, or by the hideous instrument known as the Declaration of Taking, with which the government can take your property without notice and force you to leave within 90 days.

The gate put up by the Rogerses was torn down by a Forest Service assault team and the Rogerses hauled off in chains for blocking "public access" to their private land. The Rogerses took the Forest Service to federal court, which is always a losing battle for the private property owner. For one thing, the government lives forever—and it prints the money. Then the Forest Service suggested that they sell their land to the Trust for Public Land. Bill Rogers told them, "No, because we believed that TPL would only resell the land to the Forest Service. We wanted to live on it and work our own land."

The Rogerses turned the deal down, but many property owners under attack by the Forest Service sell out. They have certain incentives: Sellers get a tax break by selling to TPL, because they get an appraisal for "highest and best use," but sell the property to TPL for a lower price and claim the difference as a tax deduction. The Trust for Public Land, because it is tax exempt, sells the land to the government for the appraised price and pockets the difference.

The Columbia Gorge

The Cascade Mountains sweep in a long straight line from Northern California to Canada, punctuated every sixty miles or so by a chain of restless stratovolcanoes poking up like warning beacons announcing: Plate Techtonics At Work. As the Pacific Basin Plate dips beneath the North American Continental Plate into the hot planetary mantle, the melted seafloor rises as magma and breaks through the crust to give us Mount Rainier (tallest of the Cascade sentinels), Crater Lake (deepest of the collapsed volcanic calderas), Goldmeyer Hot Springs (at a sixty-mile interval where a volcano should be but isn't) and side-by-side Mount Adams and Mount Saint Helens (which demonstrated conclusively in 1980 that the Cascade volcanoes are not extinct).

The Columbia River flows through the eighty-mile wide Cascades between Mount Saint Helens and Mount Hood. Geologically, it was the other way around: The Cascades pushed up across the path of the ancient Columbia. Either way, the result was a basalt-ribbed river cutting through a mountain range, which left a gorge of nicely scenic but not particularly spectacular topography—more like the gentle Ozarks than the Grand Tetons of Wyoming, with the Sugarloaf of Beacon Rock and the Yosemite-like precipice of Multnomah Falls thrown in to spice things up a little.[30]

Today the State of Washington lies to the north of the Columbia River and Oregon lies to the south. Most of the mountains that cross the Columbia River belong to the U. S. Department of Agriculture, Forest Service; the Gifford Pinchot National Forest ir Washington, the Mount Hood National Forest in Oregon. The lazy two-lane Washingto State Highway 14 winds along the north bank and high-speed Interstate 84 skirts the south. The land flanking both shores of the broad river is mostly private.

Portland, Oregon dominates the area. You can get to anywhere in the Gorge on the freeway from downtown in an hour or so. The West Hills Mafia of Portland— the town's cliquish and clanny old-money elite—has long considered the Columbia Gorge its personal playground. Members in good standing own widely spaced country estates on the bluffs overlooking the river and hire old-fashioned paddle-wheel pleasure boats to run them upstream for an intimate birthday party of a hundred guests. The fact that 41,000 fellow citizens happen to live in the twenty-three towns of the Gorge from Troutdale to The Dalles is a mere inconvenience. The towns are simply eyesores caused by lowlifes who haven't the good taste to live in the architectural contest of Portland's West Hills. For many years the people of the gorge smiled tolerantly at the snooty Portland tourists—the locals were absorbed with their own lives, working little farms and ranches, operating timber stands and sawmills, tending the hydroelectric dams and generally minding their own business.

In 1978, the U. S. Forest Service came into the Columbia Gorge town of Dodson, Oregon, population 50, and held a big public meeting. The District Ranger told everybody the Forest Service wanted to buy all their houses. They'd pay Fair Market Value because they had $5 million in their budget to buy up inholdings and the only inholdings left in this particular District of the Mount Hood National Forest were the towns. The Forest Service candidly told the citizens they were afraid that if they didn't spend the $5 million in 1978, they wouldn't get any acquisition budget at all the next year.[31]

Ordinary people in rural areas can be interested in selling out if the price is right, and the Forest Service was talking the right price. However, after the Ranger walked them through the details and the townspeople discovered they would have to sign the papers now but wait fifteen months to get their money—during the Carter inflation—they showed the Forest Service the door. In fifteen months, who could tell what the right price might be?

The Ranger tried to be as diplomatic as he could, but he was a plainspoken man and said, "Folks, you'd better sell to the Forest Service, because if you don't, the National Park Service is going to come in here and flat take it away from you."

The Forest Ranger must have been a prophet. In 1979 the National Park Service sent a team into the Columbia Gorge to do a study. Chuck Williams of the Friends of the Earth had written a letter to National Park Service Director William Whelan suggesting in the strongest terms that he should promote a new Columbia Gorge National Park to preserve the natural landscape. Whelan set the wheels in motion.

The U.S. Forest Service and the National Park Service do not get along with each other. The Forest Service belongs to the Department of Agriculture and the Park Service belongs to the Department of the Interior. Big egos have always occupied the Cabinet-level big chair in each department. The two departments have tried to absorb each other through various hostile takeover schemes and stratagems for more than a century. So when the Forest Service saw Chuck Williams guiding the Park Service around the gorge, avoiding any contact with the locals and taking pictures of *their* turf, all eyes narrowed to cunning slits and the old Machiavellian guile went to work.

Forest Service District Ranger Gene Zimmerman of the Columbia Gorge Ranger District, Mount Hood National Forest, received word from on high that because people objected to them buying up the little towns in the Gorge directly, they were going to call upon the Trust for Public Land to run interference for them. And so it was that while the Park Service did their *Study of Alternatives*, the Trust for Public Land began quietly buying up the Columbia Gorge, holding the land for subsequent purchase by the Forest Service. Sneaky, sneaky.

The Park Service report scared hell out of everybody with its alternatives, one of which was No Action, which, of course, the Park Service said, would result in the total destruction of the gorge by the people who lived there. The other alternatives were all federal action alternatives, one of which was to create a brand new type of federal entity called a National Scenic Area, which was a Greenline Park that drew a boundary around everything and imposed regulations that stopped you from using your land but didn't pay you for taking it.[32]

Chuck Williams helped form the **Columbia Gorge Coalition** in Hood River, Oregon, to take the most extreme possible government control position. Most of its members were from Portland. Its specialty became making a stink about every economic development in the gorge, no matter how small, and characterizing it as total devastation. Their motto became, "Local control can't do the job."[33]

In 1980, Multnomah County Executive Donald G. Clark, who had gubernatorial ambitions and figured that the Portland environmental vote would put him over the top, founded an environmental group called **Friends of the Gorge**. The IRS awarded FOG its tax exemption in the Spring of 1981 and the group went public, recommending creation of a Columbia River Gorge National Recreation Area, to be operated by the National Park Service and modeled after the Cuyahoga Valley National Recreation Area in Ohio. Park Service Director Whelan had made it clear before being replaced by Russell Dickinson that the gorge would never make it as a National Park because its modest features didn't qualify, but that some lesser designation might win the cachet of Congress.

Don Clark brought elegantly tailored Nancy N. Russell on board as chairman and Carol Kirschner as executive director of Friends of the Gorge, both women politically well-connected. They quickly found that Oregon didn't like the Park Service and that any proposal for them to operate a Columbia Gorge area would fail. So FOG hired Gail Achterman, an attorney formerly with the Department of the Interior, to draft the Columbia River Gorge National Scenic Area Act of 1983, with the Forest Service as the administrative agency.

Citizen opposition to the plan surfaced instantly and a long and noisy battle began. Local advocates like Esson Smith and Joe Wrabek helped form Columbia Gorge United to keep the wolves away. Chuck Cushman's National Inholders Association helped them along, staving off federalization for several years.[34]

Some puzzling hints about why FOG had been organized came out of the 1983 congressional hearing on the Gorge Bill held by Senator Mark Hatfield. The record of that hearing shows Don Clark, whose Portland environmental vote in the Governor's race had brought him in third out of a field of three, telling Senator Hatfield:

> Mr. Clark: Twenty-eight months ago, on the advice of U.S. Senator Mark Hatfield, I invited the building of a broad-based, bipartisan coalition to prepare a comprehensive and realistic approach to protect the gorge.
>
> The response was immediate and substantial. An organization was formed whose membership held little in common except a sincere desire to protect the Columbia River gorge. Because of the diversity of the group, compromise came very hard—but, it did come.[35]

The organization, of course, was Friends of the Gorge. Why would Senator Hatfield want a front group to push Gorge legislation rather than simply have his staff draft it? Let's see. One of Senator Hatfield's good friends and political supporters is John D. Gray, founder of Omark Industries, now called Oregon Cutting Systems, leading manufacturer of chainsaw equipment. Mr. Gray is also the owner and developer of the renowned Salishan Resort on the Oregon Coast.

Gray enlisted architects John Storrs and Charles Scroggin in 1964 to create the legendary Salishan coastal resort, which has won scads of Mobil 5-Star honors, Holiday Magazine Fine Dining Awards and AAA 5-Diamond Awards for its lodge and gourmet dining room, heated indoor swimming pool, a challenging 18-hole par 72 championship golf course, tennis courts, condominiums, planned private community, and tasteful upscale mini-mall shopping center.[36]

Salishan boasts a lot of thoughtful little touches, such as $300,000 worth of covered walkways—important in the Pacific Northwest's maritime climate. All this and Pacific Ocean beaches, too.[37]

Salishan is the only five-star resort on the Oregon Coast. Mr. Gray gave substantial contributions to **1,000 Friends of Oregon** and was a member of their board of advisors—and the Friends made sure statewide land use regulations outlawed any more destination resorts on the Oregon Coast. As the old joke goes, an environmentalist is a person who just got his building permit and doesn't want you to get yours.

The Columbia Gorge has always been looked upon as a great site for a destination resort. But there's this little catch: It couldn't pay for itself. As the Howard Hughes interests discovered in a 1971 study, the Gorge is just too close to Portland. You can go see everything the Gorge has to offer and get back to your downtown hotel in less than a day, no trouble. So, despite the magnetic attraction of the Gorge, the urban center would compete with any destination resort you could conceivably design. The added magnetic attraction of federal designation would almost but not quite bring enough overnighters to pay—you get an overnighter and you've sold two meals and made a little money. You could manage the construction, maintenance and operating costs, but debt service would kill you.

Besides, because state land use regulations prevented the construction of any new destination resorts, the whole idea was moot.

Unless Congress wrote a special dispensation to create a "convention center" in the Gorge and kicked in enough taxpayer money to cover the debt service.

By 1984, a new executive director named Bowen Blair, Jr., fresh out of Yale Law School, came to Friends of the Gorge, and he and Nancy Russell attracted the support of Mr. Gray and other Portland big money. Even one of the Weyerhaeuser clan signed a fundraising letter for FOG—he wouldn't mind getting rid of some of the small competition that operated timberlands and sawmills in the Gorge like William Birkenfeld's family-owned Wind River Logging Company and the 260-employee Broughton Lumber Company.[38]

On November 17, 1986 President Ronald Reagan signed the Columbia River Gorge National Scenic Area Act. It was a major victory for Bowen Blair and Nancy Russell—and the Act had all the right clauses written in.[39]

Now Mr. Gray is the owner-developer of the brand new Skamania Lodge—the Congressionally-approved "convention center"—on the brow of a hill in the National Scenic Area above Stevenson, Washington, overlooking the Gorge. Congress allocated $5 million to the project.[40]

In Stevenson, Walt's Texaco and Al's Doughnuts are closed. The Sears outlet had to move to a smaller building. The Arco station was up for sale but there were no takers. Ann's Food Fair, the town's only supermarket, ran out of boxes long ago for people who were moving out to pack their things in. The environmental movement shut down the logging that was the backbone of the local economy. The promised influx of tourists failed to materialize.[41]

Why does this remind us of the Rockefellers and Grand Teton National Park? Why hasn't anybody noticed that the idealistic preservation plans of grassroots activists like Chuck Williams of Friends of the Earth always get co-opted by big money folks like Gray and Weyerhaeuser and their Friends of the Gorge?

Twenty-three towns were included in the long, narrow 292,000-acre, six-county National Scenic Area, including Hood River and The Dalles, Oregon. The total population within the boundaries was about 41,000 Americans. Thirteen towns were greenlined as urban areas, into which all development is to be confined, and the other ten towns were presumed not to exist.

To make that presumption a reality, the Trust for Public Land was again brought to the fore.

Our friend Joe Wrabek, former mayor of the little Gorge village of Cascade Locks, Oregon, tells about the Trust for Public Land destroying those ten towns.

"Back in 1978, when the Forest Service wanted to nationalize all the private inholdings in the Mount Hood National Forest, they had one little problem. The Weeks Act of 1911 requires the Forest Service to get the permission of the state to take any property off the tax rolls, and in Oregon that approval power has been delegated to the counties by state law. The Forest Service wanted to buy the town of Wyeth, Oregon, but the Port and City of Cascade Locks complained to the Board of County Commissioners that the land, only six miles away, was the sole place their town could expand into in the future. The County Commissioners said No to the Forest Service.

"The next year, Harriet Hunt Burgess, then West Coast land trader for the Trust for Public Land [now President of the **American Land Conservancy**], dropped by one day with a sales contract and options for 550 acres that took away most of the town of Wyeth."[42]

The late columnist Warren Brookes described the deal:

> TPL was well rewarded. It bought these properties from Joseph Yoerger in two blocks. In the first, it paid a purchase price of $750,000 on August 14, 1980, at 11:22 a.m. At 11:23 a.m., TPL sold this block to the Forest Service for $944,000, a gain of $194,000. Three minutes later, TPL executed its option to purchase the second Yoerger block for $175,000, and one minute later sold it to the Forest Service for $292,000, a gain of $117,000 on a $1,000 option.[43]

Harriet Hunt Burgess was a formidable presence in TPL. She remains a leading land-nationalization lobbyist on Capitol Hill. She did a whole string of deals in the Columbia Gorge after it was declared a National Scenic Area, as we shall see below.

She was appointed by the National Academy of Sciences to its Committee on Federal Acquisition of Lands for Conservation. This committee has a congressional mandate of creating a $30 billion long-range American Heritage Trust land-nationalization program. Patrick Noonan of the Conservation Fund was also appointed, but resigned in 1991. The committee is headed by Nathaniel Reed, a wealthy Hobe Sound, Florida, environmentalist who served during the early 1970s as Assistant Secretary of the Interior for Fish and Wildlife and Parks—boss of the U.S. Fish and Wildlife Service and the National Park Service. Reed is also a trustee of NRDC, a vice chairman of the National Audubon Society and a member of the president's council for Rockefeller's American Farmland Trust.

The slow death of the Columbia Gorge has continued in like fashion since the Scenic Area was created in 1986, but now the old leaders of Friends of the Gorge have lashed up with the Trust for Public Land to help things along. Bowen Blair, Jr., found his reward for shepherding the Gorge Bill through Congress and is now the well-paid director of the Oregon Field Office of TPL, and Nancy Russell sits on the National Board of Directors.

Most recently the Trust for Public Land destroyed the town of Bridal Veil, Oregon. Built in 1872, the town came into the hands of Herschel McGriff of Bridal Veil Lumber Company—it was one of the few remaining company towns in America still occupied and functioning.

Congress put Bridal Veil in a Special Management Area so the federal government could buy or condemn all the property. The Forest Service didn't want the bad publicity of condemning and bulldozing a whole town, so they turned to the Trust for Public Land to deal with McGriff. TPL got the town from him and served eviction notices to the 27 families in Bridal Veil, ordering them to vacate by October 31, 1991—Halloween was appropriate, locals jibed, because something less than human was going to move in: The Trust for Public Land had plans to obliterate all sign of human habitation and *build a wetland on the site.*

There was no evidence that a wetland had ever existed on the site naturally, and the notion of *building* a wetland has a somewhat ridiculous ring to it, but that's what TPL planned to do. Then the local Crown Point Historical Society got the county planning board to vote the town of Bridal Veil "historic" under historic preservation laws, and thwarted the Trust for Public Land's bulldozers—for a while.

All but three of the families moved out and the empty homes are doing what any untended century-old structures would do in an area that gets 60 inches of rain a year—mouldering slowly into the ground. TPL is happy just waiting until the historic buildings are beyond restoration to bring in their demolition crews and sell the wetland to the Forest Service.

What kind of ghouls run the Trust for Public Land that could treat their fellow citizens so basely? An insider who is growing disenchanted with TPL drew us a picture:

The actual functionaries of TPL who oversee the destruction of the Columbia Gorge are the Oregon Field Office—Blair and Russell—and the Trust for Public Lands National Advisory Board. They do their dirty work together in meetings on the site.

TPL's National Advisory Board meetings, says our informant, are attended by three classes of being, the first two consisting of TPL board members: 1) the remittance men, who have the money and power; 2) the fanatics, who have the agenda; 3) the staff, including President Martin J. Rosen, which does all the work.

In the fall of 1992, the National Advisory Board held its meeting in the Columbia Gorge. This is how it went, says our informant:

Day one. The fanatics went over the facts and figures of land acquisition progress while the remittance men had a few drinks and the staff took notes and ran errands. The fanatics showed a slide show demonstrating what they had done so far and what they intended to do the next year while the remittance men had a few drinks and the staff took notes and ran errands. Here are the facts:

As of September 1, 1992, TPL had sold 8,535 acres in the Columbia Gorge for $18,634,500.00, nearly all of it to the U.S. Forest Service.

Properties remaining in the ownership of TPL comprised 161 acres with a Fair Market Value of $500,000:

The Gilbert tract (Washington), 2 acres, $30,000, acquired December 30, 1983.

Bachelder tract (Washington), 3 acres, $40,000, acquired July 9, 1984.

Leigh tract (Oregon), 5 acres, $21,000, acquired October 1, 1991.

Bridal Veil II (Oregon), 12 acres, $125,000, acquired February 15, 1991.

Camas Field (Washington), 9 acres, $50,000, acquired July 29, 1992.

Rowena I (Oregon), 130 acres, $234,000, acquired September 24, 1992, conveyed to U.S. Forest Service September 24, 1992.

The Trust held options on 6,550 acres with a Fair Market Value of $3,075,000:

The Altorfer tract (Washington) 80 acres, $75,000.

Rowena View II (Oregon), 470 acres, $750,000.

Dalles Mountain Ranch (Oregon) 6,000 acres, $2.25 million.

Grand total of TPL Gorge properties sold to the government, plus land owned or optioned for future sale to the government: 15,246 acres worth $22,209,500.

Day two: Everybody went for a bus ride to the places they saw in the slides the day before. The remittance men had a few drinks and approved everything the fanatics wanted done. President Martin J. Rosen picked up the room tab and the bar bill. Everybody went home. And left 40,000 Gorge residents to their griefs.

The Trust for Public Land's Board of Directors includes chairman Douglas P. Ferguson and other members Robert L. Armstrong, John W. Baird, Eugene Barth, Sara Brown, Robert Cahn, Robert E. Carlson, George P. Denny, William M. Evans, Jr., Francis S. Foote, Jr., Terese Tarlton Hershey, Eugene C. Lee, Richard D. Marshall, Marie Ridder, Nancy N. Russell, James D. Sano, and F. Jerome Tone.

The Burlington Northern Foundation gave $25,000 in 1989—to an outfit that promotes the wetland regulations that Marty Sevier struggled with near Seattle trying to keep the net worth of Burlington Northern lands from going to zero. Yoo-hoo! Are you asleep at the switch, BN?

The Mary Flagler Cary Charitable Trust gave $30,000 in 1990 for a Neighborhood Open Space Management Grant Program.

The Columbia Foundation of San Francisco gave $15,000 for a project designed to promote the planting of 20 million trees in California by the year 2000—but not do the actual planting, just the promotion.

The Walter and Elise Haas Fund gave $25,000 in 1989.

The Andrew W. Mellon Foundation gave $750,000 in 1990 for waterlands preservation efforts—there's the Mellon money again.

The Trust for Public Land received a stupendous $5 million grant from the **Pew Charitable Trusts** (the Sun Oil money) of Pennsylvania, for funding of "The Energy Foundation," a collaborative effort with the MacArthur and Rockefeller Foundations (who else?) to support energy efficiency and conservation throughout the United States—read "prevention of additional energy generating capacity." The Pew Charitable Trusts also gave TPL $290,000 in 1990 for a feasibility study to assess viability of developing the Philadelphia Metropolitan Opera House.

The Rockefeller Foundation gave $200,000 in 1990 towards the operating costs of the energy project mentioned above.

The Trust for Public Land has also flat stopped economic development out of sheer ideology. A low income housing project was trashed near Walden Pond in Massachusetts. TPL bought 25 acres near the historic puddle made famous by Henry David Thoreau and forced developers to scrap the project.[44]

The Trust for Public Land works hand in glove with the Sierra Club. As should be clear by now, the network of environmental groups is exceedingly complex, groups linked to government webbed to big money tied to power brokers who promote talented protégés. The Sierra Club is one of the oldest outdoor groups in America, and one of the most respected—because nobody realizes the damage it does to our economy.

Sierra Club Summation

Among its many publications, the Sierra Club puts out a newsletter, *National News Report* 26 times a year, the slick bimonthly magazine *Sierra*, and through its huge book publishing arm, Sierra Club Books, scads of Economy Trasher propaganda pieces. A few recent titles include *Adventuring in Australia; California's Wild Heritage: Threatened and Endangered Animals in the Golden State; Earth Day Source Book; Hidden Dangers: Environmental Consequences of Preparing for War;* and *Wild by Law: The Sierra Club Legal Defense Fund and the Places It Has Saved.*

The Sierra Club's Board of Directors serves without compensation and meets seven times a year and includes president Anthony Ruckel, vice president Edgar Wayburn, secretary Michele Perrault, treasurer Ann Pogue, and fifth officer Rebecca Falkenberry. Other members include Phillip Berry, Joni Bosh, Richard Cellarius, Kathy Fletcher, Joe Fontaine, Mark Gordon, Susan Merrow, Mary Ann Nelson, Jean R. Packard, and Duncan Stewart. Paid staff includes Carl Pope, executive director (salary, $77,142); Chris Thollaug is assistant secretary (71,672; Vicki Thorpe, assistant treasurer ($46,575); and Louis Barnes, assistant treasurer ($76,992).

The Sierra Club operates 57 chapters, 386 affiliate groups, and 15 field offices.

The Sierra Club Foundation is a 501(c)(3) organization established in 1960, which funds nonlegislative activities including research, public education, and publishing. It is as much of an Economy Trasher as its lobbying parent. The attorney general of New Mexico filed notice of intent to bring a civil complaint against the Sierra Club Foundation over a $100,000 gift that was not used for an intended land purchase. The money was given to the foundation in 1970 by Ray Graham III, an Albuquerque businessman. Graham wanted some land in northern New Mexico to be bought with the money, so that it could be protected from development and used for grazing. The purchase was never made and Graham separately has sued to get his money back. The foundation argued that Graham released the gift from any restrictions in 1980.[45]

The Sierra Club created a political action committee (PAC) in 1976, the Sierra Club Committee on Political Education (SCCOPE), as "the first political action committee associated with a large membership-based environmental organization" to meet "the need to enhance our legislative goals by influencing the outcome of electoral politics." Each Sierra Club member may contribute up to $5,000 annually. SCCOPE aroused some controversy between the "emerging" environmentalists and old-line conservationists. Richard Fiddler, one of SCCOPE's founders, commented that "some members didn't think we should get involved in electoral politics at all. But many of us thought that since the Club was increasingly focusing on legislative action, we should do it in a more organized manner."

The Club reports that in the ten years since SCCOPE was established, "it has evolved from a club controversy into a strong political force in local, state and national elections. SCCOPE is that entity which allows the club and its members to participate in elections, from endorsing candidates to making campaign contributions." During the 1982 elections SCCOPE endorsed candidates in 200 local races, two candidates for governor, and candidates in 183 House and 18 Senate races. Through donations from members to SCCOPE, the Club contributed more than $500,000 and thousands of volunteer hours to federal races. Looking to the future, Sierra Club political director Rose Kapolezynski has said that "we intend to make sure environmental issues are addressed by all the candidates and to encourage environmentalists to become delegates to the national nominating conventions." That sounds a lot like a plan to take over the political process.

SCCOPE contributed a total of $487,000 to candidates in 1989-1990.

The Sierra Club and its various affiliates coin money at an astounding rate. They get 37 percent of it from memberships; 29 percent from contributions and grants; 11 percent from book sales; 8 percent from advertising and renting their mailing list to commercial outfits; 7 percent from outings; 4 percent from reimbursements; and 4 percent from royalties.

Their grant list is formidable. The Sierra Club itself is ineligible for most grants, since it is a lobbying group under the Tax Code. They got around that little obstacle by incorporating the Sierra Club Foundation, as we noted above. The Foundation got $75,000 from **The Joyce Foundation** in 1990 for a Great Lakes Federal Policy

Project—how to stop all economic use of the Great Lakes; $40,000 from the **Charles Stewart Mott Foundation** in 1990 for expansion of the Multilateral Development Bank Program. The Mott Foundation also gave $30,000 for an Air Toxics Outreach Project. **The Foundation for the Carolinas** gave $10,000 in 1989. **The George Gund Foundation** gave $20,000 for the same Great Lakes Federal Policy Project that the Joyce Foundation gave $75,000 for; and another $10,000 to trash the Great Lakes economy from the **Patrick and Anna M. Cudahy Fund.**

The Sierra Club Legal Defense Fund, however, is the big winner in grantsmanship. It got $25,000 from the **Compton Foundation** in 1989; $25,000 in 1990 from the **Wallace Alexander Gerbode Foundation** "to develop an individual donor base for Hawaii," i.e. this was the seed money for a big direct mail fund raising campaign to stop all development in Hawaii. The Legal Defense Fund got $27,000 in 1990 from the **San Francisco Foundation** to represent seven plaintiffs in an anti-industry lawsuit; $125,000 from the **Public Welfare Foundation, Inc.** in 1990 to establish an office in Louisiana; $20,000 from the **Town Creek Foundation** in 1990; $23,050 from the **Charles Stewart Mott Foundation** in 1990 to establish a Great Lakes regional office so they could trash General Motors, of which Mott was a founder; $295,000 from the **Mary Flagler Cary Charitable Trust** to establish an office in Florida, and another $35,000 to fund lawsuits against developers in the Gulf Coast and Atlantic coastal area; $25,000 from the **Joyce Mertz-Gilmore Foundation** for general support; Unspecified amounts from the **New York Times Company Foundation, Inc.**; $10,000 from the **Overbrook Foundation** for general support in 1989; $10,000 from the **Prospect Hill Foundation, Inc.** for a lawsuit against National Forest Service Management Plans—a move to shut down the timber industry (1990); $50,000 from the **Scherman Foundation, Inc.** for general support in 1989-'90; $25,000 from the **William Bingham Foundation** for a matching grant for operation of a new Florida office; $100,000 from the **W. Alton Jones Foundation, Inc.** for operation of the new Louisiana office in 1989.

The Sierra Club and its many tentacles have the power to stop any economic activity in America dead in its tracks.
And they use it.

Sierra Club. Sierra Club Foundation. Sierra Club Legal Defense Fund. The Trust for Public Land.
Job killers.
Economy trashers.

Sierra Club—Footnotes

1 "From Fringe To Political Mainstream," by Michael Weiskopf, *Washington Post*, April 19, 1990, p. A1.

2 *Son of the Wilderness: The Life of John Muir*, Linnie Marsh Wolfe, Alfred A. Knopf, New York, 1945.

3 *The Life and Letters of John Muir*, William F. Bade, 2 vols., Houghton, Mifflin, Boston, 1923.

4 "Sierra Club" by Susan R. Schrepfer, *Encyclopedia of American Forest and Conservation History*, Richard C. Davis, editor, Macmillan Publishing Company, New York, 1983, p. 603.

5 *Trains of Discovery: Western Railroads and the National Parks*, Alfred Runte, Northland Press, Flagstaff, Arizona, 1984.

6 "Conflict in Preservation," Susan R. Schrepfer, *Journal of Forest History*, Vol. 24, No. 2, April 1980, p. 65.

7 *John Muir and His Legacy: The American Conservation Movement*, Stephen Fox, Little, Brown, Boston, 1981.

8 *Gifford Pinchot: Forester-Politician*, M. Nelson McGeary, Princeton University Press, Princeton, 1960.

9 "The Struggle for the Valley: California's Hetch Hetchy Controversy, 1905-1913, Elmo R. Richardson, *California Historical Society Quarterly*, 38 (1959), 249-58.

10 *John Muir and the Sierra Club: The Battle for Yosemite*, Holway Jones, 1965.

11 *Conservation and the Gospel of Efficiency: The Progressive Conservation Movement 1890-1920*, Samuel P. Hays, Harvard University Press, Cambridge, 1959.

12 *Thoughts on Conservation and the Sierra Club*, Bestor Robinson, interview conducted by Susan R. Schrepfer, San Francisco, Sierra Club, pp. 5, 49.

13 *David Brower: Environmental Activist, Publicist, and Prophet*, an oral history by Susan Schrepfer, University of California Regional Oral History Office, Berkeley, 1978.

14 *This Is Dinosaur: Echo Park Country and Its Magic Rivers*, Wallace Stegner, ed., Knopf, New York, 1955.

15 "With Friends Like These..." by Paul Rauber, *Mother Jones*, November 1986, p. 35.

16 *Storm Over Rangelands: Private Rights in Federal Lands*, Wayne Hage, Free Enterprise Press, Bellevue, Washington, 1989, pp. 95-113.

17 Foreword by Michael McCloskey, in *Clearcut: The Deforestation of America*, Nancy Wood, Sierra Club, San Francisco, 1971.

18 List provided to Ron Arnold by Michael McCloskey in his office in San Francisco, 1979.

19 "Washington in the Grip of the Green Giant," by William Symonds, *Fortune*, October 4, 1982, p. 137.

20 The Endangered Species Act is codified at 16 U.S.C., Sections 1531 *et seq.* See also *Endangered Species: Management Improvements Could Enhance Recovery Program*, U. S. General Accounting Office, December 21, 1988, pp. 13-14.

21 "Preservation Versus Elimination," by Norman D. Levin, *BioScience* 36, no. 5 (1986), p. 309.

22 "Sad finale for the Dusky," *Defenders*, July / August 1987, p. 5.

23 *The Seaside Sparrow, Its Biology and Management*, T. L. Quay, editor, North Carolina State Museum of Natural History, Raleigh, 1983, pp. 41-48.

24 "War of the Woods," by Charlie Smith, *The New Pacific* magazine, Summer 1992.

25 "Getting Credit For a Cause," by Pamela G. Hollie, *New York Times*, August 17, 1986, p. F1.

26 "U.S. Is Protesting Pollution Penalty," by John H. Cushman, Jr., *New York Times*, May

18, 1990, p. A16. See also "Coors Brewing Signs Agreement to Avert Sierra Club Lawsuit," *Wall Street Journal,* September 13, 1991, p. A4.

27 "Sierra Club vs. the Terminally Ill," *Organization Trends,* published by the Capital Research Center, Washington, D. C., July 1991, p. 5.

28 "Buying In," by Eve Pell, *Mother Jones,* April / May 1990, p. 23.

29 "The Role of Citizen Interest Groups," by Downing and Brady, in *Nonprofit Firms in a Three Sector Economy,* White, editor, p. 74.

30 "Gorgeous Gorge," by Sallie Tisdale, *Los Angeles Times,* May 17, 1992, p. MA14.

31 The section on the Columbia Gorge is based on interviews with Joe Wrabek, long-time gorge resident and currently Commissioner of Cascade Locks, Oregon. The documents, letters, reports and hearing records that back up this section are all in his possession.

32 *Study of Alternatives,* Columbia River Gorge, National Park Service, 1979.

33 "Why 'Local Control' Can't Do The Job," by John Yeon, *The Oregonian,* 1983.

34 "Senator hears protest, support," *The Enterprise,* Bingen-White-Salmon, Washington, February 17, 1983, p. 1.

35 *Columbia River Gorge Act of 1983,* Hearing before the Subcommittee on Public Lands and Reserved Water or the Committee on Energy and Natural Resources, United States Senate, 98th Congress, 1st Session, on S. 627, Portland, Oregon, March 25, 1983, p. 161.

36 "Extensive wine list educates customers at Salishan Lodge," by Mort Hochstein,*Nation's Restaurant News,* July 15, 1985, p. F16.

37 "Resort's facilities offer quiet elegance," by Ron Arnold,*Western Conservation Journal,* August-September 1979, p. 34.

38 Philip Weyerhaeuser freely admitted his anti-competitive intent in a meeting with property rights group Columbia Gorge United leader Esson Smith in 1987.

39 "The gorge," *Sunset,* May 1987, p. 72.

40 "You own the Columbia River Gorge," by Julie Wilson and Kim Walker, *Town & Country Monthly,* September 1992, p. 94.

41 "The curse of a splendid view," by James Ring Adams,*Forbes,* December 1, 1986, p. 182.

42 Personal interviews, August 1992.

43 "Land trusts or government advance men?" by Warren Brookes,*The Washington Times,* January 24, 1991.

44 "Walden Pond development project has been scrapped,"*Wall Street Journal,* August 14, 1990, p. A2.

45 *The New York Times,* May 13, 1992.

National Audubon Society ▰▰▰▰▰▰▰

National Audubon Society (Founded 1905, precursors in 1886 and 1896)
Annual budget: $40,081,591 (1992)
Staff: 315 total
Members: 542,000 individuals (1993)
Tax Status: (501)(c)(3)
Headquarters: 950 Third Avenue   801 Pennsylvania Avenue SE
New York, New York 10022   Washington, D.C. 20003
Phone: (212)832-3200   Phone: (202)547-9009
Fax: (212)593-6254   Fax: (202)547-9022

Economy Trasher Number Six. The original Audubon Society was formed in 1886 by a member of the New York elite, George Bird Grinnell. He was a fascinating and consequential man, a paleontologist by education, an anthropologist and ethnologist by inclination, publisher of the influential conservation periodical *Forest and Stream*, owner of a cattle ranch near Lander, Wyoming, a big game hunter, a thinker credited by some as the true inventor of the concept of official wilderness area designation, and one of the key figures in the 1891 establishment of the forest reserves that evolved into our present national forest system. He knew everybody in the conservation movement of his day. As publisher of *Forest and Stream*, he acted as a nexus between the rich and powerful, such as the Vanderbilts, Rockefellers, and Roosevelts, and the academic and technical such as Professor William H. Brewer of Yale, Professor Alexander Agassiz of Harvard, and Gifford Pinchot, first Chief of the U.S. Forest Service (Pinchot was both technical and rich, the scion of a wealthy Connecticut family and a European-trained forester).[1]

Grinnell's Audubon Society, however, even though it grew rapidly to 39,000 members, did not survive to become the direct lineal ancestor of the modern National Audubon Society in anything except spirit. Grinnell cranked out the first issue of *The Audubon Magazine* as a protest against overhunting of birds. The few issues of the magazine remained just about the only tangible result of the society, for the organization expired in 1888, only two years after Grinnell started it. The current incarnation of *Audubon* magazine was not to appear until after a hiatus of more than forty years. Grinnell was too busy with other matters to organize the emergent movement and give it the impetus it needed to blossom into political power. Nevertheless, he remained active in bird protection and was a member of the first board of directors when the national association was formed in 1905.[2]

Significantly for the future, Grinnell also played an active part in stopping the historic process of homesteaders privatizing the federal lands through his support of moves to prevent settlers from preempting private rights in public lands. Trashing the economy always begins with eliminating private property rights.[3]

The Massachusetts Audubon Society, formed in 1896 by a Boston Brahmin named Harriet Hemenway, became the actual progenitor of the "Audubon Movement" that eventually resulted in the formation of the National Audubon Society. The Massachusetts society "grew out of a protest movement by women seeking to stop the slaughter of Florida wading birds, whose plumes were used to decorate hats" as the *Washington Post* wrote in 1990.[4]

The use of egret feathers by millinery firms threatened the bird's existence. The same year the Massachusetts group was formed, the Pennsylvania Audubon Society was founded. In 1897, Audubon societies sprang up in New York, New Hampshire, Illinois, Maine, Wisconsin, New Jersey, Rhode Island, Connecticut, and the District of Columbia. By 1901 thirty-six state Audubon societies had been organized and worked toward government protections, not only for egrets, but also for a carefully thought-out selection of game and non-game birds. State representatives in 1901 created a loose federation, the National Committee of Audubon Societies. A succession of important personages came to the fore in this movement, among them ornithologist and writer of bird guides Frank M. Chapman, President Theodore Roosevelt, and the ever-present George Bird Grinnell, and on January 5, 1905, incorporated the National Association of Audubon Societies for the Protection of Wild Birds and Animals, Inc., shortened in 1940 to National Audubon Society.

A number of state and regional Audubon Societies have remained so independent from the national that they are affiliates virtually in name only, for example, the Maine and Massachusetts Audubon Societies.

National Audubon's first official organ, *Bird-Lore* was owned and edited by Frank M. Chapman from 1899 to 1935. (In 1941 it was changed to *Audubon Magazine* and in 1961 to *Audubon*. It was edited from 1966 to 1991 by Les Line and won numerous awards for design and reporting.)

The original founders were just a bit snooty: The "object of this organization," they wrote, was to serve as "a barrier between wild birds and animals and a very large unthinking class, and a smaller but more harmful class of selfish people," in the words of newly elected president William Dutcher. "The unthinking....ignorant class, we hope to reach through educational channels, while the selfish people we shall control through the enforcement of wise laws, reservations or bird refuges, and the warden system."[5]

Dutcher's "sanctuary and warden system" was created in 1900 when he and fellow conservationist Abbott Thayer established the "Thayer Fund" with $1,400 to pay for seven wardens to protect gull and tern colonies in Maine and eight wardens at Coast Guard stations to protect bird colonies along the lower Atlantic coast.[6]

Before there were laws to protect wildlife, Audubon developed a private system that worked quite well. That the early members were utterly dedicated to their cause is beyond question: their wardens faced known danger and several were murdered by early poachers. These martyrdoms increased public sympathy for the cause. The concept of a private conservation group finding private solutions with dedicated private individuals was the source of the National Audubon Society's original success.

Beginning with our system of wardens and sanctuaries, supplemented later by research, the NAS was and *is* unique, because we did not rely *solely* on persuasion through education, nor did we *ever* believe that simply passing laws would help conserve wildlife. We got control of land by purchase, long-term lease, bequests, or in some cases merely by verbal agreement. We put a man on that land who stood between the endangered species and the market place. Had it not been for the Audubon system of sanctuaries and wardens, many endangered species would not have survived long enough to be classified as such."[7]

The private sanctuary system remains one of Audubon's best contributions to society, with more than 250,000 acres in their private system nationwide, not counting sanctuaries owned and operated by local Audubon chapters. NAS still supports a force of 35 wardens to patrol its wildlife sanctuaries.

In private sanctuaries, productive resource extraction may continue side-by-side in harmony between man and nature. For example, Audubon developed on its 26,000-acre Paul J. Rainey Wildlife Sanctuary on the Gulf Coast in Vermilion Parish, Louisiana, six natural gas wells operated by Consolidated Oil and Gas Company and two other petroleum corporations that has pumped some $2 million a year into the Society's coffers—with no ecological harm.

The National Audubon Society is not just funded by the oil industry—taking large amounts of money from Exxon USA, the Amoco Foundation, Allied-Signal Foundation and other big oil foundations—it *is* the oil industry.[8]

Just as "Only Nixon could go to China," only on private environmentalist-owned property could such intelligent use of resource lands be accomplished without interference from an environmental group. Notwithstanding the National Audubon Society's about-face into the feudal system of state ownership and its promotion of socialistic command-and-control of resources by government, its founders deserve credit for putting into effect the vision that ecologist Garrett Hardin would not express for many years that "The tragedy of the commons is averted by private property."[9]

With those oil and gas wells pumping money into their cash register, the National Audubon Society has vigorously opposed oil and gas exploration in the Coastal Plain of the Arctic National Wildlife Refuge (ANWR). They deliberately cultivate the impression that the entire 19 million acre refuge would be devastated by oil development. In fact, only about 15,000 acres—less than a tenth of one percent of the refuge, a tiny patch located in the northernmost part of Alaska—would actually be disturbed in any fashion. At more than three-and-a-half times the size of California and with less than 2 percent of its population, Alaska hardly suffers from overdevelopment. And the lessons learned from Prudhoe Bay about building small-footprint drilling pads have made the ecologically sound development of ANWR more than feasible.[10]

The National Audubon Society wants the money from its own oil and gas operations, but doesn't want you or the rest of America to benefit from the petroleum resources of ANWR, which experts estimate as one of the largest oil reserves in the world. This ungracious posture is masked by the public image of the Society, the sweet face of the birdwatcher.

Yet the public image of the Audubon Society as just a bunch of birdwatchers who got together to protect the egret has always been a little out of focus. Even the group's name is a form of hype: John James Audubon, the society's namesake, had nothing to do with the organization and as a matter of fact killed more birds than he painted, but as the *New York Times* noted sarcastically, "the very birdness of his pictures apparently transcended that fact."[11]

Perhaps the public has forgotten that the Audubon Society itself is a ruthless bird killer. In 1971, the National Audubon Society planned to poison herring gulls occupying Tern Island in the Nantucket Sound area. The herring gulls, which are on the State of Massachusetts' protected list of seabirds, had taken over the traditional nesting grounds of the local terns, and the Audubon Society had received permission from the Massachusetts Department of Natural Resources to exterminate them from this particular island. So much for respecting the "balance of nature." The Audubon Society exterminated one species in favor of another for its own very human reasons: personal preference.[12]

Perhaps the public has forgotten this episode. There is nothing so revolutionary as a long memory. And perhaps the public is unaware that the National Audubon Society ruthlessly uses leghold traps to capture and kill mammals that predate bird nests on their sanctuaries. An Audubon sanctuary only protects you if you're the right species. This fact, when fully recognized by the animal rights segment of the environmental movement, will likely spark a civil war within the ranks. There is nothing so disillusioning as a little inside information.[13]

In the years since its inception, a sophisticated program of expanding government controls has continually underlain Audubon's birding folklore. Yet the birding identity of the National Audubon Society and its many chapters was solid as a Rockefeller. As time went on, the bird books of Frank Chapman gave way to those of Roger Tory Peterson, ornithologist, wildlife artist, author of 15 books, and Audubon officer—who became a popular icon of the organization. It may be an overstatement, but if you own a bird book, Peterson likely wrote or illustrated it or the name Audubon Society is probably somewhere in its title.

Respectability and Audubon Society became virtually synonymous. The *Washington Post* said of the organization, "It traditionally focuses on preservation of wildlife and natural resources and has a reputation for being politically moderate."

But things changed in 1985 when Peter A. A. Berle (pronounced BUR-lee, 1992 salary $178,000, benefits $$21,285) took over as National Audubon Society president and chief executive officer. He was very bottom-line oriented and he changed things accordingly. As the *NonProfit Times* put it, "Unlike Greenpeace, the National Wildlife Federation and the National Audubon Society do not have an image as confrontational organizations.... However, in the past few years, both groups have discovered that the public responds better to a tougher approach."[14]

"Better" public response means "more money."

Peter Berle, president and chief executive officer, is a lawyer. He was graduated from Harvard University and Harvard Law School, and has taught at the State University of New York and Hunter College. He founded Berle, Kass & Case, a New

York law firm that initiated a suit against the Union Carbide Corporation for the alleged pollution of underground water on Long Island with pesticides. Berle served three terms in the New York State Assembly from 1968 to 1974. From 1976 to 1979 he served as commissioner of the New York State Department of Environmental Conservation—during the era of Love Canal's toxic waste scandals. Berle sits on the board of directors of the Twentieth Century Fund, Clean Sites Inc., and the Hudson River/Black River Regulating District—this guy isn't waiting for the revolving door, he's in government and the environmental movement at the same time. And he has turned the Audubon Society into an Economy Trasher of the first rank.

Peter Berle's relentless campaign to increase Audubon's market share by destroying key resource extraction industries has not received the attention it deserves. Shortly after Berle took the helm of NAS, he held strategy sessions with top staffers to identify the campaigns that would yield the greatest dollar income and membership increase. The targets of choice were the forest products industry and the livestock industry because they are easy: Both can be made to appear unattractive by accusing them of resource damage, both are historic users of the federal lands, both continue to rely on federal lands for their survival, and both industries are easily affected by bills introduced through sympathetic members of Congress to reclassify commercial areas into non-commercial areas.

Who Is The Public?

Anything to do with federal lands can readily be used to whip up emotional frenzy by characterizing them as "public lands." Contemporary mythology looks upon Public Lands as "belonging to everybody, to you, to me, to the public, to all of us." It is a surpassingly exalted idea, but has no basis in reality.

To begin with, the term "public lands" originally referred to government lands *which were offered for sale to the public for purposes of settlement and homesteading.* What made them "public" lands was that the public could preempt them, alienate them from government ownership into private ownership. The tangled tale of how the federal government came to own those lands in the first place rewards close study.[15]

The Founding Fathers intended that all territory of the United States be sold to private parties with the exception of small parcels required for government uses such as administrative and military installations. In the late Nineteenth Century, the process of complete divestiture was slowed and then halted as Eastern special interests fought for control of the vast resources discovered in the West. Moneyed elites discovered that they could not control large enough areas through their own enterprises, and shifted to a strategy of lobbying Congress to create reserves to be retained by the federal government as a capital asset. The subsequent legislation of vast reserves to be kept by the federal government and managed in socialistic fashion as capital assets was an aberration of original intent.[16]

However, once the laws were changed, original intent meant nothing except as a historical curiosity. The pertinent fact today about the Public Lands is that what belongs to everybody belongs to nobody. If you believe that the public lands belong to you, try to do something on your public property, say build a house, or drive a jeep where there is no road, or even stand too long in one spot in a national park. Try it with a few fellow citizens. Try it with 250 million fellow citizens. It doesn't matter. Regardless who you are or how many you are, you will quickly discover that the public is everyone but you.

The public lands are exactly as public as a public restroom—you can use it if you behave, but it's not yours.

You have no title, right, control or license to the public lands, nor does anybody *except the federal government.* In actual fact, the so-called public lands are federal lands, *government lands*—owned, controlled, and policed by bureaucrats and managed according to the dictates of politicians from whom you would not likely buy a used car. Take solace from that, if you can. The public lands are not public in any meaningful way. They are the private property of the government, government lands, which means they are *political lands.*

That is a fact of which the Audubon Society—the whole environmental movement—is keenly aware. The Environmental Grantmakers Association addressed it in their Fall 1992 meeting at Rosario Resort in Washington State's San Juan Islands. "We must redefine the term *federal* lands to mean *public* lands," said session leader Debra Callahan of the W. Alton Jones Foundation. "*Federal* is government. *Federal* is bad. *Public* is all of us. It's a concept that we need to push: 'these lands that are at stake belong to all of us.'"[17]

Peter Berle and other leaders of large environmental groups do their best to make sure you are not aware that the term "public lands" is a charming fiction. Under Berle's leadership, Audubon has turned to inciting outrage against resource industries so his lobbyists can reclassify historically commercial-use federal areas into non-commercial-use federal areas. Audubon invokes the Public Lands mythology to arouse rage and hate against the timber industry and the livestock industry, as witness the belligerent titles of two films the Society commissioned: *Ancient Forests: Rage Over Trees* and *The New Range Wars.* Rage and war effectively prevent rational thought and sober reflection—two deadly enemies of environmentalism.

Forests Without People

The National Audubon Society was one of two major environmental groups which generated the much-publicized Spotted Owl controversy in the Pacific Northwest, the other being the Sierra Club Legal Defense Fund. They were joined by a host of national, local and regional groups into an effective set of coalitions and pulled out all the stops for this one. In 1987, a consortium-group called the Ancient Forest Alliance, including the Wilderness Society and the Sierra Club, submitted a petition to the U. S. Fish and Wildlife Service asking that the northern spotted owl be listed as an endangered species. The Service decided not to list. In order to force the government to do the coalition's bidding, the National Audubon Society played its part by litigating in the courts, lobbying in Congress, and dissimulating on television.

The campaign, which had been simmering on Audubon's back burner for a number of years—a "blue ribbon" panel of scientists undertook a study of the northern spotted owl for the National Audubon Society in 1986[18]—began in earnest in early

1988 when Brock Evans, NAS vice president for legislative policy—environmentalese for "lobbyist"—met with the Ancient Forest Alliance anti-industry activists for a planning session in Portland, Oregon. The goal was specific, but diffuse: Portland-based activist Randall O'Toole told *Newsweek* magazine, "Cumulatively, the environmental movement is interested in shutting down the timber industry."[19]

No, I don't want you to have your job.

A local single-purpose affiliate with national scope was established with the intention of making it look like a spontaneous grass roots eruption:

Native Forest Council (1988)
Budget: $200,000
Staff: 6
Tax status: 501(c)(3)
P.O. Box 2171
Eugene, Oregon 97402
Phone: (503)461-2156 Fax: (503)461-2156
Executive director: Timothy Hermach

The point of the entire alliance, of course, was to stop the cutting of all trees for nature's sake—devastating the lives of thousands of industry employees and leaving consumers without vital products was beside the point. But how to shut down the timber industry to save the trees? It would be tough to cripple one of the region's economic mainstays. Local opposition would certainly be intense. The tried-and-true tactic of turning a local issue into a national issue would most effectively neutralize the regional forest industry by pitting it against the whole nation, so the coalition considered potential approaches. What could appeal to the nation so strongly that they would be willing to eliminate an entire regional industry?

Clearly, the big two-hundred-fifty-year-old Douglas fir and Western hemlock forests of the Pacific Northwest—trees four feet in diameter and 200 feet tall—had great propaganda potential. It would be easy to convince the public that logging should be stopped to protect this natural legacy from being damaged. The constituent groups had done something similar in dozens of places before. But how to make it happen here, and on this scale?

The coalition settled upon a long-term, three-pronged strategy: First, to continue and magnify the litigation program they had already launched to delay timber harvest in the commercial old growth forests on federal lands; second, to conduct a carefully orchestrated "timed-release" publicity campaign that would gradually condition the public to feel that commercial old-growth forests are a lofty non-commercial value, and thus to accept the decimation of the Pacific Northwest timber industry; and third, to operate a vigorous legislative campaign to eliminate all commercial forest designations and totally stop timber harvest on federal lands forever.

"Lawsuits make news. People sitting in trees make news. Hearings in Congress make news," said Andy Kerr, conservation director of

Oregon Natural Resources Council (1972)
Members: 90 organizations and 4,000 individuals
1050 Yeon Building
522 SW 5th Avenue
Portland, Oregon 97204
Phone: (503)223-9001

the most important local environmental group in Oregon and an Audubon ally in the campaign.[20]

The three parts of the Audubon campaign were expertly planned and executed. One of the coalition members explained the in-progress litigation plan to an environmental law conference at the University of Oregon Law School in these terms:

> Here's the problem facing a litigator entrusted in delaying a federal old-growth timber sale: There is simply no specific statutory protection for old-growth forests. You can read the statutes high and low that constrain Forest Service and BLM management and you won't find the term "old-growth forest" used anywhere. To date, old growth forest has not been recognized by Congress as a resource deserving of legal protection. We hope that that changes, and, in fact, the ultimate goal of litigation is to delay the harvest of old-growth forests so as to give Congress a chance to provide specific statutory protection for those forests. That is a long-term goal.
>
> Until legislation is adopted which protects these forests, we need at least one surrogate, if you will, that will provide protection for the forests. A surrogate must have three qualities to be a good surrogate. First, it must be unique to old-growth forests; secondly, it must be measurable using scientific methods; and third, it must, of course, enjoy some amount of statutory protection.... Well, the northern spotted owl is the wildlife species of choice to act as a surrogate for old-growth protection, and I've often thought that thank goodness the spotted owl evolved in the Northwest, for if it hadn't, we'd have to genetically engineer it.
>
> It's a perfect species for use as a surrogate. First of all, it is unique to old-growth forests and there's no credible scientific dispute on that fact. Second of all, it uses a lot of old-growth. That's convenient because we can use it to protect a lot of old-growth. And third, it appears that the spotted owl faces an imminent risk of extinction. That's very important, for if it didn't, federal agencies could argue that they could continue to log old-growth and not hurt the spotted owl.[21]

One might consider that as evidence of deliberate obstructionism intended to destroy the Northwest timber industry.

The Portland Audubon Society had already filed suit on October 19, 1987, against the Bureau of Land Management in Oregon and the Seattle Audubon Society against the U. S. Forest Service questioning the ability of the northern spotted owl to survive with planned logging in the owl's habitat in Washington, Oregon, and Northern California, the perfect stalling tactic while preparing the legislative campaign.[22]

Since the U.S. Fish and Wildlife Service had decided not to list the owl as endangered, and the courts take time, it was now necessary to force that listing administratively. The National Audubon Society and its allies operated an influence campaign for the purpose. Federal agencies had continuously studied the northern spotted owl, *strix caurina occidentalis*—actually one of several subspecies, not *the whole species* of spotted owl—and found no reason to think that projected logging plans would significantly affect the owl's survival.[23] The Fish and Wildlife Service had conducted a status review in 1982 and the U. S. Forest Service prepared a draft Supplemental Environmental Impact Statement which analyzed the habitat requirements of the northern spotted owl in 1986. The BLM completed an Environmental Assessment of the northern spotted owl on February 3, 1987, found the owl would not be significantly affected by its timber harvest plans in Oregon and therefore decided not to supplement the current Environmental Impact Statement with new owl data. That was what triggered the Audubon lawsuit against BLM. Similarly, failure to specifically review whether the northern spotted owl was an endangered species triggered the Audubon lawsuit against the Forest Service.

Audubon had to make sure the Endangered Species Act itself did not lapse when it came up for reauthorization in 1988. Many groups said a lot in public about the reauthorization. But, as the *Washington Post Magazine* noted, "environmental groups may wield tremendous clout behind the scenes.... The National Audubon Society played a key role in securing last year's reauthorization of the Endangered Species Act."[24]

The lawsuits plus more behind the scenes pressure on the Bush administration yielded the desired result: On June 23, 1989, the U. S. Fish and Wildlife Service proposed listing the northern spotted owl—not as an "endangered" species, but as a "threatened" species under the Endangered Species Act.[25] Service spokesman David Klinger said a final decision would not be forthcoming for some time.

Immediately, the Audubon alliance began a mad scramble to press government to convene a policy-making panel to make the final decision and stack it with their allies.[26] On October 23, 1989, the Interagency Scientific Committee to Address the Conservation of the Northern Spotted Owl was formed to develop "a scientifically credible conservation strategy for the northern spotted owl." The Committee was established by an agreement signed by the heads of the Forest Service, the BLM, the Fish and Wildlife Service, and the National Park Service.[27] The Interagency Scientific Committee issued its Final Report in May of 1990, concluding that the lack of consistent planning strategy had resulted in a high risk of extinction for the northern spotted owl subspecies. It was practically reading from the script provided by the National Audubon Society and the Sierra Club and the Ancient Forest Alliance.[28] Despite the fact that upwards of 25,000 jobs would be killed as a result, a month later the Fish and Wildlife Service listed the northern spotted owl as a threatened species.[29]

Between March 1988 and June 1989, according to the Northwest Independent Forest Manufacturers Association, 33 medium and small independent mill shut down in Washington and Oregon, eliminating more than 2,500 mill jobs—spotted owl lawsuits and restrictions had killed their timber supply.[30] Protest demonstrations became a way of life in forest communities as loggers took to the streets carrying signs, taking a page from the early environmental movement itself.[31]

Then, flaws in every assumption behind the listing became quickly apparent. First, the premise "that there was no credible science that the spotted owl had any other habitat than old-growth forests" proved to have been a matter of oversight, not positive study. Scientists had not thoroughly searched for spotted owls in second-growth forests because they had swallowed their own dogma and didn't believe they lived there.

Industry foresters immediately hired wildlife biologists from academia to comb their privately-owned second-growth forests in Northern California and quickly discovered more than 500 spotted owls living and nesting in second growth redwood forests—in densities equal to or greater than in old-growth.[32] Subsequent studies discovered more owls in second-growth in Oregon and Washington. And the spotted owl was found in New Mexico, which threatened timber jobs there.[33]

Second, the spotted owl did not need vast areas of old growth—it used a variety of habitats, and even seemed to prefer man-altered forests.[34]

Third, the bird was not threatened with extinction after all. Counts made after its listing would not qualify it for threatened status. But the government is not about to de-list it and bring down upon their heads the wrath of powerful environmental organizations. Instead, harsh logging restrictions were imposed on the privately owned second-growth forests where owls lived.[35] That's the environmental movement: Kill jobs. Trash the economy.[36]

The battle has grown incredibly complex in the time since, with congressional actions to stop environmentalist lawsuits, counteractions, injunctions to stop logging, protests and counterprotests. Lumber prices went through the ceiling as a direct result of owl restrictions.[37] Just as the Audubon forces planned it. Their power is awesome.

The media portion of the campaign—designed to condition the public in favor of reclassifying commercial old-growth into non-commercial preserves—was designed with the same care used in the litigating campaign. Finding a respectable name for the proposed anti-timber campaign was crucial. "This is important," lobbyist Brock Evans said. "We should think about it. We need to give it a better name. Professional foresters call them 'Old Growth' forests. That sounds like me: I'm old and gray. What really are these things? These are 'Ancient Forests.' The Reagan Administration wanted to call acid rain 'unbuffered precipitation.' You have to give these things a proper name that explains it immediately, that tells you what you're talking about."[38]

Cunning. Calculated.

And so the Ancient Forest campaign was conceived with a public relations name that has no biological meaning whatever, but evokes awe, reverence—and submission to some greater power than human need for material goods. There was talk of "eight-hundred to a thousand-year-old trees," numbers picked out of a hat to sound impressive, as fewer than one percent of the trees in question grow to *half* that age. As in most environmentalist campaigns, the technique was to cut people out of the equation, to misdirect attention away from the basic needs for food, clothing, and shelter, to evoke in those who are not struggling from paycheck to paycheck a yearning to transcend their comfortable but empty lives by participating in a superindividual cause of beauty and nobility.[39] The trick is to sucker people at the top of the Needs Hierarchy into this outlook so strongly they don't care that they're putting their less fortunate neighbors out of a job.

In our increasingly non-reading, television-only society, the straightest line to the public's emotions for Audubon's Economy Trasher message was the television special. Audubon had established National Audubon Society Productions, Inc, headed by Christopher Palmer (1992 salary $101,002, benefits $16,479), a former Environmental Protection Agency official, to produce "The World of Audubon" documentary series that airs both on PBS and the TBS cable channel.

The vehicle in this series for Audubon's anti-timber television propaganda crusade was titled *Ancient Forests: Rage Over Trees*. Audubon got movie actor Paul Newman to narrate the film, purportedly for free, who begins by saying the dispute over the trees goes to "the heart of society's values." At the end, he urges viewers "to let Congress know what you want done with them." In between, the film guides viewers who know nothing about the forest through a maze of images and moods designed to damn all tree cutting and besmirch all who cut them.

Ancient Forests: Rage Over Trees is a masterpiece of deception, a model of the figure of speech known as synecdoche, the holding out of a part to stand for the whole. The art of having an item or part stand for the whole is a sublime device in poetry—and *the* classical unfair trick of debate. Audubon holds out about ten percent of the National Forests as the whole universe of discourse for their film. But the audience is not allowed to know that.

What is never discussed is that nearly ninety percent of all presently remaining "ancient forests" in America are already saved. The vast bulk of all old-growth is in some kind of protected status: national parks and monuments, national scenic areas, national recreation areas, national wild and scenic river areas, national scenic trails systems, national wilderness system areas, greenbelts, biological research areas, Native American religious sites, reserves under the National Forest Management Act of 1976, and dozens of other special classifications that prevent logging. Little by little, one area after another has been pushed off-limits to economic resource use. At the height of the "ancient forest" controversy, a *Seattle Times* article revealed the cumulative impacts on the timber industry in Washington State:

Before 1970, 28 percent of the land available for timber harvest was withdrawn for National Parks—Olympic, Mount Rainier, and North Cascades National Parks, nearly 3 million acres. After 1970, 10 percent was removed from timber harvest for Wilderness Areas—Alpine Lakes, Glacier Peak, Mount Baker, and Pasayten Wilderness Areas, another 1 million-plus acres. The United States Forest Service implemented Forest Plans under the National Forest Management Act of 1976—lobbied into existence as the result of an Izaak Walton League lawsuit—that allocated 31 percent of timber harvest lands to non-harvest uses—about 3.1 million acres. The Forest Service implemented Forest Plans that reduced the harvest level on 9 percent of the timber harvest lands—967,000 acres. The federal government's Interagency

Scientific Committee took away 10 percent of harvest lands in its Endangered Species Plan to protect the Northern Spotted Owl—997,000 acres. New designations of Critical Habitat for the Northern Spotted Owl withdrew an additional 2 percent—164,000 acres.[40]

The cumulative impact of environmentalism *in just one state* adds up to 9.3 million acres withdrawn from the original 10.3 million-acre federal forest land base. That leaves less than 10 percent of the original timber harvest land base for commodity use. It is that last tiny scrap which the National Audubon Society holds out to stand as the whole.

Getting the last piece of the forest pie is the true purpose of the Ancient Forest campaign, and that context, the fact that most "ancient forests" were long ago protected in national parks and other areas is never even mentioned. Misdirection of attention—the oldest trick in stage magic, and a most unfair trick in debate.

Ancient Forests: Rage Over Trees uses another classic deception to argue its case: It never makes clear the nature of its goal, which is to *reclassify* historically commercial forests into new non-commercial preserves. It gives the *impression* that loggers are presently going into some vague sort of existing preserves and improperly cutting down trees that should not be cut.

In fact, all the old growth Audubon wants to reclassify is presently in legitimate and historic National Forest commercial timber harvest areas where *all* the trees were intended to be eventually cut—and regenerated—according to sustained yield practices as mandated by Congress. After twenty-five years of aggressive engulfment of commercial timber into non-commercial classifications, there are not many such areas left. The trees are there. We just can't use them.

The film's appeal was to the emotions, not to sober judgment. It incited rage, as the title says. The images Audubon used in *Rage Over Trees* concentrate on the emotional contrast between soothing cathedral-like groves on the one hand and jarring aerial views of freshly cutover squares on the other. Shots taken by **LightHawk**, a New Mexico-based network of volunteer pilots donating their small planes for aerial surveillance, allow the viewer to look down upon a patchwork of open areas in the vast forest cover of the Pacific Northwest.

The impression intended is that these hideous clearcuts are permanent scars, desecrations of the timeless holy temple of the Ancient Forest. The fact is that if the pilot had flown over the same forests forty years ago he would have seen the same patchwork—but in alternate squares. Many of the areas shown were cuts made in *second-growth* forests, not in old-growth. Much of the original old-growth in the Pacific Northwest was logged off in the 1880s and '90s, especially in the lush, easily-accessible lowland and foothill areas between the Coast Range, the Olympic Mountains, and the Cascade Range. Loggers have long chuckled at the tourist who stops beside a tall thick stand of timber and says, "Wow, look at that virgin forest," to which the logger replies, "Yep, and here we are cutting those virgin trees for the second time." The fact that trees grow back rapidly is brushed aside as an irrelevant argument—*big* trees don't grow back rapidly. The fact that the overwhelming majority of big "ancient forests" are already locked away in some protective designation is carefully hidden to give Audubon's special pleading undeserved credibility.

Taking pictures of a commercial forest from the air and saying "Look at the permanent destruction!" is to hold out forestry in a false light, like singling out a still frame in what should be a movie: Commercial forests grow rapidly in the Northwest, and the pattern of cuts shifts each year around what foresters call the "working circle."

A working circle isn't a circle at all, it's the total land base a forester uses to calculate his sustained yield timber harvest. To take a round number for an example, let's say a forester has a 50,000-acre land base of old-growth blessed with an average soil quality sufficient to grow Douglas fir and its allied species to merchantable maturity in 50 years. Each year, then, the forester can progress through one-fiftieth of his forest working circle, or 1,000 acres—his annual allowable cut—with a trained logging crew and in the fifty-first year return to his starting point and find a healthy, mature merchantable stand of Douglas fir ready to harvest once more. All is well with the world.[41]

The forest provides raw materials for more than 100,000 different products, it provides direct employment for thousands—loggers, truckers, mill workers, machinists, foresters, managers and staff people—it generates secondary income that supports jobs in the wider community for doctors, grocers, teachers and department stores, it generates tax dollars to pay for roads, schools, and bureaucrats' salaries, it provides hunting, camping, motorized recreation, watershed regulation, wildlife habitat, and many other goods and services—and it lasts forever.[42]

However, if, during the tenth year of successful operations in the working circle, environmentalists pressure Congress to reclassify 5,000 of the yet-untouched acres to create a National Wilderness Area, and the next year 5,000 more unlogged acres are removed to expand a National Park, and the next year 5,000 more virgin acres are removed to establish a Wild and Scenic River, and then 5,000 more pristine acres are removed to create a National Scenic Area, and another 5,000 natural acres are removed to protect the spotted owl, then the original 50,000 acre working circle has been reduced by half to only 25,000 acres. If foresters are to stick to the sustained yield principle, they must reduce their annual allowable cut in half. It still takes Douglas fir 50 years to grow to maturity on these soils. So now the foresters can only order the cutting of 500 acres each year, producing only half the raw materials, half the finished products, half the direct employment, half the community support, half the tax revenues. They have run out of trees—not because the loggers cut them all down, but because environmentalists persuaded Congress to put them off-limits.

And that is what actually has happened on all the National Forests in America. Before the Multiple Use / Sustained Yield Act of 1960 was five years old, environmentalists lobbied the Wilderness Act of 1964 into existence and took millions of acres out of working circles. Before the multiple use principle had ten years to work, environmentalists in 1968 lobbied new National Parks, the Wild and Scenic Rivers Act, the National Trails Act, and other non-timber laws into existence and took millions of acres out of working circles. The past twenty five years has seen a steady erosion of the original sustained yield working circles across America so there is precious little commercial timber area left— but there are millions of acres of untouchable old-growth. Our natural resources have been locked up. Our economy has been locked out. And all for scant benefit.

If a LightHawk airplane were to fly over any of the remaining working circles in our peaceful and productive commercial forest, its pilot would only see the fresh clearcuts and scream, "Look at the permanent destruction!"

He would not see the tender seedlings the forester's planting crew had put in the ground the year after timber harvest.[43]

He would not see the pioneer species filling in the ecological niches in five-year-old clearcuts, the fireweed and clubmosses and huckleberries and salmonberries, feeding the deer, carpeting the ground around the growing saplings.

He would not realize that the light green blocks were ten-year-old clearcuts filling up the spaces between the Douglas fir and Western hemlock with red alders adding their root-node nitrogen to the soil.

He would not understand that the shaggy spots in the darker green forest were naturally occurring Western redcedar and Sitka spruce adding their botanical diversity in twenty-year-old clearcuts.

He would not be able to see the thinnings which foresters had taken out to remove culls and leave the soil nutrients available so the stronger final harvest trees can grow better, while the culled thinnings provide useful products as the forest grows into a thirty-year-old clearcut.[44]

He would not be able to distinguish vigorous forty-year-old clearcuts from patches of old-growth, nor be able to see the minor-products harvesters on the hidden forest floor as families picked sword ferns for florist shops, cascara bark for medical use, and a host of other little income-boosters nobody ever thinks of.

He would never recognize that nearly all the Douglas fir old-growth here grew naturally from hundred- to two-hundred year-old clearcuts made by Mother Nature—mostly devastating fires, insect and disease attacks, and avalanches in the steeper terrain.

He would not know that Douglas fir *requires* a biological clearcut environment, that it is a *subclimax species* which cannot reproduce under its own stems and can never be a self-perpetuating climax forest.

He would not know that its seed require bare mineral soil and ample sunlight, and will die in the twilight world of duff, litter, and humus on its own forest floor.

He would not know that mature Douglas fir forests are doomed to be replaced by co-dominant Sitka Spruce or Western hemlock unless some catastrophe clears the soil so they can reproduce.

Our LightHawk pilot would not know that the average natural mortality age of the Douglas fir is between 300 and 400 years, and that fewer than one percent of all Douglas firs grow to the Audubon Society's "eight-hundred to a thousand years old"—and *most* of those have been designated for protection in national parks for generations.

He would not understand that people have been harvesting and growing trees in this forest, in private forests and on national forests, living with these trees and dying with them, loving them and using them, nurturing them and being nurtured by them, for more than a century.

And even if he could see all this, he would not tell you because he is *getting money* to scream, "Look at the permanent damage!"

LightHawk (1974 part time, 1980 full time)
Budget: $713,000 (1991)
Members: 5,000
P.O. Box 8163
Santa Fe, New Mexico 87504-8163
(505) 982-9656
Michael Stewartt, executive director

Begun in 1974 as Project LightHawk, the organization went full-time in 1980 and shortened its name in 1989. It originally simply gave rides in two Cessna Turbo-210's to environmentalists to overfly clearcuts, but has expanded its activism through grassroots organizing, aerial surveys and photographs, sensational media exposure, and rapid transportation of environmental mucky-mucks who need to get someplace in a hurry. It now recruits the services of aircraft owners and pilots with at least 1,000 hours flight time and encourages them to coordinate some volunteer time with LightHawk to help fill the need for pilots and additional aircraft.[45]

LightHawk flew then-Senator Tim Wirth over Pinon Canyon in southeastern Colorado, which led to his pushing an amendment that transferred the canyon from the U.S. Army to the Forest Service, restricting all economic uses of the area.

LightHawk has an international agenda of its own: In early 1990 LightHawk convinced the government of Belize to place a 97,000-acre logging area permanently off limits and killed sustained yield forestry by creating the Bladen Nature Reserve, larger than all other parks in Belize combined.

Executive Director Michael Stewartt is also the chief pilot, having flown over 7,000 hours to trash the economy of America.

Memberships in LightHawk are $35 a year. Members receive a subscription to the quarterly newsletter, *LightHawk: The Wings of Conservation.* It includes a column on "charitable giving strategies." LightHawk peddles an eight minute videotape titled "The Ancient Forests, A Call to Action," for $14, narrated by Dennis Weaver. For an ostensibly volunteer operation, Project Lighthawk in New Mexico received a lot of money to hold out the forest in a false light:

W. Alton Jones Foundation, Inc. gave $30,000 in 1989 for Old-Growth Campaign in Pacific Northwest and similar program for environmentalists in Indonesia.

Jessie Smith Noyes Foundation, Inc. gave $10,000 in 1990, a 2-year grant for advocacy strategies using aerial surveillance to protect water resources in southern states.

Town Creek Foundation, Inc. gave $10,000 in 1990.

Funders in the Environmental Grantmakers Association gave $700,000 to LightHawk in 1992 to destroy the economy. How much more they got from whom is kept secret. LightHawk will not reveal its funding sources.

One facet of the impact of shutting down these "ancient forests" went unmentioned by Audubon: Most of the buyers of federal timber were independent small and medium sized mills, not the corporate giants such as Weyerhaeuser and Louisiana-

Pacific, which have substantial acreages of their own fee timber. Thus the net impact would be to eliminate the small and medium sized marginal operators, and, by Congressional mandate, to consolidate monopoly power in the big survivors.

But the world of television cannot deal with such niceties. If it doesn't flash colored lights or blow up, television can't handle it. As *New York Times* TV critic Walter Goodman said of *Ancient Forests: Rage Over Trees*, "The producers make their case visually, with pictures from the air of sections near Opal Creek in the state of Washington that have been opened to loggers; they are not pretty. By contrast, the camera captures the cathedral-like peace of the yet-untouched trees; a lovely swimming hole; a heaven for backpackers, where, says Paul Newman, the narrator, 'solitude can be found.' And it concludes with a camp-out and one of the environmentalists telling his children, by firelight, of the glories of the old forest. The background music gets inspirational whenever the camera catches a sun-dappled spot. The pictures are seductive; the issue becomes cast in esthetic terms."

Audubon's producers know their propaganda techniques very well. They make a gesture at giving the timber interests a hearing—cast, of course, into the invisibly precut universe of discourse focusing on the last commercial ten-percent of the National Forests Audubon now wants to shut down. Critic Goodman remarked, "Most astonishingly, the businessmen are just as clean-cut looking and plausible-sounding as the environmentalists. The difficulty is that after listening to both sides, particularly in an al fresco debate, the audience may be hard put to say whose case is closer to reality."[46]

The television debut of *Ancient Forests: Rage Over Trees* was set for September 19, 1989 on Ted Turner's TBS network and the Public Broadcasting System. The Seattle Audubon Society court case was scheduled by U.S. District Court, Judge William Dwyer for a May 1990 decision. The Ancient Forest Protection Bill was drafted and ready to run through Congress, sponsored by Indiana Democrat Jim Jontz. The three-pronged strategy was working.

Forest products companies and their employees became alarmed about the Audubon TV special when the camera crews first showed up to film them. From the beginning it was clear that the whole frame of reference of the film was biased against them. A logging equipment supplier in Bandon, Oregon, called on Charles S. Cushman of the National Inholders Association, a pro-jobs, pro-land-rights grassroots organization based in the tiny town of Battle Ground, Washington—an apt name—to organize a boycott against firms that funded the Audubon specials. NIA, as Cushman's group is known, worked with other groups and quickly cranked up its FAX network. Bill Grannell of a citizen group called The Oregon Project bolstered the spur-of-the-moment coalition, helping contact dozens of community leaders throughout the Pacific Northwest to warn of the impending Audubon hatchet job by Turner's TV stations. The activists quickly discovered that Stroh Brewery of Detroit had committed $600,000 in funding to Audubon specials through 1990. They notified the beer maker that it was sponsoring a dangerously biased program and they could easily find another brand of beer to drink.

Stroh contacted Christopher Palmer, Audubon's top production executive, requesting some changes to make the film more favorable to loggers. "They asked if we could re-edit it and shoot some new footage," Mr. Palmer said. "But I felt the film was fair."[47]

Maybe Palmer is missing a battery or something.

Palmer said after a conversation with Peter Stroh, the company's chairman and chief executive officer—who also sits on Audubon's board of directors—that it is unlikely the company will sponsor Audubon specials in the future. The company was in the middle of takeover talks and under severe financial pressure. Stroh had been a sponsor on each of its four annual TV specials since 1986.

Because of the community boycott, eight advertisers including Citicorp, Ford Motor Company, and Exxon Corporation pulled $250,000 of ads from TBS for *Ancient Forests: Rage Over Trees.* TBS agreed to run the special without commercials, and also agreed to provide Audubon with interim funding for the specials until it could line up a new sponsor. After a six-month search, Mr. Palmer got a $3 million commitment from General Electric, already a big supporter of Audubon's classroom projects. The grant was intended to fund eight hour-long specials, and GE also committed to buy commercial time when the specials appear on TBS. GE said Audubon would have complete editorial control over the specials.[48]

When word of GE's sponsorship got out, Rollo Pool, manager of public relations at Alaska Pulp Corporation in Sitka, told reporters that his company told GE "not to bid on a $3 million project to rebuild a boiler at one of our sawmills as a protest against their sponsorship of *Rage Over Trees*, and following the call for a boycott by the National Inholders Association, had instructed its purchasing officer not to buy any GE equipment unless there is no other alternative. Alaska Pulp employs 800 people and operates a pulp mill and sawmill.

"We told them we weren't interested in buying their products unless they were the last company on Earth we could buy them from," Pool said. "We get one-hundred percent of our timber from public lands, and a show like *Rage Over Trees* is a slap in the face."[49]

Blood Money

Undaunted, the environmentalists staged media followups that were incredibly powerful. In October 1992, the Environmental Grantmakers Association annual meeting heard a report on the general media campaign conducted to promote the "ancient forest" concept. It was presented to the closed meeting by no less a personage than Donald Ross, executive director of the Rockefeller Family Fund, which currently operates the EGA out its New York City offices.

Ross told the gathering of foundation and environmental executives, "I want to give a very quick description of the media campaign that has been underway for about the last nine months on the forest issues. It's complicated because there are three organizations involved, the Ancient Forest Alliance, Americans for Ancient Forests, and Western Ancient Forests, which have at various times worked very closely together and at other times had a high degree of tension between them and not a great deal of communication.

"Partly we funders are responsible for it because at the same time two separate groups of funders picked two separate horses on which to lavish large sums of money to run media campaigns. Despite great efforts to get them to work very closely together it sometimes worked not as well as one would want."

The Environmental Grantmakers Association's funder foundations were expert at secretly routing the money for this Ancient Forest effort so that it would be impossible to trace. We would never have realized that the whole years-long Ancient Forest campaign—not just this 1992 media campaign—was a synthetic artifact of EGA, had the tapes of their conference not come to our attention.

Ross said, "The funding foundations pooled their money up front for this Ancient Forest effort. It was pooled within the Wilderness Society which acted as the fiscal agent, but there was a three person board set up—with the Wilderness Society having one of the seats—to manage that money as a separate venture from the Wilderness Society. These three board members were writing the checks."

Who received the checks they wrote? "One campaign was run by David Fenton of Fenton Communications. He is a for-profit public relations firm in Washington, D.C. that has done a fair amount of activist political work over the years for mainly progressive and left wing types of organizations, foreign governments, and so forth. [Fenton ran the Alar scare campaign against apple growers for the Natural Resources Defense Council, represented the Sandinistas in Nicaragua, and was a registered foreign agent of Greece under Andreas Papandreou, Grenada under Maurice Bishop, Jamaica under Michael Manley, and the People's Republic of Angola.]

"Fenton used the media tour technique in his campaign and it was pretty effective. He gathered four or five activists: Jeff DeBonis, [a U.S. Forest Service timber sale planner who organized the

Association of Forest Service Employees for Environmental Ethics
Budget: $680,015 (1993), Jeff DeBonis salary, $30,000
Members: 2,000 within the U.S. Forest Service
P.O. Box 45
Vida, Oregon 97488
Phone: (503)484-2692 (current executive director, Andy Stahl)]

Andy Kerr [conservation director of Oregon Natural Resources Council], Michael Stewartt of LightHawk and scheduled intensive visits to major media centers in New York, Los Angeles and Washington, D.C. where they would spend two or three days with back to back meetings with editorial boards of newspapers and so forth. It produced a torrent of media.

"The other major national campaign was the Chlopak effort. Bob Chlopak [of Chlopak, Leonard and Schecter, consultants, Washington, D.C., Phone 202-296-2777] is the former head of the Democratic Senate Campaign Committee, the staff head, and had a lot of background of political campaigns working for the last several years with the Sawyer-Miller Group [Washington, D.C., Phone 202-223-1300] which is a public relations, advertising media strategy firm.

"The third effort was more grass roots, run by the **Western Ancient Forests**

Campaign and their contribution to the media portion was to take a large log on a truck throughout the country [the truck was driven, we discovered, by Mitch Friedman of the ecoterrorist group Earth First! and the log sold for $4,200 to Owl Lumber].

"The Fenton effort generated a good deal more media than the Chlopak effort partly because Chlopak's campaign was a political/legislative effort as well. The Fenton and Chlopak efforts were not coordinated, and that was a shortcoming of the ancient forest project. Chlopak produced radio ads in targeted Congressional districts and one of them was designed to counter the wise use argument about jobs. We also used the LightHawk video to help get the ancient forests issue in the presidential campaign."

In October 1992, LightHawk's clips from *Rage Over Trees* appeared in seven hundred movie theaters nationwide, narrated by Paul Newman and produced by film outfit Big Blue, asserting that "the last trees will soon be gone from the national forests, logs and jobs are being exported and recreation creates nine times as many jobs as timber harvesting." Moviegoers were asked to call 1-800-BE-A-HERO, where a donation was requested—the "charitable giving strategies" LightHawk's newsletter column talks about. You can't get a whole lot more propagandistic than the ancient forest campaign, and funders in the Environmental Grantmakers Association paid for it through the Fenton and Chlopak public relations firms.

Donald Ross continued, "The grass roots media campaign of Western Ancient Forests was paid for largely by the Chlopak effort. Chlopak spent something on the order of $600,000 beginning in January 1992 through October. The LightHawk effort I believe received about $700,000. The Chlopak effort actually received about $1.1 million but has not spent all the money. The media spending by the Western Ancient Forests grass roots group itself was relatively small. They got money from the Chlopak campaign for media.

"There is no national organization these days who can wage one of these national campaigns by itself. Chlopak's core budget for himself and his staff was $15,000 per month and that was doing it at a *pro bono* rate. Fenton's campaign was in that same ballpark [over a million dollars]. They are expensive campaigns."

Chlopak's "Americans for the Ancient Forests" front group was nothing but the artifact of big money foundations, primarily W. Alton Jones, the Pew Charitable Trusts, and the Bullitt Foundation. Their blood money did its work.

In late 1992 we got a call from Connie Gold in Hoquiam, Washington. The wife of a former logger who is now a schoolteacher, she has been a pro-timber activist fighting the environmentalists for her community.

Connie informed us, "I just called to let you know our town is in serious trouble. The pulp mill just shut down. Six-hundred mill workers in Grays Harbor County are out of work. The sawmills went last year. Our town is dying. There are plenty of trees but we can't cut them. Our food banks are empty. The logger retraining program in Olympia is finished but none of our people had the gas money to get there. The donut shop is closing down, all the little businesses that used to serve the mill guys are struggling. The churches had to scrape to get donations for needy families. We're experiencing suicides, family fights, child abuse—everybody's coming apart. A counselor for abused children didn't have access to a computer to keep track of all these new cases, so she took her case load home and made a system of handwritten files in manila folders instead. Congress won't help us. The state broke its promise of help—we couldn't even get stipends to help parents of disabled children. We don't have anywhere to go and wouldn't have the money to move if we did. We used to be solid middle class people. We're out of hope. They won. They've killed us."

No, I don't want you to have your job.

Audubon's Economy Trasher strategy was working very well.

Litigate.

Legislate.

Obfuscate.

No Home on the Range

The next target was cattle ranching on federal lands. Audubon's production company went to work trashing the livestock industry with *The New Range Wars*. The new film claimed that "cattle grazing is destroying what remains of the wide open spaces of the Southwest like New Mexico and Arizona."[50]

Again, Audubon mischaracterized the debate in *The New Range Wars* by failing to identify its actual goal, to reclassify historically commercial grazing lands into untouchable nature preserves, only this time the primary administrative agency being pressured was the Bureau of Land Management rather than the U. S. Forest Service.

Audubon vice president Graham Cox made a number of disingenuous statements to the press that his organization had taken no position against grazing on federal lands. That was patent nonsense: Audubon had long pushed for ruinous increases in grazing fees as a way to drive livestock off federal lands. Audubon was also one of many environmental groups that had used the anti-grazing slogan "Cattle Free By '93!" Audubon's Economy Trasher agenda was clear to their opponents, and plainly revealed in the television special when it was first broadcast by TBS in June 1991.

Again, the message was conveyed with emotional images rather than sober judgment. Again, the images conveyed what appeared to be damage to the resource—herds of cattle trampling the grass, areas of erosion, blowing dust. Again, the context was totally missing. Again, the land user was allowed a token response, cast, predictably, in the invisible universe of discourse created and controlled by Audubon Productions. Again, it was a hatchet job that gave the public bad emotions about every rancher that grazes cattle on federal lands and set the public at war against them.

There was no mention that the "resource damage" was a mere theatrical apparency—blowing dust, pounding cattle hooves—that belied the excellent range condition on the vast majority of federal grazing allotments. It was the same unfair debate tactic as presenting today's forest clearcut as a permanent disaster rather than tomorrow's rebirth.

There was no mention that each federal grazing permit is connected to a privately-owned "commensurable base land" ranch capable of handling the entire cattle herd for winter pasture, and that the IRS levies taxes on the base ranch *and* the federal land grazing allotment *as a single economic unit*.[51]

There was no mention that water rights in federal lands are controlled by the states, not the federal government, and are adjudicated by courts into private ownership based on the owner making "beneficial use" of the water.[52] The rancher owns the water on most federal land grazing allotments. Two states in the West, Nevada and Idaho, even have laws on their books that *forbid* the federal government from obtaining, purchasing or owning water rights.[53]

There was no mention that most of the infrastructure on federal grazing allotments is the private property of the rancher—the roads, fences, wells, pipes, stock-watering ponds, cattle chutes, corrals, barns, ranch houses, cook houses, and so on. The private rancher is not receiving a subsidy from the federal government. He pays for his own infrastructure and a stiff grazing fee on top of that, according to estate tax valuations by the IRS, a grazing fee that is twice as high as the federal grass is actually worth.[54]

There was no mention that grazing permit allotments are bought and sold with the base ranch when it is bought or sold, and that most federal grazing allotments are so well cared-for that they are passed down in families from generation to generation as a rich legacy.

There was no mention of anything that would indicate that ranchers own legitimate private rights in their federal grazing allotments or that they are among the most responsible stewards of any lands, public or private.

And there was certainly no mention of the outright fraud being perpetrated by a new generation of environmentalist zealots gaining employment in the federal agencies who purposefully insert false range condition reports in rancher files and use them to cut the number of animals the rancher can graze—an incremental tactic designed to gradually run the rancher out of business.

One of the first reactions to *The New Range Wars* was a protest from one of the Westerners who participated in its filming. Audubon Productions obtained permission to use several of country-western singer Michael Martin Murphey's songs on the sound track of *New Range Wars*. Murphey says he was assured that the film would be a "balanced piece" and not anti-rancher propaganda. But Christopher Palmer's film-makers superimposed Murphy's hit song *What Am I Doin' Here?* over scenes of cowboys wrangling cattle—clearly conveying the impression that the cowboys and the cattle should not be there—a consummate propaganda trick. It was too late to pull his permission, but Murphey—himself a member of the Sierra Club—became so angry at the misrepresentation by the National Audubon Society that he has made it a practice to pause in concerts after singing *What Am I Doin' Here?* to tell his audiences, "You're being lied to," and explaining in detail what had been done to him.[55]

Christopher Palmer told the *New York Times* that he did not set out to present a broadside attack on cattle raising when he began *The New Range Wars*.[56]

Myron Ebell, a lobbyist with Charles Cushman's National Inholders Association, disputed Palmer's assertion, saying, "It's not a documentary about Western federal lands. It's political advocacy. On the surface, they give both sides, but in terms of the imagery and the language, everything is tilted one way." The Inholders

Association organized another boycott of Audubon.

Rick McCarty of the National Cattlemen's Association said his trade group would not join the inholders boycott, but said he shared Mr. Ebell's concerns about the program being misleading and inaccurate. PBS was scheduled to repeat the TBS broadcast in July. McCarty said, "We feel that PBS is remiss if it lends its airwaves to a special-interest group, even recognizing that we're a special-interest group ourselves. I don't think we have the expectation that if we produced a program, PBS would run it. We don't think it's a level playing field."

The Inholders boycott went into gear again as it had with *Rage Over Trees,* but on a much larger scale, sending out 35,000 letters and organizing a national letter-writing and fax campaign this time. The Ford Motor Company canceled $60,000 worth of commercials that were to run during the TBS version. Ford spokesman Michael Parris said his company had pulled its commercials before it began receiving complaints. "We had already made our decision. We're not a political company. We don't want to be in the middle of a big controversy. It's not a matter of picking sides on an issue as much as it is getting out of a controversy."

But GE was the big target because of its $3 million bankrolling of the Audubon specials. Chuck Cushman said of his Inholders campaign, "We urged people to contact their local GE dealers and to boycott GE products and services. We believe that GE is funding propaganda pieces, and we want to expose Audubon as being controversial so that it will be harder for them to get advertisers."

General Electric withdrew its $3 million, 3-year funding of the Audubon Society's television specials. GE said its decision was necessitated by recession-dictated cutbacks, and that there was no connection to the protest.

Chris Palmer, Audubon's executive producer for the television specials, said that GE's decision put the series' PBS telecasts in jeopardy. "Ted Turner has told me that he will fill the gap in funding on TBS, but we will have to give up our PBS airings if we cannot find a new underwriter because GE was our sole corporate sponsor on PBS."

Peter Berle, Audubon's president, was furious. He said, "This inholders association is a right-wing group that hires itself out to oppose expansion of public parks and other conservation measures all over the country." Be that as it may, the obverse is definitely true: Audubon is a left-wing group that hires film crews to oppose grazing on federal lands and other economic measures all over the country. To Economy Trashers, more government is the answer to everything. To everybody else, government is the problem.

As one rancher from Arizona said, "I love living in this country, but I'm sick of government."[57]

Audubon relentlessly continues to destroy the livestock grazing industry.

The North Woods Scam

Without doubt Audubon's most audacious project is the grand theft of 26 million acres of New England stretching from the Downeast Maine coast to western New York state. Many environmental groups joined in this one, including the Sierra Club, the Wilderness Society and the Adirondack Council.

The Northern Forest Lands Study was authorized by Congress in late 1988 after being attached to the Appropriations Bill by Vermont Sen. Patrick Leahy without public hearings. The Study was completed in April 1990, ostensibly by an advisory group called "The Governors' Council," but in fact largely controlled by Forest Service official Stephen Harper. He told a Tufts University audience that his study "strongly suggested a conservation program and suggested a number of ways of doing that. The New England Governor's Conference passed a resolution in June [1990] supporting the proposals that are in there and suggesting Congress work with the states and the Federal agencies to advance that agenda. Conservation groups, some 18 or 20 of them, signed onto several different letters supporting this need to move ahead, obviously working together."[58]

As we shall see, Harper was playing a cat and mouse game when he said his study "strongly suggested" a conservation program. In an early draft of the Northern Forest Lands Study, he made *positive recommendations* for Greenlining and federal acquisition, but they were so controversial they were suppressed in the final draft. Harper thereafter took pains to give the impression there had never been recommendations, only "alternatives."

One of the environmental movement's most successful instruments for activating such immense campaigns is the two-day conference. Bringing the best minds together and letting the agenda develop by itself usually results in the boldest activists becoming the natural leaders and their large vision the guidepost for the rest.[59]

Brock Evans, Audubon vice president, spoke with the Forest Service's Stephen Harper at the November 4, 1990 Growth Management Forum at Tufts University in Medford, Massachusetts. Evans strongly urged that the 26 million acres of Northern Forest private land in Maine, New Hampshire, Vermont, and upstate New York be taken from its rightful owners and placed in a Northern Forest Lands preserve.[60]

The goings-on at this seminar have been loudly denied by everybody involved, but we have a tape of the entire proceedings and can prove everything we say.

Evans, who was in the area teaching a course in environmental politics at Harvard, told his audience, "For a century, I think it's safe to say, timber companies up there have owned all 26 million acres. Once it was all public domain, then it went to the private domain where it's been for a very long time. They had what you might call a social compact. That is, yes, they were going to log it and they were going to cut down the forest, but at the same time the public could use them and go and fish and hike in the legendary North Woods and have the North Woods kind of experience.

"The problem in recent years is that now the logging has intensified, it's a lot more for export. There are multinational corporations, at least in part now. They're selling off the lake front and riverside for condos and home developments as well. That's not the social compact. That's why people are upset.

"I don't agree that we can't get it all back. I don't agree that we can't get the social compact back. I don't agree that it shouldn't all be in the public domain. In fact I think it all should be in the public domain."

As in the use of "Ancient Forests" instead of "old growth," Evans urged his colleagues to mythologize the North Woods with folk tales, romanticized language and image-making. The substance doesn't matter as long as you get your way.

Brock Evans bragged about the similarities between environmentalist campaigns in the federal lands of the Pacific Northwest and their plans for the still privately owned Maine woods, boasting that the New England campaign would be even bigger. Evans said of himself: "You might say I'm a twenty-five year veteran of the forest wars in the northwest. It's the same kind of situation as here. We should get all of it. Be unreasonable. You can do it. Yesterday's heresy is today's common wisdom. It happens over and over again.

"I think you have much going for you here. You have favorable politicians, which you don't have in the Northwest. You have a long tradition of activism here in the Northeast. You have lots of strong urban centers where support comes from. So I would say let's take it back. Let's take it all back."

Evans denies saying it. We have it on tape. So do half the people who attended the forum. Tape recorders were rolling all over that room. When Evans' actual remarks came to light, *The New England Environmental Network News* published at Tufts University issued a smooth, slick, sanitized version as a coverup.[61]

The Wilderness Society was present at the Tufts gathering as well. Michael Kellett, then-Northeast Regional Director of the organization, said, "What we're really talking about here is sustainability, sustaining planetary life support systems and part of that is maintaining undisturbed ecosystems. I think it's likely this will all end up, most of this will end up being public land, preferably not by taking away— but that will probably be really the only alternative."

Sandra Lewis of the Tufts University Environmental Studies Program, told of how she had "sat down at a meeting about two years ago at the Wilderness Society and at that time most of the conservation organizations didn't have a very big vision— so I'm pleased to hear that they're at a new place.

"I don't think it unreasonable to think about 26 million acres as a possible reserve. I think it may be an absolute necessity to think in those terms for survival and for preservation of biodiversity.

"I've heard foresters say something to the effect that we don't want to turn it into a museum, as if museums were bad. I think maybe that's exactly what we should turn it into. I think there's a lot to be said for museums and I think that more and more we're going to want to preserve our past and our culture in the form of our ecological culture.

"I think it's possible. I see a scenario where environmentalists down in Washington, D. C. can really help."

Nancy Anderson, Director of the New England Environmental Network asked Brock Evans "if he could tell me how we go about going to the Congress of the United States, how we prepare a bill that would bring about the public ownership of these 26 million acres of land."

Evans told her he would be happy to draft federal legislation, but warned that "those who really want to protect these forests in New England need to sit down and get their own act together. My first recommendation is to decide basically what you want.

"Get it together. Let's go after a bill to purchase these forests, let's say to purchase half and study the other half.

"We won't worry about whether the legislation has a chance of passing now or not. The first time people see it they're going to say this is impossible, we can't do that. But we change those impossibilities, that's all. Our whole business is changing impossibilities."

Those who want to understand the vision of the environmental movement should read that paragraph again. You can expand a limited program of environmental protection to economic Armageddon with that vision. You can nationalize every last square inch of private property in America with that vision. You can enslave a nation of free people with that vision. "Our whole business is changing impossibilities."

Evans should not be regarded as a utopian dreamer for making such statements. His track record of changing impossibilities shows that he is a deeply grounded political realist. He knows what he is talking about and he can do what he says. He has trashed more of the economy and nationalized more private property with his persistent political changing of impossibilities than some socialist dictators did with tanks and guns. Being a realist, he warned his colleagues, "We have to have a process to educate all the people up there before we do anything at all."

As we shall see, that means using millions of dollars of foundation funds from the Environmental Grantmakers Association's network to carry out vast media campaigns through professional public relations firms and "grass roots" groups set up for the purpose.

Jonathan Carter, a biology professor at the University of Maine at Farmington presented a slide show to the Tufts audience critical of forestry practices, calling them "a rapid biocidal destruction of Maine's northern forest." He said, "This necessitates in my opinion an immediate move on the part of the federal government to purchase these lands."

Stephen Harper, author of the Northern Forest Lands Study, told the Tufts audience, "The process has started." As an official of the U.S Forest Service, Harper said, "The northern New England delegation got for this fiscal year an appropriation of over a million dollars to continue the Northern Forest process to identify what special tracts are highest priority."

The National Park Service also contributed two reports to the NFLS on rivers and trails to connect other areas. Terry Savage, the NPS Chief of Planning and Design in the North Atlantic Region, told a different session of the Tufts University gathering, "Some of the 32 million acres of the Northern Forest Lands would make lovely parks in case any of you are involved in that." The audience laughed. "Just a pitch," he winked. But notice how the numbers escalate—21 million acres, 26 million acres, 32 million acres. They want it all. Savage added that the NPS is "interested in developing a network of parks, not necessarily our parks, so that parks begin to be something that everybody lives and breathes every day."

However, Savage complained that resistance to environmentalist dreams was developing. "We had to cancel a bunch of studies up in Maine along the coast because the newspapers were filling up with articles about we're going to come in and gobble up the land." Erich Veyhl and Bob Voight of the Maine Conservation Rights Institute in Lubec, Maine, became volunteer crusaders for private property rights because of environmentalist inroads. Veyhl and Voight are quite effective ones at getting articles into newspapers warning the public of Mr. Savage and his ilk.[62] Savage suggested that there was a way around the problem, however.

"One of the things we've been doing is that we've held two meetings now with local conservation organizations together, just all of us in groups and began to develop a network, a computer network, a physical one-on-one network, to develop SWAT teams, if you will, to go out and look at all the different parks, to constantly monitor them.

"And if we're all talking together we're going to be a much more powerful group of people than if we're all talking individually. I think we have a wonderful future in New England for the environmental interests and preservation interests."

Your tax dollars at work, dear reader, paying a federal bureaucrat to incite the public to measures that would take private property without compensation—and ultimately destroy the societal basis of protecting private property.

Two days after the Tufts convocation, Maine voters rejected further public land acquisition in the state by a margin of 59 percent to 41 percent.

A week later, the Wilderness Society sponsored a "Maine Northern Forest Lands Activists Workshop" in Bethel, Maine. Activists included high-ranking members of the Sierra Club, National Audubon Society, Maine Audubon Society, Natural Resources Council of Maine, the Nature Conservancy, National Park Service and other organizations. Greenlining was the major focus of this workshop. One session was titled "The Greenline Game," in which the gathering broke up into subgroups to "create a greenline proposal for Maine's northern forest lands that could be implemented over the next 25 years."[63]

Brock Evans kept up National Audubon's persuasion campaign. He worked with Tom Tuckman of Senator Patrick Leahy's staff, who drafted the Northern Forest Lands Act of 1991 (which failed). Tuckman made sure the bill included a $10 million allocation for a giant four-state forest lands inventory, and Evans pushed with a 15-group coalition for a $25 million appropriation to pay for nationalizing lands under a "Forest Legacy" program that came out of the Northern Forest Lands study of 1990.

On July 15, 1991, Senator Leahy held a public hearing on the Northern Forest Lands bill in Lyndonville, Vermont, a nice out-of-the-way place, four hours' drive from populated areas, hoping that nobody would show up. The testimony panels were expected to be in favor of the bill, stacked with environmentalists. The hearing drew an angry crowd of property owners from four New England states, outnumbering the environmentalists by two to one.

National Audubon Society staffer Stephen Young, invited by Senator Leahy, got up and read with approval from the "Findings" section of Leahy's bill: "(1) The northern forest lands of Maine, New Hampshire, New York and Vermont are unique ecological resources of national significance," and "(2) The traditional forest land conservation solutions are not sufficient to protect the integrity and traditional uses of the northern forest lands for the long term."

Representative Berny Sanders, the only declared socialist Congressman, had an aide read a statement that the bill was needed to "maintain patterns of land use under increasing development pressures," claiming that developers were "turning forest into condominiums."

Senator Leahy told the audience, "The proposed Northern Forest Lands Council would have no regulatory or land acquisition authority."

Donald Gerdts, an Adirondack property rights advocate who had driven for hours from New York, got up and told the Senator he was deceiving the public, reading Leahy's own language from the bill: "The Northern Forest Lands Council shall establish a four-year plan" to include "Federal, State, local, or non-governmental land acquisition in fee simple and easements for forest land conservation purposes."[64]

At the same moment, a public hearing on the bill was taking place in Bangor, Maine, chaired by Senate Majority Leader George Mitchell and Senator William Cohen. The testimony panels there were also stacked with environmentalists, except for Bob Voight of the Maine Conservation Rights Institute. Two-hundred angry opponents from all over Maine shouted their objections to the bill. Bob Voight, whose Maine Conservation Rights Institute is a property rights protection group, told Senator Mitchell, "This is part of an ever-expanding agenda to make a wilderness park out of Maine."[65]

Carol LaGrasse of the Adirondack Cultural Foundation said of the bill, "This is a classic assault by the rich against the poor, the urban and suburban dwellers against the country folk, trying to turn our communities and homes into a park for their recreation.

"The Adirondacks are far wilder now than 100 years ago with forests grown up over open fields, homesteads and settlements for mile after mile. The Adirondackers themselves are endangered by an economy that has been choked by a national conspiracy to steal their homes and communities for hikers and canoers and by U.S. Senators who would sell out families in hundreds of small towns for the vote of a national preservationist party."[66]

The Senators tried again on October 5, 1991, but got an even worse drubbing by a crowd twice as big, with property owners outnumbering environmentalists by more than 3 to 1. Local activist Mary Adams, head of the Maine Freedom Fighters, a tax-revolt grassroots group that engineered a successful 1977 referendum repealing the statewide property tax, gave the Senators an unwelcome blast: "You guys should be like ET in the movies and 'phone home' to find out what we folks think. It's a mess down here at the grassroots. We're worried about taxes, about jobs, about survival.

"The Northern Forest Lands Council is set up to design, implement and enforce a regional comprehensive planning process identical to the state's Growth Management Law. That's a state centralized master planning-statewide zoning scheme. No, the drafts don't say that. But if a dog with a foaming mouth came into your yard and bit you once, would you do a study before you shot it the second time it came around?"[67]

The Governor of Maine didn't like the bill either.

Part of the reason may have been an outrageous project launched just before the Senators' second hearing by the Natural Resources Council of Maine and the Maine

Audubon Society to create a 10.5 million acre North Woods Conservation Area. NRCM asked the Maine Land Use Regulation Commission (LURC) to downzone the state's unorganized townships, forest plantations and coastal islands to prevent any land use other than limited forestry, restricted farming and "primitive recreation." The Council's staff attorney, Catherine Johnson, was adamant that the use rights be taken and the owners not compensated.

Paul Fichtner, a LURC commissioner, asked Johnson how NRCM intended to compensate landowners for taking away their rights to use property as they wished. Compensation was not warranted, she replied.

Michael L. Cline of the Maine Audubon Society read testimony that broadly supported the NRCM plan. He said, "The major element that must be incorporated into the new comprehensive plan is a management strategy for exclusion of developments and other conflicting uses from large tracts of forest land that possess special natural features that define the character of the North Woods."[68]

No, I don't want you to have your land.

The Natural Resource Council of Maine / Maine Audubon Society proposal to take land without compensation complemented the National Audubon Society's call for federal ownership in the North Woods—a double whammy.

With this assault fresh in their minds, Maine property owners flocked to the Senate hearings and panned the Forest Lands bill.

The Maine Times, run by flaming environmentalists, made no bones about the bill's results, editorializing, "Residential development then must be strictly curtailed. The most dangerous critter in the woods is not a man with a chainsaw but a man with a lawnmower. We must learn to accept our part in the millions of acres the public will control and give up our need to own a quarter-acre of it."[69]

Yes, Massa.

Notwithstanding the *Maine Times'* enthusiasm, the state's two Senators got the message and withdrew their support for the Forest Lands Act in early 1992. In a letter to Maine Governor John R. McKernan, the Senators said, "The comments we received, the views expressed at the public hearings and your letter have highlighted the lack of consensus in Maine on the need for the legislation. In light of these circumstances, we have decided not to pursue further efforts regarding the legislation."[70]

Before the hearings were even finished, representatives of the four New England Governors incorporated a private group funded by government to carry on the giant land grab project, the

Northern Forest Lands Council
Budget: $1,425,000 (1992) federal funds; additional partial state matching funds.
Funded by the U.S. Forest Service ($175,000)
Funded by Congress ($1,250,000)
Private not-for-profit Vermont corporation
54 Portsmouth Street
Concord, New Hampshire 03301
Phone: (602)224-6590 Fax: (603)224-6603

and began inventorying resources over the four-state region using the New York Department of Environmental Conservation and the Adirondack Park's computerized Geographic Information Systems (GIS), lashing it up to the computers of the State University of New York School of Forestry at Syracuse and those of the Northern Forest Lands Council.

The conservation commissioners of Maine and Vermont were two of the sixteen members appointed by their Governors to the Northern Forest Lands Council, but legal opinions by the Attorneys General of both states found their role in the incorporation illegal.[71]

On August 13, 1991, the Council tried to hold its first meeting in New York but was shouted down by angry property owners. Keith Van Buskirk of Queensbury, New York, served a subpoena to the meeting's organizers for using a public building for private purposes. The meeting was held at the Department of Environmental Conservation's conference room at Ray Brook—almost. About 80 local residents shouted, "Go back to the city where you belong," and "Let us sit up there and you ask us the questions."

Citizens would not listen to pleas from John Sargent, chair of the Northern Forest Lands Council, and the meeting had to be abandoned.[72]

Citizens filed a lawsuit against the Adirondack Park Agency and the New York Department of Environmental Conservation to block their further participation in the Northern Forest Lands Council. The suit pointedly noted that Peter Berle, the National Audubon Society's executive director, was the former New York Department of Environmental Quality Commissioner and had been head of the Twenty-First Century Commission that had promoted plans to destroy property rights in Adirondack State Park. Great credentials.[73]

Despite citizen objections, the Northern Forest Lands Council has continued undaunted.

The National Audubon Society has a strong network of allies taking away private property on many fronts in New England, including

American Rivers
Budget: $1,600,000
Members: 15,000
Staff: 18
Tax status: 501(c)(3)
801 Pennsylvania Avenue, S.E., Suite 400
Washington, D.C. 20003
Phone: (202)547-6900 FAX: (202)543-6142
Kevin J. Coyle, President

which came thundering into Maine to tear their hydroelectric dams down in 1989. American Rivers and the Natural Resources Council of Maine tried to take away the Federal Energy Regulatory Commission licence of the Edwards Manufacturing Company of Augusta, which sells all the electricity it generates from a dam it owns on the Kennebec River to the Central Maine Power Company. "If successful, the two organizations would then remove the dam," said John Echeverria, general counsel for American Rivers. Echeverria, by a nice coincidence, is also general counsel for the National Audubon Society. Isn't that an interesting linkage?[74]

Natural Resources Council of Maine
Budget: $1,110,488
Members: 7,000
Staff: 23
Tax status: 501(c)(3)
271 State Street
Augusta, Maine 04330-6900
Phone: (207)622-3101 Fax: (207)662-4343[75]
Everett B. Carson, Executive Director

the other dam-buster. This group is a ferocious property rights killer that we have already seen in the Nature Conservancy profile. Natural Resources Council of Maine is very good at grant writing. Some of its contributors:

The Educational Foundation of America gave $10,000 in 1990 to defend Maine's solid waste law.

The Public Welfare Foundation gave $30,000 in 1990 to draft legislation against pulp mills and industrial plants.

Town Creek Foundation gave $10,000 in 1990.

Island Foundation gave $10,000 in 1990 to implement the State's growth management plan.

Amelia Peabody Charitable Fund gave $40,000 in 1989.

Charles Stewart Mott Foundation gave $32,000 in 1990 to draft legislation against pulp mills and industrial plants.

Charles Englehard Foundation gave $15,000.

W. Alton Jones Foundation gave $10,000 in 1989 for waste control program.

Also working with American Rivers and the Natural Resources Council of Maine was the

Conservation Law Foundation (1966)
Budget: $1.8 million
Members: 5,000
Staff: 30
Tax status: 501(c)(3)
62 Summer Street
Boston, Massachusetts 02110
Phone: (617)742-2540 Fax: (617)523-8019
Douglas I. Foy, Executive Director[76]

which had pressed another anti-hydroelectric dam campaign in Maine, this one against Great Northern Paper Company. GNPC's system of 19 hydro dams on the

Penobscot River is the largest private hydro system in the country, but depends on periodic relicensing from the Federal Energy Regulatory Commission because the federal government has never recognized private rights in the use of water flow.[77] The Conservation Law Foundation intervened in GNPC's relicensing process on behalf of the Maine Audubon Society, American Rivers and the Appalachian Mountain Club to kill the private rights of the paper company.[78]

The Conservation Law Foundation is a key advocate of Greenlining. In CLF's January 1990 comments to Stephen Harper of the Northern Forest Lands Study, the organization's directors complained, "The Draft Report omits the only protection strategy which fulfills the draft's call for a comprehensive, regional effort to preserve the Northwoods: consistent land use planning within a greenline boundary. The exclusion of this well-established protection strategy, and a short discussion of its variations, is a central weakness of the Draft Report. While the University of Massachusetts study commissioned by the NFLS examines this key strategy in detail, the strategy was relegated to Appendix K of the Draft Report. This strategy must be moved to the body of the Report and become the focus of the discussion on future action to preserve the Northwoods."[79]

The Conservation Law Foundation published a vicious attack on property rights activists written by Francis Hatch, former lieutenant governor of Massachusetts— and former chairman of the Conservation Law Foundation. Hatch is a close friend of Peggy Rockefeller, and sits on the Board of Directors of the Maine Coast Heritage Trust. The Eastern Establishment is solidly behind the Northern Forest takeover.[80]

Island Foundation gave $20,000 in 1989 for litigation and advocacy to protect New England's marine resources.

The John Merck Fund gave $75,000 in 1989 for joint project with Vermont Natural Resources Council on visibility problems and acid deposition. And another $55,000 for the same project.

Joyce Mertz-Gilmore Foundation gave $20,000 in 1989 for energy project.

Charles Stewart Mott Foundation gave $75,000 in 1990 for energy efficiency project.

The Ruth Mott Fund gave two grants of $10,000 each in 1989 for fighting military pollution.

New England Biolabs Foundation gave $30,000 in 1989 to develop model for energy efficiency and conservation in electric utility industry in Massachusetts.

W. Alton Jones Foundation gave $100,000 in 1989 for promotion of source reduction, recycling and management plan for solid waste disposal in New England states.

Jessie Smith Noyes Foundation, Inc. gave $60,000 in 1990, a 2-year grant to restrict water supply sources.

James C. Penney Foundation, Inc. gave $10,000 in 1989 for energy conservation projects.

Pew Charitable Trusts gave $40,000 in 1990 for energy efficiency project in New England.

Prince Charitable Trusts gave $35,000 in 1989 for project support.

Charles H. Revson Foundation, Inc. gave $50,000 in 1989 for energy project in New York.

Rhode Island Foundation gave $25,000 in 1989 for Rhode Island Water Conservation project.

Rockefeller Family Fund gave $40,000 in 1989 for energy project.

Rockefeller Foundation gave $100,000 in 1990 for energy conservation project in Jamaica.

It is a grave insult to America that the National Audubon Society is working with all these organizations to destroy private property rights in the Northern Forest. It is an insult to America's intelligence that Audubon denies they are doing it.

It is astounding the forces Audubon can recruit to hide the fact: former Secretary of the Interior Stewart Udall wrote a hit piece for the *Los Angeles Times* against critics of the land grab, including the present authors, denying that such a plan existed. Listen to the tapes, Mr. Secretary. And read the local "alternative" newspaper, *Maine Times*, of November 27, 1992, to see how openly all the environmentalists in Maine are pushing the 26 million acre takeover. The plan exists, Mr. Secretary. We'll be happy to debate you publicly with our tapes in hand and a long list of your personal connections to the big money foundation boys behind the environmental groups. Is it a deal? Oh, you have other engagements? We don't know how to say this politely, but the Honorable Mr. Udall is blowing a little sunshine up our nose. George Orwell would love it.[81]

The National Audubon Society couldn't care less. It is forging ahead with its plans to nationalize those 26 million acres of New England. Four national groups announced in October of 1991 they were joining forces to push the Northern Forest plan—Audubon, the Wilderness Society, the Sierra Club and National Wildlife Federation. In a bid to quell outrage from the locals, the coalition said it urged a policy that addresses the "quality of life" needs, including providing for jobs, lower-priced housing, public health and education programs and social service and infrastructure needs. Christian Ballantyne, a Sierra Club official, said the plan is intended to "recognize that the citizens are an integral part of the landscape and that we will not be able to protect forests without their cooperation."[82] Perhaps the locals can learn to dress up like trees and pose for tourists.

And to hell with you all.

Audubon Strategy For The Future

In 1990 Society President Peter A. A. Berle hired Landor Associates of San Francisco to survey what came to mind when people heard the word "Audubon." The bad news was "birds." The public relations consultants added that "old-fashioned" and "exclusive" were also on the response list. Greenpeace got much higher marks. Bummer, as the *New York Times* slanged.[83]

Berle wanted to be Greenpeace without having to climb smokestacks or parachute off bridges. Mostly he wanted the money and members that Greenpeace was generating. There was nothing to do but revamp Audubon's antiquated, wheezing image. The original purpose of the National Audubon Society was officially doomed. Birds were out. The Green Ideology was in.

Well, think about it. Duke University Professor John Terborgh discovered that migratory songbird numbers were declining not because of pesticides such as DDT as Rachel Carson had warned in *Silent Spring,* and not because of forest habitat degradation caused by man's developments, but because of nest parasites such as the cowbird and nest predators such as raccoons and opossums.[84] Think of the fund raising letter you'd have to write about that: "Dear Audubon Member, please send money to help us kill the raccoons, opossums and cowbirds that are raiding the nests of the red-eyed vireo, the acadian flycatcher and other songbird species that are declining from natural causes." It lacks something, doesn't it? Bummer. Out with the birds. In with the Green Ideology. We have to stop your neighbor with the lawnmower from owning a quarter-acre of the Northern Forest. No, I don't want you to have your job. Send money.

The National Audubon Society's logo of an egret in flight was replaced by a graphic of a striped blue flag emblazoned with the words National Audubon Society, an emblem hilariously reminiscent of the Black Flag brand roach killer logo, a bit of unintentional self-parody.

Berle told his staff to refrain from overusing "bird images." He ordered them to say, "We're much more than birds. Our scientists, lobbyists, and grass-roots activists work on a variety of issues, including ancient forests, wetlands, the Platte, and the Arctic Wildlife Refuge." He didn't mention trashing the economy, nationalizing all private property and eliminating individual liberties worldwide—he's got an impressive list of international as well as domestic programs.

In March of 1991 Berle fired key staff members of *Audubon* magazine. Les Line, the magazine's top editor for 25 years, was replaced with a national tabloid managing editor, Malcolm Abrams of *The Star.* New! Improved! Supermarket checkout stand environmentalism is twice as strong! Eliminates jobs in half the time! But wait, there's more! Not only do you get these 12 brand new razor-sharp lobbyists to slice jobs to ribbons in just ten seconds, we'll also send along this environmentally-sound royal shaft to give your employed friends and neighbors!

Hype makes money. The traditionalist conservation of Les Line is too serious for Mr. Berle's cash register mentality. Line said, "Berle told me that the primary reason I had to go was my interest in nature and natural history and natural resources, and that that was not where the action was." We've seldom agreed with Les Line, but we've always respected his integrity. Malcolm Abrams? Seen Elvis riding a Spotted Owl in the North Woods lately?

Money is where the action is. Money is where Audubon is. Hey, 40 mil a year ain't hay.

The *Audubon* magazine is going for the big money glitz—eco-glitz. Money-making glitz like replacing the July 1991 cover story about the effects of the Persian Gulf war on the environment with one about the society's participation in an American-Russian effort to establish an international park across the Bering Strait. The idea appears to be to turn *Audubon* from a respected nature journal into a house organ to Bag Big Bucks for Berle.

To make sure the twentysomething, thirtysomething generation hip-hops onto

Berle's Bandwagon and pushes off the fuddy-duddy fortysomethings and fiftysomethings, Audubon is going Hollywood. Christopher Palmer of Audubon Productions and its infamous *Rage Over Trees* and *The New Range Wars* is also producing feature films and music videos. Their first made-for-TV feature film was "The Last Elephant," starring Isabella Rosellini, John Lithgow and James Earl Jones, billed as an action-adventure flick about one man's crusade to stop poachers from slaughtering elephants for their ivory tusks. At least Audubon is admitting this one is fiction.[85]

Then there are Environmentally Sound music videos featuring rock stars such as the Grateful Dead. And high-tech interactive videodisk systems for schools and institutions, and computer software and games, funded through joint ventures with Apple Computer Inc., Lucasfilm Ltd. and N. V. Philips, the Dutch electronics giant. Are your brains clean yet, kiddies?

Palmer said, "We have to reach new audiences that don't read as many books and newspapers or watch documentaries. They do watch music videos and movies—and we have to deal with the world as it is."

Environmentalism for the thinking-challenged.

But not *by* the thinking-challenged. Berle and his New Audubon crew are among the most intelligent of the Economy Trashers. They do not mind recruiting the money of the less thoughtful, but they have made sure they don't place bozos in positions of trust. And they have not tampered with Audubon's immensely powerful organizational structure. Of its organizational structure, Audubon says, "The strength of the organization lies in its 510 chapters, which are community-based Audubon societies that excel at enjoying nature's bounties while actively working to conserve them. Nine regional and five state offices coordinate chapter activities and serve as centers of environmental action." The national organization also operates 6 environmental education centers, 3 Audubon ecology camps, 9 research stations, 82 wildlife sanctuaries with major sanctuaries in 15 states.

The National Audubon Society's board of directors includes chairman Harold E. Woodsum, Jr. and other members Noel Lee Dunn, Paul R. Ehrlich, George Ellman, Charles G. Evans, James G. Hanes III, Marian S. Heiskell, Madeleine M. Kunin, Harriet M. Marble, Jan Marsh, John Peterson Myers, Carl Navaree, Donal C. O'Brien, Jr. and Edward D. Rea. They receive no compensation.

Officers include President Berle, and Senior Vice Presidents Carmine Branagan (salary $107,336, benefits $11,540), Marshall T. Case ($92,272 and $15,407), James A. Cunningham ($11,780, $17,941), Eric Fischer ($130,068, $7,256), Susan Parker Martin ($115,509, $18,387), Christopher Palmer ($101,002, $16,479), and Elizabeth Raisbeck ($86,375, $12,028). Vice Presidents include Jan Beyea ($82,503, $15,221), Graham Cox ($81,027, $1,370), Mary Joy Breton ($82,875, $11,043), and Brooks Yeager ($71,751, $12,082). John Gourlay is advertising director ($81,932, $9,970). Management cost, 1992: $3,680,496. Fundraising cost, $4,338,227.

The National Audubon Society's investments include $12,366,647 in U.S. Government obligations, $830,425 in Money Market Funds, $9,640,927 in Corporate Bonds, and $34,237,474 in Corporate Stock, a total of $57,075,473 in investments.

The National Audubon Society occupies the position in the overall environmental movement that we call the Establishment Interventionist Axis, a position it shares with the much larger National Wildlife Federation, and for the same reasons. It does not eschew owning and managing its own private wildlife areas although it acts to interfere with the property rights of others generally, and specifically acts to nationalize private land into government nature preserves. And although it acts to regulate business and stop market activities on federal lands, it does so in the interest of and with the cash of a substantial spectrum of large corporations which would benefit from less competition (holding $43 million in corporate stocks and bonds).

The following grants are to the National Society except where specific state or local Audubon chapters or independent societies are noted.

Alcoa Foundation, originally a segment of the Mellon money, gave $10,000 in 1989 to the Society of Western Pennsylvania.

Mary Reynolds Babcock Foundation, Inc. gave $20,000 in 1989 for North Carolina Coastal Islands Sanctuary Program.

The Bank of Boston Corporation Charitable Foundation gave $10,000 to the Massachusetts Society.

The Bodman Foundation gave $25,000 in 1989 for second payment on two-year pledge toward ornithological program, specifically for preservation projects focusing on species in Northeast and on Long Island.

The Bush Foundation gave $30,240 to the Minneapolis Society in 1990, a 2-year grant for wetlands education program in Minnesota.

The Champlin Foundation gave $100,000 in 1989 to make second floor of Caratunk barn usable.

The Clark Foundation gave $20,000 in 1990.

The Compton Foundation gave $15,000 in 1989 for study of environmental consequences of population growth.

Jessie B. Cox Charitable Trust gave $75,000 to the New Hampshire Society for New Hampshire Wetlands Project, education and advocacy project to protect wetlands throughout state.

The Charles E. Culpepper Foundation, Inc., gave $50,000 in 1990 toward Platte River Project.

Jessie Ball duPont Religious, Charitable and Educational Fund gave $200,000 in 1989, a 3-year grant for Florida Chapter's Leadership Development and Florida Wetlands Protection Initiative.

The Charles Engelhard Foundation gave $20,000 in 1989.

The Ford Foundation gave $125,000 in 1990, a 2-year grant for public education on sustainable development in U.S. and developing countries.

Ford Motor Company Fund gave $20,000 in 1990 for special support.

Gebbie Foundation, Inc. gave $500,000 in 1989, a 4-year grant to the Jamestown Society for capital campaign; another $15,000 for rural schools outreach program.

General Electric gave $25,000 to the New York State Society in 1989; another

$15,000 to National in 1989.

H. J. Heinz Company Foundation gave $17,500 in 1989.

Island Foundation, Inc. gave $10,000 in 1989 to the Maine Society, to identify Maine's high risk wildlife species and subsequent management planning; another $15,000 to the Medomak (Maine) Society in 1989 for interns who are monitoring reintroduction of puffins to Maine coast; another $10,000 to the Rhode Island Society in 1989 for citizens' campaign to prevent construction of Big River Dam while increasing awareness of water conservation.

W. Alton Jones Foundation, Inc. gave $20,000 to the Maine Society in 1989 for comprehensive study of pesticides in Maine; and another $150,000 to the Massachusetts Society for Belize tropical rainforest management and protection.

The Joyce Foundation gave $205,000 in 1990, a 2-year grant, for staff scientist and symposium on biotechnology issues; and another $150,000 in 1990, a 2-year grant for work on implementation of Farm Bill, especially in relation to groundwater policies.

The J. M. Kaplan Fund, Inc. gave $35,000 in 1989 "for efforts to clean up Long Island Sound through citizen mobilization campaign, including holding public hearings and conferences, publishing fact sheets and designing and monitoring implementation of plan."

The John D. and Catherine T. MacArthur Foundation gave $200,000 in 1989 for a film, Man and the Rainforest: Seeking a Balance.

Marin Community Foundation gave $160,000 in 1991, a 4-year grant for environmental education program at Richardson Bay Sanctuary.

McGregor Fund gave $25,000 to the Michigan Society in 1989 for colonial waterbird research.

Joyce Mertz-Gilmore Foundation gave $35,000 in 1989 for Global Climate Disruption Project which will inform its constituency about global warming and establish activist network that will educate elected officials and advocate constructive environmental policies.

Monsanto Fund gave $14,380 to the Massachusetts Society in 1989.

Charles Stewart Mott Foundation gave $40,000 in 1990 to the Michigan Society to investigate and measure relationship of specific toxic chemicals to biological abnormalities in Caspian Terns that result in reproductive problems and failures; another $40,000 in 1990 to National "for Foreign Assistance Action Project."

The New York Times Company Foundation, Inc. gave $10,000 in 1989 for general support and toward Adirondack Council.

Edward John Noble Foundation, Inc. gave $50,000 in 1990, a 2-year grant for Audubon Adventures programs for New York City schools.

The David and Lucile Packard Foundation gave $80,000 in 1990 for restoration and enhancement of wildlife habitat values on 550 acres in Stone Lakes area of southwestern Sacramento County, California.

The Procter & Gamble Fund gave $10,000 in 1990.

Marjorie Merriwether Post Foundation of D.C. gave $10,000 to the Massachusetts Society in 1989 for general support.

Z. Smith Reynolds, Inc. gave $20,000 in 1989 for North Carolina Coastal Islands Sanctuary Project to acquire property and implement management plans to protect state's endangered remnant populations of colonial waterbirds.

The Rhode Island Foundation / The Rhode Island Community Foundation gave $20,000 in 1989 for consultants for Thode Island Water Conservation Project.

Rockefeller Family Fund, Inc. gave $20,000 in 1989 to the Maine Society "to reorganize and expand Society's fundraising capability," i.e. this was seed money for a direct mail campaign.

The Florence and John Schumann Foundation gave $75,000 in 1989 for production costs of nature films for television; and $75,000 in 1989 for Office of Government Relations.

Town Creek Foundation, Inc. gave $25,000 in 1990.

Victoria Foundation, Inc. gave $15,000 in 1989 for workshops for elementary school teachers who lead students through hands-on and out-of-door activities of Audubon Adventures.

National Audubon Society.
Job killers.
Economy trashers.

National Audubon Society—Footnotes

1 *The Audubon Ark: A History of the National Audubon Society,* Frank Graham, Jr., with Carl W. Buchheister, Alfred A. Knopf, New York, 1990.

2 "National Audubon Society," by Susan L. Flader, *Encyclopedia of American Forest and Conservation History,* Richard C. Davis, editor, Macmillan Publishing Company, New York, 1983, p. 451.

3 *Storm Over Rangelands,* Wayne Hage, Free Enterprise Press, Bellevue, Washington, 1989, p. 63.

4 "From Fringe To Political Mainstream," by Michael Weiskopf, *Washington Post,* April 19, 1990, p. A1.

5 *Protecting the Environment: Old Rhetoric, New Imperatives,* Jo Kwong Echard, Capital Research Center, Washington, D.C., 1990, p. 153.

6 "From the Swamps and Back: A Concise History of the Audubon Society," Buchester and Graham, *Audubon,* January 1973, pp. 4-45.

7 "Interpretive Programs on Audubon Sanctuaries," Wilma Anderson, brochure, p. 1.

8 Donations from Amoco, Allied-Signal, see *Protecting the Environment: Old Rhetoric, New Imperatives,* Jo Kwong Echerd, Capital Research Center, Washington, D.C., 1990, p. 157. Donations from Exxon, see *Patterns of Corporate Philanthropy,* Marvin Olasky, Capital Research Center, Washington, D.C., 1987, p. 142.

9 *At the Eye of the Storm: James Watt and the Environmentalists,* Ron Arnold, Regnery Gateway, Chicago, 1982, p. 161.

10 "From the Editor," by Benjamin W. Patton, *NWI Resource,* Fall 1992, National Wilderness Institute, Washington, D.C., p. 1.

11 "Old Environmental Group Seeks Tough New Image," by Anne Raver, *New York Times,* June 9, 1991, page 1.

12 *New York Times,* April 15, 1971.

13 "From the Swamps and Back: A Concise and Candid History of the Audubon Movement," by Carl W. Buchheister and Frank Graham, Jr., *Audubon,* January 1973, p. 4-45.

14 *NonProfit Times,* April 1990.

15 See, for example, *The Public Lands: Studies in the History of the Public Domain,* edited by Vernon Carstensen, University of Wisconsin Press, Madison, 1968.

16 See *Storm Over Rangelands: Private Rights in Federal Lands,* Wayne Hage, Free Enterprise Press, Bellevue, Washington, 1989, particularly the chapter "Genealogy of the Federal Lands."

17 "The Wise Use Movement: Threats and Opportunities," session of Environmental Grantmakers Association meeting, October 1-3, 1992, Orcas Island, Washington.

18 In addition, Dr. Russell Lande analyzed the population demographics and viability of the northern spotted owl in 1985 and 1987; a team of Bureau of Land Management biologists prepared analyses of the northern spotted owl May 8, 1986, January 16, 1987 and May 8, 1987.

19 "Who's Who: 20 for the future," *Newsweek,* September 30, 1991, p. 62.

20 "War of the Woods," by Charlie Smith, *The New Pacific,* Summer 1992.

21 Andy Stahl, Sierra Club Legal Defense Fund, address to the Sixth Annual Western Public Interest Law Conference, "Old-Growth's Last Stand," Saturday, March 5, 1988, University of Oregon School of Law, Eugene, Oregon, transcript, p. 13-14. Complete transcript available from For The Record, Eugene, Oregon, 503-345-6168.

22 Significant cases in this tangled web are *Portland Audubon Society v. Lujan*, 712 F. Supp. 1456, 1485 (D. Or. 1989); and *Northern Spotted Owl v. Hodel*, 716 F. Supp. 479 (W.D. Wash. 1988). *Seattle Audubon Society v. Evans* 771 F. Supp. 1081 (W.D. Wash.), *aff'd*, 952 F.2d 297 (9th Cir. 1991). Seattle *Audubon Society v. Robertson*, 914 F.2d 1311 (9th Cir. 1990) *rev'd*, 112 S.Ct. 1407 (1992).

23 "Early findings link threatened owl to a related subgroup: spotted owl may be genetically identical to California owl," by William K. Stevens, *New York Times*, December 4, 1990, p. B8.

24 *Washington Post Magazine*, September 3, 1989.

25 See 54 *Federal Register* 26666.

26 "Oregon negotiations on policy to protect spotted owl snag; timber industry, environmentalists fail to agree," by John Lancaster, *Washington Post*, June 28, 1989, p. A2.

27 Incorporated into the Department of the Interior and Related Agencies Appropriations Act for Fiscal Year 1990, Pub. L. No. 101-121, 103 Stat. 701, 745-50 (1989)(Section 318).

28 "Government plans cut in logging in Washington State to save owl," *New York Times*, June 15, 1990, p. A9.

29 55 *Federal Register* 26189 (June 26, 1990). See also "Owl designated 'threatened'; impact in doubt," by Mark A. Stein, *Los Angeles Times*, June 23, 1990, p. A1.

30 "Saving endangered jobs as well as owls," column by Brad Knickerbocker, *Christian Science Monitor*, March 5, 1992, p. 17.

31 "No Hoot for Northwest Mills: Preserving an Owl's Habitat," by Richard Martin, *Insight*, June 19, 1989, pp. 18-20.

32 "New Research Shows Spotted Owl Thrives, Timber Industry Says," by Mark Stein, *Los Angeles Times*, August 18, 1989.

33 "Spotted owl dispute jolts another timber region," by Barry Meier, *New York Times*, February 1, 1992, p. 7.

34 "The spotted owl is no pussycat; but the real issue is forest management, not endangered species," editorial, *Los Angeles Times*, September 20, 1990, p. B6.

35 "Spotted owl protections expanded to private land," by Mark A. Stein, *Los Angeles Times*, July 14, 1990, p. A30.

36 "Saving owl may cost 20,000 jobs; White House said to accept proposals by scientific panel," by John Lancaster, *Washington Post*, September 7, 1990, p. A1.

37 "Owl decision pushes lumber prices up sharply," *Christian Science Monitor*, June 27, 1991, p. 8.

38 Brock Evans, National Audubon Society, untitled address to Growth Management Issues Workshop, Forestry in New England and New York: An Urgent Issue, part of A Growth Management Forum—Sustaining the Economic and Environmental Future of New England sponsored by the New England Environmental Network Environmental Citizenship Program, Lincoln Filene Center, Tufts University, Medford, Massachusetts, November 3-4, 1990.

39 Not everybody buys environmentalist arguments. See "Poll finds jobs more important than spotted owl," *Los Angeles Times*, July 4, 1991, p. D2.

40 Richard W. Larsen, associate editor, "From timber towns, a cry for compassion," *Seattle Times*, Sunday, October 6, 1991, p. A16.

41 *Forest Resource Management*, by William A. Duerr, Dennis E. Teeguarden, Neils B. Christiansen and Sam Guttenberg, W. B. Saunders Company, Philadelphia, 1979, Chapter 15.

42 "Techniques for Prescribing Optimal Timber Harvest and Investment Under Different Objectives—Discussion and Synthesis," by K. Norman Johnson and H. Lynn Scheurman, *Forest Science*, March 1977.

43 *The Yield of Douglas Fir in the Pacific Northwest*, Richard E. McArdle, Walter H. Meyer and Donald Bruce, U.S. Department of Agriculture Technical Bulletin 201, revised 1949.

44 "Economic Models for Thinning and Reproducing Even-Aged Stands," by John Fedkiw and James G. Yoho, Journal of Forestry, January 1960, pp. 26-34.

45 *The Nature Directory*, Susan D. Lanier-Graham, Walker and Company, New York, 1991, p. 95.

46 "More than Spotted Owl Is Endangered," by Walter Goodman, *The New York Times*, August 12, 1990, p. H27.

47 "Stroh Abandons Audubon," *Wall Street Journal*, September 6, 1989, p. B6.

48 "Audubon Society Hopes Music Videos And Movies Get Its 'Green' Message Out," by Laura Landro, *Wall Street Journal*, April 10, 1990, p. B1.

49 "Audubon Specials: An Endangered Species," by Jane Hall, *Los Angeles Times*, December 17, 1991.

50 "Audubon Show Irks Cattle Ranchers," by James Barron, *The New York Times*, July 31, 1991, p. C11.

51 See the Taylor Grazing Act, 48 Stat. 1269.

52 See *Cadillac Desert: The American West and Its Disappearing Water*, Marc Reiner, Viking, New York, 1986.

53 *Water Rights Laws in the Nineteen Western States*, vol. 1, Department of Agriculture Miscellaneous Publication 1206, Government Printing Office, Washington, D. C., 1971.

54 *Storm Over Rangelands: Private Rights in Federal Lands*, Wayne Hage, Free Enterprise Press, Bellevue, Washington, 1989.

55 Telephone interview with Mr. Murphy's manager in Taos, New Mexico, January, 1992.

56 "Audubon Show irks Cattle Ranchers," *New York Times*, July 31, 1991, C11.

57 "The Arizona Rancher: An Endangered Species?" by James Bishop, Jr. and Bennie Blake, *Phoenix Magazine*, June 1992, p. 57.

58 Transcript, "Forestry in New England and New York: An urgent Issue," Growth Management Issues Workshop, November 4, 1990.

59 Transcript, "Forestry in New England and New York: An urgent Issue," Growth Management Issues Workshop, November 4, 1990.

60 Transcript, "Forestry in New England and New York: An urgent Issue," Growth Management Issues Workshop, November 4, 1990.

61 "Maine's Chance to Protect Northern Forests: An Opportunity That Will Not Come Again," by Brock Evans, *New England Environmental Network News*, Tufts University, Medford, Massachusetts, Volume X, No. 1, Winter 1991.

62 "Victimized by preservationists," by Bob Voight, *Bangor Daily News*, March 22, 1991.

63 Workshop materials, Wilderness Society, November 10 and 11, 1990, Bethel, Maine.

64 "Northern Forest Lands Act hearing draws opposition," by Carol W. LaGrasse, *Adirondack Journal*, July 24-30, 1991, p. 1.

65 In-person interview in Portland, Maine, September 17, 1992.

66 Telephone interview, October 1992.

67 "Bouncing Mitchell around in Bangor," by Warren Brookes, *Washington Times*, October 16, 1991.

68 "Council wants LURC to rezone wild lands," by Andrew Kekacs, *Bangor Daily News*, September 20, 1991, p. 3.

69 "A Vision for the Forest," editorial by Jay Davis, *Maine Times*, August 23, 1991, p. 27.

70 "Forest Lands Act considered dead after Maine senators pull support," by Carol LaGrasse, *Adirondack Journal*, March 4-10, 1992, p. 1.

71 "State of Maine 'chips away' at Northern Forest Lands program," by Carol W. LaGrasse, *Adirondack Journal*, November 13-19, 1991, p. 1.

72 "Angry residents obstruct first New York meeting of No. Forest Lands Council," by Carol W. LaGrasse, *Warrensburg-Lake George News*, August 21-27, 1991, p. 1.

73 "Taxpayer lawsuit against DEC/APA evokes history of policy against local interests, say plaintiffs," by Carol LaGrasse, *Adirondack Journal*, October 9-15, 1991, p. 1.

74 "Environmentalists, dreaming of river without dam, may contest license," by Lyn Riddle, *New York Times*, February 12, 1989, p. 51.

75 1992 Annual Report, Natural Resources Council of Maine.

76 "They're environmental rangers," by Steven Krauss, *Yankee*, April, 1987.

77 "Paper mill's foes fight hydro dam, urge conservation," by Neil Springer, *Energy User News*, September 2, 1985, p. 1.

78 "Preservationist Extortion Scam," by Erich Veyhl, *Land Rights Letter*, August 1992, p. 2.

79 Cover letter, CLF to Stephen C. Harper, January 26, 1990, "On the Draft Northern Forest Lands Study Report."

80 "A Motley Crowd of Deceivers," by Francis W. Hatch, *Conservation Law Foundation Newsletter*, Winter 1992, p. 1.

81 Udall's piece was published in Maine as "Anti-ecologists do anything in order to use everything," *Maine Sunday Telegram*, August 2, 1972, p. C7.

82 "Groups join to protect northern forest's future," by Robert Braile, *Boston Globe*, October 23, 1991.

83 "Old Environmental Group Seeks Tough New Image," by Anne Raver, *The New York Times*, June 9, 1991, p. 1.

84 "Why American Songbirds Are Vanishing," by John Terborgh, *Scientific American*, May, 1992, p. 98.

85 "Audubon Society Hopes Music Videos And Movies Get Its 'Green' Message Out," by Laura Landro, *Wall Street Journal*, April 10, 1990, B1.

Humane Society of the United States

Humane Society of the United States (Founded 1954)
Annual budget:	$17.2 million (1990); $19.2 million (1991)
Staff:	124 total—72 professional, 52 support
Members:	975,000 individuals
Tax Status:	(501)(c)(3)
Headquarters:	2100 L Street, NW
	Washington, D.C. 20037
	Phone: (202)452-1100 Fax: (202)778-6132

Economy Trasher Number Seven. The Humane Society of the United States has been called "the General Motors of the animal protection industry." The *Animal Rights Reporter* said of HSUS, "It is powerful, with even the White House returning its phone calls." It is the country's largest and best known humane society. It is the best staffed, serving 37 states through eight regional offices. It is involved in every imaginable animal protection issue, using investigations, litigation, education, training programs, media campaigns, and lobbying to monitor dog racing, rodeos, wetlands, medical research, wildlife refuges, circuses, movies, cosmetics, furs, marine issues and rain forests. Through its training programs, HSUS reaches state and local Humane Societies—otherwise unaffiliated—some of which have State police power and can perform criminal investigations, searches and seizures, and secure arrests and prosecutions.

This mishmash agenda demonstrates our point about including the animal rights factions in the environmental movement: they blend not only through contacts between strict animal rights groups and strict land-air-water-wildlife savers, but also in the internal agendas of single animal protection groups such as HSUS.

HSUS has an admirable reputation. As the *Christian Science Monitor* wrote, "Although other groups, such as the Humane Society of the United States and the American Society for the Prevention of Cruelty to Animals, have long denounced the mistreatment of animals, they have usually done so in a less militant fashion than [People for the Ethical Treatment of Animals]."[1]

The broad scope of HSUS and its relative moderation have drawn fire from the radical animal rights faction which does its best to push the whole movement to the left. HSUS is thought by many activists to be not as effective as it could be if it focused on fewer tasks and goals. The *Animal Rights Reporter* said, "With its resources spread over so many issues, HSUS lacks the impact that some of the more specialized groups have."[2]

Humane Society of the United States chief executive officer John Hoyt responded, "In trying to address virtually every major animal issue that surfaces, we have in many cases minimized our effectiveness in other equally important areas of concern. We must begin to be a bit more selective about those issues we tackle in a major way, lest we lose the war altogether."

One of the HSUS's most successful focuses is humane education for children. Its Connecticut-based division, the National Association for the Advancement of Humane Education (NAAHE), started a Kids in Nature's Defense (KIND) Club in 1988 that quickly grew to more than 206,000 members, the largest children's animal protection group in the world. Matt Biondi, the famous Olympic swimmer, serves as chairman of HSUS's Children's Dolphin Campaign.

Despite its long and honorable history as an animal welfare group, but perhaps because of pressures from the animal rights left-wing, the purpose of the Humane Society of the United States has shifted away from the mere humane treatment of animals. Dr. Michael W. Fox, veterinarian and environmental-studies director of the HSUS, said in a 1988 *Newsweek* magazine interview, "Humane care is simply sentimental, sympathetic patronage."

The new direction of the Humane Society was captured in the title of Fox's 1980 book, *Returning to Eden,* an argument for the return to a simpler purified world, without suffering and civilization, where people and animals live together in perfect harmony.[3] "Human beings aren't superior, we're just different," Fox insists. "We need to think not in terms of a hierarchy, but what I call a 'holoarchy,' a seamless web of life."

This millenarian vision of perfect harmony is the common thread that binds environmentalism and animal rights into a single philosophical package: It is the embodiment of Professor Robert Nisbet's prophetic warning against the "third great wave of redemptive struggle in Western history" for the "liberation of nature from human exploitation."

Concepts such as "a seamless web of life" are quasi-religious notions, not something a naturalist or a scientist would find appropriate. The totality of actual living organisms forms a very seamy web at best, and hierarchies are found everywhere: in food chains, in the stages of embryo development, in dominance patterns among animal communities—for example, alpha males and alpha females of many species eat first, mate exclusively, act first. Nature does its business any way that works. Eco-egalitarianism is an all-too-human conceit projected onto nature by those seeking redemption, not knowledge.

The distinction between animal welfare and animal rights is critical. Animal welfare societies, which seek to avoid unnecessary suffering, have existed since the 19th century and have a minimal impact on biomedical research and the human use of animals in general. A typical animal welfare society is

The American Humane Association
Annual budget: $4 million
Staff: 40 professionals and clerical
Members: 20,000
Tax status: 501(c)(3)
9725 E. Hampden Avenue
Denver, Colorado 80231
(303)695-0811

This group was founded in 1877 to prevent neglect, abuse, cruelty, and exploitation in the treatment of animals. The association retains these goals and has drifted only slightly into the animal rights arena.

It is fascinating to note that half of this group is dedicated to the prevention of cruelty to children and the prevention of child abuse. This kind of genuine concern for humanity is what one would expect from an animal welfare society.

Lawrence Brown, executive officer of the AHA, says the animal protection division of his group is a national federation of over 3,000 local and state animal care agencies and individuals. The Association works to promote quality standards for animal shelters and to reduce euthanasia rates in those shelters. The association maintains education programs for children and adults to show them the responsible way to care for pets. The AHA/Delta Society National Hearing Dog Resource Center coordinates and distributes information on the training of unwanted dogs for deaf and hearing-impaired people.

AHA lobbies for legislation to prevent the abuse of pets, laboratory animals, zoo animals, and circus and rodeo animals. Notably, AHA does not lobby to stop such uses of animals, only to assure humane treatment of animals.

The Stuart Foundation gave $14,400 in 1989 for scholarships to National Horse Abuse Investigation Training School.

Animals rights organizations by contrast are founded upon the philosophical concept that animals have moral and legal *rights* which they may claim—with human groups as their intermediaries and enforcers. These rights include avoidance of suffering for any human reason and the right to physical liberty. Animal rights groups regard the avoidance of cruelty *per se* as a secondary issue. The primary issue is strictly moral and legal rights: confining an animal is kidnapping and slavery; consuming meat is cannibalism; sacrificing animals to spare humans from disease is the moral equivalent of the Nazis' most demented experiments.[4]

Tom Regan is the animal rights movement's leading philosopher. His 1983 book *The Case for Animal Rights* has become one of the holy scriptures of the movement.[5] He wrote:

> I regard myself as an advocate of animal rights—as part of the animal rights movement. That movement, as I conceive it, is committed to a number of goals, including:
> the total abolition of the use of animals in science;
> the total dissolution of commercial animal agriculture;
> the total elimination of commercial and sport hunting and trapping.
> There are, I know, people who profess to believe in animal rights, but do not avow these goals. Factory farming, they say is wrong—it violates animals' rights—but traditional animal agriculture is all right. Toxicity tests of cosmetics on animals violates their rights, but important medical research—cancer research, for example—does not. I used to think I understood this reasoning. Not any more. You don't change unjust institutions by tidying them up.
> What's wrong—fundamentally wrong—with the way animals are treated

isn't the details that vary from case to case. What is wrong isn't the pain, isn't the suffering, isn't the deprivation. These compound what's wrong....but they are not the fundamental wrong. What's fundamentally wrong is the system that allows us to view animals as *our resources,* here for *us*—to be eaten, or surgically manipulated, or exploited. [Emphasis in the original.][6]

Regan's views have been put into effect with a fervor that frequently erupts into violence.

The modern animal rights movement is dated by most analysts from the 1972 anthology *Animals, Men, and Morals* or Richard Ryder's 1975 book, *Victims of Science.*[7] However, Australian philosopher Peter Singer brought out a central point of the movement's belief system in his 1975 book, *Animal Liberation: A New Ethic for Our Treatment of Animals*:

> [T]he limit of sentience (using the term as a convenient if not strictly accurate shorthand for the capacity to suffer and/or experience enjoyment) is the only defensible boundary of concern for the interests of others. To mark this boundary by some other characteristic like intelligence or rationality would be to mark it in an arbitrary manner.... The racist violates the principle of equality by giving greater weight to the interests of members of his own race when there is a clash between those interests and the interests of another race.... Similarly the speciesist allows the interest of his own species to override the greater interests of members of other species.[8]

This gives us the critical philosophical structure of animal rights: The test of concern for others is their ability to feel pain, not their intelligence; to give humans moral value while denying moral value to animals is disallowed. Tom Regan capped off the belief system with his standard that "inherent value" applies to animals as well as humans: to limit "inherent value" to humans is morally wrong because these distinctions "lack rational justification." The notion that nature has inherent value apart from human beings underlies all environmentalist philosophy, not just that of the animal rights faction. And, like all ideas, that idea has consequences.

George Reisman, Professor of Economics at Pepperdine University's School of Business and Management noted a crucial consequence of the "inherent value of nature" premise in a 1990 treatise, *The Toxicity of Environmentalism*:

> While it is not necessary to question the good intentions and sincerity of the overwhelming majority of the members of the environmental or ecology movement, it is vital that the public realize that *in this seemingly lofty and noble movement itself can be found more than a little evidence of the most profound toxicity....*
> There is something which provides an explanation in terms of basic principle of why the mainstream of the ecology movement does not attack what might be thought to be merely its fringe. This is a fundamental philosophical premise which the mainstream of the movement shares with the alleged fringe and which

logically implies hatred for man and his achievements. Namely, the premise that *nature possesses intrinsic value—i.e.,* that nature is valuable in and of itself, apart from all contribution to human life and well-being.

The anti-human premise of nature's intrinsic value goes back, in the Western world, as far as St. Francis of Assisi, who believed in the equality of all living creatures: man, cattle, birds, fish, and reptiles. Indeed, precisely on the basis of this philosophical affinity, and at the wish of the mainstream of the ecology movement, St. Francis of Assisi has been officially declared the patron saint of ecology by the Roman Catholic Church.

The premise of nature's intrinsic value extends to an alleged intrinsic value of forests, rivers, canyons, and hillsides—to everything and anything that is not man. Its influence is present in the Congress of the United States, in such statements as that recently made by Representative Morris Udall of Arizona that a frozen, barren desert in Northern Alaska, where substantial oil deposits appear to exist, is "a sacred place" that should never be given over to oil rigs and pipelines. It is present in the supporting statements of a representative of the Wilderness Society that "There is need to protect the land not just for wildlife and human recreation, but just to have it there." It has, of course, also been present in the sacrifice of the interests of human beings for the sake of snail darters and spotted owls.

The idea of nature's intrinsic value inexorably implies a desire to destroy man and his works because it implies a perception of man *as the systematic destroyer of the good, and thus as the systematic doer of evil....* Indeed, from the perspective of such alleged intrinsic values of nature, the degree of man's alleged destructiveness and evil is directly in proportion to his loyalty to his essential nature. Man is the rational being. It is his application of his reason in the form of science, technology, and an industrial civilization that enables him to act on nature on the enormous scale on which he now does. Thus, it is his possession and use of reason—manifested in his technology and industry—for which he is hated. [Emphasis in the original.][9]

This simple—but not simplistic—recognition of the consequences of environmentalist thought goes a long way to explain why the animal rights factions, which as a matter of course come hard up against the question of inherent value in nature, are so prone to violence against property and people—and why the mainstream does not attack them.

Values, in the opinion of most philosophers and thinking people, are *considerations,* the product of reflective thought, not a property of physical matter. Values—considerations of good and bad, right and wrong, beautiful and ugly—exist in our heads and in our holy texts and in our laws and in our human social structure because some rational being put them there, according to this view. Religionists say the rational being was God, humanists say it was the human individual, legalists say it was juridical leaders on behalf of society, but all of this stripe agree that values are the artifact of consideration by a being that is aware of being aware.

There is nothing to prevent us, however, from believing that we can find good or bad or duty or obligation or any other value inherently residing in mountains or molecules and in eagles or atoms and in oceans or electromagnetic radiations. Scientists know that the physical universe does not contain inherent values. Mystics, philosophers, politicians, and animal rights activists, on the other hand, are free to believe what they will about the world. And they do. To project our inner psychological makeup onto the rest of the world is a quirk shared by most of us, so we should not be surprised to find it amplified to rock and roll levels by the animal rights factions.

It has not been uncommon for animal welfare societies to lose their way on this slippery psychological, philosophical and ethical ground and convert into animal rights groups. One such is:

International Fund for Animal Welfare (1969)
Annual budget: $4,916,491
Members: 650,000 worldwide
Staff: 35 professionals and clerical
411 Main Street
Yarmouth Port, Massachusetts 02675
(508)362-4944

This group was founded by Brian Davies who was trying to end the killing of baby harp seals for their white coats by Norwegian and Canadian hunters in the Gulf of St. Lawrence. His efforts were helped along by the phony Greenpeace film showing incredibly cruel killing methods of baby harp seals. Davies got to like the struggle and became a struggle junkie.

In 1971 he shifted to moving polar bears away from towns they had been raiding to prevent people from killing them. In 1978 he struggled to stop the killing of grey seals in Scotland. In 1981 he struggled to stop the killing of dogs for food in the Philippines. In 1985 he struggled to create the marine mammal sanctuary in Madeira, California. In 1987 he struggled to stop the Australian government from killing kangaroos as part of its desert management plan. In 1988 he bought a plot of land in Costa Rica to save bees. In 1989 Davies struggled to stop all animal testing of cosmetics. The concern Brian Davies felt for animal welfare lost its bearings and became a fervid zeal for animal rights, with all the attendant anti-human trimmings. His purpose statement now includes the words, "preventing and abolishing all cruelties done to them by humans." His group, unlike the American Humane Association, has no branch to prevent and abolish all cruelties done to humans.

1980 was the year in which the Humane Society of the United States began the drift from its origins as a humane society to being a camouflaged animal rights organization. In that year Society literature formally said that "there is no rational basis for maintaining a moral distinction between the treatment of humans and other animals," the core belief of the animal rights movement.[10] As

Dr. Frederick Goodwin, director of the National Institutes for Health said, "I yield to no one in my concern for animal *welfare*. But animal *rights* is a fundamental moral confusion about the relative value of human and animal life."[11]

A noted philosopher and academic once said of animal rights, "Analyzed rationally, the philosophy collapses quickly; after all, nature is bad as well as good, cruel as well as beneficent. But the emotional power of the message is enormous. Science has provided us with the means and not the ends. It gives us an atom bomb, but it does not tell us whether to drop it, or on whom. People feel cast adrift, and there's a certain comfort in the absolutism of the animal-rightists."[12]

Modern objectivist philosophers hold that much of our eco-anxiety results from "a general crisis of objectivity," the roots of which can be traced to Immanuel Kant. When Kant argued that the mind is incapable of knowing reality and that objective value judgments are impossible, asserts scientist Dr. Richard Sanford, he was sowing seeds of pure destruction. As a result of his ideas, philosophy (and to a lesser extent science) has become little more than an academic shell game in which truth is redefined to mean, not *correspondence* to reality, but *coherence* among ideas and where questions are decided (and laws passed) on the basis of authority rather than fact. He wrote, "The environmental movement is the culmination of [Kantianism], and, by rejecting reason, the ultimate effect of environmentalism will be the elimination of science and of civilized society along with it."[13]

We see the decay of reason all around us. We watch television news, or read the newspapers, and we are so assaulted by tales of doom and gloom—many of them staged by news reporters, such as NBC News's rigging of a General Motors truck to explode in a "test"—that we cannot *think*. We *feel*—we feel there are just too many people on the Earth. Worse, we feel that within a lifetime or two it will be too late to do anything about it. Resources will be gone. Nature will be gone. Hope will be gone. Such anxiety is all too easy to fan into fear and anger against *people*— particularly against the economic institutions that keep people alive—and then into the urge to liberate nature completely from human exploitation. That image of the world—false though it is—means trashing the economy and trashing the freedoms that make our economy possible.

Few listen to the voices of optimists such as economist Dr. Julian Simon, who draws a much more hopeful picture of the future: Poverty will decline. Pollution will be controlled and energy efficiency will improve. Even though population will grow, crowding will decrease as people spread more evenly over the globe. Standards of living will rise. Physical labor will shrink. More and more time will be devoted to education and the arts. Electronics will knit us together, revolutionizing both communications and entertainment. Progress will be so dramatic that a century from now life will be as improved as ours is over that of an 1893 factory worker—if environmental laws don't forbid it.[14]

Dr. Simon points out that since 1950, worldwide per-person grain production is up more than 25 percent, per-person soybean production has tripled, per-person meat production has almost doubled, and per-person fish catch has doubled.[15]

Dr. Simon made a famous bet with environmentalist doom-sayer and Stanford University professor Paul Ehrlich that the price of basic commodities such as grain or metal would fall over time, allowing the challenger to pick any date in the future. Ehrlich, who wrote the 1968 panic-mongering bestseller, *The Population Bomb*, took the bet and selected 1990 as the future date. Ehrlich lost, despite the addition of a billion people to the earth in the 1980s. The price of the five chosen metals fell. Ehrlich forked over $576.07. But he still makes his doom and gloom predictions to media adulation. Of Dr. Simon, Ehrlich said, "He's a Marxist. I'm not talking about Karl Marx, but Groucho Marx. It was Groucho who said why worry about posterity—what did they ever do for us?"

Speaking of Karl Marx, Robert Bidinotto, staff writer for *Reader's Digest* raised a cogent issue about environmentalism: "With the collapse of Communism—particularly of socialist economic theory—environmentalism has become freedom's foe for the '90s." Bidinotto noted that, "Environmentalism represents a now-denuded Marxism, stripped of all its tenets, desperately clutching its last fig leaf of mindless egalitarianism. As such, it is a purely negative, contentless "ism." It is the final rallying point for nihilistic drifters and collectivist dreamers, who are united, not by ideas, but by a hostility toward human thought; not by values, but by an aversion for human aspirations; not by some utopian vision of society, but by a profound alienation from human society."[16]

Skip the intellectual analysis: You can see what's happening to us in the telephone directory. A major city carried this Yellow Pages ad under *Books* for a store called Eco-Origins: "Mind - Body - Spirit - Earth - Growth - Healing - Recovery. Tapes - Enviro Gifts - Jewelry - Oils - Aroma Therapy & Seminars." The people who answer such an ad are not desperately clutching at fig leaves of mindless egalitarianism, nor are they nihilistic drifters and collectivist dreamers. They're probably just secretaries and salesmen and store clerks and young executives drifting in a world of intimacy lost, desperately seeking love and a sense of belonging and self-esteem—the things psychologist Abraham Maslow told us about in his Needs Hierarchy. They're clutching at hope. Hope that the Earth, if properly propitiated, will bring them wholeness. In order to treat the Earth respectfully, in order to make the Earth's blessings flow to us, they see that the only hope is to liberate nature from human exploitation. And that is a dream of religious intensity and power.

Despite the fact that HSUS refuses to call itself an animal rights organization, using the term "animal protection" instead, the Society's leadership is dominated by animal-rightists. Fox himself is only the most visible, and was put in charge of the Society's newly created Center for the Respect of Life and Environment to "let Dr. Fox direct some of his views in a channel that was an arm's length removed from the HSUS. He sometimes makes statements on biomedical research and other things that don't always reflect our view," according to HSUS chief executive officer John Hoyt.

However, the Society's official spokesman on laboratory animal issues is veterinarian Martin Stephens, who is an anti-vivisectionist, and who replaced another even more strident anti-vivisectionist veterinarian, Brandon Reines.

Hoyt himself signed a four-page 1986 "Holiday Fundraising Appeal" that described what is happening in research laboratories as "absolutely horrifying." Animals, his appeal said, "will be attached to electrodes, plunged into freezing water, or suffer through other physical or psychological experiments too horrible to describe. Please don't think this is impossible, or that I have exaggerated the situation. The truth is that *it happens just this way every day*."

Hoyt disavowed the message of the letter, but kept sending it out unchanged every year until 1991. The purpose of the letter was to raise funds to lobby state legislatures and Congress to stop the use of unclaimed pound animals in medical research. About 15 million unclaimed dogs and cats are put to death in animal pounds each year. About 2 percent are sent to research institutions instead of being killed at the pound. Thirteen states now prohibit the sale of pound animals to research facilities, which means researchers have to buy animals specifically bred for research at a cost of $400 to $600 each. Ironically, the HSUS campaign's success means that twice as many animals die—lab-bred *and* pound animals.

The Humane Society was one of several major players in lobbying the Animal Welfare Act Amendments enacted as part of the Omnibus Farm Bill of 1985—without benefit or hearings or debate in either house. Democratic niceties don't matter when it comes to environmental issues. The amendments are strongly animal rights-oriented, thanks in large part to Christine Stevens, head of the Washington-based Animal Welfare Institute. The regulations generated by these amendments fill 127 pages with fine print that tangles and strangles scientific research into a hopeless knot. Some of the provisions are innocuous, some horrendous. Institutional animal-care committees must be established. All procedures that impose even minor discomfort on test animals will be given intense scrutiny. Veterinary care, caging facilities, proper anesthesia, ventilation provisions, feeding schedules and diet are stringently regulated. Scientists are not too bothered about those requirements—other than the needless paperwork—because reputable labs already have such requirements of their own.

The mandate that has everybody baffled is "happiness," a clause requiring researchers to "insure the psychological well-being of primates" inserted by Senator John Melcher, a veterinarian from Montana who was booted out of Congress at the next available electoral opportunity, in part for his crazy animal rights votes and in part because of his crazy pro-wilderness votes. (After the voters gave him the bum's rush, Melcher packed up his Senate desk and went right to work a few blocks away for Christine Stevens in the Animal Welfare Institute.)

Primatologists have no idea what "happiness" means to a macaque as opposed to a mandrill, given the scarcity of scientific studies on the wide variety of primates and their even wider divergence in life preferences. The U. S. Department of Agriculture has driven its regulation-writers around the bend trying come up with rules that make several hundred primate species smile (and smiling is not generally a primate gesture indicating happiness anyway).

The National Institutes of Mental Health are likewise going batty trying to be sweet to primates. Primate ethologist Steven Suomi has gone on the record as saying the law will cause "chaos at best and outright harm to the animals at worst." Suomi points out that human ideas of a nifty setup don't usually match what a monkey thinks. Big cages delight some primates but scare hell out of others. Social housing calms down some primates but generates murder among others, particularly adolescent males. Ventilation keeps some primates grinning but gives others pneumonia.

The public comment period on the new animal happiness regulations generated more than 8,000 wildly contradictory responses. The government still has not finished the final regulations. When it does, the Office of Management and Budget estimates it will cost $1 billion. The Foundation for Biomedical Research thinks it more like $2 billion. The Humane Society of the United States trashes the economy again.

And the HSUS publication list contains pamphlets with such titles as *Animal Rights, Animal Welfare, and Human/Animal Relationships: An Annotated Bibliography for Higher Education*; *The Shame of Fur Campaign Packet*; *Farm-Animal Welfare and the Human Diet*; *Close-Up Report: Animal Brutality for Fun and Profit*, all of which strongly advocate animals rights viewpoints.

The programs of the HSUS are also strongly animal rights oriented. As *Animal's Voice* said, "Thanks to the efforts of the Humane Society of the United States (HSUS) leading a drive to abolish hunting and trapping on wildlife refuges through litigation and legislation, the battle is now joined. Representative Bill Green of New York State has introduced the Refuge Wildlife Protection Act (HR 1963) of 1989 into Congress and the bill is gaining support."[17] Trash the hunting economy.

HSUS also tries to destroy the fur industry. It has taken part in numerous protest demonstrations, one particularly nasty one against Saks Fifth Avenue in New York. Trash the apparel industry.[18]

HSUS also wants to eliminate parimutuel dog racing, a $3.2 billion business. Trash the sports industry.[19]

Most despicable, HSUS also works to eliminate the pet breeding industry, supporting local laws that impose stiff fees, heavy regulatory burdens, and harsh fines against pet breeders, ostensibly to control the population of unwanted pets.[20]

Hunting bans promoted by the Humane Society have led to some severe embarrassments because of its ideological failure to understand natural processes. Princeton, New Jersey, an Ivy League town as politically correct as they come, enacted a gun ban and a deer hunting ban under Humane Society pressure. With few natural predators and no hunting allowed, the deer population, of course, exploded. The township was overrun with deer.[21] That our "fragile ecosystems" ain't so fragile is one of the inconvenient facts of nature that nature lovers don't seem to grasp. Shortly, the *New York Times* ran a story under the comic headline *Bambi boom may soften Princeton's firearms ban*, chuckling that Princeton had too many deer, and was allowing deer hunting and deer birth control by dart injection.[22]

State affiliates frequently poke their noses into animal rights cases and end up red-faced. A homeless man had been caring for some horses when the Missouri Humane Society invoked its police powers to take them away from him. Lowell Rott went to court, won his case, got custody of the horses and rode off into the sunset leaving the Humane Society charged with animal abuse. Oops.[23]

The Humane Society of the United States, though, proves time and again its crass indifference to the economic welfare of its fellow Americans. In one shameful case, HSUS sued the Department of Agriculture over cattle branding, alleging it was a cruel practice that should be banned. How buyers and sellers could verify ownership without brands and carry on orderly markets was no worry of the HSUS.[24] They won, and the USDA had to suspend its branding rules. The confusion this caused in the livestock industry cost millions.[25]

The leadership of this chameleon-like outfit is quite fascinating. John A. Hoyt, chief executive officer of the Humane Society of the United States and Humane Society International since 1992, served as president since 1970. He also served as president of the London-based World Society for the Protection of Animals from 1986 to 1990. Hoyt is also president of the Society's affiliate, the National Association for Humane and Environmental Education and the Center for Respect for Life and Environment. He is a director of the Society's affiliate, the Interfaith Council for the Protection of Animals and Nature, the Global Tomorrow Coalition, and In Harmony with Nature. Hoyt earned a B.A. at Ohio's Rio Grande College and a Master of Divinity at Colgate Rochester Divinity School. Rio Grande College conferred an honorary Doctor of Divinity upon him after long service on their board of directors.[26] The religious dimension of HSUS is not without meaning.

The Religion Question

Religion does not intersect environmentalism only at the animal rights node. We observe that a proposed "wedding of spirituality and ecology" has developed in American's religious community that extends well into the mainstream of the environmental movement. For example, the Jewish Theological Seminary in New York City devoted its 1989 High Holy Day Message to the environment. The American Baptist Church and the United Methodist Church produced policy statements on the environment that urge the faithful to pursue ecologically sound lifestyles. The Presbyterian Church (USA) developed a similar statement. The Vatican's January 1990 World Day of Peace focused on the environment. The Roman Catholic Church also added "abuse of the environment" as a sin in its new universal catechism issued in 1992, the first new catechism in 426 years.[27]

In early 1990 astronomer Carl Sagan and twenty-two other well-known researchers appealed to world religious leaders to join scientists in protecting the environment. At a Moscow conference Sagan asserted "a religious as well as a scientific dimension" to the problems of global change. An appeal signed by the scientists said that "efforts to safeguard and cherish the environment need to be infused with a vision of the sacred." More than a thousand churchmen were present at the conference, which was jointly sponsored by the USSR Academy of Sciences and the Russian Orthodox Church. The religious leaders hailed the scientists' appeal as "a unique moment and opportunity in the relationship of science and religion."[28]

U.S. News and World Report commented, "A marriage between religion and environmental concern makes intuitive sense to the many people who feel the divine most keenly in a natural setting. Clark Kellogg of New York's Riverside Church says that the closest he has ever come to God was while sitting in a warm spot high in the Sierra Nevadas. 'I realized that everything was wonderful—alive and connected—and I was part of it,' he says. He is now helping to draft a declaration that would dedicate the church to environmental action."[29]

Within this hodgepodge of greening mainstream religions one can also find some rather unexpected fringes, for example, Jews for Animal Rights (we didn't make this up), which promotes vegetarianism and provides materials for celebrating bar / bat mitzvahs, confirmations, and other holidays in accordance with animal rights principles; and the International Network for Religion and Animals (we didn't make this up, either), an association of Christians, Jews, Moslems, Buddhists and Hindu believers which seeks "to apply the moral principles of these religions to human interaction with animals, especially with regard to the treatment of experimental laboratory animals, animal products used as food, and animals used for clothing and entertainment purposes;" among many other similar organizations.[30]

The greening of the Church is not a mere bandwagon effect: it reflects serious theological complications. Some churchmen such as Lynn White, Jr. have suggested that arrogance toward nature is central to Judaism and Christianity and that survival depends upon nothing less than a drastic reformulation of basic theological tenets. White made the case that the Bible causes humans to exploit nature because it sets man above nature. Genesis holds that man was created in God's image, White wrote, and that God gave man dominance over all living creatures. True stewardship of the earth, advocates claim, would require that mankind yield its claim to the central place in creation and temper the quest for personal salvation. Paul Gorman of New York City's Episcopal Cathedral of St. John the Divine said, "This is as radical a challenge to the Judeo-Christian tradition as Copernicus and Galileo."

Thus, it is not only along the animal rights axis that we find religious, moral and philosophical motivations. Even though Victor Scheffer did not posit a dimension of the sacred as one of the fundamentals in "Environmentalism's Articles of Faith," it does exist and it is powerful. It, like the environmental paradigm itself, appears to challenge rather than enhance notions of the sacred current in Western civilization.

Scandals in Protectionland

But a religious environmentalist is no more righteous than anybody else. In 1988 newspaper columnist Jack Anderson revealed that HSUS bought Hoyt's house in Maryland for $310,000 and let him and his family live there rent-free. They also reported that HSUS gave Treasurer Paul Irwin $85,000 as reimbursement for lease payments and improvements on ocean-front real estate in Maine. And, they said, the HSUS Board never authorized these transactions. An independent audit revealed the payments.[31]

In another HSUS scandal, the Washington law firm of Harmon & Weiss concluded that "excessive compensation payments" not authorized by the full board "threaten the status (of HSUS) as a charity under the federal tax law and appear to constitute a wasting of its assets." A second opinion by attorney Jacob A. Stein agreed mistakes were made, but that they were not criminal and don't threaten the society's tax-free status. Nevertheless, HSUS revised its financial policies and procedures and hired a new controller.[32]

The fallout was that John Hoyt was punished by a promotion from president of HSUS to the newly created position of chief executive officer. Treasurer Paul Irwin was punished by election as president while retaining his position as treasurer.[33] The HSUS tried to make this shuffle seem like a moderation of its animal rights agenda. An official spokesman said, "There was a perception" that the group had "gone too far [in the animal rights direction]." It was after this that HSUS replaced vociferous anti-vivisectionist Brandon Reines as the head of their lab animal issues with Martin Stephens, who seems to be seeking a truce. Stephens has said of the animal research debate, "You are either for sick children or the welfare of rats," a polarization he called "unfortunate."[34]

Paul G. Irwin, the new HSUS president, has been an officer of HSUS since 1976. He was awarded a Doctor of Letters degree from Rio Grande College; he earned Masters Degrees from Boston University and Colgate Rochester Divinity School and a baccalaureate from Roberts Wesleyan College. He also did postgraduate work and Harvard University, Andover Newton Theology School, and the Massachusetts Health Center. Irwin is an ordained United Methodist Minister, and prior to joining HSUS was engaged in ecclesiastical responsibilities in Massachusetts and New York in professional education and internship for parish ministers in affiliation with Boston University School of Theology. He initiated and administered programs focused on the enablement of the handicapped and disenfranchised. He also served a rotation in Brazil with Project Hope.

Irwin serves on the board of directors of the American Bible Society, Theodore Roosevelt National Bank, the Wilhelm Schole, the Center for Respect of Life and Environment, the National Association for Humane and Environmental Education, and the World Society for the Protection of Animals, headquartered in London.

It is clear that the Humane Society of the United States is run by two very religious, very powerful men. We are not making a sectarian argument for or against any particular religious denomination or system of beliefs by pointing this out—Hoyt and Irwin, like all Americans, have a right to their beliefs that is absolute and irreproachable. We are calling attention to the fact that two politically influential and canny men with strong religious backgrounds running an environmental group should not come as a surprise because *religion-like behavior is at the core of all environmentalism.*

Without making judgments on the preferability of one belief system over another, it is vital to the economic debate to be aware that the religious-philosophical dimension of the animal rights / animal protection segment of the environmental movement is a key nexus that ties it to the overall environmental movement at the deepest level, the level most analysts today call "Deep Ecology." Religious-philosophical beliefs are based on ideas. Ideas have consequences. In order to debate the bad effects of environmentalism, it is essential that critics and skeptics grasp the essence of those consequential ideas. Deep Ecology is the most profound idea, the root from which all the factions of the movement grow. It behooves us to know a little about it. We grasp—by reading their own books—that all environmentalists are in some fashion looking for a return to Eden, to the pure or the primitive, like HSUS's Michael W. Fox. Here is what's behind that universal urge.

The Philosophical Factions

A thoughtful sect has emerged in the environmental movement to emphasize the liberation of nature by unmaking civilization. It is known as "Deep Ecology," a term coined by Arne Naess, a Norwegian philosopher who in 1973 first suggested that two distinct environmental movements were forming, not one. The first movement, said Naess, was the large, popular, mainstream cluster of groups presided over by professionals—bureaucratic and shallow in that it merely sought reforms of pollution and resource depletion. The other was small, personal, and deep in that it envisioned a fundamental change in the way human cultures related to the natural world: the liberation of nature from human exploitation. Naess's thought influenced many others, perhaps most importantly the American environmental radicals Bill Devall and George Sessions, who picked up Naess's theme of two environmental movements, one shallow, one deep, and popularized it into a creed.[35]

Naess, born in 1912, was a professor of philosophy at the University of Oslo from 1939 to 1970, when he resigned to become a radical environmental activist. He defined a quasi-religious outlook on nature that he called "ecosophy" [ecological philosophy], an elaborate system embodying his vast expertise in empirical semantics, the philosophy of science, Gandhi's theory of nonviolence, and Spinoza's theory of freedom and ethics. It explicitly projected intrinsic value into nature. It was the precise opposite of humanistic philosophy as found, for example, in Jacob Bronowski's *The Ascent of Man*, which unfolded an unqualified reverence for man *qua* rational being.[36]

Shorn of technicalities, the essence of Naess's Deep Ecology philosophy is a complete rejection of Western humanistic civilization and all "anthropocentrism,"—human-centeredness—which is the vital link to the animal rights faction. To Naess, human beings have no special place in the universe, and no right to change the world—because it harms the habitat of other species. This belief is identical to the basic premise of the animal rights factions. Proper human behavior consists in "a more spiritual approach" to Nature, "a more sensitive openness to ourselves and nonhuman life around us." Deep questioning goes with deep ecology: Where the science of ecology would not ask what kind of society would be the best for maintaining a particular ecosystem, deep ecology does, going beyond the factual scientific level to the level of "self and Earth wisdom" and "ecological consciousness"—but one suspects that no deep questioning on those subjects is envisioned. Tolerance of opposing viewpoints is not one of environmentalism's strong points.

Bill Devall and George Sessions have elaborated Naess's ideas into a set of basic principles, stressing that everyone should arrive at his or her own deep ecology—but without straying from the following non-negotiable propositions, quoted verbatim from their book *Deep Ecology*:

1. The well-being and flourishing of human and nonhuman Life on Earth have value in themselves (synonyms: intrinsic value, inherent value). These values are independent of the usefulness of the non-human world for human purposes.

2. Richness and diversity of life forms contribute to the realization of these values and are also values in themselves.

3. Humans have no right to reduce this richness and diversity except to satisfy *vital* needs.

4. The flourishing of human life and cultures is compatible with a substantial decrease of the human population. The flourishing of nonhuman life requires such a decrease.

5. Present human interference with the nonhuman world is excessive, and the situation is rapidly worsening.

6. Policies must therefore be changed. These policies affect basic economic, technological, and ideological structures. The resulting state of affairs will be deeply different from the present.

7. The ideological change is mainly that of appreciating *life quality* (dwelling in situations of inherent value) rather than adhering to an increasingly higher standard of living. There will be a profound awareness of the difference between big and great.

8. Those who subscribe to the foregoing points have an obligation directly or indirectly to try to implement the necessary changes.[37]

Professor Reisman's point about the toxicity of environmentalism was well taken. This, as should be evident, is simply a contract tying one to the conceptual foundation of environmentalism—a belief in the intrinsic value of nature; the basic goal to liberate nature from human exploitation; the primary archetype: Nature Is Good. Humans Are Destroying Nature. Humans Are Bad. Humans Must Be Stopped.

The Utopia envisioned by Devall and Sessions is sufficiently ambiguous that it can be read by optimists as a realm of eternal peace inhabited by scattered small bands of highly educated ecologists—a sort of Yuppie Wild Kingdom—or by pessimists as a postliterate Stone Age ruled by brutal population controllers who cannot remember why they must kill all children beyond the one allowed to each couple.

But the Deep Ecologists' Ecotopia cannot be read as allowing the survival of any industry or of any civilization. And that is something most deeply to consider. Where one comes down on that issue is likely to determine the shape of the next century's politics.

Deep Ecologists feel a gut revulsion and hatred for modern industrial society, asserting that it is not necessary or conducive to spiritual and cultural growth, much less survival. Man has become a blight upon the planet, "living in an addict's dream of affluence, comfort, eternal progress, using the great achievements of science to produce software and swill," in the words of ecopoet Gary Snyder. Humans should kill off most of their population and revert to primal, tribal conditions living a life of non-egoistic self realization, introspection, balance, harmony, purification, and "a dancing celebration or affirmation of all being"—all being, that is, except Western civilization. We are to suppose that Aristotle, Sappho, St. Augustine, Mary Wollstonecraft, Michaelangelo, the Brontë sisters, Beethoven, Marie Curie, Einstein, Golda Meier, and their ilk do not qualify as "being."

The ultimate irony is that Deep Ecology's ecopoets and ecosophists are published and lionized through the great achievements of Western civilization, using swilly software (typesetting programs), petrochemicals (ink), virgin and recycled trees (paper), automotive products (book distributors' delivery trucks), electricity (to light retail book stores and power the broadcast media that publicize ecobooks), and few of them turn down the addictive royalty checks that buy affluence and comfort.

Deep Ecology means never having to say Thank You.
Its psychological roots are in all of us.

Primitivism

At the root of all environmentalism is a mindset called primitivism. Primitivism, according to scholars Arthur O. Lovejoy and George Boas, is "the belief of men living in a relatively highly evolved and complex cultural condition that a life far simpler and less sophisticated in some or in all respects is a more desirable life." Primitivism reflects the assumption "that correctness in opinion and excellence in individual conduct or in the constitution of society consists in conformity to some standard or norm expressed by the term 'nature' or its derivatives."[38]

That defining essence applies to all environmentalisms, whether philosophical, bureaucratic, deep, shallow, heavy, light, vast or half-vast.

Lovejoy and Boas studied two kinds of primitivism that are pertinent to environmentalism: Chronological primitivism and cultural primitivism.

Chronological primitivism is a kind of philosophy of history answering the question: When is the best of times, the past, the present, or the future? Chronological primitivists all answer: The past. The Theory of Decline supposes that the highest degree of excellence or happiness in man's existence came at the beginning of history. The early Greeks, for example, held that a primal Golden Age was the best of times:

First of all the deathless gods who dwell on Olympus made a golden race of mortal men who lived in the time of Cronos when he was reigning in heaven. And they lived like gods without sorrow of heart, remote and free from toil and grief: miserable age rested not on them; but with legs and arms never failing they made merry with feasting beyond the reach of all evils. When they died, it was as though they were overcome with sleep, and they had all good things; for the fruitful earth unforced bare them fruit abundantly and without stint. They dwelt in ease and peace upon the lands with many good things, rich in flocks and loved by the blessed gods.[39]

That description of The Golden Age by Hesiod, circa 700 B. C., embodies the inducements offered by all Utopias; Its outlines are clearly recognizable in modern Ecotopias. Live simply and Nature will take care of all your needs—like it used to be. Back to Nature is best, back in time. Whether back to the Golden Age of the Greeks or back to the Late Paleolithic, it's always *back*. Though they may differ on the details, all environmentalists feel that earlier times were better times. They idealize pristine America prior to European settlement. They idealize ancient societies, as we see in the goddess-worship cults growing among committed environmentalists. They are backward-looking chronological primitivists.

Cultural primitivism, on the other hand, is the discontent of the civilized with civilization. To people living in any phase of cultural development it is always possible to conceive of some simpler one. Cultural primitivism has had enduring roots in human psychology ever since the civilizing process began. As Lovejoy and Boas wrote,

It is a not improbable conjecture that the feeling that humanity was becoming overcivilized, that life was getting too complicated and over-refined, dates from the time when the cave-man first became such. It can hardly be supposed—if the cave-men were at all like their descendants—that none among them discoursed with contempt upon the cowardly effeminacy of living under shelter or upon the exasperating inconvenience of constantly returning for food and sleep to the same place instead of being free to roam at large in the wide-open spaces.[40]

Though they may differ on the details, all environmentalists feel that the simpler life of which they dream has been somewhere, at some time, actually lived by human beings. In primitive tribal societies environmentalists see living replicas of the character and life they wish to emulate. The simpler, better life *must* have existed, and present-day primitive cultures are the proof that such a life is possible. Environmentalists look not only to the past for better times, but also to extant preliterate cultures for better lives. Environmentalists are cultural primitivists.

Primitivists also look to "Nature" as the measure of all things. Only nature is good. Man can be good only by following Nature. Lovejoy and Boas found at least seven varieties of "the state of Nature" that shape primitivist belief, themes that pervade Western literature from ancient times:

1. The original condition of things, and especially the state of man as nature first made him, whatever this condition may be supposed to have been, is best. As Rousseau put it, "Everything is good when it leaves the hands of the Creator; everything degenerates in the hands of man."

2. That condition of human life is best which is most free from the intrusion of technology, where none or only the simplest practical arts were known. Thoreau is the American exemplar of this creed.

3. Natural societies should have no private property, particularly private property in land. Marx and other communist primitivists back at least to Plato have preached this doctrine.

4. Natural societies should have the simplest marital states, such as the community of wives and children; in its extreme form, sexual promiscuity, including incest. We saw quite a bit of this form of primitivism during the sexual revolution of the 1960s, but herpes and the AIDS epidemic have put something of a damper on it. Such sexual insurgency has a long history: The Greek philosopher Diogenes is reputed to have advocated the community of wives, "considering marriage to consist in nothing but the union of the man persuading with the woman consenting. And for this reason he also thought that children should be held in common."[41]

Diogenes also asserted that incest is not against nature: "Oedipus discovered that he had had intercourse with his mother and had had children by her; whereupon—when he should, perhaps, have concealed this, or else have made it lawful for the Thebans—he first of all announced it to everybody, and then reproached himself and moaned loudly that he was father and brother to the same children, and husband and son to the same woman. But cocks do not see anything wrong in such unions, nor do dogs or asses, nor yet the Persians, who are considered the best people of Asia."[42]

5. Vegetarianism is best, not on hygienic grounds but as an expression of the feeing that bloodshed in all its forms is sinful, that man in an ideal state should— and once did—live at peace with the animals as well as with his own kind. The very earliest coherent literature on earth, the Mesopotamian *Epic of Gilgamesh* presents this theme in the hero Enkidu who at first lived and grazed among the animals as one of them until seduced by a prostitute trying to lure him to the city of Uruk where his great strength could relieve the populace of the tyrant Gilgamesh. After having sex with the prostitute, Enkidu could no longer communicate with the animals. They fled from him. He was polluted because sex with his own kind had made him distinctively human. He went to the city where he abandoned his vegetarian ways and his "natural" life. Note the psychological equation, sex equals eating meat equals pollution equals human. And note that pollution is a moral and religious term, not a scientific one. Make of this story what you will, but remember, it is one of the first stories civilized people told each other.

6. Society is best without organized political government, or without any except the "natural" government of the family, clan or tribe—anarchism, in the nonpejorative technical sense of the word. Marxists believed that under pure communism, even their socialist state "would wither away," but the withering away of the Soviet Union as it actually happened wasn't quite what they had in mind. Yet environmentalist primitivists perversely never fail to recommend the most hideously bureaucratic totalitarianisms when they actually come to power.

7. Natural ethics operates when man is in unity with himself, controlled by "natural" impulses, without deliberate and self-conscious moral effort, the constraint of rules, or the sense of sin. Of course, the basic principles of Deep Ecology are assumed to be "natural" impulses, so rigid and brutal enforcement of the environmental ethic tends to be invisible to Deep Ecologists.

Primitivists through the ages have been—and continue to be—the deep reformers of the world: Equalitiarians, communists, philosophical anarchists, pacifists, vegetarians, insurgents against prevailing moral codes, propagandists of "natural" religion, all find sanction for their beliefs and programs in the supposed models of primeval man or of living primitives. (Hitler, recall, was a vegetarian, non-smoker, non-drinker, and anti-vivisectionist.) To that list we now add environmentalists.

The Board of Directors of the Humane Society of the United States includes chairman K. William Wiseman, chairman emeritus Coleman Burke, vice chairman O. J. Ramsey, secretary Amy Freeman Lee, chief executive officer John A. Hoyt, president/treasurer Paul G. Irwin, and vice president/general counsel Roger A. Kindler. Other members include H. I. (Sonny) Bloch, Anita Schoomaker Coupe, Irene Evans, Carroll Forgham-Thrift, Regina Bauer Frankenberg, Harold H. Gardiner, Alice R. Garey, Jane Goodall, Leslie R. Inglis, John Kelly, Jack W. Lydman, Virginia Lynch, Marilyn G. Seyler, Robert Sorock, John E. Taft, Terry C. Thomason, Viola Weber, Robert F. Welborn, David O. Wiebers, and Marilyn Wilhelm.

The Humane Society of the United States straddles Establishment Interventionist Axis behavior and Establishment Eco-socialist Axis, but until and unless it regains its animal welfare footing, its behavior will be preponderantly Establishment Eco-socialist Axis, which is where we place it.

The Southwestern Bell Foundation gave the Humane Society of Missouri $12,000 in 1989.

The Columbus Foundation gave the Columbus, Ohio Society $100,000 in 1990 "to support capital campaign."

The Geraldine R. Dodge Foundation, Inc. gave HSUS $11,500 in 1989 for scholarships to train animal workers.

The Grainger Foundation, Inc. gave $10,000 to the Colorado Society in 1989 "for operating fund."

William G. Selby and Marie Selby Foundation gave Florida Society $15,000 in 1990 "for rescue vehicle."

The James L. and Eunice West Charitable Trust gave the Humane Society of North Texas $10,000 in 1989 for building expansion.

None of the many other grants could be traced.

The Humane Society of the United States.
Job Killer.
Economy Trasher.

Humane Society of the United States-Footnotes

1 *Christian Science Monitor*, October 15, 1990.

2 *Animal Rights Reporter*, October 1989.

3 *Returning to Eden: Animal Rights and Human Responsibility*, Michael W. Fox, Viking, New York, 1980.

4 *America's New Extremists: What You Need to Know About the Animal Rights Movement*, David T. Hardy, Esq., Washington Legal Foundation, Washington, D. C., 1990, p. 8-9.

5 *The Case for Animal Rights*, Tom Regan, University of California Press, Berkeley, 1983.

6 "The Case for Animal Rights," by Tom Regan in *In Defense of Animals*, edited by Peter Singer, Blackwell, New York, 1985, p. 13-14.

7 *Animals, Men, and Morals: An Inquiry into the Maltreatment of Non-Humans*, edited by Stanley Godlovitch, Caplinger Publishing, New York, 1972. *Victims of Science: The Use of Animals in Research*, Richard Ryder, National Anti-Vivisection Society, London, 1975, 1983.

8 *Animal Liberation: A New Ethics for Our Treatment of Animals*, Peter Singer, New York Review distributed by Random House, 1975, p. 8-9.

9 George Reisman, *The Toxicity of Environmentalism*, The Jefferson School of Philosophy, Economics, and Psychology, Laguna Hills, California, 1990.

10 *HSUS News*, 1980.

11 Speech to Saving Lives Coalition, Washington, D.C., June 10, 1992.

12 *City Paper*, vol 5. # 51, Washington D. C., December 20-26, 1985. p. 37.

13 *Rational Readings on Environmental Concerns*, edited by Dr. Jay H. Lehr, Van Nostrand Reinhold, New York, 1992.

14 *The Resourceful Earth: A Response to Global 2000*, Julian L. Simon and Herman Kahn, eds., Basil Blackwell, New York, 1984.

15 "Is the Era of Limits Running Out? A Conversation with Garrett Hardin and Julian Simon," by Ben Wattenberg and Karlyn Keene, *Public Opinion 5*, no. 1, 1982, p. 48.

16 Speech at the Foundation for Economic Education conference of April 28, 1990 at Alderbrook Resort Inn on Hood Canal in Washington State.

17 *Animals' Voice*, December 1989. See also, "Refuge hunting: preserve use or logical harvest?" by Michael Satchell, *U. S. News and World Report*, January 12, 1987, p. 26. See also "Refused on refuges?" by Lonnie Williamson, *Outdoor Life*, October 1986, p. 39.

18 "U.S. Humane Society pickets SFA in N.Y.C.," *Women's Wear Daily*, October 4, 1988, p. 20.

19 "Hounds embody $3.2 billion business," by Garrison Wells, *Denver Business Journal*, June 21, 1991, p. 1.

20 "Once a pet peeve, now a crime," by Kristin Larson Doyle, *Insight*, February 4, 1991, p. 62.

21 "Cost of Princeton tolerance: deer protected by hunting ban, herd overruns New Jersey township," by Michael Specter, *Washington Post*, February 12, 1991, p. A3.

22 "Bambi boom may soften Princeton's firearms ban," *New York Times*, October 6, 1991, p. 30.

23 "Horse sense prevails in custody drama in rural Missouri: homeless man, it is decided, can provide better care for charges than state," by James S. Hirsch, *Wall Street Journal*, April 13, 1992, p. A13.

24 "Humane Society sues USDA over branding," *Washington Post*, April 10, 1986, p. A22.

25 "Court tells USDA to suspend cow branding rule," by Jon F. Scheid, *Feedstuffs*, April 21, 1986, p. 1.

26 *Public Interest Profiles, 1992-1993*, p. 501

27 "A new Catholic catechism," by Alan Riding, *New York Times*, November 17, 1992.

28 Seth Shulman, "Sagan appeals to world religious leaders," *Nature*, Vol. 343, 1 February 1990.

29 *U.S. News & World Report*, Nov. 27, 1989, pp. 66-67.

30 Both organizations can be found profiled in *The Encyclopedia of Associations, 27th Edition - 1993*, p. 1208. Jews for Animals Rights is entry number 10425 and the International Network of Religion and Animals is number 10422.

31 "Excessive Payments at Humane Society," by Jack Anderson and Joseph Spear, *Washington Post*, September 8, 1988,

32 "Questions of Humane Society finances," by Jack Anderson and Dale Van Atta, *Washington Post*, February 20, 1991, p. D16. See also "HSUS in hot water again," by Merritt Clifton, *The Animals' Agenda*, May 1991, p. 33.

33 "Reshuffles at HSUS," by Merritt Clifton, *The Animals' Agenda*, December 1991, p. 33.

34 "Conquering 'Animal Rights' With A Smile," by Kathleen Marquardt, Chairman, Putting People First, opinion column, Washington, D. C., June 15, 1992.

35 Arne Naess, "The Shallow and the Deep, Long-Range Ecology Movement. A Summary," *Inquiry* 16 (1973): pp. 95-100.

36 See Arne Naess, *Gandhi and Group Conflict: An Exploration of Satyagraha— Theoretical Background*, Oslo, 1974; "Spinoza and Ecology," in S. Hessing, ed., *Speculum Spinozarnum 1677-1977*, London, 1978; "Through Spinoza to Mahayana Buddhism, or through Mahayana Buddhism to Spinoza?" in J. Wetlesen, ed., *Spinoza's Philosophy of Man; Proceedings of the Scandinavian Spinoza Symposium 1977*, Oslo, 1978; "Self-realization in Mixed Communities of Humans, Bears, Sheep and Wolves," *Inquiry* 22, 1979, pp. 231-241.

37 Bill Devall and George Sessions, *Deep Ecology: Living as if Nature Mattered*, Peregrine Smith Books, Salt Lake City, 1985, particularly Chapter 6, "Some Sources of the Deep Ecology Perspective," p. 70.

38 Arthur O. Lovejoy and George Boas, *Primitivism and Related Ideas in Antiquity*, Octagon Books, New York, 1973, first published by The Johns Hopkins Press, 1935, p. 7, p. 103.

39 Hesiod, "Works and Days," in *Hesiod: The Homeric Hymns and Homerica*, English translation by Hugh G. Evelyn-White, Loeb Edition, published in the United States by Harvard University Press, Cambridge, 1914, p. 11.

40 Lovejoy and Boas, *Primitivism and Related Ideas in Antiquity*, p. 7.

41 Diogenes Laertius, VI, 72. See the Loeb Edition, *Diogenes Laertius: Lives of Eminent Philosophers*, translated by R. D. Hicks, Vol. II, published in America by the Harvard University Press, Cambridge, 1925, p. 75.

42 Dio Chrysostom, *Discourses*, X, 29-30. Edited by J. von Arnim, 1893.

Environmental Defense Fund ▮▮▮▮▮▮

Environmental Defense Fund (Founded 1967)
Annual budget: $17,394,230 (1993)
       Staff: 110 total—80 professional, 30 support
   Members: 250,000 individuals (1994)
    Tax Status: (501)(c)(3)
Headquarters: 257 Park Avenue South   1616 P Street, NW
          New York, New York 10010   Washington, D.C. 20036
          Phone: (212)505-2100   Phone: (202)387-3500
          Fax: (212)505-2375   Fax: (202)234-6049

Economy Trasher Number Eight. EDF was founded on October 6, 1967 by a group of lawyers and scientists as a single-purpose organization to ban the insecticide DDT.[1] It was the first environmental group established exclusively to "defend the environment in the nation's courts." The founding motto of this charming Economy Trasher was "Sue the bastards!" Bastards suing bastards?

It was the era of Rachel Carson's 1962 milestone antipesticide masterpiece, *Silent Spring*. Carson's alarm that Earth had reached the limits of its capacity to absorb the harmful activities of man was dramatized in her concern over the ecological impact of DDT. In particular, the insect killer was alleged to cause thinning of eggshells in wild bird populations which had ingested DDT-polluted water or food, especially raptors that ate contaminated prey species down the food chain.

Several of EDF's founding trustees worked in New York with the Brookhaven Town Natural Resources Committee, a group of students, teachers, conservation officers, laymen, scientists, and lawyers. Five members of BTNRC, Charles Wurster, Dennis Puleston, George Woodwell, Robert Smolker, and Arthur Cooley became the scientific core of the Environmental Defense Fund after struggling to ban DDT in Suffolk County. They warned the county of potential dangers in using DDT for mosquito control, but without success.[2]

By their own account, the group was "busy trying to discover new strategies to influence the political system. They concluded that conservationists were good but meek people. Greater clout was needed to save the environment."[3]

With Long Island attorney Victor Yannacone, the little gaggle of scientists took their battle to court, where they discovered "they had finally found an effective means not only to get action but to focus attention on their scientific evidence...'By suing, we had the tiger by the tail, in court, where he couldn't ignore us.'"[4] This first case against the Suffolk County Mosquito Control Commission in 1966 was financed by the Rachel Carson Memorial Fund of the National Audubon Society.[5]

It was shortly after taking this first case to court that the group gathered at Brookhaven National Laboratory and incorporated as the Environmental Defense Fund. An early statement said, "The basic aim of the EDF is to create, through litigation, a body of legal interpretations for natural resource conservation and abatement of ecologically perilous situations." Arthur Cooley, one of the founding trustees recalled, "We were trying to get DDT banned and really didn't think beyond that. But the formation of EDF changed things. People began coming to us with cases and we saw that there could be a big agenda."[6]

Part of that agenda was the transmogrification of science into a political tool. In 1969 the EDF joined with the Wisconsin chapter of the Izaak Walton League and the local Citizens Natural Resources Association in an administrative hearing on the effects of DDT in the environment by the Wisconsin Department of Natural Resources. Forming coalitions is one of the key strategies of the EDF.

Executive director Frederic D. Krupp (salary $125,000) once said, "EDF emphasizes close communications with other national, international, and state environmental groups. Much of this cooperation happens behind the scenes, as we agree on which group is best equipped to lead a joint project, for example."[7]

The Wisconsin hearing was a circus. Yannacone's histrionic techniques of cross-examination and the carefully orchestrated parade of anti-DDT scientists stole the media show. EDF received more than 19,000 column-inches of national coverage during this time. But, as Bruce Ingersoll wrote in *BioScience,* while the decision was being awaited, "round one was a time when their doubts about DDT crystallized, when their worst fears were substantiated by scientific fact. Reports of testimony against DDT and its metabolites were then disseminated across the nation by journalists clambering aboard the accelerating band wagon of environmental awareness. Many people heard the indictments and tuned out, not waiting to hear the defense."[8]

This has remained a key tactic of the Bastards Suing Bastards, not so very different from the misdirection of attention techniques that create the illusions of stage magic.

EDF lawyers used scientific studies which were selectively edited so that DDT and its metabolites DDE and DDD would show reproductive harm. The most famous, *Marked DDE Impairment of Mallard Reproduction in Controlled Studies,* was performed at the Patuxent Wildlife Center in Laurel, Maryland. It is a masterpiece of scientific hocus-pocus.

Researcher R. C. Heath and two associates spent four years, 1965-1968, experimenting on ducks to see what effect DDT, DDE, and DDD had on reproduction. They did two sets of experiments, the first, during 1965 and 1966, using controls and three experimental groups, the first experimental group fed 2.5 parts per million of DDT, the second 10 ppm DDT, and the third 40 ppm DDT daily. The second set of experiments in 1967 and 1968 used five groups of birds: controls, birds fed 10 ppm of DDE, another group fed 40 ppm DDE, one fed 10 ppm DDD, and a fifth fed 40 ppm DDD.

If the second set of experiments sounds weird, it is. DDE and DDD are *metabolites* of DDT, that is, they are *breakdown products* that occur during metabolism of DDT. The authors claimed that DDE and DDD residues are easily encountered in the natural foods of mallards, which are omnivores, but they did not bother to establish that rather important and highly debatable assumption with any evidence from the real world.

Trust me, baby.

But what was really weird about the Patuxent experiments was the crazy findings in the two control groups of the first and second set of studies. The two control groups, of course, were fed normal diets not containing DDT, DDE, or DDD, and should presumably yield identical reproductive results, or nearly so. They weren't even close. In one control group the number of eggs laid per hen was 39.2, whereas in the other it was 16.8. That much difference between two *control* groups that are supposed to provide stable baseline data would make most scientists go back to the drawing board to find out what happened, or quietly file the experiment in a bottom drawer somewhere and go on to other studies. But not the Patuxent researchers.

They did something really *really* weird. They discovered that the first set of control birds had 17 percent *less* fertilization than those fed DDT! The logical conclusion is that DDT is a powerful duck fertility drug.

Not daunted by logic, the Patuxent bunch explained away this embarrassing fact as "a variation in pen fertility." However, when the *experimental* birds on doses of 10 ppm of DDE showed 35 percent less fertilization than the controls, it was no longer "a variation in pen fertility rates," but a statistically significant "effect" attributed to DDE. However, 40 ppm of DDE "caused" only a 21 percent decrease in fertility, which makes no sense at all, because the first rule of toxicology is "the dose makes the poison," which means that the *amount* of poison determines the *power* of the effect—the dose / response curve showing how much dose it takes to create how much effect.

The Patuxent Posse could have been measuring Shirley MacLaine's past lives for all anyone knows, but they insisted on salvaging their four years of work and duly published their findings, insisting that DDT, DDE, and DDD harmed duck reproduction.[9]

The final product was a hopeless mess of data that scientists who should know better insisted upon holding up as proving DDT was harmful.

Trust me, baby.

Charles Wurster, one of the co-founders of the Environmental Defense Fund, made a virtual career of touting the Patuxent experiments and other similarly dubious studies as proof that political action was needed to ban DDT.[10]

The Era of Weird Science was born, and they didn't even need any help from Hollywood special effects wizards.

In 1972, EDF won a comprehensive nationwide ban on DDT, and politics remained an integral part of the picture. DDT was banned even though an EPA-appointed hearing examiner concluded that it "is not a carcinogenic hazard to man" and stated flatly that using DDT "under the registrations involved here" had no "deleterious effect on fresh-water fish, estuarine organisms, wild birds or other wildlife." The examiner's judgment was clear: "The evidence in this proceeding supports the conclusion that there is a present need for the essential uses of DDT." EPA administrator William D. Ruckelshaus, in issuing the ban, admitted that he had neither attended the hearings nor read the transcripts. He said, "DDT was banned for political reasons."[11]

Frederic D. Krupp became executive director of the Environmental Defense Fund in 1984 after serving as general counsel to the Connecticut Fund for the Environment, a statewide group which he helped found. He completed his undergraduate work at Yale University (where else?), received his law degree from the University of Michigan Law School and has taught environmental law at the University of Michigan and Yale University. He knows everything. Well, enough to tell you how to run your life.[12]

Like the Natural Resources Defense Council, EDF has operated a relentless Economy Trasher program since the day it was founded. Unlike NRDC, the Environmental Defense Fund employs professional economists to calculate some of the impacts of its actions, and its leaders retain at least a vestige of recognition that market incentives and property rights may be tools for ecological stewardship.

Director Krupp has argued that it is no longer sufficient for environmentalists to oppose pollution. He called for a new generation of environmental advocates who carefully consider the impact of regulation on industry, taking into account everything from economic growth and jobs to taxpayer and stockholder interests. Krupp called the new breed "Third Stage Environmentalists" and called upon them to recognize that at the bottom of most environmental problems—from pesticides to dams—are legitimate social needs. One can't just oppose the problem without finding a way to meet the need, Krupp said.[13]

EDF even presented President Bush a White House-warming gift in 1988, a report called *Project 88: Harnessing Market Forces to Protect Our Environment*. The report delivered to the Bush transition team was co-sponsored by Senators Tim Wirth (D-Colorado) and the late John Heinz (R-Pennsylvania). The best one can say about it is that performance has substantially lagged behind policy. EDF has since produced a lot of harness and not much market.[14]

Some of the harnessing of market forces EDF recommended actually made economic sense: For example, "pollution credits" that would allow total emissions in an industrial region up to a low but economically viable level. When one company cleaned up its pollution, it could market its "pollution rights" for a certain allowable tonnage of nitrogen oxides, sulfur oxides, particulates, and so forth, to another firm. Theoretically, this allowed some tightly restricted economic growth rather than simply murdering the economy with a meat-cleaver ban on pollution.[15] When the Bush administration announced its costly revision of the Clean Air Act six months after taking office, the President's acid rain provisions featured the complex emissions trading scheme outlined in the *Project 88* report. In 1991, the Chicago Board of Trade announced plans to trade pollution allowances as proposed by the Environmental Protection Agency. EPA had actually submitted new regulations to control acid rain through the buying and selling of pollution rights, first for sulfur dioxide, later for nitrogen oxides.[16]

On the other hand, some of the harnessing of market forces EDF recommended made no sense at all. Michael Oppenheimer, a staff atmospheric physicist whose work is funded by a grant from entertainment mogul Barbra Streisand, has spent a great deal of time repeating Vice President Al Gore's 1992 statement to CNN, "The biggest new market in the history of world business is the market for the new products and new processes that will make possible economic progress without environmental destruction. Millions of jobs are at stake unless we can lead the environmental revolution and create the new jobs that will come out of this revolution."

If you do your arithmetic, you'll quickly see that abandoning existing technology, retooling all our factories and diverting our expertise to go to market with unspecified new products and processes gives you a minus number. Bookkeepers call that a loss. Maybe that's too easy for an atmospheric physicist. Maybe running with Vice Presidents evaporates a physicist's common sense.

Whether EDF makes sense or not, it carries a lot of political clout.

Director Krupp has used that clout most of the time as a mainstream interventionist Economy Trasher, not an arm's-length friend of the market. EDF practically manufactured the global warming scare single-handedly. Months before global warming became front page news, EDF co-sponsored international forums on the greenhouse effect in Austria and Italy.[17] EDF has continually complained against air pollutants claimed to be connected to ozone depletion.[18]

Another characteristic of EDF's Economy Trasher behavior is its "Chemical of the Month Lawsuit" program, as some critics have dubbed it. In the specific area of filing Economy Trasher lawsuits, EDF is virtually indistinguishable from NRDC. In fact, there are some eerie similarities.

For example, the great lead scare of 1990 looked like a recycled Alar scam. It arose from a law that EDF dreamed up. The EDF had helped lobby the Safe Drinking Water and Toxic Enforcement Act of 1986 into California law—in fact, EDF lawyer David Roe wrote most of Proposition 65, the initiative that became the law.[19] California set health standards almost 50 times stricter than the Food and Drug Administration for leaching of lead from tableware.[20] Tiny amounts of lead are found in certain ceramic tablewares at such low levels that the odds of any actual harm from them leaching out are vanishingly small.

In 1990 the EDF released a lead report tricked up to make the results look horrifying, and holding up New York children as the main "victims," much like NRDC's Alar hype,[21] and the next day ran a media campaign to frighten the public away from buying ceramic tableware.[22] The *Los Angeles Times* ran a front page story saying that lead from tableware put 25 percent of Southern California children at risk.[23] They weren't too clear about whether EDF's claimed risks were real.[24] Critics of EDF pointed out that this was just another leftist political scare to tighten the interventionist screws on business and squeeze the last bit of profitability out of the economy.[25] Nevertheless, the State of California and the Environmental Defense Fund sued ten dishware firms for lack of a lead warning on their products.[26] The industry firms under attack denied that there was any lead peril from their products, but their statements were drowned out in all but a few places in the press.[27] An anti-lead referendum was even filed. The public, however, did not fall for EDF's hype as it did with NRDC's Alar scam: ceramic tableware sales remained at normal levels.[28]

The Chemical Lawsuit is ubiquitous at EDF. These days EDF sues paint manufacturers to remove methylene chloride from their paint stripper products because of "cancer risks."[29]

If it's a chemical, EDF doesn't like it. During the final weeks of the Reagan Administration, the EDF criticized indoor radon exposure guidelines as "inadequate." EDF brags that many of their recommendations were included in the final bill which requires EPA to set new health-based standards, develop building codes for new construction, monitor the nation's schools for radon, and support state programs to implement new codes and standards.[30]

Chemicals are not all. The breadth of EDF's intervention in the economy is stunning. There is hardly an area it does not reach, including Antarctica: It threatened to sue the National Science Foundation if researchers did not manage their waste to EDF's taste.[31] Scientists noted that most of the pollution in Antarctica was being caused by eco-tourists encouraged to visit the ice continent by EDF and its environmentalist colleagues.[32]

EDF jumped on the wetlands bandwagon when President Bush and his White House Council on Competitiveness tried to bring the environmentalists' rubber definition of wetlands into some economic feasibility. EDF was right there arguing that the end of the world was at hand if wetlands actually had to be wet.[33]

EDF also joined the Wilderness Society in the Ancient Forest debate, claiming that Taxol, a drug from the Pacific yew which had been found effective in treating ovarian cancer—was being kept from the market because of overlogging by big industry. In fact, logging restrictions enacted by environmental groups forbade logging where the Pacific yew was most plentiful. The shortage had been caused by environmental restrictions, not by industry, which would have been only too eager to make a buck by selling Pacific yew. Here was another example of environmentalists covering up their own great guilt by blaming industry for their own lack of vision.[34]

Perhaps EDF's biggest public relations coup was its successful campaign to convince fast-food chain McDonald's to reform its solid waste policy.[35] In an unusual alliance, EDF worked with McDonald's to conduct a study on the generation of solid waste at its restaurants and find ways to reduce garbage.[36] McDonald's subsequently set the lofty goal of reducing its solid waste by 80 percent, mostly throwaway supply packaging.[37] McDonald's began recycling its low-density polyethylene supply packaging materials.[38] Among the controversial results of its joint project with EDF was McDonald's agreement, after much hesitation and indecision, to eliminate the foam clamshell packages for its sandwich products and replace them with paper containers.[39] Customers did not like the effect of paper packaging on their food—heat loss and soggy burgers—and experts argued that the difference in recycling benefit was negligible.[40] However, McDonald's did its best to cash in on a new Green image, as reflected in its advertising and news releases.[41] The biggest benefit went to EDF's leader, Fred Krupp, who was lionized for bringing the corporate giant to its McKnees: *People Weekly* ran a feature congratulating him on "crushing the clamshell" and *Inc.* magazine touted his ability to speak capitalism.[42]

You can never outrun the Environmental Defense Fund to the left. EDF issued one of its overwrought reports slamming Green Cross Certification Company, a firm that tests products for environmental soundness—such things as recycled content or recyclability—and issues a label so that manufacturers and retailers can make environmental claims for their products with a credible source to back them up.[43] EDF accused Green Cross of being sloppy in its practices and Green Cross accused EDF of aiding its competition, Green Seal.[44] EDF's chief complaint was that Green Cross had not properly verified claims of recycled material content in plastic trash-bags. Retailers with certified claims were not concerned.[45] EDF finally had to back down and reach a truce.[46]

America has by now figured out that environmental laws do not always help the environment—and that sometimes they are a distinct hindrance. The chemical recycling industry has been hindered under the Resource Conservation and Recovery Act (RCRA) from using innovative technology to improve recycling of process chemicals, and their complaints came to a head in a March 1992 meeting of the House Subcommittee on Transportation and Hazardous Materials. The panel convened to consider reauthorization of RCRA, and, of course, EDF was there with bells on. Only now it was bells like those which one puts on the cat. When EDF lobbyists tried to ring the panel's chimes that 13 out of the 50 worst hazardous waste sites in the U. S. are chemical recycling facilities, industry representatives got up and sounded the tocsin of how it was stupid restrictions pressed upon the subcommittee years earlier that prevented chemical recyclers from doing anything about the problem, and offered a better—and cheaper—way to solve the problem.[47]

But do not underestimate the power of the EDF. Not content to merely meat-axe everything in sight as some environmental groups do, EDF's expert staff find ways to give our economy The Death of a Thousand Cuts, one of the most impressive being a computer program called Elfin. It was recycled from the EDF's late 1970s campaign against nuclear and coal plant construction. Elfin is an energy-use forecasting program developed by Dan Kirshner, an economic analyst for the EDF. The software has become the standard for California utilities applying for rate adjustments or new construction. Now that EDF has won the war against economic development and destroyed the nuclear industry's growth, Elfin has proven valuable in influencing energy planning in California where it is used as a business planning tool by the utilities that EDF defeated. The program is available in micro and mainframe versions. In this instance, EDF not only won the political war against increased energy production, but has also succeeded in creating the universe of discourse in which all energy reduction debates in California must take place.[48]

The Environmental Defense Fund gets its money from memberships and contributions (57 percent); foundation grants (27 percent); bequests and endowments (7 percent); investment income and other (5 percent); government grants (3 percent); and attorneys fees (1 percent). EDF netted $40 million worth of donated public-service advertising spots in a 3-year campaign on recycling in conjunction with the Advertising Council.

The EDF is a solid member of the Establishment Interventionist Axis of the overall environmental movement.

EDF operates 5 branch offices in Oakland, California; Boulder, Colorado; Raleigh, North Carolina; Austin, Texas; and Richmond, Virginia.

EDF's Board of Trustees consists of chairman George C. Montgomery, Jr. (Managing Director of Hambrecht & Quist, Inc., NY); vice chairmen Frank E. Loy (President of the German Marshall Fund of the United States), Christopher J. Elliman (Chairman, Adirondack Council), and Teresa Heinz (Chairman, National Council for Families & Television); treasurer Freeborn G. Jewett, Jr. (Deputy General Counsel, Inter-American Development Bank); and secretary Arthur P. Cooley (An original EDF trustee and science teacher, Bellport High School, NY). Other trustees include: Wendy Benchley (Trustee, New Jersey Environmental Federation), James W.B. Benkard (Partner, Davis Polk & Wardwell, NY), Sally Bingham (Co-chairman, Environmental Leadership Forum; chairman, San Francisco Boys Chorus), David Callinor (Science Advisor, Smithsonian Institution), John Curry (Attorney, Chapel Hill, NC), John W. Firor (Director, Advanced Study Program, National Center for Atmospheric Research), Gretchen Long Glickman (Managing Director, Haskell & Stern Associates, NY), Lewis B. Kaden (Partner, Davis Polk & Wardwell, NY), Anthony A. Lapham (Partner, Shea and Gardner, Washington DC), Gene E. Likens (Director, Institute of Ecosystem Studies), Percy Luney, Jr. (Associate Professor of Law, North Carolina Central University), Harold Mooney, Bunny Murray (Mrs. James B., activist from Earlysville, VA), Paul H. Nitze, Lewis S. Ranieri (Chairman and Chief Executive Officer, Ranieri Wilson & Co., Inc.), William T. Reed III (Partner, Reed Brothers; Founder, Conservation Council of Virginia), Irving J. Selikoff (Professor Emeritus of Environmental Medicine, Mount Sinai School of Medicine), Farwell Smith (Fundraiser, Wilderness Society), Frank Taplin, Bailus Walker, Jr. (Professor of Environmental Health and Toxicology, School of Public Health, SUNY-Albany), W. Richard West, Jr., John Hill Wilson, Robert W. Wilson (Investor), Wren W. Wirth (wife of former Senator Tim Wirth, Blaikie F. Worth (activist in Adirondacks and New York City), Charles F. Wurster (Associate Professor, Marine Sciences Research Center, SUNY-Stony Brook).

United States taxpayers helped EDF trash their economy to the tune of $344,062 in government grants in 1987, and at least $92,131 from the Department of Energy, Federal Trade Commission, Environmental Protection Agency, and Department of the Interior during 1978-1982, according to data obtained under the Freedom of Information Act.

These philanthropists helped the Environmental Defense Fund trash the economy:
The William Bingham Foundation gave $200,000 in 1990 for programs

to identify and promote means to reduce climate change and depletion of atmospheric ozone.

Carnegie Corporation of New York gave $240,000 in 1990, a 3-year grant "toward research on effects of environmentally introduced toxins on pregnant adolescents."

Robert Sterling Clark Foundation, Inc. gave $50,000 in 1990 for scientific research, economic analyses, advocacy, litigation and public education to increase government investing in recycling; $50,000 in 1989; $50,000 in 1988; $50,000 in 1987.

Compton Foundation, Inc. gave $50,000 in 1989 for California Wetland Protection.

Patrick and Anna M. Cudahy Fund gave $10,000 in 1989 for general operating support.

Geraldine R. Dodge Foundation gave $100,000 in 1989 to assist program activities in New Jersey by EDF's staff of scientists, economists and lawyers, focusing on land and water resource protection, solid waste management and acid rain/energy policy.

The Frost Foundation gave $15,000 in 1989 for efforts to improve transport and storage of nuclear waste.

The Ford Foundation gave $475,000 in 1990, a 2-year grant for supplement to expand Fund's projects on rural economy and the environment; and $100,000 in 1990 for participation by representatives of developing country nongovernmental organizations in conferences on climate change.

The Fund for New Jersey gave $20,000 in 1990 to continue work to limit heavy-metal pollution of Hudson River Estuary.

German Marshall Fund of the United States gave $35,000 in 1989 for North American-European cooperative climate-change activities.

Richard and Rhoda Goldman Fund gave $15,000 in 1990 for first payment for Computer Modeling Project.

George Gund Foundation, $35,000 in 1987.

The William and Flora Hewlett Foundation gave $225,000 in 1990, a 3-year grant "for general support of Alternative Decisionmaking Program."

W. Alton Jones Foundation, Inc. gave $75,000 in 1989 "for air quality program."

The Joyce Foundation gave $375,00 in 1990, a 3-year grant "for research, policy and education activities of biotechnology program;" also $100,000 in 1990 "for project to reduce fossil fuel combustion through market incentives;" and another $10,000 in 1990 "for work on economics of alternative technologies for solid waste management in Midwest."

F. M. Kirby Foundation, Inc. gave $17,500 in 1989 "for acid rain program;" plus $10,000 in 1989.

The Kresge Foundation gave $500,000 in 1990 "toward purchase of computer equipment and leasehold improvements."

John D. and Catherine T. MacArthur Foundation gave $600,000 in 1989, a 3-year grant "toward promoting environmentally sustainable developments in tropical countries."

Marin Community Foundation $5,000 in 1987.

Richard King Mellon Foundation gave $150,000 in 1989 "for project, Analysis of Factors Affecting Wetlands Regulation and Development of Policy for their Preservation."

Joyce Mertz-Gilmore Foundation gave $100,000 in 1989 "for global Atmosphere Program which seeks to involve industrial and Third World nations in coordinated effort to limit greenhouse gases through scientific, economic and legal means."

Eugene and Agnes E. Meyer Foundation gave $150,000 in 1987.

Charles Stewart Mott Foundation gave $75,000 in 1990 "for Toxic Chemicals Program;" and $40,000 in 1990 "to promote sustainable development in the third world."

Ruth Mott Fund gave $30,000 in 1989, a 2-year grant "for support of International Program to prevent global deforestation."

New York Community Trust gave $35,000 in 1987.

Edward John Noble Foundation, Inc. gave $20,000 in 1990 "for Toxic Chemicals Program."

The Overbrook Foundation gave $30,000 in 1989.

The Pew Charitable Trusts gave $150,000 in 1990, a 3-year grant, for work in designing early warning program to identify vanishing species.

Public Welfare Foundation, Inc. gave $200,000 in 1990 for Global Atmosphere Program and international programs which deal with global warming; $150,000 in 1988, $50,000 in 1987.

Rockefeller Family Fund, Inc. gave $35,000 in 1987.

The Rockefeller Foundation gave $85,000 in 1990 to facilitate participation by nongovernmental organizations, particularly from developing countries, in process of formulating international accord of climate change; plus $30,000 in 1990 for research project on environmental oversight of biotechnology.

The San Francisco Foundation gave $32,000 in 1990 to protect ecological and economic productivity of San Francisco Bay/Delta from combined effects of pollution and freshwater diversion; $50,000 in 1987.

The Streisand Foundation gave $250,000 in 1988 to the Streisand Chair of Environmental Studies, created under EDF's Program for the Future. Total pledges to the Program for the Future exceed $2.8 million. This money supports the work of Michael Oppenheimer, an atmospheric physicist. The Streisand Chair permanently supports part of the funding for Oppenheimer's work.

The Times Mirror Foundation gave $10,000 in 1989 for unrestricted operating support.

Town Creek Foundation, Inc. $15,000 in 1990.

Van Ameringen Foundation Inc. gave $10,000 in 1990 for Toxic Chemicals Program.

Victoria Foundation, Inc. gave $20,000 in 1989 for general support.

Environmental Defense Fund.
Job killers.
Economy trashers.

Environmental Defense Fund—Footnotes

1 *EDF Letter*, November 1987, p. 6.
2 "EDF People," *EDF Letter*, November 1987, p. 6.
3 "EDF People," *EDF Letter*, February 1989, p. 6.
4 "EDF People," *EDF Letter*, February 1989, p. 6.
5 *Ecological Sanity*, George Claus and Karen Bolander, David McKay Company, Inc., New York, 1977, p. 302.
6 "EDF People," *EDF Letter*, November 1987, p. 6.
7 "Do Environmental Groups Talk To One Another?", *EDF Letter*, November 1987, p. 3.
8 "DDT on Trial in Wisconsin—Part II," Bruce Ingersoll,*Bioscience*, vol. 19, 1969, pp. 735-736.
9 "Marked DDE Impairment of Mallard Reproduction in Controlled Studies," R. G. Heath, J. W. Spann, and J. F. Kreitzer, *Science*, vol. 162, pp. 271-273.
10 *Ecological Sanity*, p. 371-422.
11 Personal interview with William Ruckelshaus during his tenure as a vice president of Weyerhaeuser Company in Federal Way, Washington.
12 Krupp's leadership of EDF has been celebrated in major periodicals: See "Green Giants: on the front lines with two rival guardians," by Jon Bowermaster,*New York*, April 16, 1990, p. 52. See also "Fred Krupp: clean heir," by Lisa Reed, *Inc.*, September 1990, p. 164.
13 *Wall Street Journal*, column by Fred Krupp, November 1986.
14 *Industry Week*, March 19, 1990.
15 "Trading places," *The Economist*, July 7, 1990, p. 32.
16 "U. S. proposes regulations to decrease acid rain," by John H. Cushman, Jr., *New York Times*, October 30, 1991, p. A13.
17 *In These Times*, February 21, 1989.
18 See "Ozone hazards trigger call for faster R-22 phaseouts," by Anne M. Hayner, *Air Conditioning, Heating & Refrigeration News*, December 9, 1991, p. 1.
19 "You can't refuse Proposition 65," by Robert T. Grieves, *Forbes*, November 14, 1988, p. 355.
20 "California moves to limit leaching of lead from tableware," by Robert Reinhold, *New York Times*, November 13, 1991, p. A11.
21 "Many New York-area children said to have lead poisoning," *New York Times*, March 6, 1990, p. A16.
22 "Groups warns of lead poisoning," *New York Times*, March 6, 1990, p. B3.
23 "Lead levels put 25% of Southland children at risk," by Maura Dolan and Rudy Abramson, *Los Angeles Times*, March 6, 1990, p. A1.
24 "A report that may be misleading," by Eric Felten, *Insight*, April 2, 1990, p. 24.
25 "Lead scare: leftist politics by other means," column by Eric Felten,*Wall Street Journal*, June 28, 1991, p. A12.
26 "Ten dishware firms sued for lack of lead warning," by Paul Jacobs,*Los Angeles Times*, November 13, 1991, p. A1.

27 "Ceramic tableware lead levels spur California lawsuits; firms deny peril," by Charles McCoy, *Wall Street Journal,* November 13, 1991, p. B7. See also "Lead levels in China dishes called suspect," by Jay Mathews, *Washington Post,* November 13, 1991, p. A3.

28 "Lead issue not sinking sales," by Debby Garbato and Lisa D. Wendlinger, *HFD-The Weekly Home Furnishings Newspaper,* December 23, 1991, p. 52.

29 "Suits target cancer risk of paint stripper," by Paul Jacobs, *Los Angeles Times,* March 25, 1992, p. B8.

30 "New Radon Legislation Offers Better Public Health Policy," *EDF Letter,* August 1989, p. 2.

31 "Face-off forming on Antarctic ice," by William Booth, *Washington Post,* September 28, 1990, p. A25.

32 "Who's polluting Antarctica?" by Laura Tangley, *BioScience,* October 1988, p. 590.

33 "Bush announces wetlands plan, prompting debate over its reach," by Keith Schneider, *New York Times,* August 10, 1991, p. A1.

34 "Environmental groups tie Taxol shortage to logging," *Wall Street Journal,* November 21, 1991, p. B5.

35 "Mac attack on solid waste," editorial, *Christian Science Monitor,* April 22, 1991, p. 20.

36 See "McD, ecology group team up for study on fast-food garbage," *Nation's Restaurant News,* August 13, 1990, p. 1. See also, "Unusual alliance for McDonalds," by John Holusha, *New York Times,* August 9, 1990, p. C2. See also "The greening of McDonalds: fast-food giant to study ways to reduce its garbage," by Martha M. Hamilton, *Washington Post,* August 2, 1990, p. C11.

37 "Big Mac attacks trash problem," by Martha M. Hamilton, *Washington Post,* April 17, 1991, p. B1.

38 "McDonald's starts recycling low-density polyethylene," *Journal of Commerce,* April 18, 1991, p. 7A.

39 "McDonald's flip-flops again and ditches its clamshell," by Matthew Grimm, *Adweek's Marketing Week,* November 5, 1990, p. 4.

40 "McDonald's to do away with foam packages," by Michael Parrish, *Los Angeles Times,* November 2, 1990, p. A1.

41 "The greening of the golden arches," by Bill Gifford, *Rolling Stone,* August 22, 1991, p. 34. See also "The McGreening of America: environmentalist Fred Krupp speaks corporate America's language," by Craig Mellow, *Inc.,* February 1991, p. 59.

42 "Environmentalist Fred Krupp helps crush the ubiquitous fast-food clamshell," by Susan Reed, *People Weekly,* April 15, 1991, p. 61. See also "The McGreening of America: environmentalist Fred Krupp speaks corporate America's language," by Craig Mellow, *Inc.,* February 1991, p. 59.

43 "Environmental group slams Green Cross," *Los Angeles Times,* October 1, 1991, p. D2. See also "Green watchdogs battle over product claims," by David Stipp, *Wall Street Journal,* October 22, 1991, p. B1.

44 "Brave new labeling," by Will Nixon, *E Magazine,* March-April 1992, p. 7.

45 "Environmental report hits Green Cross," *Discount Store News,* October 21, 1991, p. 3.

46 "Truce seen in certification wars," by Terry Troy, *HFD-The Weekly Home Furnishings Newspaper,* November 18, 1991, p. 70.

47 "RCRA too much, too little depending on point of view," *Chemical Marketing Reporter,* March 23, 1992, p. 5.

48 "Software for political advantage," by Clinton Wilder, *Computerworld,* March 26, 1990, p. 80.

The Wilderness Society

The Wilderness Society (Founded 1935)
Annual budget: $16,093,764 (1993)
Staff: 136 total
Members: 293,000 individuals
Tax Status: (501)(c)(3)
Headquarters: 900 17th Street, NW
Washington, D.C. 20006
Phone: (202)833-2300 Fax: (202)429-3959

Economy Trasher Number Nine. Robert Marshall, son of a prominent constitutional lawyer, trained forester, federal bureaucrat, and chief architect of the Wilderness Society, was the author of a book titled *The People's Forests.*[1]

If that sounds like a socialist slogan, there's a good reason. He was a member of the Socialist Party of Norman Thomas and a zealous opponent of entrepreneurs, capitalism, and private property—an open advocate of overthrowing the American form of government. He was no proletarian rabble—his Ph.D. from Johns Hopkins University and his rich father equipped him well to destroy his own origins. He set out to eliminate profit-making lumber companies through a combination of rigid regulation and government ownership. Marshall's biographers rarely mention this or quote from his book.[2]

The closest that historians generally get to Marshall's socialist party membership and political radicalism is a conservation encyclopedia entry that mentions in passing,

> One of Marshall's leading concerns was the social management of America's forests. In February 1930, he was the youngest of the six signers of Gifford Pinchot and George P. Ahern's circular, "Letter to Foresters," which blamed the mismanagement of privately owned forestlands for "forest devastation." The needed remedies, the "Letter" said, were increased federal and state regulation of private forestry practices and expanded public ownership of forestlands. During the early Depression years, Marshall expounded upon these themes in a pamphlet, *The Social Management of American Forests* (1930), and in a book, *The People's Forests* (1933).[3]

Another Wilderness Society founder, Benton MacKaye, was a member of the Socialist Party of America that nominated Eugene Debs for President of the United States in 1920. MacKaye was to serve as president of the Wilderness Society from 1945 to 1950. Of the two men's political affiliations, Thomas' Socialist Party was the more radical, in keeping with Marshall's thinking: "Public ownership is the only basis on which we can hope to protect the incalculable values of the forests for wood resources, for soil and water conservation, and for recreation....Regardless of whether it might be desirable, it is impossible under our existing form of government to confiscate the private forests into public ownership. We cannot afford to delay their nationalization until the form of government changes."[4]

Another Wilderness Society co-founder, Aldo Leopold, was a U.S. Forest Service ranger who lobbied the world's first official Wilderness Area into law and also wrote the seminal eco-socialist tract, *A Sand County Almanac*.[5] Leopold believed fervently that "government is the proper custodian of the land, which for one reason or another is not suited to private husbandry." The Wilderness Society, since those founding days, has worked to prove that those reasons why land is not suited to private husbandry are infinitely elastic. The organization that is their legacy could accurately be characterized as The Wilderness Socialists.[6]

It all began with an article by Marshall titled "The Problem of the Wilderness" in the *Scientific Monthly* for February 1930 in which he wrote that the "one hope" to save wilderness areas was "an organization of spirited people who will fight for the freedom of the wilderness." The National Conference on Outdoor Recreation, held in 1924 with some 309 delegates from 128 national organizations and funded by a grant from the Laura Spelman Rockefeller Memorial Foundation, inspired him to this vision, but it took four years for anyone to take Marshall's "one hope" a step further.[7]

In 1934 at the Knoxville convention of the American Forestry Association, Marshall ran into three other men who shared his enthusiasm. Benton MacKaye had proposed an Appalachian Trail from Maine to Georgia in 1921, but when it actually got under way parts of the trail were crossed by new highways.[8] Harvey Broome, an outdoors-minded Tennessee lawyer and Bernard Frank, a forester with the Tennessee Valley Authority agreed with the other two on the need for a national wilderness organization.

They recruited the help of four others: Harold Anderson, founder of the Potomac Appalachian Trail Club; Ernest Oberholtzer, an advocate of the Quetico-Superior Wilderness; Aldo Leopold, originator of the U.S. Forest Service's wilderness program; and Robert Stirling Yard, executive director of the National Parks Association (see profile of National Parks and Conservation Association). Together the eight formed the Wilderness Society in January 1935 in Washington, D.C.[9]

The eight constituted themselves as the society's Organizing Committee, and when incorporation papers were filed in 1937, the governing board was called The Council, and the eight positions were increased to thirteen. Members of the society could not vote for these officers or on issues. The board was a self perpetuating oligarchy. Only true believers were wanted in the membership, and they were at first almost exclusively Easterners. Bob Marshall supported the group out of his own pocket until his death in 1939 from heart failure at the age of thirty-eight and thereafter by a generous bequest.

They wasted no time stopping developments. Following Leopold's premise that "wilderness gives significance to civilization"—as he wrote in the first issue of the society's magazine *The Living Wilderness* in September 1935—the organization fought against the drilling of an aqueduct tunnel under Rocky Mountain National Park, denounced plans for Civilian Conservation Corps truck trails in the Adirondacks, and battled the construction of a skyline parkway in the Green Mountains of Vermont.

It was not long before what has become the standard counterpoint to wilderness advocacy appeared: Herbert A. Smith, editor of the *Journal of Forestry*, denounced the "cult of wilderness," asserting they were comprised only of "urbanites in easy circumstances." The public wanted development and easy access to resources and recreation, he said. Smith's message has echoed in the wilderness debate ever since.

Yard became the principal official of the Wilderness Society, serving as editor of *The Living Wilderness* and as secretary-treasurer from 1935 to 1937. From then until his death in 1945 he was also president.

Olaus J. Murie took over as president and Howard Zahniser became executive secretary and editor, leading the society against the Echo Park dam in the 1950s. By this time most of the wilderness issues has shifted to the western states and the membership had shifted with it. Today most people have forgotten that the Wilderness Society began as an East Coast interest group and in many ways remains so.

Howard Zahniser was fated to take over as society executive director and become the leading architect of America's wilderness legislation. He emerged from the successful decade-long battle against the proposed dam in Dinosaur National Monument as an important spokesman for conservationists in Washington. He became known for his eloquent statements in formal public hearings and for informal congressional contacts.

During an era when everyone else thought wilderness legislation was impossible, Zahniser never lost faith. When people told him, "That's impossible," he just worked harder. As Brock Evans said, environmentalism means changing impossibilities. After an intricate years-long struggle, Congress finally passed the Wilderness Act in 1964, much of which was Zahniser's own words and conceptual framework. Unfortunately, Zahniser died on May 5, 1964, shortly before the final passage of the act, so he never got to savor his victory.

Zahniser was also a Johnny Appleseed, spawning new organizations and spreading the growing environmental movement. He was an organizer of the Natural Resources Council of America in 1946, where he was chairman in 1948 and '49. He was president of the Thoreau Society in 1956, and vice-chairman of the Citizen's Committee for Natural Resources in 1955. He served on the Interior Department's Advisory Committee on Conservation from 1951 to 1954.

The Wilderness Society's founders made no bones about their intent.

Today's Wilderness Society is not so blunt about it, but at least admits its eco-socialist intent. Former Society President George Frampton (salary $125,000) said in 1988, "Our only rational options are to reject privatization and commercial exploitation of our precious public resources in favor of long-range planning, careful stewardship, and protection. We must not squander our heritage or forsake our birthright."[10]

It is not too difficult to separate out the glittering generalities from the clear intent in this rhetoric. The rejection of "privatization and commercial exploitation" barely masks the Society's actual intent to eliminate all private property, not just prevent the private acquisition of federal lands, and the characterization of all free market resource use with the pejorative terms "commercial exploitation" reveals the distaste the Society retains for all free market enterprises. "Long-range planning, careful stewardship, and protection" are familiar environmentalist buzzwords meaning, respectively, "lock it up so future generations won't be able to use it either," "have armed federal rangers enforce our vision of how to use these lands," and "no private individual will engage in any market activity on federal lands." The bits about "squandering our heritage" and "forsaking our birthright" are emotive triggers designed to get a rise out of the faithful.[11]

The blurbs that go out to the uninitiate are much more innocuous sounding: "We are the specialists on public land issues: wilderness, national parks, national forests, Bureau of Land Management lands, wildlife refuges, Alaska, wild rivers and trails...over 700 million acres...one-third of America's total land surface."[12]

Acting President Karin Sheldon (salary $90,896, benefits $22,724) was vice chair of Defenders of Wildlife. Former President George T. Frampton, Jr., now a Clinton administration Interior Department sub-cabinet officer (Assistant Secretary of Fish and Wildlife and Parks) served as president of the Wilderness Society from 1986 to 1993, coming from his own law practice established in 1985, where he also served as counsel to the firm of Ennis, Friedman, Bersoff & Ewing.[13] He was a partner in the law firm of Rogovin, Huge & Lenzer from 1976 to 1984. Frampton is another Yale College graduate, got his master's degree in economics from the London School of Economics, and earned his J.D. from Harvard Law School. Ivy with a touch of Brit. Frampton served as law clerk to U.S. Supreme Court Justice Harry A. Blackmun, and as a special prosecutor on the Watergate Special Prosecution Force. He was also a fellow at the public interest law firm, the Center for Law and Social Policy. If that's not the right background to make you want to play doctor with society, nothing is.

The *Washington Post* correctly characterized the Wilderness Society: "The only mainstream group to focus exclusively on protecting the nation's public lands, the group lobbies aggressively to expand wilderness areas and safeguard biological diversity in the United States. Its membership has more than doubled since Frampton became president in 1986."[14]

Wilderness has two distinct meanings in the modern environmental debate. One is the commonsense meaning of any wild, remote, area where people go to enjoy the scenery, take Grandma for a Sunday drive, give the kids a picnic in a nice campground, or just fiddle about in nature. The other is a legal term meaning specific lands designated by Congress under authority of the Wilderness Act of 1964—Wilderness with a Capital "W"—that exclude roads and all motorized vehicles, prohibit campgrounds or any structure whatsoever, forbid timber harvest, eliminate or severely restrict livestock grazing, and even outlaw wheelchairs because they are "mechanized" transportation. Congress passed the law by creating a little over 11 million acres of Wilderness, and envisioned a final size of the Wilderness System at 15 to 20 million acres. The latest count is over 90 million acres and climbing.[15]

The costs of rangers managing Wilderness to keep it pristine amount to millions every year, yet environmentalists will not allow the smallest Wilderness entry fee to be charged, even though low income people rarely or never visit Wilderness Areas. All wilderness use is "below-cost" use. The cost of managing wilderness, paying for rangers, rehabilitation programs for fragile areas trampled by hiking boots, rerouting trails away from overcrowded camp sites and a myriad other duties, is never factored into arguments to create new wilderness. Thus, wilderness is a free lunch totally at taxpayer expense for the tiny minority of the high-income, highly-educated white physical elite. And the service is lousy. Injured hikers in Wilderness cannot even count on immediate helicopter rescue—choppers are illegal motorized vehicles and are used only as last-resort options. To boot, below-cost wilderness use doesn't even yield a product that everybody can use such as lumber and paper from "below-cost timber sales."[16]

You've never driven through a Wilderness because roads are illegal. You can't take Granny for a Sunday drive in any Wilderness whatsoever—Grannies in cars are illegal. You can't give the kids a picnic in Wilderness campgrounds because they don't exist—they're illegal. Wilderness is the most restrictive land use designation in the federal lock-up—and least visited.

Not many people have ever used Wilderness, but the situation got worse as the "baby-boomers" began to age and look for less strenuous leisure activities. Back in 1979 when backcountry use peaked, about 2.4 million people slept outside in a national park Wilderness area, but by 1988 it had declined to 1.6 million. It is worth noting that a national park is one kind of designation—it allows roads, structures, campgrounds, visitor lodging, and motorized vehicles—while Wilderness designation is another—it may be added to backcountry portions of a national park and impose all the limitations of the Wilderness Act on that part of the national park. In other words, Wilderness "protection" may be stacked onto other kinds of "protection" for a double whammy of inaccessibility.

In Yosemite, where there is some Wilderness in the high country surrounding the famous waterfall-laced valley, its use peaked in 1975 at 79,000, but that dwindled to no more than 60,000 in the highest year since. At Rocky Mountain National Park, only 32,000 people stayed in the Wilderness portion, less than half of its earlier usage. In Lassen National Park, while total visits increased 4 percent, Wilderness use dropped 12 percent. There are many Wilderness Areas not associated with national parks, and they have never been *seen,* much less used, by more than 93 percent of America's population—only about 7 percent of our population, the physical, educated and affluent elite, ever visited a Wilderness.[17]

Just protecting existing Wilderness is not the way of the Wilderness Society. It has a grandiose socialist project of "completing the American Wilderness System:"

As far as we have come since the signing of the Wilderness Act of 1964...there is an equally lengthy journey ahead if we are to fulfill their dream. More than 90 million acres of federal public lands in national parks, forests, and a small amount of other federal lands have been included in the Wilderness System. Yet another 90 million acres of wildlands, prime wildlife habitat, and fragile ecosystems (some linking existing parks and wilderness areas) are still in dispute, still unprotected, still at risk. This is the challenge that lies before us.[18]

And, of course, when that next 90 million acres is stripped of free market commodity production and classified as Wilderness System land, there will be another 90 million acres somewhere waiting to be eco-socialized.

In addition the Wilderness Society has activated programs to engage in

> Saving the Arctic National Wildlife Refuge; Protecting ancient forests in California and the Pacific Northwest; Working to reduce below-cost timber sales; Seeking designation of new wilderness and national parks on public lands in Utah, New Mexico, Arizona, and California; attempting to overturn President Reagan's lame-duck pocket veto of the Montana Wilderness Bill, a compromise painstakingly crafted by all the interests involved and passed overwhelmingly by both Houses in one of the last actions of the 100th Congress....[19]

The notion of "protecting the nation's public lands" is rather peculiar in the Wilderness Society. "Aggressively to expand wilderness areas" ultimately means to extend "no commodity use" regulations to every acre of federal land everywhere. It also means to confiscate as much existing private land as possible and turn it into public land. The Wilderness Society's tools to accomplish this dual task of "permanent protection" include laws such as the Land and Water Conservation Fund Act to nationalize private land by purchase or condemnation; and laws such as the Wilderness Act, Wild and Scenic Rivers Act, Endangered Species Act, Clean Water Act wetlands regulations, and others to stop all free market uses of public lands. The end result is a gigantic public domain that nobody can use. This organization is the Economy Trasher *par excellence*.

Marshall's brand of socialism foreshadowed today's common environmental thinking, which could accurately and technically be called eco-socialism. This is not something new that Frampton brought with him. For example, the "most important of the 1978 [Appalachian Trail] amendments authorized $90 million for federal acquisition of private property on the Appalachian Trail route. Another expanded the width of the trail corridor subject to condemnation under eminent domain to roughly a thousand feet."[20] Increase the size of the public domain and make sure it cannot be used profitably, that's always been the way of the Wilderness Society.

Typical eco-socialist programs of the Wilderness Society: In February 1989, the organization issued a report urging that $917 million from the federal Land and Water Conservation Fund be used to nationalize private land "that farming and development are threatening nationwide." Where have we heard that plea against farming and residential development before? Of course, it is The Two Nasty Things that the Rockefeller Money Axis first learned to combat to prevent the demagnetization of their Rockresorts and nearby nature preserves, and that was so well adapted by the Mellon Money Axis in the Nature Conservancy and the Conservation Fund. But don't think that it's just the Wilderness Society and the Rockefeller Money and Mellon Money Axes that are trying to stop The Two Nasty Things. The annual announcement of such recommendations to spend piles of taxpayer money from the Land and Water Conservation Fund to nationalize private land has become a favorite indoor sport among a coalition of about 20 big environmental groups. In 1989, it just happened to be the Wilderness Society's turn to issue the spearhead report.

There is a fundamental difference, however, between the Wilderness Society's programs and those of the Rockefeller Money Axis, the Mellon Money Axis and The Establishment Interventionist Axis. Despite the fact that the Society's original goals included the right to "receive, hold, convey, and transfer property of any kind,"[21] it has steadfastly rejected the acquisition and ownership of private property for its own self-management, unlike the Audubon Society and the Nature Conservancy and the American Farmland Trust. Instead, the Wilderness Society prefers to advocate only government ownership and management of natural resources. And in order to eliminate any possible free market use of natural resources, the Wilderness Society makes a career of harshly criticizing government ownership and management where the slightest chance that free market benefit might result.

Its goal seems to be to nationalize everything and have the government run everything, but to retain some measure of civilized amenity that caters to their refined preferences. The Wilderness Society falls into a distinctive Establishment Eco-Socialist Axis in the complex overall movement. The Wilderness Society is the most thoroughgoing eco-socialist in the entire movement, even including such wild cards as Greenpeace of the Radical Eco-Socialist Axis, which contains a substantial anarchist streak that simply wants to destroy all civilization no matter who runs it, government or private interests. The Wilderness Society really operates only a two-pronged strategy: to nationalize all private land possible, and to eliminate all free market use on government lands. Although talk among its leaders borrows from the Deep Ecology philosophy of unmaking all human civilization, we can identify no specific program or policy of the Wilderness Society that would result in the complete destruction of the civilized world.

A typical example of nationalizing everything is the Northern Forest Land project we examined in the National Audubon Society profile.[22] The Wilderness Society set up an office in New England for the express purpose of promoting the nationalization of 26 million acres of private land in Maine, Vermont, New Hampshire, and upstate New York.[23] The Wilderness Society, like the Audubon Society's Brock Evans, tried to confuse the issue of the private ownership of the North Woods by asking "Whose Woods These Are," saying the vast land should be "returned" to the public domain, where it had never been.[24] One of the ploys the Society used in trying to steal the North Woods was to enlist columnists to write heart-rending accounts of resource damage in the Eastern region of the United States, implying that bad logging practices were to blame—when in fact the "decimation of its trees and forests" was the result of an infestation of Gypsy moths, an epidemic that could not be fought with insecticides because other environmentalists had banned their use.[25]

A perennial Wilderness Society hand-wringing program is its annual funeral for the National Wildlife Refuge System, which has been on the verge of death every year for several decades now. Society President George Frampton said, "Our refuges are in a desperate plight yet their cry for help is barely heard. It is safe to say that the condition of our wildlife refuges is one of the great scandals of American conservation."[26] The scandal, as we shall see, is Frampton's big mouth.

In October 1988 the Society issued its list of ten "most endangered national wildlife refuges in the country."[27] The mournful cry, when investigated more closely, had little to do with the refuges themselves; it was actually a ploy to nationalize private land near the refuges. The "dangers" bemoaned by the Society for the most part did not exist *within* the boundaries of the national wildlife refuges, but on adjacent private land. Their proposed "remedial" plan called for vigorous enforcement of the Clean Water Act's anti-development wetlands regulations on neighbors of the refuges, stepped-up federal condemnation of private lands adjacent to refuges, reordered Interior Department budget priorities so that a higher percentage of limited refuge funds go to resource protection and regulation of adjacent private landowners, the passage of an Organic Act to set out more clearly in the law the environmentalist philosophy making wildlife refuges off limits to hunting or any other use, and increasing the power and enforcement authority of the Fish and Wildlife Service.

The report of the "Ten Most Endangered Refuges" was merely the jumping off point for a long media circus on the subject. Each refuge on their list offered a new Media Stunt of the Month. In February the Wilderness Society made a big fuss about agriculture and residential developers threatening a wildlife refuge in the lower Rio Grande Valley of South Texas—those Two Nasty Things again. The *Christian Science Monitor* gave the story 17 column inches.[28] In April, New Jersey's Great Swamp refuge was reported to be beset by residential development and pollution. The *Christian Science Monitor* gave the story 28 column inches.[29] If you're smart enough, you can milk one story about phony threats to ten refuges for ten months, then wait a couple of months, issue another report about the ten most endangered refuges, and turn it into an annual cottage industry.

Adding more and more wildlife refuges to the federal domain at stupendous taxpayer cost is no problem to the Wilderness Society. But let the Forest Service propose to increase reliance on private concessions to keep open campgrounds that are normally shut down much of the year for lack of federal funds, and the Wilderness Society reports it as a "disturbing trend."[30] And if someone suggests private management of a wildlife refuge, the Society cranks up the Rhetoric Organ to play such tunes as, "Why has our government so suddenly turned upon the land, the very root of our culture, the source of our strength among nations? Why, after a century of progress away from the Robber Barons, does the Secretary of the Interior, the chief conservation officer of the United States, make war on wilderness—those wild places our people have come to love so well?" Whoosh! Purple prose doesn't get a lot purpler.

The Wilderness Society also operates a perennial program of slamming Forest Service management of the National Forests.[31] The gist of every criticism is to stop or reduce the production of commodities on federal lands, to shut down or slow down timber harvest. One of its reports called "Forests of the Future?" panned the Service's entire planning process, "outlining its failures all down the line"—failures to prevent sound timber harvest and regeneration for commercial purposes.

Another, titled "The Tongass Report" allegedly "makes it clear that Alaska's Tongass National Forest is in desperate trouble as the victim of management policies that have distorted the intent of the law and threatened the health and productivity of the land and the wildlife it supports at a cost to the taxpayers of hundreds of millions of dollars." The Wilderness Society issued its report in response to a study by the Forest Service—which the Society characterized as "a chronicle of distortion and disaster."[32]

The distortions, however, were all those of the Wilderness Society, not of the Forest Service as accused: The Society deliberately ignored the whole context of the dispute, which is that only ten percent of the vast 16.78 million acres of the Tongass National Forest are scheduled to ever be logged during the next hundred years, including those portions that have been under active logging management for decades. Even though 5.7 million acres of the Tongass are lush with commercial forests, timber harvest is restricted to only 1.7 million acres over the next century, or about 17,000 acres each year (a thousandth of the Tongass) and regeneration is stunningly fast in this temperate rain forest. To complain about "the Tongass disaster" is simply a lie—Alaska's Senator Ted Stevens and Representative Don Young argued forcefully that their bill in support of continuing timber harvest on the present one-tenth of the Tongass was good for the environment, the economy and people.[33] The Wilderness Society does not want commercial logging on even the measly one-tenth of the forest to which it has always been restricted.[34]

Among the Wilderness Society's favorite Forest Service targets is the so-called "below-cost timber sale." The idea is that the taxpayer is subsidizing timber companies by selling them trees at rock bottom prices, building roads for their log trucks to get to the timber and then cleaning up the mess they leave behind—the total cost of which is below what the timber gives back to the federal treasury. The Society has said, "such timber sales impose two direct costs on the taxpayer: first, in federal spending to subsidize Forest Service timber sales; second, in expensive environmental mitigation and reforestation efforts—efforts that often fail." They are so worried about the taxpayer's pockets that they bring endless strings of lawsuits and administrative appeals against Forest Service timber sales—legal actions which cost so much that when subtracted from the other costs of a timber sale often bring it back up into the "above cost" category. Environmentalist protests account for a substantial portion of the "below-cost" problem.

Unfair accounting methods also make highly profitable timber sales appear to be "below-cost." For example, the road building cost to access a timber sale is charged solely against the logging budget of the Forest Service, when actually most roads become a permanent part of the forest's infrastructure used by wildlife managers, the recreational public, fire control crews, and many others who get the road for free at the cost of the logging budget, clearly an unfair accounting practice. In addition, in most cases the private logger pays a substantial portion of the road building costs in National Forests because the Forest Service has long had a "share-cost" road building program.

Another unfair accounting practice which gives profitable timber sales the appearance of "below-cost" problems is that of including environmental mitigation costs entirely in the logging budget rather than sharing the cost with the wildlife management budget of the Forest Service. Even in cases of salvage logging where crews come in to clean up blowdown from severe storms, the logger gets stuck with all the mitigation costs and the wildlife department gets all the benefit for free.

When a Forest Service study discovered that the "below-cost" timber sales the Wilderness Society had been criticizing actually turned a tidy profit, the Society issued a scathing refutation based on their objections to making a profit from public lands![35]

The Society operates a program called The National Forest Action Center, which publishes several newsletters:*Biweekly Update*; a bimonthly Forest Issues Bulletin; and the monthly *Ancient Forest News*. The idea is to keep the pressure on the administrative agency. Keep the pressure on. Keep the pressure on. Make sure every federal bureaucrat is looking over his shoulder to the left.

The Wilderness Society doesn't give a damn about the taxpayer. It only weeps over taxpayer cost when some activity on federal land produces a useful product or employment or a business opportunity for a private firm. When the cost is billions to nationalize private land, the Wilderness Society becomes strangely indifferent to the taxpayer's plight.

The Wilderness Society was also the third major player in the Pacific Northwest battle over the northern spotted owl described in our profile of the Audubon Society above. The Society provided several key attacks in the overall battle plan, one of the most important a report on the horrendous job loss being suffered when the owl was listed as a threatened species under the Endangered Species Act. The Society trumped up a report purporting to show that log exports and automation were the real culprits in timber job losses.[36]

The Society's study only covered large firms which owned their own timber-lands and mills, big companies which had the capital to switch from manufacturing lumber that required controversial big trees to flakeboard and other products that use small-diameter non-controversial trees grown on their own lands as their only hedge against an uncertain supplemental federal timber supply. The employment decline in these firms was indeed caused by automation and log exports, an automation driven by uncertainties over timber supply that environmentalists had created—but they were not the firms suffering from the spotted owl restrictions because they have their own timberlands.

By shifting emphasis away from the real victims—the medium and small loggers, truckers and mill owners who totally depended on federal timber because they possessed no private timber of their own—the Wilderness Society convinced a large public that there was no job loss at all caused by the spotted owl and it was just greedy robber baron timber giants that objected to stopping all logging on the federal lands to save the owl. The real victims owned no logs to export, and any federal logs they were able to buy have long been prohibited from export. The real victims were not the well-capitalized giants that could afford expensive automation, but independent family firms that had long relied on ingenuity and skill as much as on fancy equipment. The real victims were the small contract log truck drivers whose jobs could not be automated. The real victims were the little contract logging outfits that worked terrain too rough for the automated tree-snipper tractors common in the flatlands of the South, or, more often, simply could not afford to borrow for the high-priced equipment when there was no federal timber supply that could be counted on to pay back the bank loan.

The Wilderness Society ignored the real people whose jobs they killed and whose economy they trashed. The Wilderness Society misdirected the public's attention to a non-problem, created the illusion of a big-business bogeyman causing all the unemployment, in order to hide the Wilderness Society's own true and deep guilt. The Society ritually cleansed itself and its cohort of the heavy guilt any ethical person would have felt over disrupting the lives and communities of thousands of suffering timber workers they had thrown into the unemployment lines[37].

The irony is that forest products firms and those with heavy reliance upon forest products are among the Wilderness Society's most important cash contributors. *The NonProfit Times* reported, somewhat inaccurately, "The Wilderness Society has a policy of not taking money from any company involved in extraction activities on public lands."[38] Quite the contrary. The Wilderness Society is funded by Timberland Company, The New York Times Foundation, and Morgan Guaranty Trust Company of New York, all of which are involved in investments that deal in extraction activities on public lands—it's tough to print newspapers and financial documents without cutting a few trees down for the paper, and with the complex log-trading transactions from one mill to the next, how do they know their raw materials didn't come from public lands?

The question was a sore point with former Wilderness Society head George Frampton. When Timberland Company announced that it was renewing its financial pledge to the environmental group in January 1992,[39] Frampton rushed into print in the letters section of the *New York Times* claiming that his organization was "not financially dependent on Timberland company or other corporations, and thus cannot be swayed politically."[40] Frampton's letter was made so much more believable because the newspaper that published it is one that gives money to his organization. The *New York Times* Foundation is not only a major donor to the Wilderness Society, it also gives them extensive favorable news coverage and special treatment in the letters section worth countless millions.

Among the other eco-socialist efforts of the Wilderness Society are: an attempt to take over or shut down the private concessions at Yosemite National Park,[41] an attack upon the Forest Service with critical analyses of nine major forest plans, filing anti-timber comments on 56 draft and final Forest Service plans, and involvement in 30 separate administrative appeals of final plans, all of which cost millions of dollars of administrative delays. Beginning in 1986, the Wilderness Society prosecuted a long campaign to have a vast section of Southern California locked up in a proposed California Desert Protection Act that would have shut down mining operations, recreational rockhounding, motorized recreation, hunting, fishing, and practically any use except hiking.

The Wilderness Society operates 15 field offices in Anchorage and Juneau, Alaska; San Francisco, California, Denver, Colorado; Coral Gables and Marathon, Florida; Atlanta, Georgia; Boise, Idaho; Augusta, Maine; Boston, Massachusetts; Bozeman, Montana; Santa Fe, New Mexico; Portland, Oregon; Salt Lake City, Utah; Seattle, Washington.

The Wilderness Society gets 48 percent of its money from memberships; 16 percent from development contributions; 12 percent from telemarketing, 11 percent from grants; 5 percent from bequests; 3 percent from investment income; 2 percent from list rental; 1 percent from magazine advertising; and 2 percent from miscellaneous sources.

At the beginning of 1993, the Board of Directors of the Wilderness Society included chairman Alice M. Rivlin (now Deputy Director, Office of Management and Budget in the Clinton Administration); vice chairs Edward Dayton and Robert O. Blake; treasurer Thomas A. Barron; and secretary Arnold H. Bolle. The governing council also includes Edward A. Ames, Jim Baca, John C. Bierwirth, Ernest E. Day, Christopher Elliman, William D. Evers, Bert Fingerhut, Joseph L. Fisher, Stephen L. Griffith, Gary Kimble, George Marshall, Arsenio Milian, Walter C. Minnick, Gilman Ordway, Art Ortenberg, Mitchell Rogovin, John Seiberling, Wallace Stegner, Charles F. Wilkinson, Terry Tempest Williams, and Jane H. Yarn.

Alice Rivlin went to the Clinton administration as director of the Office of Management and Budget. Wilderness Society officer Jim Baca was appointed director of the Bureau of Land Management, but fired after only a year because even Interior Secretary Bruce Babbitt thought he was too extreme. George Frampton remains Assistant Secretary for Fish and Wildlife and Parks. Not a bad patronage payoff for the Wilderness Society. Power, power, power.

Total annual grants received are approximately $2.6 million.

Archer Daniels Midland Corporation, the agribusiness giant, a direct link to the Rockefeller Axis money.

The William Bingham Foundation gave $15,000 in 1990 "for program to protect ecosystems in Florida Everglades and Florida Keys."

The Clark Foundation gave $30,000 in 1990.

The Compton Foundation, Inc. gave $15,000 in 1989.

Patrick and Anna W. Cudahy Fund gave $20,000 in 1989 "for Earth Day, 1990."

Dakin Fund.

Discount Corporation of America.

The Richard and Rhoda Goldman Fund gave $10,000 in 1989.

Guardsmark, Inc.

The George Gund Foundation gave $20,000 in 1990 "for unified effort to raise international environmental priorities agenda for G-7 Economic Summit."

W. Alton Jones Foundation gave $150,000 in 1989 "for development of detailed inventory of old-growth forests in Pacific Northwest and efforts to preserve forests in region." Another grant to put the forest products industry out of business.

F. M. Kirby Foundation.

John D. and Catherine T. MacArthur Foundation.

Andrew W. Mellon Foundation.

Richard King Mellon Foundation. The Wilderness Society is closely tied to both the Rockefeller Axis money and the Mellon Axis money.

Morgan Guaranty Trust Company of New York.

National Wildlife Federation.

New York Times Foundation.

Northwest Area Foundation gave $169,000 in 1991 to the Northwest Regional Office in Portland, Oregon, "to help timber-dependent communities in Oregon and Washington develop economic diversification plans and work toward supportive policies." This shameless twaddle simply translates into "do everything you can with this grant to put loggers out of business while hiding behind a false front of pretending to help—but make sure none of the $169,000 gets into the hands of a logger's family."

The Pew Charitable Trusts gave $150,000 in 1990, a 3-year grant "for work on biodiversity impact of new forestry practices."

The Prospect Hill Foundation, Inc. gave $53,000 in 1990 "for production of two issues of wilderness magazine."

The Scherman Foundation, Inc. gave $25,000 in 1989, a 2-year grant for general support.

Sierra Club.

Timberland Company.

Town Creek Foundation, Inc. gave $100,000 in 1990.

United Conveyor Corporation.

United Sanctuary Fund.

Walker, Richer & Quinn.

Waste Management, Inc.

The Wilderness Society
Job killers.
Economy Trashers.

The Wilderness Society-Footnotes

1 *The People's Forests*, Robert Marshall, H. Smith & R. Haas, New York, 1933.

2 "The Strenuous Life of Bob Marshall," by Roderick Nash, *Forest History*, October 1966, p. 18-25.

3 "Robert Marshall," article, *Encyclopedia of American Forest and Conservation History*, Richard C. Davis, editor, Macmillan Publishing Company, New York, 1983, p. 406.

4 *The People's Forests*, Robert Marshall. p. 210.

5 *A Sand County Almanac*, Aldo Leopold, Oxford University Press, Oxford, 1949.

6 *Wilderness and the American Mind*, Roderick Nash, Yale University Press, New Haven, 1967, 3d. ed. 1982.

7 U. S. Congress, Senate, National Conference on Outdoor Recreation: *Proceedings of the National Conference on Outdoor Recreation, May 22, 12, and 24, 1924*, 68 Cong. 1 sess., 1924, S. Doc. 151.

8 "Benton MacKaye: A Tribute," by Lewis Mumford, et al., *Living Wilderness*, January / March 1976, p. 6-34.

9 "Wilderness Society," article, *Encyclopedia of American Forest and Conservation History*, Richard C. Davis, editor, Macmillan Publishing Company, New York, 1983, p. 701.

10 "Stewardship meets the bottom line," *Wilderness*, Summer 1988, p. 3.

11 *The Politics of Wilderness Preservation*, Craig W. Allin, 1982.

12 "Conservation Up Front," *Wilderness*, Winter 1988, p. 2.

13 "Frampton new Society president," *Wilderness*, Winter 1985, p. 2.

14 "From Fringe To Political Mainstream," by Michael Weiskopf, *Washington Post*, April 19, 1990, p. A1.

15 *The Quiet Revolution: Grass Roots of Today's Wilderness Preservation Movement*, Donald N. Baldwin, 1972.

16 *Wilderness Management*, John C. Hendee, George H. Stankey, and Robert C. Lucas, U.S. Department of Agriculture, 1978.

17 "Backpack: Call of the Wild Fades for Baby Boomers," by Kevin Roderick, *Los Angeles Times*, May 31, 1989.

18 Quoted from *Protecting the Environment: Old Rhetoric, New Imperatives*, Jo Kwong Echard, Capital Research Center, Washington, D. C., 1990, pp. 85-86.

19 *Wilderness Society Annual Report*, 1989.

20 "The Long Way 'Round," Donald Dale Jackson, *Wilderness*, Summer 1988, p. 17.

21 Internal Revenue Service letter of Determination to the Wilderness Society, June 4, 1948.

22 "Wilderness group proposes huge forest preserve in Maine," by Philip Shabecoff, *New York Times*, March 20, 1989, p. A15.

23 "Systems management: The Wilderness Society is now active in New England," by T. H. Watkins, *Wilderness*, Fall, 1989, p. 16.

24 "Whose woods these are: The task of saving the last of Northern New England's wildland is a puzzle of possibilities, contentions, and promise," by Norman Boucher, *Wilderness*, Fall, 1989, p. 18.

25 "Forests are still vanishing," column by Tom Wicker, *New York Times*, March 24, 1989, p. A31.

26 "Wildlife System is Reported in Deteriorating Condition," by Philip Shabecoff, *New York Times*, October 28, 1988.

27 "Society Lists Ten Most Endangered Refuges," *Wilderness*, Winter 1988, p. 3.

28 "Endangered oasis in South Texas: encroaching agriculture and developers threaten lower Rio Grand valley refuge," by Howard LeGranchi, *Christian Science Monitor*,

February 21, 1989, p. 12.

29 "Wildlife oasis needs protection: urban development and pollution threaten New Jersey's Great Swamp refuge," by Bill Breen, *Christian Science Monitor*, April 11, 1989, p. 12.

30 "Stewardship meets the bottom line," *Wilderness*, Summer 1988, p. 3.

31 "Congress should investigate Forest Service violations," *Wilderness*, Summer, 1987, p. 3.

32 "The Tongass Report: a chronicle of distortion and disaster," *Wilderness*, Spring, 1988, p. 2.

33 "The forest and the trees," letter to the editor by Ted Stevens and Don Young, *Washington Post*, October 14, 1989, p. A21.

34 *People of the Tongass: Alaska Forestry Under Attack*, K. A. Soderberg and Jackie DuRette, Free Enterprise Press, Bellevue, Washington, 1988.

35 "U. S. timber sales found profitable: wildlife group challenges the study by Forest Service," *New York Times*, December 19, 1988, p. A15.

36 "Exports, automation cited by study for slump in timber," by Michael Parrish, *Los Angeles Times*, September 26, 1991, p. D4.

37 "Society challenges timber job assumptions," by Patricia Byrnes, *Wilderness*, Winter 1991, p. 5.

38 *NonProfit Times*, April 1990.

39 "Timberland renews pledge to Wilderness Society," by Mark Tedeschi, *Footwear News*, January 27, 1992, p. 9.

40 "Environmentalists get little corporate aid," letter to the editor, *New York Times*, April 30, 1992, p. C6.

41 "At Yosemite, environmentalists compete with entrepreneurs for business," by Robert Reinhold, *New York Times*, September 23, 1990, p. 17.

The Cousteau Society ▌▌▌▌▌▌▌▌▌▌▌▌▌

Cousteau Society, Inc. (Founded 1973)
Annual budget: $17.7 million (1990)
Staff: 135 including crews of two ships
Members: 300,000 (1994)
Tax Status: 501(c)(3)
Headquarters: 870 Greenbrier Circle, Suite 402
Chesapeake, Virginia 23320
Phone: (804)523-9335 Fax: (804)523-2747

Economy Trasher Number Ten. It comes as a surprise to most Americans to learn that the Cousteau Society, Inc. has the tenth largest income of any American environmental group. It comes as an even greater surprise to learn that the distinguished French naturalist Jacques Cousteau is one of the most virulent Economy Trashers alive today, a virtual Captain Malthusian.

The Cousteau Society enjoys one of the most sterling reputations in the eco-anxiety industry. Society Founder Jacques-Yves Cousteau is an institution. He was born in 1910 at St. Andre-de-Cubzac, France, earned his *Bachelier* at Stanislas Academy in Paris (1927) and was awarded an honorary D.Sc. by the University of California at Berkeley and another by Brandeis University, both in 1970. In the interim, he served with distinction as lieutenant-commander in the French Navy during World War II, winning the Legion of Honor and the Croix de Guerre with palm. His films have earned him three Academy Awards: *The Silent World* (best documentary), *The World Without Sun* (best documentary) and *The Golden Fish* (best short film). He has produced over 70 films for television, including five series: *The World of Jacques-Yves Cousteau, The Undersea World of Jacques-Yves Cousteau, Oasis in Space, The Cousteau Odyssey Series*, and *The Cousteau/ Amazon Series*, among many others, which earned him induction into the TV Hall of Fame in 1987. His many other awards and honors would fill a room.

Dr. Cousteau's early co-invention with Emile Gagnon of the aqualung (self-contained underwater breathing apparatus, or SCUBA), his subsequent involvement with the development of submarines and underwater habitats and his filmmaking achievements gave him international preeminence as an advocate for the world's oceans for decades. Dr. Cousteau's research vessel, *The Calypso*, has been so famous for so long that fading eco-singer John Denver in his heyday wrote a top-of-the-charts song about it. Anyone who missed seeing Captain Cousteau on television can certainly still find him in reruns on Channel 92 or something.

The good Captain also has extensive business interests that don't always overjoy his neighbors. In 1985 he attempted to construct a Cousteau Ocean Center in Norfolk, Virginia, but local leaders were not thrilled by the $15.5 million bond issue to support it.[1] Dr. Cousteau's enterprises also operate the Cousteau Oceanic Park in Paris, a theme park not unlike Disneyland, but in 1991 they weren't very good at making money with it.[2] In 1991 the Cousteau Society also entered negotiations to replace a Boy Scout summer camp on Santa Catalina Island off the coast of Southern California with a Cousteau Society Education Center, which would in fact have been one of those Rockefeller-style magnetic resorts we saw in the profile of the Nature Conservancy.[3] The plans fell through and the deal was never consummated.[4]

Few of Dr. Cousteau's admirers, however, realize that he is also a hard-core Malthusian who pushes for severe controls over all industry, forced birth control worldwide, and the elimination of both national sovereignty and private property rights.

If that sounds like a wild-eyed accusation, wait until you read a few direct quotes below from the Captain himself.

Jacques-Yves Cousteau and his son Jean-Michael Cousteau direct the Cousteau Society's activities, which are entirely preoccupied with industry-bashing and, most astonishingly, with the establishment of a worldwide command-and-control eco-police force. The senior Cousteau, in the pages of the Society's journal, *Calypso Log*, has called for the creation of an eco-army he calls The Green Helmets.

In December, 1991, Captain Cousteau urged the establishment of global rules to protect the environment, and said "it is urgent to create an international entity to monitor and police" such global rules, including strict limits on human population.[5]

Dr. Cousteau's global rules are embodied in an international fund raising petition he sponsored, a "Bill of Rights for Future Generations." The old one from the United States Constitution, it seems, is simply outdated. After all, it was written two centuries ago. Our problem is not too little freedom, but too much.

To begin with, we're having too many babies. Second, we're free to engage in the unsupervised exchange of goods. "Free enterprise," expounds the Captain, "is leading to scandalous inequalities." So we need a new Bill of Rights to keep us from exercising our freedoms too much.

In among the lofty glittering generalities asserting that "future generations have a right to an uncontaminated and undamaged Earth," and "to its enjoyment as the ground of human history, of culture, and of social bonds that make each generation and individual a member of one human family," is a duty to maintain "a constantly vigilant and prudential assessment of technological disturbances and modifications adversely affecting life on Earth, the balance of nature, and the evolution of mankind in order to protect the rights of future generations."

Vague statements of that sort usually mean trouble when you read the fine print.

Dr. Cousteau's Bill of Rights urges "governments, non-governmental organizations, and individuals" to "implement these principles." He wants the Bill of Rights for Future Generations added to the United Nations charter. He wants his eco-army of Green Helmets to enforce it.

Exactly what kind of "vigilant and prudential assessment of technological disturbances" does Cousteau have in mind? It's not clear.

Exactly what kind of controls does Cousteau have in mind for "modifications adversely affecting life on Earth?" It's not clear.

But it's very clear who has the moral right to enforce these views on everybody else: Dr. Jacques-Yves Cousteau.

Nary a Not

In the February 1992 *Calypso Log* he made it even plainer: "Here I am referring to the necessity of creating an international environmental police, 'green helmets,' who would be under the direction of the United Nations. Our planet needs guardians, independent organizations, free of the constraints of profit or national sovereignty, and responsible for making up an almost daily bill of health of our common habitat, our Earth."[6]

Those "independent organizations" with totalitarian police powers, of course, include the Cousteau Society.

As David Chilton, pastor of the Church of the Redeemer in Placerville, California wryly commented, "One subtle but significant difference between the original *Bill of Rights* and Cousteau's substitute is that the old one sported a proliferation of negatives: 'Congress shall make no law...,' 'The right of the people shall not be violated,' and so on. But in Capt. Cousteau's version, there's nary a not."[7]

Despite the ambiguity, Dr. Cousteau evidently got his wish for a Green Helmet institution while attending the June 1992 United Nations Conference on the Environment and Development (UNCED)—the "Earth Summit," or as some wags called it, "the Flat Earth Summit." The Commission on Sustainable Development was created "to monitor how well individual countries pursue environmentally sound development." It operates with the long-standing Economic and Social Council and was designed to rely heavily on evidence gathered by private environmental groups such as the Cousteau Society. It sounds very much like the policing agency Cousteau had in mind, and it now exists.

William Pace, director of the Center for Development of International Law in Washington, D.C. said the agency would have no authority to directly enforce environmental law, but would "nonetheless wield considerable influence. This body has a much higher profile than a lot of countries wanted." This commission may in time turn out to be the first Green Helmet organization to actually carry guns.[8]

Jacques Cousteau has, through his film and television work, taught us to ask profound questions of nature. This is the proper place to ask some profound questions of what he has taught us about nature. He recommends that we "prudentially assess" the balance of nature—but how can we when there is no such thing as the balance of nature?

In a revision that has far-reaching implications for the way humans see the natural world and their role in it, scientists at the 1990 annual meeting of the Ecological Society of America—the nation's premier association of ecological scientists—announced they are forsaking the old stable-equilibrium model of nature. The balance of nature concept "makes nice poetry, but it's not such great science," said Dr. Stewart T. A. Pickett, a plant ecologist at the Institute of Ecosystem Studies of the New York Botanical Garden at Millbrook, New York.

Ecologists have mistakenly operated on the assumption that the normal condition of nature is an equilibrium in which organisms compete and coexist in an essentially stable steady state. The obsolete picture of nature, according to a *New York Times* reporter, went something like this: "Predators and prey—wolves and moose or cheetahs and gazelles, for instance—are supposed to remain in essentially static balance. Anchovies and salmon reach a maximum population that can be sustained by their oceanic environment and remain at that level. A forest grows to a beautiful, mature climax stage that becomes its naturally permanent condition."

The idyllic image of perfect balance led to the doctrine, enshrined by environmentalists, that nature knows best and that human intervention in nature is bad by definition. In reality, the stable, steady-state world upon which Dr. Cousteau bases his Rights of Future Generations never existed. Ecologists who study population dynamics are finding that predator-prey relationships are in a continual state of flux, never stable, always in motion. The ultra-aggressive leader of a particular wolf pack can greatly expand the pack's hunting efficiency and destabilize the ecosystem—and conversely the death of an average leader can induce instability by causing the pack to disperse, allowing rodent populations to explode. Ecological communities of plants and animals are inherently unstable, primarily because of idiosyncratic differences in behavior among communities and individuals within them.

Glib talk of protecting an imaginary "balance of nature" is only a cover for political control over resources. It is a mindstyle with no basis in reality.

This "New Ecology"—a Disequilibrium Paradigm—challenges Victor Scheffer's "Environmentalism's Articles of Faith" at the deepest level and nullifies his insistence that man must be stopped from "tampering" with Nature. Man *is* Nature in the deepest sense. Man probably *created* much of what we consider Nature.

For example, the supposedly pristine Serengeti plain of Africa with its cheetahs and gazelles is probably the direct result of ancient human-set fires that created savanna habitat which now accommodates its tremendous abundance of grazing animals and carnivore predators. The supposedly unspoiled rain forest of Latin America was shaped thousands of years ago by humans who planted and transplanted trees and other plants throughout the jungle. The world is not the place *National Geographic* TV specials and the Sierra Club's fund-raising mailers have led us to believe.

Victor Scheffer's "Environmentalism's Articles of Faith" with its imaginary idea of "Nature without Man" is simple political twaddle. The idea is indeed useful, as Mr. Scheffer asserts, but useful for what? Useful for giving ammunition to Malthusian misanthropes who want to reduce or eliminate industrial civilization—or even to eliminate the human species.

And if some actual teleology did push ecological communities toward internal equilibrium, scientists now believe that external disturbances like ice ages, variation in annual weather patterns, floods, fires, hurricanes, tornados, and disease rarely if ever give an ecological community the chance to settle into a stable state.

The question of whether humans should intervene in natural processes is moot, ecologists now say, because humans and our near-human ancestors have been doing so for eons, and ecological systems around the world have evolved with us. Humans are emerging in ecological thought as just one of many sources of ecological disturbance that keep nature in a perpetual state of uproar. Change, violence, danger are the stuff of nature.[9]

Environmentalists have considered the Darwinian concept of natural selection as virtually the sole source of the highly ordered systems we see in living things. Environmentalists have found natural selection to be a useful weapon to reduce human beings to insignificance. In a world that runs only on random natural selection, their reasoning goes, there is no such thing as a direction to evolution, so there can be no such thing as "higher" or "lower" forms of life. Therefore human beings are not "higher" on a scale of evolution than an amoeba or a grasshopper, and thus have no more meaning than an amoeba or a grasshopper.

This proposition has served environmentalists well in political battles, particularly in arguments about the loss of species caused by human action—evolution can never make up for the loss. Mankind, environmentalists exclaim, is destroying species today at a greater rate than anything in the past. And evolution to fill in the missing niches is slow as molasses, requiring geological time scales to produce new species. Extinction is forever.

Perhaps not. Ten years ago ecologists Paul Klerks and Jeffrey S. Levinton decided to test the theory that evolution works very slowly by examining the metal tolerance of invertebrates in Foundry Cove on the Hudson River in New York. Like other coves nearby, Foundry Cove teemed with life: water striders on the surface pouncing on unwary midge nymphs; oligochaete worms and insect larvae in the muddy bottom providing food for fish, crabs and prawns. The ecologists picked Foundry Cove because it has perhaps the highest concentration of toxic cadmium and nickel pollutants in the world.

Foundry Cove lies across the Hudson from Mount Storm King and West Point, and derives its name from a Revolutionary era forge which produced chains that stretched across the river to snare British warships. During the Civil War the foundry made ammunition. After World War II a battery manufacturer occupied the site. From 1953 to the 1970s industrial plants dumped more than 100 tons of nickel-cadmium waste into the cove. In the early 1980s, as much as 25 percent of the bottom sediments consisted of cadmium. There should be nothing alive there.

But Klerks and Levinton were shocked to find the place teeming with invertebrate life. Virtually all the species in nearby coves were living happily in Foundry Cove. They found that the most commonplace invertebrate in the cove was a worm that shouldn't be there. They transferred specimens of this species from a nearby cove to Foundry Cove and they died. Local specimens, on the other hand, thrived and reproduced in the pollution with perfectly normal young. The ecologists raised Foundry Cove worms in clean sediments and then put their grandchildren back in the polluted waters. They lived. There was a tolerance to cadmium in their genes.

In the words of Levinton, "The evolution of cadmium resistance could have taken no more than 30 years. In fact, the genetic variability in nearby populations, together with the high mortality we measured, indicated that the degree of metal tolerance observed could have evolved in just two to four generations—or a couple of years. To prove the conclusion, we exposed worms from an unpolluted site to cadmium-laden sediment and bred the survivors. Sure enough, by the third generation, the descendants had two thirds of the cadmium tolerance found in the Foundry Cove worms."[10]

High speed evolutionary transformations of modern species into new varieties and even species are being discovered in everything from worms to birds to mammals all over the world. The discoveries are new, and because they contradict environmentalist dogma are having a hard time finding their way into publication. But they are coming. We have held private discussions with numerous wildlife biologists who are studying this disturbing new discovery, and they tell us stories of persecution by fellow scientists worthy of the Church's persecution of Galileo. Their response is the same that Galileo made to the Inquisition when it demanded he recant his belief that the Earth moves. After he officially recanted, he is said to have muttered under his breath, "It still moves." Modern biologists are refusing to recant, and saying of the speed of evolution, "It *really* moves." Evolution works much faster than anyone dreamed. It can happen in a few generations.

The reality is that the Earth is not so fragile as environmental organizations would like us to think. Human beings are not so shortsighted as anti-free enterprisers would like us to believe. The doctrine that nature knows best and human intervention is bad is simply false. The crisis mentality is totally unjustified. There are environmental problems, but there is no environmental crisis. Most environmentalism is bad fortunetelling by professionals with enough education to know better—but without any common sense.

The New Ecology means every environmental law on the books will have to be repealed and rethought. Everything in the environmentalist articles of faith is based upon the now discredited balance of nature theory. Every environmental law in America has been based on assumptions that there was a balance of nature. For example, in the endangered species laws, legislators assumed that a balance of nature existed before humans got here and that human development is by its very nature harmful to that balance of nature. So every human development that has any impact on an endangered species must be stopped. There is no effort of any kind in current law to find solutions that allow man and nature to live together in productive harmony. None whatever. The Endangered Species Act actually *forbids* the calculation of human cost during the listing process. Now we know that's wrong because we know the underlying assumptions about the balance of nature are wrong.

Dr. Cousteau's notions of nature are full of holes. He wants to stop industrial civilization as do all the other Economy Trashers. He has issued general damnations of industrial civilization.[11] He has specifically opposed mineral exploration of Antarctica—an explorer opposing exploration, so we will never know what resources lie there under the ice.[12] He has demanded a full stop to population growth.[13]

As his vision of nature is flawed by old data, so his vision of how to protect nature is impaired by ideology—and a number of prominent scientists are now saying so.

Cousteau appeared in July 1992 on a French television FR3 feature talking about his role at the Earth Summit in Rio de Janiero. He mentioned that Henry Kendall of the ultra-left-wing Union of Concerned Scientists (see profile) had come to him for help. Kendall was beside himself that a group of scientists had put together a document called the Heidelberg Appeal which called for science to solve problems and allow population to grow, seeing people as an asset, not a liability.

The Heidelberg Appeal, coordinated by Dr. Michel Salomon (10 Avenue de Messine, 75008 Paris, France), and signed at the close of the Rio Summit by 425 scientists and intellectuals, said:

> To Heads of States and Governments:
> We want to make our full contribution to the preservation of our common heritage, the Earth.
> We are however worried, at the dawn of the 21st century, at the emergence of an irrational ideology which is opposed to scientific and industrial progress and impedes economic and social development.
> We contend that a Natural State, sometimes idealized by movements with a tendency to look toward the past, does not exist and has probably never existed since man's first appearance in the biosphere, insofar as humanity has always progressed by increasingly harnessing Nature to its needs and not the reverse.
> We fully subscribe to the objectives of a scientific ecology for a universe whose resources must be taken stock of, monitored, and preserved.
> But we herewith demand that this stocktaking, monitoring, and preservation be founded on scientific criteria and not on irrational preconceptions.
> We stress that many essential human activities are carried out either by manipulating hazardous substances or in their proximity, and that progress and development have always involved increasing control over hostile forces, to the benefit of mankind.
> We therefore consider that scientific ecology is no more than an extension of this continual progress toward the improved life of future generations.
> We intend to assert science's responsibility and duties toward society as a whole.
> We do, however, forewarn the authorities in charge of our planet's destiny against decisions which are supported by pseudoscientific arguments or false and nonrelevant data.
> We draw everybody's attention to the absolute necessity of helping poor countries attain a level of sustainable development which matches that of the rest of the planet, protecting them from troubles and dangers stemming from developed nations, and avoiding their entanglement in a web of unrealistic obligations which would compromise both their independence and their dignity.
> The greatest evils which stalk our Earth are ignorance and oppression, and not Science, Technology, and Industry whose instruments, when adequately managed, are indispensable tools of a future shaped by Humanity, by itself and for itself, overcoming major problems like overpopulation, starvation and worldwide diseases.[14]

By the time Dr. Cousteau commented on it, the Heidelberg Appeal had over a thousand signatures. The good Captain was horrified that Dr. Michel Salomon, one of his own countrymen, could raise a voice of optimism and have the temerity to issue a warning against everything for which Cousteau stands.

Dr. Cousteau mentioned on the French FR3 television program that Kendall of the Union of Concerned Scientists came to him with a serious problem: "We want to say to the world that we are going toward disaster, but we do not know how to do it and we need help."

Dr. Cousteau helped by advising Kendall to write a dire "Warning to the World," and get it signed by as many scientists as possible, then make a media circus of it (see the Media chapter for details).

Dr. Cousteau was willing to help because he holds some rather quaint views on how to control population. They are worth examining in some detail.

In particular, Dr. Cousteau told interviewer Jean Daniel, editor-in-chief of the French weekly *Nouvelle Observateur* that as more poor refugees left their homelands, "More and more people are willing to use the atomic bomb if the situation arises that one billion people are migrating toward the West."[15]

That's a direct quote. M. Daniel stands by it.

Hold on there a second, *Cher Capitaine*. Use the atomic bomb? *Mon ami*, are you nuts? Dreaming up a script for *Terminator III*? *Voulez-vous* your Green Helmets to be a nuclear power? Do we hear Professor Malthus chuckling backstage? "All the children born, beyond what would be required to keep up the population to this level, must necessarily perish, unless room be made for them by the death of grown persons...."

This is getting too weird.

But it was only a repetition of sentiments Dr. Cousteau had voiced a year earlier in an interview with the *UNESCO Courier*, where he told us what he thinks of people.

> The damage people cause to the planet is a function of demographics—it is equal to the degree of development. One American burdens the earth much more than twenty Bangladeshis. The damage is directly linked to consumption. Our society is turning toward more and more needless consumption. It is a vicious circle that I compare to cancer.
>
> The elimination of viruses seems like a noble idea, but it poses an enormous problem. Between the year 1 and the year 1400 the population was practically unchanged. Through epidemics, nature compensated to equalize births and deaths.
>
> Should we eliminate suffering, diseases? The idea is good, but perhaps not a benefit for the long term. We should not allow our dread of diseases to endanger the future of our species.
>
> This is a terrible thing to say. In order to stabilize world population, we must eliminate 350,000 people per day. It is a horrible thing to say, but it's just as bad not to say it.[16]

Stoke up the ovens, boys, here comes Dr. Fixit.

Dr. Cousteau was confronted with this quote on the French FR3 television talk show. When faced with his own statement that it was necessary to eliminate 350,000 people per day to stabilize world population, he denied that he had ever said it. Despite the published interview.

The two reporters who conducted the *UNESCO Courier* interview, Bahgat Eluadi and Adel Rifaat, assert that not only did Dr. Cousteau indeed say that to them, but that they had sent him their text for correction and he approved it. Eluadi and Rifaat say they cut out unbelievably monstrous things Dr. Cousteau had told them during the interview.

So perhaps Captain Cousteau was merely updating his *UNESCO Courier* views on population control when he suggested nuclear solutions to *Nouvelle Observateur*.

Hoo boy, Toto, this *sure* ain't Kansas anymore.

But the Cousteau Society *is* run by a man who compares humanity to a cancer on the Earth. It *is* run by a man who thinks that curing diseases is not a long term benefit for humanity. It *is* run by a man who thinks we need to eliminate 350,000 people a day to help the earth. It *is* run by a man who can envision using the atomic bomb to control population.

The total assets of the Cousteau Society for 1990 were $17,734,750. Revenues for the year were broken down as follows: Membership support $6.4 million; Membership solicitation income, $1.4 million; Films and filmstrips, $5.7 million; Contributions and grants, $597,371; Book sales, $235,876; Publishing and royalties, $823,711; Interest income, $62,337; Other, $960,331, for total revenues of $16,304,406. To raise this amount, the Society spent $1,088,384 on membership fund raising; $1,877,141 on membership solicitation; and $1,831,480 for management and other administrative expenses. It is noteworthy that the Cousteau Society spent $1.8 million in order to solicit $1.4 million worth of memberships.

The Cousteau Society, Inc. is related to two foreign organizations that subsidize it heavily: Campagnes Oceanographiques Francaises (COF), a French nonprofit research organization that provides the Society the vessel *Calypso* at no cost other than maintenance and insurance; and Found Cousteau, a French nonprofit membership organization that leases the wind propelled ship *Alcyone* to the Society at a favorable rate.

Jacques Cousteau provides his services to the U.S.-based Society without remuneration, obtaining his personal fortune from other business ventures and some income from French nonprofit organizations. As is usual in such cases, he obtains certain benefits from his organizations that do not count as remuneration: During 1990, for example, the Society spent $811,177 on renewal of films owned personally by Cousteau, and received reimbursement from him in the amount of $420,929, with the balance remaining due. No doubt he will pay up some day.[17]

Directors and officers of the Cousteau Society, Inc., are president and chairman of the board Jacques-Yves Cousteau; executive vice president Jean-Michael Cousteau; vice presidents Henri Jacquier and Richard C. Murphy; secretary Patti Buchman; assistant secretary Charles Vinick; treasurer Robert L. Steele; and other directors including Nicholas J. Coolidge; Frederick Hyman; Lee Parr McGrath; Lee Steiner; and Robert Wussler.

Coolidge is an investment banker and attorney; Hyman is an international business executive; McGrath is a partner in a New York public relations firm; Steiner is a partner in the law firm of Loeb & Loeb.

The Cousteau Society falls in the Global Eco-Socialist Axis, an international version of the Establishment Eco-Socialist Axis inhabited by the Friends of the Earth and the Wilderness Society.

The Society publishes *Calypso Log*, a bimonthly journal with a circulation of 238,000 on general environmental issues. The Society also publishes *Dolphin Log* bimonthly to a circulation of 89,000 for children ages 7 through 15, covering "all areas of science, history and arts related to the world's water system." The Society also publishes teachers' guides, brochures, books, films and filmstrips. Public relations contact: Sandy Bonds; Barbara Simpson (212)826-2940 425 E. 52nd Street, New York, N.Y. 10022. Fax (212)751-4349.

The Foundation Center lists no contributors to the Cousteau Society. Funding sources for those contributions and grants in the amount of $597,371 remain a mystery.

The Cousteau Society.
Job killers.
Economy trashers.

The Cousteau Society-Footnotes

1 "Cousteau Center divides Norfolk: $15.5 million bond issue dampens joy of some leaders," by Carlyle Murphy, *Washington Post*, July 6, 1985, p. F1.

2 "Cousteau Park latest French themer facing major financial difficulties," by Tim O'Brien, *Amusement Business*, August 5, 1991, p. 22.

3 "Scouts out at Catalina," by Ronald B. Taylor, *Los Angeles Times*, August 17, 1991, p. B1.

4 "Cousteau Society drops plans for Catalina resort," by Ronald B. Taylor, *Los Angeles Times*, October 15, 1991, p. B3.

5 "Green Helmets!," by Jacques-Yves Cousteau, *Calypso Log*, December 1991, Vol 18, No. 6., p. 3.

6 "World Bill of Rights," by Jacques-Yves Cousteau, *Calypso Log*, February 1992, p. 21.

7 "Capt. Cousteau runs Bill of Rights aground," by David Chilton, *McClatchy News Service*, January 9, 1993.

8 "New U.N. agency will keep a close eye on development," *San Francisco Chronicle*, June 9, 1992.

9. William K. Stevens, "It May Be Nice to Fool Mother Nature," *San Francisco Chronicle*, July 3, 1990.

10 "The Big Bang of Animal Evolution," by Jeffrey S. Levinton, *Scientific American*, November, 1992, p. 84.

11 "Now hear this," *Fortune*, April 24, 1989, p. 20.

12 "Captain Cousteau," by Frank Graham, Jr., *Audubon*, May 1990, p. 17.

13 *Cousteau: The Captain and His World*, by Richard Munson, W. Morrow, New York, 1989.

14 "The Heidelberg Appeal," by Dr. Michel Salomon, *Projections*, Fall, 1992.

15 "Interview," by Jean Daniel, *Nouvelle Observateur*, (special issue prepared for the Earth Summit) June 1992, p. 4.

16 "Interview," by Bahgat Eluadi and Adel Rifaat, *Courrier de l'Unesco*, November, 1991, p. 13. The original French reads:

    "Le dommage causé à la planète est fonction de la démographie, mais également du degré de développement. Un Américain fatigue la planète beaucoup plus que vingt Bangladeshis. Ce dommage est également lié à la consommation. Notre société est tournée vers une consommation de plus en plus inutile. C'est un cercle infernal, que je compare au cancer.

    "L'élimination des virus relève d'une idée noble, mais elle pose à son tour d'énormes problèmes. Entre l'an 1 et l'an 1400, la population n'a pratiquement pas changé. A travers les épidémies, la nature compensait les abus de la natalité par des abus des mortalité...

    "Nous voulons éliminer les souffrances, les maladies? L'idée est belle, mais n'est peut-être pas tour à fait bénéfique sur le long terme. Il est à craindre que l'on ne compromette ainsi l'avenir de notre espèce.

    "C'est terrible à dire. Il faut que la population mondiale se stabilise et pour cela, il faudrait éliminer 350.000 hommes par jour. C'est si horrible à dire, qu'il ne faut même pas le dire."

17 The Cousteau Society, Inc., Financial Statements and Schedule, December 31, 1990.

Natural Resources Defense Council

Natural Resources Defense Council (Founded 1970)
Annual budget: $16 million (1992); $20,496,829 (1993)
Staff: 128 total—83 professional; 45 support
Members: 170,000 individuals
Tax Status: (501)(c)(3)
Headquarters: 40 West 20th Street
New York, New York 10011
Phone: (212)727-2700
Fax: (212)727-1773

1350 New York Avenue, NW
Suite 300
Washington, D.C. 20005
Phone: (202)783-7800
Fax: (202)783-5917

Economy Trasher Number Eleven. The Natural Resources Defense Council is an artifact of the Ford Foundation, founded in 1970 with a $400,000 grant. Its purpose was to link establishment Wall Street lawyers with young, aggressive recent law school graduates who shared their interest in environmental activism. The grant was given during the early years of McGeorge Bundy's leadership of the Ford Foundation. Bundy had just come from the stardust and glamor of Washington as special assistant for national security in the Kennedy and Johnson administrations. Bundy, although a Back Bay Republican from a prominent family, came to the Ford Foundation determined to distance himself as much as possible from his role as a chief architect of the U. S. war in Vietnam, and sought to achieve high visibility for himself as a liberal domestic reformer. The creation of the Natural Resources Defense Council was one of his acts of personal redemption.

It was a time when the Ford Foundation was funding legal aid programs for many segments of society, the poor, minorities, and consumers, but contributed to these reformers with a somewhat shotgun approach. One analyst of philanthropy wrote that the Ford Foundation was giving grants "to established minority organizations such as the NAACP and the Urban League, but others went to new and inexperienced groups, even to street gangs."[1] More than one wag has suggested that the NRDC was one of those street gangs.

The three co-founders of NRDC, Richard Ayres, Gus Speth and Tom Stoel started in the cluttered offices of the Yale Law Journal. They originally intended to model an environmental law firm after the NAACP Legal Defense Fund, which had successfully used the courts to protect the civil rights of blacks.[2]

With their pile of money from the Ford Foundation, the young NRDC lawyers worked in a three-room office in New York's Bar Building learning how to sue the pants off industry. One of their first projects was done by Ayres and two aides who examined every plan filed by states to meet air quality standards required by the 1970 Clean Air Act. They found numerous flaws and tried to get the EPA to force states to correct their plans. Without luck. That is, until they used the Ford Foundation's $400,000 to sue the EPA for approving bad plans—and won case after case.

David Hawkins, an NRDC staff attorney, won a 1973 court ruling requiring states to impose a surcharge for commuter parking to discourage driving and found that Congress could undo all his legal-beagle do-gooding by passing a law prohibiting the EPA from enforcing the regulations. Hawkins said, "Without political support, opponents of change would just get your victory nullified in Congress. We realized we had to be more involved in the legislative process."

So the NRDC helped set up the National Clean Air Coalition in late 1973 to coordinate lobbying for numerous organizations—labor unions, churches and civic and public-health groups—to push for tough clean air regulations.

When Jimmy Carter won the presidency, he brought a batch of NRDC lawyers into power. Gus Speth left to join the president's Council on Environmental Quality, which he chaired during the Carter years. Hawkins became the EPA's assistant administrator for air. Other NRDC staffers joined the CEQ and the Justice and Interior departments. There are environmental activists salted all through the federal government, many of whom remained after the Carter years in Civil Service jobs to sabotage Reagan Administration free enterprise reforms. The Bush and Clinton administrations have recruited their share of environmentalists, too.

Ayres and two NRDC colleagues, David Hawkins and David Doniger, have become the most feared street gang in the environmental movement. Bill Pederson, a lobbyist for petroleum and chemical interests, told the *New York Times,* "There's no law firm, no think tank that has three people of that quality and that depth of experience."

The Natural Resources Defense Council, which even some of its members misname the *National* Resources Defense Council, has mugged both business and government with ferocious lawsuits that have cost the American economy billions in legal fees and lost productivity since 1970. They are one of the few big environmental groups that steadfastly refuses to hire an economist, regarding economics as irrelevant to environmental issues. No cost is too high. That is the motto of NRDC when it comes to protecting the environment. Zero risk. Infinite cost.

And they're very good at it, if not the best, at least the first among equals. Most of our Washington contacts say NRDC staff lawyers know the field as well or better than anyone else practicing environmental law. We've even heard a few federal attorneys in the Justice Department complain that NRDC lawyers are better informed than they are in the courtroom. A former Environmental Protection Agency attorney told the *Wall Street Journal,* "When you're up against them, you're up against the first team."[3]

Steven Schatzow, then head of pesticide regulation for EPA added that NRDC is "the most effective of the environmental groups. They are able to file good lawsuits, they're effective on Capitol Hill, they can use the media, and they're good at reacting with the agency."

A Department of the Interior official said, "It's amazing how much they drive public policy." And it's amazing how the government invites them to do it: NRDC lawyer Dan W. Reicher was appointed to a seat on the President's Council on

Environmental Quality, a heavyweight executive policymaking position for the Bush administration.[4]

On the other hand, William Wild, columnist for the *Dayton Daily News*, said, "NRDC is an organization of environmental vigilantes that is more irksome, if you can believe it, than William K. Reilly's federal Environmental Protection Agency bureaucrats."[5]

Irksome they are, to business, to the government, to jobs and the economy. Even cities have found NRDC lawyers trying to bankrupt them. Los Angeles officials argued with NRDC lawyers that the city would suffer billions of dollars worth of economic damage if NRDC's stiffer storm runoff requirements are enforced as written in the harsh provisions of the federal Clean Water Act. Almost every major city in the U. S. would be practically shut down if NRDC had its way. The law requires that even the tiniest pollutant which can be carried from one place to another by storm runoff be accounted for, isolated, treated, or handled in some other way that is either technically impossible or fantastically expensive.[6]

NRDC has developed its share of dirty tricks and skullduggery in the political wars of ecology. NRDC was behind the delay of a study of the economics of pesticide regulation at the University of California at Berkeley that would have revealed the disastrous cost of interventionism to the nation's largest agricultural producer.[7] With characteristic chutzpah, NRDC bravo Al Meyerhoff joined in a letter to the editor of the newspaper that blew the whistle on them complaining that it was not nice to expose environmentalists because they are on the side of the angels. Many farmers threatened by Meyerhoff's cohort have told me the only angel on the side of NRDC is the Angel of Death.[8]

NRDC for a time became virtually the Chemical Warfare Council—waging war against nearly every chemical used in industrial processes, an insidious way to destroy the economy without the consumer noticing until all the products vanish. NRDC has fought to ban, regulate, eliminate, limit, or destroy everything from lead (in paint and tableware),[9] refrigerants,[10] and diesel bus exhaust,[11] to obscure but vital substances such as 1,1,1-trichloroethane,[12] methylene chloride,[13] cadmium,[14] and a host of others.

NRDC wants a risk-free society, and that is not just utopian nonsense, it is physically impossible. As scientists have long known, everything is toxic in a large enough dose, including pure oxygen (too much of it blinds human infants) and chemically pure water (an overdose will dilute body electrolytes to the point that nerve conduction fails and death ensues). But if you are a political 800-pound gorilla, you can do anything you want, including interventions that totally destroy the economy.

John Hamilton Adams (salary $120,000) is the Natural Resources Defense Council's first and only executive director. He and four Yale Law School graduates—McGeorge Bundy, their benefactor, was also a Yalie, even though he later served as Dean of Harvard—founded NRDC in 1970, making him the longest surviving executive director in the environmental movement. Adams came from corporate practice and also served as assistant U.S. attorney in the Southern District of New York.

From the beginning NRDC's primary focus has been litigation. It sues businesses and government over alleged violations of anti-pollution laws, such as the Clean Water Act[15] and Clean Air Act.[16] It lobbies as well, giving testimony before Congress on pesticides,[17] water rights,[18] nuclear wastes,[19] toxic dumping,[20] and many other issues. At first NRDC was not even a membership organization. It had zero members until 1974, when its membership program began. Today it has over 170,000 members and a ton of money.

The NRDC's philosophy has always centered around a radically interventionist anti-growth ideology that endangers the free operation of business in American society. Many critics have commented that its philosophy is that "no cost is too great" to achieve whatever goal it happens to favor at the moment.[21] That cost is your job and the economy of your country.

When New York Mayor David N. Dinkins planned to build incinerators as a means of solid waste disposal, the NRDC opposed the idea.[22]

When Amoco Corporation, Exxon Corporation, and Mobil Corporation released advertisements touting their recycling programs, NRDC challenged their achievements as not being enough.[23]

When the stiff requirements of the Corporate Average Fuel Economy regulations were rolled back to reflect economic and minimal benefit realities of the auto industry, NRDC challenged the action. The eco-millenium must arrive by bicycle.[24]

The NRDC has been exceedingly successful at enforcing its views: The suits NRDC has filed and won have forced both regulators and regulated industries to spend large and unjustified amounts of money to prevent what many scientists and physicians consider minimal or insignificant risks to human health.[25] Typically, NRDC lawyer David Doniger says, "We take the view that there are rights involved here, rights to be protected regardless of the cost involved."[26]

NRDC wouldn't know how to take costs into consideration even if it believed in them without an economist to complement their staff of attorneys, scientists and resource specialists. On the other hand, the Environmental Defense Fund has more than a dozen economists who calculate costs, risks, and benefits as part of their justification for pursuing a change in public policy or a lawsuit. Even the eco-socialist Wilderness Society employs economists. John Baden of the Foundation for Research on Economics and the Environment says "Many companies find it profitable and productive to design programs in cooperation with the economic policy staff of these groups."[27]

Nobody finds anything about the NRDC profitable except its staff. An anonymous environmentalist was quoted in a *Los Angeles Times* interview complaining that NRDC is "too purist." He or she said, "The NRDC tends to be for zero risk, whereas we would be willing to accommodate a one-in-a-million risk in exchange for getting enforceable standards." The NRDC is the rigid ideologue of the Interventionist segment of the environmental movement.

The *Wall Street Journal* once described the NRDC as a kind of shadow EPA. "It has influenced laws on air pollution, water pollution, toxics, drinking water, pesticides, nuclear wastes, strip-mine reclamation, land use, energy conservation, and much more. It's hard to find a major environmental law it hasn't helped shape within Congress, the courts, and federal agencies. And often, the influence is profound."[28]

NRDC also runs its own foreign policy. It performed a major Soviet coup before the hard liners could manage it: By arrangement with the Soviet Academy of Sciences,[29] NRDC sent its scientists to the Soviet Union to observe the testing of nuclear weapons, bringing Soviet scientists here to observe U.S. nuclear tests in Nevada.[30] NRDC was also instrumental in bringing public attention to the concept of "nuclear winter," an end-of-the-world theory popularized by a team of scientists headed by celebrity astronomer Carl Sagan.[31]

The Bounty Hunters[32]

In 1982, NRDC announced the founding of its Citizen Enforcement Program to bring lawsuits against companies that are in violation of environmental statutes, on behalf of NRDC members. The program has investigated the records of thousands of companies in over twenty-five states, and prepared lawsuits against more than one hundred of the worst violators.[33]

By 1988, the NRDC could boast in its Annual Report, "The Program has enjoyed a remarkable success rate. To date, all of the suits have been concerned with violations of Clean Water Act permits that limit pollutant discharges into waterways and sewage treatment plants. Most of the companies that NRDC has sued or negotiated with have agreed to comply with their permits, and over three million dollars in penalties has been paid to the United Stated Treasury, state environmental agencies, or third party environmental organizations."

The citizen enforcement effort led to a record penalty payment from Bethlehem Steel amounting to $1.5 million, while Gwaltney of Smithfield, a Virginia meat-packing company, was assessed nearly $1.3 million in penalties. The *Gwaltney* case went to the U. S. Supreme Court, which affirmed the constitutionality of the citizen enforcement provisions of the Clean Water Act.[34]

Bethlehem was required to contribute $1 million to environmental protection projects, including $50,000 to Save Our Streams, $100,000 to the National Fish and Wildlife Federation, and $200,000 to the Trust for Public Land. NRDC won a fat $485,000 attorneys' fee award, too.

A number of legal critics have noted that the citizen enforcement actions of NRDC have operated entirely outside of Congress's intention that the provision be used by individual citizens and neighborhood groups to bring *current* violations of the law to the attention of the EPA and other enforcement agencies. Instead, big rich national organizations such as NRDC have used the provisions in a targeted and strategized manner to punish *past* violations by honest companies that have kept records of their discharges accurately enough so that a clever lawyer can come in, demand the papers, and at his leisure sift through them to see if there is some past infraction he can make into an easy case.

Michael Greve, writing for the Washington Legal Foundation said, "The NRDC had closely monitored the EPA's administration of the effluent guidelines program under the Clean Water Act, and reached the conclusion that the program would be ineffective without stringent enforcement. With the help of a seed grant that helped to fund initial citizen suits, the NRDC attempted to establish a self-sustaining Clean Water Act enforcement program by recovering attorneys' fees and using them to fund future cases."

Attorneys' fees awarded to successful litigants are almost always calculated according to the going rate for private-practice attorneys in the district in which the case is settled. In Washington or New York, for instance, this could be $250 per hour or more. According to public records, NRDC's five highest paid lawyers earn less than $82,000 per year, a bit more than the government attorneys they face in court, but far less than the corporate attorneys they see much more frequently.

The reason NRDC picked the Clean Water Act is that cases cost virtually nothing to construct and are just about the easiest cases to win in all lawyerdom. The payoff is also highest in relation to the upfront cash layout. Thus, ironically, the NRDC's citizen enforcement project is driven by economics, which NRDC says is irrelevant when it comes to the environment.

Even worse, NRDC's citizen enforcement program does virtually nothing to stop pollution. In fact, its vigilante aspect may reduce the incentives for industry to comply voluntarily with the law. NRDC's citizen suit program also impedes technological innovation by frightening companies away from trying new pollution control devices that might initially cause technical violations of the law but when the bugs are worked out could clean up pollution much better. And NRDC also drives industry to consider simply shifting their discharges from the water to the land or air.[35]

The U. S. Supreme Court recognized the abuses of the citizen suit and placed limits on what an environmental group could do with them.[36]

The Anti-Pesticide Crusade[37]

NRDC says its Pesticides Program "aims to improve public health by reducing exposures to toxic pesticides and by fostering increased public demand for safe food. A strategy combining legislative and educational efforts, as well as litigation, is proving to have a notable impact."

The most notable impact of NRDC's Pesticide Program to date was to bankrupt thousands of apple growers with its Alar scam.[38] It came to the public's attention on February 26, 1989 on the CBS News "infotainment" magazine *60 Minutes* in a segment produced by David Gelber titled "A Is For Apple." The initial image on the small screen was a big red apple plastered over with the skull and crossbones poison symbol.[39]

Ed Bradley intoned, "The most potent cancer-causing chemical in our food supply is a pesticide sprayed on apples to keep them on the trees longer and make them look better."

Not a single case of human cancer has ever been attributed to Alar—whose chemical name is daminozide—but CBS News said nothing about that. To boot, Alar is used only on about 5 percent of the U. S. apple crop. CBS News also did not reveal that it had colluded with the Natural Resources Defense Council to conceal the NRDC report *Intolerable Risk: Pesticides in Our Children's Food* from reputable scientists and made a deal with NRDC for exclusive rights to break the story.[40]

Bradley's brief introduction set up a masterpiece of manipulation. The segment went on to frame an unfavorable image of pesticides among a concerned but technologically untrained public. There was no mention of the benefits of Alar.[41] There was no mention of the honest scientific opinion that Alar-treated apples are safe for children to eat in large quantities.[42] There was no indication that EPA had already announced it was acting to ban Alar[43] as a low level cancer risk of 1 in 20,000 over a 70 year lifetime—the acceptable risk being placed at 1 cancer in a million.[44]

And there was no indication that CBS News was knowingly acting as shill for a Natural Resources Defense Council political/fundraising project designed months earlier by a hired communication consulting firm.

Bradley introduced Janet Hathaway, senior attorney for the Natural Resources Defense Council, as if CBS News had sought out NRDC rather than NRDC soliciting CBS News through consultant Fenton Communications, Inc., which is what actually happened.

Hathaway said, "What we're talking about is a cancer-causing agent used on food that the EPA knows is going to cause cancer for thousands of children over their lifetime." The science said that any cancers that might result from UDMH, a breakdown product of Alar, would occur over a 70 year life span, the vast bulk of them at the end of the span, not the beginning.[45] But the image of toddlers with cancer is terrifying and the image of an elderly grandfather with cancer is not even news, so NRDC went for the schoolchildren.[46]

Bradley then asserted that "Janet Hathaway's organization, the Natural Resources Defense Council, has just completed the most careful study yet on the effect of daminozide," but the report, titled *Intolerable Risk: Pesticides in our Children's Food*, in fact was a mere rehash of the flawed studies that had been earlier rejected by EPA's Scientific Advisory Panel. But Hathaway proceeded to make the alarming charge that from the eight pesticides her group had studied, the risk of children developing cancer is approximately 250 times the EPA acceptable risk level. EPA showed the lifetime risk fifty times lower than NRDC asserted.

"What that means," Hathaway insisted, "is that over a lifetime one child out of every 4,000 or so, of our preschoolers, will develop cancer just from these eight pesticides."

The subsequent scientific critique of NRDC's "most careful study yet" was uniformly negative.[47] Virtually every toxicologist who reviewed it rejected it as incorrect.[48] The NRDC study in fact did not meet *any* minimum scientific standards: it was not peer reviewed and it was not published in any professional journal.[49] It never had to stand the test of critical methods and thus had not even the basic characteristics of real science.

In addition, the NRDC Alar study was performed by scientists on the payroll of NRDC who could reasonably be characterized as mere bought-off hacks worried about preserving their personal incomes.[50]

The devastation to the apple industry following the *60 Minutes* broadcast was immense.[51] In Virginia, where apple growers do not use Alar on their crops, the price of apples plunged 35 percent in the weeks following the NRDC report. One cooperative in California was forced out of business entirely: its former president said, "Business dropped 100 percent. It killed us." Panicky mothers dumped apple juice down the drain, and schools pulled the fruit from lunchrooms.[52] A survey by the Wirthlin Group after the program aired found that 6 out of 10 people had heard or read something that made them think apples were unsafe.[53] Four out of 10 specifically mentioned reports linking apples to pesticides that cause cancer.[54] Calls for a total ban on Alar were immediate.[55] Washington's Yakima Valley, a $1 billion a year contributor to the state's economy, lost 40 percent of its income. Thousands of orchardists were pushed into bankruptcy, and a handful of beleaguered mom-and-pop apple growers brought a lawsuit against CBS News *60 Minutes* and NRDC for damages of more than $300 million[56]—an agribusiness trade group, the Washington State Apple Commission decided to keep a low profile and not help with the lawsuit, just the sort of industry cowardice that leaves the little guy twisting in the wind and makes business such an easy target for NRDC.[57] NRDC was later dismissed from the suit, as was CBS News *60 Minutes*. The little farmers lost big.

During the peak of the Alar furor, actress Meryl Streep testified before a Senate committee against pesticide use by America's farmers and appeared in a series of television commercials in which she washed broccoli in laundry detergent, explaining to a child actor why it was necessary. Streep represented Mothers and Others for Pesticide Limits, an NRDC front group. Outraged farmers were stunned to see how easily an ignorant but glamorous celebrity could ruin their lives with a sweep of the hand.[58]

On a later broadcast of *60 Minutes* Ed Bradley introduced Al Meyerhoff of the NRDC, and asked if the benefits of Alar have been worth the suffering caused to growers. Meyerhoff replied, "We don't have a quarrel with the apple growers. I think the growers here have been as much victims as the consumers have been victims. They're a victim of Uniroyal. They're a victim of the chemical industry selling them a bill of goods." Scientists disagreed, saying it was a bad precedent to pull apples off the market with no proof of any danger—hysteria is easy to incite but hard to quell.[59]

It was not until October 3 of 1989 that the public got an inkling of how the NRDC and *60 Minutes* had colluded to devastate the apple market. The *Wall Street Journal* editorial page that day led off a piece with this intriguing paragraph:

> After this year's stir over use of the chemical Alar on apples, political publicist David Fenton celebrated the work of his firm in a lengthy memo to interested parties. He wrote of a "sea change in public opinion" that has "taken place because of a carefully planned media campaign, conceived and implemented by Fenton Communications with the Natural Resources Defense Council."[60]

Fenton's memo is a document in arrogance well worth reading. Here is most of the text:

In the past two months, the American public's knowledge of the dangers of pesticides in food has been greatly increased. Overnight, suppliers of organic produce cannot keep up with demand. Traditional supermarkets are opening pesticide-free produce sections.[61]

The campaign was based on NRDC's report "Intolerable Risk: Pesticides in Our Children's Food." Participation by the actress Meryl Streep was another essential element.

Usually, public interest groups release similar reports by holding a news conference, and the result is a few print stories. Television coverage is rarely sought or achieved. The intensity of exposure created by design for the NRDC pesticide story is uncommon in the non-profit world.

Our goal was to create so many repetitions of NRDC's message that average American consumers (not just the policy elite in Washington) could not avoid hearing it—from many different media outlets within a short period of time. The idea was for the "story" to achieve a life of its own, and continue for weeks and months to affect policy and consumer habits. Of course, this had to be achieved with extremely limited resources.

In most regards, this goal was met. A modest investment by NRDC re-paid itself many-fold in tremendous media exposure (and substantial, immediate revenue for future pesticide work). In this sense, we submit this campaign as a model for other non-profit organizations.

Media coverage included two segments on CBS 60 Minutes, the covers of *Time* and *Newsweek* (two stories in each magazine), the Phil Donahue show, multiple appearances on Today, Good Morning America and CBS This Morning, several stories on each of the network evening newscasts, MacNeil/Lehrer, multiple stories in the *N.Y. Times, Washington Post, L.A. Times* and newspapers around the country, three cover stories in *USA Today, People,* four women's magazines with a combined circulation of 17 million (*Redbook, Family Circle, Women's Day* and *New Woman*), and thousands of repeat stories in local media around the nation and the world....

Consumer feedback devices were built into the campaign, including self-published book sales and the first use of a 900 phone number by a non-profit group....

In October of 1988 NRDC hired Fenton Communications to undertake the media campaign for its report.... The report marked the first time anyone—inside government or out—had calculated children's actual exposure levels to carcinogenic and neurotoxic pesticides. The study showed one of the worst pesticides to be daminozide, or Alar, used primarily on apples and peanuts....

[L]ast fall, Meryl Streep contacted NRDC, asking if she could assist with some environmental projects. Ms. Streep read the preliminary results of the study and agreed to serve as a spokesperson for it....

It was agreed that one week after the study's release, Streep and other prominent citizens would announce the formation of NRDC's new project, Mothers and Others for Pesticide Limits. This group would direct citizen action at changing the pesticide laws, and help consumers lobby for pesticide-free produce at their grocery stores.

The separation of these two events was important in ensuring that the media would have two stories, not one, about this project. Thereby, more repetition of NRDC's message was guaranteed.

As the report was being finalized, Fenton Communications began contacting various media. An agreement was made with 60 Minutes to "break" the story of the report in late February. Interviews were also arranged several months in advance with major women's magazines like *Family Circle, Women's Day* and *Redbook* (to appear in mid-March). Appearance dates were set with the Donahue Shows, ABC's Home Show, double appearances on NBC's Today show and other programs.

On February 26th CBS 60 Minutes broke the story to an audience of 40 million viewers.... The next morning, NRDC held a news conference attended by more than 70 journalists and 12 camera crews.

Concurrently, NRDC coordinated local news conferences in 12 cities around the country also releasing the report....

On March 7 Meryl Streep held a Washington news conference to announce the formation of NRDC's Mothers and Others for Pesticide Limits. She was joined by board members including pediatrician Dr. T. Berry Brazelton, National PTA President Manya Unger and Wendy Gordon Rockefeller of NRDC.

Coverage of Mothers and Others that week included USA Today (cover); The Today Show on NBC; The Phil Donahue Show (10 million viewers); *Women's Day* (6 million copies sold); *Redbook* (4 million); *Family Circle* (6 million); *Organic Gardening* (1.5 million); *New Woman* (1.7 million); *People Magazine*; USA TODAY Television (200 markets); Entertainment Tonight (18 million viewers); ABC's HOME Show (3 million viewers); Cable News Network and numerous radio networks, newspaper chains, broadcast chains, wire services and other media around the nation.

In addition, we arranged for Meryl Streep and Janet Hathaway of NRDC to grant 16 interviews by satellite with local TV major market anchors....

In the ensuing weeks, the controversy kept building. Articles appeared in food sections of newspapers around the country. Columnists and cartoonists took up the story. MacNeil/Lehrer, the *New York Times* and *Washington Post* did follow-up stories, as did the three network evening programs and morning shows. Celebrities from the casts of *L.A. Law* and *thirtysomething* joined NRDC for a Los Angeles news conference.

Soon school systems began banning apples (which is not what NRDC intended or recommended). Three federal agencies (EPA, USDA and FDA) issued an unusual joint statement assuring the public that apples were safe (although to children who consume a great deal, these assurances are not entirely true).

And the industry struck back. NRDC's credibility was, as expected, questioned by industry "front groups" such as the American Council on Science and Health. A major corporate pr firm, Hill and Knowlton, was hired for

$700,000 by the apple growers, which also put forward a $2 million advertising budget. Stories began appearing (including a *Washington Post* cover piece) saying that the levels of Alar in apples were below federal standards, and charging the media with exaggerating the story. This missed the whole point of the study—that children ingest so many apples for their size that the legal federal standard is unsafe....

Usually, it takes a significant natural disaster to create this much sustained news attention for an environmental problem. We believe this experience proves there are other ways to raise public awareness for the purpose of moving the Congress and policymakers.

That, as appalling as it is, was by no means the entire story. Knowing TV's preference for glitz over fact, Fenton worked with actress Meryl Streep to sidestep all factual issues. Her typical approach was illustrated in an April 1989 magazine article:

"Food is a religious, sacred thing. The [NRDC] pesticide report turns the world inside out. To think that food could hurt a child. It's weird. It upsets every corner of my existence. I went sort of wild. It's insane that we have to worry about the food we give to our children."

This "religious, sacred, sort of wild" performance was, of course, well rehearsed and meticulously followed the pre-planned NRDC script that David Fenton helped prepare. It completely short-circuits rationality, as intended.

More from the same article: "I can't do battle with the biochemists, but I don't think I have to. Though the NRDC data is solid, mothers will respond to this on an emotional level. When kids are involved, it's a completely different set of circumstances. Women will be passionate about the issue in that it affects our most vulnerable group."[62]

It was not at all clear to many in the public during the first crucial period of the campaign that Mothers and Others for Pesticide Limits was an NRDC project. Even the news media did not make the connection immediately. Everyone seemed to think that it was just the beautiful and concerned Ms. Streep and some energetic Connecticut housewives. At least one newspaper editor struck out of an opinion column the assertion that Mothers was a front group for NRDC because it could not be immediately verified. Even Accuracy In Media, a watchdog group, although its leaders assumed that such activism must be coming from a single source, did not publish anything about the connection until after the truth was generally recognized. Once it became clear to all that NRDC and Mothers were the same entity, the purpose had been accomplished. Separating the furor generated by the CBS Alar segment and the Streep announcement of Mothers was vital, as Fenton wrote above, "in ensuring that the media would have two stories, not one. Thereby, more repetition of NRDC's message was guaranteed."

The tactic worked. Streep testified before Congress that she is so intent upon avoiding pesticides that she would not mind paying three dollars for an organically grown apple.[63] The homeless sleeping on the sidewalk grates outside the hearing room would no doubt be pleased to hear of her willingness to sacrifice for the sake of principle. The mere fact that such unqualified celebrities are able to become the arbiters of scientific truth and public policy in America should give us pause.[64]

Fenton boasted in an interview published in the left-wing periodical *Propaganda Review*, "Over a two-week period, if you turned on the Today show or the evening news or Donahue you saw it. You heard it on the radio. If you opened your home town newspaper, you read about it four times. It was everywhere."

Meredith Brokaw, wife of NBC News anchorman Tom Brokaw, is listed as a director on the letterhead of Meryl Streep's Mothers and Others for Pesticide Limits. The day representatives of the EPA, the FDA, and the Department of Agriculture all told a Senate committee that it is safe to eat apples, Tom Brokaw headlined the story, "The Government takes the side of the American apple industry." He then said, "It was the U.S. Government against Meryl Streep, school officials, and an untold number of consumers worried about the use of a chemical called Alar on apples." Meredith Brokaw obviously knew the truth that the whole thing had been orchestrated as a fund raiser and political hysteria campaign by NRDC. Didn't she tell husband Tom? And if she did, why did he promote this incredible setup by NRDC, a special interest group with an obvious monetary interest in the outcome of the campaign?

This degree of sophistication is breathtaking to an apple grower in Yakima, Washington, or Winchester, Virginia, or upstate New York.[65] Or to most of us.

Even before this master stroke against the economy, NRDC was rated tops among Economy Trashers. A 1988 survey in the *Washington Monthly* named NRDC one of the best five public interest groups, saying they were "the Wall Street lawyers of the environmental movement."[66] It noted that "the NRDC pioneered the use of the lawsuit to safeguard the environment. A survey of environmental policy professionals on Capitol Hill and in the Executive Branch found NRDC rated "the most influential, most effective, most respected and credible," among those groups that lobby on environmental issues. Thirty-four Washington-based policy makers made this determination—the rest of the eighty people polled did not return their questionnaires.

NRDC gets 49 percent of its money from memberships, 42 percent from foundations; and 9 percent from fees, contracts, and other sources. It operates 3 branch offices in Honolulu, Los Angeles and San Francisco. Members in 1990 had an average annual income of $68,000 and 85 percent of them had bachelor's degrees.

NRDC publishes the *Amicus Journal* quarterly, *Newsline* bimonthly, and *tlc*, published quarterly by Mothers & Others for a Livable Planet, a project of NRDC.

NRDC's Board of Trustees includes chairman Adrian W. Dewind; and vice chairmen Robert O. Blake, Michael McIntosh and George M. Woodwell. Other members of the board include: Dean Abrahamson, Adam Albright, Leonard R. Argent, Adele Auchincloss, David Hahn Baker, Eula Bingham, Boris Bittken, Lucy Blake (California League of Conservation Voters), Charles E. Boob, Henry R.

Breck, Richard Cotton, Gordon J. Davis, Beatrice Abbott Duggan, Stephen P. Duggan, John E. Echohawk, James B. Frankel, Francis W. Hatch, Hamilton F. Kean, Burks B. Lapham, Jonathan Z. Larsen, Peter Morton, Carol R. Noyes, John B. Oakes, Franklin E. Parker, Robert Redford, Nathaniel Pryor Reed, Cruz Reynoso, John R. Robinson, Laurance Rockefeller, Thomas Roush, Christine H. Russell, Frederick A. O. Schwarz, Jr., John Sheehan, David Sive, James Gustave Speth (World Resources Institute), Frederick A. Terry, Jr, and Thomas A. Troyer. Recognize any of these names? If you don't recognize John Oakes, he's former editorial page editor of the *New York Times*. Another reason NRDC has such good press.

The Natural Resources Defense Council, although created by the Ford Foundation and heavily influenced by the Rockefeller Axis, with Laurance Rockefeller on its board and piles of Rockefeller money in its coffers, is sufficiently distinct in its policy and programs that it cannot be included in the power axis of either clique. Likewise, it does not properly fall into the Establishment Interventionist Axis along with the Audubon Society because it is too radically anti-market and rejects all economic calculation, yet NRDC does not fall comfortably into the Establishment Eco-Socialist Axis with the Wilderness Society because it is not sufficiently systematic in destroying private property. Thus it fits the Radical Interventionist Axis. If that sounds like a contradiction, examine NRDC's record again and see if it doesn't fit.

NRDC has received grants from:

Ametek Foundation, Inc., of Pennsylvania a manufacturer of water purification equipment.

Atherton Family Foundation gave $30,000 in 1989 "for endangered species stream flow coastal and groundwater protection."

Mary Reynolds Babcock Foundation, Inc. gave $60,000 in 1989, a 2-year grant "for Clean Water Program."

The William Bingham Foundation gave $300,000 in 1990 "for operation and endowment of environmental conflict negotiation program, and toward construction of headquarters building, model of energy efficiency."

Carnegie Corporation of New York gave $300,000 in 1990, a 2-year grant "toward nuclear weapons verification and data center projects."

Mary Flagler Cary Charitable Trust gave $75,000 in 1990, a 3-year grant "for project to provide long-term protection for nationally significant marine and coastal areas of Southwest and New England."

Samuel N. and Mary Castle Foundation gave $10,000 in 1989 for "environment protection project."

The Clark Foundation gave $50,000 in 1991 "for New York City Program."

Columbia Foundation gave $25,000 in 1990 for general support.

Corning Glass Works Foundation.

Dakin Corporation.

The Aaron Diamond Foundation, Inc. gave $50,000 in 1989 "for pediatric mobile lead detection unit research."

Geraldine R. Dodge Foundation, Inc. gave $100,000 in 1989 "for comprehensive program to reverse pollution of New Jersey waters from dumping at sea of garbage and coastal discharges of sewage, medical waste and oil."

William H. Donner Foundation.

The Educational Foundation of America gave $75,000 in 1990 for "waste management and reduction project."

Field Foundation.

Forbes Foundation.

Wallace Alexander Gerbode Foundation gave $50,000 in 1990, a 2-year grant for renewed support of California Pesticides Project; another $25,000 "for participation in Hawaii Public Utilities Commission Proceeding to Require Energy Utilities in Hawaii to Implement Integrated Resource Planning."

The George Gund Foundation gave $45,000 in 1990 "for United States Energy Conservation Program."

Fund for the City of New York, Inc. gave $20,000 in 1990 "to monitor implementation of New York City's recycling legislation."

The William and Flora Hewlett Foundation gave $150,000 in 1990, a 2-year grant for general support of negotiation and alternative dispute resolution activities.

The Hyde and Watson Foundation gave $10,000 in 1989 "for purchase and alteration of new facility to increase efficiency of programs."

Island Foundation, Inc. gave $15,000 in 1989 "to implement State's [Maine] growth management plan."

W. Alton Jones Foundation, Inc. gave $262,000 in 1989 "for Nuclear Weapons Data Center, international global warming reduction program and for general support of Los Angeles environmental program activities."

The Joyce Foundation gave $40,000 in 1990 "for project on implementation of acid rain provisions of Clean Air Act."

The J. M. Kaplan Fund, Inc. gave $300,000 in 1989 "for general support for effective environmental work on broadest range of issues. Urban Law Center program, which works with local community groups to protect against excessive development."

The Kresge Foundation gave $300,000 in 1990 "toward purchase of headquarters condominium."

Landels, Ripley & Diamond.

Leupold & Stevens, Inc.

Mayfair Supermarkets.

The John Merck Fund gave $50,000 in 1989 for Missile Verification and Warhead Dismantlement Project.

Joyce Mertz-Gilmore Foundation gave $100,000 in 1989 for program that will pursue national and international policy initiatives to halt global warming process and prepare for effects which are already inevitable.

Morgan Bank.

Charles Stewart Mott Foundation gave $40,000 in 1990 for promoting Environmentally Sound Energy Lending Policies; another $75,000 in 1990 to reduce toxic emissions and hazardous wastes at source points, focusing first on need for improved industrial waste management policies and practices and second, on reduction and safe management of municipal wastes including participation in model program in Northeast.

New England Biolabs.

The New York Community Trust gave $35,000 in 1990 for urban environment program.

New York Times Company Foundation.

Edward John Noble Foundation, Inc, gave $35,000 in 1990 for work in area of toxic substances and hazardous wastes.

The North Face.

The Overbrook Foundation gave $30,000 in 1989.

The Prospect Hill Foundation, Inc. gave $20,000 in 1990 "for Nuclear Weapons Databook, Volume V;" and another $20,000 in 1990 "to promote solid waste reduction."

The Prudential Foundation.

Charles H. Revson Foundation, Inc. gave $100,000 in 1989 "for New York City Urban Environment Project and Medical Waste Project."

Rockefeller Family Fund, Inc. gave $10,000 in 1989 "for National Campaign Against Toxic Hazards, which organizes at national, state and local levels to shift debate on toxic issues from control to prevention strategies."

The Rockefeller Foundation gave $95,000 in 1990 "to implement energy-efficiency demonstration project with USSR GOSSTROI, in Tallin, Estonia, and to establish nationwide database of environmental problems in Soviet Union with Socio-Ecological Union."

The San Francisco Foundation gave $30,000 in 1990 "to protect San Francisco Bay/Delta by reducing freshwater diversion and by promoting water conservation and water quality safeguards."

The Scherman Foundation, Inc. gave $70,000 in 1989, a 2-year grant "for general support."

The Florence and John Schumann Foundation gave $65,000 "for U.S.-Soviet Demonstration Project on Energy Conservation."

Streisand Foundation.

Public Welfare Foundation gave $250,000 in 1990 "for Atmosphere Protection Initiative, which deals with problems of global warming, ozone depletion and toxic air emissions."

Town Creek Foundation, Inc. gave $15,000 in 1990.

Victoria Foundation gave $30,000 in 1989 "for New Jersey Coastal Protection Project."

G. N. Wilcox Trust gave $25,000 in 1989 "for pledge payment to expand education program in the [Hawaii] preserves."

The Winston Foundation for World Peace gave $38,000 in 1989 "for renewal for satellite-photo analysis of Soviet plutonium plants."

Dean Witter Foundation gave $12,500 in 1989 for general support.

World Wildlife Fund for Nature.

The Natural Resources Defense Council.
Job killers.
Economy Trashers.

Natural Resources Defense Council—Footnotes

1 *The Golden Donors: A New Anatomy of the Great Foundations,* Waldemar A. Nielsen, E. P. Dutton, New York, p. 64.

2 "From Fringe To Political Mainstream," by Michael Weisskopf, *New York Times,* April 19, 1990, p. A16.

3 "Environmental trio uses expertise to shape debate," by Timothy Noah, *Wall Street Journal,* April 4, 1990, p. A7.

4 "Environmental lawyer to switch councils," by Ann Devroy and Thomas W. Lippman, *Washington Post,* February 13, 1990, p. A19.

5 Quoted in "The Natural Resources Defense Council: Front-Line vigilantes of Environmentalism," *Organization Trends,* Capital Research Center, Washington, D. C., May 1989.

6 "Bid for stiffer storm runoff rules falters: water quality officials rebuff environmentalists and say existing anti-pollution effort is sufficient," by Dean E. Murphy, *Los Angeles Times,* April 28, 1991, p. 1.

7 "The Green lobby's dirty tricks," by Gerald Sirkin, *Wall Street Journal,* January 2, 1991, p. A6.

8 "Retailed 'facts' unfair to NRDC," letter by Albert H. Meyerhoff, Otto C. Doering III and Alexander D. Leslie, *Wall Street Journal,* January 30, 1991, p. A11.

9 "Get the lead out, now," by Roger Morton, *School and College,* November 1991, p. 21.

10 "Environmentalists ask EPA for '95 CFC ban, 2005 phaseout for HCFCs," *Contractor,* January 1992, p. 6.

11 "EPA sets plans to curb bus exhaust," by Michael Weisskopf, *Washington Post,* September 11, 1991, p. A6.

12 "Group warns of chemical damage," by Martha M. Hamilton, *Washington Post,* June 19, 1990, p. D2.

13 "Environmental group says Kodak is major emitter of chemical," *Wall Street Journal,* June 20, 1989, p. A4.

14 "Trying to make batteries 'green,'" by John Holusha, *New York Times,* June 3 1990, p. F9.

15 "Water pollution lawsuit takes aim at chemicals," *Chemical Marketing Reporter,* November 6, 1989, p. 3.

16 "Joint group plan suit to require emissions rule," environmental groups, states, threaten EPA with lawsuit over operating permits for major air polluters', *Platt's Oilgram News,* February 11, 1992, p. 5.

17 "Bush's pesticide plan kindles debate," by Conrad B. MacKerron, *Chemical Week,*

November 8, 1989, p. 14.

18 "House committee hears opposing pleas on fate of OCS leasing moratoria," *Platt's Oilgram News*, February 26, 1986, p. 6.

19 "Trouble for DOE's reactors," by Eliot Marshal, *Science*, October 28, 1988, p. 508. See also "States seek remand of EPA waste regs," by Mark Crawford, *Science*, January 3, 1986, p. 18.

20 "Beach pollution problem is worsening, group says: sewage, not needles, closes shores this year," by D'Vera Cohn, *Washington Post*, August 10, 1989, p. A14.

21 "The Natural Resources Defense Council: Front-Line vigilantes of Environmentalism," *Organization Trends*, Capital Research Center, Washington, D. C., May 1989.

22 "Incineration plan draws criticism," by Allan R. Gold, *New York Times*, September 8, 1991, p. 38.

23 "Groups dispute oil companies' recycling ads," by Alan Kovski, *The Oil Daily*, April 24, 1992., p. 1.

24 "Settlement sought in challenge to CAFE rollback," by Helen Kahn, *Automotive News*, February 13, 1989, p. 2.

25 *Toxic Terror*, Elizabeth Whelan, 1985.

26 "From fringe to political mainstream: environmentalists set policy agenda," by Michael Weisskopf, *Washington Post*, April 19, 1990. p. A1.

27 *Wall Street Journal*, August 21, 1989.

28 *Wall Street Journal*, January 13, 1986.

29 "NRDC and Soviet Academy sign unusual test-verification pact," by William Sweet, *Physics Today*, July 1986, p. 63.

30 "Soviets allow monitoring in USSR," by Richard Monastersky, *Science News*, July 4 1987, p. 6. See also, "Nuclear test watchers feel political heat," by Eliot Marshall, *Science*, August 7 1987, p. 594.

31 "Excerpts from a roundtable at Moscow State University," by Igor Izodorovich Altschuler and Ruben Artyomovich Mnatsakanyan, *Environment*, December 1988, p. 10.

32 This entire section is derived from a report by the Capital Research Center and used by permission. Supplements from other sources are noted.

33 "Environmentalism and bounty hunting," by Michael S. Greve, *The Public Interest*, Fall, 1989, p. 15.

34 "Citizen lawsuits on environment work," letter by James F. Simon, *New York Times*, August 28, 1989, p. A14.

35 "Searching for incentives to entice polluters," by Matthew L. Wald, *New York Times*, October 8, 1989, p. F8.

36 "Citizens' suits limited on past acts of polluters," by Stuart Taylor, Jr., *New York Times*, December 2, 1987, p. 10.

37 Portions of this section are derived from *Fear of Food* by Andrea Arnold and used by permission of the Free Enterprise Press.

38 "Apple growers bruised and bitter after Alar scare," by Timothy Egan, *New York Times*, July 8, 1991, p. A1.

39 The Alar segment of 60 Minutes was transcribed by Accuracy In Media, Washington, D.C., and provided to us by AIM associate editor Joseph Goulden.

40 *Intolerable Risk: Pesticides in Our Children's Food*, Natural Resources Defense Council, New York, 1989.

41 Three years later Elizabeth Whelan of the American Council on Science and Health defended the use of Alar. See "Apples revisited," by Elizabeth Whelan, *Wall Street Journal*, March 16, 1992, p. A14.

42 "Alar controversy mirrors differences in risk perceptions," by Ann. M. Thayer, *Chemical & Engineering News*, August 28, 1989, p. 7.

43 "Alar sales in U. S. for food use halted," by Richard Seltzer, *Chemical & Engineering News,* June 12, 1989, p. 6.

44 "The EPA is Looking for a Few Bad Apples," *Newsweek,* February 13, 1989, p. 65.

45 "Apple dangers are just so much applesauce," column by Elizabeth M. Whelan, *Wall Street Journal,* March 14, 1989, p. A20.

46 "Pesticides and kids," by Leslie Roberts, *Science,* March 10, 1989, p. 1280.

47 "Scare of the Week," editorial by Daniel E. Koshland, Jr., *Science,* V. 244, No. 4900, 7 April 1989, p. 9.

48 "Alar: The Numbers Game," by Leslie Roberts, *Science,* V. 243, No. 4897, March 17, 1989, p. 1430.

49 "The pesticide scare: changing public perception" by Ellen Goldbaum, *Chemical Week,* May 3, 1989, p. 28.

50 "NRDC pesticide study was flawed, EPA says," *Chemical Marketing Reporter,* March 13, 1989, p. 5.

51 "Pesticide fears cancel US apple export order," by John Davies, *Journal of Commerce,* March 14, 1989, p. 1A.

52 "Apples: forbidden fruit?" by Janice Wright, *American Baby,* May 1989, p. 22. See also "Are pesticides poisoning our children?" by Arlene Fischer, *Redbook,* May 1989, p. 116.

53 "Stores urged to pull Alar-free apple signs," by John Mejia, *Supermarket News,* June 26, 1989, p. 1.

54 "'60 Minutes' is a Health Hazard," *AIM Report,* March-B, 1989, XVIII-6, p. 3.

55 "Alar on apples: pressures mount for a total ban," by Richard Seltzer, *Chemical & Engineering News,* May 22, 1989, p. 4.

56 "11 apple growers sue CBS program: damages sought following report on chemical alar," *New York Times,* November 1989, p. A22.

57 "Apple commission won't join '60 Minutes' suit," by Lorianne Denne, *Puget Sound Business Journal,* January 21, 1991, p. 9.

58 "Why are rats and actresses dictating U. S. food policy?" by Richard Krumme, *Successful Farming,* June 1989, p. 18.

59 "Some fear bad precedent in Alar alarm," by Malcolm Gladwell, *Washington Post,* April 19, 1989, p. A1.

60 "How a PR Firm Executed the Alar Scare," *Wall Street Journal,* October 3, 1989, p. A22.

61 The reader can find verification for Fenton's remarks in "Finding organic food," *New York Times,* July 19, 1989, p. C3. See also "Sold on organic," by Joanna Poncavage, *Organic Gardening,* June 1989, p. 42.

62 *Organic Gardening,* April, 1989.

63 "Ms. Streep goes to Washington to stop a bitter harvest," by Bonnie Johnson, *People Weekly,* March 20, 1989, p. 50.

64 "The great apple scare," by Robert James Bidinotto, *Reader's Digest,* October 1990, p. 53.

65 For an outraged cry from agriculture on the zeal and sophistication of their opponents, see "Agriculture Needs A Strategic Command," by Charlotte Sine, *Farm Chemicals,* January 1990, p. 62.

66 "The best and worst of public interest groups," by Rita McWilliams, *Washington Monthly,* March 1988, p. 19.

Clean Water Action

Clean Water Action (Founded 1971)
- Annual budget: $11,666,294 (1990)
- Staff: 1,000, 90 professional
- Members: 600,000
- Tax Status: 501(c)(4)
- Headquarters: 317 Pennsylvania Avenue, S.E.
  Washington, D.C. 20003-0884
  Phone: (202)457-1286 Fax: (202)457-0287[1]

Economy Trasher Number Twelve. This is one of the Nader Bunch. If you enjoy byzantine intrigues, you're going to *love* this profile. It's a veritable compendium of Sympathetic Constituencies in the environmental movement's web of interests and Ralph Nader is the most secretive node in that web.

Clean Water Action is a leader in the eco-pest industry that comes knocking on your door for a contribution at dinner time. But Clean Water Action doesn't work alone on its door-to-door canvassing. Its managers coordinate their canvassing with

Citizen Action
1406 W. 6th Street, 2nd Floor
Cleveland, Ohio 44113
Members: 2 million
Staff: 30
Phone: (216)861-5200

a Nader group founded in 1979 with revenues of $30 million in 1990, according to *Forbes* magazine, which published a Nader-style investigation of Nader in its September 17, 1990 issue. The *Encyclopedia of Associations*, on the other hand, which essentially publishes what groups tell them, shows a budget of $1.5 million for 1993. Under the leadership of Executive Director Ira Arlook, Citizen Action lobbies for environmental, insurance and health care legislation and supports political candidates. In its own language, Citizen Action works for "economic democracy and social justice," says its goal is "to make the concerns of the majority of Americans felt in economic, environmental, and political decision-making." It claims to only "conduct research, training and educational programs."

Citizen Action also coordinates its own and Clean Water Action's door-to-door canvassing with the **Public Interest Research Groups,** founded in 1970 with revenues of $20 million in 1990 and an estimated net worth of $8 million. The PIRGs are another Nader invention, with 25 state chapters on 90 college campuses, with state names appended up front, such as PennPIRG for Pennsylvania, WashPIRG for Washington—is Illinois PIRG called IllPIRG?. They are funded though mandatory or "negative checkoff" student fees. They sell publications, they litigate, and each state chapter has a professional lobbying staff.

United States Public Interest Research Group (1983)
Annual budget: $313,000 and net worth of $127,000
Members: 25,000
Staff: 11
215 Pennsylvania Avenue, S.E.
Washington, D.C. 20003
Phone: (202)546-9707
Gene Karpinski, executive director.

USPIRG acts as the PIRGs' Washington lobbying office.

But the **Fund for Public Interest Research** in Boston has been the headquarters for most PIRGs since 1982. In 1985 a federal appeals court declared New Jersey PIRG's mandatory fee violated First Amendment rights, and a suit against NYPIRG is pending. A UCLA student referendum barred CALPIRG from fee collecting.

Now, Citizen Action does not just coordinate its own, Clean Water Action's and the Public Interest Research Groups' door-to-door canvassing, they also coordinate **Greenpeace USA**'s—which works with another Nader group,

Public Citizen, Inc.
Annual budget: $7.7 million and net worth $3.4 million.
Supporters: 100,000
Staff: 12
P.O. Box 19404
Washington, D.C. 20036
Phone: (202)833-3000

Joan Claybrook, president. Ralph Nader's flagship organization, founded 1971, with 1990 revenues of $7.7 million and a net worth of $3.4 million.

Public Citizen does all sorts of Ralph Naderish things: Its Aviation Consumer Action Project lobbies agencies on airline industry regulation; Buyers Up peddles goods to members at discounts; Congress Watch lobbies Congress and works with Citizen Action; Critical Mass Energy Project fights for the "rapid phase-out" of nuclear power; the Health Research Group publishes *Health Letter*, a nifty newsletter with a circulation of 80,000 and sells litigation kits to plaintiff attorneys suing drug companies; the Litigation Group specializes in class action law suits.

A lot of the information used by the door-to-door kamikaze outfits appears to have been generated by the **National Environmental Law Center** (a PIRG "sister organization").

Let's see, this profile is supposed to be about Clean Water Action, isn't it? Okay, CWA reportedly got its seed money from Ralph Nader, but exactly how is not clear. David Zwick has been executive director of CWA since it was founded in 1971 and executive vice president of the allied Clean Water Fund since its founding in 1974, and he won't say.

Zwick has been employed almost exclusively as an activist of some sort for virtually his entire career. He served in the U.S. Coast Guard for four years after earning a B.S. from its academy in 1963. He holds an M.P.P. from the John F. Kennedy School of Government at Harvard University and a J.D. from Harvard University Law School. As soon as he got out of school, Zwick became a project supervisor for the Ralph Nader group **Center for Study of Responsive Law** and has been a Little Ralphie ever since. From 1975 to 1978 he was downstate coordinator and tax campaign coordinator of the **Illinois Public Action Council**. He worked with the **Environmental Policy Institute** and has acted as a consultant, lecturer, and writer.

CWA and all its Little Ralphies lobby to kill jobs and trash the economy on many issues, including "alternative" sewage treatment methods, junk-lawsuits to enforce Superfund, the Clean Water Act, the Safe Drinking Water Act, anti-pesticide activism, restriction of industrial waste treatment, groundwater "protection" which includes putting farmers out of business, source reduction of industrial pollutants by stopping the manufacture of goods, and all those other wonderful-sounding things that produce only laws that stop industry and do little or nothing on the ground except soak up vast amounts of money for little result. The group publishes *Clean Water Action News* quarterly.

Clean Water Action is definitely part of The Nader Bunch, but you mustn't say that too loudly. Ralph's Economy Trasher headquarters, the **Center for Study of Responsive Law**, will disavow all connection to Clean Water Action. So will USPIRG, except maybe admitting that it joined with Clean Water Action—*and* Citizen Action, the Environmental Policy Institute, Friends of the Earth, and the Oceanic Society—to urge a boycott of Exxon to get a rollback in gasoline prices in 1989.[2]

You'll get denials from Citizen Action, too, except maybe about having worked with CWA on a Lafayette Square demonstration against the Bush administration on water policy issues.[3]

But questions to The Nader Bunch must be phrased with extravagant care because of a pleasant pretense that there is nobody here but us chickens working in harmony and a nasty habit of accusing you of asking too many questions.

The Nader Bunch, said *Forbes* magazine about its investigation of the network, "eerily resembles nothing so much as John D. Rockefeller's original secret Standard Oil Trust. This 'shrewd and slippery device for evading responsibility,' in the words of the great muckraking journalist Ida Tarbell, 'had no legal existence. It was a force as powerful as gravitation and as intangible. You could argue its existence from its effects, but you could never prove it. You could no more grasp it than you could an eel.'"[4]

Forbes concluded, "The Nader Trust is just the same but considerably ruder."[5]

Perhaps they don't want to show any connection because The Nader Bunch relies a lot on tax-deductible money. Federal law is very touchy about using tax-deductible money to do lobbying and support political candidates, and many of the Little Ralphies do a lot of just that. If the IRS catches you intermingling funds between non-lobbying and lobbying outfits, or particularly between non-lobbying and political candidate support projects, they become surly and tend to strip you of your tax-exempt status and invite you to explain your misbehavior to a judge. The consequences can be a vacation at a clean, well-lighted federal facility long enough for you to read *Moby Dick*, *War and Peace*, Shakespeare's plays and all four volumes of Karl Marx's *Capital*—several times.

Forbes reported, "Citizen Action's Edwin Rothschild directly told FORBES that its canvassers push political candidates, a flagrant breach of their nonprofit status that Executive Director Ira Arlook was anxious to deny."

Oh, well, let's give them a break. Ralph Nader would never lie to us, would he?

Nader came to fame for writing *Unsafe At Any Speed* attacking General Motors for safety problems with their Corvair. Nader came to sainthood in 1966 when Senator Abraham Ribicoff (D-Connecticut) dragged General Motors executives before his subcommittee to confess they had set detectives on Ralphie and to issue an apology for investigating him. Nader came to power when he won a 1970 settlement of $425,000 in his invasion of privacy lawsuit against General Motors.

His quirky personal lifestyle has intrigued a generation. He seems to have taken a vow of poverty, maintaining for years that he subsisted on a mere $10,000 a year. It's gone up to $15,000 nowadays—the price of bread and water has risen shamelessly, no doubt.

Forbes says things may not be so austere for Ralphie. "Neighbors say, and have said for nearly 20 years, that Nader lives in a townhouse, worth perhaps $1.5 million and assessed at $7,400 annual property taxes, on Bancroft Place in northwest Washington, D.C. District records show the deed is held by Nader's sister Claire, who seems to work in his organization."

Ralphie denies it, and Ralph Nader would never lie to us, would he?

From tracking Ralphie's travels around the country giving speeches at the rate of 50 to 100 each year, we find that he charges on a sliding scale which reportedly hits university appearances for about $4,000 (Ron Arnold's daughter Andrea saw him while she was getting her degree at Stanford—almost nobody showed up but they paid anyway) and hotshot trial lawyer association meetings where the fee can go up to $10,000 and more. Where does all that money go? And, of course, we get the impression that Ralphie gets there on a bicycle or on foot.

Forbes says things may not be so austere for Ralphie.

"Oh, God, limousines and nothing but the best hotels," says a disillusioned former state Trial Lawyers Association official. "We got quite a bill when he was in town."

Ralphie denies it, and Ralph Nader would never lie to us, would he?

Well, maybe he has connections to Clean Water Action and maybe he doesn't. Ralphie doesn't have any connection to CNN's *Crossfire*—but ex-Nader employee Michael Kinsey is co-host. There are Little Ralphies ensconced everywhere in key positions. Clean Water Action's David Zwick is one of them. He was a leader in organizing a June 1989 "town meeting" between EPA administrator William Reilly and five eco-groups. CWA staffer Bridgit Shea said, "This event marked the first time an EPA head has met face-to-face with leaders of citizen groups whose constituencies face direct threats from pollution."[6]

Clean Water Action falls in the Establishment Interventionist Axis despite a significant constituency with eco-socialist preferences.[7] Most of its "clean water action" is directed to stopping technological progress, stopping economic growth, and killing jobs—for example, blocking the much-needed expansion of the Downington, Pennsylvania sewage treatment plant and killing Waste Management, Inc.'s ash fill permit in Bucks County so it couldn't operate a waste incinerator. Clean Water Action is not very good at making things happen, but is outstanding at stopping things from happening, like your paycheck.

CWA, like some two dozen other environmental groups, is highly effective at door-to-door and telephone fund raising—The Nader Bunch raises a staggering $48 million a year at your front door—and this is the place to see how it works. The Nader Bunch groups that prefer door-to-door canvassing are all coordinated, suggesting a far more centralized control than any one of these groups would care to admit. Clean Water Action, PIRGs all over the country, Citizen Action and the non-Nader Greenpeace USA all coordinate their canvassing through a single management network.

We could find no indication that any others join this loop. We are almost certain that the eco-group **In Defense of Animals**, which gets nearly all its money from door-to-door solicitation, never coordinates with The Nader Bunch. However, you've no doubt met somebody from The Nader Bunch at the door if you live in a moderately affluent section of a major urban area.

Why, you might ask, would environmental groups go door-to-door like a vacuum cleaner salesman, even in a recessionary economy, when direct mail is so much less hassle? As we saw in the profile of Greenpeace, even using the left's best direct mail gurus Craver, Mathews, Smith & Company, the comeback is small percentagewise, and unpredictable, and requires that the mailing list be worked assiduously over a period of time in order to pay off. Going door-to-door day to day, as unlikely as it sounds, is a steady source of predictable income, which allows eco-group leaders to plan for the future with a more assured budget.[8]

Eco-groups recruit canvassers mainly through newspaper want ads. The classified ads are the route into canvassing of more than 90 percent of all eco-pests. The ad may read, "Active Activists. Earn $2500 to $4000 this summer saving the [select one: whales, air, water, earth], up to $19K/yr. Paid Training, travel & advancement. If you work well w/people & are committed to the issues, call 1-800-ECO-CASH."

It's a way to get cheap foot soldiers and not too different from the come-ons for novice encyclopedia salesmen. In fact, the first eco-pest on record, Mark Anderson, was an encyclopedia salesman before he traded books and broadsides for a clipboard and political handouts.

The usual respondent to the eco-ad is an idealistic college student on summer break or a recent graduate just discovering that previous environmentalists made it impossible to find a real job so it becomes necessary to do something for which you are overqualified, like annoying people who just got home from work at a job that's looking a little shaky, too.

Once recruited, most eco-canvassers are briefly trained in the basics of no more than eight current issues, given a clipboard and a stack of political fliers, subjected to a song-singing pep rally, then hauled to the *turf*, i.e. the scene of the con, in the van of a group staffer and dropped off to spend four sweatshop hours interrupting people decompressing after a hard day or watching *Studs* or just sitting down at the dinner table.

The turf will most likely be the liberal suburbs of a big city, like Bryn Mawr next to Philadelphia, or if the city itself is big enough and liberal enough, like San Francisco, you may have to use your own car or take the bus to the group's designated upper middle class neighborhoods. Philadelphia has about six regular eco-pest organizations knocking on doors and San Francisco has more than twenty. Atlanta has about three regulars and Seattle two. Your name will already be on the clipboard list if the group is really efficient and uses such databases as *The Haynes Criss-Cross Directory*, which goes house by house, street by street just so direct sales people can call you by name at the door.

With so many competing clipboard carriers in America's major cities, there are occasional turf battles over whose street this is that have been known to degenerate into eco-rumbles as do-gooders slug it out for Mother Earth among the plastic flamingoes.

Once you open the door, you become a *contact*—whether you end up giving money or not, you've been contacted, so you're a contact. Then the eco-pest delivers his or her sales spiel, called a *rap*, i.e., tells you what he or she wants, just to make sure you understand that you're not going to get a set of Fuller brushes in six weeks and that you're being asked to give your money to a perfect stranger in return for nothing but hope—hope that your money will in some way result in saving the [whales, air, water, earth].

If you give one of the usual excuses, 1) I'm not interested in giving money to anybody who knocks on my door, or 2) I care about the [whales, air, water, earth] but I don't want to part with any money for [them, it], you will be *qualified*, i.e., told repeatedly what the eco-pest wants until one of two things happens: 1) You slam the door, or 2) You give in and agree to give some money.

If you select 2) You give in and agree to give some money, you will be *targeted*, i.e., haggled with to increase the amount of money you're willing to part with. For example, if you say, "Okay, here's twenty bucks." the eco-pest will target you to give thirty-six—"We ask folks to do $3 a month, Mr. Sucker."

However, just as you're writing the check, your wife or husband in the next room hears the sound of money draining away and yells, "Don't give any money to whoever's at the door, stupid, the sink just broke and we owe the plumber a thousand dollars," or some such. So the buck stops there. The eco-pest has been *spoused*, the proper fate for them all.

A sufficient number of eco-pests are *not* spoused to create a substantial cottage industry. The average environmental canvasser has a fundraising quota of $110 per four hour shift. That may sound like a great deal of money for an eco-pest to raise offering nothing more than a newsletter or political flier in only four hours of work. In fact the average take exceeds the quota by nearly half. It is not uncommon for an eco-canvasser to end the day with $200 or more.

For their bravery in facing hundreds of slammed doors during the shift, eco-pests are paid an average of $55 straight salary per day, plus a commission of 30 percent on everything they raise over the quota. Eco-pests don't get rich—the most they could expect to make is about $14,000 a year (that $19K/yr in the ad is mostly baloney), but, if you don't call out for pizza too often, you can do okay on $14,000 a year.

The telephone canvassers who will call you asking for more money in six months—your name is now the private property of the ecogroup that got money from you, and they also can and do sell it to merchandisers such as The Nature Company, Patagonia, Inc., and other mail order catalog retailing firms—can make $30,000 a year if they can stand the pressure of the telemarketing bull-pen. Telemarketing is a killer job that takes a natural motor mouth and a thick hide. But, even at $30,000 a year you don't get rich.

But the eco-groups that hire these folks do get rich. Figure the arithmetic: Most door-to-door groups have thirty or more offices nationwide. The average canvassing crew has twenty eco-pests in it. Let's say that only 20 of those groups send out only 15 canvassers a night (or afternoon, some places get better results earlier in the day). Let's say each canvasser makes only the quota—there are always slackers, even among environmental activists—and raises exactly $110 a night, five nights a week, fifty-two weeks a year. That's $33,000 a night, $165,000 a week, $660,000 a month, $7,920,000 a year.

That arithmetic is far too conservative, because the financial report that Greenpeace, Inc. (the lobbying arm of Greenpeace in America) files with New York State shows they alone took in $14,227,780 door-to-door nationwide in fiscal 1992. Their telephone solicitors brought in $1,830,939. Direct mail only brought in $36,161, as opposed to the 501(c)(3) Greenpeace Fund, which brought in $26,967,289 by direct mail that year, but only a piddling $4,348 by telephone solicitation, and a paltry $590,383 from door-to-door campaigns.

Forbes asserted that on any given summer night The Nader Bunch had 2,000 canvassers working the doors and bringing in a total of $48 million a year. The total budget of Greenpeace Fund is $48.6 million a year, Greenpeace, Inc. is $16.3 million for a total Greenpeace income of $64.9 million, and Clean Water Action is $11.6 million. Think of all that money, coming in every night in the form of $5 and $10 and $25 donations. That's no cottage industry, that's a money factory.

Is this "grassroots" activism? Are the people who gave money to a door-to-door hokum peddler a real constituency? Some are. Raising money is not the only purpose of direct canvassing. Eco-pests are educators and political triggers as well. Some of the contacts, even ones who will not give money, will take a flier and write a letter to a legislator—and yes, your Senator or Representative does pay attention to the mail, if there's enough of it. Direct door-to-door canvassing is one way to get a political message across without debate from competing viewpoints or dilution in the press by balanced reporting or fair comment. So the educational and persuasional dimension of door-to-door activism should not be discounted in counting all the money.

And speaking of all the money, where does it all go? Thirty to forty percent of what a doorstep donor gives to one of these eco-pests goes straight into the pest's pocket and stays there as his cut of the sale. The eco-groups don't admit that, because the cost of fundraising in a non-profit group is supposed to stay under twenty-five percent in order to be considered ethical. But there are no enforceable canons of ethics for the environmental movement. So Clean Water Action and Greenpeace and all the PIRGs and all the others can lie through their teeth and no one can do a thing about it.

Clean Water Action's 1989 fiscal report claimed that 26 cents of every canvassed dollar is spent fund raising, 65 cents went to lobbying and program work, and nine cents were spent on general and administrative costs. Greenpeace's report states that 38 cents of every dollar goes toward fundraising and 62 cents to the programs. Citizen Action allots 67 cents to program work and 33 cents to fund raising and overhead. None of the PIRGs, including U.S. PIRG, an independent national networking affiliate for all the states, will reveal any of their numbers, including budgets, salaries, fund raising costs, or anything else—they're a secret society, in effect. Call U.S. PIRG at 202-546-9707 and ask politely for their numbers. If they won't tell you, as they wouldn't tell us, you might think about asking the Internal Revenue Service to look into their non-profit status, because all of their numbers are supposed to be public information which they have no right to withhold.

Clean Water Action's Board of Directors includes Sophie Ann Aoki; William Fontenot; David Grubb; Peter Lockwood; Terry Reuther; Wendy Rockefeller; Patricia Schifferle; Barbara Taylor; Paul Twerdowsky; and David Zwick.

CWA claims to get 98 percent of its $11.6 million budget from door-to-door and telephone canvassing; 2 percent from other sources.

That two percent from "other sources" includes:

Mary Reynolds Babcock Foundation, Inc. gave $25,000 in 1989 for North Carolina Groundwater Protection Project.

The Boston Foundation, Inc. gave $15,000 in 1990 for education and organizing campaign for Boston neighborhood groups concerned with developing recycling programs.

Geraldine R. Dodge Foundation, Inc. gave $30,000 in 1989 for research and education in New Jersey, focusing on safe drinking water, control of toxic hazards and protection of natural resources.

The Charles Engelhard Foundation gave $20,000 in 1989.

Ruth Mott Fund gave $10,000 in 1989 for programs in selected states, national programs, and regional networking.

The Fund for New Jersey gave $10,000 in 1990 to continue Home SAFE Home education program and environmental shoppers campaigns, both aimed at helping consumers make environmentally sound choices.

Northwest Area Foundation gave $165,000 in 1989 to build capacity of public to contribute to development of groundwater policy in Minnesota.

Jessie Smith Noyes Foundation, Inc. gave $50,000 in 1990, a 2-year grant to protect groundwater by strengthening state-based advocacy and increasing collaboration among grassroots and national environmental and agricultural constituencies in Southern tier U.S.

Prince Charitable Trusts gave $25,000 in 1989 for operating support.

Public Welfare Foundation, Inc. gave $60,000 in 1990 for Grassroots Environmental Organizing Project, which will work to strengthen and expand its efforts in low-income and minority communities; plus $30,000 to the North Carolina chapter "for statewide organization that works with citizens, grassroots environmental groups and local officials to clean up and protect their surface and groundwater supplies from toxic contamination."

Town Creek Foundation, Inc., gave $10,000 in 1990.

Clean Water Action.
And all those folks who answer the door.
Job killers.
Economy Trashers.

Clean Water Action—Footnotes

1 *Public Interest Profiles 1992-1993*, Congressional Quarterly, Inc, Washington, D.C., p. 449.

2 "Six groups urge boycott of Exxon," by Philip Shabecoff, *New York Times*, May 3, 1989, p. A8.

3 "Earth Takes Center Stage," by D'Vera Cohn, *Washington Post*, April 15, 1990. p. A1.

4 *The History of the Standard Oil Company*, Ida M. Tarbell, 2 vols., McClure, Phillips & Co., New York, 1904.

5 "Ralph Nader, Inc.," by Peter Brimelow and Leslie Spencer, *Forbes*, September 17, 1990, p. 117-129.

6 *E Magazine*, September/October 1990.

7 See *Consumer Affairs Letter*, October 1988.

8 "I Was a Door-to-Door Ecopest," by David Borgenicht, *Philadelphia*, March 1992, p. 37.

Conservation International ▆▆▆▆▆▆▆▆▆▆

Conservation International (Founded 1987)
  Annual budget: $11,837,616 (1993)
    Staff: 57 total—41 professional; 16 support
    Members: 55,000 individuals
    Tax Status: 501(c)(3)
    Headquarters: 1015 18th Street, NW
       Suite 1000
       Washington, D.C. 20036
       Phone: (202)429-5660 Fax: (202)887-5188

Economy Trasher Number Thirteen. This Washington, D.C.-based environmental group was founded on February 1, 1987 as a breakaway from the Nature Conservancy, ostensibly in a dispute over protecting whole ecosystems rather than piecemeal lots. CI is another member, like the World Wildlife Fund, of the environmental movement's Global Interventionist Axis, which works to delay or prevent the development of market economies throughout the Third World with "debt-for-nature" swaps under the pretense of helping "sustainable development."[1]

Peter Seligmann, founder of CI and now its chairman of the board, did his undergraduate work at Rutgers, earned a Master's Degree in Forestry from Yale (where else?) and spent eight years as director of the California Nature Conservancy. He proved to be a stellar fundraiser, hustling $25 million to buy up private land and peddle it to the government.[2]

Because the Nature Conservancy has pretty well worked all the high-dollar contacts of the Mellon Interventionist Axis, and because California boasts its own panoply of fat cats, Seligmann became the envy of TNC's headquarters fundraising staff. Conservancy bosses William Blair and later Frank Boren wanted to tap Seligmann's California money for the national's own fundraising, and brought him to the high command in Virginia. Seligmann didn't mind going Back East, but he felt a proprietary interest in his Western domain and resisted TNC Command Central's demands, which is the real reason Conservation International broke away from the Nature Conservancy.

Seligmann took Conservancy staffer Spencer Beebe with him, along with seven or eight others, and quickly established CI as the new kid on the block with offices in Washington, D. C. Its mission was to save tropical rainforests. Beebe, a native Oregonian who came from a moneyed family, set up shop in Portland with a Conservation International Foundation operation of his own, which has subsequently broken away into a new organization called **EcoTrust** working exclusively in the Pacific Northwest. Movement power multiplies by splintering.

Seligmann is not the most dynamic leader in the environmental movement; he'd be the last person you'd notice at a Washington cocktail party.[3] His wife

Sue, on the other hand, is beautiful, outgoing, and brilliant—a Yalie like Peter—and the first person you'd notice at a Washington cocktail party. Her intelligence and ability is a good part of the reason for Peter's success.[4]

His view of environmental policy is mainstream interventionism as applied to foreign countries. We see no outright eco-socialist agenda in CI beyond the permanent nationalization of what were already government lands. For the origins of the debt-for-nature swap, see the profile of World Wildlife Fund.

Peter Seligmann's first project as CI leader was a debt-for-nature swap in Bolivia, South America's poorest nation, which typifies his approach: Part of the 3 million-acre Chimane Forest was covered by an agreement signed by Bolivia and Conservation International in July 1987 in which CI bought $650,000 of Bolivia's bank debt and the government agreed to set aside the equivalent in local currency for conservation projects. Part of the deal was an agreement by Bolivian President Jaime Paz Zamora to rezone existing timber concessions, but not revoke all timber rights, i.e., to hamper the market system, but not to nationalize it. Another part of the deal was to impose a new three-year land management plan on the Chimane Forest to specify logging practices, protection of flora and fauna, and insure participation by indigenous Indian communities. Wood exports made up roughly 5 percent of the country's total, which would be reduced by the rezone and management plan. Guillermo Mann, Conservation International's vice-president of science claimed that each of three large timber companies working the Chimane make $1.3 million in profit a year, but only pay $70,000 each to the state in taxes. "The difference is appalling," Mann said in an anti-capitalist tirade, "and has to be changed."[5]

How the country would make up for the loss of usable wood is not mentioned.

Peter Seligmann said of the deal in a *Christian Science Monitor* interview, "In the Bolivian agreement, 2 million acres are set aside as a biosphere preserve, and only the native Indians can use it. Then there's 2 million acres around it that are set aside as a sustainable-development region, the idea being let's develop it for cattle, for timber, for fisheries, for farming, for whatever can make money without destroying it."

There is no record that CI ever did any actual development on any of its debt-for-nature swaps anywhere in the world. None of its money that we could trace has ever gone to "Dirt Projects" where the money gets to the ground, but only for "Talk Projects"—consulting, planning, propaganda and the like—where the money gets turned into hot air. There will be no offices, apartments or factories in any of CI's "developments."

However, Seligmann said, "And let's develop it so it will be attractive enough that the World Bank, the Chase Manhattan Bank, and the Inter-American Development Bank will invest." CI's *modus operandi* differs somewhat from other debt-for-nature swappers in that CI frequently—but not always—establishes a local office of its own in the foreign country to receive the funds from the swap rather than contract them to an indigenous local group.

Seligmann had a pretty good idea how to get investment from those banks he mentioned because Rodolfo Silva of the Inter-American Development Bank and Francis X. Stankard, retired chairman of Chase Manhattan Overseas Bank, are members of his board of directors and able to make things happen.

One of Seligmann's early priorities was to attract a board of directors who could help with fundraising in the United States and influence in foreign countries. The CI Board of Directors includes chairman Peter Seligmann; and other members W. Stanton Avery of file-folder company fame; Michel Batisse, an environmental journalist frequently published in the *UNESCO Courier*; Skip Brittenham, Los Angeles lawyer; Yvon Chouinard, chief executive of sportswear maker Lost Arrow Corporation and of Patagonia, Inc., a mail order catalog retailing firm; Damaris Ethridge, a Florida investor; Fabio Feldmann, Brazilian congressman; Harrison Ford the movie star; Charles Hedlund a prominent businessman; Alan Hirschfield, financier who became a movie studio chief at Paramount, moved about Hollywood in several capacities, went back to the finance world, and then back into the media as Financial News Network CEO; William T. Hutton, a lawyer; Christine Jurzykowski, president of Fossil Rim Foundation, a private exotic game farm in Texas; Gordon Moore, another prominent businessman; Paulo Nogueira, an agriculturist from Sao Paulo, Brazil; F. Noel Perry, private investor in San Francisco; Leon Rajaobelina, former Minister of Finance in Madagascar; William Rogers, a Washington, D. C. lawyer; Andres Marcelo Sada, chairman of a Monterey, Mexico, company called CYDSA and director of the private environmental group Pronatura; Jose Sarukhan K., rector of the National Autonomous University of Mexico in Mexico City; Kenneth F. Siebel, Jr., president of Siebel Capital Management in San Francisco; Rodolfo Silva, special representative in Mexico of the Inter-American Development Bank in Costa Rica; Francis X. Stankard, retired chairman of Chase Manhattan Overseas Bank; Peter W. Stroh, CEO of Stroh Brewery in Detroit; Miguel Aleman Velasco, special ambassador from Mexico to lure foreign investment; Jose Koechlin von Stein, a businessman and philanthropist from Lima, Peru; and Alan N. Weeden, chairman of QV Trading Systems and president of the Frank Weeden Foundation.

Seligmann is an astute manager. Seeing that his organization had established a good network of foundation funding sources, he capped his membership at 55,000. The cost of servicing a membership is substantial. CI only *needs* enough members to maintain its tax-exempt status. The IRS requires that nonprofit organizations pass a test of "public support" five years after obtaining their 501(c)(3) status. The 501(c)(3), of course, allows contributors to deduct donations from their income tax. During this IRS test, the organization must prove that it is not the captive of any special interest, but is "publicly supported," meaning "the public support received must be from a representative number of persons within the community, and not from a few individuals or families."[6]

That means you have to have enough small donors to balance your big donors according to an IRS formula. If you pass the test, the IRS gives your nonprofit a 509(a)(1) proof of public support status. If you fail, you could be stripped of your 501(c)(3) tax exempt status, which could be a disaster for an unwary environmental group.

Seligmann determined that he could escape the treadmill of having to seek vast numbers of new members all the time without harming his operation. The effort required to keep a 55,000 membership level is substantially less than that required to grow in membership size, so he realized a significant savings which could go into his programs.

Seligmann's Bolivian deal kept to the classic Thomas Lovejoy pattern of debt-for-nature swaps, cooperating with Lidema, a private environmental group in Bolivia—working with a contract to obligate the foreign environmental group to perform the wishes of the American environmental group. CI did not take part in actual reforestation or tree-planting, nor did it ever supervise timber cutting or any other Dirt Project. However, it did "support" the Beni Forest Service by providing technical advice in forest ecology, planning, and development, according to Maria Teresa Ortiz, CI's Bolivia Program Director. In other words, no Dirt Projects, just Talk Projects.[7]

Conservation International has worked a number of debt-for-nature swaps, including a number of "firsts." In 1990, CI made a debt-for-nature swap that was the first to cancel both trade debt and bank debt—with the Central Bank of Madagascar in return for pledges to make inventories of endangered plants and animals, to generate environmentalist propaganda to the Malagasy people, to give technical and financial support to parks, preserves and other projects, to provide information for policy formation and to teach agricultural techniques that are less harmful than current slash-and-burn methods. The *New York Times* failed to note in their report on this swap that Conservation International's own office in Madagascar was the actual recipient of the funds, which were used for projects CI itself selected and negotiated.[8]

Steve Rubin, director of conservation finance at CI came up with the idea of simultaneously canceling trade credits and bank credits while doing research for a book on the economics of environmental issues, *Untying Your Money,* published in 1989 in Britain by Economist Publications. The Bankers Trust of New York Corporation holds much of Madagascar's debt to banks; a French subsidiary of the International Business Machines Corporation and Honeywell hold trade credits, with whom CI negotiated.[9]

In 1991 CI worked a deal in which, for the first time, a lending institution contributed debt directly to U. S. environmental groups, which would then turn over the debt to foreign environmental groups and institutions. BankAmerica Corporation forgave nearly $6 million of its outstanding loans to Latin American countries on condition that they negotiate with environmental groups and identify projects on which the money would be spent. Treasury Secretary Nicholas F. Brady said it was "an important development in the history of debt-for-nature swaps." Brady seemed oblivious to the fact that the mechanism was merely a ploy to fund projects of private environmental groups.

BankAmerica Chief Executive Richard M. Rosenberg said the bank would forgive the debt over a three-year period, beginning with $2 million in 1991. The debt repayments were to be made instead to the World Wildlife Fund and Conservation International and to the Smithsonian Institution. In this case, foreign debt was being used to enrich American environmental groups with no pretense of dealing through a local group in another country. The initial transaction was the transfer of $500,000 in Mexican debt to WWF and CI and $100,000 in debt of Ecuador to the Smithsonian.[10]

Bank of America also made a sweetheart deal with Conservation International to release a new series of checks to its customers, which were printed on recycled paper—and the bank would donate 50 cents to CI for each order of the new checks.[11]

Russell A. Mittermeier became president of CI in 1990, coming from the World Wildlife Fund as vice president for science from 1987 to 1989. He served as a director of four different WWF programs between 1979 and 1989. One of the few environmental group leaders who did not come through the revolving government/eco-group door, Mittermeier is a scientist of considerable repute. He earned his B.A. from Dartmouth and his Ph.D. in biological anthropology from Harvard. He has written five books and more than two hundred papers and articles. Beginning in 1977, he served as chairman of the Primate Specialist Group of the International Union for Conservation of Nature's Species Survival Commission (SSC), and as SSC's vice chairman for International Programs since 1985, and as chairman of the World Bank's Task Force on Biological Diversity in 1988 and 1989. He is also a member of the board of Wildlife Preservation Trust International and the Belize Zoo and a research associate at the Museum of Comparative Zoology at the State University of New York at Stony Brook.

CI has made considerable inroads into quieting potential controversies about debt-for-nature swaps. The problem of indigenous peoples, who are commonly locked out of national policy making, have received considerable attention from Conservation International. CI says it will not participate in any swap unless the indigenous people are an integral part of the negotiations (this does not include settlers). CI has also addressed a much more embarrassing problem: most indigenous peoples make their living by exploiting the rain forests that CI wants to save—in many cases they only object to logging or mining if they don't receive a piece of the action. CI racked its brains over how to make an income from a nature preserve to keep the Indians happy.

In Ecuador, they buttoned down the problem with buttons—made from the ivory-like tagua nut. Before plastic turned buttons into a dirt-cheap and plentiful commodity, many apparel makers used buttons made from tagua, which is common in Ecuador and Colombia. Conservation International found agents willing to revive the industry with the help of board member Yvon Chouinard, chief executive of Ventura, California-based Patagonia, Inc., who twisted the arm of Paul Hawken of Smith & Hawken Ltd., based in Mill Valley, California, another mail order catalog retail firm, to join with him in ordering tagua-nut buttons for their line of sportswear.[12] The two firms agreed to buy a million tagua-nut buttons from communities in northwestern Ecuador. The idea, bragged CI, was "to harvest a renewable crop instead of cutting down the trees for logs." No note was made that trees for logs are renewable too, especially in the fast-growing rain forests of the tropics, and income from renewable logs is vastly greater than from tagua-nut buttons—and you don't need an ideologically-attuned buyer on your board of directors to make a profit from logs. Even though CI put none of its own funds into the deal, it was the closest they have come to an actual Dirt Project. But the button makers live in an area where the annual per capita income is less than $1,000 a year, according to the Corporación de Investigaciónes para el Desarrollo Socio-Ambienta, the Ecuadoran environmental group coordinating the program. Besides Patagonia paying the button producers $80,000 to $90,000 in the first year, Smith & Hawken planned to spend $50,000 to $60,000 on the tagua. The companies also paid a combined licensing fee of $50,000 to CI. The public relations splash was worth a fortune.[13]

Conservation International also takes care of its own. In the first of its deals in Mexico, CI turned $4 million worth of foreign debt into $2.6 million in Mexican pesos to be distributed to five private environmental groups and the National Autonomous University, which operates a biological station in the Selva Lacandona, a rain forest in Southern Mexico. Jose Sarukhan K., rector of the National Autonomous University, is a board member of Conservation International. Is that self-dealing, or what?[14] A second Mexican swap for about $1.5 million was being negotiated by a private environmental group, Pronatura, according to the *Los Angeles Times.*[15] The head of Pronatura is Andres Marcelo Sada, a Monterey businessman. Señor Marcelo is a member of the board of Conservation International. Is that self-dealing, or what? Maybe it's not illegal, but is it right? It's just another example of American environmental imperialism, obligating foreign environmental groups by contract to do the bidding of American interventionists and eco-socialists.

A Bad RAP

Conservation International says it needed greater legitimacy in targeting specific areas for preservation. The save-the-rain-forest movement had no scientific answer to the question of *which* rain forests to save. So they developed an ecological SWAT-Team called the Rapid Assessment Program (RAP) to quickly survey unexplored tropical rain forest areas believed to have the greatest diversity of living species and rank them as world conservation priorities.

What really happened was that CI realized that *settlers,* the indigenous people of these foreign countries, were rushing into the most valuable lands and building homes, villages, and trails in the time-honored pattern of pre-emption that would ultimately put full title to the land in their hands. If that were allowed to happen it could immensely complicate CI's program of saving land from people who want it for themselves. Thus Slapdash Science came to the rescue in the hands of CI's Gringo Bio-Squad. Hello, Third World. We're from America and we're here to help you.

Russell A. Mittermeier, president of Conservation International, said, "RAP is cutting-edge biology that will set the conservation agenda for the next century. We know more about the surface of Mars than about these forests, the most diverse ecosystems on Earth. Now we will be able to show where the plant and animal species are concentrated while there is still time to protect them." Most of that is hyperbole—RAP, as we shall see, is hardly biology at all, and far more biologists have tromped around in tropical rain forests than on the surface of Mars, unless Mr. Mittermeier has been keeping some odd company.

There's a little problem with CI's RAP approach, however: Real science is anything but rapid, and the Rapid Assessment Program is nothing more than Bio-squads with lap-top computers running around in a few accessible developed areas of the rain-forest trying to form judgments and estimates of what's in the rest of the rain-forest. Your ten-year-old probably does a more reliable job of counting tadpoles.

Murray Gell-Mann, Nobel prize winning physicist and chairman of the MacArthur Foundation's world environment and resources committee, helped develop the RAP concept. He acknowledges the problem: "Because the accelerated research of the RAP team could be criticized for not being 'real' science," Gell-Mann told the *Christian Science Monitor*, "the use of top field biologists whose expertise could not be quarreled with is key to the program."[16]

Using reputable scientists instead of doing good science is the environmentalist equivalent to using the *ad hominem* argument in debate: If you can't present any good evidence to make your point, quote a beloved figure saying anything that sounds good.

The *Smithsonian* magazine gave us a picture of CI's top field biologists at work in a 1991 article by "To hell with you all" eco-writer Richard Conniff:

> They were like scholars in a great museum that was crashing down around them. They worked among the disappearing treasures with efficiency, dispatch and even humor, as if a lifelong student of antiquities could carefully record the exquisite details of a Greek amphora and then watch with equanimity as someone hammered it into dust; or as if the world's leading authority on Chippendale furniture could note the particulars, then stand by as side chairs and highboys were smashed to splinters around him.
>
> What these researchers were cataloging was only ostensibly less precious—one more rain forest being chain-sawed into oblivion, with no more than the usual assortment of plants and animals produced by millions of years of evolution and found nowhere else on Earth. The researchers were accustomed to this kind of destruction. They spend much of their time studying forests like this one and seeing them vanish.[17]

Now that we have the universe of discourse set up so that we have no idea what human needs are being met by this rain forest "being chain-sawed into oblivion," or what kind of management is used to regenerate the trees, and couldn't care less about the people who derive their food, clothing, and shelter from "this kind of destruction," we are ready to say "To hell with you all" and look upon the RAP researchers as unqualified heroes.

We first meet a botanist named Al Gentry, one of four permanent members of Conservation International's RAP team. Gentry, 46, is senior curator at the Missouri Botanical Garden and has the reputation of knowing more tropical plants than anyone who ever lived. The other three are Ted Parker, a 38-year-old research associate at Louisiana State University's Museum of Natural Science, an ornithologist able to identify most of the 4,000 bird species of the Neotropics—New World tropics—by their songs alone; Mammalologist Louise Emmons, 47, a Smithsonian research associate and author of *Neotropical Rainforest Mammals*; Robin Foster, 46, plant ecologist with the Smithsonian Tropical Research Institute (STRI) in Panama and known for his long-term study of rain forest dynamics on a 50-hectare plot at STRI's Barro Colorado Island station.

These experts had no other job than to make sure some local people did not claim this land for themselves. They did some unprofessionally crude guesswork based on one-shot hop-skip-and-jump sample collecting and expected people to applaud. People applauded. If you're working for an ideologically charged environmental group and your actual intended results are political— the government designation of preserves—then all the science you need is political science. These scientists gave the agenda of Conservation International's imperialism an undeserved jump into political hyperspace. We're sure they're very proud.

How could they do it better? Well, CI, take a hint from

African Wildlife Foundation (1961)
Annual budget: $4,676,000
Staff: 30
Nonmembership
1717 Massachusetts Avenue, N.W.
Washington, D.C. 20036
Phone: (202)265-8393
FAX: (202)265-2361

This outfit is not exactly an environmental group, but almost. It concentrates on the ground where the animals and people are, it does not hate human beings, it is not terribly political in its methods, and it doesn't particularly trash the economy of Africa to achieve its conservation goals. If it was a membership group and a little more rabid, its budget would qualify it as Economy Trasher Number Nineteen—it's richer than the Izaak Walton League of America and Friends of the Earth.

The African Wildlife Foundation began life as the African Wildlife Leadership Foundation and changed its name in 1982. AWF conducts programs training Africans in wildlife management and ecology. It actually established schools of wildlife management in Tanzania and Cameroon, and offers continuing support and scholarships for them. AWF also provides technical assistance in park and reserve management. And, wonder of wonders, it provides real *stuff*: vehicles, aircraft, tents, uniforms, radios and training to antipoaching patrols.

President Paul T. Schindler says his group maintains a field office in Nairobi, Kenya to monitor and administer its projects. AWF initiates and supports conservation education throughout Africa and supports management research. It works with environmental groups, but rarely takes their anti-human stance in issues and is far less political than practical. It doesn't buy up or tie up private or government land and it saves a lot of animals while trying to deal with people's problems at the same time. AWF recently found it necessary to join the ban-ivory campaign and put out a shamefully misleading mailer of the standard Economy Trasher variety, which was soundly thrashed in a fascinating newspaper hit-piece against the organization.[18]

AWF publishes *Wildlife News* three times a year, and also publishes wildlife handbooks and park guides to Africa.

Conservation International gets its funds 44 percent from foundation grants; 40 percents from individual donations and grants; 9 percent from memberships; and 7 percent from other sources.

Compton Foundation, Inc. gave $20,000 in 1989.

The Charles Engelhard Foundation gave $156,000 in 1989.

Ford Motor Company Fund gave $30,000 in 1990.

John D. and Catherine T. MacArthur Foundation gave $760,000 in 1989 for a program of collaborative conservation projects with Brazilian conservation groups in Atlantic forest, small grants program and development of Atlantic Forest Action Plan; plus $550,000 in 1989 for projects in Mexico: Selva Lacandona Project, re-opening Chajul Biological Station, conducting regional bio-geographic survey, developing management plans for Montes Azules Reserve, sustainable development projects in Chiapas and regional environmental education projects; plus $417,500 in 1989 for a program of training, field surveys and improved planning and management of reserves in Bolivia, Peru, Venezuela and Colombia. That's a total of $1,727,500 from one foundation in one year.

Joyce Mertz-Gilmore Foundation gave $20,000 in 1989 for general support.

M. J. Murdock Charitable Trust gave $78,000 in 1990 for studies on the Gulf of Alaska Ecosystem.

The Overbrook Foundation gave $40,000 in 1989.

The Prospect Hill Foundation, Inc. gave $20,000 in 1990 toward conserving Mexico's Midriff Islands in the Sea of Cortes.

Rockefeller Family Fund, Inc. gave $75,000 in 1990 to develop markets and ecologically sound production systems for tropical forest products; plus $50,000 in 1990 toward establishment of ad hoc Ecosystem Conservation Task Force to search for solutions to rapid destruction of North America's temperate rainforests.

Town Creek Foundation, Inc. gave $10,000 in 1990.

Conservation International.
Job killers.
Economy trashers.

Conservation International—Footnotes

1 "Reducing Debt, Protecting Nature," editorial, *Christian Science Monitor*, March 20, 1991, p. 20.

2 "On The Rise: Peter Seligmann, 37," by Susan Caminiti, *Fortune*, December 21, 1987.

3 See for example the lackluster interview with Seligmann in "Building economies and saving trees," by Cheryl Sullivan, *Christian Science Monitor*, January 4, 1988, p. 3.

4 See the bio on Seligmann in *Esquire* magazine, December 1989, p. 110.

5 "Bolivian Indians Protest Wrecking of Rain Forest," by James Painter, *Christian Science Monitor*, September 18, 1990, p. 4.

6 *Legal Handbook for Nonprofit Organizations*, Marc J. Lane, American Management Association, New York, 1980, p. 235.

7 "Conservation Efforts in Bolivia," letter by Maria Teresa Ortiz, *Christian Science Monitor*, August 4, 1989, p. 20.

8 Telephone interview with CI's Madagascar Project director, October 10, 1992.

9 "Agreement to Preserve Environment Provides Help for Madagascar," *New York Times*, August 28, 1990, p. C4.

10 "BankAmerica to Forgive Loans In Deal to Aid Rain Forests," by Martha M. Hamilton, *Washington Post*, June 12, 1991, p. C4.

11 "Bank of America to Donate Loans," American Banker, March 13, 1992, p. 6.

12 "2 Companies Agree to Use Product From Rain Forest," *New York Times*, September 12, 1990, p. D4.

13 "Will These Buttons Help Save the Rain Forests?" *Business Week*, September 24, 1990, p. 137.

14 "Mexican Debt Deal May Save Jungle," by Mark A. Uhlig, *New York Times*, February 26, 1991, p. A3.

15 "Mexico to Ease Debt, help the Environment," by Juanita Darling, *Los Angeles Times*, February 20, 1991, p. D5.

16 "Biologists Rate the Rain Forests," by Clara Germani, *Christian Science Monitor*, September 24, 1990, p. 14.

17 "RAP: on the fast track in Ecuador's tropical forests," by Richard Conniff, *Smithsonian*, June 1991, pp. 36ff.

18 "Crying Wolf Over Elephants: Scare tactics mislead public, yield big dollars," by Richard Bonner, *Seattle Post-Intelligencer*, February 14, 1993, p. E1, originally published in the *New York Times Magazine*.

National Parks and
Conservation Association

National Parks and Conservation Association (Founded 1919)
     Annual budget: $11,285,639 (1993)
              Staff: 43 total
           Members: 400,000 individuals
         Tax Status: 501(c)(3)
       Headquarters: 1015 31st Street, NW
                     Washington, D.C. 20007
                     Phone: (202)223-6722 Fax: (202)944-8535

Economy Trasher Number Fourteen. If ever there was a group diligent in the utter destruction of private property rights in America to expand federal control, the National Parks and Conservation Association is it. If ever there was a group diligent in eliminating visitor access to our National Parks, the National Parks and Conservation Association is it.

It is all the more shameful because NPCA was founded as the National Parks Association by Stephen Mather, the first director of the National Park Service, who created the system of private concessioners with private property rights—possessory interests—in their facilities to provide services for visitors to America's national parks.[1]

However, Stephen Mather from the very beginning intended the National Parks Association to act as a surrogate for the National Park Service, doing things for the parks that the government could not. In mid-1919, only three years after Congress founded the Park Service, Mather helped fund the startup of the Association and arranged for old Park Service colleague and publicity chief Robert Sterling Yard to be its executive director. Yard had been obliged to quit the Park Service because a new federal law prohibited the use of private funds to pay for federal work, and Mather, a wealthy Chicago borax magnate who took on the national park directorship out of personal idealism, had been paying the bulk of Yard's salary out of his own pocket. Mather politely twisted the arms of a few of his many distinguished colleagues to serve on his Association's board and give it the proper luster.[2]

As Horace M. Albright, Mather's successor as Director of the National Park Service, wrote in his autobiography:

> It was organized along the lines of the American Civic Association, with several distinguished national leaders on its board. Its president was J. Horace McFarland of the American Civic Association, and vice presidents were Nicholas Murray Butler, president of Columbia University, Congressman Billy Kent of California, Henry Suzallo, president of the University of Washington, and John Mason Clarke, chairman of the geology and paleontology section of the National Academy of Sciences. The stated purpose of the National Parks

Association was "to defend the National Parks and National Monuments fearlessly against the assaults of private interests and aggressive commercialism."[3]

The association's purpose mirrored Mather's vision of private concessions in the parks as a public utility, private companies given government monopoly status under strict regulation as a way to prevent the kind of "aggressive commercialism" he had observed in Yellowstone, where agents of competing hotels and stage companies practically dragged visitors off arriving trains to get their business. The "assaults of private interests" Mather defended against included attempts to build railroad lines in spectacular natural features, cut giant sequoias for exhibition displays and take water from parks for nearby farms or mines. Although the modern NPCA still uses Mather's words in its anti-private-property campaigns, they had a very different meaning to the founders of the organization.[4]

Bob Yard, financed by Mather's wealth, served as president of the National Parks Association until 1936 when he left to become secretary and then president of the Wilderness Society (see profile), where he remained until his death in 1945.

He was a prickly leader of the National Parks Association and, particularly after Steve Mather's debilitating stroke in 1928, made enemies in the National Park Service for his purism: he opposed recreation in the parks, feeling their mission should be educational, scientific and inspirational. Yard was the original national parks elitist. He opposed the inclusion of "inferior" areas such as the Everglades—he called it "a promoters' proposition," which infuriated Florida promoters; Jackson Hole—which infuriated the Rockefellers, who wanted control of the park concessions there; and Kings Canyon—which infuriated the Sierra Club's leaders, who wanted exclusive use of the area.[5]

Yard's purism and dictatorial style rubbed too many people the wrong way. He "retired" as National Parks Association secretary in 1934 and as its editor in 1936. After Yard departed for the Wilderness Society, the association assumed a more professional and credible tone.

As director of the park service, Horace Albright was an important member of the National Parks Association during Yard's early campaigns lobbying against dams being built in the parks, irrigation works being constructed using park waters in Yellowstone Lake, or railroad projects across park lands. The "aggressive commercialism" Mather had in mind only included truly disruptive projects, not the visitor accommodations and transportation services his Association came to oppose under later leadership.

Albright also revealed that from 1926, the National Park Association had substantial support from the Rockefeller interests, beginning with John D. Rockefeller, Jr. Albright himself sat on two Rockefeller boards of directors: Jackson Hole Preserve, Inc. (for thirty-seven years) and Colonial Williamsburg (1935-1958). When Albright left the Park Service in 1933 he became vice-president and chief operating officer of United States Potash Company, most of whose potash deposits were on leased federal lands in New Mexico. Albright's U.S. Potash offices were in Rockefeller Center, a few floors from the Rockefeller nonprofit network offices.

Albright maintained his membership in the National Parks and Conservation Association his entire long life—he wrote his autobiography at age 95. Rockefeller money remains to this day a source of major grants to the National Parks and Conservation Association.[6]

The Rockefeller-style agenda of gobbling up private land to control The Two Nasty Things, residential development and commercial agriculture, is quite visible through the nobody-here-but-us-tree-huggers facade of the National Parks and Conservation Association today. So is the old-style Rockefeller secrecy in gaining control of private land so it can be transferred to the federal government.

However, although the Rockefeller style is clearly visible, the Rockefeller interests are not the dominant policy source of the National Parks and Conservation Association. The group's financial support and policy-making influence is sufficiently fragmented that several elite family foundations—including the Mellons—NPCA's management and its board of directors share the right to call the shots. Thus we locate NPCA on the Establishment Interventionist Axis rather than the Rockefeller Interventionist Axis.

The National Parks Association's magazine had grown to be a recognized leader in the field by 1960. Its membership grew from about 5,000 in 1960 to 55,000 in 1972, a reflection of the burgeoning environmental movement. The NPA joined with other eco-groups and helped in the campaigns to block a dam proposed for the Grand Canyon, stopped a proposed Everglades jetport, and fought to stop oil development in Alaska.

The group enlarged its name to National Parks and Conservation Association in 1970, a reflection of its leaders' sense of an expanding mandate. During the 1970s, the association took active positions in support of non-park issues—more public transportation, pollution abatement, and control of human overpopulation—which generated controversy among its members and directors about the group's purpose. NPCA even joined a bizarre coalition seeking to cut off all types of illegal immigration, especially from Latin American countries.

By 1980 the National Parks and Conservation Association was convinced "that the survival of national parks is no longer a regional or national question, but perhaps even an international problem." It stood in the same ranks as the Sierra Club, the National Audubon Society and the Wilderness Society—a far different organization than its founders envisioned.[7]

NPCA has been headed since 1980 by President Paul C. Pritchard (salary, $108,000 a year), who was appointed to the position after serving as the Carter administration's deputy director of the Heritage Conservation and Recreation Service, the highest ranking career position in the U. S. Department of the Interior. There's that revolving door again. Out of government, into the environmental movement, where he could be the lobbying surrogate of the National Park Service under the mantle of the selfless nonprofit group. Pritchard holds a B.A. in humanities, a Master's in economics and natural resources, and has completed postgraduate work at Harvard University.

The Heritage Conservation and Recreation Service (HCRS) was a creation of the Carter administration. In 1978, Interior Secretary Cecil Andrus, following the environmental movement's agenda of more preservation and less recreation, abolished the old Bureau of Outdoor Recreation (BOR) and replaced it with the HCRS. It absorbed not only the activities of the BOR, but also the work of the Office of Archaeology and Historic Preservation and the National Natural Landmarks Program, both units of the National Park Service. Andrus appointed Chris T. Delaporte as director of HCRS and Paul Pritchard as deputy director.

Delaporte badly misjudged his constituency. He paid more attention to the natural landmark program, following the will of the National Parks and Conservation Association, than to historic preservation issues. He thus alienated his supporters in the historic preservation arena, who were already worried about the blurring of distinctions between natural and cultural resources. In 1980, the National Conference of State Historic Preservation Officers voted "no confidence" in HCRS and its director. Delaporte's personal behavior became the subject of scandalous revelations in the press, which hurt the agency.[8]

The presidential administration of Ronald Reagan put a swift end to the HCRS. Early in 1981 Interior Secretary James Watt—who had been director of the Bureau of Outdoor Recreation from 1972 to 1975—abolished the Heritage Conservation and Recreation Service and transferred to the National Park Service the organization and its programs, excepting only the national grant program of the Land and Water Conservation Fund, which was assigned to the Office of the Secretary. The huge array of projects that went to the park service included administration of the State portion of the Land and Water Conservation Fund, the Nationwide Outdoor Recreation Plan and State Comprehensive Outdoor Recreation planning, the Urban Park and Recreation Program, Park and Recreation Technical Services, Federal Land Planning, planning for the National Wild and Scenic Rivers System, the National Trails System, Natural Area Programs, the National Register of Historic Places, National Historic Landmarks, Historic Preservation, Technical Preservation Services, National Architectural and Engineering Record, and Interagency Archaeological Services. Pritchard, as second in command of HCRS, had direct control over many of these agencies.[9]

Paul Pritchard, we will come to realize, is one of the environmental movement's best time binders, a one-man institutional memory who has kept old environmental expansionist plans from the Carter years alive through the Reagan and Bush era and safely into the Clinton administration. He has been the movement's highest bridge over troubled waters. His power and reach are awesome. There are many items on Mr. Pritchard's agenda, and your private land is one of them.

So is your nearest national park—and all the rest of them. The National Parks and Conservation Association does everything it can to keep people out of the national parks. Odd as that may seem, it is the logical consequence of protecting the parks. From whom do you protect them? Visitors, of course. NPCA published a study in 1990 pointing with alarm at the crowds that visit parks, saying that visitors are destroying wildlife and the environment in the parks, none of which is true.[10] What NPCA really objects to is the "deterioration of the park experience," by which they mean the presence of other people, particularly those with different views about parks. It's Bob Yard's old philosophy that people were coming to the national parks for the wrong reasons—for *recreation*, heaven forbid. In 1992, NPCA went so far as to seek a ban on skiing, golf, and tennis in Yosemite National Park in California, only the latest in a long series of attacks against the public use and enjoyment of parks that evidently belong only to "everybody," who isn't a skier or golfer or tennis player.

In 1989, NPCA sponsored a private commission which recommended steps to reduce and eventually eliminate visitors from many national park areas.[11] The group sought to eradicate snowmobile trails from Voyageurs National Park,[12] to shut down a visitor airport near Glen Canyon National Recreation Area,[13] to discourage horseback riding at Manassas National Battlefield Park,[14] to keep people from viewing ancient Indian petroglyphs by blocking overnight accommodations,[15] and to stop scenic flights into the Grand Canyon with an Act of Congress.[16] NPCA even filed suit against Garfield County, Utah, for attempting to widen and pave a former stock trail that connects Capitol Reef National Park to Glen Canyon National Recreation Area, characterizing "Burr Trail" as a hiking-only trail in its magazine to convince its members that was being turned into a highway, a perception that generated dollars for its fundraising efforts.[17] NPCA's Barry Tindall testified before the House Ways and Means Committee trying to impose an excise tax on recreational vehicles that would discourage their users from visiting national parks.[18] NPCA submitted legislation to impose a departure fee on foreign visitors that would discourage them from visiting national parks.[19] The group opposed improvements in visitor access at Chickamauga.[20] The thick catalog of NPCA's anti-visitor campaigns is appalling.

Fooling the Faithful

NPCA is also aggressive in trying to create new national parks. An April 1, 1988 fundraising appeal from Paul Pritchard was headlined, Help Us Create A New Generation of National Parks While There Is Still Time. "Forty-eight potential new National Parks are located all over the American map," Pritchard wrote, "and the names stir the heart:"

> from the Tallgrass Prairie in Oklahoma to the Florida Keys; from New England's Connecticut River to California's Big Sur; from Hells Canyon in Oregon to the Atchafalaya Basin in Louisiana.

There's one little problem with most of these places with poetic names: They're somebody's private property. Pritchard couldn't care less. And he never told his members. "You and I must act now to create these new National Parks," demanded Pritchard, "because whatever we fail to save now, will be lost forever. Each of these natural areas is facing immediate threats from the outside."

Threats? From what? The answer is private ownership. People using their land to farm and to build homes and whatever else they please to do with what is rightfully theirs. That threatens Paul Pritchard. That threatens the National Parks and Conservation Association. Because they want to nationalize that private property to create new parks.

Pritchard's appeal never mentions private property. The whole four page letter just talks about natural wonders suffering irreversible effects. From what? Silence. Scenic grandeur is under pressure. From what? Silence. We are in a race against time to save these places. From what? Silence. NPCA members have no idea what their leader is asking them to do, to take private property away from its rightful owners in order that Congress may designate it a new National Park.

Pritchard's appeal, of course, had this punchline: "Will you join me in this great cause with a special contribution of $35?" Send money. Send money. Send money.

The campaign brought in hundreds of thousands of dollars. It was all used to destroy private property rights. The donors never knew. It's probably immoral to play upon peoples' gullibility and ignorance to raise bigtime donations, but it's not illegal. NPCA's power to manipulate words and symbols, to stir the fears and hopes of its members, is formidable.

NPCA also uses its power and prestige to stop development of lands *outside* national parks, saying that such activities would interfere with views from inside the parks. This landscape concept is called a "viewshed." We realize the term is vaguely ridiculous, but it has the force of law in the hands of government agencies pressured by environmental groups. It faintly resembles the notion of a watershed, with the falling water replaced by falling views. Presumably, if you stand somewhere and look around, a view gets shed upon you by the surrounding landscape. The environmentalist ideology appears to be that if anything human exists in that landscape, it hinders the view from being properly shed upon you, so it must be controlled and removed.

NPCA has acted to block petroleum exploration outside Theodore Roosevelt National Park,[21] fought an irrigation project outside the Black Canyon of the Gunnison,[22] and tried to stop developer Rex Baker from building a resort adjacent to Rocky Mountain National Park, saying it would disturb the area's ecosystem.[23] If the principle that nothing should be done that can be seen from inside a national park were to be applied to the nation as a whole, there would be no civilization at all in any of the eleven Western states and very little in the East Coast chain stretching from the Great Smoky Mountains National Park in North Carolina to Acadia National Park in Maine—which would suit NPCA policy-makers just fine.

What's Yours Is Negotiable

The gravest danger to the American way of life is the erosion of private property rights being carried out by environmental groups working with government agencies. The National Parks and Conservation Association is as dangerous as the Nature Conservancy and considerably more dangerous than the other 900 land trusts in America, since it has the best of all possible cover stories: We're Protecting *Your* National Parks.

The true story is: Your Land is Our Land.

By 1987 NPCA had targeted two million acres of private land within the parks for direct government takeover,[24] and 71.4 million acres more to expand the national park system.[25] A great deal of hunting land is included.[26] Beyond that, NPCA has targeted more than 90 million acres in the National Natural Landmarks Program, to bring them completely under land use control of the National Park Service.[27]

NPCA and the National Park Service have systematically and continuously worked together for decades to destroy private property rights through numerous programs. It is important to grasp the variety and scope of these property-taking programs, because they masquerade in charming camouflage.

How the Parks Work

In order to understand the National Parks and Conservation Association, we have to understand the National Parks.[28] Everybody has heard of national parks. There are currently 50 places called national parks. But the National Park Service, an agency of the U.S. Department of the Interior, manages a hodgepodge of 367 units (at press time) with diverse names such as national monuments, national recreation areas, national historical parks, and national seashores. The NPS divides up their 367 areas into three broad categories: Natural Areas, Recreation Areas and Historical Areas—these divisions are falling out of use within the Service, but help the outsider look in.[29]

Natural Areas include National Parks (usually large in area and protecting a variety of resources; examples: Grand Canyon and Yellowstone), National Monuments (smaller but protecting at least one major feature such as Devil's Tower in Wyoming), National Preserves (such as Big Thicket in Texas), National Environmental Education Landmarks and Registered Natural Landmarks, generally small places.

Historical Areas include National Historic Sites, National Historical Parks, National Memorials, National Military Parks, National Battlefields, National Battlefield Parks, National Battlefield Sites, National Cemeteries, and National Historic Landmarks.

Recreation Areas include National Parkways (roads such as the Blue Ridge Parkway), National Recreation Areas, National Seashores, National Lakeshores, National Scenic Trails, National Scenic Riverways and National Wild and Scenic Rivers.

Now that you're dizzy with understanding, it gets more confusing. The National Park Service also controls or exercises some form of jurisdiction over numerous classifications of land *not formally in the park system.*

Greenways: these are "linear" parks along roads, rivers, trails, anything in a line. They run through urban, suburban or rural sites and are intended to connect separate parks into a continuous system under a federal-regional web of jurisdiction.

National Natural Landmarks, a "voluntary" "cooperative" program "honoring" landowners whose property has been declared "nationally significant" by environmentalists and the National Park Service. The program was created by the Nature Conservancy in 1961 as a harmless-sounding device to incrementally bring private land first into federal recognition, then under federal control and finally into federal ownership—a simple feeder system to create new park units. The Nature Conservancy wanted to be a National Natural Landmark surrogate for the NPS, which eagerly adopted the idea.

Greenline Parks are, according to a National Parks and Conservation Association book on the subject, "a large scenic landscape area which is protected by law and regulation from being overtaken by unplanned development to the extent that it retains its natural scenic or historic attributes. The area is often in productive use by traditionally low-impact land-oriented industries like fishing, farming, ranching or timbering. The protections for a such a landscape are cooperatively arranged and managed by citizens and agencies on the local, state and federal levels, usually through a joint commission."[30]

Examples would be the Pinelands preserve in New Jersey, ruled by a joint state-federal commission and the Columbia River Gorge National Scenic Area in Washington and Oregon, ruled by a joint bi-state / federal commission.

Greenlining as a verb, the same NPCA book tells us, is "the process of establishing and maintaining a greenline park. This process includes both community and federal involvement in analyzing the landscape's resources, deciding on priorities for preservation and economic development, setting up legal and regulatory protections, and following through by managing the landscape according to an agreed-upon plan."

In December 1981, the National Parks and Conservation Association released its report, *Greenline Parks: Potential New Areas*, prepared for the President's Council on Environmental Quality. A Park Service official, J. Glenn Eugster, who was then chief of the Division of Natural Resource Planning, sent a copy of the NPCA report to a number of environmental groups along with a list of candidate areas in fourteen states, saying: "I thought the report would be of interest to you. More importantly, I feel that the greenline park concept to conservation is a technique worth investigating as we pursue our individual and collective agendas." It is noteworthy that Mr. Eugster considered the NPS and the environmental movement to have a collective agenda.[31]

What greenlining boils down to is that some environmental group which has a surrogate arrangement with the national park service decides that your landscape should be greenlined and gets various layers of government to go along with it. Then privately owned land is encircled with a boundary drawn by environmentalists—the Greenline—and the land is allowed to stay in private title, but is strictly controlled by an appointed commission overruling the choices of both the landowners and locally elected officials. That way the environmentalists get control of your land without having to pay for it—although legal challenges may change that.

In all the Greenline parks currently established, local governments have lost all of their authority and local residents have been reduced to little more than serfs. That NPCA line about "community involvement" is a joke—the only thing that resembles community involvement is normally a few local land-owning environmentalists who donate the first pieces of land, playing the Judas Goat leading their neighbors to slaughter.

The model and key example of a Greenline Park is the Columbia River Gorge

National Scenic Area, land flanking the Columbia River in Oregon and Washington. Six counties, twenty-three towns, 292,000 acres, and 41,000 Americans fall inside the Greenline, along with miles of private land. The scenic area is ruled by a commission appointed by the Governors of the two states, who had to sign a bi-state compact to ratify the Act of Congress creating the area.

In operation, the Gorge Scenic Area has proven itself a nightmare of restrictions on private property use that has stopped all economic growth and brewed antagonism nearly to the point of civil insurrection. The Park Service is not the only Greenline Land Grabber. Anybody in the federal domain can get into the Greenline act: Columbia Gorge is administered by the Forest Service, U.S. Department of Agriculture.

The uproar caused by Greenlining has led to a more recent Park Service buzzword,

Partnership Parks, whatever those are, generally presented as a friendly attempt to form local "partnerships" with NPS "technical assistance." This Partnership strategy looks like Greenlining without using the nasty G Word. It appears to mean strict protection "without total public agency ownership," while the partnership appears to actually be with environmental groups to co-opt local governments and take their authority away from them. The Partnership Park idea was explained at a Baltimore, Maryland workshop in June 1991: First, use "studies" of an area of private land to build political momentum in advance of public notification so that property owners who are aversely affected find out too late to mount an effective opposition campaign. The National Park Service Partnership Park idea was presented at a workshop sponsored by the

Rails-To-Trails Conservancy (1985)
    Annual budget: $1,544,293 (1991)
    Members: 71,600
    Staff: 25 professionals and clerical
    1400 16th Street, N.W., Suite 300
    Washington, D.C. 20036
    Phone: (202)797-5400 Fax: (202)797-5411

Another land trust, this one run by President David Burwell, along with six state groups, to establish trails on abandoned railroad rights-of-way all over the nation. What that means is that RTC advocates, legislates and regulates private land away from its proper owners in corridors of railroads whose tracks have been abandoned.

It works this way: Many early railroad rights-of-way crossed private property. The railroad rights-of-way then constituted an easement for public transportation over that private property, with the provision that the land under the rail corridor would revert back to the private owner upon abandonment. These were called reversionary property rights. The railroad used the corridor, but the landowner who had given the rail easement still owned the underlying land.

It was a good system. It was commonplace for a farmer in Missouri, for example, to watch the Missouri-Kansas-Texas locomotive hauling freight across his back forty, happy in the knowledge that his land was working to help America grow great and strong, and that when, in the course of time, his descendants might see the railroad abandon its track, they would get his land back from under those rails.

The Rails-To-Trails Conservancy has made a million-dollar business of taking those reversionary rights away from their private owners and converting the corridors to hiking and biking trails. The theory is, "It's still a transportation corridor, isn't it?" The Interstate Commerce Commission unfortunately agrees with RTC. So now hundreds of thousands of land owners have hikers and bikers wandering all over their property, not staying on the right of way, picking fruit from their orchards and vandalizing their homes.

And because Interstate Commerce Commission rulings have virtually extinguished owners' reversionary property rights through a number of key cases brought by environmentalists, citizens rarely get just compensation for the theft of their land, which now amounts to 242 trails covering more than 3,100 miles of what should be private property.

The federal government also refuses to enact good-citizen laws on hikers and bikers to make them responsible for their intrusions or the damage they do to private property.

It's just another demonstration of the overwhelming power the environmental movement has to destroy private property anywhere it pleases.

The Rails To Trails Conservancy works in more than thirty states with many of the other 900 land trusts in America, and with the Sierra Club.

RTC has over 71,000 members, with chapters in Illinois, Michigan, Ohio, Pennsylvania and Washington State. It issued a 1990 historical study, *Railroads Recycled: How Local Initiative and Public Support Launched the Rails-to-Trails Movement, 1965-1990.* It is an economy trasher *par excellence.* Read it and you'll see how the environmental movement will do anything to keep land out of private ownership.

The National Park Service has helped to fund the activities of the Rails To Trails Conservancy, particularly a traveling seminar series titled, "Creating Trails from Abandoned Railroad Corridors." RTC publishes activist and legal guides to defeat private land owners. Its quarterly newsletter, *Trailblazer,* comes with membership dues of $18, and the periodic *Guide to America's Rail-Trails* is a directory of trails RTC has taken from private owners.

RTC, like the Sierra Club, offers members a VISA affinity group card. RTC receives $10 for each new account opened and a percentage of every retail sale made with the card.

RTC plans to take every last mile of abandoned railroad right-of-way in America and kill the reversionary property rights to prevent the land from returning to its rightful owners.

Among the grants:

Patrick and Anna M. Cudahy Fund gave $26,950 to establish office in Illinois.

Geraldine R. Dodge Foundation, another fraction of the Rockefeller money, gave $35,000 in 1989 for efforts in New Jersey, coordinated by northeastern field office in Morristown, to convert abandoned rail lines into publicly owned corridors for hiking, biking, horseback riding and other recreational activities.

The Richard King Mellon Foundation gave $200,000 in 1989 toward a challenge grant to help establish new state-wide chapters.

M. J. Murdock Charitable Trust gave $10,000 in 1990 to establish Washington State Chapter.

The San Francisco Foundation gave $11,500 in 1990 to explore incorporating abandoned railroad corridors in Bay Area's network of trails and greenways.

When the National Park Service gets involved with one of these rails to trails deals, it's an example of a Partnership Park.

We know this is getting thick, but the latest attempt by environmentalists to increase the power of the National Park Service is the **Heritage Conservation Act**, which would create a new category of lands under federal control called "National Heritage Areas," declared by NPS to be "nationally significant." Congress has not yet accepted the idea, but the National Parks and Conservation Association and others are lobbying steadily, year after year, to get it passed—eventually.

Key concepts include authorizing the National Natural Landmark Program mentioned above; *Buffer Zones* surrounding all NPS sites; an official list of *Endangered Sites* intended to justify emergency powers; the power of injunction; fines up to $25,000 per day and jail terms for disobedient landowners; emergency acquisition procedures that classify every landowner a "willing seller" whether they are willing or not. A version of the bill was introduced into the Senate in late 1990 as a trial balloon that sank, and a refined version (S. 2556) was introduced on April 8, 1992 by Sen. Dale Bumpers (D-AR), which also failed to develop. It appears to be another legislative campaign like that surrounding the 1964 Wilderness Bill crusade: environmentalists doggedly pushed it year after year, evolving and refining its details until it passed.

The Empire Builders

In case you haven't figured it out already, the national parks are not just a system of wonderful places that the government is protecting for all of us and future generations.

The parks are legally owned and managed by the National Park Service. It's a bureaucracy. And bureaucracies grow. Empire Building is the chief occupational disease of bureaucrats, and the National Park Service is not immune to infection.[32]

Park Service, Park Service, how does your garden grow?
Taking people's private land by all the tricks we know.

How does the Park Service take peoples' land? Since only Congress has the power to designate new units for inclusion in the park system, the Park Service needs new land control devices and private citizen surrogates to forward its interests and lobby Congress—and the National Parks and Conservation Association was founded by the first Director of the National Park Service to be that surrogate. Other groups, such as the Nature Conservancy and Conservation Fund, later volunteered as surrogates for their own reasons, mostly money and power.

The first few national parks were carved from the federal domain—Yellowstone, Mount Rainier, Yosemite, Grand Canyon, and all the other grand old natural areas we all think of when we say "national park." Later units were the result of donations by wealthy philanthropists such as the Rockefeller gifts of the Grand Tetons in Wyoming and Acadia National Park in Maine. Some were combined state and private donations, such as the Great Smoky Mountains and Shenandoah.

The Park Service had a problem with private land from the outset: original settlers whose valid claims, homesteads and villages were surrounded by new parks—inholders, people owning private land within or near the boundaries of a government area. Shortly after the National Park Service was founded in 1916, its "Creed" instructed park officials to go after those private inholdings and nationalize them as rapidly as possible.[33]

Some of the most horrendous stories of federal abuse came from the 1930s land condemnations in Shenandoah National Park, including helpless old ladies in handcuffs being dragged off their land by law officers.

But most of the truly magnificent federal areas had been protected by the 1930s, and the NPS lust for Empire Building hadn't even got a good start yet. Park Service Director Horace M. Albright, one of the founding members of the National Parks and Conservation Association, recommended that the Park Service take jurisdiction over the military sites and national monuments previously under other agencies.[34] Secretary of the Interior Harold L. Ickes agreed and arranged a cozy meeting with President Franklin D. Roosevelt at President Hoover's camp on the Rapidan River in Virginia.[35] Albright said what he wanted, FDR asked no questions and ordered it done. On June 10, 1933, a couple of months before Albright left government to be executive of U.S. Potash Company, FDR signed Executive Order 6166 reorganizing the National Park Service, which transferred the military sites and national monuments to the NPS. Things are simple if you belong to the Aristocracy of Pull.[36]

After a couple of decades, just about all the federal areas available had been absorbed into the Park Service. The U.S. Forest Service had thwarted losses of national forest acreage to the Park Service by giving their scenic lands special recreation or preservation status.[37] In the 1950s it became clear that if the Park Service Empire was to grow, the Emperor had to take private land, and those historical parks Albright had brought in made an attractive costume to hide the Emperor's naked hankering.

Documenting the Scandal

The first taking of all-private land for a federal park happened near Boston, Massachusetts. It was ostensibly intended to commemorate the locale where the American Revolution began.

We would never have known what really happened if it was not for Erich Veyhl. He has been documenting abuses by the National Park Service for many years—because he's suffered the abuses himself. Erich is a slim, bespectacled young man who lives in Concord, Massachusetts and owns a residence in Maine, where he hopes to move one day. He's the quintessential engineer. Very bright. Very logical.

Very methodical. Works for a Boston-area high-tech firm.

Erich learned the hard way that you have to organize politically if you want to protect your basic rights, such as life, liberty and property. The National Parks and Conservation Association and several other environmental groups elbowed their way into Maine and promoted all kinds of land control projects, and one project, a new national park, threatened to take Erich's home site by condemnation—along with another million acres or so.

A 1980 study by the National Park Service recommended a comprehensive review of the park system and NPCA jumped in and made recommendations to create 86 new National Parks, including four in Maine. NPCA President Paul C. Pritchard said, "Our goal was to find lands of national significance, the criteria used by Congress when it creates parks."[38]

One of NPCA's proposals, a "Bold Coast National Park," affected Erich Veyhl's land in the Cutler Coast area: take 17 miles of shoreland running along the Grand Manan Channel to Quoddy Head State Park, along with over a million inland acres, and make it into a National Park. Dave Simon, a resource specialist with NPCA, said, "The proposals we have made are open to discussion now. What we have tried to do is to identify areas that are nationally significant and would make fine additions to the national park system. Whether they are eventually included in the park system is another story. We now will wait to see if the ideas develop some momentum. The next step for the areas in Maine is to open up discussions with Maine residents and conservation groups and see if there is any interest or motivation to move ahead."[39]

So Erich Veyhl helped found the Washington County Alliance to fight back.

When you get the Alliance in one room, and you can—a hundred people isn't many—you see a lot of homeowners, some businesspeople—a small town motel owner, for example—and a few folks with a vacant lot where they'd like to build a home some day. No mall developers or subdivision brokers or apartment house builders—there are few such developments anywhere in Washington County and none on the coast. Strictly amateur stuff.

But the Alliance was very professional in its approach to fighting back against big organizations that do nothing but take peoples' property away from them. They brought in Chuck Cushman of the National Inholders Association, a private property protection group based appropriately in Battle Ground, Washington. Cushman is so effective in helping people all over the nation organize against environmentalists that they sneeringly call him Mr. Rent-A-Riot. Cushman wears the insult like a badge of honor.

He helped Erich Veyhl's ragtag little group learn the ropes of political clout, and things have never been the same since. One of the tools Cushman put in their hands was the Freedom of Information Act, which gives citizens access to certain kinds of federal documents even if the agency doesn't want to reveal them. They took advantage of it, realizing that the only weapon they had was the truth, and the only way to get at the truth in politics is *to get the records.*

Erich Veyhl has spent years using the Freedom of Information Act, writing to government agencies, talking to Members of Congress, digging out memos, correspondence, secret reports, all kinds of evidence. His files would impress a computer engineer—because Veyhl *is* a computer engineer. And he uses his files in congressional testimony, letters to the editor and challenges to environmental group leaders.

Because he lives close to the first all-private land national park, he took more than his usual care in documenting how it really happened. This is the true story of Minuteman National Historical Park.

The Feds Are Coming! The Feds Are Coming!

What was really going on near Boston during the early 1950s was that wealthy estate owners in the vicinity, especially around the upscale suburb of Lincoln, began to get worried about commercial strip developments, offices, even a military housing project planned for the northern part of town where the riffraff lived—immigrant farmers and other lowlifes who didn't count. The elite's interests in controlling the rabble coincided with the Park Service's imperial expansion strategy.

Thus, after appropriate quiet lobbying with the aid of the National Parks Association, Congress created the Boston National Historic Sites Commission in June 1955. The commission included Mrs. Louise du Pont Crowninshield, Dr. Walter Muir Whitehill, Dr. John P. Sullivan, along with Representative Thomas P. O'Neill, Jr. and Senator Leverett Saltonstall and Park Service Director Conrad L. Wirth.[40]

The commission's interim report delivered in June 1958 stated:

> The Boston National Historic Sites Commission recommends the creation of a national historical park embracing portions of the traditional setting along the route in Lexington, Lincoln and Concord, Massachusetts, that was traversed by the British on the epoch-making 19th of April, 1775, and used by the Minute Men and Provincial Militia to turn their retreat into a rout. Part of the route in Lexington and Lincoln was also covered the night before by Paul Revere on his famous ride and includes the site of his capture.
>
> The proposed park would be made up of two principal units. The larger, of 557 acres, would form a continuous stretch of slightly more than four miles of road and roadside properties from Route 128 in Lexington to Meriam's Corner in Concord. The smaller unit, at the celebrated North Bridge in Concord, would embrace 155 acres inside maximum boundaries.
>
> Of the 557 acres in the proposed larger unit, 524 acres of private properties would need to be acquired. In the smaller unit, 142 acres. The current market value of the total of 666 acres of private properties proposed for acquisition in both units is $4,838,100. Of this amount, $503,400 would satisfactorily initiate an urgent program to acquire 310 acres, consisting of the total of 294 acres of vacant parcels in both units and 16 acres of improved parcels of almost equal priority at the North Bridge....
>
> This Commission is mindful and appreciative of the solicitude and concern

of the Secretary of the Interior [Fred Seaton], who has indicated his intention of invoking the authority granted to him under the Historic Sites Act approved August 21, 1935, (49 Stat. 666) in order to designate and establish the parcels thus saved as a national historic site."[41]

This 1958 report appeared only in *House Document No. 57, 86th Congress,* and was never published or mentioned in the media. Such supposedly "public" documents have a way of conveniently vanishing from sight unless you know exactly where to look in a federal repository library. From the beginning the plan was to nationalize virtually all of the private property at Minuteman—but nobody knew it except the commission, the National Park Service and a handful of local boosters who were let in on the details.

In April of 1959, after slight adjustments in the boundaries, 745 acres of choice Massachusetts private land was designated as Minuteman National Historic Site. Designation as a National Historic Site did not take the property away from its owners. However, locals previously kept in the dark discovered that the House Public Works subcommittee was considering a proposal to change the site into a park.

A few alarmed land owners immediately began a petition campaign to stop the new designation. Harry Cook, a farmer in Lincoln, complained to state Rep. James DeNormandie, saying the chief trouble was that no one in government had talked over the details with citizens. Walter E. Beatteay of Lexington road in Concord organized land owners in a petition campaign against "socialized history." He complained that it took four months for the Park Service to answer his inquiries and then the answer was evasive.[42]

Park Service Director Conrad Wirth promoted park status, telling a reporter that "the Federal Government's power to take land by eminent domain would be used only to prevent abuse of the park's purposes, and in absence of abuse, owners are not compelled to sell to the government."

Rep. DeNormandie, elected by the rich constituency of Lincoln and himself a driving force behind the park campaign, added his reassurances: "An owner, in fact, can have life occupancy if he wishes, and in fact can even leave the property to his children. There is no restriction on the owner until the government buys the land, and the government only buys unused land to prevent commercialization."

On September 21, 1959, Congress changed the classification to a National Historical Park, subjecting the land to condemnation. In 1961, the Park Service began a program of pressuring property owners to sell. Harry Cook and Walter Beatteay were targeted for especially rough treatment for years. Harry Cook died of a heart attack under the stress. Beatteay was a ship's master and the Park Service relentlessly harassed his wife while he was at sea. He suffered frequent nightmares about his wife's suffering during his extended absences. He finally gave in and sold to the Park Service—a typical "willing seller."[43]

After a decade of Park Service deceit, an article in the *Minute-Man Supplement* from May 1975 tells the whole story in a nutshell:

The National Park Service will close its land acquisition office for the Minuteman National Historical Park next month and homeowners within the park boundaries who refuse to negotiate a sale would be subject to condemnation proceedings....There are 16 [of the original 267] privately owned tracts remaining to be purchased there....The land officer said the land acquisition program was 95 percent complete and funds are available to purchase the remaining tracts.[44]

The Park Service completed its condemnations in 1988, then announced a new expansion of the park to take more private land. What began with unctuous promises that no land would be taken ended with total nationalization. It became the pattern of virtually all subsequent additions to the national park system. The deceptions behind this first overt taking of all-private property to create a federal park are worthy of a book of their own.

It is one of America's great ironies that the federal government nationalized private land through blatant lies to make a commemoration site for the American Revolution. It reminds us why we fought the Revolution in the first place.

A whole spate of nationalized private property parks followed Minute Man: Piscataway Park (Maryland, 4,216 acres, 1961); Cape Cod National Seashore (Massachusetts, 44,600 acres, 1961); Point Reyes National Seashore (California, 65,299 acres, 1962); Fire Island National Seashore (New York, 19,356 acres, 1964); Ozark National Scenic Riverways (Missouri, 79,587 acres, 1964); Delaware Water Gap National Recreation Area (Pennsylvania, 47,676 acres, 1965); Assateague Island National Seashore (Maryland, 39,630 acres, 1965); Cape Lookout National Seashore (North Carolina, 28,400 acres, 1966); Indiana Dunes National Lakeshore (Indiana, 12,534 acres, 1966); St. Croix National Scenic River (Wisconsin, 62,695 acres, 1968); Appalachian National Scenic Trail (Maine to Georgia, 52,034 acres, 1968); Buffalo National River (Arkansas, 94,126 acres, 1972); many, many more.

During the 1960s the Park Service agenda was dominated by three great expansion projects: "Mission 66," a program to rehabilitate facilities and double ("round out") the park system at a cost of $786 million;[45] the 1962 Outdoor Recreation Resources Review Commission (ORRRC), which recommended a separate vast expansion program for the national parks;[46] and the Land and Water Conservation Fund created in 1964 to provide funds for park expansion.[47] All three had long-term consequences.

Of the three, the ORRRC had the most immediate fallout in terms of innovative land-taking programs. It was in large part a Rockefeller artifact, prompted by Joseph W. Penfold, conservation director of the Izaak Walton League of America (see profile) and orchestrated and chaired by Laurance Rockefeller. It consisted of four senators, four representatives, seven presidential appointees, advised by a council of fifteen bureaucrats and twenty-five representatives of various interests. The massive multi-volume ORRRC report was edited by Henry L. Diamond, Laurance Rockefeller's personal counsel on environmental issues, who also served as the commission's legal counsel. Diamond was born in Chattanooga, Tennessee, May 24, 1932, graduated from Vanderbilt in 1954 and, after military service, took his law degree at Georgetown University. He has remained a Rockefeller agent all his life, a longtime board member of the American Conservation Association, Jackson Hole Preserve, Inc. and Resources For The Future.[48]

A great shift in Park Service policy came in the 1960s, as described by Ronald Foresta, environmental commentator, in *America's National Parks and Their Keepers*:

> In 1964, the Land and Water Conservation Fund was established in large part to enable the Park Service and other federal land managing agencies to acquire recreation land from private owners, by condemnation and at prevailing market prices if necessary. During the halcyon, recession-free days of the early and mid-1960s, that seemed reasonable. The American economy looked like a great, unflagging money machine, and to what better use could the wealth be put than expanding the National Park System? Ambitious, expensive thinking characterized open space studies conducted during the 1960s and even well into the 1970s, before new realities caught up with planning dreams. For example, in 1972, the NPFF [National Parks For the Future] study group concluded that too much of the nation's land had passed into private ownership. The solution? Buy it back. The cost? One hundred billion dollars. The group proposed a large national bond issue for land acquisition, capital development, and improvement of the national, state, city, and county park systems. Such a scheme would allow the public to "buy back America."
>
> Even during the Kennedy and Johnson years, however, it was apparent that direct acquisition alone would not do—too much had to be preserved. Therefore, in 1962 the National Landmarks Program was established. This program allowed an official designation of nationally significant status to be conferred on important natural areas held by state and local governments, conservation organizations, and private owners. These lands were entered on a National Registry of Natural Areas, and although the registry designation conferred no formal protection on the natural areas, it was hoped that owner pride and the high public visibility that registration prompted would make more specific and expensive measures unnecessary.[49]

The Landmark Flimflam

Both the "endless acquisition" and "landmark designation" approaches were formalized in National Park Service planning procedures. In 1969, Interior Secretary Walter Hickel promulgated a policy guideline "on the need to identify and fill gaps in the National Park System." The park service used both approaches in the 1972 National Park System Plan that resulted from Hickel's policy.

The endless acquisition mentality actually lasted longer than commentator Foresta suggests: As an Interior Department internal analysis noted, "In fact Congress was so committed to this strategy that it mandated in 1976 the National Park Service to study and present to Congress no less than twelve new additions to the system each year. This later became known as the Park-A-Month program." The Park-A-Month plan was hung as a Christmas Tree Ornament on the Act that created Sawtooth National Recreation Area in Idaho, Public Law 95-625.[50]

But it was the Natural Landmarks Program "to fill gaps" that presaged a new direction and an even more serious threat to private property everywhere. It is the environmental counterpart to the National Historic Landmark Program. With the land control device of the National Natural Landmark (NNL), the Park Service eventually found itself able to enter private land without the knowledge or consent of the owner, evaluate that land for "national significance" despite objections of the owner, and form a backlog of candidate areas for future designation as national parks—an ingenious low cost method to gain control of private land without taking the title and having to pay for it.

The origins of the NNL concept have been obscured by Park Service mythology, but a careful reading of the 1966 *National Registry of Natural Landmarks Handbook* tells us:

> Efforts to establish a Natural Landmarks Program began in late 1960 within the division of Natural History. The Nature Conservancy and the American Geological Institute assisted greatly both in formulating criteria and guidelines for selection of sites and in compiling an extensive list of sites for consideration.
>
> Guidelines were developed for evaluating sites as to their quality, and feasibility. Four sites were recommended for registration in March and an additional three in November 1963. Mianus River Gorge in New York States became the first Registered Natural History Landmark on April 1, 1964, followed by Corkscrew Swamp Sanctuary, Florida; Rancho La Brea, California; Wissahickon Valley, Philadelphia, Pennsylvania; Elder Creek, California; Fontenelle Forest, Nebraska; and Berge-Byron Swamp, New York.
>
> To reduce confusion between this program and the Registry of National Historic Landmarks Secretary Udall approved a change in the title of the program from National Registry of Natural History Landmarks to National Registry of Natural Landmarks on February 26, 1965.[51]

The Introduction of this Park Service handbook says the legislative authority for the Landmarks Program "stems from the provisions of the Historic Sites Act of August 21, 1935," and that NPS Director Conrad Wirth recommended the program to Secretary Stewart Udall by memorandum of March 9, 1962 and Udall gave his approval on May 18, 1962.

We get some insight from this twenty-five-year-old document into how the National Park Service gives itself powers and hides its surrogates in the environmental movement.

The Historic Sites Act of 1935 made no mention whatever of preserving natural areas for any reason; it referred strictly to "historic and archaeological sites, buildings and objects" for inclusion in the Historic Landmarks Program. The Park Service simply found, according to an internal 1962 memo, that "The Historic

Landmarks Program has established a pattern, many parts of which are appropriate to the proposed geology-ecology program," and conveniently borrowed the authority from the Historic Sites Act without the knowledge, oversight or approval of Congress.[52]

It was in essence a magic incantation conjuring up an authority that did not exist. However, the Solicitor General of the Interior Department gave a legal opinion in 1964 that said the Secretary was acting within his authority, using a phrase from the Historic Sites Act authorizing the Secretary to designate and protect "objects of national significance" as justification. Thereafter, the two words "national significance" became the NNL jargon.[53]

It is clear that two Park Service surrogates, the Nature Conservancy and the American Geological Institute, conceived the natural landmark program, not the Park Service. The environmental movement created the concept. It is also clear that the program was in operation for a year within the NPS Natural History division before Secretary Udall "established" it. And if you have a really sharp memory, you'll recall that Mianus Gorge was a property of the Nature Conservancy (re-read their profile). The Conservancy was acting as the Judas Goat to get the program rolling.

Then the Park Service began a five-step procedure to recognize and designate natural areas. First came "theme studies," an idea that originated in a 1969 memorandum from Secretary of the Interior Walter Hickel to National Park Service Director George Hartzog. The themes are derived from broad categories of ecological and geological features such as eastern barrier islands or boreal forests. Regional study teams, usually scientists in academia that are recognized experts in the topic and working under contract to the Park Service, survey a physiographic province and make recommendations as to which sites appear to be of Natural Landmark caliber.[54]

Second, a scientist from a local university goes onto the property and makes an on-site evaluation—with or without the knowledge or consent of the landowner.

Third, the on-site report is reviewed by a Park Service team of three scientists, also hired from universities.

Fourth, approved evaluations go to the Interior Secretary, who designates the site as a National Natural Landmark and it is added to the National Registry of Natural Landmarks list.

Fifth, the NNLP staff contacts the landowner, informing him of the NNL designation and asking him to enter into an agreement to manage the site in a manner that will prevent the deterioration of its nationally significant values. If the landowner agrees, he receives a certificate and plaque from the Park Service in recognition of his voluntary participation. If he doesn't agree, he faces relentless and endless harassment from the National Park Service.

When the Carter administration created the Heritage Conservation and Recreation Service in 1978, Director Chris Delaporte launched the landmark program in a new direction. He ordered a task force to prepare a proposed "National Heritage Policy Act of 1979," which was introduced into Congress.[55]

This bill called for two new "registers:" one, for "Natural Areas," one of "Historic Places," all to be designated by the Secretary, under criteria he would prescribe. The "Natural Areas include lands and waters of ecologic and geologic significance," as Assistant Secretary Robert Herbst told Congress.[56]

In October 1979 HCRS sent its legislative request to Congress to authorize the Natural Landmarks Program and in November 1979 promulgated without notice "Interim Regulations" for its landmarks program. The regulations defined a "natural landmark" as "A specific area designated...which contains a representative example(s) of the nation's natural history." As its authority, HCRS invoked the Historic Sites Act of August 21, 1935, as had the 1966 handbook.[57]

In November 1980 Congress enacted a different bill, H.R. 5496, specifically refusing to authorize the natural landmark program. The House Committee report said, "This amends the National Historic Preservation Act of 1966—only. This does not contain the natural area provisions contained in related bills considered." The report continued that the new law's "definition of 'historic property' or 'historic resource' is not intended to expand the definition beyond its usage in the 1966 Act to include natural areas—the term 'prehistoric' is only intended to be used in the context of human prehistory."[58]

Indeed, a U.S. District Court in Richmond, Virginia discovered that the Historic Sites Act of 1935 itself was being used to violate the rights of land owners. In August of 1980, the court set aside the designation of the Historic Green Springs District as a National Historic Landmark and its placement on the National Register of historic Places "as violative of plaintiffs' due process rights under the Fifth Amendment, U.S. Const. Amend. V, and of the Administrative Procedure Act."[59]

After Congress rejected HCRS's request for authorization of natural landmarks, in December 1980, the waning days of the Carter administration, the agency promulgated "Final Regulations" for the natural landmarks, which became known as The Midnight Regulations. The final regulations were virtually identical to the interim regulations, and made no alterations to meet serious objections that had come from the public during the comment period.. They required continual Federal "monitoring" of landmarks designated, to make sure they "have retained those values which initially qualified them."

The *Federal Register* shows that The Midnight Regulations said:

Landmark designation may trigger application of Federal, State, or local statutes which may discourage public and private development activities. For example, specific legal consequences of landmark designation may include:

(a) Section 102(c) of the National Environmental Policy Act, requiring Agencies to ascertain and explain the effects that any proposed undertaking would have on the environment of a designated natural area, and to permit only proposals, or alternatives to them, having the least adverse effect.

(b) Section 8 of General Authorities Act of 1976 requiring Interior to report to Congress any historic or natural landmark subject to any known or anticipated damage or threat to its quality.

(c) Section 9 of the Mining in the National Parks Act of 1976, directing that whenever Interior finds a historic or natural landmark may be damaged by surface mining, to so tell the person causing it and seek the Advisory Council's advice on how government can prevent that damage.[60]

HCRS, again asserting its authority as the 1935 Act in these regulations, did not address the legal question of whether that 1935 Act, and 1976 provisions referring back to it, is statutory authority for Federal designation of large, privately-owned natural or other areas and Federal artifices to prevent their private development.

Immediately after the program was established, a number of environmental groups applied political pressure to the academics doing the studies, seeking to get their favorite examples of other peoples' property listed as NNLs. By 1982 the pressure had grown so intense that a Yale University "theme study" paid for by the Park Service contained these interesting remarks:

Politics: There are definitely pieces of the landscape which have been included in our list at least partially for political reasons. By political we mean that given a choice of more or less equivalent areas we chose the one that someone really wanted us to include. We have definitely seen examples of knowledgeable people strongly suggesting areas that, if recommended, would get in the way of "undesirable activities"—dams, power plants, roads, etc. etc. Politics also works in the opposite direction in that some owners don't want their lands recognized as nationally significant since such a recognition may get in the way of their plans for using the land.

Secrecy: Secrecy is probably one of the most frustrating aspects of our decision making process. Many recommendations were made to us "in confidence" and we have included some of them which met the rest of our criteria. The question of secrecy and of publicity is a hot topic which will undoubtedly come back to haunt us over the years if this document becomes generally available to the public. We have had some interesting and complex discussions and interpersonal interaction on this subject, especially in the Adirondack region.[61]

The secret surrogacy by environmental groups such as the Nature Conservancy became a major feature of national park expansion when the Reagan administration came to power in 1981 and tried to put an end to the endless condemnation of private land that had resulted from the Park-a-Month program.[62]

Interior Secretary James Watt abolished the Heritage Conservation and Recreation Service on May 31, 1981, by Order No. 3060. President Ronald Reagan deleted all Heritage's previously-requested funds for designating any new natural landmarks, which Congress approved.[63]

The chief lawyer of the Interior Department, William H. Coldiron, issued a memo in October 1981, specifically stating that the 1935 Act does not authorize the National Natural Landmark Program. The question arose over the proposed designation of a "Susquehana Piedmont Gorge National Natural Landmark" in

Pennsylvania. After five pages of detailed explanation why he was rejecting the designation, Solicitor Coldiron wrote generally and absolutely, "The 1935 Act does not authorize designation of a large land and water 'area' a 'natural landmark.'"[64]

A 1982 policy release under Interior Secretary James Watt described how the park system had matured and was "richly representative of our cultural heritage," concluding that it was "no longer assumed that preservation and public appreciation are best assured by Federal ownership."[65]

Did this official deauthorization of the program stop the environmentalists or the park service? Not in the slightest. The National Park Service went forward with the National Natural Landmark Program without missing a beat.

The secrecy factor came back to haunt the park service in quite a few reports on targeted National Natural Landmarks. Consider this paragraph from page 72 of the 1989 evaluation of the Bristol Cliffs in Vermont, performed under NPS contract by the University of Vermont:

> The largest landowners in the North Unit are Harvey, Paul, and Lawrence Farr, and Robert and Ramona Fuller, all of Bristol. These and other landowners were not contacted due to a concern that premature contact in the initial stages of this NNL evaluation could jeopardize efforts to secure local support for the proposed landmark. Again, this concern stems from negative local sentiment towards federal interference which surfaced during the establishment of the Bristol Cliffs Wilderness Area. Land owners should be contacted only if future efforts are made to designate the Bristol Cliffs Cheshire Formation as a National Natural Landmark.[66]

This report had already been sent to Washington and the site was in the pipeline for designation when property owners accidentally discovered it through the Freedom of Information Act while looking for something else. The stink was big and instant. Everybody in every bureaucracy tried to cover up the deliberate secrecy. When Ted Nelson, Town Manager of Bristol, Vermont demanded an explanation from the State of Vermont Agency of Natural Resources, a staff assistant wrote back:

> The reason landowners were not contacted in the Bristol Cliffs case is because the area has not been recommended for designation. That some landowners were identified by name in the Severson report appears to be merely to make it easier to contact them later, should the recommendation proceed. As I said earlier, the recommendation is stalled at an early stage.[67]

Hey, Pinocchio, how's your nose? Then Vermont State Representative John A. Hise wrote to Senator James M. Jeffords demanding an explanation and got this fascinating response:

> The Park Service admits that they made a mistake. According to the Park Service, the review in question was conducted by a University of Vermont

graduate student doing gratis work for ⠂ Park Service for graduate credit.

The Park Service reassures me that the National Natural Landmark Program is strictly voluntary, with absolutely no restrictions on land use unless the landowner wants to participate in the program. If a landowner objects, there is no National Landmark designation. I am also assured that the review process for the National Natural Landmark Program has absolutely no bearing on the process for identifying new National Park or Wilderness areas.[68]

You believe that, don't you? When Representative Hise sent the same demand for an explanation to Secretary of the Interior Manuel Lujan, National Park Service Director James Ridenour replied:

The onsite evaluation report for the Bristol Cliffs Wilderness was prepared by graduate students at the University of Vermont under an agreement with the National Park Service's North Atlantic Regional Office in Boston. Our agreement with the university allows students to choose unique natural areas to study for academic credit as part of their undergraduate curriculum and under the direction of a tenured professor. The Bristol Cliffs area is identified as a "recommended National Natural Landmark" in the natural region theme study, "Potential Ecological and Geological Natural Landmarks of the New England-Adirondack Region," prepared under contract for the NPS in 1982.

Students conducting onsite evaluations are provided copies of the NNL evaluation guidelines and program regulations (36 CFR 62). However, since the students are not under contract to the Government, their reports are not governed by the requirements of 36 CFR 62. The language that appears on page 72 of the Bristol Cliffs report would not appear in a study report paid for by the Government.[69]

I'm not responsible, said the Government. You're telling *us* you're not responsible?

The potential damage to private property rights from the National Natural Landmark project was clearly recognized by its advocates, and even discussed in scholarly journals. Russell A. Cohen, an environmental law expert and champion of the landmark system, wrote in a law review article in 1982,

Designation of private land as an NNL triggers several federal statutes....First, the endangered landmarks may be considered for acquisition by the Park Service. In those cases in which the Park Service chooses to acquire and the landowner sells or donates the land willingly, the landowner will have little to complain about. (If, however, he is unwilling to part with the property, the Park Service could invoke its eminent domain power.) Second, if the list of endangered landmarks is publicized it could lead to an outpouring of public sympathy for a particular landmark and spark a local effort to stop whatever activity is putting the natural feature in danger. If the landowner himself was engaged in that activity he might be enjoined by a court, denied necessary development permits, have his property condemned by the local government, etc. ....

The registry technique is usually relied upon to keep a foot in the door with landowners who are unwilling to part with any interest in their land at the present time. In the meantime, the landowner is periodically reminded of the natural significance of his property by the certificate on his wall and check-up calls from the registry staff.

These [land control] devices include the acquisition of a fee simple or conservation easement through purchase, bargain sale or outright gift (called dedication in some states), leases, remainders, management agreements, and rights of first refusal. While many of the techniques (including registration) are relatively weak in themselves, when used in conjunction with other devices they can have a fairly strong cumulative effect....

The Ohio Natural Landmark Program, started in 1977 and modeled largely after the federal program, tries to incorporate a right of first refusal into its owner agreements....the Mississippi Natural Heritage Law of 1978 provides for a right of first refusal....Maine required owners of sites listed on the state Critical Areas Registry to notify the Office of State Planning of any proposed alteration in the use or character of the site at least 60 days before the alteration.

In addition, The Nature Conservancy and other private conservation organizations use the information generated by the NNLP to assist them in setting priorities for natural area acquisition efforts....

The National Parks and Conservation Association (NPCA) has been one of the most outspoken supporters of the NNLP, and has helped to publicize both the Program itself and the various natural and historic landmarks designated under it, especially those that are threatened with destruction.[70]

What publicity there was went almost entirely to NPCA members in direct mail campaigns. The general public didn't know. The Park Service kept on keeping the NNL program secret from landowners.

Agents of the Agency

Environmentalist land trusts knew all about the National Natural Landmark Program, however, because they were part of it. This brings up the serious concern that private environmental groups are working in such close complicity with the National Park Service to destroy private property rights that they have become *de facto* agents of the federal government without public knowledge.

The correspondence files of the National Park Service are full of secret letters to and from environmental groups plotting ways to take private land for additions to the federal park system. In 1984, the National Parks and Conservation Association began work on a comprehensive plan for expanding the park system in ways that could get around the Reagan administration's safeguards for private property. But all the land trusts in the environmental movement had to get behind this effort for it to have any effect.

The Conservation Foundation, then headed by Rockefeller protégé William K.

Reilly, who edited *The Use of Land: A Citizen's Policy Guide to Urban Growth*, issued a 1985 report, *National Parks for a New Generation*, saying,

> The park service already has worked closely with land trusts in several areas to protect threatened parcels before Congress appropriated funds for their acquisition by the government. Despite these efforts, however, the full potential of land trusts has yet to be realized by the park service. Several parks are now considering the use of private land trusts as part of their land protection initiatives, a trend that should be encouraged through experiments at several units. The service might also stimulate the creation of land trusts and support their work—for example, by offering them technical assistance. And park service staff might sit on the advisory boards of groups working near parklands or encourage 'Friends of...' organizations to expand their roles to encompass land acquisition.[71]

The Conservation Foundation was pressuring both park service officials and environmental group leaders to work together even more closely. Their pressure paid off the next year. A park service associate director sent a memo to all regional directors acknowledging their collaboration: "The National Parks and Conservation Association has been working for the past two years on a 'comprehensive plan' for the National Park System. Their report, scheduled for completion in 1987, will include recommendations for additions to the system to fill 'gaps' and boundary adjustments for existing units." The writer assigned a task to his underlings to be completed by April of 1987:

"Prepare an inventory of existing new area studies and produce a brief summary of legislative action or current status. This would be a separate document from any 'plan' update and would not be intended for release to the public."[72]

Secrecy and complicity, secrecy and complicity—the two main themes run through hundreds of park service memos. When the Sierra Club submitted a suggested expansion plan for the park system in 1986, one Park Service associate director wrote to another that "The response to the Sierra Club should, I think, take advantage of the memories of all of those [with] a knowledge of the involvement of outside groups, i.e., the Wilderness Society and NPCA."[73]

The same letter said, "The National Natural Landmarks Program has been compiling new park recommendations derived from natural region theme studies since 1971. The last revision is attached for your review. However, it is our belief, and I suspect yours too, that any contemplated revision of the 1980 revised Plan should exclude any information on actual sites recommended to fill gaps. This subject, as you know, is very sensitive, which is why the attached compilation has never been distributed outside of National Park Service."

Secrecy and complicity. NPCA published a nine-volume study in 1988 called *Investing in Park Futures: A Blueprint for Tomorrow*. Volume 8 was titled "New Parks: New Promise," of which Part III was called *Expanding the National Park System Vision*, and the third major heading was titled "National Landmark Programs: 'Ladies in Waiting.'"

NPCA saw the NNL program entirely as a feeder program for new national parks. Its "Ladies in Waiting" section said:

> The landmarks still constitute the largest potential source of additional historical and natural areas needed to fill existing gaps in the national park system....The NPCA position is that the candidate sites and landscapes have already been identified—they are long overdue for protection....
>
> An exhaustive program of inventory and site identification in the major physiographic provinces of the country is nearly complete. Funded by about $2 million of Park Service contracts, university scientists have conducted "theme studies" for each physiographic region, surveying thousands of sites. Thirty-one of thirty-three theme studies are complete; the remaining two (regions of Alaska) are half finished. More than 3,000 locations were recommended for landmark status.
>
> In the past, the national natural landmark program was a major factor in identifying potential new units of the national park system. The National Park Service has even compiled a list of over 400 sites that were considered the best candidates for the national park system by the ecologists and geologists who prepared the thirty-one natural region theme studies. When the Park Service was still preparing the portions of the annual reports that dealt with proposed new areas, the registry of natural landmarks was a frequent source of candidates. Though Congress has declined to fund a consistent new areas study program since 1981, the candidate landmarks remain—ready to become parks of the future.
>
> Landmarks seem to differ from the types of units in the national park system. In philosophy and management approach they should favor preservation over recreation and access. The nature and level of visitor uses should be more strictly controlled, and greater emphasis placed on compatible education and research activities.
>
> There is ample precedent for landmarks making the leap to national park status, and such sites needn't be labeled "national parks." Both Congaree River Swamp, South Carolina, and John Day Fossil Beds, Oregon were first NNLs prior to their designations as national monuments.
>
> Candidates for national park system ecological reserves, or formally affiliated reserves, can be found on the public lands, the lists of candidate and designated landmarks, and in the priorities of organizations such as the Nature Conservancy....
>
> And in fact, in many respects, the detailed resource inventory approach utilized by The Nature Conservancy surpasses the designation process of the natural landmark program for identifying critical ecosystem preservation needs. At any rate, the National Park Service should be concerned with the protection priorities of the Conservancy, lend assistance where possible, and be possibly involved with the ultimate disposition of particularly valuable Conservancy lands.[74]

The National Park Service used this NPCA document not as a recommendation for planned expansion, but as a stepping stone for an unprecedented new vision of limitless expansion. In a breathtaking memo from the chief of NPS interagency resources to the chief of park planning shortly after NPCA released its *Investing in Park Futures* report, we see:

You should be aware of the existence of a List of 385 recommendations for potential units of the National Park System derived from complete natural region theme studies conducted with government contracts during the period 1970-86. This List, and the actual letters of recommendation we have on file which were used to compose it, is not widely known about even in NPS. This List could be given more visibility in our agency, but should be put in a more presentable format. This List represents the best data we have for identifying potential candidate sites for addition to the National Park System. It should not be incorporated in the 1980 document update, but remain a separate in-house compilation. It can best be used and interpreted by staff familiar with the nature of the theme studies they were derived from, and the nature of the sites themselves.

We understand that the NPS Plan proposed by NPCA goes well beyond the simple notion of gaps and how to fill them. Regardless of what NPCA proposed, a real NPS plan goes beyond anything the Service has yet considered or talked about, or probably NPCA, and must take into account, for example, issues such as management of land adjacent to the National Park System, i.e., buffer zones, corridors, etc. This topic deserves discussion at the highest levels of the Service, which we would be glad to participate in, and in collaboration with staff of the Associate Director, Natural Resources, if they wish.[75]

Eleven months later, the "highest levels of the Service" had finished their collaboration and adopted the NPCA plan as the National Park Service's official "springboard for discussion and action." In a letter to NPCA Executive Director Paul Pritchard, National Park Service Director William Penn Mott said:

I offer my congratulations and thanks to you, Destry Jarvis and the others whose understanding of, and obvious deep concern for, the Service and the System are so clearly reflected in the Summary.

To begin the process by which we may put the Plan to use, I called for a review of the Executive Summary by each member of the Service's Washington and Field Directorate. Although I gave them a very short turnaround time, their response was very strong. They, as I, agree with many of the plan's contentions and recommendations; disagree with others; and cite a number of errors and omissions. Overall, their response was positive and highly appreciative. Each noted a number of items that already have been accomplished or are in progress....

The errors that were noted may have resulted from the steadily increasing speed with which the Service has moved ahead - often, in the direction suggested by the Plan - during the several years in which the Plan was being prepared. That progress has been guided, to a large extent, by the 12-Point Plan in whose development you participated.

I have selected Boyd Evison, Regional Director, Alaska, to lead the review of the NPCA Plan, and the development of a process to make its agreed-upon features integral to the direction of the Service in the future. He will have my full support, and will encourage input from as wide an array of National Park Service employees as possible....

I understand that publication of the full 9-volumes will be complete in the next several months. It is my intention that every National Park Service employee will have access to the full set, and feel free to comment on it. To assure thorough and effective treatment, each Associate Director in our Washington Office will provide explicit responses to those contents of the Plan and gaps in it that relate to their areas of responsibility. Our Office of Policy Development will furnish staff support to Boyd. Boyd will also coordinate comments from the Regional Directors.

As we proceed with analysis of the Plan, and follow-up on it, we hope to have NPCA's continuing participation in each step. Again, I commend you for this springboard for discussion and action. It will play a significant part in shaping the Service and the System, and in working for the health of the global ecosystem of which we are a part.[76]

It is hard to imagine how a private organization could be made more of a *de facto* federal agency. The park service spent thousands of federal dollars buying copies of the expensive NPCA report and hundreds of thousands studying it and incorporating it into federal policy. No federal dollars went into the preparation of the NPCA report—it wasn't necessary because the costs were made up by government purchases after publication. We estimate that at least half a million taxpayer dollars went into its distribution and application.

Conversely, alternative park system plans submitted by property rights advocates were totally ignored. The National Inholders Association had to file a lawsuit in federal court against the President's Commission on Americans Outdoors because NIA members were being physically ejected from decision-making meetings held by Commission members, Park Service personnel, and other Interior Department officials.

Property rights advocates were thrown out. Environmental groups were made agents of the agency.

In March of 1990, syndicated columnist Alston Chase exposed the National Natural Landmark Program in a scathing report. The resulting public outcry was horrendous. The park service was forced to admit that the NNL program had actually been a front to supply candidate sites for expanding the National Park System. When demands were filed to make public the NNLs that had become part of the park system, the past secrecy and complicity came back to haunt the park service. An April 1990 memo from one NPS official to another reveals the embarrassed disarray:

As you know, recent inquiries about the National Natural Landmarks (NNL) Program have necessitated that we examine our records regarding the Program's relationship to the National Park System. The attached chart has been prepared to answer inquiries.

We sent this chart to you informally very recently. However, we have had to revise this chart as new information has been found. We now believe that 15 designated NNLs were later incorporated in units of the National Park System. In other words, 15 NNLs existed before the National Park System unit was created, which subsumed the NNL. If you have information that will improve upon what we know to date, please let us know.[77]

The accompanying chart listed NNLs from Point of Arches added to Washington State's Olympic National Park to Congaree River Swamp in South Carolina and from Gulf Hagas in Maine's Appalachian National Scenic Trail to Pinhook Bog in Indiana Dunes National Seashore. Private property had been trampled to extinction. The Park Service still does not know with certainty all of the NNLs that have been "subsumed" into units of the National Park System. And they have even less account of the NNLs that did not go into the park system but were designated without notifying the private property owner.

The National Parks and Conservation Association's ten-volume *Investing in Park Futures* report was originally offered for sale to the general public for about $80 a set. When public outcry arose over the NNL program as a result of Alston Chase's column, the NPCA mysteriously ran out of copies when critics ordered them. Ann Corcoran, publisher of the *Land Rights Letter*, couldn't get a copy at all. Even though she's a *member* of NPCA, they absolutely refused to sell her one.

The NNL program finally came under question in 1991 by the top cop of the Interior Department, the Inspector General. Peter Rich of the Office of the Inspector General scoured the National Park Service for evidence of harm to private land owners. Charles M. McKinney III of the National Natural Landmarks Program had become deeply concerned about private property abuses, and wrote this memo to Rich:

It is rather difficult to document specific details where private landowners have been adversely affected because most private owners remain unaware (even today) that their lands are involved with this government program. In addition, those known private landowners who have been subjected to adverse effects as a direct result of NNLP activities, require direct contact to ascertain the details and degree of adversity inflicted. Further, some landowners are reluctant to discuss these matters out of fear of reprisals being taken against them....

The process which creates harm (adverse affects) to private landowners began during the data gathering process associated with the creation of natural theme studies. Thematic studies were conducted by the NNLP throughout the 1970s and early 1980s on each of the 33 physiographic natural regions and provinces nationwide. These natural area studies are heavily relied upon by all Federal, State and municipal government agencies, plus numerous private national, regional and local conservation organizations. The studies are utilized by these public and private agencies to focus on those lands possessing natural features (geological and ecological) which, in their opinion, should be preserved even without regard for the negative impact imposed on private landowners and the obvious degradation of private property rights. Furthermore, the theme study recommendations specify which natural areas should be considered as NNLs. Secret documents were also submitted by each theme study contractor regarding which natural areas should become new units of the National Park System.

Whether a particular natural area is eventually inactivated, whether it remains a potential NNL, or whether it is ultimately designated as an NNL is not the critical factor. No, what is critical is the conduct of the entire NNLP process that private landowners object to—the absence of accountability and deliberate deception directly associated with the program.

No amount of revised regulations, rehashed internal handbooks, lists of owners, or an infusion of additional funding can erase the past and present mismanagement of this program. This blatant breach of public trust can only slowly be reversed with full disclosure of past wrongdoing and total openness with private landowners. This is the only path to regain public confidence and program credibility.[78]

Secrecy. Collusion. Reprisals. Deliberate deception.

What country is this?

The Inspector General's investigation had been prompted by the Alston Chase exposé we mentioned above. Chase wrote his devastating critique from a number of his own sources and with the help of government documents and memos obtained by Erich Veyhl. Chase's widely published March 5, 1990 column asserted that National Natural Landmark designation is "a deception subjecting these lands to many federal and state restrictions and making them prime targets for federal takeover as part of national park system expansion."

He offered a number of specific examples and revealed what we have already seen, that the National Parks and Conservation Association was a surrogate acting as a *de facto* agent of the National Park Service. Chase also discussed the proposed National Heritage Conservation Act, the environmentalist land grab that we discussed above.[79]

To the general public, it was an explosive exposé. Most Americans have no idea that the environmental movement does such things. Nor did Mr. Chase have the space to include the extensive damning documentation we have included here—he simply made the assertions based on records he saw with his own eyes.

National Parks and Conservation Association President Paul Pritchard, not realizing that Chase had based his column on a tall stack of documents, issued a lengthy denial to the Universal Press Syndicate which distributes Chase's columns to over 50 newspapers. Mr. Pritchard's response is worth quoting unedited and in its entirety. Knowing what we know, it's entertaining. And it's enough rope.

Those of us in the environmental community can count on Alston Chase to raise issues that warrant public concern and attention. Sometimes his columns are well-researched and accurate. However his recent column, "Secret targets of landmark stealth," March 5, in which he claims the National Park Service and the environmental community are engaged in a massive conspiracy to secretly take over lands of thousands of Americans, may read like a shocking expose, but it is so chockful of factual inaccuracies, misstatements and misinformation that it warrants response.

Mr. Chase's column is based on allegations made by Erich Veyhl of the Washington County Alliance, a small group of Maine landowners. The column fails to mention that Mr. Veyhl's group is strongly associated with an anti-national park group called the National Inholders Association. One of the more notable targets of this group has been the proposed American Heritage Trust Act, which seeks to provide a stable source of funding for local, state and federal conservation and recreation programs. This group also routinely disseminates false information and half-truths and distorts the facts in order to panic landholders, mostly those who live in the vicinity of national parks or other federal areas, into thinking that the federal government is out to "take" their land.

Mr. Veyhl's concern is not so much over the National Natural Landmarks Program as over a specific proposal advanced by National Parks and Conservation Association more than two years ago, which would establish a new national park in Maine. The proposal involved a National Natural Landmark, and it stirred up a hornet's nest of controversy, due largely to misinformation from Mr. Veyhl's organization. We believe, despite the scare tactics used by Mr. Veyhl's group, that the majority of the American people and Maine residents want to see their coastline preserved and not commercially exploited by land sharks and residential developers.

Mr. Chase takes issue with procedures of the NNLP and asserts that Mr. Veyhl has uncovered a "scam," which he, Mr. Chase, has dubbed "Greengate." Nonsense. For years, NPCA has raised concerns about the NNLP's management with the National Park Service. And we agree there indeed is need to reform designation procedures and administrative guidelines. However, there is no "scam," no "coverup." Environmental groups certainly are not "red faced with embarrassment" over the landmarks program, as Mr. Chase alleges.

Here are the facts regarding Mr. Chase's claims:

First, the park service does not hire scholars to conduct "secret" theme-studies of geographic regions. Because they are government documents, all such studies are available to the public. Once areas are identified as worthy candidates for landmark designation, property owners are notified. There have been a few isolated cases in which the NPS inadvertently has neglected to give proper notification to a landowner; action has been taken to rectify these situations. But it is blatantly false to assert, as Mr. Chase does, that landmark properties are routinely designated without owners' knowledge or consent.

Second, Messrs. Chase and Veyhl confuse the official park theme-study process with NPCA's recent 10-volume study, "The National Park System Plan:

A Blueprint for Tomorrow." Contrary to Mr. Chase's innuendo that NPCA is a government "agency," NPCA is not. I repeat, it is not an "agency" of the federal government. NPCA is a national, non-profit organization with more than 100,000 active citizens who are concerned about our national park system. Our study received no federal funding. Furthermore, our "System Plan," report is not a "secret" document. It was released nearly two years ago with a great deal of national publicity. Anyone may purchase a copy from us or from any environmental publisher.

Third, Mr. Chase asserts that our report describes landmark properties as "ladies in waiting," referring to a landmark's potential of someday becoming a national park unit. Mr. Chase doesn't state that the report consistently refers to the "potential" for the national park system. There are more than 1,900 National Historical Landmarks and more than 600 National Natural Landmarks. All are deemed "nationally significant." Few are "suitable and feasible," to quote NPS guidelines, for national park designation.

Further, new national park units are created by act of Congress only after public and congressional hearings. They are not established by agency landmark designation.

Fourth, Mr. Chase makes an erroneous claim that there is a "web" of federal and state restrictions on landmarks once they are designated. This is not the case: No federal law affects a National Natural Landmark in private ownership. Only a handful of states enacted regulations, usually voluntary tax incentives, designed to protect landmarks.

Finally, Mr. Chase makes a preposterous claim that the proposed National Heritage Conservation Act (which has yet to be introduced into Congress because conservationists still are exploring strategies to address the landmark and national park threat issue) would provide criminal penalties of $25,000 a day for homeowners who do things that "affect landmarks adversely." The legislation will avoid another crisis such as the one that occurred at the Manassas National Battlefield a few years ago when Congress had to step in to stop construction of a massive shopping mall next to the national battlefield.

Yes, members of the National Heritage Coalition are concerned about the growing list of federally designated "threatened" national parks and landmarks. We shall continue to work to find an agreeable, legislative solution to the plight of our national parks and landmarks.

> Paul Pritchard
> President
> National Parks and Conservation Association
> Washington[80]

Is that great standup comedy, or what? Now that we've stopped laughing, we can see that Mr. Pritchard's defense is somewhat—how shall we say this charitably?—whimsical. Paul, babe, you're no Shakespearean, but you read that script wonderfully. You're hot! You've got the part.

Still, there's this nagging little detail about Mr. Pritchard:

How could he not be aware that National Natural Landmarks were targets for condemnation and addition to the National Park System?—*he was second in command of the NNL program himself* while deputy director of the Heritage Conservation and Recreation Service during the Carter administration and had seen the secret memos with his own peepers.

Oops.

Punching Out Property Rights

National Park Service Director James M. Ridenour did nothing to stop these abuses and has lied to Congress trying to lead them to believe that he has. He supposedly placed a "moratorium" on the NNL program in November 1989 pending a "review." Interior Department Inspector General James R. Richards began an audit of the NNL program—which Ridenour's National Park Service tried to stop with its own review—and dug into the facts. The National Park Service review was a farce, as an NPS memo of January 1990 admitted: "Nothing has happened to correct program deficiencies."

The Inspector General's audit was released in December of 1991 and found that "NPS may have violated the property rights of over 2,800 private landowners because the evaluation, nomination, and designation of natural landmarks may not have been conducted with landowner knowledge or consent." The audit noted possible "trespass violations" by government agents in efforts to collect information on potential landmarks and complaints by landowners of being "harassed by conservation groups," and recommended suspending all 587 landmark sites since not all landowners had been notified that their properties had been designated in the presumably voluntary program.

Audacious as ever, NPCA President Pritchard joined with Wilderness Society President George T. Frampton to write to Interior Secretary Manuel Lujan and NPS Director Ridenour urging the agency to "throw its full support behind this worthy program" and concluding "we look forward to assisting you in any way."

They further wrote Ridenour, "We strongly recommend against the adoption of regulations that would permit landowner objections to thwart the evaluation process." Pritchard and Frampton suggested that the National Park Service initiate a dual listing procedure to allow evaluations and inventorying to proceed while giving the appearance of landowner consent.

"An acceptable compromise," Frampton and Pritchard wrote, "would be to maintain two lists. The principal list, the National Registry of Natural Landmarks, would consist of sites where a landowner, or a majority of multiple owners, consent to the designation. Sites determined nationally significant, but not designated due to owner objection, should be placed on a separate, publicly available list of 'Properties Determined Nationally Significant.'" Some ruse. And that's exactly what got into the current draft regulations.

Nobody in the National Park Service has lost their job over this scandal—except Charles M. McKinney III, the bureaucrat who saw the need to reform the program whose memo we quoted above, who was scapegoated.[81]

None of the unrepentant bureaucrats or environmentalists involved have been fired or gone to prison. Hardy Pearce, NNL Chief from 1986 to 1990, although relieved of responsibilities for the program, still received merit pay raises, according to a 1991 report. Land owners whose property rights have been damaged by the NNL program have never obtained justice. Justice will probably never be done.[82]

Perhaps most indicative of the utter contempt that the National Park Service holds for private property rights is the following conversation between NPS Director James Ridenour and members of the National Parks Advisory Board at their October 1991 meeting. The subject under discussion was the National Natural Landmarks Program. A tape of the meeting was obtained and transcribed by Erich Veyhl and published by Ann Corcoran in the *Land Rights Letter*—but these passages were deliberately cleaned up and omitted from the official minutes of the meeting.

> *Ridenour*: I can't overemphasize how emotional this issue has become. I will say that there are people who are making their living opposing this program and they have stirred people's emotions to the point that being a National Natural Landmark means that the Park Service is coming to take your land.
>
> *Unidentified woman*: Yeah.
>
> *Ridenour*: This past year we probably have spent a couple of hundred thousand dollars reacting to a situation on the coast of Maine, for example, where the State was looking at some Natural Landmarks that they wanted to name up along the coast of Maine. [Ridenour was lying to his own advisory board: The State of Maine did no such thing—it was entirely a National Park Service project and Ridenour knew it.] So there is an intense letter writing campaign, and they write to Congress almost on a daily basis, certainly a weekly basis. I think a little of the steam has gone out of it for the moment because the fellow went too far and called some of the senior Senators from Maine socialists and communists, or something like that, in his newsletter.
>
> [Erich Veyhl challenged Ridenour under the Freedom of Information Act to produce evidence that the alleged "socialists and communists" namecalling ever took place, and Ridenour, after much stalling, admitted he had no basis for this accusation.][83]
>
> *Unidentified woman*: Oooh!
>
> *Ridenour*: So this has become a very intense issue. And I would compliment [Associate Director] Gene [Hester] for the restraint he's used [audience laughter] during the past year for not tracking down some of these people who are spreading these stories [more laughter] and punchin' 'em out [more laughter] which is something I might want to do. But in any event this is an important project and your input's going to be very important to us.[84]

Private property rights are obviously very funny to Mr. Ridenour and the National Parks Advisory Board.

The Bush administration caved in to the National Parks and Conservation Association in October 1991 at the National Parks 75th Anniversary Symposium, and agreed to resurrect a 1970s program to add a dozen new parks to the system each year—The Park-A-Month Plan. Paul Pritchard had brought forward the old eco-dream from the Carter administration—he was the environmentalist bridge over troubled waters.

Business As Usual

The National Parks and Conservation Association is one of the slickest big-business organizations of the environmental movement. Of its total $8.7 million income for 1991, direct mail accounted for $1,493,246 and telephone solicitation campaigns brought in $593,131. NPCA received $432,833 in foundation grants and $119,872 in corporate donations (they are not required to report which corporations gave the contributions). NPCA also has a taxable subsidiary called 31st Street Georgetown Associates, acquired as a 50 percent interest in a real estate limited partnership investment company that owned a building at 1015 31st Street, N.W. in Washington, D.C., with year end 1991 assets of $4,163,606. The partnership was "unprofitable" and NPCA took a $609,939 loss on it in 1991. The Estate of Philo Higley donated a bequest of $901,250 reported in 1991.

What did NPCA do with all this money?

Paul Pritchard received a salary of $108,228, while association controller Davinder Khanna was paid $52,129; fund raising director Eliot Gruber got $45,998; editor Sue Dodge got $45,434; membership director Terry Vines got $45,170; and conservation director William Lienesch got $34,190. Other salaries and wages cost $1,193,629. Members also paid $257,159 for the staff pension plan. NPCA spent $2.5 million on postage and shipping and $2.4 million on printing and publications. Lobbying expenses were $55,331, with total lobbying between 1988 and 1990 of $134,059. Oh, yes, "park preservation and expansion" got $692,013.

Yep, we're just a little grass-roots outfit hugging a few trees. We told you it was great standup comedy.

NPCA is a master at disguising its true power. On September 28, 1990, all assets of the Association's Land Acquisition Revolving Fund were transferred, at carrying value of $1,004,293, to the National Park Trust, a very quiet separate 501(c)(3) land-buying organization. NPT is a captive instrumentality of the NPCA: Paul Pritchard and two of NPCA's board members hold similar positions with National Parks Trust. It was an impressively sophisticated maneuver. Now NPCA's land buying can be carried on by NPT, thus deflecting criticism from the main organization.[85]

Yep, we're just a little grass-roots outfit hugging a few trees. Yuk, yuk.

To get some idea of how slick and cold-blooded NPCA has become, examine the contract they gave to a professional fund-raising outfit, Public Interest Communications, Inc. Here's the proposal from PIC that was accepted and signed by NPCA's director of operations:

The responsibilities and procedures will be as follows:
1. High Dollar Telemarketing Campaign. Subject to the terms and conditions hereinafter set forth, NPCA hereby retains Public Interest Communications (PIC) to conduct a High Dollar Telemarketing Campaign to contact 15,000

prospects from NPCA's $50-plus donor file supplied to PIC by the NPCA. The responsibilities of PIC shall include the following functions:

a) Training the telephone callers with informational materials approved by NPCA.

b) Writing the script used by the callers in their presentations.

c) Creating the NPCA follow-up billing letters.

d) Researching the phone numbers of all donors on the list provided to PIC for calling.

e) Managing the production of all letters used in this program, and handling negotiations and arrangements with printers, mailing houses, and other production operations.

f) Managing and supervising the day-to-day telephoning and verification efforts.

g) Providing daily reports during the calling and a final report at the conclusion of the program.

h) Designing and implementing a random telephone followup as a safeguard to: (1) ensure the accuracy of the sales reports and (2) to maintain a quality check on the sales approach to the callers.

i) Managing the fulfillment of all pledges, hedges, and no answers.

j) Generating follow-up second bills to those who have pledged, but did not pay within four weeks of the conclusion of the program.

k) Preparing installment billings to individuals four weeks after they pay their initial installment.

l) After three days of calling, reevaluate the program to insure that the effort is attaining desired goals.

m) Supplying you with a summary of comment sheets to help determine the attitudes of a portion of NPCA's constituency.

2. Compensation of PIC. The cost of the program will be $7.00 per completed decision (defined as a phone contact with a prospect) for all negotiations beginning at $1,000, $6.00 for negotiations beginning at $250 and $4.50 for negotiations with the initial ask of twice the individual's highest previous gift. The cost includes our creative charges, the management of the program, clerical costs and the long-distance telephone bill.[86]

NPCA signed a similar deal with Outreach Affiliates, Inc. on April 1, 1992 for general non-high-dollar fund raising.

Well, folks, this is what your nobody-here-but-us-tree-huggers NPCA looks like before putting on its conservationist costume. Sifting through their financial reports is kind of like walking in on an acquaintance and finding them naked.

The Board of Directors of the National Parks and Conservation Association includes chairman Norman G. Cohen; vice chairs Nancy Lampton, Deborah MacKenzie, and Nancy Wheat; secretary James Matson; and treasurer Thomas W. Markowsky.

Other members of the board include: Eugene Brown, W. L. Lyons Brown, Carl

Burke, Dorothy Canter, Donald S. Downing, William M. Hassebrock, F. Ross Holland, Charles Howell III, Daniel P. Jordan, Wilbur F. LaPage, William Leedy, Betty Lilienthal, James MacFarland, Stephen M. McPherson, Robert Mendelsohn, W. Mitchell, John B. Oakes (formerly of the *New York Times*), Jean Packard, William B. Resor, Elvis Stahr (former head of the National Audubon Society), Charles D. Stough, Lowell Thomas, Jr., Carol Trawick, Frederick C. Williamson, Sr., Ted L. Wilson, Robin Winks.

Do any of these people have the faintest idea what their Association is doing?

National Parks and Conservation Association receives its major large grants from the Rockefeller and Mellon interests:

American Conservation Association gave $50,000 in 1989 for general support and another $50,000 for budget of chapter in New York.

Mary Flagler Cary Charitable Trust (substantially derived from Standard Oil money and Florida real estate) gave $22,400 in 1990 for Delaware and Hudson Canal Heritage Corridor Project of New York State Chapter.

Andrew W. Mellon Foundation gave $75,000 in 1986 and $270,000 in 1987.

First National Bank of Boston (a Mellon bank) gave $285,886 in 1987.

National Parks and Conservation Association.
Job killers.
Economy Trashers.

National Parks and Conservation Association-Footnotes

1 *Stealing the National Parks*, Don Hummel, Free Enterprise Press, Bellevue, Washington, 1987.

2 *Steve Mather of the National Parks*, Robert Shankland, Alfred A. Knopf, New York, 1951.

3 *The Birth of the National Park Service: The Founding Years, 1913-33*, Horace M. Albright as told to Robert Cahn, Howe Brothers, Salt Lake City, 1985, p. 106.

4 See the chapter on the Mather-Albright principles of concessions in *Stealing the National Parks*, Don Hummel, Free Enterprise Press, Bellevue, Washington, 1987.

5 *National Parks: The American Experience*, Alfred Runte, University of Nebraska Press, Lincoln, 1979.

6 See the grant list at the end of this profile.

7 "National Parks and Conservation Association," by Alfred Runte, *Encyclopedia of American Forest and Conservation History*, edited by Richard C. Davis, Macmillan Publishing Company, New York, 1983, p. 463.

8 "Bureau of Outdoor Recreation," by David A. Clary, *Encyclopedia of American Forest and Conservation History*, edited by Richard C. Davis, Macmillan Publishing Company, New York, 1983, p. 54.

9 "Department of the Interior," *The United States Government Manual 1981/82*, Government Printing Office, Washington, D.C., 1981, p. 317.

10 "Crowds in parks: a growing issue," by John Lancaster, *Washington Post*, November 23, 1990, p. A29.

11 "Study tells of growing threats to national parks," by Philip Shabecoff, *New York Times*, March 19, 1989, p. 13.

12 "NPCA seeks to block park snowmobile trail," *National Parks*, November-December 1990, p. 15.

13 "NPCA contests airport near Glen Canyon," *National Parks*, November-December 1990, p. 16.

14 "Stables expansion at Manassas defeated," *National Parks*, September-October 1991, p. 14.

15 "NPCA files suit to protect petroglyphs," *National Parks*, July-August, 1991, p. 13.

16 "Park overflight bill passes both Houses," *National Parks*, September-October 1987, p. 6.

17 "NPCA blocks attempt to widen Burr Trail," *National Parks*, March-April 1992, p. 24.

18 "RV excise tax urged by national parks group," by Stephen Landrigan, *RV Business*, May 25, 1990, p. 1.

19 "Group proposes departure fee to raise funds for national parks," *Travel Weekly*, September 30, 1991, p. 3.

20 "NPCA against widening highway at Chickamauga," *National Parks*, November-December 1987, p. 9.

21 "NPCA appeals leasing near Teddy Roosevelt," *National Parks*, March-April 1992, p. 20.

22 "Water project above Black Canyon approved," *National Parks*, May-June 1992, p. 14.

23 "Developers stake claims next to US parks," by Scott Armstrong, *Christian Science Monitor*, September 12, 1988, p. 3.

24 "Missing pieces: two million acres of parkland are privately owned; NPCA's National Park Trust is working to change that," by Frances H. Kennedy, *National Parks*, September-October 1987, p. 30.

25 "National parks face five major threats," *National Parks*, November-December 1991, p. 9. See also *Investing In Park Futures: A Blueprint for Tomorrow*, National Parks and Conservation Association, Washington, D.C., February 1988.

26 "They're after our hunting land: a private organization of park enthusiasts has set its sights on your valuable hunting land," by Lonnie Williamson, *Outdoor Life,* September 1988.

27 *Investing In Park Futures: A Blueprint for Tomorrow*, National Parks and Conservation Association, Washington, D.C., February 1988.

28 For the story of the national parks see these standard histories: *Our National Park Policy: A Critical History*, John Ise, Resources For the Future, Johns Hopkins University Press, Baltimore, 1961; *National Parks: The American Experience*, Alfred Runte, University of Nebraska Press, Lincoln, 1979; *Mountains Without Handrails: Reflections on the National Parks*, Joseph Sax, University of Michigan Press, Ann Arbor, 1980; *Parks, Politics and People*, Conrad L. Wirth, University of Oklahoma Press, Norman, 1980; *The National Park Service*, William C. Everhart, Westview Press, Boulder, Colorado, 1972, 1983; *The National Parks: Shaping the System*, U.S. Department of the Interior, Washington, D.C., 1991; See also *The National Parks: Index 1993*. This useful index is revised almost every year.

29 Number of park units provided by National Park Service, December 1992.

30 *Greenline Parks: Land Conservation Trends for the 'Eighties and Beyond*, edited Marjorie R. Corbett, National Parks and Conservation Association, Washington, D.C. 1983.

31 J. Glenn Eugster to Conservation Interests, memo on National Park Service letterhead, Mid-Atlantic Region, Philadelphia, Pennsylvania, dated March 14, 1982.

32 Serious students of National Park Service empire building must examine *History of Legislation Relating to the National Park System through the 82nd Congress*, 108 volumes, Edmund B. Rogers, Departmental Library, U.S. Department of the Interior; *Administrative History: Organizational Structures of the National Park Service 1917-1985*, Russell Olsen, National Park Service, Washington, D.C., 1986; and *Laws Relating to the National Park Service, the National Parks and Monuments*, Hillory A. Tolson, GPO, 1933.

33 Franklin K. Lane to Stephen Mather, May 13, 1918, National Archives.

34 *Administrative History: Expansion of the National Park Service in the 1930s*, Harlan D. Unrau and G. Frank Williss, National Park Service, Denver Service Center, Denver, 1983.

35 *The Autobiography of a Curmudgeon*, Harold L. Ickes, Reynal and Hitchcock, New York, 1943.

36 *Origins of National Park Service Administration of Historic Sites*, Horace M. Albright, Eastern National Park and Monument Association, Philadelphia, 1971.

37 *History of Natural Resources Agencies and Proposals for their Reorganization*, unpublished internal document, U.S. Department of the Interior, Departmental Library, 1977.

38 "Bold coast national park urged; Proposal gets mixed reaction Down East," by Bob Cummings, *Maine Sunday Telegram*, June 12, 1988.

39 "National Park status proposed for Cutler to Lubec coastline," by Marie Jones Holmes, *The Quoddy Tides*, April 8, 1988, p. 1.

40 Public Law 84-75, Chapter 144, S.J. Res. 6, approved June 15, 1955.

41 *The Lexington-Concord Battle Road*, Interim report of the Boston National Historic Sites Commission to the Congress of the United States, June 16, 1958, p. 3.

42 This section relies on "Minute Man Park Plan Running Into Opposition," by Wilfrid C. Rodgers, *Boston Daily Globe*, August 12, 1959.

43 Interview with Erich Veyhl from his Minuteman Park file.

44 "Land acquisition office to close at Minuteman Park," by Dick Solito, *Lincoln Supplement*, Lincoln, Massachusetts, May 1975, p. 1.

45 *Mission 66: To Provide Adequate Protection and Development of the National Park System for Human Use*, National Park Service, U.S. Department of the Interior, January, 1956. See Also, "The Mission Called 66," by Conrad L. Wirth, *National Geographic*, Vol. 130, No. 1, July 1966, p. 7.

46 *Outdoor Recreation for America*, A Report to the President and to the Congress by the Outdoor Recreation Resources Review Commission, GPO, January, 1962.

47 The story behind the Land and Water Conservation Fund is byzantine and requires substantial study to grasp even its outlines. The fund was essentially a ransom negotiated by Senator C. P. Anderson to get the Wilderness Act out of the House Interior and Insular Affairs Committee in 1964 after it was held hostage for years by Chairman Wayne Aspinall, who also obtained approval for his pet project, the Public Land Law Review Commission, as part of his price for releasing the wilderness legislation that he feared. Aspinall thought the fund, with its provisions to purchase non-wilderness land for public use, would relieve pressure by environmentalists to designate endless wilderness areas, but he failed to see that the same pressure would be applied to private property through the fund with even worse impact to the economy. See *Conservation Politics: The Senate Career of C. P. Anderson*, Richard A. Baker, University of New Mexico Press, 1965. See also "The National Forests and the Campaign for Wilderness Legislation, " by Dennis Roth, *Journal of Forest History*, Vol. 28, No. 3, July 1984, p. 112. See also *National Parks for a New Generation: Vision, Realities, Prospects*, Conservation Foundation, sponsored by the Richard King Mellon Foundation, Washington, D.C., 1985, p. 233.

48 Diamond is listed in *Who's Who In The East*.

49 *America's National Parks and Their Keepers*, by Ronald Foresta, Resources For The Future, Washington, D.C. [Baltimore] distributed by the Johns Hopkins University Press, 1984, p. 237-38.

50 *An Organizational Trend Analysis of the National Park System between 1960 and 1980*, by Ric Davidge, internal study, U.S. Department of the Interior, p. 31.

51 *National Registry of Natural Landmarks Handbook*, U.S. Department of the Interior, National Park Service, Release No. 2, August 18, 1966, p. 2. Released by C. P. Montgomery, Assistant Director.

52 Memo from Howard R. Stagner, Chief Naturalist, to Director Wirth, February 5, 1962.

53 49 Statutes 666 (1935).

54 The Nature Conservancy, *Preserving Our Natural Heritage*, brochure, 1976.

55 H.R. 6804, National Heritage Policy Act of 1979, introduced in the House September, 1979.

56 U.S. Congress, House Report No. 96-1456. pp. 54, 58.

57 36 Code of Federal Regulations 1212.

58 U.S. Congress, House Report No. 96-1457, pp. 22-23, 45.

59 *Historic Green Springs, Inc., v. Bob Bergland, et al.*, Civil Action No. 77-0230-R, August 11, 1980, U.S. District Court, Richmond, Virginia. See "Judge Overturns Historic Status of Section of Louisa County, Va.," by Peter Elkind, *Washington Post*, August 18, 1980.

60 45 *Federal Register* 81185.

61 *Potential Ecological and Geological Natural Landmarks of the New England-Adirondack Region*, Thomas G. Siccama, William A. Niering, Gail Kalison, Ann M.H. O'Dell, Elizabeth B. Speer, Yale School of Forestry, 1982, p. 7.

62 *At the Eye of the Storm: James Watt and the Environmentalists*, Ron Arnold, Regnery Gateway, Chicago, 1981.

63 H.R. 4035.

64 Memo, Solicitor William H. Coldiron to Assistant Secretary for Policy, Budget and Administration (Robin West), October 9, 1981, p. 5.

65 *History and Prehistory in the National Park System and the National Historic Landmark Program*, National Park Service, Washington, 1982.

66 *Evaluation of Bristol Cliffs Natural Landmark*, Jeff Severson, University of Vermont, Botany Department, 1989.

67 Charles W. Johnson to Ted Nelson, June 12, 1989, on letterhead of State of Vermont Agency of Natural Resources, Department of Forests, Parks and Recreation.

68 James M. Jeffords to John A. Hise, Jr., June 12, 1989.

69 James M. Ridenour to John A. Hise, Jr., June 21, 1989.

70 "The National Natural Landmark Program: A Natural Areas Protection Technique for the 1980s and Beyond," by Russell A. Cohen, *UCLA Journal of Environmental Law and Policy*, Vol. 3, Fall 1982, Number 1, p. 120ff.

71 *National Parks for a New Generation*, p. 268-69.

72 Associate Director for Planning and Development (Dave Wright) to Regional Directors, NPS memo dated December 9, 1986.

73 Jerry Rogers (associate NPS director, cultural resources) to Dave Wright (associate NPS director, planning and development) internal memo, draft version, July 17, 1986, finished version August 4, 1986.

74 "National Landmark Programs: Ladies in Waiting," *Investing in Park Futures: A Blueprint for Tomorrow*. Volume 8, "New Parks: New Promise," National Parks and Conservation Association, Washington, D.C. 1988, p. III-54-III-59.

75 NPS memo, chief, interagency resources division to chief, park planning and special studies division, May 7 1987.

76 William Penn Mott to Paul Pritchard, April 12, 1988.

77 Chief, wildlife and vegetation division to National Natural Landmarks Program Regional coordinators, NPS memo, April 26, 1990.

78 Charles M. McKinney III to Peter Rich, June 24, 1991.

79 "Secret target of landmark stealth," by Alston Chase, *Washington Times*, March 5, 1990. See also the follow-up column, "National landmark cover-up continues," Alston Chase, *Washington Times*, March 21, 1990.

80 See Letters to the Editor, *Washington Times*, March 23, 1990, p. A9. See also "National Parks Association President and Chairman of the Washington County Alliance Battlelt Out on National Stage," *Downeast Coastal Press*, April 3, 1990, p. 19.

81 "Landmarks lassitude?" by Alston Chase, *Washington Times*, December 14, 1991.

82 "Reward for park misdeeds," by Alston Chase, *Washington Times*, April 16, 1991.

83 Veyhl to Ridenour, March 27, 1992. Veyhl to Ridenour, May 4, 1992. Ridenour to Veyhl, May 20, 1992. Veyhl to Ridenour, May 29, 1992. George Berklacy, NPS Office of Public Affairs, to Veyhl, June 4, 1992, stating, "Your repeated requests have not produced the evidence you seek because it does not exist."

84 "NPS Director Ridicules Critics," *Land Rights Letter*, April 1992, p. 7.

85 *NPCA New York Annual Financial Report*, June 30, 1991, p. 1, Financial Summary, Line 19, "Other Changes in Fund Balances."

86 Letter of Proposal and Agreement, from PIC to Judy Graziano (NPCA), September 4, 1991. New York Department of State, Office of Charities Registration.

People for the Ethical Treatment of Animals

People for the Ethical Treatment of Animals (Founded 1980)
Annual budget: $11,700,000 (1993); $9,800,000 (1992)
Staff: 103 total
Members: 500,000 contributors
Tax Status: 501(c)(3)
Headquarters: P. O. Box 42516
Washington, D.C. 20015
Phone: (301)770-7444 Fax: (202)770-8969

Economy Trasher Number Fifteen. People for the Ethical Treatment of Animals (PETA) is one of the more rabid and radical—and influential—environmental groups on the scene today. The *Animal Rights Reporter* called PETA "the most influential organization in the animal rights movement." PETA "has established an impressive track record of orchestrated events which bring it media attention, movement respect, and member donations." PETA "has grown in size and scope, resembling a small corporation more than the cutting edge of a social movement."[1]

As an advocate of animal rights philosophy, PETA has agitated to eliminate the meat industry ("we're absolutely opposed to breeding animals for humans"); abolish the use of furs from fur farms or wild animals; stop all hunting ("there's something fundamentally wrong with a person who feels that it's acceptable to go out into the woods, and for fun, slaughter") and fishing ("fishes suffocate"); eliminate the use of animals in entertainment, medical research and military research; prevent the use of all animal products such as wool ("we don't need wool") and silk ("silkworms can feel pain"); and stop the ownership of animals as pets—all of which is a reflection of its "vegan" ideology.[2]

PETA promotes *veganism*, an animal rights philosophy far more radical than vegetarianism. Veganism, as well as it can be represented accurately, is the ideal that no animal food be consumed in any way, not even milk or eggs, and that no harm of any sort be done by humans to any animal because there is no moral difference between humans and animals. Examples: PETA co-director Ingrid E. Newkirk asserted about those who eat meat, "I would think it's primitive, barbaric, arrogant, unnecessary."[3]

Production of milk or even honey is immoral since it involves "exploitation." Newkirk explained, "Most supermarket milk comes from cows raised in intensive factory farms. They stand on concrete most of their lives, they are inside most of the time, they are artificially inseminated, their young are taken away from them when they are one or two days old, they go on to become veal."[4] She agreed with an interviewer that pet ownership is the moral equivalent of slavery, unless the animal needed shelter to begin with. The very word "pet" is offensive, since it "connotes a demeaning attitude of master versus thing."[5]

The notion of animal rights is something relatively new, something alien to animal welfare, and brimming with an agenda of disaster for people.[6] This program was explicated by Australian philosopher Peter Singer in his 1975 book *Animal Liberation,* which challenged the notion of human dominance over other animals and contemptuously reviled animal welfare and humane treatment as just another form of "speciesism." Singer asserted, "Human beings have come to realize that they [are] animals themselves, It can no longer be maintained by anyone but a religious fanatic that man is the special darling of the whole universe, or that other animals were created to provide us with food, or that we have divine authority over them, and divine permission to kill them."[7]

The core of the animal rights philosophy is the dismissal of differences between people and animals—language, reason, morality, free will—as ethically irrelevant. Animal rights asserts equal moral status to all living things based on the ability to feel pain. In this ethic, all human use of animals, for food, clothing, sport, companionship, medical research, is "speciesism," the moral equivalent of racism.[8]

The movement's theoretician, Tom Regan, clearly recognized one place the philosophy is taking us: to the crippling of medical science. He wrote in his 1983 book, *The Case for Animal Rights,* "Even granting that we face greater harm than laboratory animals presently endure if research on these animals is stopped, the rights view will not be satisfied with anything less than total abolition. The practice remains wrong because unjust.

"If abandoning animal research means that there are some things we cannot learn, then so be it.... We have no basic right...not to be harmed by those natural diseases we are heir to."[9]

PETA is even against dissection in medical schools.[10] The *Washington Post,* which gives money to environmental groups, became alarmed and wrote an editorial worrying that hard-line animal activists will completely outlaw anatomy instruction with animal specimens in schools.[11] It sounds to us like PETA leaders have had brain surgery by doctors trained in PETA medical schools.[12]

As expert economy trashers, PETA activists have developed highly sophisticated attacks on industry. They use slick media campaigns and rock stars, they peddle T-shirts, sports watches and videos. They generally try to give the animal rights movement a degree of hipness that appeals to the youth market. In one campaign, Canadian singer k.d. lang made a beef-against-beef television spot in an effort to destroy the meat and animal husbandry industry.[13]

Trashing the fur economy has been a growth industry for PETA. This animal rights group thrusts their views on big names in the fashion industry. PETA has pressured modeling agencies, photographers, and stylists to refuse to work with furs. PETA protesters staged a nasty demonstration at a 1991 Oscar de la Renta fur show.[14] Three major fashion designers have stopped using furs: Bill Blass, Georgio Armani, and Norma Komali, but deny PETA had anything to do with it.[15] PETA pressure probably did, however, if Merv Griffin Enterprises' example is instructive: They sent PETA a letter stating that fur coats will no longer be given as prizes on television's "Wheel of Fortune." The syndicated show had a policy of using only ranch-raised furs, but Griffin Enterprises President Robert Murphy told PETA that all fur gifts had been eliminated.[16] The pressure against wearing fur was so intense it sparked a near-violent backlash at a Hollywood fund raiser for animal rights.[17]

Fortune magazine flippantly described British-born PETA co-director Ingrid Newkirk as "the Mother Teresa of rabbits," but acknowledged that she has imposed PETA's ethics on companies such as Benetton and Noxell "the same way trains impose themselves on stalled sedans." Running over industry roughshod is a favorite pastime of environmentalists. Companies are like trees in the sense which John Muir once complained that "trees cannot run away; any fool can destroy them." The same is true of companies. They cannot run away either, and any fool can destroy them with a little persistence. PETA has the persistence.[18]

PETA's protests against animal testing of cosmetics, applying cosmetics to animals' eyes or skin to test for toxicity and safety, caused Avon so much distress that the company announced in June 1990 it would suspend the tests—with no reliable alternative to determine the safety of their products to their customers.[19] PETA also constrained Tonka to stop safety testing Play-Doh on rabbits. Other companies that have stopped safety tests because of PETA demands include Revlon, Faberge, Mary Kay Cosmetics, Amway, Mattel Toys, and Hasbro. Even though each of these companies denies that PETA agitation had anything to do with their decision to stop safety testing, there was no other reason for them to stop.[20] In addition, a PETA Catalog offers a video of product testing on rabbits at Biosearch, a Philadelphia laboratory, claiming the exposé by "one of our undercover investigators" to have been "instrumental in the banning of these cruel tests by major companies including Avon, Revlon, Benetton, and Estee Lauder."[21] The National Institutes of Health and the American Medical Association have expressed concern over what PETA and other animal rights groups are doing to public health and safety.[22]

Zoological societies are also under attack by PETA, which seems to want all zoos shut down.[23]

To PETA, *homo sapiens* seems to be the only species that may be abused. Ingrid Newkirk said about people, "We're the biggest blight on the face of the earth," and in the same interview volunteered the macabre thought, "Human euthanasia would be a great step if there were no abuses."[24] Medical research to save children's lives is improper, since "you have no right."[25] PETA certainly deserves honorary membership in *Wild Earth's* Voluntary Human Extinction Movement: PETA's Newkirk declared in a now-famous 1986 interview the oft-reprinted quote, "I don't believe human beings have the 'right to life.' That's a supremacist perversion. A rat is a pig is a dog is a boy." Even the truculent environmentalist *Audubon* magazine panned Newkirk for such virulent misanthropy.[26]

It hardly needs saying, but devaluing human life and deifying animals is a dangerous development in a society into which, as P.T. Barnum once observed, "There's a sucker born every minute." Self-loathing is a time-honored indoor sport among us human beings. The trouble is, when reduced to a plan of action in a gullible society, the game of self-loathing usually divides into two camps, loathors and loathees, one of which staffs the ovens while the other goes up in smoke. Our most recent animal rights regime was run by one Heinrich Himmler, whose immortal thoughts on Jews, Gypsies, Blacks and homosexuals echo down to us through the years: "We Germans, who are the only people in the world who have a decent attitude toward animals, will also assume a decent attitude toward these human animals." The audience applauded.

It couldn't happen here? It *is* happening here. *PETA* is happening here. As the human advocacy group Putting People First said in court records about PETA: "In their eyes, those who do not share their philosophy—animal trainers, hunters, fishermen, cattlemen, grocers, and indeed all non-vegetarians—are the moral equivalent of cannibals, slaveowners, and death-camp guards, and must be dealt with accordingly."[27] Barnum was right. To the Egress.[28]

Most PETA supporters do not know about the group's vegan agenda and follow the group because they believe it is effective in pushing the cause of humanity to animals. Here we see a pattern common to American environmental groups: The leaders have a radical agenda, but the followers do not, yet help them with money and memberships anyway.[29] As H. L. Mencken said, "No one ever went broke underestimating the intelligence of the American public."

Critics, however, have a way of making things clear: Ted Nugent, rock star and bowhunter, was quoted by the Texas Wildlife Association as saying, "These animal rights freaks are to wildlife what Jim and Tammy Bakker were to religion."[30]

PETA was the brain-child of doctor's-son Alex Pacheco, who was raised from infancy in Mexico and grew up in Ohio, where he graduated from high school and entered Ohio State University, planning to become a Catholic priest. Pacheco says that his interest in animal rights originated during a 1978 stay with a friend in Toronto during which he visited a slaughterhouse, a visit which traumatized him so much he became a vegetarian on the spot. His visit was followed by indoctrination by "two brilliant activists," one a founder of **American Vegetarians** and the other an "artist, feminist, and animals rights activist."[31] He got a copy of Peter Singer's *Animal Liberation*. The die was cast. Pacheco quickly founded a campus animal rights group and hasn't stopped since.[32]

But there's more to it. The ancestry of Pacheco's People for the Ethical Treatment of Animals can be traced in a roundabout fashion to 1962 England and the **Hunt Saboteurs Association**. HSA specialized in "hunt sabs," disrupting fox hunts by spraying artificial fox scent designed to throw the hounds off the trail and also vandalizing hunters' vehicles—tire slashing, windshield smashing, and the like. The HSA created the pattern that would dominate animal rights activism to this day: It operated as a loosely organized underground attack group, but worked in tandem with an aboveground group, the **League Against Cruel Sports**, which conducted aboveground lobbying and public relations campaigns just far enough away from the HSA to avoid prosecution.

The HSA was one of a number of early British animal rights groups, the most important of which was the **Animal Liberation Front**, founded in 1976 by convicted animal rights criminal Ronnie Lee upon his parole after serving one year of a three-year prison sentence for a series of firebombings against laboratories as a member of the **Band of Mercy**. Lee had founded the Band of Mercy in 1972 as a splinter from the HSA, which Lee saw as being insufficiently direct.

Lee joined with thirty supporters to form the

Animal Liberation Front
Domestic terrorists, United Kingdom and USA
Membership secret and underground
Budget secret, aided by above-ground groups such as PETA
FBI lists ALF among America's Top Ten Terrorist organizations

and immediately returned to vandalism and arson. Lee said, "The attack on the Charles River Laboratories was the first ALF activity; vehicles were damaged, and several thousand pounds' worth of damage was caused."[33] In its first year of operations, ALF inflicted a quarter-million pounds sterling in damage. Its targets included any institution in any way connected with animals. Butcher shops, furriers, animal breeders, chicken and beef farmers, fast food outlets, and horse racing tracks were all hit. ALF smashed the windows of several halal [Islamic] butcher shops in Bedfordshire; smashed the windows of six shops in Banbury for displaying circus posters; planted a bomb under the car of a cancer researcher.[34]

Even the dead were not safe from Animal Liberation Front terrorism, which set out to shock the public out of its apathy about animal mistreatment. In January 1977 three ALF activists broke into the graveyard of St. Kentigern's Church in the small Lake District village of Caldbeck to desecrate the grave of Robert Peel, the legendary huntsman and most English of folk heroes, who had lain there a hundred and twenty-three years. They smashed his headstone and dug up the grave. The activists, who did not bill the desecration as an ALF raid, even called the media to report they had exhumed Peel's remains and thrown them in a cesspit. The police found no evidence of this, but discovered a stuffed fox's head in the dug up grave. One of Ronnie Lee's colleagues, Mike Huskisson, and two other activists were captured and sentenced to nine months in jail for the desecration.[35]

There followed a decade of increasing violence as the animal rights movement radicalized in the United Kingdom. In 1982, the **Animal Rights Militia**, actually ALF members using another name, sent letter bombs to the Prime Minister and the leaders of three political parties, with one exploding and injuring an office worker; firebombs were hurled at the homes of four staff members of the Willcome Foundation's laboratories and the homes of two directors of the British Industrial Biological Research Association. The cars of two BIBRA staff members were bombed. In 1984 Scotland Yard established a special squad and an Animal Rights National Index for the protection of researchers and investigation of animal rights terrorism.[36]

More recent acts of Animal Liberation Front terrorism in the U.K. include firebombing of numerous fur-selling department stores,[37] firebombing of medical research universities,[38] and the bombing of researchers' cars[39]—one of which bombs permanently injured an infant.[40]

In 1979, just before Alex Pacheco founded PETA, he got a summer job on the *Sea Shepherd*, the ship financed by Cleveland Amory's Fund for Animals and operated by defrocked Greenpeacie Paul Watson (see profile of Greenpeace and subprofile of the Sea Shepherd Conservation Society above; see also the profile of Fund for Animals below). *Sea Shepherd* Captain Paul Watson was at that time obsessed with destroying a particularly infamous whaling boat, the *Sierra*. He caught up with the vessel off the coast of Portugal and rammed it. The whaler was towed into Lisbon harbor for repairs where Sea Shepherd supporters later blew it up with a naval bomb. Watson had already scuttled the first *Sea Shepherd* in Leixoes harbor to prevent it from being sold to pay for his damages to the *Sierra*.

Some romanticized stories say that Alex Pacheco was part of the ramming crew and was briefly jailed in Portugal, but there were only three men on the *Sea Shepherd* when it attacked the *Sierra*, and Pacheco was not one of them.

Pacheco actually went straight to England, where he joined the Hunt Saboteurs Association. There he learned the ways of animal-rights ferocity with gusto. "I had a lot of fun," Pacheco said of his Saboteur experience. "There was a lot of excitement."

Part of Pacheco's English excitement was meeting Kim Stallwood, a young and politically savvy animal rights journal editor with the traditionalist **British Union for the Abolition of Vivisection**.[41] Stallwood himself was far more radical than BUAV's somewhat genteel and graying membership, openly supporting ALF with sympathetic coverage in his periodical, *Liberator*. Another one of those aboveground-belowground relationships. Six years later, Stallwood was to have every member of BUAV's executive committee he disapproved of removed, a slick trick accomplished by bussing two-hundred black-clad radicals to an election meeting long remembered for its cries of "Fuck the rich!" which reduced the "menopausal old bitches," as one young firebrand called some of the elderly members, to tears.[42] Stallwood was later to become a key player in PETA.

Pacheco returned to the United States and transferred to George Washington University where he became a political science major. While volunteering at a local dog pound he met Ingrid Newkirk, who worked there. He shared with her his copy of *Animal Liberation* and gained a new convert.[43] He incorporated People for the Ethical Treatment of Animals as a Delaware corporation in July, 1980, with co-director Ingrid Newkirk. Newkirk had previously been a deputy sheriff, a Maryland state law enforcement officer—evidently all in animal control capacities—and chief of Animal Disease Control for the District of Columbia's Commission on Public Health.[44] She, like Pacheco, is one tough cookie. Now America had an animal rights group run by a doctor's son turned Sab and a cop gone sour.

PETA assembled a core-group of eighteen members that met in a Takoma Park, Maryland basement. PETA's first operations were in 1980 picketing a poultry slaughterhouse in Washington. In April 1981 the group demonstrated at the National Institutes of Health against animal research. A month later PETA began its now-infamous attack against Dr. Edward Taub, a behavioral scientist of national standing, whose work was largely devoted to the rehabilitation of stroke and head injury victims. A fellow scientist told a *Baltimore Sun* reporter, "In addition to his landmark studies of the recuperative potential of damaged nervous systems, Dr. Taub's contributions to the relatively new discipline of biofeedback have vast and immediate therapeutic implications in such diverse areas as psychiatry, neurology, cardiology, and gastroenterology...in fact, to speak merely of his 'contributions' is to minimize his efforts, as Dr. Taub is actually one of the founding fathers of this field."[45]

Dr. Taub came to the attention of PETA because Alex Pacheco found his name on a list of government research grant recipients, he was the closest researcher to Pacheco's Takoma Park home, just a short distance away in Silver Spring, Maryland, and because Taub used monkeys in research to help stroke and head injury victims regain use of paralyzed limbs.

Dr. Taub at the time was studying deafferentation, the loss of all sensation in a body part—although some control over movement returns, in practice, most affected limbs atrophy and become useless. Through research with monkeys, Dr. Taub discovered that paralysis in surgically deafferented arms and legs was only temporary, and that the monkey could thereafter be trained to use the limbs. Dr. Taub discovered the crucial fact that in humans, the loss of use was not the direct result of stroke or injury, but of frustration and inability to learn to use a limb that cannot be controlled through the instinctive sense of feel. The benefits patients have received from this discovery are beyond measure.[46]

Alex Pacheco infiltrated Dr. Taub's laboratory, posing as a student interested in his research. He seems to have been following the action plan recommended in the animal-rights manual *Love and Anger* by Richard Morgan. "Since most researchers don't think there's anything wrong with what they're doing, they might even be willing to discuss their research with you, as long as you approach them innocently."[47] Dr. Taub suspected nothing.

Pacheco ingratiated himself with Dr. Taub, volunteering to work at night, and Taub gave him the keys to the place. Pacheco secretly took pictures of conditions in the lab that he thought were "horrifying," and took them to New York animal rights groups. Cleveland Amory, who had financed the *Sea Shepherd* ramming of the *Sierra* in 1979, gave Pacheco money to buy a better camera and some walkie-talkies, which enabled Pacheco to photograph inside the lab while staying in touch with a sentry posted outside to warn of any unexpected visitors.[48]

When Dr. Taub went on vacation for two weeks in August, 1981, he left the monkeys in the care of lab assistants with whom Pacheco had struck up a friendship. One day, one of the lab assistants improperly lashed an experimental monkey known as Domitian to a "chairing" device in a shocking quasi-crucified pose. While the lab assistant was out of the room, Pacheco took pictures of the setup.[49] He later used one of the photos in a poster emblazoned with the motto: "This Is Vivisection. Don't Let Anyone Tell You Different." Thus a photo of an improper setup became the emblem of the animals rights movement against animal suffering.

While Taub was on vacation, two graduate student lab assistants mysteriously failed to show up for work to clean the cages or feed the animals on certain days. John Kunz, the graduate student left in charge of the place, said, "Both of them stopped coming in. They called in with different excuses. I didn't come down on them hard. In hindsight, maybe they were taking advantage of that situation."[50] On days when the lab was improperly staffed and in disarray through no fault of Dr. Taub, Pacheco brought in sympathetic academics and animal rights activists, including members of the Humane Society, on unauthorized "tours" of the lab.[51]

Pacheco then obtained affidavits from his "tourists"—as a lawyer described it, he "covered himself with paper"—stating that the monkeys were living in poor and unhealthful conditions. He took the photos and affidavits to local law enforcement agencies, who agreed to obtain a search warrant to raid the lab and seize Taub's animals—but not before animal rights activists spent days building cages to house the 17 monkeys that would be seized. The night before the raid, Pacheco and Newkirk smuggled in one final witness, veterinarian Richard Weitzman, who did not agree that the animals were in any danger and said his reaction was, "Why didn't you confront the gentleman and tell him what's wrong and have him fix it?" Pacheco and Newkirk did not inform Weitzman of the next morning's raid. When Weitzman heard about the raid on the news, he said, "I knew there was something not too right about this. I felt they were people who were against the research more than anything else."[52]

Police executed a search warrant and seized the monkeys on September 11, 1981. PETA promptly ran a large fundraising ad based on the story. Readers were exhorted to "be part of a historical first" by sending money. Contributors were told "Money is urgently needed for civil legal costs, expert witnesses, other professionals, etc. for this on going project," although the only legal action pending was one brought by the State.[53]

The prosecuting attorney, Roger Galvin, brought a 17-count information against Dr. Taub, of which 11 counts were dismissed at trial, 5 ended in acquittal, and the one remaining was overturned and dismissed upon appeal.[54]

The single residual charge was failure to provide adequate veterinary care for six of the animals. Seven veterinarians gave testimony on that count regarding the advisability of bandaging nerve-severed limbs. Five had expertise in deafferentation, and supported Taub's decision not to use bandages. Two vets with no specific expertise held that he had been negligent in omitting bandages. The court sided with the two dissenting opinions and found Taub guilty of one charge of animal cruelty. His conviction was overturned on appeal and four scientific societies also exonerated him in independent investigations.

Roger Galvin, however, may not have been the impartial official he was supposed to be: He shortly helped to found the California-based **Animal Legal Defense Fund**, which began working in cahoots with PETA.[55]

PETA paid no attention whatever to Dr. Taub's inconvenient acquittal—they continue to fundraise on the case to this day, peddling a $15 videotape in their PETA Catalog (Item No. 6506), *The Silver Spring Monkeys,* which smears Dr. Taub as if he had been convicted. The sales blurb said, "Alex Pacheco narrates the story of the first-ever police raid on a research laboratory...and the first and only U. S. criminal conviction of an experimenter on charges of cruelty to animals."[56]

Cleveland Amory, founder of The Fund for Animals, got in on the Taub case and wrote a tidy little hatchet piece in the *New York Times* headlined, "Needless Cruelty to Animals," which reinforced PETA's misrepresentation of Dr. Taub's work and conviction.[57]

The Taub case put PETA on the map. It was only the beginning. A year later, the Animal Liberation Front burglarized laboratories at the University of Pennsylvania Head Injury Clinic which were developing therapies for serious head injuries based on research using baboons—research which helped develop antitoxins that counteract the effects of stroke or trauma and greatly limit the damage.[58] The ALF stole 6 years worth of research data in their first break-in, including videotapes of the injuries and treatment, also doing extensive vandalism to computers and medical equipment. ALF during its second break-in stole animals being used in research on arthritis and Sudden Infant Death Syndrome. PETA immediately distributed ALF news releases attacking the research and making it look as bad as possible.[59]

The ALF had uncovered something serious in the Penn case, unlike the Taub farce. From the 60 hours of videotape ALF stole, PETA edited down a 26 minute indictment of technicians making crude remarks while performing non-sterile surgery on inadequately anesthetized baboons. The tape had been shot by the researchers themselves. The evidence was incontrovertible.

The reaction was overwhelming. PETA members staged a sit-in at National Institutes of Health on Rockville Pike in Washington, D.C. Secretary of Health and Human Services Margaret Heckler suspended funding for the Penn project. The NIH slapped Penn with a citation for "material failure to comply with Public Health Service policy for the care and use of laboratory animals." The U. S. Department of Agriculture, which is responsible for enforcing the Animal Welfare Act, stuck Penn with a $4,000 civil penalty. Ultimately, the Head Injury Clinic was closed.[60]

As the *Daily Pennsylvanian* reported, "The incident gained national press attention, culminating in an appearance on the Phil Donahue Show by People for the Ethical Treatment of Animals' co-founder Ingrid Newkirk.... The University remained the center of controversy when the California-based Animal Legal Defense Fund threatened to file suit."[61]

PETA still fundraises from copies of the tapes ALF stole, hawking in its catalog a $15 videotape titled *Unnecessary Fuss* described as "rare and stunning footage, filmed by researchers themselves" which gives "a unique and in-depth view of how experimenters abused baboons."[62]

PETA forwarded copies of the documents stolen by the Animal Liberation Front— PETA says it does not accept stolen materials for legal reasons, but does accept copies of them—to the Animal Legal Defense Fund for legal consideration. ALDF's annual report brags that it was involved in defense of activists facing "criminal charges arising from the break-in at the University of Pennsylvania Head Injury Laboratory and the showing of the videotape... After the receipt of 60 hours of head injury videotapes by PETA, ALDF attorneys began a series of FOIA requests." The annual report also notes ALDF's victory in preventing grand jury testimony relating to the break-in, and in five of their attorneys overseeing "the highly successful NIH sit-in, which is credited with forcing the final closing of the head injury laboratory."[63]

Within a short time, animal rights terrorism surged in the United States. PETA made no effort to hide its encouragement of this activity. A November, 1983 *Washington Post* article on Ingrid Newkirk, who had just resigned from the D. C. Animal Disease Control Division, noted that during her five years in that Division, "Newkirk has endorsed—and on occasion served as intermediary for—a clandestine group called the Animal Liberation Front, whose members have stolen research animals from Howard University and a U. S. Navy lab in Bethesda."[64] One of PETA's *Factsheets* stated:

> The Animal Liberation Front's activities comprise an important part of today's animal protection movement just as the Underground Railroad and the French Resistance did in earlier battles for social justice. Without ALF break-ins at the University of Pennsylvania Head Injury Clinic, the City of Hope in Los Angeles, and at many other facilities that had successfully sealed their atrocities from public scrutiny, many more animals would have suffered....
>
> What you can do:
>
> Offer a permanent home to rescued [i.e., stolen] animals: contact PETA for information. Support PETA's *Activist Defense Fund*, which helps pay legal fees of individuals accused of liberation-related activities. Blow the whistle on facilities where animals are forced to suffer. You may now be working in such a place, or be willing to take a job to keep a particular laboratory or animal supplier under surveillance. All contacts are kept in strict confidence.[65]

It was clear that PETA had established itself as the aboveground lobbyist parallel to ALF as the underground terrorist exactly on the British model.

In July 1989, ALF burglars broke into and entered the laboratories of Dr. John Orem at Texas Tech University Health Sciences Center. ALF burglars stole his personal records, his research animals, spray-painted his walls, and destroyed more than $50,000 worth of equipment. Dr. Orem had been investigating Sudden Infant Death Syndrome. "SIDS is the leading killer of babies in the first year of life," according to Dr. John Remmers, a leading pulmonologist. "We have no idea how to prevent it or treat it. We need to understand the activity of the nerve cells in the brain that regulate breathing during sleep. Until this happened to Dr. Orem, he was the only one in the world getting at the fundamental causes of SIDS."[66]

Orem had trained a small number of cats through behavioral conditioning to hold their breath briefly so he could monitor brain-cell activity during apnea, or breathing interruption. He implanted electrodes into the brains of the cats with such sophisticated painless techniques that they carried on normal lives in his lab, playing, eating, sleeping, roaming around at will. His data-gathering capabilities were equally sophisticated, allowing him to obtain meaningful information with a minimum of experimental animals, fewer than ten each year. The National Institutes of Health said Orem's veterinary practices were a model of excellence and federal inspectors consistently found his lab exemplary.

PETA immediately used the felonious raid as a basis for fundraising, touting the burglary in its newsletter, interviewing two of the ALF burglars,[67] and giving out Dr.

Orem's home address, urging readers to "write polite, respectful letters," but also enabling PETA members to harass him.[68] PETA also offered a $15 video (Item No. 6509) titled *No Gravy for the Cat*, which their sales pitch described as "An exposé of John Orem's ride on the federal grant gravy train and the story of five cats slated for death in his laboratory at Texas Tech and how they escaped with their activist liberators on the underground railroad."[69]

Also in 1989, on April 3 the Animal Liberation Front broke into three buildings at the University of Arizona, stole more than a thousand animals being used in medical studies, vandalized equipment to the tune of $300,000 and destroyed two research laboratories, a research center, and an off-campus office by gasoline fires.[70]

> Twenty-four hours later, ALF released a videotape of the destruction, filmed by its own crew, to one local TV station, Channel 9. Transmitted via satellite from the headquarters of People for the Ethical Treatment of Animals (PETA) in Washington, D.C., to Channel 9 [in Tucson, Arizona] the tape was shown on the three major television stations as the lead story on their evening news reports the day after the attack.[71]

As a result of these raids, the FBI has formally classified ALF as a terrorist organization. The FBI considers ALF responsible for more than a hundred criminal attacks, including three classified as domestic terrorism.[72] PETA, the aboveground ally of underground ALF, provides aid and comfort, publishing full-page ads in PETA's journal, with photographs of stolen animals and proclamations that "All these animals were rescued by the Animal Liberation Front" and the "ALF Credo," which includes the commitment "To economically sabotage the industries of animal exploitation."[73] Alex Pacheco has stated bluntly, "Damaging the enemy financially is fair game."[74]

The animal rights movement is doing a good job of trashing the economy while getting rich itself. The 1980s saw the establishment of at least seventy animal rights groups and an increasing shift of traditional animal welfare organizations toward animal rights causes. By the end of the decade, Fund for Animals had an income of $1.8 million and assets of over $2 million; Animal Protection Institute had a $2.6 million income; Animal Welfare Institute had $404,998; Friends of Animals brought in $3.4 million. Just these five outfits commanded an income of more than $15 million atop assets of nearly $7 million.[75]

Legal action—lobbying and litigating—has shut down research projects worth hundreds of millions of dollars.[76] Laws restricting the use of pound animals in medical research have raised costs prohibitively, killing projects in transplant and cardiovascular research requiring dogs and cats.[77] Illegal action has taken an even worse toll. Over the past ten years, raids have caused more than $10 million in damage in the United States. But the moral bankruptcy of the movement has wrought truly dreadful human costs, with raids delaying and stopping research projects on SIDS, infant blindness, cancer, AIDS, and many other diseases that plague both people and animals.[78] PETA not only condones such attacks, it offers a legal pamphlet about them.

PETA published a pamphlet, *Activism and the Law*, counseling that there may come a point in any public struggle when "a law once obeyed reluctantly or uncritically is discredited," and suggests that "more and more people" are "deciding there is a higher law than that written by those who subjugate the helpless." It counsels that while the decision to undertake "illegal actions" may be unpopular, "no struggle against exploitation has been won without them."

The pamphlet also makes it clear that the "discredited" laws PETA activists may disobey are not just municipal ordinances against sit-ins, but also the statutes prohibiting burglary, arson, and grand larceny. PETA further points out that "today's legal system is a nightmare for the police officer: a poker game in which all the best cards seem to be in the defendant's hand," since "judges dismiss cases for cryptic, technical reasons." The message, evidently written by Ingrid Newkirk from her law enforcement experience, is not a "Law and Order" complaint. It is virtually legal advice for potential lawbreakers: "PETA urges all activists contemplating or fearing brushes with the legal justice system to do their 'homework,' & offers this pamphlet as a brief introduction to encounters with the law."[79]

The pamphlet gives legal counsel to prospective criminals and others in the form of a sample hypothetical case: "Brown and his female companion are stopped by the police at 8 pm as they are walking on the public road in the vicinity of the burglary of a primate research center. Brown is carrying a backpack." PETA activists are advised how to deal with the legal situation of suspect Brown after he and his companion are stopped:

> The officers ask the couple who they are and what they are doing. Brown responds that they are just out for a walk. As he reaches into a coat pocket to pull out a wallet, one of the officers spins him around, pats down his clothing, and pulls out the sole contents of the other pocket: a map of the research center with the surveillance camera and burglar alarm locations clearly marked.
> The officers order Brown to open his pack. Brown refuses to do so, stating that the pack contains only camping gear. The officers arrest Brown, search his pack and discover burglary tools and stolen research files.
> Brown's female companion has provided identification, but refuses to answer any of the officers' questions. They tell her she must accompany them to the station. At the station, Brown's companion is told by police that Brown has admitted his involvement in the crime—although he has not done so—and that the judge will go easy on her if she doesn't complicate the case. She confesses.
> Meanwhile, Brown is not read his rights until being interrogated six hours later at the police lock up. During questioning he admits that he broke into the center.

The pamphlet, PETA said, "should assist the reader in answering" a set of 14 legal questions, including, "Will the frisk be upheld by the courts?" and "Was the discovery of the map sufficient to warrant Brown's arrest?" and "Does Brown's companion's refusal to answer questions count against her?" and "Is her confession admissible?" With major headings such as "Silence is a Suspect's Best Friend," "Probable Cause," "Police Orders," and "Stop and Frisk," the pamphlet tells how to deal with misdemeanor charges ("painting slogans on a butcher's truck" or "interrupting a fur show") and felony charges ("burning a laboratory building" or "liberating animals valued at over $100").

Here we have a non-profit organization providing a written legal primer concerning the commission of a crime. PETA complains when animal-rights criminals are prosecuted.[80]

PETA goes a step further: it pays the legal expenses of animal rights criminals when apprehended and arrested. In the case of Roger Troen, who was arrested for taking part in an October 1986 burglary and arson at the University of Oregon, PETA paid his legal fees of $27,000, and informed its members in January of 1989 of the payment. After Troen's conviction in January 1988 of theft, burglary, and conspiracy, he was ordered to pay restitution of $34,900. PETA defector Gary Thorud said of Troen in a sworn deposition, "We were illegally funding this individual with money solicited for other causes, and Ingrid [Newkirk] was using that money, bragging to the staff that she had spent $25,000 in the case." PETA sued Thorud for making this and other anti-PETA statements, and vigorously denies that the use of such funds was illegal.[81]

Another animal rights activist, Fran Stephanie Trutt, was convicted of possessing pipe bombs and successfully prosecuted for attempting to murder the president of a medical laboratory with a radio-controlled, nail-studded bomb.[82] PETA's Form 990 Return of Organization Exempt From Income Tax for the fiscal year beginning August 1, 1988, shows that PETA contributed $7,500 to her legal expenses.

Biomedical researchers are perplexed at finding themselves polarized at one end of the spectrum of debate on the issue of animals and research, although they do not represent extreme views. *The Journal of the National Cancer Institute* commented, "At the other end are those who truly do represent extreme, radical views—[People for the Ethical Treatment of Animals] or any number of active groups."[83] The polarization has put all medical scientists who use animals at risk.

PETA has a long memory and seems never to forgive an opponent: In January 1990, ALF burglarized the office of University of Pennsylvania veterinary scientist Dr. Adrian Morrison, stole his personal correspondence and vandalized the room.[84] His offense? He had testified on Dr. Taub's behalf nine years earlier, and spoke up for the value of Dr. Orem's work, and—sin of sins—criticized PETA.

As the *Philadelphia Inquirer* reported of a PETA demonstration at Penn, "Morrison's office was broken into January 14. The militant Animal Liberation Front took credit. Yesterday, PETA released what it said was a 'preliminary examination' of copies of documents taken in the break-in. The review concluded that Morrison had written letters supporting other researchers and that he planned to oppose certain 'animal protective' legislation."[85]

When *Village Voice* published a story on animal rightist objections to Morrison's research, PETA sent out copies of it to a number of people who lived near Morrison, along with a letter saying, "Please see the enclosed *Village Voice* cover story involving your neighbor Adrian Morrison who lives at [home address]," enabling readers to harass him.[86] PETA's newsletter bragged: "Tired out from the ALF raid on his Penn lab, Adrian Morrison got a grant to spend a month in Italy this summer visiting fellow cat-electrode implanter Pier Permeggani at the University of Bologna. See how tight funds are? Sure there were sightseeing trips, expensive dinners and vivisection stories swapped, but the real highlight of Morrison's trip was being discovered, exposed and picketed by Animal Amnesty, a PETA contact group. Thanks to the activists, there really *is* no rest for the wicked."[87]

Alex Pacheco brought Kim Stallwood to the United States in 1986 to serve as executive director at a salary of $41,000 (1989). PETA members and supporters began a corporate takeover campaign against animal humane groups similar to the coup which Stallwood had pulled off in England with the British Union for the Abolition of Vivisection. According to the *Boston Globe*, "A PETA consultant won control of the Toronto Humane Society, endowed with $14 million, last fall through a proxy fight. One of her employees recently was arrested for possession of explosives and weapons, and vandalizing a restaurant that served chicken."[88]

PETA activists also took over the $8 million-endowed New England Anti-Vivisection Society in a two-fisted proxy fight. The *Boston Globe* reported, "The wife of Gary Francione, a PETA executive and a Pennsylvania attorney, walked into the Anti-Vivisection Society's Boston headquarters a few months ago and purchased 300 voting memberships for $3,000 in cash.... A surge of several hundred applications for voting membership arrived at the headquarters in bulk...."

Alex Pacheco set up the Action Campaign Fund to subsidize or pay full airfare to Boston for voting activists all over the nation. According to the *Boston Globe*, "One activist from a Midwestern state described how more than two dozen tickets had already been reserved with PETA's permission."[89] PETA's Alex Pacheco and Ingrid Newkirk, along with Dr. Neal Barnard of PETA-ally, Physicians Committee for Responsible Medicine, were voted onto NEAVS's board of directors, thereby giving them access to the $8 million fund balance.

To prevent the same thing from happening to themselves, PETA made sure that their organization does not have 325,000 members as claimed, but exactly *three*: Chairman Alex Pacheco, director Ingrid E. Newkirk, and secretary/treasurer Sue Brebner. This three-member board of directors of PETA in 1987 voted themselves the only "members" of the organization. The move has a simple explanation: under Delaware non-profit corporation law, "members" have a right to vote for the board, remove directors for cause, and examine the corporate books. By amending their original Articles of Incorporation, the three-member board was able to convert their "members" into mere contributors, and the board into a cozy little self-perpetuating multi-million dollar trio.[90]

In 1990, PETA boasted an income of $6,793,809, of which slightly over $1.1 million was spent on fundraising.[91] Its operations were backed by nearly $2 million dollars in assets and a staff of sixty-five employees.[92]

Throughout America PETA activists have blocked laboratory entrances, picketed rodeos demanding an end to all cowboy sports, released gory video footage of health and safety test animals, broken up stockholder meetings, tried to shut down zoos, and sued in the courts to stop all health and safety testing on animals. PETA has successfully shut down at least 10 animal research labs.[93]

To gain access to corporate stockholder meetings, PETA has bought more than $40,000 worth of stock in a dozen major corporations that sell animal products or use animals in health and safety tests. PETA has introduced animal rights resolutions at annual meetings of IBM, Procter & Gamble and Gillette. Frankie J. Trull, president of the Washington-based Foundation for Biomedical Research, which supports the use of animals in health and safety research because alternative methods are less reliable, says "PETA or groups like PETA have intimidated researchers."[94]

In twenty years of investigating and analyzing the environmental movement, Ron Arnold says he has never seen anything like the climate of terror created by the animal rights movement. He has never seen his sources demand anonymity with such genuine fear for their lives. The absolute devotion, the fervor, the willingness of animal rights activists to use violence for The Cause is frighteningly reminiscent of the rise of Nazi Germany.

Where does PETA get its money? Contributions and donations make up 92 percent of its income; merchandise and other sales, 4 percent; fundraising, 2 percent; investments and royalties, 1 percent; program activities and other, 1 percent. Its fundraising power has been elevated to a science, as we shall see.

Perhaps the most interesting campaign of this organization was carried out against a highly popular animal act on the Las Vegas Strip: Bobby Berosini's Orangutans. Berosini is a ninth generation entertainer, considered one of the best animal trainers in the world. His love and care in working with animals is legendary. He raised some of his orangutans since they were babies. He feeds them and cares for them. He virtually lives with them. In the last 20 years he has never been away from them for more than a day. His skill in handling outbursts of violence among his animals without resorting to abuse has served as a model for many animal handlers. He knows his orangs intimately; instantly recognizes physical signs that the animals are frightened or agitated, such as hair raising, goose pimples, wrinkled skin, moving from side to side, and looking around nervously for the source of a sound. Each of his orangutans cost $40,000 and are fully licensed in his possession by the federal government as endangered species. Bobby Berosini's act has always emphasized the need to protect orangutans in the wild. His facilities for the orangs' care and comfort are the best available anywhere.

This is the man whose lifetime accomplishments and reputation were systematically destroyed by People for the Ethical Treatment of Animals in conjunction with another rabid animal rights group, the **Progressive Animal Welfare Society** (PAWS). To protect his ability to keep working, Bobby Berosini was forced to spend more than $2 million to take PETA and PAWS to court on charges of defamation and invasion of privacy.[95]

He had good reason to take legal action. PETA and PAWS were engaged in a campaign to destroy Berosini's reputation. The cold, calculating premeditation of PETA in planning to defame Bobby Berosini is chilling. This is no figment of our imagination: Everything you are about to read came from court records in the case Bobby Berosini filed against PETA. Of course, PETA vehemently denies everything you are about to read, but, as well shall see, the jury agreed with Bobby Berosini.

Here is what the court record says: In 1987, Linda Levine, PETA's state representative on the Nevada Federation of Animal Protective Organizations, met with PAWS president Pat Derby in Las Vegas to discuss the use of animals in entertainment. PETA and PAWS solicited help from Dart Anthony, who was the president of the Humane Society of Southern Nevada. Levine and Derby told Anthony that PETA and PAWS wanted to create problems for entertainers who used animals in shows on the Las Vegas Strip, and they wanted to put an end to the use of animals in entertainment everywhere. They specifically mentioned Berosini as well as Siegfried and Roy of the famous big cat act as intended targets. Mr. Anthony declined to assist in the plan, much to the credit of himself and the Humane Society, which has its own problems.

PETA and PAWS, faced with the necessity of operating their campaign without Humane Society aid, fell back on their traditional tactics: To mount an attack in the form of direct mail fund-raising appeals. Both organizations knew that if they could cause the right kind of trouble, it would mean millions of dollars in fund-raising donations for their coffers.

In the spring of 1989 PETA began a fund-raising campaign based on the theme *Animals in Entertainment.* The campaign's mail package design was approved in PETA's Washington, D.C. headquarters and thousands of fund-raising solicitations went out from PETA's contract mail house. The solicitations urged members to "rush PETA the most generous special contribution you can." The campaign targeted Bobby Berosini's Orangutans, an act that had been playing for years at the Stardust with the Lido de Paris show.

It was the beginning of a three-year nightmare for Bobby Berosini and his wife Joan.

In April of 1989 PETA contacted Alison Kravenko, a former Lido dancer whose boyfriend, Ottavio Gesmundo, was still employed as a dancer at the Lido. PETA also contacted Michael Bradshaw, the Lido dance company manager who left his job after a confrontation with Berosini. Bradshaw had been on close terms with both Gesmundo and his girlfriend Kravenko. The three were brought into the unfolding PETA campaign to destroy Bobby Berosini's reputation.

Once these contacts had been recruited and PETA's *Animals in Entertainment* campaign had gotten under way, Berosini began having frequent problems backstage at the Stardust. The dancers, prompted by Gesmundo, began to systematically harass the orangutans. First they made disturbing noises offstage and onstage to upset the orangutans while they waited for their act in a private holding area with Berosini, blocked off by a curtain adjacent to the stage.

The dancers hissed. They yelled. They imitated animal noises, particularly chimpanzee sounds. They stomped their feet. They slammed doors. They billowed the curtains of the holding area. The fire dancers in the spectacular Lido act even held their flaming torches near the curtains to terrorize the orangutans.

It worked. Berosini's orangs became nervous, fidgety and upset. Bobby Berosini saw the danger signals, hair raising, goose pimples, swaying from side to side. He felt total outrage that anyone would be so monstrous as to deliberately upset his animals. He concentrated on keeping them in control, never realizing he was being set up.

Orangutans are large and extremely strong animals, as much as ten times stronger than humans. They can attack viciously when provoked or frightened. The dancers were well aware of this fact. They also knew that when faced with upset animals, Berosini would have to use restraining measures to prevent real and serious danger to himself, his assistants, the dancers and even the audience. Berosini's last resort measure, the dancers knew, was to strike an unruly orangutan with a light wooden dowel—similar to the perch in a birdcage—wrapped in black tape. The orangs were not hurt by the stick, but brought back to their senses and under control.

Once the pattern of unpredictable disturbances by the dancers had been established, Rachel Carpenter, a Las Vegas PETA member, made arrangements with another Lido dancer, Lucy Boling, to secretly make a film for PETA of Berosini in the holding area, trying to catch him using the stick to restrain the orangutans when the dancers frightened them. Carpenter and Boling could not find a place to hide the camera where Berosini would not detect it, so they gave up the filming plan.

The next day Gesmundo hid in the rafters at the Stardust to videotape a staff meeting attended by Berosini, hoping to get something inflammatory for PETA. There was nothing much, just insider talk about the act of no use to PETA—but it would have meaning to another dancer. Gesmundo was an inept spy. He got caught in the rafters, lied his way out of the pickle, went home and used his video equipment to dub a copy of the tape. He gave the copy to former dancer Seamus Brennan, who showed it to his girlfriend Simone Turner, one of the Lido dancers. She was readily recruited into the campaign and began deliberately making hissing noises during the act to upset Berosini's orangs. Turner was caught harassing the orangutans and summarily fired. When she left the Stardust, she vowed revenge against Berosini.

Things were not going well for PETA's campaign, so in late May, 1989, they stepped up the action. A new PETA employee at Washington headquarters, Debra Larson, using the alias Debra Jordan for her PETA work, received personal instructions from PETA chief investigator Jeanne Roush to call a Las Vegas PETA contact, Janie Greenspun, to discuss using the media in the anti-Berosini campaign.

Chief investigator Roush also contacted Gesmundo directly by telephone from Washington, telling him that a camera had to be hidden somehow to get videotape of Berosini actually striking an orangutan. Everything depended on hiding that camera, regardless how risky it was. Roush gave Gesmundo complete advice about what needed to be done to make the videotape useful.

In June, things unexpectedly began to go PETA's way: All Lido dancers had their regular contract reviews, and as usual, the Stardust decided not to renew some of the contracts, including Gesmundo's. The ousted dancers had thirty days' work left on their contracts. Now, with little to lose, they stepped up their harassment of Berosini to unbearable levels. And Gesmundo found a way to hide his video camera in a hatbox on a shelf overlooking Berosini's private holding area. The setup to destroy Bobby Berosini's reputation was complete.

Now things got out of hand. During July the Lido dancers went to ridiculous lengths to upset the orangutans night after night. Gesmundo himself created an unauthorized "monkey dance" during the Lido show's African Scene, when Berosini and his orangutans were in the private holding area adjacent to the stage. It got him fired, but not before he got several nights worth of footage showing Berosini desperately trying to get his orangs under control with the wooden dowel.

On the night of July 17, 1989, when Gesmundo was fired for disrupting the show, he was overheard backstage talking about the secret tapes, making threats that the Lido show was "going down," that he would blackmail Berosini with the tapes, that he would edit the separate tapes together to make it look like Berosini was a madman who routinely beat his animals, even to the point of adding a new sound track of orangutan danger and pain cries.

The very next day PETA received the tapes from Gesmundo. Now their plan went swiftly into action. PETA sent numerous copies of the tapes with form letters to experts sympathetic to PETA causes, signed by Roush and Larson/Jordan. The form letters were written to obtain maximum impact on the experts and solicited maximum condemnation of Berosini. PETA's letter to an expert named Galdikas stated that PETA "desperately" needed an expert opinion "strongly condemning such abuse." One form letter stated that Berosini's "abusive treatment clearly indicates that the beatings are daily and routine." Another form letter stated that Berosini "repeatedly" beat the orangutans with a steel bar. Yet another said that the videotape showed that "assistants are restraining the young orangutans while the trainer beats them with his fist and with an object which we have been told is a steel pipe covered with electrical tape." The experts came to the conclusion that Berosini was abusing his animals.

With condemnatory affidavits from numerous experts in hand, Roush and Larson/Jordan traveled to Las Vegas ready to spring the trap. They first hired a law firm, part of PETA's normal procedure when entering a community for an "investigation." Then they met with Gesmundo to have his VHS format videotape enhanced by Las Vegas video expert Alan Kartes. Before they had the enhancement done, Gesmundo obtained Roush's agreement that PETA would pay all his legal fees when Berosini sued. Kartes then dubbed the tapes together and copied them onto 3/4 inch format, creating a broadcast quality product. Kartes electronically enhanced both video image and sound track, making the final version more sensational.

PETA then hired a private investigator and set up surveillance of the Berosini family home, where the orangutans were housed, hoping to gather more evidence for their fund-raising campaign. Roush, Larson/Jordan, and the investigator watched the Berosini home 24 hours a day for three days, but were unable to see anything when the orangutans were taken out of the bus in which they were transported and moved into the house.

Now an unexpected complication nearly unraveled the campaign. Pat Derby, president of PAWS, somehow came into possession of a copy of Gesmundo's tape as enhanced by Kartes. Derby realized that PAWS had been scooped by PETA in what was supposed to have been a cooperative deal. It was clear that whichever of the two animals rights organizations was perceived by the public as being responsible for "exposing" the animal abuse "scandal" on the Las Vegas Strip would reap millions of dollars in contributions. Literally millions of dollars were at stake.

PETA quickly found out that PAWS had acquired a copy of its broadcast quality tape. Both organizations realized that the other would do anything to be first to break the story. It became a feeding frenzy—two environmental groups competing in The Dash For Cash.

PAWS contacted the national television show *Entertainment Tonight* less than 24 hours after obtaining the tape, even though PAWS had only the tape and not the condemnatory expert affidavits—or any other evidence. When PETA found out that PAWS had given the tape to *Entertainment Tonight*, they rushed immediately to a television network affiliate and released the tape and their affidavits.

Simultaneously PETA set up prearranged pickets outside the Stardust, complete with copies of the videotape, a tape player and television monitor to show passersby their "evidence" of animal abuse, and handed out prepared literature on the *Animals in Entertainment* campaign. PETA's Dash For Cash was done against the advice of its own Las Vegas attorney who advised the group to wait until the investigation was complete.

Now the massive direct mail campaign against Bobby Berosini was launched. PETA and PAWS both attacked Berosini in the media daily with barrages of name-calling and accusations. PETA and PAWS accused Bobby Berosini of criminal animal abuse, saying that he beat his orangutans with a steel pipe, stating that his beatings were routine and unprovoked. The setup was perfect. Bobby Berosini was crushed under the onslaught of self-righteous environmentalism.

"I just want to die," he told his wife Joan. His hard-earned reputation was destroyed overnight.

But he and his wife fought back. Bobby went on television and announced that any member of the public could inspect his orangutans to determine whether they were abused. Two animal rights picketers responded to the invitation and personally inspected the orangutans at Berosini's home. They found no signs of abuse and disgustedly quit the picket line, feeling they had been had by unscrupulous leaders. Neither Roush nor Derby took up Berosini's offer. Roush stated on television that she had "no intention" of looking at the orangutans.

The public clamor brought a government clamor. Local and federal bureaus with jurisdiction over his animals investigated Berosini. First came the Humane Society of Southern Nevada—which, gratefully, had refused to be part of this character assassination—and inspected the animals on July 30, 1989 and found no signs of abuse. When PETA and PAWS first went public in their attack on Berosini, PETA member Janie Greenspun contacted the Humane Society and asked them not to investigate, evidently fearful that PETA's early attempt to recruit the Humane Society into the conspiracy would be revealed. Roush also contacted the Humane

Society on behalf of PETA to find out if Greenspun had called to request that they not investigate. During that call, the Humane Society warned Roush that she was moving too fast without looking at the animals. Roush responded that she "had to do that" because *Entertainment Tonight* was about to release her tape under the aegis of PAWS.

The Humane Society also imposed its statutory police power by putting the animals on protective custody status. For more than 60 days the Humane Society monitored the animals at home and at the Stardust. No evidence of abuse was ever discovered.

Berosini's orangutans were also inspected by the United States Department of Agriculture, which has federal jurisdiction over the animals. On August 2, 1989, the U.S.D.A. issued a report stating that there were no signs of abuse on the orangutans.

Bobby Berosini was cleared by both state and federal authorities.

Did that deter PETA and PAWS?

Not in the slightest. Both environmental groups kept up a relentless barrage of attacks, milking the fund-raising possibilities of the setup. PETA wrote a headline in its *PETA News* saying "Berosini Busted," as if Berosini had been arrested for criminal animal abuse, when in fact no such thing had happened.

In the 12 months immediately following the release of the Berosini tapes, PETA's massive fund-raising efforts yielded a $2 million increase in gross income, from about $6 million to about $8 million.

That is what the court record said.

The court record exists because Berosini finally realized he must take legal action and filed suit against PETA and PAWS and several of the individual campaigners. While the case was pending before the lower court, journalist Katie McCabe wrote an article titled "Beyond Cruelty" in the *Washingtonian* magazine. It dared to criticize PETA. PETA struck back with a $3 million libel action, claiming invasion of privacy (holding out in a false light), tortious interference with business relations (namely contributions), and trade libel. Evidently Pacheco's dictum that "damaging the enemy financially is fair game" protects only environmentalists and not their critics.

Even more appalling, as soon as the lawsuit against the *Washingtonian* had been filed, PETA sent letters to the National Association for Biomedical Research, American Fur magazine, the Coalition for Animals and Animal Research, and the Incurably Ill for Animal Research, notifying them that PETA was seeking $3 million in damages, enclosed a copy of the complaint, and demanded that they "immediately inform your members that publication or distribution of 'Beyond Cruelty' can result in a personal action against them."[96] Again, freedom of speech is only for environmentalists. There can be no debate.

The Washingtonian settled the lawsuit out of court, published an apology and a series of corrections and clarifications, and donated a sum of money (rumored among Washington insiders to be $100) to an unidentified animal group (rumored to be a local humane society).[97]

PETA also brought lawsuits against two witnesses in the Berosini trial, Gary Thorud and Sam Alston, who had voluntarily come forward to testify, just as they had earlier acted as "whistleblowers" to federal authorities regarding PETA's alleged unlawful conduct, and as informants to Katie McCabe for her *Washingtonian* article.[98]

Despite everything PETA could do, Bobby Berosini won his case. After two years of preparation and 74 witnesses in 22 days before the jury, he won a trial court judgment in the amount of $3.2 million from the animal rights groups. We wrote the court record portion of this profile from the 8,600-page trial transcript and the appeal documents.[99]

PETA is appealing the jury's verdict to the Nevada Supreme Court.[100]

A September 1992 report by the National Charities Information Bureau (NCIB) determined that PETA does not meet several standards for acceptable charities. NCIB said PETA spends too much on fundraising and too little on programs. With 42 percent of PETA's organizational expenses devoted to fundraising, it couldn't possibly meet the standard requiring at least 60 percent of all expenses be spent on programming. NCIB also reported that only 20 percent of PETA's budget is directly tied to "research and investigations" of "animal cruelty," which means that PETA's mailing might mislead donors by inferring that donations will be used to help animals, when nearly half of the money collected is used to raise more money. PETA's board of directors consists of only three members, violating the standard of a minimum of five members. Board President Alex Pacheco's salary, paid by PETA, also violates NCIB guidelines.[101]

PETA has become the target of grand jury investigations in Michigan, Oregon, the state of Washington and elsewhere. *U.S. News and World Report* wrote, "The PETA leaders are bracing for what their lawyers fear will be indictments issued under the Racketeer Influenced and Corrupt Organizations Act which could bring jail terms up to 25 years, millions of dollars in fines and forfeiture of assets—penalties that would put PETA out of business."[102]

The FBI has questioned dozens of PETA members about the activities of Newkirk and Pacheco, and at least 10 were granted immunity and required to testify before grand juries. Pacheco told a reporter, "It's political. They failed to get the ALF, so they're coming after us."

And that should tell us something about the ethics of People for the Ethical Treatment of Animals.

People for the Ethical Treatment of Animals.

Job killers.

Economy trashers.

People for the Ethical Treatment of Animals—Footnotes

1 *Animal Rights Reporter*, September 1, 1990.

2 Quotes from *City Paper* Interview and *PETA News*. "Vegan" commentary from Alston Chase column, *Washington Times*, August 7, 1990.

3 *City Paper* Interview, p. 47.

4 *City Paper* Interview, p. 43.

5 *City Paper* Interview, p. 42. For extended commentary on pets, see "The Dreaded Comparison: Race and Animal Slavery," book review of Marjorie Spiegel's *The Dreaded Comparison*, in *PETA News*, January/February 1989, p. 11.

6 "Activist Ingrid Newkirk fights passionately for the rights of animals, some critics say humans may suffer," by Susan Reed, *People Weekly*, October 22, 1990, p 59.

7 *Animal Liberation: A New Ethics for Our Treatment of Animals*, Peter Singer, New York Review distributed by Random House, 1975.

8 "Are animals people too? Close enough for moral discomfort," by Robert Wright, *The New Republic*, March 12, 1990, p. 20.

9 *The Case for Animal Rights*, Tom Regan, University of California Press, Berkeley, 1983.

10 "Animal rights activism threatens dissection," by Constance Holden, *Science*, November 9, 1990, p. 75.

11 "The dissection debate," editorial, *The Washington Post*, May 3, 1991, p. A24.

12 "Tactics turn rabid in dissection war," by Gayle Hanson, *Insight*, September 23, 1991, p. 18.

13 "Big stink in the beef belt," *Time*, July 16, 1990, p. 51.

14 "What's new in fashion? Stripped-down protesters," by Woody Hochswender, *The New York Times*, May 14, 1991, p. B7.

15 "Furor over fur coats heats up: rights groups are using aggressive tactics to demand more humane treatment of animals," by Elizabeth A. Brown, *Christian Science Monitor*, January 17, 1990, p. 12. See also "Grand illusions: as the controversy over wearing fur rages on, there are—at last—some stunning fakes," by Candace Bushnell, *Health*, September, 1989, p. 72.

16 *Washington Post*, July 16, 1990.

17 "Revolt of the fur bearers," by Nina Darnton, *Newsweek*, January 6, 1992, p. 49. See also "Champions of synthetic fiber, angry human stars make the fur fly at a benefit for animal rights," *People Weekly*, March 6, 1989, p. 266.

18 *Fortune*, January 1, 1990. See also "The outlook for veal parmigiana, the honesty industry, double taxation at 3 a.m., and other matters," by Daniel Seligman, *Fortune*, March 27, 1989, p. 163.

19 "Avon's move to halt its animal testing wins qualified praise from protesters," by Jeffrey A. Trachtenberg, *The Wall Street Journal*, June 23, 1989, p. A9.

20 "Revlon, Inc. calls a halt to all animal testing," *The Wall Street Journal*, July 3, 1989, p. 11. See also, "Animal testing feels the heat," by David Christian Smith, *The Christian Science Monitor*, October 15, 1990, p. 12.

21 PETA Catalog, no date, Washington, D. C. , p. 27.

22 "Animal rights vs. research? A question of the nation's scientific literacy," by Dennis L. Breo, *The Journal of the American Medical Association*, November 21, 1990, p. 2564.

23 "Just too beastly for words: zoos are becoming an endangered species, beset by financial crises and targeted by animals rights activists," by Jesse Birnbaum, *Time*, June 24, 1991, p. 60.

24 *City Paper* Interview, p. 42.

25 *City Paper* Interview, p. 44.

26 "Fuzzy-Wuzzy Thinking About Animal Rights," by Richard Conniff, *Audubon*, November 1990, p. 127.

27 *Brief of Amicus Curiae, Putting People First*, in the case People for the Ethical Treatment of Animals v. Bobby Berosini, in the Supreme Court of the State of Nevada, No. 21580, September 27, 1991. A summary of the full brief was allowed in the appeal.

28 One of Barnum's legendary impostures was a sign in his most crowded circus exhibit building, "To the Egress." His eager mass of customers hurried their leisurely stroll past the bearded lady and Siamese twins to see what kind of exotic creature an Egress might be, not knowing it was an overglorious synonym for "Exit."

29 "Animal Worship II: the threat to U.S. health and welfare mounts," by Robert M. Bleiberg, *Barron's*, November 13, 1989, p. 9.

30 *Texas Wildlife, Newsmagazine of the Texas Wildlife Association*, December, 1991, Vol. 7, No. 8.

31 "The Silver Spring Monkeys," by Pacheco and Francione, in *In Defense of Animals*, edited by Peter Singer, Blackwell, New York, 1985, p. 135.

32 "The Great Silver Spring Monkey Debate," by Peter Carlson, *Washington Post Magazine*, February 24, 1991, p. 17.

33 *Animal Warfare*, David Henshaw, Fontana Paperbacks, London, 1989, p. 191.

34 *Animal Warfare*, David Henshaw, Fontana Paperbacks, London, 1989, p. 53-54.

35 *Animal Warfare*, David Henshaw, Fontana Paperbacks, London, 1989, p. 57.

36 *Daily Telegraph*, November 17, 1986, p. 2.

37 "Animal rights activists jailed for store bombs," *The Independent*, London, June 8, 1989.

38 "Animal rights terrorists bomb university," by Paul Stokes, *The Daily Telegraph*, February 24, 1989.

39 "Two Bomb Attacks on Scientists in the U.K.," by Jeremy Cherfas, *Science*, June 22, 1990, p. 1485.

40 "Woman in bombing condemns attackers," *The Times* (London), June 12, 1990.

41 Deposition of Alex Pacheco, in the case of Berosini v. People for the Ethical Treatment of Animals, et al., at Las Vegas, Nevada, March 9, 1990.

42 *Animal Warfare*, David Henshaw, Fontana Paperbacks, London, 1989, p. 160-164.

43 "Are animals people too? Close enough for moral discomfort," by Robert Wright, *The New Republic*, March 12, 1990, p. 21.

44 *Public Interest Profiles, 1991-1992*, p. 555.

45 *Baltimore Sun*, November 11, 1981.

46 See Taub, "Somatosensory Deafferentation Research with Monkeys: Implications for Rehabilitation Medicine," in *Behavioral Psychology in Rehabilitation Medicine: Clinical Applications*, 1980.

47 *Love and Anger: An Organizing Handbook for Activists in the Struggle for Animal Rights and In Other Progressive Political Movements*, Richard Morgan, second edition, Westport, Connecticut, Animal Rights Network, 1981.

48 *Washington Post*, October 11, 1981, p. B7. See also *Washington Post Magazine*, February 24, 1991, p. 18.

49 Draft of "Correction and Clarification," reached by the Multi-Door Dispute Resolution Division of the District of Columbia Superior Court, David R. Anderson, Esquire, mediator, the in case Alex Pacheco v. Katie McCabe, Civil Action 90-0A01627, February 15, 1990.

50 *Washington Post Magazine*, February 24, 1991, p. 18.

51 *Science*, December 11, 1981.

52 *Washington Post Magazine*, February 24, 1991, p. 18.

53 Paid advertisement by PETA, *Washington Post,* September 20, 1981.

54 *Taub v. State,* 296 Md. 439, 463 A.2d 819 (Md. 1983).

55 *Brief of Amicus Curiae, Putting People First,* in the case of PETA v. Berosini, Appeal to the Supreme Court of the State of Nevada No. 21580, September 27, 1991.

56 PETA Catalog, no date, Washington, D. C., p. 27.

57 "Needless Cruelty to Animals," by Cleveland Amory, *New York Times,* September 17, 1989, p. E23.

58 "Stroke Therapy," Zivin & Choi, *Scientific American,* July, 1991.

59 *New York Times,* June 15, 1984, p. A1.

60 "Protesters prompt halt in animal research," by Jennie Dusheck, *Science News,* July 27, 1985. See also "HHS halts animal experiment," by Barbara J. Culliton, *Science,* August 2, 1985.

61 *Daily Pennsylvanian,* January 15, 1990, p. A4.

62 PETA Catalog, no date, Washington, D. C., p. 26.

63 "University of Pennsylvania Head Injury Laboratory," in *Newsletter, 1985 - The Year In Review,* Animal Legal Defense Fund Newsletter No. 1, 1986, p. 2. See also, "Protesters prompt halt in animal research," by Jennie Dusheck, *Science News,* July 27, 1985, p. 53.

64 *Washington Post,* November 13, 1983, p. A1.

65 "The Animal Liberation Front: Army of the Kind," *PETA Factsheet* Miscellaneous #5, no date, Washington, D. C.

66 Telephone interview, June 1992. See relevant comments in "Blood feud: researchers begin fighting back against animal-rights activists," by Deborah Erickson, *Scientific American,* June 1990, p. 17.

67 "ALF Talks!" *PETA News,* November / December 1989, p. 17.

68 "Bloody Good Work," *PETA News,* May / June 1990, p. 4

69 PETA Catalog, no date, Washington, D. C., p. 26.

70 "Battling the Animal Liberation Front," by Assistant Chief Harry R. Hueston II, University of Arizona Police Department, Tucson, in *The Police Chief,* September 1990, p. 52.

71 Ibid.

72 *Terrorism in the United States, 1989,* Terrorist Research and Analytical Center, Counterterrorism Section, Criminal Investigative Division, U. S. Department of Justice, Federal Bureau of Investigation, Washington, D. C., December 31, 1989.

73 *PETA News,* Washington, D. C.

74 "Raiders of the Research Ark," by Elizabeth Carpenter, *City Paper,* Washington, D. C., December 18, 1987, p. 14.

75 Data from New York and West Virginia Departments of State 1989 registrations for respective groups.

76 "Behind the laboratory door," by Peter Haskell Bresnick, *The Progressive,* March 1990, p. 20.

77 "Animal research: ten years under siege," by Christopher Vaughan, *BioScience,* January 1988, p. 10.

78 "No longer dismissed as weirdos, animal-rights groups are now threatening medical research," by Fred Barnes, *Vogue,* September 1989, p. 542.

79 *Activism And The Law: A Legal Primer,* PETA flyer, no date, two sides of one sheet, Washington, D. C.

80 "U. S. accused of trying to smear animal rights group: members say felony trial of leaders is due to pressure from medical, research interests," by Paul W. Valentine, *Washington*

Post, December 7, 1989, p. A17.

81 Deposition of Gary Thorud in the case *Berosini v. PETA*.

82 "A Bombing Is Thwarted In Norwalk," by Robert D. McFadden, *New York Times*, November 12, 1988, p. 29. "Woman in Bomb Case Gets 3-Year Probation," by The Associated Press, *New York Times*, January 9, 1990, p. B3.

83 *Journal of the National Cancer Institute*, May 22, 1989.

84 "Animal rights group ransacks professor's office at Vet School," by Jeremy Selwyn, *The Daily Pennsylvanian*, January 15, 1990.

85 *Philadelphia Inquirer*, February 4, 1990, p. 2B.

86 Letter on PETA letterhead dated May 8, 1990, addressed to a resident of the same street as Morrison and signed by "Ann Chynoweth, Researcher."

87 "PETA Smells a Lot of Bologna," *PETA News*, September / October 1990, p. 26.

88 *Boston Globe*, April 10, 1987, p. 23.

89 *Boston Globe*, April 10, 1987, p. 23.

90 Certificate of Amendment of Certificate of Incorporation of People for Ethical Treatment of Animals, Inc., filed March 16, 1987.

91 New York State Department of State financial report summary for PETA.

92 New York State Department of State financial report summary for PETA, and Better Business Bureau report, June 1989.

93 "Protesters prompt halt in animal research," by Jennie Dusheck, *Science News*, July 27, 1985, p. 53. See also "Picketers ride animal rights full tilt to the rodeo arena," by Glenn Emery, *Insight*, April 16, 1990, p. 20. See also, "Animal rightists raid USDA lab," by Constance Holden, *Science*, September 4, 1989, p. 1099.

94 "Behind the laboratory door," by Peter Haskell Bresnick, *The Progressive*, March, 1990, p. 20. See also, "Animal research: ten years under siege," by Christopher Vaughan, *BioScience*, January, 1988, p. 10.

95 "Spectacle, complete with apes, in Vegas courtroom," by Kevin Roderick, *Los Angeles Times*, August 8, 1990, p. A1.

96 Letters dated February 27, 1990 to Ms. Frankie L. Trull of the National Association for Biomedical Research; March 28, 1990 to Editor, American Fur; April 13, 1990 to Mr. William Greenough and Mr. Robert Emmens, all signed by Alex Pacheco.

97 "Magazine apologizes in 3rd suit," by Howard Jurtz, *Washington Post*, October 17, 1991, p. C1.

98 *PETA v. Gary D. Thorud and Sam Alston*, Law No. CL910516 in the Circuit Court for the City of Alexandria, Virginia.

99 "Ape trainer wins suit against rights group," *The New York Times*, August 13, 1990, p. A12.

100 "Orangutan trainer is awarded $4.2 million. Bobby Berosini receives money for invasion of privacy and defamation damages," *Los Angeles Times*, August 12, 1990, p. A3.

101 Reported in *People's Bulletin*, by Kathleen Marquardt, December 20, 1992, p. 2.

102 "Pursuing PETA," Michael Satchell, *U.S. News & World Report*, September 21, 1992.

Defenders of Wildlife ▀▀▀▀▀▀▀▀▀▀▀▀▀▀▀▀▀

Defenders of Wildlife (Founded 1947)
Annual budget: $5,004,042 (1992)
          Staff: 31 total—18 professional, 13 support, also part timers and interns
     Members: 75,000 members plus 13,000 contributors
   Tax Status: 501(c)(3)
Headquarters: 1244 19th Street, NW
                    Washington, D.C. 20036
                    Phone: (202)659-9510 Fax: (202)833-3349

Economy Trasher Number Sixteen. Its logo is a howling wolf. Defenders of Wildlife was founded during the 1940s as a reactionary anti-livestock group opposed to steel-jawed leghold traps to control predators. It was originally called Defenders of Furbearers and superseded the Anti-Steel-Trap League, founded in 1925. The group's founders proposed "alternative non-lethal predator control methods," such as capturing wolves and coyotes by hand and removing them from the area—a marvellous plan to trash the livestock economy by shifting the dangers from one ranch to the next.

The group was intended to protect a range of animals, including the gray wolf, red wolf, Florida panther, grizzly bear, Western yellow-billed cuckoo, desert tortoise and Kemp's Ridley sea turtle. Its programs have tended to reintroductions of wolves in former habitats and outlawing poisons and pesticides that might affect wildlife, but have included marine debris control programs to reduce mammal entanglements, and a perennial effort to enlarge the national wildlife refuge system.

Defenders sponsored the 1985 "Wolves and Humans" exhibit in Yellowstone National Park and at Boise, Idaho. More than 250,000 visitors saw the exhibit, which won the Natural Resources Council of America Award of Achievement and Education.

DOW has a substantial lobbying operation for a tax exempt organization ($713,346 in the 4-Year Averaging Period 1989-1992). In 1988 it pressured Congress to appropriate $10 million to expand the Lower Rio Grande National Wildlife Refuge in Texas, $2 million to nationalize private property for the new Sacramento River National Wildlife Refuge in California and $1 million for additions to the Rachel Carson National Wildlife Refuge in Maine.[1]

Another 1988 achievement: Defenders coordinated the establishment of a network of more than 120 wildlife viewing areas on public and private land in Oregon, a measure to help justify state investments in wildlife protection. In the same year Defenders trashed the economy of Nevada by forcing a ban on livestock grazing on more than 10,000 acres of ranch-permit BLM land designated as desert tortoise habitat.

The major program of wolf reintroduction is paralleled by efforts of stop predator poisoning. Defenders has pressed several states to establish a livestock guard dog program as an alternative to poisons. The Agriculture Department Cooperative Extension Service's pest management program has also listened to Defenders' demands for nonlethal wildlife control. Defenders has also insinuated itself into the operation of EPA's "Poison Patrol" hotline, which takes anonymous calls from anyone suspecting pesticide killing of wildlife.

Rodger Schlickeisen (1992 salary $104,121; benefits $10,412) took over as president of the Defenders of Wildlife in 1991 after Malcolm Rupert Cutler was assailed by extremists who wanted to push Defenders into a more aggressive anticivilization posture. Schlickeisen came from employment as chief of staff to Senator Max Baucus (D-Montana) and was associate director for economics and administration in the Office of Management and Budget during the Carter administration. Damn! There's that revolving door *again!* Out of government, into the environmental movement.

But it was the same with Cutler before him: Rupe Cutler, Ph.D., served as a subcabinet officer of the U.S. Department of Agriculture during the Carter administration. He is currently Director of Education at Virginia's Explore Park in Roanoke. The same revolving door was enjoyed by an earlier president of Defenders of Wildlife, Joyce M. Kelly, currently executive director of the Wildlife Habitat Enhancement Council—Kelly was director of wilderness, recreation and cultural programs for the Interior Department's Bureau of Land Management, deputy division director of the E.P.A.'s Safe Drinking Water Program and associate director of President Reagan's Commission on Americans Outdoors.

But now back to Schlickeisen, who received his undergraduate degree in economics from the University of Washington, his master's in business administration from Harvard University, and his doctorate from George Washington University. The most noteworthy aspect of Mr. Schlickeisen's pre-Defenders career is the fact that he was chief executive officer of Craver, Mathews, Smith & Company, purveyors of left wing public relation programs and direct mail gurus to the environmental movement (see Greenpeace profile).

The noisy controversy that dethroned Rupe Cutler and brought Rodger Schlickeisen into the leadership of Defenders of Wildlife is worth examining for its entertainment value alone. *E Magazine,* a slick environmentalist periodical, published an article in early 1990 titled "Our Incredible War on Wildlife," written by Jude Reitman. It led readers to believe that Defenders had gone soft on hunting.

An irate letter to the editor followed in the next issue from a notable who fumed, "As a former member of Defenders of Wildlife, who served on the Board of Directors for nine years, I was embarrassed—but not surprised—by the pro-hunting comments of M. Rupert Cutler, President of Defenders, set forth in 'Our Incredible War on Wildlife.'"[2]

The article and letter were only the latest in a long string of pressure moves by animal rights activists to push Defenders to the left. In mid-1988, in fact,

Animals' Voice, a radical publication trying to push Defenders into its camp, wrote, "By the early 1970s, Defenders of Wildlife (80,000 members), while never officially opposed to hunting, had compiled a rather strong record on the issue of protecting wild animals. The organization called for a ban on the steel-jaw leghold trap and led some aggressive anti-predator control campaigns.

"But while it once seemed the organization might step into the anti-hunting camp, that hope has disappeared. Now, the organization has become so moderate that it even refuses to back the Refuge Wildlife Protection Act (H. R. 2724), which would ban hunting and trapping on national wildlife refuges—areas originally designated as 'inviolate sanctuaries' for wildlife."[3]

The "moderate" organization had actually been working on its own favorite Economy Trasher project, the reintroduction of wolves to the Yellowstone ecosystem, a move that would serve to decimate ranching and farming in the entire area surrounding the national park. Local residents had fought such suggestions from animal rights extremists for years, but by 1989, as the *Washington Post* wrote, "the pro-wolf side has gained the upper hand politically.

"That is largely due to the private group Defenders of Wildlife, which has worked to change attitudes of ranchers near the park. The organization paid for visits by a group of ranchers to Minnesota, where wolf packs have had little effect on ranches near their range. It also established a private fund, now totaling $40,000, to reimburse stockmen who lose animals to wolves.

"As a result, opposition has been reduced somewhat, and some local members of Congress have cautiously agreed to reintroduction. A key convert is Sen. James A. McClure (R-Idaho), who has endorsed reintroduction as long as the wolves lose their protection as endangered species if they threaten stock.

"Under strong pressure from Congress, the Interior Department is due to issue a report on wolf reintroduction before the end of this year. The study is not final but officials familiar with it say it will recommend bringing the wolf back to Yellowstone."[4]

Why did the *Washington Post* give Defenders of Wildlife such wonderful reviews? It could have been the result of skills Defenders learned from the federal government. The latest instruction session for environmentalists came in June 1992 when the U.S. Fish and Wildlife Service and the National Park Service held a closed-door media workshop for groups supporting wolf reintroduction to Yellowstone National Park, including Defenders of Wildlife. What went on in there? Nobody knows. It was closed-door. *Only* wolf supporters were allowed in. Others were physically ejected. *Only* pro-wolf members of the press were allowed in. Others were physically ejected.

The federal government holding secret meetings for the benefit of the environmental movement is nothing new. The Center for the Defense of Free Enterprise sued the President's Commission on Americans Outdoors in 1987 because they were throwing Wise Use supporters out of decision-making meetings that were supposed to be open to the public. The Center was thrown out of court because it filed too late, but the congressional General Accounting Office investigated the accusations and issued a report vindicating all our allegations.[5]

But in the Yellowstone wolf case, government by the dark of night angered local Wise Use advocates. Troy Mader, a leader of the Abundant Wildlife Society of North America, which opposes wolf reintroduction, led a protest against the secret meeting.

He told reporters, "Our purpose is to make people aware that wolves will cause severe impacts on recreation and multiple-use, hunting around Yellowstone, as well as on livestock and pets. Wolves are not warm, cuddly animals. They're frighteningly efficient predators. If people were told the truth about wolves, they wouldn't be in favor of bringing them back."

The conference was held at a national park in public facilities paid for with taxpayer dollars. Two featured speakers were U.S. Fish and Wildlife Service biologist Ed Bangs, leader of the Wolf Environmental Impact Statement (EIS) team and Dr. David Mech, another USFWS biologist. Both are advocates of wolf reintroduction.

Mader of AWS said in his protest statement that wolves are not actually endangered, despite government claims. "There are 60,000 wolves in North America alone," Mader said. AWS added that wolves never naturally existed in Yellowstone in the first place. The records of early explorers such as Jim Bridger and later Northern Pacific Railroad scouts contain no mention of wolves in Yellowstone. Even if they are introduced, visitors are never likely to see them— they're shy of humans and quite elusive. But wolf reintroduction will cost taxpayers millions and create nothing but problems for everybody who lives for many miles around Yellowstone.[6]

So Defenders was not exactly a friend of the ranching economy—they clearly understood the threat to rancher survival that wolf reintroduction actually posed. Defenders was also operating a particularly virulent campaign against ranchers, accusing them of overgrazing and failing to provide forage for wildlife at their own expense, a campaign which would end up taking range rights away from ranchers throughout the West.

Nevertheless, the *E Magazine* exchange about Defenders carried on into its next issue with two letters, one from I. B. Sinclair of Media, Pennsylvania, who wrote, "Defenders of Wildlife has lost its moral compass and its reason for existing. Founded to defend wildlife and to abolish the leghold trap, it has made a deal with the devil and now compromises constantly in an effort to offend no one, particularly hunters.

"The hunters," said Mr. Sinclair, "have won the battle for the soul of Defenders. Pro-wildlife staff have been fired, key representatives in the field cut adrift, historic issues abandoned, and those board members who fought against trapping and hunting have departed.

"Defenders is now irrelevant to the cause of defending and protecting wildlife.

It now belongs with the group of pseudo wildlife groups that are pro-hunting and deplore [squeamish] individuals they dub as 'humaniacs.' I want my dollars to benefit those who still fight the good fight. As Henry Cabot Lodge once said, 'We do not compromise with evil,'"

The "evil" guy, Malcolm Rupert Cutler, president of Defenders of Wildlife, shot back, "Mr. Sinclair's response is a clear misrepresentation. Both he and the author of the article in question erroneously label Defenders of Wildlife as pro-hunting. As Mr. Sinclair knows, and as author Jude Reitman was plainly told, our board has no overall position on hunting.

"Defenders was founded in opposition to the steel-jawed leghold trap and we continue to oppose its use. Further, our official policy states: 'Defenders advocates policies which are in the best interests of all wildlife, by analyzing wildlife management programs to determine the appropriate response. Hunting is evaluated by this standard on a case-by-case basis.'

"It works this way: Defenders campaigned for successful passage of a law preventing a proposed deer hunt in Loxahatchee National Wildlife Refuge. And at Defenders' urging, the Montana Department of Fish, Wildlife and Parks is withdrawing plans for a sandhill crane hunting season for 1990.

"With so many threats to wildlife today, we should steer away from confrontation and, instead, work together toward what all sincere conservationists know is top priority—ensuring the survival of diverse, abundant and naturally occurring populations of wildlife."

Cutler was certainly no marshmallow and no friend of the American economy. He had joined with the leaders of five other environmental groups in early 1990 to assail President Bush with a letter asserting, "White House Chief of Staff John Sununu is the nation's chief environmental foe." The environmentalists asked to meet with Mr. Bush "to air their growing concerns about the administration's commitment to the environment and Mr. Sununu's role in decisions."[7]

In addition, Defenders sued the federal government in 1991 in an effort to speed up wolf reintroduction into Yellowstone National Park.

Foray into Free-Market Environmentalism

Under Schlickeisen, Defenders has given a tiny part of its operations over to a carrot and stick approach to protecting wildlife—which shows more promise than just the stick: The organization has established a wolf reward program that will pay a private landowner $5,000 for showing that a litter of wolf pups has been successfully reared on his property. The U.S. Fish and Wildlife Service will verify the location of den sites and the presence of wolves.

In addition, Defenders of Wildlife, under a program directed by Montana environmentalist Hank Fischer, pays Western ranchers for any losses of livestock due to wolf predation. Defenders has raised $100,000 for its compensation fund. Since 1987, however, only $12,000 has actually been paid out to ten different ranchers.

Hank Fischer said, "These two programs shift the economic responsibility of wolf recovery away from the individual livestock producer and toward those people who seek wolf restoration." Fischer called the programs "a foray into free-market environmentalism."[8]

The notion of free-market environmentalism has more merit than the command and control environmentalism most groups espouse—and Defenders of Wildlife by no means relies in any major way on free-market programs such as Fischer runs in Montana. Free-market environmentalism condones the trashing of the commodity economy, but simply requires environmentalists to pay for their economic damage with their own non-profit dollars—or, on government lands, envisions all taxpayers bearing the cost of protecting wetlands, endangered species or other programs that have had their costs shoved off onto private citizens under current law.

At its worst, free-market-environmentalism demands that federal land permittees behave as if they were on private land—a premise clearly false to the facts. This is the egg-headed viewpoint that insists that ranchers with grazing permits on federal lands pay the same fee to the federal government as they would to graze on private lands.

The free-market environmentalist blockheads who demand this "return to free enterprise standards" and "an end to subsidized grazing" neglect all the economic facts of the case: The private rancher with a federal grazing permit already owns the water and all economic infrastructure on the so-called "federal" lands they graze. Only a feebleminded or malicious person would insist that such permittees pay higher fees to use what they already own. As we noted in the National Audubon Society profile, it is the rancher permittee who is paying the federal government a subsidy in the form of grazing fees that are already higher than the value of the top of the dirt and the grass, which is all the federal government owns on a "federal land" ranch. The private permittee already owns the water rights, the roads, the fences, the stockwatering ponds, pipes and springs, the cattle chutes, barns, corrals, bunk houses, cook houses, ranch houses and the base commensurable ranch without which no federal grazing permit can be obtained. So, free market environmentalism is still very much environmentalism—the opinion of some white-collar authoritarian who thinks he knows how to play doctor with your private sector better than the people who actually make it work.

But back to Defenders of Wildlife and their wolf payment program. If a rancher takes cash for the cattle he loses to environmentalist-caused wolf predation, the carrying capacity of his ranch has been diminished permanently by the continual presence of wolves. Cash cannot change that basic reality. The paid-off rancher thus runs a smaller herd on the same land, produces less food and shoeleather, and employs fewer people. In an economy with sufficient surplus to afford non-profit donations to pay cash for free-market environmentalism, the real costs can be covered; however, there is a limit to how much damage our goods-producing capacity can tolerate, even with compensation, before we begin to miss the goods.

This is particularly true in the case of takings of private property: How much land can we nationalize even with full high-dollar compensation before America becomes a thoroughgoing socialist state by the simple fact that there is only a mere scrap of private land left? No matter who pays for it, free-market environmentalism is still environmentalism. It still kills jobs and trashes the economy—it just trades cash for damaged goods.

But Defenders of Wildlife is in no danger of becoming a free-market environmentalism champion. The vast majority of its projects are standard command and control interventionist environmentalism: impose demands from the top.

Typically, Defenders formed a "Nongame Coalition" in 1987 to lobby for funding of the Nongame Act which protects wildlife species not hunted, trapped or fished—nor officially endangered. They wanted to impose $50 million per year in taxes on equipment used by birdwatchers, wildlife photographers, and nature sightseers, those who most actively benefit from preservation of nongame species.[9]

In 1990 Defenders won an appeals court ruling that essentially created a Global Endangered Species Act: The 8th U. S. Circuit Court of Appeals ruled in favor of Defenders of Wildlife in its claim that the Endangered Species Act applies not just to wildlife within the United States but to plants and animals anywhere in the world if they are threatened by projects funded by the federal government. Even though the ruling did not apply to private organizations abroad independent of federal programs, it brought such private interests within reach of civil suits filed by environmentalists if they harmed habitat in which endangered species live. Here is another example of environmentalists pushing the cost of their desires onto others who do not share their beliefs—straight command and control environmentalism.[10]

Defenders of Wildlife helped to engineer one of the most appalling deceptions in the history of environmentalism in the fascinating case of the Louisiana Black Bear. Working with a joint landowner-conservationist group called the Black Bear Conservation Committee, Defenders presented itself as a friend of private property and jobs in a cooperative effort to preserve the creature.

Hiding behind this appealing rhetoric and pretending to resist federal interference in what was essentially a local effort, Defenders quietly filed a lawsuit against the U.S. Fish and Wildlife Service demanding that the black bear be listed under the Endangered Species Act—Louisana landowners were totally unaware of the treachery. Then, still pretending to oppose federal intervention, Defenders threatened to sue the U.S. Fish and Wildlife Service because it had not designated "critical habitat" for the black bear. Worried landowners contacted the Center for the Defense of Free Enterprise in early 1994 and asked Ron Arnold to come investigate the situation. Working with local attorneys, Arnold and the landowners discovered the role of Defenders. Arnold gave talks at community organizing meetings, and helped activate the citizenry to attend a federal hearing on critical habitat. More than 600 people showed up for the hearing, where opponents outnumbered supporters by more than 20 to 1. *The New Orelans Times-Picayune* wrote, "A speech by Ron Arnold, the table-thumping evangelist of the national property-rights movement, drew a standing ovation."

Membership dues and contributions, 88 percent; legacies and bequests, 4 percent; investment income, 4 percent; other, 4 percent.

Defenders of Wildlife operates 3 regional offices. It publishes a bimonthly magazine, *Defenders*, and an activist newsletter, *Wolf Action*.

The Board of Directors of Defenders of Wildlife includes chair Brenda T. Moorman; vice chair Karin Sheldon; treasurer Alan W. Steinberg; and secretary Terry Pelster. Other members include: Kenneth Berlin; Thomas C. Brokaw (an investor, not the television newsman); Oliver Houck; Freeborn G. Jewett, Jr.; Huey Johnson; Richard Katz; Stephen R. Kellert; William M. Kennedy; Robert Larsen; Maxine McCloskey; Brian B. O'Neill; Lisa Peterfreund; John Raimondi; Leslie D. Schilling; and Charles F. Wurster.

Defenders of Wildlife is funded by:

Ford Motor Company Fund gave $35,000 in 1990.

Town Creek Foundation gave $15,000 in 1990.

Defenders of Wildlife.
Job killers.
Economy trashers.

Defenders of Wildlife—Footnotes

1 *The Nature Directory*, by Susan D. Lanier-Graham, Walker and Company, New York, 1991, p. 52.

2 Letter to the editor, *E Magazine*, May/June 1990.

3 *Animals' Voice*, July/August, 1988.

4 *Washington Post*, August 23, 1989.

5 *Center for the Defense of Free Enterprise v. President's Commission on Americans Outdoors*, Case No. C97-32C, March 31, 1987, and "The President's Commission on Americans Outdoors Violated the Federal Advisory Committee Act," 1988, General Accounting Office.

6 "Wolves Real and Imagined," by Kathleen Marquardt, *Washington Report*, Putting People First, September 22, 1992.

7 "Environmentalists try to cut Sununu down to size," by Michael Weiskopf, *Washington Post*, February 22, 1990, p. A21.

8 "Wolves in the Marketplace," Terry L. Anderson, *Wall Street Journal*, August 12, 1992, opinion page.

9 "Bird in the hand worth more than in the bush?" *Environment*, January / February 1987, p. 22.

10 "A Global Endangered Species Act?" by Sean Kelly, *Washington Post*, August 16, 1990, p. A21.

Center for Marine Conservation

Center for Marine Conservation (Founded 1972 as the Center for Environmental Education; name changed in 1989)
   Annual budget: $5.6 million
      Staff: 38 total—28 professional, 10 support, plus interns
      Members: 110,000 individuals
     Tax Status: 501(c)(3)
   Headquarters: 1725 DeSales Street, NW, Suite 500
      Washington, D.C. 20036
      Phone: (202)429-5609 Fax: (202)872-0619

Economy Trasher Number Seventeen. The Center for Marine Conservation calls itself "The only major environmental group dedicated exclusively to ocean issues"—notwithstanding the Cousteau Society's omnipresence on that scene. But with Cousteau spreading out into the Green Helmet business and population control, the CMC's claim is valid.

The CMC is one of the few remaining environmental groups that still occupies a cluster of messy offices staffed by people clad mostly in shorts and Birkenstock sandals—in the heart of Washington, D. C. They have garnered most of their media attention from beach cleanup campaigns in which volunteers walk along the strand and pick up trash. Despite its gentle aging-hippy ambience, CMC basks in hard-won respect in Washington, despite hearty disgust from Greenpeace and some other environmental groups of strong opinion. Few other groups in the mid-range of the environmental movement pack such an Economy Trasher wallop in the political ring. CMC was instrumental in the coalition stopping offshore oil exploration and development along several of the nation's coasts—trashing a multi-billion dollar industry with grassroots and federal lobbying.

The center's lobbying, research, and grassroots efforts have made the difference in creating a Monterey Bay National Marine Sanctuary.[1] Dan Haifley of **Save Our Shores**, a Santa Cruz, California-based environmental group, said, "They are the prime movers behind the Monterey Bay sanctuary designation. They have been a constant presence, shadowing the project even during the dark years of the Reagan Administration." Action on new sanctuaries was suspended for five years because there was no money to take care of the units already in the system, much less pay for the taking of private property and expansion of the federal bureaucracy required by designating new sanctuaries. There still isn't the money, but organizations such as the Center for Marine Conservation can push the designation through Congress with sheer political clout. As the sanctuary designation clanked its way through the maze of federal agencies, CMC was there adding the lubricant of pressure and power at every sticking point. "It is the center who is calling the shots on moving it through the system," said Haifley.[2]

In 1986, CMC helped establish the world's first whale sanctuary, the Silver Bank Humpback Whale Sanctuary near the Dominican Republic.[3]

Marine sanctuaries form only one segment of the center's advocacy for stopping economic use of the oceans. The center has been at it for twenty years, twisting arms among federal and state legislators to enforce endangered species fines and imprisonment, to choke offshore oil drilling and shipping to death, to stop commercial fisheries with a strangling net of regulations—and cleaning up beaches in nicey-nicey garbage pickup campaigns.

In 1987 the Center began a joint program with the National Oceanic and Atmospheric Administration (NOAA) and the Society of the Plastics Industry to educate the merchant shipping, commercial fishing and plastics manufacturing industries about the hazards of marine debris, now expanded to include recreational fishermen and boaters.

CMC turns nasty, though, when its Economy Trasher ideology gets in gear. The center joined with three environmentalist powerhouses—the National Wildlife Federation, the National Audubon Society, and the Environmental Defense Fund in claiming that Mexico and Japan had illegally slaughtered tens of thousands of endangered and threatened sea turtles. The four demanded that the Bush Administration impose economic sanctions against the two countries, although the claims of damage they presented were all prepared by their own hired scientists and not verified with any physical evidence.[4]

The Center is adept at forming coalitions with much bigger, more powerful groups to do its lobbying. It joined in January 1992 with the World Wildlife Fund, the third-richest Economy Trasher, to "comment on petitions to designate the northern offshore spotted dolphins as depleted under the Marine Mammal Protection Act and as threatened under the Endangered Species Act" to Dr. Nancy Foster, Director of the Office of Protected Resources of the National Marine Fisheries Service.[5]

The Center really got revved up in the lobbying campaign for the International Dolphin Conservation Act of 1992 before the Senate Committee on Commerce, Science, and Transportation, joining a coalition of 25 environmental groups. When tuna boat owners offered an alternative method of saving dolphins rather than the devastating measures supported by the Center for Marine Conservation, it enraged the group so much that CMC lobbyist Suzanne Iudicello telephoned the tunamen's Washington representative on October 6, 1992 and spewed forth a torrent of threats to destroy the tuna industry. These environmentalists can get vicious when aroused.[6]

The Center also turned the lights off in Florida, pressuring the U.S. Fish and Wildlife Service to force citizens to turn off beachfront lighting that adversely affected the nesting of sea turtles.

The center conducts its own research through government contracts, foundation grants and industry gifts, maintaining a National Marine Debris database in a high-powered computer network. Its research findings are distributed in a series of self-published pamphlets. A few typical titles: *The Exxon Valdez Oil*

Spill: A Management Analysis; Marine Wildlife Entanglement in North America; Citizen's Guide to Plastic in the Ocean: More Than a Litter Problem; Shipping Safety and America's Coasts; and *Sea Turtle and Shrimp Fishing Interactions: A Summary and Critique of Relevant Information.*

The center stretches its $5.6 million budget with volunteers, particularly in the initial data-gathering stages of research projects. As the left-wing *Utne Reader* reported, "Using volunteers' data and observations, [the center's] scientists conduct further experiments and document results that can influence government and business policy."

As an example, the *Utne Reader* pointed out that scientists suspected that several kinds of marine life were threatened by plastic litter. "Animals were dying when they became entangled in, or tried to eat, plastic and other marine trash. The Center for Marine Conservation helped organize an annual national beach cleanup to determine the kinds and amounts of marine trash involved; 100,000 volunteers in coastal and Great Lakes states participated.... The data gathered by volunteers showed that more than 60 percent of marine litter is plastic, and that it causes the death of some 100,000 marine mammals every year. The facts and the ensuing bad publicity have encouraged plastics manufacturers to work harder toward recycling these materials."[7]

Such major news weeklies as *U. S. News & World Report* covered the beach trash pickup with favorable comment.[8] Even the stolid *Wall Street Journal* nodded with approval in a story titled, "Beach sweep turns up everything, even sink."[9] Who could object to cleaning up a beach?

Nobody, of course. But that's not all there is to it. The center works to regulate the shipping and recreational boating industry into oblivion, blaming it for a substantial amount of that beach litter. Only readers of trade publications would even know there was an Economy Trasher dimension to this story.[10] The center works to eliminate the balloon industry, because latex and mylar balloon remains choke seabirds.[11] The center also publishes a list of common beach pollutants in order to put political pressure on their manufacturers—but does nothing to politically pressure the consumers who put the pollutants on the beaches.[12] Moreover, the center continues to use beach pollution as a critical fundraising issue even though the National Oceanic and Atmospheric Administration reported finding that U. S. waters were generally cleaner in the 1980s than previously.[13]

The CMC doesn't publicize its pressure to eliminate the tourist trade in whale and dolphin-watching excursions. The center pushed for a regulation against feeding marine mammals in the wild, using the usual nature-knows-best and man-is-bad arguments to prevent interested people from coming in intimate contact with whales and dolphins.[14]

Environmentalists seldom crack a smile, but one of the fallouts of their Don't-Watch-The-Whales campaign makes everybody else laugh out loud: "Whales and other sea mammals," reported the Associated Press in 1992, "are often so sociable that they seek out charter boats, making proposed national rules restricting approaches to the creatures unworkable, charter operators say."[15]

Gray whales migrating off Washington's coast sometimes rub up against a charter boat and allow tourists to pet them. Westport, Washington charter operator Bill Hoffman said, "as soon as you start petting them, they don't want you to leave."

Hoffman and 17 others testified on whale watching at a hearing conducted by NOAA at its Seattle office. Thomas W. O'Brien of Seattle, representing Special Expeditions, Inc., a nature-tour operator which conducts whale-watching trips, said at the hearing there are "numerous occasions when whales violate the proposed regulatory distances in order to closely interact with a vessel. Who's going to regulate the whales?"

Regulate the whales? CMC, of course!

Whales like people better than the Center for Marine Conservation likes people. We knew it all along.

The whale watching tourism operators said that environmentalists' rules are unnecessarily rigid and could be financially devastating to tourism-dependent towns such as Westport.

This is one of the hidden dangers of the environmental movement's network aspect: While groups such as the Sierra Club and National Audubon Society killed thousands of timber jobs in the forests around Westport and used as their cover story that tourism would make up for the lost timber jobs, the Center for Marine Conservation comes along on their heels and destroys the tourist industry.

The proposed regulations would bar vessels from approaching within 100 yards of whales and 50 yards of dolphins and porpoises. Aircraft would be barred from operating within 1,000 feet of those animals.

Perhaps the most devastating thing the CMC has done, though, is to successfully pressure the Bush Administration into slapping a moratorium on oil exploration on the Outer Continental Shelf until the year 2000.[16] Despite the excellent safety record of the undersea oil drilling industry, political pressure was enough to stop it, in practical terms, forever—as business analyst Peter Drucker has pointed out, "In business, anything over eight years is permanent." Even more devastating, CMC is pushing to eliminate oil tankers from American waters. Their argument is simple: As long as tankers carry petroleum into American ports, sooner or later there will be a major oil spill.[17]

President Roger E. McManus previously served as vice president of programs and as director of the group's Endangered Species Program. Before joining CMC in 1981, he served on the staff of the President's Council on Environmental Quality during the Carter and Reagan administrations, and with the U.S. Fish and Wildlife Service—oops, there's that wicked revolving door again. Out of government, into the environmental movement.

A general membership in CMC costs $20 and gets you a subscription to *Marine Conservation News*, the quarterly newsletter. You also get a discount on merchandise peddled in the Whale Gifts catalog. The Center also publishes *Entanglement Network Newsletter*.

The Center gets 59 percent of its money from memberships, 27 percent from grants, 9 percent from contracts, 4 percent from royalties and publications, and 1 percent from bequests.

The Center has regional offices in California, Florida, Texas, Virginia, and England.

The Center's Board of Directors includes chairman Anthony R. Lapham; vice chairman Cameron H. Sanders, Jr.; treasurer Bonnie R. Cohen; and secretary Cecily Majerus. Other members include Susan K. Beck; Payton Lee; Feodor Pitcairn; Norman C. Roberts; and George Woodwell.

The Center for Marine Conservation is funded by:

The German Marshall Fund of the United States gave $10,000 in 1989 to provide substantive preparations for meeting of Convention on International Trade in Endangered Species of Wild Fauna and Flora.

Richard and Rhoda Goldman Fund gave the San Francisco office $20,000 in 1990 for California Debris Reduction campaign.

Island Foundation gave $10,000 in 1989 for research and education to designate Stellwagon Bank in Massachusetts Bay marine sanctuary.

W. Alton Jones Foundation, Inc., gave $50,000 in 1989 for research program on conservation of marine biological diversity.

Knight Foundation gave $50,000 in 1990 for Adopt-A-Shore and Coastal Cleanup Program in Florida.

John R. McCune Charitable Trust gave $25,000 in 1989 for general support.

The David and Lucile Packard Foundation gave $50,000 in 1990 to provide leadership for Fisheries Management Program, and $35,000 in 1990 to conduct first major study on conserving marine biological diversity.

The San Francisco Foundation gave $20,000 in 1990 to co-sponsor California Coastal Clean-up, and to develop Marine Debris Action Plan.

Town Creek Foundation gave $25,000 in 1990.

Center for Marine Conservation.
Job killers.
Economy Trashers.

Center for Marine Conservation—Footnotes

1 "Protecting Monterey Bay," letter to the editor by Michael Weber, *Los Angeles Times*, March 18, 1990, p. M6.

2 See *Santa Cruz Sentinel*, July 9, 1990.

3 *The Nature Directory*, by Susan D. Lanier-Graham, Walker and Company, New York, 1991, p. 52.

4 *Public Interest Profiles, 1992-1993*, p. 443.

5 Nina M. Young and Suzanne Iudicello of CMC to Dr. Nancy Foster, National Marine Fisheries Service, January 16, 1992, statement for the public record.

6 Davis Wright Tremaine to Suzanne Iudicello, October 6, 1992, correspondence discovered in the documents of a dolphin-related lawsuit.

7 *Utne Reader*, March/April 1991.

8 "Coastal cleaning," by Jo Ann Tooley, *U. S. News & World Report*, September 17, 1990, p. 8.

9 "Beach sweep turns up everything, even sink," column by David Stipp, *Wall Street Journal*, June 8, 1990, p. B1.

10 "Two views on pollution solutions," by John De Gaspari, *Boating Industry*, July 1989, p. 12.

11 "Balloons blamed for wildlife deaths," *Los Angeles Times*, January 15, 1992, p. A8.

12 "Dirty dozen beach pollutants listed," *Los Angeles Times*, May 24, 1991, p. A43.

13 "Is coastal pollution ebbing?" by William Booth, *Washington Post*, January 30, 1991, p. A1.

14 "Don't feed the whales and dolphins," by Brad Matsen, *National Fisherman*, November 1990, p. 55.

15 "Charter skippers say whales won't stay away," *Bellevue Journal American*, October 30, 1992, p. A6.

16 "No more drilling: read my lips," by Patricia A. Parker, *Sea Frontiers*, September-October 1990, p. 12.

17 "Major oil spill called inevitable," by Larry B. Stammer, *Los Angeles Times*, March 22, 1990, p. A3.

Environmental Law Institute ▰▰▰▰▰▰

Environmental Law Institute (Founded 1969)
Annual budget: $4.3 million
Staff: 59 total—52 professional, 7 support
Members: 1,900 associates
Tax Status: 501(c)(3)
Headquarters: 1616 P Street, NW
Washington, D.C. 20036
Phone: (202)328-5150 Fax: (202)328-5002

Economy Trasher Number Eighteen. Environmental lobbying and litigation is one of the few growth industries in The Age of Economy Trashers. There are now 22,000 American lawyers who claim to be practicing environmental law, a number that seems so high it couldn't grow any worse. But grow it does, and the Environmental Law Institute, a non-profit research and educational organization with an interdisciplinary staff of lawyers, economists, scientists, and journalists, fertilizes the weeds. ELI was an offspring of the Conservation Foundation and remains a Rockefeller-dominated institution. ELI does not litigate or lobby, but it is nothing more or less than a support institution for the organized environmental movement that does lobby and litigate. ELI's board of directors is fully loaded with heavyweights from pressure groups, Brock Evans, chief lobbyist of the National Audubon Society and Gus Speth, executive director of World Resources Institute, for example.

ELI is the information generator of the environmental movement, publishing books, important professional journals and two key authoritative journals, the looseleaf—and astronomically expensive—*Environmental Law Reporter* and *The Environmental Forum*. The *Environmental Law Reporter* analyzes environmental law issues and prints news of all major judicial, legislative, and regulatory developments, including pending litigation. The monthly journal includes a separately bound *News & Analysis* section, containing articles written by experts, and weekly *Update* sheets. The *Environmental Law Reporter* is available on the computer database service LEXIS and the computerized research service WESTLAW.

The Environmental Forum is the publication of ELI's associates program, whose membership is composed of environmental group leaders across the country. This bimonthly journal is a cross-fertilization periodical that publishes the best ideas of the best minds in how to trash the economy with environmental law, thinking up fiendishly clever devices to abrogate private property rights, criminalize business and industry, and remove all market uses from the federal lands. You have to read it to believe it.

ELI also publishes the bimonthly *National Wetlands Newsletter*, one of the most potent private property destroyers in print. It contributors include the National Wetlands Technical Council, a group of policy-oriented wetlands scientists employed by environmental groups and governments that want to take your property without paying for it.

One of the surest signs that environmental law has gotten totally crazy is the advent of *training courses for judges* in environmental law. *The Christian Science Monitor* reported, "Responding to the growing thicket of environmental suits and legislation, a Massachusetts state agency and two legal institutions are developing a training course for judges caught in the brush.

"Ever increasing state and federal regulations are forcing judges to become more expert on environmental issues, says William Futrell, president of the Environmental Law Institute (ELI). The institute will help develop the program."[1]

Futrell was quoted as saying, "We have just had an explosion of environmental statutes. It's a highly complex mix of law and science and it is an area where Congress continues to legislate."

The Massachusetts judge training school was assisted by the Flaschneer Judicial Institute of Boston, operating on a grant from the Jesse B. Cox Charitable Trust, and the Massachusetts Department of Environmental Affairs.

The Environmental Law Institute is no stranger to such training programs: it has given them to more than 25,000 lawyers and environmental administrators since its founding in 1969. ELI's policy research and technical assistance teams serve as the handmaiden of the environmental movement, providing expert data and advice on how to win lawsuits against industry in air and water quality litigation, how to legislate restrictive hazardous waste and toxic substance regulations, the prevention of surface mining, how to stop private owners from using their own wetlands and coastal zone property, how to defeat private property rights using the Endangered Species Act, and the removal of market uses from government lands. ELI performs basic research on environmental economics and maintains a number of special programs to destroy industry and stop economic development, including the Wetlands Program, the Center for Surface Mining, and the Toxics and Groundwater Program.

ELI's Center for State Environmental Programs works with private environmental groups and state officials to devise economy trasher programs and rigid enforcement techniques. The state center conducted 24 courses in state environmental regulation in 13 states during 1988 alone.

The Environmental Law Institute, according to President J. William Futrell is supported "by publication and conference fees, government research contracts, foundation and public agency grants, and individual and corporate contributions. ELI is a member of the Environmental Federation of America, an organization of 18 environmental groups that raises money for environmental concerns through work place fund raising drives, such as the annual Combined Federal Campaign."[2]

This last remark of Futrell's has provoked a firestorm of outrage. Critics have expressed disgust over environmental groups getting their grubby paws on public charity funds such as the Combined Federal Campaign and United Way. "Fossil" Bill Kramer, who writes the syndicated column, "The Angry Environmentalist," says, "These funds are intended to work for community needs such as hospitals, food banks, cultural organizations and the Girl Scouts, not to line the pockets of environmental lawyers and ideologues." Kramer wrote a scathing newspaper column after an interview with Environmental Federation of America executive director Cal Stein in which Mr. Stein bragged that environmental groups were getting $5 million a year from community charity funds.

When Kramer went public with Stocks' statement in his newspaper column, the United Way of America angrily denied giving any funds to environmental groups and demanded a retraction. Kramer stuck by his guns, and when the United Way of America insisted he provide proof, Kramer correctly stated that the burden of proof was theirs as a public agency, not his. Kramer demanded instead that United Way provide him with the records of every United Way program in the United States so he could publish a detailed list of names and amounts. United Way then backed off, and not only dropped its demand for a retraction, but also refused to provide the records of all the United Way campaigns throughout the U.S., saying they were all independent and that United Way of America could not speak for them.

However, Kramer did obtain a list of 27 environmental groups that get money from the Combined Federal Campaign, a community charity donated by federal employees. The account is called Earth Share: "One gift supports all 27 agencies listed below, protecting America and the world's health and natural resources, now and forever." (Not to mention trashing the economy and killing jobs.) The groups are: African Wildlife Foundation; American Farmland Trust; American Forestry Association; American Rivers; Center for Marine Conservation; Clean Water Fund; Defenders of Wildlife; Environmental Action Foundation; Environmental Defense Fund; Environmental and Energy Studies Institute; Environmental Law Institute; Friends of the Earth; Izaak Walton League of America; National Audubon Society; National Coalition Against the Misuse of Pesticides; National Parks and Conservation Association; National Toxics Coalition; National Wildlife Federation; Natural Resources Defense Council; The Nature Conservancy; Rails-to-Trails Conservancy; Sierra Club Legal Defense Fund; Trust for Public Land; Union of Concerned Scientists; the Wilderness Society; World Resources Institute; and the World Wildlife Fund. Give them a big handout, America. If you give to your community charity or the Combined Federal Campaign, you have no choice.[3]

President J. William Futrell was professor of law at the University of Georgia and the University of Alabama before joining the Environmental Law Institute. Prior to that he worked as an attorney in private practice and served as president of the Sierra Club. There's another common revolving door: out of one environmental group and into another. Former Sierra Club lobbyist Brock Evans (who also sits on ELI's board) switched to the Audubon Society for better career advancement opportunities—these are just two of many insider revolvers.

It is not fanciful to say that the environmental movement could not do without the Environmental Law Institute. It is without question the single most important source of information to the movement about environmental law. No one who does not read the *Environmental Law Reporter* can credibly claim to be well informed on the issues. ELI research and advice to activist environmental organizations is absolutely indispensable to the success of the movement. The Institute is as close to being a one-stop-shopping center for environmental policy research and development as one could imagine.

The Environmental Law Institute falls on the Establishment Interventionist Axis.

The Institute's funding sources come from publications (27 percent); federal and state grants or contracts (24 percent); research contracts (21 percent); foundations (12 percent); associates and individuals (12 percent); interest and royalties (3 percent); and conferences (1 percent).

The Institute's Board of Directors is an environmental law powerhouse. It includes: Alvin Alm; Frederick Anderson; Michael Bean; William L. Bondurant; Leslie Carothers; Anthony Celebrezze, Jr.; David Challinor; Richard Dewling; Carol E. Dinkins; Brock Evans (Audubon Society); Frank Friedman; J. William Futrell; David Hayes; Nancy Maloley; Langdon Marsh; Craig Mathews; James Moorman; Edmund Muskie; Owen Olpin; Helen Petruskas; Ann Powers; John Quarles; B. Suzi Ruhl; David Sive; Allen Smith; Turner Smith; James Gustave Speth (World Resources Institute); Robert Stafford; Donald Stever; Roger Strelow; Lee Thomas; Grover Renn; Nicholas Yost; and David Zoll.

ARCO Foundation gave $10,000 in 1989 for environmental policy analysis.

Ford Motor Company Fund gave $25,000 in 1990.

General Electric Foundation gave $25,000 in 1989.

The Andrew W. Mellon Foundation gave $250,000 in 1990 for Center for East European Environmental Programs.

Joyce Mertz-Gilmore Foundation gave $15,000 in 1989 for Atmospheric Pollution Program which addresses nitrogen oxide emissions, ozone reduction and global warming.

Edward John Noble Foundation, Inc. gave $20,000 in 1990 for general support.

Town Creek Foundation, Inc. gave $10,000 in 1990.

Environmental Law Institute.
Job killers.
Economy Trashers.

Environmental Law Institute—Footnotes

1 *Christian Science Monitor*, August 7, 1990.
2 "Institutions: Environmental Law Institute," by J. William Futrell, *Environment*, September 1989, p. 45.
3 Data from the Combined Federal Campaign recipient records, Washington, D.C.

Union of Concerned Scientists ■■■■■

Union of Concerned Scientists (Founded 1969)
Annual budget: $3.7 million
        Staff: 32 total—25 professional, 7 support
    Members: 100,000 individuals "including thousands of scientists."
  Tax Status: 501(c)(3)
Headquarters: 26 Church Street   1616 P Street, NW, Suite 310
              Cambridge, Massachusetts 02238 Washington, D.C. 20036
              Phone: (617)547-5552   (202)332-0900
              Fax: (617)864-9405   (202)332-0905

Economy Trasher Number Nineteen. A Union of Concerned Scientists fund raising letter dated September 1992 began, "Our global environment is under a severe threat because of a failure of American leadership." It was a variation on the main theme of UCS since its founding in early 1969: Bash America.

The organization most relentlessly critical of America in the environmental movement, the far-left-wing Union of Concerned Scientists began not as an environmental group at all. It was convened in early 1969 by a faculty group of 48 professors at the Massachusetts Institute of Technology to act as the sponsor of a one-day research work stoppage to protest against the Vietnam War.

In late January of 1969, the magazine *Science* gave prominent coverage of the proposed protest: "Scientists Plan Research Strike at M.I.T. on March 4." Faculty and students got together and sponsored the event, which was far more like an ordinary campus conference than a strike. Numerous distinguished figures spoke at the March 4 conference, including Rep. George Brown of California; Francis E. Low, later MIT provost; Hans Bethe, Nobel laureate and professor of theoretical Physics at Cornell University; Bernard T. Feld, subsequently editor of the *Bulletin of Atomic Scientists*; and William McMillan, of the RAND Corporation.

Also on the program were radical activists such as Eric Mann of the Weatherman faction of Students for a Democratic Society; Father Anthony Mullaney, one of the "Milwaukee 14" draft resistance organizers, who served a prison term for his anti-Vietnam war activism; and the noted leftist, Noam Chomsky, MIT Professor of Linguistics who tagged himself "an active critic of American society."

For those unfamiliar with Eric Mann's Weather Underground, originally called the Weathermen—after the lyrics of an anti-war song by folksinger Bob Dylan—it split with the relatively nonviolent SDS in 1970 over the use of terror tactics, which the Weathermen felt were their only effective weapons in their "armed struggle against the state." The group was forced underground when its "bomb factory" in Greenwich Village exploded. The group engaged in a terror campaign culminating in the bombing of the U.S. Capitol in 1971 in protest of "the Nixon involvement in Laos." Most of its known members have been arrested at one time or another.

The conference called for "concrete action" against the ABM (antiballistic missile) system, the dismantling of MIT's $90 million-a-year Draper Laboratory where largely classified research was performed, and a change in MIT policy to reject all future classified research contracts. The Union of Concerned Scientists helped to make all those things happen in later years.

The underlying tone of the March 4 conference was captured by Jonathan Kabat, a key organizer of the campus group Science Action Coordinating Committee and chairman of the panel titled "Proposals for Further Action," who said: "It's not a question of a few reforms, it's not a question of just saying that we oppose this aspect and that aspect and this aspect. You've got to say 'no' to capitalism. You've got to say 'no' to a system that is based on the profit motive and reduces humanity to nothing. You've got to say, 'No, we want capitalism to come to an end.'"[1]

The Union of Concerned Scientists' sponsorship statement at the top of the March 4 conference agenda began: "Misuse of scientific and technical knowledge presents a major threat to the existence of mankind. Through its actions in Vietnam our government has shaken our confidence in its ability to make wise and humane decisions."

This anti-Vietnam war rhetoric has conveniently vanished from UCS's current literature; only the first sentence of that paragraph survives. In fact, it appears to have suffered the fate of those famous pages of the now-defunct Great Soviet Encyclopedia which were periodically cut out and replaced by the Central Committee so that history would reflect the current party line.

It is fascinating to read accounts of the origin of the Union of Concerned Scientists written twenty years later. The magazine *Technology Review*, published at MIT, ran a 1989 editorial titled "March 4, 1969" commenting on talks held to commemorate the twentieth anniversary of the event. Editor Jonathan Schlefer 1) failed to mention that the original meeting was a work stoppage; 2) didn't acknowledge that it was an anti-Vietnam war protest; and 3) didn't bother to mention the overt anti-capitalist rhetoric that drenched UCS's kickoff meeting. But you can count on the Union of Concerned Scientists for objectivity and intellectual integrity, right, Charley?[2]

The huge media coverage of the March 4 conference turned on a light for the 48 MIT faculty members who called themselves the Union of Concerned Scientists: they had a constituency which could turn into money and influence. The ad hoc group became permanent, got its own offices in Boston, and grew into a multi-million dollar activist center. Three of the original March 4 sponsors still sit on the board of directors of UCS today: James A. Fay, Professor of Mechanical Engineering, MIT, now Emeritus; Kurt Gottfried, Chairman, Department of Physics, Cornell University (he was a Visiting Professor at MIT in 1969); and Victor F. Weisskopf, Institute Professor of Physics, now Emeritus, MIT.

The membership of Union of Concerned Scientists has always consisted of less than 10 percent scientists and more than 90 percent generic America-bashers. UCS has spent most of its time since 1969 shutting down American nuclear power reactors, trying to eliminate the American defense establishment and generating America-bashing propaganda dressed up in scientific garb by people with Ph.Ds behind their names and all their anti-capitalist allegiances sticking out in front.

UCS's first membership recruitment campaigns turned up few scientists but many anti-war protesters. For its first few years, the UCS said very little about the environment, focussing upon draft resistance, opposition to weapons research, and general anti-war activism. They worked hard to push through the ABM Treaty of 1972, which stopped what the faculty statement had called the "ill-advised and hazardous" antiballistic system. As a later era found, having no way to stop incoming nuclear warheads was ill-advised and hazardous to America. Its absence was one of the chief reasons that the Strategic Defense Initiative (SDI), better known as Star Wars, was later proposed.[3]

When the Vietnam war ended, UCS turned to anti-nuclear activism on two fronts, one to shut down all 111 American nuclear energy generation plants, the other to entirely dismantle the American nuclear defense capability.

You've got to say, "No, we want capitalism to come to an end."

The defense-dismantling program of the Union of Concerned Scientists has been carried out with the intelligence you'd expect of an organization of America-bashers presided over by a board of noted scientists. The cleverest thing they did was in the fall of 1982—when the leaders of the nuclear freeze movement were still buoyed by what they considered a popular tide—UCS introduced to America's schools the subject of nuclear war, and their favorite way to prevent it, i.e., bash America. It was part of a campaign to make "peace" or "nuclear war" education a part of the short list of subjects which all children must study. They succeeded in convincing states such as Oregon, and municipalities from New York and Milwaukee to Pittsburgh and Los Angeles to legally require such a unit of instruction.

The Union of Concerned Scientists wrote a teaching unit for junior-high-school students under a lucrative contract with the teachers union, the National Education Association. The unit was called *Choices: A Unit on Conflict and Nuclear War*. It was a masterpiece of fear and hate mongering—fear America, hate America.

The authors of *Choices* instructed teachers, "It is also important for you to admit your fears about nuclear war. This may help students more freely admit their own fears."

Lesson 1 of *Choices* began with a picture of a mushroom cloud distributed to all students. The teacher asks what it means to them. The teacher then goes to the first exercise, "The First Atomic Bomb," reading "one factual and one personal account of the dropping of the atomic bomb on Hiroshima." The "factual" account gives no background to World War II, and doesn't even mention who started it. The "personal account" includes a child's description of the devastation.

Then the class is divided into groups of four or five students, who are asked to discuss their feelings about the Hiroshima accounts. Then the groups list three or four things they felt after hearing these accounts, which a spokesperson from each group presents to the class. Plenty of time is allowed to discuss their thoughts and feelings about Hiroshima and the atomic bomb. As an option, the teacher distributes the book *Unforgettable Fire*, "pictures drawn by atomic-bomb survivors 30 years after the event."

Lesson 2 goes through the same exercise with radiation sickness, particularly with bomb victims who do not die immediately. Students are encouraged to start a private journal in which they write about their new-found fears, sense of national guilt, disgust with being a creature which would do such a thing to others.

Finally, teachers give a map of their city to students who do the exercise "Ground Zero" showing the effects of a one-megaton bomb at different distances from "the point on the earth's surface on or above which a nuclear weapon explodes." The Union of Concerned Scientists pointed out in their instructional materials that should the teacher "choose to have students draw the concentric circles on the maps, they will need compasses." The Union of Concerned Scientists is nothing if not thorough.

There you have it. That is the history of World War II according to the Union of Concerned Scientists. It generated in millions of young students exactly what UCS intended: pity for the Japanese, disgust for America.

It was another brick added to the edifice of self-loathing, first for America and then for all things human, that an entire generation of American students learned from our educators.[4]

Needless to say, young people emerging from such brainwashing would hardly be eager supporters of national defense measures.

The Union of Concerned Scientists did everything it could to take the American defense establishment apart.

In 1985 the Union of Concerned Scientists sent a message to Soviet General Secretary Mikhail Gorbachev asking for a joint prohibition of all development and testing of space arms, as well as a moratorium on further testing of antisatellite weapons. In the political context of the arms control negotiations of the time, in which the U.S. was attempting—according to some analysts—to raise the hardware ante so high that the Soviets would no longer be able to compete, the UCS appeal clearly favored Soviet interests. A gushingly friendly letter from General Secretary Gorbachev to Union of Concerned Scientists Chairman Henry W. Kendall did little to allay the suspicions of such analysts.[5]

In 1986 the Union of Concerned Scientists tried to kill the Strategic Defense Initiative as they helped kill the antiballistic missile system in 1972. UCS hired Washington, D.C-based pollsters Peter D. Hart Research Associates, Inc., to telephone 549 members of the 37,000 members of the American Physical Society and ask whether they thought SDI was "a step in the wrong direction for America's national security policy." Respondents answered by a ratio of 54 percent against SDI to 29 percent for SDI. UCS concluded that their survey showed "profound and pervasive skepticism toward SDI in the scientific community."[6]

The Union of Concerned Scientists predictably complained that the B-2 Stealth bomber was unnecessary and too costly.[7]

You've got to say, "No, we want capitalism to come to an end."

The Union of Concerned Scientists' anti-nuclear power program has been most impressive. In 1987 the UCS petitioned the Nuclear Regulatory Commission to shut down 8 "unstable" reactors of the Three Mile island design until they could be made more stable. UCS cited 30 accidents at the eight plants, of which 10 were considered especially troubling. UCS also asked for public hearings to revive the hysteria of the 1979 reactor accident at Three Mile Island as a fund raising event. NRC spokesman Joe Fouchard said the information presented by the Union of Concerned Scientists was "generally out of date" and there was "no reason at all" to close the plants or order hearings.[8]

When new reactor designs promised to make nuclear power politically acceptable in 1988, the Union of Concerned Scientists reacted warily. Having called for the phase out of all existing reactors, new safer reactors presented a serious threat to the group's ideology. By this time the scientific prestige of UCS's board of directors had made the organization the most respected of anti-nuclear groups, and that public esteem had to be safeguarded. No knee-jerk diatribes would appear. A spokesman said only that the group wanted to be shown that the new generation of nuclear reactors live up to the claims made for them, something even a customer would want before buying. One new model, UCS conceded—a gas-cooled reactor—"sounds eminently workable," said staffer Robert Pollard.[9]

The UCS did its best to head off a resurgence in nuclear power by publishing a 1990 report critical of three new safer nuclear plant designs, by General Electric, Westinghouse and General Atomics. While applauding with faint praise some of the new safe designs, UCS found countervailing disadvantages. Minor, who oversaw the study for UCS, said, "Even with looming questions of safety, new reactors might be ordered later in this decade. But unless the issues are resolved, the second generation will be few in number and short lived."[10]

The Union of Concerned Scientists operated a 1991 petition campaign to shut down Yankee Rowe nuclear power plant, which had one of the best operating records in the U.S. nuclear industry.[11] Led by staffer Robert D. Pollard, an ultra-left wing activist and disgruntled former employee of the Nuclear Regulatory Commission, the Union of Concerned Scientists complained to the NRC that the reactor containment vessel in Yankee Atomic's plant at Rowe, Massachusetts, weakened by 31 years of atomic bombardment, would only withstand a force measured at 35 foot pounds, when NRC regulations specify it must be able to withstand 50 foot pounds.[12]

The NRC rejected the Union's petition to close Rowe, recognizing there were items that needed routine repair during the scheduled refueling shutdown the next April.[13]

After relentless pounding by UCS in the press that a meltdown was imminent, fear campaigns in the neighborhood of Rowe and arm twisting of the NRC technical staff, Yankee Atomic voluntarily shut down the Rowe plant on October 1, 1991. It was barely voluntary: The NRC technical staff had been heavily lobbied by UCS members and were set to recommend the shutdown.[14]

As soon as Yankee Rowe shut down, UCS went to work on the Surry nuclear power plant operated by Virginia Power. A computer-based statistical survey of the plant turned up a pipe design unique to the Surry plant that had a 1-in-a-thousand probability of failure that could lead to a meltdown and release of radiation into the environment. The computer, capable of devising billions of possible combinations of events, ran across a Rube Goldberg lashup of 28 different possibilities and tied them together in a worst-case-scenario: A gravity-fed water pipe from the James River *could* break, which *could* flood a building housing electrical equipment, which *could* short it out, which *could* disable a critical safety system, which *could* shut down the reactor's cooling system, which *could* lock out other safety systems, which *could* last for hours, which *could* give the two nuclear cores time to melt—and then you'd be in deep neutrons.

Virginia Power said the risk analysis forced upon them by the computer model was so contrived and exaggerated the actual danger so greatly it could not be realistically assessed: Since there was no precedent for such a large cooling system leak anywhere in the world, not even in the Chernobyl disaster, which was the result of a deliberate if foolish operator decision, Virginia Power had to feed the computer its best-guess estimates based on smaller leaks combined into one big leak.

However, America-basher Bob Pollard of UCS struck again—he, of course, had been an early advocate of computer-based risk analysis rather that reality-based design and performance data—and said the reactor should be shut down immediately. "It's an unacceptable situation where a single pipe rupture could cause a meltdown," he said, knowing full well the actual unlikelihood of such an event. He pouted, "The utility should be not able to disavow its own numbers on the likelihood of an accident. They're the ones who chose the numbers."[15]

Robert D. Pollard knew perfectly well that the risk assessment was unrealistic. After a six-year tour in the nuclear Navy and four years at Syracuse University to earn a bachelor's degree in electrical engineering, he was hired in 1969 by the Atomic Energy Commission, the NRC's predecessor agency. By 1974 he was coordinating design and safety reviews for seven plants. He left to join the Union of Concerned Scientists in 1976. UCS gave Pollard the title senior nuclear safety engineer and sent him to work in their Washington, D.C. office.

Pollard, 53, has goaded regulators for years into writing new rules, performing inspections and making other changes at power plants, usually by filing petitions with the Nuclear Regulatory Commission with charges that its regulations were not being met and then personally influencing the technical staff of NRC, holding the threat of adverse publicity over their heads if they do not comply with his wishes. Knowing the ropes in the bureaucracy, he can apply quiet pressure to a few key points and get big results.[16]

You've got to say, "No, we want capitalism to come to an end."

As the environment became a viable fund raising vehicle for UCS, the program emphasis shifted to such issues as energy policy and global warming. UCS Staffer Bob Pollard served on the Blueprint Steering Committee for the 1988 *Blueprint for the Environment*, rubbing shoulders with top environmental group leaders as an equal.

The first ploy was a Union of Concerned Scientists report in late 1989 that said the U.S. could double renewable energy's share of the supply mix, from 7.5 percent today to 15 percent in the year 2000. And by 2020, it said, renewables could provide half of the country's energy needs.

To achieve those goals, government would have to offer "market incentives" and sponsor intensive research and development.

UCS noted that wind turbines, solar collectors, thermally efficient building designs, and biomass-derived ethanol have become more competitive with fossil fuels in the past decade despite the downturn in oil prices.

The final recommendation was a command and control masterpiece: Replace all energy systems in government facilities to renewables; require all utilities to convert to "environmentally benign technologies," whatever that means.

This, beamed UCS, would reduce acid rain and air pollution, lower U.S. oil imports and discourage future oil price increases, and raise employment by shifting jobs from conventional energy industries to more labor intensive renewable energy industries. It makes one wonder whether any UCS scientist has ever worked on a farm where they grow renewable energy biomass, because the need for farm labor has historically fallen through increased efficiency to the point that the children of farmers are being forced more and more into other occupations—aside from the comical picture of the government forcing a nuclear power plant engineer to don a pair of bib overalls at gunpoint or a Texas petroleum refinery technician being sentenced to thirty years driving a tractor in North Dakota.

UCS said, "These steps would cost the government no more than about $10 billion a year by 2000, mainly in reduced tax revenues, and could be paid for by a modest increase in taxes on fossil fuels or a reduction in government subsidies for conventional energy technologies."[17]

That's what they said about President Bush's Clean Air Act, which is costing so much that critics are losing count at about $110 billion a year.

UCS in 1989 commissioned Republican Party pollster Vince Breglio and his firm Research/Strategy/Management to conduct a poll on global warming and protection of the environment.

More than 70 percent of those surveyed called for the United States to lead the fight against global warming and not wait until there is international agreement.

Breglio said of his findings, "The environment is becoming a political issue with some bite. Politicians will have to be more careful and demonstrate their seriousness about the issue because American voters are more serious about the issue."[18]

In fact, that growing awareness is what convinced the Union of Concerned Scientists to make their mark as a distinctly environmental group.

The energy issue was a natural because of UCS's long anti-nuclear experience. Several recent projects have been virtually free rides. For example, UCS picked up an existing report, "Recipe for an Effective Campus Energy Conservation Program," by Walter Simpson, an expert in college campus energy efficiency, and distributed it to campus and environmental groups.[19]

In a radical departure from the group's normal radical departures, UCS held a brainstorming session in Washington D.C. in 1991 to develop some new ideas for extinguishing the oil well fires in Kuwait set by the retreating Iraqi military under orders from Saddam Hussein. Novel methods such as air cannons and huge sleds to set off unexploded land mines were presented to enthusiastic oil company fire fighting experts. It was a pleasant contrast to other environmental groups quarreling against government reports that the pollution from the desert fires wasn't going to bring the world to an end.[20]

In 1990 the Union of Concerned Scientists gathered 49 Nobel laureates and 700 members of the U.S. Academy of Scientists to sign an appeal sent to President Bush for action against global warming.

The appeal was publicized in press releases by UCS and the eco-group called U.S. Council for Energy Awareness. The groups' statement listed five key policy objectives:

1) A steady increase in motor vehicle fuel economy standards, while the search continues for fuels and other technologies that mitigate carbon dioxide impact.

2) A substantial increase in Federal funding for research on energy efficiency technologies, as well as Federal activities to enhance the adoption of more efficient energy use.

3) Development, demonstration, and commercialization of renewable energy technologies on a massive scale.

4) A nuclear energy program that emphasizes protection of public health and safety, resolution of the problem of radioactive waste disposal, and stringent safeguards against the proliferation of nuclear material and technology that can be applied to weapons construction.

5) Full consideration of environmental, social and economic impacts in the establishment of Federal subsidies and regulatory standards for development of energy sources.

Translated out of scientificese, that means:

1) Make fuel standards so tough that American automobile manufacturers can no longer produce their best selling models, the full size car that the American public favors. Bash America.

2) Centralize government control of energy so that no private sector innovations can be developed on the free market. Bash America.

3) Here's some eyewash making it look like we favor plentiful energy sources, but when Kansas farmers start converting corn to methanol or ethanol for automobile fuel and actually solve the problem, we'll invent all kinds of terrible things it does to the environment so you can't use that either. Bash America.

4) We want to sound like we might be in favor of nuclear power, but we're actually working to shut all existing nuclear reactors down as soon as possible. Bash America.

5) Hedge free market development of new energy sources with so many restrictions and disincentives that it becomes uneconomic to even try, leaving American with no energy sources at all. Bash America.

The nuclear power industry was silly enough to think this publicity stunt represented thinly-veiled support for nuclear power plants. It wasn't, which they found out the hard way.[21]

The Union of Concerned Scientists became just another environmental group in 1992 as it promoted its Earth Citizen Program. The idea was that the Earth Summit in Rio de Janiero was a lead-balloon failure, and that the only good to come of it was that "Over 20,000 scientists, environmentalists, and advocates of poor nations came together," said a slick direct mail fund raising solicitation. "We joined together in a new movement to save our planet from the looming threats of global warming, environmental degradation, overconsumption, and population growth.

"This movement cannot succeed unless there is also a committed set of citizens who will lend support when we encounter political opposition or entrenched special interests."

Here's what Earth Citizens are supposed to do, according to their fund raising letter:

> Energy consumption in the US is so high that the 250 million Americans consume as much as all four billion people in developing nations. Because energy use plays a critical role in food production, and greatly affects the economy and the environment, any reduction in the American consumption of energy and other resources will have a multiplied effect throughout the ecosystem of Earth.
>
> This means that UCS—and the members of our activist networks—must play an important role in dealing with population issues. We must address the excessive consumption of resources by the industrialized world and develop a vigorous new program to educate Americans about the links between population growth and environmental damage. And we must begin to reduce the resource depletion that results from American overconsumption.

> The solutions to the problems of rapid population growth are clear and well understood, but it may be difficult to achieve the popular support necessary to achieve them.
>
> Most developing countries have recognized that rapid population growth harms their development. A majority have adopted population policies and family planning programs—despite the US refusal to finance the United Nations Fund for Population Activities and to provide sufficient financial support for family planning.
>
> But there is still a need to increase substantially the availability of information and assistance on voluntary family planning. Much can be achieved just by providing contraceptive options for those who cannot obtain them due to financial, social, or political restrictions.
>
> More fundamentally, we must deal with the economic and social prob-

lems that are the root causes of high fertility rates: widespread poverty and the oppression of women.

When women everywhere have control over their own reproductive decisions, fertility rates drop. That means that, in addition to its justice, promoting women's equality and greater access to health care and education will help produce declining fertility and eventual stabilization of population. Furthermore, women must be able to play a full, empowered role in the determination of development policy at all levels.

Attacking poverty must include redressing the imbalance between North and South by providing developing nations with the resources that will allow them to move toward prosperity—rather than draining them of resources to promote overconsumption in the rich nations, as is now the case.

The rich nations must deal with poverty-induced migration not by throwing up walls, but by helping to solve the economic, political, and social problems that are its root cause. Supporting sustainable development in impoverished areas is not altruism on the part of the North, but enlightened self interest.

But the reality is that none of this will happen without positive American leadership. And that will require a major change in the attitudes of the American people about this whole interlinked set of issues.

The bottom line, of course, was Send Money.

Because we are small [Is $3.7 million a year small?], it is extremely important to us that you decide to become a Sponsor but the tax-deductible contribution you make does not have to be large. Just $20 or $30 or even less will go a long way because we operate so efficiently. Of course, for those who are able, $100 or even $1000 will help us tremendously!

Before you send your thirty bucks to help the Union of Concerned Scientists build Utopia, think through what they just asked you to do. The first thing they asked you to do was Stop Using Everything—"energy and other resources." Did you notice? We did.

It's all very vague, but somehow it doesn't just sound like "use what you need to live a full life and find conserving ways to do it." There's that high and mighty word "overconsumption." "Over" in whose opinion? Where does "consumption" become "overconsumption?" Is a Big Mac and fries "overconsumption" because some vegetarian junta doesn't want you eating meat? And will the Green Helmets drop the atomic bomb on you if you "overconsume?"

Or will the Eco-Police shut down all power plants, nuclear and otherwise, to stop our wasteful "overproduction?" We've got some people with very strong views on how you should live your life writing this fund raising letter. They don't sound too easy to live with.

Then there's that tired old America-bashing argument that the U.S. uses more energy and other resources than everybody else. Well, we *produce* more energy and other resources than everybody else, which is why we can consume them. That sounds suspiciously like what the Union of Concerned Scientists really objects to. The fact that we're so damn productive and successful and happy consuming what we produce just makes them mad enough to—to what?

Now drop down the fund raising letter a few paragraphs. Well, it would certainly be nice to eliminate poverty and to empower women—and all other minorities, while we're at it. But somehow this sounds like special pleading to the potential contributor's political correctness, not a terribly realistic goal that your thirty bucks would put a big dent in. Give your thirty bucks to a poor person or a woman; it will do more to eliminate poverty and empower women than the Union of Concerned Scientists would, betcha.

Now, let's grapple with the really troublesome part of this donation letter: "redressing the imbalance between North and South by providing developing nations with the resources that will allow them to move toward prosperity." What does that mean, exactly? Transplant the American spirit of free enterprise to all foreign countries and teach people to take dangerous risks today in the hopes of reaping rich rewards in the future? With the environmentalist dogma of no-risk and the left-wing dogma of no-rich, fat chance. More likely it is the tattered old plan to shift the money around until everybody is equally poor— Take America's wealth and give it to Somalia and Angola and Guatemala and India and everybody else until the entire world is poverty stricken.

And that bit about "draining [poor countries] of resources to promote overconsumption in the rich nations"—at least it comes with a transaction price so the seller gets paid something, however inadequate. It beats the environmentalist plan to dam up all resources so that nobody can consume any of them anywhere, ever.

At root, the Union of Concerned Scientists just doesn't like people. Their bottom line is plain fear-mongering:

> As a result of the impact of all these people, valuable plant and animal species are disappearing every single day and there is a very real possibility that major ecological systems will suffer irreversible damage, food supplies could crash, and civil strife could arise in many nations.

Threaten us with civil strife, why don't you, Union of Concerned Scientists? In fact, if any civil strife in excess of our present abundant supply comes along, it's far more likely to be aimed against self-righteous environmentalists who keep people away from every resource so nothing can ever be used by anyone. The only way you could get the American food supply to crash is to cut off its electricity by shutting down power plants, cut off its raw materials such as chemical fertilizers and pesticides, and hamper its ability to manage by imposing bureaucratic restrictions on wetlands, by endangered species designations, and by hundreds of other wrong-headed eco-laws, all of which the Union of Concerned Scientists is busy doing.

The Union of Concerned Scientists is just a bunch of plain old Economy Trashers who have been educated beyond their intelligence. And remember, they have a lot more generic America-bashers than they do scientists, so they may not even be that educated.

Executive director Howard C. Ris, Jr. took the position in 1984, coming from employment as head of the University of Southern California's Nuclear Arms Program. He has also worked for the New England River Basins Commission and the Massachusetts Executive Office of Environmental Affairs. Ho-hum, there's that revolving door again. Out of government and into the environmental movement.

The Union, which falls on the Establishment Eco-socialist Axis, gets its money from individuals (68 percent); foundations (16 percent); bequests and memorials (5 percent); interest (2 percent); publications sales (2 percent), and miscellaneous (7 percent).

The Board of Directors consists of chairman Henry W. Kendall and other members: Alvin Duskin (President, The Bering Company); James A. Fay; Daniel S. Fisher (Professor of Physics, Harvard University); Kurt Gottfried; Leonard Meeker (Former Legal Advisor to the U.S. State Department); Claudine Schneider (Director, Artemis Project, former U.S. Representative); Adele Simmons (President, John D. and Catherine T. MacArthur Foundation); Ellyn Weiss (environmental attorney); Victor Weisskopf; and Richard Wright.

The George Gund Foundation gave $25,000 in 1990 for Global Warming and Energy Policy Program.

The Florence and John Schumann Foundation gave $50,000 in 1989 for efforts to mobilize scientific community on issue of global warming.

Union of Concerned Scientists.
Job killers.
Economy Trashers.

Union of Concerned Scientists—Footnotes

1 *March 4: Scientists, Students, and Society*, edited by Jonathan Allen, The MIT Press, Cambridge, Massachusetts, 1970.

2 "March 4, 1969," by Jonathan Schlefer, *Technology Review*, April, 1989, p. 2.

3 "Non-Nuclear Umbrella," by Shirley Hobbs Scheibla, *Barron's*, July 15, 1985, p. 9.

4 "The Scandal of 'Peace Education,'" by Andre Ryerson, *Commentary*, June, 1986, p. 37.

5 "Outer Space Should Serve Peace," by Mikhail Gorbachev, *Soviet Life*, October, 1985, p. 2.

6 "How Physicists Feel about SDI," *Science News*, April 12, 1986, p. 233.

7 "Full B-2 Cost Put at $155 Billion As Congressional Opposition Mounts," by Patricia A. Gilmartin, *Aviation Week & Space Technology*, April 2, 1990, p. 22.

8 "Group Urges Closing of 8 'Unstable' Reactors," *New York Times*, February 11, 1987, p. A24.

9 "Taking Fear Out Of Nuclear Power," by Edmund Faltermayer, *Fortune*, August 1, 1991.

10 "New Ideas Changing Nuclear Debate," by Matthew L. Wald, *New York Times*, July 22, 1990, p. E5.

11 "A-Plant Closure Urged Over Safety of a Weld," by Matthew L. Wald, *New York Times*, June 5, 1991, p. A25.

12 "NRC Schedules Hearing on Safety of Oldest Nuclear Power Plant," by Thomas W. Lippman, *Washington Post*, July 3, 1991, p. A10.

13 "NRC Rejects Bid to Shut Site in Massachusetts," by John R. Wilke, *Wall Street Journal*, August 1, 1991, p. B4.

14 "Oldest U.S. Nuclear Plant Shut Down," by Thomas W. Lippman, *Washington Post*, October 2, 1991, p. A3.

15 "NRC Investigating Surry Nuclear Plant," by D'Vera Cohn, *Washington Post*, October 26, 1991, p. B1.

16 "Turning Off The Juice," by Matthew L. Wald, *New York Times*, October 6, 1991, p. F4.

17 "Those other energies," by Roger Vielvoye, *Oil & Gas Journal*, December 4, 1989, p. 25.

18 "Warming to the Idea of Leadership," Maralee Schwartz, *Washington Post*, December 6, 1989, p. A10.

19 "New Equation for Saving Energy," by Teresa L. Waite, *New York Times*, April 7, 1991, p. 4A.

20 "Advice on well kills," by Patrick Crow, *Oil & Gas Journal*, April 8, 1991, p. 30.

21 "Concerned Scientists have cause for concern," editorial, *Modern Power Systems*, March 1990, p. 17.

Friends of the Earth

Friends of the Earth (Founded 1969, reconstituted 1990)
Annual budget: $2,467,775 (1993)
Staff: 45 total—38 professional, 7 support
Members: 50,000 individual
Tax Status: 501(c)(3)
Headquarters: 218 D Street, SE
Washington, D.C. 20003
Phone: (202)544-2600 Fax: (202)543-4710

Economy Trasher Number Twenty. The furthest to the political left of mainstream groups, according to the *Washington Post*.[1] FOE senior staffer Dale Jones agrees that most of the membership is on the left. Actually, the Union of Concerned Scientists is probably farther out in left field; compare the profiles and see what you think.

In 1990, the original Friends of the Earth merged with the Environmental Policy Institute and the Oceanic Society to form the new and improved Friends of the Earth. Under the merger, which was approved by the respective boards of directors in January 1989, Friends of the Earth is the membership organization, the Friends of the Earth Foundation was "folded into" the Environmental Policy Institute and maintained its 501(c)(3) tax status, and the Oceanic Society maintained its own 501(c)(3) tax status.

The reorganization came after a rancorous battle over the direction being taken by the original Friends of the Earth. *Newsweek* magazine headlined the story, "Environmentalists in a Family Fight." Founder David Brower, who had lost his job as the Sierra Club's first executive director in a 1969 fracas, had been in and out of court fighting the governing board of FOE over a planned move from its San Francisco headquarters to Washington. Brower opposed the move to close the venerable San Francisco office, laying off 18 of 21 experienced staffers, ceasing publication of its monthly newspaper *Not Man Apart*, and downplaying its controversial emphasis on nuclear-arms control in favor of more traditional concerns.[2]

The whole story of Friends of the Earth (FOE for short) is similarly colorful, reflecting the personality of David Ross Brower, who was born in Berkeley, California, July 1, 1912. From the day in New York in July 1969 when Brower created the scattered, impetuous, feisty little outfit in his own image, FOE has pushed the limits of environmentalism to one extreme after another. FOE, with its main office in San Francisco, agitated to save the whales, kill the supersonic transport, kill nuclear power (including the Clinch River breeder reactor in Tennessee), kill valid leases of coal and oil fields on federal lands and lock up all of Alaska in no-use designations, among other things.[3]

Brower has a knack for spotting hot issues early and sensing which are likely to fall between the cracks of other environmental groups' programs. His penchant for adopting ever more radical eco-socialist projects has alienated old friends by the dozen. It is a pattern of Brower's life to attract admirers, make them cherished friends for a while and end up turning them into bitter enemies.

Brower ran Friends of the Earth as president for ten eventful years. The group's newsletter, *Not Man Apart*, reached outside the membership and gave FOE a reputation beyond its small size—about 20,000 members. The staff grew from 25 to 60 people. Projects came first, the money to pay for them second. Debts began to pile up.

Parenthetically, it is worth noting that Robinson Jeffers provided Brower with the name of the newsletter, *Not Man Apart*. It came from a poem titled "The Answer:"

> ...Integrity is wholeness, the greatest
> beauty is
> Organic wholeness, the wholeness of life and things, the divine
> beauty of the universe. Love that, not man
> Apart from that, or else you will share man's pitiful confusions,
> or drown in despair when his days darken.[4]

It is instructive to see the constituency Brower was cultivating, that would respond to Jeffers' misanthropy. Jeffers' poetry inspired two generations of environmentalist intellectuals with a loathing for all things human that is unimaginable to a healthy soul. These lines from his "Original Sin" are archetypal:

> ...As for me, I would rather
> Be a worm in a wild apple than a son of man
> But we are what we are, and we might remember
> Not to hate any person, for all are vicious
> And not be astonished at any evil, all are deserved;
> And not fear death; it is the only way to be cleansed.[5]

No, it's not a raving lunatic, it is one of America's most revered nature poets. The voice of Robinson Jeffers has touched many members of Friends of the Earth, even those who know neither his name nor his poetry, with a cool, considered and detached abhorrence of humanity that makes To Hell With You All Richard Conniff look like Mother Teresa.

Brower picked a string of executive directors to manage Friends of the Earth and each fell afoul of his imperious manner. The executive director would give the staff their daily marching orders in the morning, Brower would take them to lunch at noon and they would come back with new tasks in the afternoon. Over the years, four FOE executive directors resigned, citing obstinate interference. Management—hand picked by Brower—began to build up a seething resentment against the man who was at once their mentor and tormentor.

However, the Sierra Club gave Brower their John Muir Award in 1977 and elected him honorary vice-president.

Brower stepped down as president of FOE in November of 1979. He remained chairman of the board—and kept pestering people and sending memos. He tapped Edwin Matthews to succeed him as president, but it didn't work out. Matthews was a corporate lawyer who split his time between the megabuck firm of Coudert Bros. in downtown San Francisco and the North Beach office of Friends of the Earth. Staffers grumbled that Matthews usually came in just as they were going home at five. Matthews was dismissed by the executive committee after only a year, but remained on the FOE board.

In 1980 Rafe Pomerance became president of FOE. The founder of the Clean Air Coalition—and a media hound known for asking reporters to mention him in their articles—Pomerance led the group in impressive campaigns against acid rain, the MX missile, the Synfuels Corporation, and James Watt, the Interior Secretary environmentalists loved to hate—Watt was their best fund-raiser until he resigned under fire in 1983.

Pomerance managed to build FOE membership by 50 percent, peaking in 1983 at 30,000. However, business ratios in the world of environmentalism say that wasn't enough to support the staff FOE had sprouted. Pomerance, being a good manager, calculated that his organization was overstaffed by twice and began a series of staff cuts in 1984.

Brower interfered, as usual, sneaking a full-page ad into *Not Man Apart* asking members to "Save the Team." Pomerance was so furious he impounded the entire print run and dumped it in the recycling bin. Pleading in the newsletter was no way to build membership. Direct mail, the proper approach, was neglected. Pomerance said, "There was very little attention paid to it internally. The direct-mail campaign was very poorly run."

With the usual 30 percent annual dropout rate of environmental groups, FOE membership fell off to about 16,000. Brower told his staff, "Don't compromise on your programs. The money will come from somewhere." It did. It came from borrowings from loyal members who never saw their money again, leading to a budget deficit of $700,000 and a lot of angry members.

The board of directors of a non-profit corporation has as much fiduciary trust responsibility as that of a for-profit: They may not act with financial irresponsibility. FOE's board did the right thing: They cut back programs to fit the vanishing budget.

Typically, Brower responded with a bumper sticker remark: "It's nice to be in the black, but it's more important to be in the green." He wasn't thinking about the color of money.

FOE's directors were not amused: They kicked him off the board in July 1984 during a six-hour marathon conference call. The Sierra Club scenario was playing itself out again. But this time, Brower went to court and won his seat back.

He held on for a tense sixteen months. Then on November 23, 1985, the anti-Brower board of directors voted to move the FOE office to Washington, D.C.—if they couldn't dump Brower, they could at least move away from him.

Brower saw this as heresy, a drift toward Friends of the Earth being just another lobbying group, no longer the early warning system of the environmental movement. He tried to force a vote of the membership over the move, but failed. He then went to court again to force an early board election, but canceled when he found that he would be in court before the same judge on the same day against the Sierra Club, which he was suing as a member of their board of directors to force a vote on the funding of an antinuclear weapons project he supported.

Brower requested a recall of the governing board majority and offered five candidates for open positions at the regular election of the board by the membership in April of 1986, threatening to resign from the organization he had established 17 years earlier if he lost.

Some 5,613 members voted on the recall. Brower lost by 180 votes. The anti-Brower directors won every seat. They summarily booted the Archdruid off the board of both the FOE and the FOE Foundation. Brower took his marbles—along with a left-wing constituency of grassroots environmentalists—and incorporated Earth Island Institute.

Brower's recent two-part biography, *For Earth's Sake*, doesn't talk about any of this. He told a reporter for *Modern Maturity* magazine, "I don't like to dwell on that. We've made up. All the wounds have healed." They haven't.[6]

While the wounds were still fresh, Brower spake a dire prophecy, "If they go ahead with the move, I don't think the FOE will last much longer." Wrong again.

Friends of the Earth moved to Washington and is doing quite well without their Archdruid, thank you. Anti-Brower board member and former conservation director Geoffrey Webb became Acting Director and carried on in a businesslike manner. The fracas cost FOE some members, but the ones that remained were intensely loyal.

Rafe Pomerance had bailed out of Friends of the Earth and gone to work in Washington for Gus Speth at the World Resources Institute as congressional liaison.[7]

Part of the reason for FOE's success is the 1989 merger that brought the Environmental Policy Institute (EPI), the Oceanic Society, and FOE together—the new leadership created the first environmental organization to deliberately reject specializing in narrower issues such as wildlife preservation and wilderness protection and choose the whole planet as its "niche."

Geoff Webb said of his merged group, known at first as EPI/FOE, "It's an ambitious plan, and it's a bit of a gamble. We're trying to build an environmental group for the 1990s."[8]

The merger actually represented a reunion for FOE and EPI, which was established in 1972 by former FOE staff members who were dissatisfied with the direction that FOE founder David Brower set—Brower has a long history of alienating former associates. EPI President Michael Clark said, "It's a remarriage. But it recognizes that we're dealing with different forces now. We're increasingly dealing with global problems."

One of their first projects was to work with government officials of Nicaragua and Costa Rica to establish a "peace park" along their shared border.[9]

Friends of the Earth enjoyed a global advantage during its split: wide name-recognition abroad as the U.S. affiliate of Friends of the Earth International, a network of 33 organizations—now grown to 44—around the world. The Right Livelihood Awards Foundation presented its 1988 $100,000 prize to Friends of the Earth leader Sahabat Alam of Malaysia for work on rainforest preservation, shared with a physician and a housing expert. It was presented in Stockholm the day before the Nobel Prize ceremonies.[10]

The new FOE is making piles of money, but its spirit remains relentlessly Economy Trasher, even without David Brower.

Officials of all three groups were candid about the fact that finances had been part of the motivation to merge. Oceanic Society President Clifton Curtis said, "We all see the need to depend less on foundation money. There is intense competition for limited funds, and I could count on two hands those foundations that know coastal issues."

Geoff Webb candidly admitted that the foundation community had been unwilling to touch Friends of the Earth with a ten foot pole for the past two years because of David Brower. He looked forward to New York money starting to come in, and an $80,000-a-year golden donor who will keep up payments. In addition, a sizeable bequest came their way after the move to Washington.

FOE Executive Director Michael S. Clark took his position in 1990, coming from the presidency of the Environmental Policy Institute which he had headed since 1986. Clark was formerly a private consultant specializing in nonprofit organizations. From 1982 to 1984 he was president of the Northern Lights Institute, a support group for small environmental groups in Idaho, Montana and Wyoming. Before that Clark served as president of the Highlander Research and Education Center in New Market, Tennessee. He earned an undergraduate degree from Berea College.

The reincarnated Friends of the Earth dumped Brower's flagship publication, *Not Man Apart*, and with the October 1990 issue began a newsmagazine called simply *Friends of the Earth*. Not very imaginative, but very decisive in repositioning the group: Brower's intense personality still clung to Friends through this distinctive and highly respected magazine. The new leadership said the "sexist overtones" of the name *Not Man Apart* affected their decision to scuttle the name, which nobody believed. The left-wing *Utne Reader* gave the new magazine high marks, calling it an "upgraded, readable, and very informative publication."[11]

The new improved FOE wasted no time scrambling for publicity. They convinced rock icon Paul McCartney to promote Friends of the Earth on a 1989 world tour. In his first tour in 13 years, McCartney played in nine European countries before heading for Asia and North and South America. The former Beatle agreed to promote FOE in the concert brochure distributed to all ticket holders, and FOE's literature and merchandise, including T-shirts, were available at all concerts. McCartney said, "Basically, we are just trying to save the planet. It is boring, but unfortunately if we don't get boring we're going to get dead." Linda McCartney, who toured with her husband, said the family uses biodegradable products, keeps many animals on their organic farm near Rye in southeast England, and are vegetarians. But think of all the petroleum that gets used up making the compact discs and audio cassettes that made McCartney rich. Being an environmentalist means never having to say thank you. So Friends of the Earth got a big bang and a bunch of bucks from a bygone Beatle.[12]

FOE kept up its relentless industry-bashing, even improving upon David Brower's stunt-of-the-month tactics. The London office of Friends of the Earth initiated an annual "Green Con Award," flagellating industries for claiming to be environmentally sound. The first winner was British Nuclear Fuels for saying that nuclear plants, unlike conventional plants, don't pollute the air. A Friends of the Earth official said they wanted to trash "companies jumping on the green bandwagon when in fact they are talking gibberish." A British Nuclear spokesman said their corporate campaign was truthful. "We maintain nuclear power could contribute to lessening the greenhouse effect." He expressed amusement at the award, and said they would have displayed the trophy in the press office, "but it's so hideous nobody wanted it." They put it in the recycling bin.[13]

And another prize in the Don't-Bother-Me-With-Facts category went to Friends of the Earth after the Gulf War for their response to a team of U.S. atmospheric scientists who said they expected the Kuwait oil fires to have only minimal effect on global climate and limited effects even in the Persian Gulf region. The National Science Foundation's assistant director for geosciences said, "The preliminary findings don't suggest there will be major disruptions to global weather or climate." Brent Blackwelder, a Friends of the Earth vice president, held a news conference two hours after the science foundation's news conference ended. FOE had sent its own observation team to Kuwait, Blackwelder said, and accused the U.S. government of deliberately minimizing the environmental damage from the fires because it would detract from the "glitz and glitter of smashing Iraq." Ah, yes, we can't allow anything less than total disaster into the minds of our donors. They might start asking whether FOE was deliberately exaggerating the environmental damage from the fires because the truth would detract from the glitz and glitter of their fund raising campaign.[14]

On a bit more pragmatic note, the Canadian section of Friends of the Earth went after some of the green (dollar-bill green) by endorsing a line of private-label food products carried by Loblaw Companies, a big Canadian food distributor. The "Nature's Choice" line is intended to appeal to consumers concerned about health and the environment. Friends of the Earth endorsed Loblaw's green-line baking soda and gets a royalty, said executive director Julia Langer. Friends of the Earth gets to enclose a leaflet in each package telling how to use baking soda "instead of environmentally harsh cleaners and drain unpluggers." And how to join Friends of the Earth, of course.[15]

FOE's Board of Directors includes chairman Herman Warsh (an influential moneybags who resigned after the merger with EPI); vice chairs Linda Heller

Kamm and John Roberts; treasurer Frances Hart; and secretary Janet Welsh Brown. Other members include: Bob Allen; Robert Alvarez; Leslie Barclay; Robert Cahn (a noted environmental author); Clarence Ditlow; John Dougherty; Marion Edey (long a stalwart of the League of Conservation Voters); Michael L. Fischer (Sierra Club); Alan Gussow; Michael J. Herz; Alvin Josephy; Ed Marston; Helen Mills; Katherine B. Mountcastle; Josephine Murray; Avis Ogilvy; Robert Redford (The Sundance Kid); Marie Ridder; Anthony Robbins; Dave Dive; Dick Trudell; and Dave Zwick (Clean Water Action, Washington, D.C.).

Even though FOE no longer publishes *Not Man Apart,* it puts out *Atmosphere* (a quarterly ozone newsletter), *Community Plume* (a quarterly chemical safety newsletter), *Friends of the Earth* (10 times a year) and *FOELink*, an international newsletter issued periodically through electronic mail.

Affiliated organizations are active in Europe, Australia, Canada, Mexico, South America, South Pacific, Japan and Hong Kong.

Contributors to Friends of the Earth include:

American Conservation Association, Inc., the Rockefeller money.

American Railroad Association.

Beldon Fund.

Bullitt Foundation, Inc., the broadcasting fortune of the founders of KING-TV in Seattle.

The Morris and Gwendolyn Cafritz Foundation gave $15,000 in 1990 for Chemical Safety Projects. Grant shared with Environmental Policy Institute.

Carnegie Corporation of New York gave $25,000 in 1988 (EPI).

Compton Foundation, Inc.

Charles A. Dana Foundation, Inc. gave $50,000 in 1987 (EPI).

Hillsdale Fund.

Ittleson Foundation, Inc.

The Joyce Foundation gave $50,000 in 1990 for implementation of multiphase effort to reorganize board, staff, membership and programs in order to strengthen participation of minority communities in environmental issues.

German Marshall Fund of the United States.

Charles Stewart Mott Foundation gave $40,000 in 1990 to increase interest of Multilateral Development Banks in investing in projects that will reduce tropical deforestation and arrest global warming; plus $400,000 to the Friends of the Earth Foundation for challenge grant for institutional capacity building; plus $50,000 in 1990 to the Foundation for technical and scientific assistance to coastal-focused citizen groups working to protect the nation's oceans and coastal ecology from toxic pollutants and other environmental threats.

New-Land Foundation.

Jessie Smith Noyes Foundation, Inc. gave the Foundation $20,000 in 1990, a 2-year grant to protect groundwater and encourage sustainable agriculture by providing technical assistance to and encouraging advocacy by grassroots organizations in Southwestern, Southcentral and Southeastern states; also gave $40,000 in 1988 (EPI).

James C. Penny Foundation, Inc. gave $10,000 in 1989 for Global Warming, Ozone Depletion and Energy Use Project, which educates citizen and consumer groups about initiatives they can take to reduce threats to global environment.

Public Welfare Foundation gave $150,000 in 1988 (EPI).

Recreational Equipment, Inc.

Rockefeller Brothers Fund gave $100,000 in 1990, a 2-year grant for project to monitor lending policies and practices of Asian Development Bank; plus $45,000 in 1990 toward Nuclear Non-Proliferation Project.

Rockefeller Family Fund, Inc. gave $40,000 in 1987 (EPI).

Warsh-Mott Legacy gave $15,000 in 1990 for program addressing international crisis in conservation of plant gene plasm; plus $10,000 in 1990 toward travel expenses of delegates to organizational meeting of World Fund for Conservation of Domestic Animal Genetic Resources and translation of meeting's materials.

Youth Project.

Friends of the Earth.
Job killers.
Economy Trashers.

Friends of the Earth—Footnotes

1 "From Fringe To Political Mainstream," by Michael Weiskopf, *Washington Post,* April 19, 1990, p. A1.

2 "Environmentalists in a Family Fight," by Gerald C. Lubenow, *Newsweek,* January 27, 1986, p. 7.

3 Much of this section was derived from "With Friends Like These..." by Paul Rauber, *Mother Jones,* November 1986, p. 34.

4 "The Answer," by Robinson Jeffers, in *Such Counsels You Gave to Me,* Random House, New York, 1937, p. 107.

5 "Original Sin," *The Poems of Robinson Jeffers,* Vintage, New York, 1963.

6. "Man of the Earth," by Lee Green, *Modern Maturity,* April - May 1991, p. 22.

7 "Lobbyist for the earth," by Dale Russakoff, *Washington Post,* July 27, 1989, p. A21.

8 "An Alliance in the War for the World," by Cass Peterson, *Washington Post,* February 10, 1989, p. A25.

9 *E Magazine,* January / February 1990.

10 "'Alternative' Nobels," by Constance Holden, *Science,* November 25, 1988, p. 1123.

11 "New Magazines," by Laurie Ouellette, *Utne Reader,* January / February 1991, p. 128.

12 "McCartney Plans World Ecology Tour," *New York Times,* July 29, 1989, p. C26.

13 "Introducing the Annual 'Green Con Award'" by David Stipp, *Wall Street Journal,* April 3, 1990, p. B1.

14 "U.S. Scientists Play Down Effect of Fires In Kuwait, Angering Environmentalists," by Bob Davis, *Wall Street Journal,* June 25, 1991, p. A3.

15 "Loblaw Pushes Activist-Endorsed Line Aimed at Issue-Conscious Consumers," by Michael T. Malloy, *Wall Street Journal,* May 1, 1989, p. B6.

Izaak Walton League of America

Izaak Walton League of America (Founded 1922)
Annual budget: $2,074,694 (1993)
Staff: 23 total—14 professional, 9 support
Members: 52,700 individuals
Tax Status: 501(c)(3)
Headquarters: 1401 Wilson Boulevard, Level B
Arlington, Virginia 22209
Phone: (703)528-1818 Fax: (202)528-1836

Economy Trasher Number Twenty-One. The Izaak Walton League of America was organized in Chicago in 1922 by a group of 54 sportsmen to combat water pollution and other environmental abuses in order to halt a decline in hunting and fishing. Publicist Will H. Dilg is recognized as its founder and was its first president. He was a fiery speechmaker and persuasive writer. It has been said that IWLA was "born with its fists doubled," declaring itself the "Defender of Woods, Waters, and Wildlife." A left jab and the economy is down for the count.

The group was named after Izaak Walton, 17th century English angler-conservationist and author of the classic *The Compleat Angler*. One of the most famous quotes from that venerable tome says, "What is everybody's business is nobody's business." Mr. Dilg evidently never read his book, or he'd have known Walton was talking about the privately owned fishing rights in British streams. The IWLA spends a lot of time making somebody's land and water into nobody's land and water and making everybody's land and water into nobody's land and water.

The Izaak Walton League introduced the three-level organization form to the conservation movement, divided into national headquarters, state groups, and local chapters. Because of Dilg's zeal and the work of many volunteers, IWLA became influential shortly after it was founded. Dilg, never afraid of exaggeration, boasted that the league would soon have a million members, but at peak it was only about 100,000.

However, Dilg was good at making his little outfit look big: He enlisted the aid of the Illinois governor to outlaw the sale of black bass, and a colleague wrote of his campaign with his seven state chapters, "Dilg made them look like 700."

But Dilg rubbed a lot of people the wrong way. When he gave a Pennsylvania audience some flatly wrong information, Seth Gordon, who later became the league's conservation director, took him to task. Dilg retorted, "Why worry? They'll never know the difference."[1]

To hell with you all.

Dilg was replaced in 1926, but not before his group lobbied to keep roads out of Superior National Forest in the locale later to become the Boundary Waters Canoe Area. They also lobbied to have the private property within the area nationalized.

The league stopped industrialist E. W. Backus from building dams for flood control and development in the boundary lakes of Minnesota and Ontario. The league also carried out the nation's first official water pollution survey in 1927 at the request of President Calvin Coolidge, and campaigned for years until finally convincing Congress to pass the Water Pollution Control Act of 1948.

In the 1940s they also fought to take range rights away from ranchers on the federal lands, promoted wilderness designations to prevent any commodity use of federal lands, and urged the creation of wild and scenic rivers to remove residents from the banks of their favorite fishing streams.

A great deal of the league's growing effectiveness was the result of one man: Joseph Weller Penfold, first as its western representative in Denver (1949-1957) and subsequently as its conservation director in Washington, D.C. His 1952 exploit in taking Congressmen Wayne N. Aspinall and John P. Saylor on a floating and camping trip in Colorado and Utah areas threatened by dam construction won him access to both men when they came to positions of power. Aspinall became chairman of the House Interior and Insular Affairs Committee and Saylor was its ranking minority member. The two of them killed the dams planned for Echo Park and Split Mountain in Dinosaur National Monument.

During the late 1950s, Penfold and Edward C. Crafts, assistant chief of the U.S. Forest Service, together with a few other colleagues, determined that a high-level commission was needed to promote outdoor recreation (and extend their power empire). They found an ally in Laurance S. Rockefeller, who encouraged their idea for his own reasons. The two drafted enabling legislation and convinced key legislators including Aspinall and Saylor to support their bill. Aspinall, however, sensed that this commission might become a permanent agency of government, so he made sure the act directed it to dissolve within seven months of submitting its final report, due at the end of January, 1962. Thus, on June 28, 1958, President Dwight D. Eisenhower signed the act creating the Outdoor Recreation Resources Review Commission (ORRRC). Laurance Rockefeller was appointed chairman.

The ORRRC was in large part a Rockefeller artifact, consisting of four senators, four representatives, seven presidential appointees (including Penfold, of course), advised by a council of fifteen bureaucrats and twenty-five representatives of various interests. The massive multi-volume ORRRC report was edited by Henry L. Diamond, Laurance Rockefeller's personal counsel on environmental issues, who also served as the commission's legal counsel. Diamond was born in Chattanooga, Tennessee, May 24, 1932, graduated from Vanderbilt in 1954 and, after military service, took his law degree at Georgetown University. He has remained a Rockefeller agent all his life, a longtime board member of the American Conservation Association, Jackson Hole Preserve, Inc. and Resources For The Future.[2]

The commission wrote fifty-two very specific recommendations that changed the face of America forever and set the stage for the evolution of the environmental movement in the next decade. The ORRRC neatly sidestepped its own mandated termination by recommending the establishment of the Bureau of Outdoor Recreation to plan for the nation's recreational needs permanently, and Congress agreed in 1962.

The BOR would become a vehicle to power for Paul Pritchard, later of the

National Parks and Conservation Association. ORRRC also led to the passage in 1964 of the Land and Water Conservation Fund Act which has spent millions to take millions of acres away from private property owners in the name of nature preservation—some were willing sellers and some the victims of condemnation, but all swelled the growing domain of nationalized land. Many others pieces of environmental legislation that came later, such as the National Scenic Trails System and the National Wild and Scenic Rivers System were originally recommendations of this commission in which the Izaak Walton League of America was so influential.

The League gained its loyal following among hunters and fishermen because it recommended that hunting and fishing regulations should be set by trained fish and wildlife agency personnel rather than by legislative decree.[3] The League has also defended hunters by running programs to improve their public image through improving their outdoor behavior.[4]

Those avid hunters and fishermen are probably unaware that it was their Izaak Walton League which brought the 1973 lawsuit that nearly shut down the whole forest products industry in America. The Izaak Walton League brought suit against the Forest Service complaining that it was harvesting too much timber and demanding that an obscure law from the 19th Century be followed to the letter. Feeling compelled for lack of clear Congressional intent to adhere to the literal language of the 1897 Organic Act, the U.S. Court of Appeals at Richmond, Virginia upheld the U.S. District Court for the Northern District of West Virginia in *Izaak Walton League v. Butz*. In one fell swoop we threw out 75 years of accumulated scientific knowledge and practice.

How ironic that the League wanted hunting and fishing regulations set by trained fish and wildlife agency personnel, but wanted forestry regulations set by the courts rather than trained foresters.

The ruling forbade any future sales of timber in the Monongahela National Forest of West Virginia unless the sale was of "dead, matured or large growth of trees...marked and designated" and removed from the site. The Izaak Walton League was in effect arguing that "You should only cut Ancient Forests"—as a ploy to stop timber operations. A decade later when another tack was required to kill the forest industry, the Izaak Walton League decided that its earlier position was inconvenient and aligned itself with the "Don't cut Ancient Forests" faction. Strange how the League's moral high ground shifts so easily.

Subsequently, the Forest Service administratively applied the Monongahela decision to the nine national forests in Virginia, North Carolina, South Carolina and West Virginia. Volumes planned for sale in those states plummeted 90 percent. The Chief of the Forest Service, John McGuire, warned that if the decision were applied to all 155 national forests, it could reduce the harvest by as much as 75 percent per year, from 12 billion board feet to 3 billion board feet.

The Forest Service shut down timber sales all over the nation until Congress could pass the National Forest Management Act of 1976 specifically allowing clearcut logging in appropriate places. The League trashed the forest economy, killing thousands of jobs and stopping the flow of wood products—because they thought cutover land wasn't picture pretty.

Clearcutting, a principal environmentalist target, is a scientifically based system of silviculture, as foresters explain—one that nature herself uses, albeit with less discretion, by means of fire, storm and insect infestation. Since 1910, Forest Service research has shown again and again that shade-intolerant species—including many southern, northern and western pines, Douglas fir, white oak, yellow birch, black walnut, yellow poplar, sweet gum, bald cypress, larch, tamarack and black cherry—must be harvested by clearcutting if they are to be reproduced successfully. That is the only way foresters can manage forests on a high-level, sustained yield basis.

Clearcutting is biologically sound, based on keen observation of natural processes, and when combined with modern industrial replanting and reseeding programs, brings back forest regrowth much faster and healthier than unaided nature. As Sir Francis Bacon said centuries ago, "Nature, in order to be commanded, must be obeyed." Environmentalists are offended by such success—the dogma is that man cannot possibly improve upon nature—and fall back on arguments that it is not pretty. That's true. Neither is the aftermath of a forest fire or a hurricane, but catastrophe is necessary for these species to reproduce. It's going to happen one way or another. If we stop all logging, nature will destroy those forests sooner or later anyway, and humanity gets no benefit. If we use clearcutting judiciously where appropriate, we will get the benefit of the wood for human use as paper, as homes, as thousands of other needs.

Perhaps the greatest insult the Izaak Walton League hurls at our intelligence is retorting with the question, "Well, what will happen when all the forests are clearcut?" It's hard to tell if the League asks such a thing out of stupidity or deliberate malice to misdirect attention away from the real issues.

Nothing will happen when all the forests are clearcut because no one has proposed to clearcut all the forests. In fact, foresters are careful to point out that not only is clearcutting prescribed solely where it makes biological sense, but also that timber harvest of any kind is envisioned only where commercial stands are both suitable and available. The national parks and wilderness areas are not targeted for clearcutting or timber harvest of any kind by anyone, because both systems are properly off limits by law. Private timber companies often maintain their own preserves, never to be harvested, because a particular stand is unique or surpassingly beautiful or more valuable for recreation than for growing timber crops.

Environmentalists also assert that replanted forests are monocultures—only one species of tree in a whole forest, which destroys biodiversity. Such critics have obviously never walked the ground in industrial forests. "Volunteers," sprouts and seedlings of the original forest mix pop up among the replanted species in vast numbers—in addition to the fact that industrial tree nurseries grow numerous species for outplanting. In addition, many forest types end up being virtual monocultures all by themselves—the Tongass National Forest, for example, is dominated by only two species, Sitka spruce and Western hemlock, co-dominants that cover millions of acres in Southeast Alaska, with pockets of Western redcedar and very few other species clumped in a few favored places. The mighty Douglas fir, which crowds both spruce and hemlock into submission further south, is totally absent, even though the soils and temperature are perfect—the Pacific storm track dumps so much rain on the Tongass that forest fires can't open up the bare mineral soil and bright sunlight they need for regeneration. No natural clearcuts, no Douglas fir.

Well, forget the science. The Izaak Walton League doesn't give a damn about the facts today any more than Will Dilg did in the 1920s—"Why worry? They'll never know the difference."

They don't give a damn about you having wood products or about responsible foresters and loggers having stable jobs or about the survival of the timber industry.

To hell with you all.

Most interesting, this organization that takes the federal government to court gets substantial funding from the federal government, in particular from the Department of Agriculture and the U. S. Fish and Wildlife Service.

It's a stretch from their usual schemes, and it took a lot of doing, but the Izaak Walton League of America found a way to cash in on the global warming scare. Laury Marshall-Forbes wrote the League's report titled "Unprecedented Risks: The Effects of Global Climate Change on U.S. Wildlife Resources," which blamed the industrial economy for horrendous future disasters. Upon close reading, however, one discovers that the hyphenated author did not perform a *study* at all, which would have required actual fieldwork to ascertain whether or not the risks were real, but instead wrote a *report*, which was little more than a literature search in a library with some interpretation thrown in.

Ms. Marshall-Forbes said of her report, "Global climate change could cause a number of problems for wildlife, including habitat loss, endangerments and possible extinction. We must recognize these potential threats and begin to take steps now to protect wildlife in the future."

The studies cited by the League's report are all based on computerized predictions that resulted from assumptions made by the scientist doing the study. Because of very measurable increases in certain "greenhouse gases" such as carbon dioxide that trap heat in the atmosphere, and the laboratory rate of warming these gases ought to cause, the computer estimated that a temperature rise of 2 to 10 degrees ought to occur over the next century. Unfortunately, the real world refuses to cooperate. Those increased greenhouse gases, the result of the industrial revolution, have been growing for more than a century, but so far, the planet has warmed by a degree at most, and many scientists doubt even that, including Dr. Robert White, head of the National Academy of Engineering, because the temperature measurements are highly questionable.

Well, let's not allow a little thing like reality to interfere with some good old fund raising worry, worry, worry. The Izaak Walton League of America wants you to fear that several types of species may be particularly vulnerable to climate change impacts, including species in "island" habitats, such as national wildlife refuges and national parks. How convenient that these species are in areas that may be particularly vulnerable to changes in the political climate.

"Why worry? They'll never know the difference."

The most important part of the announcements about this report are those magic words, "send a $5 check, made payable to the Izaak Walton League of America."[5] And let's not forget that the League used its efforts to get a $20,000 grant from the Joyce Mertz-Gilmore Foundation in 1989 for its Global Warming and Wildlife Project.

It was virtually the same ploy the League used to cash in on the acid rain scare. The League's Upper Mississippi regional representative Paul Hansen put together another "report" on the population decline of the Black Duck, asserting that acid rain may be playing a role in waterfowl decline.[6] It was just a library study, a search of the existing literature; Hansen did no field work to demonstrate whether or not the purported link to acid rain was real. The factual gaps in Hansen's report were big enough to drive a tank through: He made no effort to show whether the acid lakes had always been acidic—the half-billion dollar National Acid Precipitation Assessment Program found fewer than 300 of the 7,000 lakes studied to be acidic in any biologically serious degree. Most of those lakes were found to be naturally acidic due to surrounding soil acidity, and not from industrial pollution deposition. With very little to go on, the Izaak Walton League opportunistically pushed Green Guilt with their virtually meaningless report. Oh, yes, and don't forget to send money for your copy of the report, because we need it to pay our lobbyists—who spent hundreds of hours on Capitol hill in 1988 working for harsh Economy Trashing controls on industry.[7]

"Why worry? They'll never know the difference."

The League sponsors a number of environmental programs including Wetlands Watch, Outdoor Ethics Information Center,[8] Save Our Streams (written up in *Boys' Life*, no less),[9] Acid Rain Project, Chesapeake Bay Program, and a syndicated weekly television program, *Make Peace With Nature*.

It sounds very Sweetness and Light until you realize that the League routinely bashes industry as a fund raising gimmick—and joins eco-socialist groups in their bashing sprees. For instance, in 1992 the League joined with the Sierra Club and Natural Resources Defense Council to file a complaint with the Federal Trade Commission against Amoco Corporation, Exxon Corporation and Mobil Corporation for misleading the public in advertisements featuring their oil recycling programs. The groups accused the oil companies of burning their waste oil instead of rerefining it, which the Sierra Club claimed was as dangerous as dumping waste oil.[10]

None of the environmental group charges had any merit. Amoco and Exxon had both given large amounts of money to the Izaak Walton League in previous years, and these accusations to the FTC may have been a reminder that a healthy contribution would be in order. But if you were a League member, you almost certainly got hit up for a healthy contribution to help pay for this vital eco-project, which cost virtually nothing. Anyone can file a complaint with the FTC against any company for any imaginary violation and it costs nothing but the effort to write the complaint. Worse, and there's nothing the company can do about it except pay an army of lawyers to fight the complaint. If they are cleared, the Izaak Walton League doesn't apologize, it goes on to another job-killer scheme to raise some more money.

"Why worry? They'll never know the difference."

The League participated in the *Blueprint for the Environment* project in 1988, donating the services of former Executive Director Jack Lorenz (salary $75,000) to the Blueprint Steering Committee and Conservation Director Maitland Sharpe chaired the Grazing Policy Task Force to trash the Western rancher. The Izaak Walton League remains particularly antagonistic to the livestock industry as it did in the 1940s, campaigning on Capitol Hill for ruinous increases in grazing fees, elimination of permittees' cattle from federal range-lands, and seizure of private streams and waterways from ranchers without compensation.

"Why worry? They'll never know the difference."

The League contains some 400 local chapters, 20 state divisions, an Upper Mississippi regional office, and a national headquarters in Washington, D.C. The Izaak Walton League of America Endowment Million Dollar Club is a separate corporation established to acquire and protect unique natural areas. The Endowment receives no portion of the League's membership dues; all funding comes from individual foundations and corporate contributions.

The League's publications include *Outdoor America* (quarterly outdoor magazine), *Outdoor Ethics* (quarterly newsletter for outdoor writers, natural resources managers, hunter safety instructors, and recreation groups); *Splash* (quarterly Save Our Streams newsletter); *League Leader* (quarterly newsletter to keep the 2,000 chapter and division officers in touch with the national office).

In 1961 the Izaak Walton League absorbed the Friends of the Land.

Executive Director Maitland Sharpe (salary $76,052, benefits $5,617), former Conservation Director, took over from Jack Lorenz in 1993. Lorenz was a more interesting man—he joined the League in 1973 as editor of *Outdoor America*, its monthly magazine. The next year he was appointed executive director. Lorenz previously worked in the environmental affairs department of the Falstaff Brewing Company in St. Louis and served as president of the American League of Anglers from 1982 to 1984. Here's the odd fish: a revolving door from business to the environmental movement—and the beer business at that! Lorenz is on the advisory board of the National Freshwater Fishing Hall of Fame and is an active member of the Outdoor Writers Association of America. Lorenz graduated from the University of Tulsa with a degree in journalism.

IWLA's Board of Directors includes honorary president William D. Ruckelshaus; president Donald C. Freeman; vice president Charles Wiles; secretary Mel Sneed; treasurer Francis Satterlee; executive board chairman Donald L. Ferris; and executive board vice chairman Timothy W. Reid. Other members of the executive board include: Stan Adams; Ethyl Bloch; Dale Brentnall; Fred A. Cooper; H. Nick Frost; Delmer H. Miller; Paul Toren; Howard S. White (general counsel); and Fred Widlak.

The Izaak Walton League of America fits solidly in the Establishment Interventionist Axis.

Funding sources include: 54 percent from contributions and grants; 3 percent from interest income; 40 percent from membership dues; and 3 percent from sales and bequests. Contributors listed below in some cases have contributed because their executives at times past have entered into League fishing tournaments and other outdoor sports events, and may not be intentionally supporting the group's Economy Trasher efforts.

Amoco Foundation.
Anheuser-Busch.
ARCO Foundation.
Baltimore Gas and Electric.
Bowater Southern Paper Corporation.
Beldon Fund.
Bell Foundation.
Burlington Resources.
Chevron, USA.
Deluxe Check Printers
Gaylord and Dorothy Donnelly Foundation.
E. I. du Pont de Nemours & Company. In February 1987, du Pont joined with the League to co-sponsor the second annual Chesapeake Bay Conservation Awards program.
Edison Electric Institute.
Exxon Company.
FMC Corporation.
The Grand Rapids Foundation gave $25,000 in 1989 for building a winterized lodge.
George Gund Foundation.
International Business Machines
Joyce Foundation.
Louisiana-Pacific Corporation.
Richard King Mellon Foundation.
Joyce Mertz-Gilmore Foundation gave $20,000 in 1989 for Global Warming and Wildlife Project.
Missouri Department of Conservation.
National Fish and Wildlife Foundation.
National Marine Manufacturers Association.
National Taxidermists' Association.
Northwest Area Foundation.
Pennzoil.
Phillips Petroleum Foundation.
Procter & Gamble
Laurance Rockefeller Charitable Trust.
The Procter & Gamble Fund gave $10,000 in 1990.
Steelcase Foundation gave $13,000 in 1989 for building winterized lodge.
Tenneco.
3M Company.

Town Creek Foundation.
U.S. Department of Agriculture.
U.S. Fish and Wildlife Service.
Unocal Corporation.
Virginia Environmental Endowment gave $35,000 in 1991 to continue promotion, training and technical support for expansion of Save Our Streams in Virginia; plus $20,000 in 1991 to continue development and expansion of Save Our Streams in West Virginia.
Weyerhaeuser Foundation.
Charles A. Weyerhaeuser Foundation.

"Why worry? They'll never know the difference."

Izaak Walton League of America.
Job killers.
Economy Trashers.

Izaak Walton League of America—Footnotes

1 "Izaak Walton League of America," by William Voight, Jr., *Encyclopedia of American Forest and Conservation History*, Richard C. Davis, editor, Macmillan Publishing Company, New York, 1983, p. 319.
2 Diamond is listed in *Who's Who In The East*.
3 *Animals' Agenda*, July / August, 1988.
4 "A question of ethics," by George Reiger, *Field and Stream*, January 1992, p. 14.
5 "Global Climate Change Could Threaten U.S. Wildlife," by Mary Kadlecek, *The Conservationist*, July - August 1991, p. 54.
6 "Acid rain, the real culprit in decimating wildfowl populations," column by Howard Brant, *Shooting Industry*, July 1987, p. 22.
7 "Black Duck Decline: An Acid Rain Link," by Jon R. Luoma, *Audubon*, May 1987, p. 19.
8 "Stream Stewardship: materials to show you how," by Janet Essman, *Conservationist*, July - August 1991, p. 54.
9 "Stream savers," by Pat Durkin, *Boys' Life*, July 1991, p. 7.
10 "Groups dispute oil companies' recycling ads," by Alan Kovski, *The Oil Daily*, April 24, 1992, p. 1.

The Fund for Animals

Fund for Animals (Founded 1967)
Annual budget: $1.8 million
   Staff: 23 total
   Members: 200,000 individuals
   Tax Status: 501(c)(3)
   Headquarters: 200 West 57th Street   850 Sligo Avenue, Suite LL2
              New York, New York 10019   Silver Spring, Maryland 20910
              Phone: (212)246-2096   (301)585-2591
              Fax: (212)246-2633   (301)585-2595

Economy Trasher Number Twenty-Two. One of the most wild-eyed anti-hunting, anti-rodeo, anti-people animal rights groups in the business—led by some of the brightest, most literate, most intellectual activists in the movement.

If you still think that environmentalism is mere emotionalism promoted by uninformed, misled, poorly-read people who don't understand how things work, this group's profile will disabuse you of that belief once and for all.

The Fund for Animals was founded by writer and commentator Cleveland Amory, whose books have influenced several generations of opinion leaders. Amory was born in Nahant, Massachusetts in 1917. He earned an A.B. from Harvard in 1939 and was a reporter on the Nashua New Hampshire *Telegraph* and the *Arizona Daily Star* in Tucson, later the managing editor of the Prescott, Arizona *Evening Courier*. He was associate editor of the *Saturday Evening Post* and editor of *Celebrity Register* for five years. He knows everybody who shaped the America we know today.

Amory's books, *The Proper Bostonian, Who Killed Society?, Mankind? Our Incredible War on Wildlife,* and *The Cat Who Came for Christmas,* to name but a few, have shaped opinion in America since the 1940s. He is a member of the elite Harvard Club of New York City and of the toney New York Athletic Club, as well as president of the New England Anti-Vivisection Society that PETA leaders Alex Pacheco and Ingrid Newkirk won in a proxy fight in 1987, which says something about the degree of connection between PETA and Fund for Animals.

Cleveland Amory is living proof that intellect and erudition do not necessarily promote calm and rational wisdom, but may have the diametrically opposite result—ferocious radical zealotry. He wrote a savage anti-hunting piece titled "They are bloodthirsty nuts" in *U.S. News & World Report* so nasty it would curdle holy water.[1]

As part of his sedulously radical activism, Cleveland Amory and his Fund for Animals paid for the original eco-pirate ship, the *Sea Shepherd* (see the PETA profile), which was captained by former Greenpeace director Paul Watson, allegedly given his walking papers by the organization due to differences of opinion over non-violent versus violent protest. The original vessel was scuttled in 1980 in the belief that authorities intended to seize it. Sailing on the vessels was a manner of initiation ritual.

The crew "reportedly paid Paul Watson $1,000 each in order to enjoy being a part of the historical adventure."[2]

Amory's main emphasis is on the absolute elimination of all hunting and fishing, although his animals rights agenda extends to stopping all human use of animals for any purpose whatsoever.[3] The Fund opposes "the cruelty of bullfighting, the clubbing of baby seals, use of the leghold trap, sport hunting, laboratory animals, greyhound racing, and dog fighting."[4]

The Fund for Animals has stirred an interesting controversy that threatens to split the environmental movement from the inside. Its rabid opposition to the leghold trap has seriously troubled land-trust environmental groups which operate their own nature preserves such as the Nature Conservancy and the National Audubon Society. The nature preserve-operating organizations have used leghold traps for many years to keep raccoons, opossums and other mammals from predating bird nests. The National Audubon Society on its Rainey Wildlife Sanctuary in Louisiana uses leghold traps to keep nutria—a huge ratlike rodent transplanted from South America—from devastating its nesting migratory birds. The Fund for Animals wants them to stop using the leghold trap. The only alternative for predator control would be poison baits, which, on a wildlife preserve, would very likely kill non-target species. That and all other alternatives to the leghold trap are unacceptable to the Audubon folks. This battle is still brewing on the back burner, but look for a knock-down, drag-out in the near future.

Amory's Fund for Animals has been a high-profile player in the Wild Horse controversy on Western federal lands. The Interior Department's Bureau of Land Management (BLM) is responsible for administering the Wild Horses and Burros Protection Act of 1971, which essentially pushed the cost of upkeep for wild free-roaming horses off onto the permittees who have grazed their cattle on this land for a century.

The BLM's Wild Horse Bureau was run by John Boyles in 1990, when a large roundup of wild horses was under way to protect the range condition of BLM's 170 million acres in the American West. At that time over 10,000 wild horses were penned in federal corrals, available for "adoption," that is, purchase for $125 by private owners who would give them a suitable home at their own expense.

The Fund for Animals did not like the conditions in the pens and complained loudly against the roundup. Cleveland Amory made one of his typically razor-tongued remarks: "Ronald Reagan once said that the best thing for the inside of a man is the outside of a horse. There hasn't been an administration since Rutherford B. Hayes's that has done less for wildlife, and particularly wild horses, than this President."

Doing something for wild horses is an activity Amory hasn't much direct experience with—he's more comfortable in the Harvard Club than on a horse. Nevada rancher Demar Dahl, on the other hand, knows a lot about wild mustangs out in the sagebrush and chaparral, and sits a horse more than most workers sit a desk. He watched an unculled herd of 100 mustangs expand to over 700 in a decade and put him out of business. The herd had expanded because ranchers could no longer shoot them when their numbers began to compete for water and grass—the 1971 law forbade it.

Dahl told *U.S. News & World Report*, "There was no vegetation left, and they ruined the springs—did incredible damage." The writer, Michael Satchell, who doesn't know a lot about wild horses, either, printed that much. But he neglected to say that the springs those horses had ruined were the private property of Mr. Dahl, as was all water on his grazing allotment, and that the grass and forbs the mustangs ate Mr. Dahl had paid for in grazing fees several times higher than their real worth.[5]

But the 1971 law had pushed the cost of supporting all of the uncontrolled wild horses onto him. He could not deny them access to the wells and stock watering ponds he had built at his own expense. He could not prevent them from drinking the water he owned. He could do nothing to stop them from eating the grass he struggled to conserve to maximize the value of his range. He could not stop the mustangs from competing his cattle into smaller and smaller numbers. He could not thin their numbers by shooting, trapping, removing or chasing them. And the range damage they did went on his Range Condition Report in BLM files as if he had caused it by poor cattle grazing methods.

Enough ranchers were facing financial ruin from wild horse increases to give the Interior Department a serious political headache. The Reagan administration's privatization program had been stopped cold by the existence of ranchers' rights in federal lands. The federal government couldn't privatize by auction what was already private. The government couldn't sell what it did not own. Ranchers, the federal government discovered, held *de facto* and *de jure* rights to water, minerals, and the range that the agencies had held to be mere privileges that could be revoked at any time. In order to prevent a showdown that could conceivably unravel the entire federal domain—all over the issue of wild horses—the BLM began to round up the wild horses and pen them up.

Wild Horse Bureau chief John Boyles said, "The intent of Congress is to preserve some symbols, not expand their herds."

The Fund for Animals didn't like that. But they too quietly realized that going to the mat over wild horses would raise some very disturbing questions over who really owns the "federal" lands. So they directed their wrath toward the pens and complained loudly about humane conditions. They wanted more money spent on keeping the horses properly—the cost to taxpayers was then passing $10 million a year. But the Fund for Animals didn't offer any of its budget to solve the problem.

Today the horses remain penned. And the wild horse problem on the range grows worse. And the Fund for Animals remains vocal. But not generous with its funds.

But the Fund for Animals' main target is the elimination of all hunting and fishing. Sport hunting and fishing alone—not counting commercial fishing—generates something like $6 billion a year worth of economic activity. The Fund for Animals wants to see that vanish.[6]

Cleveland Amory and his Fund have some very intelligent ways of making it happen, one of which is taking advantage of the opposition's misfortunes. Their strategy to eliminate hunting in California is a case in point:

The Fund for Animals had filed a lawsuit to stop bear hunting in California. They had been unsuccessful with state agencies at trying to impose their views on the hunting minority. Under the California Environmental Quality Act, the department of fish and game must provide documents to the court to prove the species can tolerate cropping. Gathering such data requires the work of an army of biologists, wildlife managers and department staff. Therefore, anything that would reduce the number of these people keeping track of animal populations would open the hunting season to a court challenge and stop it completely.[7]

It works like this: The Fund for Animals had successfully stopped the bear hunt in 1989 and came into court to stop the 1990 hunt. Their lawyers came into court armed with arguments that had proven successful in past cases on bears, tule elk and mountain lions—specifically, that the environmental document prepared by the department to justify the hunting season under CEQA was inadequate.

The Fund prevailed in the bowhunting portion of the hunt by successfully arguing that the department did not adequately consider all of the data on the wounding of bears with bowhunting equipment. This was a violation of Section 203.1 of the Fish and Game Code, which mandates the department and commission to consider an individual animal's welfare when setting hunting seasons. Sacramento Superior Court Judge Cecily Bond ruled for the Fund, stating specifically it was because of a technicality: "This court was not passing judgment on the legality or propriety of bowhunting, but only that the respondents did not meaningfully consider all the data in making their decision."

At the same time that the court was considering this case, Fund for Animals supporters, along with numerous other environmentalists, took another tack to destroy hunting. They lobbied to chop the budget of the department of fish and game in 1990. The sale of hunting and fishing licenses had declined because earlier environmentalists had not only stopped specific hunts, but also put numerous hunting and fishing spots off limits. The decline in hunting license sales meant that the Fish and Game Preservation Fund, an account made up of license fees, came up with a projected deficit of $12.6 million. It costs a lot to monitor wildlife.

The California Assembly did the easy thing: It simply hacked the $12.6 million shortfall out of the budget and, under the tutelage of helpful environmentalists, specified where the cuts were to occur. Wildlife management got chopped $5 million, or 22.8 percent of the department's budget.

The predictable result? Nearly every field-level wildlife biologist was targeted for layoff. These, of course, are the very people who gather the annual data used by the courts to justify hunting seasons. Without the annual data, any halfwit lawyer could file a successful legal challenge to close the hunting season.

What did Cleveland Amory say when he heard about the budget cuts? "I don't mean to be gloating about someone's financial hardship, but it gives us an opportunity to stop some of this cruel activity. I think it's very exciting that the shortfall is there."[8]

Let's ponder that sentiment a moment. Let's assume that Mr. Amory is playing square with us and that he really doesn't mean to gloat about someone's financial hardship. Fair enough. No gloat.

But look what he does with it. "It gives us an opportunity to stop some of this cruel activity." The financial hardship of those wildlife biologists is an "opportunity." Mr. Amory doesn't gloat over their unemployment, *he gets excited about it.*

Now let's think this through. Remember, any human use of animals is "cruel" to Mr. Amory and his Fund. He wants to end *all* human use of animals. When he has caused the next industry, sport fishing, to collapse, what is he likely to do? He won't gloat. The financial hardship of sport fisherman outfitters is an "opportunity." He'll get excited about it.

When he has caused the next industry, commercial fishing, to collapse, what is he likely to do? He won't gloat. The financial hardship of commercial fisherman is an "opportunity." He'll get excited about it.

When he has caused the next industry, meat, livestock and poultry, to collapse, what is he likely to do? He won't gloat. The financial hardship of farmers and ranchers is an "opportunity." He'll get excited about it.

When he has shut down all the rodeos, circuses, animal acts and medical research laboratories using animals, he won't gloat. He'll get excited about it and see it as an opportunity to shut down the next industry.

If there's a next industry left by then.

Mr. Amory has afforded us a view into the secret heart of hearts of the true environmentalist. He gets excited about economic hardship. He's honest when he says it's not gloating. It's something so obscene there's not even a word for it.

Think about that when *your* job goes up in environmentalist smoke. Economy Trashers will get excited about it.

They got something to really be excited about in late 1992. One of the Bush administration's final actions was an out of court settlement of a lawsuit brought against the U. S. Department of the Interior's Fish & Wildlife Service, agreeing to speed up the process of listing endangered and threatened species. The victory was extraordinary, said director Wayne Pacelle. The settlement officially recognized environmentalist demands to take a "multispecies, ecosystem approach" to listing plants and animals. In effect, whole ecosystems would be examined and everything protected at once. The economic devastation this would bring about might be the shortest way to getting the endangered species act repealed—the rehabilitation of New York City to restore Atlantic salmon populations in all the short-run streams on Manhattan Island would require the removal of every human structure from Harlem to the Staten Island ferry.[9]

Fund for Animals national director Wayne Pacelle was appointed in 1988. He was previously president of the Animal Rights Alliance and associate editor of *The Animals' Agenda*, published by the Animal Rights Network, Inc. in Rochester, Vermont—he still serves on the magazine's board of directors. Pacelle is a graduate of Yale University.

Pacelle led a crowd of about 120 demonstrators carrying signs and chanting slogans against hunting outside the Texas Wildlife Expo 92 in Austin, Texas in October 1992. It turned out to be one of the stupidest things they could have done. Pacelle "strutted back and forth like a little Hitler," according to J. C. Van Kirk, president of the American Hunting and Fishing Ethics Bureau and founder of the Texas Sportsmen's Legal Fund, groups that defend the right to hunt. One of Pacelle's demonstrators carried a placard that read "Conserve Hunters. Harvest One Today." Expo visitors chanted back, "Get a life."

A Fund for Animals demonstrator displayed a life-size effigy of baseball great Nolan Ryan—an avid bowhunter—with arrows impaled through its heart and crotch. "This is a bad move on the Fund's part," said Van Kirk. "Not only do a lot of hunters in Texas love this man, but millions of non-hunters as well."[10]

A firestorm of negative public opinion erupted. Pacelle was stunned by the reaction and did everything he could to deny the incident in a letter to the editor of the *Austin American Statesman*, saying it had been a setup. The Texas Sportsmen's Legal Fund and other hunting groups offered a $1,200 reward for the identity of the demonstrator holding the offensive mutilated effigy. Photos revealed that the woman standing next to the guilty demonstrator turned out to be none other than Ingrid Newkirk of People for the Ethical Treatment of Animals.

The woman displaying the effigy was found to be Patty Garcia of Live Oak, Texas, a well known animal rights activist and member of a group called Voice for Animals.

The Fund for Animals also joined in a coalition to get an anti-hunting initiative on the Colorado ballot in November 1992. Amendment 10 would have stopped the spring black bear hunt. Although the front group for the initiative, calling itself Coloradans United for Bears (CUB), claimed that the measure was crucial "to protect Colorado's black bears from extermination," it was a total falsehood, but has become a routine claim in anti-hunting literature.[11]

State bear hunts, like all game animal hunts in the United States, are strictly regulated by state wildlife departments and black bears in Colorado are not in the slightest danger. Bag limits and seasons are determined by wildlife biologists, as in the California case. Skilled biologists track the population closely. When numbers go down, the game department reduces the number of hunting licenses for sale or even stops them if needed. Conversely, when biologists see game animals reaching population limits as indicated by sightings of dead and starving animals, extensions of seasons may be authorized.

The Fund for Animals also participates in hunt sabotage, much as the original British Hunt Saboteurs Association did (see PETA profile). In particular, Fund national outreach director Heidi Prescott has made a career of interfering with hunters and getting arrested for it.

Prescott is the daughter of a Methodist minister turned counselor and a graduate of Pennsylvania's Edinboro State College. She is a vegetarian whose diet includes no dairy products—the "vegan" we discussed in the PETA profile. She does everything she can to force you to do the same, which in her case is little more than to assert the moral authority of civil disobedience, showing the courage of her convictions when convicted for interfering with hunts and serving jail time.[12]

She's been arrested for harassing hunters and scaring game animals away seven times, and spent 13 days in jail in a Maryland conviction rather than pay a $500 fine. She claims she refused to pay for moral reasons, but her Fund for Animals salary of $14,000 probably didn't have $500 stretching room.[13]

She was arrested with two other Fund for Animals members on November 26, 1992 at the McKee-Besher Wildlife Management Area in Montgomery County, Maryland and charged with failure to obey law enforcement officers. Aaron Medlock, staff lawyer for Fund for Animals, said the activists were trying to prevent ducks from flying into the range of hunters.[14]

However, the example of Prescott and the Fund for Animals may be inciting unbalanced followers to lawbreaking somewhat in excess of civil disobedience— doing what that Texas demonstrator's placard recommended. In Ohio, Michigan and Indiana, eight sportsmen have been murdered between the dates of April 1989 and April 1992 by a sniper while alone in remote areas, according to the *Cleveland Plain Dealer*. All the slayings occurred during hunting season. The FBI and county law enforcement investigators have not ruled out an animal rights anti-hunting motive, but until a suspect is apprehended they cannot confirm it, either. Five of the victims were hunters, two fishermen, one simply walking in a hunting area. Authorities think one person was responsible for all eight murders. The phenomenon of hunters becoming the hunted has made headlines in the nation's biggest papers.[15]

Although the Fund for Animals does not overtly support it, the Rocky Mountain Humane Society has advocated hunter harassment including shooting in the vicinity of hunters in order to stop hunts and to scare off game.

A book titled *A Declaration of War: Killing People to Save Animals and the Environment* and written under the pseudonym "Screaming Wolf," is sold by the Good Shepherd Foundation.

In England, Bernard Levin quoted a leader of the Hunt Retribution Squad in the *London Times* as saying "the next stage then would be to actually take a hunter out completely."[16]

It is not clear whether the Fund for Animals is itself drifting in the direction of committing such acts of violence. It is all too clear that its executive director led a demonstration in Texas which displayed a placard recommending the murder of hunters, and was accompanied by the leader of People for the Ethical Treatment of Animals.

The Fund for Animals has also taken part in boycotts of fur and animal products in Canada,[17] attempted to assert "non-hunters' rights,"[18] and has attacked the commodity uses of the national forests, including timber harvest, livestock grazing, and hunting—stating its case that the U.S. Forest Service had "a poor record in forest conservation which includes an alliance with the timber industry, subsidies for cattle grazing, and cooperation with hunters." The Fund for Animals refuses to acknowledge that timber management, livestock grazing and hunting are each conservation activities—misuing the term "conservation" as if it meant "preservation only."[19]

The Board of Directors of the Fund for Animals includes president and chairman Cleveland Amory; vice president Michael Kilian; and treasurer-secretary Marian Probst. Other members include Richard Carlson; Priscilla Cohn; Del Donati; Judith Ney; Kathryn Walker; Amory Winthrop; and Gretchen Wyler.

Fund for Animals.
Job killers.
Economy Trashers.

The Fund for Animals-Footnotes

1 "They are bloodthirsty nuts," by Cleveland Amory, *U.S. News & World Report*, February 5, 1990, p. 35.
2 *Seal Wars*, Janice Scott Henke, Breakwater, Saint John's, Newfoundland, 1985, p. 130-136.
3 "Cut to the chase," *The Economist*, November 10, 1990, p. 33.
4 *Encyclopedia of Associations, 27th Edition, 1993*, entry number 10413.
5 "The final roundup for America's wild horses?" by Michael Satchell, *U.S. News & World Report*, March 2, 1987, p. 69.
6 "An interview with Luke Dommer, founder of the Committee to Abolish Sport Hunting," (interview) by Wayne Pacelle, *The Animals' Agenda*, September 1991, p. 12.
7 "When the nonhunting majority speaks, government agencies don't listen," by Wayne Pacelle, *The Animals' Agenda*, January-February 1990, p. 19.
8 "The Domino Effect," by Jim Matthews, *Outdoor Life*, March 1991, p. 61ff.
9 "Imperiled species to get swifter protection," *Washington Post*, December 15, 1992.
10 "Nolan Ryan Effigy Mutilated by Animal Rights Activists at Texas Wildlife Expo," by Kathleen Marquardt, *People's Bulletin*, Washington, D.C. October 10, 1992.
11 "Hunting and the Endangered Species Act: Hunting is one of the major causes of animal extinction," by Wayne Pacelle, *The Animals' Agenda*, June 1992, p. 22.
12 "Courage of her convictions," by Coleman McCarthy, *Washington Post*, August 11, 1990, p. A21.
13 "Heidi Prescott: hunt saboteur," by Phil Maggitti, *The Animals' Agenda*, November 1991, p. 8.
14 "Activists Arrested for Disrupting Hunt," by Kathleen Marquardt, *People's Bulletin*, December 1, 1992, p. 4.
15 "New twist in animal rights: hunter is the prey," *New York Times*, November 26, 1990, p. A11.
16 "Sportsmen being murdered," by Kathleen Marquardt, *People's Bulletin*, October 20, 1992, p. 1.
17 "Canada's fur trade feels chill," by Mary Williams Walsh, *Los Angeles Times*, November 6, 1990, p. A1.
18 "Wildlife mis-management," by Wayne Pacelle and Dan Namowitz, *The Animals' Agenda*, September 1991, p. 12.
19 "A clear cut case of government abuse: a look at the U.S. Forest Service," by Wayne Pacelle, *The Animals' Agenda*, June 1991, p. 40.

Earth Island Institute ■■■■■■■■■■

Earth Island Institute (Founded 1982)
    Annual budget: $1.5 million
          Staff: 18 total, some full-time, some part-time
      Members: 32,000 individuals
    Tax Status: 501(c)(3)
  Headquarters: 300 Broadway, Suite 28
              San Francisco, California 94133
              Phone: (415)788-3666 Fax: (415)788-7324

Economy Trasher Number Twenty-Three. This is David R. Brower's latest organization. Brower, of course, is the Archdruid, as he was tagged in John McPhee's 1971 biography.[1] This much-lionized idol of the environmental movement is a self-proclaimed militant environmentalist, regarded by many to be the movement's most visionary spokesman.[2]

The source of Brower's honorific title is significant: Charles Fraser, a real estate developer who sought to build vacation homes on Cumberland Island, off the coast of Georgia, was thwarted by Brower and his ilk. Fraser said, "Ancient druids used to sacrifice human beings under oak trees. Modern druids worship trees and sacrifice human beings to those trees." Being the most willing to sacrifice humans, Dave Brower became the Archdruid.[3]

David Ross Brower was born in Berkeley, California, July 1, 1912. An avid amateur naturalist from his youth, Brower joined the Sierra Club as a young man and worked his way up the hierarchy to become its first executive director in 1953 (See the Sierra Club profile). After more than fifteen years of running afoul of the Club's volunteer leadership, he was thrown out of the Club in an acrimonious 1969 board meeting. Brower founded Friends of the Earth on the rebound (See the Friends of the Earth profile). After years of running afoul of his own Friends of the Earth board of directors, they gave him the heave-ho in 1985. Brower then founded this third group, which has not yet kicked him out.

If you have been skipping around in this book, make sure to read the profiles of the Sierra Club and Friends of the Earth before going any further with Earth Island Institute. Otherwise, this profile will make a good deal less sense.

Brower himself says, "The Sierra Club made the Nature Conservancy look reasonable. I founded Friends of the Earth to make the Sierra Club look reasonable. Then I founded Earth Island Institute to make Friends of the Earth look reasonable. Earth First! now makes us look reasonable. We're still waiting for someone else to come along and make Earth First! look reasonable."[4]

Brower himself has not changed his lifelong habit of never even trying to look reasonable: The Archdruid told a *Christian Science Monitor* reporter in 1991, "I'd like to declare open season on developers and shoot them all. Not kill them, just tranquilize them." This is the same man reputed to have once said, "Childbearing should be a punishable crime unless the parents hold a government license" (Brower had three sons and a daughter without a government license). He is also said to have offered a modest proposal to require internal passports for all Americans in order to travel within the United States.[5]

Earth Island Institute reflects Brower's latest thinking, that environmental groups "have to get together with peace and justice groups," and the movement "has to globalize." In its earliest years Earth Island worked primarily with a volunteer staff, concentrating on projects such as the first Conferences on the Fate of the Earth, publication of special editions of *Earth Island Journal*, making films about native peoples with a Western-civilization-bashing theme, and a trip to the former Soviet Union's Lake Baikal.

In 1986 Earth Island Institute opened a small office which provided services for The Brower Fund, *Earth Island Journal*, the Environmental Project on Central America, International Marine Mammal Project, the Dolphin Project, International Rivers Network, and Rainforest Action Network. Outside the office it supported such efforts as the Ladakh Project, Sacred Land Film Project, and Information for the Public Trust. As the name-styles indicate, all very left-wingish stuff.

EII has expanded its offices twice since 1987, now occupying a rear second floor space in a commercial office building on San Francisco's Broadway just below the Live Nude Girls porno palaces and just above the toney Embarcadero sushi bars. Two of Earth Island's projects have spun off into separate new organizations of note: Rainforest Action Network (see profile) and International Rivers Network. The office houses more than 20 projects such as the Sea Turtle Restoration Project and the Urban Habitat Program—which received $50,000 from the San Francisco Foundation in 1991—the latter which, oddly enough, acknowledges that people are part of the environment.[6]

Earth Island Institute is run by co-executive directors John A. Knox and David C. Phillips. They do not split up the projects between themselves, but operate in a unique joint-action collegial style. Eighty-year-old David Brower has little to do with the day-to-day operation of the Institute and mostly travels the college circuit as senior guru. But like Brower, both Knox and Phillips are dedicated Economy Trashers and their organization could fairly be placed in the Radical Eco-socialist Axis, although a few of their programs are interventionist in impact and Earth Island has been known to rub shoulders with the establishment and perform a few economic calculations now and then.

For example, their Environmental Justice project does give priority to the economic lives of racial and ethnic minorities. As described in *Race, Poverty & the Environment,* an EII publication emphasizing the need to develop environmentalist constituencies among people of color, the project uses the rhetoric of Bernsteinian "social democracy," i.e., redistribution of property, capital and political power to a collectivist state that leaves some of the private sector intact but under heavy regulation. Eco-socialist or not, this project, along with Earth Island's Urban Habitat Program, could end up giving a human conscience to eco-leaders more accustomed to communing with trees than people.

Trashing the Tuna Industry

Earth Island Institute's main claim to Economy Trasher shame is destroying the American tuna fishing industry in the Eastern Tropical Pacific.

EII did it through its Dolphin Project, which pressured tuna processors into the commercial "Dolphin Safe" program. Earth Island's project was an eco-fraud not too different from the phony Greenpeace seal-slaughter campaign. Their primary tool was what has become known as the LaBudde Videotape—a rigged visual jolt of fishermen who appear to be heartlessly killing hundreds of dolphins—surreptitiously taken by environmentalist Sam LaBudde who signed on as a mechanic and cook with the worst tuna boat he could find, a salvaged wreck with an inexperienced crew, then edited the footage as deceptively as the Greenpeace seal film and asserted it was typical of all tuna boats.[7]

Because of Earth Island's campaign, Congress passed a "Dolphin Safe" law in 1992 that has turned into a bureaucratic nightmare. The tangle of senseless regulation means Americans buy smaller, more expensive cans of tuna filled with lower quality, blander fish liberally stuffed with "tuna helper"—a gelatine hydrolized protein filler which expands the internal structure of the fish to fool you into thinking you have a full can—and it also includes the flavor enhancer monosodium glutamate (MSG) to which many people are allergic.

The irony of it is that the Big Three tuna industry firms, StarKist, Bumble Bee and Chicken of the Sea, got rid of quite a bit of U.S. and Latin American competition by going "Dolphin Safe" in the Eastern Tropical Pacific where the big yellowfin tuna swims in association with dolphins. They simply shifted their canning and purchasing operations to other oceans not covered by "Dolphin Safe" rules: the Western Pacific, Indian and Atlantic. There the canneries now pay rock-bottom labor rates and their dolphin mortality rate with foreign fleets is ten times higher than before. Thus the self-righteous "Dolphin Safe" movement contains a glaring commercial anti-competitive dimension, as we shall see in detail below.

The "Dolphin Safe" program of the Big Three tuna processors also forced the U.S. fleet, which invented canned tuna, to move at great expense to the Western Pacific where ships pay higher operating costs to catch lower quality fish—skipjack, which usually does not associate with dolphins and which sells for considerably less than the blacklisted yellowfin. With canneries buying nothing but the cheaper skipjack, tuna prices paid to fishermen sunk to their lowest levels in twenty years— but the retail price of tuna went up very quietly as the Big Three slightly reduced the size of the can. With its high wages and operating costs, the U.S. fleet will be the first to go broke while the Big Three laugh all the way to the bank.

And the Big Three appear to be systematically underfilling their cans. This means consumers are not getting the fish they are legally entitled to, which leaves an artificially induced surplus of tuna, which drives the fish price down and penalizes the fishermen. The American Tunaboat Association has filed a complaint with the U.S. Food and Drug Administration alleging that canners are disregarding "pressed weight" standards and underfilling cans. The FDA has also received many complaints from Congressmen passing on protests from their constituents about the quality of the "Dolphin Safe" tuna pack. The FDA is investigating.

Adding to the tragedy, millions of immature tuna including females and babies that should be building up the breeding stock are being needlessly killed by "Dolphin Safe" methods, which threatens the long-term survival of the world's tuna schools.[8] The Dolphin-Safe bureaucracy has thrown more than ten thousand people in tuna-related jobs out of work in the Americas.[9] The Dolphin-Safe bureaucracy is threatening to eradicate the lowest cost protein source for millions of people in the Third World.[10] Mexico and numerous other Latin American nations accuse the United States of using environmentalism as a front to prosecute a trade war against the Third World.[11]

How did Earth Island Institute achieve this economic and ecologic debacle? It's a fascinating story. And it all revolves around the videotape taken by Sam LaBudde.[12]

The *Atlantic* Article

Sam's story was eloquently told in a 1989 issue of the prestigious *Atlantic Monthly* by equally prestigious writer Kenneth Brower.[13] LaBudde has personally assured us it is correct in all details.[14]

Kenneth David Brower—author of many articles and books including *The Starship and the Canoe, Song for Satawal,* and *One Earth*—was born in San Francisco November 15, 1944. His father is David Ross Brower, founder of Earth Island Institute, which may explain why his *Atlantic* article reads like a press release for Earth Island Institute. *Atlantic* made no mention of that rather key relationship. Hmm....

Any *Atlantic Monthly* article written by an author Doing It For Daddy deserves close scrutiny. "The Destruction of Dolphins" by Kenneth Brower was a masterpiece. It had everything. It was thrilling. It was funny. It was heart-rending. It was stylish. It was pulse-pounding. It was lyrical. It was passionate. It filled you with rage against the U.S. tuna fleet. It was stainlessly credible.

You would have to do a great deal of detective work and interview everyone involved in the story to discover that Kenneth Brower's "The Destruction of Dolphins" was actually a calculated political deception.

Thanks to Teresa Platt, Hector Eribez, Arturo "Tury" Acevedo and Steve Medina of the non-profit Fishermen's Coalition, that detective work and those interviews got done.

When Kenneth Brower wrote his article, Sam LaBudde had already shown his rigged videotape to the Senate Committee on Commerce, Science, and Transportation on behalf of Earth Island Institute and claimed, "the events that I filmed are tragically representative...the things you will see on this film happen every day...I would like to say that I feel that what is shown on the film is representative of the U.S. Fleet."[15]

LaBudde was not under oath. Neither was Kenneth Brower when he wrote his *Atlantic* article.

But their deception worked. As Earth Island co-director David Phillips gloated after his campaign destroyed the American fleet, "We stuck it to the U.S. tuna industry."[16]

Brower began his *Atlantic* article logically enough with a page about the life of dolphins which introduces us to the lovable creatures, including a graphic account of dolphin sex practices. "Dolphin" and "porpoise" are common names for various kinds of small whales, we learn. Porpoises are generally chubbier in shape and smaller than dolphins, with a blunt rather than beaklike snout. Porpoises are not known to associate with tuna. There are seven species in the family of porpoises (Phocaenidae).

The family of dolphins (Delphinidae) contains 14 genera and 32 species of dolphins, three species of which regularly associate with yellowfin tuna. However, experts argue whether porpoises are part of the dolphin family or a distinct family. Almost everyone, including scientists, uses the terms "porpoise" and "dolphin" interchangeably. Just to confuse matters further, there is a *fish* known as a dolphin, also called the dorado or mahimahi.

Brower did not bother to explain that the U.S. tuna industry began about 1900, based on five major types: bluefin (a prized gamefish), skipjack, albacore, yellowfin and bigeye. But Brower did note that since at least the 1940s, a primary U.S. and Latin American tuna fishery in the Eastern Tropical Pacific—an eight million square mile region splayed from California to Chile to the Hawaiian Islands— involved searching out dolphin that travel in mysterious symbiosis above the meaty 35- to 150-pound yellowfin.

As Brower noted, no one knows why spotted, spinner and common dolphins swim above big schools of choice yellowfin tuna, but this unlikely association is common throughout the Eastern Tropical Pacific. Tuna fishermen learned by experience that dolphin accompanied just the perfect fish that should be harvested to keep the oceans healthy: clean catches of primarily large fish that had assuredly spawned many times, with minimal waste or "bycatch" of other fish species. If you find any of these three kinds of dolphin, you most often—but not always—find mature yellowfin tuna under them.

The original tuna fishery caught yellowfin swimming beneath dolphin by "chumming"—throwing bucketfuls of bait fish called "chum" into the water, which caused the tuna to rise to the surface in a feeding frenzy. The dolphin usually spread out away from the thrashing tuna. The crew then cast lines into the mass of fish, snagged them with hooks, and yanked them out of the water over their heads onto the boat deck. It was not very efficient, and it tended to deplete the fish used as chum. Occasionally a dolphin would get snagged as well.

As foreign competition and demand increased in the early 1960s, purse seine nets came into use to catch the fish more efficiently. Tunaboats would scout for dolphin, send out small speedboats to herd the dolphin into one place, then drop the end of the net in the water and slowly swing the big tunaboat around to encircle the dolphin and the rich harvest of tuna beneath them. The net mesh then hung from the floats straight down into the water like a circular fence—purse seines are called "fence nets" in Mexico—surrounding the catch. The net would finally be gathered shut at the bottom, like an old-fashioned purse, and the catch hauled (or "brailed") aboard while the dolphin escaped.

When purse seine nets were first used, dolphins accidentally got caught under side billows of the net mesh, and, being air-breathing sea mammals, drowned before anyone could do anything about it. This incidental dolphin kill was a completely unwanted side-effect of tuna fishing, not some perverse killer-macho badge of honor, as Kenneth Brower and Sam LaBudde made it out in the *Atlantic* article.

The real situation is quite the opposite. Fishermen need the dolphin to escape quickly so they can haul their fish catch out of the hot tropical waters and into refrigerated wells as soon as possible to keep product quality high. Most importantly, fishermen *need* the dolphin to escape unharmed so they can lead the boats to more schools of tuna. You don't intentionally hurt your scouts.

Brower also did not mention that fisheries experts immediately began working on new kinds of purse seine nets and concerned captains devised new setting techniques to assure dolphin escape. The tuna industry developed the fine-mesh "Medina panel"—named after its inventor Harold Medina—which was soon used on all boats to prevent dolphin noses and fins from snagging in the normal wide mesh of the tuna net and help them escape. Tuna captains devised an engine-reversal procedure called "backdown," which warps the net with enough force to sink a controlled portion, creating a channel for the dolphins to escape while keeping the tuna in the net.

As the new technology was being developed it is likely that more than a hundred thousand dolphins were killed annually by the U.S. fleet. Estimates of dolphin mortality from 1960 to 1972 were based on small samples and resulted in vastly overblown estimates. After 1972, figures were based on better observations as more observers kept tabs and the estimates steadily improved. Dolphin mortality figures collected by 1979, when the mortality count came in at 21,426, are regarded as reliable by virtually every marine scientist.[17]

Atlantic writer Kenneth Brower, of course, tried for effect to stretch the numbers into the millions and the fishermens' malice to infinity.

Dolphin mortality rates fell as fishermen became more skillful and as they devised more techniques to release the mammals from the nets. U. S. fisherman spread the new ways to other nations by word of mouth at first. The Inter-American Tropical Tuna Commission (IATTC) educated fishermen more formally. It was formed in 1949 by treaty between Costa Rica and the United States as a scientific conservation body to monitor the health of the fish stocks in the Eastern Tropical Pacific. It conducted gear and equipment research projects and fishermen's educational programs.

Not satisfied with these advances in dolphin safety, in the early 1970s environmentalists characterized tuna fishermen as uncaring barbarians and began to lobby Congress to pass the Marine Mammal Protection Act of 1972, which stated: "It shall be the immediate goal that the incidental kill or incidental serious injury of marine mammals permitted in the course of commercial fishing operations be reduced to insignificant levels approaching a zero mortality and serious injury rate."[18]

The law required that the goal be reached in the Eastern Tropical Pacific by establishing a schedule for decreasing the allowable dolphin kill each year, funding a research program for the development of dolphin-saving equipment and techniques, requiring a license to come into contact with a dolphin, and an observer program to assure the law was working. The Inter-American Tropical Tuna Commission was given the task of monitoring this new law, expanding to include dolphin conservation programs.

It is worth noting that in 1981 Congress amended the Act to include "the goal of zero mortality shall be satisfied in the case of incidental taking of marine mammals in the course of purse-seine fishing for yellowfin tuna by a continuation of the applications of the best marine mammal safety techniques and equipment that are economically and technologically practicable." Clearly, Congress never intended to put fishermen out of business by this law.[19]

Keep in mind that this law applied *only* to the Eastern Tropical Pacific.

The demand to approach zero mortality was typical of the "Zero Risk" mentality emerging in the entire environmental movement at the time, and was based upon Environmentalism's Articles of Faith rather than biology. It's their same old standard for industrial civilization: "If you can't do it perfectly, you mustn't do it at all."

By 1984, the percentage of captured dolphins released alive had gone up to 99.23, and in 1992 stood at 99.8 percent—a tribute to the success of the law and the efforts of the fishermen.[20]

Although tuna populations can sustain harvests of between 20 percent and 40 percent of the reproductive population each year, the maximum safe depletion rate of dolphins is probably much less than ten percent. The International Whaling Commission believes that the most conservative estimate of the annual reproduction rate of dolphins is two percent. Thus any level of dolphin mortality below that would have absolutely no effect on the survival of the species. Dolphin populations are not being depleted.[21]

But, as we have already seen in many of the profiles above, environmental organizations need never-ending perceptions of crisis in order to fundraise and continue their appearance of legitimacy, and these dolphin safety facts were buried in a carefully orchestrated campaign of lies.

Earth Island Institute claimed that tuna fishing was decimating dolphin populations, that there were only a million or so individuals left. In fact, dolphin are neither endangered nor threatened. There are nearly ten million in the Eastern Tropical Pacific alone. In order to change public perception to one of crisis, numerous environmental groups have lobbied for years to have dolphin listed as "threatened" under the Endangered Species Act using the stratagem of dividing up species into subspecies, locales—even single herds—so that a perception of crisis can be legitimated.

Scientists at the National Marine Fisheries Service and Scripps Institution of Oceanography count the total dolphin population of the Eastern Tropical Pacific at some 9.5 million individuals.[22] In other words, speaking in strictly biological conservation terms and apart from humane considerations, an incidental kill of less than two percent—the reproduction rate—or under 190,000 animals each year, would not affect the populations. In humane terms, fishermen strive to keep dolphin mortality to the lowest numbers possible, preferably zero. Remember too that dolphins are their scouts, and the commercial incentive to keep them alive and healthy is powerful.

In the past decade, only one year showed an increase in dolphin mortality to more than 100,000 animals, the result of an influx of foreign vessels which were quickly equipped with the proper gear and their crews trained in the backdown procedure.[23]

During 1992, dolphin mortality in the Eastern Tropical Pacific was well below 1 percent. The actual number was 0.28 percent, which is sustainable by anyone's definition, including Greenpeace's.

Kenneth Brower also failed to mention that before Earth Island's Dolphin Project, the U.S. tuna fleet was faced with two huge economic setbacks during the 1970s, one political, the other regulatory: First, the countries of the Latin American coast extended their sovereign limits to 200 miles, from which U.S. fishermen were subsequently excluded. Second was a massive relocation of U.S. canneries to places such as Puerto Rico and American Samoa, where labor rates and regulatory costs are lower—another example of capital flight with a component resulting directly from environmental regulatory overkill. In 1979, five huge tuna canneries worked in California. Today only one survives, Pan Pacific Fisheries on Terminal Island near Long Beach.

These two upheavals shrunk the U.S. tuna fleet in the Eastern Tropical Pacific from 101 vessels in 1979 to 65 in 1987—before Sam LaBudde and Earth Island Institute destroyed it completely. The U.S. tuna fleet was owned mostly by families who've been in this business for generations. These are Americans largely of Italian and Portuguese descent who have a tradition of hanging on by their fingernails when times get bad, believing with all their hearts that things will get better. With environmentalists like Kenneth Brower, Sam LaBudde and Earth Island Institute around, things will never get better.

The Eco-Spy

After telling us a little about dolphins, Kenneth Brower's *Atlantic* article brings into focus "The Undercover Man," Sam LaBudde. Mr. LaBudde appears first as a boyish and impulsive nature lover who just happened to fall into the dolphin videotape project and subsequently to make a career of hawking it as an omen of apocalypse.

Brower made quite a point of it: "Many of LaBudde's projects have begun in impulse. Impulsiveness lies alongside wanderlust in a spot close to his heart."

Brower depicts LaBudde as "a spy" who took his videotapes surreptitiously at the risk of his life. This disarming description nips in the bud any suspicion that LaBudde's adventures might have been deliberately and systematically designed to destroy the U.S. tuna fleet.

It's not quite that simple.

Samuel Freeman LaBudde, we learn, was born in Madison, Wisconsin on July 3, 1956 to a family of natural scientists, his father Norwegian, his mother Cherokee. His last name, incidentally, is pronounced as if it were "LaBuddy." Kenneth Brower wrote in *Atlantic* of Sam LaBudde, "If his life had any direction, he thinks, it was movement away from humanity. He liked nature better than man."[24] A key signature of the true environmentalist.

The *Atlantic* article, incidentally, is by no means the only eco-exploitation of Sam's videotapes. They have become virtual fixtures on television newscasts as file footage illustrating how nasty tuna fisherman are. LaBudde also won the Goldman Prize, which comes with $60,000 cash, for environmental action in 1991 for his video efforts.[25] More recently, *National Geographic* ran a story titled "Dolphins in Crisis" just before a key Congressional vote that destroyed the last remnants of the U.S. tuna fleet—a story with a sidebar reading: "Armed with a video camera, Samuel LaBudde got a job as a cook on a Panamanian tuna boat and came home with images of wholesale dolphin slaughter.... LaBudde's tapes for Earth Island Institute galvanized the drive for "dolphin safe" tuna. Now most nations ban the import of tuna caught by the encirclement of dolphins."[26] On the heels of the *National Geographic* story, ABC News *Prime Time* presented LaBudde's videotapes to a wide national television audience, keeping the phony five-year-old images alive.

What really happened?

Kenneth Brower's *Atlantic* article goes into substantial detail about how Sam LaBudde came to take those gruesome videotapes. Brower gives us a thorough preliminary biography, in fact. LaBudde, we are told, grew up in southern Indiana, completed high school, took a couple of semesters of college and then dropped out to bum around the West Coast for a while, spending a year in San Francisco. LaBudde worked for four years as a commercial tree planter in the Cascades— where, he said, "the country was all just bombed and gutted."[27]

LaBudde doesn't mention it, but these industrial forests were so "gutted" that their owners were paying him high wages to regenerate every freshly logged site. Forest firms support a thriving economy of tree-planting contractors. Many of them are little counterculture-communes that moved in the 1970s from San Francisco's Haight-Ashbury to form tree planting cooperatives in Oregon. They tend to have quaint names such as The Hoedads—after the hoedag, a pick-like tree-planting tool. From about 1977, these little tree-planting outfits were a commonplace on the Oregon scene, living apart from society in tent communities, big on anti-capitalist revolutionary-chic but not known for keeping regular work hours, although once they showed up in the brush they did a respectable job of planting trees and achieved good seedling-survival rates. Former co-op members we interviewed think they recall seeing LaBudde working now and then, but nobody is sure.

In 1981 Sam LaBudde moved to Alaska for four years, where, in Brower's words, he "worked as a machinist's apprentice, a marine engineer, a commercial fisherman, and a seismic crewman."

Kenneth Brower doesn't tell us, but what that really means is that LaBudde worked for a short time at Otto Kilcher's Machine Shop in Homer, Alaska learning to do light repair work such as replacing bent propellers, then drifted down the street to work at Jim Niemehla's Fish Dock Services for six months. The State of Alaska has no record that LaBudde ever held a marine engineer's license at all. Jim Niemehla says LaBudde was a hard worker and helped with minor repairs such as spot welding, but never tested his skills with anything serious like an engine teardown.[28]

And that commercial fisherman experience? It was necessary for the credibility of the later story to make Sam look like a seasoned old salt, so Kenneth Brower rhapsodized that "Much of LaBudde's career has been spent at sea."

Well, not really. The "four years as a commercial fisherman in Alaska" LaBudde later bragged about actually shrinks down to exactly two trips as a deck hand on Jim Niemehla's boats *Fanta Sea* and *Voyager* out of Homer into the Gulf of Alaska during mild Spring weather—three months on a crab boat, one month on a halibut boat. A total of four months.

"Much of LaBudde's career has been spent at sea."

Hmm....

Yoo-hoo! Where are you, *Atlantic* fact checkers? Brower's story is getting the bow mixed with the rudder in quite a few places.

All this seafaring adventure must have given Sam an itch for a wee bout of shore leave, since he returned to Indiana in 1984 and two years later, at age 30, completed a Bachelor of Arts degree in biology at Indiana University at Bloomington on December 31, 1986, with a quite respectable grade point average of 3.3.[29]

After being graduated, LaBudde wintered in the Florida Keys, in and around Tavernier on Plantation Key, waiting tables at nearby watering holes from January to March of 1987. But, Brower wrote, "The heat and the boredom of the Keys triggered an outburst of resumes, and one of these landed him a job as a National Marine Fisheries Service observer aboard a Japanese trawler in the Bering Sea." Brower did not mention what time of year LaBudde spent in the Keys; sure, it doesn't freeze often, but the *heat* in the dead of winter?

Why did Brower want to misdirect our attention by making it sound like *heat* drove LaBudde from Florida? Could it be because the Florida Keys have long been a gathering ground for dolphin activists such as Rick Trout, a former dolphin trainer for the U.S. Navy who became an animal rights advocate based on Lowe Street, Tavernier, Florida?[30] Sea Shepherd and Greenpeace activists also frequented the Florida Keys before, during and after the time LaBudde was there.

In fact, the book *Eco-Warriors* openly mentions that a member of Paul Watson's Sea Shepherd Conservation Society "tells a story of asking for contributions in a Key West bar while the group was preparing for its 1989 voyage to the Pacific. Four college students began querying her, and when she told them that she was sailing on a ship that was going to attempt to stop the slaughter of dolphins by tuna fleets, they took her tin can and panhandled for her."[31]

Was Sam LaBudde in Florida getting a little indoctrination that wasn't so impulsive?

But what's really interesting is that Brower repeats proudly in numerous later paragraphs that LaBudde had been an employee of the National Marine Fisheries Service.

Wrong.

Yoo-hoo! *Atlantic Monthly* fact checkers? This is your wake-up call. LaBudde was never a National Marine Fisheries Service employee.

And he didn't act on impulse in this "outburst of resumes." He was carefully calculating and sent his resume to Frank Orth Company & Associates in Bellevue, Washington, a nationally-known fisheries consultant whose exclusive business is providing observers for fishing vessels.[32]

Orth hired LaBudde and placed him in a short three-month NMFS observer assignment on a Japanese factory trawler, April through June of 1987. Life as an observer on a giant Japanese factory trawler is a relatively comfortable entry-level job. The main qualification is an undergraduate degree in a biological science. This brief stint nearly doubled LaBudde's time at sea.

Sam LaBudde was not an employee of the National Marine Fisheries Service, but of Frank Orth Company contract employers.[33]

It sounds more impressive to say you worked four years doing dashing fishery things in Alaska and that you were a National Marine Fisheries Service observer than to say you worked four months on a couple of short fishing trips and were a temporary contract employee of Frank Orth Company & Associates—but what a skillful tissue of perfect little details Brower is weaving to make LaBudde's story credible.[34]

After being released from the Frank Orth Japanese factory trawler job—and they never hired LaBudde again, although he applied for another observer job with them in January 1988[35]—he zigzagged from Seattle "in his battered Volkswagen Rabbit," climbing mountains and other neat stuff on the way to San Francisco with his last $800, where he looked for work in the environmental establishment. There he visited Earth Island Institute's offices and, while waiting to talk to someone, picked up an issue of *Earth Island Journal*. Here is Kenneth Brower's report of the encounter:

> "It was the dolphin issue, with the purple cover," LaBudde says. "I was just amazed. I was a fisherman, a biologist. I thought I was informed about environmental things. I knew about the depletion of the ozone layer before most people did, and about the destruction of the rain forests. But I had thought whales and dolphins were sacrosanct species, above abuse. Nobody had told me they were being captured in nets, with speedboats and explosives and helicopters."
>
> Why, LaBudde asked, weren't they telling anyone? They were trying, David Phillips and Todd Steiner, of Earth Island, protested. (They had, after all, produced the very article that this stranger was holding in his hand.) Earth Island had the facts on the slaughter, Phillips and Steiner said. They had a lot of dry documentation. What they needed was film. Well, LaBudde wondered,

couldn't someone get on a tuna boat? He himself was a former fisherman and NMFS observer; he could probably get aboard.

Phillips and Steiner sent LaBudde to see Stanley M. Minasian, executive director of the

> **Marine Mammal Fund** (1970) Originally incorporated as Save the Dolphins, Inc., name changed in 1979 to Marine Mammal Fund.[36]
> Annual budget: $131,539 (1989).[37]
> Members: 8,000
> Fort Mason Center, Historical Building E-205
> San Francisco, California 94123
> Phone 415-775-4636

The Marine Mammal Fund occupies a couple of cluttered offices in historic Fort Mason on San Francisco's North Beach, next to the tourist traps of Fisherman's Wharf. Its leader, Stan Minasian, has a long history of malice toward the tuna fishing industry.

While Minasian was a student at the University of California at Berkeley in the 1960s, he paid a visit to August Felando, then-executive director of the American Tunaboat Association in San Diego. Felando recalls, "Mr. Minasian told us we shouldn't be fishing for tuna in association with dolphins. He told us in no uncertain terms that he was going to stop it."[38]

Minasian started Save the Dolphins, Inc. out of a San Francisco apartment in 1970, obtaining his non-profit tax exempt status from the IRS in 1973. His group derived most of its income selling dolphin trinkets, T-shirts and the like. Of the Marine Mammal Fund's 1989 income, $112,069 came from sale of such goods.

The Tunaboat Association heard from Stan Minasian again in 1971. He filed a lawsuit trying to get some film from the National Marine Fisheries Service. It had been taken by a naval scientist aboard a commercial tuna boat as part of scientific experiments to develop techniques to reduce dolphin mortality. The tunaboat captains were authorized to deliberately perform "disaster sets" on dolphins so the scientist could film their behavior under stress, studying them from underwater and from the vessel. The resulting footage was assembled by the National Marine Fisheries Service into a 20-minute instructional presentation. It showed the worst of the worst—so captains could avoid it.

Stan Minasian found out about the film and filed suit to get it. He wanted to use it to promote his cause. The Tunaboat Association intervened in the lawsuit, realizing that this young man was ready to make good on his threat to put them out of business. The judge ruled that Minasian could have the film—minus the parts revealing trade secrets, *and* providing that every frame contained a disclaimer stating that the scene was taken under experimental conditions and not typical of commercial practice.

Tunaboat Association leader Felando said, "Minasian arranged to use the film and even had a celebrity narrate it, Dick Cavett, as I recall. It didn't have much impact with the disclaimer in every frame. But we saw twenty years ago that Minasian clearly recognized the value of film."[39]

Minasian spent years spoiling for some film *without* disclaimers. When Sam LaBudde walked through the Marine Mammal Fund doorway and told him what he had told Phillips and Steiner, Minasian saw his Francis Ford Coppola and envisioned his *Dolphin Apocalypse Now!* winning the Congressional Academy Awards.

Brower wrote that William Perrin, the noted biologist who had first brought the tuna-dolphin problem to world attention back in the 1960s, conferred with LaBudde. "He warned me about ending up in concrete galoshes."

Writer K. Patrick Conner further embroidered this story in a 1990 article which appeared in *This World* magazine: "Perrin, in San Diego, worried about what might happen to LaBudde if he were caught. 'Perrin warned me,' said LaBudde, 'that I might end up in concrete galoshes.'"

Can you hear the ominous music on the sound track?

If not, it's because Perrin never said that. What really happened? LaBudde made a phone call to Dr. Perrin—Perrin did not "confer with LaBudde"—and asked about the dolphin program, basically researching. LaBudde said he was going to try to get on a tuna boat, but did not explain that he was planning to film anything, and asked for general advice. Perrin was not worried that Sam might get caught because Sam never told him he was planning anything to get caught with. Perrin gave him the standard "young pup" speech to fresh college graduates, warning Sam that it was hard, hard work and that fishermen were a rough bunch—rough in the sense of unrefined, not in the sense of violent. Perrin said that he based his remark to LaBudde on his own experience in the early days of observers when the fishermen would not even talk to him, which is very stressful when you have to share a boat with them for extended periods. Perrin neither said nor implied anything about ending up in concrete galoshes.[40]

Author Kenneth Brower never contacted Dr. Perrin to verify the statement.

Atlantic fact checkers never contacted Dr. Perrin to verify the statement.

Now Kenneth Brower gets to the meat of his article: How LaBudde got on a tuna boat and took the incriminating footage. Brower tells us that neither Earth Island Institute nor the Marine Mammal Fund had the money to help fund the exploit of getting on a fishing vessel.

"But if he succeeded," wrote Brower, "then they might be able to get a video camera to him, but that was the most they could do for him."

Strange that Brower should say that, because Earth Island's financial reports for 1988 and 1989 show they paid $12,000 directly to Sam LaBudde in independent contractor wages plus $3,000 travel reimbursement. Now, $15,000 may not be much to Kenneth Brower, but that's a respectable personal payoff for most of us.

Earth Island's financial reports also show they spent $327,475 in 1988 on the Dolphin Campaign: "education of the public on the incidental killing of the dolphin by the tuna industry in the eastern tropical pacific," and $195,558 in 1989 on the International Marine Mammal Project for the same purpose.[41]

That's a total of $538,033 Earth Island Institute spent on dolphin stuff in just a little more than a year.

How much of the Marine Mammal Fund's $114,333 total payouts in 1989 went into Sam LaBudde's pocket we could not discover. Their financial reports are not as revealing as Earth Island Institute's.[42]

Between the two organizations, it's clear they could do better than a lousy video camera. But Kenneth Brower knows it excites sympathy to poormouth about Daddy's organization.

Next scene in Brower's Bogus Bulletin: Undaunted by such impending poverty, LaBudde walks determinedly out the door and into history. We follow him across the Mexican border in his battered old Volkswagen to Ensenada, where he sleeps on the beach flats south of town. He sneaks onto the docks looking for work every day for three weeks. He finally lands a job on the *Maria Luisa*, a boat of Panamanian registry.

Wait a minute. There's a loose thread in this story: Does LaBudde just leave his beloved battered old Volkswagen in Ensenada and sail off into the sunset? Well, no. It seems that "a friend had driven his car back to the States." Friend? What friend? Just an Earth Island staffer assigned to get LaBudde to Ensenada and drive his VW back to San Francisco?

Here's Brower's version of how LaBudde got the tunaboat job:

> The tuna captains were curious: why would a former Alaskan fisherman like him, a man who could make $4,000 a month in Alaska, want to work on an Ensenada boat for 30,000 pesos a week—about $15. Because he was tired of American life, LaBudde would answer. He was burned out on the United States and wanted to go to the Andes. On a tuna boat he could work his way closer to those mountains while learning Spanish and practicing a trade he knew. It was not a bad story—there was more than a little truth in all its parts—and LaBudde's resume was fairly impressive. He had been a commercial fisherman and a machinist. As a mechanic, he pointed out, he had the advantage of literacy in English, the language of the manuals for the American outboard motors that powered the seiner speedboats.

Well, that's a nice fish story, but *Maria Luisa* crewman Adolfo Ochoa Nunez says it went a little differently. Ochoa had seen LaBudde hanging around Ensenada, on the dock and in local *taquerias* with generic names like Lupe's and Mario's, living on fish tacos and soup for a couple of bucks a day. Well-outfitted tuna boats occupied almost every slip, with excellent nets equipped for dolphin release neatly racked out on the docks, properly equipped with Medina panels. Nobody recalls LaBudde even talking to the captains of those vessels.

The *Maria Luisa*, on the other hand, was an old tub with a French-made net totally illegal for Eastern Tropical Pacific tuna fishing with dolphin. The vessel had been built in France as the *Biscaya*, had fished African waters for years, changed flags to Mexico in 1980 as the *Olmeca I*, and had laid idle at anchor off Ensenada since April 1981, its machinery growing old and rusty for six years.

Hector Eribez of South Bay Diesel in San Diego, whose business has taken him to service boats in Ensenada for years, says, "Everyone remembers the *Olmeca I*. It was anchored offshore for years, not going fishing. Then sometime in January 1987 strangers from Spain came and started taking pictures of it. Everybody figured it must have been sold, because work started being done on it."[43]

Indeed it had been sold. Ignacio Azkue Larranaga, a Basque poultry businessman from the port town of Bermeo, in Vizcaya Province, Spain, bought it for the bargain price of $60,000 and fitted it out because family business associates had told him there was money to be made in tuna fishing and were ready to invest in the venture. His relatives owned interests in tuna canneries in Spain and thought they could all get rich in the tuna fishing business.

Azkue immigrated to Venezuela where he worked with some small baitboats, close-to-shore operations, while hungering for the bigtime. An agent in Mexico offered him the *Olmeca I*, and despite warnings from experienced fishermen that the boat was too old and would bankrupt him, he dreamed of riches with a big tuna vessel and made the deal.

Azkue, known to friends and employees by the nickname Ñaki, intended to register the boat in Venezuela and fish the Caribbean. While the boat was being refitted in Ensenada, Azkue took the interim step of reflagging the boat in Panama in mid-February, 1987, and named the vessel *Maria Luisa I*, after his beautiful young wife. Azkue took a small apartment in Panama City from which to manage the boat's business while remaining based in Venezuela.[44]

Captain Gilberto Novelo in Ensenada acted as port engineer for the refitting of the *Maria Luisa*. The average investment required for an efficient tuna boat is about $2 million. A new net alone can cost upwards of $300,000, and the *Maria Luisa's* refitting did not amount to half what a new net would cost.

Azkue kept the old net that had come with the *Maria Luisa*, even though it had been designed for Atlantic, mostly African fisheries, had a wide mesh that would snag dolphin fins and snouts and trap them, was bright red, which agitates dolphins, and had no dolphin release devices at all. Everybody on the *Maria Luisa* called it "The African Net" because it didn't belong in the Americas. A boat of U.S. or Mexican registry fishing on dolphin with such a net would be subject to a horrendous fine. But the *Maria Luisa* was registered in Panama.

Not exactly your typical tuna boat.

With a bucket this sorry, getting a crew was a real problem for the new owner. Nobody with any experience would work on such a junker. The only captain that Azkue could find was a Peruvian named Pedro del Solar Novoa, who had never served as captain before, but had a good reputation as deck boss in the Caribbean, and was glad to get the opportunity.[45]

The only navigator Azkue could find was Oscar de Jesus Iriarte Navarro, a Mexican born in Topolobampo who had completed four years of navigator training school in Mazatlan—he had worked three smaller vessels but had never navigated a big tuna boat like the *Maria Luisa*. Iriarte was barely 23 years old.[46]

The First Mate was Jose Ramon Esnal Sarriegui, one of Azkue's brothers-in-law. The chief engineer was a Venezuelan, Luis Arrambari, a co-owner with Azkue who agreed to work for shares of the company. The assistant engineer was Juan Carlos Esnal Sarriegui, Azkue's other brother-in-law.

The deck crew and speedboat drivers were picked up from the docks at Ensenada, which usually had good men looking for work. Captain del Solar himself hired a Peruvian named Wider A. Otario Delgado, and Mexicans Ricardo Gutierrez Mendez, Estaban Edmundo Valdez, Alejandro Camacho Ortiz, and Miguel A. Jurado Solis. No cook could be found at all. Azkue hired a homeless Spaniard named Juan Francisco Renduelas Costales as dishwasher, and the unlucky fellow was reluctantly pressed into service as chief of the galley.

So here was a newcomer using his relatives and a co-investor as first mate and engineers, a deck crew from eight different nations, men who had never worked together, a cook who was a dishwasher, a 23-year-old navigator and a commander who had never served as captain before in his life.

Not exactly your typical tuna boat crew.

But it was exactly the kind of boat LaBudde was looking for—a dolphin disaster waiting to happen. Sam saw the *Maria Luisa* and went straight to it. Ochoa says he was amused over that bit about Sam reading English—no mechanic worth half a centavo has to look at a manual while working on an engine. "Sam was useless with the speedboat engines," said Ochoa. "When we had to take an engine apart once, Sam just watched helplessly. He didn't know anything about engines."

But Brower continues to weave his tissue of details:

> The *Maria Luisa's* captain finally gave LaBudde an unequivocal no, in spite of [his impressive resume]. (The man had good instincts, perhaps.) The boat's owner, a Basque lawyer from Panama, was visiting at the time, and LaBudde went over the captain's head to this man. On the one hand, the move was a good one, for the owner hired him immediately. On the other hand, the captain never forgave him and for the next six weeks at sea hardly spoke to him.

This setup is designed to add a little false tension to the story. But in fact, Pedro del Solar, the captain in question, got along perfectly well with LaBudde until they had been out to sea for a while and Sam began to make a habit of stripping naked to sunbathe on the nets. Navigator Oscar Iriarte said, "The whole crew was offended. Maybe in the U.S. that's okay, but in Latin America people look upon male nudity with suspicion."[47]

But in the beginning, del Solar was tolerant of the Anglo coming out on the dock every day, offering to work for food, falling all over himself trying to be helpful. Del Solar fed him, but didn't think he'd make much of a crewman. However, there wasn't any unequivocal no, and there wasn't any going over the captain's head. Azkue said he paid no attention at all to the bumbling LaBudde and left the crew hiring to del Solar. The captain finally gave in and hired Sam as a speedboat driver and mechanic while they were talking with Azkue on the dock together ten days before the boat sailed.

Owner Ignacio Azkue (who *is* Basque, but *not* a lawyer—Yoo-hoo! Does *Atlantic* use Mickey Mouse for a fact checker? No, Mickey wouldn't be so sloppy)—had his brother-in-law and co-owner, Jose Ramon Esnal, walk LaBudde to a six-man room on the boat so he wouldn't have to sleep on the beach any more. Crewman Rigoberto Chaverra Pino, one of several who shared the room with LaBudde, says del Solar treated the strange gringo like any other crewman.

There is a peculiar quirk in Kenneth Brower's writing for this *Atlantic Monthly* story that is not found in his other work: He makes absolutely no mention of the *names* of anybody associated with the *Maria Luisa I*. It is impossible to verify anything about LaBudde's story with eyewitness accounts—short of the full scale investigative reporting project we had to mount with Teresa Platt's Fishermen's Coalition. The only reason you're seeing these names here is that our network located and talked to them. Kenneth Brower, conversely, gives the captain's *nickname* and his successor's *first name* in three paragraphs each. *No other names.* Not of anybody with the *Maria Luisa I*, not the owner, not the captain, not the navigator, not any of the crew. And the editors at *Atlantic* let Brower get away with it.

Hmm....

But readers never notice the absence of names in the hypnotic flow of Brower's crafty prose. He next treats us to a dramatic account of how LaBudde got his videocamera. It is a monument of action writing:

> Twenty-four hours before the boat's departure LaBudde caught a bus to the border, rode the trolley into San Diego, and called Stan Minasian in San Francisco. "Stan, listen, I think I can swing a video camera," he said. "It's got to be small, and it's got to be here in San Diego early tomorrow." Minasian replied that he already had a camera picked out, an eight-millimeter Sony Camcorder. He would buy it the next morning and airfreight it down. LaBudde got a room at the Y and took a cab the next morning to the airport. The camera was supposed to arrive at noon, but it missed the first flight. The second flight was supposed to get in at 2:00, but that flight was delayed.
>
> "I was bouncing off the walls," LaBudde remembers. "It was getting late, and I still had a hundred miles to go back to Ensenada. I called Stan and asked him to wire some money. I was going to have to take taxis all the way back to Mexico."
>
> The plane finally arrived at 3:45 and then sat for a time on the field. At the airfreight desk a friendly man from Trinidad and Tobago had just come on shift, and LaBudde explained his problem in some detail. Perhaps the West Indian had always liked the dolphins around Trinidad and Tobago. Perhaps he just liked spy stories. He waved LaBudde aboard his pickup, and they intercepted the baggage cart on the tarmac, just as it was about to disappear into the catacombs of the terminal. The man lifted off LaBudde's package and drove him out front, where LaBudde caught the first of his cabs

to Ensenada. He arrived at the dock eighteen minutes before the *Maria Luisa* was to sail. The port authority was completing its final review.

Wow! What a rush! What a piece of writing! What a crock!

According to LaBudde's messmates, *he had a video camera when he first arrived before he was hired.* Doesn't it seem a little fishy that LaBudde waited for *ten days* after he'd been hired and berthed on the *Maria Luisa* to ask Minasian for a camera? But, of course, *Brower didn't tell us* how long it had been. Brower never checked the *Maria Luisa's* crew list to see when LaBudde signed on. Hell, Brower never checked *anything*—he was just Doing It For Daddy.

Adolfo Ochoa, one of LaBudde's roommates, said, "Sam was a strange one. He said he had little money, but he came aboard in late September with an expensive video camera. A couple of days before we were to leave Ensenada, it was stolen. Sam was very upset. He kept saying over and over, 'I've got to get another camera.' He kept calling San Francisco to get another camera—told us he was calling his father. He left and came back with another expensive video camera before the boat sailed. It was bigger than the first one."[48]

Benito Acosta, a Paraguayan bunked in the same room, said, "Sam's father must be rich."

Well, the half-million Earth Island spent on its Dolphin Project in 1988 and '89 is a good start on rich.

According to the port register, the *Maria Luisa* received its Ensenada clearances on Friday, October 9, 1987, and set out for the fishing grounds the next day, Captain Pedro del Solar commanding, Navigator Oscar Iriarte at the helm.

"The African Net," a purse seine with 4 1/4" red mesh, had been reworked to put in a temporary "dolphin netting," close-mesh panels to stop dolphins from getting caught in the net, one strip deep on each side of the net. The approved Medina panel is two strips deep, but the *Maria Luisa's* panel was only one strip deep. The corkline was incorrectly strung with French chain which can snag dolphin beaks. Dolphin safety panel markers and closed hand holds were missing. The African Net was completely unlike any other being used to fish for tuna on dolphins. And it was totally illegal by U.S. standards.

Not exactly your typical tuna boat net.

The *Maria Luisa's* ship's log shows no IATTC observer on board. Oscar Iriarte told us the navigation equipment was so shot there were several times he had to navigate by the stars.

And the vessel was originally bound for the Caribbean, not the Eastern Tropical Pacific. The Venezuelan government announced that tuna delivered to its territory would be paid for with 60 percent U.S. dollars and 40 percent local currency based on the official dollar-bolivar exchange rate. To obtain hard currency, vessel owners would have to buy dollars on the open market at double the official government rate. That's why Azkue ordered the dolphin panels installed on The African Net and changed the Maria Luisa's destination to the Eastern Tropical Pacific—so he could fish for tuna and sell his catch in a nation that did not burden fishermen with such onerous monetary restrictions. If the Venezuelan government had not imposed this policy, Sam LaBudde would never have been able to shoot his phony footage.

Not exactly your typical tuna boat voyage.

Brower tells us how LaBudde got his first videotape:

> In the job he had signed on for, LaBudde never did do well, and he did not last long in it. "I was a speedboat driver. I was supposed to go out and help round up dolphins with bombs. In the speedboats you have headsets on, and the captain can talk to all the drivers. But my Spanish wasn't good enough. I couldn't understand the captain, especially when he got mad. His name is Perico [Pedro del Solar], which means a little bird, a canary. He'd get mad and start screaming, and I wouldn't understand a word that was coming out of his mouth."
>
> That Perico's squawks confused LaBudde was just as well, for in a speedboat he had no way to accomplish his secret mission. He was transferred to deck duty, which served his purposes better. "We went out for a month, and made only one set on dolphins. The set was an absolute disaster. I wasn't going to film the first dolphin set. I hadn't been filming much with the camera—I wanted to sit on it and try to keep it cool. I couldn't very well bring the camera out the first time we made a set on dolphins. Except that I did. It turned into a disaster set so fast. I got out the camera, and stood there next to the first mate [Jose Ramon Esnal], who was a Basque, the brother-in-law of the owner. He'd turn around and look at me, and I'd drop the camera down and act real casual. I'd give him a look like, Isn't this amazing? Then I'd put the camera back up."

Brower then writes a Point-Of-View (POV) scene as if he were the video camera, *all in italics* so we'll know it's stylish writing:

> *Scene shift: Speedboats are inscribing white semicircles on a calm ocean, herding dolphins. The camera is steady and sure now. Scene shift: the dolphins are massed inside the net. At least a thousand are in the school, maybe two thousand. At the moment they seem reasonably calm They are spinner dolphins. Their triangular fins break the surface by the score and then cut back under. Scene shift: the dolphins are in a panic, hundreds of them canopied in the middle portion of the net. The net is all white explosive spray and chaos. At this distance no once can be sure what sort of animals are roiling the sea. It looks as if someone were trying to drown a regiment of cavalry. White gulls hover, excited. A frigate bird drops down to have a closer look.*

Brower then wrote,

"The camera was moving around," LaBudde says of this first footage. "I had to do real short hits on stuff. I was on the deck crew, twenty people were running all over the place, and I had to go down and start pulling dolphins out of the net. I got good shots of the canopy, but I didn't get a lot of it."

One to two hundred eastern spinner dolphins died, trapped under the canopy, in that first set. When the carcasses had been disentangled from the net and dumped, shark bait, the crew had their catch-a single yellowfin tuna.

End of account. We are left with the impression that this is an everyday thing that happens on all tuna boats. And we are left with the impression that this was all there was to it. Not quite....

Indeed LaBudde did not last long in his first job. "Sam drove speedboat like a girl," groused roommate Adolfo Ochoa. And those "bombs" LaBudde couldn't throw very well are heavy-duty firecrackers, not military artillery as implied—and are illegal for U.S. vessels. Captain del Solar reassigned LaBudde as deck hand, where Navigator Oscar Iriarte, the young Mexican, took a special liking to the inept crewman. Although Sam was by this time thirty-one years old, he still retained the boyish face and gangly body of a teenager, and did not reveal his true age. Iriarte said, "I felt sorry for him. He was just a kid. He needed a friend."

Iriarte found that LaBudde was from San Francisco. "Hey, my wife Gloria is living near there in San Jose with her family," Oscar told Sam. "I'm going to live there for a while after this trip." LaBudde said, "We'll have to get together." He began to cultivate the navigator with recruitment in mind.

Another thing: LaBudde's filming was no big secret. He had openly shown the camera around even before his first one was stolen. An article in *This World* magazine said of LaBudde's filmmaking, "in the kind of crude humor the crew could appreciate, he occasionally burst into the bathroom to photograph men relieving themselves."[49] Both of Azkue's brothers-in-law, Jose Ramon Esnal and Juan Carlos Esnal were aware of the video camera but were too naive to have any suspicions.

In fact, the edited tape that LaBudde showed to Congress contains the sequence "when he had to go down and start pulling dolphins out of the net." Congress saw Sam LaBudde heroically untangling dolphins in that scene.

Who was holding the camera?

That time it happened to be the cook.

Big secret.

Captain del Solar realized The African Net was not suited to tuna fishing long before the disaster set took place. He had made two practice sets with the *Maria Luisa* before trying a real one. "I had seen these red nets before in the Caribbean, and knew they had problems," he said. He brought the vessel to port in Panama only three weeks after leaving Ensenada—a transit ticket shows the *Maria Luisa* making a northbound transit of the Panama Canal on November 1, 1987. Suppliers in Panama City remember the *Maria Luisa* as the worst tuna boat they had ever seen.

Captain del Solar in Panama argued with owner Ignacio Azkue that The African Net was not suitable for tuna fishing. Azkue argued with del Solar over the fact that he had caught no fish to pay the bills. There would be no money for a new net or modifications to The African Net. Azkue sent them out again. That's when LaBudde got his first film, off the coast of El Salvador.

In the disaster set on the thousand dolphins, as soon as Captain del Solar realized The African Net was not pursing at the bottom as it should, and was instead billowing like a canopy, pushing the dolphins upward and trapping them in the edge folds, he ordered a backdown procedure and aborted the set. Navigator Iriarte performed the reversal as ordered.

LaBudde edited the backdown procedure out of his finished videotape. The public never saw the speedboat crew rushing to chase the dolphins out of the net and succeed in rescuing more than 95 percent of them. Five hours of such missing tape is probably laying around Earth Island Institute somewhere unless they have destroyed it. We'd like to see all five hours of it made public.

And that single yellowfin LaBudde commented on was one of about 30 tons of tuna that was in the net before Captain del Solar aborted the set. When he saw the net was not operating properly, the captain released both dolphins and tuna. He had no intention of sacrificing dolphins for even a good catch of tuna.

The most experienced crew members say that fifty dolphins maximum died in that disaster set. And they were spotted dolphins, not "rare Costa Rican spinners" as LaBudde claimed, a fact that Navigator Iriarte noticed while reviewing the videotape with us and scientific experts later confirmed. The crew were not crass about the deaths, but complained bitterly to Captain del Solar, who now called back to Panama and flatly told the owner he would not set on dolphins again until the net was fixed.

Brower then wrote,

> The seiner's luck did not improve. The *Maria Luisa* passed schools of skipjack but did not bother to set on them. Those schools were small fry. The quest was for *aleta amarilla*. "There's no status or honor to catching anything besides the big yellowfin with dolphins," LaBudde says. "There's this big machismo associated with dolphin fishing. The smaller species of tuna, even though you get almost as good money for them these days, are just 'trash.'"

The crew disagrees. In separate interviews with Captain del Solar and Navigator Iriarte, both independently recalled that on November 23 the *Maria Luisa* made a set on skipjack off Costa Rica, but The African Net ripped and they got no fish.

Kenneth Brower never asked the owner to see the ship's log. We could find no evidence that he ever checked a thing LaBudde told him. Swallowed it whole.

There's no point even asking about *Atlantic's* fact checkers any more. Obviously, the facts don't matter to them when they're acting as propagandists.

On November 26 Captain del Solar returned to Panama to have the net repaired. He had now come back twice with no fish and this time with a damaged net. On December 3, Azkue fired him. Four experienced Mexican deckhands left the crew after getting no pay—two jumped ship, one pretended appendicitis and only one formally resigned for non-payment. Engineer Luis Arrambari likewise resigned: even though he was a co-owner of the vessel, he could see that his shares in the catch were equal to zero.

LaBudde still did not have the tape he needed. He only had footage of one aborted set on dolphins trapped in the water. The trip would be a total loss if he couldn't get something more dramatic: dolphins being hauled up in nets and dying on the deck.

By this time LaBudde was no longer working as a deck hand, but as ship's cook. Brower sets up the transition in typically fanciful form, walking the reader through a situation with a bad cook, a Spaniard nicknamed Juan Papas (John Potatoes), "because we got two kinds of potatoes with every meal." This is Juan "Johnny" Costales, as he was actually known, the homeless man signed on as dishwasher.

Then, so Brower tells us, Juan Papas took a day off and LaBudde volunteered to fill in, making a hit with the bummed-out crew, learning on the spot to cook icky red meat—"I was a vegetarian. I'd go down to the freezer and I'd see these twenty-pound hunks of dead animals frozen solid. I don't even know what animal it comes from, or what part it is, or anything about what to do with it, except you've got to thaw it out and cut it." But LaBudde was a natural whiz with food and a great success, he says, attributing it to his days waiting table in the Florida Keys.

It was also a strategic move, because, "As cook, LaBudde would have locked cabinets in which to secure his video camera. As cook, he would have no duties on deck during sets on dolphins, which would free him to film the sets."

But the new captain, "A giant son of a bitch," according to LaBudde, wanted a new cook. Brower wrote:

> His popularity with the crew, fortunately, was such that he was given a two-day trial run as cook for the big Basque. He rose to the challenge, and the two days proved enough. "I did my best to keep the captain out of the kitchen," he says of the uneasy truce that followed. "Took coffee and rolls up to him on the bridge every morning. Keep him up there. If he didn't have to come downstairs for coffee, I never had to see him."

The owner and crew remember it differently. It was true enough that nobody liked the cooking of Johnny Costales. He gave them the same meal every day twice a day: chicken, rice and potatoes. He even put potatoes in *ceviche*, a marinated raw fish appetizer in which potatoes do not belong. He was doing the best a homeless dishwasher could, but even pity has its limits. As Navigator Oscar Iriarte recalls, Captain del Solar killed two birds with one stone: First Mate Esnal had been complaining to him that LaBudde was as worthless a deckhand as he had been a mechanic and, realizing the crew was grumbling over the food, the captain assigned LaBudde as assistant cook to help Juan Papas. LaBudde gradually assimilated the cook's job without any formal promotion.

Then, after del Solar was fired, the new captain took over, a seasoned Atlantic fisherman and a Basque from Bermeo, Spain, like Azkue: Joseba Santamaria Bilbao (also registered in the Castilian form of his name, Jose Antonio Santamaria). It is common for everyone's job to be open to termination when a new captain takes command. Owner Azkue saw no reason to pay for a real cook—"I did not recommend LaBudde and did not know or care if he could cook or not. It was the captain's problem," he said.[50] Santamaria simply formalized the arrangement he found: LaBudde doing the main cooking and Juan Papas gratefully assuming the duties of dishwasher as he had wanted in the first place.

But Brower had to dress things up to make it appear that Santamaria was against LaBudde:

> The navigator, a 300-pound Mexican, became a fierce advocate of LaBudde as cook, and the rest of the crew were rooting for him.

The 300-pound Mexican navigator, of course, is Oscar Iriarte. He's closer to 250. He told us he liked LaBudde but had no reason to be an advocate of his cooking, nor did the rest of the crew: Sam's food wasn't much better than Juan Papas'.

Maria Luisa—Mrs. Azkue—took LaBudde under her wing while they were docked in Panama, helped him stock the ship's pantry at local shops, taught him the rudiments of fry cooking in the galley, and wished him well when the *Maria Luisa* went out again on December 17.[51]

However, since LaBudde proved to be just about as lousy a cook as Johnny Costales, they let him go after putting up with his meals for a month. By that time, however, LaBudde had filmed two more dolphin sets, both off Costa Rica, one on January 1, 1988, the other on January 9, and got what he needed—grisly footage of dolphins being hauled up from the sea in the red net, crushed in the winch block and flopping around dying on the deck, and this time they were spinner dolphins.[52]

Both of these sets were not only illegal, they were also stupid. Spinner dolphins usually associate with smaller schools of tuna or carry none at all, but Captain Joseba Santamaria set on them anyway, demonstrating his lack of experience in the Eastern Tropical Pacific. In the January 9 set, Captain Joseba Santamaria failed to order the backdown maneuver, required even though fewer than fifty dolphins were in the net. Navigator Iriarte protested in the strongest terms. The captain was obligated to remove all live dolphins from the net before hauling it aboard, which he did not do. A U.S. boat, if caught with dolphins in the net, would be subject to a $1,500 general fine plus $500 for each animal. In addition, a dolphin falling out of a net being hauled up the twenty-foot-high power block could seriously injure any deckhand working below. Things were so bizarre that Navigator Oscar Iriarte kept a private log of the trip listing the infractions.

Not exactly your typical tuna set.

Brower, of course, gives us the most heart-rending edition imaginable of the carnage against perhaps twenty dolphins that got caught in Santamaria's net and were hauled aboard. Captain Joseba, as they called Santamaria, is a Basque, part of an ancient Iberian culture that does not see things as others do. Brower reveals the difference in a monologue by LaBudde from a few minutes after filming the bloody deck scene:

> "I walk back out on deck, and here's our captain filleting a dolphin on the deck of the ship. An animal with a brain almost as large as his own, and he's cutting it up to eat it. Something snapped in me. *I couldn't do anything.* Anything I could have done would have been self-destructive. Except filming. So I went back and got the camera. I walked out on deck and pointed the camera at the captain. I thought, If he looks up, I'm dead. He sliced about fifteen seconds more, using a little three-inch penknife."

Consider that warning in California about concrete galoshes.

Hear the ominous music on the sound track?

LaBudde is feeding us the fake Perrin line again, but he was in no danger of walking the plank—in fact, everybody felt rather protective of him, as long as he kept his clothes on. They just didn't like his cooking or his sunbathing. Certainly Captain Santamaria was no sweetie-pie, but he had no sense that his fileting the dolphin should be hidden from the little pest's camera. Unlike the Greek and Roman sailors of antiquity who revered dolphins, the Basques have historically regarded them as a staple source of food, just as the Northwest Indians hunted and ate whales and seals as a staple source of food for millennia, and as far-northern cultures still do. Basques do not regard eating dolphins as a sacrilege any more than a vegetarian regards eating apples as a sacrilege. Joseba Santamaria behaved no differently than generations of Basques before him, but Kenneth Brower does not enlighten us in their traditions. He writes further of that evening,

> "...the crew ate dolphin for dinner. The cook did not partake of it. "I had a terrible lapse in my ability to understand Spanish," LaBudde says. "The galley boy had to prepare the dolphin. I wasn't going to do it."

That was a sop for LaBudde's *Atlantic Monthly* public. In a sworn statement—something Mr. LaBudde has avoided about his *Maria Luisa* experience—his roommate Rigoberto Chaverra Pino said, "Mr. LaBudde says in his film that when he saw so many porpoises die he felt like crying, but when I saw him butchering a porpoise he did not feel like crying. He himself prepared the porpoise because he was the cook, he gave it to the captain and he also ate it himself. When we consider Mr. LaBudde upon seeing him eat the porpoise and later we see him on television protesting because he says there was a slaughter, we know it is not as Mr. LaBudde states it."[53]

Deck boss Victor Carlos Fuentes gave this statement: "I personally accuse Mr. LaBudde of being a liar. He claims he suffered when he saw dolphins slaughtered. He opens up the porpoise in the afternoon and he himself cooks it, which we all ate, including himself."[54]

In fact, one person who didn't eat the dolphin that evening was Navigator Oscar Iriarte. Captain Joseba offered him a piece, saying, "Here, try some dolphin steak, it's good." Iriarte says he held out a big jar of red hot Mexican peppers to the captain and replied, "Here, try some jalapeños, they're good."

But Sam LaBudde, the whole crew says, cooked Flipper and chowed him down with Captain Joseba.

Ah, yes, the magnificent Samuel LaBudde, whose great purpose in life is to serve dolphins. Medium rare, hold the salsa.

The burger flipper of Flipper burgers himself admitted to Kenneth Brower that he is a master of artful deceit:

> "For months everything I did, in every moment, was calculated for effect. I needed a cover or to diffuse fears or intuitions that I wasn't on the level. I like to think that's contrary to my nature. I'd just come out of college. I was trying to become a biologist. I believed that working on yourself, and who you are, should be a constant process throughout your life. To have to start pretending so hard, for so long, is really contrary to that. It's easy to lose track of yourself."
> "But were you good at it?" I asked.
> "I was great at it."

We know, Sam.

Congress believed you. America believed you.

You were great at it.

After LaBudde had all his tape, the *Maria Luisa* docked at Taboga Island off Panama on January 23, 1988, where Captain Santamaria threw a party in the galley. At least he had caught a little fish during this trip and made a little money for the crew.

There LaBudde showed his tapes to all and sundry, even to Azkue. The owner recalls viewing a short segment showing the net being set off the stern of the vessel, which did not interest him or arouse any suspicion about why LaBudde was filming the operation. Azkue also recalls that an engineer from another vessel remarked after viewing the tape, "That was sure a disaster set. Who was the captain of this rig?"

Kenneth Brower tells us that Sam LaBudde soon sent the videotapes by courier from Panama. Ignacio Azkue says otherwise. While the *Maria Luisa* was docked in Panama, a woman came to the boat saying she was Sam LaBudde's girlfriend. Azkue says Earth Island Institute sent her, a staffer named Brenda Killian. He believes the videotape was transferred to her, not sent by any courier service. Perhaps Brenda will show the public her passport? Probably not.

Kenneth Brower tells us Sam thought about going out on another trip with the *Maria Luisa* to get more film, but got a call from San Francisco saying they had enough footage, so he jumped ship. To the best of Navigator Iriarte's recollection, Sam was not invited to stay on board because the captain decided it was time to hire a decent cook.

On January 29, 1988, LaBudde flew from Panama to San Francisco. Before he left, he exchanged telephone numbers with Oscar Iriarte, who was to leave the boat two weeks later. Iriarte was unhappy with the poor pay of fishing life and had plans to go to diesel mechanic school in San Diego after joining his wife. "Call me when you get to San Jose," said LaBudde. "I may have some work for you."

Shortly after Iriarte went to live with his wife's family in late February, he made the call. Sam came to San Jose the next day. Oscar Iriarte tells what happened:

"Sam sat in my living room and explained everything, what the video camera was really for, why he was there. He told me about Earth Island and what they were going to do to the U.S. tuna industry. He asked me to testify. He wanted me to go to the U.S. legislature and back up his film.

"I told him, 'Sam, I'd like to help you. We've been friends. But I can't testify. It's not right to say that's the way things happen tuna fishing. If I testified I'd never work on a fishing boat again, not that I intend to. I can't do this work for you. It's not right, Sam. It's not right.'"

Kenneth Brower ended his sensational *Atlantic* article with a burst of creative writing: "Three days after LaBudde jumped ship, the *Maria Luisa* went out with one bad generator. She made one more set on dolphins and then the main engine blew up, killing two men."

The ship's log shows no such event. The voyage went on uneventfully. The main engine never blew up. Nobody ever died from an accident on the *Maria Luisa*.

Atlantic published Brower's article without adult supervision.

Sam LaBudde and Earth Island Institute edited five hours of raw footage from the *Maria Luisa* into a silent 11-minute illusion. They spliced the thousand-spotted-dolphins-in-the-water disaster set of Pedro del Solar together with two different castings of Joseba Santamaria showing a dozen spinner dolphins suspended in The African Net, and a single spinner dolphin crushed in the block. This footage was intercut with deck scenes of half-a-dozen spinner dolphins being untangled and slid down the shark chute, with the clip of Santamaria slicing one animal, all in a sequence to make it appear that a vast number of dolphins had been killed out of sheer malice and macho.

Would you like to see the other five hours of the LaBudde Videotape made public?

In March 1988, the eleven-minute-fabrication aired on CBS, ABC and CNN. LaBudde said, "the events that I filmed are tragically representative...the things you will see on this film happen every day...I would like to say that I feel that what is shown on the film is representative of the U.S. Fleet."

He was great at it.

Nobody even tried to fact-check the story.

It swept away years of honest effort to reduce dolphin mortality.

When LaBudde's rigged tape hit the media in Central America, the Bank of Bilbao shut off Azkue's credit. He tried to reflag the *Maria Luisa* in Venezuela, but Panamanian creditors would not release it until the mortgage was paid in full. Azkue had to stop operating the vessel and tied it up, a ruined man. Basque boat owners in Venezuela gave him shoreside work managing their vessels, feeling he'd gotten a raw deal. Azkue sold the *Maria Luisa* in 1989. It was renamed the *Guadalete* and fished regularly until it sank without casualties off the coast of Mexico August 1, 1992. It went out with a whimper, not a bang.[55]

Pedro del Solar worked for a while in American Samoa and then returned to Peru. Joseba Santamaria is again based in Africa, operating in the Atlantic. Oscar Iriarte became a diesel mechanic and works on trucks. He never returned to navigating.

Many crew members remain unidentified because they fear reprisals from the environmentalists.

Going Dolphin Safe

LaBudde's phony film began to do its work.

With the long-needed weapon now in hand, Dave Phillips of Earth Island Institute and Stan Minasian of the Marine Mammal Fund set out to destroy the tuna fishing industry. In April 1988 the two groups filed a lawsuit against the U.S. Department of Commerce, charging that it had failed to uphold the Marine Mammal Protection Act.[56]

Earth Island's half-million-dollar publicity machine went into high gear. In June 1989 Dave Phillips and Sam LaBudde used the International Whaling Commission annual meeting in San Diego as a stage for a series of high-profile protests on the docks of the remaining U.S. tuna fleet's home port.

At one of many showings of the LaBudde videotape, Ani Moss, a fashion model and wife of recording industry magnate Jerry Moss, viewed the graphic footage and wept. She introduced herself to LaBudde and said she wanted to help. Back home in Los Angeles, Moss and two other women, Maggy Howe and Lise Snyder, quickly formed a nonprofit called **The Dolphin Connection**. One of its first projects was the "Dolphin Awareness Evening," a posh Hollybash replete with limousines, valet parking, a buffet featuring toasted seaweed and vegetarian sushi, and a thousand celebrities about to become aware of dolphins.[57]

The fundraiser was held on November 16, 1989, at Jerry Moss's A&M Records sound stage. Among the myriad Hollywood denizens that showed up was director Richard Donner, who accepted an award for the gratuitous scene in his megahit, *Lethal Weapon II*, in which Danny Glover's screen family berates him for eating a tuna sandwich and lectures him about the Dolphin Safe issue.

Stan Minasian of the Marine Mammal Fund gave an impassioned speech. Dave Phillips of Earth Island Institute gave an impassioned speech. Sam LaBudde of the phony videotape gave an impassioned speech. LaBudde urged his audience to boycott tuna, particularly Heinz's StarKist brand.

StarKist is the only major brand of tuna on the U.S. market owned by an American company, H. J. Heinz. Heinz controlled 35 percent of the domestic market and had annual revenues of approximately $160 million in 1989. Van Camp Seafood Company—Chicken of the Sea—is owned by the P. T. ManTrust of Indonesia. Bumble Bee Seafoods, Inc. is owned by the Unicord Company of Thailand. Earth Island later extended its boycott to Bumble Bee.[58]

Dave Phillips got Herb Chao Gunther of the Public Media Center, a left-wing

San Francisco public interest advertising agency, to place full-page ads attacking Heinz in the *New York Times* and other major newspapers. They orchestrated letter-writing campaigns that resulted in school children sending in boxes of letters to Heinz protesting the killing of dolphins. They ran a media campaign, convincing Herb Caen of the *San Francisco Chronicle* to write a column about the boycott that produced hundreds of supportive letters.

The boycott had no commercial effect whatever. Surveys showed that consumers weren't willing to pay more for dolphin-safe tuna.[59]

In fact, Heinz enjoyed revenues that climbed by 10 percent in 1989. The *New York Times* observed, "Consumer boycotts rarely hurt a target company's sales. StarKist revenue and profit actually grew during the two years of the boycott called by the Earth Island Institute and other groups."[60]

Jerry Moss of A&M Records, who, after making Hollywood aware of the dolphin-safe issue, took great pains to arrange a private lunch with Heinz chairman of the board Anthony O'Reilly. "Rather than garrison shouting at garrison, lunch was more of a joint tutorial," O'Reilly told the *New York Times*. What they taught each other is not clear.

What is clear is that Mr. Moss is a shrewd businessman capable of seeing a commercial advantage for Heinz in going dolphin-safe and capable of explaining such advantages to Mr. O'Reilly. Mr. O'Reilly appears to have grasped the message immediately.

On April 12, 1990, Jerry and Ani Moss, along with Dave Phillips and Sam LaBudde, were flying to Washington, D.C. on a Heinz corporate jet to announce that StarKist had agreed to a four-point Earth Island Institute demand: 1) An immediate ban on any tuna caught with dolphins or in drift nets; 2) worldwide compliance with the ban extending to Heinz's canneries in Puerto Rico, Samoa and elsewhere, and including all Heinz's products, specifically Weight Watchers entrees and pet food; 3) a ban on the purchase of tuna caught by any vessel without official observers on board; and 4) active lobbying support for legislation introduced to Congress by Representatives Barbara Boxer (D-California) and Senator Joseph Biden, (D-Delaware) that would require warning labels on all tuna caught with dolphins in the Eastern Tropical Pacific.[61]

Within hours of StarKist's announcement, Chicken of the Sea brand's Van Camp Sea Food Company and Bumble Bee Company followed suit.[62]

The Big Three had gone dolphin-safe. Together they accounted for about 70 percent of the domestic market.[63]

It was a great victory for Sam LaBudde and Earth Island.

Two weeks later, on April 26, Van Camp announced the closure of its Puerto Rico tuna cannery, which shut its doors in June. Over two-thousand jobs killed.

It was a great victory for Sam LaBudde and Earth Island.

The same day Bumble Bee Seafoods announced the elimination of second shift operations in Puerto Rico. Eight-hundred jobs killed.

It was a great victory for Sam LaBudde and Earth Island.

The three remaining smaller tuna processors, Pan Pacific in California, Mitsubishi and Neptune in Puerto Rico, were forced to go dolphin-safe by environmentalist threats. Neptune closed its processing operations in August. Six hundred jobs killed.

It was a great victory for Sam LaBudde and Earth Island.

By April 15, 1992, Alfredo Salazar, Jr., Puerto Rico's administrator of economic development told the U.S. International Trade Commission that the job loss due to contraction of tuna canning employment since the boycott was 7,590 jobs. Salazar told the Commission, "The 4,850 jobs remaining in the tuna canneries are important to the Puerto Rican economy, which is the poorest region of the U.S. economy. Per capita income in Puerto Rico is less than one-third of the U.S. average and less than one-half of that in the poorest state in the Union."[64]

It was a great victory for Sam LaBudde and Earth Island.

Mike Dunn of Mitsubishi Canneries told us that the estimate of 10,000 jobs lost because of the dolphin-safe move by the Big Three was far too low.

It was a great victory for Sam LaBudde and Earth Island.

In April, 1991, Sam LaBudde was awarded the Goldman Prize for environmental action. He was declared a savior of the planet and given $60,000. Ten thousand people he put out of work never heard of him.[65]

It was a great victory for Sam LaBudde and Earth Island.

But it wasn't great enough.

Earth Island Institute had filed suit in 1990 to restrict tuna imports from Third World nations caught by foreign fleets whose fishing methods harm dolphins.[66] The United States government imposed the embargo in the Eastern Tropical Pacific, and Mexico protested it to the General Agreement on Tariffs and Trade (GATT).

The U.S. position at the GATT forum concerning dolphin-related tuna fishing was, "This type of association has not been observed in other areas of the World, consequently intentional encirclement of dolphins with purse seine nets is used as a tuna fishing technique in the ETP (Eastern Tropical Pacific).

"The U.S. measures were limited to the ETP because it was only there that the unique linkage between yellowfin tuna and dolphins occurred, so it was only there that danger to dolphin from commercial fishing existed."

Oh, really?

As scientist Frank Alverson told the UC-MEXUS conference in San Diego in 1992, "The tuna-dolphin association is found throughout the world's oceans. The contention by the government of the U.S. that the tuna-dolphin association is unique to the ETP is a canard."[67]

The National Research Council's recent publication "Dolphins and the Tuna Industry," agrees: "This association has been observed and used by fishermen in other oceans," followed by 18 similar references cited on the same page.[68]

GATT ruled that the U.S. policy was not "environmental protection," but instead a "trade barrier." It was illegal under international law. Mexico, having won its case, then changed its fishing law to include a ten-point dolphin-safety program.[69]

Environmentalists were not satisfied. They pressured the U.S. government to disregard the GATT ruling. In January 1992, U.S. District Court Judge Thelton Henderson in San Francisco ordered the U.S. Department of Commerce to impose a secondary embargo on 27 nations that import tuna from Mexico and Venezuela, confirming that nations who buy un-dolphin-safe tuna from other nations will find *all* of their tuna shut out of U.S. markets.[70]

It was on this occasion that Earth Island's Dave Phillips told the *San Diego Union-Tribune*, "We stuck it to the U.S. tuna industry," and added: "You can stick a fork in Mexico. It's done."[71]

Mexican President Carlos Salinas de Gortari threatened to go once again to GATT and ask that Henderson's ruling be declared a violation of international trade pacts. He had many allies waiting to join him in his complaint about the unfair trade war being waged by the United States. Among the nations facing the secondary embargo were Japan, Italy, France and Spain.

The National Research Council in early 1992 released a detailed study of the dolphin-tuna issue that rejected the idea of banning tuna encirclement in favor of training boat captains. The study had been mandated by Congress as part of the reauthorization of the Marine Mammal Protection Act and sponsored by the U.S. Commerce Department's National Oceanic and Atmospheric Administration.[72]

The Inter-American Tropical Tuna Commission's member nations met shortly afterward to forge a practical solution to the problem at their La Jolla, California, headquarters. The Agreement of Nations that came out of the meeting proposed to use international cooperation and self-determination to reduce dolphin mortality to nearly zero by the turn of the century, instead of the unilateral bludgeoning used by the United States on the tuna countries today.

Not good enough for Environmentalism's Articles of Faith.

Earth Island Institute and a coalition of twenty-four other environmental groups pushed for the passage of the International Dolphin Conservation Act of 1992, introduced by Massachusetts Congressman Gerry Studds as H.R. 5419. Dave Phillips of EII gave testimony before Congress on behalf of all 25 groups in July 1992.[73] Studds' bill used wording nearly identical to the news release of H. J. Heinz Company when it announced the Dolphin Safe program, almost as if the Heinz legal department had drafted the bill. The law would impose a global moratorium, effective March 1, 1994, on any tuna purse seine fishing that might even remotely harm any marine mammal. The ban would cover every ocean, not just the Eastern Tropical Pacific Ocean.

StarKist later issued comments that perhaps the "every ocean" clause needed a bit of fine tuning—it was getting a little too close to their own self-interest: "We have one concern regarding a provision of the Bill that we would like to record in the event consideration of this or similar legislation takes place in the future.

"The potential for unnecessary detriment to the tuna industry without a concomitant benefit to marine mammal safety exists in the Bill as passed by the House of Representatives. Empowering the U.S. Secretary of Commerce to determine unilaterally that there exists a regular and significant association between marine mammals and tuna in an area of an ocean outside the eastern tropical Pacific could lead to significant unwarranted disruption in tuna fishing."[74]

Make that "disruption in *our* tuna fishing."

StarKist has no doubt forgotten that it sponsored a study of tuna-dolphin fishing in the Atlantic in 1959 that was written up in 1961. Dr. Gilbert Winfield Bane, Jr., conducted an exploratory fishing survey off Ghana on the West Coast of Africa, and wrote, "frequently, when swimming and feeding in association with tuna, porpoise, leaping high into the air, were spotted from a distance of about ten miles on a clear day."[75] Shortly after the study was completed, StarKist sponsored a purse seiner to fish in the Atlantic off West Africa for tuna in association with dolphin.

An odd fact: The National Marine Fisheries Service allows two thousand dolphins—four percent of the population—to be killed in the course of fisheries off the New England coast—where Congressman Studds is from—and does nothing to stop it. Yet they won't permit a smaller percentage mortality in the Eastern Tropical Pacific where mortality reduction was being pursued with great success. Their rationale is that the New England deaths are accidental and not the result of deliberately surrounding dolphins. Is there something besides ecology going on here?

Senator John Breaux of Louisiana introduced a bill that would turn the IATTC Agreement of Nations into law, but the House passed the Studds bill in late 1992 and adjourned. The Senate, left without a conference committee, approved the House version, which became law in late 1992.

In the interim, filmmaker Richard *Lethal Weapon* Donner had threatened in a letter to Senator Breaux that unless the Studds bill became law he would blame Breaux personally and impose a Hollywood boycott on Louisiana as a film location, which would cost the state's economy tens of millions of dollars. Bang! Bang! You're dead. Environmentalism is quite a Lethal Weapon, hmm?[76]

There was one little hitch: A slip-knot in the Studds bill required at least one other nation with more than 20 purse seine tuna boats to sign on to the deal in order for the moratorium on tuna/dolphin fishing to go into effect. That's only Mexico and Venezuela. Neither are suicidal, so neither has come forward.

Even if the moratorium doesn't go into effect, a perfect catch of tuna by encirclement with zero dolphin mortality cannot be sold in the United States—just because it was caught by encirclement. Total control of the market by the "Dolphin Safe" Big Three.

The battle rages on.

Some Questions

Why was Heinz so eager to go dolphin-safe so suddenly, when it had long supported the tuna industry as it came into compliance with the Marine Mammal Protection Act? Did chief executive Anthony O'Reilly foresee the damage it would do to his two major competitors? Did the Big Three companies realize the economic harm they would do to the Third World? What's going on here?

The popular Mexican television program *60 Minutos*—similar in format to the CBS News *60 Minutes* program, but unaffiliated—broadcast an hour-long segment, "The Tuna War," in December 1992 asking exactly that question.

Their answer:

> ANNOUNCER: The United States government has declared two embargoes against Mexican tuna. They accuse Mexico of causing a high dolphin mortality while tuna fishing in the Pacific Ocean. The Mexican tuna industry has lost $50 million due to the embargoes. Most of the U.S. fleet fishes now in the Indian and Atlantic Oceans, claiming they do not cause dolphin deaths.[77] Reality is quite different. Several scientists say that in both oceans the dolphin mortality is ten times higher than that in the Eastern Pacific. Behind the U.S. embargoes there are only economic, not environmental interests.[78]
>
> JORGE CASTAÑEDA, REPORTER: The dolphin safe policy was put in place first by StarKist and followed by Bumble Bee and Chicken of the Sea, the most powerful tuna companies in the U.S., which have clearly benefitted from the embargoes. This has been the policy in the last two years and has caused a good portion of American, European and Asian consumers to buy canned tuna only if marked Dolphin Safe. It harms particularly the Mexican tuna that sells in those markets. Mexico has the world's largest tuna fleet.
>
> Most tragic, an important source of nutrition for the world's poorest families is being threatened. Millions of people in the Third World depend on the protein in an inexpensive can of tuna.

So, it appears that the U.S. tuna industry is trying to destroy its competitors to the South. And Earth Island Institute is their catspaw sticking the Economy Trasher fork in Mexico.

The *60 Minutos* program was centered on the UC-MEXUS conference held in San Diego by the University of California in July 1992. It dealt with separating fact from fiction.

> JORGE CASTAÑEDA, REPORTER: The Earth Island Institute has claimed that dolphin populations in the Eastern Pacific were not even one million specimens. But reality is different.
>
> MARTIN HALL, INTER-AMERICAN TROPICAL TUNA COMMISSION (IATTC), TUNA-DOLPHIN PROGRAM: The most recent estimate of population is a bit over 9.5 million dolphins.
>
> JORGE CASTAÑEDA, REPORTER: Another argument on which Earth Island Institute bases its position and U.S. legislation about the embargo is that two of the dolphin species that associate with tuna were endangered species. The species are whitebelly, spotted and common. It was said that the population of those three species had decreased by 40 percent in the last 5 years. But according to experts the species mortality is not over one percent.
>
> WILLIAM PERRIN, NATIONAL MARINE FISHERIES SERVICE: In the past 5 years the killing for all stocks has declined to somewhere on the order of 1 percent or less. We think that these levels are sustainable. So the future of the populations seems assured. [This is the same prestigious biologist who did not warn LaBudde about concrete galoshes.]

JORGE CASTAÑEDA, REPORTER: Earth Island Institute based its position on the high mortality rate of dolphins in the major tuna fishing fleets, mainly the Mexican.

GUILLERMO COMPEAN JIMENEZ, PROGRAMA NACIONAL PARA EL APROVECHAMIENTO DEL ATÚN Y LA PROTECCIÓN DE LOS DELFINES: In the statistics that I showed we can see that 70 percent of the current castings of the Mexican fleet at zero mortality. This number has been growing constantly. We can still do more. The results show that 99.6 percent of dolphins encircled during fishing operations are freed unharmed and with no mortality in these groups.[79]

JORGE CASTAÑEDA, REPORTER: Earth Island Institute indicates that most American tuna boats a majority of which belong to the big three companies that imposed the dolphin safe policy are able to sell their tuna because they moved their ships to the Atlantic and Indian Oceans.

DAVID PHILLIPS, EARTH ISLAND INSTITUTE: In these areas tuna can be sold as free of danger to dolphins in the Dolphin Safe markets of the United States, Thailand and other places. It reflects a very important fleet movement to an area where they can operate without harming the dolphin.

JORGE CASTAÑEDA, REPORTER: The dolphin safe policy is based exclusively on the fact that tuna fish in seas other than the Pacific do not involve killing dolphins. But reality is very different from the assumptions of Earth Island Institute and the United States government.

FELIPE CHARAT, CÁMERA NACIONAL DE LA INDUSTRIA PESQUERA (CANAINPES): Dolphin safe is a hoax. All the tuna eaten in the U.S. in one way or another has killed dolphins, but nobody acknowledges it because it is commercially unacceptable. If we do the mathematics we will see that in the Eastern Tropical Pacific two out of 1,000 dolphins die while in the Indian ocean two out of 100 die. So the mortality in the Indian ocean is ten times higher than that of tropical eastern pacific.

FRANKLIN ALVERSON, PORPOISE RESCUE FOUNDATION: Let's leave behind once and for all the myth that the association between dolphins and tuna only happens in the Eastern Pacific. Next time you buy a can of tuna ask yourself whether it was really fished protecting the dolphin.

DOUG DE MASTER, NATIONAL MARINE FISHERIES SERVICE: I agree that there is no way of fishing that is totally free of trapping other fish and sometimes there is also capture of dolphins. In the widest sense of dolphin safe there is no way of capturing tuna without dolphins.

JORGE CASTAÑEDA, REPORTER: For those reasons the San Diego conference concluded that the law that imposed the embargoes and the dolphin safe policy have no scientific or ecological basis. They only do serious harm to Mexican tuna ships and those from other Latin American countries.

It is very clear that the U.S. government has no real environmental concern with the problem. It is clear that their only concern is the strong economic interest of the three big tuna companies.[80]

Is the environmental concern really just a front for a trade war by U.S. companies suppressing Latin American fisheries? Is the U.S. government selectively protecting dolphins only in places that will harm Latin American fisheries?

Have Heinz or the other two big tuna companies given money to Earth Island Institute or to any of the other 24 environmental groups in the Dolphin Conservation Act coalition? The answer is unequivocally Yes. We can trace $15,000 from Heinz in 1989 to the Conservation Foundation (merged with the World Wildlife Fund) in Foundation Center records.

The results of Earth Island Institute's Dolphin Project have been manyfold:

The U.S. flag purse seine tuna fleet has been virtually eradicated from the Eastern Tropical Pacific: many ships have been sold off to foreign owners and reflagged or retired. Two have sunk.

Loss of mortality-reduction skills in purse seine crews as boats refit to fish without dolphin.

Migration of vessels to the Western Pacific, Indian and Atlantic Oceans where dolphins are being killed in large numbers because existing dolphin safe regulations apply only to the Eastern Tropical Pacific.

Depletion of immature tuna breeding stock from school-tuna and high bycatch mortality rates, particularly of sharks.

Massive loss of cannery production in the United States and Puerto Rico.

Loss of shipbuilding jobs in Seattle and San Diego as tunaboat orders vanish.

Virtual loss of the National Marine Fisheries Service observer program as U.S. vessels disappeared from the Eastern Pacific.

Endangerment of the IATTC observer program as tuna revenues decline and program funding vanishes.

A trade war and serious friction between the governments of the United States and Latin American countries.

Over ten thousand jobs killed.

The Law of Unintended Consequences?
Not likely.

Earth Island Institute goes on its merry way Trashing the Economy and raising funds from foundations and members to do it. Like most other environmental groups, EII uses professional fundraising groups. In 1990 they used Herb Chao Gunther's Public Media Center for a year-long membership development project at a cost of $33,000. Wiltshire/Associates ran a foundation fund raising campaign at a cost of $18,300, and Kathryn Knight did some foundation fund raising at a cost of $2,000.

Wiltshire/Associates was contracted in 1989 to raise funds for EII's Dolphin Project under a Foundation Grants Cultivation Program. Services provided included researching potential funders, developing a list of the "20 best bets," production of the proposal packet to the foundations, "attempt to find connections between potential funders and EII staff, board and other supporters," arrange meetings between foundations and Earth Island staff, and to "devise strategy with

EII to further promote proposals after they've been placed on a funder's docket." Earth Island is extremely secretive about their funding sources.

Kimery Wiltshire is president of Wiltshire/Associates, which, since 1985 has been providing fund raising consulting services to environmental groups. Her clients have included SIERRA NOW, Green Seal, the Planning and Conservation League, Mono Lake Committee and the Oregon Natural Resources Council. Wiltshire is also the Co-Director of the Illilouette Fund (a member of the Environmental Grantmakers Association) and Executive Officer for the Quality of Life Amendment. She serves as the Vice-President of the Mountain Education Program and is a board members of the Environmental Federation of California.

Kathryn Knight has been a fund raiser in the environmental movement for a dozen years, with Wiltshire/Associates since 1989, consulting for Earth Island Institute, Californians Against Waste and Citizens for a Better Environment.

Earth Island Institute income breakdown: Membership and contributions, 60 percent; foundation grants, 35 percent; other, 5 percent.

Earth Island Action Group is a non-profit but not tax-deductible group that specializes in legislative advocacy. Earth Island Voters is a political action committee.

Earth Island Institute's Board of Directors includes chairman David R. Brower; president Carl Anthony (10 hours per week, compensation $2,664.67 in 1990); vice president Elizabeth Robinson Gunther (Vice-President of the law firm Heller, Ehrman, White & McAuliffe); secretary Ellen Manchester; treasurer Denise Fort; counsel Peter Winkler. Other members include: Linda Blackner; Arlene Blum; Patricia J. Cummings; Judy Diamond; Kendra Ellis; Claire Greensfelder; Michael Hathaway; Randall L. Hayes; John A. Knox; David Phillips; Tim Such; and Robert C. Wilkinson.

Wallace Alexander Gerbode Foundation gave $15,000 in 1990 for organizational development.

Julian Price gave $75,000 in 1986.

Earth Island Institute. Marine Mammal Fund.
Job killers.
Economy Trashers.

Earth Island Institute—Footnotes

1 *Encounters with the Archdruid,* John McPhee, Farrar Strauss and Giroux, New York, 1971.

2 "A longtime gadfly still stings," by Catherine Foster, *Christian Science Monitor,* April 8, 1991, p. 14.

3 "With Friends Like These..." by Paul Rauber, *Mother Jones,* November 1986, p. 35.

4 *E Magazine,* January / February 1990.

5 "A longtime gadfly still stings," *Christian Science Monitor.*

6 Personal interview by Ron Arnold with co-director John Knox in Earth Island Institute offices in San Francisco, October 15, 1992.

7 "Tunamen fight back," Dennis Potter, *Fishing Boat World,* June 1992, p. 14.

8 "Dolphin Safe - An Analysis," American Tunaboat Association, February 20, 1992.

9 Submission of the government of the Commonwealth of Puerto Rico by Mr. Alfredo Salazar, Jr., Administrator of the Commonwealth Economic Development Administration, before the U.S. International Trade Commission, Investigation 332-313.

10 "La Guerra del Atún," (The Tuna War), *60 Minutos,* broadcast on Mexican television December, 1992.

11 "The Tuna/Porpoise Fishery of the Eastern Tropical Pacific Ocean and its Impact on Relations Between the United States and Mexico," by Franklin Alverson, UC-MEXUS Conference, University of California, San Diego, July 24-25, 1992.

12 "Biologist honored for saving dolphins," *Los Angeles Times,* April 23, 1991, p. B8.

13 "The Destruction of Dolphins," by Kenneth Brower, *The Atlantic Monthly,* July 1989, pp. 35-58.

14 Telephone interview by Ron Arnold with Sam LaBudde, October, 1992.

15 "Statement of Sam La Budde, Earth Island Institute, accompanied by Dave Phillips, Co-director, Earth Island Institute," Hearings before the National Ocean Policy Study of the Committee on Commerce, Science, and Transportation, U. S. Senate, 100th Cong., 2d sess., on The Reauthorization of the Marine Mammal Protection Act, April 13 and May 19, 1988, pp. 98-99.

16 "A Catch-twenty-tuna," by S. Lynne Walker, *San Diego Union-Tribune,* February 9, 1992, p. A3.

17 *Dolphins and the Tuna Industry,* National Research Council, Committee on Reducing Porpoise Mortality from Tuna Fishing, Robert C. Francis, Chairman, National Academy of Sciences, National Academy Press, Washington, D.C., 1992, p. 4.

18 Marine Mammal Protection Act, 16 U.S.C. 1361 *et seq.*

19 Marine Mammal Protection Act Amendments, 16 U.S.C. 1361 *et. seq.*

20 Dolphin release figures provided from observer records as analyzed by the Porpoise Rescue Foundation.

21 *Dolphins and the Tuna Industry,* National Research Council, Washington, D.C., 1992, p. 70.

22 Prepublication Draft:*Estimates of Cetacean Abundance in the Eastern Tropical Pacific,* Paul R. Wade and Tim Gerrodette, submitted to International Whaling Commission, 1992, Volume 43, Document SC/44/0 18.

23 Inter-American Tropical Tuna Commission dolphin mortality records.

24 "The Destruction of Dolphins," by Kenneth Brower, *The Atlantic Monthly,* July 1989, p. 35.

25 "Saviors of the planet," *Time,* April 29, 1991, p. 66.

26 "Dolphins in Crisis," by Kenneth S. Norris, *National Geographic,* September 1992, p. 15.

27 Telephone interview by Ron Arnold with LaBudde, October 1992.

28 Teresa Platt telephone interview with Niemehla, October 1992.

29 Admissions records, Indiana University.

30 "One Trainer Talks," by Rick Trout, *PAWS News*, May 1990, p. 65.

31 *Eco-Warriors: Understanding the Radical Environmental Movement*, Rik Scarce, The Noble Press, Inc., Chicago, 1990, p. 108.

32 LaBudde job application to Orth Company dated March 23, 1987, giving a Tavernier, Florida address.

33 Orth Company can be reached at (206)455-9693.

34 Employment records of Samuel LaBudde, Frank Orth Company & Associates, Seattle, Washington, verified October 8, 1992.

35 Correspondence, Frank Orth and Associates to Samuel F. LaBudde, January 21, 1988.

36 IRS Letter dated July 31, 1979.

37 IRS Form 990 Return of Organization Exempt From Income Tax, 1989.

38 Telephone interview, Ron Arnold with August Felando, September 1992.

39 Telephone interview, Ron Arnold with August Felando, October 1992.

40 Teresa Platt interview with William Perrin, January 1993.

41 Annual Financial Report, New York State Department of State, Earth Island Institute, for year ended 12/31/88 and 12/31/89. New York State requires nonprofits soliciting funds within their jurisdiction to disclose substantially more public information than the IRS.

42 Marine Mammal Fund, Internal Revenue Service Form 990, 1989, p. 1.

43 Interview by Ron Arnold with Eribez in San Diego, October 1992.

44 Interview with Ignacio Azkue by Doug Souter in Panama City, August 16, 1992.

45 Interview with Pedro del Solar by Teresa Platt, August Felando and Doug Souter at La Jolla, California, August 12, 1992.

46 Acta de Nacimiento (birth certificate) No. 289958, Oscar de Jesus Iriarte Navarro, Officio del Registro Civil de Topolobampo, Sinaloa, Mexico, dated May 1, 1965.

47 Interview by Ron Arnold and Teresa Platt with Iriarte in Los Angeles, January, 1993.

48 Interview by Teresa Platt with Ochoa in Ensenada, December 1992.

49 "The Conversion of StarKist," by K. Patrick Conner, *This World*, June 17, 1990, p. 10.

50 Interview with Ignacio Azkue by Doug Souter in Panama City, August 16, 1992.

51 Interview with Mrs. Azkue by Doug Souter in Panama City, August 16, 1992.

52 The ship's log shows a "porpoise" set on January 1, 1988 that lasted only 20 minutes and no catch and another on January 9 from 0930 hours to 1240 hours with a catch of 8 tons of yellowfin.

53 Affidavit of *Maria Luisa* crew member Rigoberto Chaverra Pino, before Attorney Ramon Gonzalez and Secretary Elisa de Ayarza, March 22, 1990, Balboa, Panama.

54 Affidavit of *Maria Luisa* crew member Victor Carlos Fuentes, before Attorney Ramon Gonzalez and Secretary Elisa de Ayarza, March 22, 1990, Balboa, Panama.

55 Sinking recorded in "Changes in the IATTC fleet list recorded during July 8 through September 28, 1992," Table 7.

56 "Drive to stop killing by tuna fleets is given new impetus," by Scott Armstrong, *Christian Science Monitor*, April 14, 1988, p. 3.

57 "The Conversion of StarKist," by K. Patrick Conner, *This World*, June 17, 1990, p. 11.

58 "Earth Island, Bumble Bee wage ad war over dolphins," by David Kiley, *Adweek's Marketing Week*, December 10, 1990.

59 "Stores unfazed by tuna boycott," by Emily DeNitto, *Supermarket News*, January 7, 1991, p. 32.

60 "'Epic debate' led to Heinz tuna plan," by Anthony Ramirez, *New York Times*, April 16, 1990, p. C1.

61 News Release: "StarKist Announces New Tuna Policy—First Company to Sell Only 'Dolphin Safe' Tuna," April 12, 1990, StarKist Seafood Company, Long Beach, California, datelined New York.

62 "Efforts to save dolphins are set by tuna canners," *Wall Street Journal*, April 13, 1990, p. B3.

63 "Big tuna canners act to slow down dolphin killings; 70% of market affected; 3 concerns will also stop buying fish caught in nets that are trapping mammals," by Philip Shabecoff, *New York Times*, April 13, 1990, p. A1.

64 Submission of the government of the Commonwealth of Puerto Rico by Mr. Alfredo Salazar, Jr., Administrator of the Commonwealth Economic Development Administration, before the U.S. International Trade Commission, Investigation 332-313.

65 "Ecologists honored for their work," by Connie Koennen, *Los Angeles Times*, April 22, 1991, p. E1.

66 "Suit is filed to restrict tuna imports," by Michael Parrish, *Los Angeles Times*, June 26, 1990, p. D3.

67 "The Tuna/Porpoise Fishery of the Eastern Tropical Pacific Ocean (ETPO) and its Impact on Relations Between the United States and Mexico," by Franklin Alverson, University of California MEXUS Conference, July 24-25, 1992, San Diego, p. 4.

68 *Dolphins and the Tuna Industry*, National Research Council, Washington, D.C., 1992, p. 48.

69 "Mexico wins battle over US tuna ban, but backs off to save image, trade talks," by David Clark Scott, *Christian Science Monitor*, September 27, 1991, p. 8.

70 "Judge upholds ban on tuna," *New York Times*, January 29, 1992, p. C7.

71 "A Catch-twenty-tuna," by S. Lynne Walker, *San Diego Union-Tribune*, February 9, 1992, p. A3.

72 "Dolphin Study Rejects Ban on Tuna Nets," by Michael Parrish, *Los Angeles Times*, February 28, 1992, p. A1.

73 The coalition consisted of: American Cetacean Society; American Humane Association; American Society for the Prevention of Cruelty to Animals; Animal Protection Institute; Center for Marine Conservation; Cetacean Society International; Committee for Humane Legislation; Defenders of Wildlife; The Dolphin Project; Dolphin Connection; Earthtrust; Earth Island Institute; Environmental Investigation Agency; Friends of Animals; Humane Society of the United States; Humane Society International; International Fund for Animal Welfare; International Wildlife Coalition; Marine Mammal Fund; New England Anti-vivisection Society; Progressive Animal Welfare Society; Society for Animal Protection Legislation; Whale and Dolphin Conservation Society; World Wildlife Fund-US. Conspicuously absent is Greenpeace.

74 Letter from Richard H. Wamhoff, President and Chief Operating Officer, StarKist, Long Beach, California, to Hon. John F. Kerry, U.S. Senate, October 8, 1992, in *Congressional Record*, October 8, 1992.

75 "Distribution and Abundance of Tunas and Tuna/baitfishes in the Gulf of Guinea," by Gilbert Winfield Bane, Jr., unpublished master's thesis, Cornell University, 1961.

76 "Washington Report," *Journal of Commerce*, October 19, 1992. Teresa Platt telephone conversations with Donner's office, November, 1992.

77 The *60 Minutos* announcer should have read, "U.S. *canners now purchase tuna* in the Indian and Atlantic Oceans, claiming they do not cause dolphin deaths." The U.S. fleet fishes in the Western Pacific on skipjack tuna, a fact which scientists stated correctly

later in the program. This initial misreading of the fleet for the canners does not affect the argument of the report, which is otherwise factually correct.

78 See "Tuna Purse Seine and Gill/Drift Net Fisheries in the Oceans of the World and Their Relationship to Tuna/Dolphin, Tuna/Whale and Tuna/Whale Shark Associated Schools," by Franklin G. Alverson, Sección Especializada en Pesca de Atún Programa Atún-Delfin. Cámera Nacional de la Industria Pesquera, Mexico, 1991.

79 Dr. Compean's remarks have been updated with the dolphin release figure for 1992.

80 *60 Minutos*, "La Guerra del Atún" (The Tuna War), broadcast on Mexican television December 1992.

National Toxics Campaign

National Toxics Campaign 1,400 groups; (Founded 1984)
    Annual budget: $1.5 million
            Staff: 35—28 professional, 7 support
        Members: 1,400 labor, environmental and citizen groups
     Tax Status: 501(c)(4)
    Headquarters: 37 Temple Place, 4th Floor
                Boston, Massachusetts 02111
                Phone: (617)232-0327 Fax: (617)232-3945

Economy Trasher Number Twenty-Four. One of the most virulently anti-industry organizations in the entire environmental movement. Also one of the most aggressive in direct anti-industry confrontation tactics. The NTC is the grass roots center of the environmental movement, representing as it does 1,400 separate but similar local groups, each with members who have a personal quarrel with a local industry. It is here in the environmental movement where we see personal belief systems activated most strongly.

The self-righteous zeal of these activists is quite breathtaking and quite immune to reason. National toxics campaign is actually a network of some 100,000 individual members and about 1,400 community and activist groups throughout the United States. You're looking at over a thousand environmental groups in this one organization.[1]

As a group of groups, NTC is adept at finding allies, training leaders, and cementing coalitions. One writer noted, "The National Toxics Campaign usually makes its first contact with a group in one of three ways: staff hear about a toxics problem and approach the community...; a local group calls NTC for help on a particular issue; or John O'Connor, the Campaign's dynamic executive director, comes across a group...on one of his sweeps across the country as a 'roving organizer.' Once first contact is made, the Campaign has 9 regional offices, all of which work with groups in their areas showing people ways of identifying toxic hazards, how to get issues in the media, and ways of fighting local polluters....NTC's main focus, however, is on leadership development."[2]

The NTC is expert at locating health problems, looking around for a nearby industrial operation, then making presumptive assertions that pollution of some kind from the industry caused the health problems. Accused industries trying to prove that they did not cause the health problems find it is virtually impossible—as every student of logic knows, you can never prove a negative. If an industry exists and health problems are found nearby, the industry must have done it, right?[3]

When you take such assertions to court, it is astounding how far you can go— the burden of proof is thrown upon the industry, not the complaining party. And if the NTC can't find real evidence, they sue the industry *for hiding evidence*— without having to prove the evidence was hidden.

For example, the National Toxics Campaign's western office in Denver, Colorado, began assisting the residents of the Friendly Hills subdivision just outside Denver in 1984 to fight Martin Marietta and the Denver Water Board. Anti-industry activists claimed that there were large numbers of deaths, cancers, birth defects, and diseases occurring in the community. They examined the records of Martin Marietta's industrial discharges and tracked every entry of a pollution incident— which the company had dutifully kept since the 1950s. The records did not match those of the Denver Water Board. So, the National Toxics Campaign filed charges against Martin Marietta and the Denver Water Board on behalf of the residents and in early 1990 the U.S. District Court ruled that there was substantial evidence of a conspiracy between the defense contractor and the water board to cover up evidence about the pollutants, thereby depriving the activists of their civil rights.[4]

No proof of causing deaths, cancers, birth defects, diseases. Not even any *evidence* of causing such harms. Not even proof of a *conspiracy*. Just *substantial evidence* of a conspiracy. And that was enough to get a ruling of depriving the activists of their civil rights. The case had not even gone to trial, yet this preliminary ruling was enough to destroy the reputation of an industry and a utility just as badly as if every claim against them had been proven beyond a reasonable doubt.[5]

The tactic of accusing an industry of causing harm just by the fact that it exists has been used to get huge multi-million-dollar settlements from big deep pockets corporations with no evidence at all. The National Toxics Campaign's Texas affiliate, Texans United, brought suit against Exxon USA on behalf of approximately 200 residents of Highlands, Texas alleging the company's Liberty Waste dumpsite was bad *just because it was there*. After lengthy negotiations and reams of studies done by both the National Toxics Campaign and Exxon, the company agreed to an $11 million settlement in 1990. It was cheaper to pay off the accusers than to go to trial.[6]

Confrontation Politics

If the environmental movement can be divided into two factions, one willing to compromise with polluters and one sworn to confrontation, the National Toxics Campaign is the archetype of the confrontationists.

When the Environmental Grantmakers Association accepted Chevron Company into its inner sanctum of high-dollar donors, National Toxics Campaign West Coast director Michael Picker screamed "Blood money!" He was livid with rage that EGA, a group composed of foundation executives who bankroll a wide spectrum of environmental groups and play a key role in determining the tactics and goals of the environmental movement, would allow "the largest industrial air polluter of the San Francisco Bay area" to join. Picker asserted that it was the latest example of how U. S. business plays the old game: If you can't beat 'em, buy 'em.[7]

Picker said, "Chevron is a company that skimped on repairs at its Richmond refinery, resulting in severe toxic emissions to the community. It failed to maintain pressure in its pipes, resulting in burns to workers and a fine by OSHA. It profiteered off the Mideast oil crisis and poured the profits into defeating the Big Green initiative." The Big Green was a voter initiative that would have restructured the failing economy of California to such a drastic extent it lost at the polls by four to one.

National Toxics Campaign is similar in constituency to numerous confrontational groups in the Hazardous Substances and Waste segment of the environmental movement:

Citizens' Clearinghouse for Hazardous Wastes
Budget: $680,000
Staff: 13
Membership: 20,000
Chapters: 20
P.O. Box 926
Arlington, Virginia 22216
Phone: (703)237-2249
Lois Marie Gibbs, Executive Director

CCHW was originally organized around the Love Canal incident in New York. Organizing director Will Collette said of Chevron's admission to EGA that it was "a deliberate effort on the part of large corporate polluters to drive a wedge between mainstream environmentalists and the grass-roots environmental movement, which has given polluters such a headache throughout the eighties. The way I look at it, there are two sources of power, money and people. The grassroots movement has the people, so the corporations are using the money."

The National Toxics Campaign is particularly anti-military. It has devised a direct mail fund raising gimmick they call the Grassroots Environmental Evaluation of Federal Facilities Report Card. This report card rates military bases on base cleanup, toxic use, and their record of informing the public on toxics issues. The report card is part of a membership recruitment package called the Military Toxics Starter Kit to show activists how to organize against military bases and demand change—and raise piles of new membership money for the National Toxics Campaign.[8]

"We have to turn the wastes of war into a war on wastes," said Gary Cohen, NTC policy director.[9]

NTC also bashes America in general, condemning Operation Desert Storm against Iraq and operating a media campaign asserting there were high levels of toxic substances in the Kuwait oil fire smoke that resulted from Iraqi sabotage of the fields during their precipitous retreat. Marco Kaltofen, NTC laboratory director, claimed to have found five toxic hydrocarbons in the smoke from burning oil wells in Kuwait that exceeded American standards. NTC obtained samples taken in Jubail, Saudi Arabia, about 175 miles downwind from the burning wells in Kuwait. While other analyses looked for garden-variety pollutants, such as soot, carbon monoxide and ozone, NTC found 1,2- and 1,4-dichlorobenzene at twice the maximum concentrations allowed in Massachusetts, and diethyl phthalate and dimethyl phthalate, two substances so exotic that no American standards exist. Napthalene was found at levels below American standards. Mr. Kaltofen admitted that short term exposure to these chemicals posed no risk to health, but "chronic exposures could result in human health impact."[10]

After Operation Desert Storm, Cohen said, "We're asking the U.S. Department of Defense to spend $10 billion a year for the next 10 years and launch Operation Toxic Storm." NTC had released a report claiming that 14,000 sites at more than 1,500 military bases nationwide were polluted with everything from solvents, oils and heavy metals to PCBs, photographic chemicals, refrigerants and medical wastes.[11]

National Toxics Coalition forms alliances with larger groups to build its power and credibility. In 1989 NTC joined with Greenpeace USA in threatening to sue the Environmental Protection Agency for what it called "lax regulation of toxic incinerators." Note how the rhetoric identifies the incinerators as "toxic" in the reader's mind. The EPA encouraged incineration as a safe means of disposal, saying it found no evidence of a risk to health or environment. However, NTC called for a moratorium on all new incinerator permits until the EPA further investigated the effects of burning of heavy metals and other substances on the environment and public health.[12]

Stop everything. Turn it all off. Kill jobs. Trash the Economy.

National Toxics Campaign is one group which actively pursues coalitions with Sympathetic Constituency groups in the web of environmental movement interests. For example, NTC in 1991 joined the Biotech Working Group, a coalition of eighteen environmental, farm, consumer and church organizations. It studies the use of biotechnology to make agricultural crops and forest trees genetically more resistant to pests and tries to stop any such improvement. To make their obstructionism sound more palatable to the public, NTC calls such biotechnology "making plants more tolerant of herbicides," playing on fear of chemical pesticides. "Herbicide-tolerant" plants sounds horrifying; "pest-resistant" sounds good. NTC's actual intent is to revoke the 20 percent federal tax credit given to private companies involved in pest resistance genetic research and to pass laws forbidding *all* chemical pesticides. If you have to raise money by scaring people, you do whatever works. NTC is one of the country's worst crop pests.[13]

If you wonder why church organizations belong to this coalition, consider that several denominations, including the Roman Catholic Church in its new 1992 catechism, regard genetic engineering of any sort as a sin.[14]

One of the most disturbing facts to NTC is the good record of industries in complying with water pollution control requirements—so good that now it is municipal sewage treatment plants that have the worst pollution records and are dragging their feet the most. That, of course, defies the anti-capitalist Environmentalist Articles of Faith. Thus, National Toxics Coalition came up with a 1990 report recommending that "industrial polluters" pay a higher rate per gallon of discharge than householders—because pollution control laws finally came home to roost in Boston, where NTC's main offices are located. The Boston Harbor cleanup project was under way at a cost of $6.1 billion when NTC realized that the average Boston household would be paying $1,000 in annual water and sewer fees by 1999 when the project must be completed under the Clean Water Act of 1972. There is no way NTC would ever grasp that householders are polluters, too, or even recognize that what goes down the toilet at home smells as sweet as what goes down the toilet at work—and at work, the stockholders have installed and paid for their water pollution control devices years ago.

Sanford Lewis, NTC staffer and co-author of the report said the municipal authority "should make the polluters pay dearly for their toxics discharge into the sewers." Lewis's "polluters," of course, were only the "top 20 polluting industries" and not those million polluters who regularly take a dump at home.[15]

The National Toxics Campaign assails companies to sign "good neighbor" agreements not to pollute—after carefully studying the technological limits of each company and then writing their agreements deliberately just beyond technical possibility. Companies thick enough to sign such rigged documents uniformly find themselves hauled into court for violating the agreement.[16]

National Toxics Campaign has developed stunning clout in the marketplace. Realizing that grocers were most vulnerable to consumer pressure, they orchestrated media campaigns about pesticides on food that frightened consumers out of their wits.[17]

Five small supermarket chains in the U. S. and Canada—Bread and Circus Wholesale Supermarkets in Massachusetts, Petrini Meat, Inc. in San Rafael, California, Raley's in Sacramento, Abco Markets in Phoenix, and Provigo Inc. in Montreal—caved in to the pressure and announced an agreement with NTC to disclose all pesticides used on fruits and vegetables, and agreed to pressure food growers to eliminate 64 pesticides identified by the EPA as possibly cancer-causing but for which there was no proof. The Environmental Protection Agency called the NTC program "irresponsible," as did food industry trade associations and the National Agricultural Chemicals Association. Using fear to eliminate crop protection chemicals is an outstanding way to Trash the Economy.[18]

It was the year of the Alar scare and the great cyanide grape scare, both of which were rigged to create hysteria.[19] *The Wall Street Journal* responded to the National Toxics Campaign's orchestration of the grocer agreement with a reminder that nature is generous with its own carcinogens and noted, "many environmentalists cling to their theology, which holds that as we move further from some ideal natural state, life becomes more threatened. Given this almost religious belief in nature's goodness, we'd like to pose a philosophical question: How come nobody has explained why a natural carcinogen is morally superior to an artificial one? Indeed, how is it that the urban press's eco-evangelists scarcely acknowledge the existence of natural carcinogens?"[20]

You know the answer to that one. The next year, NTC special projects director Craig Merrilees operated an assault against grocers that sell products which make environmental claims the environmentalists don't agree with. In concert with Greenpeace, Public Interest Research Groups and Clean Water Action, NTC pressured four Western supermarket chains—Ralph's, Raley's in Northern California, Fred Meyer in the Northwest and Abco in Arizona—to set up standards on environmental claims and ask manufacturers to support those claims. Merrilees told the supermarket managers that environmental groups would commission and publish a survey of retailers' efforts dealing with environmental claims. NTC pressured New York Attorney General Robert Abrams to investigate and prosecute false and misleading environmental claims. The prosecutions, of course, would never be made against environmental groups making false environmental alarms.[21]

Yes, Massa.

The central problem of the National Toxics Campaign is its insistence that managing toxic wastes can be *replaced* with reductions at the source. Industries commonly design products for least-input manufacturing as a cost control and design excellence measure; the NTC claim that industries simply don't care how much hazardous material they use in manufacturing is mere rhetoric. "Stopping pollution at its source" is inevitably a political war-cry, and not a technical possibility short of stopping all manufacturing at its source.

National Toxics Campaign's executive director John O'Connor spelled out his group's agenda, which gives us a fair indication that his organization is not trying to clean up pollution, but is playing doctor with your private sector and trying to create his version of Ecotopia. Here are his "four ideas that, if implemented, may save our skin and the planet we live on:"

1) Transition to the carbohydrate economy. "The material basis of society must be changed to a renewable, sustainable, less-polluting form." This means no use of oil, coal and natural gas. Only soybeans, corn, cotton and other plants are to be used as fuel.

2) Pollution prevention: bans and plans. "The worst classes of chemicals must be banned and all emitters of toxic pollution must develop plans to substantially reduce the use of toxic material." The use of chlorinated chemicals and pesticides are to be cut in half by 1995.

3) Superfund for workers. "As we make the transition from a poisonous to a nonpoisonous economy, workers who lose jobs in the transition should be guaranteed income, education, or new jobs."

4) Real sustainable agriculture. "Soil conservation and low-chemical agriculture must be combined with adjustments in farm economics that guarantee farmers 'fair price' at the marketplace."[22]

Yes, Massa.

NTC operates the Citizens' Environmental Laboratory, which provides low-cost testing of samples brought in by activists—if they join the National Toxics Coalition. The lab is equipped to analyze water, soil, air and waste samples and, its literature claims, can quantify 56,000 different pesticides. Its finding are completely objective and unbiased, if you're an anti-industry activist.[23]

Executive director John O'Connor is one of the group's founders, and previously worked for Massachusetts Fair Share and was coauthor of the Massachusetts Right-to-Know law. He wrote *Fighting Toxics: A Manual for Protecting Your Family, Community and Workplace.* His group also publishes *A Practical Guide to Protecting Your Drinking Water; Organizing to Win; Corporate Campaigns; Using the Media;* and *Researching and Obtaining Information.*

NTC operates 10 offices: in Livingston, Alabama; Sacramento and San Francisco, California; Denver, Colorado; Baton Rouge, Louisiana; Litchfield, Maine; Raleigh, North Carolina; Oklahoma City, Oklahoma; Dallas and Houston, Texas. NTC is affiliated with another 501(c)(3) organization, the National Toxics Campaign Fund; with Texans, Unlimited; and with West County Toxics Coalition in California.

NTC's Board of Directors consists of: president Kaye Kiker; vice presidents Ted Smith and Patty Frase; secretary Catherine Garula; and treasurer Richard Regan. Other members include: Marilyn Ayers; Martha Bailey; Norine Brodeur; Peter Cervantes-Gautchi; Pam Erikson; Irene Gillis; Charles Griffith; Grace Klinger; Pam Tau Lee; Lauri Maddy; Sandra Mayeaux; Richard Moore; Patsy Oliver: Diane Takvorian; Cora Tucker; Baldemar Velasquez; and Ernie Witt.

Compton Foundation, Inc. gave $20,000 in 1989 for Citizens Environment Laboratory.

The Educational Foundation of America gave $75,000 in 1990 for waste management and reduction project.

Island Foundation, Inc. gave $10,000 in 1989 for toxic waste research and public education of pollution sources and prevention around Boston Harbor.

Charles Stewart Mott Foundation gave $40,000 in 1990 to provide low-cost, reliable testing for community groups endangered by toxic contamination.

Jessie Smith Noyes Foundation, Inc. gave $60,000 in 1990, a 2-year grant to protect groundwater and encourage pollution prevention in the South U.S. by strengthening state-based organizing and advocacy; plus $60,000 in 1990, another 2-year grant to protect groundwater from toxics produced, used, and disposed of by the Department of Defense and its military contractors by strengthening grassroots advocacy and organizing to improve policy; plus $50,000 in 1990, yet another 2-year grant for training and skills building among organizers working in communities of color in U.S.; plus $20,000 in 1990, yet a fourth 2-year grant to strengthen grassroots and national activists by convening key networks concerned about military toxics produced, used, and disposed of by the Departments of Energy and Defense to improve national policy and federal compliance. A total of $190,000 in grants in 1990.

Public Welfare Foundation, Inc. gave $75,000 in 1990 to provide grassroots groups with technical assistance in development and implementation of toxic prevention policies.

Z. Smith Reynolds Foundation, Inc. gave $20,000 in 1989 for North Carolina Toxics Prevention project which will provide organizing and technical assistance to grassroots group, build statewide network of community organizations working on toxics issues, assist in developing statewide policies for waste reduction and toxics and produce report on North Carolina companies that emit ozone-destroying chemicals.

Rockefeller Family Fund, Inc. gave $30,000 in 1989 for National Campaign Against Toxic Hazards, which organizes at national, state and local levels to shift debate on toxic issues from control to prevention strategy.

Town Creek Foundation, Inc. gave $10,000 in 1990.

The Winston Foundation for World Peace gave $12,500 in 1989 to investigate and publicize radioactive-waste scandals at Rocky Flats nuclear weapons plant.

National Toxics Campaign.

Job killers.

Economy Trashers.

National Toxics Campaign—Footnotes

1 *Public Interest Profiles, 1992-1993*, p. 536.

2 *Making A Difference*, Summer 1989.

3 "EPA cites 10 billion lbs. of toxic pollution: ecology activists to use report as an organizing tool," by Joe Feuerhard, *National Catholic Reporter*, April 28, 1989, p. 6.

4 *The Nature Directory* by Susan Lanier-Graham, Walker and Company, New York 1991, p. 110. See also *A Consumer's Guide to Protecting Your Drinking Water*, National Toxics Campaign, Boston.

5 "Report calls military nation's worst polluter," *New York Times*, March 17, 1991, p. 18.

6 *Fighting Toxics: A Manual for Protecting Your Family, Community and Workplace*, John O'Connor, National Toxics Campaign, Boston.

7 "Oiling the Works," by Eve Pell, *Mother Jones*, March / April 1991, p. 39.

8 "Huge Cleanup Awaits Arms Plants," by Brad Knickerbocker, *Christian Science Monitor*, March 15, 1991, p. 3.

9 *E Magazine*, July / August 1990.

10 "High Levels of Toxic Substances Found in Kuwait Oil Fire Smoke," by Matthew L. Wald, *New York Times*, July 16, 1991, p. A3.

11 "Huge Cleanup Awaits Arms Plants," *Christian Science Monitor*, March 15, 1991.

12 "Sharp Curb on Incineration of Toxic Waste Sought," *New York Times*, August 18, 1989, p. A16.

13 "The attraction is chemical," by Jim Schwab, *Nation*, October 16, 1989, p. 416.

14 "A new Catholic catechism," by Alan Riding, *New York Times*, November 17, 1992.

15 "Harbor Cleanup Moves Forward," by Catherine Foster, *Christian Science Monitor*, February 23, 1990, p. 6.

16 "Critics Rap Incinerator Proposals," by Catherine Foster, *Christian Science Monitor*, August 23, 1989.

17 *E Magazine*, January / February 1990.

18 "Grocers Plan Their Own Ban On Pesticides," by Rose Gutfeld, *Wall Street Journal*, September 11, 1989, p. B1.

19 *Fear of Food*, by Andrea Arnold, Free Enterprise Press, Bellevue, Washington, 1990.

20 "The State of Nature," editorial, *Wall Street Journal*, September 22, 1989, p. A12.

21 "Group to Target Environmental Safety Claims," by Jesus Sanchez and Michael Parrish, *Los Angeles Times*, April 13, 1990, p. D1.

22 "Toxic Logic," by John O'Connor, *Mother Jones*, April / May 1990, p. 49.

23 *Researching and Obtaining Information*, National Toxics Campaign, Boston, no date.

Environimental Action ▇▇▇▇▇▇▇▇▇▇▇

Environmental Action, Inc. / Environmental Action Foundation (Founded 1970)

Annual budget:	$1.3 million
Staff:	22 total—19 professional, 3 support
Members:	16,000 members
Tax Status:	Environmental Action, 501(c)(4)
	EA Foundation, 501(c)(3)
	EnAct/PAC (founded 1980), political action committee
Headquarters:	1525 New Hampshire Avenue, NW
	Washington, D.C. 20036
	Phone: (202)745-4870 Fax: (202)745-4880

Economy Trasher Number Twenty-Five. Environmental Action was founded "by the organizers of the first Earth Day, held on April 22 1970, with the mission of carrying on the spirited citizen activism that sprung up around the nation."[1]

Environmental Action may be taking a little more credit than it is due, even though EA folks did help staff the National Teach-In Office on P Street in Washington back in 1970. Leafing through the leftovers from 1970, however, one has trouble believing *anybody* organized The First National Environmental Teach-In, which was the official name of the first Earth Day. Anti-Vietnam War campus teach-ins provided the model. College ecology groups with nifty names such as Nature's Conspiracy and Foes of Pollution (FOP) had been active for more than a year on dozens of campuses. The University of Michigan at Ann Arbor sprouted a group called ENACT (Environmental Action for Survival Committee) which scheduled its teach-in for March rather than April and by dint of being ready sooner, its plan became the "Blueprint for a Teach-In" that spread all over the U.S.[2]

Some say the idea for Earth Day actually originated with Senator Gaylord Nelson (D-Wisconsin), now counselor to the Wilderness Society, who first conceived the event as an environmental teach-in along the lines of the anti-Vietnam War teach-ins. It is also rumored that part of the funding for the teach-in came from a $200,000 personal grant from Robert O. Anderson, who carries a lot of Rockefeller baggage—he was then president of Atlantic Richfield Corporation, president of the Aspen Institute for Humanistic Studies, and was close with Robert Maynard Hutchins, a zero-population growth guru at the University of Chicago.[3]

But when you look back at radical chic writings from the era, you can find a lot of environmental groups cleverly pandering to campus activists well before the fact—Ballantine Books rushed into print with a Friends of the Earth book edited by Garrett De Bell, *The Environmental Handbook*, and Pocket Books hauled up the Sierra Club's medley *Ecotactics* just in time for the teach-in.[4]

Thousands of Americans participated in environmental rallies, demonstrations, and other activities, among them the destruction and burial of a new car in a symbolic effort to bury what they viewed as America's polluting, materialistic lifestyle. Not everyone went along with the jollity: a group of black students picketed the festivities saying that resources, instead of being wasted in such a conspicuous fashion, should be used to improve the lot of the poor.[5]

According to Environmental Action's tenth anniversary newsletter, its original express purpose was "to lobby Congress."[6] Environmental Action was also the first environmental group to promote eco-terrorism and violence against industry—long before Earth First! came on the scene. Shortly after its inception, EA sponsored an "Ecotage" contest to compile vandal tactics against industry and in 1971 published the Pocket Book *Ecotage!,* which, among many other cute tricks, recommended dumping a corporation's effluent on the white rug in the lobby of its headquarters, sealing off factory chimneys and the like. Ecotage was somewhat whimsically defined in this manual as "the branch of tactical biology that deals with the relationship between living organisms and their technology. It usually refers to tactics which can be executed without injury to life systems." *Chicago Daily News* columnist Mike Royko lionized "The Fox" of Kane County, Illinois, for sabotaging steel mill drains—an ecoteur widely believed to be an Environmental Action leader.

A typical entry in *Ecotage!* came from a California group:

> The best way to slow down or stop a road or a recreation development is to disrupt the survey.... Tools needed are hammers, small folding shovels, and cut brush to erase the original survey sight. If the road is going through private property, you must be careful not to get caught trespassing and be very sure not to cut fences or leave gates open. Slick-bottomed boots should be worn so that no identifiable foot marks are left. If the road is going through public lands, they cannot keep you out; just be careful no one sees you carrying your equipment in. Backpacks are very good for carrying tools in and stakes out of the area....
>
> Each time part of the project has to be resurveyed, the costs go up. If you are careful and quick, you can tie up a project for many months and buy time for other actions that will stop it.[7]

It is hard to imagine a more straightforward statement of intent to trash the economy. EA's public statements since then have tried to put on a less malignant face.

EA was founded as "a two-part experiment," said a newsletter. "First, we wanted to find out if a citizens lobby could affect the government's decisions. Second, we wanted to experiment with a more 'humane' office structure—no bosses, no secretaries and shared decision making. Thus, we don't have a chairman of the board. In fact, we don't have an outside board of directors. All staff members are directors and each has an equal vote at weekly staff meetings. We want to share this information because we're proud of our non-hierarchical structure. We think it's helped us to be more productive and satisfied with our work." That bit of eco-socialist chic didn't last long. EA abandoned its egalitarian pay scale and decision-making approach in favor of a staff hierarchy and pay scale like most other organizations. But the change didn't rate headlines in the newsletter.[8]

EA's Congressional agenda from the beginning was a scatter-formation of left-wing issues: They lobbied against the mobile MX missile and nuclear power, they opposed budget cuts for Amtrak, they "busted open" the Highway Trust Fund and diverted appropriations to mass transit, they pushed for a national bottle bill to require deposits on returnable bottles, they pushed for heavier penalties against industry in amendments to the Occupational Safety and Health Act, they lobbied to impose fines and prison sentences on clean air and toxic waste violators, they tried to ban all crop protection chemicals. If it could possibly hurt the economy, Environmental Action has done it.

The constituency of Environmental Action is particularly vigorous in trashing the economy. Resources for the Future, the Washington, D.C.-based think tank, did a study of six environmental groups and found that members of Environmental Action were the most politically active against industry. Seventy-one percent said they had written or called their representative in Congress on an environmental issue during the preceding year.

Environmental Action rates high in intelligent attack methods. Its most famous "stunt of the month" technique was established in 1972: digging into legislative voting records and company pollution records and publishing lists labeled "the dirty dozen."[9] The Dirty Dozen campaign is a biennial effort in which EA sends full-time organizers to 12 Congressional districts to help defeat the incumbents by publicizing their "atrocious" voting records. As the *Washington Post* commented, "No member of Congress wants to end up on Environmental Action's 'Dirty Dozen' list of worst voting records."[10]

A 1977 spin-off of the Dirty Dozen was the Filthy Five campaign which attacks the steel, chemical, paper, coal, utility, and other industries. "Charter members" of the group were the American Petroleum Institute, Manufacturing Chemists Association, American Iron and Steel Institute, American Paper Institute, and Edison Electric Institute. By destroying just these five sectors, Environmental Action reasoned that it could bring down the entire American economy. Every American uses petroleum products, chemicals, steel, paper and electricity every day.

EA is also very good at getting the taxpayer to finance their attacks on industry: One researcher used the Freedom of Information Act to ferret out at least $538,466 in grants from the federal Environmental Protection Agency and Department of Energy during 1979-1981 to Environmental Action Foundation in single amounts as high as $179,644. However, the purposes of these huge grants were not made public. Taxpayer-funded environmentalism by the dark of night.[11]

Corporate and foundation funding also supports Environmental Action. R. Shep Melnick, associate professor of politics at Brandeis University, wrote in *Philanthropy*, "A vast array of environmental groups [including] Environmental Action has arisen to challenge the power and policies of business. These groups provide members of Congress with new issues, offer reporters dramatic stories and pungent quotations, help organize local citizen groups, and file lawsuit after lawsuit. Their effect on environmental policy has been enormous. And many of these environmental organizations have received significant support from foundations and even corporations. Indeed, philanthropists deserve part of the credit for their vitality. Hence, they must examine critically the current role of these organizations."[12]

Environmental Action Executive Director Ruth N. Caplan (salary $35,000) took her post in 1985, rising from a position as EA's lobbyist on federal energy matters. She is also executive director of the Environmental Action Foundation. Before coming to EA, she served as a consultant to the New York State Consumer Protection Board and as chair of the Sierra Club National Energy Committee. She holds a Masters in Public Administration from Syracuse University.

Caplan brings a unique perspective to the environmental movement. "As environmental and consumer issues merge, an organizational marriage, despite turf differences, may follow," she said.

The *Consumer Affairs Letter* (March 1990) wrote that hers may be "the only environmental group to embrace consumerism as part of its self-defined mission.... Caplan, who has been a major player in the Energy Conservation Coalition along with Steve Brobeck of the Consumer Federation of America, called for more coalition building among groups."[13]

EA works in conjunction with its non-membership foundation and its political action committee, EnAct/PAC. Environmental Action is a membership lobbying group organized under Section 501(c)(4) of the U.S. Tax Code, and contributions to it are therefore not tax deductible. Environmental Action Foundation, on the other hand, is organized as a 501(c)(3) educational foundation, and contributions to it are tax deductible. Tax law requires that such organizations remain strictly separate. All 501(c)(3) organizations must file with the Internal Revenue Service an annual Form 990 "Return of Organization Exempt from Income Tax" detailing information about contributions, income, expenditures, and grants.

Even though the 1983 Environmental Action Foundation Form 990 lists Environmental Action as a grant recipient, it claimed it has "no relationship." However, despite this disclaimer, in 1982 EA stated that "Our sister organization, the Environmental Action Foundation...engages in education and organizing while we carry out lobbying and political action. The tax laws prevent the two organizations from merging, but our programs in energy and pollution control are complementary; the onslaught of the Reagan years has led us to work even more closely together than in the past." Tax law also forbids 501(c)(4) lobbying organizations from participating in political action to influence elections. Perhaps the IRS should ask Environmental Action exactly what its statement means.

EAF is affiliated with the Energy Conservation Coalition. EA publishes a bimonthly magazine *Environmental Action* printed "by labor union on recycled paper." Oh, so politically correct. *Power Line* is EAF's bimonthly newsjournal and *Waste Line* its quarterly newsletter.

Environmental Action gets its money from membership dues (42 percent); contributions and bequests (32 percent); educational grants (17 percent); publications (3 percent); and other (6 percent) including peddling posters, decals, and T-shirts.

Direct mail is the lifeblood of Environmental Action, as with most environmental organizations. With an annual drop-off rate of 30 percent, EA has to recruit 5,000 members a year just to stay in the same place. Ruth Caplan estimates that her group has lost 10,000 members in a five year period just because of its failure to find the winning combination of direct mail pitches and lists. "Some of it," she told *Mother Jones*, "is just luck."[14]

Environmental Action Foundation gets its money from program grants (67 percent); membership dues (16 percent); Combined Federal Campaign (11 percent); publications (4 percent); and other (2 percent).

EnAct/PAC "supports pro-environmental candidates." EnAct/PAC states that it "does not make dollar contributions to campaigns." However, Federal Election Commission reports show that EnAct/PAC makes substantial election cycle disbursements, $26,365 in 1985-86, for example.

The staff of Environmental Action is its Board of Directors. They refused to say who is on the staff. The Board of Directors of Environmental Action Foundation consists of David Cohen; Nancy Hirsh; James Overton; David Post; Andrew Stevenson.

These philanthropists helped Environmental Action Foundation trash the economy:

Bauman Family Foundation, unspecified amount.

Beldon Fund, unspecified amount.

Bread and Roses Community Fund, unspecified amount.

Bright Charitable Trust, unspecified amount.

Compton Foundation, Inc. gave $25,000 in 1989.

Fund for Friendship and Justice, unspecified amount.

Gund Foundation, unspecified amount.

John A. Harris IV, unspecified amount.

Jewish Communal Fund of New York, unspecified amount.

Joyce Foundation, unspecified amount.

McColl-Batts Foundation, unspecified amount.

McIntosh Foundation, unspecified amount.

The Overbrook Foundation gave $10,000 in 1989.

Public Welfare Foundation, Inc. gave $35,000 in 1990 for Toxics Education, Action and Mobilization Campaign to get facilities using toxic chemicals to comply with reporting requirements of federal law and to reduce use of those chemicals.

Ann R. Roberts, unspecified amount.

Alida Rockefeller, unspecified amount.

Rockefeller Family Fund, Inc. gave $25,000 in 1989 for general support for public education and advocacy on plastics reduction, especially in the South.

Tides Foundation, unspecified amount.

Town Creek Foundation gave $10,000 in 1990.

Working Assets, unspecified amount.[15]

Environmental Action / Environmental Action Foundation.
Job killers.
Economy trashers.

Environmental Action—Footnotes

1 Environmental Action membership brochure.
2 *Ecotactics: The Sierra Club Handbook for Environment Activists*, edited by John G. Mitchell and Constance L. Stallings, Pocket Books, New York, 1970.
3 Personal conversations by Ron Arnold with 1970 Earth Day organizers.
4 *The Environmental Handbook, prepared for the first national environmental teach-in*, edited by Garrett De Bell, Ballantine Books, Inc., New York, 1970.
5 *Progress and Privilege: America in the Age of Environmentalism*, William Tucker, Garden City, Doubleday, 1982, p. 37.
6 "Happy Birthday to Us," *Environmental Action*, April 1980, p. 2.
7 *Ecotage!*, edited by the staff of Environmental Action, Pocket Books, New York, 1971, p. 87.
8 *Protecting the Environment*, Jo Kwong Echerd, Capital Research Center, p. 129.
9 *Washington Times*, April 19, 1990.
10 *Washington Post*, April 19, 1990.
11 *Protecting the Environment*, Jo Kwong Echerd, Capital Research Center, p. 129.
12 *Philanthropy*, Philanthropic Roundtable, March-April, 1990.
13 *Consumer Affairs Letter*, May 1990.
14 "With Friends Like These..." by Paul Rauber, *Mother Jones*, November 1986, p. 47.
15 Sources: *National Guide to Funding for the Environment & Animal Welfare*, The Foundation Center; Environmental Action Foundation Form 990 for years 1983-1989; all entries of "unspecified amount" listed in *Protecting the Environment*, Jo Kwong Echerd, Capital Research Center, p. 129.

Non-Membership Organizations

Five important non-membership environmental groups also do their best to trash the economy with conferences, studies, and other intellectual assaults:

World Resources Institute (Founded 1982)
Annual budget: $10.0 million
Staff: 98 total
Tax Status: (501)(c)(3)
Headquarters: 1709 New York Avenue, NW
7th Floor
Washington, D.C. 20006
Phone: (202)638-6300 Fax: (202)638-0036

The richest of the nonmembership Economy Trashers. An artifact of the John D. and Catherine T. MacArthur Foundation with substantial financial and policy participation by the Rockefeller Brothers Fund and its directors. It is a research organization engaged in "policy research and analysis addressed to global resource and environmental issues," according to the *Research Centers Directory, 17th Edition - 1993.*

The areas of study of the World Resources Institute perhaps offers us the most transparent view into the agenda of the Global Interventionist Axis: "freshwater resources, agricultural lands and desertification, genetic diversity and species conservation, tropical deforestation, fisheries and ocean resources, inadvertent climate modification, (including buildup of carbon dioxide in the atmosphere), ozone depletion, energy resources and nonfuel minerals, multipollutants in the atmosphere, resource management needs of Africa, role of economic incentives and subsidies in shaping resource management in less developed countries, impact of the debt crisis on resource management programs in less developed nations, technology transfer, and loss of plant and animal habitats."

This menu is sufficiently broad to entangle any nation, developed or undeveloped, in a web of unrealistic obligations which would compromise their independence, their productivity and their dignity. The Institute generally argues through its key research leaders that national economies must be controlled by interventionists and that natural resources should not be used at all.[1] The Institute's highly impressive studies generally ignore the costs of environmentalism, the value of private property and individual liberty.[2] The intellect this Institute brings to bear to stop development throughout the world is equaled only by its financing.

The World Resources Institute has enjoyed enormous financial support from the major American internationalist foundations, including two huge grants from the MacArthur Foundation in the late 1980s, one for $10 million, the other for $15 million, plus an $800,000 grant from the Andrew K. Mellon Foundation. The Institute's literature says "Core financial support provided through a grant from the John D. and Catherine T. MacArthur Foundation," and identifies its sources of support as "foundations, industry, U.S. and foreign governments, international agencies, and individual gifts."

President James Gustave Speth was formerly chairman of the U.S. Council on Environmental Quality and chairman of the President's Task Force on Global Resources and Environment. The revolving door again. Out of government and into the environmental movement. Gus Speth was once a professor of law at Georgetown University, and was a cofounder of the Natural Resources Defense Council. Speth got his undergraduate and law degrees from Yale University and earned a B. Litt. in economics from Balliol College, Oxford University, where he was a Rhodes Scholar. If the world had to be divided into two halves, Dummies and No Dummies, this guy is No Dummy. He is without doubt one of the most effective environmentalists alive and one of the most skilled Economy Trashers. To boot, he's a Laurance Rockefeller protégé and sits on the board of directors of the Natural Resources Defense Council and the Environmental Law Institute.

Speth directs a staff of 35 research professionals, 30 supporting professionals, 5 officers and 28 support and clerical. His organization maintains a library of 10,000 volumes on the environment and natural resources run by librarian Sue Terry.

The interventionist ideology of the Institute is virtually a carbon copy of the Rockefeller Brothers' Fund environmental program, "One World: Sustainable Resource Use." The Institute's researchers are very intelligent and take pains to misdirect attention away from their severe biases against market economies, private property ownership, population growth, technological development and individual liberty. The Institute's studies drown the reader in stories of resource abuse so intently that no room is left to appreciate industrial civilization's growth.[3]

For example, in a brilliant article published in *Scientific American*, Institute research director on economics and the environment Robert Repetto demonstrates how "A country can cut down its forests, erode its soils, pollute its aquifers and hunt its wildlife and fisheries to extinction, but its measured income is not affected as these assets disappear," with the stunning conclusion that "Impoverishment is taken for progress."[4]

Having created a universe of discourse based upon those assumptions, Dr. Repetto trashes classical and neoclassical economists by complaining they did not consider "externalities" such as pollution and resource depletion as an economic cost. In fact, he is characterizing the conversion of natural objects into usable resources as "destruction" and demanding that national accounts subtract a damage quotient from the productivity gained.

The idea of "taking account" of resource depletion in the measurement of a nation's economy is the central thrust of WRI's current programs. This is the technical side of the "sustainable development" slogan being used as a method to stop all population growth and economic development.[5]

By boring in on such arguments as "Deforestation has destroyed more than a quarter of Costa Rica's remaining forest since 1970. The loss of this asset has damaged the nation's earning potential, especially as the value of some tree species has quadrupled in recent decades," Dr. Repetto convinces us that rapacious industries have ruined Costa Rica, reaping resources at unsustainable rates and convincing us that this is a capital loss resulting in a reduction in income. His argument is hypnotic.

Almost literally: it rivets our attention on maps and graphs so effectively that we lose consciousness of the flaws in his tale. He enthralls us with the notion of sustainability. He tells us that while we may want the wood to be in our barn rather than standing in the forest, once it has entered the economy with the value of a barn, we do not subtract the value of the tree that is no longer standing in the forest from our economy.

Wait a minute, Toto. I don't think we're in Costa Rica anymore.

No, it's Ecotopia. It's where you have to pay twice for every natural resource you use. Once for the labor and capital to get the natural object into the economy so you can use it, and once again to satisfy an environmentalist who wants to play doctor with your private sector.

Dr. Repetto makes us forget our common sense.

The price we pay for the tree is a direct measure of how much we're willing to have a hole in the forest where the tree used to be, which Dr. Repetto is not able to accept as an economic decision. The cost of a tree from an industrial tree farm includes the cost of management—replanting, fire protection for the new forest, foresters to tend the regrowing forest, training new loggers to harvest the new trees when they come mature in thirty years or so, and all the other trappings of good conservation.

If the tree had any value just standing in the forest that really mattered to the economy of a nation like Costa Rica, or anyplace else, someone would buy it on an open market and keep it for its intrinsic value—without fobbing the cost of maintenance off onto government through slick debt-for-nature swaps or outright government ownership, thus forcing all the taxpayers to keep it there whether they wanted to or not. Or the government would simply put the tree in a "patrimony account" as France does with certain natural resources. Dr. Repetto's notions of sustainability totally blank out the market economy. He never lets us see that rather vital fact.

But let's ask ourselves: What happened to the land that was deforested? What happened after the trees were gone? Dr. Repetto doesn't say. But he leaves us with the impression that it was simply abandoned to soil erosion, wrack and ruin.

In fact, most of it is regrowing trees vigorously under industrial management practices, but the value of those new trees is absent from Dr. Repetto's complaints and calculations. Some tracts are growing trees for pulp mills using a tropical variety that matures to market size in only eight years, and can sustain enormous production in eight year rotations forever, but Dr. Repetto doesn't seem to think pulp and paper are important, even though his research career is totally dependent upon cutting trees to make pulp and paper to give him something on which to write his condemnations of the forest products industry.

In addition, a smaller fraction of that deforested land has become farms, orchards and plantations of cash crops under private ownership. Dr. Repetto does not include the value of those crops or the capital asset value of the private property constituted by those farms. What's more, a remaining fraction of that deforested land is included in new towns and cities. Dr. Repetto does not include the tax base this land creates, or ground rents, or capital asset values of urban real estate.

In other words, Dr. Repetto totally condemns anything that smacks of capitalism, private property and individual liberties. He gives us ideological arguments that recount the details of deforestation with no context. He doesn't want to create a new market in privately owned and managed nature preserves, he wants to force everybody to pay for his moral and aesthetic preferences. And yet the glittering generalities and scary buzzwords liberally sprinkled through his masterful article— "sustainability," "external liabilities," "rapid erosion," "resource depletion"—give us the impression that Dr. Repetto has seen a new, bigger global context, has seen through old capitalist blinders to a new understanding. Lenin gave us that impression, too.

Well, indeed Dr. Repetto has, but he doesn't tell us that what he has seen is the truth that if you want to control an economy by non-market means such as propaganda and command-and-control government regulation, you had better produce very seductive propaganda and very compelling reasons to install command-and-control government regulation.

And Dr. Repetto does not even bring up the use of non-renewable resources such as petroleum and other fuel minerals which by definition cannot be sustained indefinitely. Oil pools are finite and we will run out someday. The question is: Shall we use these resources in an open market from one generation to the next so that actual supply and demand governs oil prices over time, or shall we let environmentalists rule resource use with artificial restraints, stopping new exploration to create artificial scarcity and then doling out smidgins of artificially high priced oil to each of several successive generations so that all are equally poor? Dr. Repetto doesn't ask that question.

The World Resources Institute is expert at building the intellectual framework required to convince mass audiences that we are entering an environmental crisis. Their numerous policy analyses all show how bad things are going to be. They produce dozens of research reports every year, each overwhelmingly professional, technical and convincing. The conclusion, of course, is that they, having seen the problems before the rest of us, are perfectly suited to administer all these resources for all mankind.

Whoops. Wait a minute. Maybe we missed something in there. Wasn't individual choice part of that equation once?

In 1992 the Institute released a report calling for a vast American tax structure called "Green Fees," environmental taxes on fossil fuels, household waste and traffic congestion that could remove $100 billion to $150 billion from Americans' pockets "to stimulate the economy." The logic is not very logical, but Institute director Gus Speth put it this way: "We can shift some of the tax burden in America from the things we want to encourage, like working, saving and investing, onto the things we want to discourage, like pollution, inefficiency and congestion."

The study was led by two Institute staffers, Robert Repetto, whom we have already met, and Roger Dower. They calculated the effects of Green Fees on the American economy and concluded:

A nationwide program of curbside recycling and a pay-by-the-bag system for household waste disposal could generate annual revenue of $6.3 billion and a net saving of $432 million after payment of recycling costs.

A fuels' tax based on carbon content could bring in $35 billion yearly and provide the United States its least expensive method of reducing carbon-dioxide emissions.

Rush-hour congestion tolls could not only ease traffic jams but produce revenue of $98 billion per year.

Dower said of his study, "A better system could place more of the tax burden on activities that make the economy unproductive and that should be discouraged: resource waste, pollution and congestion, for example." Dower estimated that if all his Green Fee recommendations were enforced, they could account for 10 percent of U.S. revenue.

Just what we needed. More taxes. To stimulate the economy. The Clinton recipe.

Of course, the study did not calculate the direct damage to the economy such a system would wreak, such as millions of marginally employed people being priced out of their job by stiff commute fees—low-wage burger flippers, for example. Or those odd little costs of conservation such as saving on water at home—the lowered water flow very often results in the accumulation of debris resulting in clogged kitchen sink drain pipes and big plumbing bills—an environmentalist's idea of stimulating the economy.

Among the World Resources Institute's mind-warping Economy Trashers are:

A study that said World Bank and International Monetary Fund lending policies contribute to the environmental crisis—because they don't tie funding to population control requirements.[6]

A recommendation by Institute vice president Jessica Matthews that oil prices be artificially raised to curb U.S. demand. Playing doctor with your private sector.[7]

A report which asserted that federal farm policies reward practices that harm the environment, i.e., they still allow pesticides and other crop protection chemicals to be used.[8]

A study asserting that timber harvest constituted depletion of natural resources in pursuit of rapid economic growth and should be stopped.[9]

A study claiming that fuel efficiency in new cars was being negated by the glut of cars and trucks, so that ever tougher emissions standards should be imposed until it destroys the car and truck market. The report's two authors, staffers James J. Mackenzie and Michael P. Walsh, concluded "that tougher fuel economy standards are needed along with higher fuel prices to help control consumption."[10]

To help control consumption. Think about that phrase. It's telling you something. Two guys who work in a Washington, D.C. think tank pulling down bigtime salaries and rolling in lush budgets want to control your consumption. They want to control your consumption of transportation by artificially pricing you out of the market. Their moral and aesthetic preferences shall rule over your individual decisions, over your ability to make decisions, your power of choice, your dignity. You like that, don't you?

A World Resources Institute study blamed the Third World for contributing to global warming through burning of rice fields, clearing forests for agriculture to grow food, urging an end to economic growth.[11]

An environmental study claimed that pesticides cause illness to farmers and farm laborers, and their use should be stopped.[12]

A large report stated that humans were totally destroying the environment.[13]

The Institute recommended a carbon tax on fossil fuels to cut carbon dioxide emissions, tied to carbon content—despite other studies indicating that a carbon tax large enough to achieve carbon dioxide control would reduce productivity and the gross national product.[14]

Executive director Gus Speth told an executive group they would be forced to put the environment on their agenda or be forced out of business.[15]

Engineering global social change is a difficult task requiring patience and foresight. WRI has it in spades. Gus Speth realizes his movement's goals will not be achieved overnight. He said of the 1992 Earth Summit in Rio de Janiero, "It is not precisely what happens in Rio that's critical, it's Earth Summit process, beginning now and going maybe two years after, where a lot of proposals are being surfaced, a lot of governments are facing up to the things they haven't heard about before" that will be critical to a change in thinking about the way environmental problems are handled internationally.

Speth organized the New World Dialogue, a group of 25 prominent Western Hemisphere politicians, economists, environmentalists and businessmen in 1991, which released its model for the international imposition of environmental restrictions, largely based on doomsday assumptions about global warming. The model is called The New World Compact and calls for "eight multilateral initiatives to protect forests, increase energy efficiency, slow pollution, reduce poverty, stabilize population growth, enhance scientific and technical capacity, promote trade and investment, and provide financial resources."

Michael Patrick, a University of Virginia professor of environmental sciences who has been one of the chief debunkers of the global warming theory, dismissed the compact as ideological garbage.[16]

"This is one of a series of documents to shame the US into assisting in a massive wealth transfer and there will be more as we pass the Rio Summit," said Patrick.

"I ask how much would there be to this report if there were not a popular vision that climatic apocalypse is at hand," Patrick said. "I suspect it wouldn't stand up."

The World Resources Institute's board of Directors is comprised of chairman Matthew Nimetz; vice chairman John E. Cantlon; and other members: John H. Adams (Natural Resource Defense Council); Robert O. Anderson; Robert O. Blake; John E. Bryson; Pamela G. Carlton; Ward B. Chamberlin; Richard M. Clarke; Edwin C. Cohen; Louisa C. Duemling; Alice F. Emerson; John Firor; Michio Hashimoto; Cynthia R. Helms; Curtis A. Hessler; Martin Holdgate; Thomas E.

Lovejoy (Smithsonian Institution); C. Payne Lucas; Alan R. McFarland, Jr.; Robert S. McNamara; Scott McVay; Paulo Nogueria-Neto; Thomas R. Odhiambo; Saburo Okita; Ruth Patrick; Alfred M. Rankin; Roger Sant; James Gustave Speth; M.S. Swaminathan; Mostafa K. Tolba; Russell E. Train (World Wildlife Fund); Alvaro L. Urquidi; and George M. Woodwell.

World Resources Institute received grants from the following:

Compton Foundation, Inc. gave $25,000 in 1989 "for research project, Redefining Peace."

Geraldine R. Dodge Foundation, Inc. gave $24,000 in 1989 "to complete third volume of Guides to the Environment, series of short action-oriented books aimed a dispelling confusion about global climate change, deforestation and energy."

The Ford Foundation gave $100,000 in 1990, a 4-year grant, "for two issues of World Resources, series of reports focusing on national and global environment and sustainable development."

German Marshall Fund of the United States gave $37,500 in 1989 "for conference in Europe on approaches linking Third World debt relief to conservation. Grant shared with Conservation Foundation."

The Joyce Foundation gave $60,000 in 1990 "to complete and publish research on economics of sustainable agriculture."

Joyce Mertz-Gilmore Foundation gave $40,000 in 1989 "for Solving the Greenhouse Warming Problem: Building Consensus for Action project."

Charles Stewart Mott Foundation gave $500,000 in 1990 "for Institute's Global Challenge Endowment Fund, established through $15 million MacArthur Foundation challenge grant;" plus $45,000 in 1990 "to strengthen institutional capacities of developing-country nongovernmental organizations and other indigenous groups."

The Overbrook Foundation gave $15,000 in 1989.

The Pew Charitable Trusts gave $75,000 in 1990 "for From the Ground Up program to increase capacity of indigenous and foreign institution to foster sustainable development in Africa."

Rockefeller Brothers Fund gave $300,000 in 1990 "to enable economists in Mexico and India to collaborate with World Resources Institute on introducing into national income accounts adjustments that reflect natural resource exploitation."

The Florence and John Schumann Foundation gave $75,000 in 1989 "to produce series of laymen's guides to environment;" another $25,000 in 1989 "for planning costs of project to develop environmental indicators."

Public Welfare Foundation, Inc. gave $100,000 in 1990 "to provide policymakers around world with information and support regarding efforts to slow global warming."

Resources for the Future (Founded 1952)
             Annual budget: $7.8 million
                     Staff: 85 total
               Tax Status: (501)(c)(3)
            Headquarters: 1616 P Street, NW
                              Washington, D.C. 20036
                              Phone: (202)328-5000 Fax: (202)939-3460

RFF is less of an Economy Trasher than most in this book, doing a great deal of quite objective research without people-bashing. However, the group engages in occasional advocacy with a point of view heavily influenced by the big money interests, currently the Mellon Money Axis because of personal connections between their leaders—no different from the usual Malthusians—and has done its share of thoroughgoing Economy Trashing.

The origins of Resources for the Future are virtually a miniature of movement dynamics: it coalesced from numerous forces all going more or less in the same direction. But the driving force was Horace M. Albright, the second Director of the National Park Service (1929-1933) and later executive of U.S. Potash Company (see Nature Conservancy and National Parks and Conservation Association profiles). Albright had been working in 1948 with a number of conservation groups trying to interest the Ford Foundation in giving them financial support. Because Albright knew Chester C. Davis and Rowan Gaither of the Ford Foundation executive board, he was asked to head a delegation to Pasadena, California to meet with foundation people. At a lunch with Ford Foundation bigwigs, Albright convinced Davis that the foundation should help conservation and Davis asked him to prepare a funding proposal and obtain the endorsement of about twenty-five national conservation leaders.

One of those was William S. Paley, president of Columbia Broadcasting System, who had been chairman of President Truman's Materials Policy Commission, which delivered its report on natural resources and minerals availability in the waning days of the Truman administration. Paley had formed an organization called Resources for the Future to try to follow up on his commission's recommendations, but it existed only on paper, so he offered to turn it over to Albright's coterie as the group to be funded. The Ford Foundation gave them $100,000 seed money.

While they were getting organized, Ford Foundation officials suggested RFF hold a White House conference on natural resources and gave RFF $150,000 more to cover conference expenses—a fairly clear demonstration of the kind of policy power foundations maintain over their clients. Twenty-five conservation leaders came forward to co-sponsor the conference, and Albright was elected RFF's first president.

Making the kick-off conference happen took some doing: the incoming Eisenhower administration did not like the Ford Foundation because they were New Dealers. Albright squabbled with White House Chief of Staff Sherman Adams and Ike refused to allow the title of White House Conference. Albright's RFF held the conference anyway the first week of December 1953 at the Shoreham Hotel in

Washington and called it The Mid-Century Conference on Resources for the Future. Eisenhower showed up and made some welcoming remarks, then departed. However, 1,600 people attended and the hugely successful bash launched Resources for the Future as the nation's premiere conservation group, a title it held only briefly.

Soon after the conference Albright resigned the presidency in favor of Reuben Gustavson, chancellor of the University of Nebraska, but stayed on as chairman of the board until 1962.[17]

RFF for the ensuing twenty-five years was supported by grants from the Ford Foundation.[18]

RFF became something of a cassandra in its earliest days. Its researchers issued warnings on the problems of oil and gas supply and the downsides of nuclear power long before public awareness was ready for it. During the early 1960s RFF pounded air and water pollution with studies that formed the basis of worldwide opinion for many years. During the 1970s RFF publicized environmental problems with soil erosion and pesticide use, but by that time they had lost their leadership position. RFF also performed early studies that shaped the future debate on the economics of outdoor recreation and environmentalism.

RFF studies gave shape to the idea of "amenity economics," the concept that a landscape untouched had monetary value for its tourism and recreation benefits—but not necessarily to the landowner who was forced to provide the pristine "viewshed" by government mandate without compensation.[19]

RFF operates its research program through four units: Energy and Natural Resources Division, Quality of the Environment Division, Center for Risk Management, and National Center for Food and Agricultural Policy. RRF tends to concentrate on "the social sciences aspects of problems associated with the development, conservation, and efficient use of natural resources, including fundamental and applied studies on basic resources of land, water, minerals, and air, goods and services derived from them, environmental quality, and energy policy," according to its literature.[20]

RFF research is grounded in economics and follows multidisciplinary methods. Research reports are commonly the work of a team of economists, ecologists, engineers, political scientists, sociologists, physicists, and other specialists. RFF's research plan follows two strategies: Tracking long-term trends, and detailed analysis of specific problems. Its many publications in the first category are well known to environmental scholars and sport such dry titles as *The Long-Term Adequacy of World Timber Supply* or *America's Renewable Resources: A Historical Perspective on Their Use and Management* or *World Metal Demand: Trends and Prospects*. The detailed analyses are much spicier: *Economics and Episodic Disease: The Benefits of Preventing a Giardiasis Outbreak* or *Nuclear Imperatives and Public Trust: Dealing with Radioactive Waste.*[21]

Robert W. Fri took over as president of Resources for the Future in 1986 after serving as president of the Energy Transition Corporation, deputy administrator of the Environmental Protection Agency, and a principal with McKinsey & Company.

Damn, there's that revolving door between government and the environmental movement again. And does McKinsey & Company ring any bells? It's the international management consulting company that Nature Conservancy leader John Sawhill came from. Fri and Sawhill were partners in the same firm. Sawhill's wife Isabel, a senior fellow at Washington's Urban Institute, is on RFF's board of directors. Mellon money significantly supports both the Nature Conservancy and RFF. For a number of years Robert O. Anderson of Atlantic Richfield Company and his associate Laurance S. Rockefeller served on the board. Arco and Rockefeller money still supports RFF. Linkages, linkages.

You can't tell the players without a scorecard, and the environmental movement is not eager for you to know all this stuff.

RFF joined with the National Wildlife Foundation to build the Resources and Conservation Center as a joint venture, a complex of two office buildings, one new, one renovated, at 1616 P Street, N.W. in Washington, D.C. in 1987. Each group contributed $15 million worth of land and advanced $1 million to develop the project, valued at $70 million. You figure out what kind of capital assets RFF has. Tenants include the National Planning Association, the American Civil Liberties Union, the Union of Concerned Scientists, the Environmental Defense Fund, the National Women's Law Center and the Center for Law and Social Policy. Is that a subtle combination, or what?[22]

RFF's staff is more impressive than its building: 55 research professionals, 22 supporting professionals, 2 visiting scholars, 15 clerical employees. They spend $7.5 million a year on research. They publish a quarterly journal *Resources*, and *Policy Briefs*, an occasional release. RFF maintains a library of 15,000 volumes.

RFF also holds periodic seminars and symposia on current research, provides research and policy briefings for members of Congress, and press briefings and conferences. The organization offers research fellowships supported by the Andrew W. Mellon Foundation and the W.K. Kellogg Foundation.

More than most other eco-think tanks, RFF works quietly with industries to find real solutions to real problems—they helped the Environmental Protection Agency and Amoco to find ways to reduce wastes from oil refineries and make economic use of them.[23]

In 1988, the Coalition on Superfund, a group of hazardous waste producing corporations and their insurers, hired former two-time E.P.A. chief William Ruckelshaus to lead a multimillion-dollar "study" of Superfund law that it had failed to amend during its five-year reauthorization in 1986. The Coalition also hired Resources for the Future, the Environmental Law Institute, and the Conservation Foundation (while William K. Reilly was still there) to scope out areas for the next try at making the law more reasonable.[24]

Resources for the Future took a moderate position on Superfund: It was clear that the law was not working, but rather than call for prior restraints in the form of mandated pollution-prevention infrastructure investments that would impair the manufacturing economy—as did Envirosearch-East President Joel S. Hirschhorn— RFF Vice President and Senior Fellow Paul R. Portney called for alternatives through federal financing or a private sector cleanup trust.[25]

Rather than recommend a specific anti-technological fix, RFF came out with a number of options for industry that would help solve the vast bureaucratic mess of Superfund.[26]

RFF's Center for Risk Management founded in April 1987 does crystal ball gazing of a certain utility, addressing how risks are managed by government and industry, how society decides which risks are most important, how to account for the real but hard-to-quantify values behind those decisions, and how to weigh those values against numerical risk assessments.

Resources for the Future gets 40 percent of its funding from endowment income; 30 percent from government grants and contracts; 15 percent from foundations; and 15 percent from corporations.[27]

Financial support for RFF's forest economics and policy programs has come from the Ford Foundation, the Forest Service and the Weyerhaueser Company Foundation.

RFF's Board of Directors includes chairman Lawrence E. Fouraker and other members Henry L. Diamond (boards of Jackson Hole Preserve, Inc., American Conservation Association); James R. Ellis; Robert W. Fri; Darius W. Gaskins, Jr.; John H. Gibbons; Robert H. Haveman; Bohdan Hawrylyshyn; Donald M. Kerr; Thomas J. Klutznick; Frederic D. Krupp (Environmental Defense Fund); Henry R. Linden; Thomas E. Lovejoy (Smithsonian Institution); Laurence I. Moss; Isabel V. Sawhill; Barbara S. Uehling; Macauley Whiting; and Mason Willrich.

Aetna Foundation, Inc. gave $10,000 in 1989 for "Center for Risk Management."

ARCO Foundation gave $25,000 in 1989 for "Center for Risk Management."

Burlington Northern Foundation gave $11,000 in 1989.

Ford Motor Company Fund gave $15,000 in 1990.

General Electric Foundation gave $25,000 in 1989.

The William and Flora Hewlett Foundation gave $150,000 in 1990, a 2-year grant "for general support."

Kraft General Foods Foundation gave $10,000 in 1989.

The Merck Company Foundation gave $25,000 in 1989.

The Rockefeller Foundation gave $40,000 in 1990 "toward activities of International Policy Council on Agriculture and Trade."

Union Pacific Foundation gave $10,000 in 1989 "to establish Center for Risk Management."

United States-Japan Foundation gave $120,000 in 1989 "for research and policy studies on U.S.-Japan cooperative leadership for environmental protection and economic development."

T. Unger Vetlesen Foundation gave $50,000 in 1989.

Weyerhaeuser Company Foundation gave $60,000 in 1989.

The Keystone Center (Founded 1975)
Annual budget: $4.1 million
      Staff: 39 total—30 professional; 9 support.
Tax Status: (501)(c)(3)
Headquarters: P.O. Box 606   2033 M Street, NW
                Keystone, Colorado 80435   Suite 900
                Phone: (303)468-5822   Washington, D.C. 20036
                Fax: (303)262-0152   Phone: (202)872-0160
                                     Fax: (202)785-0892

This Economy Trasher has developed approaches not nearly so Malthusian as some other non-membership environmental organizations—particularly negotiation between environmentalists and industry. But, as we shall see, that is not necessarily a good thing.

Robert Wallace Craig, president, founded the Keystone Center after serving as executive director and vice president of the Aspen Institute for Humanistic Studies (1954-64); as a vice president of Unimark International Design, Inc., an industrial design consulting firm (1965-71); the principal of Robert Craig & Associates (1973-75); a partner in the planning consulting firms Genesis, Inc. (1971-73) and Rieben & Craig in Denver (1973-75). He sits on several boards, including Colorado Outward Bound, the Santa Fe Institute and the American Alpine Club.

Craig is a noted mountain climber, having led or participated in numerous expeditions to the world's highest mountains. He is co-author with Charles Houston and Robert Bates of *Storm and Sorrow in the High Pamirs* and *K-2, The Savage Mountain*. Craig received a B.A. in philosophy and a B.S. in biology from the University of Washington. He took an M.A. in philosophy and completed Ph.D. work at Columbia University but was not awarded the doctorate.

The Keystone Center is a think tank and educational organization located in a popular ski area in Colorado. Its research is centered about facilitating "the development of effective policy and the resolution of environmental and natural resource disputes by providing a forum, the Science and Public Policy Program, for information exchange between individuals in the private sector, environmental community, academia, and government."[28]

The Center's activities focus on "negotiations for policies in the fields of energy, environment, and science / technology, including energy future, the role of oceans in hazardous waste management, ocean incineration, superfund, RCRA, product liability, biotechnology regulation, toxic waste, public utilities, drug safety, food safety and science and technology policy."[29]

The Keystone Center is virtually invisible in the media. The best profile came from the *New Orleans Times-Picayune* in 1987.

    The Keystone Center is a nonprofit organization that focuses on problems involving the environment, science and technology. The Center, outside of Denver among some of the country's highest, most majestic mountains, takes people who are used to fighting in the courts or in Congress and brings them together far away from both.

When problems can't come to Keystone, the staff goes where the problems are. That has paid off in Louisiana, which is struggling to find a solution to the proposed dumping of contaminated gypsum into the Mississippi River above New Orleans....

"The kind of problem-solving the center does is the wave of the future," said Joy Bartholomew, the assistant secretary at the state Department of Environmental Quality who oversees the task force. "Keystone Center associate director Michael Lesnick has kept the task force going, and we've been able to discuss issues with the idea of getting more information, not just winning a fight."...

"Industries and environmental groups are used to digging foxholes and lobbing grenades at each other during the congressional process, and political stalemates are guaranteed," said Leslie Dach, a Washington lobbyist for the National Audubon Society who has been involved in Keystone projects since 1978....

"Sometimes the system works and sometimes it doesn't. Several elements of a project on guidelines for waste site cleanups were incorporated into federal law. One Keystone effort on clean air legislation failed because the legislation passed before the effort was complete.

"The reports have some value, but I think the interaction between people has had a far greater impact nationally," said Blake Early, a Washington lobbyist for the Sierra Club. "You get people to set aside other issues and focus on one problem for a sustained period and that so rarely happens anymore."

Officials at the nation's major chemical corporations agree that less confrontational solutions to environmental problems, such as those offered at the center, are essential.

"Keystone offers the best hope for talking about issues before they become so heated that everyone's position is laid out," said Dave Sigman, an attorney for Exxon Chemical in Houston. "The adversarial process has not been very efficient."[30]

Keystone Center has held numerous conferences on biotechnical issues, reflecting the makeup of the center's board of directors—its chairman is executive of a biotech firm. Conferences such as "Gene Expression in Neuromuscular Development," and "Molecular Basis of Oxidative Damage by Leukocytes" are practically self-serving.

Because executives of three large environmental groups also sit on Keystone's board—Berle of the National Audubon Society, Krupp of the Environmental Defense Fund and Speth of the World Resources Institute—the Center's reports overrepresent Economy Trasher viewpoints: *Biological Diversity on Federal Lands: Report of a Keystone Policy Dialogue* contained no arguments challenging the nonscientific and political nature of the notion of biodiversity, only quibbles about how to achieve it. *The Keystone Financial Responsibility Project Final*

Report reflected no efforts to make environmentalists pay for the economic damage they do to individuals, business or communities.

Although the Center touts itself as a conciliator, the net result of the Center's policy dialogues, facilitation and mediation is unfortunately the suppression of technology and industry—killing jobs and trashing the economy.

The reason we make this assessment lies in the nature of conflict itself. As labor negotiators well know, a conflict is not ripe for negotiation unless it has reached an impasse in which neither side believes it can prevail entirely with the passage of time. The fact that a Keystone negotiating effort on clean air legislation failed because the legislation passed before the effort was complete, as remarked by Leslie Dach of the National Audubon Society, was no accident. Audubon Society lobbyists were pushing to win that bill for all they were worth and negotiating in bad faith while frittering away the time and effort of their opponents, who should have been fighting, not negotiating.[31]

If either side feels it can eventually win the whole game, it will only come to the negotiating table as a tactic to achieve that total victory—as a stall for time to gather strength, as a way to gain concessions without expending political or financial capital, or as an outright trick to disarm an opponent while vigorously prosecuting the conflict.[32]

To boot, the situation in any environmentalist-industry conflict is stacked against the industry side: An industry comes to the table with millions of dollars in assets, the livelihood of thousands of personnel and the fate of dozens of dependent communities at stake. The environmental group comes to the table with only demands, an organized constituency and the threat of political battle, public embarrassment and vexatious lawsuits.

In such a situation, there can be no compromise. Compromise implies a trade of value for value. In a compromise, each side gets some benefit and accepts some cost. In the outcome of an environmentalist-industry conflict, the environmentalists deliver no benefit to industry and bear no cost. Industry delivers all the benefits and bears all the costs. In a negotiation, environmentalists have nothing to offer industry and nothing to lose except one fundraising campaign among many. Environmentalists give up nothing to industry. Such a situation is not susceptible of compromise.

The only outcomes possible for industry are 1) surrender peaceably and save the expense of battle; 2) fight and lose. The context is much the same as the protection racket.

And the result is not as honorable as you get from the Mafia: when the *next* gang of eco-thugs swaggers into corporate headquarters with its list of demands, your former negotiating partner will not escort them out of the neighborhood and explain things to them.

The National Audubon Society and the Sierra Club were perfectly aware that they could win almost any political battle against those industries they negotiated with at the Keystone Center. They also knew that if they could manage to pry just a small concession out of the industry, the Friends of the Earth or the Union of Concerned Scientists would soon come knocking with more demands. Sooner or later the whole victory is achieved.

Industry does not seem to notice any of this.

You can size up the Keystone Center in a single sentence: Environmentalists at a negotiating table have nothing to offer industry except threats. What's so thrilling about surrendering without a fight? The cost of losing is less? That we'll admit.

Mr. Sigman of Exxon never gained anything from the Sierra Club or the National Audubon Society or any other environmental group through the Keystone Center's process. Exxon gave and the environmental groups took.

Mr. Sigman of Exxon may be pleased that his company gave away the store without having to go to court or to lobby Congress for the privilege.

We'll admit it's cheaper, but will Exxon admit it's still a loss? Or perhaps they're pretending to fight regulations that would be so expensive that only large well-capitalized firms such as Exxon could afford to comply? It certainly *looks* like a good faith effort on Exxon's part. But perhaps the Federal Trade Commission should find out for sure.

The Center publishes a quarterly newsletter, *Consensus*; *Keystone Science School Newsletter* (semiannually), and its annual report. The center also operates the American Indian / Business Roundtable as a clearinghouse for information between tribes, business and financial interests.

The Keystone Center receives 40 percent of its funding from corporate contributions; 28 percent from foundation grants; 15 percent from government grants and contracts; 12 percent from tuition to the Keystone Science School; and 5 percent from individual gifts.

The Center is a 501(c)(3) organization and is affiliated with the Keystone Center Foundation and Keystone Symposia on Molecular and Cellular Biology.

The Keystone Center's Board of Directors includes chairman Ralph E. Christoffersen (executive of Ribozyme Pharmaceuticals Inc., a biotechnology company); vice chairmen Ronald E. Cape (a distinguished scientist), James E. Crowfeet, and Hazel Rollins O'Leary; and founder-president Robert W. Craig. Other members include Peter A.A. Berle (National Audubon Society); William P. Bishop; Edward Bleier; Harold R. Bruno, Jr.; David T. Buzzelli; Philip Carroll; Alvin L. Cohen; Charles T. Condy; Harold J. Corbett; Douglas M. Costle; Pedro Cuatrecasas; Charles B. Curtis; Paul A. Downey; David K. Fagin; J. William Futrell; M. Eugene Gillis; LaDonna Harris; N. Berne Hart; Charles D. Hollister; Martin Jischke; Robert Trent Jones, Jr.; Frederic D. Krupp (Environmental Defense Fund); Klaus L. Mai; Joan D. Manley; Paul A. Marks; Robert A. Maynard; R. Garrett Mitchell; Leah Knapp Patton; James L. Peterson; Walter R. Quanstrom; George B. Rathmann; Gresham Riley; James Gustave Speth (World Resources Institute); and Lynn R. Williams.

Alcoa Foundation gave $10,000 in 1989.

Amoco Foundation, Inc. gave $20,000 in 1989.

ARCO Foundation gave $25,000 in 1989 "for policy analysis on global climate change."

W. Alton Jones Foundation, Inc. gave $50,000 in 1989 "for international Dialogue series on Plant Genetic Resources."

Eastman Kodak Charitable Trust gave $25,000 in 1989.

Monsanto Fund gave $20,000 in 1989.

The Pew Charitable Trusts gave $35,000 in 1990, a 1 1/2 year grant "for Policy Dialogue: A Scientist to Scientist Advocacy Colloquium on National Research Goals."

Shell Oil Company Foundation gave $10,000 in 1989 "for dialogue on climate change and energy policy;" and another $50,000 in 1989 "for operating support."

Rocky Mountain Institute (Founded 1982)
>   Annual budget: $1.2 million
>   Staff: 37 total—25 professional; 12 support
>   Tax Status: (501)(c)(3)
>   Headquarters: 1739 Snowmass Creek Road
>   Old Snowmass, Colorado 81654
>   Phone: (303)927-3851 Fax: (303)927-4178

Amory Lovins founded this think tank in 1982 with his lawyer wife L. Hunter Lovins, who now serves as its president and executive director. Amory, who serves as the Institute's research director and vice-president, was educated at Harvard and Oxford and sports the bushy moustache and horn-rimmed glasses look and feel of the quintessential intellectual. Hunter previously served for six years as assistant director of the California Conservation Project, which she helped found. She earned two B.A. degrees, one in political science and the other in sociology, from Pitzer College, and her J.D. from Loyola University Law School. She occasionally works evenings as deejay and bouncer at a local cowboy bar and plays lacrosse on horseback—"polocrosse"—as a sanity safeguard.

Known to environmentalists as the prophets of the soft path, the Rocky Mountain Institute emphasizes increased energy efficiency rather than increased energy production. Program director Michael Kinsley, a former Colorado county commissioner, said, "What RMI is about is least-cost, demand-side analysis."[33]

The Institute hires itself out as a consultant through their Competitek project and boasts clients including the U.S. Small Business Administration, the Tennessee Valley Authority, Xerox, Apple Computer, Marriott and Boeing. RMI's board of directors includes the head of Pacific Gas & Electric's demand-side activities and the head of strategic planning for the London Stock Exchange.

The essential message of RMI is "sustainable use of resources and energy efficiency"—the Lovinses prefer "energy efficiency" to "energy conservation" because it sounds less austere—which they believe "can be achieved through market forces without undue stress on the American lifestyle."[34]

Program director Kinsely said, "What a real free market does is search for efficiencies."[35]

That siren song is best listened to after lashing yourself securely to the mast. There are a few rocks in that big blue sky.

For example, RMI put out an admirable little searching-for-efficiencies booklet titled "Practical Home Energy Savings," which recommended turning off the pilot lights on your stoves and lighting burners with matches to save energy. Southern California Gas Company received more than 10,000 calls asking for technicians to come out and do just that after the *Los Angeles Times* ran excerpts from the booklet.[36]

The utility pointed out that not only could such a practice void the warranties on stoves and that it was a violation of the National Fuel Gas Code set by the American Gas Association, but it was also an efficacious way to blow yourself to Mars or thereabouts.[37]

Oops.

RMI agreed to remove the recommendation from its booklet.

Then there's that other problem—looking for energy efficiencies and forgetting to look for energy sources. It eventually leaves you with terrific equipment that just sits there.

Developing solar energy, biomass fuels, wind farms, tidal dams, small hydro-electric generators, and all that other soft path stuff is a great idea.[38] Along with conventional sources such as oil, coal and nuclear power. Not instead of.[39]

Soft path advocates such as RMI have this little *instead of* problem. Perhaps it's only sensible to avoid taking the Concorde from New York to Paris, but would you really like to try it on a bicycle?

Perhaps the most troublesome aspect of the soft path is that it can serve as a smiling mask for a frowning anti-industry agenda. Rocky Mountain Institute appears ambivalent. Hunter Lovins has been known to preach anti-war sentiments and typical anti-technology attitudes as part of the RMI message: "If we had a world where nuclear commerce and power production were no longer common, it would be very difficult to undertake nuclear-bomb programs."[40]

Amory Lovins has voiced clearly anti-production sentiments, particularly against the Bush administration's National Energy Strategy (NES): "Reading the NES, one has the feeling of having just wandered into a hidden valley populated by creatures long thought to have become extinct."[41]

His complaint was against the NES's emphasis on conventional fuels. Beth Miller of the Bush Energy Department said "We feel very strongly that it's a well-balanced strategy. We are enthusiastic about conservation and renewables and alternative fuels, but we believe that conventional fuels are going to be around for some time longer and that we can't ignore the supply side of the equation, that we're not going to get there looking exclusively at demand reduction."

That puts the problem with the Rocky Mountain Institute in a nutshell. It doesn't just ignore the supply side. It complains about those who don't.

Amory once told a *Christian Science Monitor* reporter, "I don't have much affection for corporate socialists who hide behind market rhetoric in order to promote their favorite turkey." He didn't say how he felt about eco-socialists who hide behind market rhetoric to promote their favorite turkey, like neat pilot light tips.

The Lovins' biggest fans are the mainstream environmental movement's biggest mouths, such as Interior Secretary Bruce Babbitt, formerly of the League of Conservation Voters, who thinks Amory is coming into his own as a world expert—

and who also wrote his constituency that the environmental movement's political opponents ought to be "driven into oblivion."[42]

Nonetheless, RMI can be reasonably located on the Establishment Interventionist Axis rather than among the radicals. Its emphasis on economics is genuine, if obsessed with the demand side.

Rocky Mountain Institute's achievements on the demand side are nicely showcased at the organization's headquarters some 16 miles west of Aspen in Snowmass, Colorado, an experimental building that serves as the residence of Amory and Hunter Lovins and the office of their staff of 22 research professionals and 8 support people. The 4,000 square foot building uses superinsulation, renewable energy sources (including wood stoves), and a greenhouse. The walls are 16 inches thick, the windows are argon-filled "heat mirror" material twice as efficient as triple glazing, solar design, compact fluorescent bulbs and many other energy-saving measures. The electric bill for the residence wing is only $5 a month and $15 in the office wing.[43]

The problem lies in the half-million-dollar price tag for the structure, or about $130 a square foot—a bit dear for the average home owner. Compared with usual construction for the Rocky Mountain area and conventional fuels, the building saves about $7,000 a year, which means it would take 40 years to cover the cost of the building with fuel savings alone—not bad, if you've got the half mil.

RMI publishes *Rocky Mountain Newsletter* three or four times a year. In addition to the regular staff, RMI employs 9 contractors and visiting scholars. Amory and Hunter Lovins have published half a dozen books together as well as sharing bylines on numerous articles and papers. Amory goes on the speaking circuit and the talk show trail while Hunter runs the business.

The Rocky Mountain Institute gets 41 percent of its funding from consulting fees; 26 percent from restricted foundation grants; 12 percent from unrestricted personal contributions; 11 from unrestricted foundation grants; 5 percent from publishing revenue; 2 percent from unrestricted in-kind corporate contributions; and 3 percent from unrestricted corporate grants, contributed facilities, and restricted personal grants.

The RMI Board of Directors includes chairman Michael Stranahan and other members Irvin C. Bupp; Carolyn M. Child; John Fox; Dana Jackson; Amory Lovins; Hunter Lovins; James T. Mills; Carol Noyes; Peter Schwartz; and Bardyl Tirana.

The William and Flora Hewlett Foundation gave $200,000 in 1990, a 3-year grant, "for general support."

Charles Stewart Mott Foundation gave $50,000 in 1990 "for Global Energy Efficiency Project to reduce global carbon dioxide emissions from fossil fuel combustion through encouraging energy efficiency investments."

The Pew Charitable Trusts gave $350,000 in 1990, a 2-year grant "to promote implementation of energy-efficiency program by utilities in Colorado and other Rocky Mountain States."

The Rockefeller Foundation gave $25,000 in 1990 "to meet preliminary research and administrative expenses of Phase I of Bombay Efficient Lighting Large-Scale Experiment (BELLE), managed in U.S. by Institute."

Foundation on Economic Trends (Founded 1977)
　　　　Annual budget: $1 million (estimated)
　　　　　　　Staff: 9 total—7 professional, 2 support
　　Tax Status:　　501(c)(3)
　　Headquarters:　1130 17th Street, NW
　　　　　　　　　Suite 630
　　　　　　　　　Washington, D.C. 20036
　　　　　　　　　Phone: (202)466-2823 Fax: (202)429-9602

The Foundation on Economic Trends classifies itself as a "social change" organization.[44] Its policy director is Andrew Kimbrell, but the real motor is President Jeremy Rifkin—also president of the Greenhouse Crisis Foundation (1989). Rifkin has been a sedulous Economy Trasher for nearly two decades. He is a veteran 1970s New Left anti-Vietnam War agitator turned environmentalist. He says he converted to vegetarianism 15 years ago after three bites into a spoiled hamburger—it was blue-gray, he recalls—the rest of which he threw away along with his beef eating habit. The reformed beefaholic found his path to prominence winding first through the labyrinths of biotechnology—he took on the biotech industry in a high-profile war against genetic engineering.

In 1985, FET brought a suit that halted the construction of a controversial aerosol testing facility in Dugway, Utah. In 1987, Rifkin forced the U.S. Defense Department to conduct an environmental impact assessment of the entire Biological Defense Research Program, which is carried out at major universities. He went back to court on this issue in 1990 to suspend programs rated in the analysis as of higher risk.[45]

In 1989 FET went to court to prevent experiments injecting gene-altered cells into humans, designed to improve an experimental cancer treatment.[46]

In 1990 Rifkin sought to suspend FDA review of all new recombinant DNA products until safety measures could be proven.[47]

The nub of Rifkin-Think is contained in a dire warning he issued about the dangers of biotechnology in 1983: "People want healthier babies, more efficient plants and animals, a better GNP, and more security for their offspring. All of which biotechnology offers."

Oh, no! Healthy babies? We can't have *that!* At least Rifkin lets everyone know just where he stands in expressing his horror of a bright future for humanity. Not many environmentalists are so blunt in spelling out the logical implications of their goals—sicker babies, less productive plants and animals, a worse GNP, and less security for our offspring. In short, fewer of us.

Rifkin is a true nature mystic and makes no bones about it. "Humanity seeks the elation that goes with the drive for mastery over the world. Nature offers us the sublime resignation that goes with an undifferentiated participation in the world around us." Resignation to a sovereign nature is the theme of all mainstream environmentalism, as Victor Scheffer's *Environmentalism's Articles of Faith* noted in its "Nature knows best" dogma, but environmental leaders seldom say it so clearly.

Jeremy Rifkin was described by *Time* magazine as "the environmental movement's most prominent polemicist." He is expert in forming coalitions with bigger, more powerful environmental groups to get his preferences turned into policy. "In the field of public policy, no one is better than Rifkin in the martial arts of social activism: lawsuits, petitions, debates, lectures and media manipulation," said *Time*. Rifkin does most of his work for the Foundation on Economic Trends appearing on talk shows, but occasionally gives testimony before congressional committees. He earned a B.S. in economics from the Wharton School of Finance and Commerce, University of Pennsylvania, and an M.A. in international affairs from the Fletcher School of Law and Diplomacy, Tufts University.[48]

FET is quite an active Economy Trasher for a non-membership think-tank. It tried to stop the launch of the space shuttle Discovery in 1990 with its payload of the nuclear-powered Ulysses probe.[49] It assailed the use of the growth hormone BST in milk cows in an effort to shut down the dairy industry.[50]

There are only three people on FET's Board of Directors: Jeremy Rifkin; Edward L. Rogers; and Elliot Stein.

Rifkin's big chance to get into the environmental movement came in the 1970s after biologists discovered recombinant DNA technology, transferring genes from one organism to another.[51] Some biologists had doubts about the safety of recombining genes—Michael Crichton's marvellous science-fiction epic *The Andromeda Strain* brought the point home in a best-selling novel and a box-office smash movie. The *New York Times Magazine* even published an article depicting the escape of a cancer-causing bacteria from a biotech lab and wiping out the whole population. Rifkin ran with the issue. He began organizing protests and filing lawsuits to stop biotechnology experiments.[52] In the process he won the support of such diverse web of interest constituencies as the National Council of Churches and politicians such as Vice President Albert Gore back when he was a senator.[53]

Rifkin won many of his lawsuits, and in the process killed technology that could have healed the environment he says he loves. As critic Ronald Bailey noted, "His successes include halting the first field-test of bacteria bioengineered to prevent crops from freezing. Most recently he has scared five major supermarket chains, including Kroger and Safeway, into withdrawing milk produced from cows treated with bovine somatotropin (BST). BST boosts milk production and is completely harmless to human beings.[54] Nevertheless, two states, Wisconsin and Minnesota, have banned BST for at least a year and bioLuddite Rifkin can claim some of the credit. (So can Wisconsin farmers alarmed at the prospect of falling milk prices.)"[55]

So can Consumers Union, publisher of *Consumer Reports,* which joined the attack.[56]

Rifkin's latest book *Beyond Beef: The Rise and Fall of the Cattle Culture* (New York, E.P. Dutton) is an Economy Trasher classic, arguing for the total elimination of the cattle industry worldwide. It is full of bull about beef. Part of Rifkin's reasoning—if it can be graced with such a name—is that cows contribute to the greenhouse effect by releasing methane in their flatulence. Most ranchers who hear this news for the first time respond incredulously, "He's worried about *cow farts?*" He is.

Beyond Beef, better titled *Beyond Belief*, is beyond redemption. Dennis Avery, director of Global Food Issues for the Hudson Institute, an Indianapolis think tank, said, "*Beyond Beef* is about the worst book I've ever read."

Rifkin's books usually get panned—Harvard's Stephen Jay Gould wrote in a review of *Algeny* that it was "a cleverly constructed tract of anti-intellectual propaganda masquerading as scholarship....I don't think I have ever read a shoddier work."

Beyond Beef is shoddier. In its pages Rifkin offers an amateurish hodgepodge history of the "human-bovine" relationship culled from library materials without consultation with experts and without any expertise in the historiography of the subject. Beef is a metaphor of all that is rotten in the modern world, which Rifkin attributes to "the loss of our sacred relationship to nature," said *Time* magazine.

Rifkin told Joan Mooney of *Publishers Weekly*, "I was surprised at the extent to which we owe western culture to this animal. We have built much of western civilization on its back, from our early theological explorations to colonial adventures to our unfolding consciousness." Because cattle have indeed played a prominent role in ancient mythology and their haunting images in prehistoric cave paintings linger in our unconscious, they are powerful tools for Rifkin's talents as a fear merchant.

Rifkin's book of bull about beef was intended to do more than generate big sales profits. He used the book to launch an Economy Trasher campaign to slash worldwide beef consumption by 50 percent over the next decade, then eliminate it altogether. He and his wife Carol assembled a Washington, D.C. coalition powerful enough to make Jeremy's Cow Jihad happen, filing lawsuits and raising hell in 20 countries with members including: The Rainforest Action Network, which blames cattle for "killing the Amazon;" the Fund for Animals, which criticizes ranchers for using poisons and traps to control coyotes that eat calves; the International Rivers Network that complains against cows using scarce water resources; and Food First, a veteran anti-agriculture lobby that denounces the use of feedlots for fattening cattle with grain that could be eaten by humans. It is a high profile campaign that could wreak billions of dollars worth of devastation to the world cattle industry and put thousands of family ranches into bankruptcy, as well as leaving many developing countries without their major source of protein.[57]

Rifkin justifies his Economy Trashing with numerous accusations against cattle. "The average cow eats its way through 900 pounds of vegetation every month," he says. "It is literally a hoofed locust." That "hoofed locust" epithet is colorful imagery, but not Jeremy Rifkin's colorful imagery—John Muir coined the expression in the 1880s, only his hoofed locusts were sheep, not cows. However, it doesn't take originality to destroy the ranching economy, just colorful images that turn people against ranchers.

It should be noted in all fairness to Jeremy Rifkin that he never personally visited a ranch or a meat-packing plant at any time during the research on *Beyond Beef*, so he can plead ignorance about the nonsense he wrote.

Here are the arguments Rifkin marshals in *Beyond Beef* to destroy the cattle industry:

Cattle ranchers are destroying tropical forests: There is no doubt that many tropical forests in the Americas gave way during the past few decades to farms, ranches, and homesteads. It was the pattern of economic development in the early United States. Forests were cleared for food production and homestead space. Our cities and farms are there now. The countries of Central and South America did the same while developing their economies. Rifkin makes it sound like this is an endless process that will destroy every square foot of tropical forest everywhere, but that is no more true of tropical countries than it was of the United States, which today has more than a third of its total area in forests, remarkable since the Great Plains and the Great American Desert take up another third.

In Latin America, "most of the pastureland that was easily cleared of forest has already been cleared," said Daniel Janzen, a biologist with the University of Pennsylvania. Tropical forests are becoming more valuable for timber production and foresters in most tropical nations are managing them for sustained yield of timber, for watershed protection, and for wildlife. Where tropical forests are cleared for slash-and-burn subsistence agriculture, which may include a few cows, the settlements typically last only a few years, then move on, after which the forest reclaims the clearing. Net loss of tropical forests to large scale cattle grazing has slowed to a virtual halt because most of the suitable places are already in pasture. There is no crisis. Cattle ranching is not destroying tropical forests. But Jeremy Rifkin's public is ready to believe any evil of human beings.

Beef is contaminated with COW AIDS. Rifkin is playing Stephen King with this accusation—a horror story that's total fiction. He says that beef is contaminated with viruses, including a bovine immunodeficiency virus that he calls "Cow AIDS." There is no evidence that any such contamination is present in any significant area, or that the virus he's talking about can infect humans, or that even if it could, it would have any effect on the human immune system. This charge is so easy to dismiss that it appears to have been added to the manuscript as a filler.[58]

Cows contribute to global warming. This is the cow fart theory. Rifkin notes that cows harbor bacteria in their four-chambered stomachs that break down the cellulose in grass and make it digestible. Methane is a natural by-product of ruminant digestion, and methane is a heat-trapping "greenhouse gas" like carbon dioxide. Worldwide, the earth's cattle generate 60 tons of methane each year and release it into the atmosphere. That, says Rifkin, is a disaster and the cattle industry must be shut down to save us from global warming.

But the fresh waters of the world put 5 million tons of methane into the atmosphere each year, the oceans release 10 million tons per year, termites give off 40 million tons, rice paddies generate 70 million tons, and wetlands release 115 million. Shall we shut them down, too? And the result of all this is so scant that scientists cannot agree that global warming *from all causes* is even happening, much less that methane release is any kind of real threat to global survival. But many Americans swallow Rifkin's arguments whole and are ready to sacrifice their neighbors in the ranching business because it's noble to sacrifice.

Beef inspection is shoddy and a danger to public health. In this section Rifkin treats us to a description of how cattle are handled from birth to butcher in terms that would gag even a grizzled cowpoke. How Rifkin knows any of this is puzzling, because he's never seen a slaughterhouse. Nonetheless, it makes a great platform to generate righteous indignation among gullible readers. The U.S. Department of Agriculture flatly denies this charge.

About 100 cases of infection from beef contaminated with E. coli bacteria occur each year, most of them caused by restaurant workers who fail to wash their hands after using the toilet, not failed inspection. The 1993 Jack In The Box food poisoning episode in which more than 300 people were infected with E. coli 0157:H7 from contaminated beef was so extraordinary it got headlines for weeks, and more than one law enforcement agent suspected sabotage by Animal Liberation Front terrorists.[59] Beef in your supermarket is so safe that most people cannot recall the last time they heard of anyone dying of contaminated beef, or even getting sick from it.

Cattle overgraze rangeland and cause irreparable desertification. Rifkin talks about years of uncontrolled grazing that transformed seas of grass into desert. He cites the statistics of the U.S. Forest Service and Bureau of Land Management that half the land under their control is in poor condition. This poor range condition proves that ranchers should be removed from federal lands. Rifkin, however, does not reveal that a huge portion of those range condition reports are false, systematically inserted in the files of grazing permittees by federal employees who revolved from the environmental movement into the land managing agencies. The truth that actual range condition is much better than the false reports indicate is emerging from documents and depositions taken in the course of several key lawsuits now before the courts. Only now, as ranchers are beginning to take the government to court over these falsified reports, is the full extent of the imposture becoming known.

Most ironic, removing cattle from the federal lands would actually make the ecological situation worse: Ranchers who own grazing permits have improved the range condition so that wildlife originally absent has been able to thrive.

To illustrate, a century ago a number of tribes in the Great Basin of the West were known by the contemptuous name of "Digger Indians" because their diet consisted mainly of roots, seeds, and nuts. It wasn't because they didn't like venison. There weren't any deer. But after the ranchers came and established extensive permanent operations, managing the grasslands for greater productivity, the range condition improved so much that huge deer herds now throng the Great Basin, deliberately introduced by the ranchers.

As range ecologists well know, cows don't just eat the grass, in return they deposit tons of the old-fashioned organic fertilizer we call manure. Cows serve to enrich, not impoverish the range. Ranchers with long-term interests in the land—grazing permits are inherited with the base ranch and pass from generation to generation—will not cheat their own posterity by being poor stewards. But city dwellers who know nothing about ranching or ecology other than what Jeremy

Rifkin tells the media are ready to destroy a whole sector of our economy and a whole community of our society, and all for illusion and false fear.

The grain we feed to cows should feed people. The bulk of the grain fed to cattle in America is milo maize and grain sorghum, which are delicacies that most city folk would shun forever if they had ever tasted them, which they haven't. They don't serve it at Spago. But the average urban dweller who reads Rifkin's book has no idea what cows really eat or how the beef industry really works. Very little human-quality grain goes into a cow, but you'd never know that reading Jeremy's joke book. And, as a matter of fact, the U.S. cattle inventory is down to about 100 million head from its level in the early 1980s of 115 million. So there are less cows eating grain of any kind in America. The same is true worldwide—beef output is contracting per capita.

Beef is unhealthy and gives people heart disease and cancer. High cholesterol, the medical profession generally agrees, is a leading cause of heart disease—but that does not necessarily mean beef is bad for you. In the first place, not all beef is well-marbled high-fat roasts and steaks—low-fat beef is very much in vogue—and in the second place, your genetic inheritance plays the biggest role in determining whether your heart is susceptible to elevated cholesterol levels, not how much red meat you eat. Many Americans are playing it safe by eating less red meat, but the national heart disease rate is not declining as a result.

There's red meat even in the new U.S. Department of Agriculture's "Eating Right Pyramid" that has replaced the "basic four" food-groups wheel that has been a fixture on classroom blackboards since the 1950s. After a year of study and $855,000 spent on comprehensive tests to answer concerns raised by nutritionists and health-care profession-als, the Feds endorse grains, fruits and vegetables, dairy, meat and fats-oils-and-sweets in declining order of consumption. Meat is a readily available complete protein which contains the 10 essential amino acids that the human body is unable to manufacture by itself.

Giving up meat means taking great care to insure daily access to a wide variety of grains, vegetables and fruits, since they do not individually contain all the needed amino acids that make up a complete protein. It takes substantial knowledge to be a properly nourished vegetarian—or adherence to a traditional culture's cuisine proven by genera-tions of survivors.

Those who eschew meat for religious, philosophical or political reasons certainly have no right to deny meat to those who want it. Maybe it's the lack of red meat in their diet that makes them so self-righteous.

Cows use resources that should go for other uses. Rifkin charges that a pound of beef requires in the input of 2,464 pounds of water, compared to only 480 pounds of water per pound of soybeans. That's a waste of valuable water resources, he charges. But not, it should be noted, of Jeremy Rifkin's valuable water resources, or anybody else's. Ranchers own the water their cows drink. It is theirs to dispose of as they wish. Water rights are fundamental in the world of agriculture—they are not the political property of some urban ideologist who raises public fears for a living.

It should also be noted that cows pee a lot, so the water goes back into the soil for recycling, and returns fertilizing nitrogen in the form of ammonia—but reading Rifkin you'd think that every pound of beef has 2,464 pounds of water in it.

Another Rifkin accusation is that countries like Egypt and Mexico have switched the use of farmland from growing staples for human consumption to growing grain for beef that only the wealthy can afford. The argument is that cattle growing makes the poor hungry. The evidence says otherwise. The poorest countries like China have experienced an increase in beef consumption along with overall improvements in diet.

Among Rifkin's allies is the American Farmland Trust. And why would a Rockefeller-funded land trust be interested in Jeremy Rifkin's weird science? Well, remember from our profile of AFT under The Nature Conservancy above that one of AFT's big donors is Archer Daniels Midland, a giant agribusiness that has just come out with a new line of vegetable-based fake meat products. Their version of the tofu-burger is called the harvestburger. Could there be a little profit for the Rockefeller Money Axis in putting the family rancher out of business using Jeremy Rifkin as a catspaw? Is there anybody out there who'd like to ask the Federal Trade Commission if the Sherman Anti-Trust Act applies?

Where's the beef? It's all turned to bull. And bull is what *Beyond Beef* and Jeremy Rifkin are full of.

The Arca Foundation gave $20,000 in 1989 "to publish Greenhouse Crisis Citizens' Guide to minimize damage to environment."

Mary Reynolds Babcock Foundation, Inc. gave $40,000 in 1989, a 2-year grant, "for Electronic Pollution Project which assists with costs of litigation to require Department of Defense (DOD) to prepare environmental impact statements before testing begins."

No assessment of the front rank of Economy Trashers would be complete without a bow to the premier non-group in the environmental movement.

Earth First! (Founded 1980)
       Annual budget: $109,000
                Staff: Secret, claims to be all volunteer
             Members: Secret, claims to be a "movement," not a group
          Tax Status: None. Not incorporated.
       Headquarters: P.O. Box 5871
                            Tucson, Arizona 85703
                            Phone: (602)622-1371
Affiliate Earth First Foundation is a (501)(c)(3).
            Foundation: P.O. Box 5176
                            Missoula, Montana 59806
                            Phone: (406)728-8114 Fax: None

As we went to press, Earth First! was in disarray, so the phone numbers may or may not get you anybody.

The exclamation point behind Earth First! is *de rigueur*, part of the guerilla chi-chi that devoted Economy Trashers love so much.

But is Earth First! otherwise for real? Probably not.

Defectors from the environmental movement have told us that Earth First! founder Dave Foreman was approached by the Sierra Club and his employer, The Wilderness Society, in 1979 with an offer to fund a new extremist point group for the movement. It would serve the function of making their own demands look more reasonable. Foreman brought together four dissident environmentalist friends grown tired of mainstream ineffectuality to form the original group: Michael Roselle, Howie Wolke, Bart Koehler and Ron Kezar.

Environmental analyst Rik Scarce wrote, "Earth First! mythology has it that Kezar and the others created Earth First! while in the desert or while reveling in a whorehouse. That mythology is vitally important, as essential to Earth First!ers as founders' resumes are to mainstream environmental organizations. Cynics might say that myths cover up lies or unpleasantness. But for Earth First!ers they are concentrated truths, mixtures of reality, fantasy, and wisdom. The Earth First! creation myths are flavorful, rich and evocative of the sort of image that the macho cowboys wanted to propagate."[60]

Did Earth First! result from a wilderness hiking trip in the sunny Pinacate Desert of Mexico or during a visit to a cheap, bawdy border brothel? Defectors say that Foreman made the deal by himself in a comfortable Wilderness Society office, and accepted the offer on the condition that funding would be steady and adequate, and that his participation was a limited-term ten-year deal, and only then began looking for a model that would attract an appropriate cult following.

Is it true? We have no reason to disbelieve it or to believe Earth First!'s own propaganda about its origins. So the whole Earth First! thing is very possibly synthetic, deliberately designed by the mainstream to push the goalpost to the left as far as possible.

The structure of Earth First! would have to be informal to avoid prosecution. From the beginning it was called a "movement," never an "organization." The founders made much of Plains Indian tribalism as a cover for the strange arrangement, touting autonomous groups that shared the same beliefs. There would be no bureaucracy, no lobbyists, no organizational spokespeople. There would be only unpaid grassroots activists (as far as anyone knew). No organization. No membership. No list of names. Only anarchy. It would drive law enforcement nuts.

But the "movement" had to have a kickoff event to attract adherents. Foreman organized a July 4th, 1980 gathering in Moab, Utah, and called it a "rendezvous," like the Indians and the Mountain Men of the Jeremiah Johnson ilk used to hold. Bart Koehler is said to have added the "Round River" appellation to the party, after the allegorical river which flows into itself that wilderness advocate Aldo Leopold had mythicized. The first Round River Rendezvous took place four days after Foreman left the Wilderness Society, and the shindig attracted 200 people.

Foreman found a suitable model for his new group in Edward Abbey's industry-killer novel, *The Monkey Wrench Gang*, which was enjoying great popularity on college campuses in the West. Reviewers at the *Denver Post* said of the book, "If you ever dreamed of destroying a bridge that spoils a pristine gorge, *The Monkey Wrench Gang* is for you," and the National Observer, "It'll make you want to go out and blow up a dam." For some readers, they were right.[61]

Abbey's fictional sabotage—"ecotage"—gang presented the perfect paradigm for a point group that could create a legend sufficiently powerful to drag the whole environmental movement leftward. Counting on the American love of the crafty outlaw with a heart of gold—a Jesse James or Butch Cassidy and the Sundance Kid—Foreman pulled off a few stunts such as yanking up oil company road survey stakes—"monkeywrenching," their vandalism was called in honor of Abbey's book title—and then gave speeches boasting of his exploits. One of his favorite lines from early podium-pounders was delivered in a conspiratorial tone to avid listeners: "I'm not advocating illegal activity unless you're accompanied by your parents, or at night."[62]

In the beginning, Earth First!'s actions were largely symbolic and theatrical rather than destructive. In 1981, shortly after the group's founding, EF! "cracked" Glen Canyon Dam by unfurling a 300-foot-long plastic banner over the top of the dam that appeared, at first glance and from a distance, to be a crack.

Foreman and Koehler took the inaugural Earth First! "Road Show" across the nation in the fall of 1981 to publicize the "tribe." Lovers of Gary Snyder's poetry were enthralled, along with students, little old ladies in cleated tennis shoes, weird lifestyle types, and sundry hangers-on.

In 1985 EF!ers sat on treetop platforms eighty feet above the ground for nearly a month to protest logging in Willamette National Forest in Oregon. In 1986 EF! blockaded Fishing Bridge in Yellowstone National Park to pressure the Park Service into closing off visitor access. Nineteen EF!ers were arrested at the demonstration. In October 1986 Texas EF!ers chained themselves to tree crushers to protest logging at Four Notch. In 1988 a group of EF!ers parachuted into British Columbia to disrupt the Canadian government's aerial wolf hunt. They chained themselves to equipment in 1990 to protest construction of Austin's Outer Loop, saying the freeway was being built without having jumped through all the federal environmental hoops it should have.

Members of Earth First! who had all this stagey glory to bask in took a greener-than-thou look down their noses at other environmentalists, who squirmed under the glare. *The New York Times* said, "Earth First! members have little use for tactics of the Sierra Club and other mainstream groups—they call them 'couch potato environmentalists'—who concentrate on letter-writing campaigns, lobbying and lawsuits."[63]

Foreman's wit and nimble ability to elude the law brought him and his eco-commandos quick notoriety and began to pressure the mainstream environmental groups to step up their rhetoric to avoid looking unconcerned.

It worked. Then in 1984 the lethal form of ecotage called tree spiking came into play—driving long, blade-shattering nails into trees to deter loggers.[64] A chainsaw that hit such a spike would kick back on the logger and cut him in half. Earth First! assembled a book from its early instruction sheets titled *Ecodefense* describing the tree spiking strategy, which an Earth First!er used to nearly kill sawmill worker George Alexander.[65]

A spike driven according to Earth First! instructions hit the bandsaw of a log headrig in Calpella, California, and shattered it into deadly shrapnel. Alexander, an offbearer working next to the bandsaw, came within half an inch of death when a sawblade fragment nearly severed his carotid artery. Other fragments sliced him almost to hamburger. He lived, but the doctors gave him a new face. If his children didn't recognize him any more, they were at least not fatherless. But that doesn't matter to Earth First!ers, who dismiss such violence cavalierly. If George Alexander had died, so much the better. To them, the fewer people the better. Worship trees, sacrifice people. Law enforcement officers followed several leads in the near-fatal tree spiking, but were unable to apprehend the criminals.

Earth First! has forced the entire environmental movement perceptibly to the left by saying the unthinkable—wouldn't it be fun to destroy industrial civilization—and getting millions to think along the same lines. Taking direct action to burn livestock auctions,[66] blow up nuclear reactor facilities,[67] shoot privately-owned cattle grazing on federal allotments,[68] and threatening the lives of corporate executives proved to be great guerilla theatre,[69] pulling supportive comments from call-in talk radio listeners and even mainstream periodicals and television news reporters. Trashing the economy through violence became the equivalent of a polite parlor game. Many in industry were totally baffled at the support this eco-terrorist group got from the media.

Earth First! was baffling because it drew upon a hodgepodge of Deep Ecology cliques, coteries and cabals. Some adherents were merely recycled specimens from the disintegrating Far Left. They called themselves by such quaint names as Social Ecologists, Eco-Feminists, the Left Green Network. Their ranks were swelling with recruits tormented by the collapse of Marxian socialism. Richard Darman, director of the Office of Management and Budget told a 1990 Harvard audience that the term "environmentalist" was "a green mask under which different faces of politico-economic ideology can hide," and "now that East-West conflict is in decline, the green mask is one under which competing ideologies will continue their global struggle."[70]

Earth Day 1990 in Washington, D. C. provided a grotesquely funny illustration of Darman's point:

> Earth Day was a beautiful day. The planners gave thanks—to the Sun, the Earth, the Trees—anything that wasn't human. During the prayer I kept my eyes open and was glad to see that, despite rousing incantations coming from the loudspeakers, most everybody was chatting about their favorite Hollywood celebrity and the suntan they would be getting.
>
> This indifference seemed to worry the planners. Perhaps they really believed that, at day's end, people would abandon their consumer-driven city—and their cars. A lady with a "Mao More Than Ever" T-shirt, selling books on *The Truth about the Constitution*, was indignant that "these people came only for the music." Occasionally, a fun-loving collegiate would complain that the music was interrupted too often for sermons; only to be hushed by more earnest peers with reminders of their Purpose.

As the sun declined, I added up the score: Mikhail Gorbachev lavishly praised for his initiation of a "Green Cross" to heal, not the oppressed peoples under his control, but a symbolic Mother Earth; Reagan and Bush condemned, of course, as enemies of the Cause.

Then came the grand finale: I was looking at the Washington Monument, wondering how many times our first President had rolled over in his grave, when a singer with a powerful, moving voice began singing the Internationale. There was the Capitol dome bathed in golden sunlight. There was the Senate and the House. There on the lawn, were Americans. And there was the communist anthem booming over all. Only in America.[71]

The lady in her *Mao More Than Ever* T-shirt and the singing of *The Internationale* were emblematic of the American Left's wistful turn to the environmental movement as the last great hope of the all-powerful centralized collectivist state, the ultimate soapbox upon which to vent its envy and hatred of free enterprise, and Earth First! was one of their favorite steps up to the microphone.

Some elements of the Far Left Environmentalists which supported Earth First! were not interested in making society do a better job of protecting the environment. They were interested in *Remaking Society*, the title of a book by Murray Bookchin, founder of the Institute for Social Ecology in Burlington, Vermont, and a thirty-year veteran of anti-capitalist environmental activism. Bookchin does not try to cloak his radicalism in reformist rhetoric as many mainstream organizations still do, but goes straight to the often hidden heart of the ideological debate. Yet Dave Foreman took Bookchin to task for not being radical enough.[72]

Bookchin frankly argues that "a humane solution to the modern environmental crisis will require a revolution that replaces capitalism with an ecological society based on nonhierarchical relationships, decentralized communities, and eco-technologies like solar power, organic agriculture and humanly scaled industries."[73] As with most ecobabble, exactly what that means is hazy, but it most certainly does not describe a society in which you could find a General Motors car, Boeing airplane factories, private property, New York City, the right to keep and bear arms, a McDonald's hamburger, or perhaps even a voting booth. Ideas have consequences.

Barry Commoner, guru of the 1970s environmental movement, has resurfaced to reprise Murray Bookchin's theme—and candor—in *Making Peace With the Planet*. Explaining that "the ideological issue can no longer be evaded," Commoner now states openly the underlying beliefs that he has held all along but would not utter: Capitalism—the free market and modern technology—is the earth's principal enemy. His book is built around three points: First, modern technology is bad; second, only a socialist system can manage an environmentally benign society; and third, militarism is the primary cause of the capitalist, anti-environment system, so only disarmament can lead to peace with the planet.[74]

It is an amusing joke on Commoner that disarmament and peace appears to be rising with the fall of socialist—not capitalist—societies, and even real communists of communism, Soviet commentators emphasized that centralized societies commit the worst sins against the environment. For example, Anatoly Gorelov, a D.Sc. in philosophy, wrote in the Soviet magazine *New Times*, "Centralization and production planning geared to the single purpose of 'overtaking and surpassing America,' combined with collectivization which led to mismanagement in agriculture and land degradation, with public opinion nonexistent and with the ruling quarters' arbitrary rule unopposed by the totally passive masses—all this leads to an ecological catastrophe much faster than capitalist anarchy does."[75]

It is sardonic that the centrally planned socialist system is being rejected by nearly everyone in the world except environmentalists.

Eco-feminists such as Carolyn Merchant repeat the Far Left anti-free enterprise theme with a different slant: the ecological ethic is essentially a feminist ethic, something many Earth First!ers believe from top to toe.[76] Ecology assigns equal importance to all parts of an ecosystem—air, water, soil, organisms—feminism asserts the equality of the sexes. Ergo, a new political system must enforce that equality.[77] Also, since the production of commodities ties up energy, and nature cannot continue to provide free goods and services for profit-hungry humans, good eco-feminists should cooperate with each other and share appropriate-technology "use-values" instead of competing for resources and owning things.[78] Exactly what this eco-prattle means is also vague, but it is definitely not friendly to industrial civilization or free enterprise.

Andrae Collard and Joyce Contrucci, co-authors of *Rape of the Wild: Man's Violence against Animals and the Earth*, take a much harder line, linking male exploitation of the earth with male exploitation of women in an impassioned plea for a feminist ecological revolution. Although they stress the necessity of kinship with nature, Collard and Contrucci blast science, industry, and capitalism with such shrill rhetoric they sound like vengeance is more necessary than kinship.[79]

Eco-feminists assert that the feminine principle is peaceful, and that ancient cultures ruled by goddess-worship rather than male-dominated god-worship were happy cultures where "celebration of life is the leading motif," and images of warfare and male aggression are strikingly absent.[80]

The "postpatriarchal" society is what they strive for. They neglect to mention that their ideal matriarchal nature-goddess cultures in historical fact were most commonly centered around grisly human sacrifice. Death-dealing violence is not absent from eco-feminism; it is turned inward to ritual murder rather than outward in the form of war.

In addition, nature-worshipping cultures institutionalize a dark and hopeless view of the world. As mythologer Joseph Campbell wrote about human sacrifice cultures, "In the primitive ritual...which is based on the viewpoint of the species rather than on that of the individual, what for us is "accident" is placed in the center of the system—namely, sudden, monstrous death—and this becomes therewith a revelation of the inhumanity of the order of the universe."[81]

It seems prudent to not take assertions about the inherent peacefulness of any ideology or social system too seriously. Earth First! is certainly not inherently peaceful.

Deep Ecology gurus such as Earth first!'s Dave Foreman assert that the mainstream Sierra Club, National Wildlife Federation, Wilderness Society, and the others, are "shallow," seeking only reform. On the other hand, the "deep" movement's professed ideal, according to Bill Devall and George Sessions, as we saw in the profile of the Humane Society of the United States above, is a complete return to Nature, the destruction of industrial civilization, a drastic killoff of human population, a return to Late Paleolithic conditions—the kind of hunter-gatherer, earth goddess-worshipping, shifting-agriculture economies of tribal peoples.[82]

Deep Ecologists Devall and Sessions argue passionately for non-totalitarian methods to achieve these goals, but they cannot specify what those methods might be, and for a good reason. There is no non-totalitarian way. Reasonable people will not vote for their own extermination.

Numerous thinkers concerned with ecological philosophy, such as John Passmore, Richard Watson, and Rudolp Bahro, have concluded that a "holistic" ecological ethic would inevitably result in a brand of totalitarianism they call "ecological fascism." For all the Deepies' intellectualized ecological consciousness that encourages "introspection, purification and harmony, and a dancing celebration or affirmation of all being," their demands remain *demands*. Industry must go. Civilization must go. Humans must go. They brook no disagreement. Their philosophy is *politically correct*, and that is that. Everything must be sacrificed to it. That is the essence of the totalitarian mystique.

Although they talk about government by democratic consensus, Deep Ecologists deny the doctrine of individual human rights and believe that only the species matters. Democracy without individualism is a contradiction in terms. Without respect for the individual and without fundamental rights that cannot be legislated away, democracy is just talk. And, although Deep Ecologists seem blind to the fact, the basic spirit of their philosophy, like the nature-worshipping cultures they wish to emulate, requires perennial human sacrifice.

Utopias throughout history have been based upon visions of deep reform—and are inherently totalitarian. Plato's *Republic*, for example, is admired by Deep Ecologists as an example of the naturalistic "perennial philosophy" which places humans in the wider scheme of things. This is not surprising because Plato was an idealist, a philosopher who believed in intrinsic values in nature. Yet the *Republic* of Plato is a thoroughgoing totalitarianism. Perhaps Deep Ecologists hope that their average reader will not be aware of that fact.[83]

The doctrine of Deep Ecology gave a rationale for the eco-terrorist network Earth First! Some Earth First!ers, including founder Dave Foreman, consider themselves to be the action arm of Deep Ecology (yes, that pesky exclamation point in Earth First! makes written English look like it has hiccups). Foreman and bright young environmental radicals such as Christopher Manes, former associate editor of the journal *Earth First!* (hiccup!) and author of *Green Rage*, lend further credence to Professor Nisbet's cassandra cry. With slogans such as "visualize industrial collapse," Earth First!ers preached "the unmaking of civilization" and gathered a small but fanatic cult, particularly among students.[84]

Their exclamatory self-righteousness knows no bounds. Their zeal to "liberate nature from human exploitation" is total. Most notable, members of America's influence community took the unmaking of civilization seriously, particularly critics reviewing *Green Rage*.[85]

Earth First! and kindred radicals do what they can to blast us back to the Stone Age. They wreck industrial infrastructure and threaten the lives of industrialists in the name of Nature.[86] Men and women of Earth First! blow up logging equipment, blow up power stations, sabotage oil exploration roads, dynamite mine shafts, torch livestock auction buildings, drive spikes into trees to make logging too dangerous to risk, kill livestock on the range, sabotage farm vehicles, occupy treetops to stop logging,[87] and commit other ecovandalism.[88]

Eco-terrorists act in stealthy bands under cover of night, scanning police frequencies to avoid the law, using theatrical code names such as "Desert Avenger," "Pine Marten," and "Mother Earth."[89] It is great fun for them, but their criminal attacks cost industry an estimated $25 million each year and the amount is growing annually.[90]

Edward Abbey once sent Ron Arnold a little scrap of a note—typed on a snaggletoothed non-electric machine, of course—taking him to task for calling his monkeywrenching "eco-terrorism" in an article Arnold wrote for *Reason* magazine. Since monkeywrenchers directed their violence only to objects and not to living organisms, Abbey argued, it was merely property that was being damaged to frighten people, and therefore monkeywrenching was a form of social protest, not properly terrorism. Right. Give us a break, Eddie. Abbey's lame rationalization was low comedy, unintentional self-parody.

Today Edward Abbey is dead. His disciples, lacking his moral authority, care nothing for life, routinely massacring livestock on federal grazing lands, and their tactics have escalated toward murder. Radicals may assert that to call Earth First! terrorists is to cheapen the meaning of the word, but the expression is precisely accurate: Their death threats and arsons and shootings of livestock and injuries of people have terrorized many. We have spoken to a number of corporate Chief Executive Officers who receive frequent calls from Earth First!ers threatening to kill their wives and children and reciting the locations of the executives' homes and private retreats to make it clear they can do it.

While law enforcement officers take their violence and death threats seriously, many find it difficult to take Earth First!ers' stated goals seriously—they know that Deep Ecology's warriors themselves, largely overeducated and underproductive freeloaders, would be among the first casualties of industrial collapse. To most Americans, eco-terrorism is simply an entertaining form of guerilla theatre that lets them vicariously get even with The System. To believe that the Deepies really intend to destroy industrial civilization is not credible to most.

The appeal of redemptive struggle should never be underestimated. Zealots more conservative than the loony-tunes Voluntary Human Extinction Movement are loudly calling for environmental jihad, self-immolation in the name of Nature: Douglas Scott, co-chairman of Environmental Action for Survival exhorted, "We

Douglas Scott, co-chairman of Environmental Action for Survival exhorted, "We will stop the destruction of the planet even at the cost of our own futures, careers, and blood."[91]

Today, Earth First! has 13 U.S. offices, some 75 local groups and 12 international groups. Since Dave Foreman quit, Northern California activist Judi Bari and cofounder Mike Roselle are considered the group's leaders, even though EF! ostensibly has no formal hierarchy. The staff, which once included Christopher Manes, author of *Green Rage: Radical Environmentalism and the Unmaking of Civilization*, publishes *Earth First! The Radical Environmental Journal* 8 times a year, and there are 25 local group newsletters. The group holds an annual conference of sorts, the Round River Rendezvous, at various outdoor spots on federal lands. The outfit also peddles T-shirts, patches, bumper stickers, window stickers and audio cassettes—while destroying the industries that make such things.

For a decade, Foreman and Earth First! outraged industry supporters and inspired people-haters and other environmentalists.[92] Then things began to go wrong. Foreman's initial panache and let's-live-on-the-run lifestyle began to pale on him after a while. His intellectual roots in the posh Establishment Eco-socialist Wilderness Society urged him into the philosophizing game, and he wrote extensively trying to justify eco-terrorism by melding it with Deep Ecology, an ivory-tower back-to-nature faction of the environmental movement that somewhat nearsightedly believes in blasting humanity back to the stone age and reducing the human population to Late Paleolithic levels—massive genocide. To save nature, of course. Foreman wrote, "We advocate bio-diversity for bio-diversity's sake. That says man is no more important than any other species...It may well take our extinction to set things straight."[93]

All sorts of intellectualized rationalizations for such mass murder were offered by Deep Ecology writers such as Bill Devall and George Sessions, but it never played in Peoria. And the counterculture followers Foreman had attracted found his theorizing tiresome. They wanted to dance to an ecstatic drum beat and sack corporate America, man. The Frankenstein Effect began to set in.

The violence got out of hand. And Foreman lost his edge. The "Redwood Summer" of 1990-91 was supposed to be Earth First!'s crowning achievement, stopping the harvest of old-growth redwoods forever.[94] Instead, it turned into the Rotten Egg Summer.[95] As the left-wing *Utne Reader* noted of Earth First!, "while leading the charge in the redwoods it was facing a whole slate of divisive problems: ideological splits within the organization, a rash of death threats from outside, FBI infiltration, the arrest of leader Dave Foreman and three other members on charges of conspiracy to sabotage nuclear reactor facilities, and a car bombing that severely injured two of its leading organizers."[96]

Foreman bailed out of Earth First! in 1990.[97] The media implied that he couldn't stand the following he had attracted any more. "I don't believe that muddying the issues with a lot of class-struggle rhetoric or weird-lifestyle stuff works," he told *U.S. News and World Report*. "Generally, you are the most effective when you remain part of society."[98] How much of that was Dave Foreman and how much was the FBI looking over his shoulder after his arrest is difficult to say.

Foreman told *E Magazine*, "I'm a member of the Sierra Club, the Wilderness Society and the Nature Conservancy. Quite frankly, I think those groups are more important than Earth First!, because they have been at it for a longer time, and because they have more power. Earth First! has opened up more issues and redefined the parameters of the debate, but it's so easy for radicals to get this 'holier than thou' attitude and to not appreciate the hard work that the more mainstream groups do."[99]

Earth First! lost its guiding spirit with the departure of Dave Foreman. Nymphs and shepherds, dance no more...

Sic transit gloria...

Foreman, with his FBI watchdogs not far out of sight, went on to co-found

The Cenozoic Society, Inc.
68 Riverside Drive, #1
Canton, New York 13617
Phone (315)379-9940

Board members are: John Davis (New York), Dave Foreman (Arizona), David Johns (Oregon), Tom Butler (Vermont), Reed Noss (Oregon), and Kris Sommerville (Colorado). The Cenozoic Society publishes the journal *Wild Earth*, of Voluntary Human Extinction Movement fame. The Cenozoic, for the geologically challenged, is the third and latest great era of earth history in which mammals and flowering plants appeared beginning about 65 million years ago. It is not clear how far back into the Cenozoic Era the Cenozoic Society's leaders want to blast us.

Today Earth First! has intertwined with Greenpeace to such an extent that in places the two have the same representative—Suzanne Pardee in Seattle, for instance. Greenpeace carries out joint actions with Earth First! and shares substantial numbers of activists, according to Barry Clausen, Washington State private investigator who infiltrated Earth First! on behalf of timber, mining and ranching interests. In addition a substantial number of Earth First! activists have blended into a new group calling itself the Native Forest Network. From what we see of their activist lists, NFN virtually *is* EF! merely using a different name.

Mike Roselle, one heir apparent to the Earth First! leadership, is a pale imitation of Dave Foreman. He lacks both the brains and style of Foreman, and his prospects to revitalize the network are mediocre at best. The most visible member of EF! is West Coast iconoclast Judi Bari, who, with Earth First! organizer Darryl Cherney, was severely injured in the San Francisco car bomb explosion mentioned above. Police arrested Bari after the incident because evidence pointed to an accidental explosion of a device intended for another target, evidence that subsequently vanished. Charges against Bari were dropped.

Bari, now recovered enough to stage occupations of industrial forestry sites, works out of Ukiah in Northern California, primarily against the forest products industry, and writes occasional diatribes in local newspapers. Her actions, she says, are funded in large part by the carpenter's union, the United Brotherhood of

Carpenters, which is still carrying on a grudge boycott because of a series of strikes a decade ago that got affiliate Lumber Production and Industrial Workers decertified at 19 West Coast plants belonging to Louisiana-Pacific Corporation.

Bari has told a number of our informants that Earth First! is just her current struggle, that if it wasn't Earth First! it would be something else. We term this the "Struggle Junkie Syndrome," and have found it typical of personalities addicted to activism. It also fosters a certain hypocrisy and artificiality which is clearly visible in Bari's behavior, too shrill on this issue, too mellow on that, always a bit off key, unlike the dead-on certainty Dave Foreman brought to the part.

Earth First! has suffered a serious internal split since Foreman's departure. Roselle and Bari, along with seven local branches in Northern California and the Northwest have renounced tree spiking, a seminal trademark of Earth First!

Judi Bari says that, "Earth First! has been so successful in working and strategizing with timber workers that the alienation caused by tree-spiking, not to mention the danger, be it real or imagined, was harming our efforts to save this planet."[100]

Michael Lewis of Earth First! Alaska is unhappy with Bari and having none of it. He told the *E Sheet*, an environmental news service, "The people who kill trees and destroy wildlife habitat for a living choose to do so each and every day of their lives. If they feel their bosses are not protecting them adequately from foreign material in the saw blades, they can choose to follow some other line of work. The fact that the chainsaw crowd is pissed off at Earth First! protests of their destruction merely reveals the effectiveness of EF! tactics. To fold up tent at this point and sneak off for a tryst with the eco-rapers is a copout."

Paul Watson of the Sea Shepherd Conservation Society entered the fray by claiming that he was the inventor of tree spiking and defending its use. Of course, Paul Watson claims to have invented everything useful, including fire, the wheel and zippers (yes, that's parody you detect).[101]

The original monkeywrenching mystique devised by Foreman is still what draws 'em in. Earth First! environmentalism has always depended on the thin line between direct action and violence for its appeal.

Bari was a good lieutenant, but she's not the zingy high-power charismatic intellectual leader Dave Foreman was. Mike Roselle is just an also-ran. Earth First! is growing detectably moribund; it hasn't had a new idea for years now. Ideas have consequences. Lack of ideas does too.

Unless some real talent shows up, unless somebody with the brains of strategist Christopher Manes assumes the mantle, its song is about sung.

The closest thing to an idea that Earth First! has had recently is talk about creating a wilderness system in the Lower 48 States of 716 million acres, about one-third of the total land area. This Great American Wilderness would allow no permanent human habitation, no roads, no mechanized equipment, no industry, removal of all non-indigenous species, reintroduction of all original species, destruction of all existing roads, dams, towns, cities, power lines, irrigation ditches—and no over-flights of any commercial aircraft at any altitude. We don't even need to unfurl a roll of plastic to see the cracks in that one.

Critics who dismiss Earth First! as a failed radical group don't grasp that it almost certainly originated as a clever strategic feint by the mainstream in the first place. When Dave Foreman quit the group he founded—and that mainstream environmentalists almost certainly funded under the table—he had effectively achieved what he was hired to do: make violent radical environmentalism a fact to contend with, and make the mainstream's demands seem more reasonable.[102]

Patagonia, Inc. gave $10,000 in 1989. We have a witness.

All of the above.
Job killers.
Economy trashers.

Non-Membership Organizations—Footnotes

1 These conclusions are examined in "Fact file," by Vicky Hutchins, *New Statesman & Society*, May 10, 1991, p. 19.

2 See comments, for example, in "Government Policies That Hurt the Environment," *The Futurist*, May / June, 1990, p. 54.

3 The media cover WRI reports with such headlines as "The Fall of the Forest: Tropical tree losses go from bad to worse," by Richard Montgomery, *Science News*, July 21, 1990, p. 40.

4 "Accounting for Environmental Assets," by Robert Repetto, *Scientific American*, June 1992, p. 94.

5 "Natural-Resource Losses Reduce Costa Rican GNP Gains," by David R. Francis, *Christian Science Monitor*, December 18, 1991, p. 7.

6 "Lending spawns Third World crisis, study says," by Michael Ross, *Los Angeles Times*, August 31, 1992, p. D2.

7 "Higher prices would curb U.S. demand," *Platt's Oilgram News*, April 16, 1991, p. 3.

8 "Federal policies distort farming practices," by Bette Hileman, *Chemical & Engineering News*, April 15, 1991, p. 13.

9 "Wood for the trees," by Nigel Holloway, *Far Eastern Economic Review*," January 24, 1991, p. 49.

10 "Study: improved fuel efficiency negated by glut of cars, trucks," by Martha M. Hamilton, *Washington Post*, December 13, 1990, p. E3.

11 "Greenhouse redesign: shifting some blame to the Third World," by Betsy Carpenter, *U.S. News & World Report*, June 18, 1990, p. 47.

12 "Tougher stance urged on pesticide use," by Peter Osterlund, *Christian Science Monitor*, July 15, 1985, p. 3.

13 "Documenting the destruction of the environment," by Emily T. Smith, *Business Week*, May 19, 1986, p. 115.

14 "Group proposes carbon tax for control of CO2," by Alan Kovski, *The Oil Daily*, August 12, 1992, p. 5.

15 "The environmental agenda for leaders," by James Gustave Speth, *Directors & Boards*, Summer 1991, p. 5.

16 "A New Model for Environmental Protection," by Clara Germani, *Christian Science Monitor*, October 28, 1991, p. 9.

17 *The Birth of the National Park Service*, by Horace Albright as told to Robert Cahn, Howe Brothers, Salt Lake City, p. 327-329.

18 "Resources for the Future," article, *Encyclopedia of American Forest and Conservation History*, Richard C. Davis, editor, Macmillan Publishing Company, New York, 1983, p. 319.

19 *The Economics of Natural Environments*, John V. Krutilla and Anthony C. Fisher, Resources for the Future, Washington, D.C., distributed by Johns Hopkins University Press, 1975.

20 *Research Centers Directory, 17th Edition-1993*, entry number 8567.

21 "Institutions," Robert W. Fri, *Environment*, vol. 30, no. 1, January / February 1988, p. 5

22 "Non-profits join to build complex," by Beth Schwinn, *Washington Post*, March 2, 1987, p. B56.

23 "EPA, Amoco join forces to ferret out ways to cut refinery wastes," *Chemical & Engineering News*, July 8, 1991, p. 10.

24 "Superfund," *Nation*, March 27, 1989.

25 "What will it cost?" by Joel S. Hirschhorn and Paul R. Portney, *Institutional Investor*, July 1990, p. E15.

26 "Study offers Superfund liability options," by Lois Ember, *Chemical & Engineering News*, June 15, 1992, p. 14.

27 RFF Annual Report, 1990; and *Corporate Community Relations Letter*, April, 1990.

28 *Research Centers Directory, 17th Edition-1993*, entry number 9191.

29 *Encyclopedia of Associations*, 1993, entry number 6995.

30 *Times-Picayune*, New Orleans, 1987, quoted in *Public Interest Profiles, 1992-1993*, p. 520.

31 *Community Conflict*, James S. Coleman, The Free Press, New York, 1957, p. 3.

32 *Power, Strategy and the Process of Community Conflict: A Theoretical Framework*, Gerald Cormick, unpublished Ph.D. dissertation, University of Michigan, 1971, p. 39.

33 "Along the soft path," by Jim Scwab, *Planning*, September 1990, p. 26.

34 "Finding oil in doors and lights," by Matthew L. Wald, *New York Times*, May 16, 1988, p. 21.

35 "Sustainability," by Brad Knickerbocker, *Christian Science Monitor*, October 16, 1990, p. 13.

36 "Homes, Businesses Plug In to Savings on Power Costs," by Michael Parrish, *Los Angeles Times*, March 27, 1991, p. A1.

37 "Gas Company Warns Against Pilot Light Tip," *Los Angeles Times*, March 29, 1991, p. D2.

38 "Energy Conservation Back on Front Burner," by Jill Stewart, *Los Angeles Times*, August 9, 1989, p. 3.

39 "Gone with the Wind," by Jacob V. Lamar, Jr. and Michael Riley, *Time*, January 20, 1986, p. 23.

40 "Prophets of an energy revolution," by James R. Udall, *National Wildlife*, December-January 1991, p. 10.

41 "Think Tank on the Efficient Energy Trail," by Brad Knickerbocker, *Christian Science Monitor*, July 26, 1991, p. 10.

42 League of Conservation Voters direct mail enclosure, 1990.

43 "By showing consumers how to save energy, Amory and Hunter Lovins put the (solar) heat on high-cost power," *People*, by Michael Small and Mary Chandler, October 19, 1987, p. 119.

44 *Encyclopedia of Associations*, 1993, entry number 16328.

45 "New suit targets university laboratories," by Seth Shulman, *Nature*, vol 344, April 19, 1990, p. 696.

46 "Groups seek human gene-transfer delay," by Rick Weiss, *Science News*, vol. 135, February 4, 1989, p. 68.

47 "Tryptophan under suspicion," Diane Gershon, *Nature*, vol. 346, August 30 1990, p. 787.

48 *Time*, December 4, 1989.

49 "Group Seeks to Prevent Nuclear Space Probe," *New York Times*, September 30, 1990, p. 28.

50 "Stores bar milk linked to a drug: five big chains take action—U.S. calls process safe," by Keith Schneider, *New York Times*, August 24, 1989, p. A1.

51 "Science debates using tools to redesign life," by Keith Schneider, *New York Times*, June 8, 1987, p. 1.

52 "Into the unknown," by William Pat Patterson, *Industry Week*, May 18, 1987, p. 24.

53 "Administration offers policy statement on biotechnology," by Gordon S. Carlson, *Feedstuffs*, June 1, 1992, p. 8.

54 "BST battle heats up: opponent of growth hormone will ask processors to join boycott," by Alan Levitt and Ellen Dexheimer, *Dairy Foods*, November 1990, p. 15.

55 "Raining in Their Hearts," by Ronald Bailey,*National Review,* December 3, 1990, p. 32.

56 "Consumers Union, FET attack BST," by Jon F. Scheid,*Feedstuffs*, December 10, 1990, p. 1.

57 "Battling biofundamentalists," *The Economist*, June 27, 1987, p. 87.

58 "AIDS-like cow virus found at unexpectedly high rate," by Keith Schneider,*New York Times*, June 1, 1991, p. 8.

59 "E. coli outbreak spreads to Nevada," by Warren King,*Seattle Times*, January 26, 1993, p. C1.

60 *Eco-Warriors: Understanding the Radical Environmental Movement*, Rik Scarce, The Noble Press, Inc., Chicago, 1990, p. 60ff.

61 "Earth First!ers wield a mean monkey wrench," by Michael Parfit, *Smithsonian*, April 1990, p. 184.

62 "Eco-warrior Dave foreman will do whatever it takes in his fight to save Mother Earth," by Susan Reed, *People Weekly*, April 16, 1990, p. 113.

63 *New York Times*, June 19, 1990.

64 "Pranks and protests over environment turn tough," by Ronald A. Taylor, *U. S. News & World Report*, January 13,, 1986, p. 70.

65 *Ecodefense: A Field Guide to Monkeywrenching*, edited by Dave Foreman and Bill Haywood, Ned Ludd Books, Tucson, Arizona, 1985.

66 "Monkey wrenching for planet earth," by Tim Vanderpool,*The Progressive*, September 1989, p. 15.

67 "Protector or provocateur? Dave Foreman, co-founder of the radical group Earth First!, faces trial for conspiracy," by Douglas S. Looney, *Sports Illustrated*, May 27, 1991, p. 91.

68 "Nature's avengers," by Lauren Tarshis, *Scholastic Update*, April 19, 1991, p. 20.

69 "The earth's guerilla army," by David Petersen, *Mother Jones*, February-March 1986, p. 8.

70 "The Talk of the Town" (editorial), *The New Yorker*, June 18, 1990, p. 25.

71 Phillipe Chamy, "The Idealogues," *CEI Update*, May, 1990, Number 5, Competitive Enterprise Institute, Washington, D.C., p. 3.

72 "Ecology wars: social ecologists vs. deep ecologists," by Richard Hill, *Omni,* August 1989, p. 25.

73 *Remaking Society: Pathways to a Green Future*, Murray Bookchin, South End Press, 1990.

74 *Making Peace With The Planet*, Barry Commoner, Pantheon, New York, 1990. We are indebted to the phrasemaking of Mark Mills who reviewed Commoner's book in *Fortune*, May 21, 1990, pp. 159-160.

75 Anatoly Gorelov, "Ideology against pure water," *New Times*, No. 20, 1990, Moscow (English language edition), p. 46.

76 See, for example, "The Power and the Promise of Ecological Feminism," by Karen J. Warren, *Environmental Ethics*, 12:1, Summer 1990, p. 125-126.

77 "The Ecology of Feminism and the Feminism of Ecology," by Ynestra King, in*Healing the Wounds: The Promise of Ecofeminism*, Judith Plant, editor, New Society, Philadelphia, 1989.

78 Carolyn Merchant, "Feminism and Ecology," in Bill Devall and George Sessions,*Deep Ecology: Living as if Nature Mattered*, Peregrine Smith Books, Salt Lake City, 1985, pp. 229-231. See also *The Death of Nature: Women, Ecology, and the Scientific*

Revolution, Carolyn Merchant, Harper & Row, San Francisco, 1980.

79 *Rape of the Wild: Man's Violence against Animals and the Earth*, Andrae Collard with Joyce Contrucci, Indiana University Press, Bloomington, 1989.

80 *The Language of the Goddess: Unearthing the Hidden Symbols of Western Civilization*, Marija Alseikaite Gimbutas, San Francisco, Harper & Row, 1989.

81 Joseph Campbell, *The Masks of God, Volume One: Primitive Mythology*, Penguin Books, 1976, first published by The Viking Press 1959, p. 181.

82 *Deep Ecology*, Devall and Sessions, particularly Chapter 6, "Some Sources of the Deep Ecology Perspective," pp. 79-108.

83 "Exploring the new ecologies: social ecology, deep ecology and the future of Green political thought," by Brian Tokar, *Alternatives*, November - December 1986, p. 30.

84 "New leftist crusade: radical cultists are trying to fill the growing emptiness," editorial by Michael Brody, *Barron's*, March 5, 1990, p. 11.

85 *Green Rage: Radical Environmentalism and the Unmaking of Civilization*, Christopher Manes, Little, Brown and Company, Boston, 1990. p. 237.

86 "Trying to take back the planet: radical environmentalists are honing their militant tactics and gaining followers," by Jennifer Foote, *Newsweek*, February 5, 1990, p. 24.

87 "Showdown in the treetops: conservation activists stage a high-altitude sit-in to save the ancient forests," by Michael D. Lemonick, *Time*, August 28, 1989.

88 See Dave Foreman and Bill Haywood, editors, *Ecodefense: A Field Guide to Monkeywrenching*, second edition, A Ned Ludd Book, Tucson, Arizona, 1987, for a compendium of industrial sabotage techniques used by eco-terrorists.

89 *The Monkeywrench Gang*, Edward Abbey, J.B. Lippincott, New York, 1972.

90 *Green Rage*, p. 186

91 *Green Rage*, p. 52.

92 "In the presence of giants," by June Jordan, *The Progressive*, August 1990, p. 11.

93 "Earth First! and Foremost," M. John Fayhee, *Backpacker*, September 1988, p. 21.

94 For the circumstances leading up to Redwood Summer, see, "Redwood radicals: is environmental extremism doing the cause more harm than good?," by Betsy Carpenter, *U. S. News & World Report*, September 17, 1990, p. 50. See also, "Redwood Summer wins big for big trees," *The Animals' Agenda*, October 1990, p. 32.

95 "Eco-Activist summer: Earth First! vs. the loggers in California," by Bill Barol, *Newsweek*, July 2, 1990, p. 60.

96 See also, "It's still sabotage, for earth's sake," by Richard Martin, *Insight*, August 7, 1989, p. 22.

97 "Eco-terrorist seeks higher ground," by Valerie Richardson and Siobhan McDonough, *Insight*, March 25, 1991, p. 20.

98 *U.S. News & World Report*, September 17, 1990.

99 *Washington Post*, April 19, 1990.

100 "Under the Gun," by David Steinman, *Reader, Los Angeles's Free Weekly*, April 24, 1992.

101 "In Defense of Tree Spiking," *Earth First!*, September 22, 1990, p. 8.

102 "Government first, earth last!: lessons from the Earth First! trial," by Charles Bowden, *E Magazine,* January - February 1992, p. 56.

Specialized Organizations

Worldwatch Institute (Founded 1974)
     Annual budget: $3 million
          Staff: 32 professional and support.
    Non-membership
       Tax Status: 501(c)(3)
       Headquarters: 1776 Massachusetts Avenue, N.W.
            Washington, D.C. 20036
            Phone: (202)452-1999 Fax: (202)296-7365

WWI, according to its brochures, was created by the Rockefeller Brothers Fund to "alert policy makers and the general public to emerging global trends in the availability and management of resources—both human and natural." Here's another bigtime segment of the Rockefeller Interventionist Axis with more than a touch of Professor Malthus in its agenda.

It's a research organization that works to "encourage a reflective and deliberate approach to global problem-solving," according to information it supplied to the *Encyclopedia of Associations* for the 1993 edition. Translated out of foundationese, that means "we're going to slow down progress in the Third World as much as possible, and make life as tough as we can for the industrialized world while we're at it."

The chairman of the board is former Secretary of Agriculture Orville Freeman, but he has little role in actual policy making for the institute. President Lester R. Brown has been hawking the Rockefeller line at Worldwatch for many years and is the brains behind the outfit—along with the ranking members of the Rockefeller Brothers Fund.

The premier publication of WWI is the annual *State of the World*, a slick and very expensively printed compendium of doom, gloom and anti-industry rhetoric that retails for a heavily subsidized $10.95. It is used as a textbook in over 900 courses at nearly 600 universities in the United States—that's influential! Sales in recent years have reached 200,000 copies, and this Economy Trasher is printed in Arabic, Chinese, French, German, Indonesian, Italian, Japanese, Polish, Portugese, Spanish and Russian, in addition to English.

Lester Brown is still peddling the same pap he was spouting a decade ago, only updated: "The nineties may be our last chance to reverse the trends that are undermining the human prospect. If we fail, environmental deterioration and economic decline may begin to feed on each other, making an effective response to these threats impossible. Effective action depends on reliable information. That's what *State of the World* is all about." That's what he said about the eighties. And seventies.

Repent, for the end of the world is on hold.

The fundamental premise of Worldwatch Institute's output is that development is using up all the resources and our economies are collapsing as a result. They never seem to notice that new technologies make resources out of what was once useless—like petroleum before anyone knew it could be made into fuel and chemical stocks for a million products: it was just this awful black goo that seeped out of the ground and ruined your farm. Worldwatch and its anti-technology outlook will make sure there's no new technology so the world's economies can never grow.

In 1988, Worldwatch Institute received $825,000 in foundation grants, nearly all of which was earmarked for the new magazine World Watch, which hucksters the same anti-industry rhetoric as *State of the World*, only on a bimonthly basis. The Institute also puts out *Worldwatch Papers* six to eight times a year for an annual subscription of $25 or $5 each, each one a research report describing some devastation in terms so biased against technology that so solution seems possible. The Institute also publishes books in what it calls the *Alert Series*.

In a joint effort with the producers of the Nova series at WGBH-TV in Boston, Worldwatch Institute stage-managed a ten-part series based on *State of the World* for public television in the fall of 1990.

Winthrop Rockefeller Trust gave $75,000 in 1989.

Public Welfare Foundation gave $300,000 in 1990 for research analysis and information dissemination regarding global warming and other critical environmental problems.

Geraldine R. Dodge Foundation gave $125,000 in 1989 for program of monitoring environmental destruction and its consequences for economy and quality of life throughout globe.

Edward John Noble Foundation gave $80,000 in 1990 for general support.

The George Gund Foundation gave $55,000 in 1990, a 2-year grant to expand international availability of World Watch Magazine and begin publication of World Watch Environmental Reader.

W. Alton Jones Foundation gave $150,000 in 1989 for new World Watch magazine.

Worldwatch Institute.
Job killers.
Economy Trashers.

INFORM, Inc. (Founded 1974)

Annual budget:	$1.5 million
Staff:	26 total—12 professional, 14 support
Members:	1,000 individuals
Tax Status:	501(c)(3)
Headquarters:	381 Park Avenue South
	New York, New York 10016
	Phone: (212)689-4040 Fax: (212)447-0689

An environmental research group that trashes the economy with information of the "social responsibility" type. For those unfamiliar with this submovement, it operates primarily by rifling through the records of publicly held corporations—

which are open to anyone—to find anything that could possibly cost the company money and public embarrassment. Anything their investigators find in corporations' public disclosure statements about lawsuits, disputes over alleged violations of pollution standards, or legal disputes over regulations is then fund raising fodder for the "social responsibility" group, loudly hawked in news releases, reports and "studies" that attack the company for being socially irresponsible. The intent of such groups, including INFORM, is not really to improve industry, or they would take the issue up with their victims privately and quietly help to find solutions rather than attacking the company as part of a public fund raising campaign.

Typically INFORM will perform a statistical analysis of some industry and use their data to complain that companies are not doing well enough. For example, INFORM studied garbage and came up with the facts that the U.S. produces 157 million tons of garbage a year of 432,000 tons of garbage a day. Three percent of garbage goes into incinerators, six percent goes to waste-to-energy plants, 11 percent gets recycled, and 80 percent goes into landfills. This, of course, was part of a campaign against landfills. The best solutions, waste-to-energy plants, are commonly opposed by INFORM's allies among environmental activists.[1]

President Joanna D. Underwood founded INFORM with two colleagues, before which she was co-director of the **Council on Economic Priorities** in New York, the premier "social responsibility" industry-bashing conclave, from 1970 to 1973. She also taught environmental studies courses at New York University and Adelphi University. She serves on the boards of the New York State Energy Research and Development Authority, Planned Parenthood of New York City, and the Hampshire Research Institute. She served as an advisory board member of the congressional Office of Technology Assessment. Underwood received her undergraduate degree from Bryn Mawr College and a diploma in French civilization from the Sorbonne.

Underwood began INFORM with a primary focus on air pollution in New York City and grew to encompass its present four major topics: hazardous waste reduction, solid waste management, urban air pollution and land and water conservation. The group is beginning to focus on natural gas and methanol motor fuels.[2] INFORM does not lobby or litigate, but does present testimony at congressional hearings.[3]

INFORM's first project was a research publication titled *A Clear View*, released in 1975. It was essentially a guide for local groups, describing methods to investigate industrial pollution and how to punish industries that pollute. It has found its way into over a dozen universities as a textbook. The Environmental Defense Fund uses it as a reference as did Shell Oil and International Paper, both large funders of the environmental movement, in writing their new corporate air pollution guides.[4]

Relying heavily on the influence of its funders in the Rockefeller, Mellon and Pew foundations, INFORM conducted a three-year research study beginning in 1982 on toxic waste practices in the chemical industry. The 530-page report, *Cutting Chemical Wastes*, was intended to establish strict regulation over all chemicals used in industry, and INFORM and its web of interests succeeded in orchestrating the creation of EPA's Office of Pollution Prevention.[5]

An article in the *Sierra Club Bulletin* about INFORM's findings boosted

INFORM's 1985 project slapping industry for polluting the Hudson River in New York.[6]

INFORM also conducted studies of new technologies for the cleaner burning of coal, surveying what was available to see what could be enforced as regulations. The group also hit the U.S. copper industry with a study of workplace health and safety derived mainly from OSHA records, which was coordinated with their publication of a directory listing clinics across the United States that specialize in treating job-related illnesses and injuries.

The real estate business has received its share of attention from INFORM: The group has published a number of consumer manuals for retirement lot buyers in the Sunbelt showing how to tell phony claims from true.

Farmers in the Southwest came in for their share of INFORM criticism about wasting water, even though new drip irrigation and other advanced technologies have steadily improved their water efficiency records. INFORM took credit for spurring work in new water technology that has been carried on by the U.S. Soil Conservation Service with a grant from the California Energy Commission.[7]

Underwood and her staff make frequent radio and television appearances to bash industry. The group also runs an active outreach program to the general public and also delivers presentations and national and international conferences and workshops. INFORM published a 1991 interview with Joanna Underwood in a special advertising section of *Barron's*, the prestigious business periodical.[8]

A typical interview with Underwood finds some way to bash industry:

> Although then-Gov. Thomas H. Kean, in his 1988 state-of-the-state message, called waste prevention the state's No. 1 waste management priority, little has been done to promote the objective, says Joanna D. Underwood, executive director of INFORM, the New York-based non-profit research organization. "We have not found in the point of view of prevention, which is the area that we look at, that New Jersey has been any more creative than any of the states we look at," says Underwood, whose organization looks at how companies can operate in a cleaner fashion, using state-of-the-art methods to meet environmental mandates.[9]

Waste-reduction advocacy remains INFORM's biggest business.[10]

Their new book *A Citizen's Guide to Promoting Toxic Waste Reduction* is a how-to-trash-you-local-industry instruction manual. INFORM also offers access to computerized data bases for money.

INFORM's $25 annual dues gets members a one-year subscription of their quarterly newsletter, *INFORM Reports*, which has a circulation of 2,000. One of their fund raising gimmicks is giving $50 donors a string shopping bag and calling them an "INFORMed Shopper." Cute. For giving a hundred bucks, you also get a discount on new INFORM studies. The group has done over 40 major studies to date, including such titles as *Business Recycling Manual, Managing Irrigation with Gypsum Blocks: A Step-by-Step Guide for Farmers*; *Toxics in Our Air*; and *Trading Toxics Across State Lines*, and intends to continue cranking them out.

INFORM receives its money from foundations (65 percent); corporations (15 percent); individuals (13 percent); other (7 percent).

The Board of Directors includes chairman Kenneth F. Mountcastle, Jr. and vice chairman Kiku Hoagland Hanes (a vice president of Patrick Noonan's Conservation Fund). Other members include James B. Adler; Christopher J. Daggett; Michael J. Feeley; Barbara D. Fiorito; Jane R. Fitzgibbon; C. Howard Hardesty, Jr.; Lawrence S. Huntington; Sue W. Kelly; Martin Krasney; Jay T. Last; Jospeh T. McLaughlin; Charles A. Moran; Susan Reichman; Frank T. Thoelen; Grant P. Thompson; Joanna D. Underwood.

INFORM, Inc. was funded by:

Geraldine R. Dodge Foundation gave $50,000 in 1989 for renewed support of research and education in New Jersey on air pollution and reduction-at-the-source for both solid waste and toxics.

The William and Flora Hewlett Foundation gave $180,000 in 1990, a 3-year grant for general support of Alternative Decisionmaking Program.

W. Alton Jones Foundation, Inc. gave $50,000 in 1989 for program to reduce production of hazardous waste.

The Joyce Foundation gave $150,000 in 1990, a 3-year grant for chemical hazard prevention program including research and outreach to grassroots groups in Midwest.

Joyce Mertz-Gilmore Foundation gave $20,000 in 1989 for efforts related to pollution of Hudson River and solid waste disposal.

Richard King Mellon Foundation gave $375,000 in 1989, a 4-year grant for program support.

Morgan Guaranty Trust Company of New York Charitable Trust gave $10,000 in 1989 for capital and operating support.

The New York Community Trust gave $40,000 in 1990 to promote effective solid waste agenda for New York City, for outreach activities and workshops.

The Overbrook Foundation gave $12,000 in 1989.

The Pew Charitable Trusts gave $120,000 in 1990, a 3-year grant for urban air quality and energy efficiency program.

The Prudential Foundation gave $10,000 in 1989 for sustainable agriculture project.

The Rockefeller Foundation gave $70,000 in 1990 toward outreach project in Mexico to introduce leaders from industry, government and nongovernmental organization to concepts of industrial toxic waste reduction.

The Scherman Foundation, Inc. gave $45,000 in 1989, a 2-year grant for general support.

Victoria Foundation, Inc. gave $25,000 in 1989 for public education campaigns to disseminate research and information on how to reduce industrial toxic wastes, how to more effectively manage garbage crisis through increased recycling and waste reduction, and how to reduce urban air pollution largely caused by vehicle emissions.

INFORM, Inc.
Job killers.
Economy Trashers.

League of Conservation Voters (Founded 1970)
        Annual budget: $1.3 million
                Staff: 67 total—12 professional, 55 field staff
             Members: 60,000 individuals
          Tax Status: Political Action Committee (PAC)
        Headquarters: 1707 L Street, NW, Suite 550
                       Washington, D.C. 20036
                       Phone: (202)785-8683 Fax: (202)835-0491

An Economy Trasher political action committee of stupendous power—and arrogance. Its former president Bruce Babbitt once wrote in a League Scorecard of candidates, "We must identify our enemies and drive them into oblivion"—and he is now Secretary of the U. S. Department of the Interior, driving his enemies into oblivion.[11]

A wonderful piece of gallows humor came out of the Senate confirmation hearings when nominee Babbitt, a former Governor of Arizona, was questioned by the Senate Committee on Energy and Resources about having urged his League of Conservation Voters to drive his mostly Republican enemies into oblivion. After Babbitt gave a glib answer touting his ability to separate his advocacy from his administrative duties, Senator Frank Murkowski (R-Alaska) asked Chairman Bennett Johnston (D-Louisiana) for the floor to address the nominee. This is what the Congressional Records shows:

SEN. MURKOWSKI: Thank you, Mr. Chairman. After making a reference to the terminology oblivion relative to the rating of some of us on this side of the aisle, as a consequence of your previous association, why, I'm not coming forth necessarily from oblivion. But I'm sensitive to the question, Governor, because....

SEN. JOHNSTON: Would you yield at that point.[12]

Even though the League is technically non-partisan, it is run exclusively by Democrats and has formally endorsed only Democratic tickets. In 1986 the League contributed $100,000 to candidates and helped elect seven pro-environmentalist Democratic senators: Wirth (Colorado); Graham (Florida); Fowler (Georgia); Mikulski (Maryland); Reid (Nevada); Conrad (North Dakota); and Daschle (South Dakota). It has also endorsed a few individual Republicans, notably Senator John H. Chafee of Rhode Island.[13]

This PAC was created in 1970 by the Friends of the Earth because FOE's tax status would not permit raising funds for political purposes. Marion Edey, a House Committee staffer, was selected as its first leader. Although it is a non-membership organization, LCV claims about 15,000 active supporters.[14]

Executive Director James D. Maddy has held his position since 1987. From 1985 to 1987 he was on the presidential campaign staff of former Arizona Governor Bruce

Babbitt. Before that he was president of the Western Governors' Association. From 1977 to 1981 Maddy served in the administration of West Virginia Governor Jay Rockefeller as governor's assistant for energy and environmental policy and as assistant for intergovernmental relations. During this time he also served as director of the State Energy Office, the Coal Development Authority, the Office of Employment and Training, and was assistant director of the Office of Economic and Community Development. Well, there's that old revolving door, out of government into the environmental movement. Maddy earned his M.A. in economics from West Virginia University in 1974 where he also served as associate director of the Regional Research Institute. Interior Secretary Bruce Babbitt (a multiple revolver), when he was president of the League, did a considerable amount of electioneering on its behalf.[15]

There is no formal membership, but a $25 donation gets you the *National Environmental Scorecard*, along with other special publications. LCV publishes *Election Reports* (post-election); *National Environmental Scorecard*; and *Presidential Profiles* during presidential election years. The Scorecard is available to non-members for $5.[16]

The League contributed more than $250,000 in 1990 in direct and in-kind contributions to more than 100 House and Senate candidates. It contributed $150,000 to 76 House and Senate candidates in 1988, up from $100,000 in 1986.[17]

In addition, the League is also known for the staff it can provide to candidates for field organizing. The League canvasses door-to-door handing out political leaflets on such issues as household toxic chemicals and the Clean Air Act.

The League's Scorecard garnered 34 members of Congress in 1990 who could boast a 100 percent score on environmental votes. The League has used its Scorecard as a potent weapon against lawmakers who protect jobs and the economy.[18]

Individual contributions constitute the sole source of income for the League of Conservation Voters, the same as all political action committees. The League has 2 branches in New Hampshire and one in Rhode Island. Its official statement on affiliates is "The League has no local chapters, although there are independent state organizations who share the League's name in 12 states."

The Federal Election Commission (FEC) says the League of Conservation Voters (LCV) went bankrupt in 1991 and so may not give more than $1,000 to a single candidate.

A selected list of contributors to LCV in 1991 as provided by the Federal Election Commission included:

James B. Arnold of La Jolla, California (University of California at San Diego) $1,000; Charles M. Bagley, Jr. of Seattle (doctor) $780; Harvey G. Baker of Daytona Beach, Florida (retired) $500; Anne Bartley of Washington, D.C. $1,800; Frances Beinecke of New York (NRDC) $5,000; Ruth Berlin of Southport, Connecticut (retired) $1,000; David Binns of Estes Park, Colorado $250; Robert Blake of Washington, D.C. (retired) $1,000; Elizabeth E. Bramhall of Tisbury, Massachusetts (housewife) $250; Thomas C. T. Brokaw of Wilmington, Delaware (investor) $4,000; Nancy L. R. Bucher of Boston (Boston University School of Medicine)

$3,000; Sonya L. Burgher of Rochester, New York (retired) $500; Carole A. Burnett of Mill Valley, California (housewife) $250; Richard H. Crawford of Davis, California (University of California) $1,000; Leo A. Drey of St. Louis (tree farmer) $500; John E. Earhart of Laguna Beach, California (private investor) $5,000; Mary Gibbons $500; Ralph J. Gunderman of North Tarrytown, New York (actor) $300; Charles Haber of Carmel Valley, California $300; John A. Harris IV of Berwyn, Pennsylvania (retired) $5,000; Lawrie Ryerson Harris of Berwyn, Pennsylvania $5,000; A. John Holden, Jr. of Montpelier, Vermont $250; John Hunting $1,000; Elise F. Jones of Newtown, Pennsylvania (demographer) $500; Goran Klintmalm of Dallas $300; Gueta Mezzetti of Washington, D.C. (consultant) $1,000; Mrs. J. Cliff Miller III $500; Roger Milliken Jr. of Cumberland, Maine (Baskenhagan Company) $1,000; Jan Montgomery of Santa Barbara, California $300; Josephine L. Murray of Cambridge, Massachusetts (retired) $1,000; Richard Patterson of Streetsboro, Connecticut (retired) $500; Jonathan Reiss of New York $250; Laurance Rockefeller of New York (NRDC) $5,000; Wendy G. Rockefeller of New York (NRDC) $5,000; Fannette Sawyer of Buffalo (homemaker) $4,000; Robert Schumann of Delray Beach, Florida (retired) $300; W. Ford Schumann of Scottsdale, Arizona (retired) $1,500; David Strauss of New Paltz, New York $300; Gordon G. Wallace of Washington, D.C. (retired) $5,000 (April), $4,000 (May); Robert B. Wallace of Washington, D.C. $5,000; John H. Watts III of Brooklyn $5,000; John M. Woolsey, Jr. of Cambridge, Massachusetts (lawyer) $500; R. Lyman Wood of Hampden, Massachusetts (store owner) $1,000; Robert Worth $250; John Yates of Buffalo $250.

The League's Board of Directors consists of chairman Brent Blackwelder (Friends of the Earth) and president Bruce Babbitt (until his 1993 confirmation as Interior Secretary in the Clinton administration), along with other members: Albert Andrews, Jr.; Richard Ayres (Natural Resources Defense Council); Frances Beinecke (NRDC); Thomas C. T. Brokaw; Syd Butler; Ruth Caplan (Environmental Action); Charles Clusen; Paul Elston; Brock Evans (Audubon Society); Sharon Francis; David Gardiner (Sierra Club); John Hunting; Rafe Pomerance, Jr.; Paul Pritchard (National Parks and Conservation Association); William Roberts; Claudine Schneider; Maitland Sharpe (Izaak Walton League of America); Charles Warren; John Watts; Vim Wright.

League of Conservation Voters.

Job killers.

Economy Trashers.

Zero Population Growth (Founded 1968)
> Annual budget: $1.3 million
>> Staff: 12 total
>> Members: 30,000 individuals
>> Tax Status: 501(c)(3)
>> Headquarters: 1400 16th St. N.W., Suite 320
>>   Washington, D.C. 20036
>>   Phone: (202)332-2200 Fax: (202)332-2302

Zero Population Growth was founded by Stanford University Professor Paul R. Ehrlich, king of the wild Malthusians. His book *The Population Bomb* set the tone of scholarly hysteria that pervades this segment of the environmental movement. Ehrlich is witty and—except for his unassailable political correctness—has a certain charm for an Economy Trasher. The good professor's arguments that population growth will destroy the earth and all life on it are a bit overdrawn, but, then, academia and common sense have never been on intimate terms.

Paul and Anne Ehrlich, an exceptional husband-wife team something like Amory and Hunter Lovins, see population issues within a global ecological context. What matters most to them is the relationship between a population and the resource base that supports it. If a population cannot be sustained without depleting the resource base and degrading the environment, an area is overpopulated.

The Ehrlichs argue that affluence, not poverty, is the fundamental human problem. The impact of a population on the environment results from three factors: (1) the size of the population; (2) affluence, measured as the amount of natural resources the average person consumes; and (3) technology, or the environmental disruption involved in producing or disposing of the goods consumed: Environmental impact = Population x Affluence x Technology.

By this formula, a baby born in America represents twice the destructive impact on the Earth's ecosystems and resources than one born in Sweden, 3 times that for one born in Italy, 13 times that in Brazil, 35 times that in India, 140 times that in Bangladesh or Kenya, 280 times that in Chad, Rwanda, Haiti or Nepal.

Do you feel guilty yet?

The clear solution to population problems based on the Ehrlich formula is extreme poverty for everyone. Except Paul and Anne Ehrlich, who live in a posh home near Paul's tenured professorship at palatial Stanford University, and whose personal impact on the Earth's ecosystems and resources is infinitely greater than that of a child born in Somalia.

The development approach to population is anathema to the Ehrlichs. The advances that lead to a natural lowering of fertility rates—achieving better nutrition, sanitation, basic health care, education, and equal rights for women—also leads to craving for the amenities brought with greater resource use.

Ehrlich's recommendations that we prevent all technology from falling into the hands of the Third World lest it become fruitful and multiply and—horror of horrors—prosper, extend to everything except birth control technology. Zero Population Growth has fallen afoul of the Catholic Church and the Protestant Religious Right by "working to safeguard such things as population education, voluntary family planning, and the right to chose an abortion." Catholic dogma usually runs in harmony with environmentalism—Francis of Assisi was canonized as the patron saint of ecologists—but on the population issue they part company rather decisively, an interesting twist and an object lesson against generalizing about the environmental movement.

Susan Weber, executive director, says her organization has seven local groups. Volunteers at the local level participate in three organized programs: Action Alert Network, Roving Reporter and Growthbusters. Growthbusters?

What do they do, walk up to developers and slug them? Walk up to little kids and shout "Stay Small"?

ZPG publishes reports throughout the year with titles such as "Abortion in America," "Combating Teen Pregnancy: An Introductory Guide to Programs and Resources," and all sorts of fact sheets on Airborne Poisons, Traffic Congestion, The Garbage Crisis, Population and the Greenhouse Effect, World Hunger, Recycling, Deforestation, Loss of Wildlife, and Water Wars—something to offend everyone.

Diane Sherman, communications director, says ZPG plans to strengthen its work at the grassroots level to increase public awareness of population issues. ZPG will also continue to focus on issues such as urbanization and local growth, global warming, sustainability, transportation, family planning, and the fast-changing issues of immigration, population and foreign aid legislation.

ZPG also pressures the World Bank and White House officials to consider population policies in their international development strategies. ZPG lobbies Congress to "protect reproductive freedoms, to expand birth control services, and invest in new contraceptive technology."

ZPG also brainwashes 'em early and often with classroom kits for the kiddies. The group sponsors teacher training workshops to provide educators with the skills, information, and materials they need to include population studies in their classrooms. For children in grades six through ten, they have "For Earth's Sake Teaching Kit," which introduces students to the relationship between population and the environment and includes activity modules, a teacher's guide, population data sheets, a resource list and a list of ways for individuals to help. For secondary students, they have the "Global 2000 Countdown Kit," containing fourteen modules and resources. The "USA by Numbers Teaching Kit" has hands-on activities that, claims ZPG, "help develop skills in critical thinking, deductive reasoning, chart reading, data interpretation, graphing, and communication at all levels." You believe all that, don't you?

Isn't it interesting that there is no module presenting another view of the population issue? Oh, well, what's fairness in the classroom anyway? Professor Ehrlich knows all the answers.

ZPG acts as an information clearinghouse. It compiles and disseminates population statistics to the media and the public; observes population trends in the U.S. and around the world; offers information and referral services; monitors and reports on legislative and judicial activity affecting population-related issues; observes media coverage and interpretation of population issues; expresses its views before Congress and the media.

Publications: Annual Report. *Media Targets,* bimonthly. *ZPG Reporter,* 6 times a year, a newsletter providing commentary concerning international and domestic population-related issues, including reproductive rights, economic growth, environment, and natural resources. It carries interviews, information on resources available, and humorous items. It also includes a calendar of events, legislative news and member news. The price is included in membership dues of $20 per year. Circulation 15,000.

During the 1989 Combined Federal Campaign, ZPG raked in nearly $90,000 and gained over 500 new members, and has remained with the campaign every year since.

Zero Population Growth.

Job killers.

Economy Trashers.

The Rainforest Action Network (Founded 1985)

> Annual budget: $1.2 million
>> Staff: 10 total
>> Members: 35,000 members
>> Tax Status: 501(c)(3)
>> Headquarters: 300 Broadway, Suite 28
>> San Francisco, California 94133
>> Phone: (415)398-4404 Fax: (415)398-2732

Operates out of the same building as David Brower's Earth Island Institute, and was originally a project of Friends of the Earth that went independent. Director Randall L. Hayes founded RAN in 1985, coming from a career in documentary filmmaking—he produced the award winning film *The Four Corners, A National Sacrifice Area?* Hayes is a long-time activist and Economy Trasher on the lecture circuit, and sits on the board of directors of Earth Island Institute. RAN absorbed People of the Earth in 1988, an environmental-peace-justice group that had been established in 1981.

Its literature says, "The group works to bring the plight of the rain forest to the public's attention in countries where there are no tropical rain forests." In fact, it merely trashes the economies of countries where there are rain forests and where there aren't.

For example, RAN's first direct action campaign was a 1987 nationwide boycott of Burger King "to protest the importation of cheap beef from countries where rain forests are clear-cut to make room for cattle." The boycott killed 12 percent of Burger King's sales. Burger King, under pressure of the boycott, canceled $35 million worth of Central American beef contracts.

Bravo, Rainforest Action Network! You proudly destroyed $35 million worth of desperately needed exports from struggling Central American economies and bankrupted dozens of responsible, well-managed ranches in Guatemala and Costa Rica—ignoring that 83% of logs cut in the Third World are for household cooking fuel, not ranching or development, a plight that could be cured by industrialization.

That thirty-five million bucks had supported *thousands* of jobs in poor developing countries. Rainforest Action Network killed them all. Not bad for an outfit with a budget of only $1.2 million to kill $35 million worth of business to poor countries. A lot of bang for the buck. Charming folks, RAN.

The slash-and-burn culture of poverty-stricken villagers who *do* clear-cut rain forests to make room for their scrawny cattle was untouched by the boycott and continues to go from patch to patch every couple of years as the soil plays out and the forest begins to close in and take over. Rainforest Action Network, whose economy will you kill next?

Randall Hayes did his best to destroy timber harvest in Malaysia by fabricating a story that the Penan of Sarawak were being raped and beaten by loggers using customary tribal forests. In a fund raising letter dated July 28, 1993, Hayes urged RAN members to donate a minimum of $25 to RAN to support his "Sarawak cause." Hayes claimed to have visited a Penan blockade against the loggers and interviewed the "victims." However, reporters for the *New Straits Times* checked with the tour company which brought Hayes to Kuching, Malaysia, and found he had not visited any blockades during his two-week safari trip there. When Eric Hansen, author of *Stranger in the Forest* upbraided Hayes for fabricating the story, Hayes was unrepentant, and refused to do anything to correct the lies. In addition, Hayes said none of the money raised would go to the Penan people, but only pay his expenses.[19]

RAN is now actively trying to ban all world trade in tropical timber products. RAN wants to totally destroy the timber industry in South and Central America and Southeast Asia by making it illegal to import any tropical wood into the United States.

RAN is also working on making it illegal to use timber from any "lowland temperate rainforest in the United States." Well, that's just about every forest below 2,000 feet in elevation—if there's no rain, there's no forest, so every forest is a rainforest. Whose economy will RAN kill next? America's, of course.

RAN gets its money from contributions (41 percent); membership dues (31 percent); grants (13 percent); merchandise sales (13 percent); special events, investment income and list rental revenue (2 percent). RAN maintains a small but intensive library and runs a speakers bureau that presents a slide show on the rainforest ecosystem.

Its monthly publication, *Action Alert*, is primarily a bulletin on immediate action issues that need grass roots response such as letters and telephone calls to legislators. It includes addresses of target individuals in government and policy groups so readers will know where to send protests or approval. Their quarterly, *World Rainforest Report*, is published in conjunction with Friends of the Earth, Maylaysia and Rainforest Information Centre. It contains progress reports on RAN programs, a list of education materials and a calendar of events.

RAN also publishes numerous fact sheets and distributes a teacher's packet and booklet. Among their fact sheets is a lengthy list of "Things to To," including boycotting tropical wood products, sending letters to leaders of countries where tropical wood is harvested and grown such as Maylaysia, writing to the president of the World Bank urging that institutions halt the funding of rain forest dams and divert the monies to small projects for inhabitants of the forests, and writing to the Secretary General of the United Nations to demand that development be stopped.

RAN claims there are 150 Rainforest Action Groups (RAGs) in the U.S. and Europe informally associated with RAN. Hayes claims they receive support materials but no funding. RAN receives electronic mail and conducts interesting conversations on the electronic bulletin board Econet if you happen to know their password. They also operate a toll-free number, 1-800-989-RAIN.

The Board of Directors includes president Randall L. Hayes; treasurer James Hupp; secretary Michael Marx; and other members: Catherine Caulfield; Chris Desser; Michael Roselle (Earth First!); David Weir.

Rainforest Action Network.

Job killers.

Economy Trashers.

Specialized organizations—Footnotes

1 "The garbage barge," by Blayne Cutler, *American Demographics*, July 1989, p. 16.

2 "Experts see natural gas as future fuel," by Gene Smith,*The Oil Daily*, September 20, 1989, p. 1. See also, "Gas 'most promising' fuel, research group contends," *The Oil Daily*, July 6, 1989, p. 6.

3 See "Waste reduction: a new strategy to avoid pollution," by Kirsten U. Oldenburg and Joel S. Hirschhorn, *Environment*, March 1987, p. 16.

4 "Chemical giants push green image," *Journal of Commerce*, November 4, 1991, p. 13A.

5 "Toxic-waste cutback effort seen as weak; industry group differs with private report," by Cass Peterson, *Washington Post*, January 8, 1986, p. A3.

6 "Chemical stream: toxics in the Hudson," *Sierra Club Bulletin*, November-December 1985, p. 12. See also "Hudson River toxics get a closer look," by Laurie A. Rich and Joseph F. Dunphy, *Chemical Week*, August 14, 1985, p. 11.

7 "Using gypsum to save water," *Environment*, September 1988, p. 23.

8 "Prevention and cure: striking a new balance," *Barron's* April 22, 1991, p. 30.

9 *Business Journal of New Jersey*, May 1990, as quoted in *Public Interest Profiles-1992-1993*, p. 512.

10 See "Waste reduction's good news," by Mimi Bluestone and Laurie Rich, *Chemical Week*, January 15, 1986, p. 10.

11 1991 Environmental Scorecard of Congress, signed by Babbitt, League of Conservation Voters, quoted in "Clinton's Cabinet Gets Greener," by Michael Fumento *Investor's Business Daily*, December 28, 1992, p. 1.

12 As quoted in "Alaska Ear," *Anchorage Daily News*, January 24, 1993, p. B2.

13 *New York Times*, October 7, 1988.

14 Entry in *Encyclopedia of American Forest and Conservation History*, Richard C. Davis, editor, Macmillan Publishing Company, New York, 1983, p. 343.

15 "Babbitt hitting the trail to stump for environment," by Maralee Schwartz and Christopher B. Daly, *Washington Post*, February 10, 1991, p. A6.

16 See "Presidential candidates' records rated," *Facts on File*, February 6, 1992, p. 78; "Conservation League gives Bush 'D' on environment," by Elizabeth A. Brown, *Christian Science Monitor*, March 19, 1991, p. 7; "Activists challenge lawmakers' claims on environment," by Maralee Schwartz and Dan Balz, *Washington Post*, April 22, 1990, p. A9; "Conservationists toughen demands on two candidates," by Bill Stall, *Los Angeles Times*, August 26, 1990, p. A3.

17 *Newspaper*, June 14, 1990.

18 "Lawmakers graded on the environment," by Maralee Schwartz and Jay Mathews, *Washington Post*, October 17, 1990, p. A6.

19 "US group lies about Penan to raise funds," by James Ritchie, *New Straits Times*, October 11, 1993, p. 1.

Money

Back in 1889, Andrew Carnegie wrote in *The Gospel of Wealth* that, "Of every thousand dollars spent in so-called charity today, it is probable that nine hundred and fifty dollars is unwisely spent." Nothing has changed.

Corporate donations and grants from non-profit private and corporate foundations are the most important sources of funding for the environmental movement. With the money comes policy-making power. That fact should give us pause. The significance of the nation's richest corporations and most elite family foundations setting the agenda of the environmental movement is unnerving. By deciding who gets how much funding, these money sources determine the political issues that will get on the menu from which Congress chooses legislation.[1]

Although membership money from the troops makes up about half of all the funding of the overall environmental movement, it does not represent policy-making power. Only a few of the big environmental groups have voting memberships that actually elect policy makers to the board of directors, and few of those memberships can honestly be said to have real policy-making power, certainly nothing like the foundation or corporation that chips in a hundred thousand here and fifty-thousand there—or ten million now and then.

Funds received from membership dues also do not represent the expendable income of environmental groups. Dues rarely cover the cost of servicing the member—newsletters, magazines, answering telephone enquiries, and such almost always cost more than the member pays in dues. Members primarily provide legitimacy—numbers, not wealth.

Wealth, real expendable wealth, comes from other sources, mainly contributions and grants. However, foundations and corporations do not simply impose policy obligations on environmental groups with their money, they also bring benefits in the form of influential connections. Foundations and corporations link movement leaders to sources of great power, sources that provide not only more money, but also personal cultivation and grooming for leadership in top political circles. By lifting the lid on this teeming nest, we can see clearly the web of money, power and influence behind the popular movement.

The Foundation Center, an organization formed by John Gardner and James Perkins of the Carnegie Corporation to break down the walls of self-imposed secrecy surrounding philanthropy after a mid-1950s set of congressional investigations, is today one of the best sources of information about foundation grants. (The Carnegie Corporation, incidentally, is actually a nonprofit foundation, not a business firm as its name seems to imply: Andrew Carnegie called it that because he had run out of names, having already established a Carnegie Foundation, a Carnegie Trust, a Carnegie Endowment and a Carnegie Institute for various specialized purposes.)

The Foundation Center keeps track of many of the more than 32,000 active private and community foundations in America that awarded over $7 billion in grants to nonprofit organizations across the country and abroad in 1992. It is less informative about direct corporate contributions, but does monitor some company-sponsored foundations—corporate giving amounted to approximately $5.9 billion. Corporate and foundation donations represent only a small fraction of total philanthropic giving in the U.S., but they are a key source of environmental group funds.[2]

The Foundation Center listed 2,937 grants to environmental groups of $10,000 or more with a total value of $237,744,080 made by 429 foundations in 1989 and 1990. The Environmental Data Research Institute of Rochester, New York, keeps a database of more than 10,000 grants awarded since 1988 by several hundred U.S. independent and community foundations. *The Chronicle of Philanthropy*, a periodical that tracks the world of donors, published figures for 1990 that showed the top 12 environmental groups alone to have combined incomes of $519 million, over half a billion dollars. Money magazine estimated the income of the environmental movement in 1991 at $2.5 billion.[3]

	The Top Ten Environmental Grantmakers for 1990 Source: Environmental Data Research Institute		
Rank	*Foundation*	*Number of grants*	*Dollar award*
1	Richard King Mellon Foundation	15	$23,573,476
2	John D. and Catherine T. MacArthur Foundation	101	$23,299,137
3	The Pew Charitable Trusts	70	$14,554,709
4	The Ford Foundation	140	$12,933,761
5	The Rockefeller Foundation	85	$10,913,360
6	The David and Lucile Packard Foundation	29	$8,440,225
7	W. Alton Jones Foundation, Inc.	97	$7,468,610
8	W.K. Kellogg Foundation	23	$7,436,577
9	The Andrew W. Mellon Foundation	25	$6,267,900
10	National Fish and Wildlife Foundation	69	$5,955,100

Most foundations that make grants to environmental groups have an officer or staff member whose sole duty is to work with environmental groups. The foundation itself usually has an environmental agenda and actively seeks out, cultivates and monitors the nonprofits to whom it gives money.

Even the Combined Federal Campaign, the government employees' charity, donated $19.1 million between 1989 and 1991 to the Environmental Federation of America, a consortium of 27 environmental groups.[4]

Grant money, although most revealing of the patterns of power that network the environmental movement together, is, of course, not the whole picture any more than membership money. We must not forget the sale of goods and commercial services, which provides probably a quarter of the whole movement's funding. We must take into consideration the book sales of the major organizations and the mailing list rental income, royalties from use of group logos on T-shirts and various other do-dads—for an anti-business movement, environmentalists are quite good at peddling wares. These amounts were listed in the individual organization profiles above.

The tax-exempt foundations that give money to the environmental movement are not necessarily motivated by the misanthropic, anti-civilization urges that drive environmentalist grant recipients. Many are, but many are not. In fact, most foundations are benevolent to a point seldom appreciated by the average American.

One political theory of giving tax-exempt status to foundations, and thus a taxpayer subsidy, is that private foundations can excellently perform social, educational, cultural and other services that the government would otherwise have to provide. Another is that government would not necessarily perform these services at all, but since the benefits are real, charities should receive favored tax treatment because they do good that would otherwise remain undone. Few who investigate the actual performance of foundations with even a cursory glance would deny them their tax benefits. All foundations on this list should be assumed to be well-disposed toward the economy unless specific comments appear to the contrary.

Which does not mean that all are innocent when it comes to the anti-business agenda of the environmental movement. Some foundations are directed by people who also serve on the boards of directors of environmental groups. Other foundations do not have such incestuous relationships, but are guided by people who wish business no good—or at least *other peoples'* business no good.

It is nearly impossible to find anyone in the environmental movement with the faintest grasp of the fact that capitalism is what made their lush foundation grants possible. As Henry Ford II wrote in resigning from the board of trustees of the Ford Foundation because of its left-wing beneficence, "The foundation exists and thrives on the fruits of our economic system. The dividends of competitive enterprise make it all possible. It is hard to discern recognition of this fact in anything the foundation does. It is even more difficult to find an understanding of this in many of the institutions that are the beneficiaries of the foundation's grant programs." Nothing has changed.

Corporations that give to environmental groups are another matter. Corporate executives, far from being the monolithic conservatives they are commonly thought to be, direct seven out of every ten public affairs dollars from their firms and corporate foundations to organizations that act to destroy business and industry—non-profit organizations demanding more government regulation, more nationalization of private property, more power for statists in the public policy arena.[5]

Corporations do not give money just to do good. The three most compelling forces behind corporate giving, according to University of Texas analyst Marvin Olasky, are 1) personal connections between the executive—or more usually the executive's spouse—and a recipient group's charismatic leadership, connections usually made on the cocktail party circuit; 2) ideology (there are many limousine liberals among the corporate conservatives); and 3) the calculated professional judgments of public relations managers of which vocally critical groups need to be placated. In the lists we showed in the profiles above, we tried to make evident which corporations are trying to placate environmental groups and which corporate executives' wives think more of an environmental group than of their shareholders' equity.[6]

To this we would add another motive: Large well-capitalized companies attempt to destroy their medium and small competition by systematically supporting environmental groups which conceive, draft, lobby, and test in the courts new environmental laws so stringent that only large well-capitalized companies can afford to comply. In addition, new eco-businesses created by the enactment of environmental laws require ever-spreading regulation in order to increase their market size.[7]

We have listed the corporations supporting specific environmental groups in the profiles above and will not repeat them here.

Before we look under the hood of the environmental movement's foundation money, we must comment on how difficult it was to uncover all the corporate and foundation information revealed here. Compilations such as the Foundation Center's *National Directory of Corporate Giving*, and *National Guide to Funding for the Environment & Animal Welfare* are incomplete and contain massive errors. The Environmental Data Research Institute's *Environmental Grantmaking Foundations* contains entries for most of the foundations in the Environmental Grantmakers Association, but provides only a few sample grants from each foundation rather than a complete compilation. The *Taft Corporate Giving Directory* contains only a small sample of corporate giving grants, usually edited by company public relations flaks to hide their ideology. *Patterns of Corporate Philanthropy* by Marvin Olasky was an excellent source for revealing who was placating whom, but was out of date. Corporate foundations must file an annual Internal Revenue Service Report called a Form 990-PF, available to the public, which is usually handwritten, unreadable, incomplete and unrevealing. However, some corporations give directly to environmental groups rather than through their foundations and in that case may not report anything to anyone. We spent literally months on the telephone prying and probing to get much of the information that follows.

Corporations and foundations are not eager to divulge to whom they are giving money, and are particularly uneasy about telling how much they are giving to whom. We think this is wrong. Environmental groups are not obligated to reveal the source of their donations, and they uniformly refuse to reveal the sources and amounts of their corporate donations, and often will not even reveal the amounts and sources of their foundation grants. We think this is wrong.

If this book has but one policy consequence for American law, it should be to require full disclosure of all money going into and out of every environmental group—period. There is nothing private about groups that devote their entire efforts to initiating, shaping and changing public policy. Take the mask off. End the secrecy. Let the sun shine in.

Command Central

Although the environmental movement, like all movements, is a SPIN—Segmentary, Polycephalous, Ideological Network—and has no central control point, since 1985 an increasingly influential conglomeration of funders and recipient groups has coalesced into a genuine power center. A group of 160 key foundations and corporations now determines the plans, strategies and tactics of much of the mainstream environmental movement to an astonishing degree. The name of this group is the

Environmental Grantmakers Association (1985)
Budget: $40,000
Staff: 1
Tax status: See below
1290 Avenue of the Americas
New York, New York 10104
Phone: 212-373-4260 Fax: 212-315-0996
Pam Maurath, Assistant Coordinator.

The Environmental Grantmakers Association can only be characterized as the cartel of eco-money. There is nothing else like it. It does not give money to environmental groups. It does not get money from corporations and foundations except to pay for its own annual meetings. It is not a pass-through that funnels money from corporations and foundations to environmental groups.

Yet EGA is the most important money and power center in the entire environmental movement with 160 member corporations and foundations (1993) and their hundreds of environmental group grant recipients. It is the planning, coordination and monitoring center for hundreds of millions of dollars worth of environmental grant money. In its closed meetings, funders discuss their agendas and activist organizations discuss their tactics and together they plan and coordinate most of the movement's programs. As *Mother Jones* commented on EGA, "By deciding which organizations get money, the grant-makers help set the agenda of the environmental movement and influence the programs and strategies that activists carry out."[8]

EGA, like the Nader Bunch profiled above, resembles nothing so much as John D. Rockefeller's original secret Standard Oil Trust. To repeat ourselves, this "shrewd and slippery device for evading responsibility," in the words of the great muckraking journalist Ida Tarbell, "had no legal existence. It was a force as powerful as gravitation and as intangible. You could argue its existence from its effects, but you could never prove it. You could no more grasp it than you could an eel."[9]

The Environmental Grantmakers Association is located in mid-town Manhattan, but its telephone is not listed with New York City Directory Assistance; it is not recorded with the New York Department of State's Charities Registration Office; it is not incorporated. But you *can* prove that it exists and it's not really secret at all, just damn near invisible.

It is currently an adjunct of the Rockefeller Family Fund, Inc. doing business as the Environmental Grantmakers Association. The EGA uses the 501(c)(3) of the Rockefeller Family Fund and EGA's Coordinator of the Secretariat is Donald K. Ross, director of the Rockefeller Family Fund.

The EGA got its start quite casually. Five big-money foundation leaders interested in environmental issues happened to be talking one day in 1985 to Donald Ross of the Rockefeller Family Fund and found they were all going to be in Washington D.C. the following week. One of them said, let's all get together Saturday.[10]

So they all stayed at the same hotel and spent a day talking about environmental grantmaking. At the end of their session they said, this was so great we ought to do it at least once a year and plan on it. The next year they had maybe twenty people. By 1988 EGA had evolved into a vigorous but loose-knit organization. It came to a point where the members decided they needed a secretariat and Jon M. Jensen volunteered to take on the job at his newly established Pew Scholars Program in Conservation and the Environment at the School of Natural Resources of the University of Michigan, where they could umbrella under the University's tax exemption (The Pew Scholars Program, incidentally, is a project established in 1988 by the Pew Charitable Trusts of Pennsylvania—the name is no coincidence). The Environmental Grantmakers Association set up a nine-member managing committee with rotating chairmanships and terms of office.

At EGA's 1988 meeting in Princeton, New Jersey, Waste Management, Inc.'s public affairs director Dr. William Y. Brown was invited to attend the private sessions and his firm joined EGA over the objections of some of its foundation members who wanted nothing to do with a donor it considered a polluter. WMI had been hit with more than $30 million in fines between 1982 and 1987 and a criminal conviction for price-fixing. Brown has very frankly stated WMI's motivation for joining, saying that "stricter legislation is environmentally good and it also helps our business." He did not mention that it also squeezes his smaller competition out of business, something it is reasonable to think WMI might contemplate, considering their price-fixing conviction. It is strange how anti-competitive actions seem to be okay as long as they're green.

By 1989 EGA had developed into *the* recognized power center of the environmental movement. At meetings, funders held frank, detailed discussions about the activists they were considering for support grants, and funders listened to the plans and tactics of environmental groups. The movement's whole program began to be laid out at each EGA meeting.

In 1989, when Chevron Corporation was admitted to EGA, managing committee member Betsy Taylor of the Ottinger Foundation in New York opposed the oil company's membership. She told a reporter, "There's a lot of discomfort here. Some of us feel troubled to be supporting a group fighting Chevron and sitting next to Chevron, talking strategy."

She doesn't seem to have noticed that the Pew money, which at the time was the EGA umbrella, was oil money, and that the Rockefeller Family Fund, whose Don Ross had been in on the creation of EGA in the first place, was also oil money.

Greenpeace USA, which accepts no corporate contributions, but does take foundation money, picketed the Environmental Grantmakers Association's November 1989 meeting in San Francisco (the EGA meeting was paid for with the help of a grant of $18,327 from the San Francisco Foundation). Greenpeace's placard carriers warned EGA not to compromise with polluters such as Waste Management, Inc., and to throw the rascals out. However, Barbara Dudley, executive of a grantmaking foundation in attendance at the anti-Wise Use session of the 1992 EGA retreat, subsequently became executive director of Greenpeace.

By 1989 the organization got so big that Jon Jensen couldn't handle it anymore and Don Ross volunteered to handle it out of the Rockefeller Family Fund offices. In April, 1990, an EGA committee set up to screen out unacceptable members ousted Waste Management, Inc., citing "a pattern of abusive corporate conduct" and "endangering and degrading the environment." Chevron was considered for expulsion, too, but it had no criminal record.

However, Joe Kilpatrick of the Z. Smith Reynolds Foundation said he wanted to avoid sitting in judgment of members. "The EGA as a matter of policy wants to be inclusive of all grant makers. I appreciate and respect the frustrations of toxics groups arising from their dealings with Chevron. But even if their grievances against Chevron are legitimate, it doesn't follow that Chevron's corporate donor program should be excluded."[11]

In November 1990 Pam Maurath came on board as half-time paid staff and became full-time paid staff in January 1991.

The Environmental Grantmakers Association is governed by a nine-member Management Committee: Chairman, Jon Jensen, Pew Scholars Program in Conservation and the Environment; John Powers, Educational Foundation of America; Jane Rogers, San Francisco Foundation; Fred Silverman, Apple Computer; Jenny D. Russell, Island Foundation; Dan Martin, MacArthur Foundation. At press time three members were scheduled to be replaced in a committee election; Tom Deans, New Hampshire Charitable Fund; Ann Fitzgerald, Compton Foundation; Maureen H. Smyth, Charles Stewart Mott Foundation.

The Environmental Grantmakers Association's meetings are beyond question the power focus of today's mainstream movement. The October 1992 Fall Retreat at Rosario Resort on Orcas Island in Washington State's San Juan Islands revealed the tremendous political clout that EGA can pack into three days.

Attendees included executives of member foundations and corporations and executives of environmental organizations. The few guests had been carefully screened and the meetings were not open to the public.

The program included plenary sessions in the island resort's shoreline convention center and breakout sessions held in separate rooms, some in private accommodations up the hill from the center.

The plenary sessions were open to all registrants. Speakers included foundation executives, environmental movement leaders and outside experts.

The breakout sessions were closed door meetings between specific donors and related environmental group grant recipients. Here the environmental groups not only presented proposals for future funding to their foundation and corporate mentors, but also gave their report cards on what they did with Daddy's money last year. This relationship was so close that each environmentalist wore a name tag with two identities printed on it: the name of the environmental group they worked for, such as the National Audubon Society, and the name of a dedicated philanthropic foundation they were getting money from, such as the Victoria Foundation.

The three-day program EGA put on was stellar. It began on Thursday, October 1, with noted Canadian television naturalist David Suzuki's talk titled *2000: The Challenge Ahead.* It was more of an inspirational pep talk by a big name than a substantive analysis but it was followed by twenty-four in-depth talks covering the entire near-term agenda of the environmental movement. The titles are instructive:

North American Forests: Coping with Multiple Use and Abuse.
Population and the Environment
Growth Management: An Approach to Sustainability
Sustainability Agriculture: Does It Help or Hurt Rural Economics?
Great Waters: Collaborative Efforts
Strengthening the Linkage Between Community Development & Environment
Energy Policy is Environmental Policy
Toxics and Solid Waste: Goodbye to Garbage?
The Former Eastern Bloc: Challenge and Opportunity for Funders
Exploring the Benefits of Diversity
Environmentally Responsible Investing
Economy and the Environment: Truth and Consequences
Great American Water Revolution
1993, Year of Indigenous Peoples
Trade and the Environment
Environmental Education, K-12
Environmental Legislation: Opportunity for Impact & Change
Pollution Prevention
Building an Environmental Majority
Media Strategies for Environmental Protection
Transportation: An Issue for the 1990s
Environment and Spirituality
The Wise Use Movement: Threats and Opportunities

Individual audio tapes of these sessions can be purchased for $11.00 each from Conference Recording Service, 1308 Gilman Street, Berkeley, California 94706, Phone; (510)527-3600, Fax: (510)527-8404. The complete conference audio set is available in a vinyl binder for $150 including shipping. Anyone who wants to see how the environmental movement really works behind closed doors should listen to these tapes.

The final session, *The Wise Use Movement: Threats and Opportunities*, was conducted by Debra Callahan of W. Alton Jones Foundation, Charlottesville, Virginia, seventh largest money source for the environmental movement in 1990. Callahan is currently Director of the Jones Foundation's Environmental Grassroots Program. Prior to that, she worked with a variety of environmental and political organizations as a consultant, activist, advocate and lobbyist including a stint as Executive Director of Americans for the Environment and New England Political Director for the League of Conservation Voters.

Callahan told her audience that the Jones Foundation had put together a report early in 1992 containing its initial impressions of the Wise Use Movement. The Jones Foundation continued assessing the threat the Wise Use Movement posed to the organized environmental movement by conducting surveys throughout America in mid-1992. The actual research was done by MacWilliams Cosgrove Snider, a media, strategy and political communications consulting firm and the report preapred under the direction of the Wilderness Society and its then-president, George Frampton.

The conclusion: The Wise Use Movement is a broad backlash against the environmental movement because of economic harms environmentalism has inflicted upon people. The Wise Use Movement is growing in all fifty states. It is not a West Coast phenomenon repeating the old Sagebrush Rebellion, but is, if anything, stronger East of the Mississippi. Wise Use groups are mushrooming in New England against threats of nationalizing 26 million acres of private land in the Northern Forest Land Study area. They consist of shrimpers and fishermen in Florida, Louisiana and Texas who are unhappy with turtle exclusion devices that decrease their catch. They include farmers in the Midwest unhappy over wetland designations. They are strong in every state in the Union.

The Wise Use Movement is demographically a cross-section of the general American public on all dimensions, male-female, young-old, blue collar-white collar, high school-college educational levels. It is not a front for big corporations, contrary to the fund raising letters and magazine stories put out by various environmental groups. It is a true grass roots movement of ordinary people, many of whom have formed their own Wise Use organizations because of actual harms done by environmentalists and without knowledge that the Wise Use Movement existed. The Wise Use Movement poses a grave threat to the survival of the environmental movement that must be countered by smear campaigns and by more attention to grass roots organizing by environmentalists.

The questions from the audience revealed that this surprisingly astute analysis stupefied most of the conference members. Some questioners simply could not grasp the unwelcome message. Others seemed to be struggling to suppress guilt feelings for harming the jobs and lives of innocent people—now that one of their own had squarely faced that fact. A few swallowed hard and adjusted their thinking.

The tape of this hour-long session is a stunning view into the environmental movement's real attitudes about killing jobs and Trashing the Economy. It contained the classic remark, "No, I don't want you to have your job." It should be required listening for everyone interested in the environment.

MacWilliams Cosgrove Snider must be given credit for one of the most brilliant strategic analyses we have ever seen from the environmental movement. Despite the unpleasant facts that they had to face from their surveys, they did not simply sweep them aside, as nearly all environmentalists do, they faced them squarely and concluded correctly what it all meant. Callahan admitted during her EGA presentation that some of her information had come from environmentalists such as the San Francisco-based Center for Investigative Reporting infiltrating Wise Use meetings, groups and conferences. Regardless how unethical her spying may have been, she untangled a mass of information and got it right.

The complete list of foundations and corporations in the Environmental Grantmakers Association is:

A Territory Resource
Abelard Foundation West
The Abell Foundation, Inc.
The Acorn Foundation
Alaska Conservation
  Foundation
Jennifer Altman Founda-
  tion
American Conservation
  Association, Inc.
American Express Founda-
  tion
American Gas Foundation
Apple Computer, Inc.
ARCO Foundation
The Asia Foundation
Mary Reynolds Babcock
  Foundation, Inc.
The Bauman Foundation,
  Inc.
L. L. Bean, Inc.
Beldon Fund
Ben & Jerry's Foundation
Beneficia Foundation
The Betterment Fund
The William Bingham
  Foundation
Kathleen Price & Joseph
  M. Bryan Family
  Foundation
The Bullitt Foundation
Patrick & Aimee Butler
  Family Foundation

C. S. Fund
Mary Flagler Cary
  Charitable Trust
Changing Horizons
  Charitable Trust
The Chevron Companies
The Chicago Community
  Trust
Columbia Foundation
Compton Foundation, Inc.
Conservation, Food &
  Health Foundation, Inc.
S. H. Howell Foundation
Jessie B. Cox Charitable
  Trust
The Mary A. Crocker Trust
Crystal Channel Founda-
  tion
The Nathan Cummings
  Foundation
Damien Foundation
Davis Conservation
  Foundation
Geraldine R. Dodge
  Foundation, Inc.
Donner Canadian Founda-
  tion
The Elizabeth Ordway
  Dunn Foundation, Inc.
The Educational Founda-
  tion of America
El Paso Community
  Foundation

The Energy Foundation
The Bert Fingerhut Family
  Foundation
Flintridge Foundation
Foellinger Foundation, Inc.
Ford Foundation
Foundation for Deep
  Ecology
The Fund for New Jersey
Fund of the Four Directions
The Gap Foundation
The Fred Gellert Foundation
General Service Foundation
The Wallace Alexander
  Gerbode Foundation, Inc.
The German Marshall Fund
  of the United States
Global Environmental
  Project Institute
Golden Rule Foundation
The Goldman Environmen-
  tal Foundation
Walter and Duncan Gordon
  Charitable Foundation
Great Lakes Protection
  Fund
The George Gund Founda-
  tion
HKH Foundation
The Hall Family Founda-
  tions
Harder Foundation
Hawaiian Electric Industries

Foundation

William Randolph Hearst Foundation

Clarence E. Heller Charitable Foundation

The William and Flora Hewlett Foundation

The Homeland Foundation

The Illilouette Fund

Island Foundation, Inc.

Ittleson Foundation, Inc.

The Richard Ivey Foundation

The Henry M. Jackson Foundation

W. Alton Jones Foundation, Inc.

Joy Foundation for Ecological Education and Research

The Joyce Foundation

W. K. Kellogg Foundation

Henry P. Kendall Foundation

Robert S. and Grace B. Kerr Foundation, Inc.

Laidlaw Foundation

LaSalle Adams Fund

The Lazar Foundation

The Max and Anna Levison Foundation

The Lifeworks Foundation

Lyndhurst Foundation

The John D. and Catherine T. MacArthur Foundation

Maki Foundation

Marpat Foundation, Inc.

The Martin Foundation, Inc.

The McIntosh Foundation

The McKnight Foundation

The Giles W. and Elise G. Mead Foundation

The John Merck Fund

Merck Family Fund

J. P. Morgan Charitable Trust

The Moriah Fund

Charles Stewart Mott Foundation

Ruth Mott Fund

The Curtis and Edith Munson Foundation, Inc.

National Geographic Society Education Foundation

New England Biolabs Foundation

The New Hampshire Charitable Fund and Affiliated Trusts

The New York Community Trust

Andrew Norman Foundation

North Shore Unitarian Universalist Veatch Program

Mary Moody Northen, Inc.

Jessie Smith Noyes Foundation, Inc.

Oshun Fund

Ottinger Foundation

The David and Lucile Packard Foundation

Patagonia, Inc. (former member)

Amelia Peabody Charitable Fund

The William Penn Foundation

James C. Penney Foundation

The Pew Charitable Trusts

Pew Scholars Program in Conservation and the Environment

Philanthropic Group— Florence V. Burden Foundation & Rivendell Foundation

Philip Morris Companies, Inc.

The Procter and Gamble Fund

Prospect Hill Foundation, Inc.

Recreational Equipment, Inc.

Z. Smith Reynolds Foundation, Inc.

Smith Richardson Foundation, Inc.

Roberts Foundatioin

Rockefeller Brothers Fund, Inc.

Rockefeller Family Fund, Inc.

Rockefeller Financial Services, Inc.

The Rockefeller Foundation

The San Francisco Foundation

The Florence and John Schumann Foundation

Sequoia Foundation

The Shalan Foundation, Inc.

Thomas Sill Foundation

Stern Family Fund

The Sudbury Foundation

The Summerlee Foundation

The Summit Foundation

Surdna Foundation, Inc.

Edna Bailey Sussman Fund

Threshold Foundation

The Tides Foundation

The Tinker Foundation, Inc

Tortuga Foundation

Town Creek Foundation

True North Foundation

The Trust for Mutual Understanding

Turner Foundation, Inc.

Vancouver Foundation

Victoria Foundation, Inc.

Virginia Environmental Endowment

WMX Environmental Grants Program

Wallace Genetic Foundation, Inc.

Weeden Foundation

Whitecap Foundation

Wilburforce Foundation

Winslow Foundation

Margaret Cullinan Wray Charitable Lead Annuity Trust

A few very large family foundations have exerted extraordinary influence on the environmental movement long before the Environmental Grantmakers Association came to power. Here are the most influential:

Rockefellers. The various Rockefeller foundations have their fingers in more environmental pies than any other philanthropic misanthropes. The accumulator of the Rockefeller family wealth, of course, was John D. Rockefeller, Sr. and his magisterial empire, the Standard Oil Trust. It is one of the undying ironies of American history that our most generous, efficacious, and innovative philanthropist was also *the* most grasping, monopolistic, and savage Robber Baron of the Nineteenth Century. Not that he was any more rapacious or corrupting than Cornelius Vanderbilt or Andrew Carnegie or Andrew Mellon or any of the others. He was just bigger and better at it. None of these corporate capitalists had the slightest concern for free enterprise. John D. saw free competition as wasteful and made sure he had no competitors—if he had to buy judges, fix journalists, bribe legislators, or even maintain a private army to shoot recalcitrant workers or competitors, well, that was just a cost of doing business.[12]

But from the very beginning of his wealth in the 1870s and 1880s, he always gave to various causes from his corporate monies, mostly to church interests in the beginning, because he was very religious, then for the transformation of the University of Chicago into one of the nation's greatest centers of learning, then to create a highly successful medical program to eradicate hookworm in the southern states.

The Rockefeller Foundation (current assets, $2.1 billion) was chartered in 1893, one of the oldest private foundations in the United States and one of the few with strong international interests. With professional managers after 1901, it set about becoming the most effective charity we have yet seen. By the end of the 1920s the Rockefeller Foundation had achieved worldwide prestige, with numerous scientists and doctors on its staff. During the Depression 1930s the foundation's International Health Division, the Medical Sciences Division, and the Division of Natural Sciences all made great contributions to the well being of the nation. During World War II, the foundation rescued leading scientists and intellectuals from Hitler's Fortress Europe. The foundation was so successful that after World War II the newly emergent United Nations organized its World Health Organization on the Rockefeller model and the National Science Foundation closely patterned its program on the Rockefeller's methods of supporting research, scholarship, and institutional development.

The foundation went through a shakeup in 1952 as John D. Rockefeller, Jr. retired and John D. Rockefeller III took over as chairman, with long-time staffer George Harrar elected president. Harrar had been head of the foundation's agricultural program in Mexico and convinced the board to adopt his new funding guidelines based on a "problem" approach: Identify problem areas for future action and then create or foster institutions to work on solutions. Harrar's first agenda contained five priority problems to solve: world hunger, control of world population, strengthening selected universities and research centers in the underdeveloped countries, achieving equal opportunity for all Americans, and aiding cultural development. The "conquest of hunger" program resulted in the Green Revolution that developed new plant varieties of much greater yield, rice in the Philippines, a Maize and Wheat Improvement Center in Mexico, and research stations in Nigeria and Colombia.

Toward the end of Harrar's career in 1971, he added an environmental program to the five priority problems. However, Harrar's Rockefeller Foundation staff did little more than make a few grants, all of them with a strong technical or training emphasis.

The foundation's Global Environmental Program was established in 1986, with four major fields of donation interest: energy conservation, sustainable development, natural resource use, and agroforestry.

In 1990 the Rockefeller Foundation began funding it with a stupendous $50 million commitment. The global environmental program has the "ambitious aim of curbing ecologically damaging practices of industrial and poor countries," reported the *New York Times*. Do we hear Professor Malthus back there somewhere?[13]

The foundation, said the *Times*, sought to "encourage efforts to build environmental protection into governments' long-range economic planning. Other major elements would promote the drafting of international treaties to deal with forest, land and water preservation, and hazardous waste disposal."

Dr. Kenneth Prewitt, senior vice president of the foundation in charge of the huge project, with Director Al Binger managing the day-to-day work, told the *Times* they were working to form a global network, "seeking key individuals who can be architects of future policy in development and the environment." You could hardly ask for a more straightforward statement of intent to form a worldwide private Permanent Green Government.

Beyond this program, the Rockefeller Foundation in 1990 awarded 96 environmental grants to the tune of $7,819,360.

North Carolina State University's International Institute got $900,000, and the University of Tennessee—Vice President Al Gore's favorite school—got $13,700 for an environmental study that will no doubt end up in some environmental group's publicity campaigns. The New York Rainforest Alliance, Inc. got $40,000 to stop timber harvest in Southeast Asia.

The Rockefeller Brothers Fund, Inc. (current assets, $275,262,103), founded in 1940 by John D. Rockefeller, Jr. and his five sons and one daughter: John D., III; Nelson; Laurance; Winthrop; David; and Abby. The Rockefeller Brothers Fund has been one of the two Mother Ships of the environmental movement for decades, the other being Laurance Rockefeller's American Conservation Association.

The Rockefeller Brothers Fund is primarily the vehicle of Laurance S. Rockefeller, one of the five sons of John D. Rockefeller, Jr. The Fund gave out $4.5 million in environmental grants in 1990. The Conservation Law Foundation got $100,000, The Institute for Research on Public Policy in Ottawa, Canada, got $50,000 (for an examination of the political barriers to environmental policy reform), and the Southern Environmental Law Center of Charlottesville, Virginia got $225,000.

It gave $100,000 to the Friends of the Earth in 1990 to monitor the lending policies and practices of the Asian Development Bank, and another $45,000 toward a nuclear non-proliferation project. They gave $300,000 to the World Wildlife Fund/Conservation Foundation in 1990, a 3-year grant for a project to evaluate the success of community-based initiatives in developing countries to manage resources on a sustainable basis, and another $35,000 for their Eastern European Environmental Program to help strengthen the management of environmental institutions in the region, to promote technology transfer and environmentally sound foreign investment, and to build support in the United States for the project.

The Fund's environmental program is titled, "One World: Sustainable Resource Use." Global topics include "development, biodiversity, women and population, agriculture and biotechnology, information and technical assistance." Climate change and security are described as "two foci."

More money for environmental organizations has poured out of this foundation over the years than any other single source, but that well-known fact is masked to some extent by its habit of channeling funds through related foundations, such as:

Jackson Hole Preserve, Inc., also incorporated in 1940, the donors of which are John D. Rockefeller, Jr., Laurance S. Rockefeller, and the Rockefeller Brothers Fund. This was originally the nonprofit holding company for the Grand Teton scam in which the Rockefellers bought up Wyoming land under a phony Salt Lake City front group, then obtained the concession to the resulting Grand Teton National Park. It has since evolved into a general purpose environmental funding philanthropy. Its present officers and trustees are president George R. Lamb, vice president Gene W. Setzer, secretary Franklin E. Parker, treasurer Ruth C. Haupert, and other members include Nash Castro, Henry L. Diamond, William M. Dietel, Clayton W. Frye, Mrs. Lyndon B. Johnson, Howard Phipps, Jr., Laurance S. Rockefeller, Fred Smith, and Conrad L. Wirth.

The Rockefeller Family Fund, Inc., incorporated in 1967 by members of the Rockefeller family, principally the grandchildren of John D. Rockefeller, Jr. The Family Fund concentrates on action-oriented programs that yield tangible results. It concentrates on four areas of giving, the environment being a principal focus. In 1990 it gave the Audubon Society of Maine $20,000 as seed money for direct mail fund raising; $25,000 to the Environmental Action Foundation for a plastics reduction project; $30,000 to the National Toxics Campaign Fund to shift the debate from a waste-control to a prevention strategy, i.e., how to kill the packaging industry; $10,000 to the Natural Resources Defense Council to pay for Meryl Streep's "volunteer" Mothers and Others for Pesticide Limits front in the Alar scam. The Fund, as we have well noted, is also host to the Environmental Grantmakers Association, a not insignificant facet of its activities.

Environmentalists also receive large amounts of money from the Winthrop Rockefeller Foundation and the Winthrop Rockefeller Trust. **The Winthrop Rockefeller Trust** of Little Rock, Arkansas (Assets $86,438,344), gave The American Farmlands Trust $50,000 and gave Worldwatch Institute $75,000.

The real Rockefeller doozy is:
The American Conservation Association
30 Rockefeller Plaza, Room 5402
New York, New York 10112
Telephone (202) 649-5822
Professional staff: 4

Incorporated in New York in 1958, the ACA is the other Mother Ship of the environmental movement. Its *sole* purpose is to pump money, vast amounts of Rockefeller money, into the environmental movement. The ACA's donors are Laurance S. Rockefeller, Laurance Rockefeller, the Rockefeller Brothers Fund, and Jackson Hole Preserve, Inc. Every year for more than thirty years it has given out about $2 million, sometimes more. It typically receives a large annual contribution from the Jackson Hole Preserve, Inc. In 1990 it gave out a total of 58 grants amounting to $2,117,500, the highest $150,000, the lowest $5,000, average grant about $50,000. In 1991 it disbursed a total grant amount of $1,846,000 and received $2 million in contributions.

The American Conservation Association's governing body includes: President Laurance Rockefeller; Executive Vice President George R. Lamb; Vice President Gene W. Setzer; Secretary Franklin E. Parker; and Treasurer Ruth C. Haupert. Other members of the board are: John H. Adams (Natural Resources Defense Council); Frances G. Beinecke; Nash Castro; Charles H. Clusen; William G. Conway; Dana S. Creel; Henry L. Diamond; Mrs. Lyndon B. Johnson; Fred I. Kent III; W. Barnabes McHenry; Patrick F. Noonan (Conservation Fund); Story Clark Resor; David S. Sampson; Cathleen Douglas Stone; Russell E. Train (World Wildlife Fund); William H. Whyte, Jr.; Conrad L. Wirth (retired Director of the National Park Service).

In 1990 ACA gave $220,000 to the Natural Resources Defense Council; $150,000 to the Open Space Institute, Inc.; $150,000 to Scenic America; $120,000 to Scenic Hudson, Inc.; $100,000 to the Rails to Trails Conservancy; $100,000 to the Wilderness Society; $75,000 to the Adirondack Council, Inc.; $90,000 to the Sierra Club Legal Defense Fund; and $25,000 to the Conservation Law Foundation of New England.

The Ford Foundation, of course. The environmental movement would be much poorer without it. The Ford Foundation was one of the prototypes of American philanthropy. It funded the earlier conservation movement generously, for example, Resources For the Future in the 1950s, but its entry into the liberal cause business that led to its huge environmental grants came about with the arrival of McGeorge Bundy in 1966. The Ford Foundation was his golden parachute out of Washington in the Johnson administration, where his adventures in foreign and military affairs and his support of escalation policies in Vietnam led the Ivy League-Council of Foreign Relations crowd to provide him a soft landing after public service. Having earlier been a popular dean at Harvard University, Bundy quickly won the staff's loyalty through his nimble mind and receptivity to new ideas. But he came with a personal agenda: he wanted to cut a figure as America's most politically activist foundation manager.

He did it, but in the process overspent his first year's income by $100 million. It got worse in later years. Even though the huge size of the Ford Foundation's fortune led a suspicious public in the late 1960s to worry about "thought control" by foundations—and foundation members have privately bragged about "creating" the Civil Rights Movement through the power of their purse—Bundy's bungling financial management soon brought the great Ford Foundation nearly to ruin and made community fears almost laughable.

Bundy approved the $400,000 grant that started the Natural Resources Defense Council in 1977. Systematic grants to other environmental groups followed.

When Bundy retired in 1979 he had funded some spectacular programs but left a financial disaster behind him that took more than a decade to straighten out. Franklin A. Thomas, a black lawyer who had once been an assistant U.S. Attorney in New York replaced Bundy, but he was as glacial in getting things going as Bundy had been precipitous. He at least stemmed the money hemorrhage, but could not come up with innovative programs of his own for some time. His major thrust, once it materialized, tended toward social programs such as teen pregnancy problems and moving welfare recipients off of public assistance and into regular jobs.

Frank Thomas is still president of the Ford Foundation and has long since found his feet. He supported the turn toward global grants for environmental purposes during the 1980s—heavy giving for Africa, the Middle East, Asia and Latin America—and appears ready to continue into the 1990s.

In recent years the Ford Foundation gave: $125,000 to the National Audubon Society; $575,000 to the Environmental Defense Fund; and $25,000 to the Friends of the Earth, Ghana.

Thought control by foundations is not so laughable any more.

The Pew Charitable Trusts are another one of the environmental movement's biggest donors. The Pews of Philadelphia have been very rich for over a hundred years. Their fortune was based mostly on oil, the Sun Oil Company in particular. The Pew who made the money, Joseph Newton Pew, and all his relatives were fundamentalist Presbyterians, as five generations of Pews in America had been before them, back before the Revolution.

The Pew philanthropy at first was dictated by the conscience of the givers and was devoted exclusively to "good works." Until 1948 the Pew gifts were distributed as personal donations. They went to hospitals, schools and cultural institutions in the Philadelphia area; to Presbyterian Church activities; and to conservative organizations and publications. Period. J. Howard Pew, head of the family business from 1912 to 1947, was a rock-hard capitalist, detested government regulation of business, didn't drink, lived deliberately plainly and called the U.S. government "the wickedest racket the world has ever seen."

Up through the 1970s the Pews simply sent checks to institutions of their preference without planning, processing, evaluation or follow-up. In 1977, Robert Smith, a bright young vice president of the oil company, took over management of the Pew philanthropy and brought professional direction to the grant program.

All the Pew charity money is managed through the Pew's private profit-making bank, Glenmede Trust Company. Even though its basic fortune is not the biggest in the United States, its philanthropy has more money than any other except the Ford Foundation, over $3 billion in 1990. There are seven separate Pew charitable trusts: the original Pew Memorial Trust, plus six smaller trusts set up by family members; these include the Mary Anderson Trust, the Mabel Pew Myrin Trust, the J. N. Pew, Jr. Trust, the Knollbrook Trust, the J. Howard Pew Fund for Presbyterian Uses, and the J. Howard Pew Freedom Trust. The Glenmede arrangement is very efficient, run by a tight family group of directors, giving the Pew charities a much lower cost of administration than comparable philanthropies.

By the 1980s, the grants to conservative policy groups had virtually vanished. Environmental groups have become a prominent feature of the Pew Charitable Trusts grant list.

In 1991 Keith KcKeown became communications director. He formerly served in that capacity for the Aspen Institute and as media director for the Center on Budget and Policy Priorities.

Pew gave in 1990:

Environmental Defense Fund $150,000; Inform, Inc. $120,000; Keystone Center $35,000; National Wildlife Federation $100,000; Rocky Mountain Institute $350,000; Trust for Public Land $5 million plus $290,000; Wilderness Society $150,000; World Resources Institute $75,000; grants to more than 90 other environmental groups.

Charles Stewart Mott Foundation is one of the Golden Donors of America, a giant philanthropy with nearly a billion dollars in assets ($929,505,650 in 1990). It is derived from the vast fortune of its namesake, Charles Stewart Mott, who owned business interests in General Motors, U.S. Sugar, several banks, a number of municipal water supply systems, and cattle ranches. His fortune at the time of his death in 1973 (at the age of ninety-seven) amounted to a billion dollars. In his youth, just as automobile sales began to boom, he took over his father's unprofitable wheel factory in the East and moved it to Flint, Michigan, and later traded it for a substantial block of General Motors stock and a vice-presidency in the new automobile firm. He was always munificent, but also had a reputation for extreme frugality; as one writer noted, "friends called him the world's most generous pennypincher."

For many years he ran his foundation as a one-man show, giving primarily to education and community development organizations in Flint. But after the Tax Reform Act of 1969 Mott, in failing health, installed a new president, William S. White, the son-in-law of his son Harding Mott—this son Harding served as chairman of the board and chief executive officer. White, a fastidiously professional man, developed a highly sophisticated program philosophy complete with mission statements, flow charts, and other trappings of business planning. Willard Hertz, White's vice-president for programs, took another approach: "Oh, forget the mission statements: They're meaningless when you are trying to determine how to spend money."

The Mott Foundation gives generously but not extravagantly—with a few exceptions—to environmental groups. In 1990 it gave $67,800 to Rockefeller's American Farmland Trust; $23,400 to American Rivers. There is a pattern of two grants to one group: Two grants to the Environmental Defense Fund, one $75,000, the other $40,000; $450,000 to Friends of the Earth—$400,000 in one grant to the Friends of the Earth Foundation and $50,000 in another; $60,000 in one grant to the National Wildlife Federation and $40,000 in another; $40,000 went to the Natural Resources Defense Council in one grant and $75,000 in another; $67,000 to the Nature Conservancy in one grant and $63,000 in another; two grants to the Sierra Club Foundation, one for $30,000, another for $40,000; and $23,050 to the Sierra Club Legal Defense Fund; the MacArthur Foundation's World Resources Institute also received two grants, one for $45,000 and a rather extravagant one for $500,000. The World Wildlife Fund received $50,000.

There are quite a few heirs and relatives of Charles Stewart Mott in the philanthropy business, many of whom give to environmental groups.

The C. S. Fund of Freestone, California, (Assets $466,542) is a private operating foundation acting as a "pass through" fund for annual gifts of donor Maryanne T. Mott and others. The "C. S." stands for Charles Stewart (Mott), whose fortune was inherited by Maryanne Mott, who in her turn has managed and diversified the fortune and is the primary donor of the C. S. Fund. Herman E. Warsh, a director of the C. S. Fund and the Ruth Mott Fund (see below), was until recently the chairman of the board of Friends of the Earth (see profile)—he came to the position from the Environmental Policy Institute, which merged with Friends of the Earth in 1990. He resigned from Friends of the Earth's board in 1991. The Foundation Center lists Mr. Warsh as one of the donors of the C. S. Fund as well as its president, but the Fund denies both statements, and was emphatic about his having resigned his chairmanship of Friends of the Earth. This case is an interesting connection between a donor foundation and a recipient environmental group. The C. S. Fund gave the Pesticide Action Network of San Francisco $15,000 for its Dirty Dozen Campaign, which maligns companies with allegations of toxic problems.

Ruth Mott Fund of Flint, Michigan (Assets $2,249,107 in 1990) gave the American Farmland Trust two $10,000 grants in 1989. Herman E. Warsh, onetime chairman of the board of the Friends of the Earth, sits on the board of directors of this foundation, too.

Warsh-Mott Legacy of Freestone, California, (Assets $4,616,998), is another fraction of the Charles Stewart Mott-General Motors money. The donor is Maryanne T. Mott; the Legacy's president is Herman E. Warsh (again). The Legacy in 1990 gave $15,000 to the Friends of the Earth for a program addressing the international crisis in conservation of plant germ plasm, and another $10,000 to pay travel expenses of delegates to the organizational meeting of the World Fund for Conservation of Domestic Animal Genetic Resources and the translation of the meeting's materials. It is fairly clear from the above that Mr. Warsh is or was tight with the Friends of the Earth.

The William and Flora Hewlett Foundation of Menlo Park, California, (Assets $559,792,927 in 1990) was incorporated in 1966, the first major new foundation based on wealth acquired in high technology. Donor William Hewlett's partner in the hugely successful Hewlett-Packard Company, David Packard, established another. The two met as engineering students at Stanford University and borrowed $538 in capital from a Palo Alto bank in 1939 to set up their first "plant" in a small local garage. They built an audio oscillator designed by Hewlett and marketed by Packard—it was the best damn audio oscillator the world had seen. Hewlett was always the technological genius, Packard the businessman. Today Hewlett-Packard is one of the legendary success stories of American industry, at its peak employing more than 70,000 people and making annual sales of more than $4 billion. It also has a **Hewlett-Packard Company Philanthropic Grants** division (total giving in 1990, $67,300,000 including $3,200,000 in grants) that gives money to environmentalists.

William Hewlett was not one of the archetypal American entrepreneurs of limited education and rugged individualism. He was born a doctor's son and never wanted for anything. He was well-educated, socially aware, and active in social and cultural affairs. For ten years before starting his own foundation he sat on the money-dispensing committee of the San Francisco Foundation, and thus had a clear idea how to run his own philanthropy when the time came, unlike most wealthy people.

From the beginning, the Hewlett Foundation gave money for environmental purposes: William Hewlett has always been an outdoorsman, a skier, mountain climber, fisherman, nature photographer, and amateur botanist. However, he has not yet seen the Economy Trasher aspect of environmentalism goring his ox, so he continues to subsidize the goring of other peoples'. It is thus not surprising that in 1990 his foundation made 31 substantial grants to environmental groups: $150,000 to the American Farmland Trust for general support; $100,000 for American Rivers to take private river property; $225,000 to the Environmental Defense Fund for support of an Alternative Decisionmaking Program; $180,000 to Inform, Inc., for general support; $150,000 to the Land Trust Alliance to put more private land out of production; $150,000 to the Natural Resources Defense Council for negotiation and alternative dispute resolution programs; $250,000 to One Thousand Friends of Oregon for general support to throw monkey wrenches in as many industries as possible, mostly the forest products industry; $150,000 to Resources for the Future for general support; $200,000 to the Rocky Mountain Institute for general support; and $20,000 to Trout Unlimited to design a Watershed Conservancy Program that would endanger private property.

The David and Lucile Packard Foundation of Los Altos, California, (Assets $227,512,098) is not one of the giant philanthropies like the Hewlett Foundation, but it is big enough to be influential in Trashing the Economy. David Packard remains chairman of the foundation's board of directors, which includes numerous other Packards and old Stanford buddies. In 1990 they gave $50,000 to American Rivers for nationalizing 2,000 rivers by the year 2000; $80,000 to the Audubon Society of California to buy 550 acres in the Stone Lakes area of Sacramento County; $50,000 to the Center for Marine Conservation for a fisheries management program to stop commercial fishing and another $35,000 for a major study on marine biological diversity; $30,000 to the Conservation Foundation for implementing wetlands policy to destroy private property rights; $200,000 to the Nature Conservancy in San

Francisco for purchase of Parrott Ranch.

As we can see from these brief sketches and the profiles above, foundations have been very influential in creating and supporting new environmental groups, shaping policy in ways the public is unaware of: The Richard King Mellon Foundation reinvented the Nature Conservancy and created the Conservation Fund with Patrick Noonan; The Rockefellers helped put a number of groups on the map, including the Conservation Foundation and the American Farmland Trust. The Ford Foundation helped establish Resources for the Future and the Natural Resources Defense Council; the MacArthur Foundation created the World Resources Institute.

The Golden Rule still applies: Who has the gold rules.

The following is a representative but very incomplete cross-section of the money behind the environmental movement, in alphabetical order.

Abell Foundation of Baltimore, Maryland (Assets $118,383,000 in 1990). Gave the Nature Conservancy $200,000 to increase their permanent revolving capital fund to buy private land on Maryland's Natural Heritage Program's priority list for preservation (see also National Parks and Conservation Association profile for details of insidious related programs).

The Amoco Foundation, Inc. of Chicago (Assets $57,982,053) gave $46,000 to the National Wildlife Federation; $100,000 to the Nature Conservancy.

Archer-Daniels-Midland Foundation of Decatur, Illinois, gave American Farmland Trust $35,000 in 1989.

Arco Foundation of Los Angeles, California, (Assets $221,858) gave the American Farmland Trust $10,000; the Conservation Foundation, $35,000; the Conservation Fund, $10,000; the Environmental Law Institute, $10,000; the Nature Conservancy, Baton Rouge, Louisiana, $25,000 to buy White Kitchen Wetlands; the Nature Conservancy, San Antonio, Texas, $25,000 to buy Clymer Meadow; the Nature Conservancy, Arlington, Virginia, $10,000; the Nature Conservancy, Arizona Chapter, $15,000 to buy streams; the Nature Conservancy, California Chapter, $15,000; the Nature Conservancy, Washington Chapter, $10,000 for Skagit Bald Eagle habitat purchase and education; Resources for the Future, $25,000 for a Center for Risk Management; Trout Unlimited, $15,000 for Embrace-a-Stream program.

Ashland Oil Foundation, Inc. of Kentucky gave the Nature Conservancy of Frankfort, Kentucky $10,000 in 1989.

The Atherton Family Foundation of Honolulu (Assets $52,027,856) gave $30,000 to the Natural Resources Defense Council for endangered species stream flow coastal and groundwater protection.

The Metropolitan Atlanta Community Foundation, Inc., of Atlanta (Assets

$88,315,842) gave $35,000 to the National Audubon Society.

Baton Rouge Area Foundation of Baton Rouge, Louisiana (Assets $7,391,000 in 1990). Gave the Nature Conservancy $25,000 in 1989 to buy Bluebonnet Swamp.

The Beinecke Foundation, Inc. of Rye, New York (Assets $35,986,799) was established in 1966 with donations made by Sylvia B. Robinson.

In 1990 it gave $251,826 to the Natural Resources Defense Council; $200,000 to Open Space Institute, Inc.; $15,000 to Yale University; $1,000 each to the Connecticut Fund for the Environment, Greater Yellowstone Coalition, and the Nature Conservancy headquarters.

The Greater Birmingham Foundation of Birmingham, Alabama (Assets $27,028,165) gave $10,500 to Friends of Animals in New York City in 1989.

The James G. Boswell Foundation of Los Angeles (Assets $55,373,116, which came primarily from farming in California's Central Valley) gave to the Nature Conservancy, California, $30,000 for Santa Cruz Island Reserve; the Nature Conservancy, Idaho, $25,000 to buy Garden Creek.

The Lynde and Harry Bradley Foundation of Milwaukee, Wisconsin (Assets $370,691,611 in 1990). Gave $133,000 in 1989 to Ducks Unlimited; $50,000 to the Nature Conservancy.

The Buchanan Family Foundation of Lake Forest, Illinois, (Assets $34,956,302) gave $20,000 to the Nature Conservancy.

Burlington Northern Foundation of Forth Worth, Texas (Assets $8,795,290). Gave $25,000 to the Nature Conservancy of Helena, Montana; $25,000 to the Nature Conservancy of Tucson, Arizona; $20,000 to the Nature Conservancy of Seattle, Washington; $10,000 to the Nature Conservancy of Minneapolis, Minnesota; $25,000 to the Trust for Public Land; $11,000 to Resources for the Future.

The Morris and Gwendolyn Cafritz Foundation of Washington, D.C. (Assets $205,516,893) gave $15,000 to the Friends of the Earth for their Chemical Safety Projects. The grant was shared with the Environmental Policy Institute.

The California Community Foundation of Los Angeles, (Assets $92,825,075) the trustees of which are the Security Pacific National Bank, City National Bank, First Interstate Bank, Trust Services of America, and Wells Fargo Bank, gave $10,000 to the Natural Resources Defense Council.

The Mary Flagler Cary Charitable Trust of New York (Assets $102,454,198) got its money from the will of Mary Flagler Cary, the late heiress daughter of Henry Morrison Flagler, who made his fortune with John D. Rockefeller in Standard Oil after 1870, and subsequently built a railroad, steamship, and resort hotel empire in

Florida—his name is plastered everywhere in the state. Mrs. Cary's maternal line came from the Lamonts of the Bankers Trust Company fortune, but current trustees do not know how much, if any, of the Cary Trust's funds originated there. The Rockefeller connection and Standard Oil are usually credited as the historical source of the Cary Trust's assets. The Cary Trust gave $22,400 to the National Parks and Conservation Association in 1990; $75,000 to the Natural Resources Defense Council for a New England coastal project; $295,000 to the Sierra Club Legal Defense Fund in 1990 to help establish a new office in Florida, and another $35,000 for lawsuits against developers along the Gulf Coast and Atlantic coasts; $30,000 to the Trust for Public Land for the same Gulf Coast and Atlantic project, and another $50,000 for a Neighborhood Open Space Management Grant Program.

Collins Foundation of Portland, Oregon gave $150,000 to the Trust for Public Land and $40,000 to the Nature Conservancy in 1989 to buy up private land in the Columbia Gorge.

The Columbia Foundation of San Francisco, (Assets $38,236,240) the donors of which are Madeleine H. Russell and Christine H. Russell, gave $25,000 to the Natural Resources Defense Council and $15,000 to the Trust for Public Lands for a tree planting program; $25,000 to the Natural Resources Defense Council for general support in 1990. The donors funded the Columbia Foundation in major part from the sale of stock in Levi Strauss Company that they held—they are heirs to the blue jean fortune.

The Compton Foundation, Inc., of Menlo Park, California, (Assets $62,534,943) is funded by members of the Compton family, heirs to the Ralston-Purina fortune. Their foundation is a major source of environmentalist money: In 1989-'90 they gave the American Farmland Trust $31,000 to buy New York farms; $25,000 to American Rivers; $15,000 to the National Audubon Society for population study; $10,000 to the Conservation Fund; $20,000 to Conservation International; $10,000 to Earth Day 1990; $25,000 to Environmental Action Foundation; $50,000 to the Environmental Defense Fund for California wetlands regulation; $20,000 to the National Toxics Campaign Fund; $50,000 to the Nature Conservancy for its Latin American Division, and $10,000 in San Francisco for general operating support, $38,000 in Honolulu for general operating support, and $30,000 to the Colorado Field Office of the Conservancy for "Rivers of the Rockies" program; $25,000 to the Sierra Club Legal Defense Fund; $15,000 to the Wilderness Society; $25,000 to the World Resources Institute for a research project called Redefining Peace.

The Cooke Foundation, Ltd., of Honolulu (Assets $16,236,976) gave $200,000 to the Nature Conservancy for Islands for Life Campaign.

Jessie B. Cox Charitable Trust of Boston, Massachusetts (Assets $51,000,000 in 1990). Gave Audubon Society of New Hampshire $75,000 in 1989 for wetlands project. Gave One Thousand Friends of Oregon $40,000 in 1989 for participation of three New England statewide groups in a National Growth Management Leadership Project. Illustrates how foundations help link regional groups across great distances, spread ideas and political skills.

Charles E. Culpepper Foundation, Inc. of Stamford, Connecticut, (Assets $118,633,965) gave $50,000 to the National Audubon Society to the Platte River project.

Arthur Vining Davis Foundations of Jacksonville, Florida (Assets $111,190,438), was originally founded in 1952 by Mr. Davis, who was president and later chairman of the board of the Aluminum Company of America (Alcoa)—which was one of the Mellon interests. Arthur Vining Davis was successful in real estate investments and had many other business interests. His first foundation, now known as "Number 1" was joined by two more after his death in 1952, known as Foundations No. 2 and No. 3.

In 1990 the Arthur Vining Davis Foundations made only two environmental grants: they gave the Nature Conservancy $100,000 to expand Key Deer Refuge on Big Pine Key, Florida; and $30,000 to WGBH Educational Foundation of Boston for the television program *The Wilderness Idea.*

Geraldine R. Dodge Foundation of Morristown, New Jersey (Assets $145,060,184 in 1990). The Foundation was established in 1974 by the will of Geraldine R. Dodge, who died in 1973. She was the niece of John D. Rockefeller, founder of Standard Oil Company, and the wife of Marcellus Hartley Dodge, chairman of the Remington Arms Company. Mrs. Dodge was known for her devotion to animals.

Gave $100,000 to Environmental Defense Fund, same amount to Natural Resources Defense Council in 1989. Gave the Trust for Public Land $75,000; Inform, Inc. $60,000; Conservation Foundation $50,000; American Farmland Trust $25,000; World Resources Institute $24,000; Humane Society of the United States $11,150.

Du Pont Corporate Contributions Program of Wilmington, Delaware (Total giving $33,264,550 in 1991). Does not report specific amounts. "America's worst polluter" gave large amounts of money to the National Wildlife Federation, the Izaak Walton League of America, and many other environmental groups.

Sarita Kenedy East Foundation of West Virginia gave $200,000 to Renew America in 1989.

The Educational Foundation of America of Westport, Connecticut (Assets $98,517,440) gave $30,019 to the Association of Forest Service Employees for Environmental Studies of Eugene, Oregon, for production and printing of a quarterly newspaper and bi-monthly activist newsletter—activists for stopping all timber production on the national forests and the destruction of thousands of timber jobs; $75,000 to the National Toxics Campaign Fund of Boston for a "Citizen's

Environmental Laboratory" which provides low cost "unbiased" testing to communities "endangered" by toxic contamination; $75,000 to the Natural Resources Defense Council for a waste management and reduction project.

The Frost Foundation, Ltd. of Denver (Assets $20,961,855) gave the Environmental Defense Fund $15,000 "for efforts to improve transport and storage of nuclear waste"—in fact it was to stop such transport altogether.

General Electric Foundation of Fairfield, Connecticut (Assets $15,359,675)—the sole donor is the General Electric Company—gave $25,000 to the Audubon Society of New York and $15,000 to the National Audubon Society; $25,000 to the Conservation Foundation; $25,000 to the Environmental Law Institute, and $25,000 to Resources for the Future.

The Wallace Alexander Gerbode Foundation of San Francisco (Assets $39,786,703)—the donors are members of the Gerbode family, who got their money originally as missionaries in Hawaii and owned sugarcane and pineapple plantations—gave $15,000 to Earth Island Institute for dolphin preservation programs that destroyed the American tuna fishing industry; $50,000 to the Natural Resources Defense Council for the California Pesticides Program and $25,000 to their Honolulu office for a lawsuit against the Hawaii Public Utilities Commission to implement "Integrated Resource Management," a way to stop commodity production and kill jobs; $25,000 to the Sierra Club Legal Defense Fund as seed money for a direct mail donor solicitation campaign.

The German Marshall Fund of the United States of Washington, D.C. (Assets $88,330,351) gave $10,000 to the Center for Marine Conservation to provide substantive preparations for meeting of Convention of International Trade in Endangered Species of Wild Fauna and Flora; $35,000 to the Environmental Defense Fund for North American-European cooperative climate-change activities; $25,000 to the World Resources Institute for North American-European cooperative climate-change activities; $327,500 to the World Wildlife Fund for a conference in Europe on approaches linking third World debt relief to conservation. Grant shared with Conservation Foundation.

The Ann and Gordon Getty Foundation of San Francisco, (Assets $2,212,747) the money coming from Gordon P. Getty, gave $50,000 to the Nature Conservancy and $65,000 to the World Wildlife Fund.

Richard and Rhoda Goldman Fund of San Francisco (Assets $5,800,430) gave $20,000 to the Center for Marine Conservation; and $15,000 to the Environmental Defense Fund, the first payment for a Computer Modeling Project; and $10,000 to the Wilderness Society to campaign for the Cranston bill to make a huge national park out of the Southern California Desert, killing thousands of jobs.

The Grainger Foundation, Inc. of Skokie, Illinois (Assets $62,293,523) gave $10,000 to the radical Northwest Coalition for Alternatives to Pesticides for its operating fund; $25,000 to the pirate Sea Shepherd Conservation Society for special program fund.

The George Gund Foundation of Cleveland, Ohio (Assets $310,698,000 in 1990) was established in 1952 by George Gund (1888-1966), a businessman and philanthropist with a lifelong interest in education and the institutions he attended. Gives to a wide variety of environmental groups through its Environmental Quality program. Gave $20,000 in 1990 to The Earth Day Coalition; $30,000 in 1990 to National Coalition Against the Misuse of Pesticides; $45,000 to Natural Resources Defense Council; $25,000 to the Scientists Institute for Public Information, Inc.; $20,000 to the Sierra Club Foundation; $25,000 to the Union of Concerned Scientists; $20,000 to the Wilderness Society; $26,500 to World Resources Institute.

Walter and Elise Haas Fund of San Francisco (Assets $69,875,000) gave $15,000 to the Trust for Public Land.

The H. J. Heinz Company Foundation of Pittsburgh, Pennsylvania (Assets $5,895,000 in 1990). Gave $17,500 to Audubon Society of Western Pennsylvania in 1989; $15,000 to the Conservation Foundation.

The James Irvine Foundation of San Francisco (Assets $506,745,921 in 1990) is another of the giant philanthropies that subsidizes environmentalists Trashing the Economy. The money came from James Irvine, a Scotch-Irish immigrant who had made a small fortune in groceries and gold mining in California and then assembled a big fortune in an 88,000 acre ranch in Orange County between what are now the cities of San Diego and Los Angeles. When he died in 1886 his son James Irvine II took over, changing from livestock production to field crops and eventually to citrus groves—keeping some of the land in cattle grazing. Son James established the foundation in 1937, mostly as a tax dodge, in the opinion of the late Congressman Wright Patman who studied the case carefully. The foundation was given majority ownership of Irvine's ranch company and instructions that it should keep its shareholdings intact and control the company's operations. Such arrangements give rise to suspicions that the principals might be self-dealing, which under present laws could conceivably result in felony charges. The Tax Reform Act of 1969 prohibited control by a foundation of a profit-making corporation, and that changed things in the Irvine Foundation.

Today the Irvine Foundation is a respectable and influential philanthropy with 9 full-time professional staff members and 9 full-time support employees. In 1989 it gave $225,000 to the Nature Conservancy for the Carrizo Plain preserve that destroyed half a dozen fine ranches and reduced their shortgrass prairie to blowing dust and tumbleweeds.

George Frederick Jewett Foundation of San Francisco (Assets $23,556,015) gave $10,000 to the World Wildlife Fund for general support.

W. Alton Jones Foundation of Charlottesville, Virginia (Assets $173,128,158). It was established in 1944 by "Pete" Jones (b. 1891), from his oil fortune. The Foundation's mission is "to protect the Earth's life-support systems from environmental harm and to eliminate the possibility of nuclear war." It gave $13.1 million in grants in 1990.

Jones Foundation gave American Rivers $50,000 in 1989; Audubon Society of Maine $20,000; Audubon Society of Massachusetts $150,000; Center for Marine Conservation $50,000; Environmental Defense Fund $75,000; Inform, Inc. $50,000; Keystone Center $50,000; Natural Resources Defense Council $262,000; Northwest Coalition for Alternatives to Pesticides $20,000; Project LightHawk $30,000; Sierra Club Legal Defense Fund $100,000; Wilderness Society $150,000; World Wildlife Fund $990,000; Worldwatch Institute $150,000.

The Joyce Foundation of Chicago (Assets $319,313,724) gave the National Audubon Society $205,000 for a staff scientist and symposia on biotechnology issues and another $150,000 for work on implementation of groundwater policies; $375,000 to the Environmental Defense Fund for research, policy and education activities of biotechnology program, and $100,000 to the EDF project to reduce fossil fuel combustion through market incentives, and another $10,000 for work on economics of alternative technologies for solid waste management in the Midwest; $50,000 to Friends of the Earth Foundation to try to get minorities involved in environmental issues; $375,000 to the National Wildlife Federation for the National Biotechnology Policy Center, another $56,000 for work on state level implementation of model water quality standards; $40,000 to the Natural Resources Defense Council for an acid rain project; $75,000 to the Sierra Club Foundation for the Great Lakes federal policy project; $150,000 to the World Resources Institute for work on "strategies for reducing carbon emissions through energy pricing, developing renewable energy alternatives and exploring transportation alternatives"—in other words, how to get cars off the road, and another $60,000 to complete and publish research on the economics of sustainable agriculture.

Peter Kiewit Foundation of Omaha, Nebraska (Assets $219,831,687 in 1990) funded by the construction giant. Gave the Nature Conservancy Omaha Chapter $24,500 in 1989 to establish their natural heritage inventory program in Nebraska.

The Fred Maytag Family Foundation of Newton, Iowa (Assets $21,259,955 in 1990. Gave the Nature Conservancy Iowa Chapter $50,000 in 1990.

John D. and Catherine T. MacArthur Foundation of Chicago. Incorporated in 1970, assets in 1990, $3,077,581,000. One analyst of the philanthropy scene described the MacArthur Foundation as "the biggest, most bizarre, riotously quarrelsome, disorganized, in some respects even dubious, of the new and very large American foundations." The donor, John D. MacArthur was the youngest of seven children. His mother died when he was a boy and his farmer father became a wandering evangelist. His education ended with grade school. He died in 1978 at the age of eighty the richest man in America.

His fortune began when he bought a bankrupt Chicago insurance company in 1935, Bankers Life and Casualty, for twenty-five hundred dollars. It did well, allowing him to invest in Florida real estate and buy up a dozen other insurance companies. He hated government so much he once said, "The only thing that will save this country is a paper shortage." The foundation based on his fortune may yet create a paper shortage by funding environmental groups that shut down all the forests.

John D.'s son, J. Roderick, had to fight the first board of directors for control of the foundation in a spate of nasty lawsuits. He lost—not in court, but to pancreatic cancer which cut his fight short in 1984—but managed to shape the foundation's mission as "being the cutting edge of social change."

One the agents for social change has been the MacArthur Foundation's environmental program, influenced most heavily by Nobel Prize scientist Murray Gell-Mann, who served as chairman of the foundation subcommittee that dealt with environmental grants. Rod MacArthur had his quarrels even with the distinguished Dr. Gell-Mann, citing him in a lawsuit for taking nearly $270,000 in part-time fees from the foundation between 1979 and 1983.

Whatever truth there may be to these pocket-lining allegations, Dr. Gell-Mann served the foundation effectively in helping to engineer the first debt for nature swap by the Nature Conservancy and Conservation Foundation / World Wildlife Fund and many other environmental grants.

Adele Simmons, President of the MacArthur Foundation, is a board member of the ultra-left-wing Union of Concerned Scientists, which may give us a clue to the foundation's political orientation.

The merged Conservation Foundation / World Wildlife Fund received $735,000 "for a program linking conservation and sustainable development in seven priority areas in Colombia, Peru and Ecuador," scheduled for 1989. The Nature Conservancy received $375,000 for "the Parks in Peril program in seven high priority national parks in Bolivia, Colombia, Ecuador and Peru." The Audubon Society received $200,000 in 1989 for a film, "Man and the Rainforest: Seeking a Balance." Conservation International received three huge grants in 1989, one for $760,000, one for $550,000 and another for $417,500, all involving debt for nature swaps. The Environmental Defense Fund received $600,000 in 1989 for work in tropical countries. This pattern of grants clearly shows the foundation's commitment to imposing American-style environmental interventionism on the Third World.

Robert R. McCormick Tribune Foundation of Chicago (Assets $470,292,080 in 1990). Gave the Nature Conservancy $500,000 in 1989 for conservation activities in the metropolitan Chicago area.

The Andrew W. Mellon Foundation (1990 Assets $1.6 billion) was formed in 1969 by the consolidation of two foundations established by the children of Andrew W. Mellon: the Old Dominion Foundation (created in 1941 by Paul Mellon) and the Avalon Foundation (created in 1940 by Alisa Mellon Bruce). The foundation has a program in Conservation and Environment including "the preservation of natural areas and the support of organizations concerned with increasing man's understanding of his natural environment, his relation to it, and the effects of this activities upon it." Through the early 1970s, a substantial fraction of grants supported land acquisition.

Between 1974 and 1979 the foundation moved into mainstream environmental grants as well, but continues to "invest in land preservation through The Trust for Public Land," which it gave $750,000 in 1990.

The foundation gave Cornell University $700,000 in 1990 which will certainly fund studies that end up in environmental group propaganda sheets because of rabid anti-pesticide advocate/scientist David Pimentel of Cornell. The Mellon Foundation also gave $450,000 to Yale University's School of Forestry and Environmental Studies, which has cranked out a notable portion of the current environmental movement's leaders.

They also gave $250,000 to the Environmental Law Institute for its Center for East European Environmental Programs.

Richard King Mellon Foundation of Pittsburgh, Pennsylvania (Assets $836,121,061 in 1990). It was established in 1947 by Richard King Mellon (1899-1970), President and Chairman of the Board of Mellon National Bank and Trust Company, and founder and president of T. Mellon and Sons. Since 1988 the Foundation has focused its grantmaking on the environment.

The Mellon money does a lot more than drive the Nature Conservancy. It gave a total of $37,596,076 in 1990. Over $21 million of that went to the Foundation's own Land Conservation Program in donations of land amounting to more than 100,000 acres to public agencies on condition the land be preserved as wildlife refuges, parks or national historic areas.

The RKM folks in 1990 gave $700,000 to Pat Noonan's Conservation Fund; $50,000 to the Conservation Foundation; $150,000 to the Environmental Defense Fund; $375,000 to Inform, Inc.; $225,000 in 1989 and $300,000 in 1990 to the Izaak Walton League of America; $200,000 to the Rails to Trails Conservancy; much more—over $31 million in grants in 1990.

Marin Community Foundation of Larkspur, California, (Assets $482,431,000) was created by the will of Beryl Buck in 1973, was administered by the San Francisco Foundation through 1986, when it was transferred to the present foundation. It gave $160,000 to the National Audubon Society for environmental education; $75,000 to Environmental Action Committee of West Marin.

Monsanto Fund of St. Louis (Assets $4,197,929 in 1990). Corporate charity of the chemical company, gave the Audubon Society of Massachusetts $14,300 in 1989.

Margaret T. Morris Foundation of Prescott, Arizona (Assets $19,244,689) gave Nantucket Conservation Foundation, Nantucket, Massachusetts, $10,000 toward land purchase in 1989.

M. J. Murdock Charitable Trust of Vancouver, Washington (Assets $213,451,475 in 1990). Gave $20,000 to Cascade Holistic Economic Consultants (Randall O'Toole runs this outfit, the man who told *Newsweek*, "Cumulatively, the environmental movement is interested in shutting down the timber industry."); $78,000 to Conservation International Foundation of Portland, Oregon—Spencer Beebe's outfit, now reorganized as EcoTrust, which is working with Northwest timber-dependent communities trying to find jobs for timber workers who were put out of work by other environmentalists.

National Geographic Society Education Foundation of Washington, D.C. (Assets $38 million in 1991). We have seen that the 10-million-member National Geographic Society is an environmental group, but we have not seen that it is also a funding source for environmental grants. Its 1991 environmental grants authorized amounted to $2,200,000, as reported to the Environmental Grantmakers Association. All of NGSEF's grants "are related to geography and the world environment." Most go to classroom projects for grades K-12 "that relate geography to an enhanced understanding of our physical, cultural, and natural environments." The range of grants is $5,000 to $50,000, with a mean of $30,000. Some real heavyweights sit on the board of directors including Sir David Attenborough and filmmaker George Lucas. Lucas is interested in the high-tech National Geographic Society Kids Network, a computer-based telecommunications project designed for grades 4-6, which enables students around the world to exchange information on environmental topics such as acid rain (one curriculum unit included in the series) through maps, charts, and letters. Technical Education Research Centers of Cambridge, Massachusetts is developing other curriculum units with partial funding from the National Science Foundation.

NGSEF's program of grantmaking includes the Geographic Alliance Network, a forty-six state school network that puts on curriculum conferences, summer institutes on regional geography and in-service workshops for teachers.

A typical grant was for $15,000 in 1991 to Tennessee Geographic Alliance in Knoxville, which is asking for long-term support through the National Environmental Education Act.

Northwest Area Foundation of St. Paul, Minnesota (Assets $237,574,602 in 1991). A highly influential foundation that has supplied leaders to activist groups. Gives large grants for cutting edge projects. Gave the Wilderness Society, Northwest Region, $169,000 in 1991 to "help eight timber-dependent communities in Oregon and Washington develop economic diversification plans and work toward supportive policies." Translation from foundationese: "Here's some money to run projects which will convince the national public that you're concerned about all the timber jobs you killed and now you'll teach loggers how to wait tables and clean toilets in motels for tourists who never show up."

Patagonia, Inc. for the past five years has employed Paul Tebbel as Environmental Affairs Director working with environmental groups, corporate environmental programs and public issues from the local to the national level. Tebbel has degrees in biology and zoology and field experience working on coyotes, bobcats, grouse, deer and ducks throughout the northern United States and Canada.

Patagonia commits 10 percent of its pre-tax profits to worthy charitable causes.

"Since 1984, our tithing program has distributed funds to over 350 different organizations. Rather than dilute the impact of our donations by spreading them thinly to a variety of causes, we have chosen to aim our dollars directly toward environmental issues. Patagonia products are designed for outdoor use and we feel a strong responsibility and commitment to keep the environment in its natural state for future generations. We are particularly interested in supporting environmental groups which operate at the most basic grassroots levels and which share our concern and sense of urgency about the state of the Earth."

Patagonia gave $660,000 in 1991. $5,000 went to New Mexico Citizens for Clean Air and Water, Los Alamos. "NMCCAW takes conglomerate polluters to court and wins." $3,500 went to American Wildlands, Hamilton, Montana. "The Foundation has been supporting the concentrated efforts of Dan Heinz who has been working since 1986 to stop improper national forest roads and timber sales in Montana." $10,000 went to the Alliance for the Wild Rockies, Missoula, Montana. "Covering the Northern Rockies plus Alberta and British Columbia, the Alliance now has thirty-nine member organizations all dedicated to preserving the wilderness of the Wild Rockies against the immediate threat of short-sighted economic policies." Translation: Your Rocky Mountain job is dead, logger, miner, trucker, rancher, farmer.

Patagonia gave $10,000 to Earth First!

Pew Scholars Program in Conservation and the Environment at the School of Natural Resources, University of Michigan in Ann Arbor was established in 1988 "in response to the critical need to identify and support a new generation of scholar-scientists who would apply their special knowledge and skills directly to finding solutions to pressing environmental problems." Can you read between those lines? The Board of Directors of the Pew Charitable Trusts set up the Program with an initial three-year commitment of $5.5 million. Under the program, ten outstanding scholars are selected annually, each receiving $150,000 fellowships over a three-year period. The first group of scholars was chosen in June 1990.

The Program under Director James E. Crowfoot, Ph.D., gave away $1,500,000 in 1991. Where does this annual mil and a half show up as income to the environmental movement? Nowhere. It's just out there in the hands of ideologues with fancy degrees using it to find better ways to Trash the Economy. Associate Director Jon M. Jensen is the chairman of the Environmental Grantmakers Association. Among the ten 1991 winners of $150,000 three-year grants were:

Carl Safina, Ph.D., National Audubon Society, New York, for protection of cranes and endangered species on the Platte River; fisheries management; marine conservation; establishing a Marine Scientific Policy Center and a Marine Advocacy Network to enhance interchanges among scholarly scientific knowledge, public information, policy, and politics.

Russell Greenberg, Ph.D., Smithsonian Institution Environmental Research Center, Edgewood, Maryland, for vertebrate behavior and ecology, tropical ecology and conservation biology.

Donella Meadows, Ph.D. (lead author of the Club of Rome's *Limits to Growth*),

Dartmouth College and the Balaton Group, Hanover, New Hampshire, for systems analysis and the integration of nature; advancing the international Balaton Group.

Constance Millar, Ph.D., Institute of Forest Genetics, United States Forest Service, Placerville, California, for advancing the Center for the Conservation of Genetic Diversity (CCGD); new forestry practices; physiochemical processes of the adaptation of trees; ways in which tree species can adapt to global climate change.

You can bet none of these Ph.Ds will use their $50,000 a year stipend to recommend commodity production or full employment as a "solution to pressing environmental problems."

Prince Charitable Trusts in Chicago received their original bequests from Frederick Henry Prince and Abbie Norman Prince, his wife. Both had fortunes. Frederick grew wealthy in the Chicago stockyards with a firm called Central Manufacturing District, while Abbie's fortune came from her family's Norman Water Works in Rhode Island. They donate $10,000 to $35,000 grants to about 16 environmental groups.

Public Welfare Foundation, Inc. of Washington, D.C. (Assets $244,146,780) gave $35,000 to the Environmental Action Foundation of Washington, D.C. for Toxics Education, Action and Mobilization Campaign to get facilities using toxic chemicals to comply with reporting requirements of federal law and to reduce use of those chemicals; $200,000 to the Environmental Defense Fund for Global Atmosphere Program and international programs which deal with global warming; $250,000 to Friends of the Earth for continued support for outreach and technical assistance to state and local environmental groups; $250,000 to the Natural Resources Defense Council for Atmosphere Protection Initiative, which deals with problems of global warming, ozone depletion and toxic air emissions; $125,000 to the Sierra Club Legal Defense Fund to establish an office in Louisiana; $100,000 to the World Resources Institute to provide policymakers around the world with information and support regarding efforts to slow global warming; $300,000 to Worldwatch Institute for research and analysis and information dissemination regarding global warming and other critical environmental problems.

The San Francisco Foundation of San Francisco (Assets $226,099,459) gave $15,000 to the American Farmland Trust to buy farmland in Contra Costa County; $20,000 to the Center for Marine Conservation to develop the Marine Debris Action Plan; $20,000 to the Conservation Fund for greenway demonstration projects in Northern California; $32,000 to the Environmental Defense Fund; $18,237 to Environmental Grantmakers Association; $30,000 to the Natural Resources Defense Council to restrict private water use; $27,000 to the Sierra Club Legal Defense Fund to represent seven environmental groups in a lawsuit.

The Harry and Grace Steele Foundation of Newport Beach, California, (Assets $41,335,080) gave $500,000 to the Nature Conservancy for continued support.

The Times Mirror Foundation of Los Angeles (Assets $18,183,490)—the donor is the Times Mirror Company, publisher of the *Los Angeles Times*—gave $10,000 to the Environmental Defense Fund for operating budget; $50,000 to the Nature Conservancy to buy Carrizo Plain; $15,000 to the World Wildlife Fund for annual support.

Town Creek Foundation of Oxford, Maryland (Assets $25,608,501 in 1991). Edmund A. Stanley, donor. This foundation gives over a million dollars a year to environmental groups and related "peace" groups, typically in $10,000 to $25,000 chunks to many groups, including American Rivers, National Audubon Society, Clean Water Fund, Environmental Action, Defenders of Wildlife, Environmental Defense Fund, Environmental Law Institute, Greenpeace USA, LightHawk, National Coalition Against the Misuse of Pesticides, National Toxics Campaign, National Wildlife Federation, Natural Resources Defense Council, the Nature Conservancy, the Public Lands Foundation, Sierra Club Legal Defense Fund, and the Wilderness Society.

In 1990 it gave an unusual $85,000 grant to Chesapeake Bay Foundation, Inc.

US West Foundation of Englewood, Colorado (Assets $13,853,913) gave $15,000 to the Nature Conservancy to buy Waldron Island property.

Victoria Foundation, Inc. of Montclair, New Jersey (Assets $149,900,000 in 1991) was established in 1924 by Hendon Chubb of the Chubb Insurance Company family. It gave a total of $609,500 in 16 environmental grants in 1990, including $20,000 to Environmental Defense Fund; $20,000 to Pinelands Preservation Alliance to start up a new organization to mobilize support for stopping development in the Pinelands.

Vulcan Materials Company Foundation of Birmingham, Alabama (Assets $2,665,690), gave the Nature Conservancy in Baton Rouge, Louisiana, $20,000.

Waste Management, Inc., a world-wide conglomerate with an annual gross income of more than $3 billion and nearly 900 subsidiaries, depends upon strict waste-control laws for its income. WMI bought into the Environmental Grantmakers Association and gives substantial grants throughout the environmental movement. From 1987 to 1990, WMI gave $900,000 to the National Wildlife Federation, the National Audubon Society and the Trust for Public Land.

Dean Witter Foundation of San Francisco (Assets $6,813,026) gave $12,500 to the Natural Resources Defense Council for general support.

All of the above:
Job killers.
Economy Trashers.

Money—Footnotes

1 For a pre-environmental-movement analysis, see *Foundations, Their Power and Influence*, René A. Wormser, Devin-Adair, New York, 1968.

2 Waldemar A. Nielsen, *The Golden Donors: A New Anatomy of the Great Foundations*, E. P. Dutton, New York, 1985, p. 30.

3 *Grants for Environmental Protection and Animal Welfare, 1991-1992*, The Foundation Center, New York, 1992. "The Philanthropy 400," Special Report, *The Chronicle of Philanthropy*, November 19, 1991, p. 1. "Best Charities," *Money*, December, 1992, p. 122-123.

4 Office of Personnel Management data.

5 Donald H. Rumsfeld, Preface to *Patterns of Corporate Philanthropy*, Marvin Olasky, Capital Research Center, 1987, p. *iv*.

6 *Patterns of Corporate Philanthropy*, Marvin Olasky, Capital Research Center, 1987.

7 "Buying in: how corporations keep an eye on environmental groups that oppose them— by giving big wads of money," by Eve Pell, *Mother Jones*, April-May, 1990, p. 23.

8 "Buying In," by Eve Pell, *Mother Jones*, April / May 1990, p. 25.

9 *The History of the Standard Oil Company*, Ida M. Tarbell, 2 vols., McClure, Phillips & Co., New York, 1904.

10 This background was provided in an interview with Pam Maurath in December 1992.

11 "Oiling the works," by Eve Pell, *Mother Jones*, March / April 1991, p. 39.

12 *The Age of the Moguls*, Stewart H. Holbrook, Doubleday & Company, Inc., Garden City, N.Y., 1956.

13 "Rockefeller Foundation Starts Ecology Effort," by Kathleen Teltsch, *New York Times*, July 24, 1990, p. C10.

Media

1952: Movie magnate Samuel Goldwyn said, "If you want to send a message to the public, call Western Union."

1992: Greenhouse guru Stephen Schneider wrote in the *Boston Globe*, "It is journalistically irresponsible to present both sides of environmental issues as though it were a question of balance."

We're definitely not in Kansas anymore, Toto.

Hey, dudes, it's Eco-Oz, where all the media are Western Union.

Take music: The most expensive garage band in history—Sting, Bruce Springsteen, Paul Simon, Don Henley, Bruce Hornsby, Branford Marsalis, Herbie Hancock, Paulino, Danny Kortchmar and Danny Quotrocchi—raised a million bucks at a Beverly Hills bash in early 1990 for the Environmental Media Association and the Rainforest Foundation. At a thousand dollars a ticket and $50,000 for the top table, the unemployed loggers and miners didn't show, but the cause *du jour* brought out Tom and Jillie Selleck, Jeff and Susan Bridges, Don Johnson, Grant Tinker, Peter Gruber, Jane and Michael Eisner, Bonnie Raitt, Lakers forward A.C. Green, Jayni and Chevy Chase, Casey and Ted Danson, Lilly and Brandon Tartikoff, Goldie Hawn, Billy Crystal (he was emcee), former governor Jerry Brown, Dianne Feinstein and Lynn and Norman Lear. Sting sang "Fragile;" Springsteen sang "The River;" Henley "The End of Innocence;" Simon "Slip Sliding Away;" American Indian Red Crow performed an Indian song; the whole group did "You Don't Know What You've Got Till It's Gone."[1]

A mil is a lot of bread for such a short set, man.

In another eco-coup, Willie Nelson sang "It's a Wonderful World" in a two-minute movie spot that was seen in 1991 on more than 1,200 screens owned by AMC Entertainment, Inc. Steve Hayden, chief executive officer and creative director of BBDO in Los Angeles made the public service announcement using lavish nature footage—emerald forests, ranging rivers, sawtooth mountain peaks, rainbow-clad waterfalls, the whole nine yards—deliberately showing no people. There's Victor Scheffer and Environmentalism's Articles of Faith again—nature is the world without people.

Didn't John Denver used to do that shtick once?

Well, Willie's music wowed 'em, and Steve's Western Union made 'em feel great. Near the tail of the PSA, four short titles appeared on the screen:

Last year by recycling paper you save 600 million trees.

22% of you carpooled, keeping millions of tons of pollutants out of the air.

You recycled 50 percent of all the aluminum cans produced, saving energy and land.

And by buying dolphin-safe tuna, you saved 50,000 dolphins.

Music down. Moonrise shot. Fade to black. End title.

You're making a world of difference.

Audiences applauded themselves. And people who hadn't done any of those things found themselves wanting to be included in the "You." Clever. And very upbeat for an environmentalist message. But very calculated.

Hayden has done a lot of *pro bono* advertising for Earth Day activities. He usually socks you with a downer. "Sometimes you need to do something much more hard hitting to break through," he explains. Why just pretty pictures and happy talk with Willie's music? "The danger is that unless a balance is struck, viewers can be lulled into a sense of despair."

Lulled into despair? Is that like being bludgeoned into joy? Oh, well, a Hollywood flak's verbal reach should exceed his grasp, else what's a metaphor?

Just follow the yellow brick road to Eco-Oz.

Singer/movie director Barbra Streisand used the $6 million HBO paid for the broadcast rights to her 1986 political fund raising concert—a Hollywood do that brought in $1.5 million for the campaign coffers of Democratic Senators Alan Cranston, Tom Daschle, Tom Harkin and Pat Leahy, along with former Representative Bob Edgar—as startup money for

The Streisand Foundation.
10536 Culver Blvd., Suite E
Culver City, California 90232
Telephone (310)836-6536

As of year end 1990, the Streisand Foundation had assets of $4,118,997, gave 34 grants totaling $502,750, high $50,000, low $250 (what putz got a lousy $250?), average $10,000-$20,000.

Margery Tabankin, executive director; Mildred Lewis, administrative director. Trustees: Richard Baskin, Alan Bergman, Marilyn Bergman, Marvin Goldberger, Jason Gould, Page Jenkins, Stanley Sheinbaum, Barbra Streisand, Paula Weinstein.

The Streisand Foundation subsequently hosted a conference on the environment in Washington and began handing out grants and endowments to environmental groups. The Environmental Defense Fund was endowed with the Streisand Chair of Environmental Studies with total pledges from the foundation of $2.8 million. EDF staffer and global warming doomsday prophet Michael Oppenheimer gets most of his support from this endowment. You can Trash the Economy a lot just singing.

Western Union calling....

Message, Spock?

Take the movies: It's not just Admiral James T. Kirk and the Starship Enterprise crew stopping off in the 20th Century to save the whales on *The Voyage Home (Star Trek IV)*. It's not just blatantly environmentalist flicks such as *Medicine Man, At Play in the Fields of the Lord* and the animated kiddie Economy Trasher *FernGully*, none of which did much box office. It's that scene in blockbuster hit *Lethal Weapon II* when the L.A. cop played by Danny Glover is attacked by his family for eating a tuna fish sandwich—"We're boycotting tuna to save the dolphins!" In a movie where human life is so expendable, why were the hamfisted writers so worried about dolphins?

The reason is **Earth Communications Office** (ECO), run by Bonnie Reiss, a former attorney to the elite—her stable included up-and-coming stars Kirstie Alley, Mimi Rogers and Robert Englund. Reiss now rallies Hollywood behind environmental messages. Although she is strictly leftish in her personal beliefs—she was floor manager of the 1980 Democratic National convention and co-founder of the powerful Hollywood Women's Political Caucus—she's no dummy when it comes to getting industry conservatives to listen to her environmental message. When she started up ECO in 1986 she brought key Republicans Ron Howard and Arnold Schwarzenegger into her eco-tent. Howard was an early supporter and board member. Country singer Rosanne Cash opened an ECO office in Nashville.

Reiss came to environmentalism through a sudden conversion. "I had this great awareness," she told the *New York Times*. "It was like 'Field of Dreams.' If you do this, it will happen. I was at this global warming conference in Washington [the one put on by the Streisand Foundation] and after listening to them all for three days, I finally raised my hand and said, 'Excuse me. This is overwhelming. You're telling me that the globe is going to warm more in the next 50 years than it has in the past 10,000, and the hole in the ozone is now the size of the United States of America, and we're losing the rain forests at the rate of one football field a second—wouldn't one mention of any of this on "The Cosby Show" do more than all your scientific books combined?'"[2]

Reiss became the Aimee Semple McPhersonesque eco-evangelist to the stars. In 1989 she ran a fact-finding trip to the Amazon with the likes of Tom Cruise, Mimi Rogers and John Ritter. She sought out the mid-level industry types for her 90-person board at $5,000 a hit. ECO's board of directors looks like the invitation list for the annual Academy Awards ceremony: Glenn Close, Dudley Moore, David Zucker, Dean Stockwell, Jeff Bridges and Michael Keaton, to name but a few. Producer and director Richard Donner is a friend—and *Lethal Weapon II* was *his* movie.

With influence like that, it doesn't take much to put a tuna fish sandwich-bashing scene in a bigtime hit.

Donner was given an award for the scene at a "Dolphin Awareness Evening" on November 16, 1989 sponsored by Earth Island Institute and The Dolphin Connection, which is a nonprofit put together by Maggy Howe, Lise Snyder and Ani Moss. Moss was a former fashion model for the Eileen Ford Agency and married to Jerry Moss, who had formed A&M Records with Herb Alpert in the early 1960s. Ani Moss met Sam LaBudde at a meeting in San Diego and watched his trumped up videotape, weeping when it was done. Moss told LaBudde she wanted to do something to help, and The Dolphin Connection was it, designed to bring the issue to people in the entertainment industry. One of its first projects was the Dolphin Awareness Evening, and a thousand celebrities came to become aware of dolphins. As we said in the Earth Island Institute profile, Stan Minasian of the Marine Mammal Fund gave an impassioned speech. Dave Phillips of Earth Island Institute gave an impassioned speech. Sam LaBudde of the edited videotape gave an impassioned speech. LaBudde urged his audience to boycott Heinz's StarKist brand tuna. If Danny Glover's family can do it, so can yours.

Western Union calling....

Today Reiss's ECO has grown to an organization of more than 1,500, with members ranging from studio heads to the unknowns who write television scripts for TV potboilers like *Doogie Howser, M.D.* or *Beverly Hills, 90210.*

ECO has made itself felt in hundreds of ways, most of them small, unobtrusive and palatable. New musical releases by Barbra Streisand, Olivia Newton-John, Quincy Jones and Belinda Carlisle carried an eco-message on the packaging scripted by ECO. Goldie Hawn and Mel Gibson lent their talents to TV public service announcements for ECO.

The big East Coast environmental outfits were not long in muscling in on this burgeoning Hollywood action. The Natural Resources Defense Council opened a West Coast office in Los Angeles and the Environmental Defense Fund began elbowing its way into the celebrity racket with the aid of

The Environmental Media Association
Budget: $602,870 (1993)
Staff: 5
10536 Culver Blvd.
Culver City, California 90232
Phone: (310)559-9334 Fax: (310)838-2367

Hollywood's *premiere* Economy Trasher, dahling. The very Wizard of Eco-Oz. It runs out of the same address as the Streisand Foundation.

One version of its origins has it organized by three pregnant wives of three moguls: Lyn Lear, married to producer Norman Lear (*All in the Family, Maude*); Cindy Horn, wife of Alan Horn, co-founder and managing partner of Castle Rock Entertainment (which produced the Billy Crystal - Meg Ryan hit *When Harry Met Sally*), and Susie Field, whose husband, Ted Field, is chairman of Interscope, a company that produces movies, television shows and records. The wives all realized their incubating offspring might be suffering from bad food, air and water and would be born into a world beset with environmental trauma.

"Thanks to our husbands," said Ms. Horn, "who have access to some of the most influential media people, we decided to put together EMA."

Another version of the origins of the Green Screen Queen is that it was an offshoot of Bonnie Reiss's Earth Communications Office. Norman Lear and wife Lyn, originally colleagues with ECO, split away over differences in their vision of the group's future. Lear wanted to go the high-priced route while Reiss was a little more grass-rooty. This version has Norman and Lyn conceiving EMA in April 1989 and unveiling it at their Brentwood home.[3]

Whatever the truth may be—and in Eco-Oz, who can tell reality from special effects?—Lear hustled 35 industry high-rollers onto their board at $10,000 to

$25,000 a pop—the champagne-bottle pop as opposed to ECO's $5,000 beer-can phht. Some came in for more, some less, but all came in to stay (total 1993 assets, $738,186). $25,000: Norman Lear; Robert Daly; Warner Bros; Mellon Bank; Conde Nast Publications; Sony Pictures; Davis Oil Company. $10,000: Grant Tinker; HBO; NBC; 20th Century Fox; Creative Artists Agency; Environment Now; Fairchild Publications; TBS Productions. Guess Inc.: $325,000. That's a lot of jeans.

Lyn Davis Lear is a power to contend with as a co-founder and board member of EMA. She received her Ph.D. in clinical psychology at the Professional School of Psychological Studies in San Diego, has practiced counseling at New York's Foundation for Manic Depression and Depression, and was in private practice in psychotherapy in Beverly Hills. She's poked around inside the heads of Hollywood's best.[4]

EMA began operations in June 1989 out of a set of offices at Lear's ACT III operation in Culver City (that's why Barbra's foundation has the same address—Lear houses all sorts of leftish funk at this mail box).

EMA isn't run by some liberal lawyer who happened to have an environmental epiphany one day, but by veteran heavy hitters within the entertainment industry with a long-term commitment, intended to outlast the usual Hollywood "issue of the month"—Disease of the Month (AIDS, breast cancer), Justice of the Month (spouse abuse, gay rights), Stigma of the Month (child molesting, conservatism)—whatever.

EMA's board of directors is strictly top cabin: Brandon and Lilly Tartikoff (NBC); Barry Diller (Fox); Michael and Jane Eisner (Walt Disney); Bob and Susan Iger (ABC); Michael and Judy Ovitz (Creative Artists); Norman Lear, Grant Tinker, Robert Redford, that sort. You get the picture.

Julia Phillips had it easy. Logger, you'll never eat lunch *on this planet* again.

EMA has a staff of five and ran on a nonprofit operating budget of $602,870 in 1993. President Andy Spahn (salary, $94,374, benefits, 0) is a long-time politico who knows his way around the shark-infested arm-twisting circuit. He left a post as chief of staff to California state controller Gray Davis to run EMA. Lauren McMahon (salary, $48,453, benefits, 0) is his right-hand person. Their outfit puts on breakfasts, lunches, and dinners—often showing producers what other shows have done on the environment and why haven't you, babe? Love ya'.[5]

There are so many of these let-me-lecture-you-about-global-warming-over-some-fava-beans-and-a-nice-Chianti sessions that one producer said, "If you're out of work, you can live off the environment in this town. Every day of the week there's a breakfast, lunch and dinner."

Speakers from bigtime environmental groups have become a commonplace at these eco-feeds, including John Adams of the Natural Resources Defense Council and Amory Lovins of Rocky Mountain Institute. EMA even brought in William K. Reilly back when he was head of the Environmental Protection Agency, Vice President Al Gore back when he was a Senator and Senator Tim Wirth back when he was a Senator. Many a lovely home and many a fine restaurant donated for the occasion featured toxic waste with the appetizer, recycled garbage with the entree and rain forest sawdust with dessert.

There are movie bigwigs who don't need an ECO or an EMA to convince them to slam human achievement with high-priced talent, masterful business organization, state-of-the-art equipment and high-tech special effects. *Star Wars* creator George Lucas talked about it in an hour-long feature showing clips from all three episodes of his famous trilogy, *From Star Wars to Jedi: The Making of a Saga.* "One of the more fascinating aspects of that project was the human spirit," said Lucas, "the human element, being able to withstand an onslaught of high technology. And how the high technology had failed."

Mark Hamill, who played hero Luke Skywalker in the trilogy, narrated *The Making of a Saga.* He observed wryly, "*Star Wars*' central irony: It uses high-tech movie making to state an anti-technology theme."

That is the central irony behind all of the Green Screen: It uses high-tech tools to state an anti-technology theme. Hollywood has gone stark raving stupid. It makes media that incite audiences to trash the economy that makes media possible.

I don't think we're in Hollywood anymore, Toto.

When EMA first cranked up back in 1989, it wasted no time getting its agenda on the screen, large and small. EMA took Allan Margolin, media director for the Environmental Defense Fund (see profile) to MTM studios in September to brief about 25 MTM executives, producers and members of the studio's creative staff. They heard all about the global environmental crisis. We're not going to be here in ten years. So let's shut everything down.[6]

Western Union calling....

The following day EMA hit the creative staff at Warner Brothers. Same message.

In October, EMA sponsored a forum with the Writers Guild of America where members heard Michael Oppenheimer, EDF's Streisand Chair scientist. Same message.

Then seminars at Columbia Television, Amblin, and Creative Artists Agency. Same message.

How to show it on the screen? A range of pitches from centering on the environment as the main plot device, making it the preoccupation of a lead character, or merely the presence of a recycling bin on the set or a National Wildlife Federation T-shirt on an extra's chest. Show 'em everything from throwaway lines about garbage to twenty lines on the importance of trees to entire episodes on aerosol cans.

How can you do a whole episode on aerosol cans? Joey Harris, played by Greg Evigan, one of the title characters on the NBC comedy series *My Two Dads*, threw away all the aerosol sprays in the house, lectured his daughter on styrofoam cups and went to jail for dumping sludge from a polluted beach into the toilets of an oil company's headquarters. "If they're going to treat our world like a toilet, I'm going to treat their toilets like they treat our world," pronounced the character from his cell. Anything for a laugh, NBC.

How about anything for a buck? David Simon, a producer of *My Two Dads*, hedges his bets. He had an episode about killing cockroaches without using pesticides. "What if the sponsor were Raid?" Simon asked rhetorically. "You color all of your product references, you make indirect statements—you have to protect where the buck is. This is a capitalist society." Gee, Dave, for how long?[7]

Once EMA has acted as the catalyst to get script changes and incorporate such environmental themes, it offers new ideas, brainstorming and further research. It acts as a liaison with its pet environmental organizations for writers and producers who have become interested.[8]

Soon *Murphy Brown* was tackling recycling, *Designing Women* dealt with fur and disposable diapers, and extraterrestrial *Alf* lobbied to stop production of chlorofluorocarbons (CFCs), alleged perpetrator of the alleged ozone problem. Flip the channel. A streetwise cop is telling another how many trees it takes to print an edition of *The New York Times*. Hmm, maybe those trees *should* be saved.[9]

Ed Zwick, executive producer of *thirtysomething* introduced an environmental organizer as a new character as well as making one of the leads, Hope, an environmental activist. Using EMA's contacts with the Environmental Defense Fund, Zwick and his writers settled on municipal waste incineration for a drubbing on the small screen.[10]

Executive producer Steve Downing of ABC's *MacGyver* was inspired to base an episode on a case presented at an EMA seminar in which a particular rain forest flower in danger of extinction was the sole medicine that could save a relative's life. The presenter? Dr. Jay Hair of the National Wildlife Federation. He said, "You've got to get the masses in the most fundamental way possible, realizing that when they get involved, they will begin to see the greater complexities and dimensions of the problems."[11]

Oh, yes. And send money.

Take television—please

Everybody in the small screen industry remembers the famous incident where the Fonz on ABC's *Happy Days* goes into a library and gets a library card. It had nothing to do with the plot, literacy was just the cause of the week and the producers stuck the scene in out of charity. The next day millions of kids deluged the nation's libraries to get a library card. The libraries were swamped. They couldn't meet the demand. That's the kind of reach the TV medium has.

Jay Hair, president of the National Wildlife Federation drooled, "The environmental movement needs to be reaching people in every possible medium, and television is the most important. If programmers can hit home that environmental quality of life is an integral part of the cultural agenda, then they have really achieved something."[12]

Right up there with sex, lies, and videotape.

Larry Kopald, creative director for the prestigious advertising agency Foote Cone & Belding said, "Television is the most powerful tool available to foster good or bad, and build or destroy societal values. TV is also used to perpetuate mass merchandising. I am part of that. I understand it. But I believe there should be conscience and balance in what I do. If I can sneak in there and use the power of the media to make people feel responsible, I'll go to sleep at night."

Hmm. Maybe we were watching the wrong channels.

Kopald produced a commercial for Mazda with a guy driving to a recycling center. "The idea is to make it seem natural and a part of life without calling attention to it," Kopald said.[13]

If the environmental movement was about recycling, that would be a great commercial. But the environmental movement is not what it seems. Maybe Kopald's next 60-second spot will be a guy driving to the unemployment office. Make it seem natural. A part of life.

Bruce Nachbar, co-producer of the mega-hit television series *The Wonder Years*, found out about Earth Communications Office and invited Bonnie Reiss to visit the set of the show and speak to the cast and crew. She gave them her standard speech about being more environmentally conscious. Use reusable mugs instead of plastic cups. Stop using paper plates. On-screen and off. She won over everybody, including the show's young stars Fred Savage and Josh Savanio.

Nachbar introduced scripts with an environmental theme. One episode carried a plot line featuring characters Kevin, Winnie and Paul fighting to save fictional Harper's Woods from nasty developers. To give the story a lasting punch, writers had the novice environmentalists lose their fight in the closing scene with a flashforward to show the strip mall that had replaced Harper's Woods. A *Brady Bunch* ending would have been too upbeat for the environmentalist worldview. Ennui. Despair. Pessimism.

On NBC's *Hunter*, the crime-fighting heroes take on a chemical company, investigating the head of the plant for murder after a child dies from breathing toxic gas when cyanide waste is illegally dumped in a neighborhood sewer.[14]

MCA/Universal hired ecologist Garrett De Bell as a consultant in 1990 to help put ecological themes in their Earth Day productions. De Bell is a recycled environmentalist left over from the first Earth Day—he edited Friends of the Earth's 1970 hodgepodge collection called *The Environmental Handbook*.

Ted Turner did a Save the Earth Week extravaganza including the Audubon Society Special *"The Great Plains,"* which painted a loathsome picture of farmers as rapers and exploiters who do not take care of their land. Certainly TV moguls and actors and movement activists can do a better job. Audubon leader Peter Berle would look *tres chic* wading in the cow manure behind a plow. It's *you*, Peter!

Ted Turner and Jane Fonda have done their best to mold the Turner Broadcasting empire into the child recruitment arm of the Small Green Screen. The Turner "Save The Earth" campaign taught children to pressure their parents into supporting the Economy Trashers. In February 1992, Turner used his cable and satellite superstation WTBS to premiere his new green scene shows.

Captain Planet and the Planeteers is an animated eco-comic strip. Good and evil fight it out to save the Earth from industry. There's this little problem, however. The parents of the kids who watch this show work for those nasty industries. What's little Kevin or little Kelsey going to think about that? Daddy hates the Earth, I know, Captain Planet tells me so.

One Child—One Voice, a scary sequence of vignettes designed to frighten kids out of their wits, presented children discussing issues such as global warming, wetlands, endangered species, biodiversity and acid rain. We're all going to die in ten years. In one sequence a huge axe sped toward the legs of a little girl. Her legs turn into small trees at the last possible second.

Are your brains clean yet, children?

ABC presented a two-hour Earth Day Special featuring Quincy Jones, Bette Midler, Meryl Streep and Kevin Costner, among other stars. MTV featured animated public service announcements to appeal to young viewers. Incidentally, don't write off MTV as the bubble gum channel—have you ever noticed that the commercials on MTV are substantially more creative and better produced than those on the big networks? Or that music videos are where some of the best new technical ideas are seen first?[15]

Paramount produced a pilot for CBS called *The Elite*, the first environmentally themed series. The two hour action-adventure featured a team of scientific experts who form an ecological crime-fighting team. It didn't fly. That business about *The Elite* and the environmental movement in the same breath made a lot of folks nervous.[16]

It made people even more nervous when Paramount hired Chris DeRose, founder of the radical animal rights group, Last Chance for Animals (LCA), to produce and host animal-issue segments of its TV show *Hard Copy*. On April 21, 1988, DeRose and seven other LCA activists broke through a locked door at the UCLA Brain Research Institute to videotape cats in a variety of neurological studies. DeRose released the tapes to local news programs, which repeated his false charges of cruelty and abuse. DeRose is also a spokesman for the eco-terrorist Animal Liberation Front and repeat offender for criminal trespass at Cedars Sinai Medical Center. He once told the *Los Angeles Times*, "If the death of one rat cured all diseases, it wouldn't make any difference to me." Thousands of members of the citizen group Putting People First ran a letter-writing campaign informing Paramount of DeRose's criminal background, which led to *Hard Copy* firing him. Upon conviction for his latest offense, DeRose took up residency in the Los Angeles County Jail for a spell to think about the UCLA break-in.[17]

In October of 1991 EMA presented their first Environmental Awards fete on a soundstage at Sony Studios in Culver City. Robert Redford gave the keynote address and Diane Sawyer acted as emcee for the awards honoring television, film and music productions that promote environmental themes. The award, called an EMA, was a baseball-size bronze sculpture designed by artist Robert Graham, went to winners in ten categories. Best feature film was *Dances With Wolves* (Orion Films). Best television episodic drama: *Shannon's Deal* (NBC) for the "Inside Man" episode. Best television comedy: *The Simpsons* (Fox) for the "Two Cars in Every Garage, and Three Eyes on Every Fish" episode. Music video: "Yakety Yak—Take It Back" (A Vision Entertainment). Ongoing commitment: (tie) *MacGyver* (ABC) and *Captain Planet and the Planeteers* (TBS).[18]

EMA made the big time the next month. President George Bush included the outfit in the honorees for his first round of Environment and Conservation Challenge Awards. Andy Spahn picked up the award in a Rose Garden ceremony at the White House. Spahn gracefully accepted the award with an insult for Bush. "President

Bush and the U.S. Congress are lagging behind the American public in their response to the environmental crisis." You can never outrun the EMA to the left, Toto.[19]

Or Ted Turner. However, Turner's *Network Earth* has the distinction of being the only CNN program so far to examine Wise Use viewpoints and other counter-arguments to the Economy Trashers. Ron Arnold enjoyed working with Sharon Collins, *Network Earth* producer and on-camera correspondent, whose crew followed him around for a week, coming to the Bellevue, Washington headquarters of the Center for the Defense of Free Enterprise to film a high level training conference for Wise Use movement leaders, going on to San Diego where they filmed him doing community organizing, and following him through the Texas woods, allowing Ron to explain the outstanding methods of a large forest products firm.

The edited product had the usual genuflections to the green ideology, but it at least offered opposing viewpoints, something rarely allowed to creep into the eco-media.

Occasionally Green Screen rhetoric backfires. Box office idol Tom Cruise gave a stirring speech at an Earth Day gathering, challenging the audience to make a difference. Some of the environmentalists present recalled that he was the star of *Days of Thunder*, 120 minutes of glorious gas-guzzling cars spewing various hydrocarbons, CO_x molecules and other pollutants into the air. He got bad reviews at Earth Day.

Just leave your picture and a resume at the door and we'll get back to ya, Tom.

There is a delectable irony in stars who jet back and forth across the country on a whim and get to work in long limousines telling the rest of us to live the simple life. Most of those studio benefits for the rain forest are held on sound stages built of tropical woods. There's more to life than getting a good table at Spago—but movie folk can't recall what.

Maybe they'd come down a little closer to earth if the environmental movement did to them what it does to ordinary mortals. For example, singer Dan Fogelberg maintains a secluded 600-acre ranch in Colorado and a rustic retreat in Maine. He goes on tour to promote the Endangered Species Act along with his recordings. He says "I've gone farther and farther from society and closer and closer to nature. I'm attracted to the wilderness, where man's inroads have yet to destroy." And John Denver has his famous Starwood compound in Aspen. And George Lucas owns Skywalker Ranch on Lucas Valley Road west of San Rafael, California. And all the other big stars have their little piece of nature.

How about if the National Parks and Conservation Association in cahoots with the National Park Service "honors" their land with National Natural Landmark designation, forbidding any new construction of recording studio space or filmmaking structures? Then we could transfer control of their property to the National Park Service and finally just take it away from them by national condemnation, bulldoze their structures to the ground and build an open space, public land preserved for future generations. Then Fogelberg and Denver and Lucas can live in the wilderness—there's no room service to make inroads and they can keep warm by rubbing two starlets together. Those rich celebrities ought to donate all their land to the public anyway—the public trust doctrine says so.

Or maybe we should ration the manufacturing stock of petroleum-based compact discs and the wood-based stock of motion picture film and videotape. Who needs entertainment? It's not essential. It doesn't feed, clothe or shelter us. All it does is make us squander our hard-earned money on frivolity and use up resources wastefully. Let's forbid the media from access to all raw materials. We could write the list of products entertainment moguls are forbidden to purchase by listing the industries they bash on their movies, going from most-bashed to least, starting with chemicals, then petroleum, then logging, then mining, and so on. Say what, dahling? You *like* free enterprise after all? Show us on the screen, babe.

All the News That Fits We Print

Take the newspapers: When it comes to reporting on the environment, the Intellectual Giants of the Press turn into micro-mind Print Pygmies.

Consider a seemingly factual, unbiased Associated Press report that went out over the A Wire to newspapers all across America in mid-November, 1992. Most of them ran it with headlines saying something to the effect that "1,575 scientists issue warning," and a subhead reading, "Human misery, mutilation of Earth expanding too fast, they say."[20]

It was datelined Washington, D.C. and the lead was, "No more than a few decades are left to reverse a trend toward vast human misery and mutilation of the Earth, a worldwide collection of 1,575 scientists said today."

The story tells us that 99 Nobel Prize winners were among the signatories. The statement said that "Human beings and the natural world are on a collision course." It listed ozone depletion, air pollution, waste of water, poisoning of the ocean, damage to farmland, deforestation, loss of plant and animal species and population growth as the greatest dangers.

The average reader would first be shocked.

"The Earth is finite," the scientists said. "Pressures from unrestricted population growth put demands on the natural world that can overwhelm any efforts to achieve a sustainable future."

The average reader would be horrified, then terrified.

We are eight paragraphs into this shocking, horrifying, terrifying statement of reputable scientists before the anonymous AP writer announces, "The appeal was coordinated by Henry Kendall, a U.S. physicist who won the Nobel Prize two years ago and now chairs the Union of Concerned Scientists."

Oh.

Now we see.

This "World Scientists' Warning to Humanity" was written and rigged by an environmental group leader, Henry Kendall of the Union of Concerned Scientists.

If you will recall our profile of the Cousteau Society, Jacques Cousteau reported in July 1992 during a French television FR3 feature on his role at the Earth Summit in Rio de Janiero that Henry Kendall of the Union of Concerned Scientists had come to him for help. Kendall told Cousteau, "We want to say to the world that we are going toward disaster, but we do not know how to do it and we need help."

Henry Kendall, recall, encountered his problem at the Earth Summit in Rio. It was the Heidelberg Appeal, a pro-technology statement signed by more than 1,000 scientists and intellectuals throughout the world saying that the gloom and doom Malthusians such as Cousteau and Kendall are themselves the problem.

Cousteau told Kendall to organize the "Warning to Humanity" and hold a big news conference to get the word out. The media, being loyal ideological environmentalists themselves, would do the rest.

Cousteau was right.

There was not a hint by the Associated Press that its story was a publicity gimmick by an environmental group. The Associated Press dutifully reported Kendall's knowingly false assertion that "there is an exceptional degree of agreement within the international scientific community that natural systems can no longer absorb the burden of current human practices."

Kendall knew there was no such exceptional degree of agreement. Kendall's warning was in fact a reaction to exceptional *disagreement*, the Heidelberg Appeal.

The Associated Press made no mention of the opposing Heidelberg Appeal. In fact, the Associated Press *obtained no opposing comment of any description.*

Kendall had the stage all to himself. The Associated Press wrote in some detail what the "World Scientists" who signed the "Warning to Humanity" wanted. AP did not mention that it was the Union of Concerned Scientists' routine agenda: Control the use of oil and coal, stop timber harvest everywhere and stop "poor farm practices;" use energy and materials "more efficiently" (translation: "stop producing things and conserve what we have now"); "stabilize" the population; reduce and eventually eliminate poverty; equality for women, including ensuring they can obtain abortions; reducing violence and the threat of war.

The Union of Concerned Scientists has been peddling this technology-bashing agenda for years.

Look behind those environmental headlines the next time you read a newspaper or watch a television news broadcast. Keep this book ready to hand to see what's really going on in those stories. Get to know the players so you can recognize their names and identify their agendas when you see them mentioned in "news" stories.

The media are hiding things from you.

The media are lying to you.

Don't trust them.

The Associated Press gave the Union of Concerned Scientists a free ride without so much as a peep that anybody disagreed with Kendall and his Malthusian Mob.

Why did they do that?

Part of the reason is that quite a few media luminaries are Economy Trashers themselves.

Recall from our profile on the World Wildlife Fund the huge media bash sponsored by the Smithsonian Institution in September 1989 titled, "Global Environment: Are We Overreacting?" Although the conference was co-chaired by the Chief Executive Officers of ABC, NBC, CBS, Turner Broadcasting, Time, Warner and the *L.A. Times* and many prominent journalists participated, the only report that saw the light of day appeared in *The Wall Street Journal* on October 5, written by David Brooks, a *Journal* editorial writer who was there, as noted by the watchdog group, Accuracy In Media.

AIM's Report of October 1989 said:

> Brooks was appalled by the absence of any balance on the panels. He said, "Through the entire conference, not a single disagreement deflected the steady breeze of alarmism. Perpetual apocalyptics such as Lester Brown and Paul Ehrlich rattled off their anthems of doom....Speakers and panels moved briskly on and off the podium: an acid rain crisis, a toxics crisis, a famine crisis, a population crisis. The result was a smorgasbord of apocalypse." Journalists participating were also awesomely one-sided.
>
> Brooks reports that one panelist, Charles Alexander, declared, "As the science editor of *Time* I would freely admit that on this issue we have crossed the boundary from news reporting to advocacy." For that he was applauded by journalists and experts alike. Andrea Mitchell, who covers Congress for NBC News, agreed, saying "clearly the networks have made that decision now, where you'd have to call it advocacy."
>
> Executive editor Ben Bradlee of *The Washington Post* chastised the other journalists for being so public with their bias. [C-SPAN was taping the conference for delayed broadcast.] Bradlee said, "I don't think there's any danger in what you suggest. There's a minor danger in saying it because as soon as you say 'To hell with the news, I'm no longer interested in news, I'm interested in causes,' you've got a whole kooky constituency to respond to, which you can waste a lot of time on."
>
> Brooks wryly noted, "Mr. Bradlee is right. Probably a lot of 'kooks' believe in objective journalism. But why shouldn't reporters lose their self-discipline when discussing the environment? Practically everyone else has. Somehow the idea has gotten around that the environment isn't a normal political issue, but a quasi-religious crusade. As a result, public discussion of the environment has been about as rigorous as one expects from a jihad."

Nobody even asked the question, "Global Environment: Are We Overreacting?" To environmentalists in journalists' clothing, there's no such thing as overreacting to their issues.

We don't have media anymore.

We have Western Union.

Eco-Oz.

A few media producers still have a sense of journalistic ethics. One is Tom Farmer, senior producer for Larry King Live on CNN. When then-Senator Al Gore released his book *Earth in the Balance*, he was invited to appear on the King show January 27, 1992. As the commentator counterpoint to Gore, producer

Farmer selected S. Fred Singer, Ph.D., Director of the Washington, D.C.-based Science and Environmental Policy Project. Dr. Singer is well-known as one of a growing number of scientists attempting to counter the Economy Trashers' claim of "scientific consensus" on environmental issues. Singer is also a debunker of Economy Trasher pseudo-science, with which Gore's book was crammed full. Dr. Singer prepped for the show, writing an opening statement, three main discussion points, and answers to a series of tough questions that his associate Candace C. Crandall could throw at him.

Just before the show was to be broadcast, Irene Williams, Al Gore's publicist, notified Farmer that our illustrious Vice President refused to go on the show if Dr. Singer was to be the commentator. Williams wanted to submit Farmer a list of "approved" commentators.

Like all Economy Trashers, Vice President Gore did not want credible dissenting voices challenging his phony alarmist agenda. Today he's a heartbeat away from the Oval Office.

Environmentalists usually insist upon, and get, the opportunity to speak unchallenged. The media have thus acted as knowing pimps to the most shameless prostitution of science. Larry King's producer Tom Farmer refused and simply cancelled Gore's spot.

The Big Green Screen

The movies are another story. Animal rights activists in particular have gotten a stranglehold on what you see in the movies. Screenwriter John Milius, who collaborated with Francis Ford Coppola on the dark and surreal Vietnam War epic *Apocalypse Now*, joked, "You can't make a movie about a tiger eating peasants unless you're on the side of the tiger."

The American Humane Association gained access to movie sets after the 1980 box-office disaster *Heaven's Gate* generated widespread criticism of director Michael Cimino for his rough treatment of animals while filming his panoramic Western. The original mission was to safeguard the animals used in films, but now the Humane Association has become a new Breen Office, censoring scenes they don't like on the grounds they might offend animal lovers. It's just a new breed of eco-bigots enforcing their moral standards on the whole society.

For example, when Walt Disney studios filmed *White Fang*, an action adventure based on the Jack London novella, the original script, true to the London story, contained a scene showing a wolf attacking a man. Betty Denny Smith, director of the Humane Association's Los Angeles office, told the *Los Angeles Times*, "I was very concerned about that being an anti-wolf statement."

Peddling the image that nature is perfectly benign and as safe as a visit to Disneyland is a top priority of the Economy Trashers. If you can divert all attention away from nature's harshness, you can direct public anger and hatred against human technology alone and thus achieve your political objectives. To the Economy Trashers, the facts don't matter. Smith, who has no direct knowledge of wolves in the wild, demanded and got a script change. Disney rewrote London's story so the attack takes place off-screen and allowed the environmental group Defenders of

Wildlife to add a disclaimer in the tail credit crawl saying that healthy wolves do not attack humans. Whoo, boy, Toto! I don't think we're on *Earth* any more.

Healthy wolves do indeed attack humans, as farmers and ranchers have seen with their own eyes in so many places for so many years they could hardly believe that Walt Disney would deliberately lie to its audiences. What would happen if some unsuspecting urban youngster took the disclaimer on faith and during a vacation to some nature spot approached a wolf only to be mauled to death? Dozens of upset rural-dwelling Americans contacted Mountain States Legal Foundation in Denver, asking that legal action be taken against Disney, the Defenders of Wildlife, and the Humane Association.

William Perry Pendley, president of Mountain States Legal Foundation, contacted a number of sources for verification of wolf attacks on humans, found abundant evidence, then urged Disney Chairman Michael Eisner to remove the disclaimer, "for factual accuracy, as well as for the sake of those children who come in contact with animals."[21]

Adam Merims, production executive on the film for Disney's Buena Vista Pictures, said, "What we tried to do was minimize the violence of the scene and yet preserve the underlying story. As film makers we tend to be pro-environmental." What film makers tend to do is cave in to environmentalist pressure groups. What Disney did on *White Fang* was negate the realism of Jack London's story and the truth about nature in order to pander to a political power and pressure lobby.

Part of the reason the disclaimer was not removed was that Disney CEO Michael Eisner is a board member of the Environmental Media Association.

Media Money

As we have seen in the profiles above, all kinds of media folks give cash donations to environmental groups. Newspapers do it for the big eco-groups. The Streisand Foundation does it for them too. What about television and radio? It's often invisible, but tends to take the form of such things as

The Bullitt Foundation
1011 Boren Avenue, Suite 821
Seattle, Washington 98104
Assets (1991): $9,122,034
1991 grants: $564,837

This grantmaking foundation was established in 1952 by Dorothy S. Bullitt, whose family was in the broadcasting business, owners of the Seattle NBC affiliate KING-TV along with KING-AM and KING-FM and related stations in Portland, Oregon and Spokane, Washington. Although located in the Pacific Northwest and focused on local and regional issues, the Bullitt Foundation gave plenty to big East Coast eco-groups in 1990: the Natural Resources Defense Council, $40,000; Center for Marine Conservation $25,000; The Nature Conservancy, Washington Field Office, $25,000.

Bullitt also gave $5,000 to Friends of the Columbia Gorge to "support an Education Outreach Program to educate community members and to encourage citizens to resist intimidation." A fancy way of saying "We gave money to the group that lobbied a vast Greenline Park onto 40,000 people in the Columbia Gorge National Scenic Area so they could "educate" the people they encircled—and to teach eco-group members how to avoid fistfights with thousands of angry people whose property had been regulated into uselessness."

The Disney clan doesn't Mickey Mouse around about environmentalism. Not only is Michael Eisner, CEO, one of the big money linchpins of Environmental Media Association, but the late Frank G. Wells, President and Chief Operating Officer of The Walt Disney Company since 1984, also started a private foundation called

Environment Now Foundation
450 Newport Center Drive, Suite 570
Newport Beach, California 92660
Assets 1990: $10,007,808

with his wife Luanne in 1989. It's funded with $10 million of Wells' own money and devoted to "protecting, preserving and restoring the environment." Wells was previously vice chairman of Warner Brothers, Inc., and a partner in the Hollywood law firm of Gang, Tyre and Brown. Wells sat on a number of boards of trustees, was director of the American Himalayan Foundation and co-authored a book about his mountaineering adventures, *Seven Summits*, published in 1986. Wells was killed in a helicopter crash in 1994.

Wells' lieutenant Paul Heeschen takes grants applications and the ENF board of directors consists of Wells' widow; Luanne Wells, President; Shari Kimoto, Secretary.

Richard S. Luskin is executive director. He practiced environmental law from 1986 to 1990 with the San Francisco firm of McCutchen, Doyle, Brown & Enersen. He was Administrator of Squaw Valley Ski Area, Planner for Kirkwood Ski Area, river guide, and Backcountry Ranger for the National Park Service at Glacier National Park and for the U.S. Forest Service at Truckee.

Hang on to your Mouse Ears, folks, they're all you're going to have left after the Disney crowd is through.

If it's any comfort, the Environmental Media Association's ultimate goal, according to a news release, is "To inspire the creation of a global network of similar organizations harnessing the power of the media for the environment."

No, it wasn't a gag for *Famous TV Bloopers*.

Harness the power. The Power. Power.

When you have them by the balls, their hearts and minds will follow.

Yes, Massa.

The *New York Times* broke with conventional wisdom and asked an impolite question we thought we'd never hear: Should Stars Set the Agenda? Reporter

Richard Bernstein noted that a group of celebrities who formed what they call the Creative Coalition is pushing a number of causes, the environment being one of the biggest. "The actor Richard Dreyfuss speaks on peace in the Middle East. The actress Meryl Streep promotes organic food with her organization Mothers and Others for a Livable Planet. The pop singer Sting fights for the South American rain forest. The rock star Don Henley works to protect Walden Woods in Massachusetts from developers. Mr. Henley and Mr. Dreyfuss have hired full-time aides to coordinate their activities."

Don Henley has a full-time aide on Walden Woods? All he wants to do is dance.

Then, wonder of wonders, reporter Bernstein asked, "Stars like Christopher Reeve, Richard Dreyfuss, Sting, Barbra Streisand, Don Henley, Ted Danson, Ron Silver, Sinead O'Connor and other new-breed show-business activists may be brilliant performers, but are they qualified to guide Americans on complex political and social questions? And does their presence make a media circus out of what should be sober reflection on complicated problems?"[22]

Hollywood's answer: Aunt Em—Hate Kansas, hate you, taking the dog, Dorothy.

Don't say you weren't warned. You watch for them there Western Union calls from Eco-Oz, now, you hear?

Sam Goldwyn said it best: Include me out.

See you at the eco-movies.
And on eco-television.
And eco-radio.
And in the eco-newspapers.

Job killers.
Economy trashers.

Media—Footnotes

1 "Mega-Style Back-Yard Benefit for Earth's Sake," by Jeannine Stein, *Los Angeles Times*, February 14, 1990, p. E2.

2 "Turning Stars into Environmentalists," by Anne Taylor Fleming, *New York Times*, October 25, 1989, p. C8.

3 "A Hollywood Effort for the Environment," Nina J. Easton, *Los Angeles Times*, April 15, 1989.

4 "The Environment Goes Prime Time," by Norman and Lyn Lear, *Almanac, The Annual of the International Council of NATAS*, 1990, Special Tenth Anniversary Issue.

5 Media Kit, Environmental Media Association, 1992.

6 "EMA busy making film, TV pitches," by James Ulmer, *The Hollywood Reporter*, September 11, 1989.

7 "The Environment: TV Comes Down to Earth," by Diane Haithman, *Los Angeles Times*, February 10, 1990.

8 "TV shows plug environment," by Sandy Smith, *Nashville Tennessean*, March 7, 1991.

9 "Hollywood groups flex power," by Alan Janson, *Daily Breeze*, January 22, 1990, p. C1.

10 "And Now a Message From an Advocacy Group," by Richard Stevenson, *New York Times*, May 12, 1990.

11 "Hair Rallies Showbusiness Exex To Support Environmental Issues," by Jane Lieberman, *Variety*, June 21, 1990.

12 "Saving the Earth—With the Help of Film and TV Characters," by Daniel B. Wood, *Christian Science Monitor*, July 25, 1990.

13 "In Hollywood They're Making the Green Scene," by Gayle Hanson, *Insight*, November 1990, p. 7.

14 "The Environment: TV Comes Down to Earth," by Diane Haithman, *Los Angeles Times*, February 10, 1990.

15 "TV's environmental impact statement," by Ray Richmond, *Orange County Register*, April 15, 1990, p. 1.

16 "Hollywood's new subplot: Environment," by Anite Manning, *USA Today*, February 5, 1990.

17 "A Desperate ALF Lashes Out," by Kathleen Marquardt, *From the Trenches*, November 11, 1992, p. 2.

18 "'Wolves,' 'Simpsons' Lauded at Environmental Awards Fete," by Bill Higgins, *Los Angeles Times*, October 2, 1991.

19 "Bush Honors H'w'd Environmental Org," *Variety*, November 1, 1991.

20 "1,575 scientists issue warning," Associated Press, no byline, as published in the *Seattle Times*, November 18, 1992, p. A12.

21 "Animal Activists, Environmentalists Eye Film Industry," Terry Pristin, *Los Angeles Times*, as reprinted in the *Albuquerque Journal*, Saturday, February 15, 1992, p. B1.

22 "Should Stars Set the Agenda?" by Richard Bernstein, *New York Times*, March 10, 1991, p. 11.

Bibliography

Books and Studies

Edward Abbey, *The Monkeywrench Gang*, J.B. Lippincott, New York, 1972.

Horace M. Albright as told to Robert Cahn, *The Birth of the National Park Service: The Founding Years, 1913-33*, Howe Brothers, Salt Lake City, 1985.

Horace M. Albright, *Origins of National Park Service Administration of Historic Sites*, Eastern National Park and Monument Association, Philadelphia, 1971.

Jonathan Allen, editor, *March 4: Scientists, Students, and Society*, The MIT Press, Cambridge, Massachusetts, 1970.

Craig W. Allin, *The Politics of Wilderness Preservation*, 1982.

Paul K. Andersen, comp., *Omega: Murder of the Ecosystem and Suicide of Man*, W. C. Brown, Dubuque, Iowa, 1971.

Andrea Arnold, *Fear of Food: Environmentalist Scams, Media Mendacity, and the Law of Disparagement*, The Free Enterprise Press, Bellevue, Washington, 1990.

Ron Arnold, *At the Eye of the Storm: James Watt and the Environmentalists*, Regnery Gateway, Chicago, 1982.

Ron Arnold, *Ecology Wars: Environmentalism As If People Mattered*, Free Enterprise Press, Bellevue, Washington, 1987.

William Ashworth, *The Encyclopedia of Environmental Studies*, Facts On File, Inc, New York, 1991.

William F. Bade, *The Life and Letters of John Muir*, 2 vols., Houghton, Mifflin, Boston, 1923.

Donald N. Baldwin, *The Quiet Revolution: Grass Roots of Today's Wilderness Preservation Movement*, 1972.

Richard A. Baker, *Conservation Politics: The Senate Career of C. P. Anderson*, University of New Mexico Press, 1965.

Doug Bandow, *Ecoterrorism: The Dangerous Fringe of the Environmental Movement*, The Heritage Foundation Backgrounder, Washington, D.C., April 1990.

Sandra S. Batie, *Soil Erosion: Crisis in America's Croplands?*, The Conservation Foundation, Washington, D.C., 1983.

Michael J. Bennett, *The Asbestos Racket: An Environmental Parable*, The Free Enterprise Press, Bellevue, Washington, 1991.

Murray Bookchin, *Remaking Society: Pathways to a Green Future*, South End Press, 1990.

Joseph Campbell, *The Masks of God, Volume One: Primitive Mythology*, Penguin Books, 1976, first published by The Viking Press 1959.

Vernon Carstensen, *The Public Lands: Studies in the History of the Public Domain*, edited by University of Wisconsin Press, Madison, 1968.

Alston Chase, *Playing God in Yellowstone: The Destruction of America's First National Park*, Harcourt Brace Jovanovich, New York, 1987.

George Claus and Karen Bolander, *Ecological Sanity*, David McKay Company, Inc., New York, 1977.

James S. Coleman, *Community Conflict*, The Free Press, New York, 1957.

Andrae Collard with Joyce Contrucci, *Rape of the Wild: Man's Violence against Animals and the Earth*, Indiana University Press, Bloomington, 1989.

Peter Collier and David Horowitz, *The Rockefellers: An American Dynasty*, 1976.

Barry Commoner, *Making Peace With The Planet*, Pantheon, New York, 1990.

T. Allan Comp, editor, *Blueprint for the Environment: A Plan for Federal Action*, Howe Brothers, Salt Lake City, 1989.

Conservation Foundation, *National Parks for a New Generation: Vision, Realities, Prospects*, sponsored by the Richard King Mellon Foundation, Washington, D.C., 1985.

Marjorie R. Corbett, editor, *Greenline Parks: Land Conservation Trends for the 'Eighties and Beyond*, National Parks and Conservation Association, Washington, D.C. 1983.

Lewis Coser, *The Functions of Social Conflict*, The Free Press, New York, 1956.

Richard C. Davis, editor, *Encyclopedia of American Forest and Conservation History*, Macmillan Publishing Company, New York, 1983.

Garrett De Bell, editor, *The Environmental Handbook*, Ballantine Books, New York, 1970.

Bill Devall and George Sessions, *Deep Ecology: Living as if Nature Mattered*, Peregrine Smith Books, Salt Lake City, 1985.

Robert Dorfman and Nancy S. Dorfman, editors, *Economics of the Environment: Selected Readings*, W. W. Norton & Company, New York, 1977.

Dio Chrysostom, *Discourses*, X. Edited by J. von Arnim, 1893.

Diogenes Laertius, VI, Loeb Edition, *Diogenes Laertius: Lives of Eminent Philosophers*, translated by R. D. Hicks, Vol. II, published in America by the Harvard University Press, Cambridge, 1925.

William A. Duerr, Dennis E. Teeguarden, Neils B. Christiansen and Sam Guttenberg, *Forest Resource Management*, W. B. Saunders Company, Philadelphia, 1979.

Jo Kwong Echard, *Protecting the Environment: Old Rhetoric, New Imperatives*, Capital Research Center, Washington, D.C., 1990.

Encyclopedia of Associations, 27th Edition, 1993, New York.

Environmental Action staff, editors, *Ecotage!*, Pocket Books, New York, 1971.

Richard A. Epstein, *Takings: Private Property and the Power of Eminent Domain*, Harvard University Press, 1985.

William C. Everhart, *The National Park Service*, Westview Press, Boulder, Colorado, 1972, 1983.

Marilyn Ferguson, *The Aquarian Conspiracy*, J. P. Tarcher, Los Angeles, 1980.

Dave Foreman and Bill Haywood, editors, *Ecodefense: A Field Guide to Monkeywrenching*, Ned Ludd Books, Tucson, Arizona, 1985.

Ronald Foresta, *America's National Parks and Their Keepers*, Resources For The Future, Washington, D.C. [Baltimore] distributed by the Johns Hopkins University Press, 1984.

Raymond B. Fosdick, *The Story of the Rockefeller Foundation, 1913 to 1950*, Harper & Bros., New York, 1952.

The Foundation Center, *Grants for Environmental Protection and Animal Welfare, 1991-1992*, New York, 1992.

The Foundation Center; *National Guide to Funding for the Environment & Animal Welfare*, New York, 1992.

Michael W. Fox, *Returning to Eden: Animal Rights and Human Responsibility*, Viking, New York, 1980.

Stephen Fox, *John Muir and His Legacy: The American Conservation Movement*, 1981.

644   Trashing the Economy

Ernst Freund, *The Police Power, Public Policy and Constitutional Rights*, 1904.

Luther Gerlach and Virginia Hine, *People, Power, Change: Movements of Social Transformation*, Bobbs-Merrill, Indianapolis, 1970.

Luther Gerlach and Virginia Hine,*Lifeway Leap: The Dynamics of Change in America*, University of Minnesota Press, Minneapolis, 1973.

Marija Alseikaite Gimbutas, *The Language of the Goddess: Unearthing the Hidden Symbols of Western Civilization*, San Francisco, Harper & Row, 1989.

Stanley Godlovitch, editor, *Animals, Men, and Morals: An Inquiry into the Maltreatment of Non-Humans*, Caplinger Publishing, New York, 1972.

Alan Gottlieb, *The Gun Grabbers*, Merril Press, Bellevue, Washington, 1986.

Alan Gottlieb, editor,*The Wise Use Agenda*, Free Enterprise Press, Belleuve, Washington 1988.

Frank Graham, Jr., with Carl W. Buchheister, *The Audubon Ark: A History of the National Audubon Society*, Alfred A. Knopf, New York, 1990.

Joseph Gughemetti and Eugene D. Wheeler, *The Taking*, Hidden House Publications, Palo Alto, California, 1981.

Wayne Hage, *Storm Over Rangelands*, Free Enterprise Press, Bellevue, Washington, 1989.

Edith Hamilton, *Mythology*, Little, Brown & Company, Boston, 1940.

David T. Hardy, Esq., *America's New Extremists: What You Need to Know About the Animal Rights Movement*, Washington Legal Foundation, Washington, D.C., 1990.

Edith Hamilton, *Mythology*, Little, Brown & Company, Boston, 1940, p. 14.

Samuel P. Hays, *Conservation and the Gospel of Efficiency: The Progressive Conservation Movement 1890-1920*, Harvard University Press, Cambridge, 1959.

John C. Hendee, George H. Stankey, and Robert C. Lucas, *Wilderness Management*, U.S. Department of Agriculture, 1978.

Janice Scott Henke, *Seal Wars*, Breakwater, Saint John's, Newfoundland, 1985.

David Henshaw, *Animal Warfare*, Fontana Paperbacks, London, 1989.

Hesiod, "Works and Days," in *Hesiod: The Homeric Hymns and Homerica*, English translation by Hugh G. Evelyn-White, Loeb Edition, published in the United States by Harvard University Press, Cambridge, 1914.

Stewart H. Holbrook, *The Age of the Moguls*, Doubleday & Company, Inc., Garden City, N.Y., 1956.

Don Hummel, *Stealing the National Parks*, Free Enterprise Press, Bellevue, Washington, 1987.

Robert Hunter, *Warriors of the Rainbow: A Chronicle of the Greenpeace Movement*, Holt, Rinehart and Winston, New York, 1979.

Harold L. Ickes, *The Autobiography of a Curmudgeon*, Reynal and Hitchcock, New York, 1943.

John Ise,*Our National Park Policy: A Critical History*, Resources For the Future, Johns Hopkins University Press, Baltimore, 1961.

Holway Jones, *John Muir and the Sierra Club: The Battle for Yosemite*, 1965.

John V. Krutilla and Anthony C. Fisher, *The Economics of Natural Environments*, Resources for the Future, Washington, D.C., distributed by Johns Hopkins University Press, 1975.

Marc J. Lane, *Legal Handbook for Nonprofit Organizations*, American Management Associations, New York, 1980.

Susan D. Lanier-Graham, *The Nature Directory*, Walker and Company, New York, 1991.

P. F. Lazarsfeld and F. N. Stanton (eds.), *Radio Research 1942-43*, Duell, Sloan and Pearce, New York, 1944.

Dr. Jay H. Lehr, editor, *Rational Readings on Environmental Concerns*, Van Nostrand Reinhold, New York, 1992.

Aldo Leopold, *A Sand County Almanac*, Oxford University Press, Oxford, 1949.

David L. Lindt, *Ding: The Life of Jay Norwood Darling*, 1979.

Arthur O. Lovejoy and George Boas, *Primitivism and Related Ideas in Antiquity*, Octagon Books, New York, 1973, first published by The Johns Hopkins Press, 1935.

John Maddox, *The Doomsday Syndrome*, McGraw-Hill, New York, 1972.

Christopher Manes, *Green Rage: Radical Environmentalism and the Unmaking of Civilization*, Little, Brown and Company, Boston, 1990.

Robert Marshall, *The People's Forests*, H. Smith & R. Haas, New York, 1933.

Abraham H. Maslow, *Motivation and Personality*, Second Edition, New York, Harper & Row, 1970.

M. Nelson McGeary, *Gifford Pinchot: Forester-Politician*, Princeton University Press, Princeton, 1960.

John McPhee, *Encounters with the Archdruid*, Farrar Strauss and Giroux, New York, 1971.

Donella H. Meadows, Dennis L. Meadows, Jørgen Randers, and William W. Behrens III, *The Limits to Growth*, Universe Books, New York, 1972.

Carolyn Merchant, *The Death of Nature: Women, Ecology, and the Scientific Revolution*, Harper & Row, San Francisco, 1980.

Ludwig von Mises, *Human Action*, Yale University Press, Hartford, 1949, revised edition 1963, third revised edition published by Henry Regnery Company in 1966.

John G. Mitchell and Constance L. Stallings, editors, *Ecotactics: The Sierra Club Handbook for Environment Activists*, Pocket Books, New York, 1970.

Richard Morgan, *Love and Anger: An Organizing Handbook for Activists in the Struggle for Animal Rights and In Other Progressive Political Movements*, second edition, Westport, Connecticut, Animal Rights Network, 1981.

David E. Morine, *Good Dirt*, Globe Pequot Press, Chester, Connecticut, 1991.

Richard Munson, *Cousteau: The Captain and His World*, W. Morrow, New York, 1989.

Arne Naess, *Gandhi and Group Conflict: An Exploration of Satyagraha—Theoretical Background*, Oslo, 1974.

Roderick Frazier Nash, *The Rights of Nature*, University of Wisconsin Press, Madison, 1989.

Roderick Nash, *Wilderness and the American Mind*, Yale University Press, New Haven, 1967, revised edition 1973.

National Parks and Conservation Association, *Investing In Park Futures: A Blueprint for Tomorrow*, Washington, D.C., February 1988.

Natural Resources Defense Council, *Intolerable Risk: Pesticides in Our Children's Food*, New York, 1989.

Jim Neumann, *State Growth Management Legislation: A Comparative Analysis of Legislative Approaches and Administrative Provisions*, Woodrow Wilson School of Public and International Affairs, Princeton, New Jersey, June, 1991.

Waldemar A. Nielsen, *The Golden Donors: A New Anatomy of the Great Foundations*, E. P. Dutton, New York, 1985.

Robert A. Nisbet, *Prejudices: A Philosophical Dictionary*, Harvard University Press, Cambridge, 1982.

Nancy Newhall, editor, *A Contribution to the Heritage of Every American: The Conservation Activities of John D. Rockefeller, Jr.*, 1957.

John O'Connor, *Fighting Toxics: A Manual for Protecting Your Family, Community and Workplace*, National Toxics Campaign, Boston.

Marvin Olasky, *Patterns of Corporate Philanthropy: Public Affairs Giving and the Forbes 100*, Capital Research Center, Washington, D.C., 1987.

Stan Olson, Ruth Kovacs & Suzanne Haile, editors, *National Guide to Funding for the Environment and Animal Welfare*, The Foundation Center, New York, 1992.

William Ophuls, *Ecology and the Politics of Scarcity Revisited: The Unraveling of the American Dream*, W. H. Freeman and Company, New York, 1992.

Ellen Frankel Paul, *Property Rights and Eminent Domain*, Transaction Books, New Brunswick, 1987.

Lester B. Pearson, *Partners in Development*, Praeger, New York, 1969.

Judith Plant, editor, *Healing the Wounds: The Promise of Ecofeminism*, New Society, Philadelphia, 1989.

Mark K. Pollot, *Grand Theft and Petit Larceny: Property Rights in America*, Pacific Research Institute, San Francisco, 1993.

Public Interest Profiles 1992-1993, Congressional Quarterly, Inc, Washington, D.C.

T. L. Quay, editor, *The Seaside Sparrow, Its Biology and Management*, North Carolina State Museum of Natural History, Raleigh, 1983.

Dixy Lee Ray, *Trashing the Planet*, Regnery Gateway, Chicago, 1990.

Tom Regan, *The Case for Animal Rights*, University of California Press, Berkeley, 1983.

William K. Reilly, editor, *The Use of Land: A Citizen's Policy Guide to Urban Growth*, A Task Force Report Sponsored by the Rockefeller Brothers Fund, New York, Thomas Y. Crowell, 1973.

Research Centers Directory, 17th Edition-1993.

Marc Reiner, *Cadillac Desert: The American West and Its Disappearing Water*, Viking, New York, 1986.

George Reisman, *The Toxicity of Environmentalism*, The Jefferson School of Philosophy, Economics, and Psychology, Laguna Hills, California, 1990.

Alfred Runte, *National Parks: The American Experience*, University of Nebraska Press, Lincoln, 1979.

Alfred Runte, *Trains of Discovery: Western Railroads and the National Parks*, Northland Press, Flagstaff, Arizona, 1984.

Richard Ryder, *Victims of Science: The Use of Animals in Research*, National Anti-Vivisection Society, London, 1975, 1983.

Joseph Sax, *Mountains Without Handrails: Reflections on the National Parks*, University of Michigan Press, Ann Arbor, 1980.

Rik Scarce, *Eco-Warriors: Understanding the Radical Environmental Movement*, The Noble Press, Inc., Chicago, 1990.

Victor B. Scheffer, *The Shaping of Environmentalism in America*, University of Washington Press, Seattle, 1991.

Richard Schlatter, *Private Property: The History of an Idea*, Rutgers University Press, New Brunswick, New Jersey, 1951.

Robert Shankland, *Steve Mather of the National Parks*, Alfred A. Knopf, New York, 1951.

Carl D. Shoemaker, *The Stories Behind the Organization of the National Wildlife Federation and Its Early Struggles for Survival*, 1960.

Georg Simmel: *Conflict*, an essay originally Chapter Four of *Soziologie* (1908), translated by Kurt H. Wolff the third edition (1923), published in *Conflict* and *The Web of Group-Affiliations*, The Free Press, New York, 1955.

Julian L. Simon and Herman Kahn, eds., *The Resourceful Earth: A Response to Global 2000*, Basil Blackwell, New York, 1984.

Peter Singer, *Animal Liberation: A New Ethics for Our Treatment of Animals*, New York Review distributed by Random House, 1975.

Holly Sklar, editor, *Trilateralism: The Trilateral Commission and Elite Planning for World Management*, Black Rose Books, Montreal, 1980.

K. A. Soderberg and Jackie DuRette, *People of the Tongass: Alaska Forestry Under Attack*, Free Enterprise Press, Bellevue, Washington, 1988.

Wallace Stegner, ed., *This Is Dinosaur: Echo Park Country and Its Magic Rivers*, Knopf, New York, 1955.

Edith Carol Stein, *The Environmental Sourcebook*, Lyons & Burford, New York, 1992.

Ernest F. Swift, *A Conservation Saga*, National Wildlife Federation, Washington, D.C. 1967.

Ida M. Tarbell, *The History of the Standard Oil Company*, 2 vols., McClure, Phillips & Co., New York, 1904.

Christopher G. Tiedeman, *A Treatise on the Limitations of Police Power in the United States*, 1886.

Thaddeus C. Trzyna with the assistance of Ilze M. Gotelli, editors, *World Directory of Environmental Organizations*, Third Edition, California Institute of Public Affairs in cooperation with the Sierra Club and IUCN—The World Conservation Union, 1990.

William Tucker, *Progress and Privilege: America in the Age of Environmentalism*, Garden City, Doubleday, 1982.

J. Peter Vajk, *Doomsday Has Been Cancelled*, Peace Press, Culver City, California, 1978.

Paul Watson as told to Warren Rogers, *Sea Shepherd: My Fight for Whales and Seals*, W. W. Norton & Company, New York, 1982.

Elizabeth Whelan, *Toxic Terror*, 1985.

Conrad L. Wirth, *Parks, Politics and People*, University of Oklahoma Press, Norman, 1980.

Linnie Marsh Wolfe, *Son of the Wilderness: The Life of John Muir*, Alfred A. Knopf, New York, 1945.

Nancy Wood, *Clearcut: The Deforestation of America*, Sierra Club, San Francisco, 1971.

World Commission on Environmental and Development, *Our Common Future*, Oxford University Press, Oxford and New York, 1987.

René A. Wormser, *Foundations, Their Power and Influence*, Devin-Adair, New York, 1968.

Government Reports and Documents

Administrative History: Expansion of the National Park Service in the 1930s, Harlan D. Unrau and G. Frank Williss, National Park Service, Denver Service Center, Denver, 1983.

Administrative History: Organizational Structures of the National Park Service 1917-1985, Russell Olsen, National Park Service, Washington, D.C., 1986

Columbia River Gorge Act of 1983, Hearing before the Subcommittee on Public Lands and Reserved Water or the Committee on Energy and Natural Resources, United States Senate, 98th Congress, 1st Session, on S. 627, Portland, Oregon, March 25, 1983.

Dolphins and the Tuna Industry, National Research Council, Committee on Reducing Porpoise Mortality from Tuna Fishing, Robert C. Francis, Chairman, National Research Council, National Academy Press, Washington, D.C., 1992.

Endangered Species: Management Improvements Could Enhance Recovery Program, U. S. General Accounting Office, December 21, 1988.

Environmental Legislation: The Increasing Costs of Regulatory Compliance to the City of Columbus, The Environmental Law Review Committee, May 13, 1991, Columbus, Ohio.

History and Prehistory in the National Park System and the National Historic Landmark Program, National Park Service, Washington, 1982.

A History of Early Land Acquisition for Kipahulu Valley as an Extension of Haleakala National Park, Mark Tanaka-Sanders, District Ranger, Kipahulu Valley, Maui, Hawaii, 1991.

History of Legislation Relating to the National Park System through the 82nd Congress, 108 volumes, Edmund B. Rogers, Departmental Library, U.S. Department of the Interior.

History of Natural Resources Agencies and Proposals for their Reorganization, unpublished internal document, U.S. Department of the Interior, Departmental Library, 1977.

Laws Relating to the National Park Service, the National Parks and Monuments, Hillory A. Tolson, GPO, 1933.

The Lexington-Concord Battle Road, Interim report of the Boston National Historic Sites Commission to the Congress of the United States, June 16, 1958.

Mission 66: To Provide Adequate Protection and Development of the National Park System for Human Use, National Park Service, U.S. Department of the Interior, January, 1956.

National Registry of Natural Landmarks Handbook, U.S. Department of the Interior, National Park Service, Release No. 2, August 18, 1966.

An Organizational Trend Analysis of the National Park System between 1960 and 1980, by Ric Davidge, internal study, U.S. Department of the Interior.

Outdoor Recreation for America, A Report to the President and to the Congress by the Outdoor Recreation Resources Review Commission, GPO, January, 1962.

Paying for Federal Environmental Mandates: A Looming Crisis for Cities and Counties, compiled for the United States Congress by Municipality of Anchorage, Alaska, Tom Fink, Mayor, September, 1992.

Potential Ecological and Geological Natural Landmarks of the New England-Adirondack Region, Thomas G. Siccama, William A. Niering, Gail Kalison, Ann M.H. O'Dell, Elizabeth B. Speer, Yale School of Forestry, 1982.

Terrorism in the United States, 1989, Terrorist Research and Analytical Center, Counterterrorism Section, Criminal Investigative Division, U. S. Department of Justice, Federal Bureau of Investigation, Washington, D. C., December 31, 1989.

U. S. Congress, Senate, National Conference on Outdoor Recreation: *Proceedings of the National Conference on Outdoor Recreation, May 22, 12, and 24, 1924*, 68 Cong. 1 sess., 1924, S. Doc. 151.

Water Rights Laws in the Nineteen Western States, vol. 1, Department of Agriculture Miscellaneous Publication 1206, Government Printing Office, Washington, D. C., 1971.

The Yield of Douglas Fir in the Pacific Northwest, Richard E. McArdle, Walter H. Meyer and Donald Bruce, U.S.Department of Agriculture Technical Bulletin 201, revised 1949.

Theses and Dissertations

Bane, Gilbert Winfield, Jr., *Distribution and Abundance of Tunas and Tuna/baitfishes in the Gulf of Guinea*, unpublished master's thesis, Cornell University, 1961, 119 pages.

Gerald Cormick, *Power, Strategy and the Process of Community Conflict: A Theoretical Framework*, unpublished Ph.D. dissertation, University of Michigan, 1971.

What The Media A

Ron Arnold and Alan Gottlieb have money,
millions of angry Americans.

There's not much you can teach Ron Arnold and Alan Gottlieb about environmental activism. But Arnold and Gottlieb are activists with a difference...
—People Magazine

Arnold warned that unless the environmental movement is brought to heel, "public hysteria is going to destroy industrial civilization..." Arnold's organization has published a "wise-use agenda" spelling out an opposing series of goals.
—The Washington Post

Mr. Arnold and Mr. Gottlieb say they have borrowed from the early tactics of the environmental movement—newsletters with ominous overtones, direct-mail fund-raising to a very specific audience, the threat of lawsuits—and are just now hitting stride. *—The New York Times*

The direction of the Center for the Defense of Free Enterprise is determined by two men, Alan Gottlieb and Ron Arnold. Arnold, who confesses to a brief history as a Sierra Club activist, has been described as the movement's "philosopher." Gottlieb, on the other hand, is the money man. *—Sierra*

The principal organizer of the Wise Use Movement is Alan M. Gottlieb...
—Harrowsmith Country Life

Ron Arnold...is gaining increasing national stature and political influence as the arch-druid of the burgeoning movement against environmentalism.
—The Boston Globe

Legislatively, Arnold has had a remarkable degree of success. He and Gottlieb organized support for a stringent anti-regulatory bill...
—Buzzworm: The Environmental Journal

Alan Gottlieb and Ron Arnold. The two men are the gurus of the Wise Use Movement. Ron Arnold [is] a former Sierra Club activist who has torn whole chapters from the textbook of grass-roots activism... *—National Parks*

Wise Use has no formal command structure. Any cohesion the movement has comes from a few pivotal figures—notably Ron Arnold [and] Alan Gottlieb... *—Audubon*

Arnold is now a fixture on the anti-environmental lecture circuit. *—Greenpeace*

Gottlieb, a shy direct-mail genius...Arnold, who looks like an Amish Santa Claus after a Slim Fast diet, goes to work as the eco-slayer.
—E, the Environmental Magazine

If you have enjoyed Trashing the Economy, you'll want to own these other exciting titles from The Free Enterprise Press.

It Takes A Hero: The Grassroots Battle Against Environmental Oppression, by William Perry Pendley. 346 pages, paperback, $14.95.

The Asbestos Racket: An Environmental Parable, by Michael J. Bennett 256 pages, paperback, $9.95.

Storm Over Rangelands: Private Rights in Federal Lands, by Wayne Hage, 288 pages, paperback, $14.95.

Stealing the National Parks: The Destruction of Concessions and Public Access, by Don Hummel, 428 pages, hardcover, $19.95.

Ecology Wars: Environmentalism As If People Mattered, by Ron Arnold, 182 pages, paperback, $14.95.

The Wise Use Agenda, edited by Alan Gottlieb, 168 pages, paperback, $9.95.